SEVEN SEAS ENTERTAINMENT PRESENTS

SAZAN & COMET GIRL

story & art by YURIKO AKASE

TRANSLATION
Adrienne Beck

ADAPTATION
Ysabet MacFarlane

LAYOUT AND LETTERING
Karis Page
Gwen Silver

COVER DESIGN
Nicky Lim

PROOFREADER
Danielle King

PREPRESS TECHNICIAN
Rhiannon Rasmussen-Silverstein

PRODUCTION MANAGER
Lissa Pattillo

MANAGING EDITOR
Julie Davis

ASSOCIATE PUBLISHER
Adam Arnold

PUBLISHER
Jason DeAngelis

Sazan and Comet Girl
© Yuriko Akase 2018
Originally published in Japan in 2018 by LEED PUBLISHING CO., LTD, Tokyo.
English translation rights arranged with LEED PUBLISHING CO.,LTD, Tokyo,
through TOHAN CORPORATION, Tokyo.

S0-CEY-111

Seven Seas press and purchase enquiries can be sent to Marketing Manager
Lianne Sentar at press@gomanga.com. Information regarding the distribution
and purchase of digital editions is available from Digital Manager CK Russell
at digital@gomanga.com.

Seven Seas and the Seven Seas logo are trademarks of
Seven Seas Entertainment. All rights reserved.

ISBN: 978-1-64505-299-9

Printed in Canada

First Printing: August 2020

10 9 8 7 6 5 4 3 2 1

FOLLOW US ONLINE: *www.sevenseasentertainment.com*

READING DIRECTIONS

This book reads from **right to left**, Japanese style.
If this is your first time reading manga, you start
reading from the top right panel on each page and
take it from there. If you get lost, just follow the
numbered diagram here. It may seem backwards at
first, but you'll get the hang of it! Have fun!!

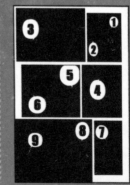

AFTERWORD

Thank you so much for picking up and reading *Sazan and Comet Girl.* This manga was originally only going to be a ten or fifteen-page one-shot, but my editor said it was a concept we could expand to a mid-length story. At first I wasn't sure I could stretch it out that far, but then I thought, "Well, I did want to do this and that, and if I have the space..." I thought back on all the fun and exciting times in my life and put everything that had moved me into the story.

I'm very grateful to Torch WEB for agreeing to publish an unknown newcomer like me in this fashion. I thoroughly enjoyed working on this manga, although I'll admit it wasn't easy going at the start. I had a lot to learn about how to work in watercolors and how to bring my characters to life.

I was fortunate that I had a lot of people supporting and helping me. My editor, Atsushi Nakagawa, was always there to listen to what I had to say and work with me every step of the way. My sister, Yumi, who came and helped me after her own job several times each month, provided both a shoulder to lean on and an extra pair of hands to help with the work. All of my friends who were there for me, all of the staff in the editorial department who helped me, and everyone else who was involved in creating this manga. And last but by no means least, you, the reader. Thank you so much.

I dream of the day when we might meet through the pages of a manga once again.

Yuriko Akase
3/2018

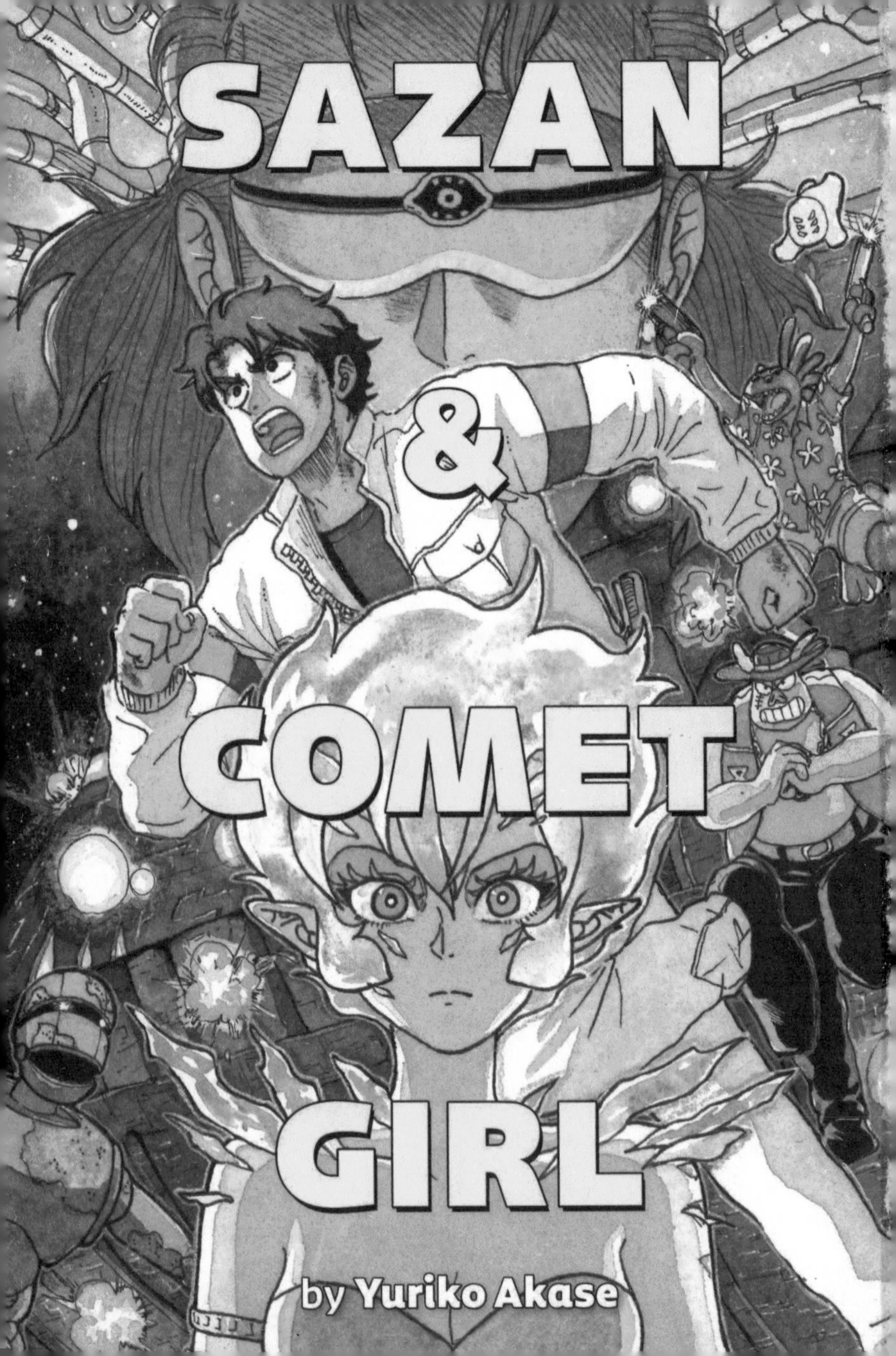
SAZAN
&
COMET
GIRL
by Yuriko Akase

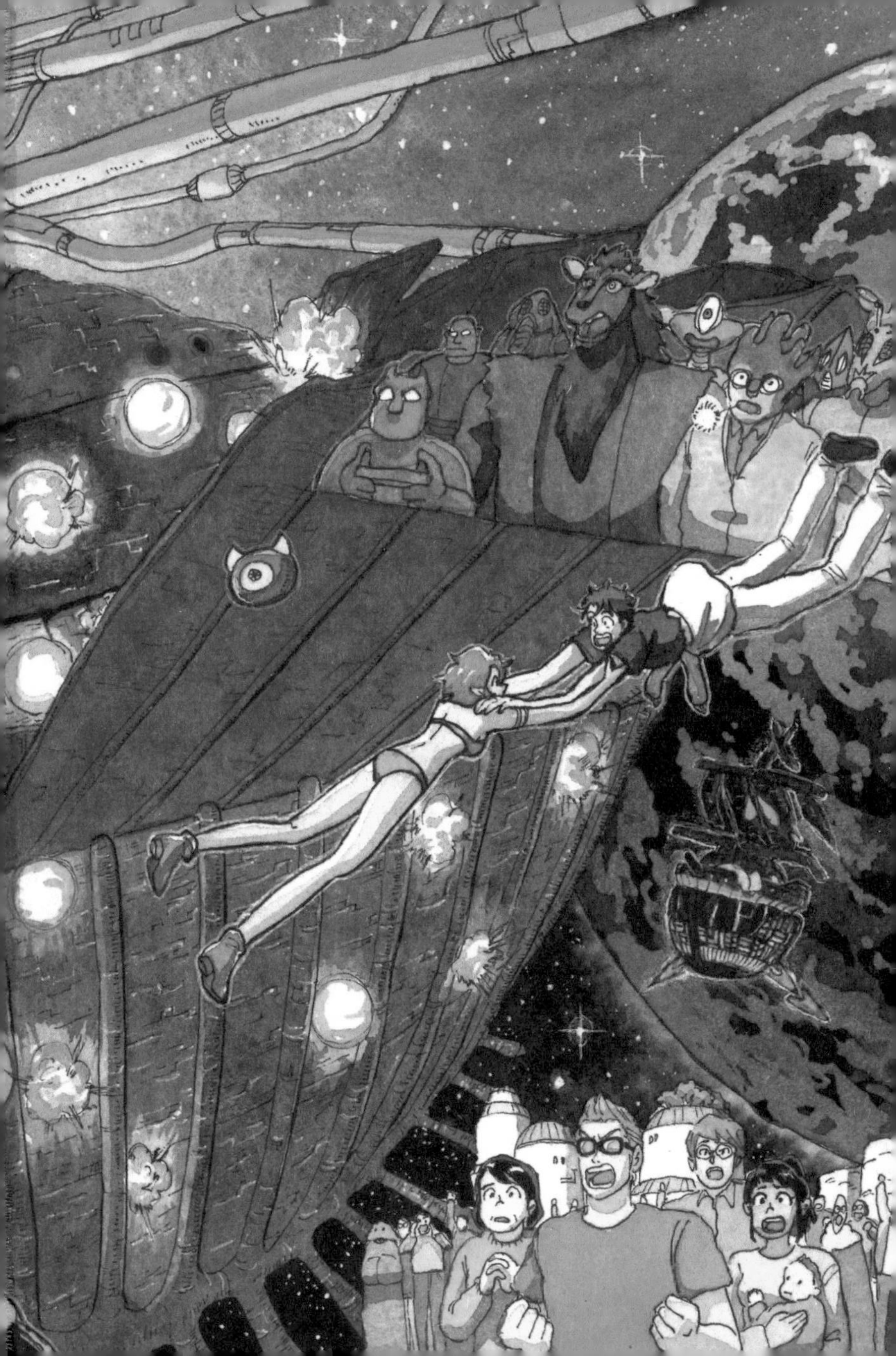

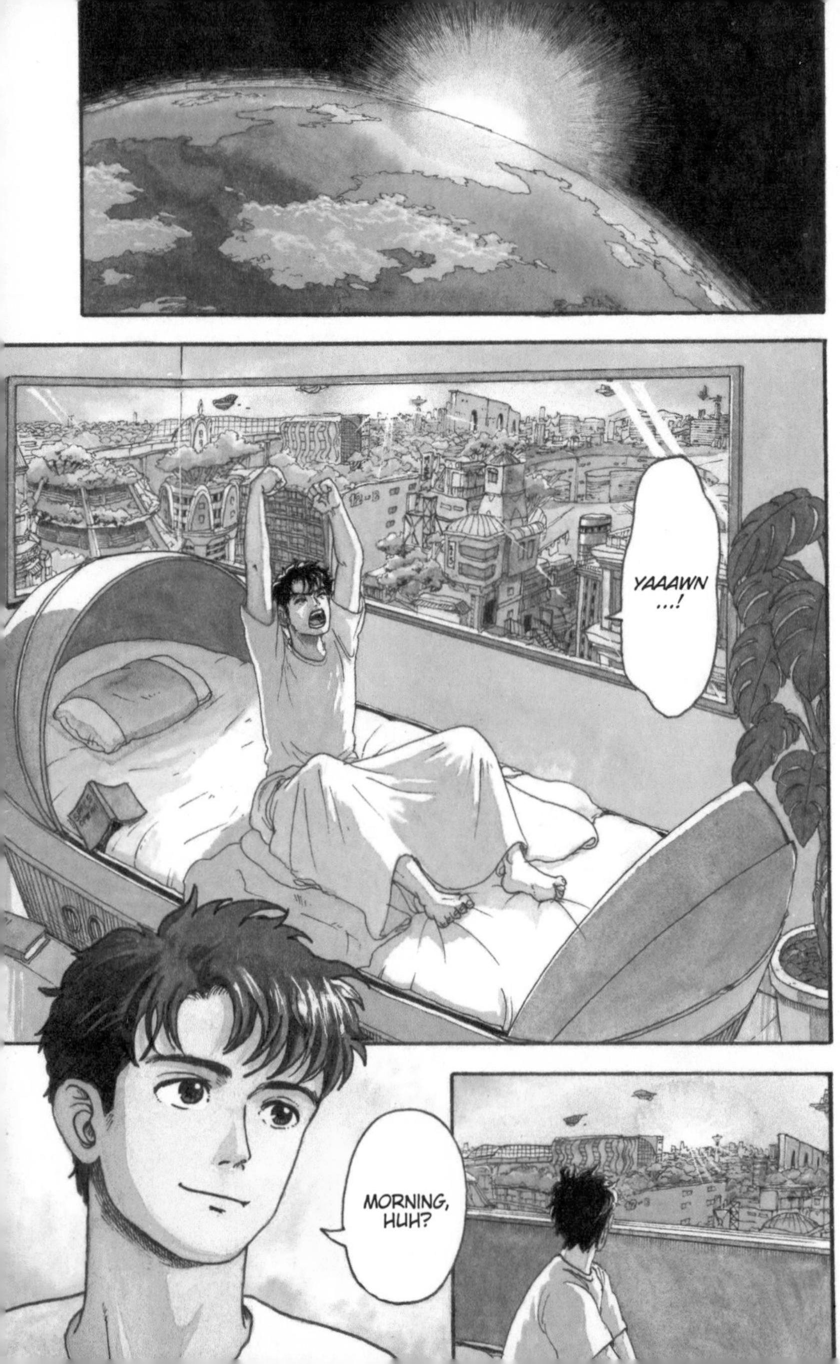
YAAAWN ...!
MORNING, HUH?

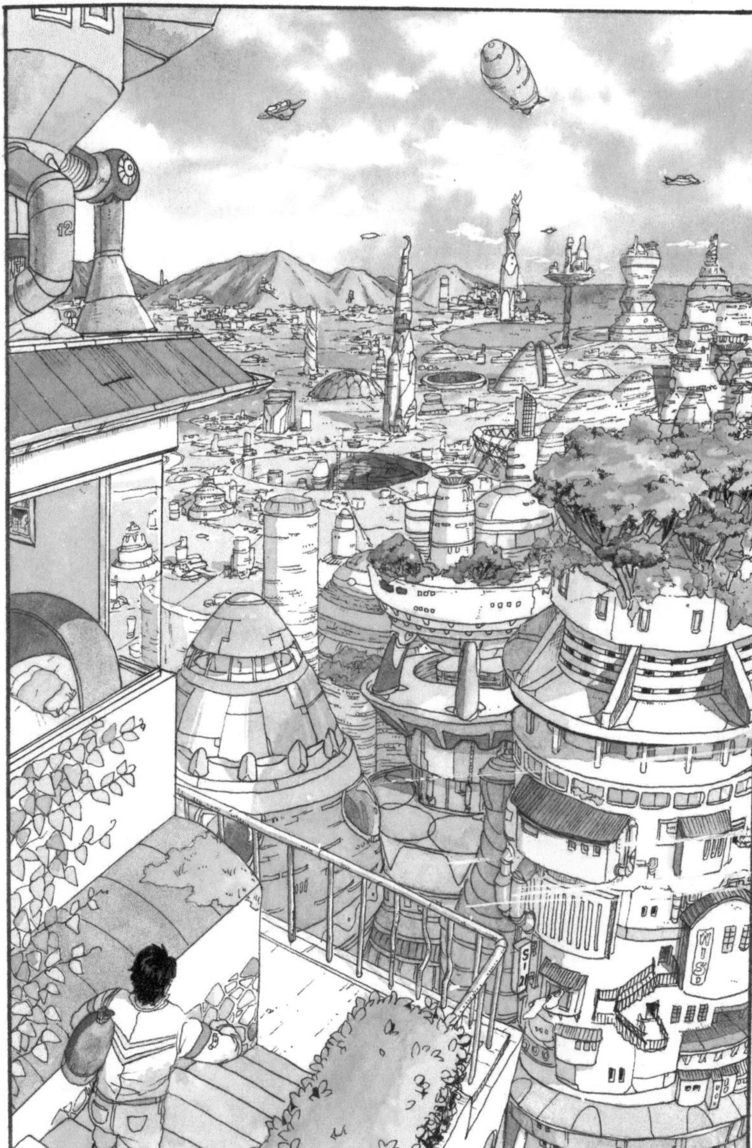

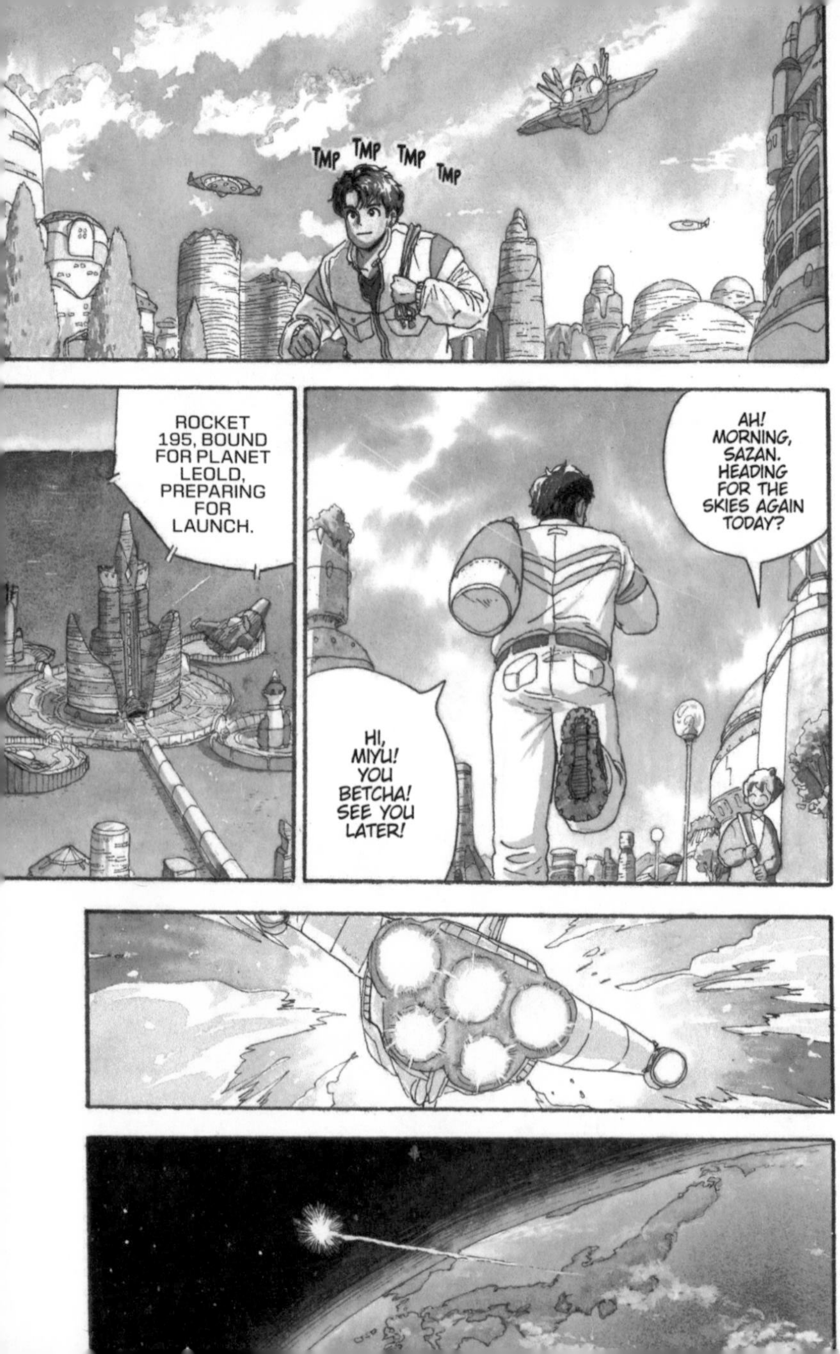
TMP TMP TMP TMP
AH! MORNING, SAZAN. HEADING FOR THE SKIES AGAIN TODAY?
HI, MIYU! YOU BETCHA! SEE YOU LATER!
ROCKET 195, BOUND FOR PLANET LEOLD, PREPARING FOR LAUNCH.

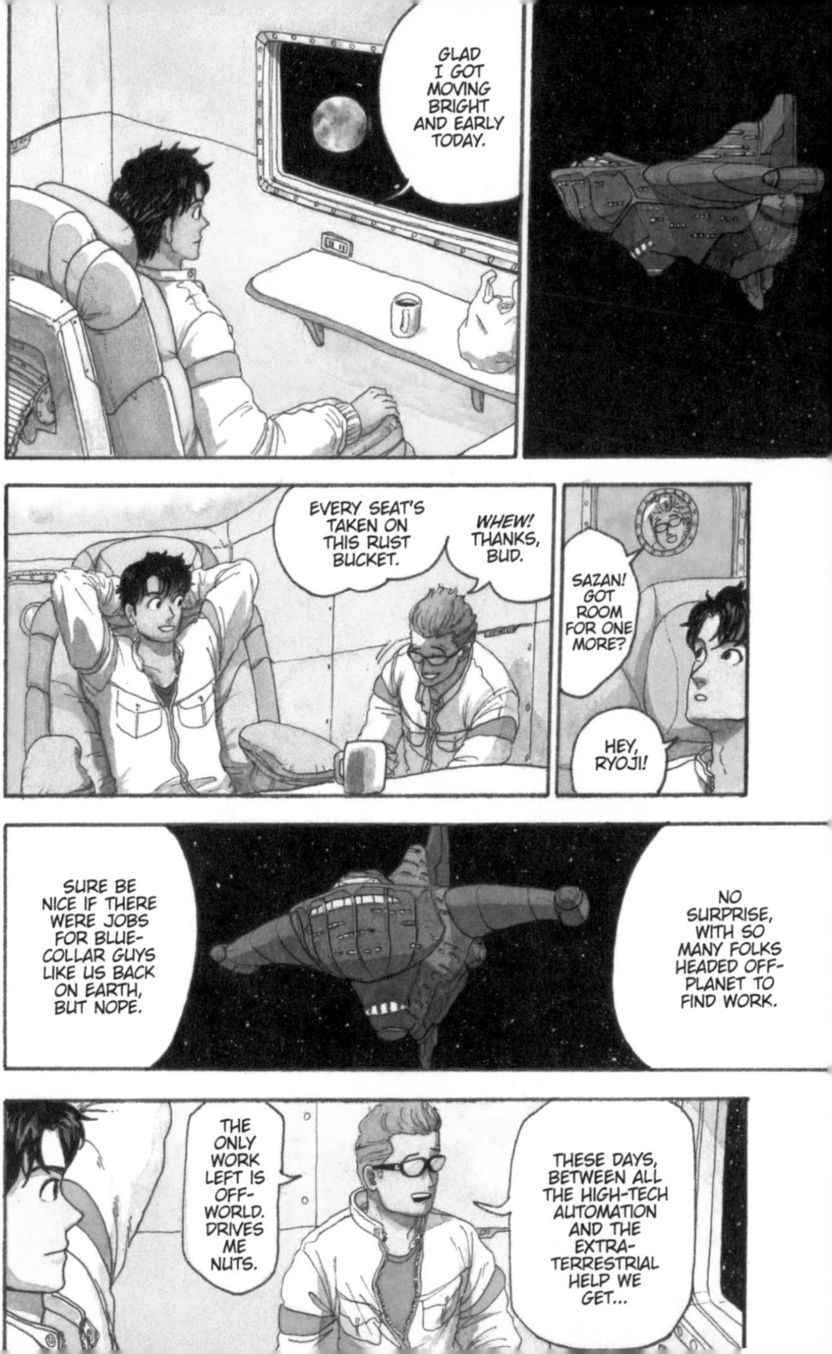

GLAD I GOT MOVING BRIGHT AND EARLY TODAY.
SAZAN! GOT ROOM FOR ONE MORE?
HEY, RYOJI!
EVERY SEAT'S TAKEN ON THIS RUST BUCKET.
WHEW! THANKS, BUD.
NO SURPRISE, WITH SO MANY FOLKS HEADED OFF-PLANET TO FIND WORK.
SURE BE NICE IF THERE WERE JOBS FOR BLUE-COLLAR GUYS LIKE US BACK ON EARTH, BUT NOPE.
THESE DAYS, BETWEEN ALL THE HIGH-TECH AUTOMATION AND THE EXTRA-TERRESTRIAL HELP WE GET...
THE ONLY WORK LEFT IS OFF-WORLD. DRIVES ME NUTS.

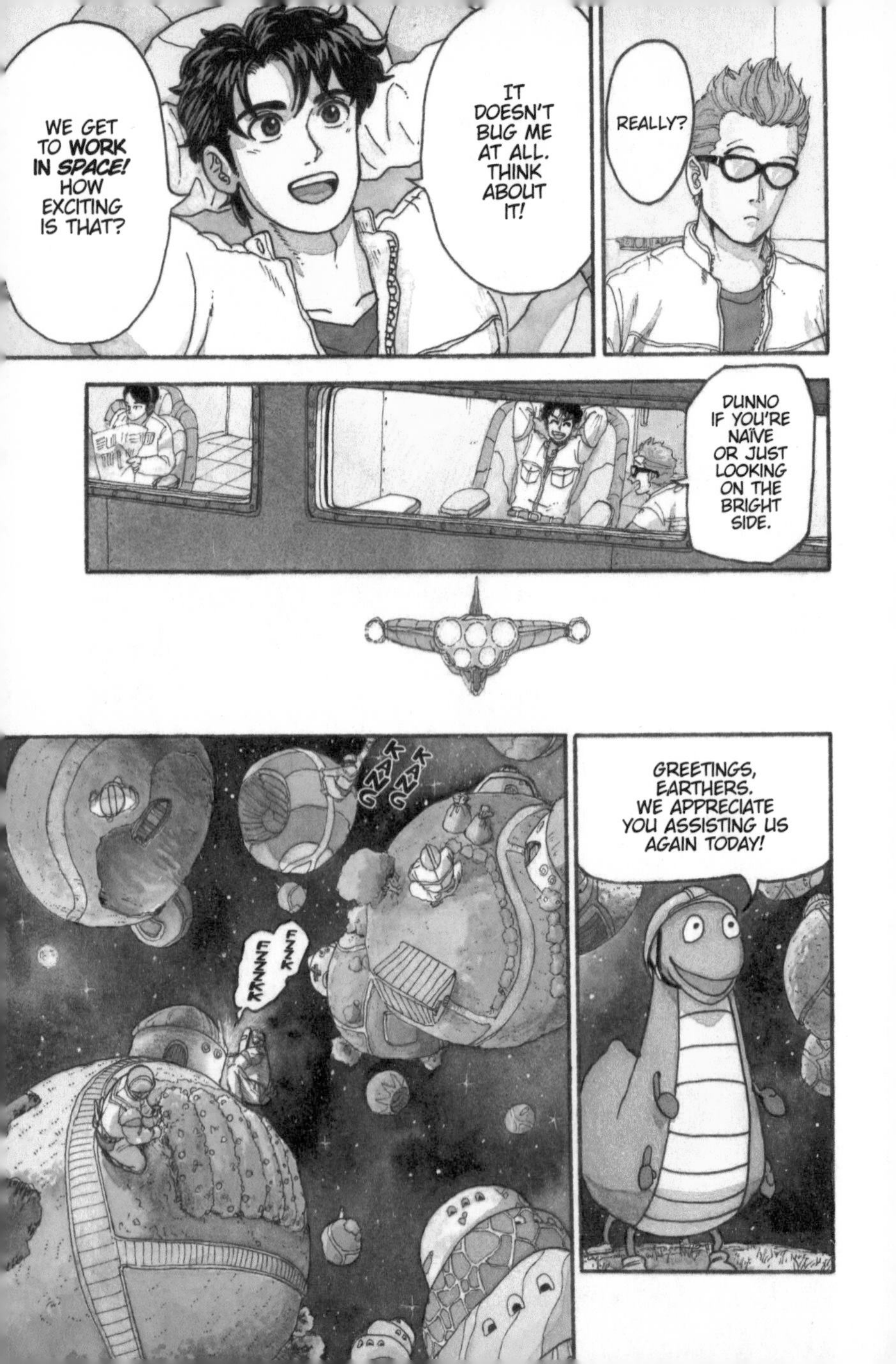

REALLY?
IT DOESN'T BUG ME AT ALL. THINK ABOUT IT!
WE GET TO **WORK IN *SPACE!*** HOW EXCITING IS THAT?
DUNNO IF YOU'RE NAÏVE OR JUST LOOKING ON THE BRIGHT SIDE.
GREETINGS, EARTHERS. WE APPRECIATE YOU ASSISTING US AGAIN TODAY!
GZZAK GZZAK
FZZK FZZZKK

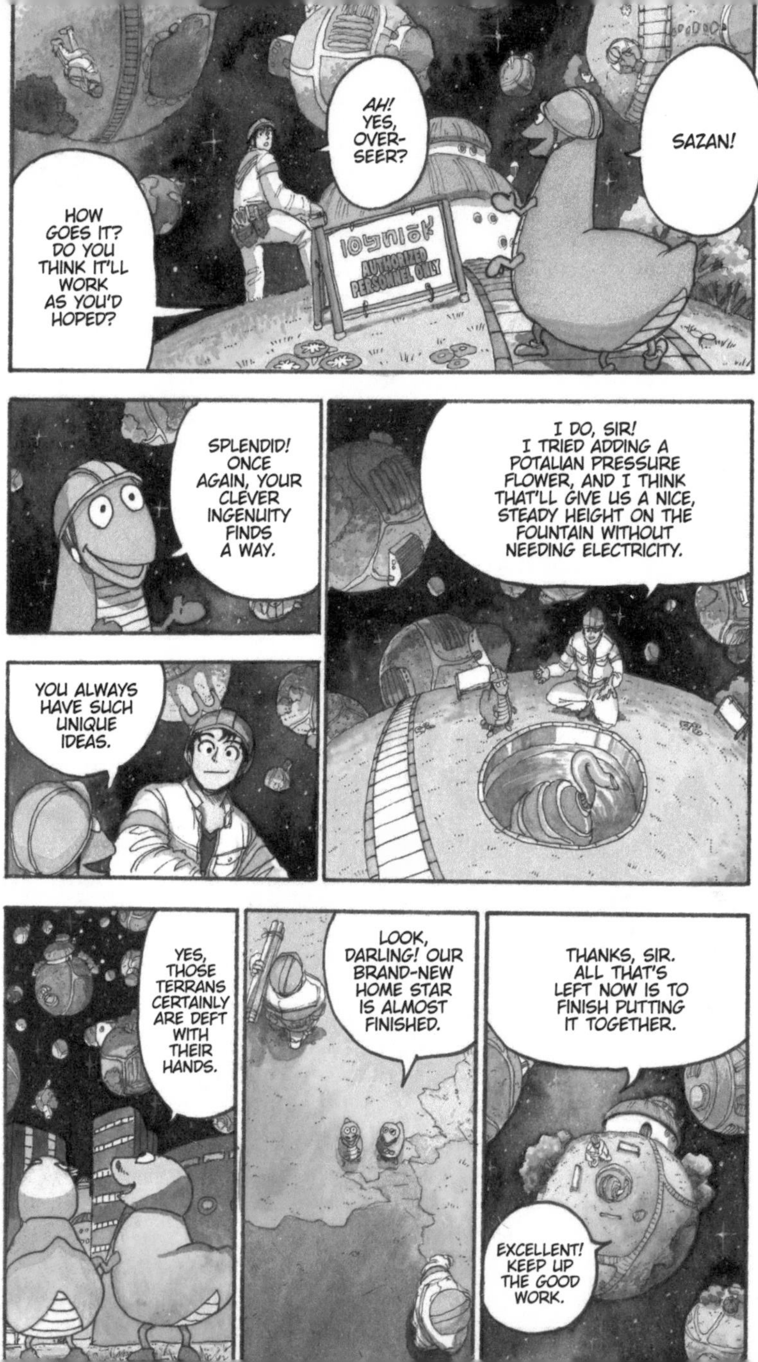
SAZAN!
AH! YES, OVER-SEER?
AUTHORIZED PERSONNEL ONLY
HOW GOES IT? DO YOU THINK IT'LL WORK AS YOU'D HOPED?
I DO, SIR! I TRIED ADDING A POTALIAN PRESSURE FLOWER, AND I THINK THAT'LL GIVE US A NICE, STEADY HEIGHT ON THE FOUNTAIN WITHOUT NEEDING ELECTRICITY.
SPLENDID! ONCE AGAIN, YOUR CLEVER INGENUITY FINDS A WAY.
YOU ALWAYS HAVE SUCH UNIQUE IDEAS.
THANKS, SIR. ALL THAT'S LEFT NOW IS TO FINISH PUTTING IT TOGETHER.
EXCELLENT! KEEP UP THE GOOD WORK.
LOOK, DARLING! OUR BRAND-NEW HOME STAR IS ALMOST FINISHED.
YES, THOSE TERRANS CERTAINLY ARE DEFT WITH THEIR HANDS.

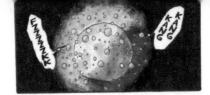

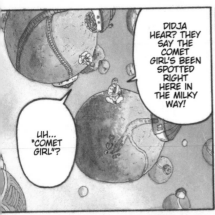

KANG KANG
FZZZZZKK
HEY, SAZAN?
YEAH?
DIDJA HEAR? THEY SAY THE COMET GIRL'S BEEN SPOTTED RIGHT HERE IN THE MILKY WAY!
UH... "COMET GIRL"?
WHAT, A BIG SPACE GEEK LIKE YOU HASN'T HEARD ABOUT COMET GIRL? EVERYBODY KNOWS SHE'S A HARBINGER OF DISASTER!
SEE, RUMOR HAS IT THAT THE COMET GIRL HOLDS *INCREDIBLE* AMOUNTS OF ENERGY INSIDE HER BODY.
ALL THAT POWER'S A SWEET TARGET FOR ALL KINDS OF NE'ER-DO-WELLS, SO SHE'S CONSTANTLY GETTING CHASED ALL ACROSS THE UNIVERSE, LEAVING CHAOS AND DESTRUCTION EVERYWHERE SHE GOES. HARBINGER OF DISASTER, SEE?

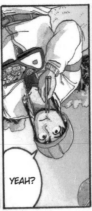

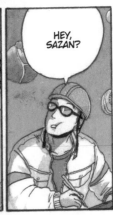

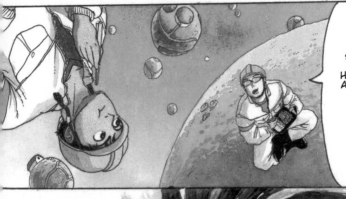

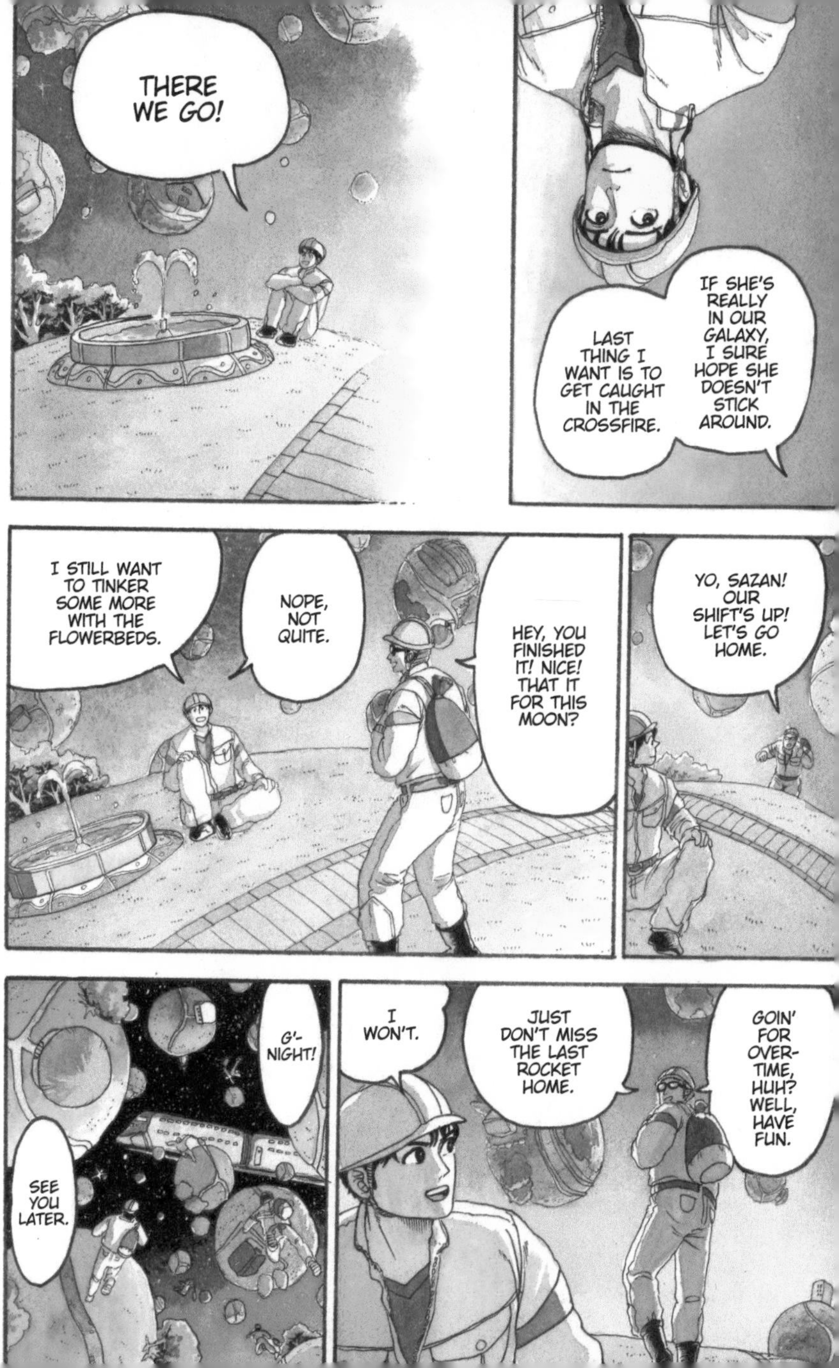
IF SHE'S REALLY IN OUR GALAXY, I SURE HOPE SHE DOESN'T STICK AROUND.
LAST THING I WANT IS TO GET CAUGHT IN THE CROSSFIRE.
THERE WE GO!
YO, SAZAN! OUR SHIFT'S UP! LET'S GO HOME.
HEY, YOU FINISHED IT! NICE! THAT IT FOR THIS MOON?
NOPE, NOT QUITE.
I STILL WANT TO TINKER SOME MORE WITH THE FLOWERBEDS.
GOIN' FOR OVER-TIME, HUH? WELL, HAVE FUN.
JUST DON'T MISS THE LAST ROCKET HOME.
I WON'T.
G'-NIGHT!
SEE YOU LATER.

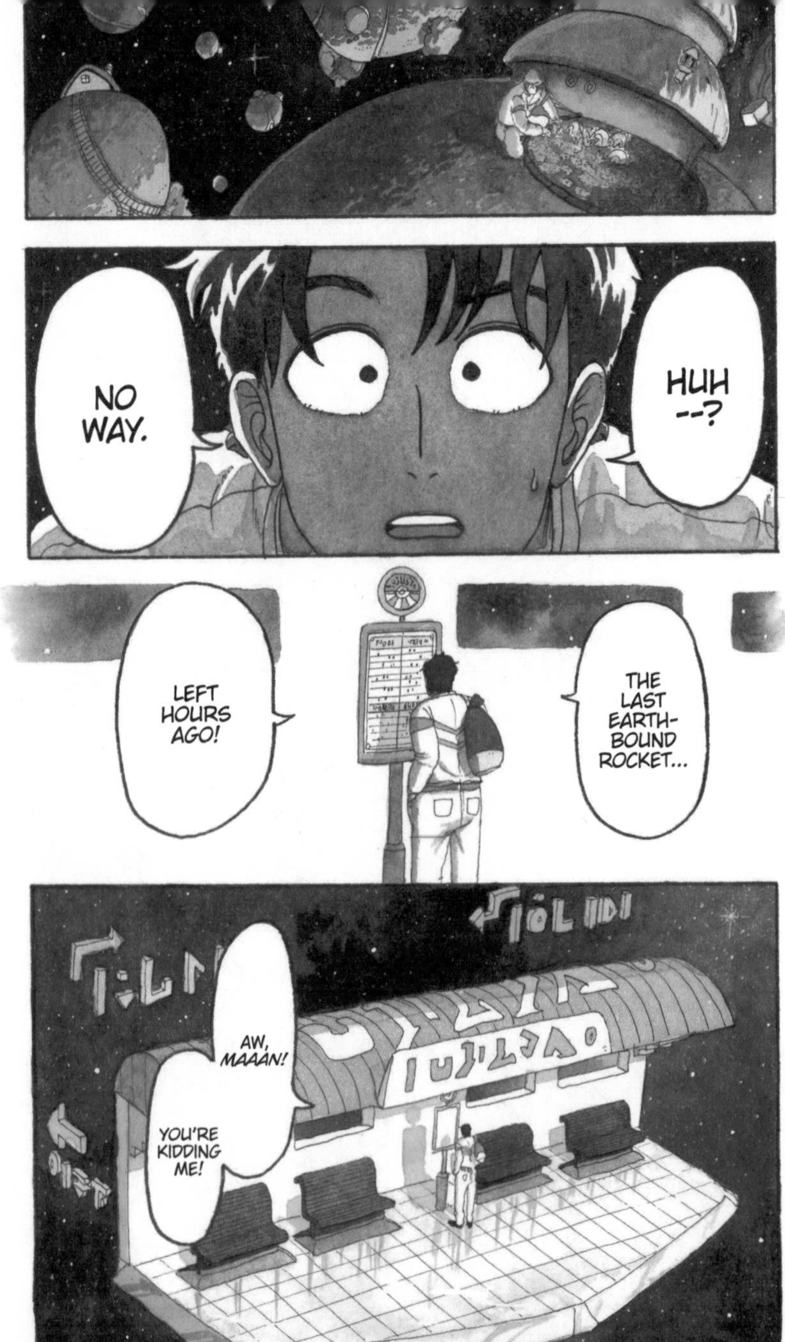
HUH --?
NO WAY.
THE LAST EARTH-BOUND ROCKET...
LEFT HOURS AGO!
AW, MAAAN!
YOU'RE KIDDING ME!

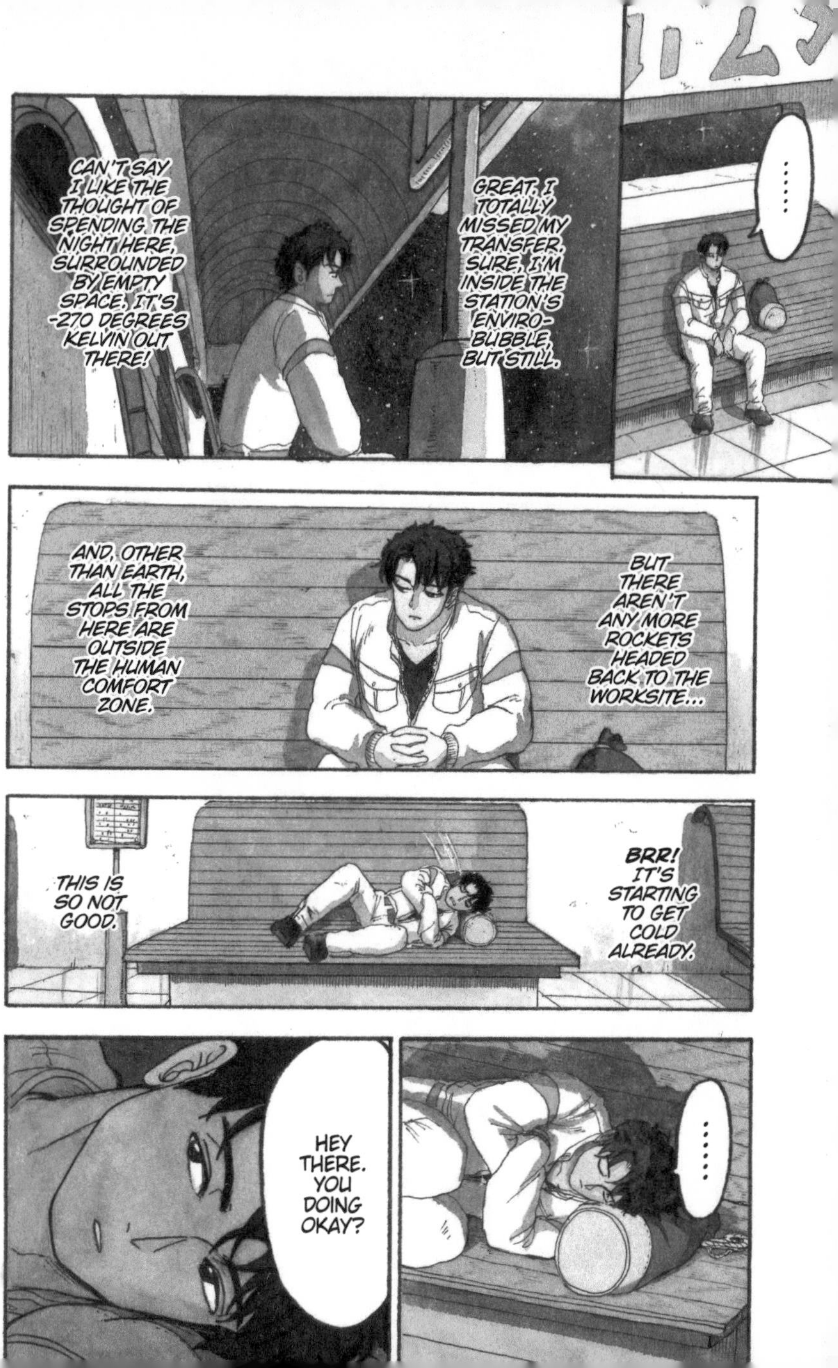
......
GREAT, I TOTALLY MISSED MY TRANSFER. SURE, I'M INSIDE THE STATION'S ENVIRO-BUBBLE, BUT STILL.
CAN'T SAY I LIKE THE THOUGHT OF SPENDING THE NIGHT HERE, SURROUNDED BY EMPTY SPACE. IT'S -270 DEGREES KELVIN OUT THERE!
BUT THERE AREN'T ANY MORE ROCKETS HEADED BACK TO THE WORKSITE...
AND, OTHER THAN EARTH, ALL THE STOPS FROM HERE ARE OUTSIDE THE HUMAN COMFORT ZONE.
BRR! IT'S STARTING TO GET COLD ALREADY.
THIS IS SO NOT GOOD.
......
HEY THERE. YOU DOING OKAY?

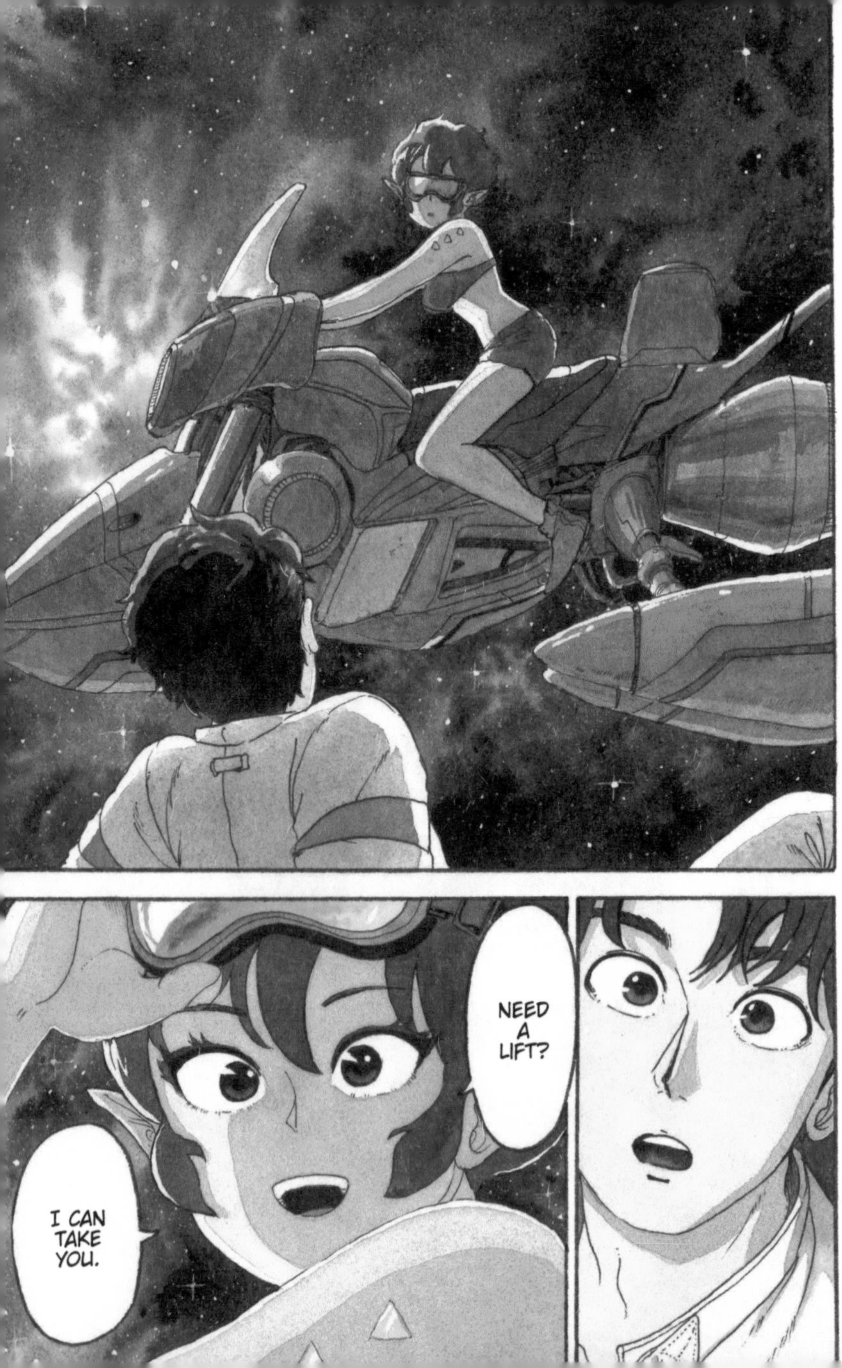
NEED A LIFT?
I CAN TAKE YOU.

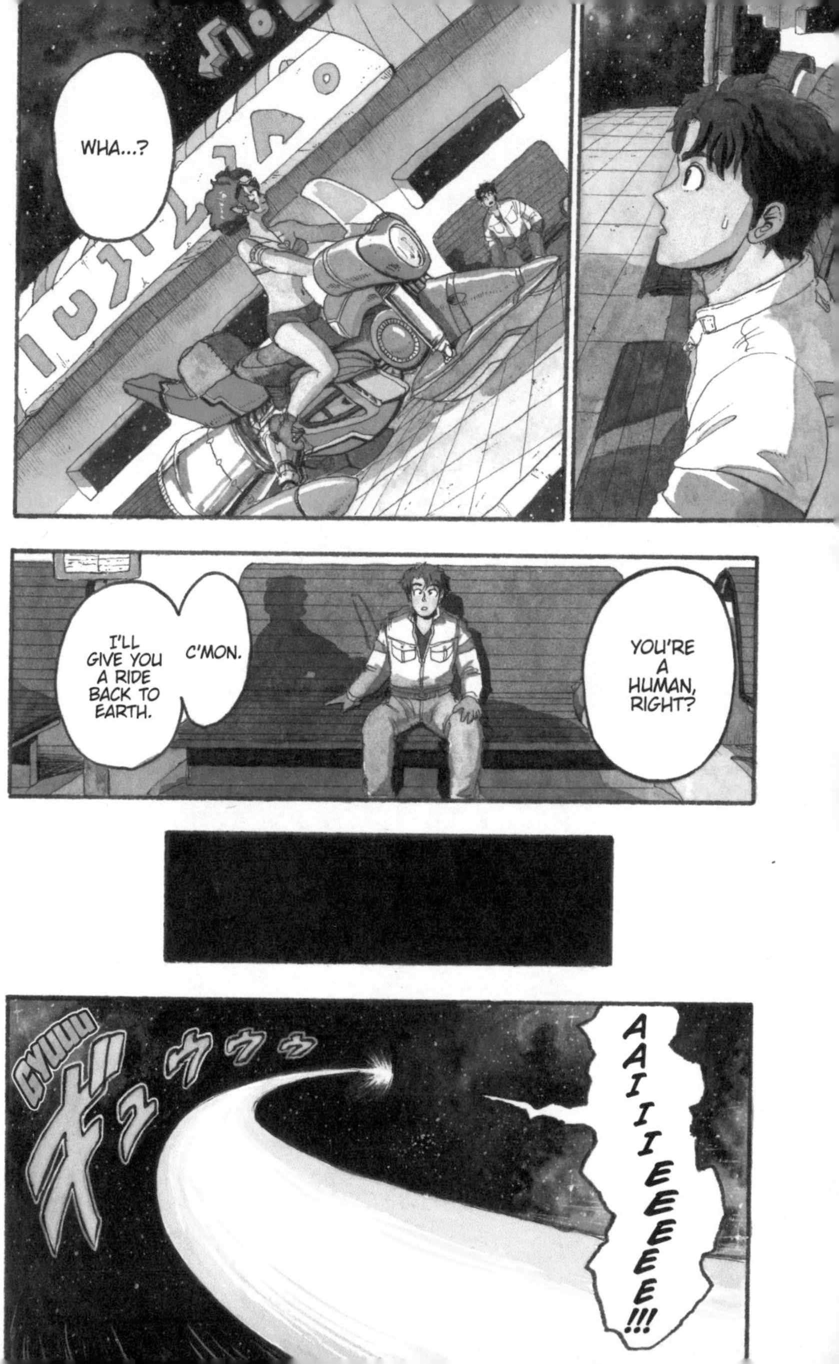
WHA...?
YOU'RE A HUMAN, RIGHT?
C'MON.
I'LL GIVE YOU A RIDE BACK TO EARTH.
AAIIIEEEEEE!!!
GYUUU
ギュウウウ

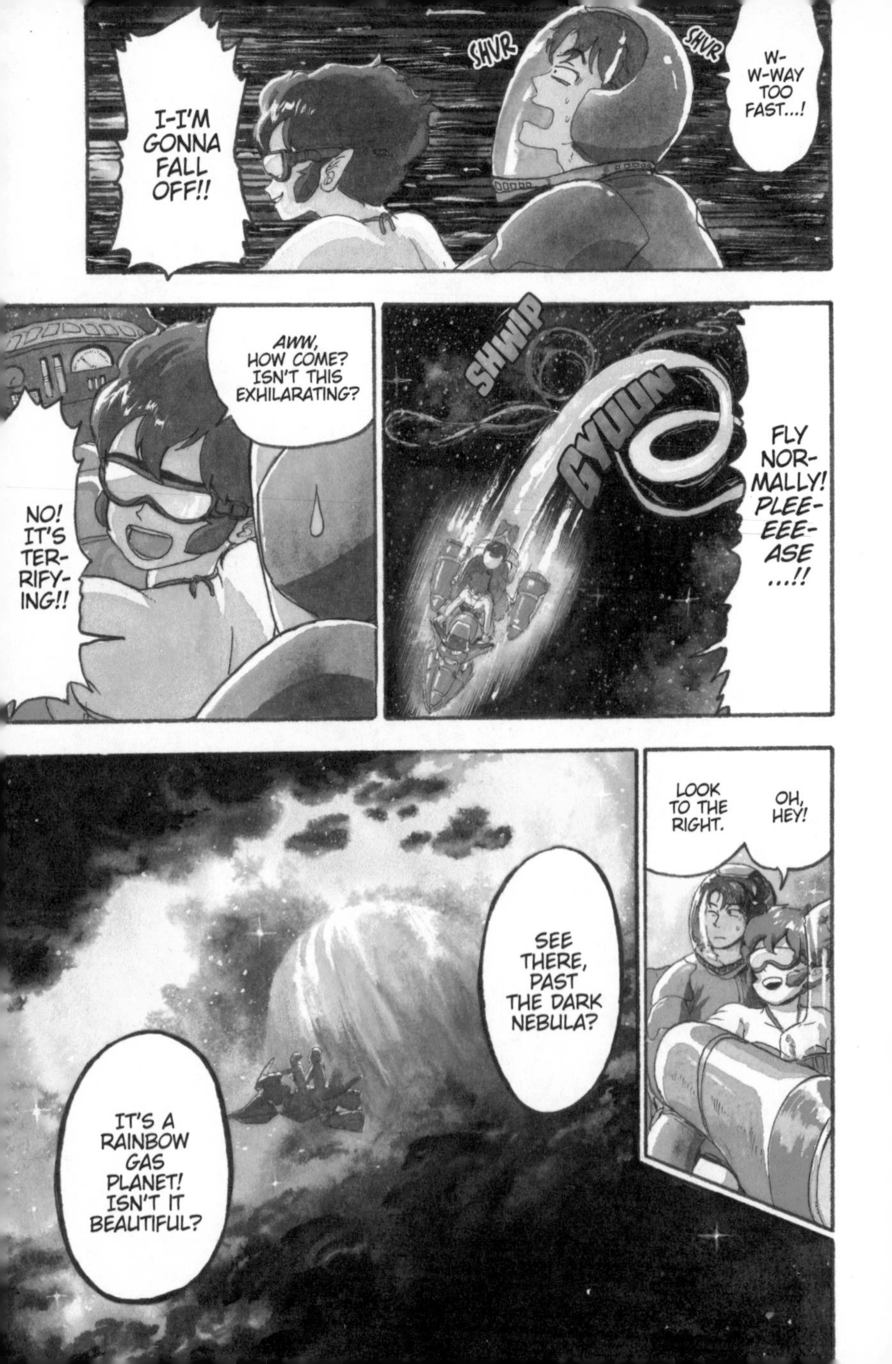
SHVR
W-W-WAY TOO FAST...!
SHVR
I-I'M GONNA FALL OFF!!
SHWIP
GYUUN
FLY NORMALLY! PLEEEEEASE...!!
AWW, HOW COME? ISN'T THIS EXHILARATING?
NO! IT'S TERRIFYING!!
OH, HEY!
LOOK TO THE RIGHT.
SEE THERE, PAST THE DARK NEBULA?
IT'S A RAINBOW GAS PLANET! ISN'T IT BEAUTIFUL?

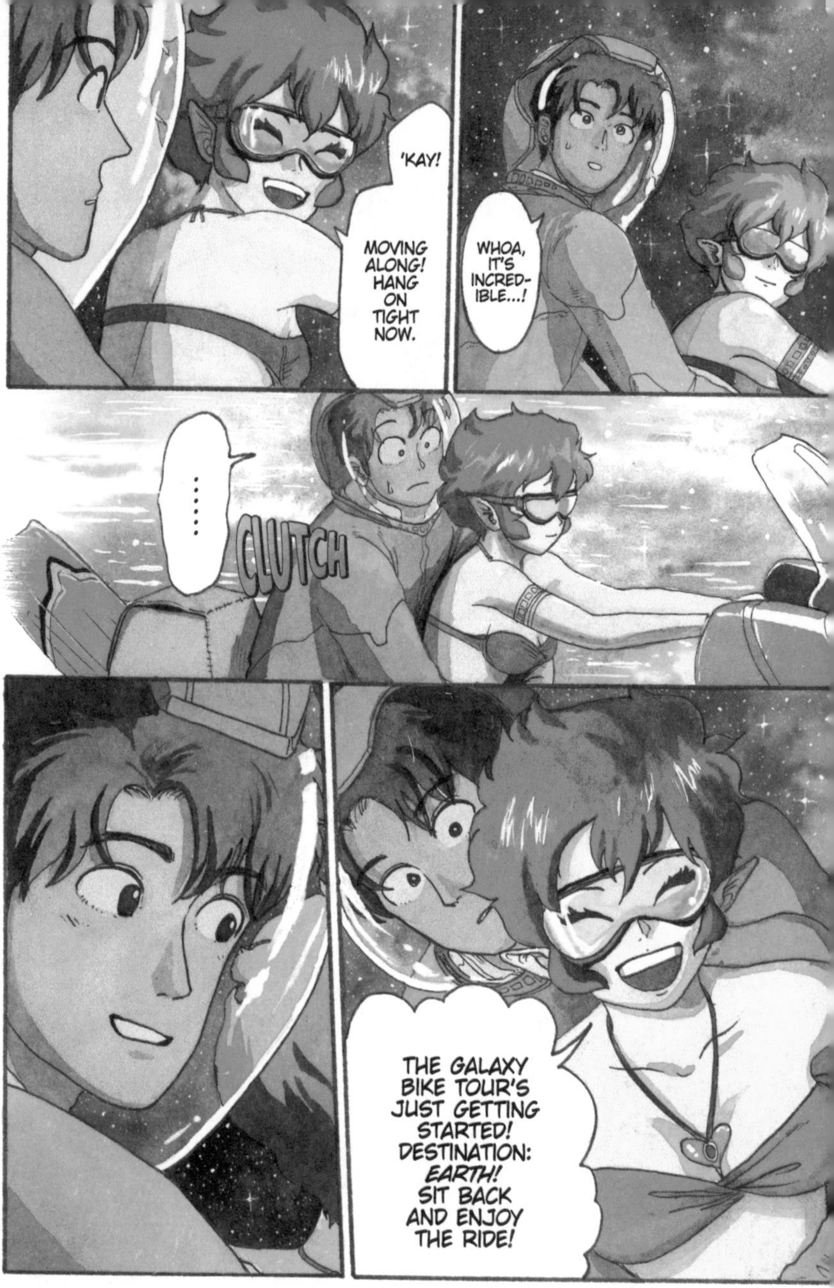
WHOA, IT'S INCREDIBLE...!
'KAY!
MOVING ALONG! HANG ON TIGHT NOW.
......
CLUTCH
THE GALAXY BIKE TOUR'S JUST GETTING STARTED! DESTINATION: *EARTH!* SIT BACK AND ENJOY THE RIDE!

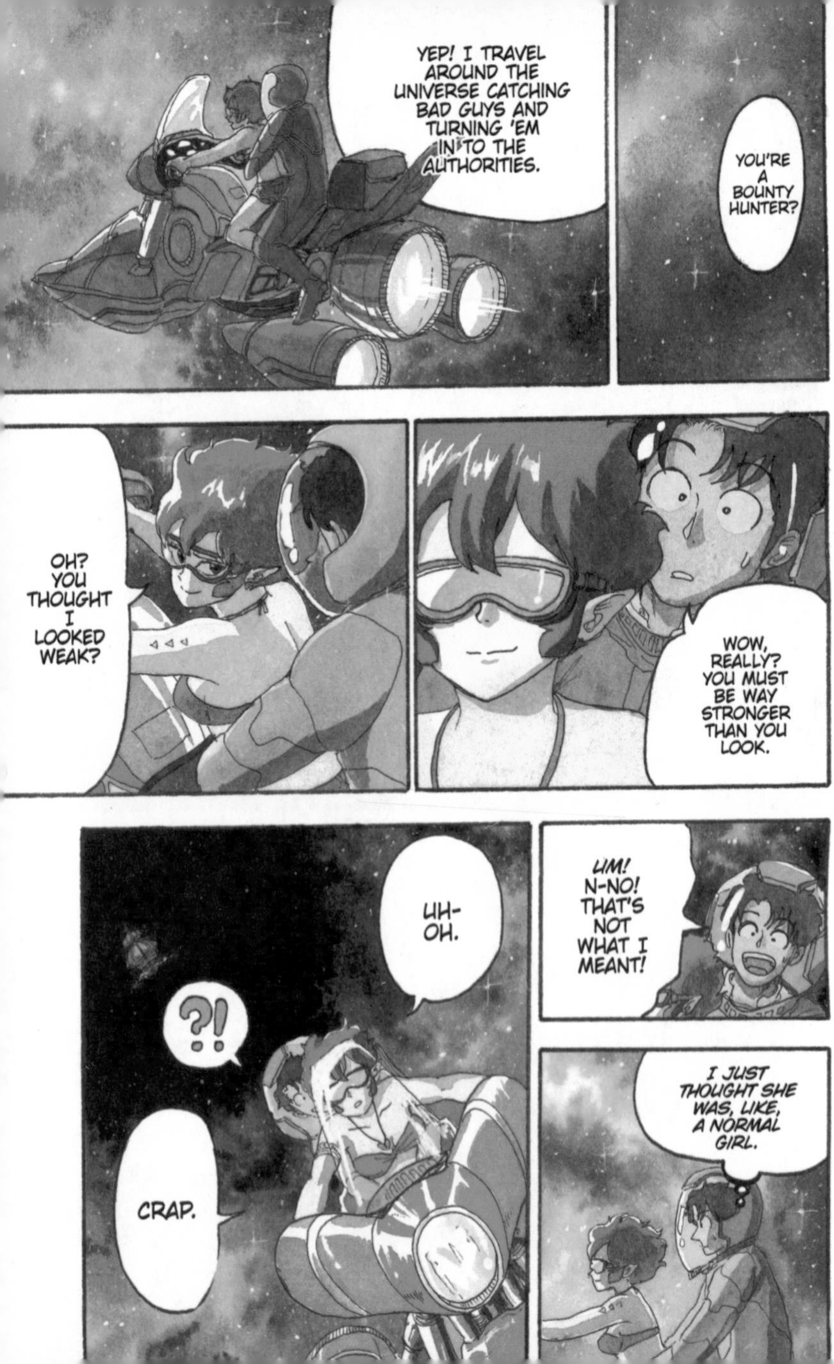
YOU'RE A BOUNTY HUNTER?
YEP! I TRAVEL AROUND THE UNIVERSE CATCHING BAD GUYS AND TURNING 'EM IN TO THE AUTHORITIES.
WOW, REALLY? YOU MUST BE WAY STRONGER THAN YOU LOOK.
OH? YOU THOUGHT I LOOKED WEAK?
UM! N-NO! THAT'S NOT WHAT I MEANT!
I JUST THOUGHT SHE WAS, LIKE, A NORMAL GIRL.
UH-OH.
?!
CRAP.

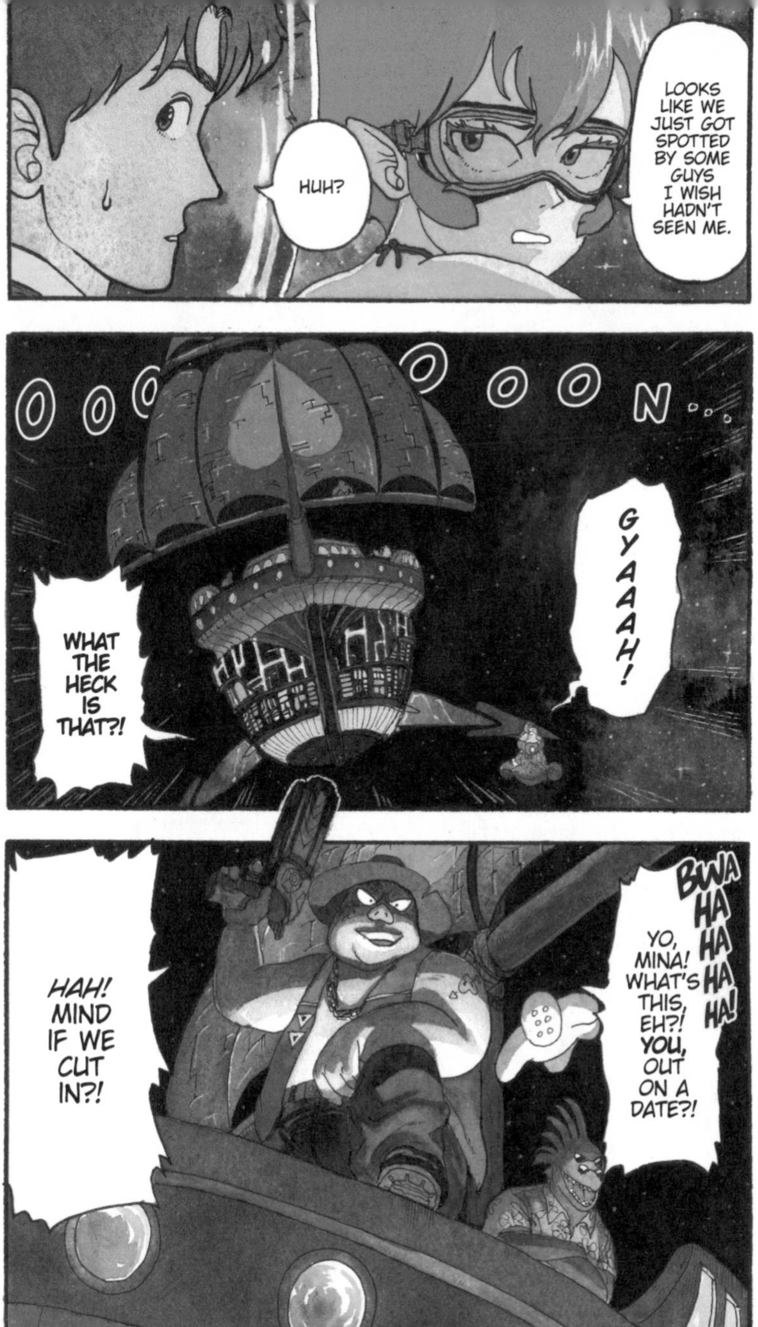
LOOKS LIKE WE JUST GOT SPOTTED BY SOME GUYS I WISH HADN'T SEEN ME.
HUH?
OOOOOOOON...
GYAAAAH!
WHAT THE HECK IS THAT?!
BWA HA HA HA HA HA!
YO, MINA! WHAT'S THIS, EH?! YOU, OUT ON A DATE?!
HAH! MIND IF WE CUT IN?!

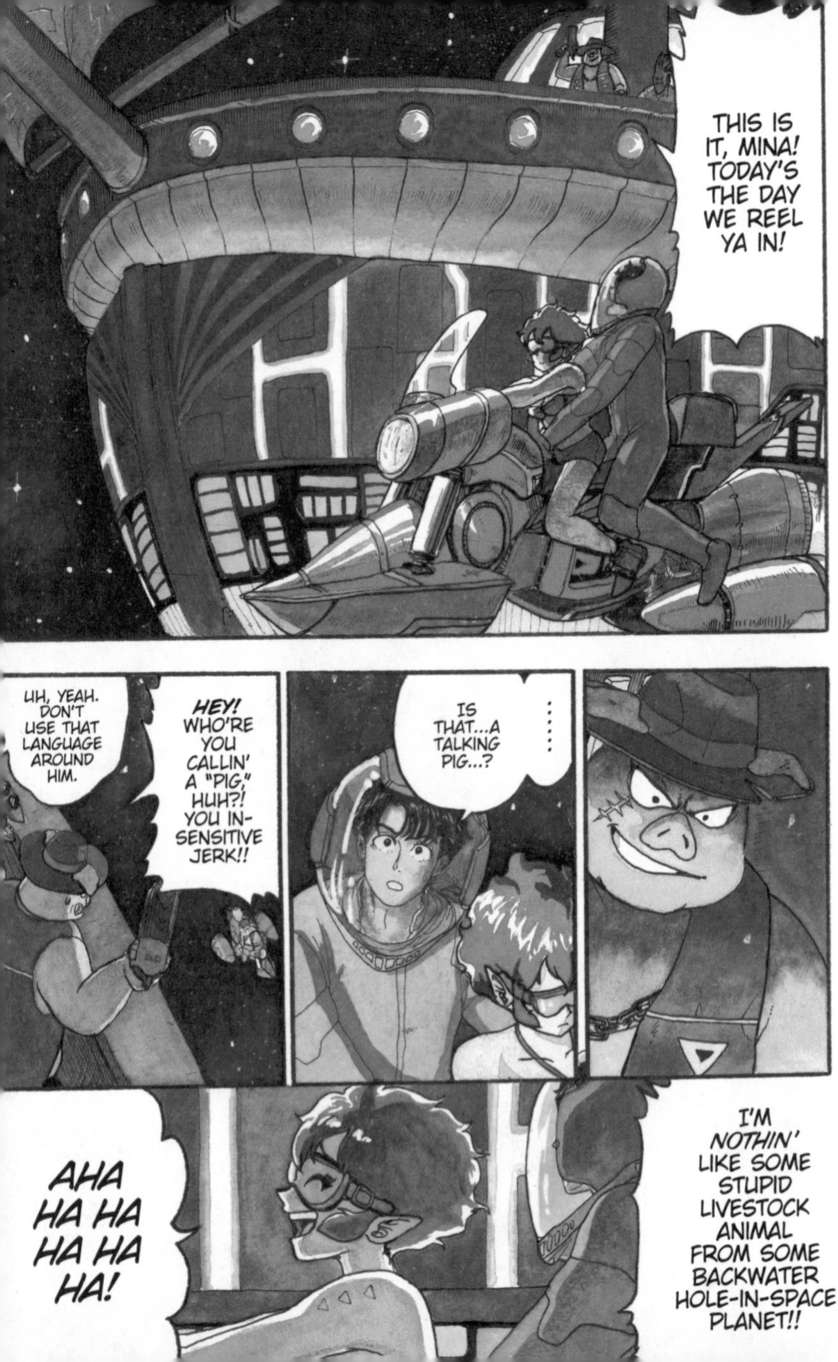
THIS IS IT, MINA! TODAY'S THE DAY WE REEL YA IN!
......
IS THAT...A TALKING PIG...?
HEY! WHO'RE YOU CALLIN' A "PIG," HUH?! YOU IN-SENSITIVE JERK!!
UH, YEAH. DON'T USE THAT LANGUAGE AROUND HIM.
I'M *NOTHIN'* LIKE SOME STUPID LIVESTOCK ANIMAL FROM SOME BACKWATER HOLE-IN-SPACE PLANET!!
AHA HA HA HA HA HA!

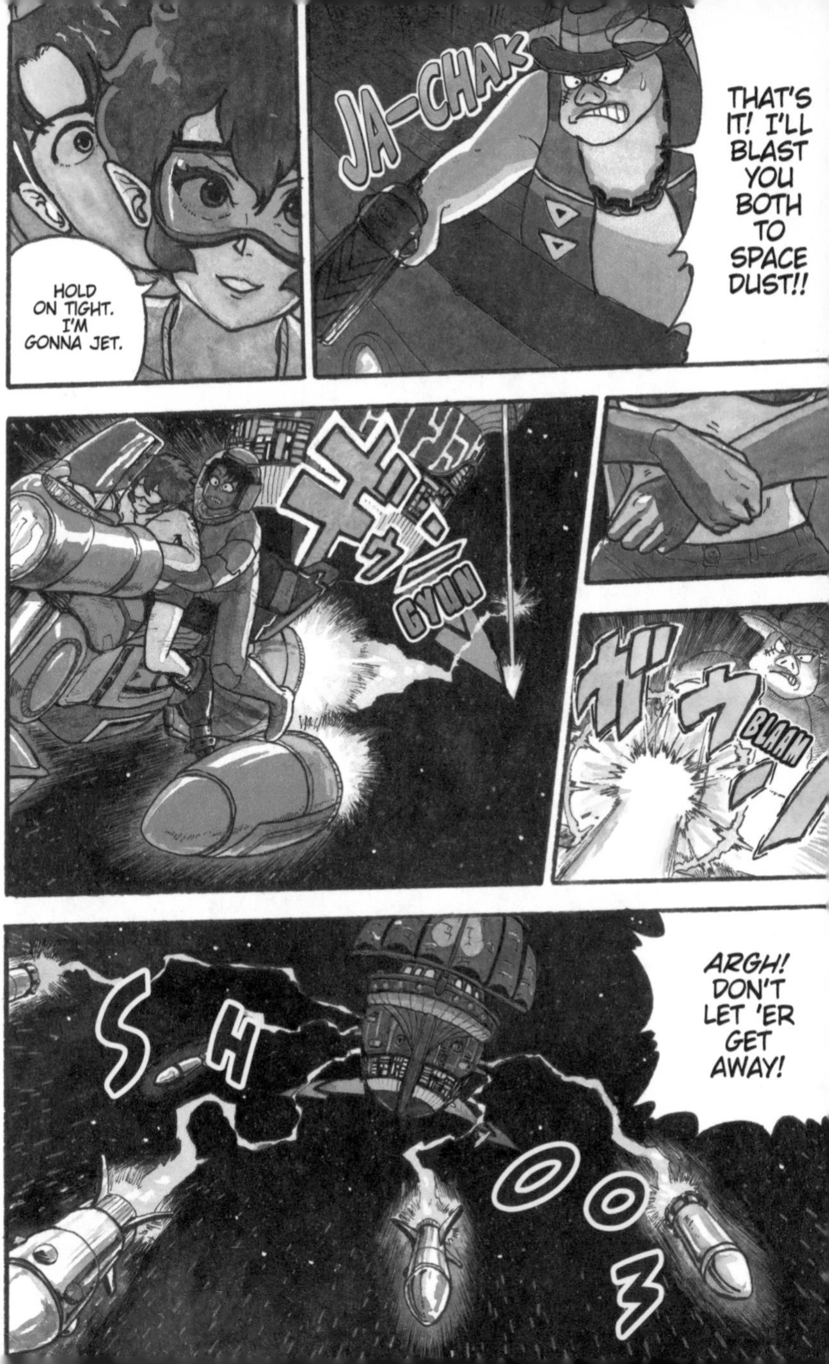
JA-CHAK
THAT'S IT! I'LL BLAST YOU BOTH TO SPACE DUST!!
HOLD ON TIGHT. I'M GONNA JET.
BLAAM
GYUN
ARGH! DON'T LET 'ER GET AWAY!
SHOOOM

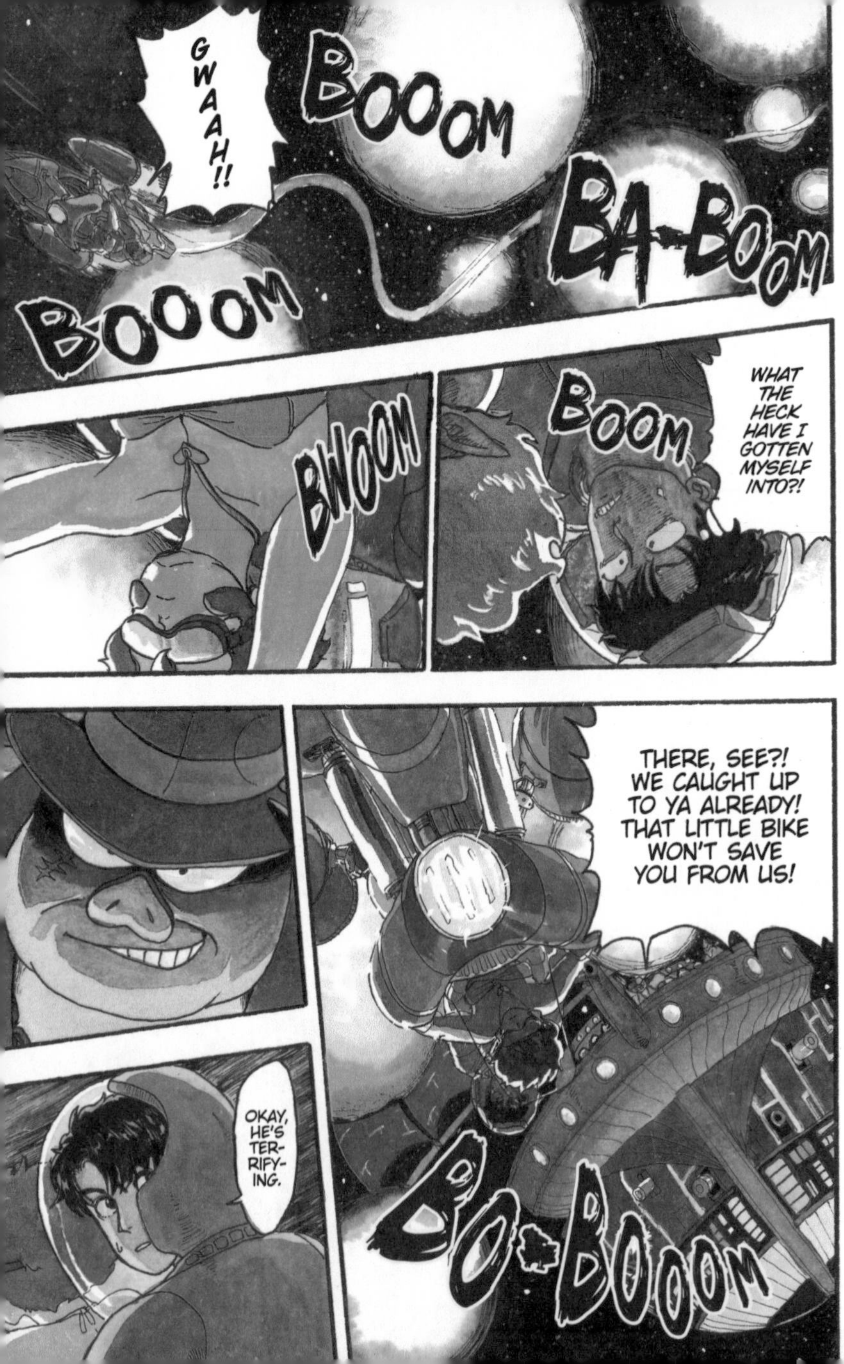
BOOOM
GWAAAH!!
BA-BOOM
BOOOM
WHAT THE HECK HAVE I GOTTEN MYSELF INTO?!
BOOM
BWOOM
THERE, SEE?! WE CAUGHT UP TO YA ALREADY! THAT LITTLE BIKE WON'T SAVE YOU FROM US!
BO-BOOOM
OKAY, HE'S TER-RIFY-ING.

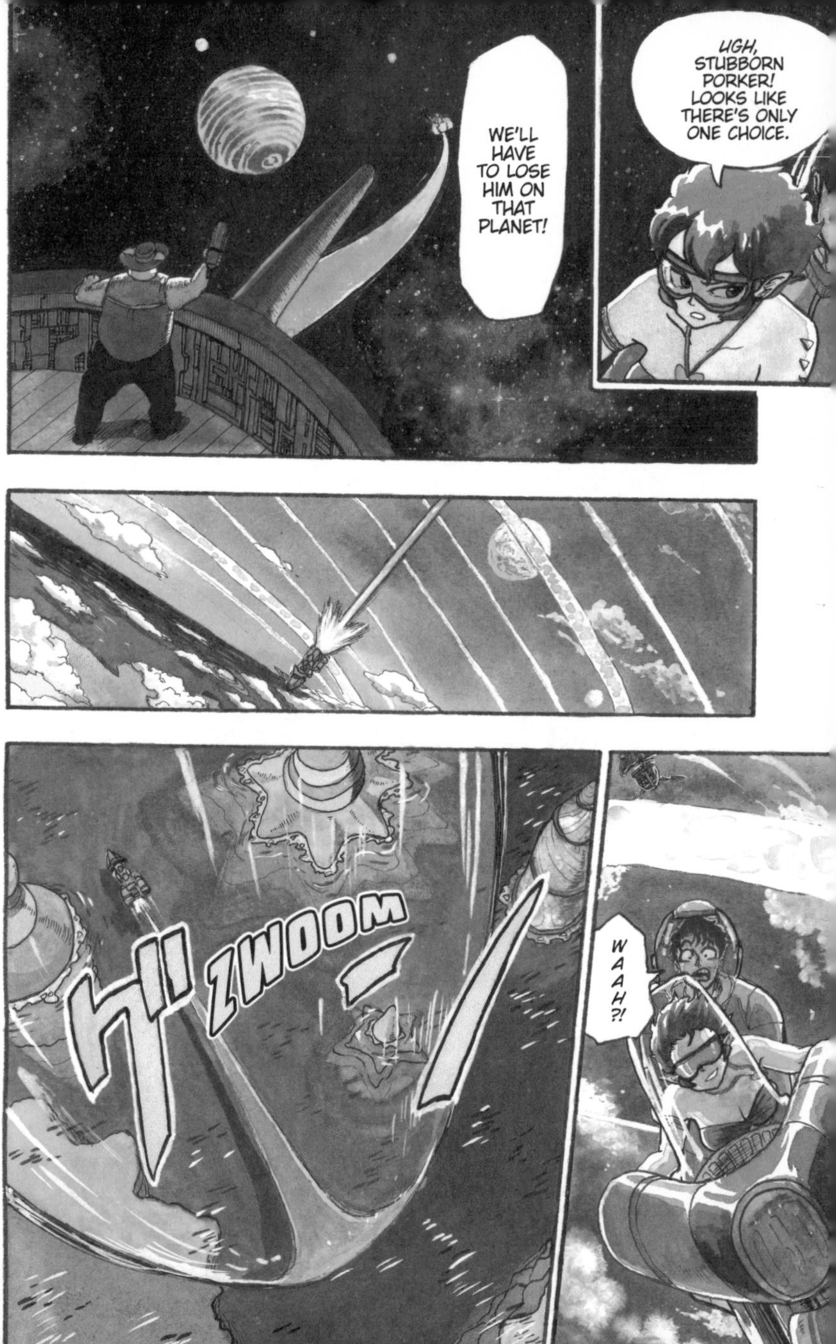
UGH, STUBBORN PORKER! LOOKS LIKE THERE'S ONLY ONE CHOICE.
WE'LL HAVE TO LOSE HIM ON THAT PLANET!
WAAAH?!
ZWOOM

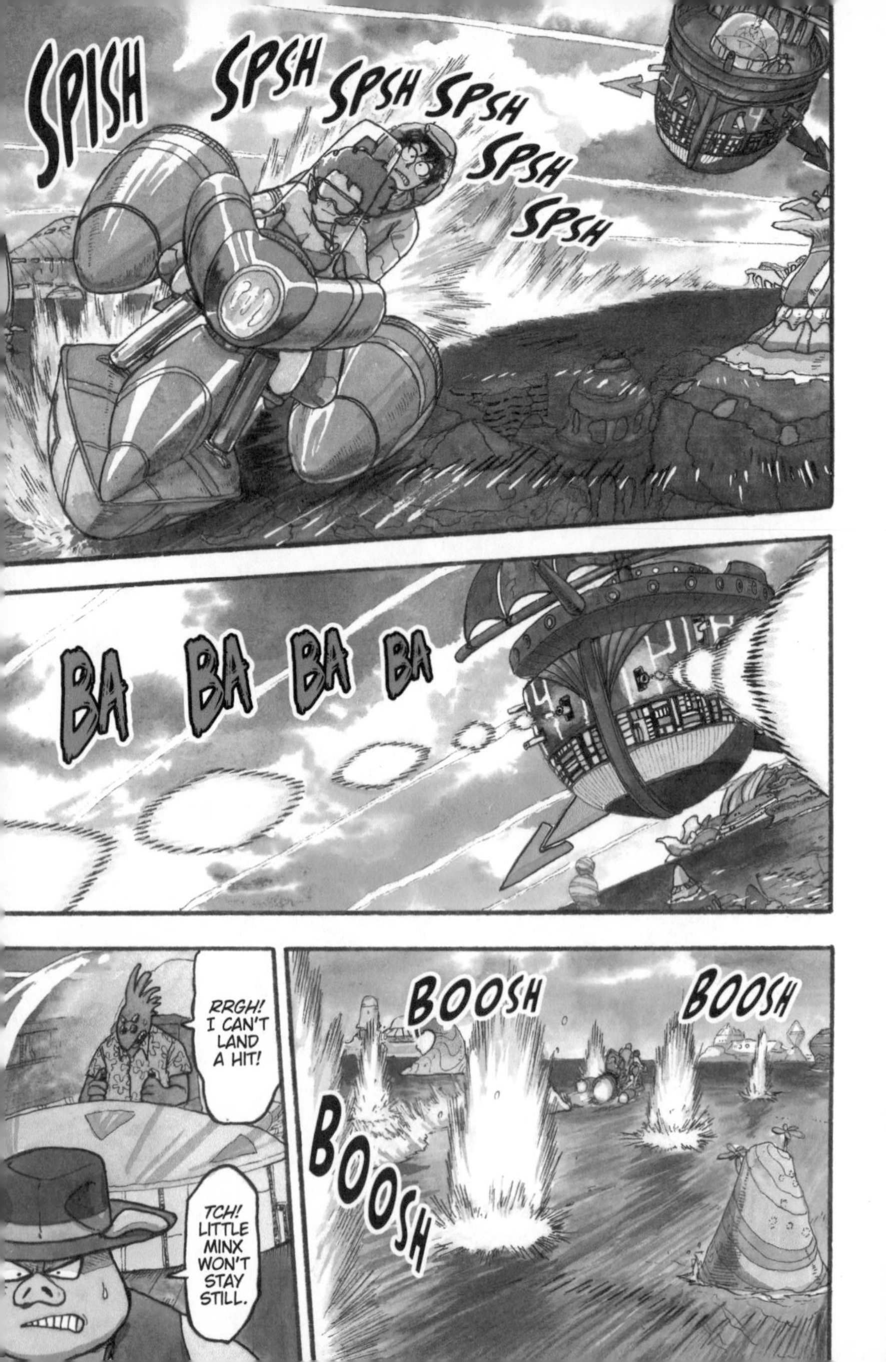
SPISH SPSH SPSH SPSH SPSH SPSH
BA BA BA BA
BOOSH
BOOSH
BOOSH
RRGH! I CAN'T LAND A HIT!
TCH! LITTLE MINX WON'T STAY STILL.

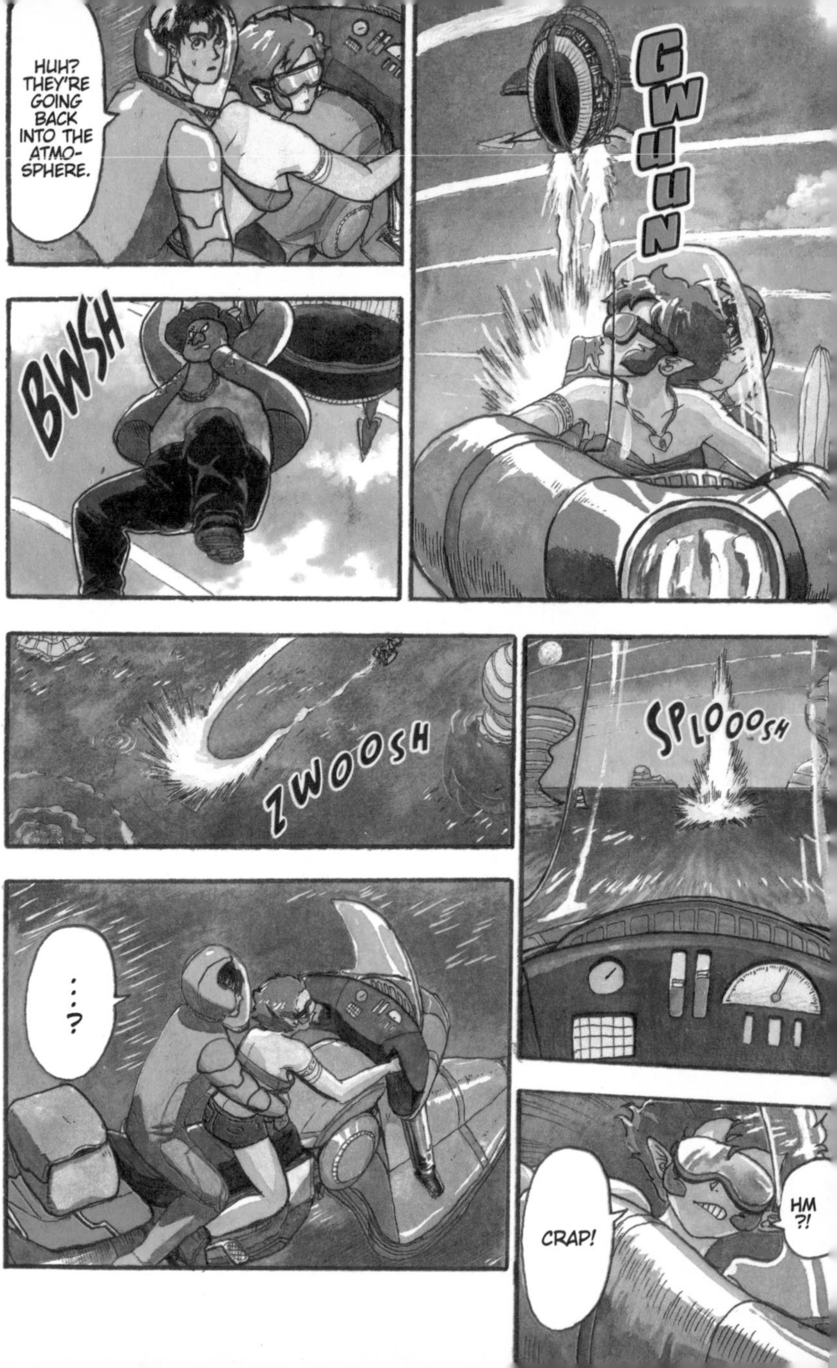
GWUUN
HUH? THEY'RE GOING BACK INTO THE ATMOSPHERE.
BWSH
SPLOOOSH
ZWOOSH
HM ?!
CRAP!
...?

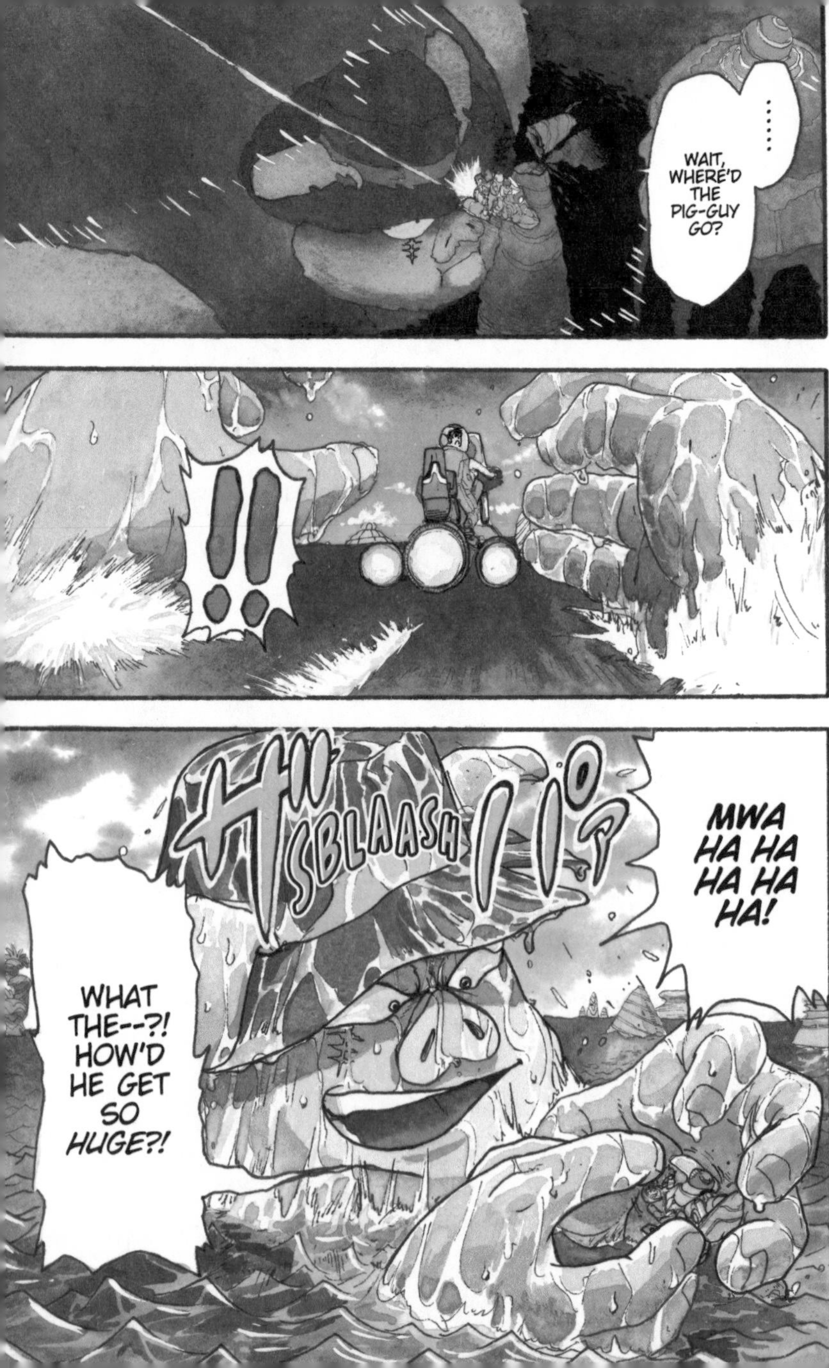
......
WAIT, WHERE'D THE PIG-GUY GO?
!!
SBLAASH
MWA HA HA HA HA HA!
WHAT THE--?! HOW'D HE GET SO HUGE?!

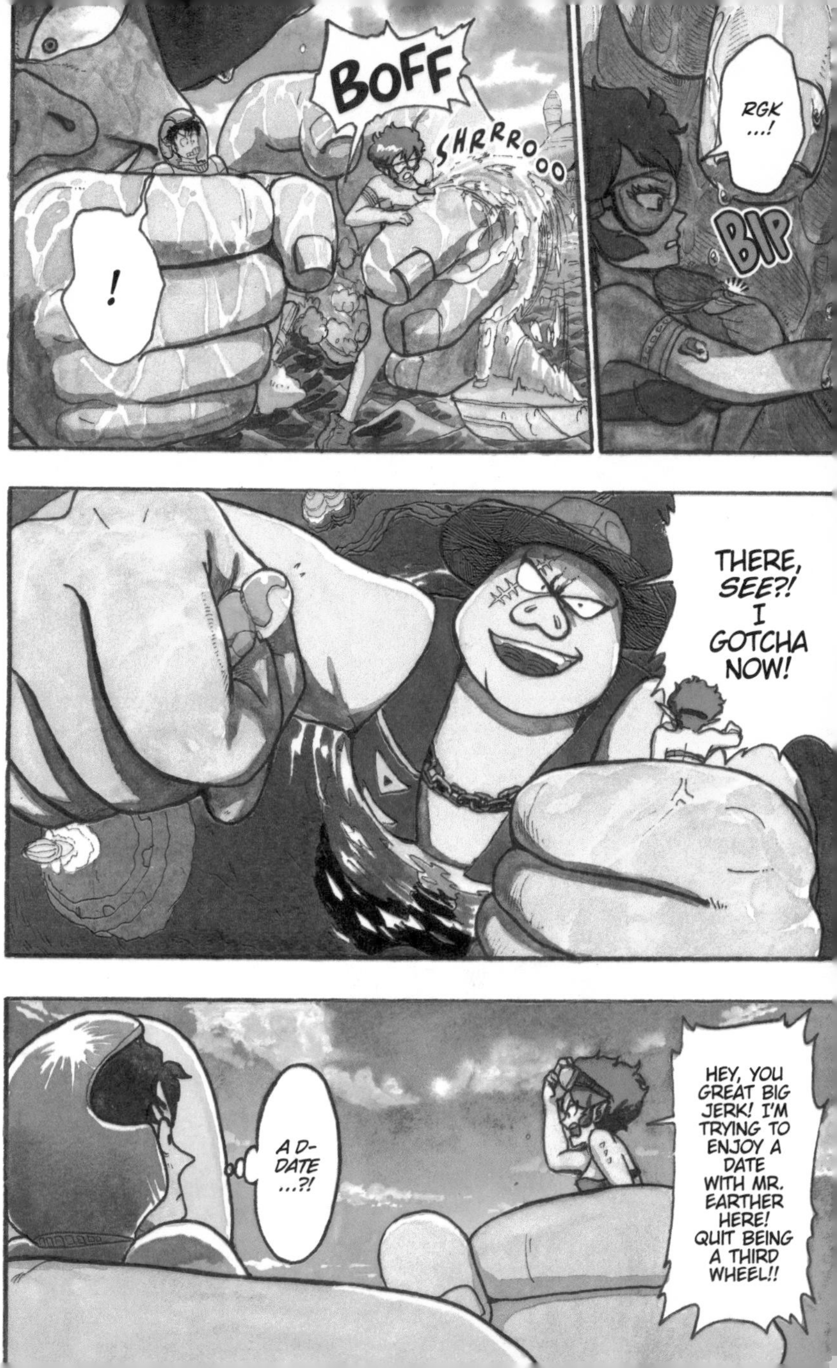
RGK ...!
BIP
BOFF
SHRRROOO
!
THERE, SEE?! I GOTCHA NOW!
HEY, YOU GREAT BIG JERK! I'M TRYING TO ENJOY A DATE WITH MR. EARTHER HERE! QUIT BEING A THIRD WHEEL!!
A D-DATE ...?!

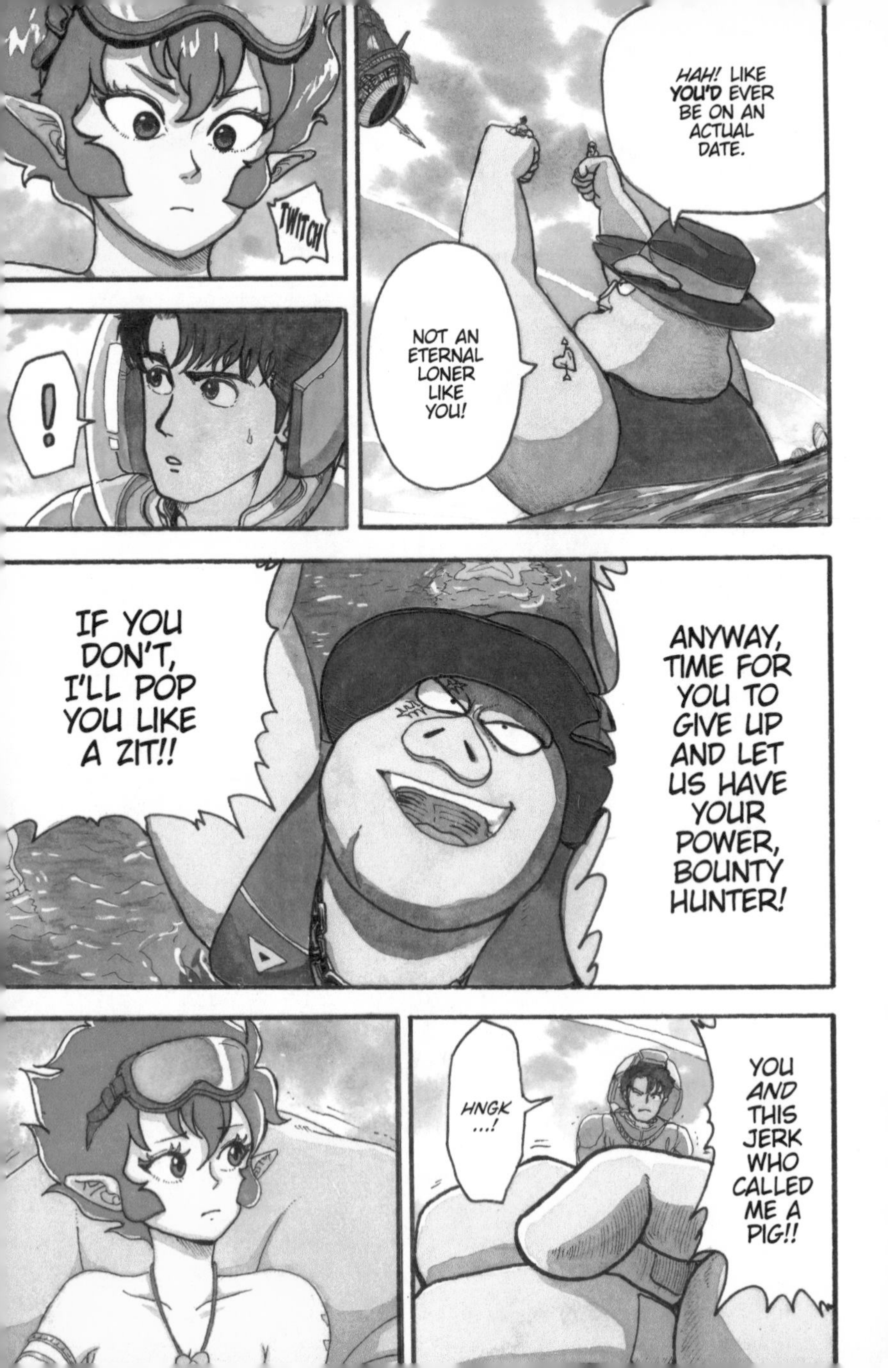
HAH! LIKE YOU'D EVER BE ON AN ACTUAL DATE.
NOT AN ETERNAL LONER LIKE YOU!
TWITCH
!
ANYWAY, TIME FOR YOU TO GIVE UP AND LET US HAVE YOUR POWER, BOUNTY HUNTER!
IF YOU DON'T, I'LL POP YOU LIKE A ZIT!!
YOU AND THIS JERK WHO CALLED ME A PIG!!
HNGK ...!

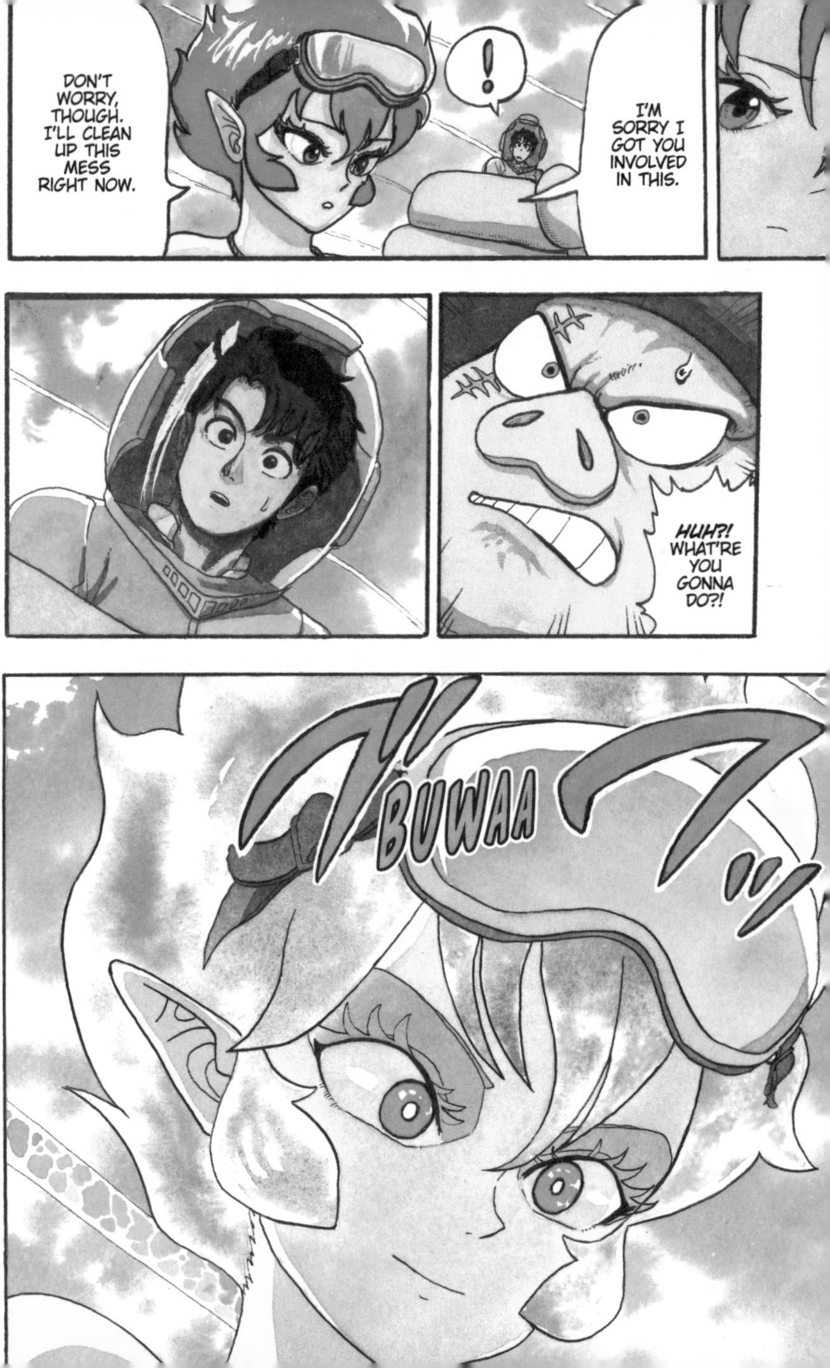
I'M SORRY I GOT YOU INVOLVED IN THIS.
!
DON'T WORRY, THOUGH. I'LL CLEAN UP THIS MESS RIGHT NOW.
HUH?! WHAT'RE YOU GONNA DO?!
BUWAA

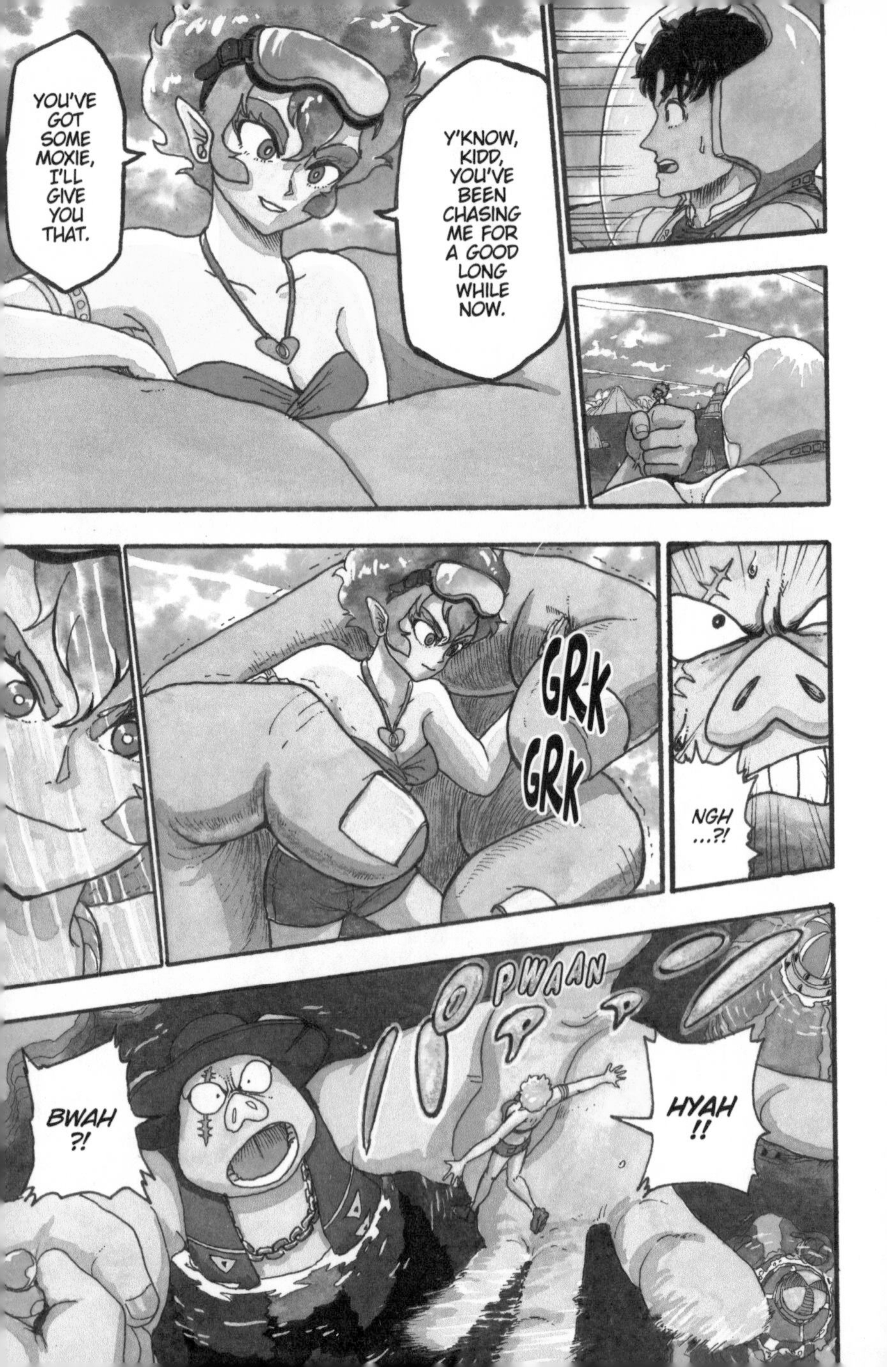
Y'KNOW, KIDD, YOU'VE BEEN CHASING ME FOR A GOOD LONG WHILE NOW.
YOU'VE GOT SOME MOXIE, I'LL GIVE YOU THAT.
NGH ...?!
GRK GRK
HYAH !!
PWAAN
BWAH ?!

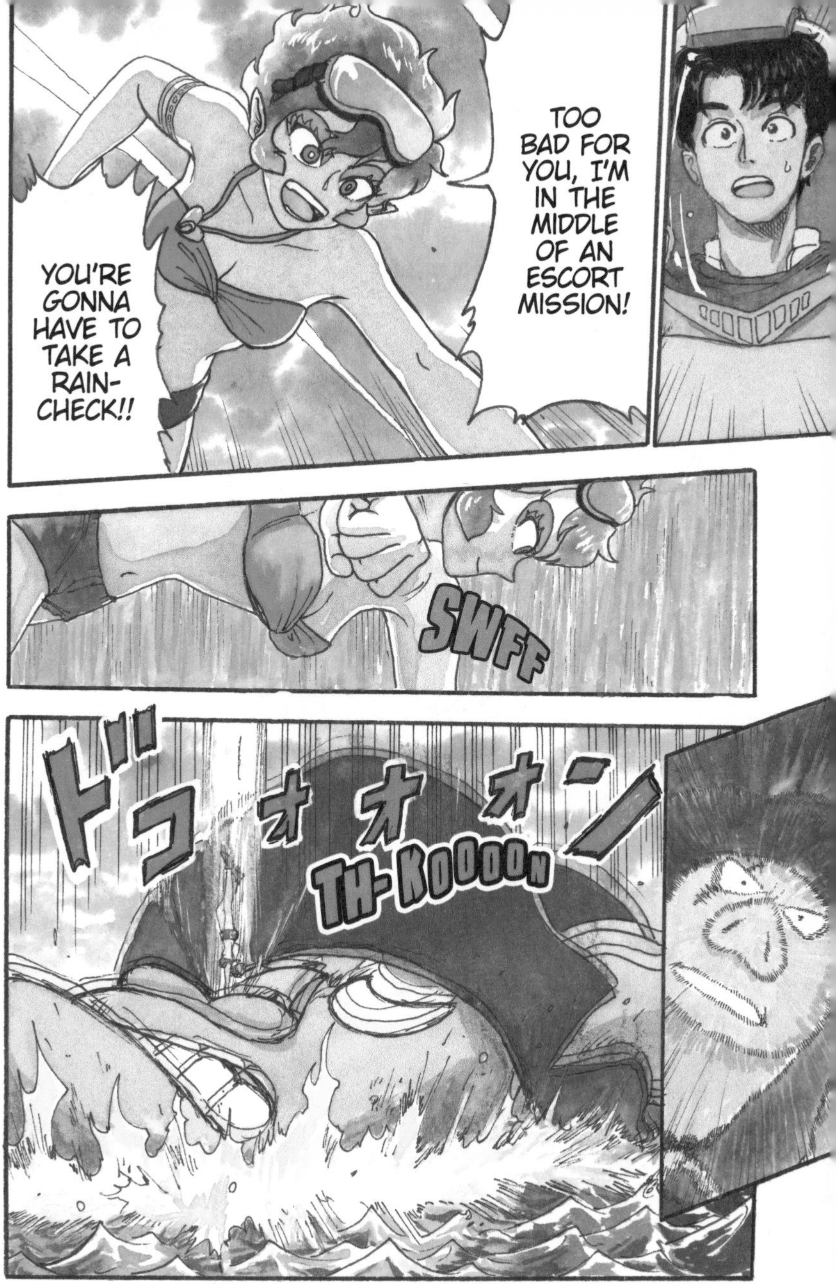
TOO BAD FOR YOU, I'M IN THE MIDDLE OF AN ESCORT MISSION!
YOU'RE GONNA HAVE TO TAKE A RAIN-CHECK!!
SWFF
ドコォオオン
TH-KOOOON

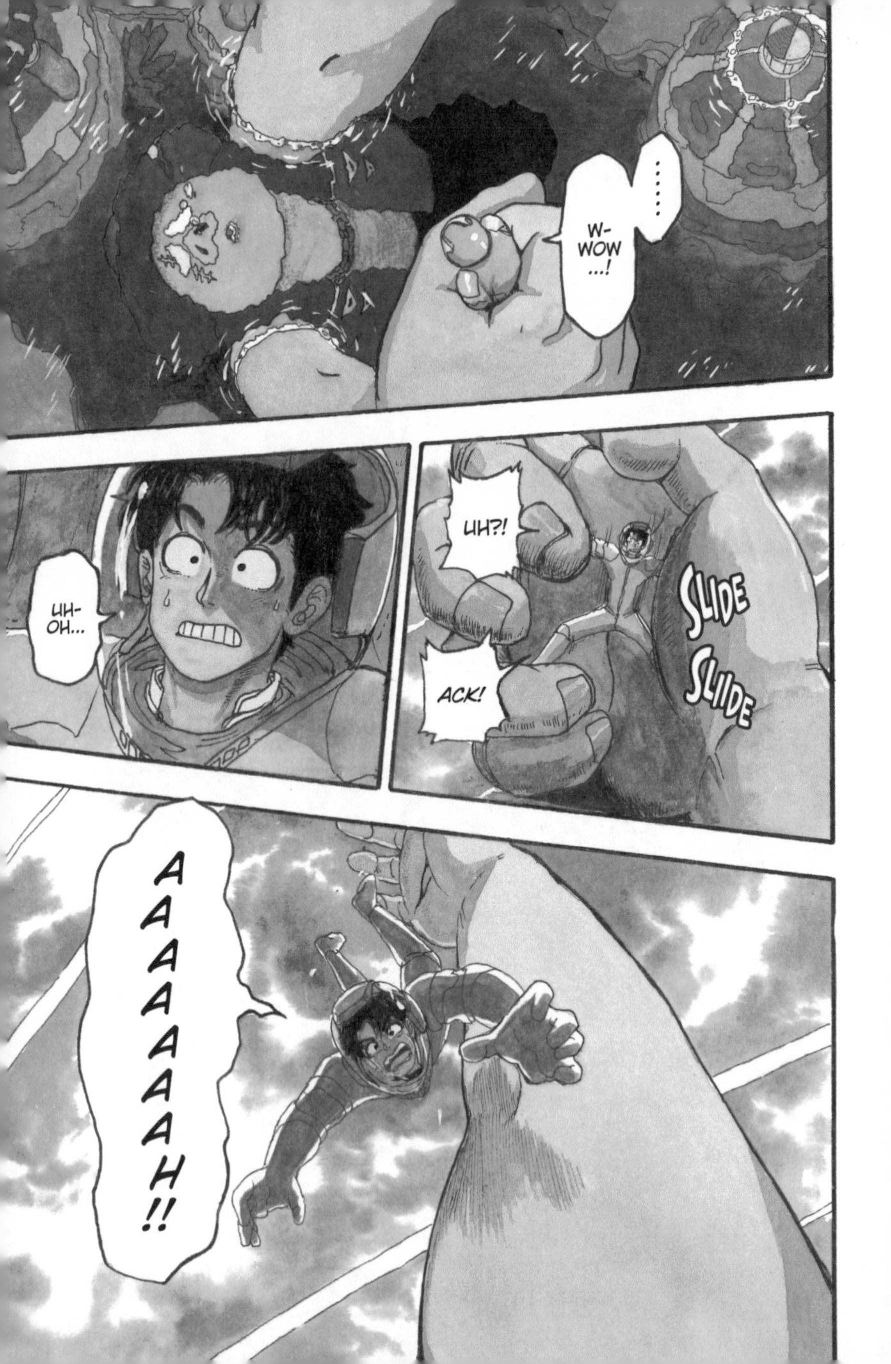
......
W-WOW ...!
UH?!
SLIDE
SLIIDE
ACK!
UH-OH...
AAAAAAAH!!

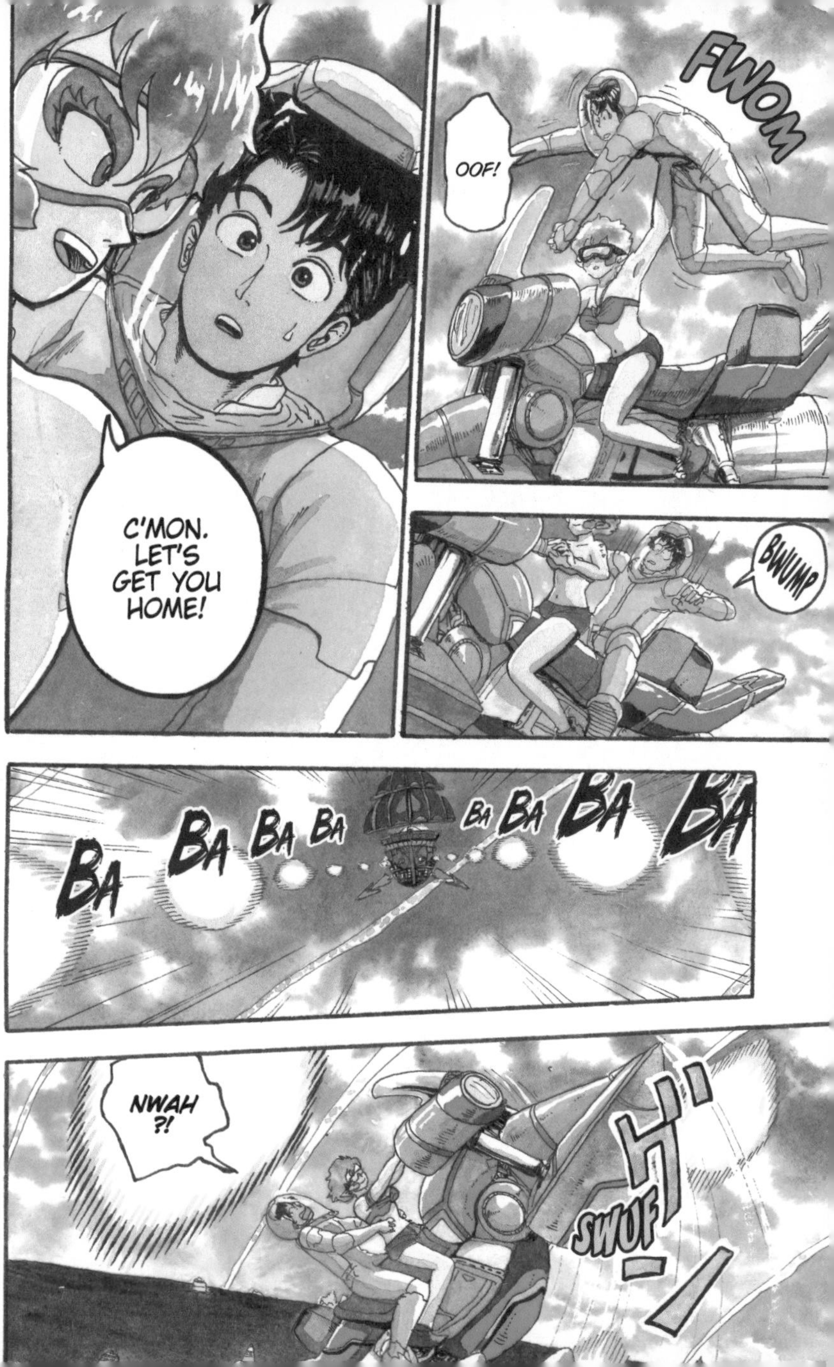
FWOM
OOF!
BWUMP
C'MON. LET'S GET YOU HOME!
BA BA BA BA BA BA BA BA
NWAH ?!
SWUF

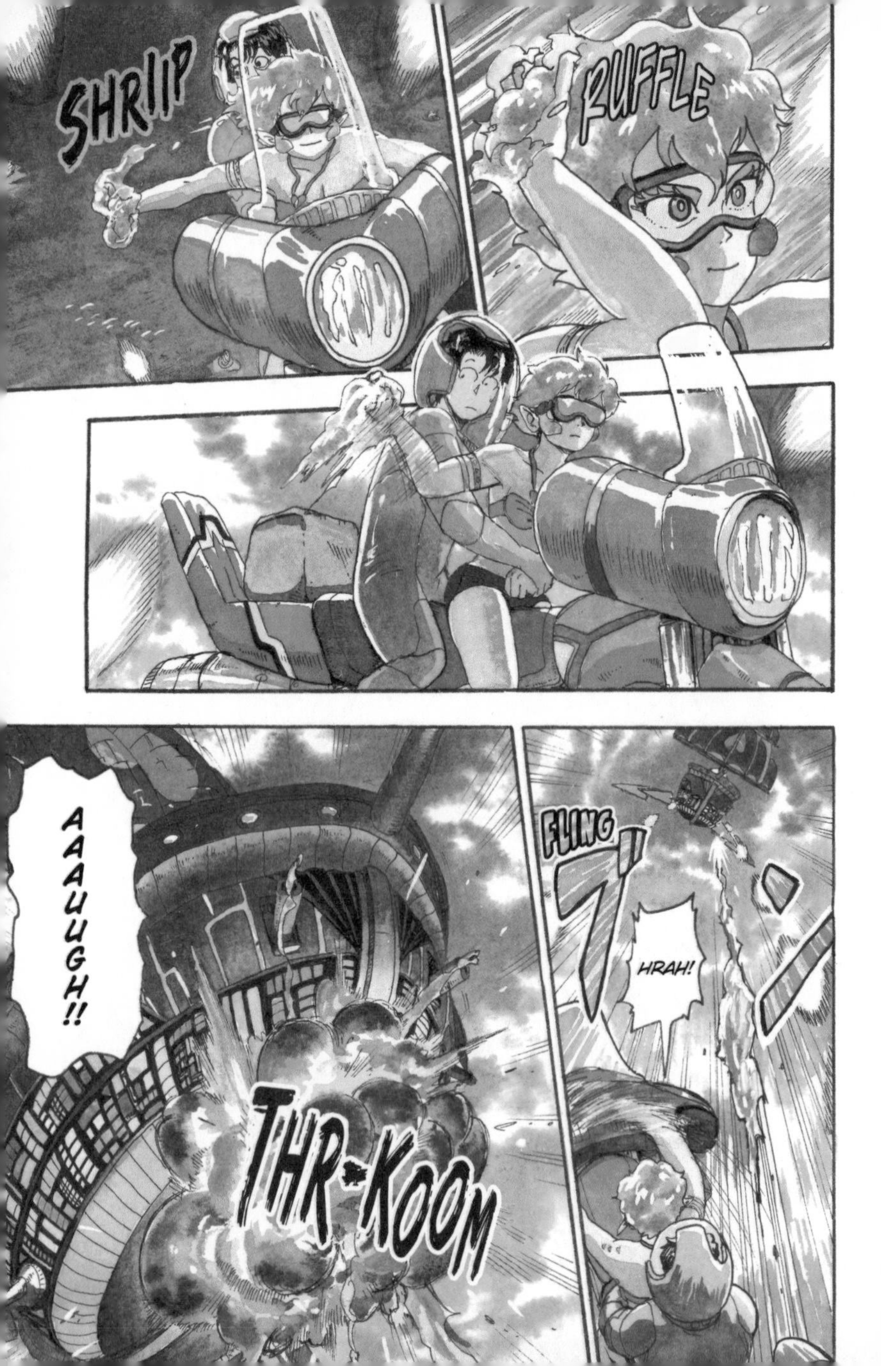
RUFFLE
SHRIIP
FLING
HRAH!
AAAUUGH!!
THR-KOOM

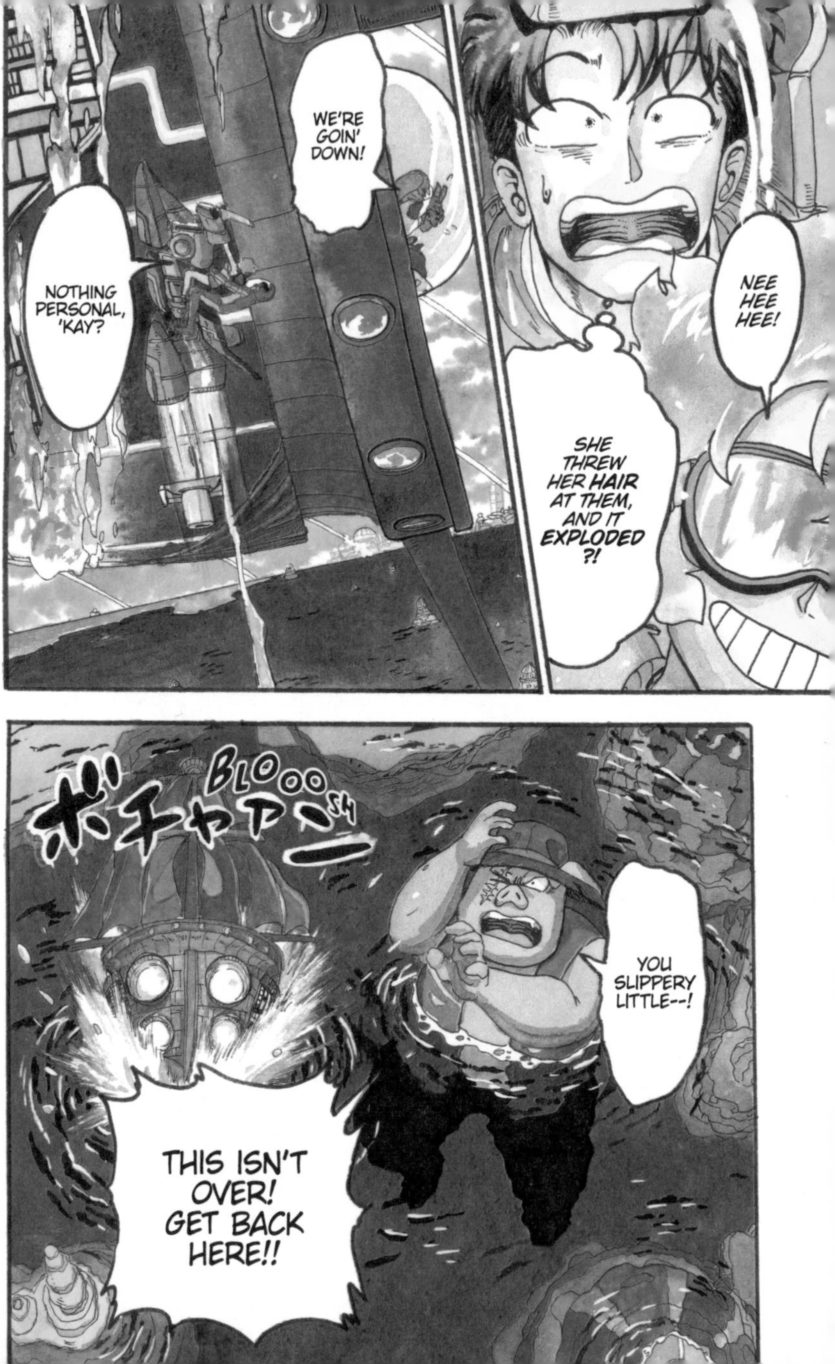
NEE HEE HEE!
SHE THREW HER HAIR AT THEM, AND IT EXPLODED?!
WE'RE GOIN' DOWN!
NOTHING PERSONAL, 'KAY?
ボチャァー
BLOOOOSH
YOU SLIPPERY LITTLE--!
THIS ISN'T OVER! GET BACK HERE!!

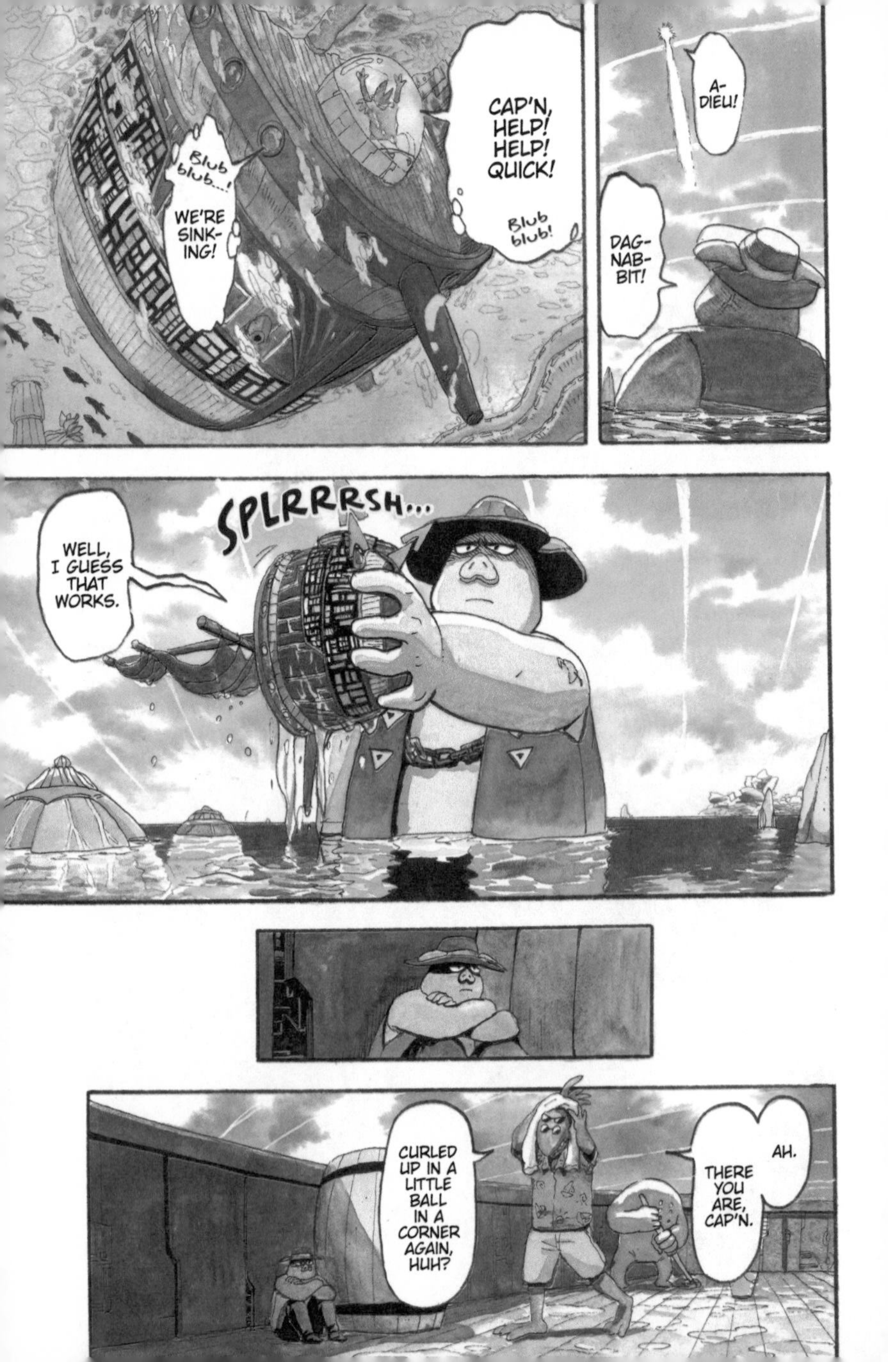
A-DIEU!
DAG-NAB-BIT!
CAP'N, HELP! HELP! QUICK!
Blub blub!
Blub blub...! WE'RE SINK-ING!
SPLRRRSH...
WELL, I GUESS THAT WORKS.
AH. THERE YOU ARE, CAP'N.
CURLED UP IN A LITTLE BALL IN A CORNER AGAIN, HUH?

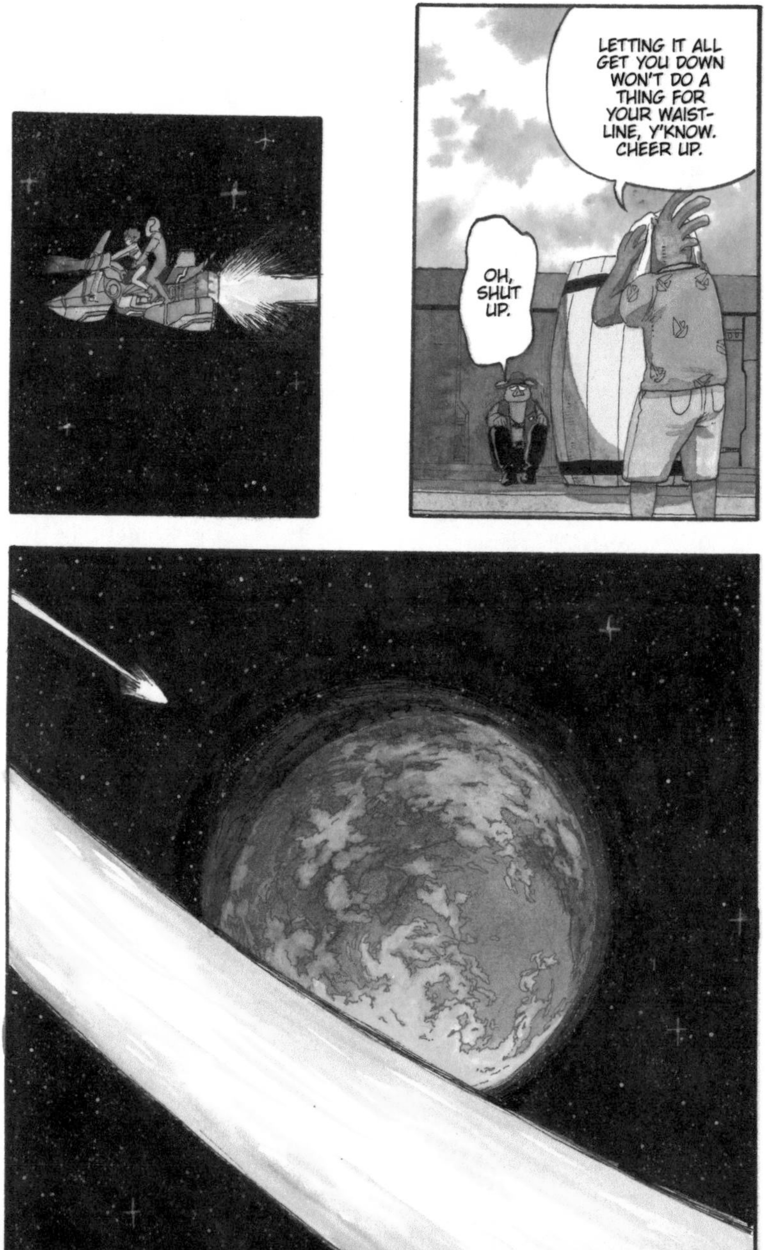
LETTING IT ALL GET YOU DOWN WON'T DO A THING FOR YOUR WAIST-LINE, Y'KNOW. CHEER UP.
OH, SHUT UP.

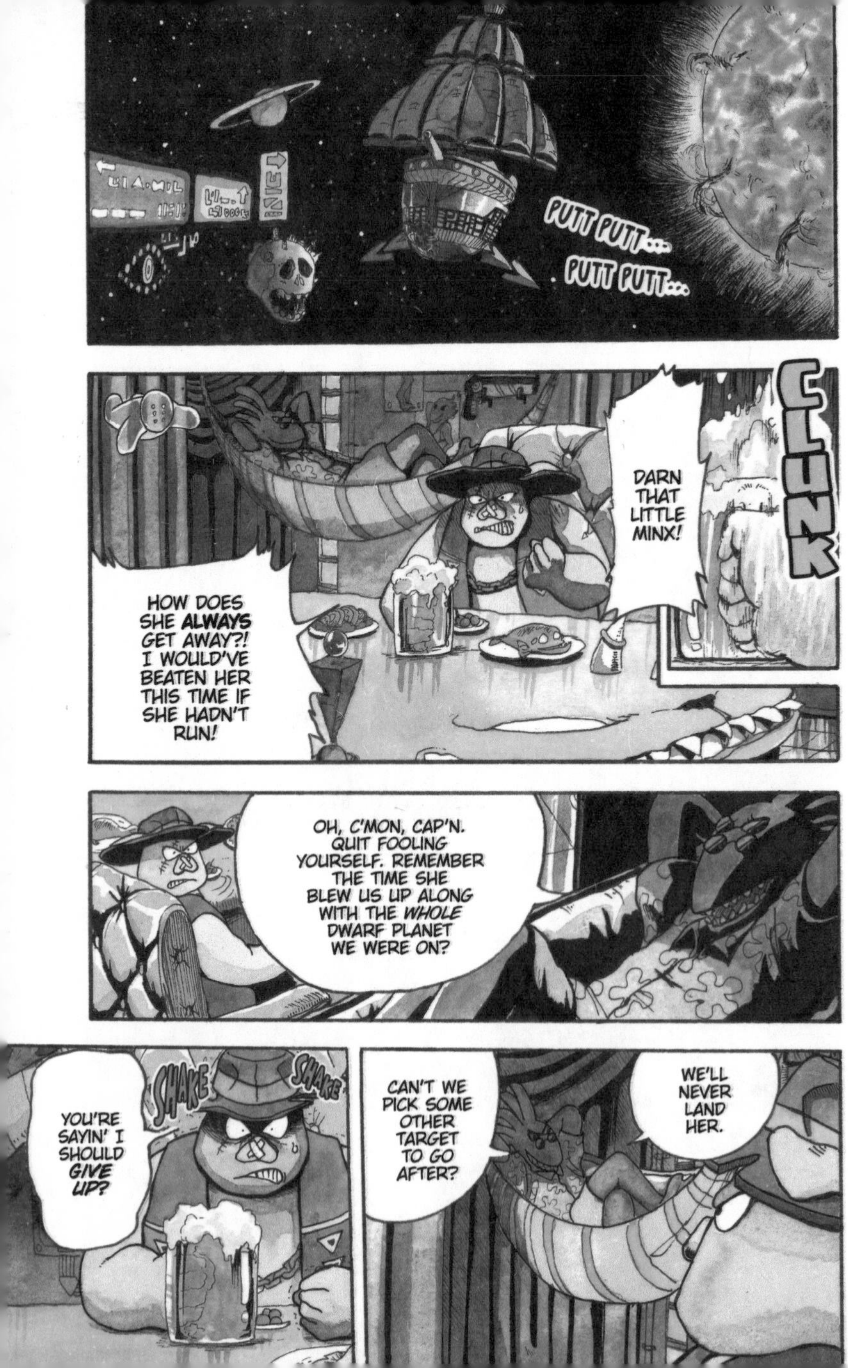
PUTT PUTT...
PUTT PUTT...
CLUNK
DARN THAT LITTLE MINX!
HOW DOES SHE **ALWAYS** GET AWAY?! I WOULD'VE BEATEN HER THIS TIME IF SHE HADN'T RUN!
OH, C'MON, CAP'N. QUIT FOOLING YOURSELF. REMEMBER THE TIME SHE BLEW US UP ALONG WITH THE *WHOLE* DWARF PLANET WE WERE ON?
WE'LL NEVER LAND HER.
CAN'T WE PICK SOME OTHER TARGET TO GO AFTER?
SHAKE
SHAKE
YOU'RE SAYIN' I SHOULD ***GIVE UP?***

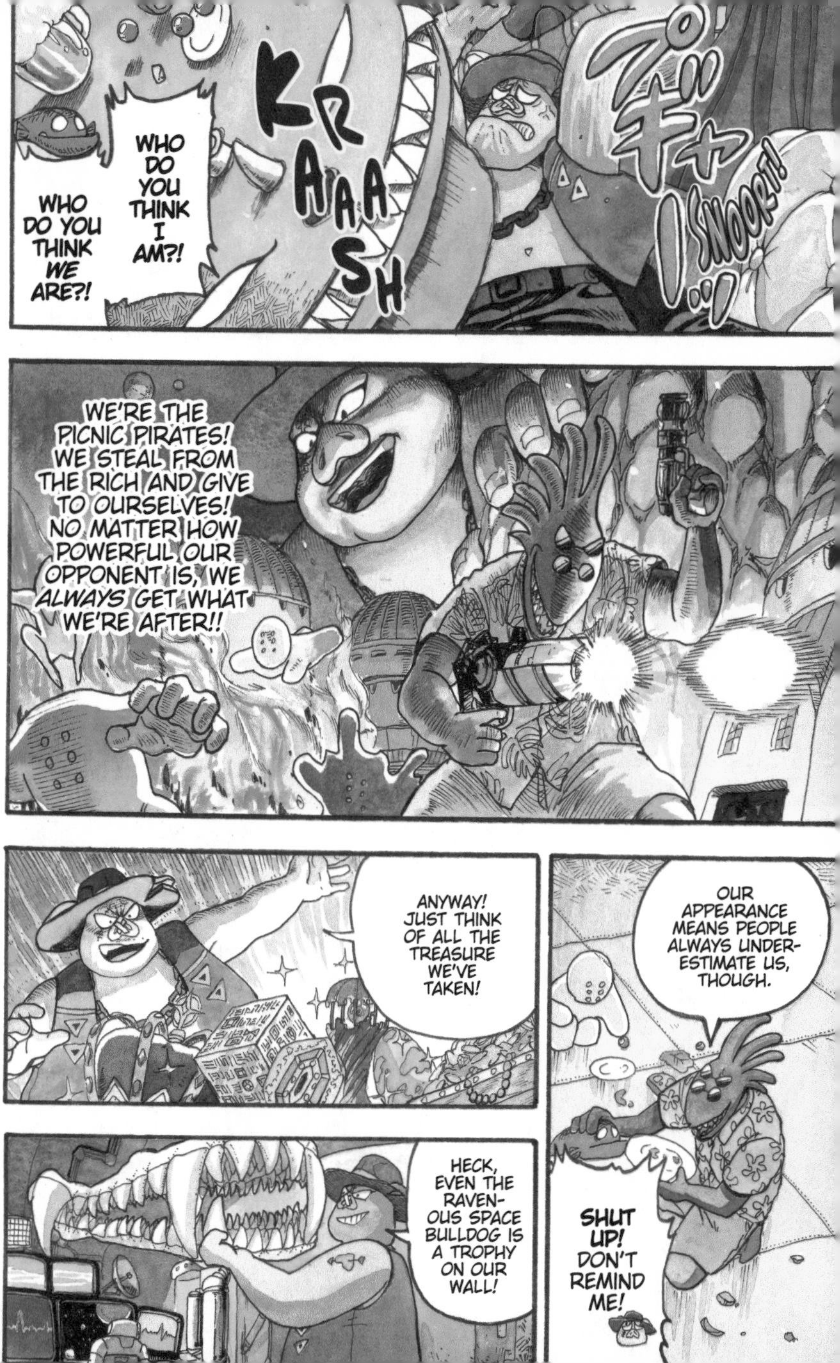
SNOORT!!
KRAAASH
WHO DO YOU THINK I AM?!
WHO DO YOU THINK *WE* ARE?!
WE'RE THE PICNIC PIRATES! WE STEAL FROM THE RICH AND GIVE TO OURSELVES! NO MATTER HOW POWERFUL OUR OPPONENT IS, WE *ALWAYS* GET WHAT WE'RE AFTER!!
OUR APPEARANCE MEANS PEOPLE ALWAYS UNDER-ESTIMATE US, THOUGH.
SHUT UP! DON'T REMIND ME!
ANYWAY! JUST THINK OF ALL THE TREASURE WE'VE TAKEN!
HECK, EVEN THE RAVEN-OUS SPACE BULLDOG IS A TROPHY ON OUR WALL!

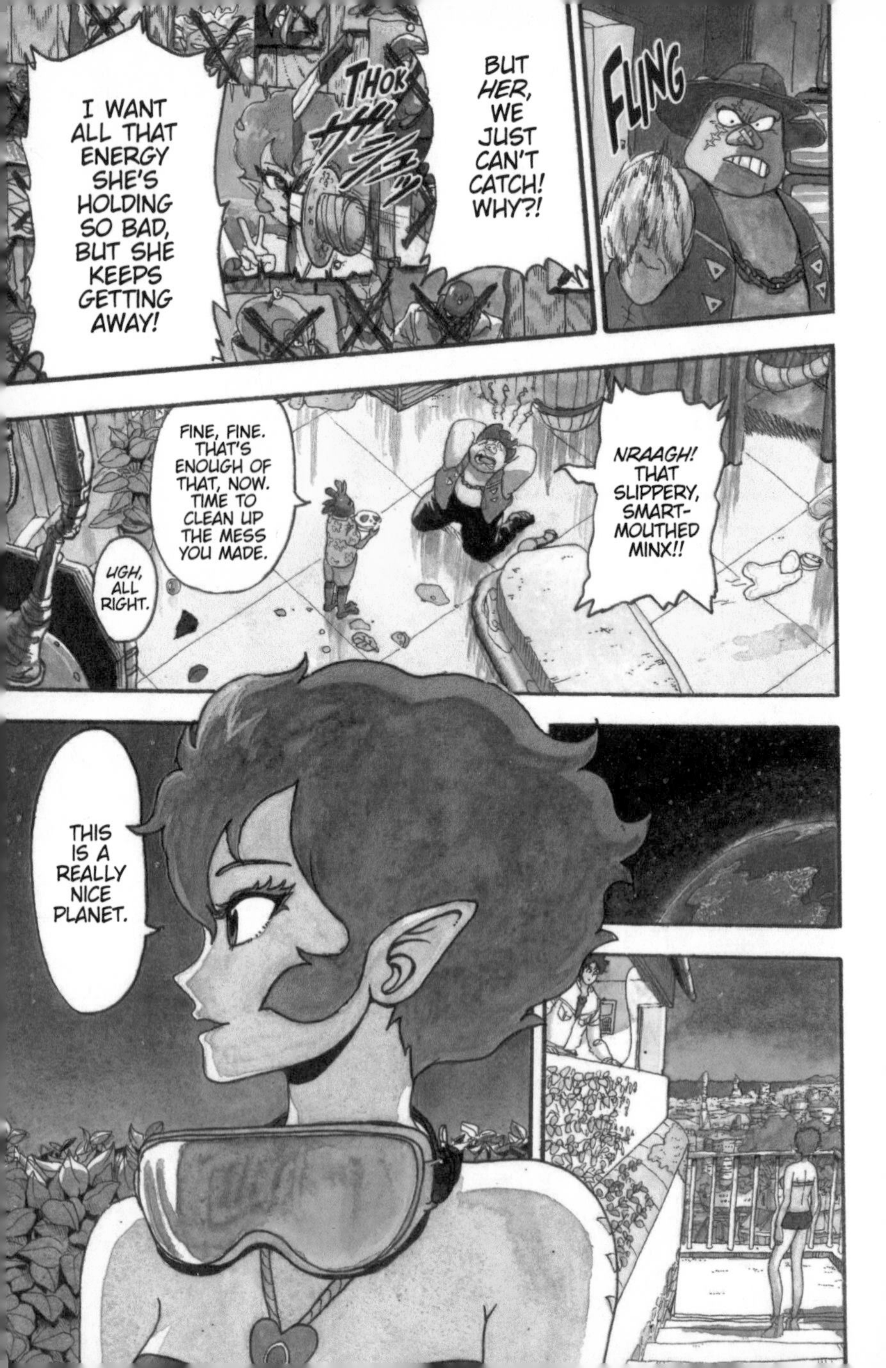
FLING
THOK
BUT HER, WE JUST CAN'T CATCH! WHY?!
I WANT ALL THAT ENERGY SHE'S HOLDING SO BAD, BUT SHE KEEPS GETTING AWAY!
NRAAGH! THAT SLIPPERY, SMART-MOUTHED MINX!!
FINE, FINE. THAT'S ENOUGH OF THAT, NOW. TIME TO CLEAN UP THE MESS YOU MADE.
UGH, ALL RIGHT.
THIS IS A REALLY NICE PLANET.

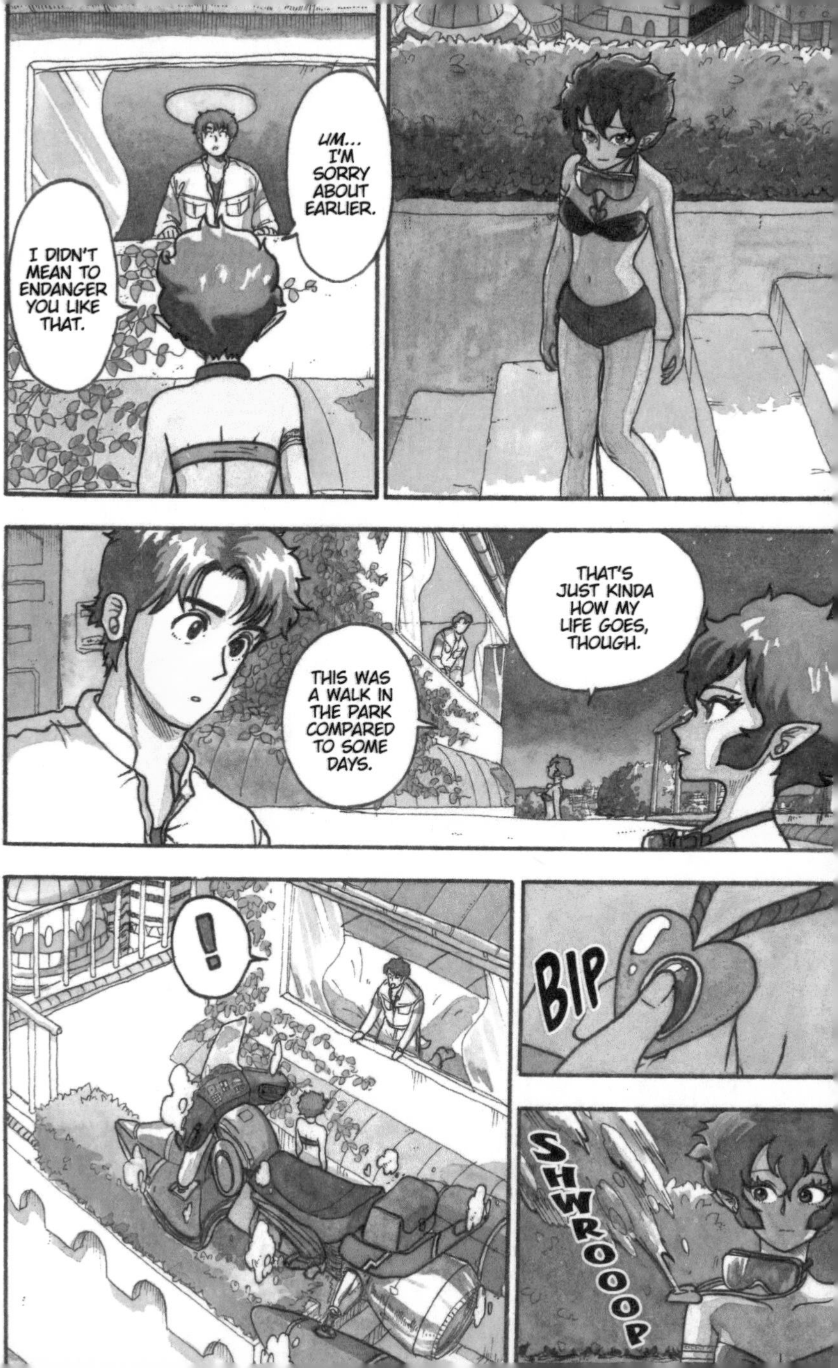
UM... I'M SORRY ABOUT EARLIER.
I DIDN'T MEAN TO ENDANGER YOU LIKE THAT.
THAT'S JUST KINDA HOW MY LIFE GOES, THOUGH.
THIS WAS A WALK IN THE PARK COMPARED TO SOME DAYS.
BIP
SHWROOOP
!

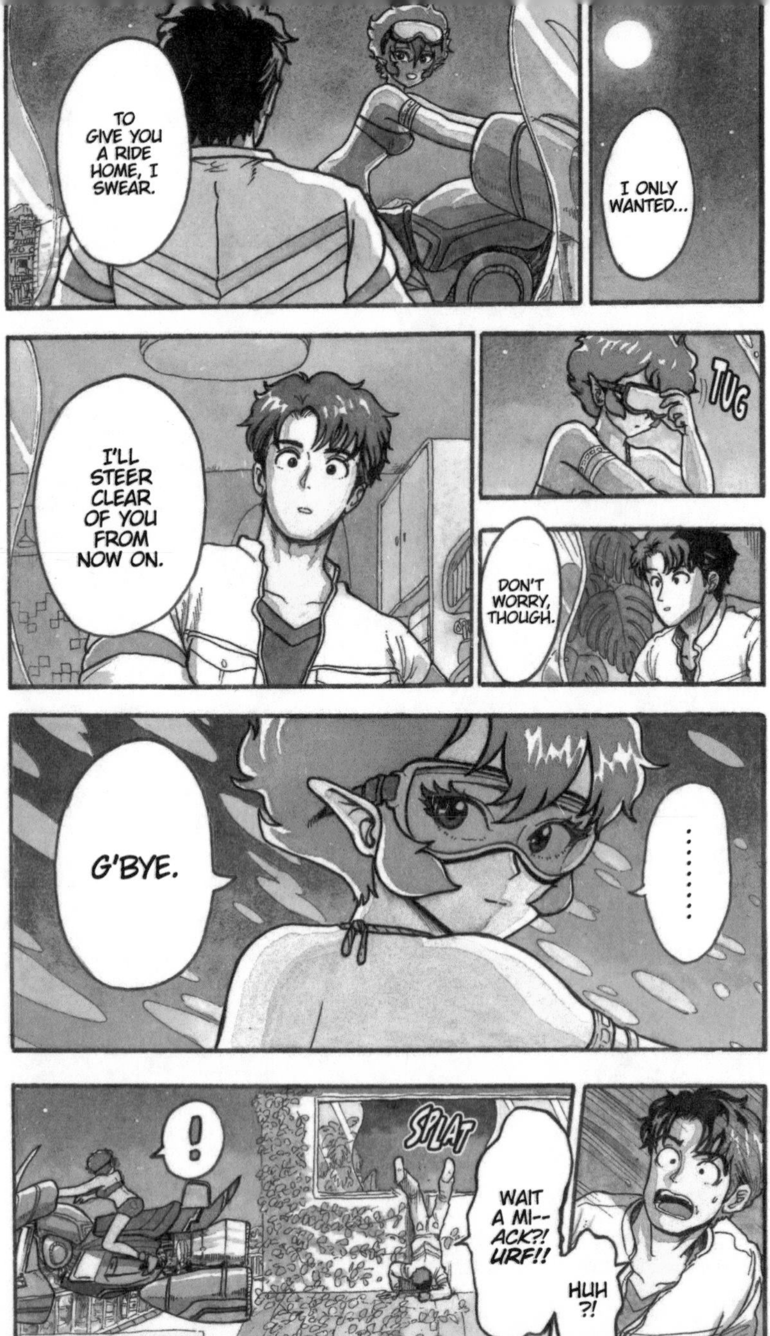
I ONLY WANTED...
TO GIVE YOU A RIDE HOME, I SWEAR.
TUG
DON'T WORRY, THOUGH.
I'LL STEER CLEAR OF YOU FROM NOW ON.
......
G'BYE.
HUH ?!
WAIT A MI-- ACK?! URF!!
SPLAT
!

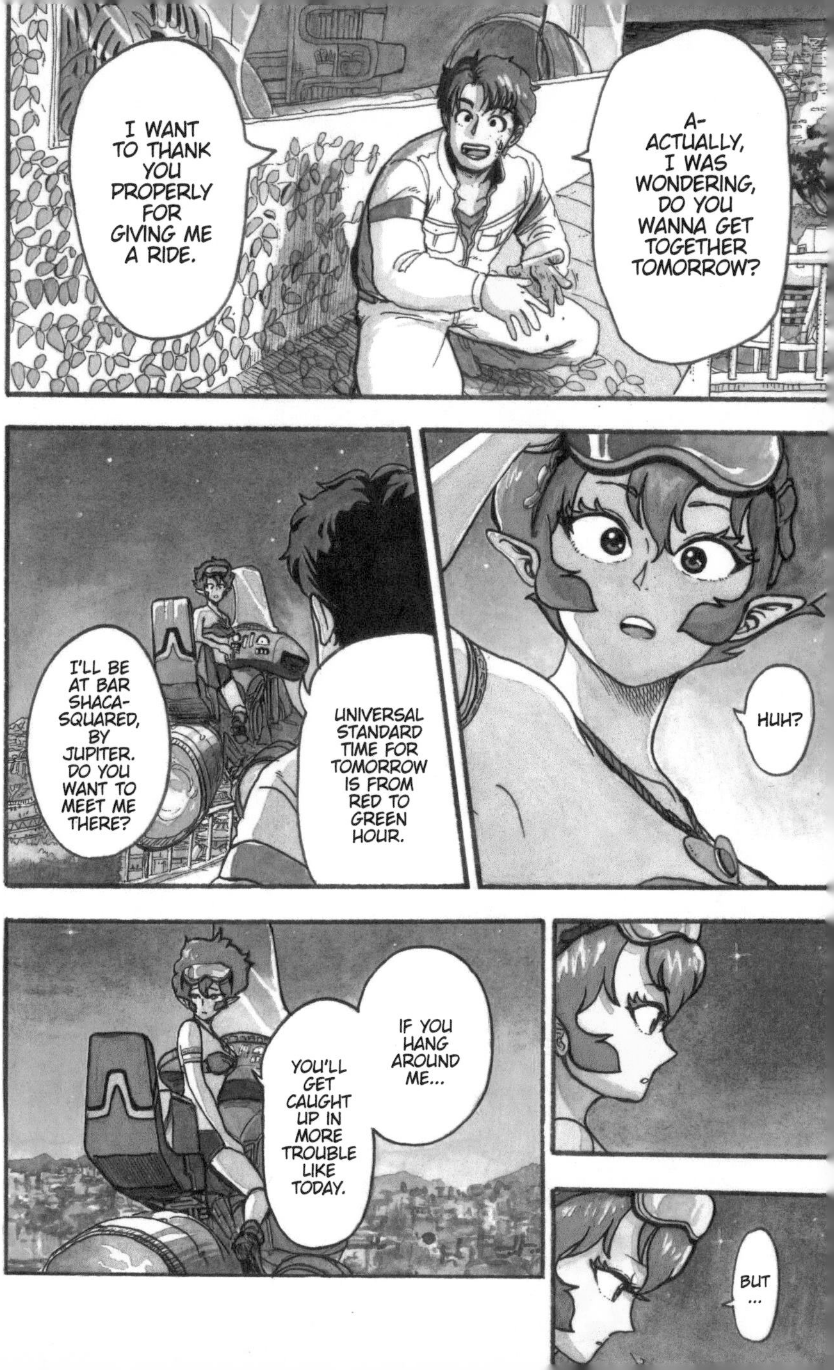
A- ACTUALLY, I WAS WONDERING, DO YOU WANNA GET TOGETHER TOMORROW?
I WANT TO THANK YOU PROPERLY FOR GIVING ME A RIDE.
HUH?
UNIVERSAL STANDARD TIME FOR TOMORROW IS FROM RED TO GREEN HOUR.
I'LL BE AT BAR SHACA-SQUARED, BY JUPITER. DO YOU WANT TO MEET ME THERE?
BUT ...
IF YOU HANG AROUND ME...
YOU'LL GET CAUGHT UP IN MORE TROUBLE LIKE TODAY.

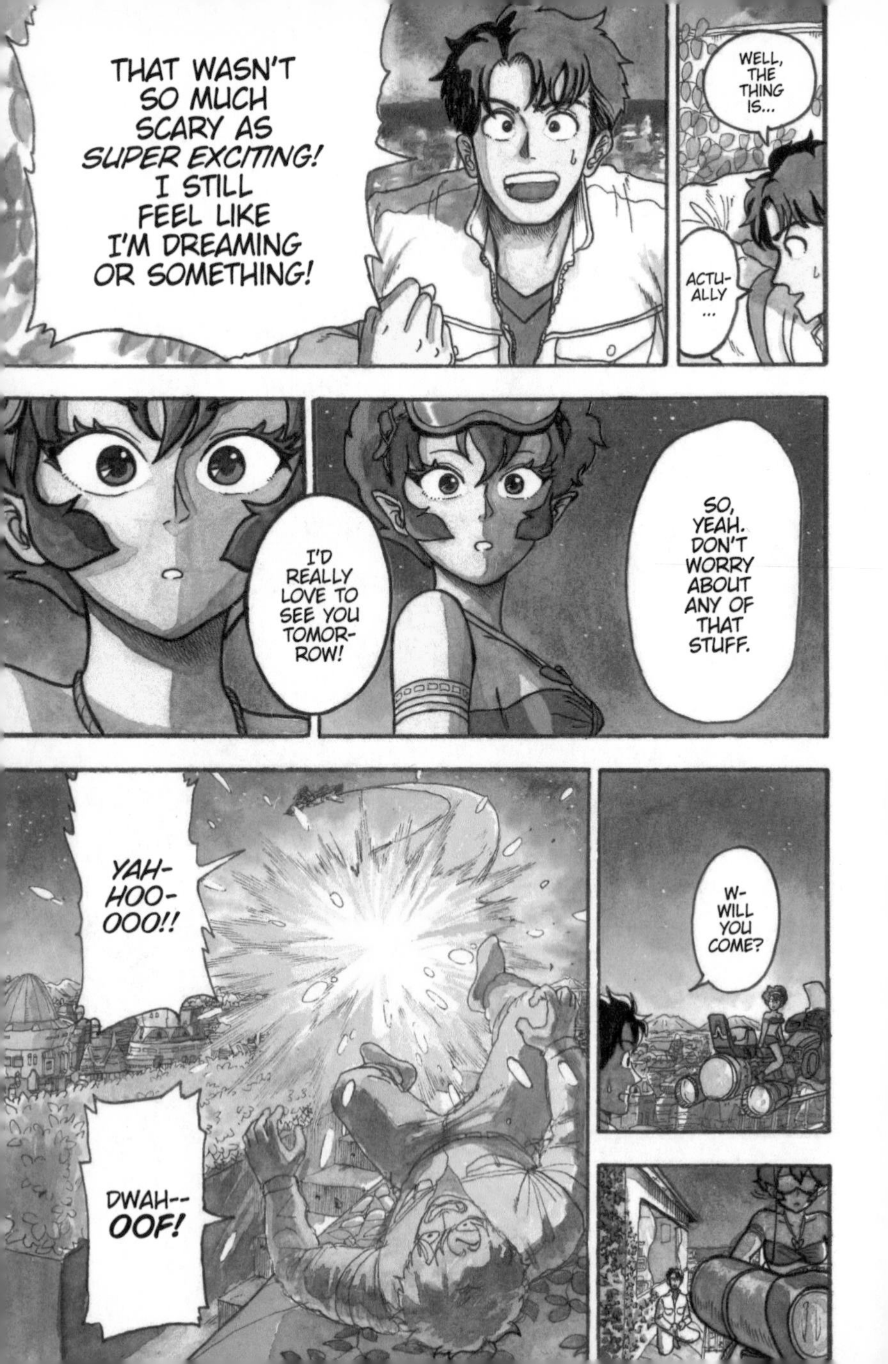
WELL, THE THING IS...
ACTUALLY...
THAT WASN'T SO MUCH SCARY AS SUPER EXCITING! I STILL FEEL LIKE I'M DREAMING OR SOMETHING!
SO, YEAH. DON'T WORRY ABOUT ANY OF THAT STUFF.
I'D REALLY LOVE TO SEE YOU TOMORROW!
W-WILL YOU COME?
YAH-HOO-OOO!!
DWAH--OOF!

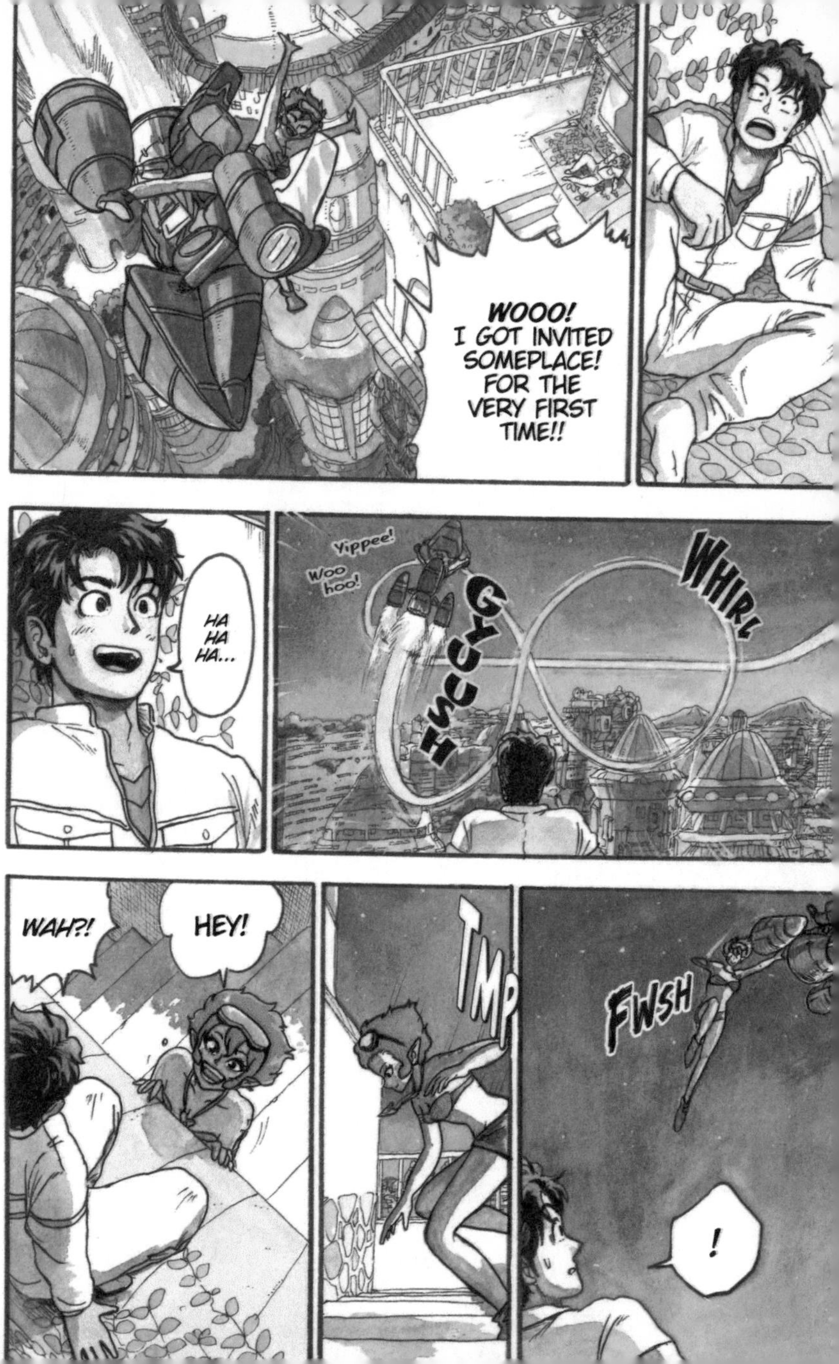
WOOO! I GOT INVITED SOMEPLACE! FOR THE VERY FIRST TIME!!
Yippee!
Woo hoo!
WHIRL
GYUUSH
HA HA HA...
FWSH
!
TMP
HEY!
WAH?!

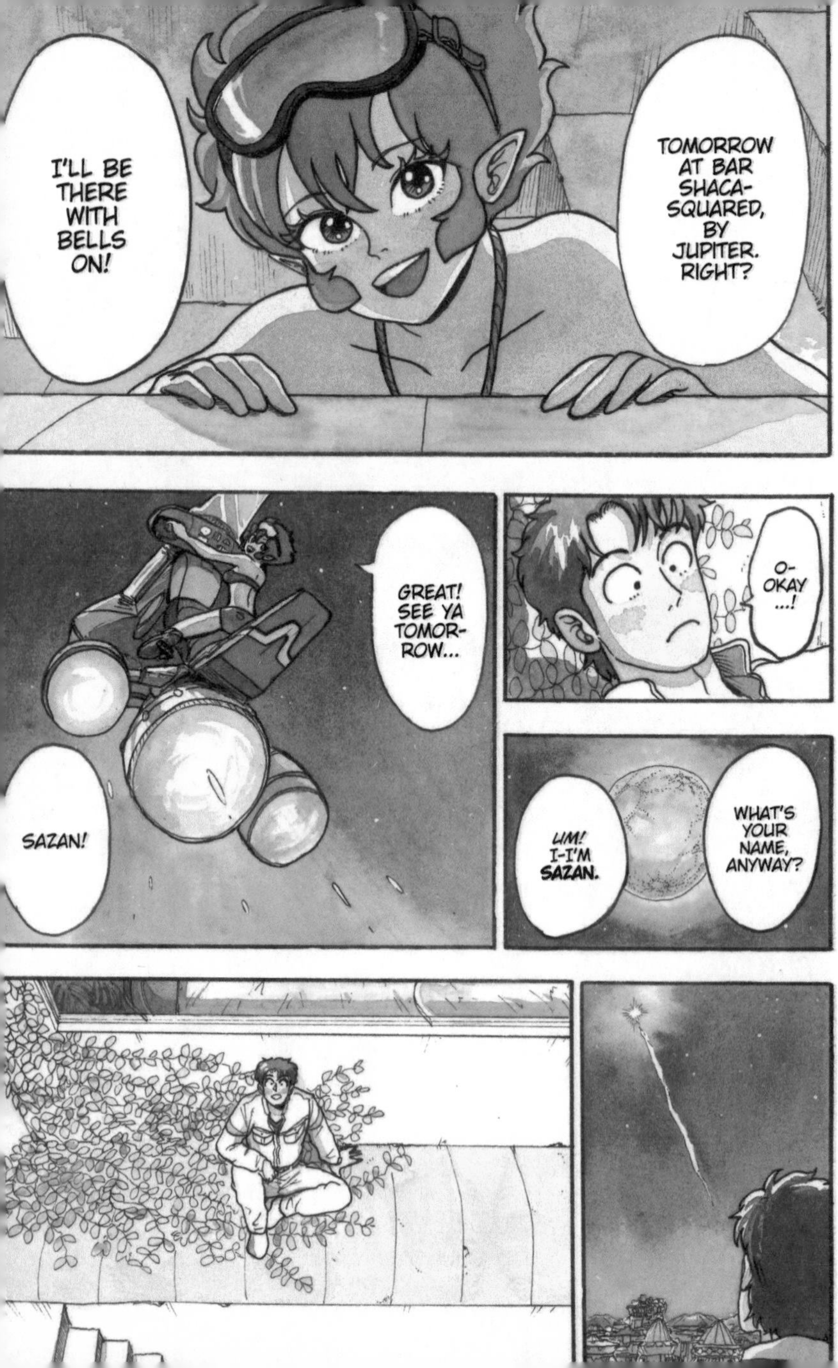
TOMORROW AT BAR SHACA-SQUARED, BY JUPITER. RIGHT?
I'LL BE THERE WITH BELLS ON!
O-OKAY ...!
WHAT'S YOUR NAME, ANYWAY?
UM! I-I'M SAZAN.
GREAT! SEE YA TOMORROW...
SAZAN!

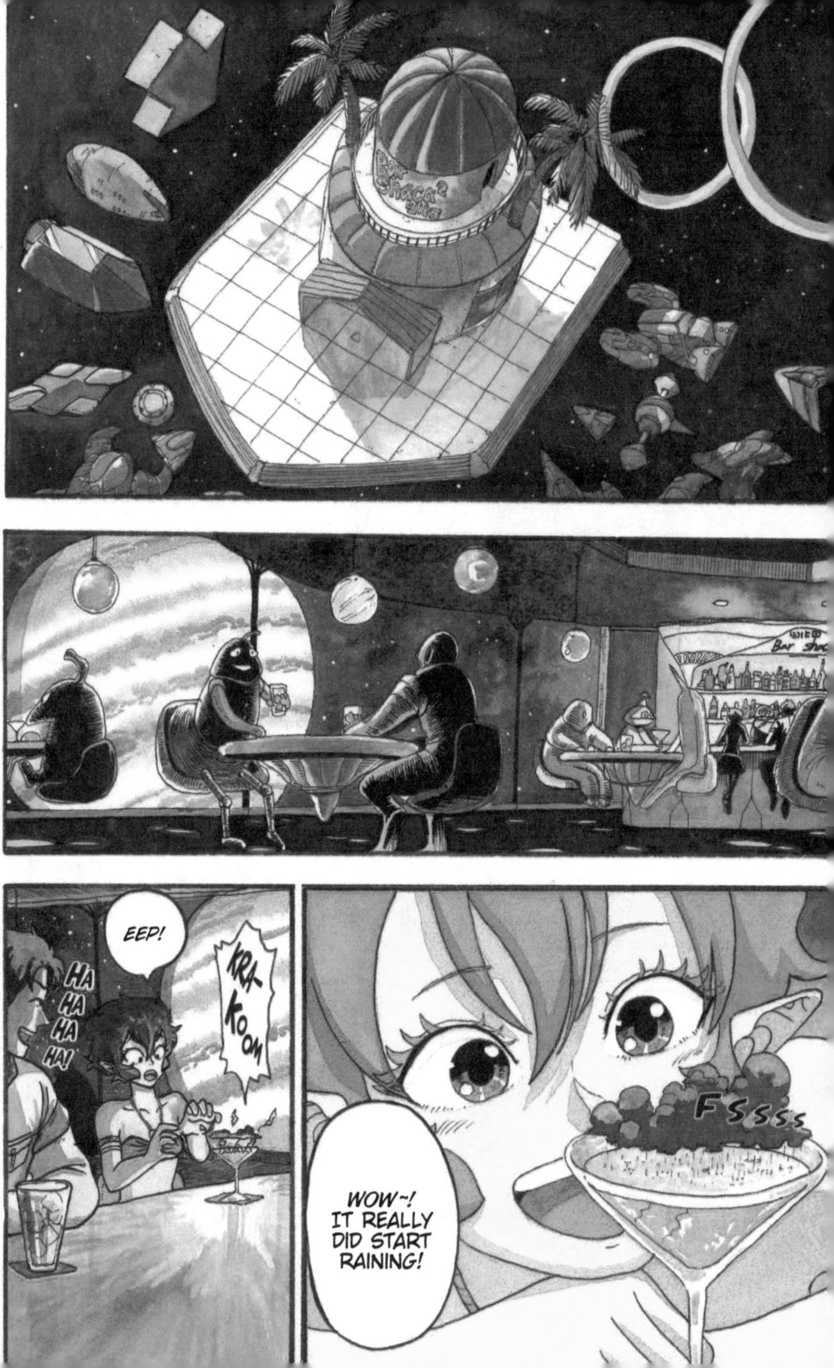
FSSSS
WOW~! IT REALLY DID START RAINING!
EEP!
KRA-KOOM
HA HA HA HA!

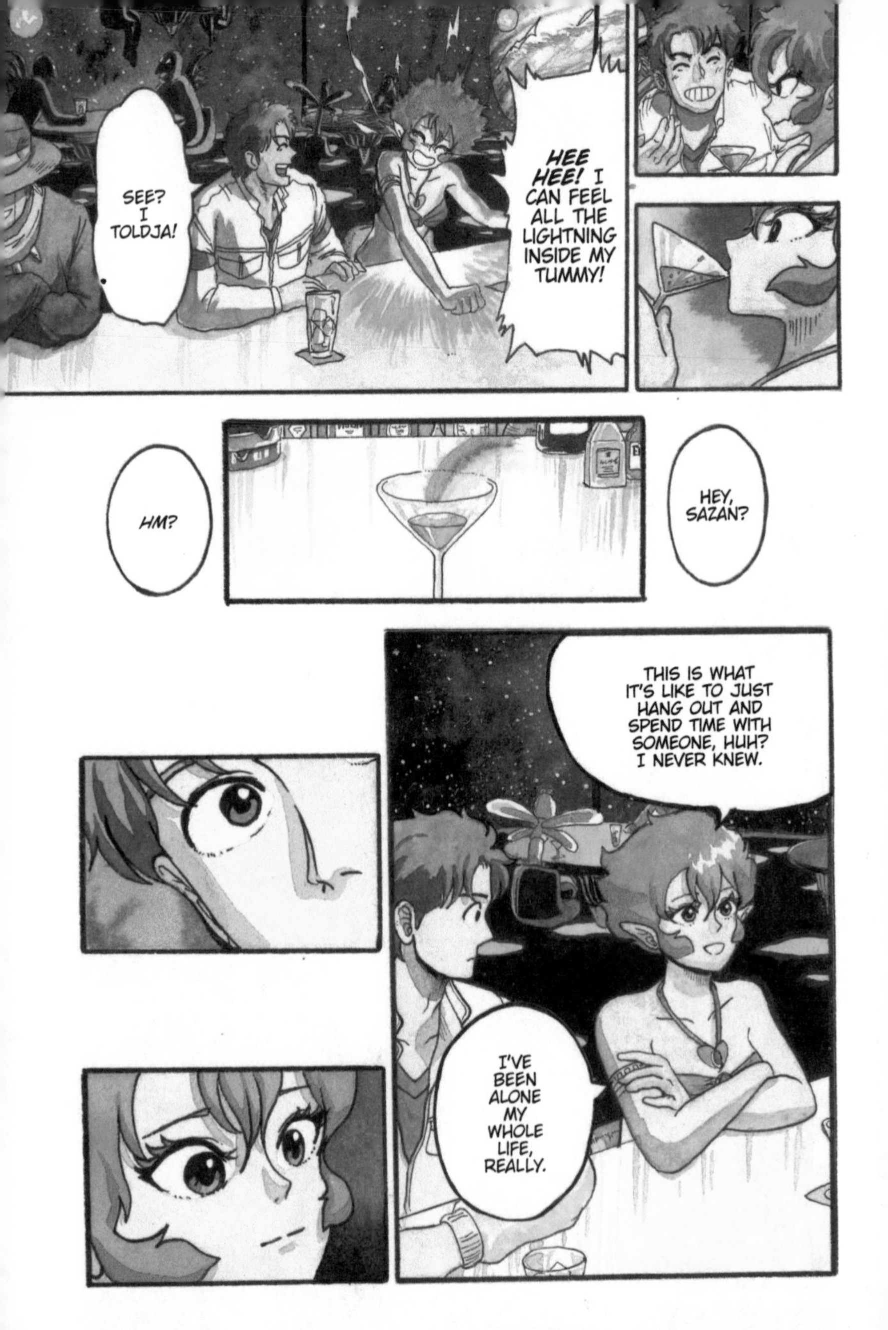
HEE HEE! I CAN FEEL ALL THE LIGHTNING INSIDE MY TUMMY!
SEE? I TOLDJA!
HEY, SAZAN?
HM?
THIS IS WHAT IT'S LIKE TO JUST HANG OUT AND SPEND TIME WITH SOMEONE, HUH? I NEVER KNEW.
I'VE BEEN ALONE MY WHOLE LIFE, REALLY.

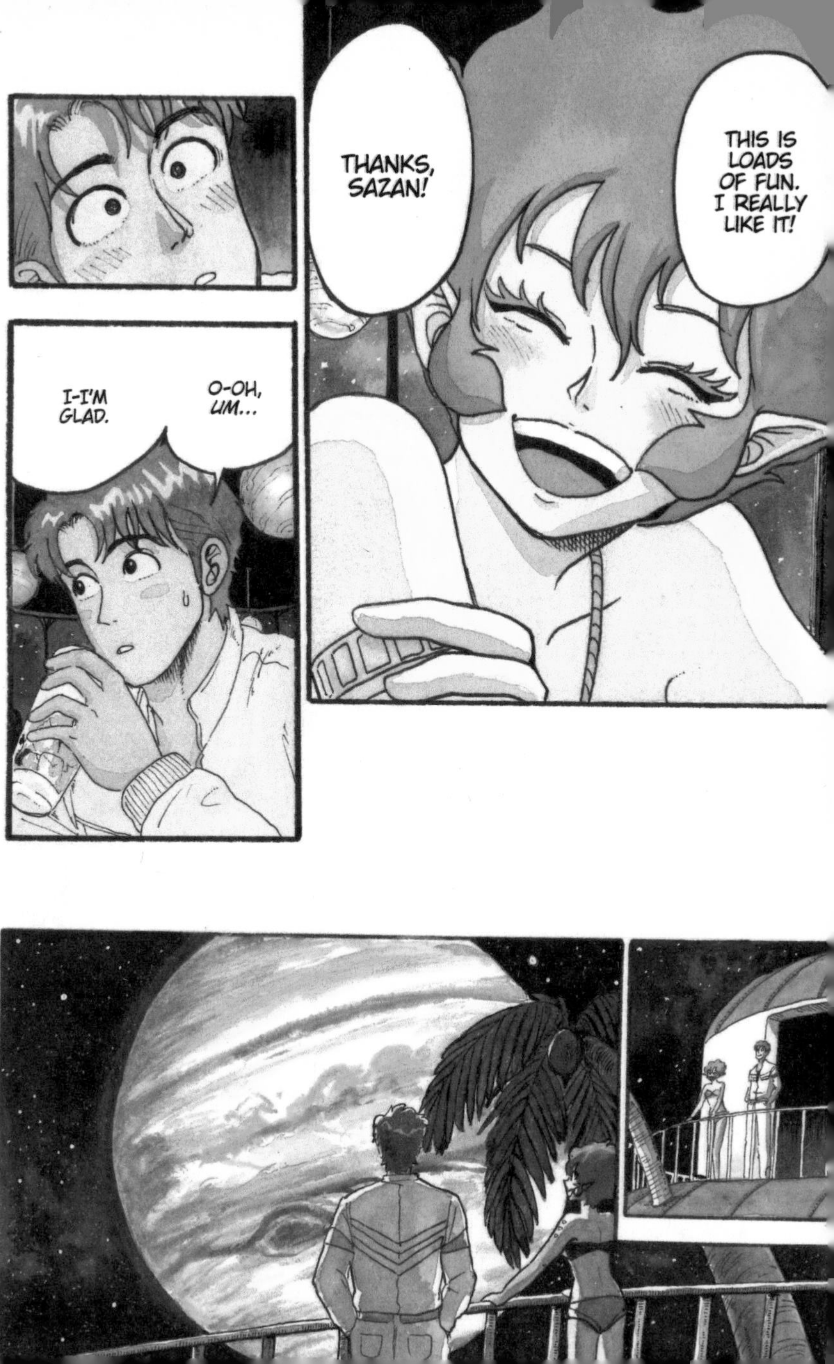
THIS IS LOADS OF FUN. I REALLY LIKE IT!
THANKS, SAZAN!
O-OH, UM...
I-I'M GLAD.

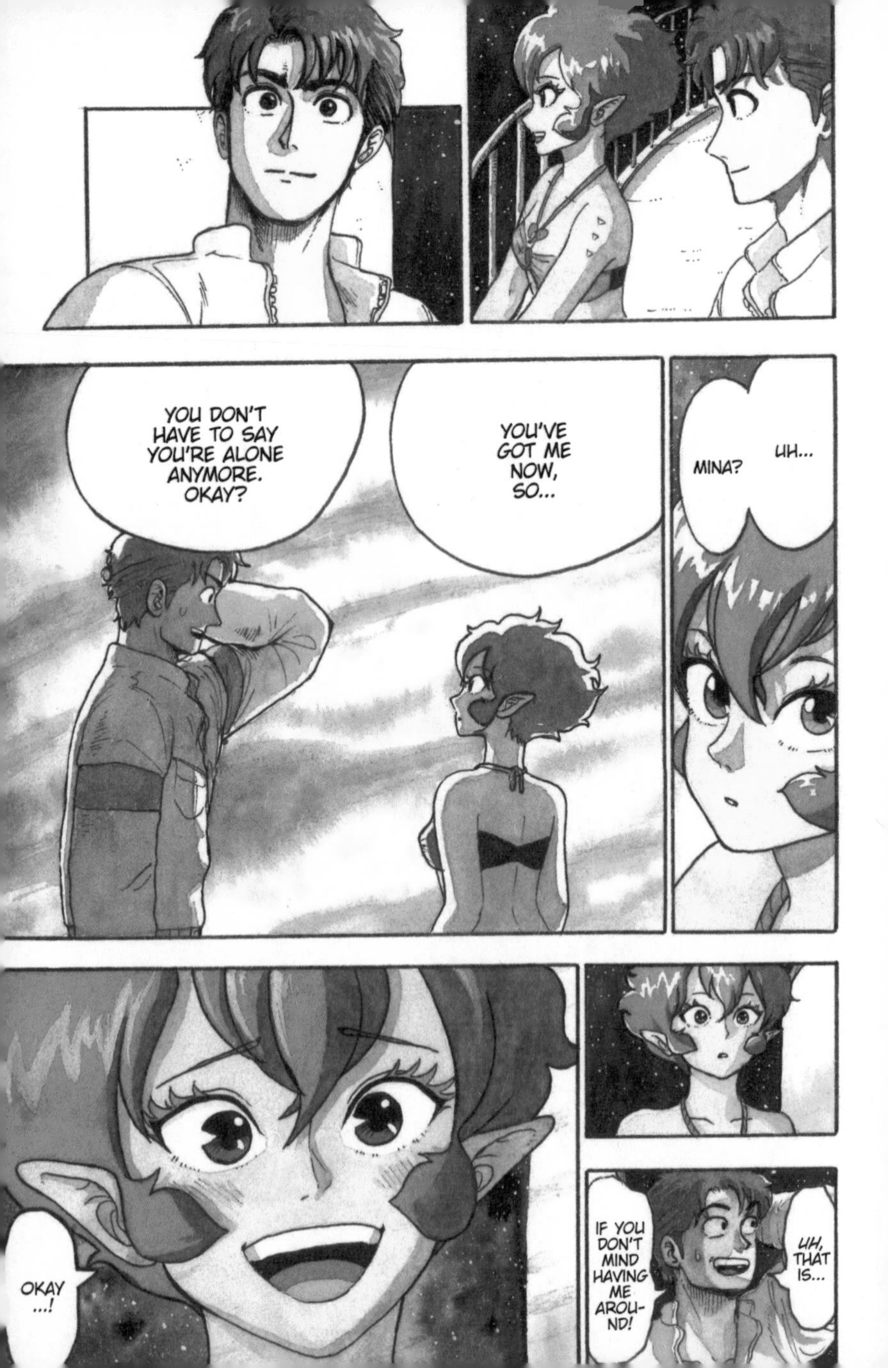
UH...
MINA?
YOU'VE GOT ME NOW, SO...
YOU DON'T HAVE TO SAY YOU'RE ALONE ANYMORE. OKAY?
UH, THAT IS...
IF YOU DON'T MIND HAVING ME AROU-ND!
OKAY ...!

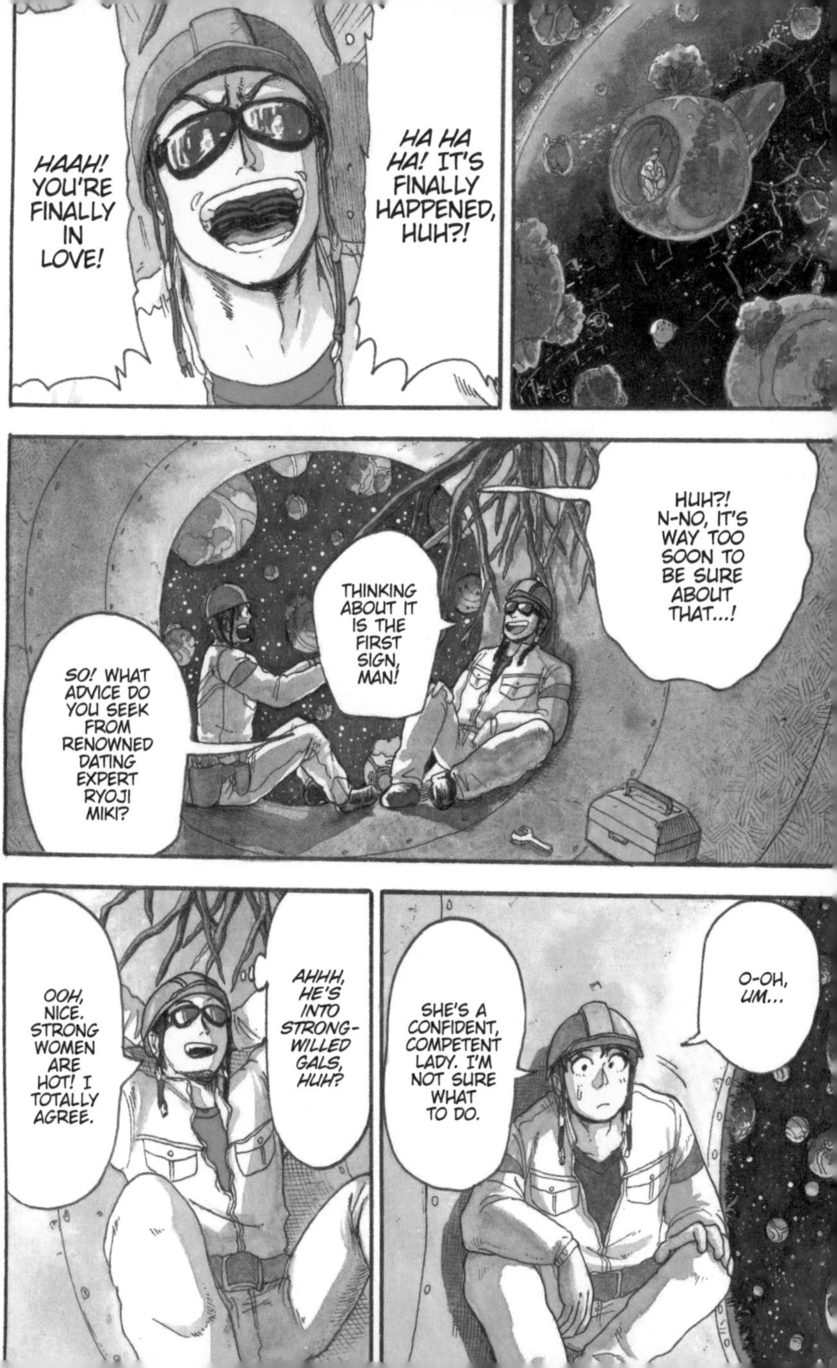
HA HA HA! IT'S FINALLY HAPPENED, HUH?!
HAAH! YOU'RE FINALLY IN LOVE!
HUH?! N-NO, IT'S WAY TOO SOON TO BE SURE ABOUT THAT...!
THINKING ABOUT IT IS THE FIRST SIGN, MAN!
SO! WHAT ADVICE DO YOU SEEK FROM RENOWNED DATING EXPERT RYOJI MIKI?
O-OH, UM...
SHE'S A CONFIDENT, COMPETENT LADY. I'M NOT SURE WHAT TO DO.
AHHH, HE'S INTO STRONG-WILLED GALS, HUH?
OOH, NICE. STRONG WOMEN ARE HOT! I TOTALLY AGREE.

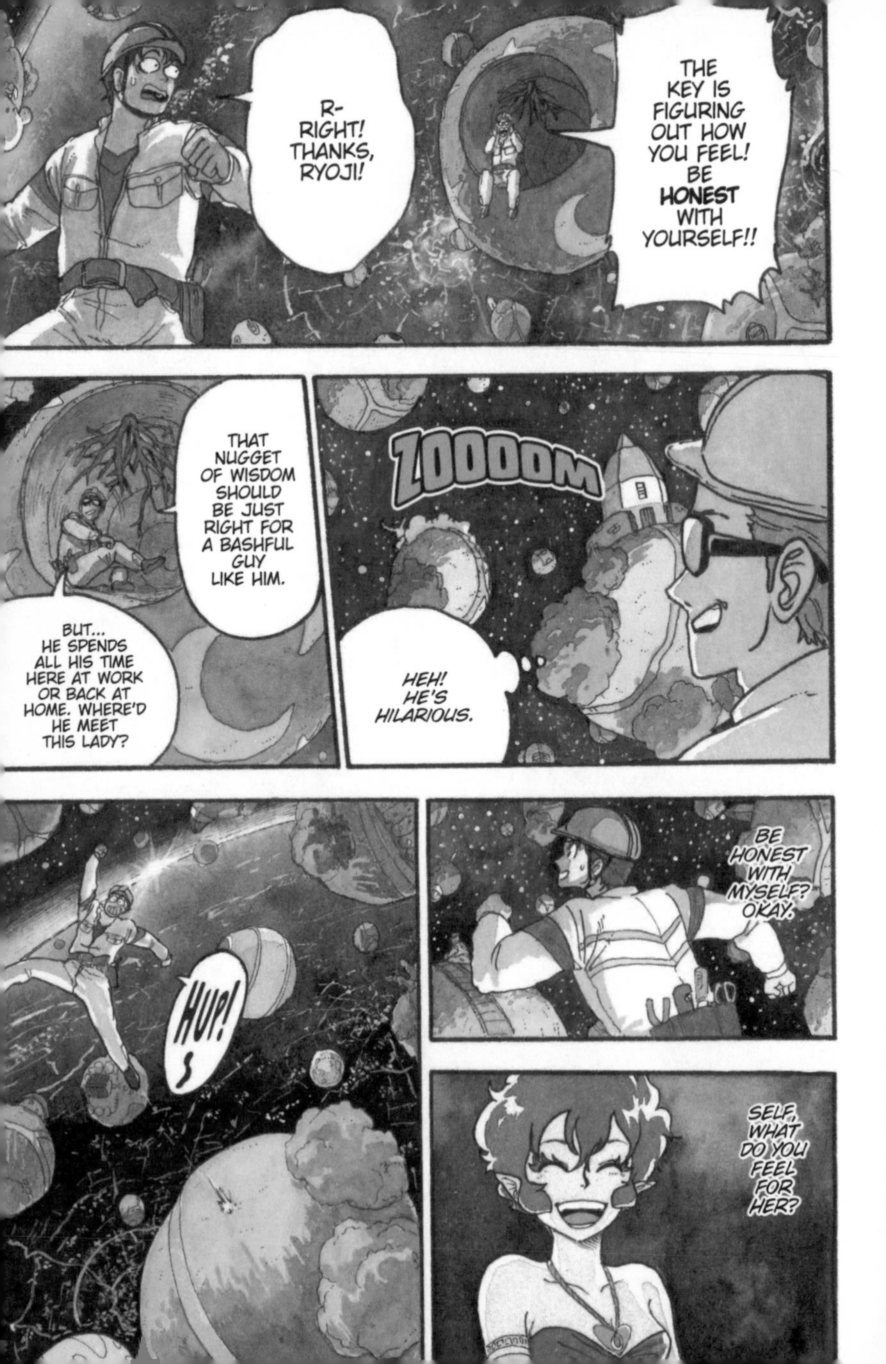
THE KEY IS FIGURING OUT HOW YOU FEEL! BE **HONEST** WITH YOURSELF!!
R-RIGHT! THANKS, RYOJI!
ZOOOOM
HEH! HE'S HILARIOUS.
THAT NUGGET OF WISDOM SHOULD BE JUST RIGHT FOR A BASHFUL GUY LIKE HIM.
BUT... HE SPENDS ALL HIS TIME HERE AT WORK OR BACK AT HOME. WHERE'D HE MEET THIS LADY?
BE HONEST WITH MYSELF? OKAY.
SELF, WHAT DO YOU FEEL FOR HER?
HUP!

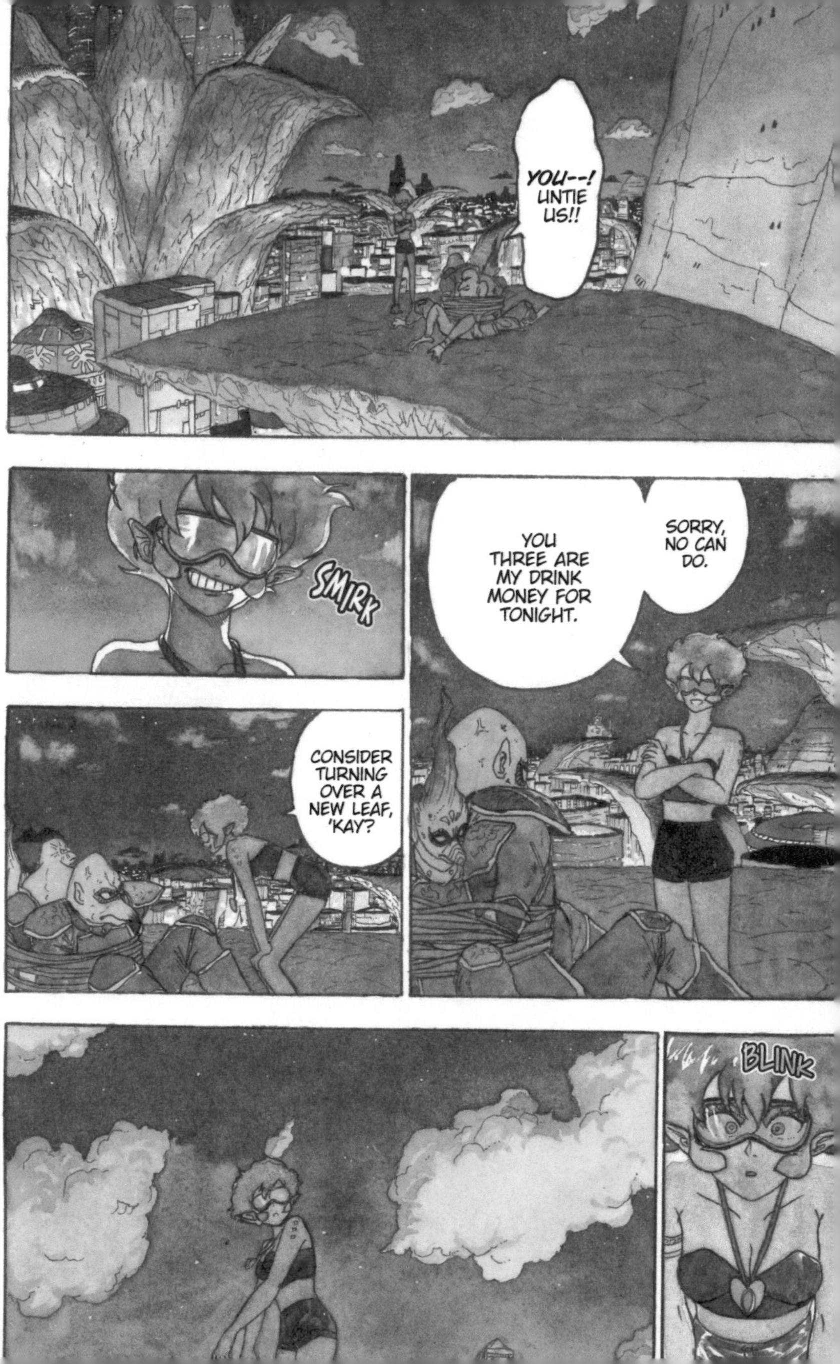
YOU--! UNTIE US!!
SORRY, NO CAN DO.
YOU THREE ARE MY DRINK MONEY FOR TONIGHT.
SMIRK
CONSIDER TURNING OVER A NEW LEAF, 'KAY?
BLINK

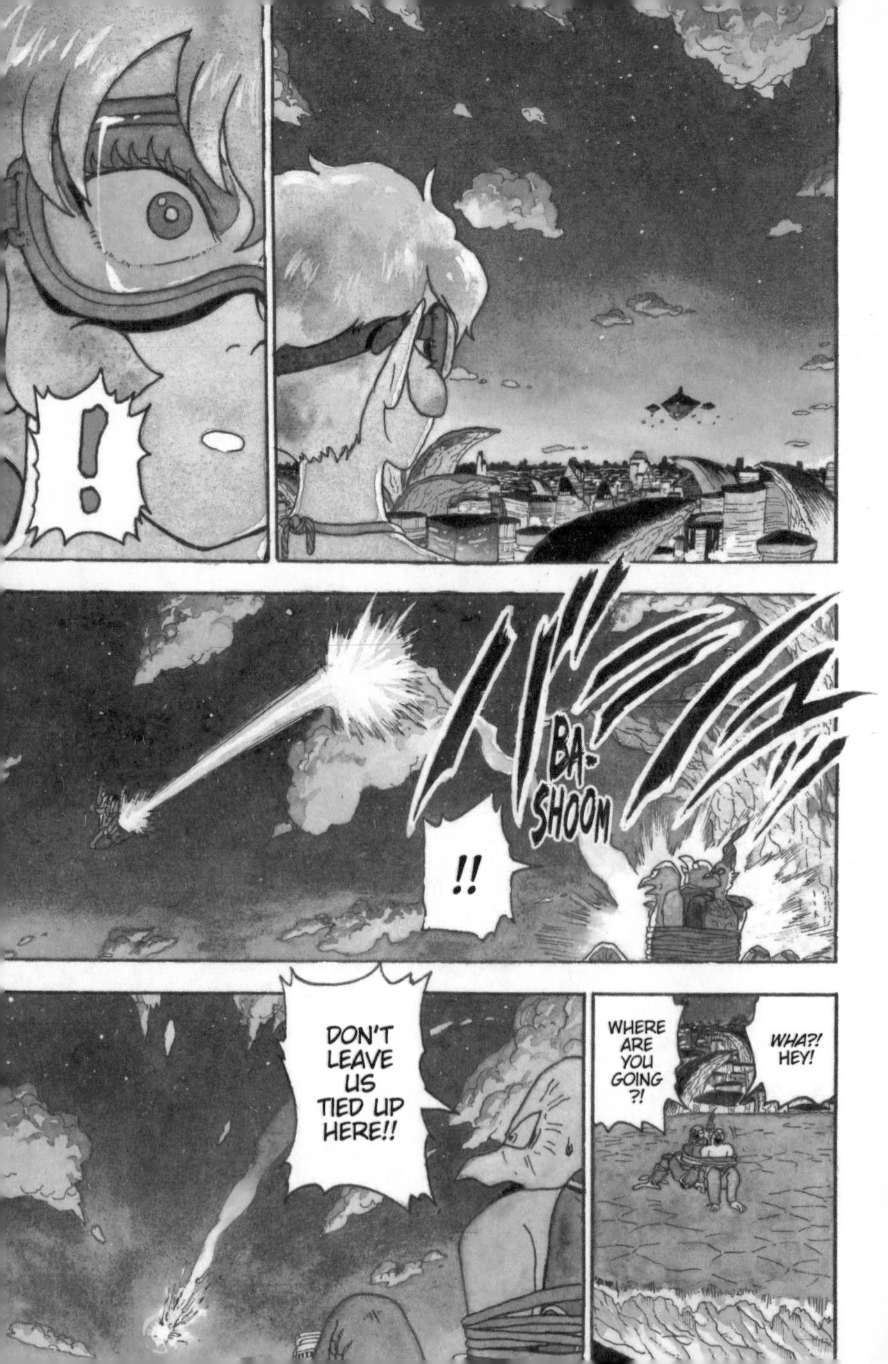
!
BA-SHOOM
!!
WHA?! HEY!
WHERE ARE YOU GOING ?!
DON'T LEAVE US TIED UP HERE!!

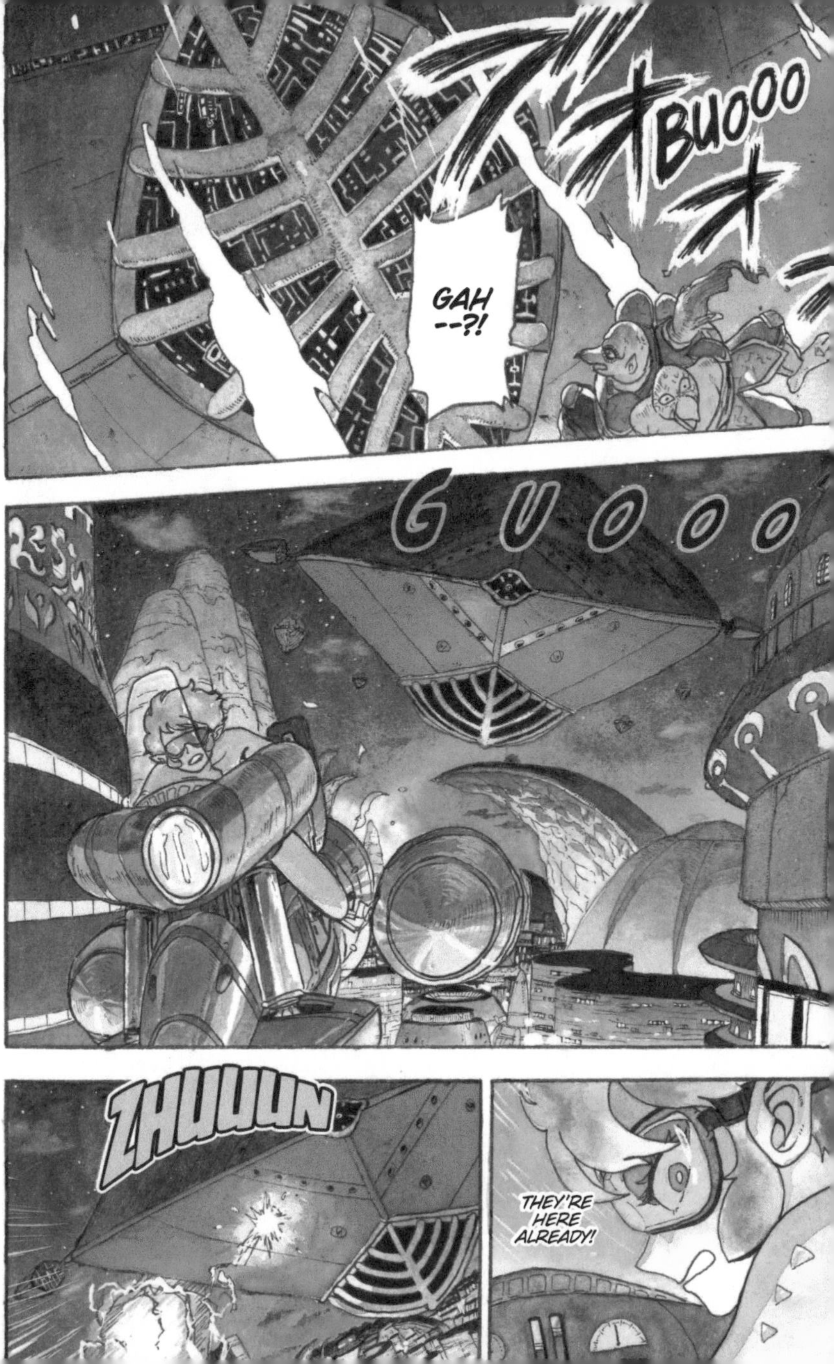
BUOOO
GAH --?!
GUOOO
THEY'RE HERE ALREADY!
ZHUUUN

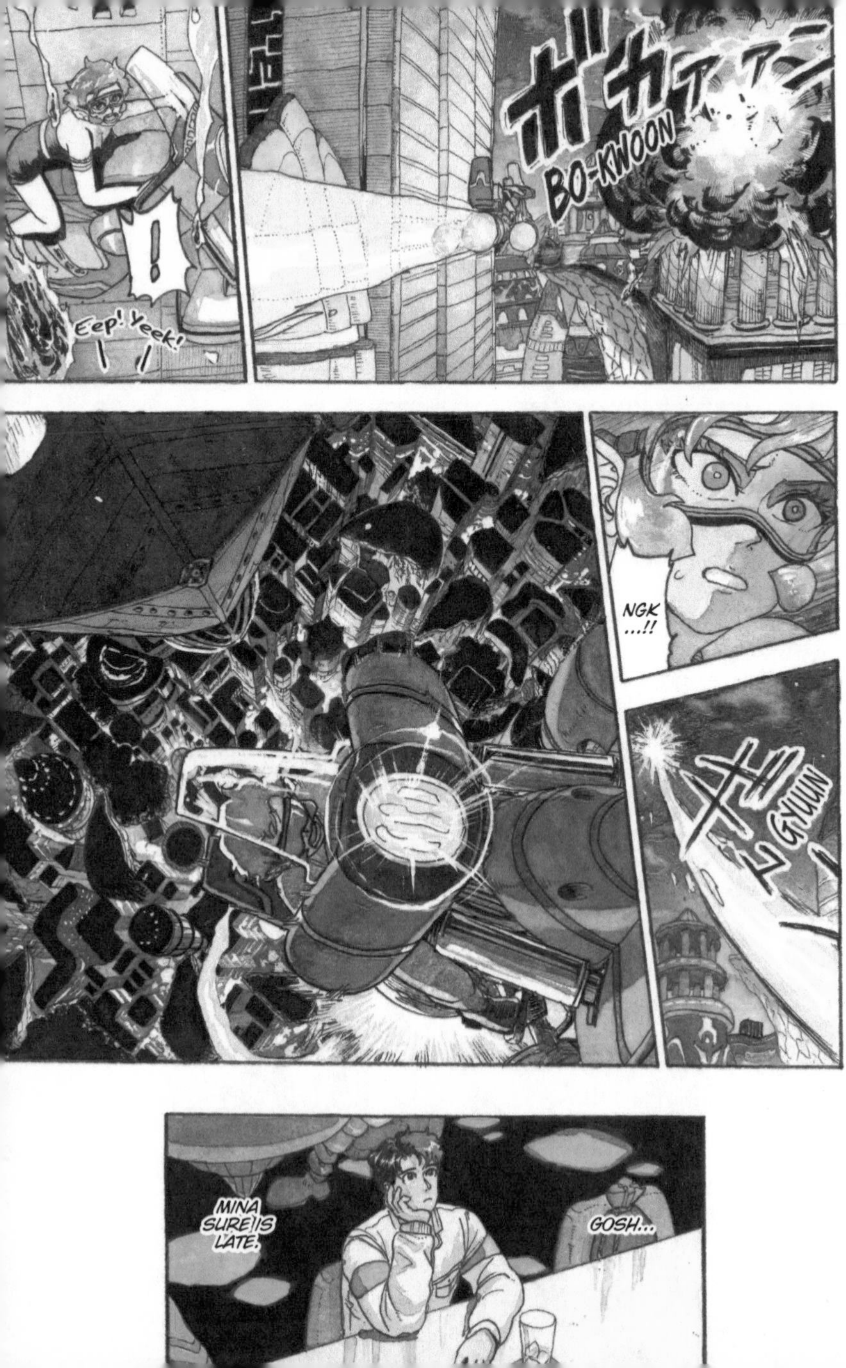
BO-KWOON
!
Eep! Yeek!
NGK ...!!
GYUUN
GOSH...
MINA SURE IS LATE.

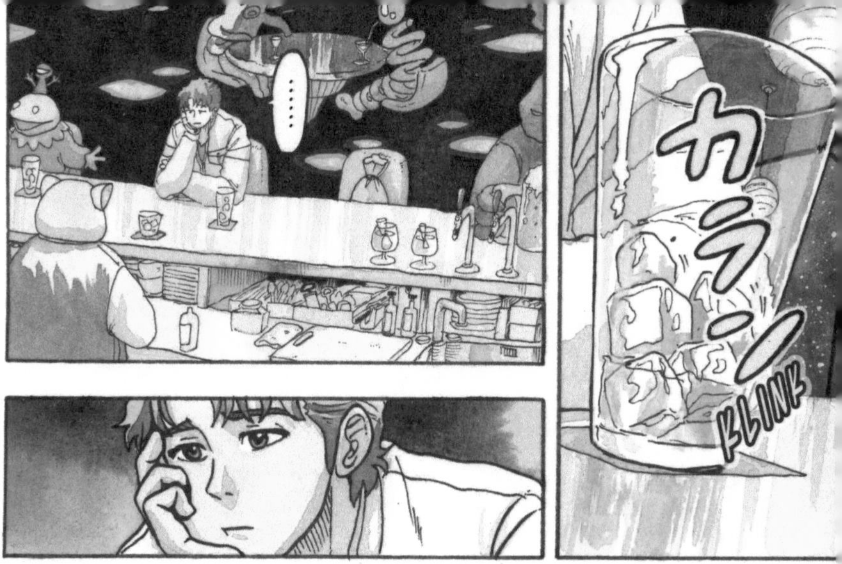
カラーン
KLINK
……
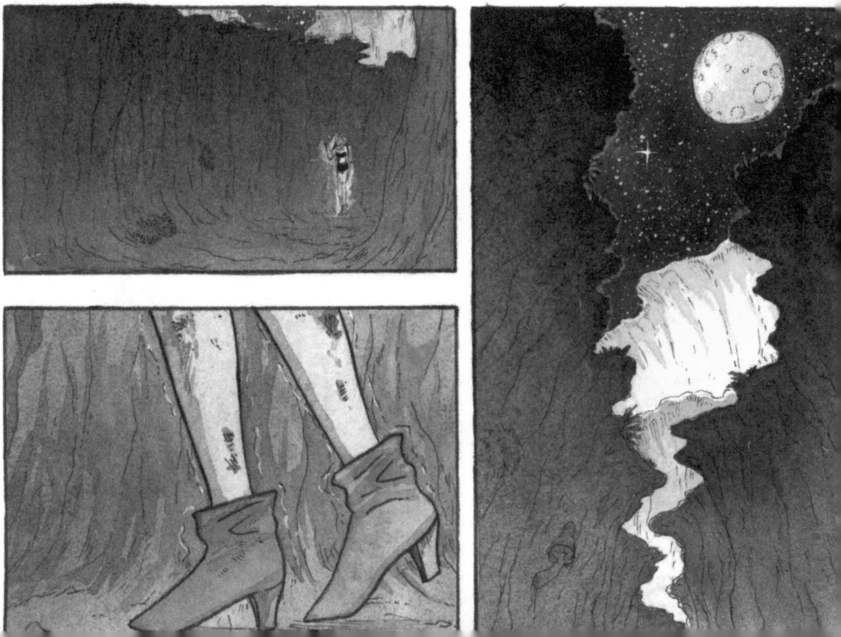

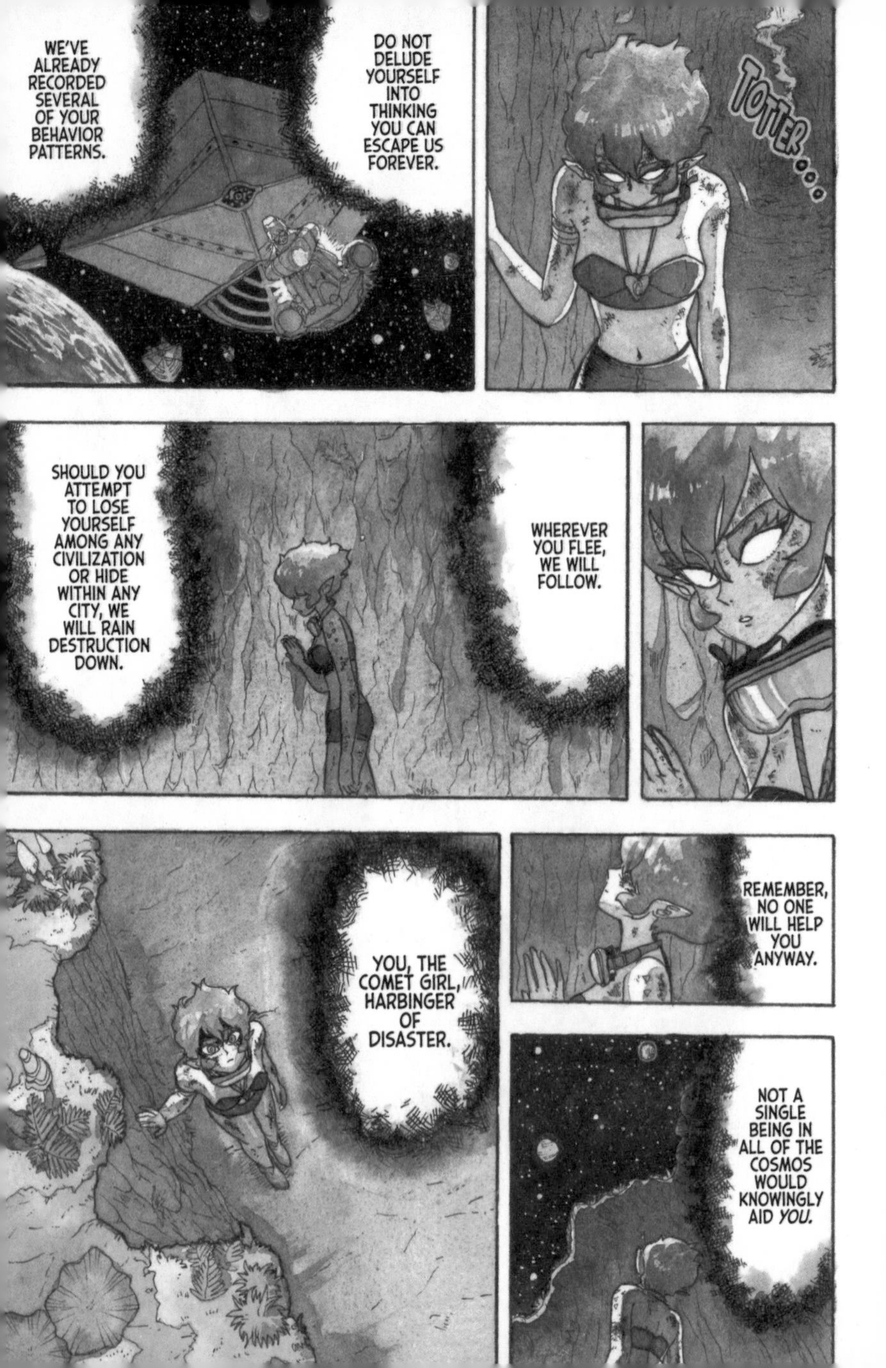
TOTTER...
DO NOT DELUDE YOURSELF INTO THINKING YOU CAN ESCAPE US FOREVER.
WE'VE ALREADY RECORDED SEVERAL OF YOUR BEHAVIOR PATTERNS.
WHEREVER YOU FLEE, WE WILL FOLLOW.
SHOULD YOU ATTEMPT TO LOSE YOURSELF AMONG ANY CIVILIZATION OR HIDE WITHIN ANY CITY, WE WILL RAIN DESTRUCTION DOWN.
REMEMBER, NO ONE WILL HELP YOU ANYWAY.
NOT A SINGLE BEING IN ALL OF THE COSMOS WOULD KNOWINGLY AID *YOU.*
YOU, THE COMET GIRL, HARBINGER OF DISASTER.

BARKEEP, GIMME ANOTHER.

I WAITED AND WAITED, BUT MINA NEVER SHOWED.

YOU'RE RIGHT. CHECK, PLEASE.

YEAH...

......

BUT I THINK YOU'VE HAD ENOUGH FOR TONIGHT.

SORRY, SAZAN...

WOBBLE...

Bar Shaca

MINA...!

I JUST COULDN'T MAKE MYSELF STEP INSIDE.

I'M SORRY. I TRIED TO GO IN, BUT...

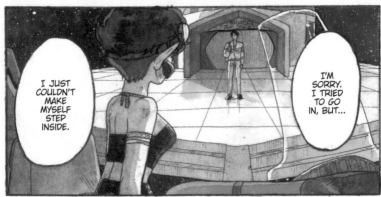

LISTEN TO ME, OKAY?

SAZAN...

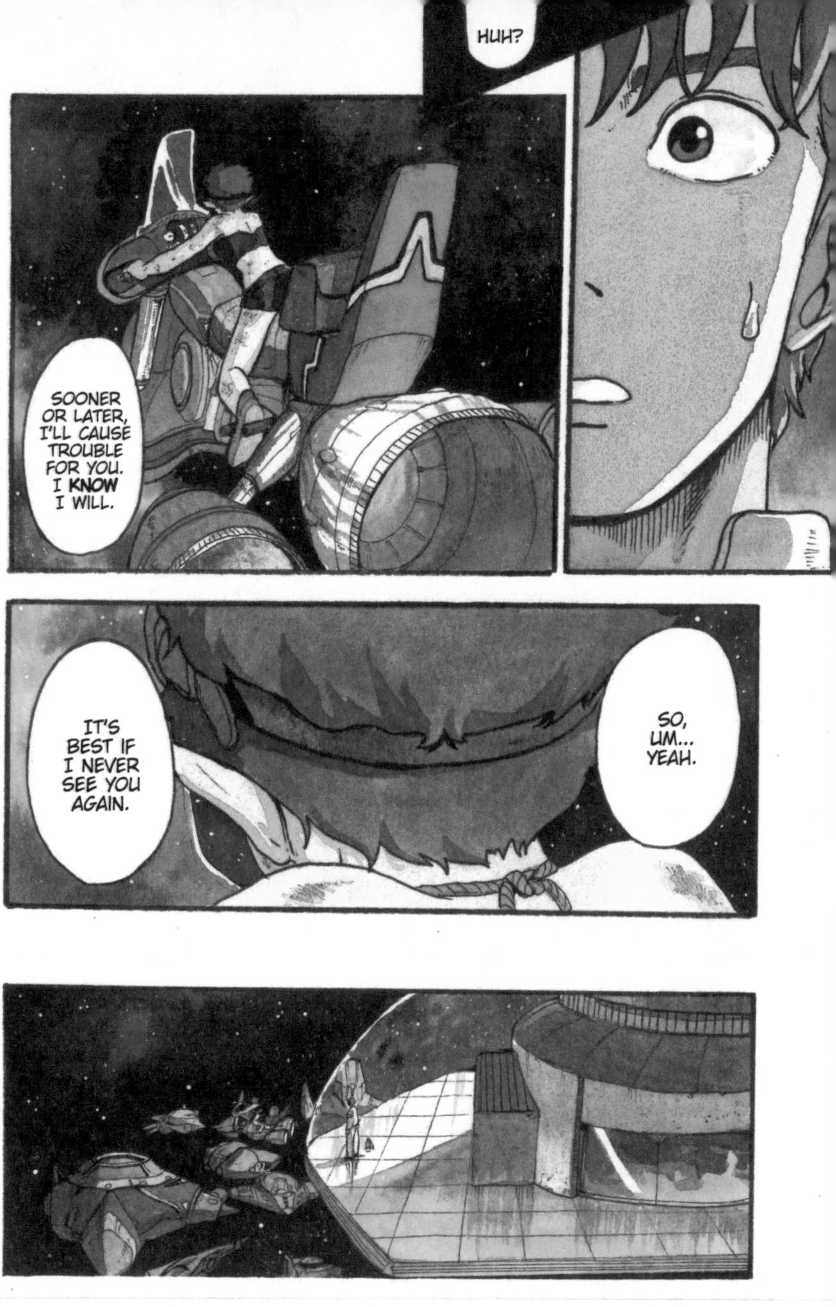
HUH?
SOONER OR LATER, I'LL CAUSE TROUBLE FOR YOU. I **KNOW** I WILL.
SO, UM... YEAH.
IT'S BEST IF I NEVER SEE YOU AGAIN.

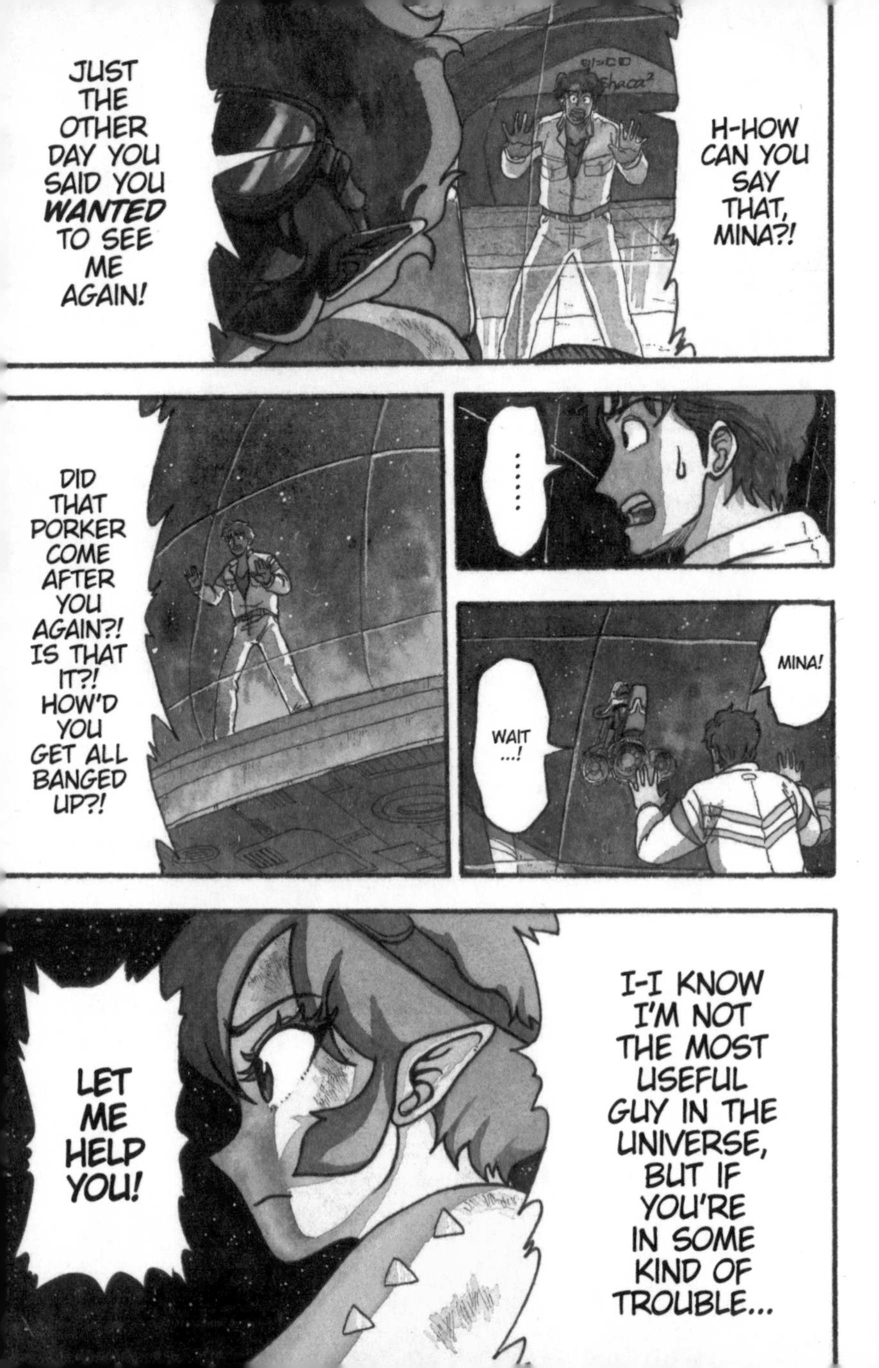
H-HOW CAN YOU SAY THAT, MINA?!
JUST THE OTHER DAY YOU SAID YOU WANTED TO SEE ME AGAIN!
......
MINA!
WAIT ...!
DID THAT PORKER COME AFTER YOU AGAIN?! IS THAT IT?! HOW'D YOU GET ALL BANGED UP?!
I-I KNOW I'M NOT THE MOST USEFUL GUY IN THE UNIVERSE, BUT IF YOU'RE IN SOME KIND OF TROUBLE...
LET ME HELP YOU!

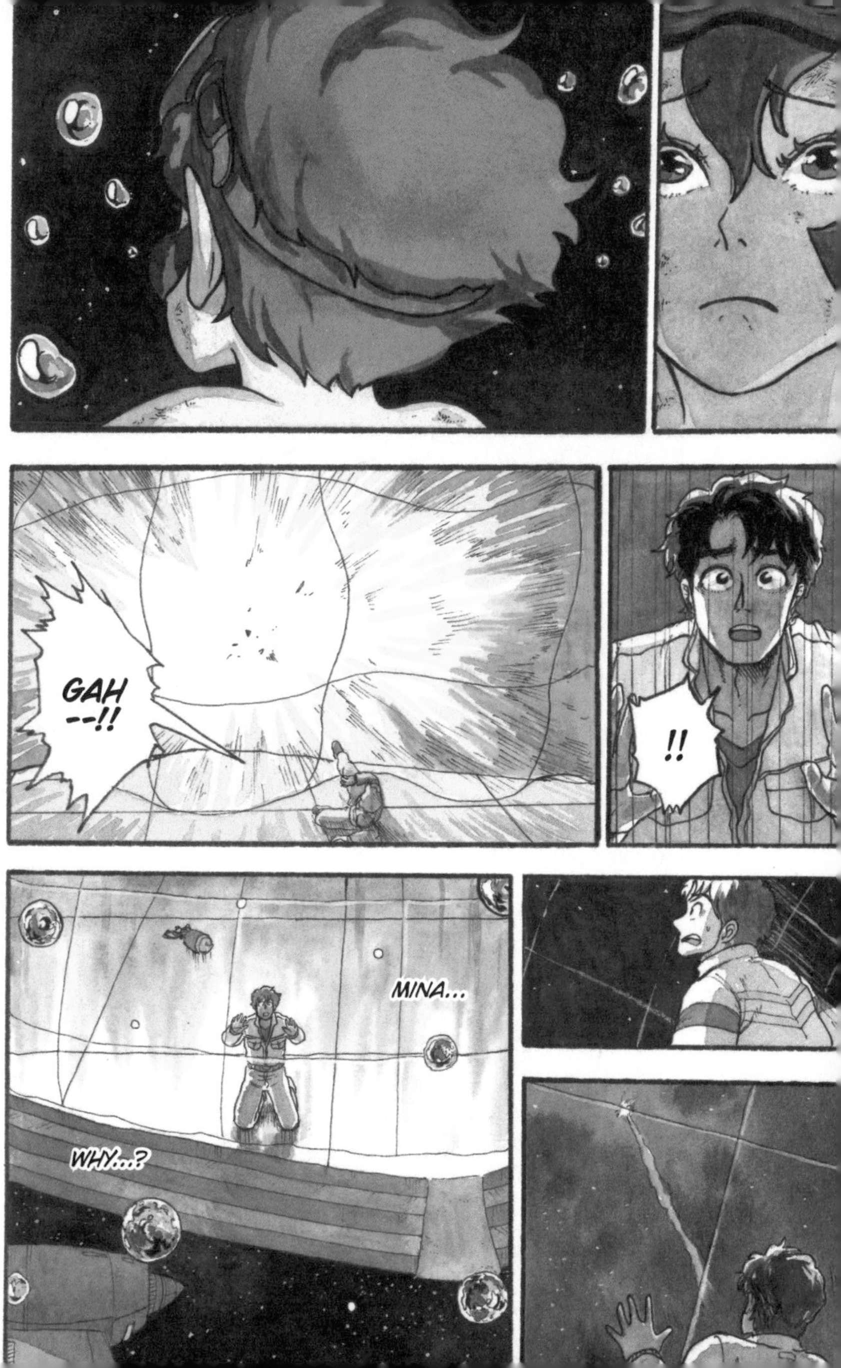
!!
GAH --!!
MINA...
WHY...?

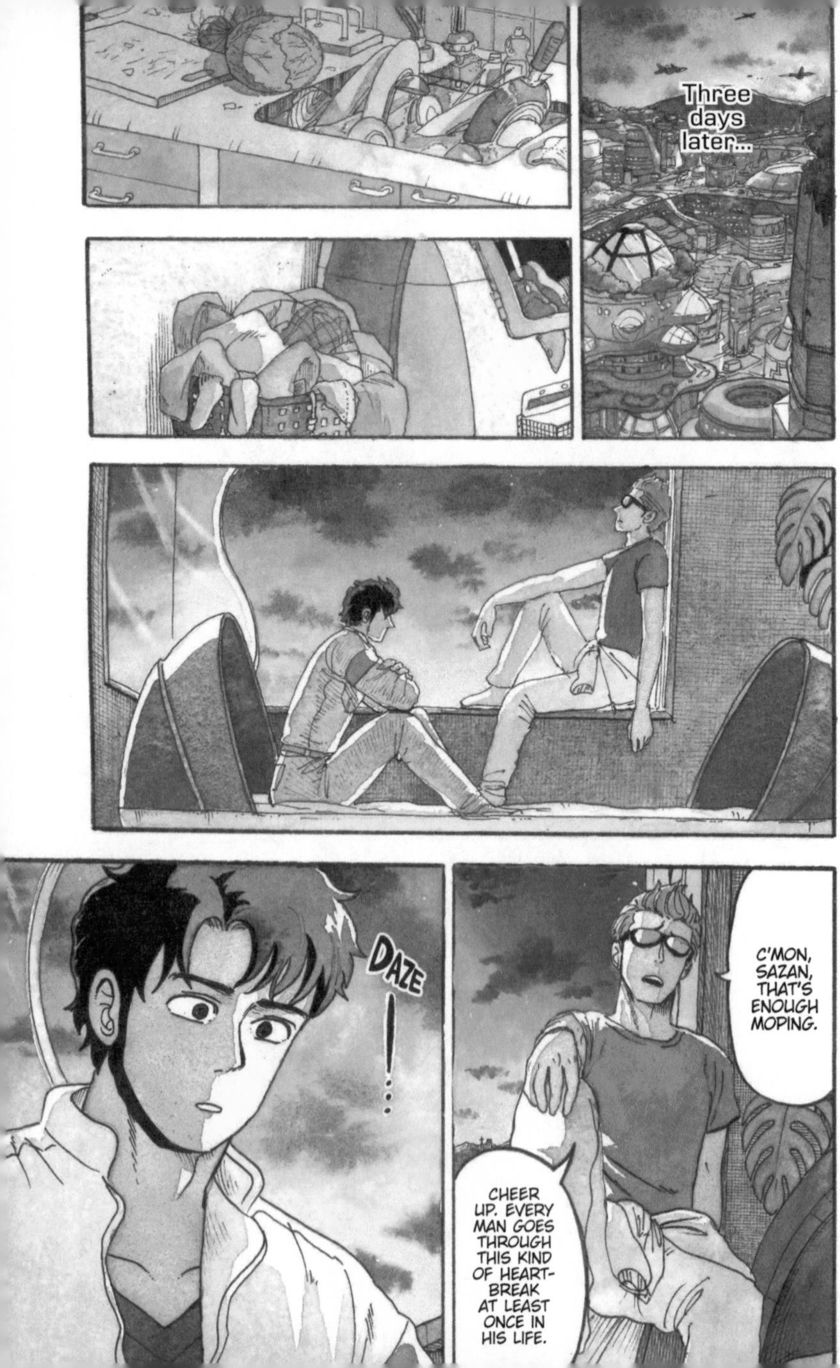
Three days later...
C'MON, SAZAN, THAT'S ENOUGH MOPING.
CHEER UP. EVERY MAN GOES THROUGH THIS KIND OF HEART-BREAK AT LEAST ONCE IN HIS LIFE.
DAZE
!

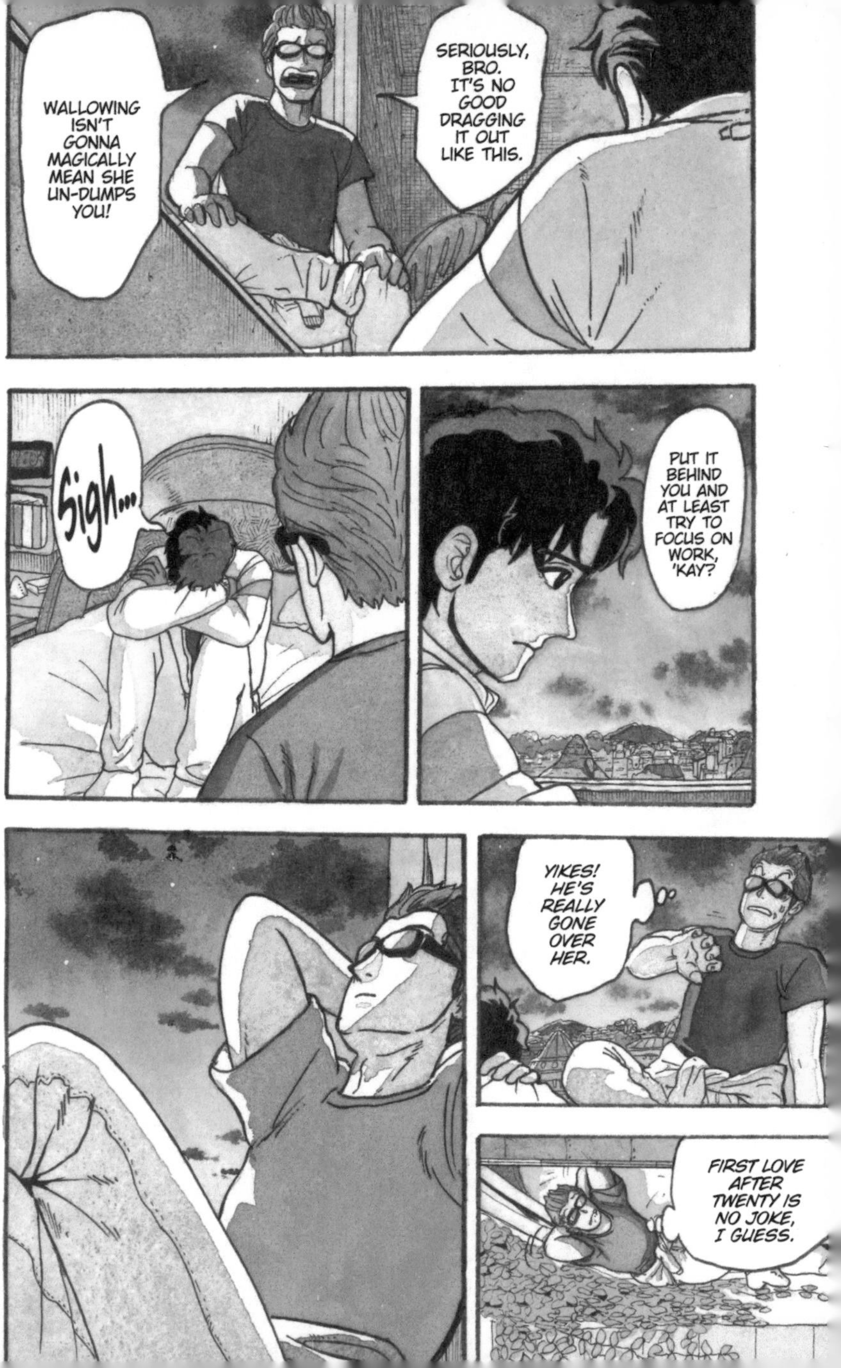
SERIOUSLY, BRO. IT'S NO GOOD DRAGGING IT OUT LIKE THIS.
WALLOWING ISN'T GONNA MAGICALLY MEAN SHE UN-DUMPS YOU!
PUT IT BEHIND YOU AND AT LEAST TRY TO FOCUS ON WORK, 'KAY?
Sigh...
YIKES! HE'S REALLY GONE OVER HER.
FIRST LOVE AFTER TWENTY IS NO JOKE, I GUESS.

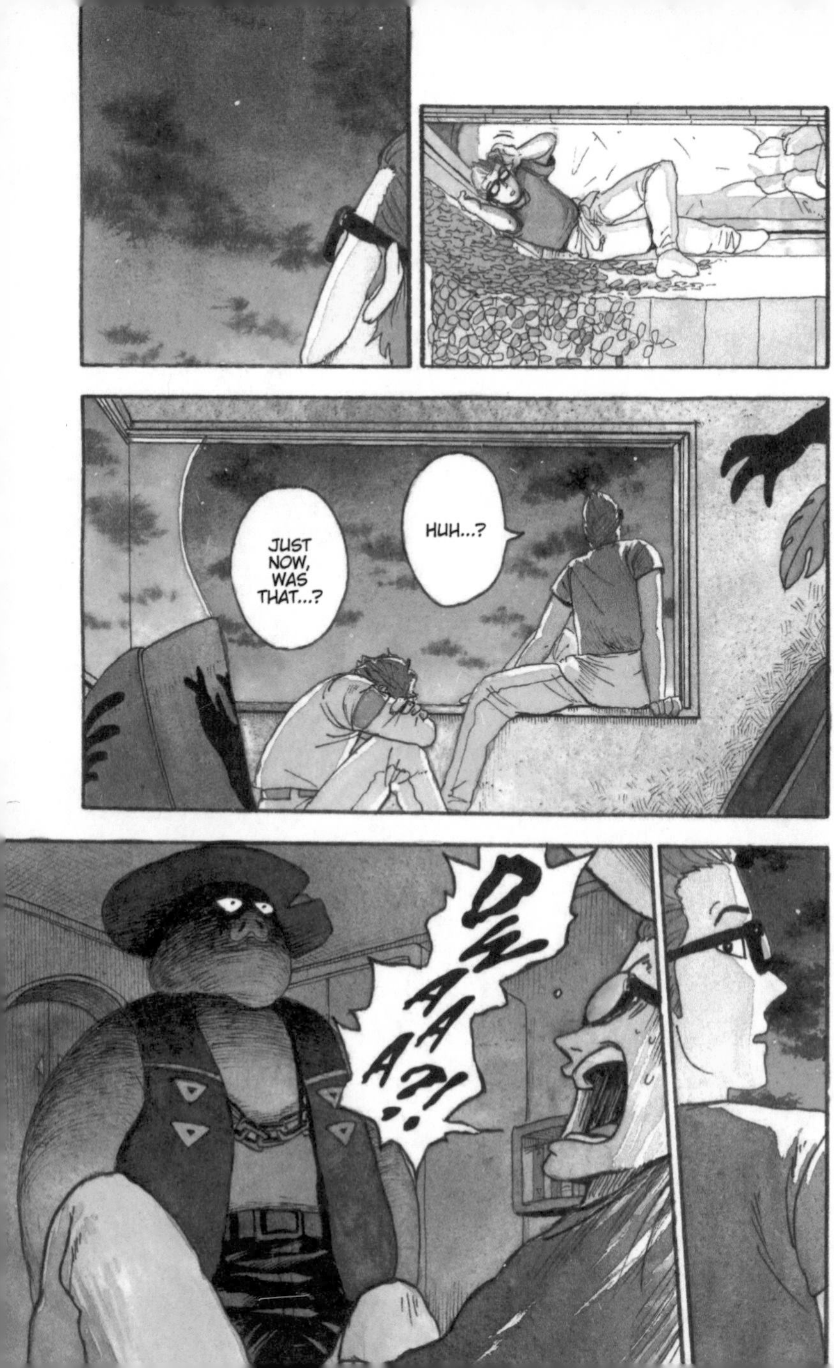
HUH...?
JUST NOW, WAS THAT...?
DWAAAA?!

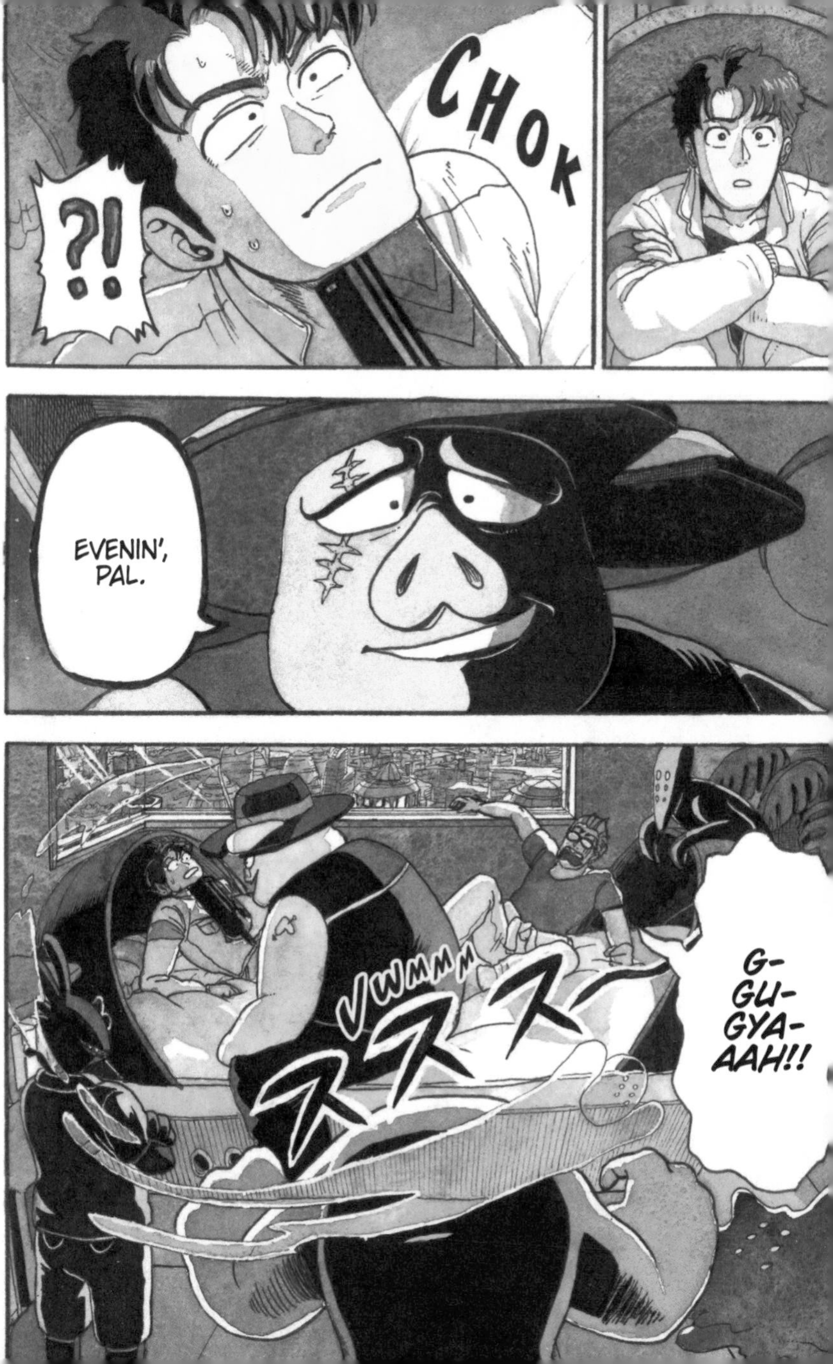
CHOK
?!
EVENIN', PAL.
VWMMM
G-GU-GYA-AAH!!
スススス

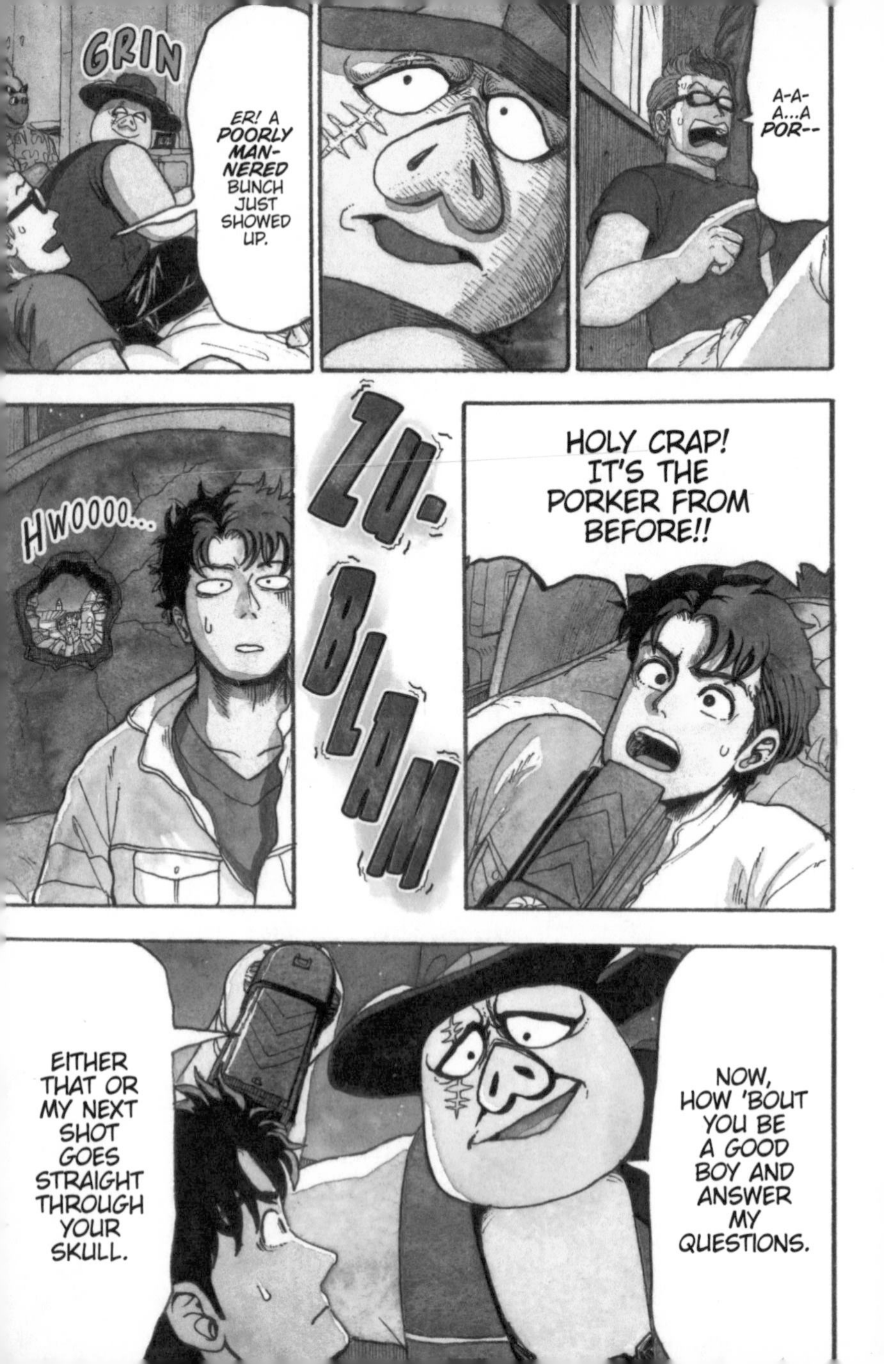
A-A-A...A POR--
GRIN
ER! A POORLY MAN-NERED BUNCH JUST SHOWED UP.
HOLY CRAP! IT'S THE PORKER FROM BEFORE!!
ZU-BLAM
HWOOOO...
NOW, HOW 'BOUT YOU BE A GOOD BOY AND ANSWER MY QUESTIONS.
EITHER THAT OR MY NEXT SHOT GOES STRAIGHT THROUGH YOUR SKULL.

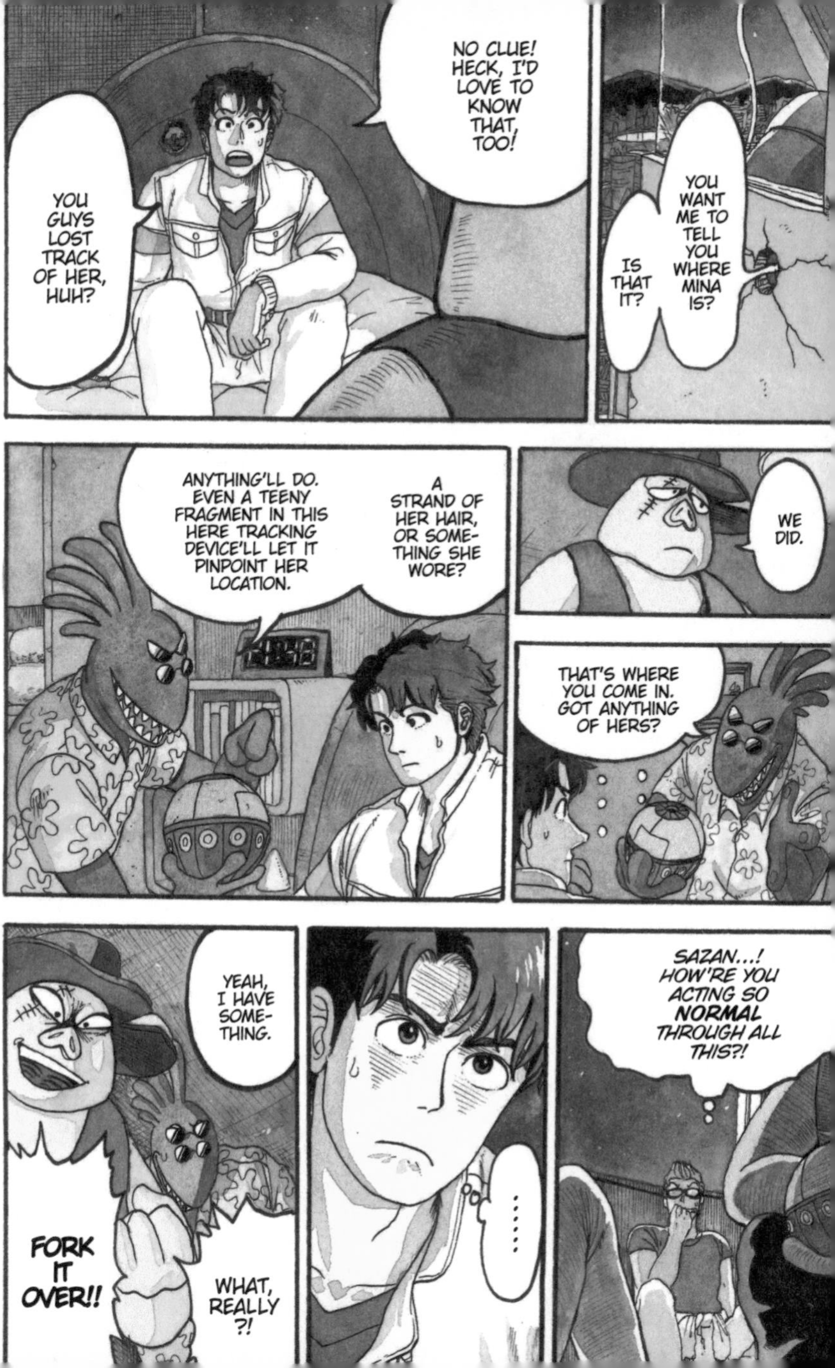
YOU WANT ME TO TELL YOU WHERE MINA IS?
IS THAT IT?
NO CLUE! HECK, I'D LOVE TO KNOW THAT, TOO!
YOU GUYS LOST TRACK OF HER, HUH?
WE DID.
THAT'S WHERE YOU COME IN. GOT ANYTHING OF HERS?
A STRAND OF HER HAIR, OR SOME-THING SHE WORE?
ANYTHING'LL DO. EVEN A TEENY FRAGMENT IN THIS HERE TRACKING DEVICE'LL LET IT PINPOINT HER LOCATION.
SAZAN...! HOW'RE YOU ACTING SO **NORMAL** THROUGH ALL THIS?!
......
YEAH, I HAVE SOME-THING.
WHAT, REALLY ?!
FORK IT OVER!!

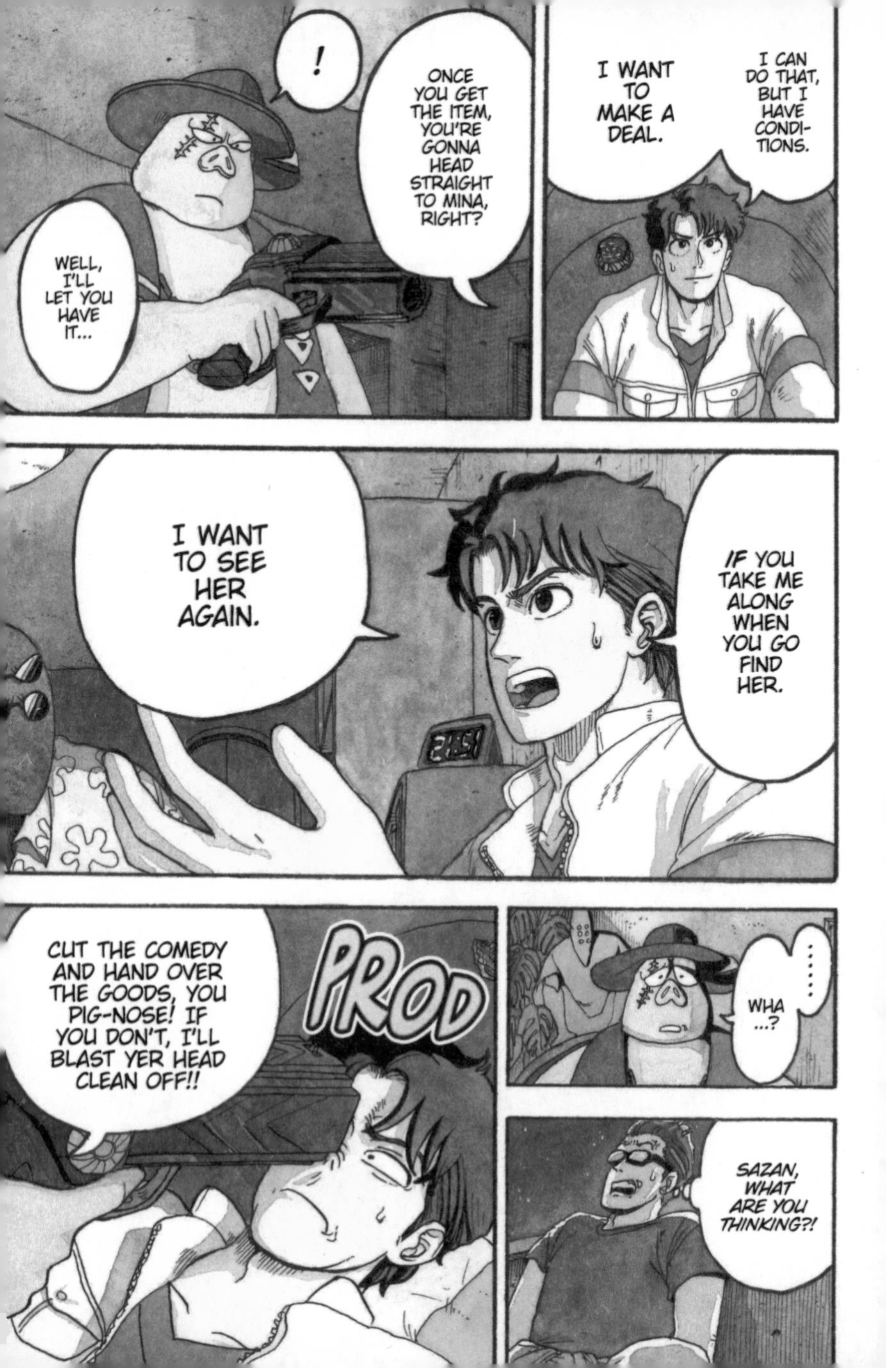
I CAN DO THAT, BUT I HAVE CONDITIONS.
I WANT TO MAKE A DEAL.
ONCE YOU GET THE ITEM, YOU'RE GONNA HEAD STRAIGHT TO MINA, RIGHT?
!
WELL, I'LL LET YOU HAVE IT...
IF YOU TAKE ME ALONG WHEN YOU GO FIND HER.
I WANT TO SEE HER AGAIN.
......
WHA ...?
SAZAN, WHAT ARE YOU THINKING?!
PROD
CUT THE COMEDY AND HAND OVER THE GOODS, YOU PIG-NOSE! IF YOU DON'T, I'LL BLAST YER HEAD CLEAN OFF!!

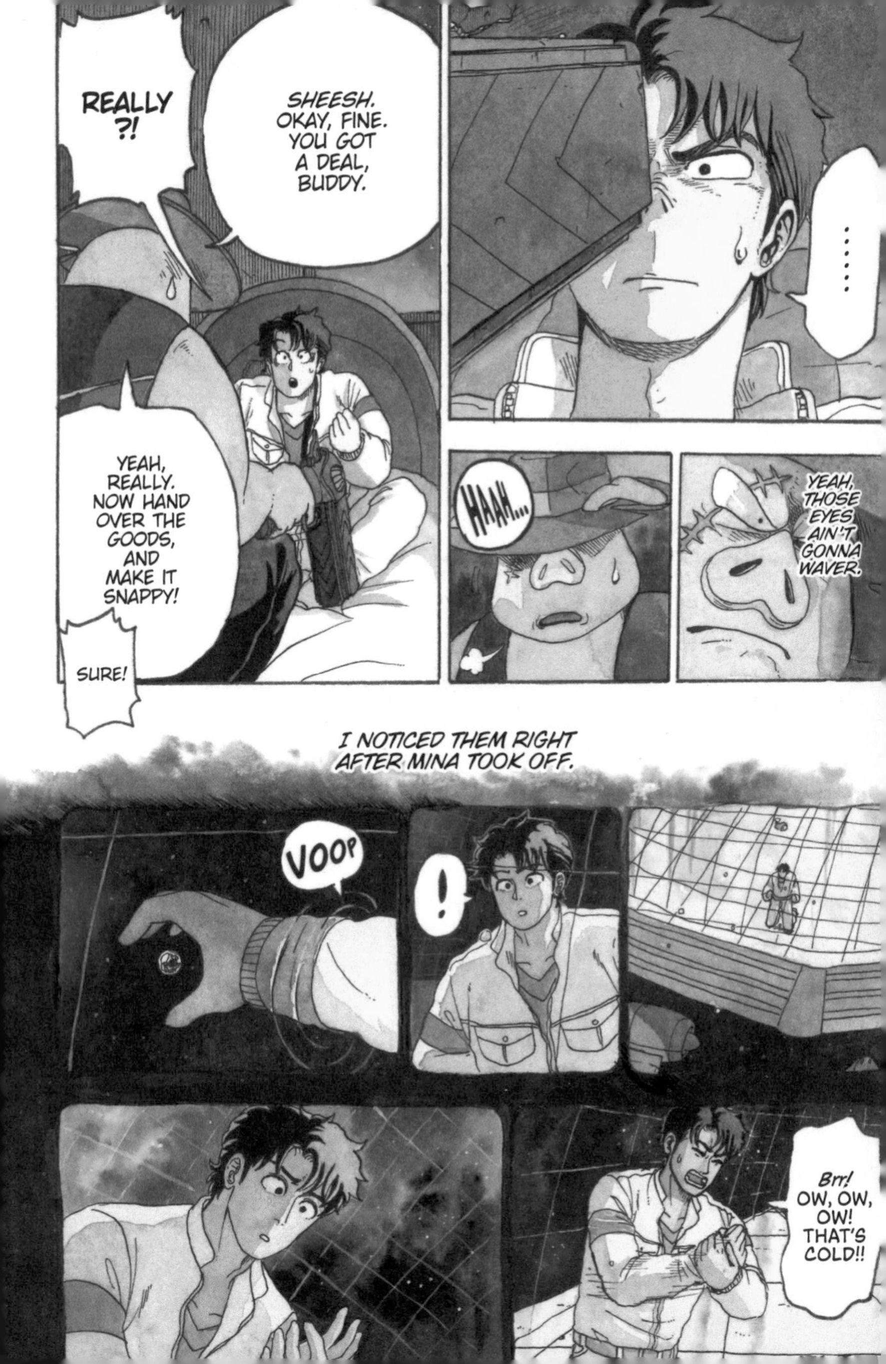
......
YEAH, THOSE EYES AIN'T GONNA WAVER.
HAAH...
SHEESH. OKAY, FINE. YOU GOT A DEAL, BUDDY.
REALLY ?!
YEAH, REALLY. NOW HAND OVER THE GOODS, AND MAKE IT SNAPPY!
SURE!
I NOTICED THEM RIGHT AFTER MINA TOOK OFF.
!
VOOP
Brr! OW, OW, OW! THAT'S COLD!!

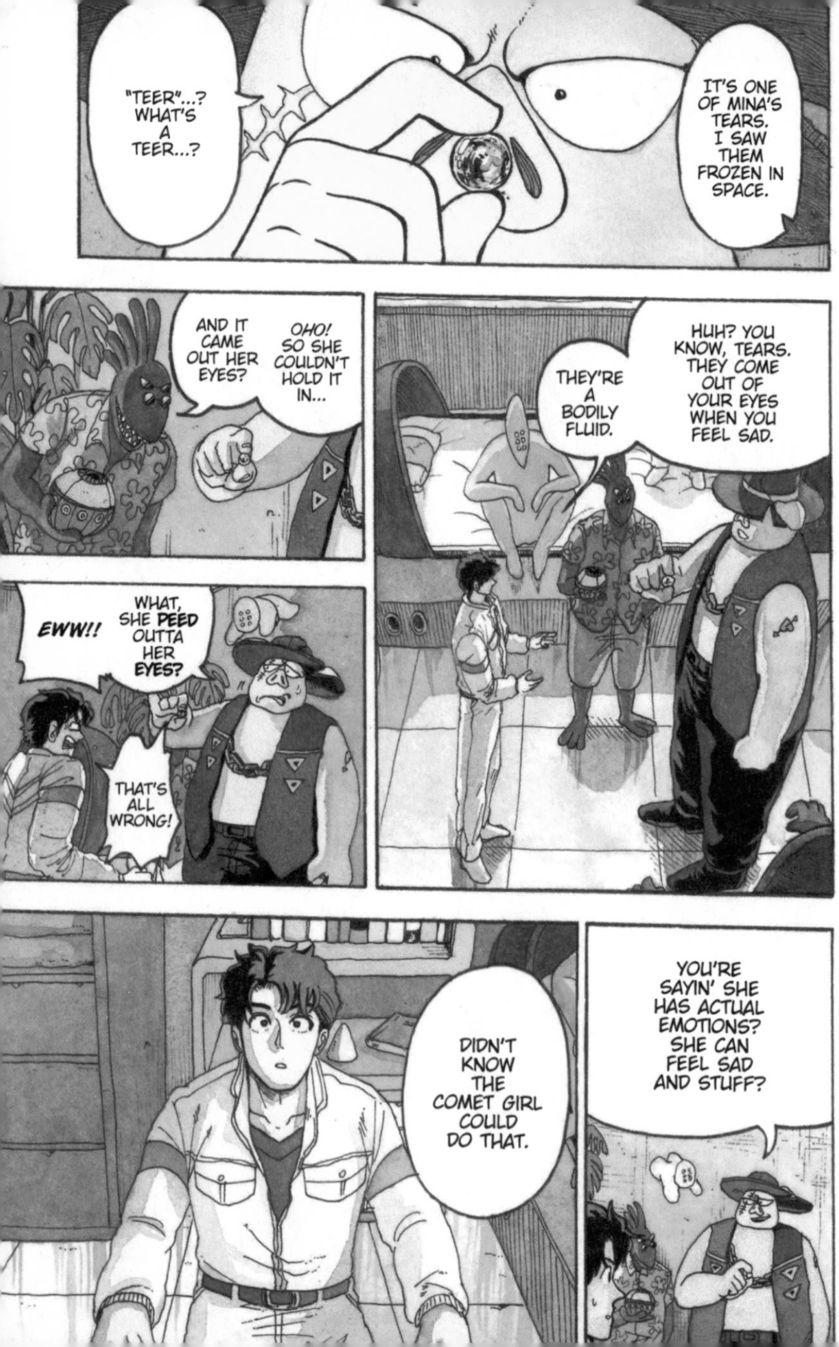
IT'S ONE OF MINA'S TEARS. I SAW THEM FROZEN IN SPACE.
"TEER"...? WHAT'S A TEER...?
HUH? YOU KNOW, TEARS. THEY COME OUT OF YOUR EYES WHEN YOU FEEL SAD.
THEY'RE A BODILY FLUID.
OHO! SO SHE COULDN'T HOLD IT IN...
AND IT CAME OUT HER EYES?
WHAT, SHE **PEED** OUTTA HER **EYES?**
EWW!!
THAT'S ALL WRONG!
YOU'RE SAYIN' SHE HAS ACTUAL EMOTIONS? SHE CAN FEEL SAD AND STUFF?
DIDN'T KNOW THE COMET GIRL COULD DO THAT.

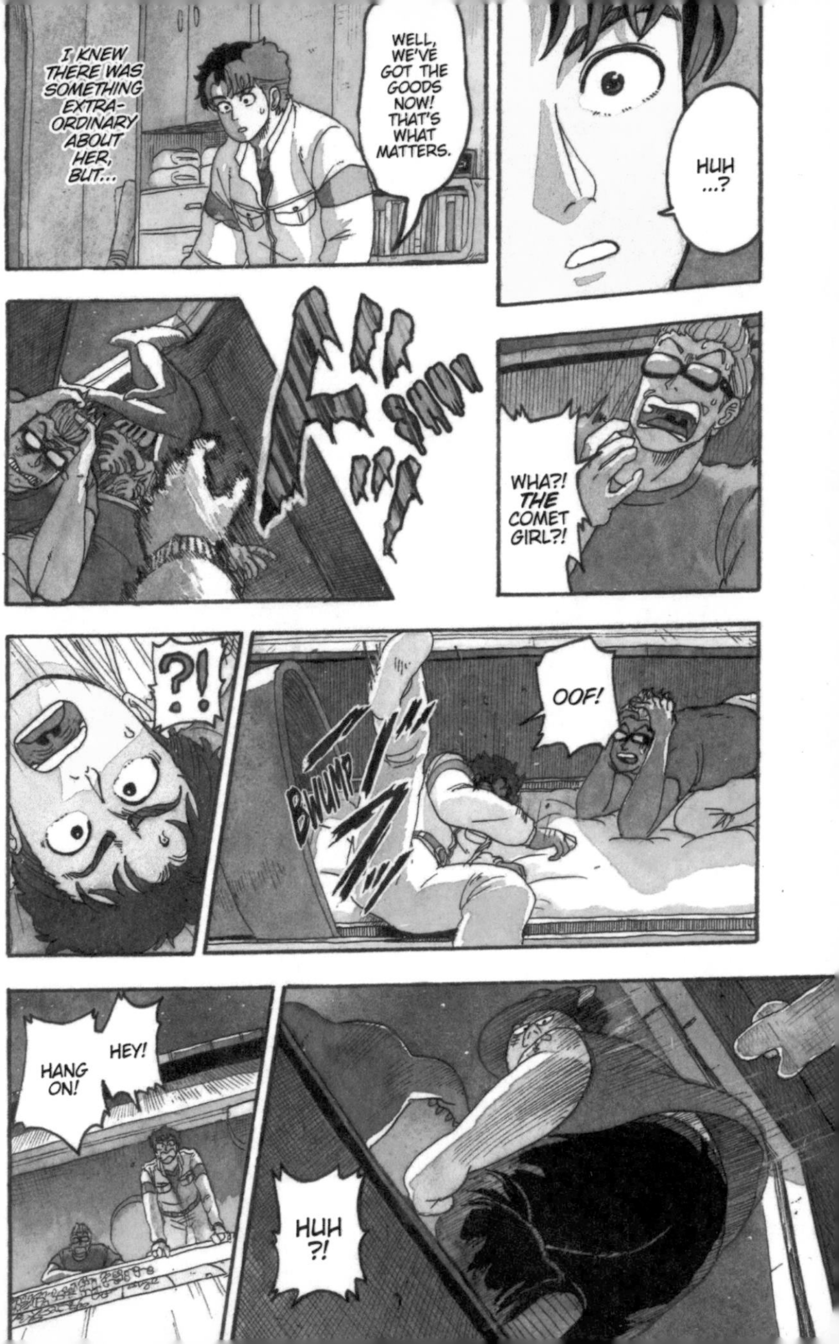
HUH ...?
WELL, WE'VE GOT THE GOODS NOW! THAT'S WHAT MATTERS.
I KNEW THERE WAS SOMETHING EXTRA-ORDINARY ABOUT HER, BUT...
WHA?! THE COMET GIRL?!
OOF!
BWUMP
?!
HUH ?!
HEY!
HANG ON!

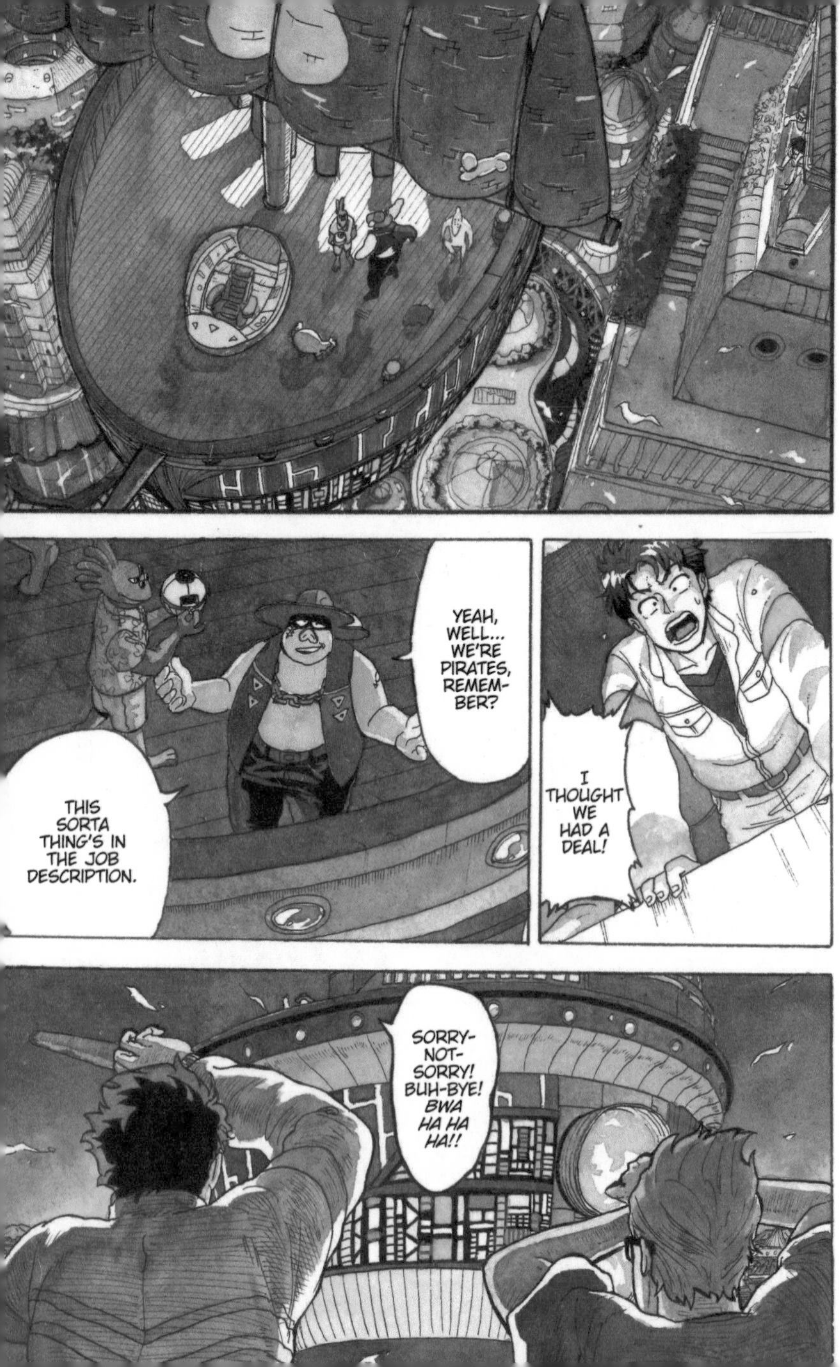
I THOUGHT WE HAD A DEAL!
YEAH, WELL... WE'RE PIRATES, REMEMBER?
THIS SORTA THING'S IN THE JOB DESCRIPTION.
SORRY-NOT-SORRY! BUH-BYE! BWA HA HA HA!!

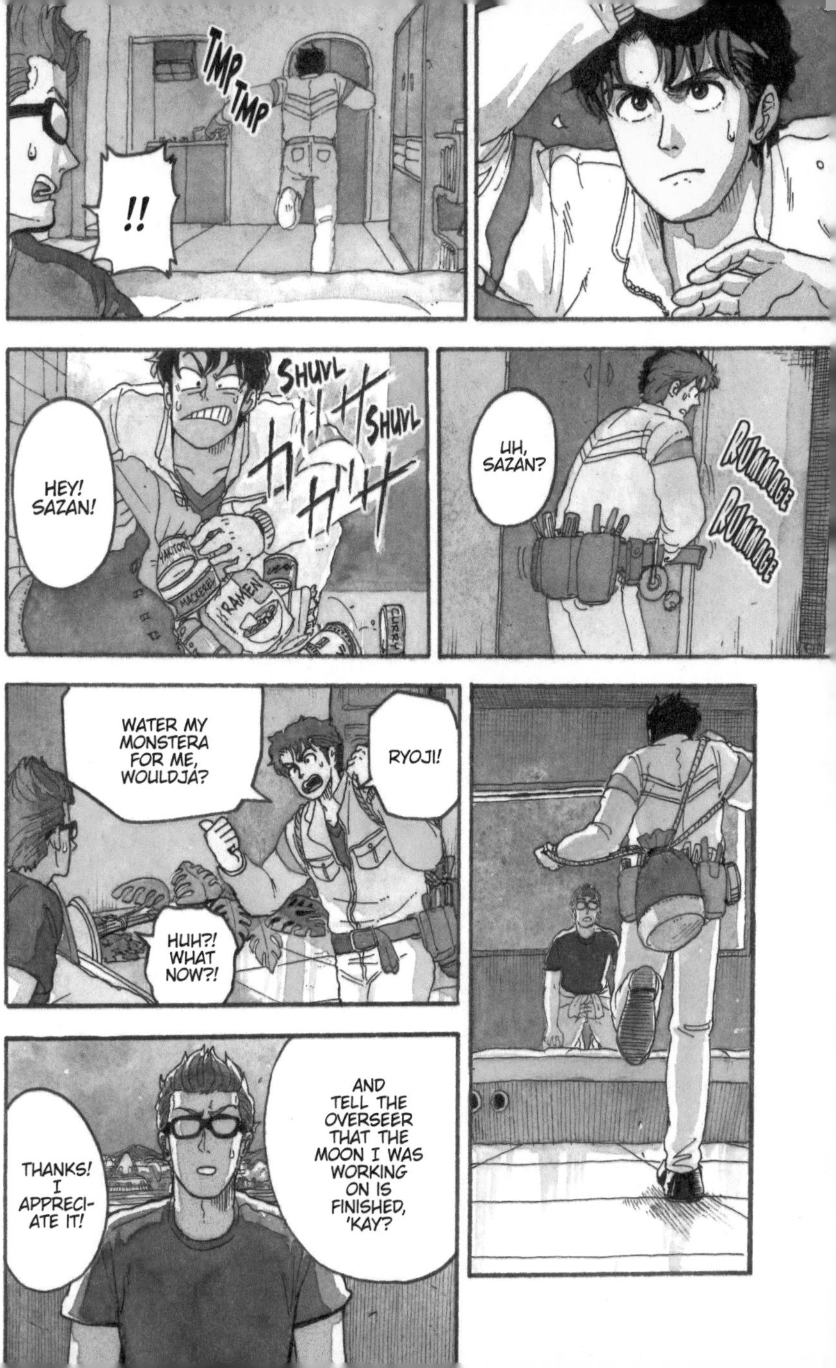
TMP TMP
!!
UH, SAZAN?
RUMMAGE RUMMAGE
HEY! SAZAN!
SHUVL SHUVL
YAKITORI
MACKEREL
RAMEN
CURRY
RYOJI!
WATER MY MONSTERA FOR ME, WOULDJA?
HUH?! WHAT NOW?!
AND TELL THE OVERSEER THAT THE MOON I WAS WORKING ON IS FINISHED, 'KAY?
THANKS! I APPRECIATE IT!

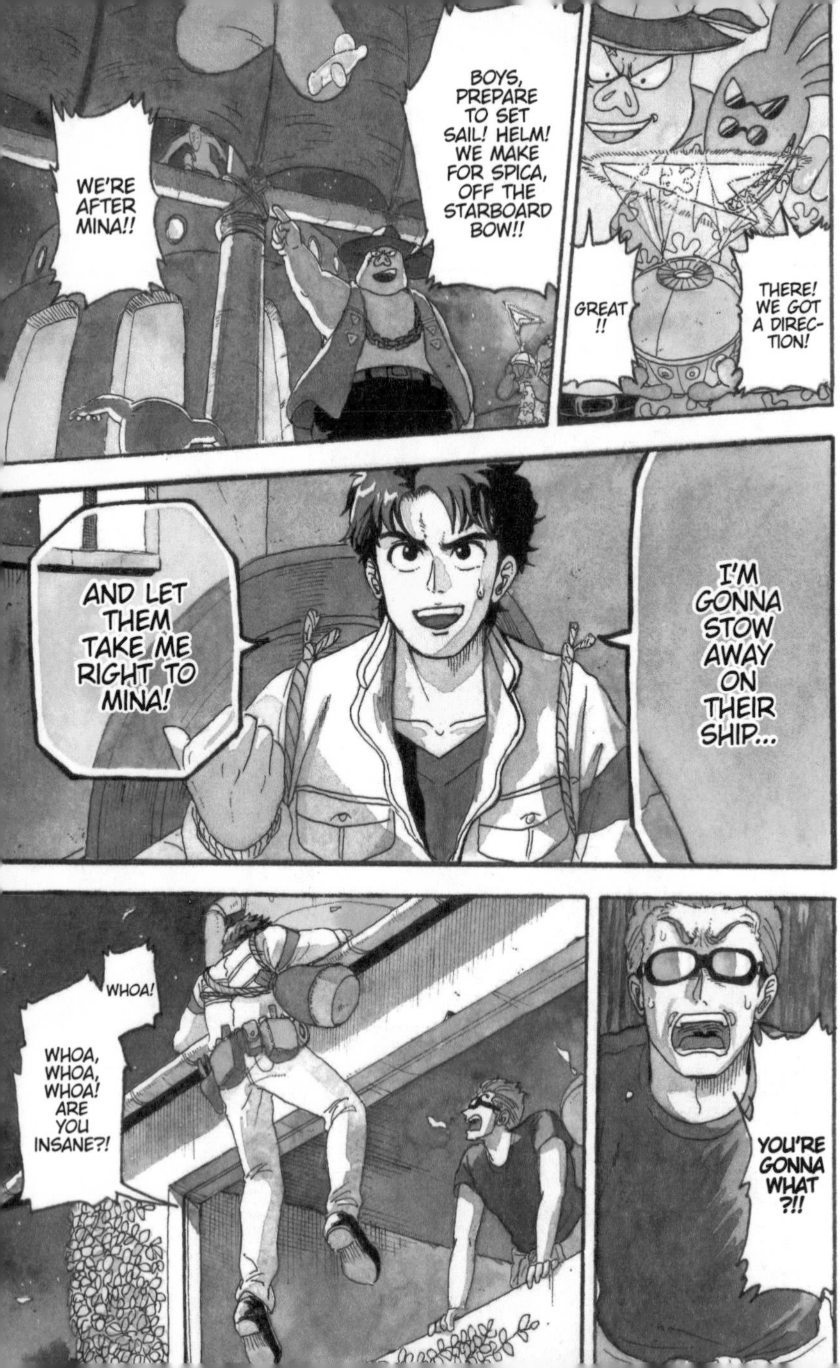
THERE! WE GOT A DIRECTION!
GREAT!!
BOYS, PREPARE TO SET SAIL! HELM! WE MAKE FOR SPICA, OFF THE STARBOARD BOW!!
WE'RE AFTER MINA!!
I'M GONNA STOW AWAY ON THEIR SHIP...
AND LET THEM TAKE ME RIGHT TO MINA!
YOU'RE GONNA WHAT?!!
WHOA!
WHOA, WHOA, WHOA! ARE YOU INSANE?!

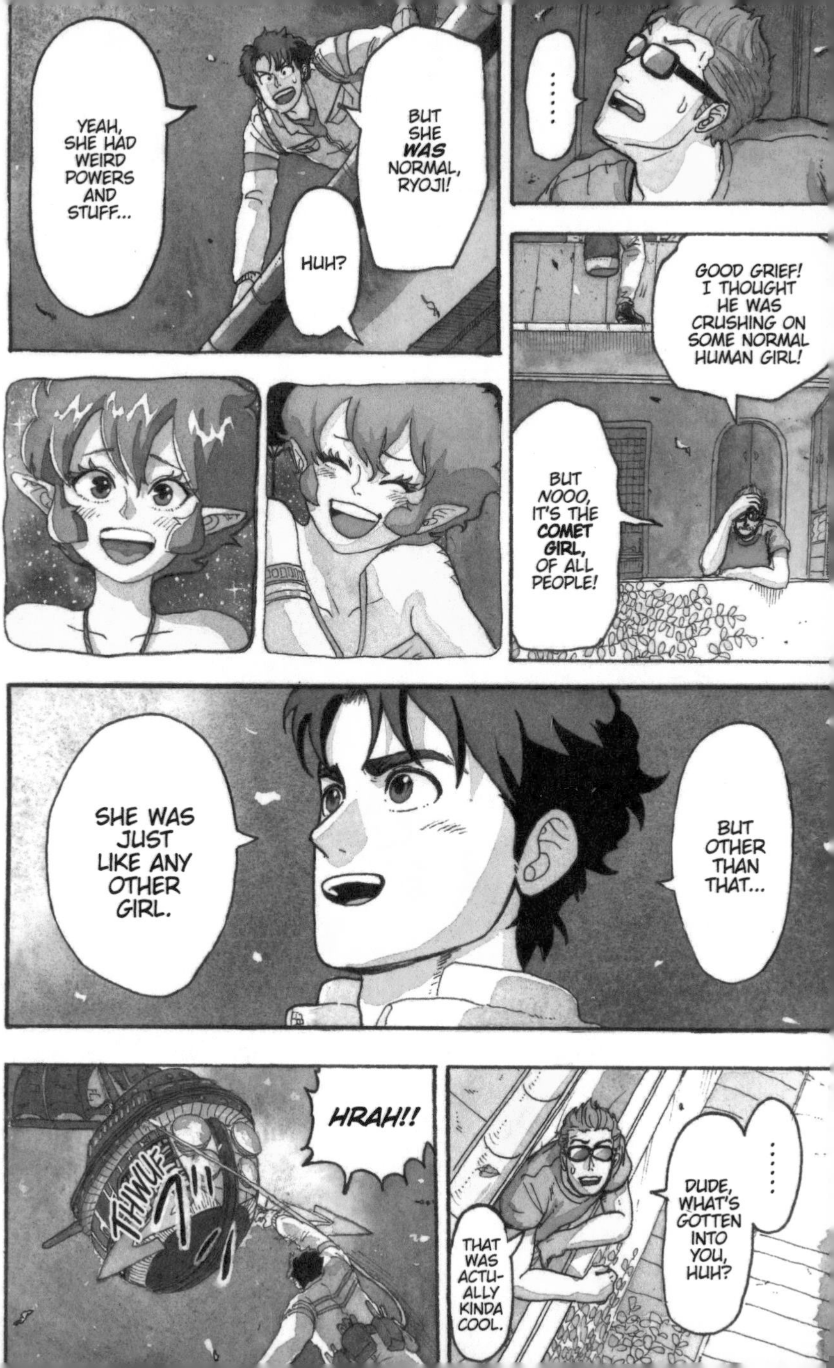
......
YEAH, SHE HAD WEIRD POWERS AND STUFF...
BUT SHE **WAS** NORMAL, RYOJI!
HUH?
GOOD GRIEF! I THOUGHT HE WAS CRUSHING ON SOME NORMAL HUMAN GIRL!
BUT *NOOO*, IT'S THE **COMET GIRL**, OF ALL PEOPLE!
BUT OTHER THAN THAT...
SHE WAS JUST LIKE ANY OTHER GIRL.
......
DUDE, WHAT'S GOTTEN INTO YOU, HUH?
THAT WAS ACTU-ALLY KINDA COOL.
HRAH!!
THWUP

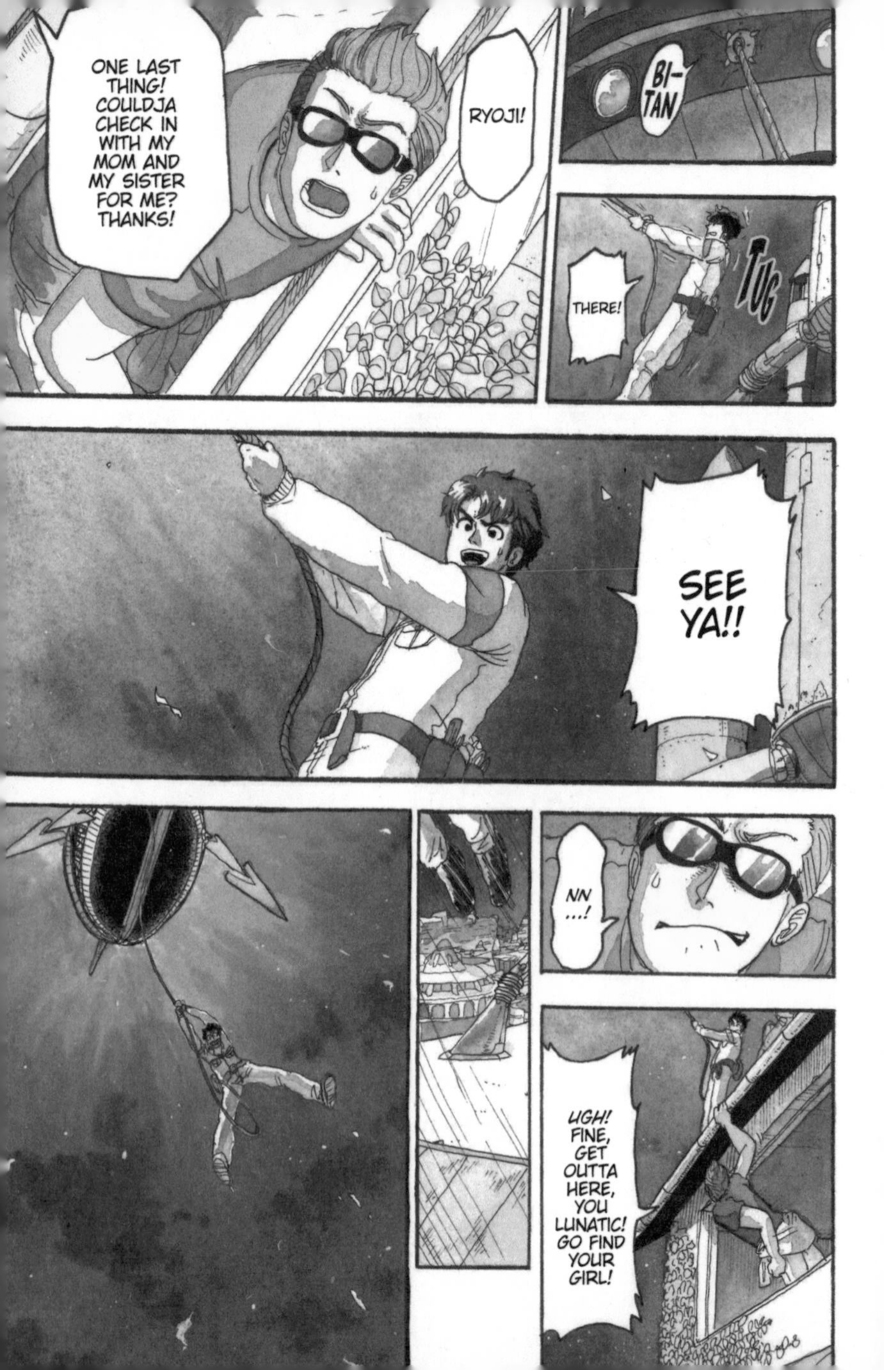
BI-TAN
THERE!
TUG
RYOJI!
ONE LAST THING! COULDJA CHECK IN WITH MY MOM AND MY SISTER FOR ME? THANKS!
SEE YA!!
NN ...!
UGH! FINE, GET OUTTA HERE, YOU LUNATIC! GO FIND YOUR GIRL!

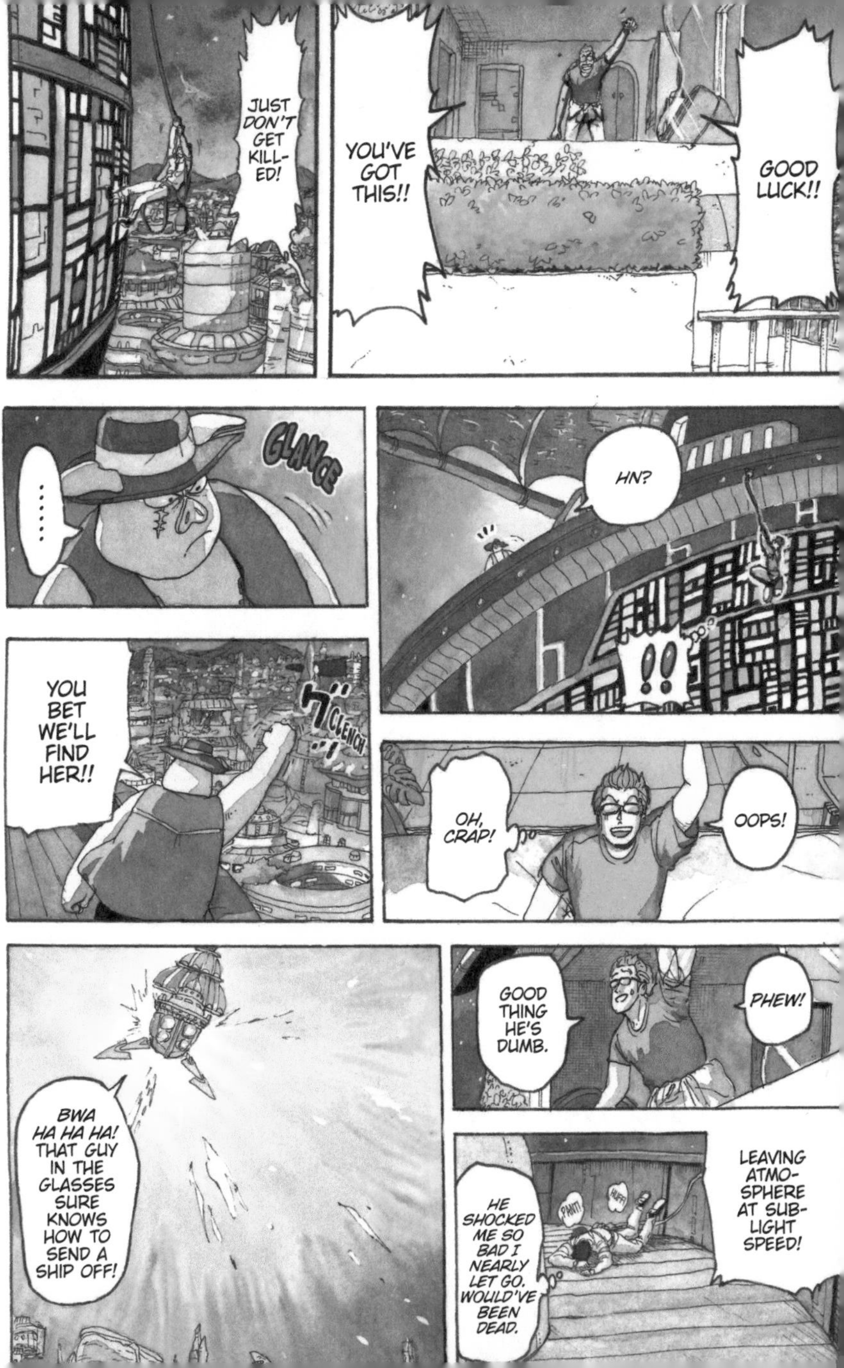
GOOD LUCK!!
YOU'VE GOT THIS!!
JUST DON'T GET KILL-ED!
HN?
!!
......
GLANCE
OOPS!
OH, CRAP!
YOU BET WE'LL FIND HER!!
ヴ
CLENCH
PHEW!
GOOD THING HE'S DUMB.
LEAVING ATMO-SPHERE AT SUB-LIGHT SPEED!
HUFF
PANT
HE SHOCKED ME SO BAD I NEARLY LET GO. WOULD'VE BEEN DEAD.
BWA HA HA HA! THAT GUY IN THE GLASSES SURE KNOWS HOW TO SEND A SHIP OFF!

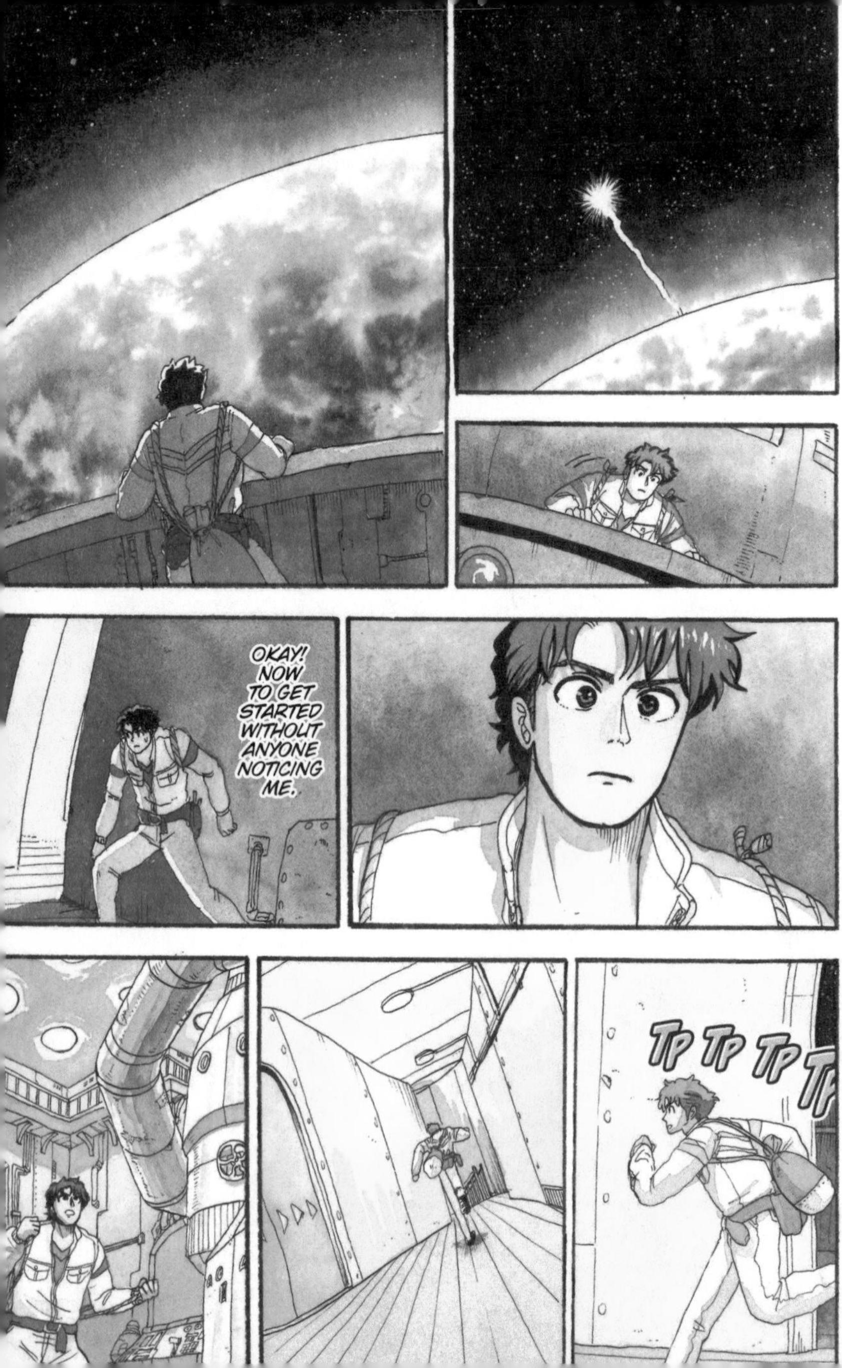

OKAY! NOW TO GET STARTED WITHOUT ANYONE NOTICING ME.
TP TP TP TP

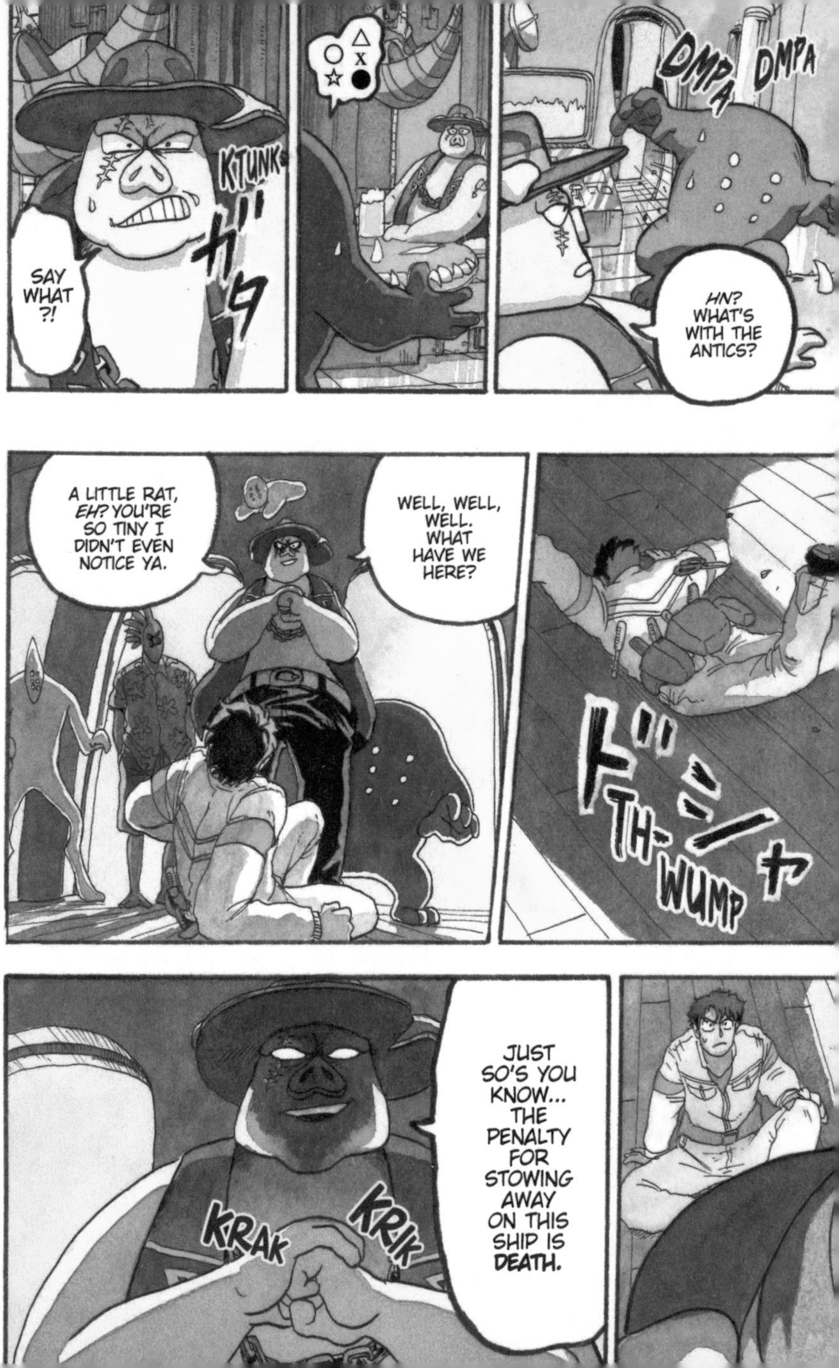
DMPA DMPA
HN? WHAT'S WITH THE ANTICS?
KTUNK
SAY WHAT?!
TH-WUMP
WELL, WELL, WELL. WHAT HAVE WE HERE?
A LITTLE RAT, EH? YOU'RE SO TINY I DIDN'T EVEN NOTICE YA.
JUST SO'S YOU KNOW... THE PENALTY FOR STOWING AWAY ON THIS SHIP IS DEATH.
KRIK
KRAK

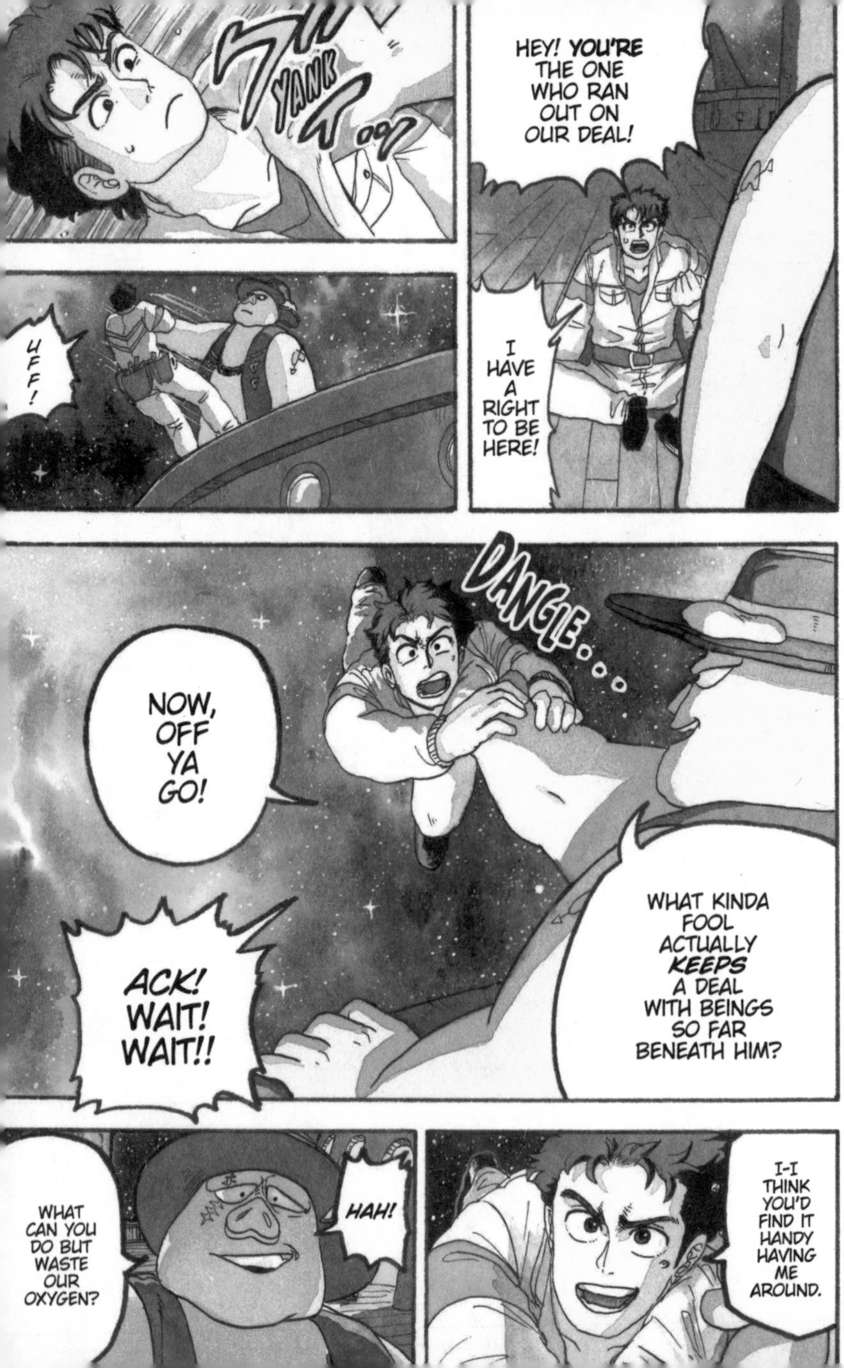
HEY! YOU'RE THE ONE WHO RAN OUT ON OUR DEAL!
I HAVE A RIGHT TO BE HERE!
YANK
UFF!
DANGLE...
WHAT KINDA FOOL ACTUALLY KEEPS A DEAL WITH BEINGS SO FAR BENEATH HIM?
NOW, OFF YA GO!
ACK! WAIT! WAIT!!
I-I THINK YOU'D FIND IT HANDY HAVING ME AROUND.
HAH!
WHAT CAN YOU DO BUT WASTE OUR OXYGEN?

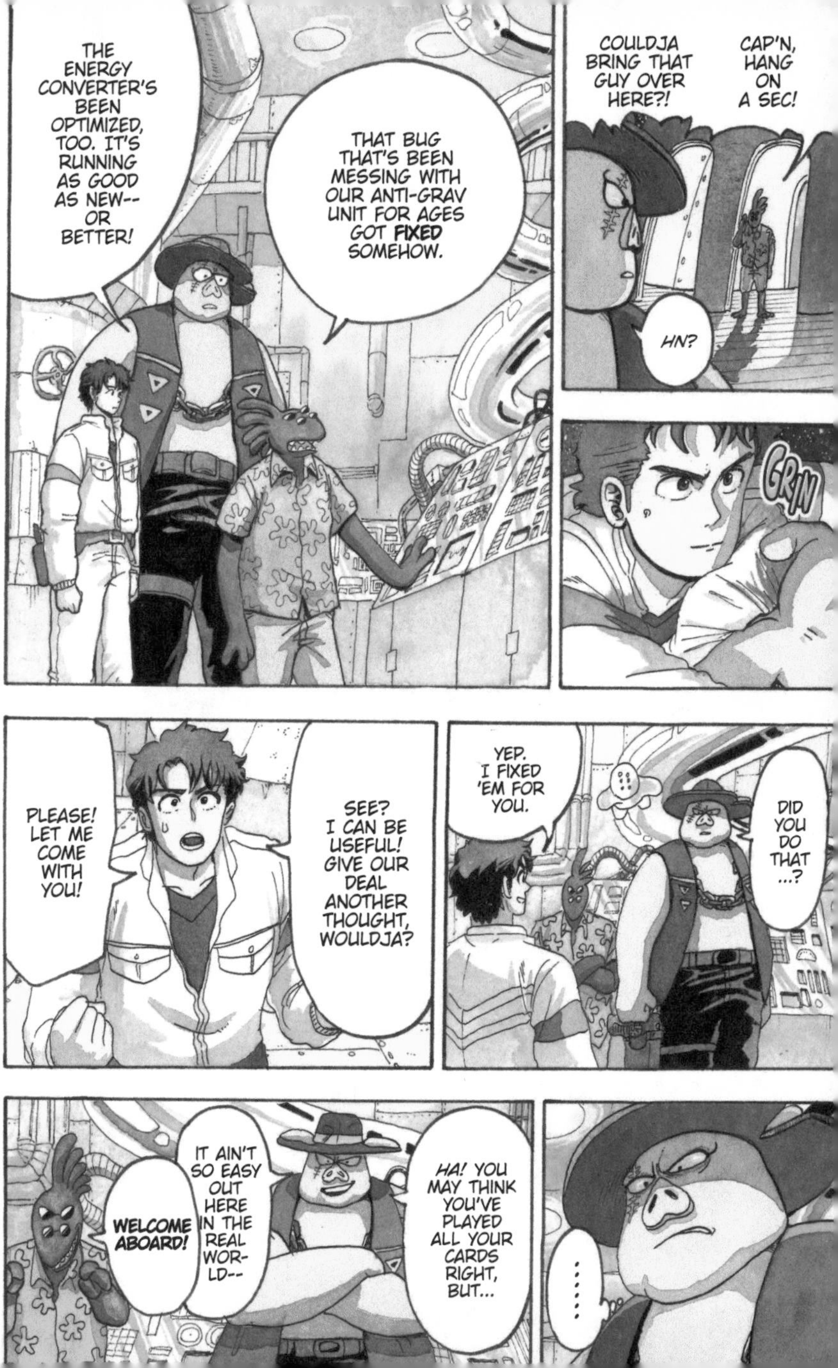
CAP'N, HANG ON A SEC!
COULDJA BRING THAT GUY OVER HERE?!
HN?
GRIN
THAT BUG THAT'S BEEN MESSING WITH OUR ANTI-GRAV UNIT FOR AGES GOT **FIXED** SOMEHOW.
THE ENERGY CONVERTER'S BEEN OPTIMIZED, TOO. IT'S RUNNING AS GOOD AS NEW--OR BETTER!
DID YOU DO THAT ...?
YEP. I FIXED 'EM FOR YOU.
SEE? I CAN BE USEFUL! GIVE OUR DEAL ANOTHER THOUGHT, WOULDJA?
PLEASE! LET ME COME WITH YOU!
......
HA! YOU MAY THINK YOU'VE PLAYED ALL YOUR CARDS RIGHT, BUT...
IT AIN'T SO EASY OUT HERE IN THE REAL WOR-LD--
WELCOME ABOARD!

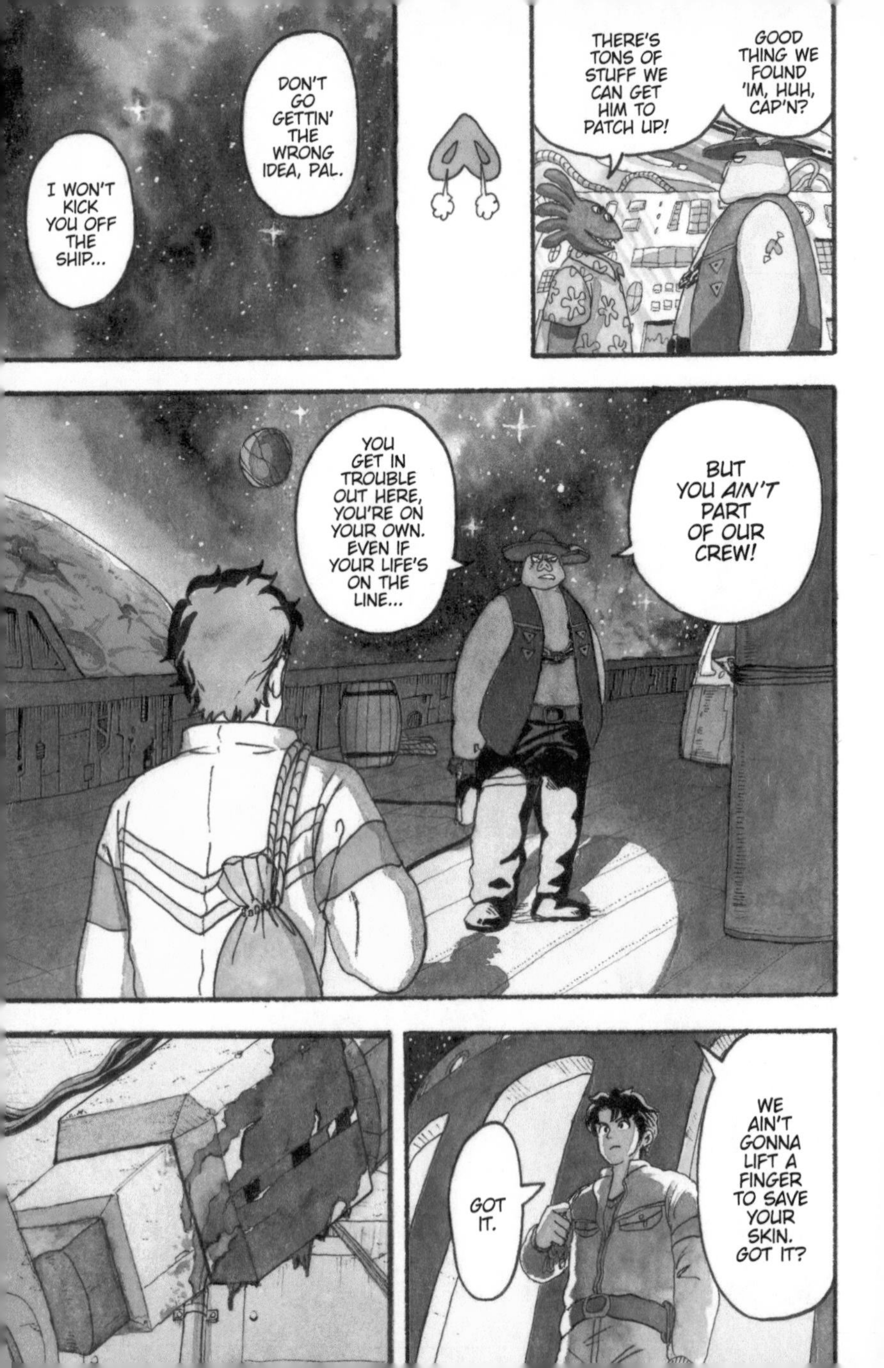
GOOD THING WE FOUND 'IM, HUH, CAP'N?
THERE'S TONS OF STUFF WE CAN GET HIM TO PATCH UP!
DON'T GO GETTIN' THE WRONG IDEA, PAL.
I WON'T KICK YOU OFF THE SHIP...
BUT YOU *AIN'T* PART OF OUR CREW!
YOU GET IN TROUBLE OUT HERE, YOU'RE ON YOUR OWN. EVEN IF YOUR LIFE'S ON THE LINE...
WE AIN'T GONNA LIFT A FINGER TO SAVE YOUR SKIN. GOT IT?
GOT IT.

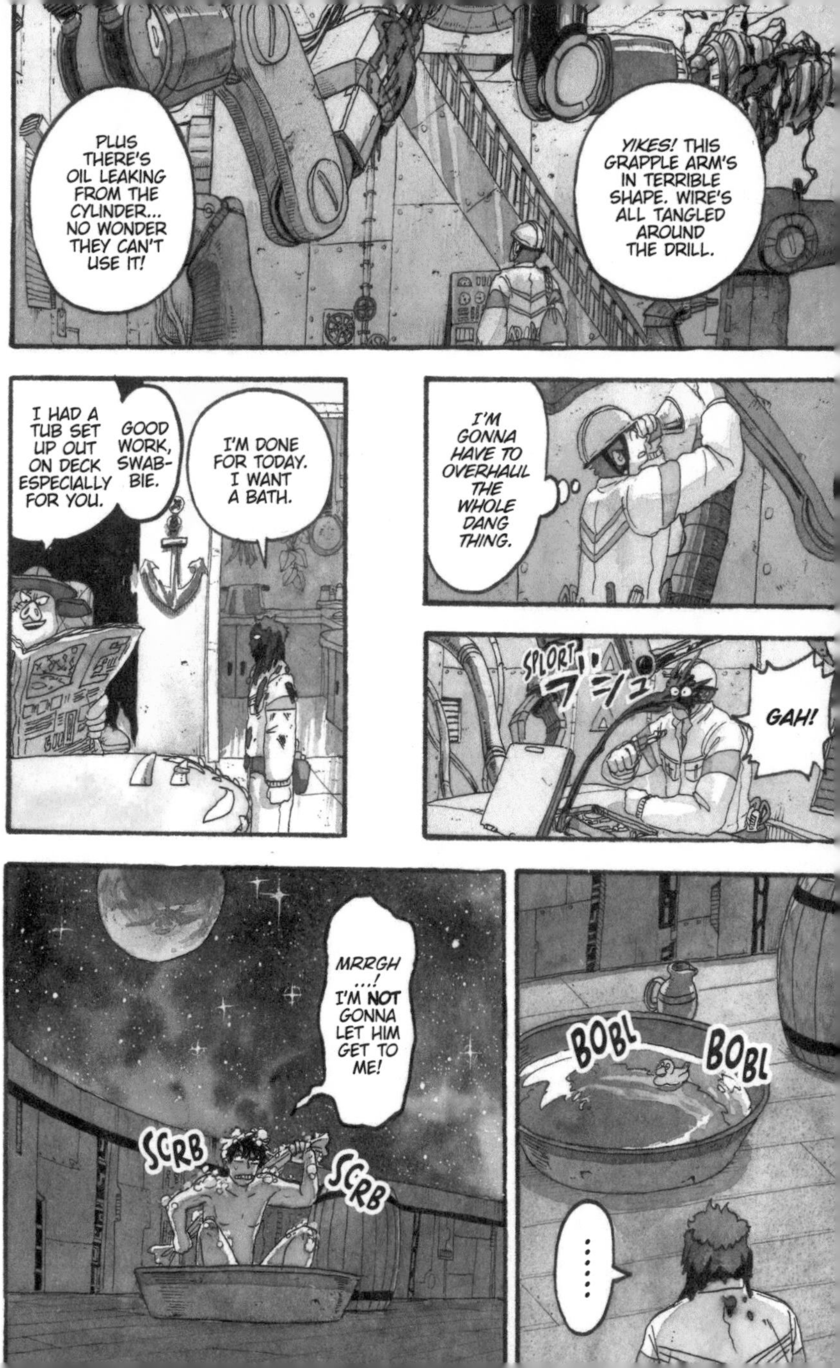
YIKES! THIS GRAPPLE ARM'S IN TERRIBLE SHAPE. WIRE'S ALL TANGLED AROUND THE DRILL.
PLUS THERE'S OIL LEAKING FROM THE CYLINDER... NO WONDER THEY CAN'T USE IT!
I'M GONNA HAVE TO OVERHAUL THE WHOLE DANG THING.
SPLORT
ブシュ
GAH!
I'M DONE FOR TODAY. I WANT A BATH.
GOOD WORK, SWAB-BIE.
I HAD A TUB SET UP OUT ON DECK ESPECIALLY FOR YOU.
BOBL
BOBL
......
MRRGH ...! I'M NOT GONNA LET HIM GET TO ME!
SCRB
SCRB

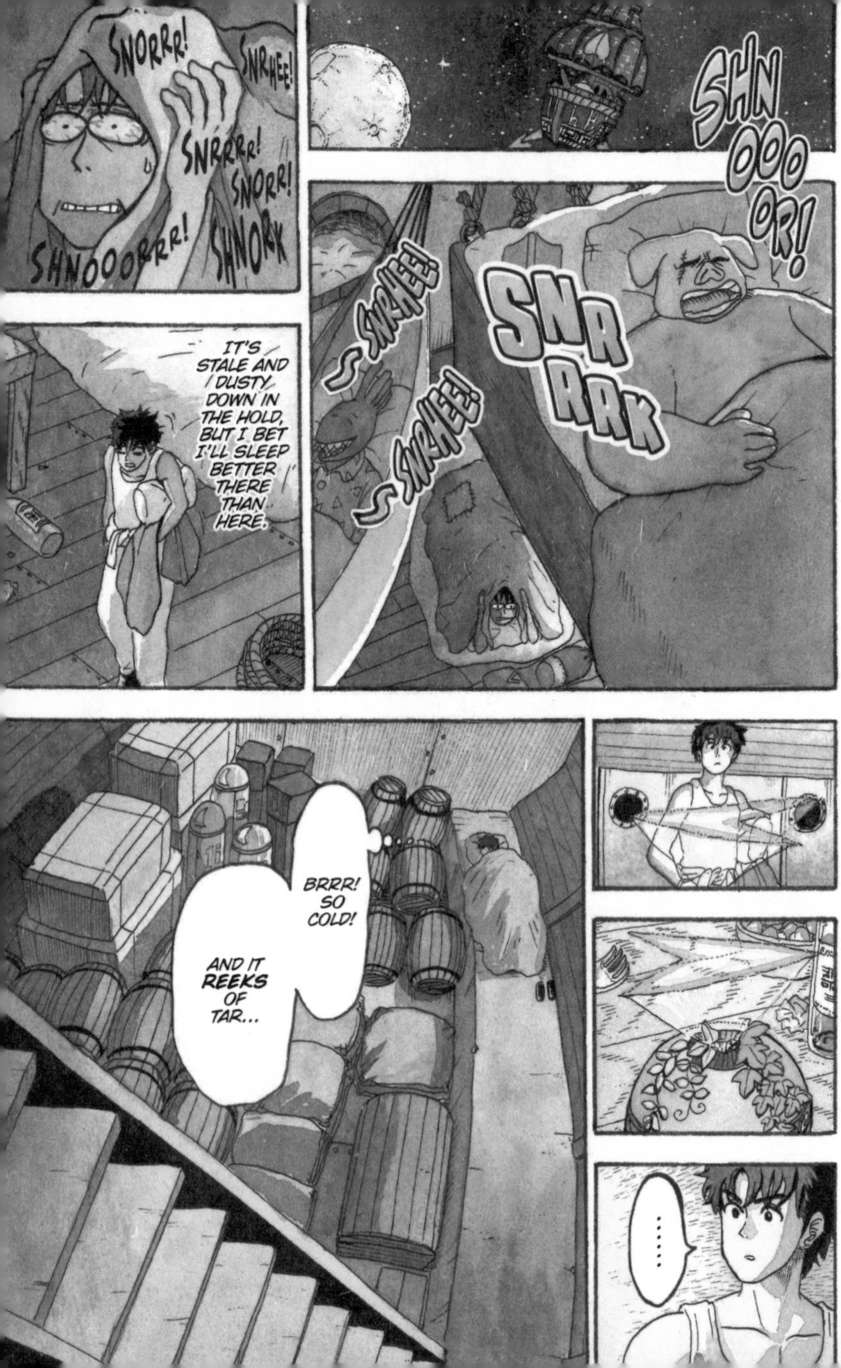
SHNOOOOOR!
SNRRAK
~SNRHEE!
~SNRHEE!
SNORRR!
SNRHEE!
SNRRRR!
SNORR!
SHNORK
SHNOOORRR!
IT'S STALE AND DUSTY DOWN IN THE HOLD, BUT I BET I'LL SLEEP BETTER THERE THAN HERE.
......
BRRR! SO COLD!
AND IT REEKS OF TAR...

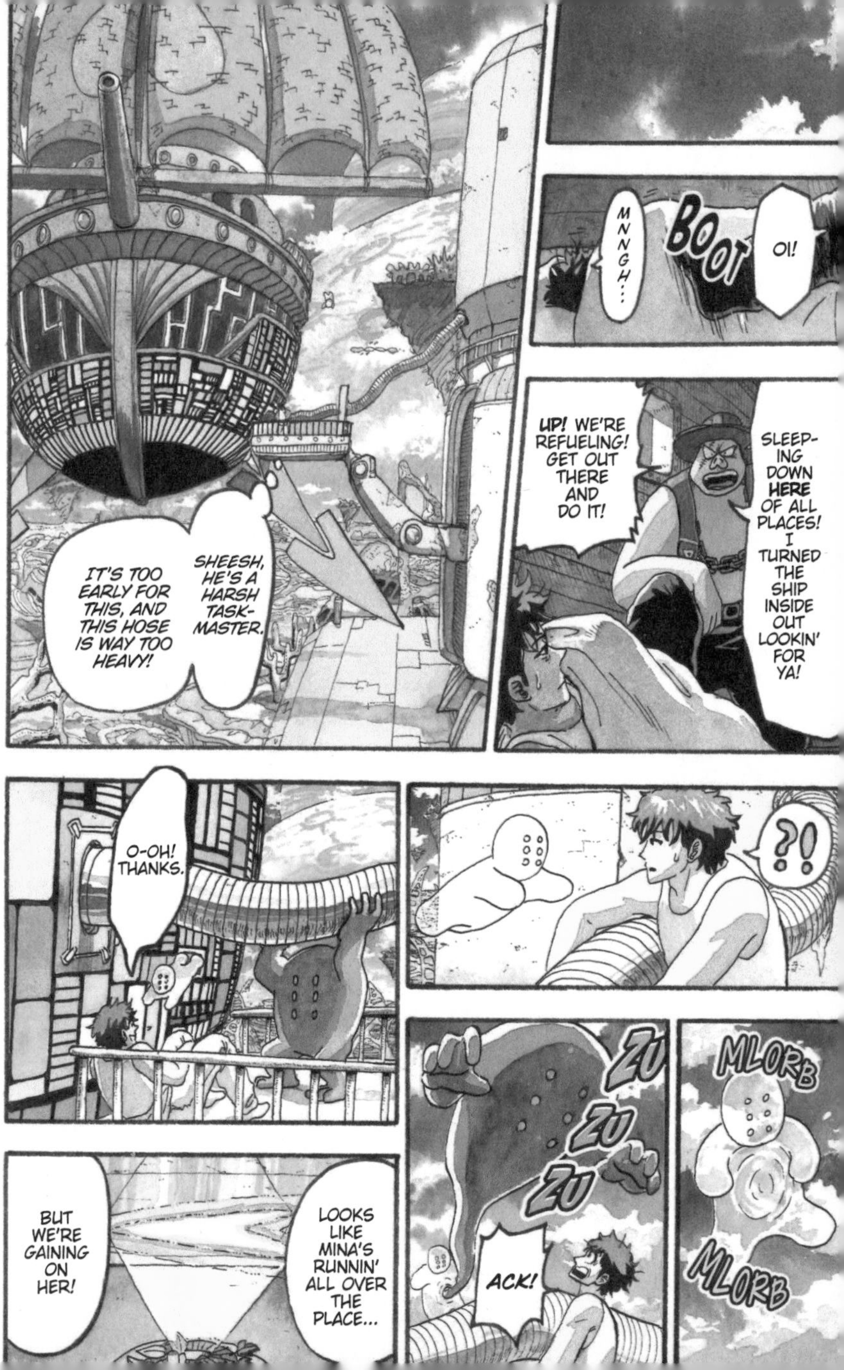
OI!
BOOT
MNNGH...
SLEEP-ING DOWN HERE OF ALL PLACES! I TURNED THE SHIP INSIDE OUT LOOKIN' FOR YA!
UP! WE'RE REFUELING! GET OUT THERE AND DO IT!
SHEESH, HE'S A HARSH TASK-MASTER.
IT'S TOO EARLY FOR THIS, AND THIS HOSE IS WAY TOO HEAVY!
?!
O-OH! THANKS.
MLORB
MLORB
ZU
ZU
ZU
ACK!
LOOKS LIKE MINA'S RUNNIN' ALL OVER THE PLACE...
BUT WE'RE GAINING ON HER!

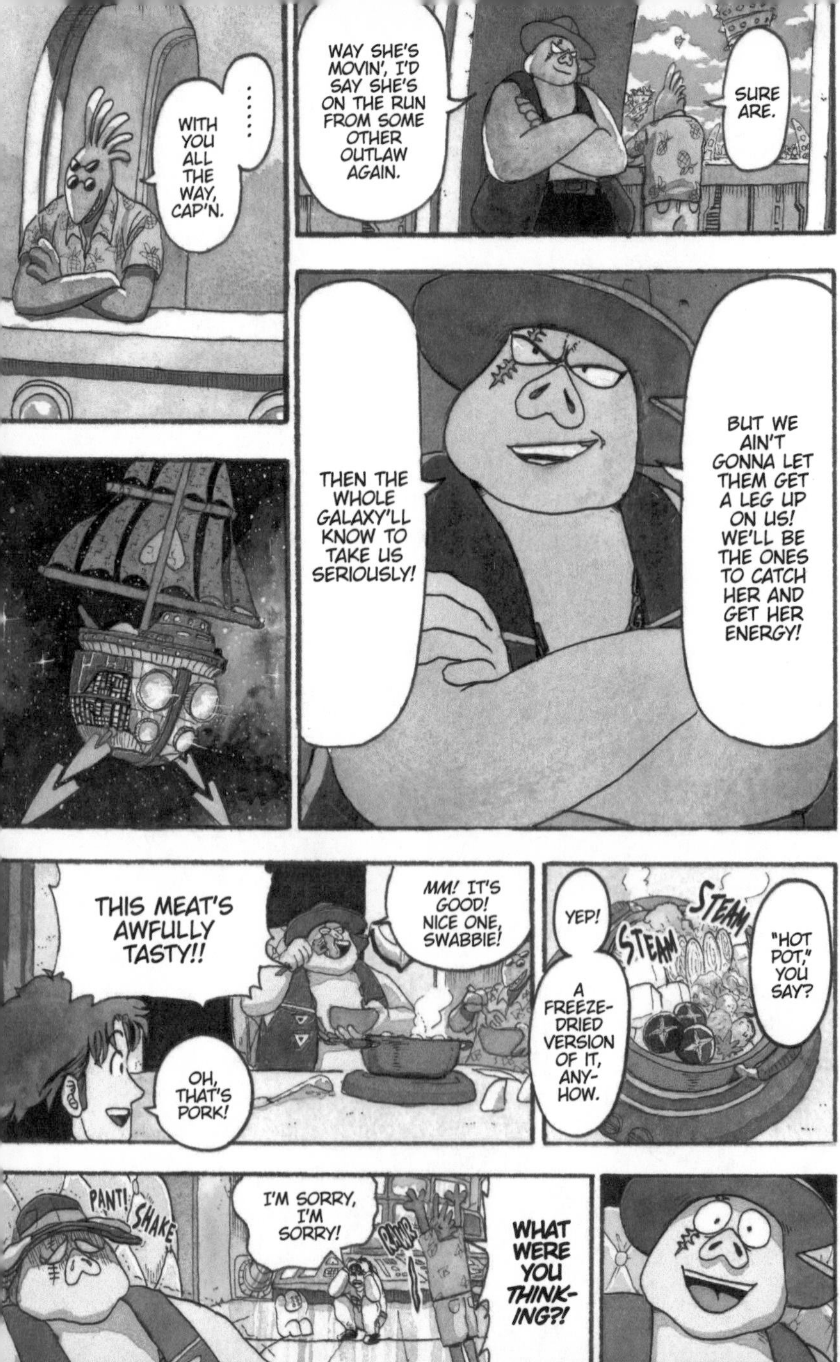
SURE ARE.
WAY SHE'S MOVIN', I'D SAY SHE'S ON THE RUN FROM SOME OTHER OUTLAW AGAIN.
......
WITH YOU ALL THE WAY, CAP'N.
BUT WE AIN'T GONNA LET THEM GET A LEG UP ON US! WE'LL BE THE ONES TO CATCH HER AND GET HER ENERGY!
THEN THE WHOLE GALAXY'LL KNOW TO TAKE US SERIOUSLY!
"HOT POT," YOU SAY?
STEAM
STEAM
YEP!
A FREEZE-DRIED VERSION OF IT, ANYHOW.
MM! IT'S GOOD! NICE ONE, SWABBIE!
THIS MEAT'S AWFULLY TASTY!!
OH, THAT'S PORK!
WHAT WERE YOU THINKING?!
I'M SORRY, I'M SORRY!
PANT!
SHAKE

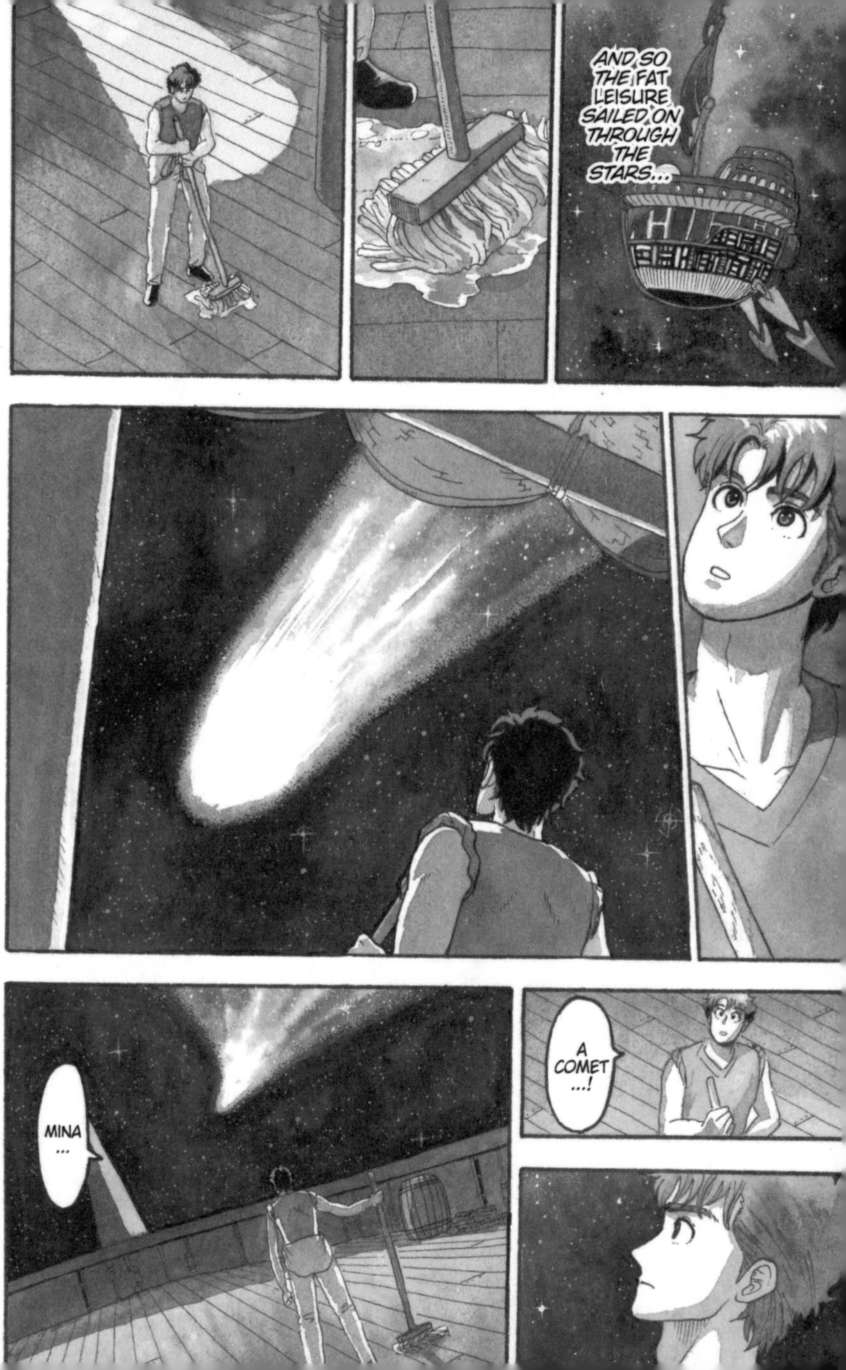
AND SO THE FAT LEISURE SAILED ON THROUGH THE STARS...
A COMET ...!
MINA ...

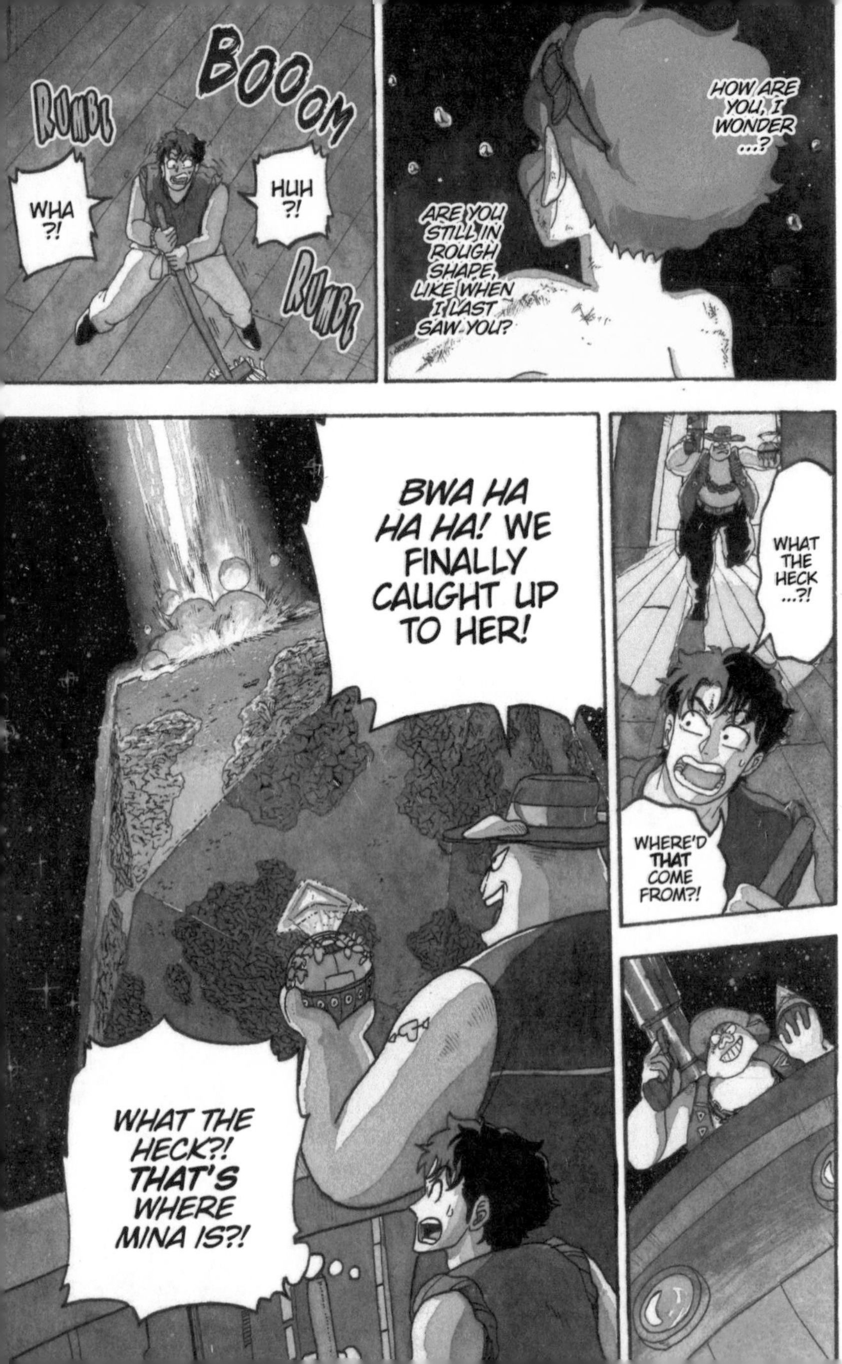
HOW ARE YOU, I WONDER ...?
ARE YOU STILL IN ROUGH SHAPE, LIKE WHEN I LAST SAW YOU?
BOOOM
RUMBL
HUH ?!
WHA ?!
RUMBL
WHAT THE HECK ...?!
WHERE'D THAT COME FROM?!
BWA HA HA HA! WE FINALLY CAUGHT UP TO HER!
WHAT THE HECK?! THAT'S WHERE MINA IS?!

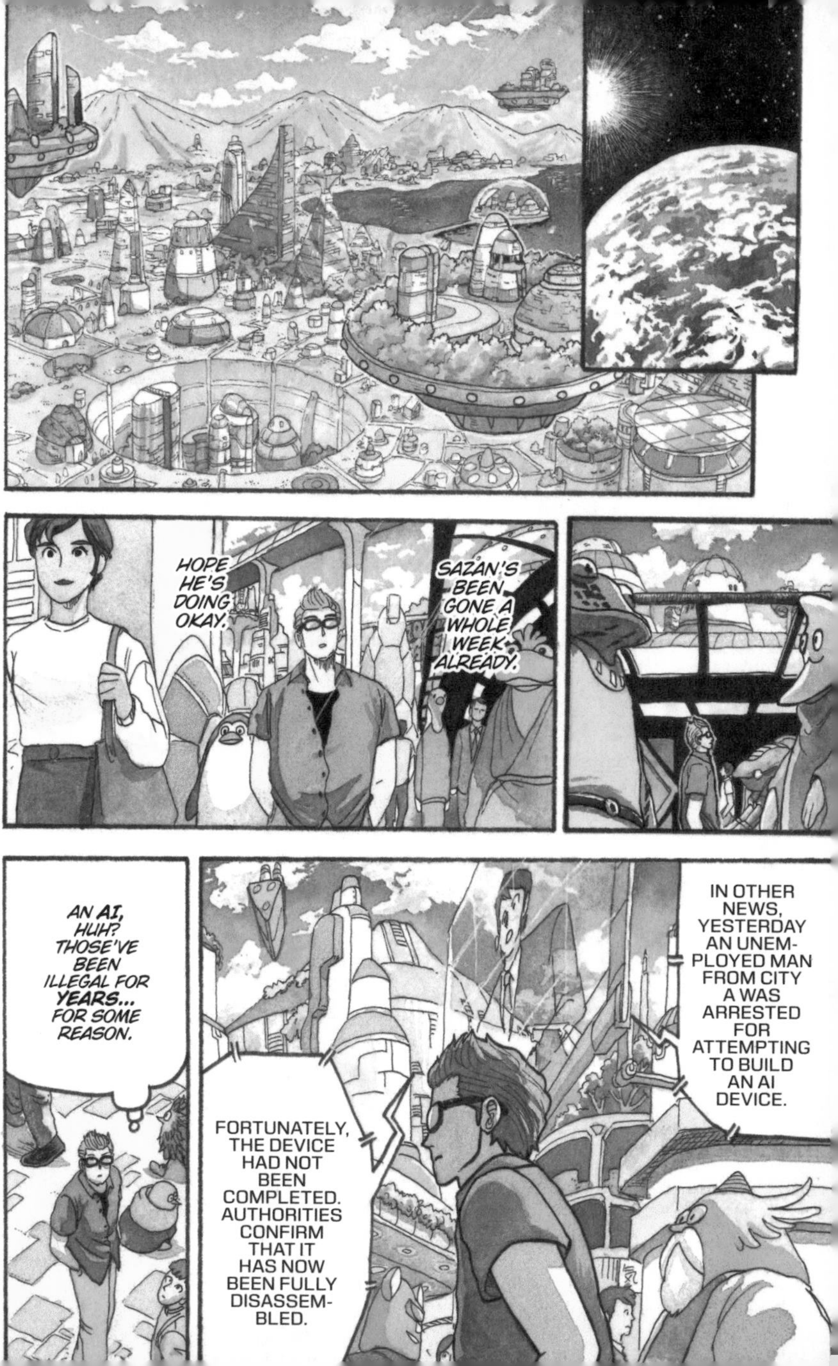
SAZAN'S BEEN GONE A WHOLE WEEK ALREADY.
HOPE HE'S DOING OKAY.
IN OTHER NEWS, YESTERDAY AN UNEM-PLOYED MAN FROM CITY A WAS ARRESTED FOR ATTEMPTING TO BUILD AN AI DEVICE.
FORTUNATELY, THE DEVICE HAD NOT BEEN COMPLETED. AUTHORITIES CONFIRM THAT IT HAS NOW BEEN FULLY DISASSEM-BLED.
AN **AI**, HUH? THOSE'VE BEEN ILLEGAL FOR **YEARS...** FOR SOME REASON.

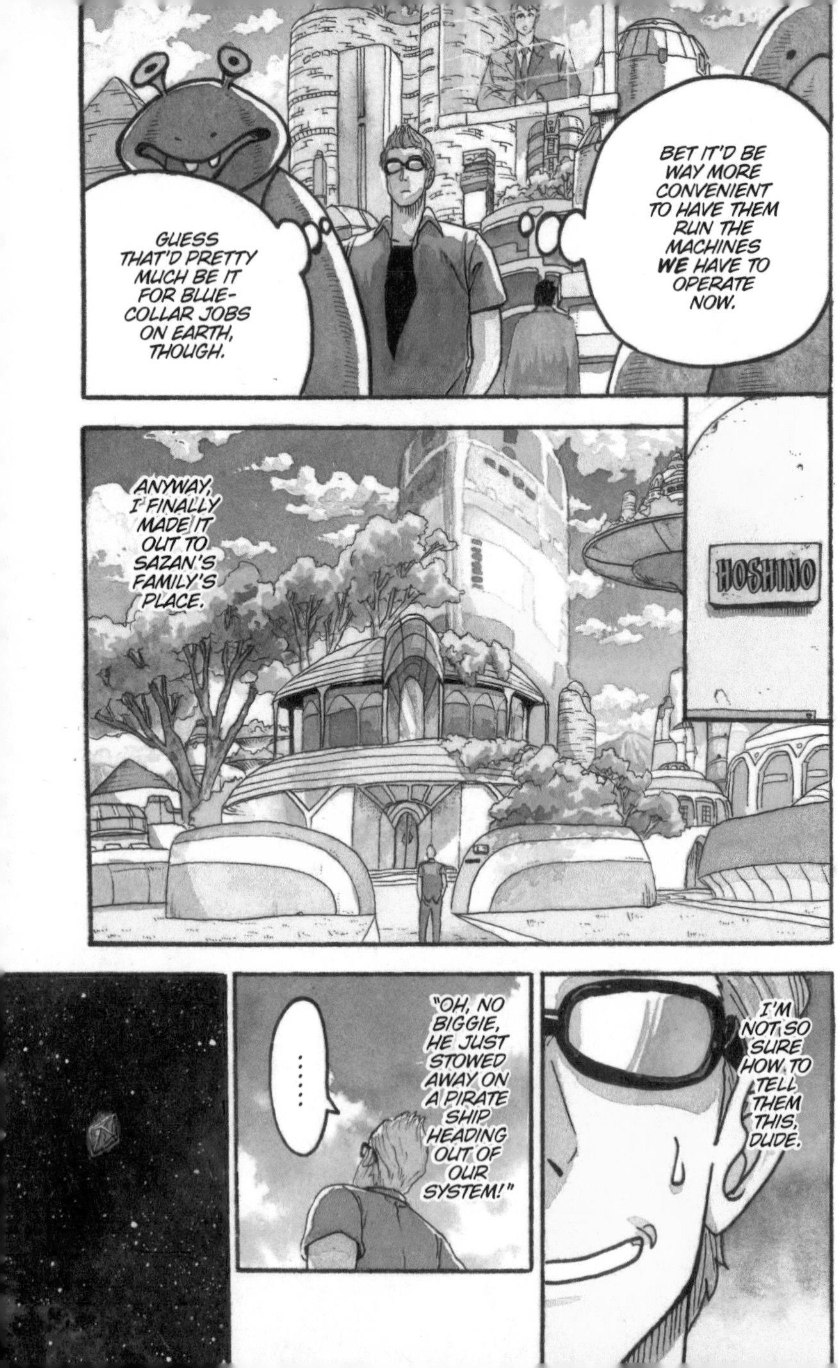
BET IT'D BE WAY MORE CONVENIENT TO HAVE THEM RUN THE MACHINES WE HAVE TO OPERATE NOW.
GUESS THAT'D PRETTY MUCH BE IT FOR BLUE-COLLAR JOBS ON EARTH, THOUGH.
HOSHINO
ANYWAY, I FINALLY MADE IT OUT TO SAZAN'S FAMILY'S PLACE.
I'M NOT SO SURE HOW TO TELL THEM THIS, DUDE.
"OH, NO BIGGIE, HE JUST STOWED AWAY ON A PIRATE SHIP HEADING OUT OF OUR SYSTEM!"
......

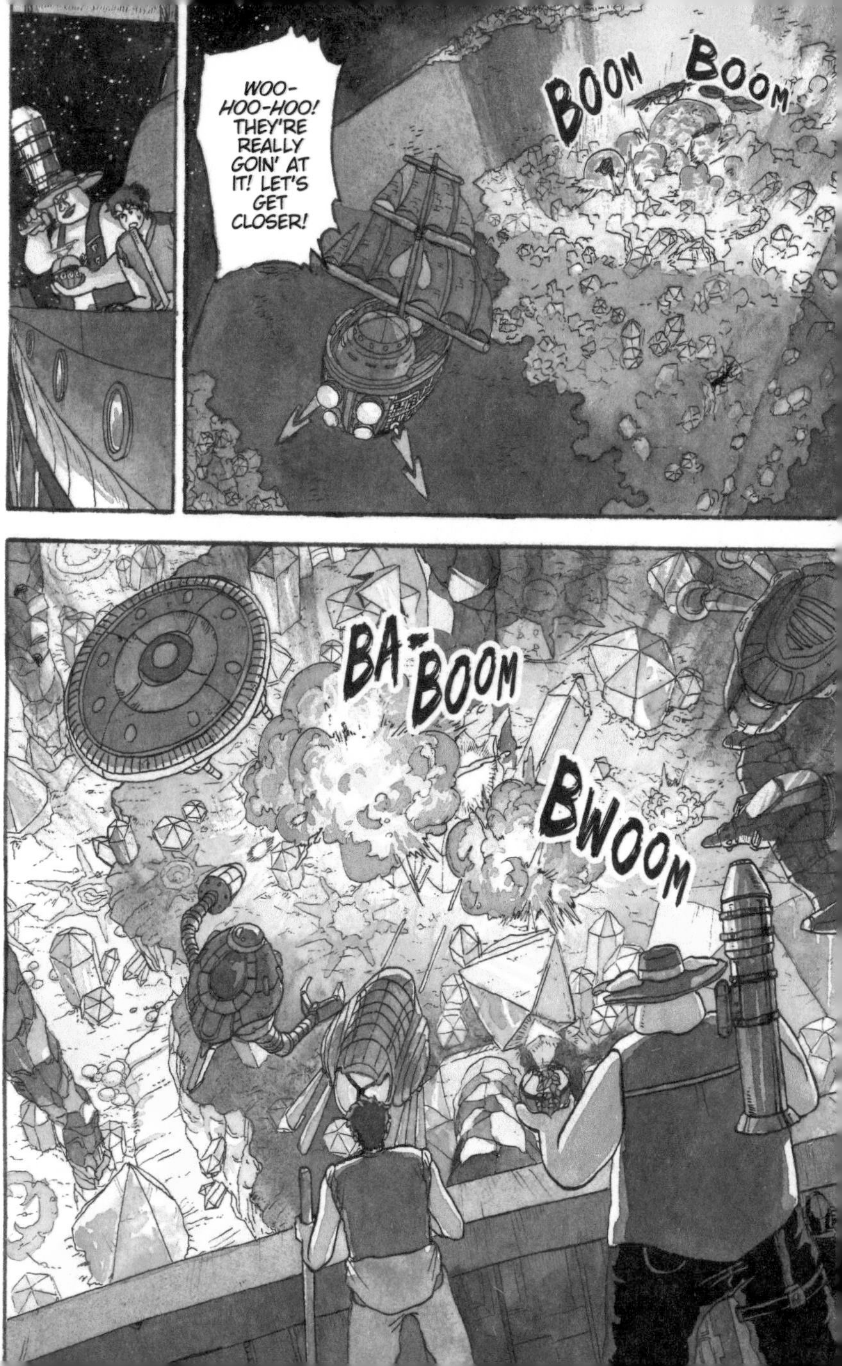
BOOM BOOM
WOO-HOO-HOO! THEY'RE REALLY GOIN' AT IT! LET'S GET CLOSER!
BA-BOOM
BWOOM

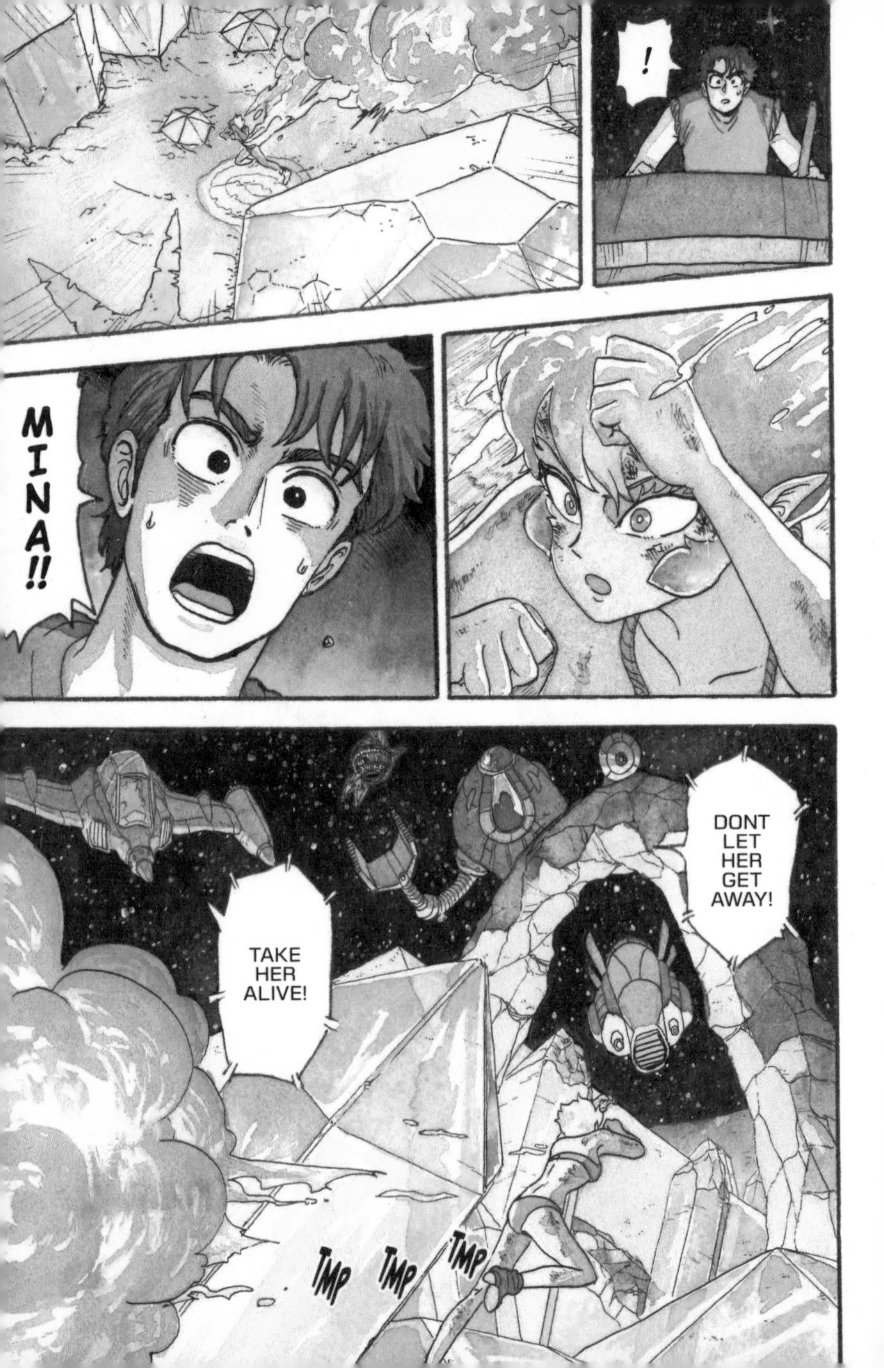
!
MINA!!
DONT LET HER GET AWAY!
TAKE HER ALIVE!
TMP TMP TMP

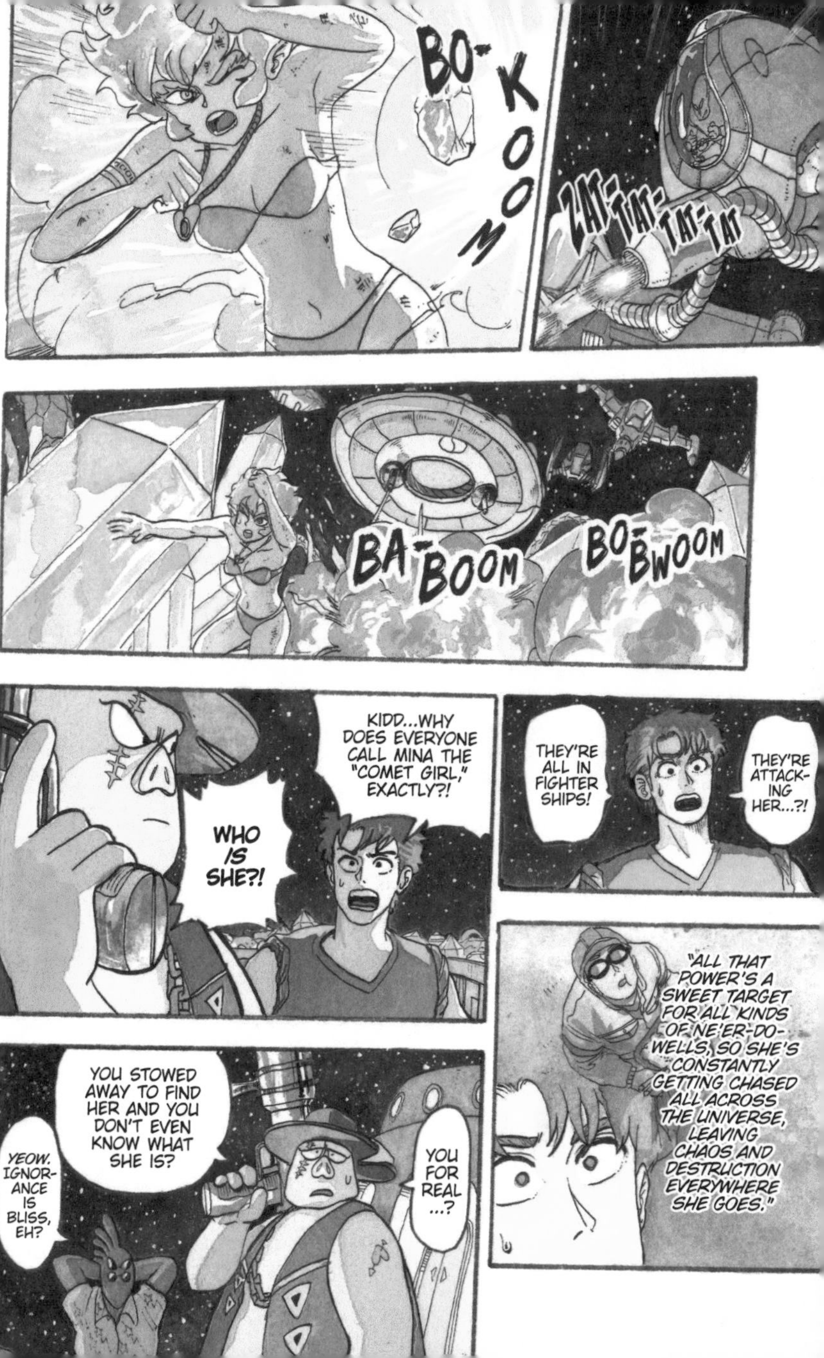
ZAT-TAT-TAT-TAT
BO-KOOOM
BO-BWOOM
BA-BOOM
THEY'RE ATTACKING HER...?!
THEY'RE ALL IN FIGHTER SHIPS!
KIDD...WHY DOES EVERYONE CALL MINA THE "COMET GIRL," EXACTLY?!
WHO IS SHE?!
"ALL THAT POWER'S A SWEET TARGET FOR ALL KINDS OF NE'ER-DO-WELLS, SO SHE'S CONSTANTLY GETTING CHASED ALL ACROSS THE UNIVERSE, LEAVING CHAOS AND DESTRUCTION EVERYWHERE SHE GOES."
YOU FOR REAL...?
YOU STOWED AWAY TO FIND HER AND YOU DON'T EVEN KNOW WHAT SHE IS?
YEOW. IGNORANCE IS BLISS, EH?

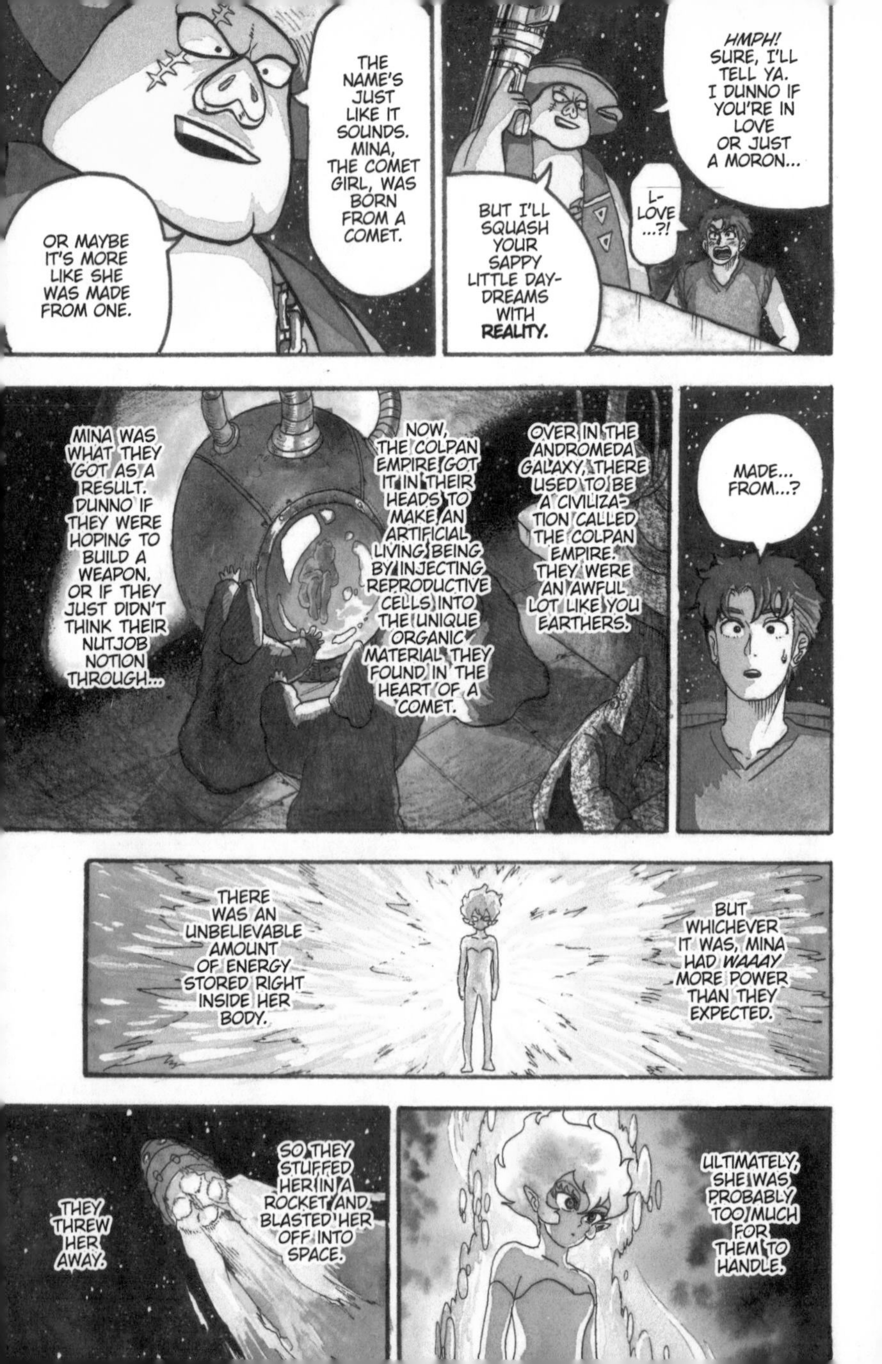
HMPH! SURE, I'LL TELL YA. I DUNNO IF YOU'RE IN LOVE OR JUST A MORON...
L-LOVE ...?!
BUT I'LL SQUASH YOUR SAPPY LITTLE DAY-DREAMS WITH **REALITY.**
THE NAME'S JUST LIKE IT SOUNDS. MINA, THE COMET GIRL, WAS BORN FROM A COMET.
OR MAYBE IT'S MORE LIKE SHE WAS MADE FROM ONE.
MADE... FROM...?
OVER IN THE ANDROMEDA GALAXY, THERE USED TO BE A CIVILIZA-TION CALLED THE COLPAN EMPIRE. THEY WERE AN AWFUL LOT LIKE YOU EARTHERS.
NOW, THE COLPAN EMPIRE GOT IT IN THEIR HEADS TO MAKE AN ARTIFICIAL LIVING BEING BY INJECTING REPRODUCTIVE CELLS INTO THE UNIQUE ORGANIC MATERIAL THEY FOUND IN THE HEART OF A COMET.
MINA WAS WHAT THEY GOT AS A RESULT. DUNNO IF THEY WERE HOPING TO BUILD A WEAPON, OR IF THEY JUST DIDN'T THINK THEIR NUTJOB NOTION THROUGH...
BUT WHICHEVER IT WAS, MINA HAD *WAAAY* MORE POWER THAN THEY EXPECTED.
THERE WAS AN UNBELIEVABLE AMOUNT OF ENERGY STORED RIGHT INSIDE HER BODY.
ULTIMATELY, SHE WAS PROBABLY TOO MUCH FOR THEM TO HANDLE.
SO THEY STUFFED HER IN A ROCKET AND BLASTED HER OFF INTO SPACE.
THEY THREW HER AWAY.

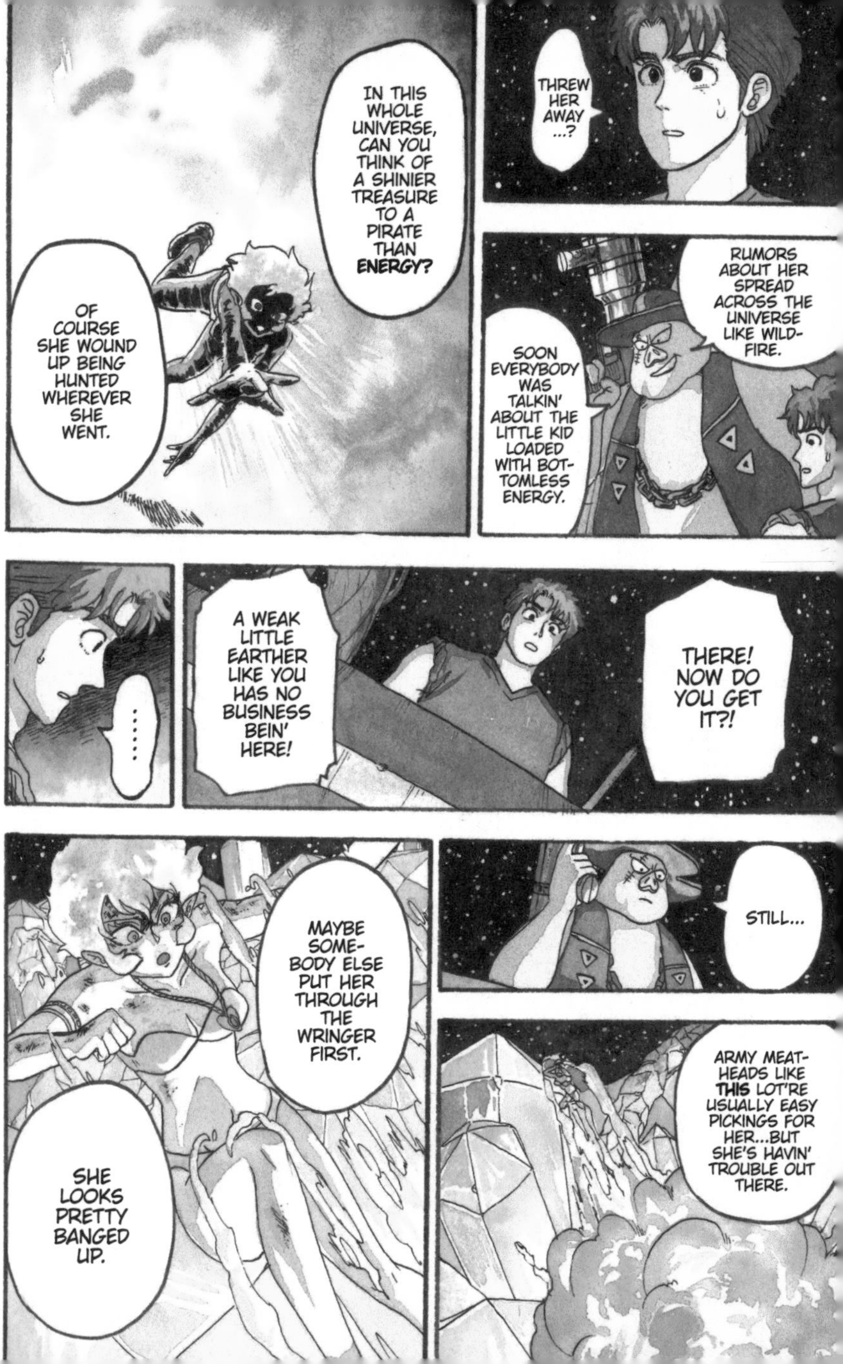
THREW HER AWAY ...?
RUMORS ABOUT HER SPREAD ACROSS THE UNIVERSE LIKE WILDFIRE.
SOON EVERYBODY WAS TALKIN' ABOUT THE LITTLE KID LOADED WITH BOTTOMLESS ENERGY.
IN THIS WHOLE UNIVERSE, CAN YOU THINK OF A SHINIER TREASURE TO A PIRATE THAN **ENERGY?**
OF COURSE SHE WOUND UP BEING HUNTED WHEREVER SHE WENT.
THERE! NOW DO YOU GET IT?!
A WEAK LITTLE EARTHER LIKE YOU HAS NO BUSINESS BEIN' HERE!
......
STILL...
ARMY MEATHEADS LIKE **THIS** LOT'RE USUALLY EASY PICKINGS FOR HER...BUT SHE'S HAVIN' TROUBLE OUT THERE.
MAYBE SOMEBODY ELSE PUT HER THROUGH THE WRINGER FIRST.
SHE LOOKS PRETTY BANGED UP.

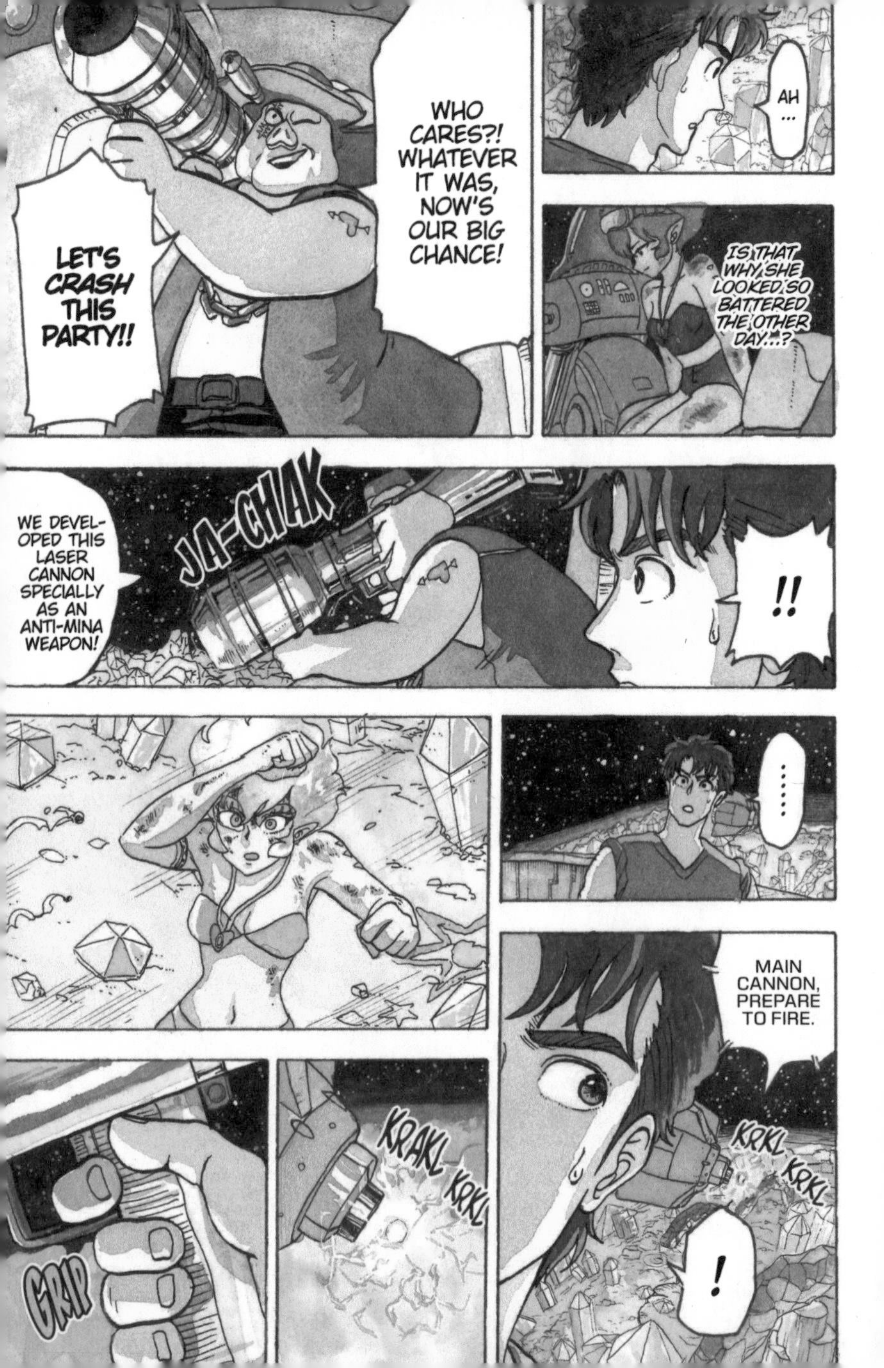
AH ...
IS THAT WHY SHE LOOKED SO BATTERED THE OTHER DAY...?
WHO CARES?! WHATEVER IT WAS, NOW'S OUR BIG CHANCE!
LET'S CRASH THIS PARTY!!
!!
JA-CHAK
WE DEVELOPED THIS LASER CANNON SPECIALLY AS AN ANTI-MINA WEAPON!
......
MAIN CANNON, PREPARE TO FIRE.
KRKL
KRKL
!
KRAKL
KRKL
GRIP

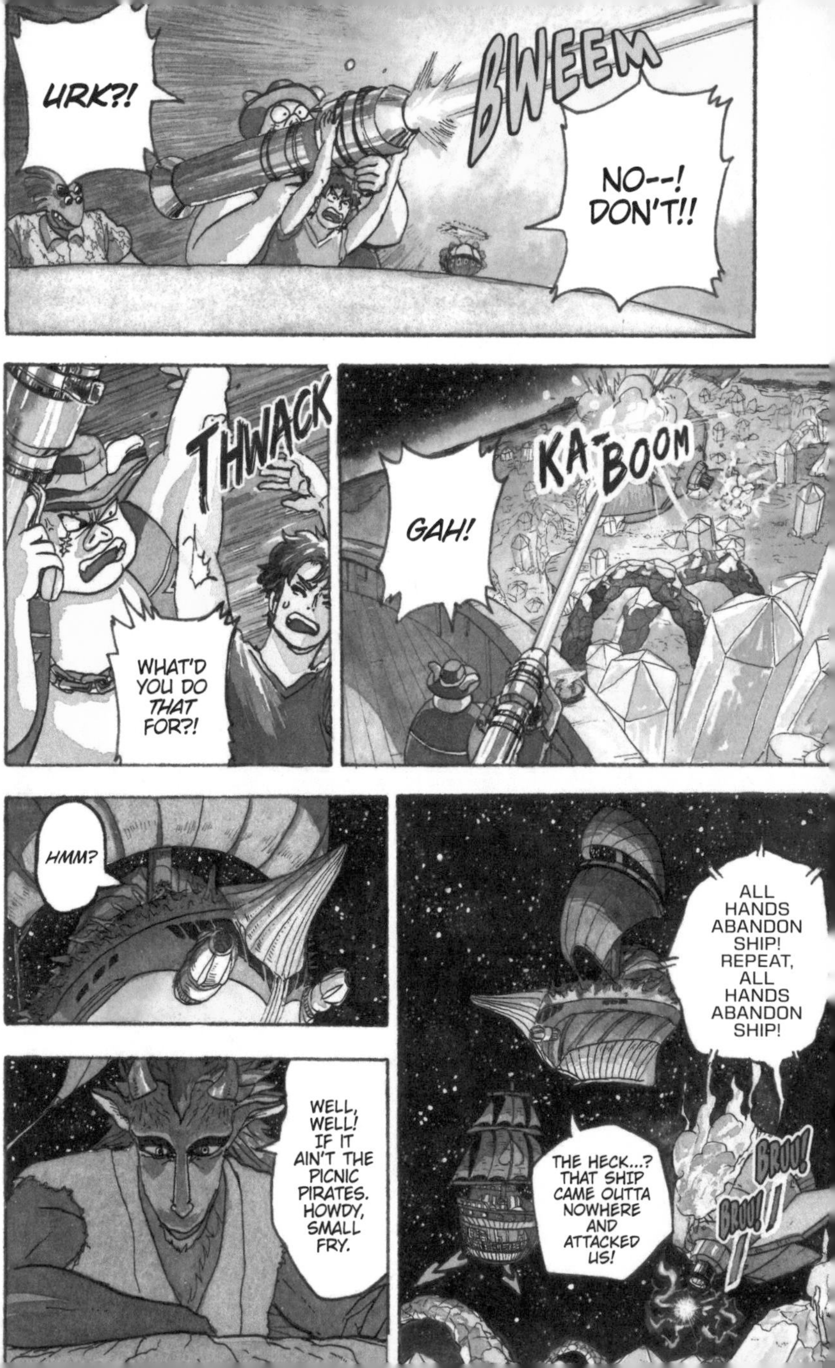
BWEEM
NO--! DON'T!!
URK?!
KA-BOOM
GAH!
THWACK
WHAT'D YOU DO *THAT* FOR?!
ALL HANDS ABANDON SHIP! REPEAT, ALL HANDS ABANDON SHIP!
BRUU!
BRUU!
THE HECK...? THAT SHIP CAME OUTTA NOWHERE AND ATTACKED US!
HMM?
WELL, WELL! IF IT AIN'T THE PICNIC PIRATES. HOWDY, SMALL FRY.

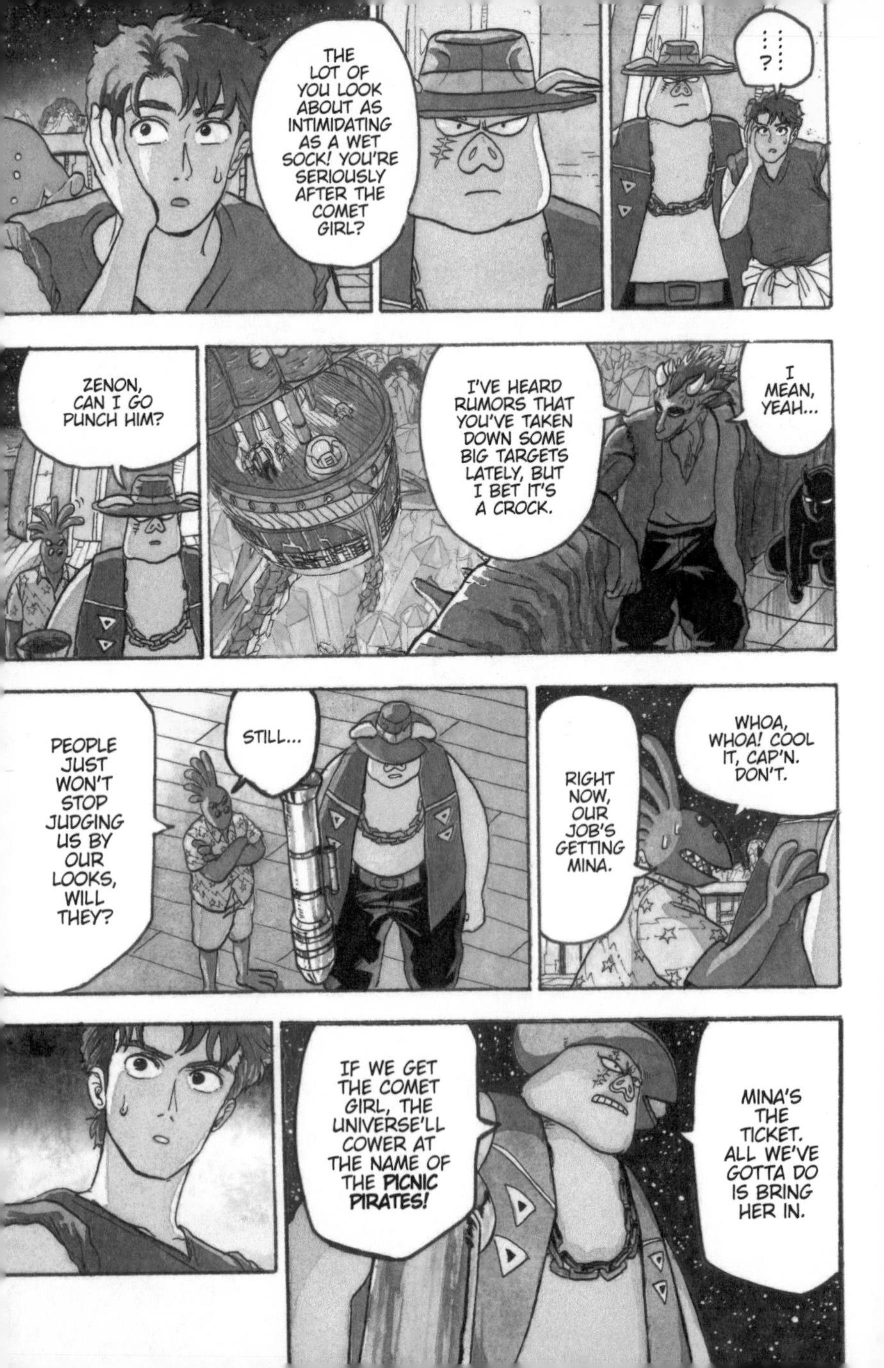
......?
THE LOT OF YOU LOOK ABOUT AS INTIMIDATING AS A WET SOCK! YOU'RE SERIOUSLY AFTER THE COMET GIRL?
I MEAN, YEAH...
I'VE HEARD RUMORS THAT YOU'VE TAKEN DOWN SOME BIG TARGETS LATELY, BUT I BET IT'S A CROCK.
ZENON, CAN I GO PUNCH HIM?
WHOA, WHOA! COOL IT, CAP'N. DON'T.
RIGHT NOW, OUR JOB'S GETTING MINA.
STILL...
PEOPLE JUST WON'T STOP JUDGING US BY OUR LOOKS, WILL THEY?
MINA'S THE TICKET. ALL WE'VE GOTTA DO IS BRING HER IN.
IF WE GET THE COMET GIRL, THE UNIVERSE'LL COWER AT THE NAME OF THE **PICNIC PIRATES!**

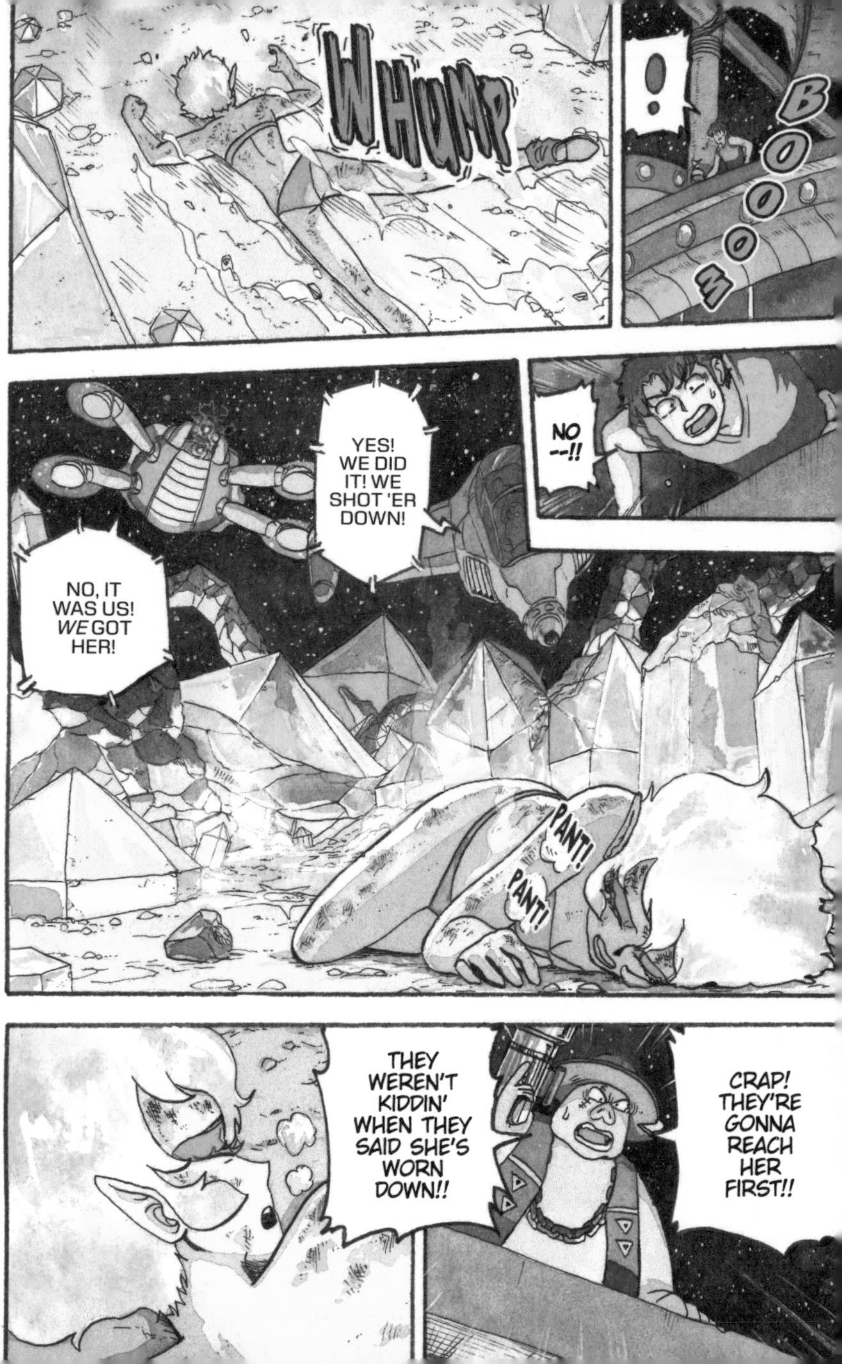
!
BOOOOOM
WHUMP
NO --!!
YES! WE DID IT! WE SHOT 'ER DOWN!
NO, IT WAS US! *WE* GOT HER!
PANT!
PANT!
CRAP! THEY'RE GONNA REACH HER FIRST!!
THEY WEREN'T KIDDIN' WHEN THEY SAID SHE'S WORN DOWN!!

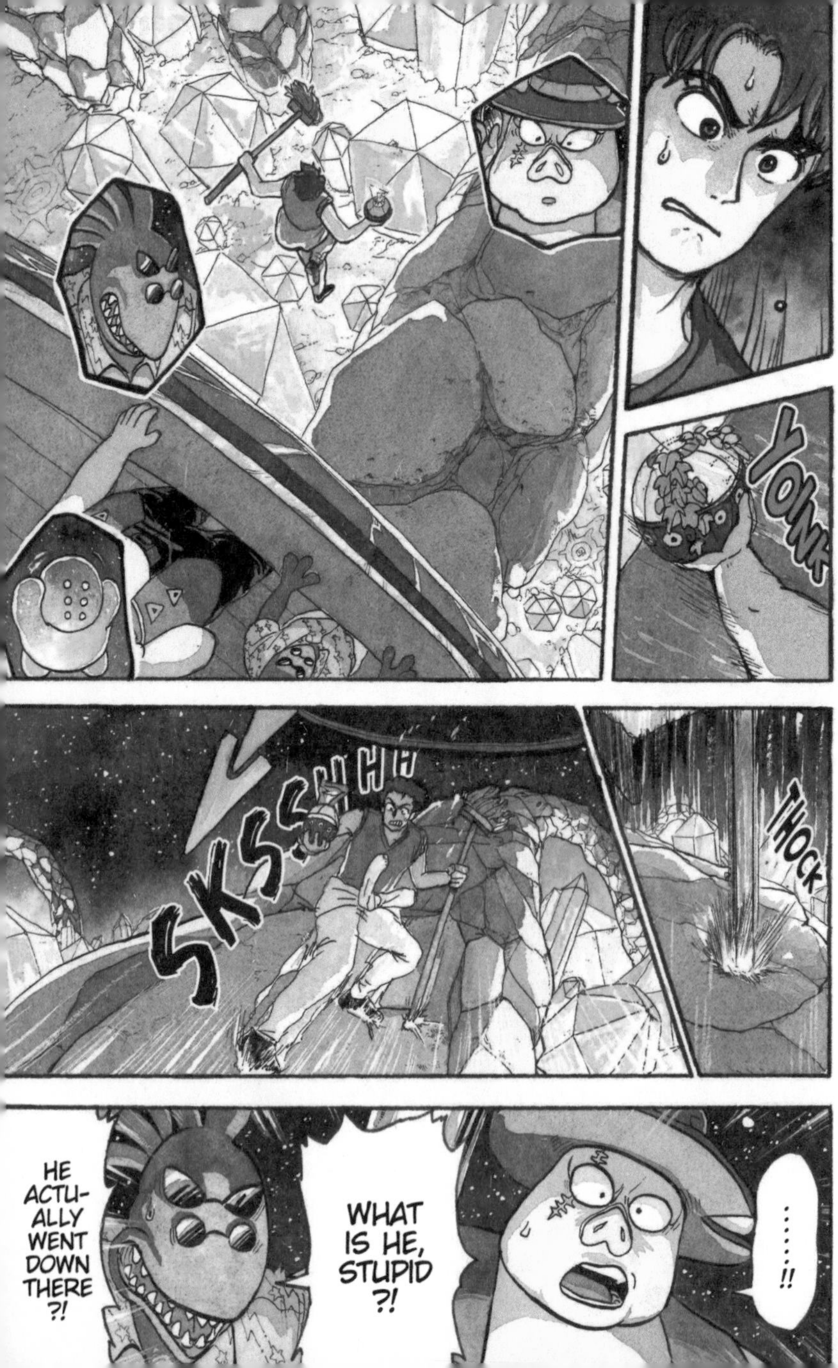
YOINK
THOCK
SKSCHH
......!!
WHAT IS HE, STUPID ?!
HE ACTU-ALLY WENT DOWN THERE ?!

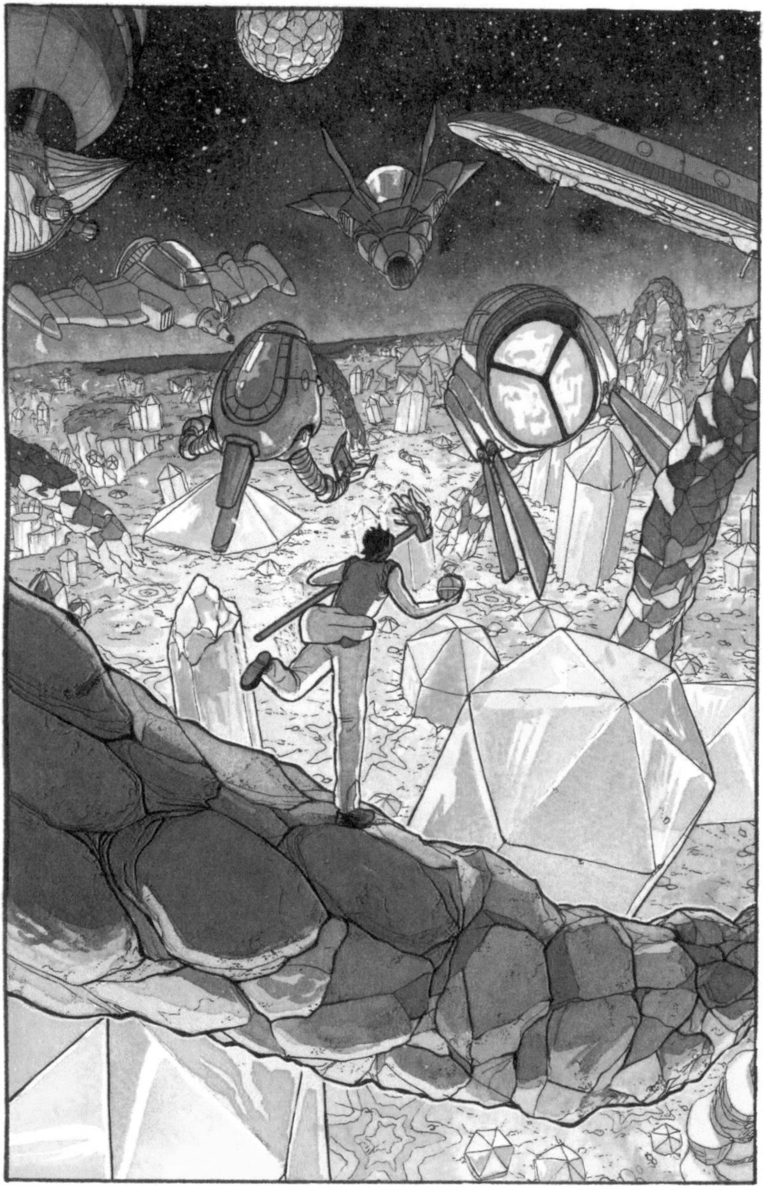

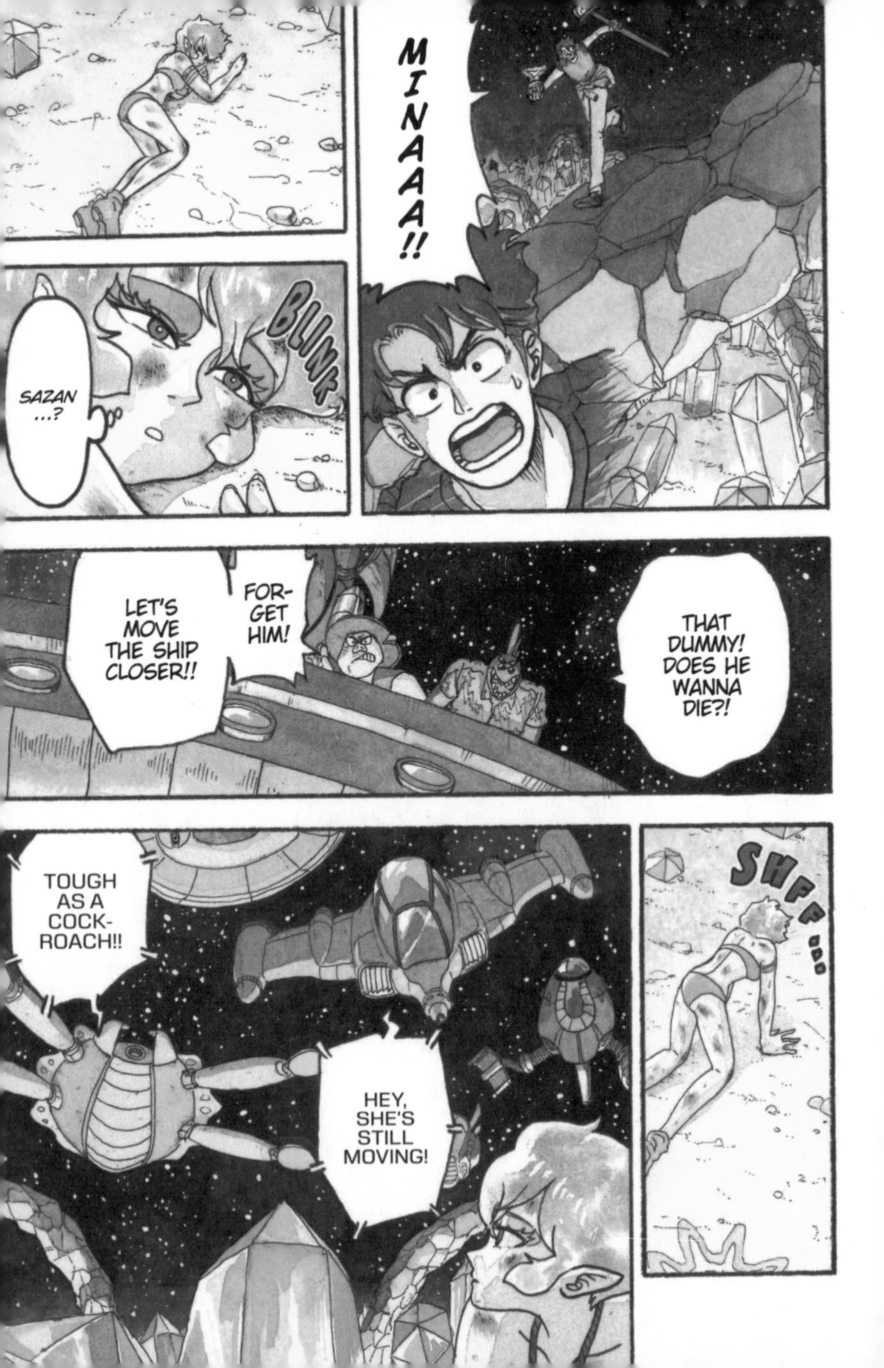
MINAAAA!!
BLINK
SAZAN ...?
THAT DUMMY! DOES HE WANNA DIE?!
FOR-GET HIM!
LET'S MOVE THE SHIP CLOSER!!
SHFF...
HEY, SHE'S STILL MOVING!
TOUGH AS A COCK-ROACH!!

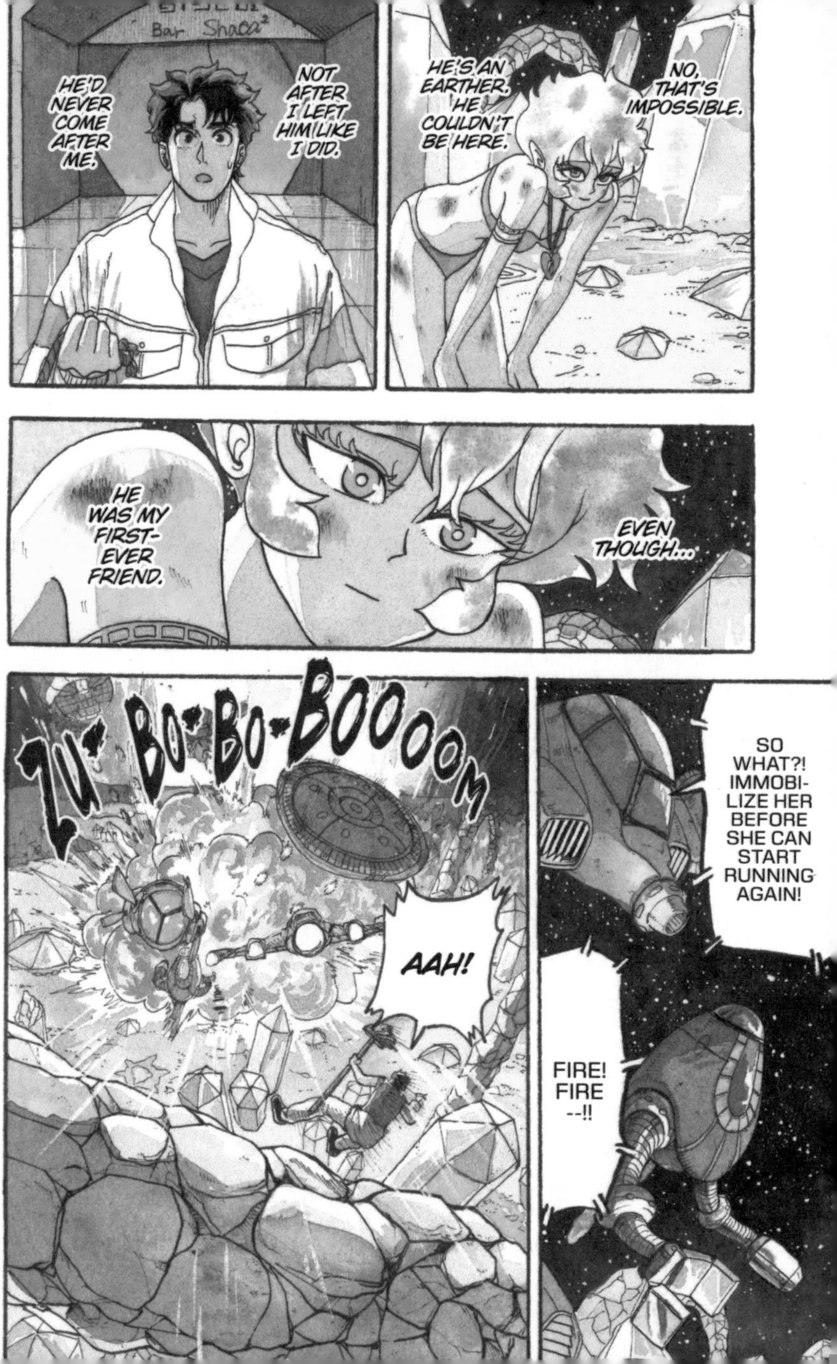
NO, THAT'S IMPOSSIBLE.
HE'S AN EARTHER. HE COULDN'T BE HERE.
Bar Shaca^2
NOT AFTER I LEFT HIM LIKE I DID.
HE'D NEVER COME AFTER ME.
EVEN THOUGH...
HE WAS MY FIRST-EVER FRIEND.
SO WHAT?! IMMOBILIZE HER BEFORE SHE CAN START RUNNING AGAIN!
FIRE! FIRE --!!
ZU-BO-BO-BOOOOOM
AAH!

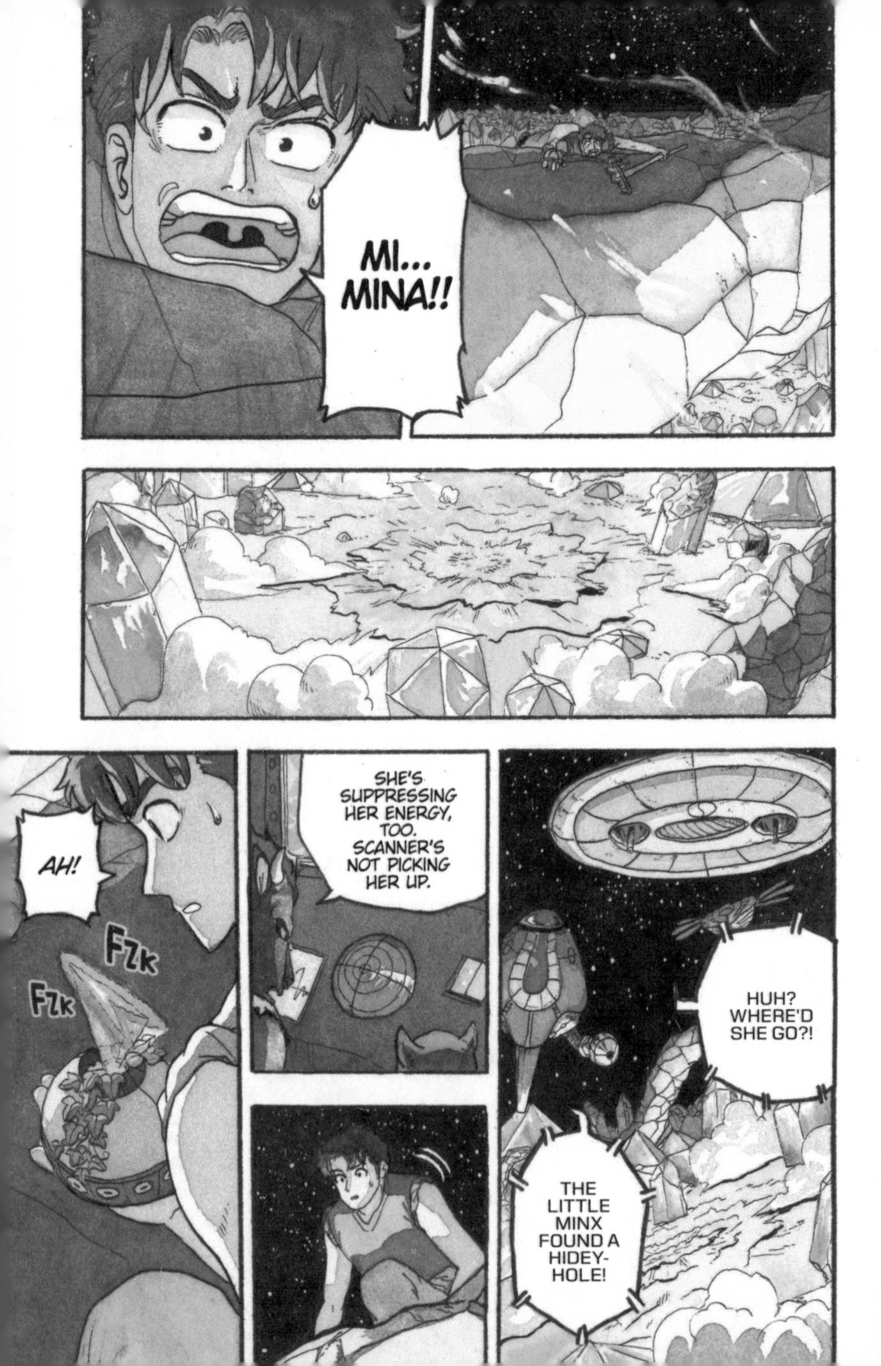
MI... MINA!!
HUH? WHERE'D SHE GO?!
THE LITTLE MINX FOUND A HIDEY-HOLE!
SHE'S SUPPRESSING HER ENERGY, TOO. SCANNER'S NOT PICKING HER UP.
AH!
FZK
FZK

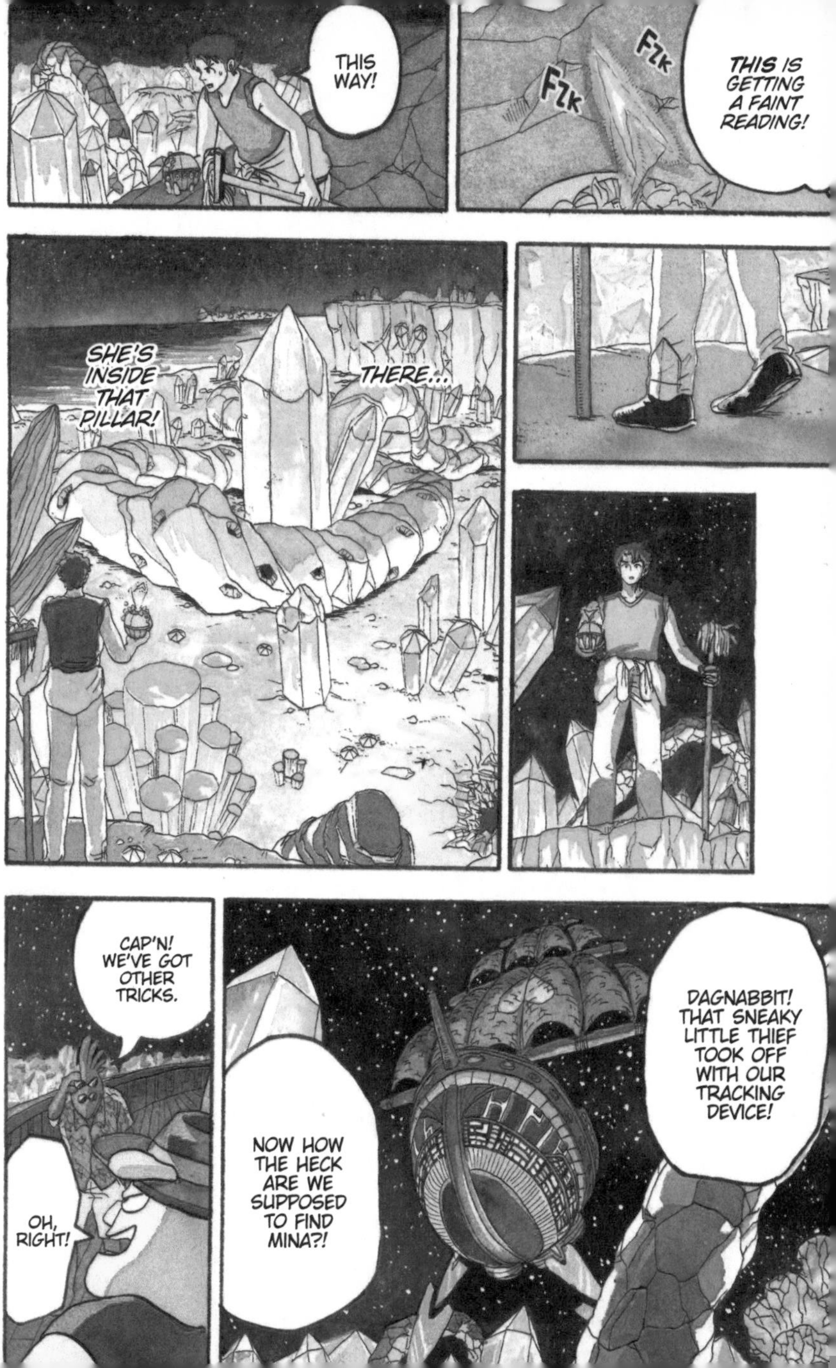
FZK
FZK
THIS IS GETTING A FAINT READING!
THIS WAY!
THERE...
SHE'S INSIDE THAT PILLAR!
DAGNABBIT! THAT SNEAKY LITTLE THIEF TOOK OFF WITH OUR TRACKING DEVICE!
NOW HOW THE HECK ARE WE SUPPOSED TO FIND MINA?!
CAP'N! WE'VE GOT OTHER TRICKS.
OH, RIGHT!

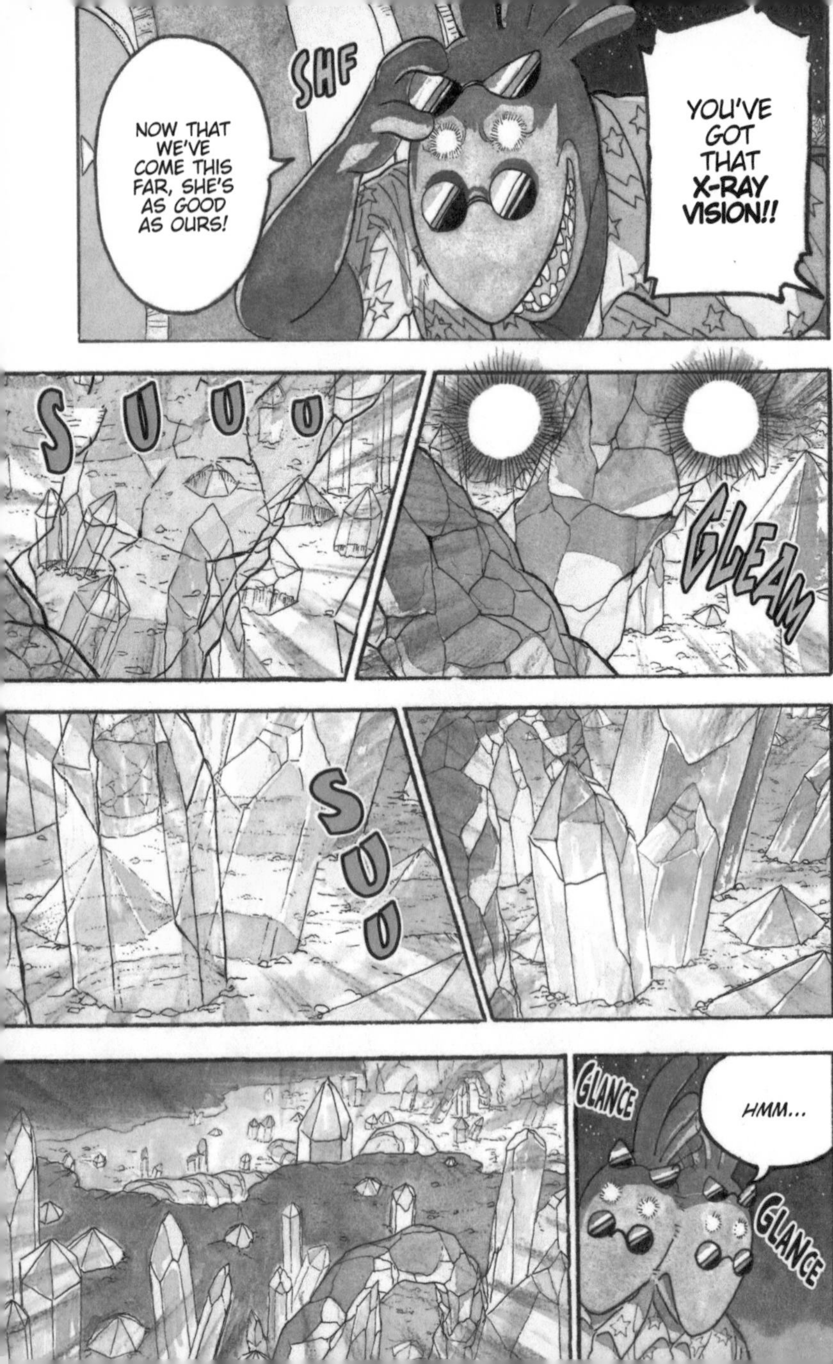
YOU'VE GOT THAT **X-RAY VISION!!**
SHF
NOW THAT WE'VE COME THIS FAR, SHE'S AS GOOD AS OURS!
GLEAM
SUUU
SUUU
GLANCE
HMM...
GLANCE

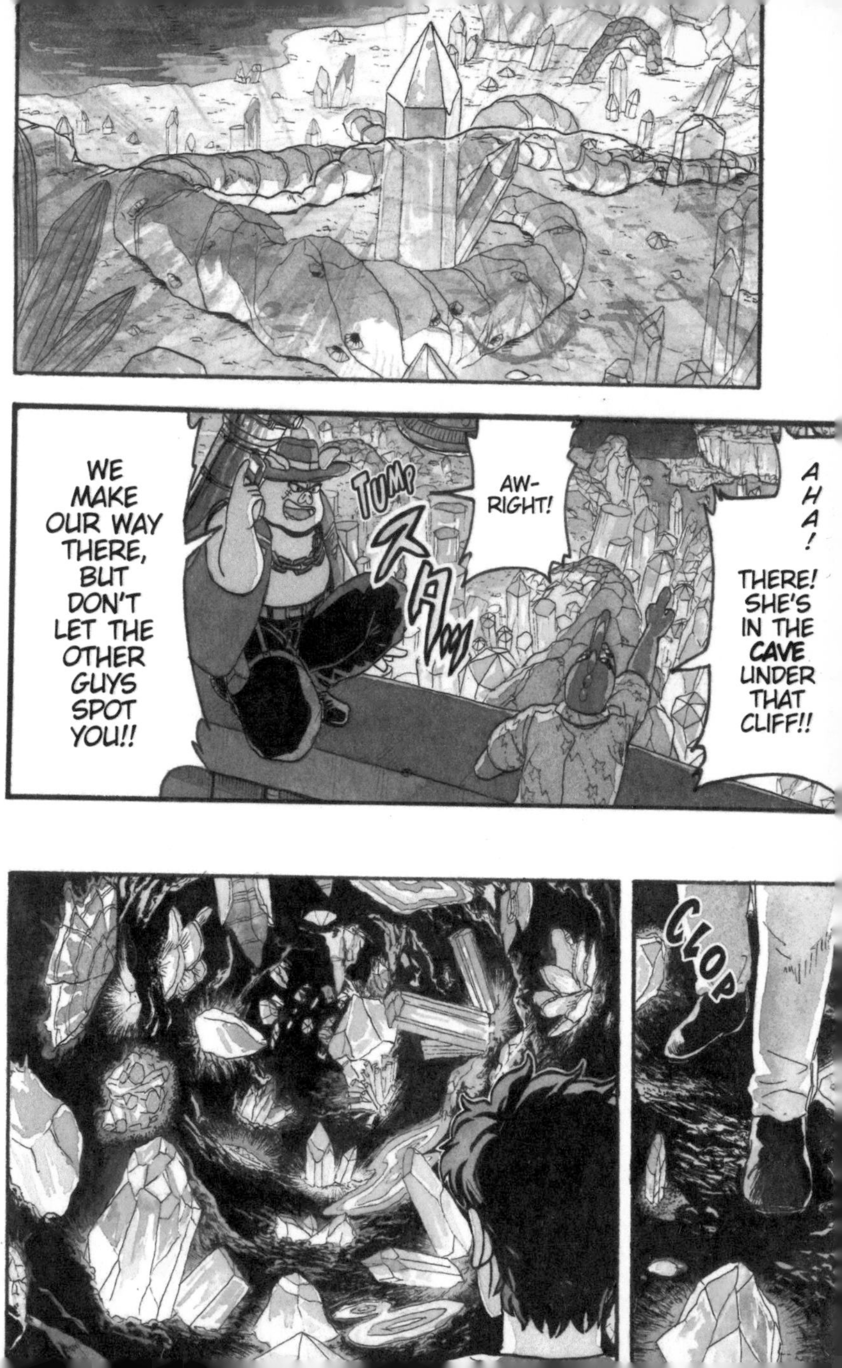
AHA!
THERE! SHE'S IN THE CAVE UNDER THAT CLIFF!!
AW-RIGHT!
TUMP
WE MAKE OUR WAY THERE, BUT DON'T LET THE OTHER GUYS SPOT YOU!!
CLOP

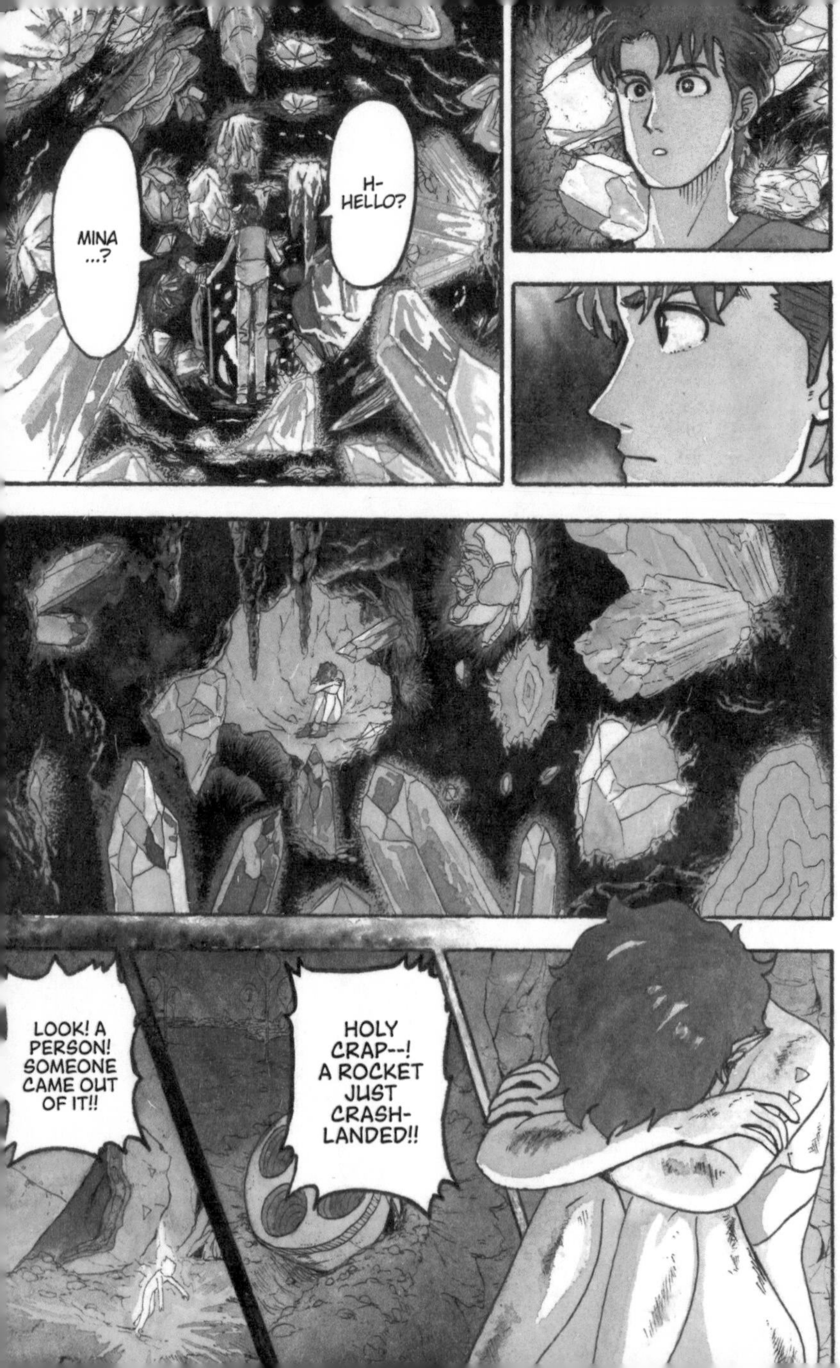
H- HELLO?
MINA ...?
HOLY CRAP--! A ROCKET JUST CRASH-LANDED!!
LOOK! A PERSON! SOMEONE CAME OUT OF IT!!

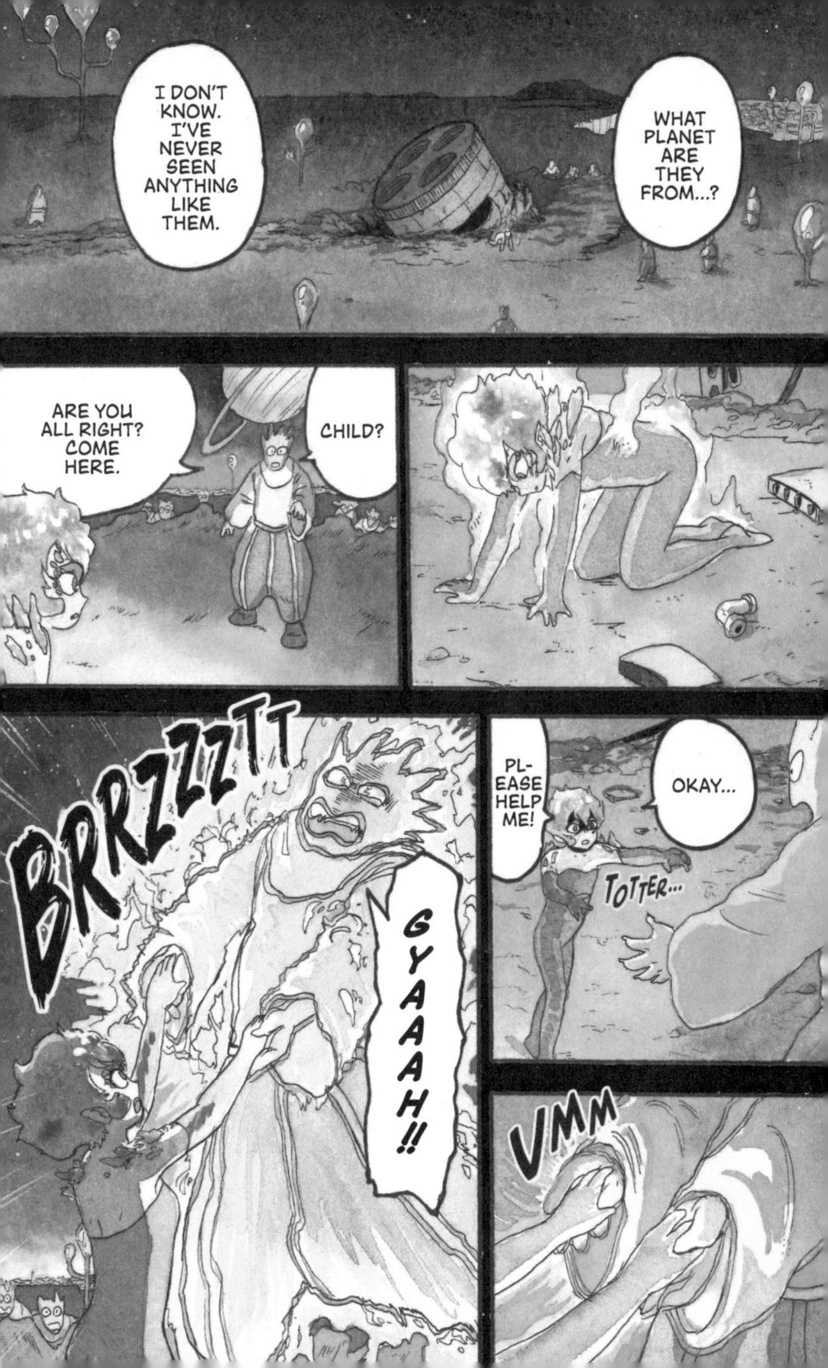
WHAT PLANET ARE THEY FROM...?
I DON'T KNOW. I'VE NEVER SEEN ANYTHING LIKE THEM.
CHILD?
ARE YOU ALL RIGHT? COME HERE.
OKAY...
PL-EASE HELP ME!
TOTTER...
VMM
BRRZZZTT
GYAAAAH!!

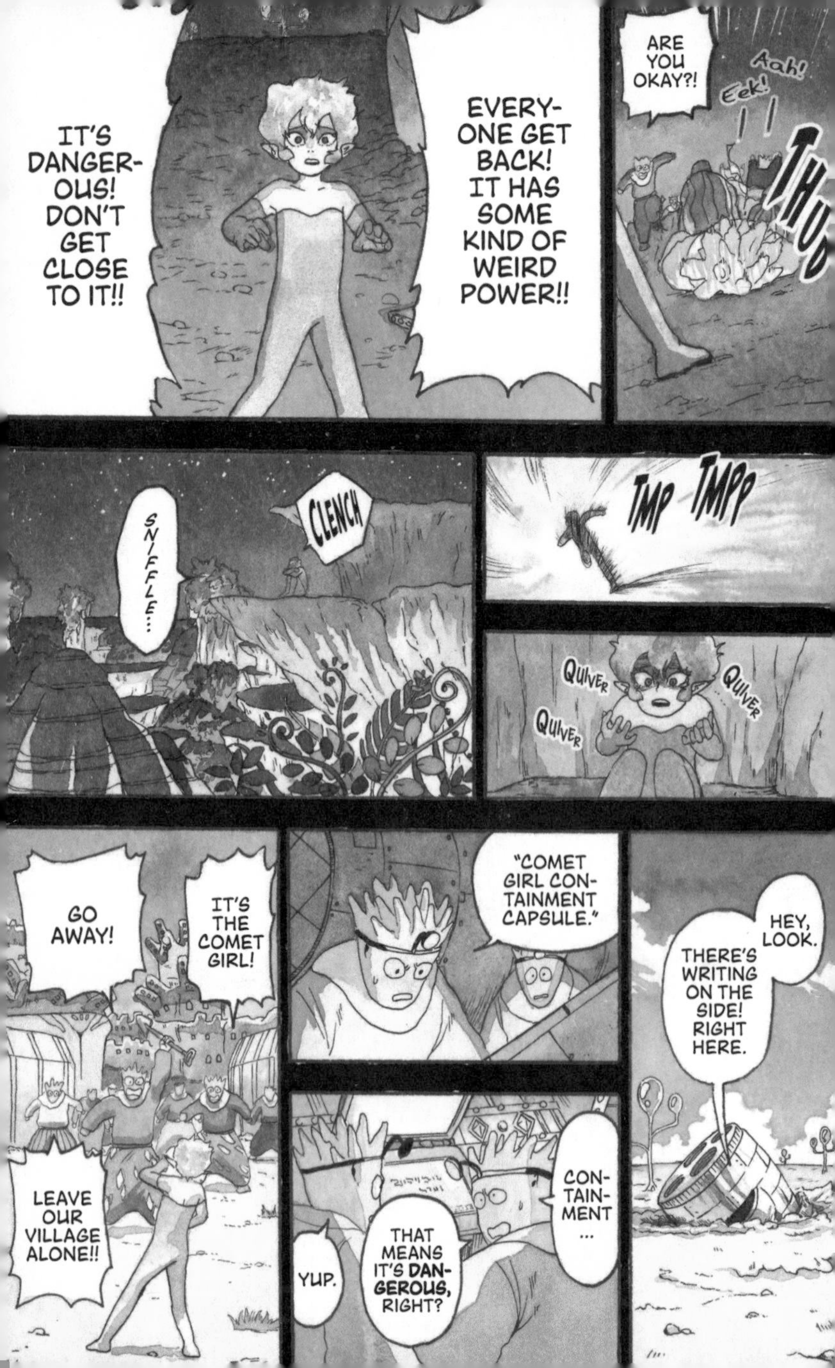
ARE YOU OKAY?!
Aah!
Eek!
THUD
EVERYONE GET BACK! IT HAS SOME KIND OF WEIRD POWER!!
IT'S DANGEROUS! DON'T GET CLOSE TO IT!!
TMP TMPP
QUIVER
QUIVER
QUIVER
CLENCH
SNIFFLE...
HEY, LOOK.
THERE'S WRITING ON THE SIDE! RIGHT HERE.
"COMET GIRL CONTAINMENT CAPSULE."
CONTAINMENT...
THAT MEANS IT'S DANGEROUS, RIGHT?
YUP.
IT'S THE COMET GIRL!
GO AWAY!
LEAVE OUR VILLAGE ALONE!!

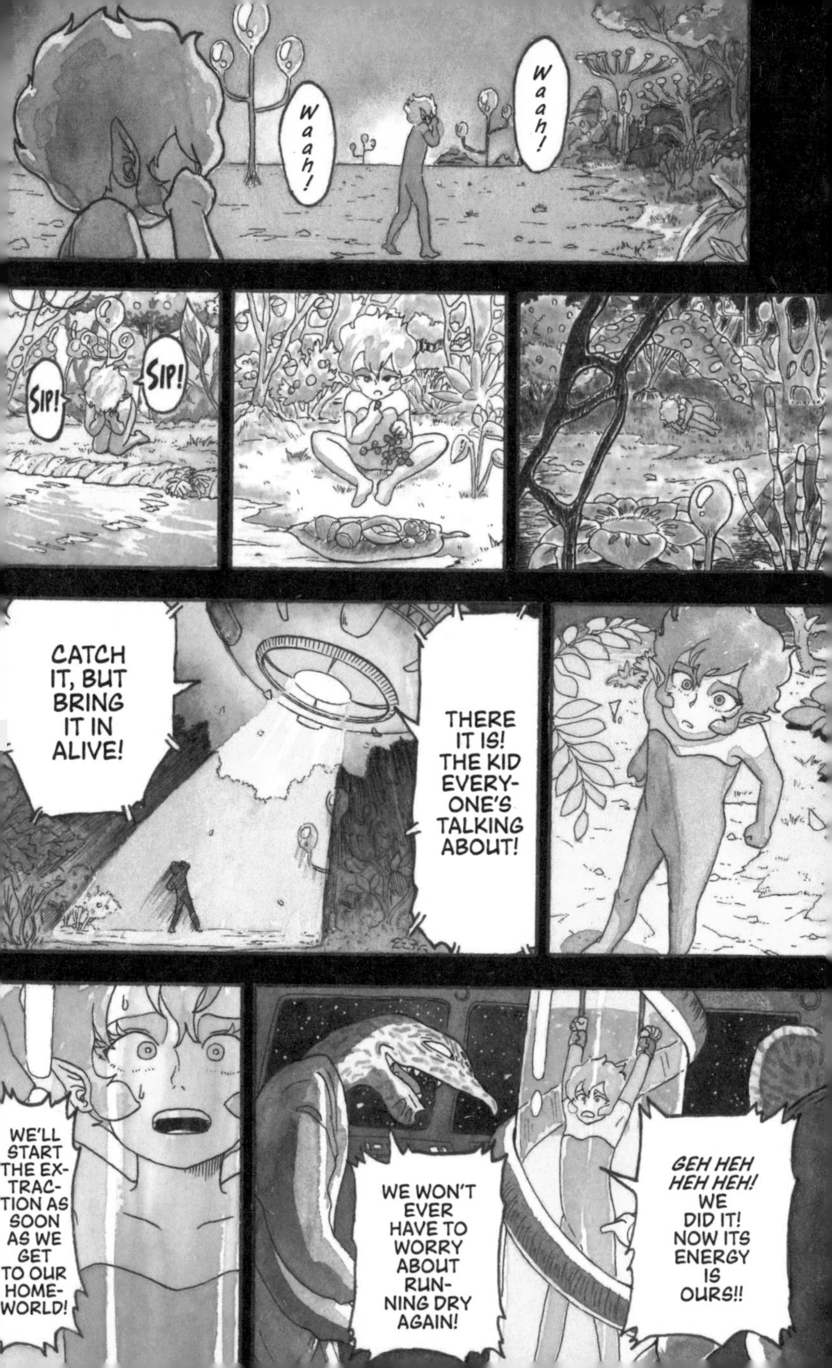
Waaah!
Waaah!
SIP!
SIP!
THERE IT IS! THE KID EVERYONE'S TALKING ABOUT!
CATCH IT, BUT BRING IT IN ALIVE!
GEH HEH HEH HEH! WE DID IT! NOW ITS ENERGY IS OURS!!
WE WON'T EVER HAVE TO WORRY ABOUT RUNNING DRY AGAIN!
WE'LL START THE EXTRACTION AS SOON AS WE GET TO OUR HOMEWORLD!

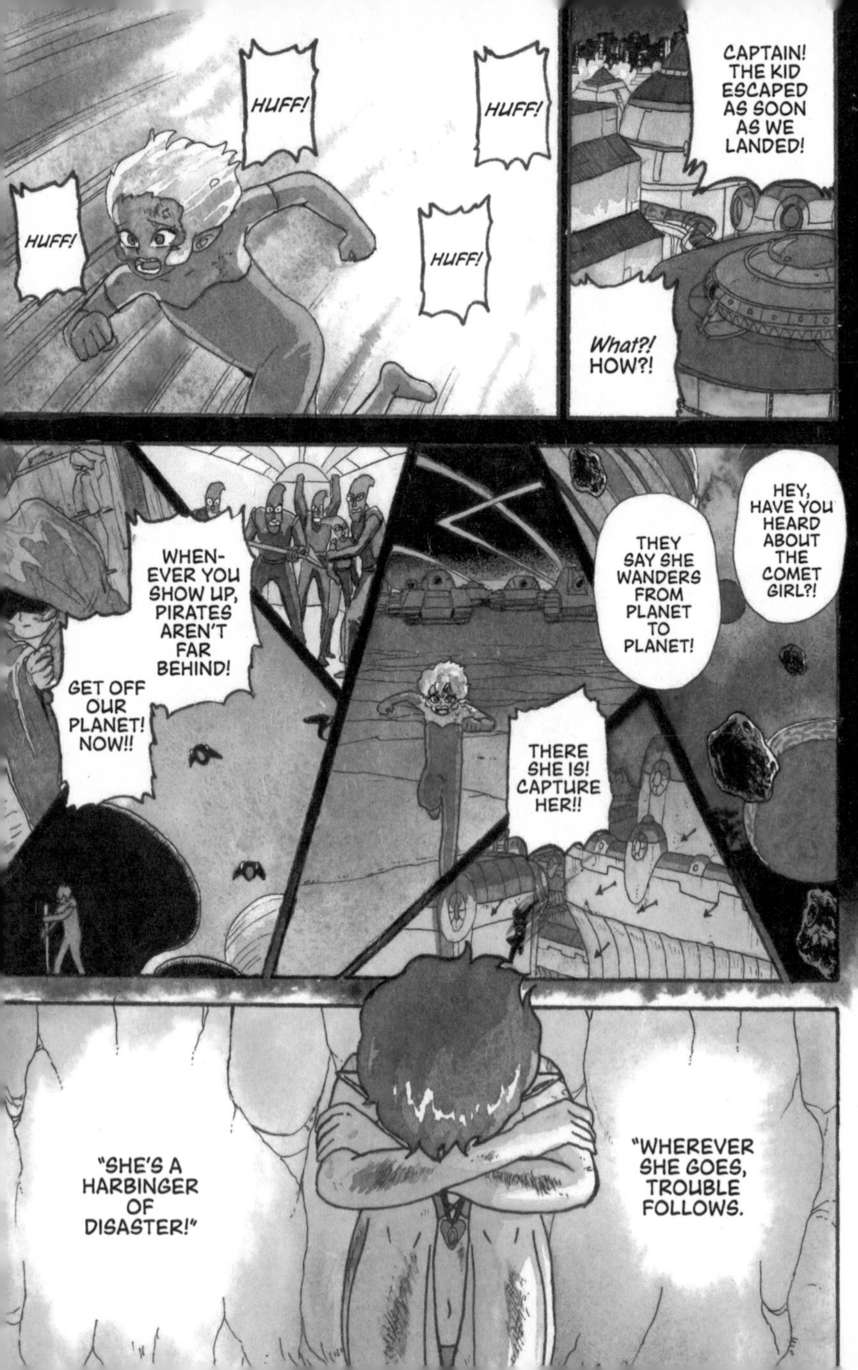

CAPTAIN! THE KID ESCAPED AS SOON AS WE LANDED!
What?! HOW?!
HUFF!
HUFF!
HUFF!
HUFF!
HEY, HAVE YOU HEARD ABOUT THE COMET GIRL?!
THEY SAY SHE WANDERS FROM PLANET TO PLANET!
THERE SHE IS! CAPTURE HER!!
WHEN-EVER YOU SHOW UP, PIRATES AREN'T FAR BEHIND!
GET OFF OUR PLANET! NOW!!
“WHEREVER SHE GOES, TROUBLE FOLLOWS.
“SHE'S A HARBINGER OF DISASTER!”

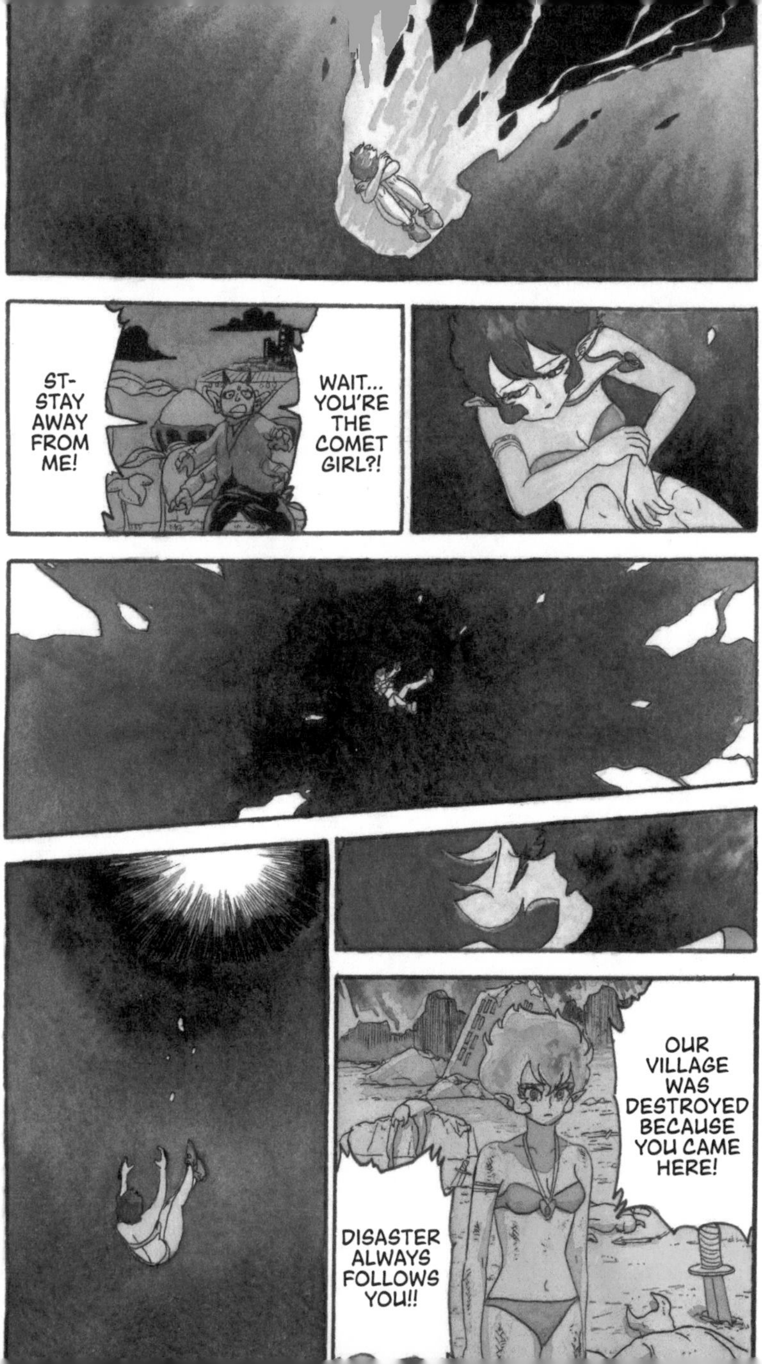
WAIT... YOU'RE THE COMET GIRL?!
ST-STAY AWAY FROM ME!
OUR VILLAGE WAS DESTROYED BECAUSE YOU CAME HERE!
DISASTER ALWAYS FOLLOWS YOU!!

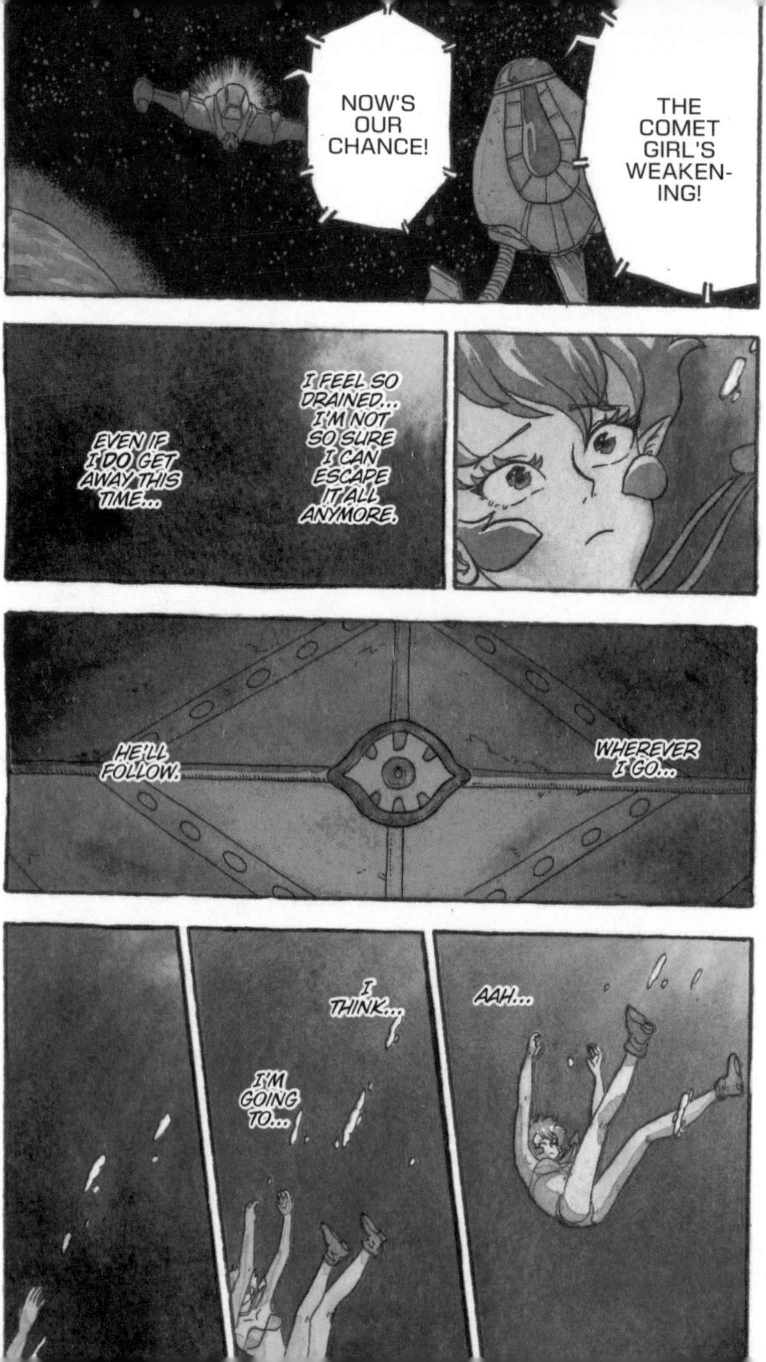
THE COMET GIRL'S WEAKEN-ING!
NOW'S OUR CHANCE!
I FEEL SO DRAINED... I'M NOT SO SURE I CAN ESCAPE IT ALL ANYMORE.
EVEN IF I DO GET AWAY THIS TIME...
WHEREVER I GO...
HE'LL FOLLOW.
AAH...
I THINK...
I'M GOING TO...

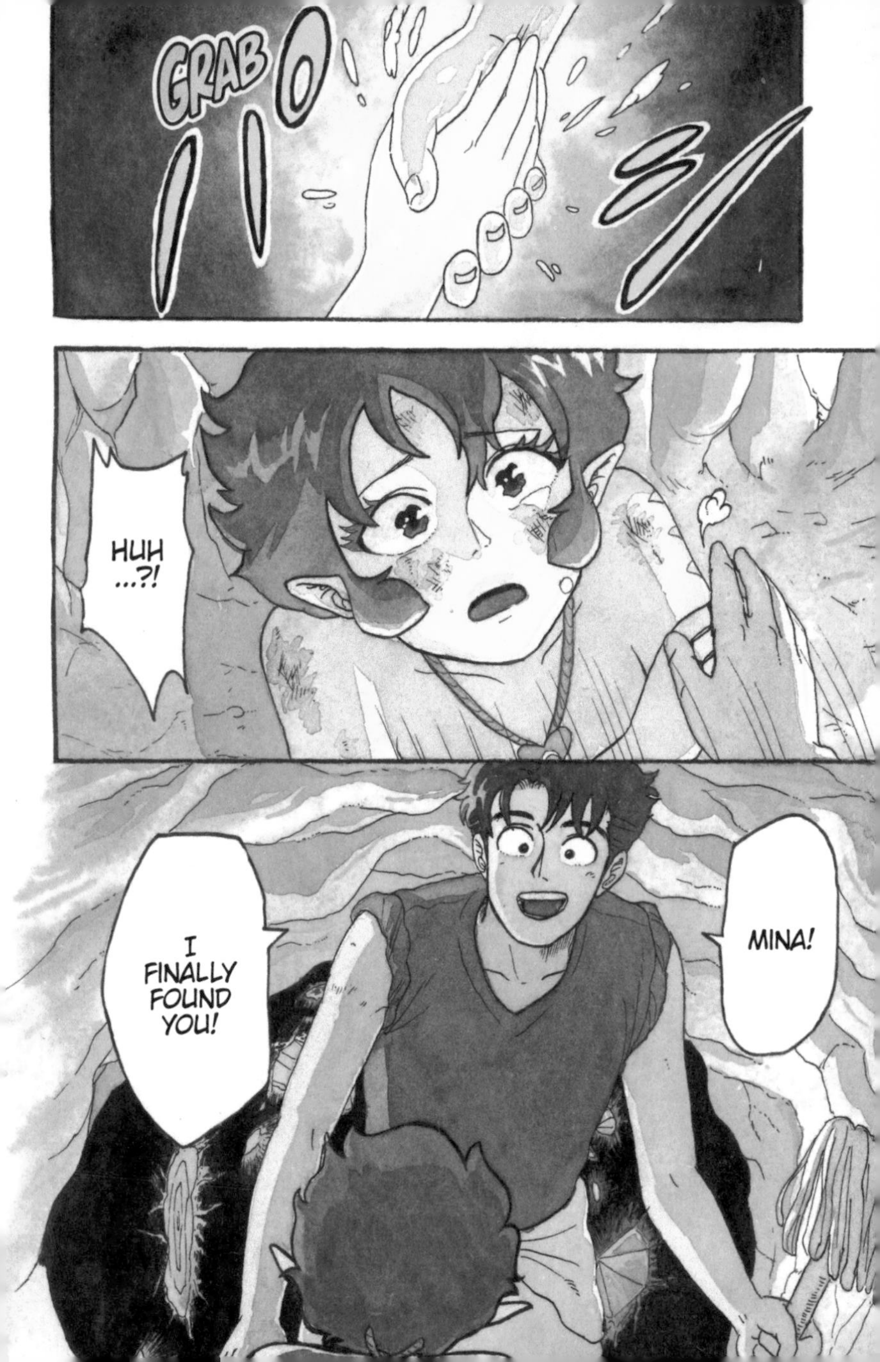
GRAB
HUH ...?!
MINA!
I FINALLY FOUND YOU!

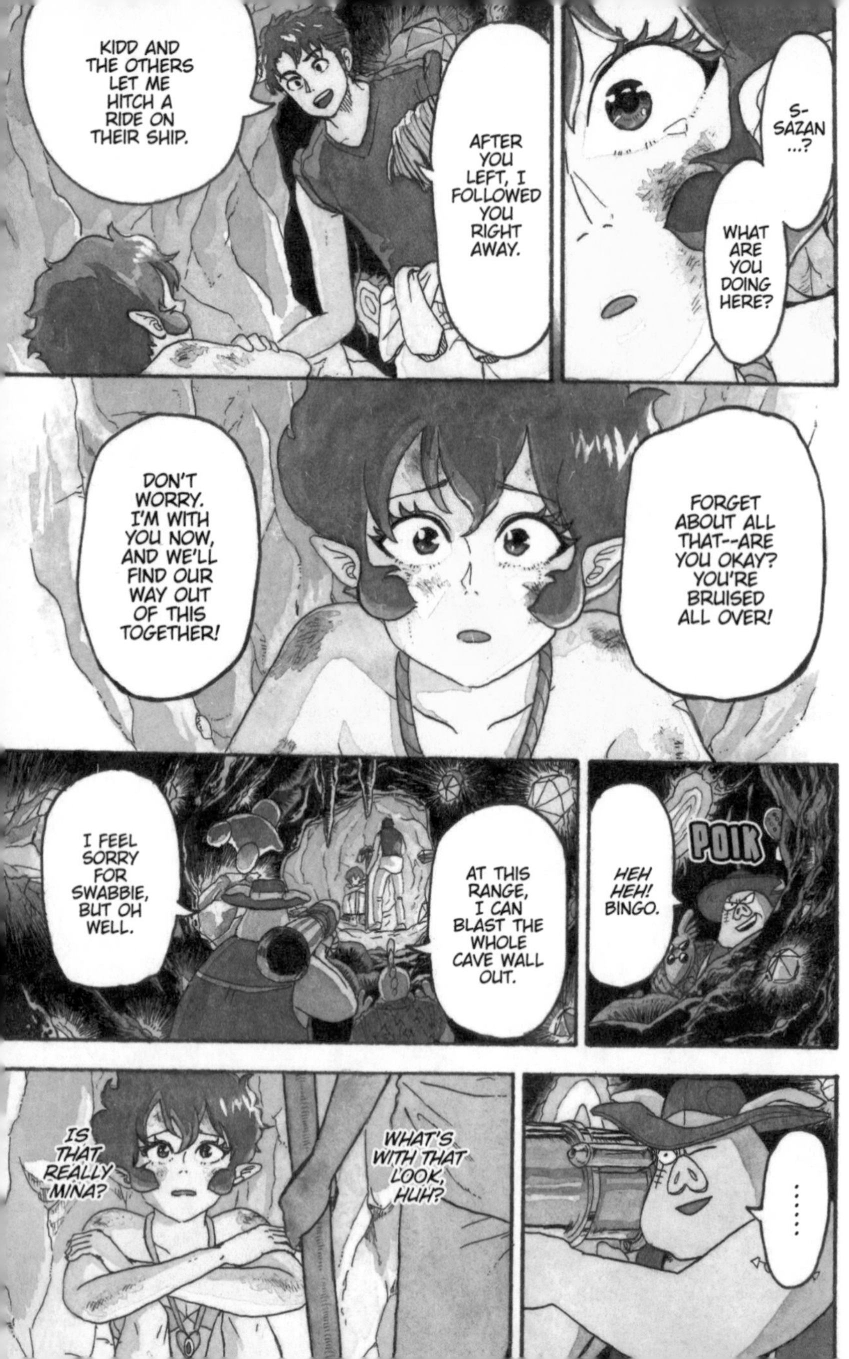
S-SAZAN...?
WHAT ARE YOU DOING HERE?
AFTER YOU LEFT, I FOLLOWED YOU RIGHT AWAY.
KIDD AND THE OTHERS LET ME HITCH A RIDE ON THEIR SHIP.
FORGET ABOUT ALL THAT--ARE YOU OKAY? YOU'RE BRUISED ALL OVER!
DON'T WORRY. I'M WITH YOU NOW, AND WE'LL FIND OUR WAY OUT OF THIS TOGETHER!
POIK
HEH HEH! BINGO.
AT THIS RANGE, I CAN BLAST THE WHOLE CAVE WALL OUT.
I FEEL SORRY FOR SWABBIE, BUT OH WELL.
......
WHAT'S WITH THAT LOOK, HUH?
IS THAT REALLY MINA?

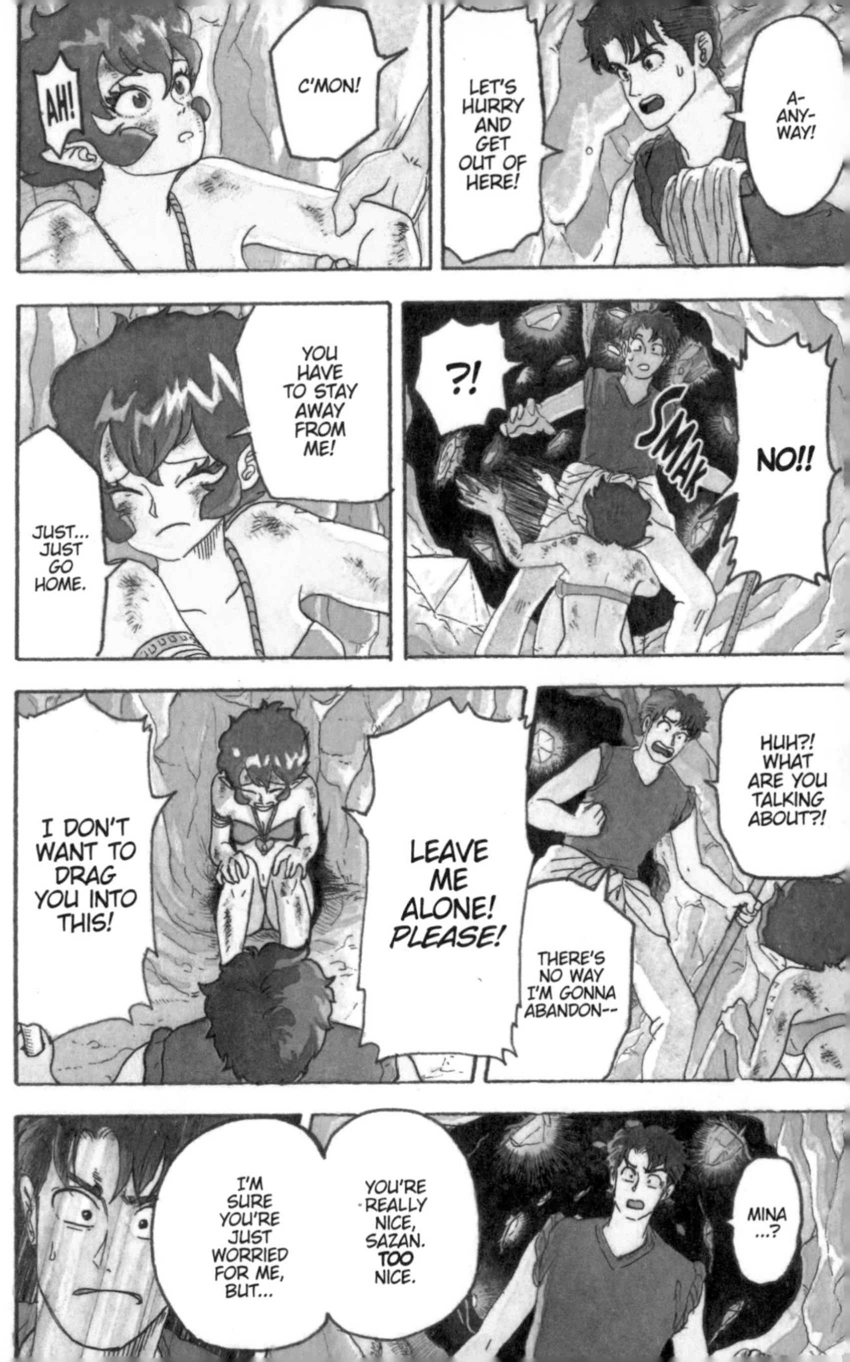
A-ANY-WAY!
LET'S HURRY AND GET OUT OF HERE!
C'MON!
AH!
NO!!
SMAK
?!
YOU HAVE TO STAY AWAY FROM ME!
JUST... JUST GO HOME.
HUH?! WHAT ARE YOU TALKING ABOUT?!
THERE'S NO WAY I'M GONNA ABANDON--
LEAVE ME ALONE! *PLEASE!*
I DON'T WANT TO DRAG YOU INTO THIS!
MINA ...?
YOU'RE REALLY NICE, SAZAN. **TOO** NICE.
I'M SURE YOU'RE JUST WORRIED FOR ME, BUT...

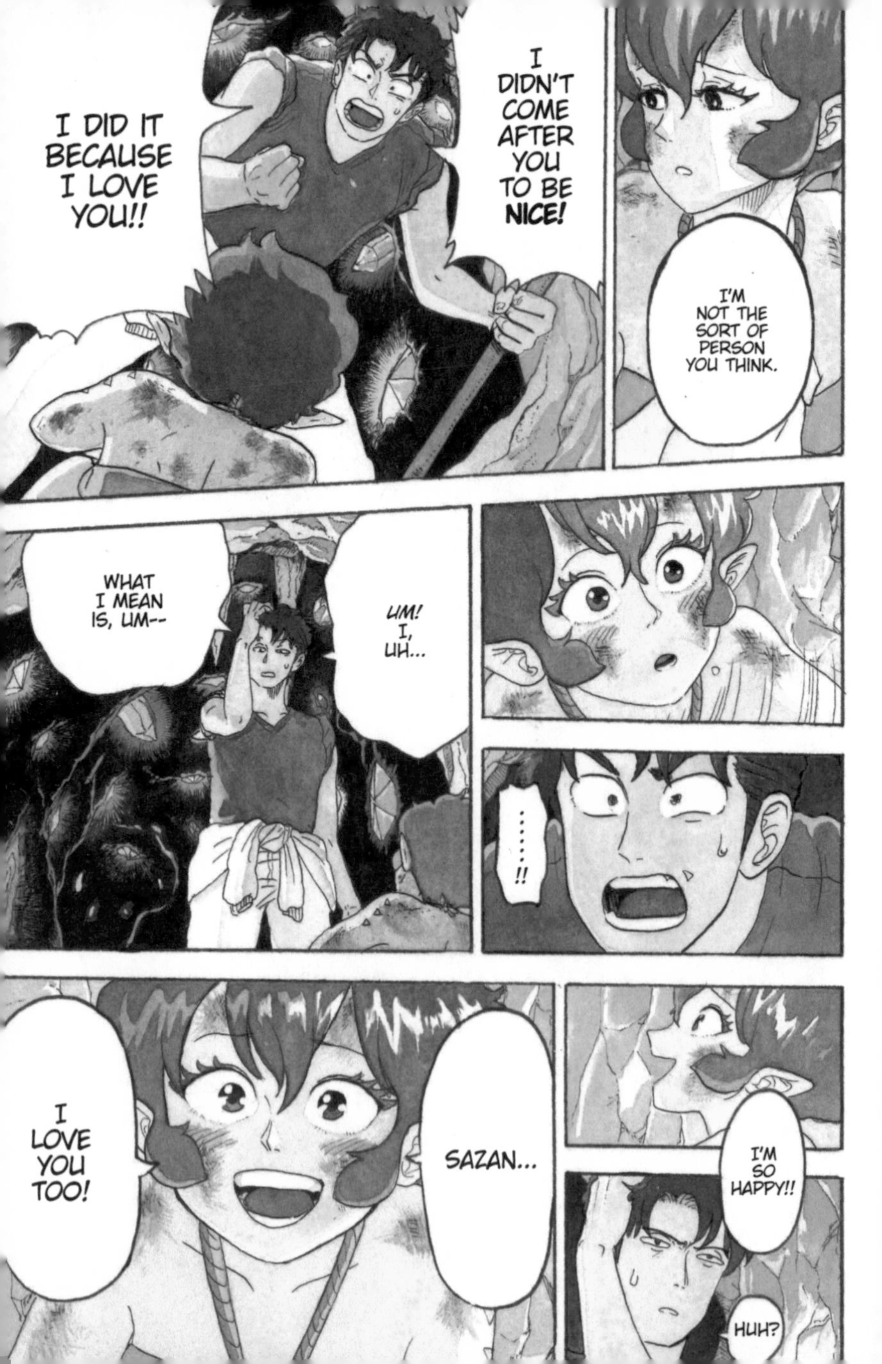

I'M NOT THE SORT OF PERSON YOU THINK.
I DIDN'T COME AFTER YOU TO BE **NICE!**
I DID IT BECAUSE I LOVE YOU!!
......!!
UM! I, UH...
WHAT I MEAN IS, UM--
I'M SO HAPPY!!
HUH?
SAZAN...
I LOVE YOU TOO!

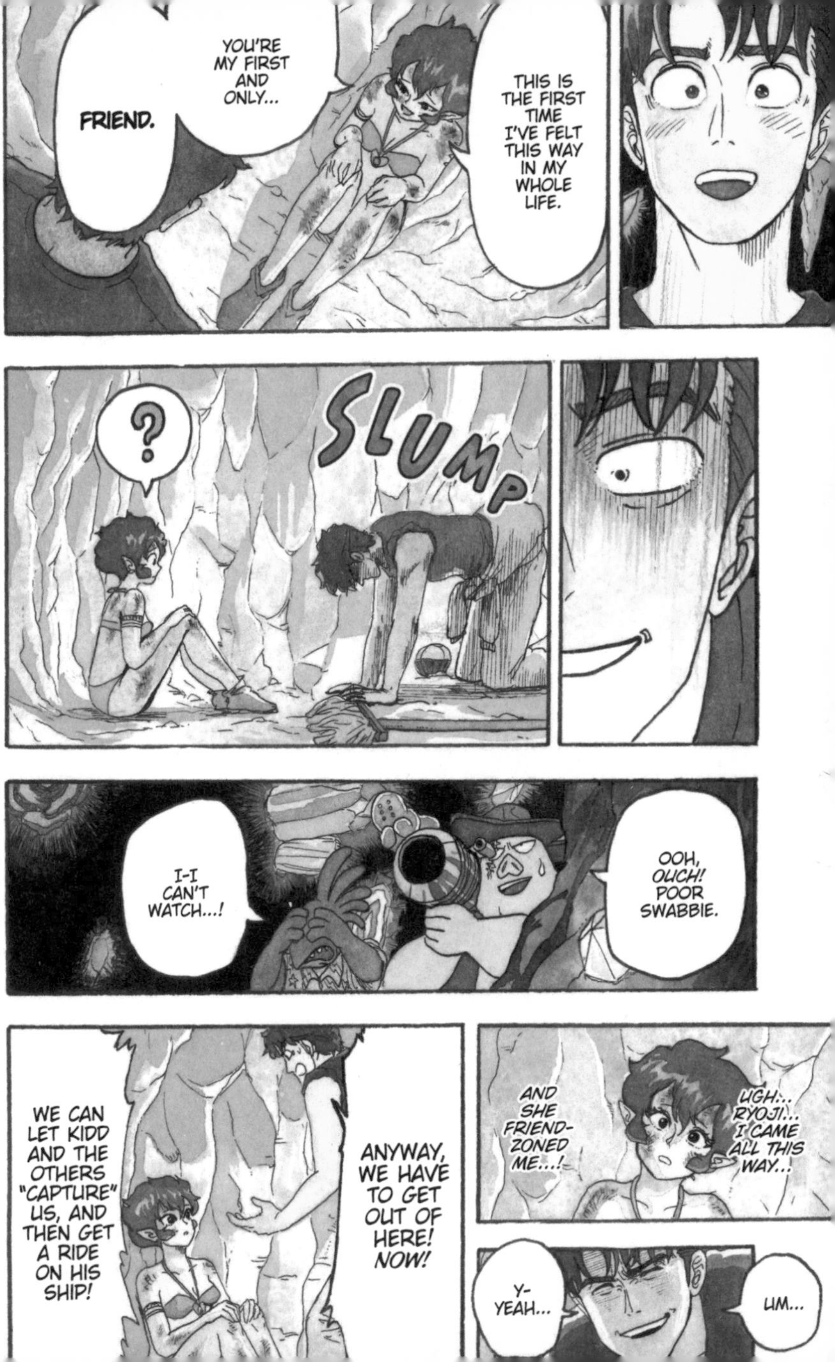
THIS IS THE FIRST TIME I'VE FELT THIS WAY IN MY WHOLE LIFE.
YOU'RE MY FIRST AND ONLY...
FRIEND.
SLUMP
?
OOH, OUCH! POOR SWABBIE.
I-I CAN'T WATCH...!
UGH... RYOJI... I CAME ALL THIS WAY...
AND SHE FRIEND-ZONED ME...!
UM...
Y-YEAH...
ANYWAY, WE HAVE TO GET OUT OF HERE! NOW!
WE CAN LET KIDD AND THE OTHERS "CAPTURE" US, AND THEN GET A RIDE ON HIS SHIP!

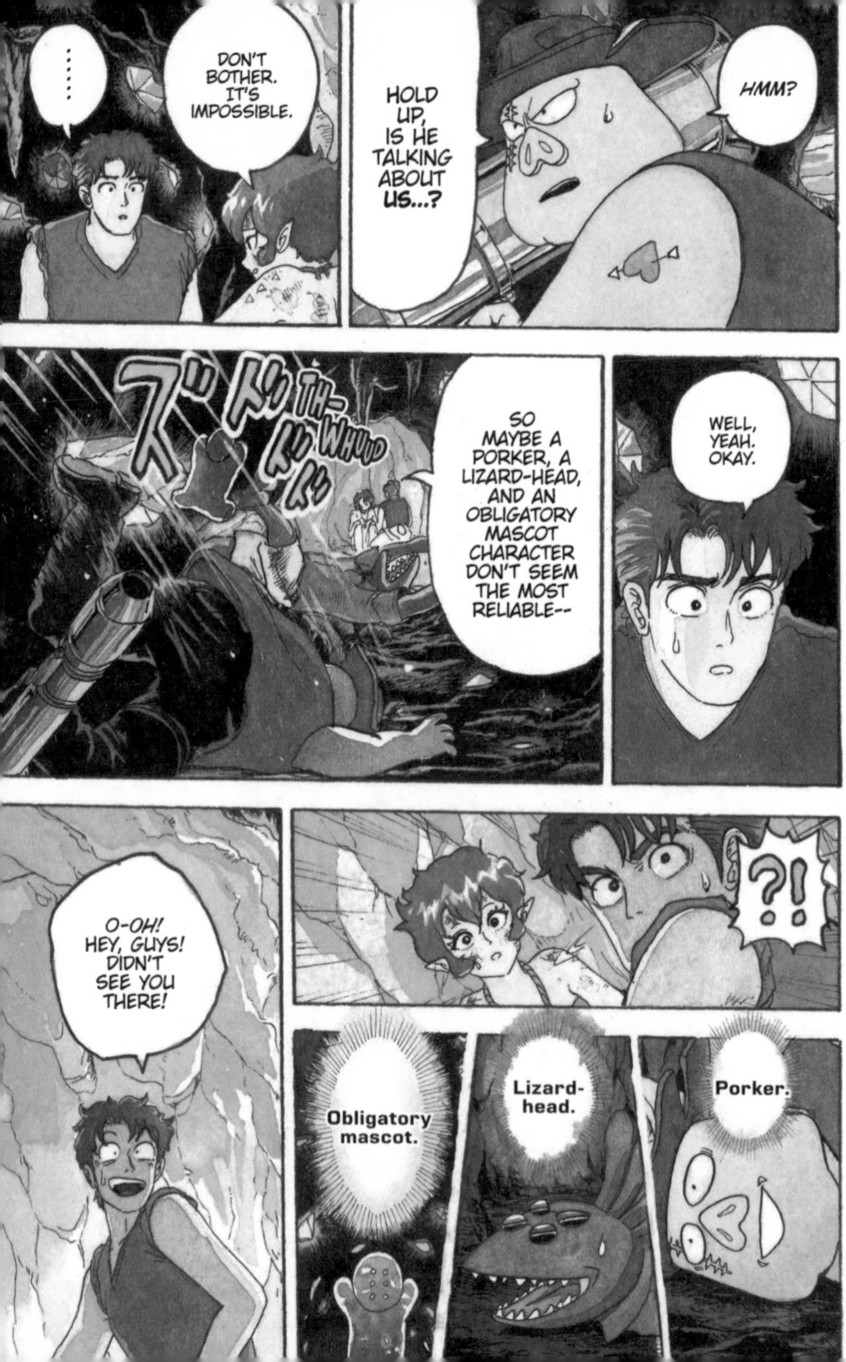
HMM?
HOLD UP, IS HE TALKING ABOUT US...?
DON'T BOTHER. IT'S IMPOSSIBLE.
......
WELL, YEAH. OKAY.
SO MAYBE A PORKER, A LIZARD-HEAD, AND AN OBLIGATORY MASCOT CHARACTER DON'T SEEM THE MOST RELIABLE--
TH-WHUUD
?!
Porker.
Lizard-head.
Obligatory mascot.
O-OH! HEY, GUYS! DIDN'T SEE YOU THERE!

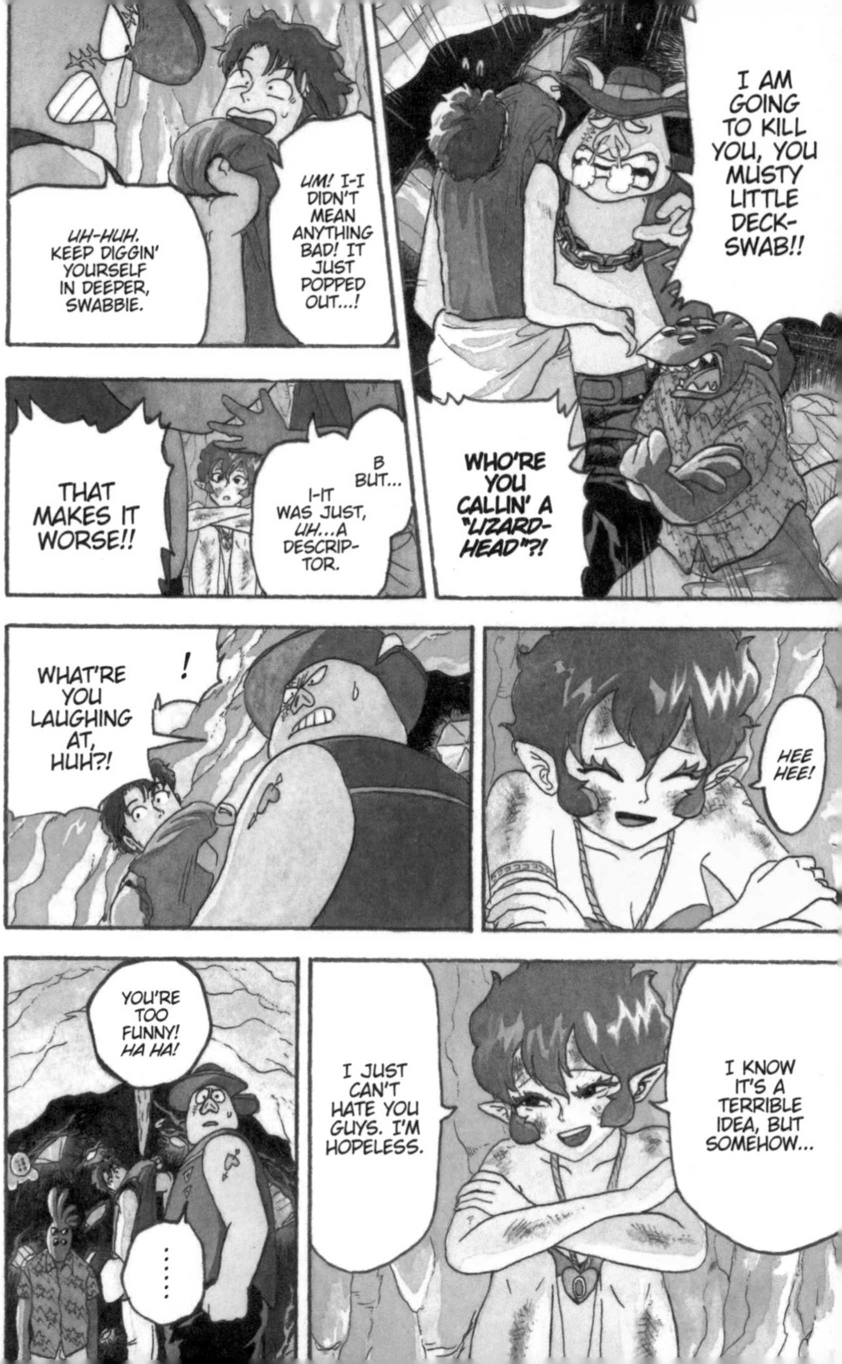
I AM GOING TO KILL YOU, YOU MUSTY LITTLE DECK-SWAB!!
WHO'RE YOU CALLIN' A "LIZARD-HEAD"?!
UM! I-I DIDN'T MEAN ANYTHING BAD! IT JUST POPPED OUT...!
UH-HUH. KEEP DIGGIN' YOURSELF IN DEEPER, SWABBIE.
B BUT... I-IT WAS JUST, UH...A DESCRIP-TOR.
THAT MAKES IT WORSE!!
HEE HEE!
!
WHAT'RE YOU LAUGHING AT, HUH?!
I KNOW IT'S A TERRIBLE IDEA, BUT SOMEHOW...
I JUST CAN'T HATE YOU GUYS. I'M HOPELESS.
YOU'RE TOO FUNNY! HA HA!
......

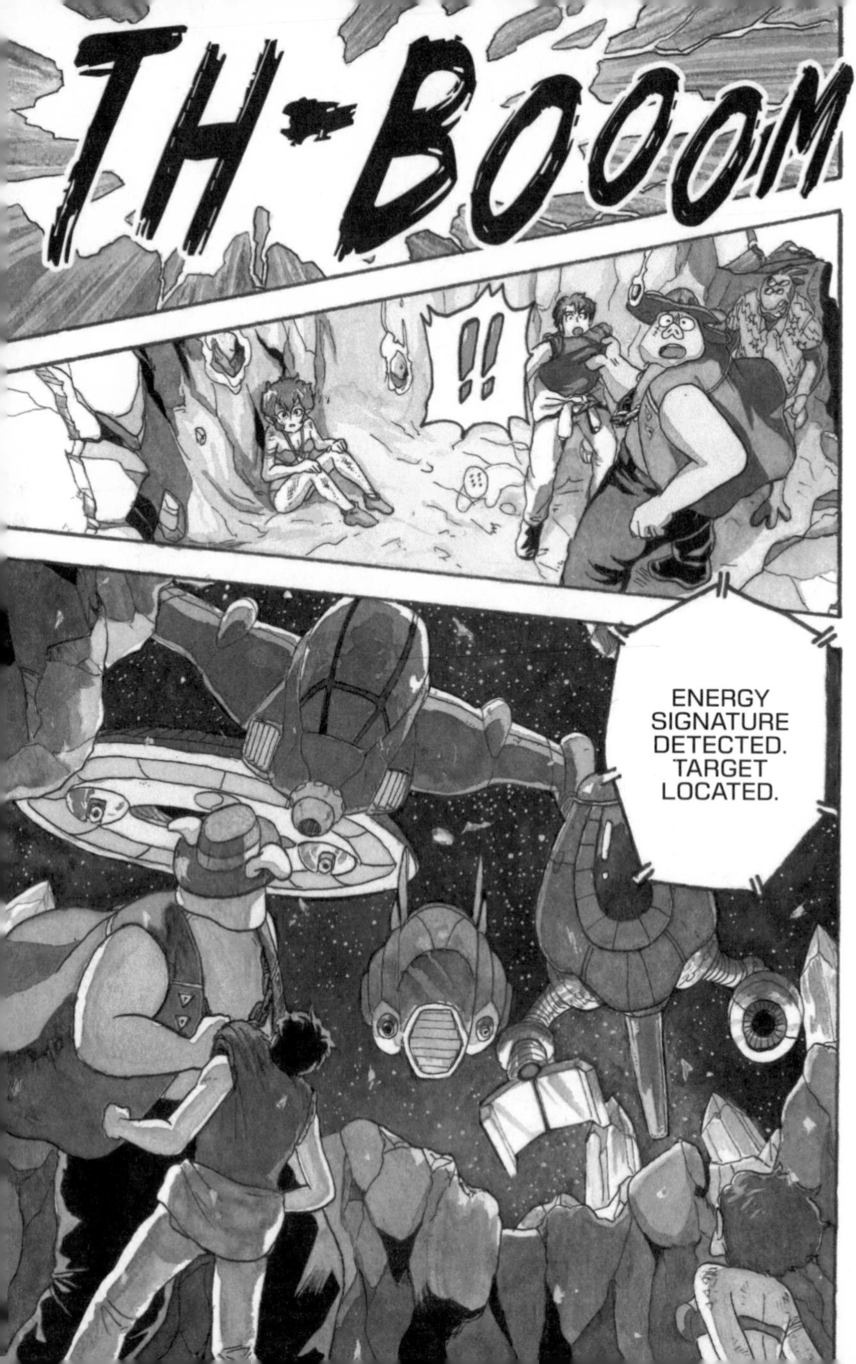
TH-BOOOM
!!
ENERGY SIGNATURE DETECTED. TARGET LOCATED.

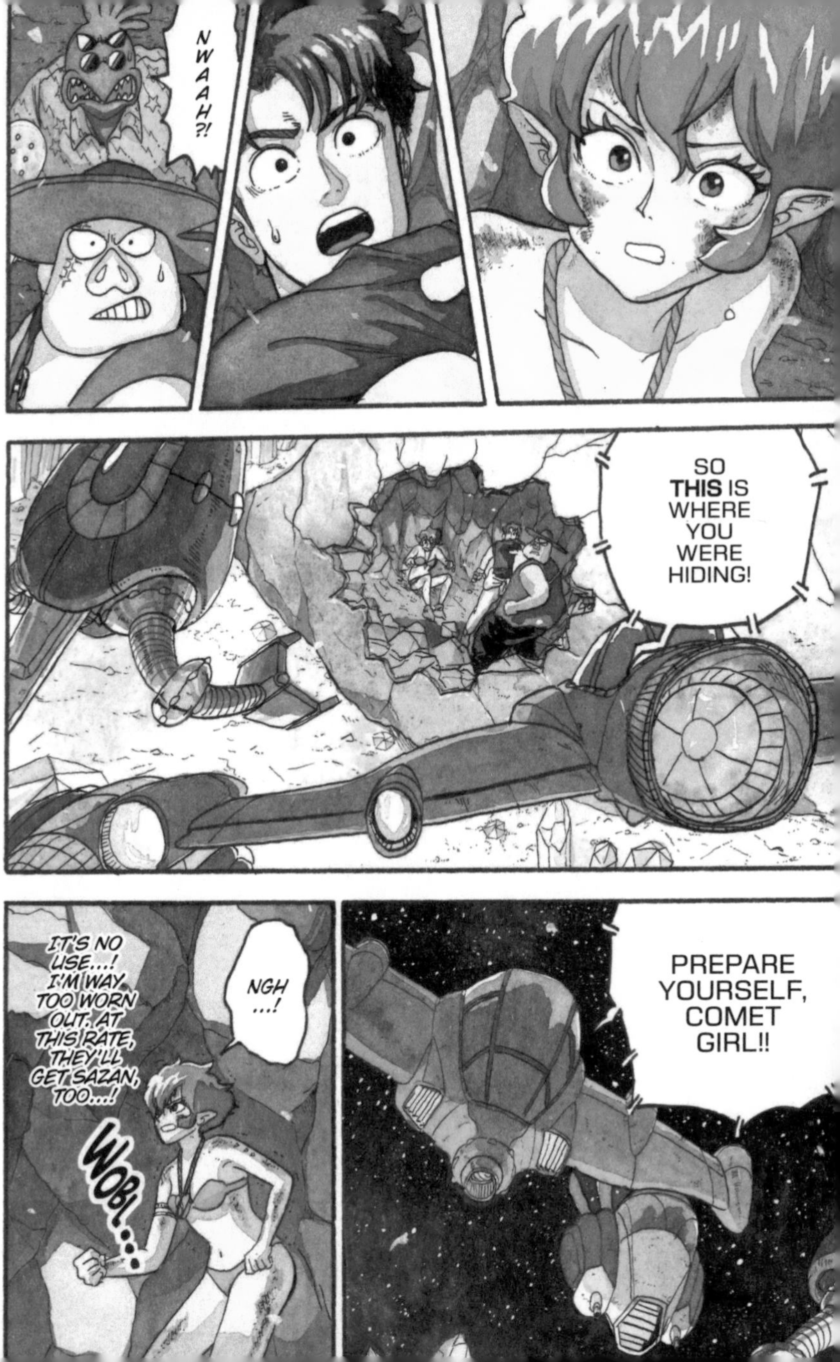
NWAAAH?!
SO **THIS** IS WHERE YOU WERE HIDING!
PREPARE YOURSELF, COMET GIRL!!
NGH ...!
IT'S NO USE...! I'M WAY TOO WORN OUT. AT THIS RATE, THEY'LL GET SAZAN, TOO...!
WOBL...

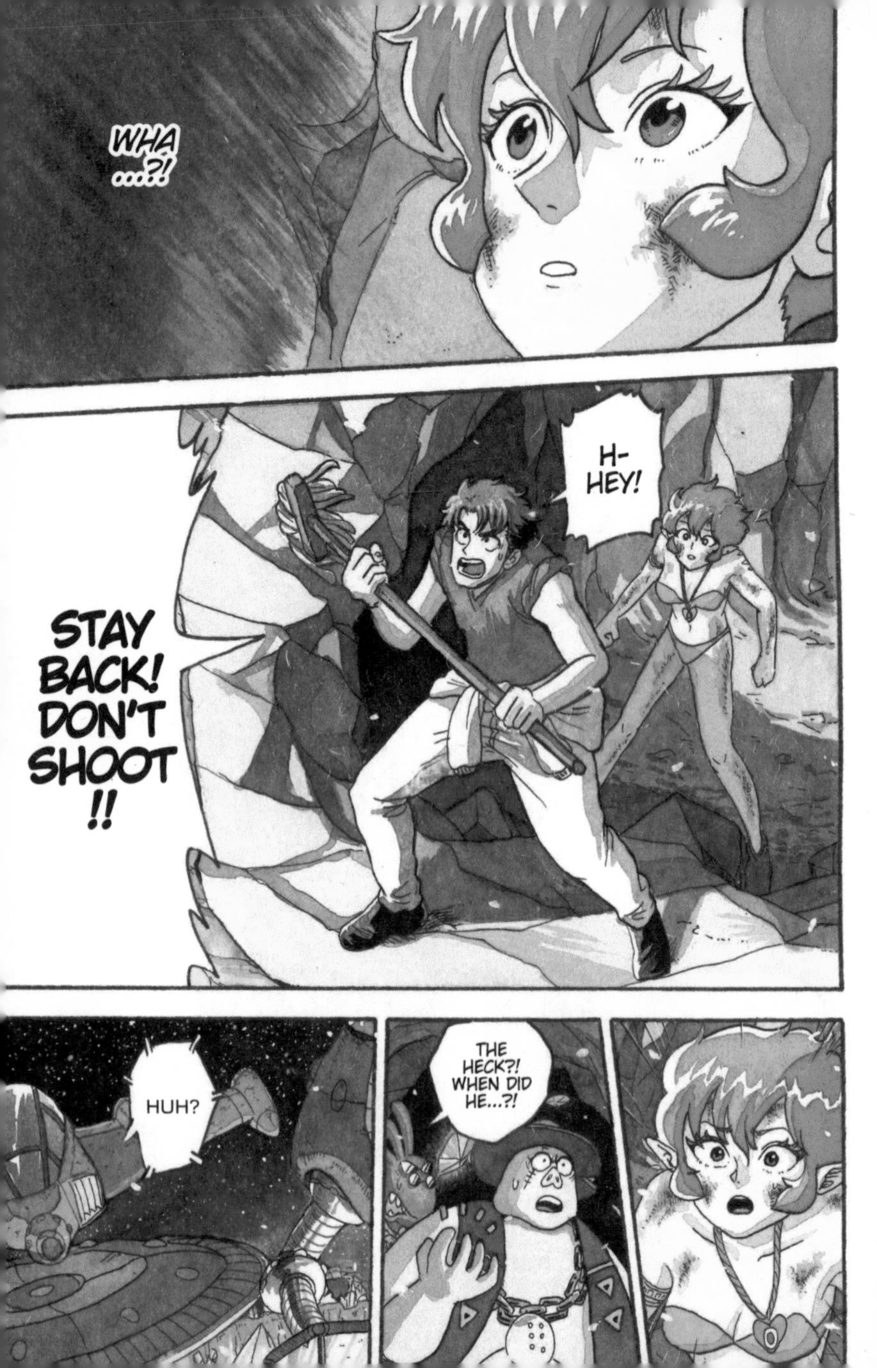
WHA ...?!
H- HEY!
STAY BACK! DON'T SHOOT !!
THE HECK?! WHEN DID HE...?!
HUH?

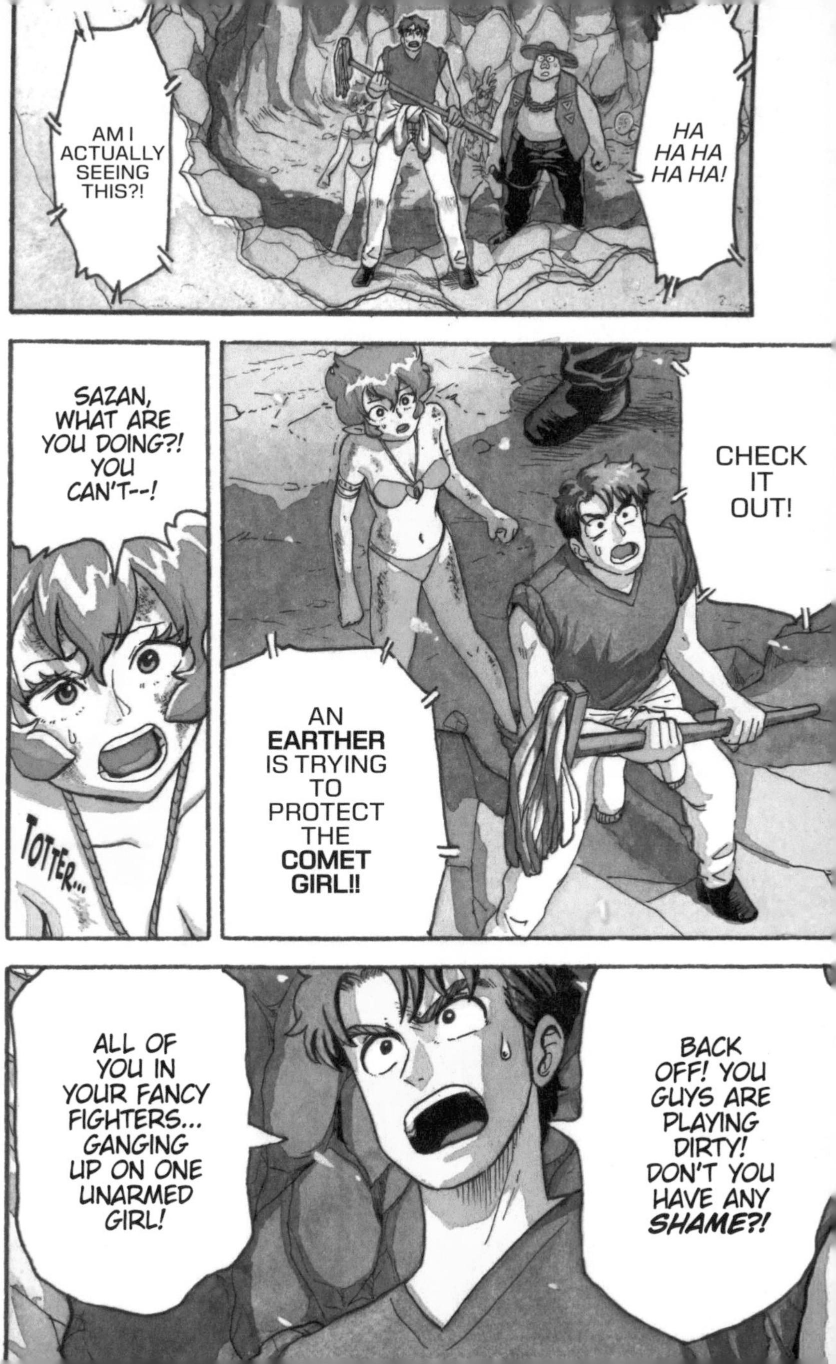
HA HA HA HA HA!
AM I ACTUALLY SEEING THIS?!
CHECK IT OUT!
AN **EARTHER** IS TRYING TO PROTECT THE **COMET GIRL!!**
SAZAN, WHAT ARE YOU DOING?! YOU CAN'T--!
TOTTER...
BACK OFF! YOU GUYS ARE PLAYING DIRTY! DON'T YOU HAVE ANY ***SHAME?!***
ALL OF YOU IN YOUR FANCY FIGHTERS... GANGING UP ON ONE UNARMED GIRL!

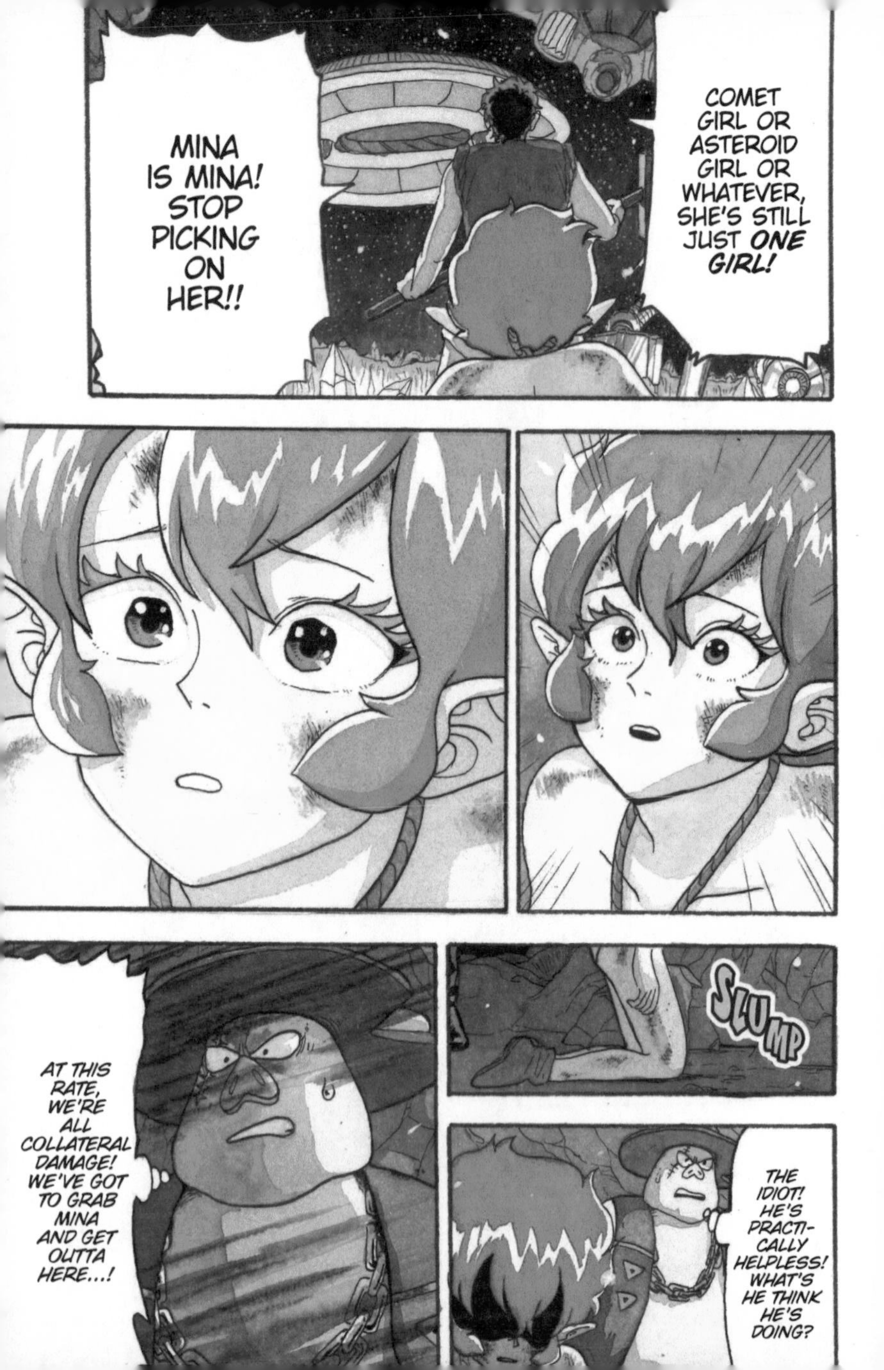
COMET GIRL OR ASTEROID GIRL OR WHATEVER, SHE'S STILL JUST ONE GIRL!
MINA IS MINA! STOP PICKING ON HER!!
SLUMP
THE IDIOT! HE'S PRACTI-CALLY HELPLESS! WHAT'S HE THINK HE'S DOING?
AT THIS RATE, WE'RE ALL COLLATERAL DAMAGE! WE'VE GOT TO GRAB MINA AND GET OUTTA HERE...!

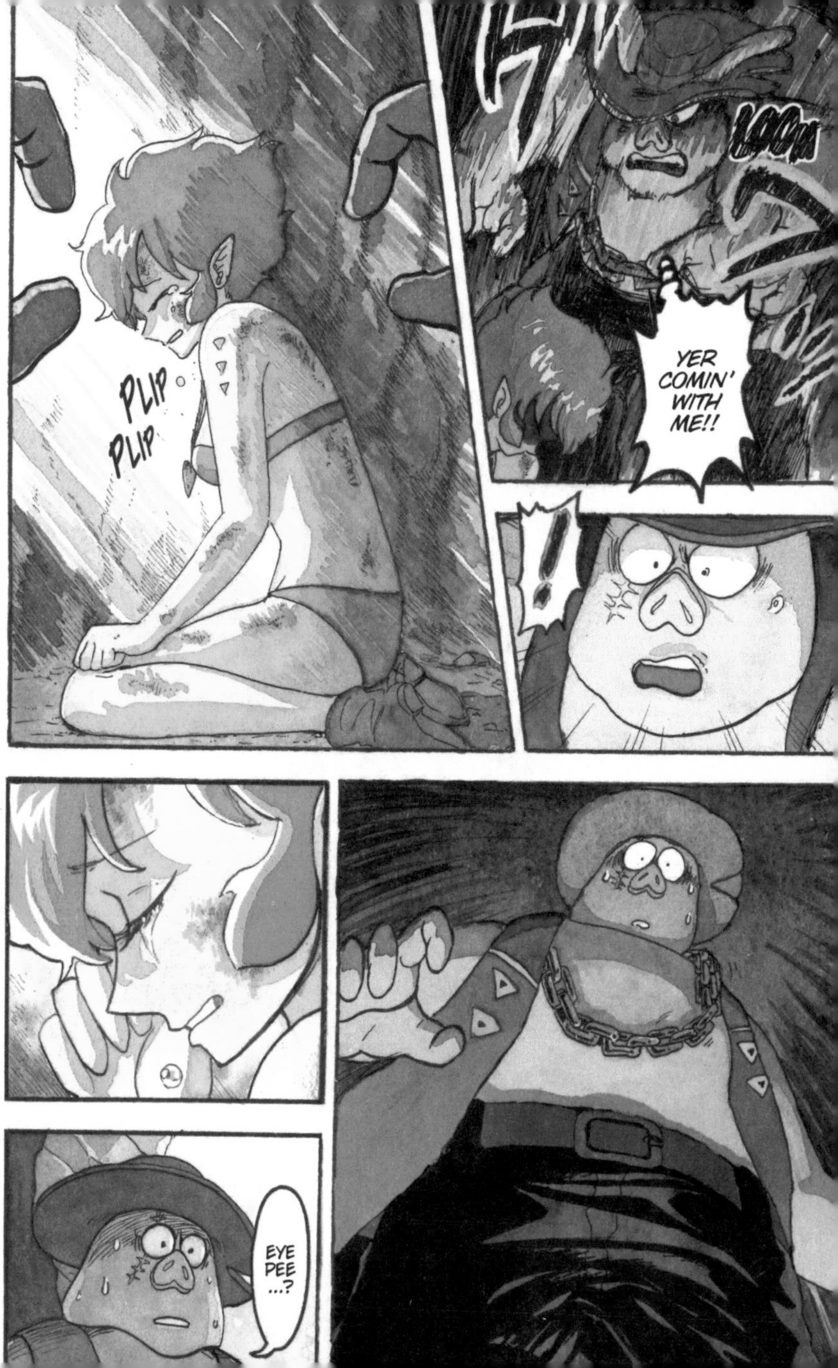
YER COMIN' WITH ME!!
!
PLIP PLIP
EYE PEE ...?

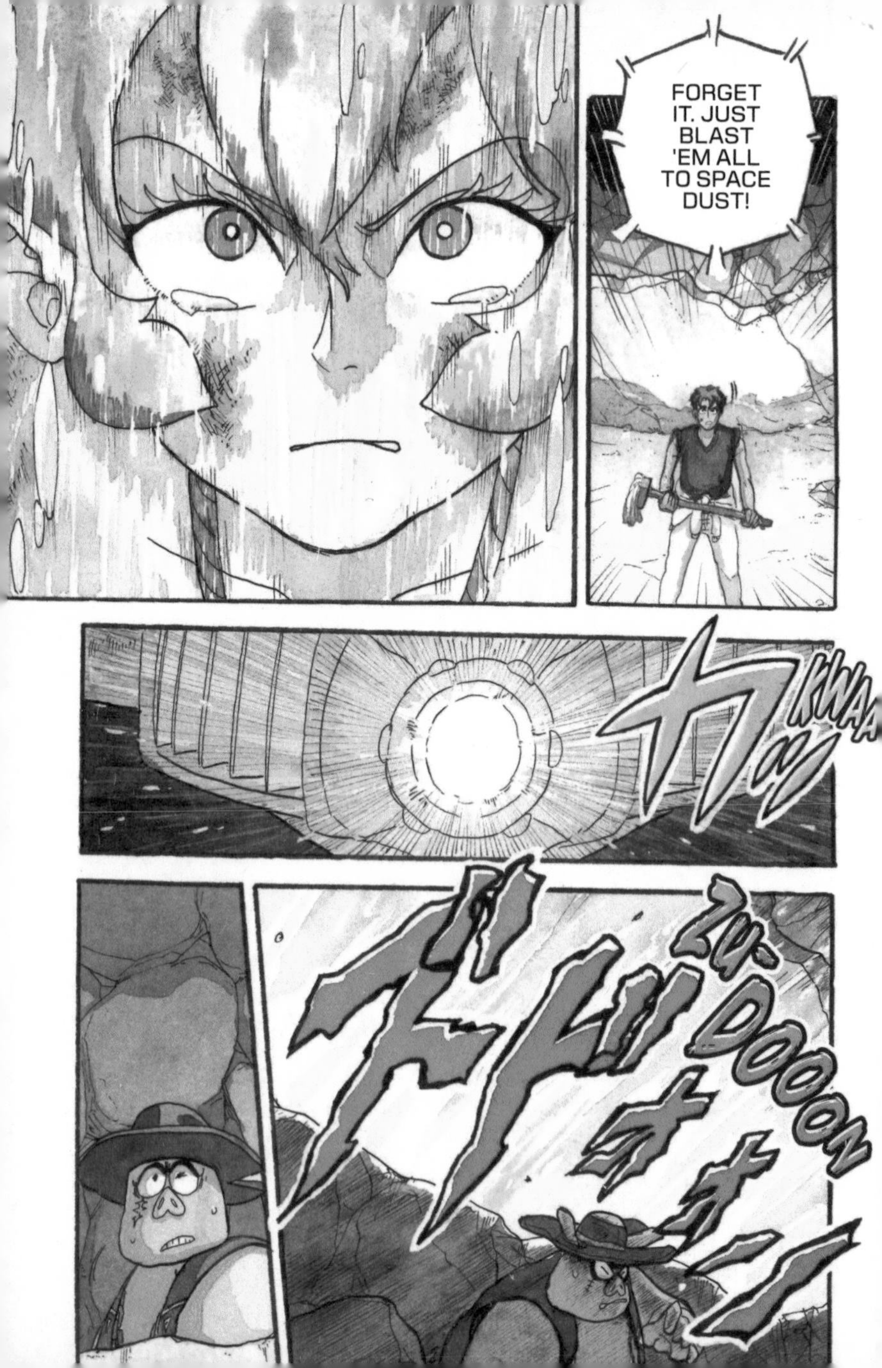
FORGET IT. JUST BLAST 'EM ALL TO SPACE DUST!
KWAA
ZU-DOOOON

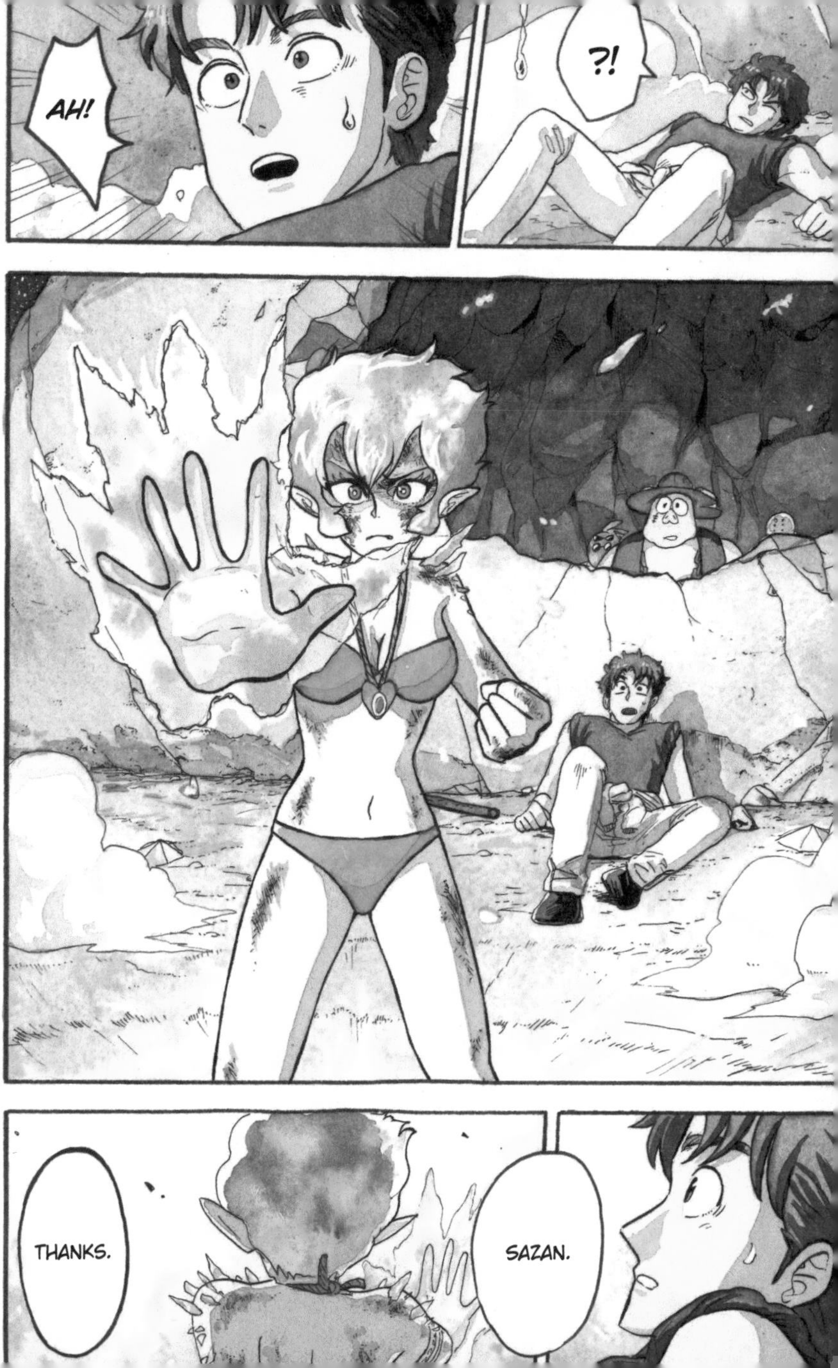
?!
AH!
SAZAN.
THANKS.

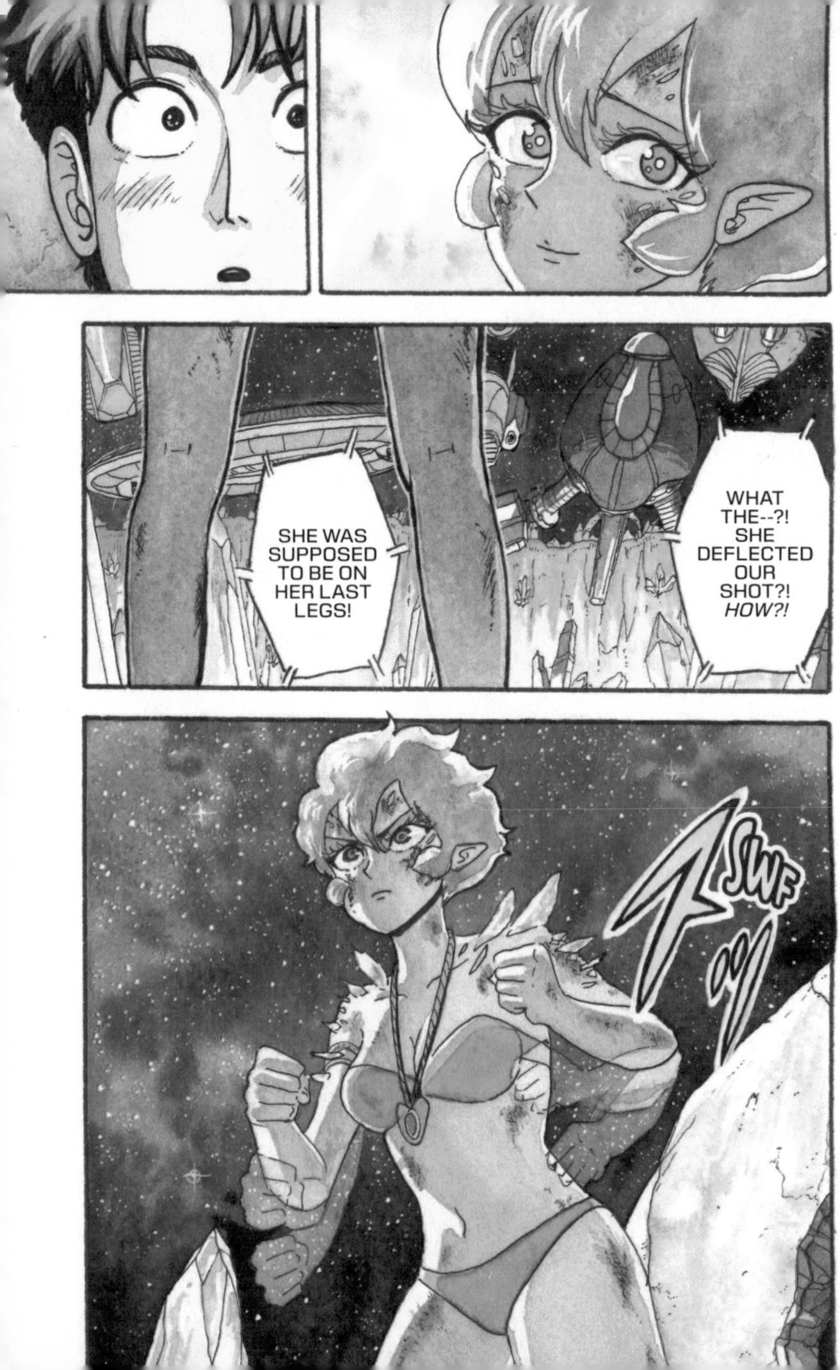
WHAT THE--?! SHE DEFLECTED OUR SHOT?! *HOW?!*
SHE WAS SUPPOSED TO BE ON HER LAST LEGS!
SWF

SHE'S BLUFFING! SHE'S TOO DRAINED TO DO ANY-THING! *FIRE!!*

GA-SHUNK

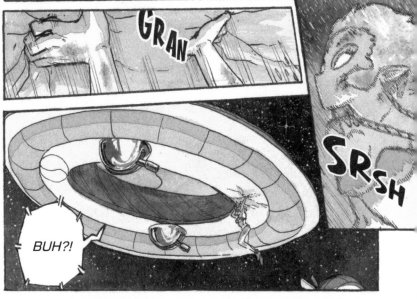

GRAN

SRSH

BUH?!

HEAVE

HNN--!!

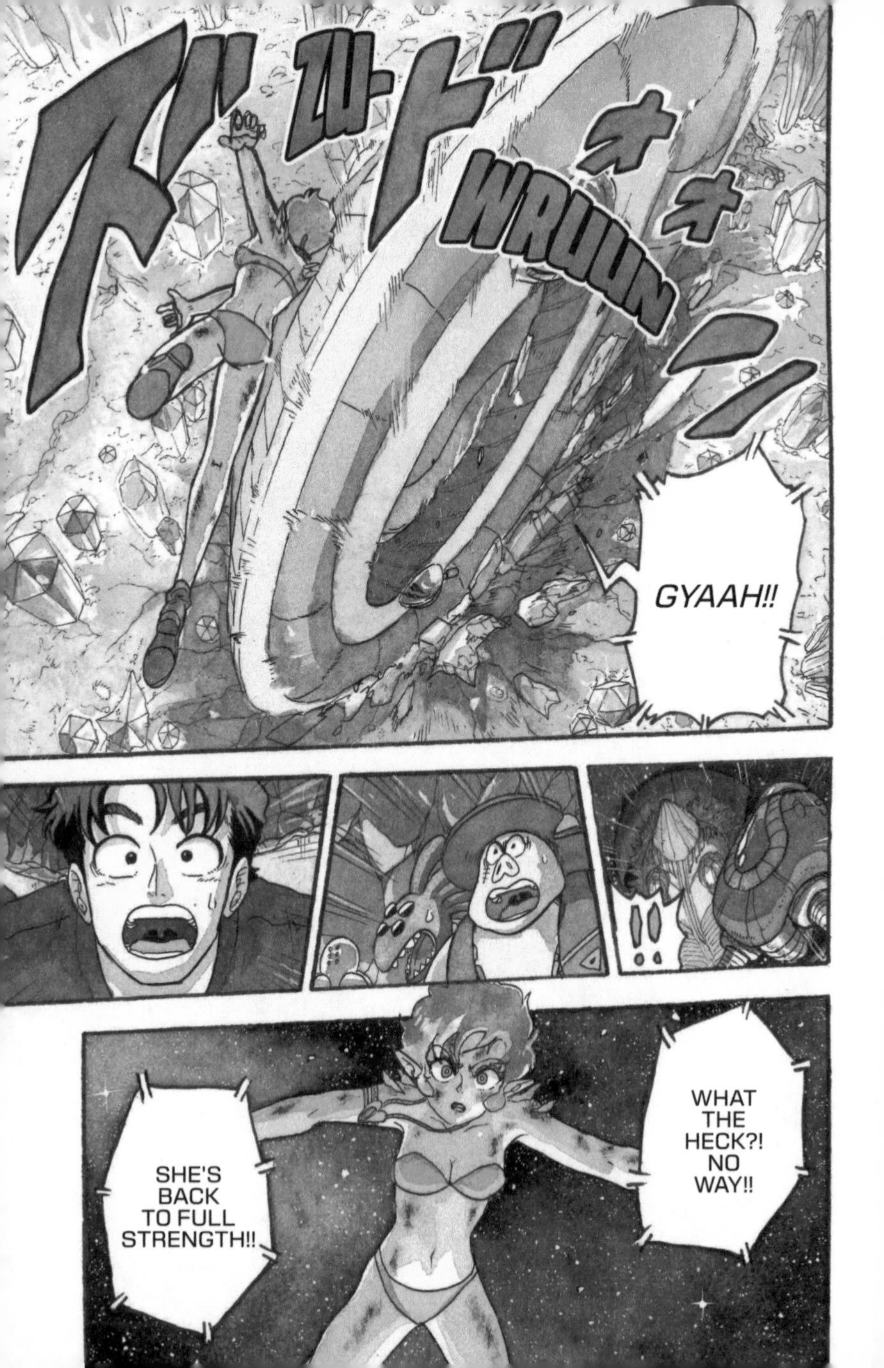
ZU-
WRUUN
GYAAH!!
!!
WHAT THE HECK?! NO WAY!!
SHE'S BACK TO FULL STRENGTH!!

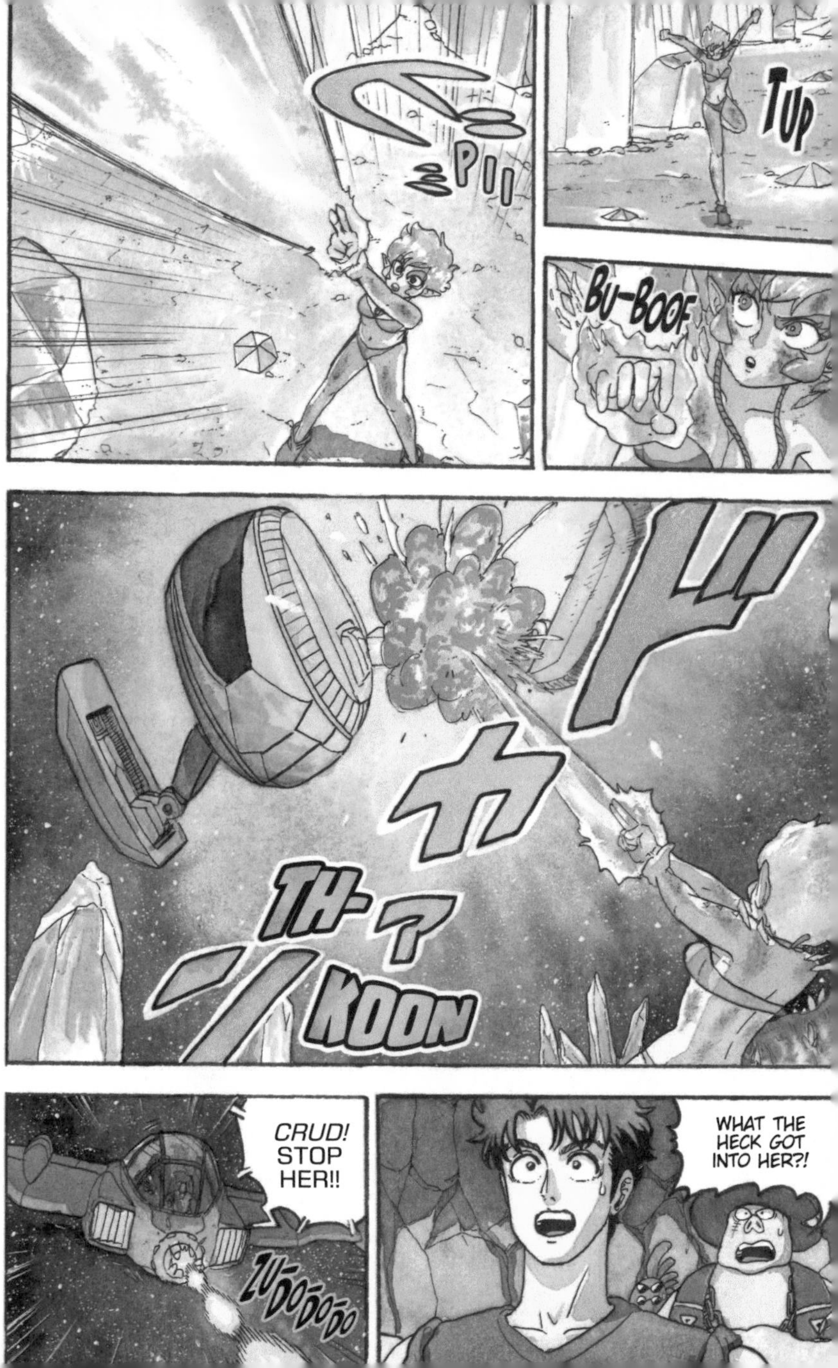
TUP
BU-BOOF
PII
TH-
KOON
WHAT THE HECK GOT INTO HER?!
CRUD! STOP HER!!
ZU-DŌ-DŌ-DO

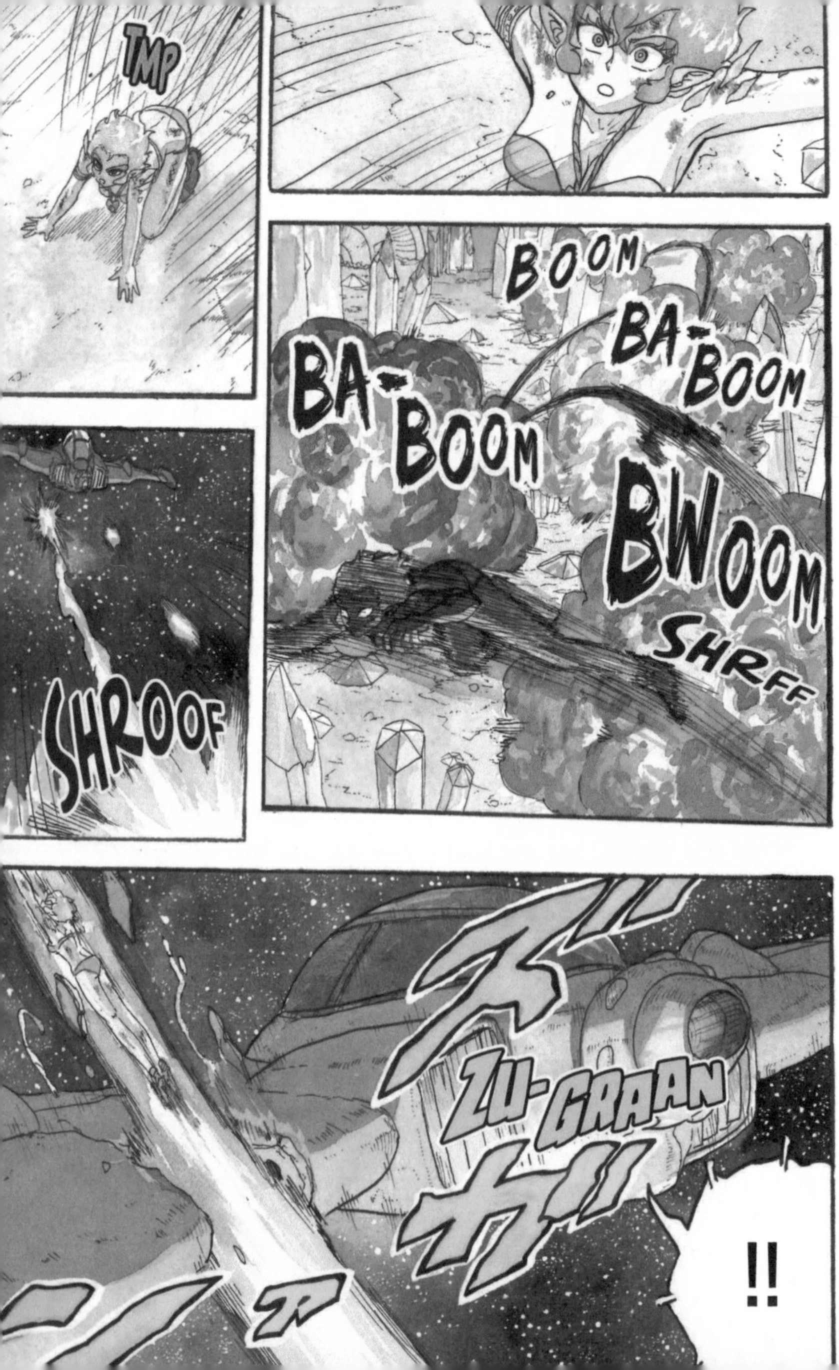
TMP
BOOM
BA-BOOM
BA-BOOM
BWOOM
SHRFF
SHROOF
ZU-GRAAN
!!

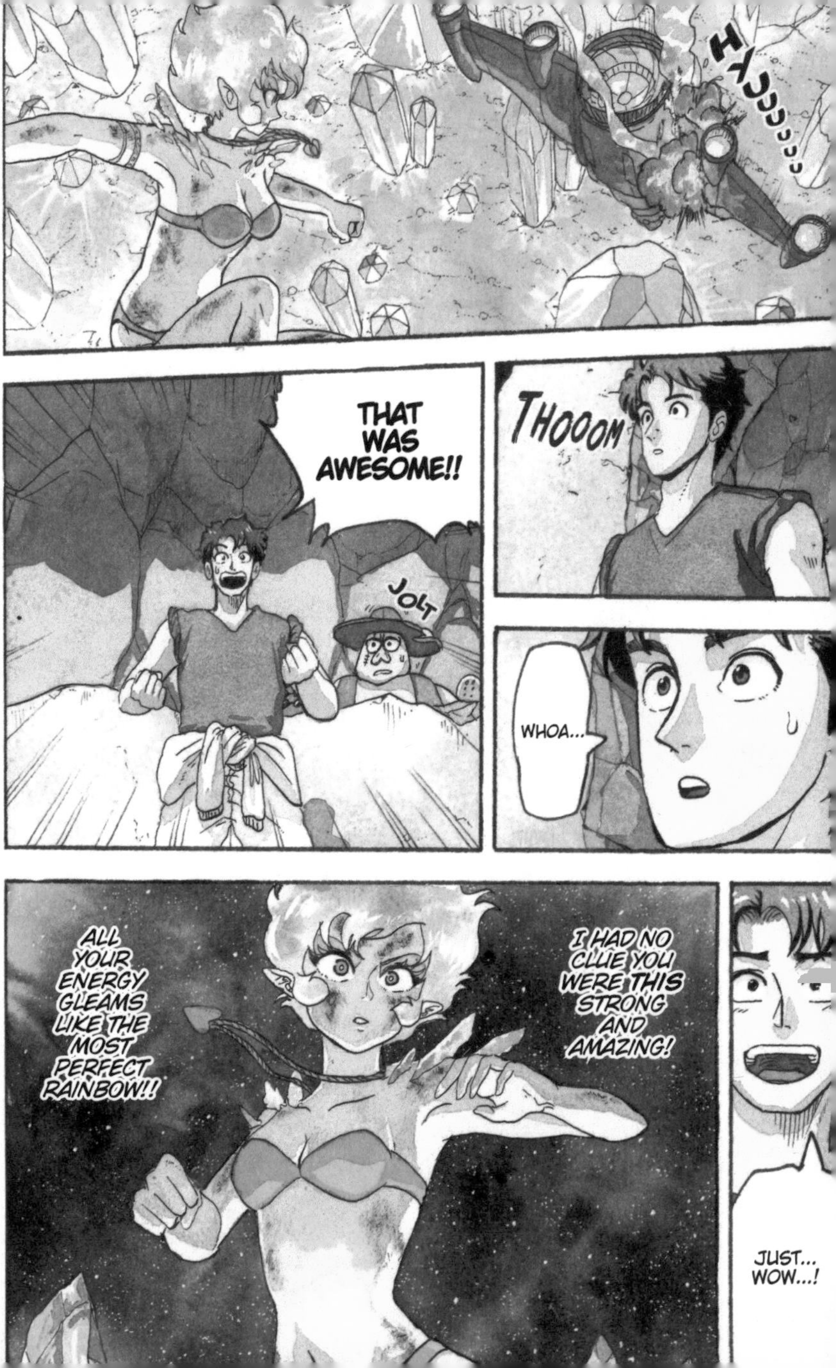
HYUUUUUU
THOOOM
WHOA...
THAT WAS AWESOME!!
JOLT
JUST... WOW...!
I HAD NO CLUE YOU WERE THIS STRONG AND AMAZING!
ALL YOUR ENERGY GLEAMS LIKE THE MOST PERFECT RAINBOW!!

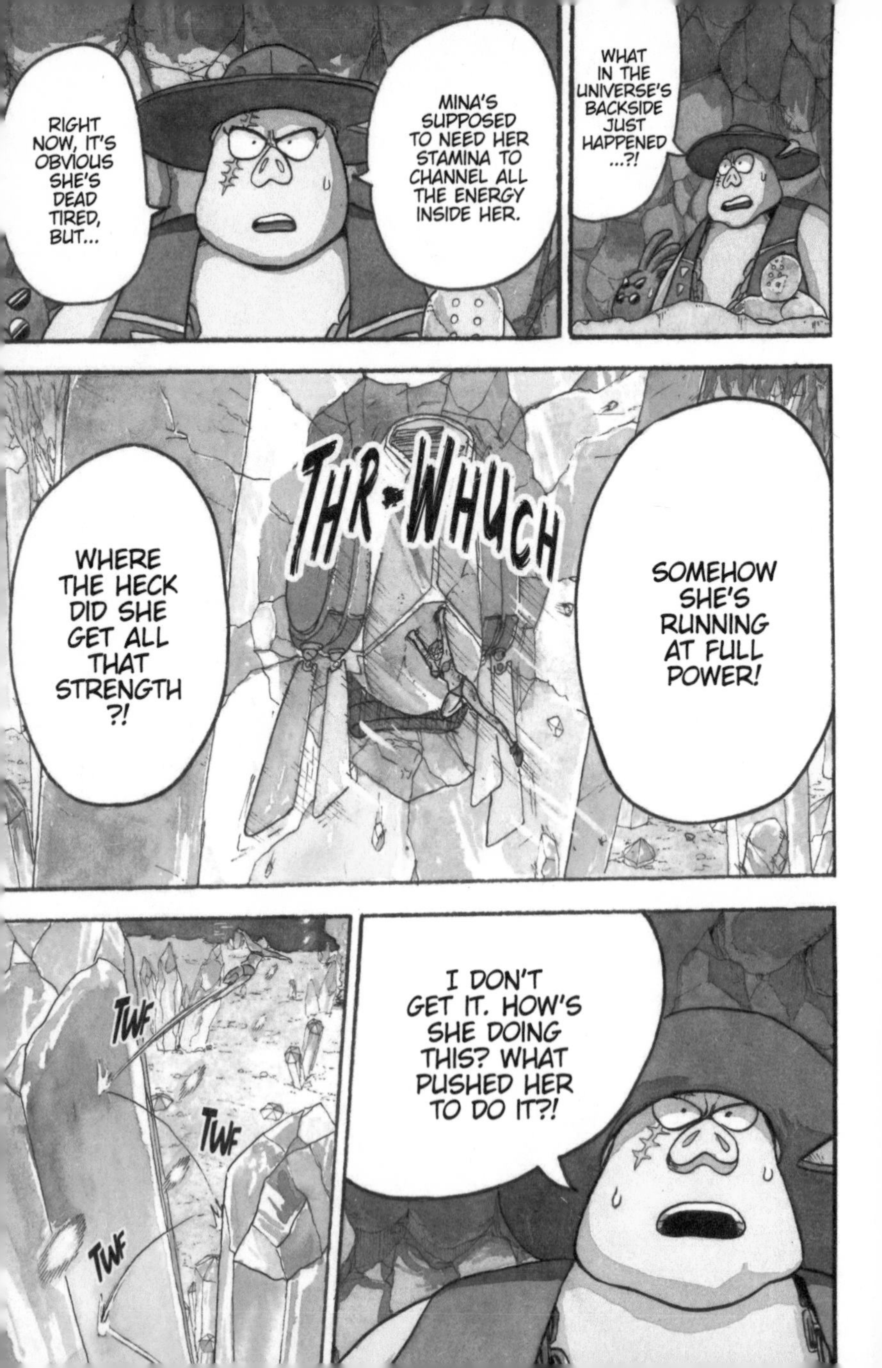
WHAT IN THE UNIVERSE'S BACKSIDE JUST HAPPENED ...?!
MINA'S SUPPOSED TO NEED HER STAMINA TO CHANNEL ALL THE ENERGY INSIDE HER.
RIGHT NOW, IT'S OBVIOUS SHE'S DEAD TIRED, BUT...
SOMEHOW SHE'S RUNNING AT FULL POWER!
THR-WHUCH
WHERE THE HECK DID SHE GET ALL THAT STRENGTH ?!
I DON'T GET IT. HOW'S SHE DOING THIS? WHAT PUSHED HER TO DO IT?!
TWF
TWF
TWF

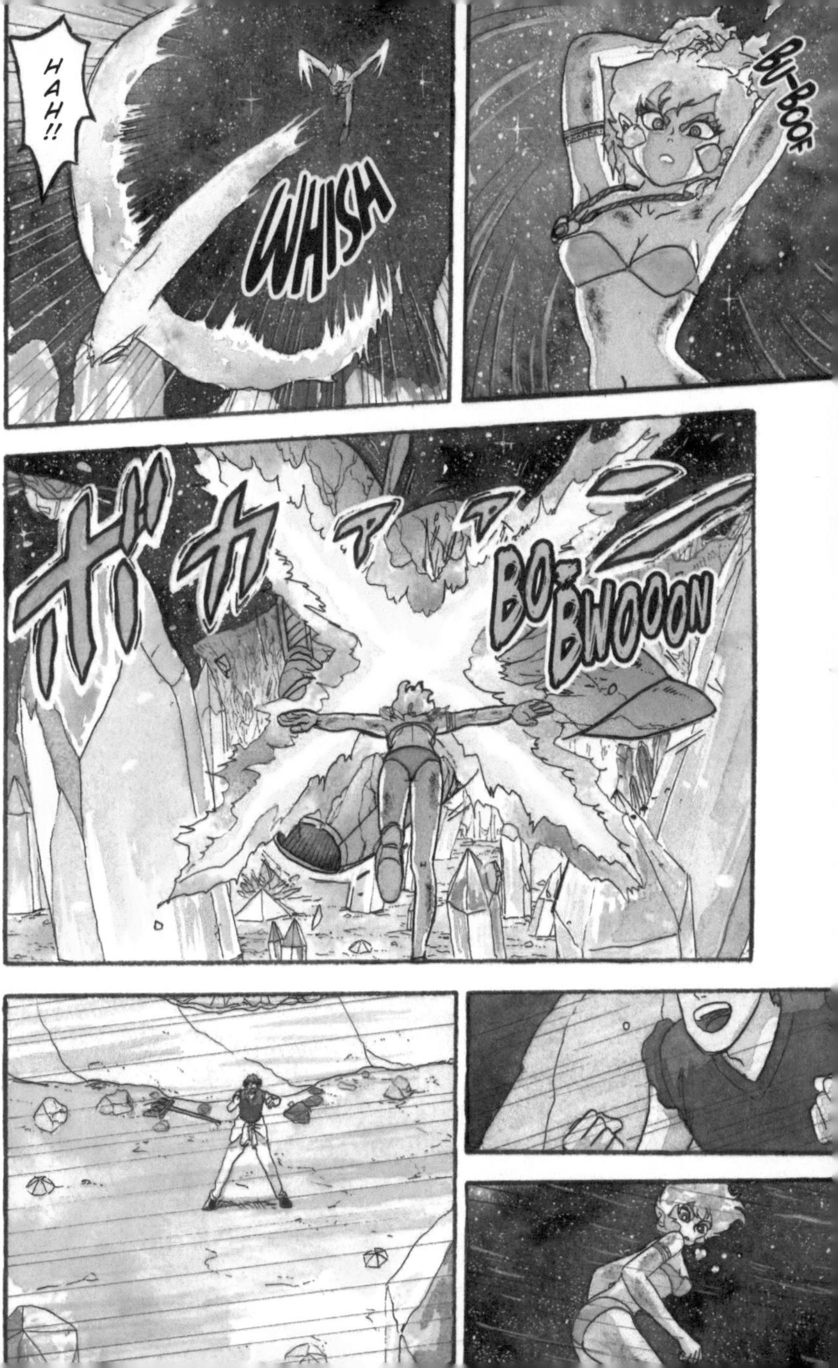
BU-BOOF
HAH!!
WHISH
BO-BWOOON

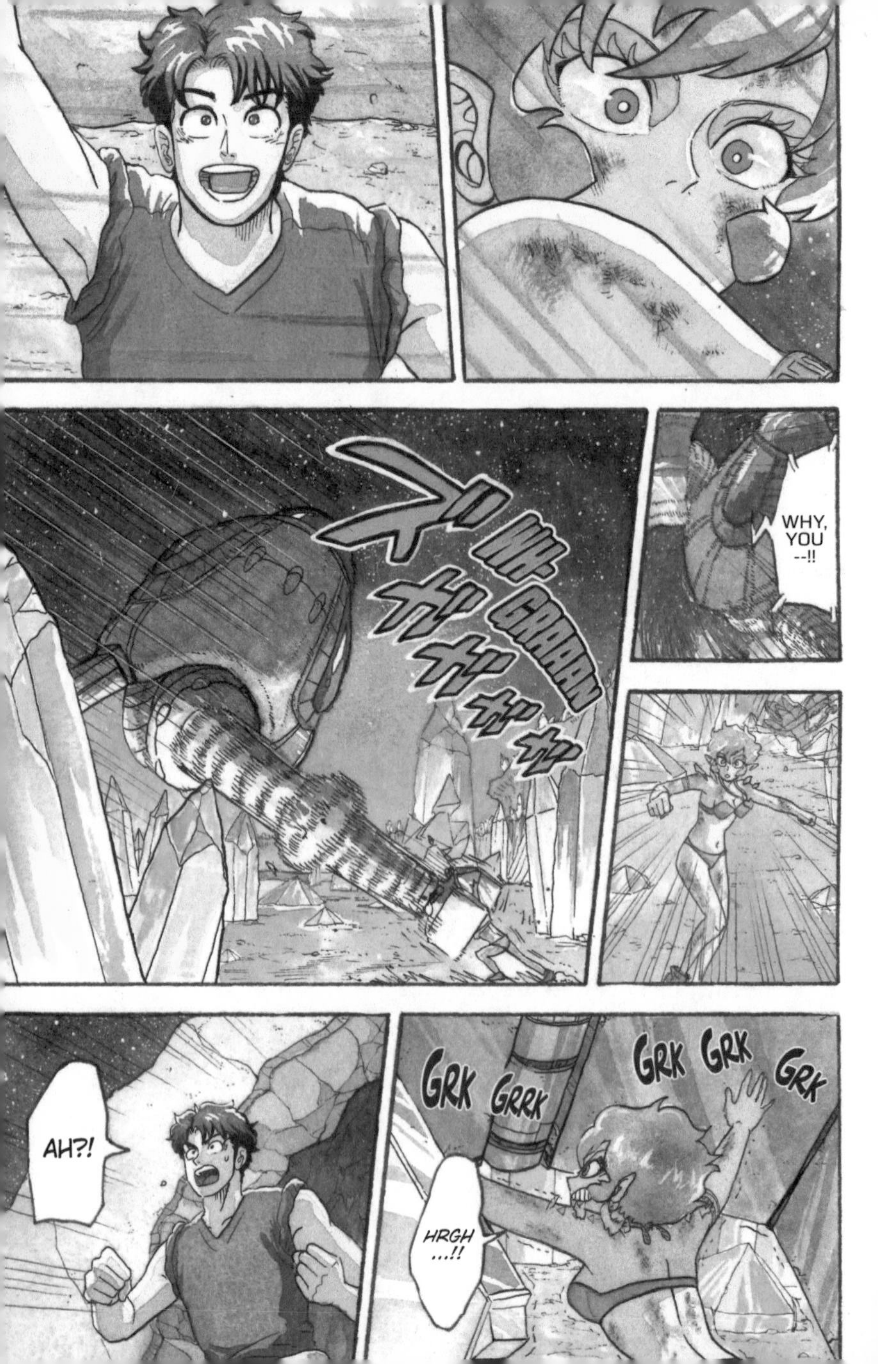
WHY, YOU --!!
GRAAAN
GRK GRK GRK
GRK GRRK
HRGH ...!!
AH?!

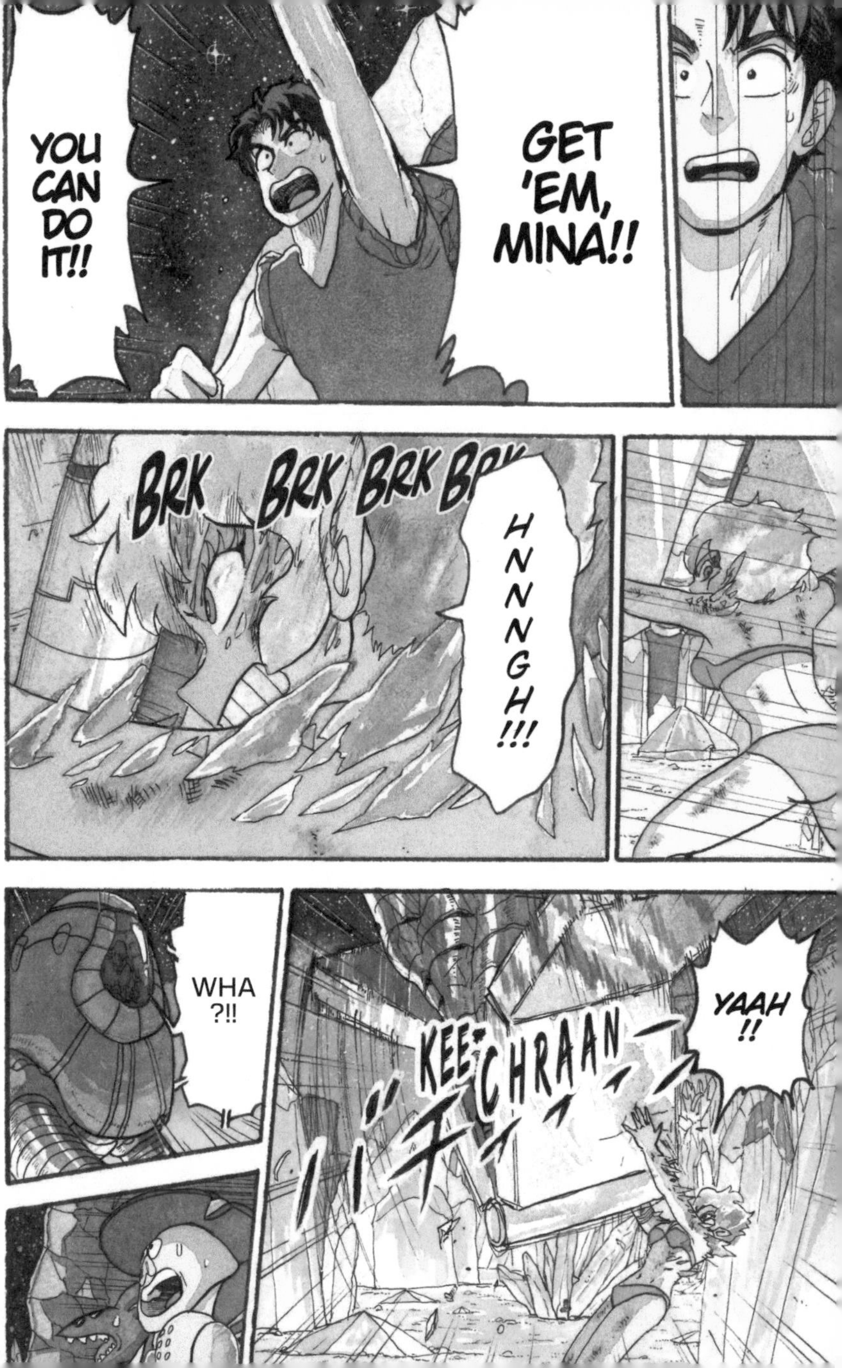
GET 'EM, MINA!!
YOU CAN DO IT!!
BRK BRK BRK
HNNNNGH!!!
YAAH!!
KEE-CHRAAN
WHA?!!

HYAAAH!!

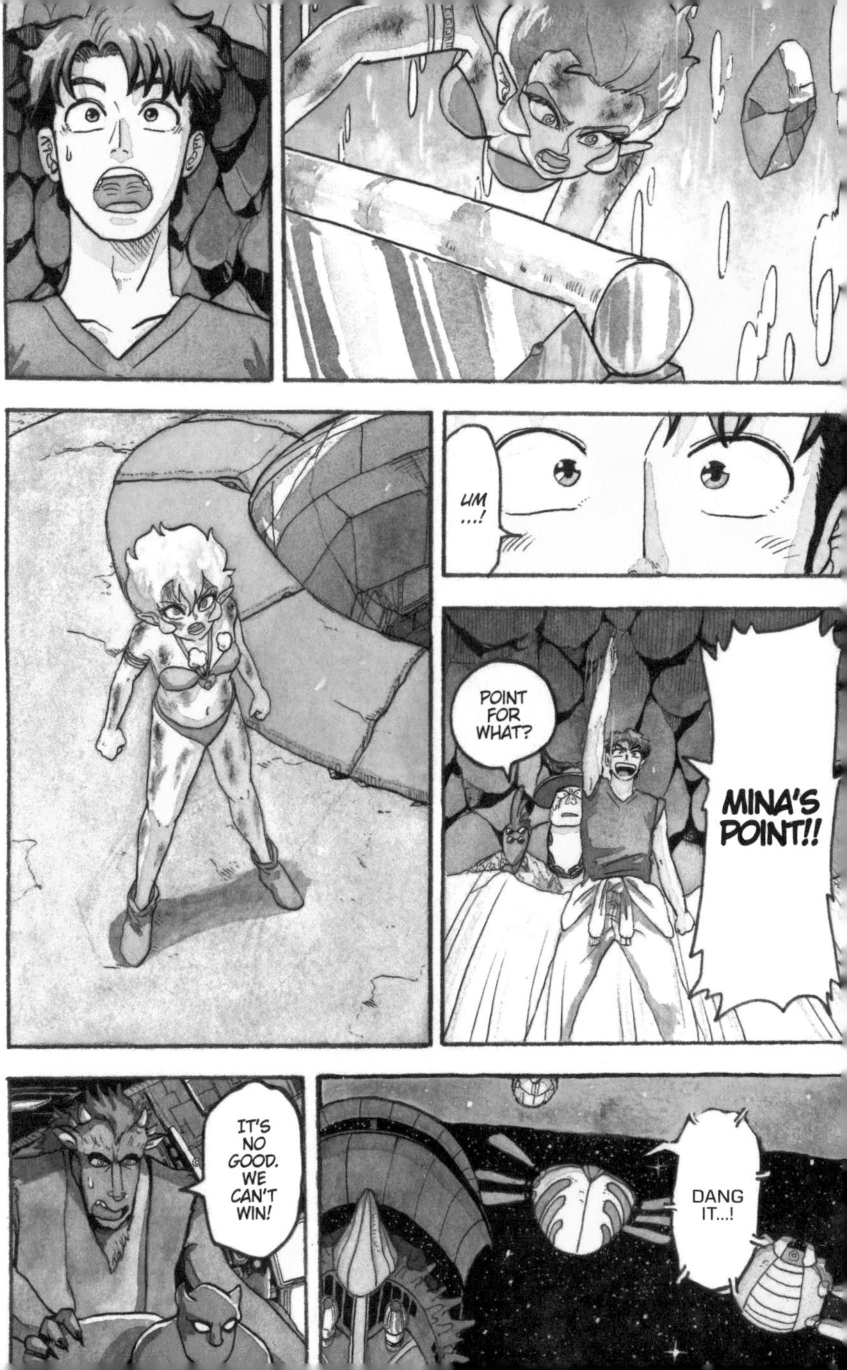
UM ...!
MINA'S POINT!!
POINT FOR WHAT?
DANG IT...!
IT'S NO GOOD. WE CAN'T WIN!

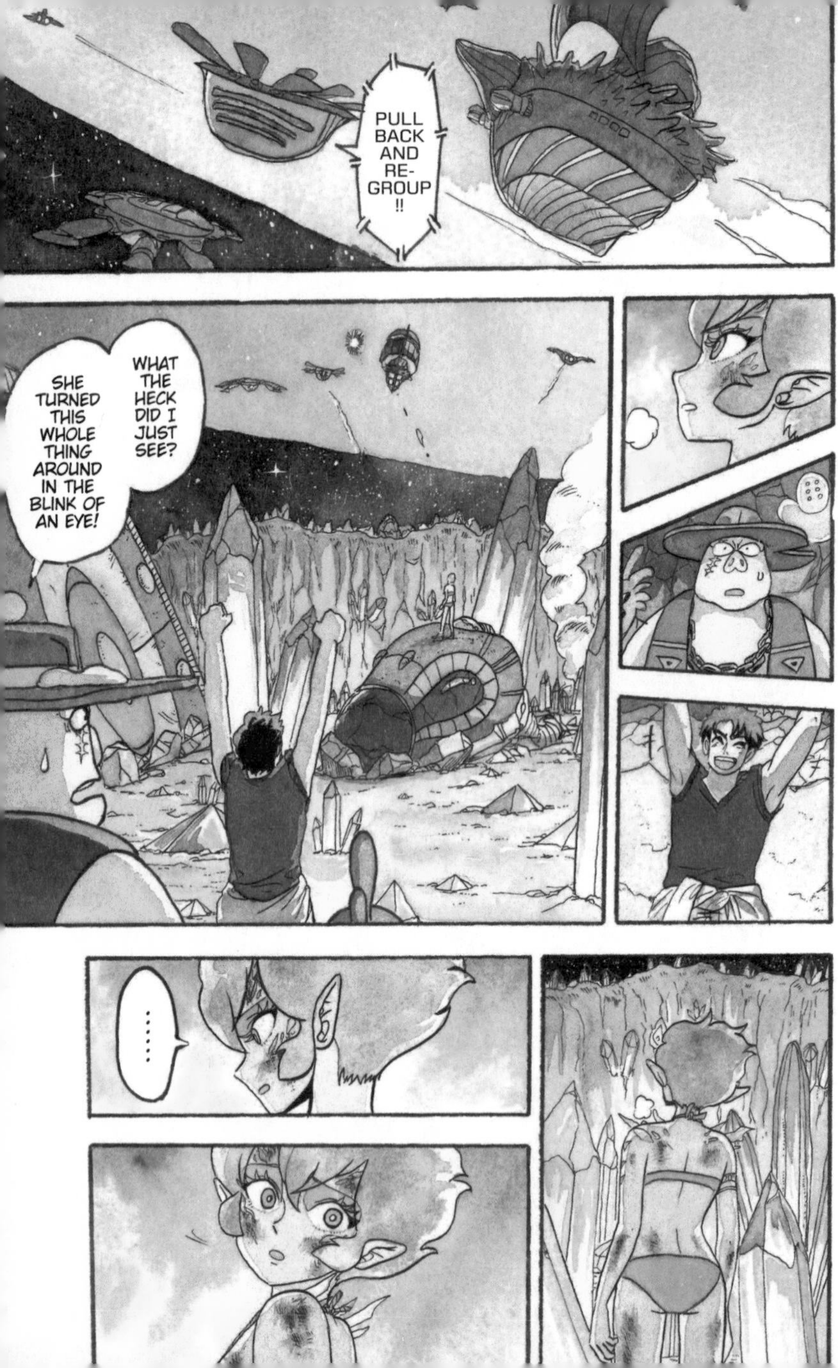
PULL BACK AND RE-GROUP!!
WHAT THE HECK DID I JUST SEE?
SHE TURNED THIS WHOLE THING AROUND IN THE BLINK OF AN EYE!
......

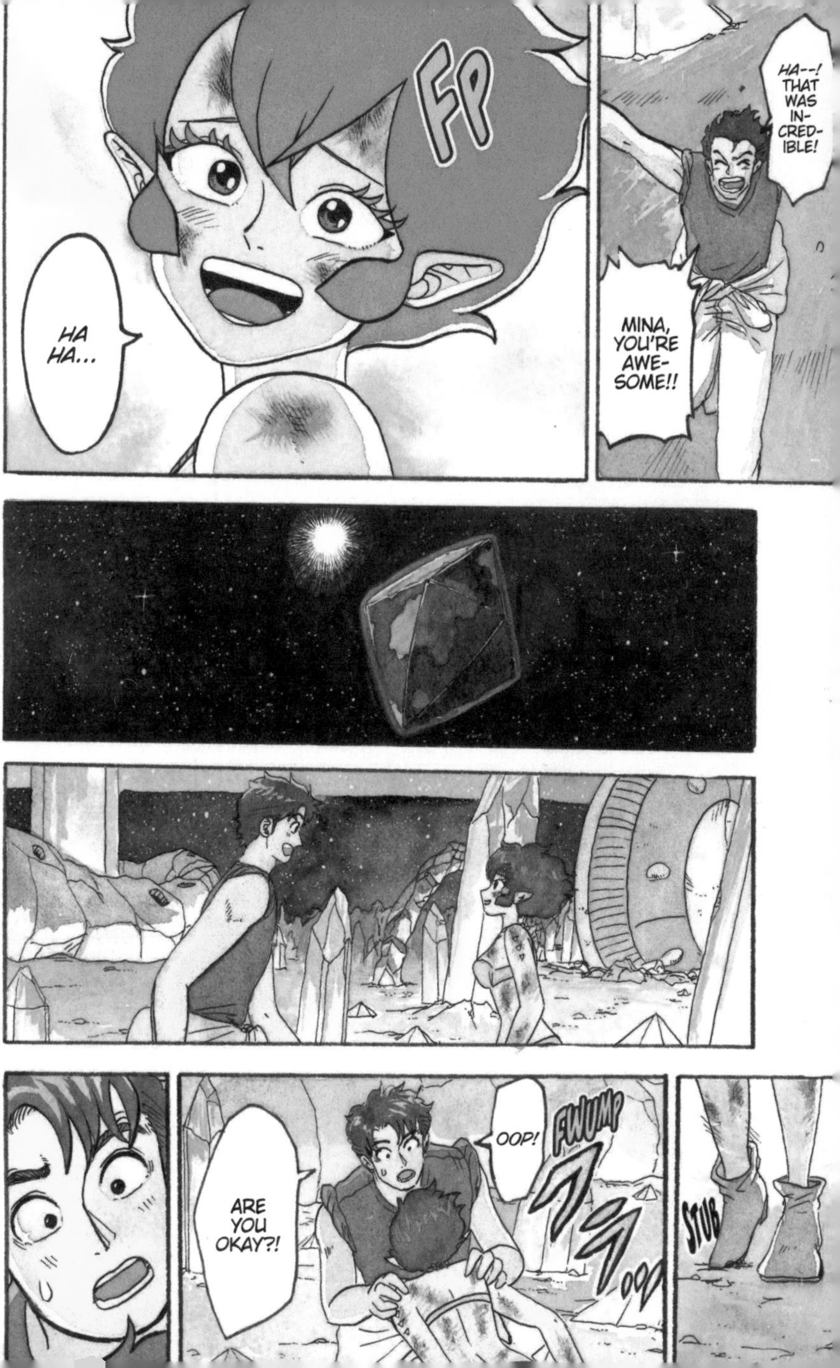
HA--! THAT WAS IN-CRED-IBLE!
MINA, YOU'RE AWE-SOME!!
FP
HA HA...
STUB
FWUMP
OOP!
ARE YOU OKAY?!

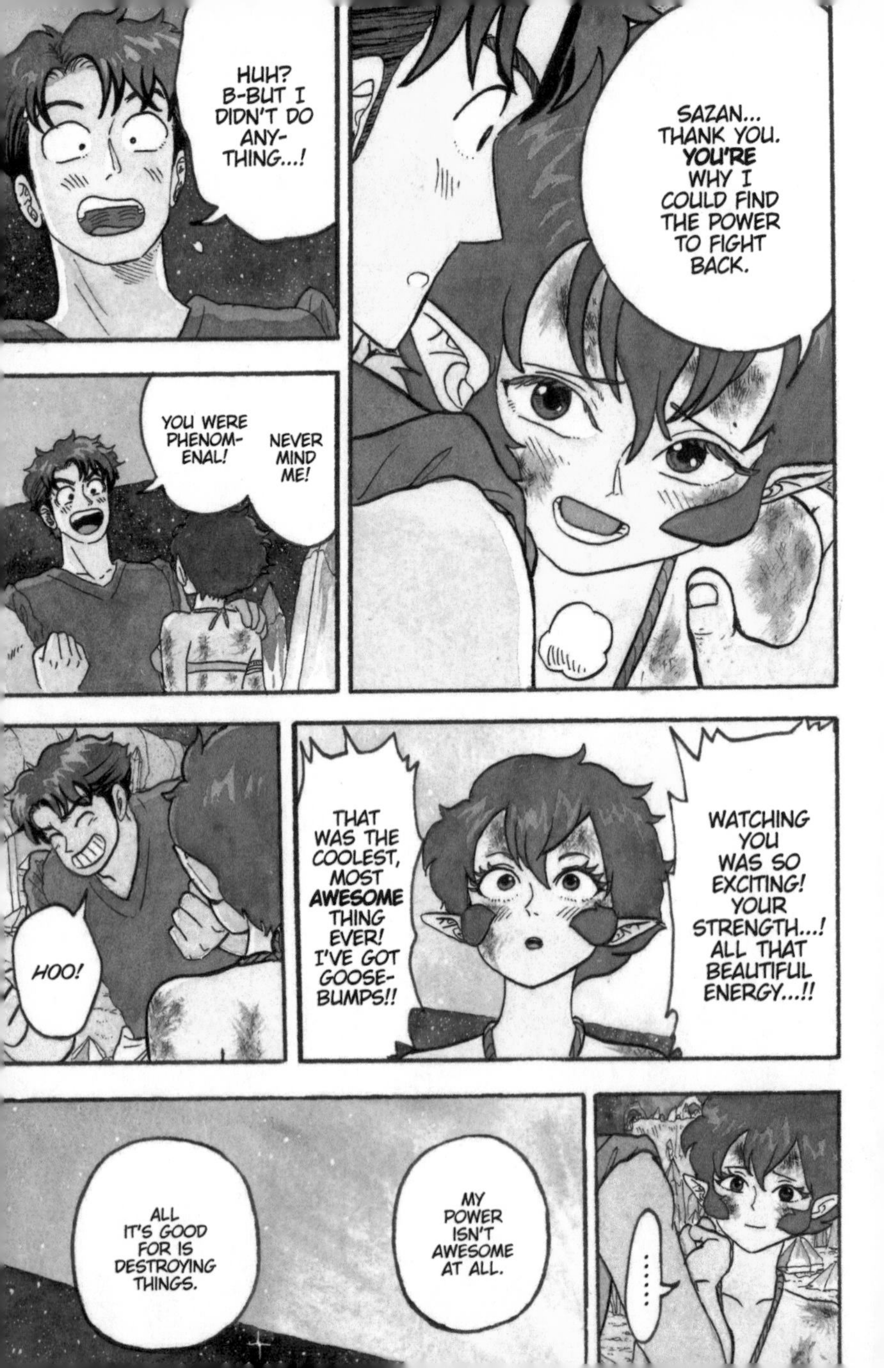
SAZAN... THANK YOU. **YOU'RE** WHY I COULD FIND THE POWER TO FIGHT BACK.
HUH? B-BUT I DIDN'T DO ANY-THING...!
NEVER MIND ME!
YOU WERE PHENOM-ENAL!
WATCHING YOU WAS SO EXCITING! YOUR STRENGTH...! ALL THAT BEAUTIFUL ENERGY...!!
THAT WAS THE COOLEST, MOST **AWESOME** THING EVER! I'VE GOT GOOSE-BUMPS!!
HOO!
......
MY POWER ISN'T AWESOME AT ALL.
ALL IT'S GOOD FOR IS DESTROYING THINGS.

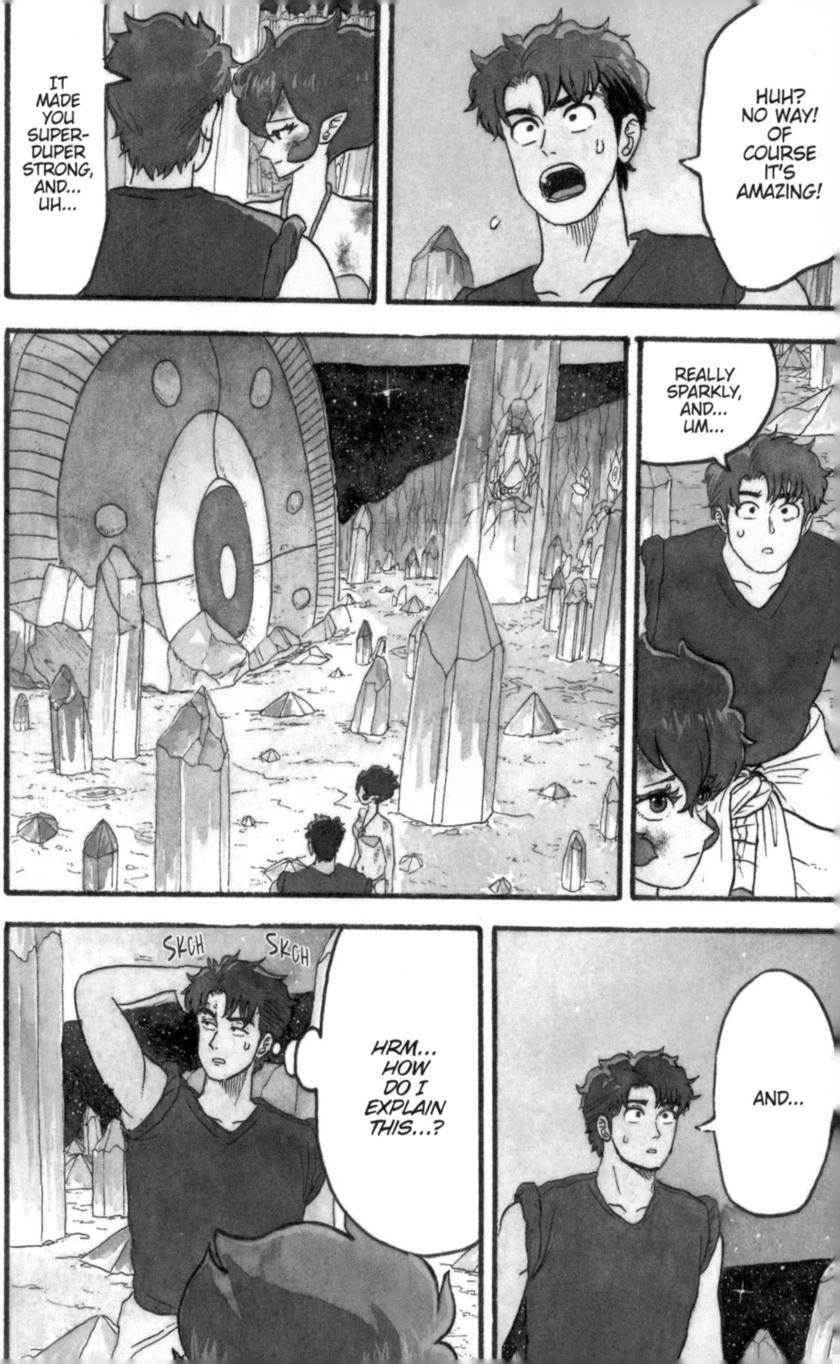
HUH? NO WAY! OF COURSE IT'S AMAZING!
IT MADE YOU SUPER-DUPER STRONG, AND... UH...
REALLY SPARKLY, AND... UM...
AND...
SKCH SKCH
HRM... HOW DO I EXPLAIN THIS...?

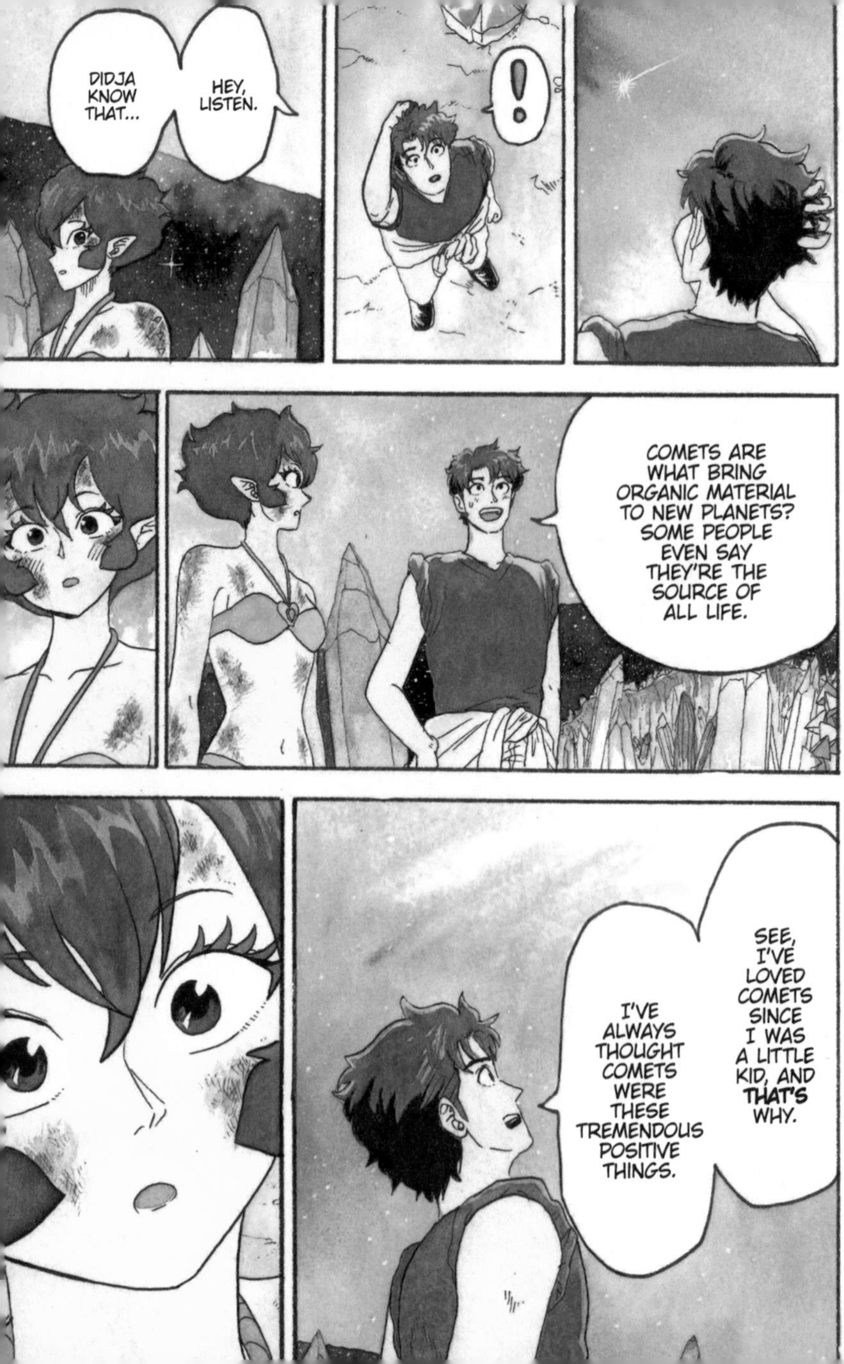
!
HEY, LISTEN.
DIDJA KNOW THAT...
COMETS ARE WHAT BRING ORGANIC MATERIAL TO NEW PLANETS? SOME PEOPLE EVEN SAY THEY'RE THE SOURCE OF ALL LIFE.
SEE, I'VE LOVED COMETS SINCE I WAS A LITTLE KID, AND **THAT'S** WHY.
I'VE ALWAYS THOUGHT COMETS WERE THESE TREMENDOUS POSITIVE THINGS.

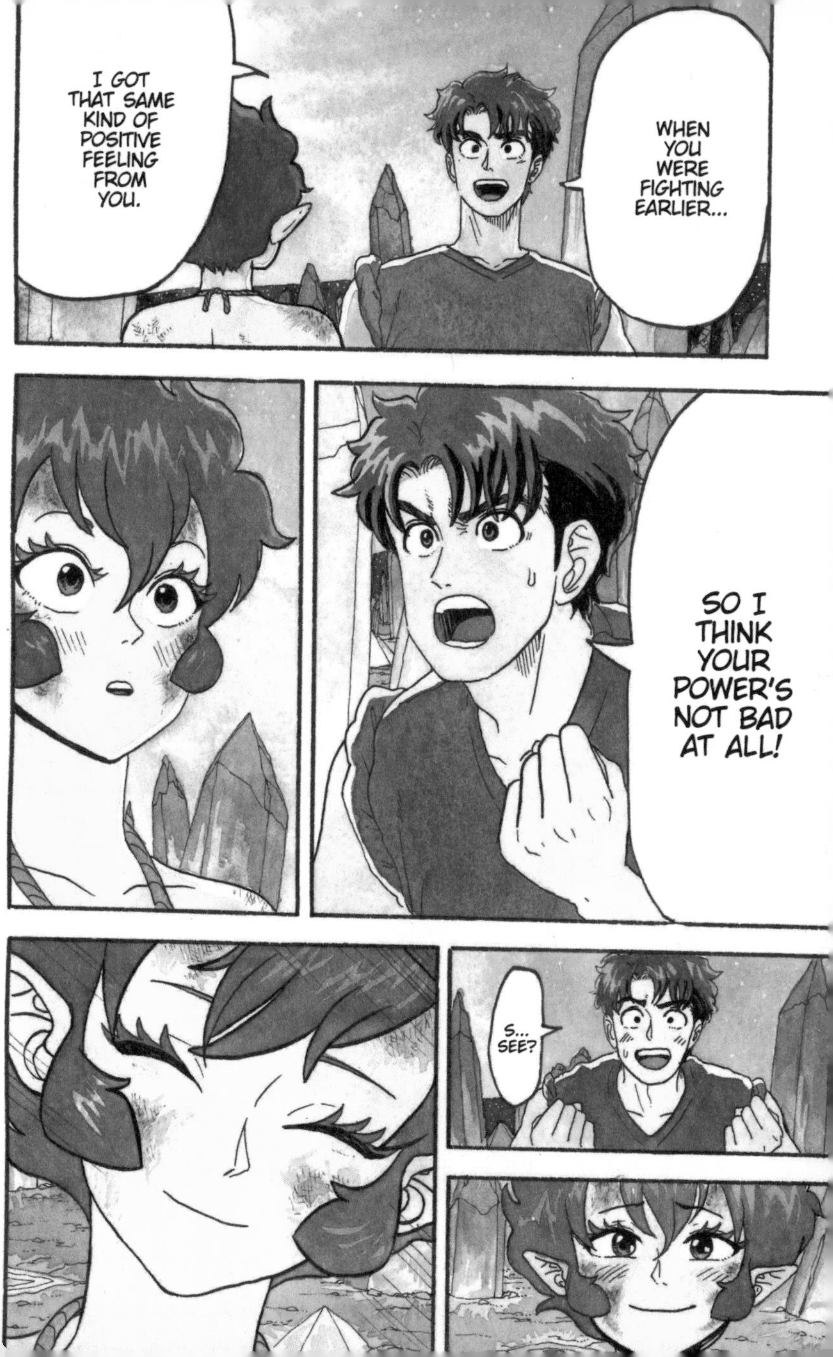
WHEN YOU WERE FIGHTING EARLIER...
I GOT THAT SAME KIND OF POSITIVE FEELING FROM YOU.
SO I THINK YOUR POWER'S NOT BAD AT ALL!
S... SEE?

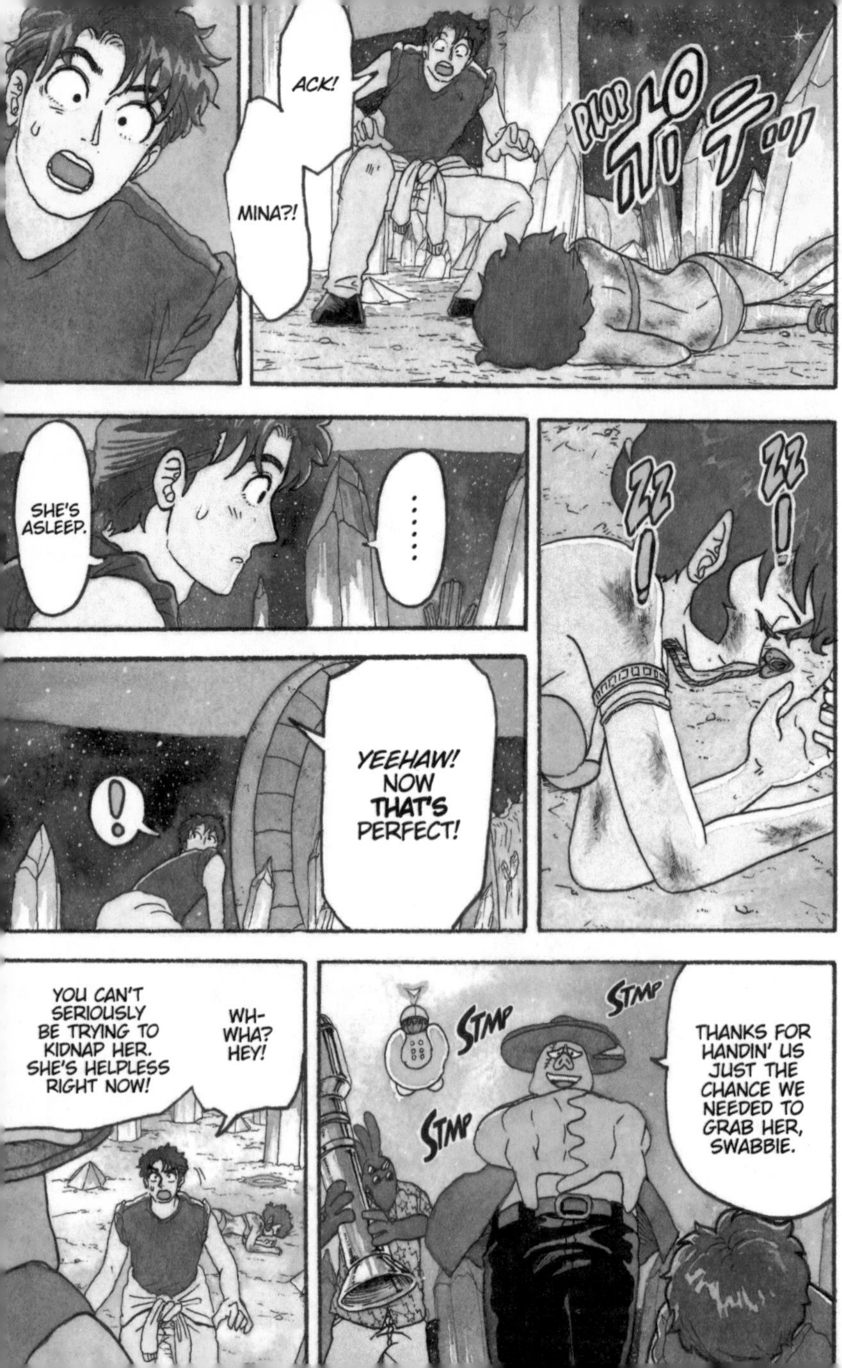
PLOP
ACK!
MINA?!
ZZ
ZZ
......
SHE'S ASLEEP.
YEEHAW! NOW THAT'S PERFECT!
!
STMP
THANKS FOR HANDIN' US JUST THE CHANCE WE NEEDED TO GRAB HER, SWABBIE.
STMP
STMP
WH- WHA? HEY!
YOU CAN'T SERIOUSLY BE TRYING TO KIDNAP HER. SHE'S HELPLESS RIGHT NOW!

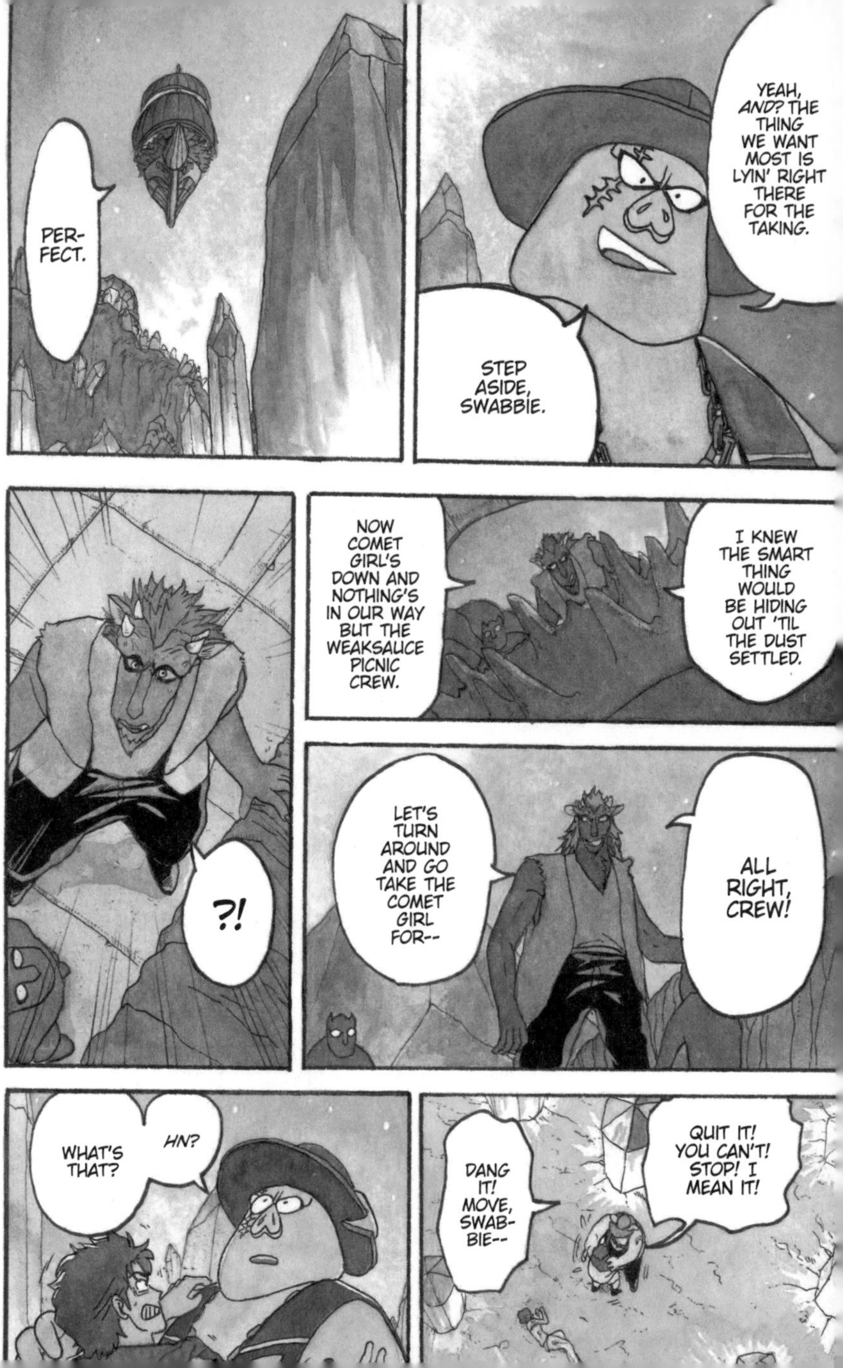
YEAH, AND? THE THING WE WANT MOST IS LYIN' RIGHT THERE FOR THE TAKING.
STEP ASIDE, SWABBIE.
PER-FECT.
I KNEW THE SMART THING WOULD BE HIDING OUT 'TIL THE DUST SETTLED.
NOW COMET GIRL'S DOWN AND NOTHING'S IN OUR WAY BUT THE WEAKSAUCE PICNIC CREW.
ALL RIGHT, CREW!
LET'S TURN AROUND AND GO TAKE THE COMET GIRL FOR--
?!
QUIT IT! YOU CAN'T! STOP! I MEAN IT!
DANG IT! MOVE, SWAB-BIE--
HN?
WHAT'S THAT?

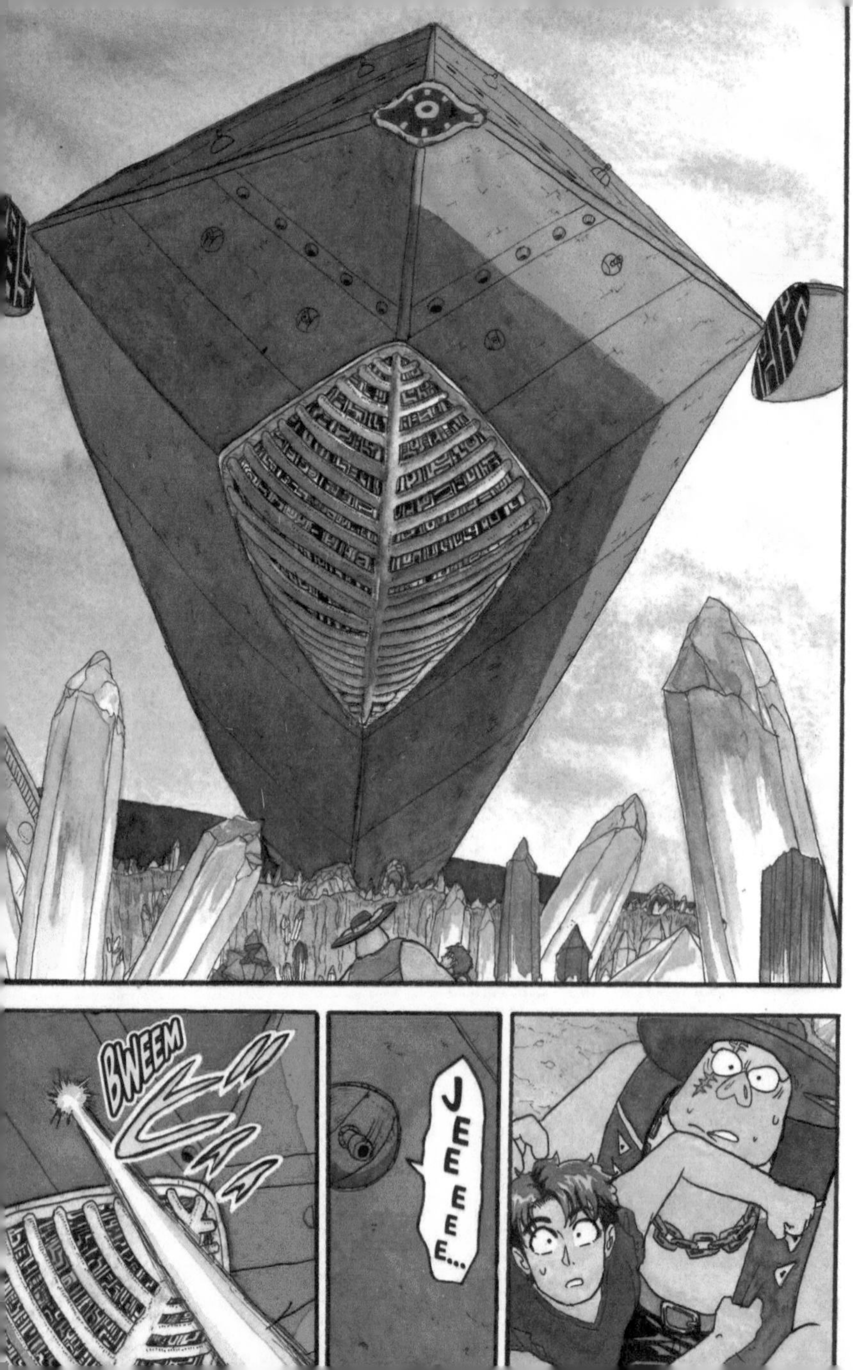
JEEEEE...
BWEEM

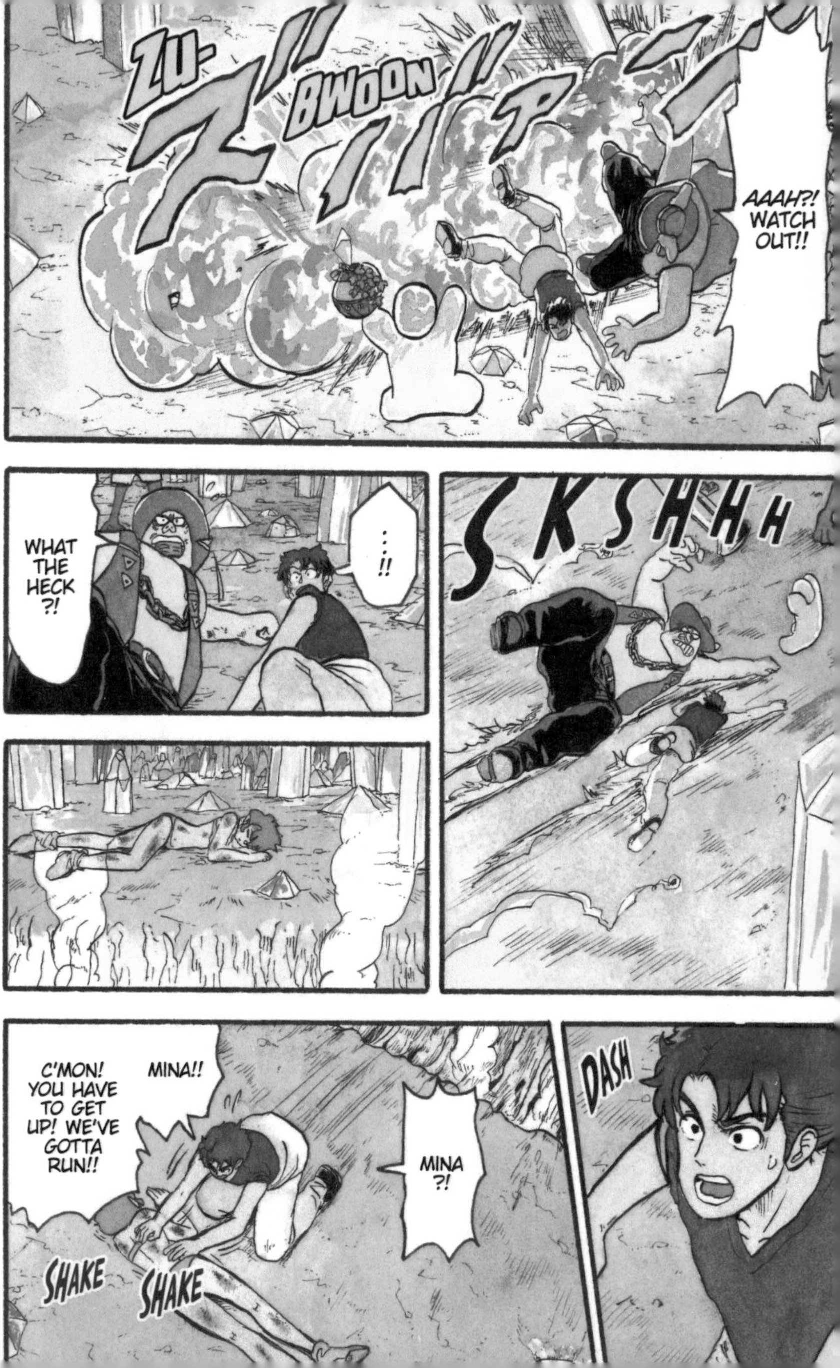
ZU-
BWOON
AAAH?! WATCH OUT!!
SKSHHH
...!!
WHAT THE HECK ?!
DASH
MINA ?!
MINA!!
C'MON! YOU HAVE TO GET UP! WE'VE GOTTA RUN!!
SHAKE
SHAKE

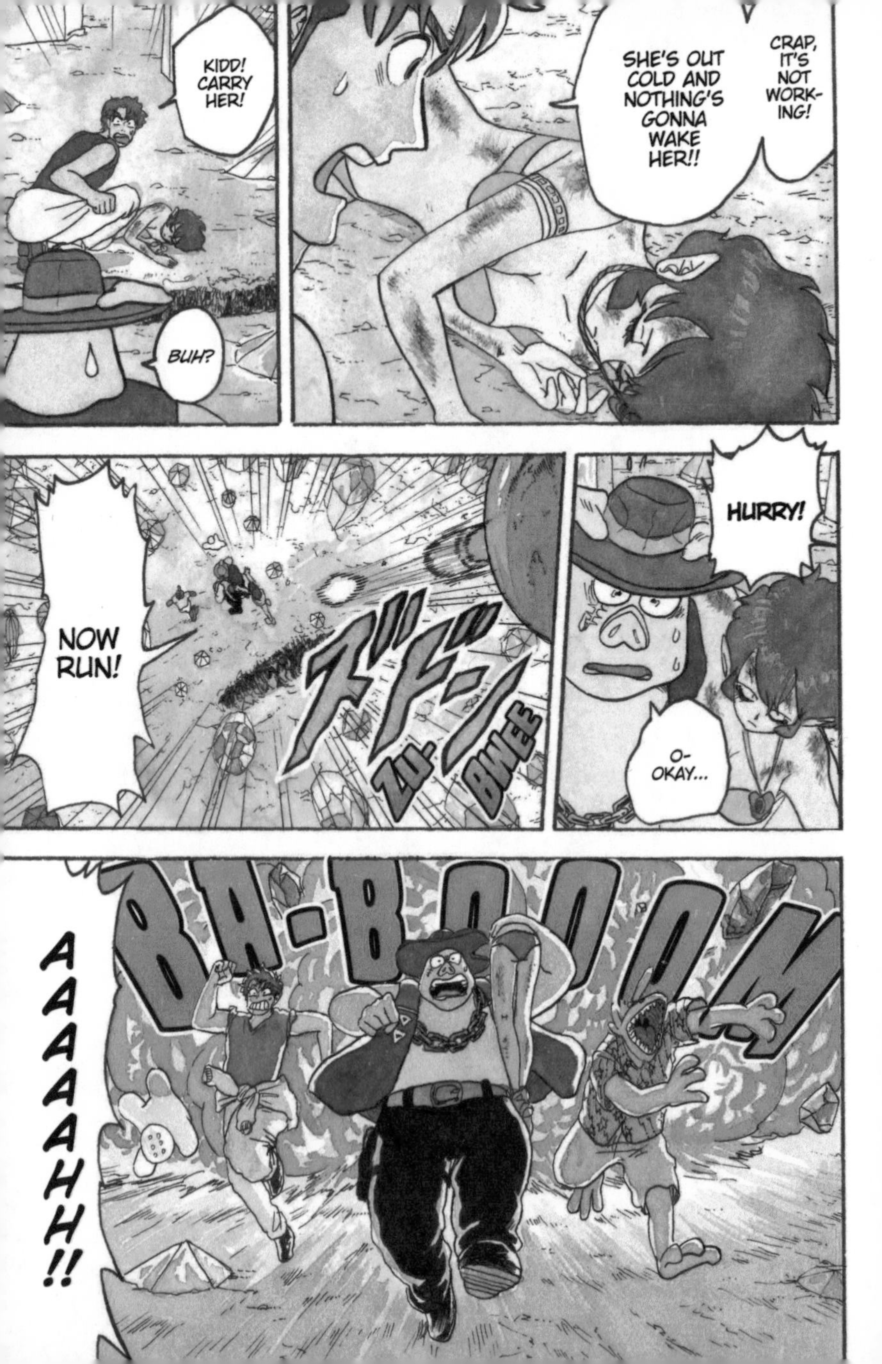
CRAP, IT'S NOT WORKING!
SHE'S OUT COLD AND NOTHING'S GONNA WAKE HER!!
KIDD! CARRY HER!
BUH?
HURRY!
O-OKAY...
NOW RUN!
ZU-
BWEE
BA-BOOOM
AAAAAAHH!!

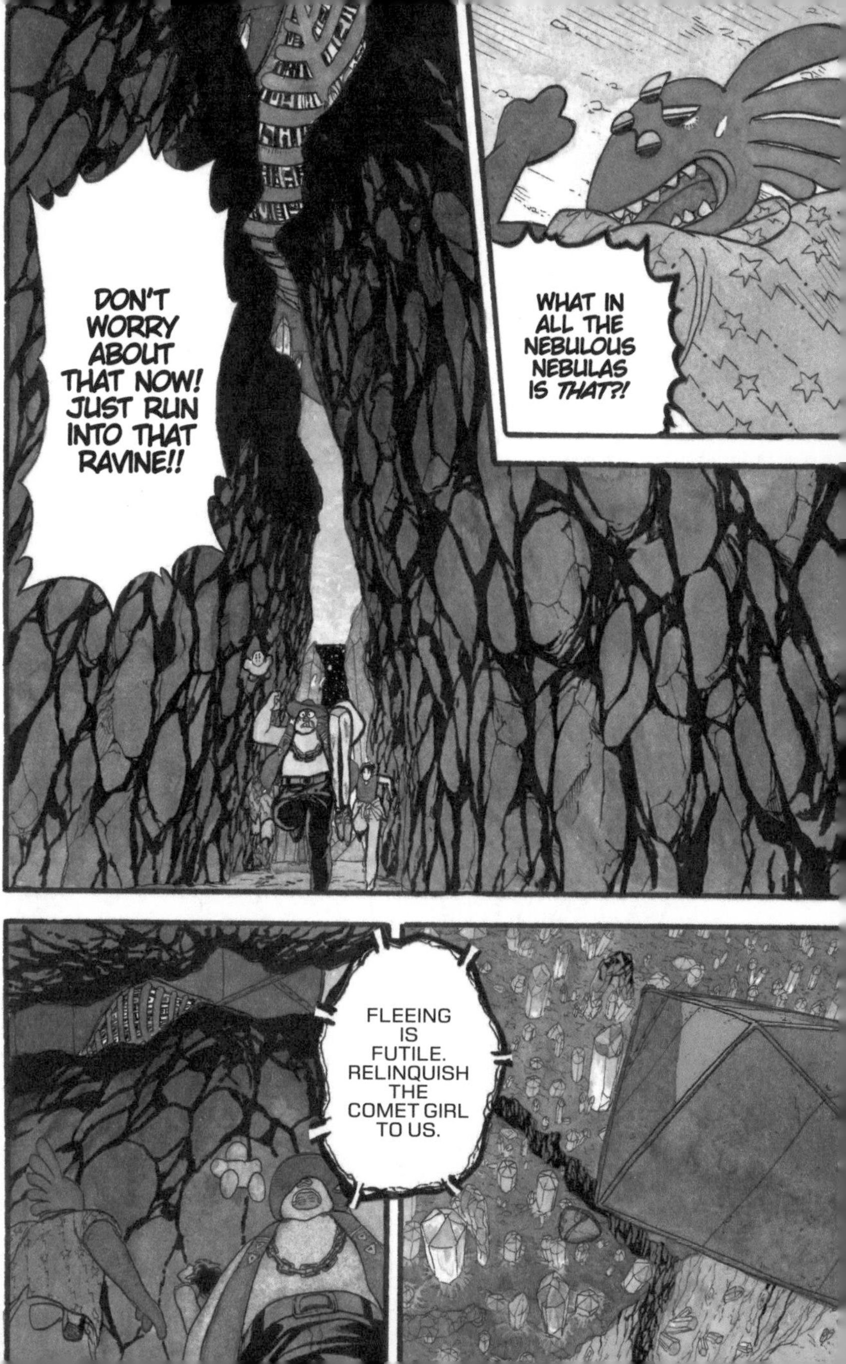
WHAT IN ALL THE NEBULOUS NEBULAS IS *THAT*?!
DON'T WORRY ABOUT THAT NOW! JUST RUN INTO THAT RAVINE!!
FLEEING IS FUTILE. RELINQUISH THE COMET GIRL TO US.

CLAPPU!

ZWIIP

BWOOMP

WAH?!

GET US TO THE *FAT LEISURE* !!

SHONK

LET'S GO!!

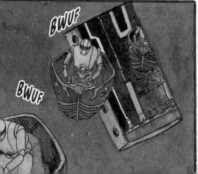

BWUF

BWUF

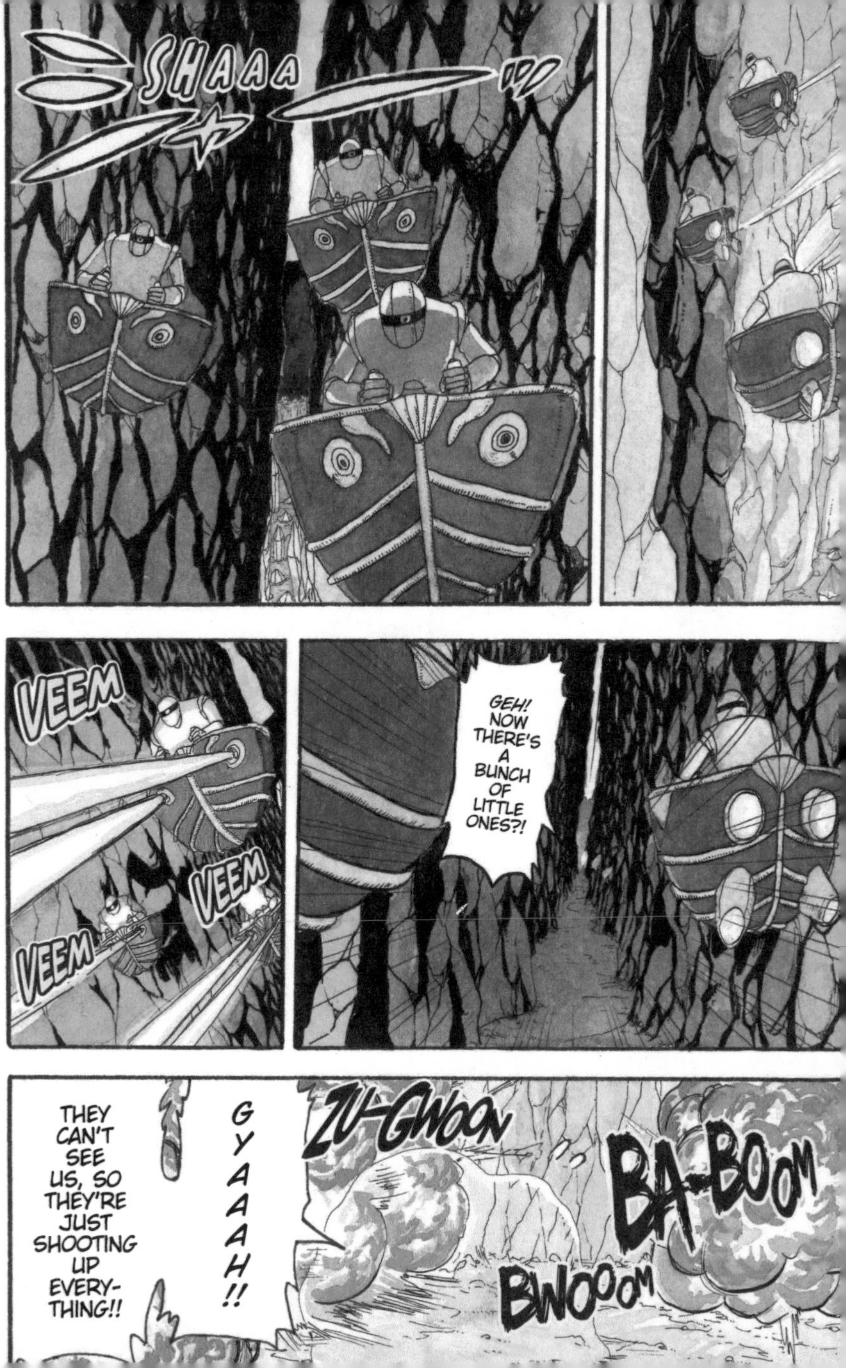
SHAAA
GEH! NOW THERE'S A BUNCH OF LITTLE ONES?!
VEEM
VEEM
VEEM
BA-BOOM
ZU-GWOON
BWOOOM
GYAAAAH!!
THEY CAN'T SEE US, SO THEY'RE JUST SHOOTING UP EVERY-THING!!

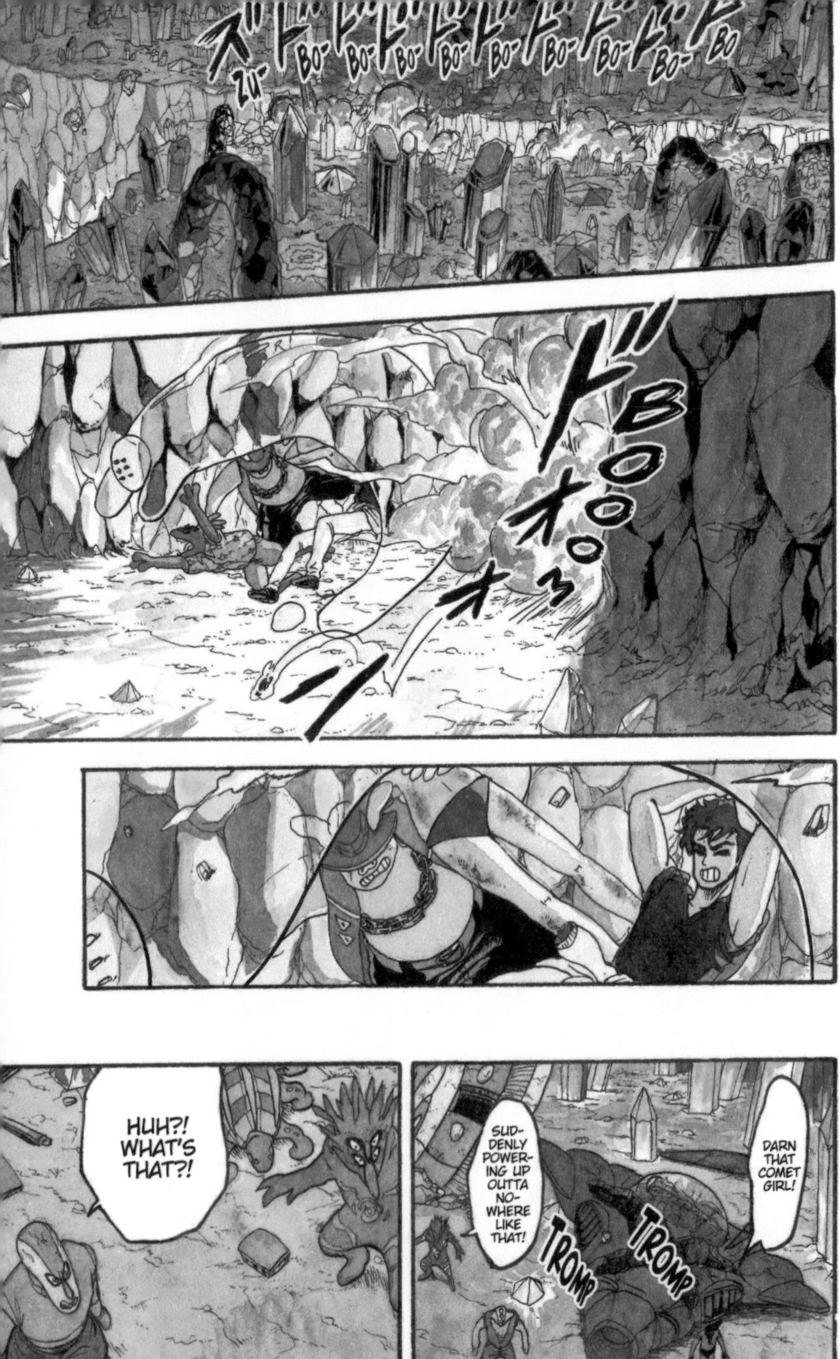
ZU- BO- BO- BO- BO- BO- BO- BO- BO- BO
BOOOM
DARN THAT COMET GIRL!
SUD-DENLY POWER-ING UP OUTTA NO-WHERE LIKE THAT!
TROMP
TROMP
HUH?! WHAT'S THAT?!

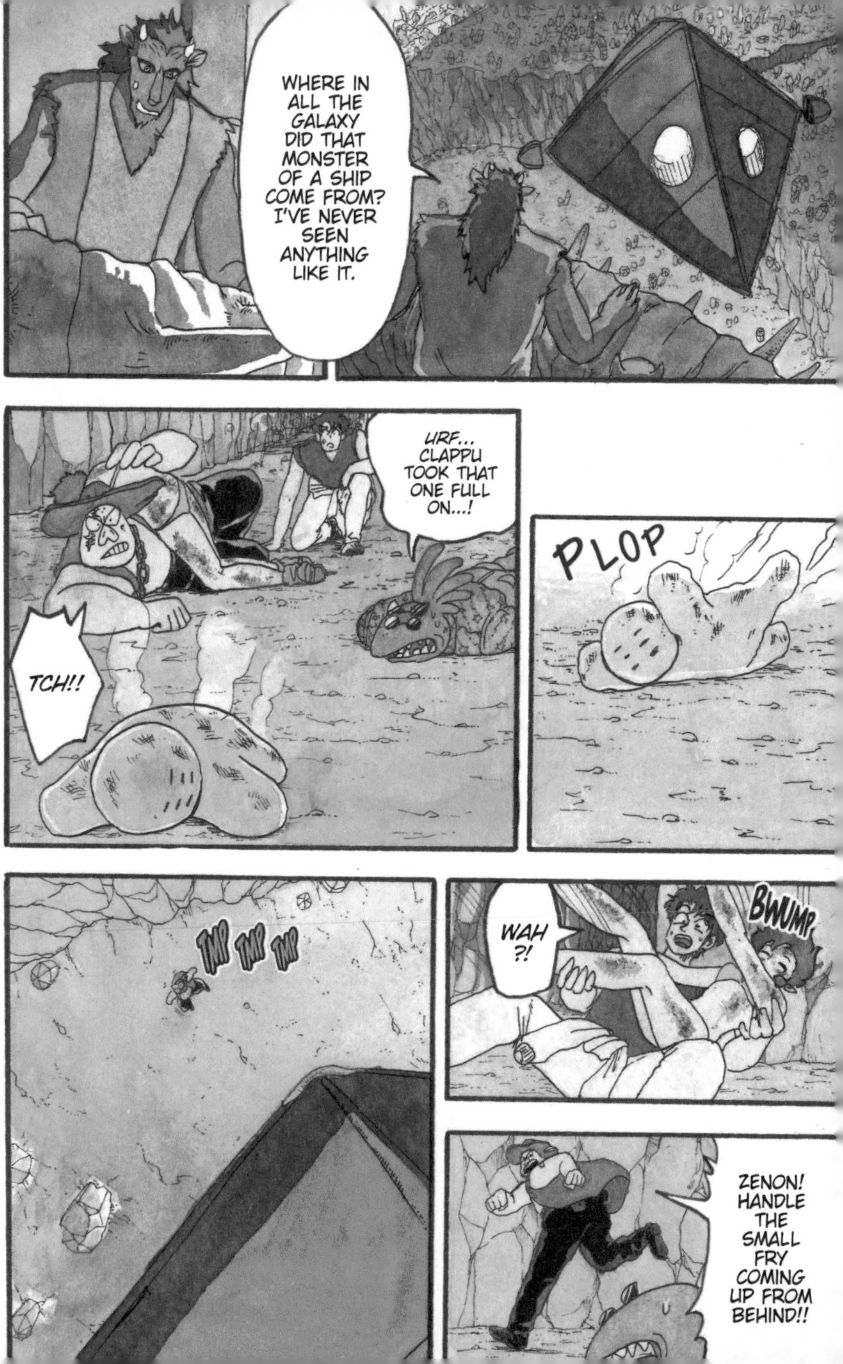
WHERE IN ALL THE GALAXY DID THAT MONSTER OF A SHIP COME FROM? I'VE NEVER SEEN ANYTHING LIKE IT.
PLOP
URF... CLAPPU TOOK THAT ONE FULL ON...!
TCH!!
BWUMP
WAH ?!
ZENON! HANDLE THE SMALL FRY COMING UP FROM BEHIND!!
TMP TMP TMP

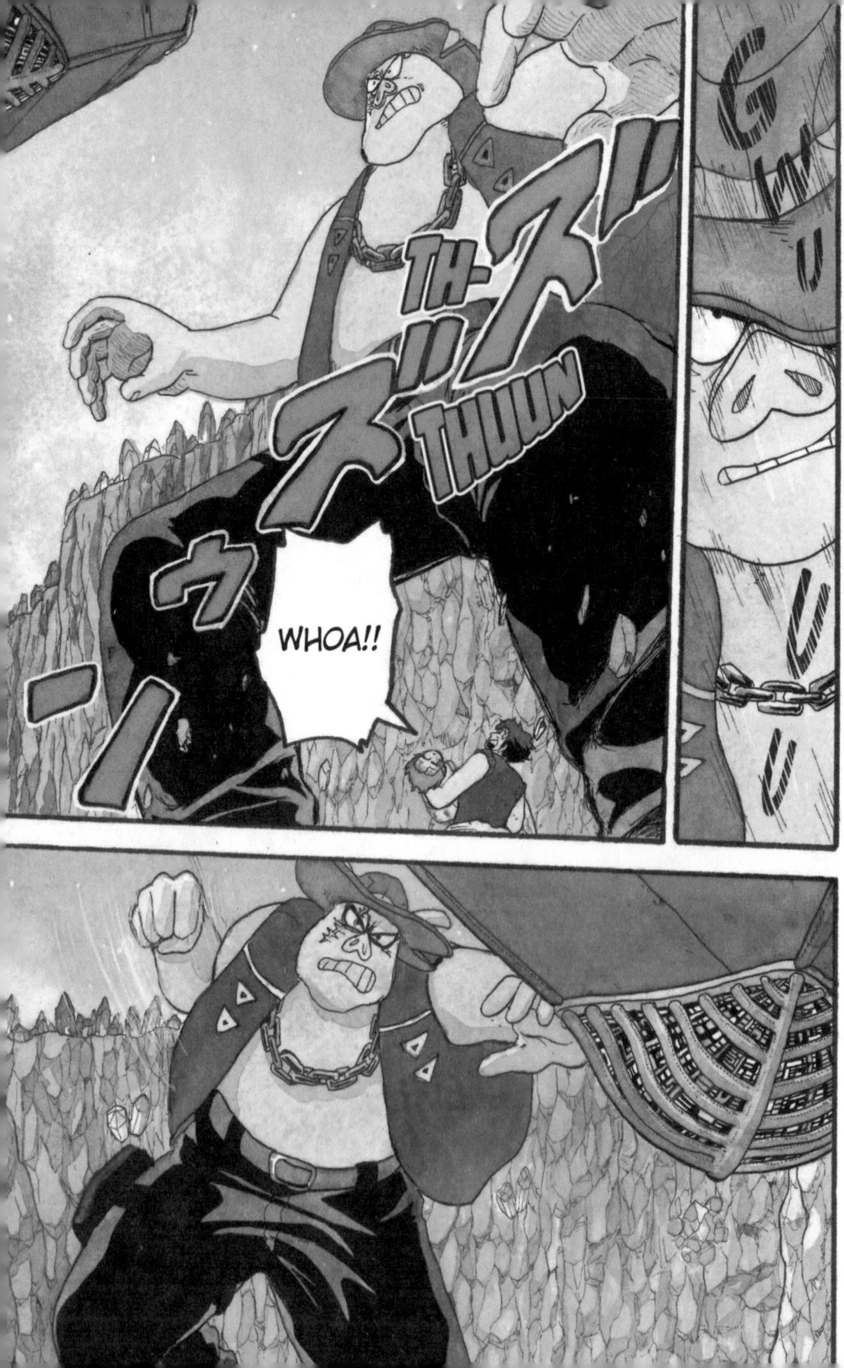
GUUU
TH-THUUN
WHOA!!

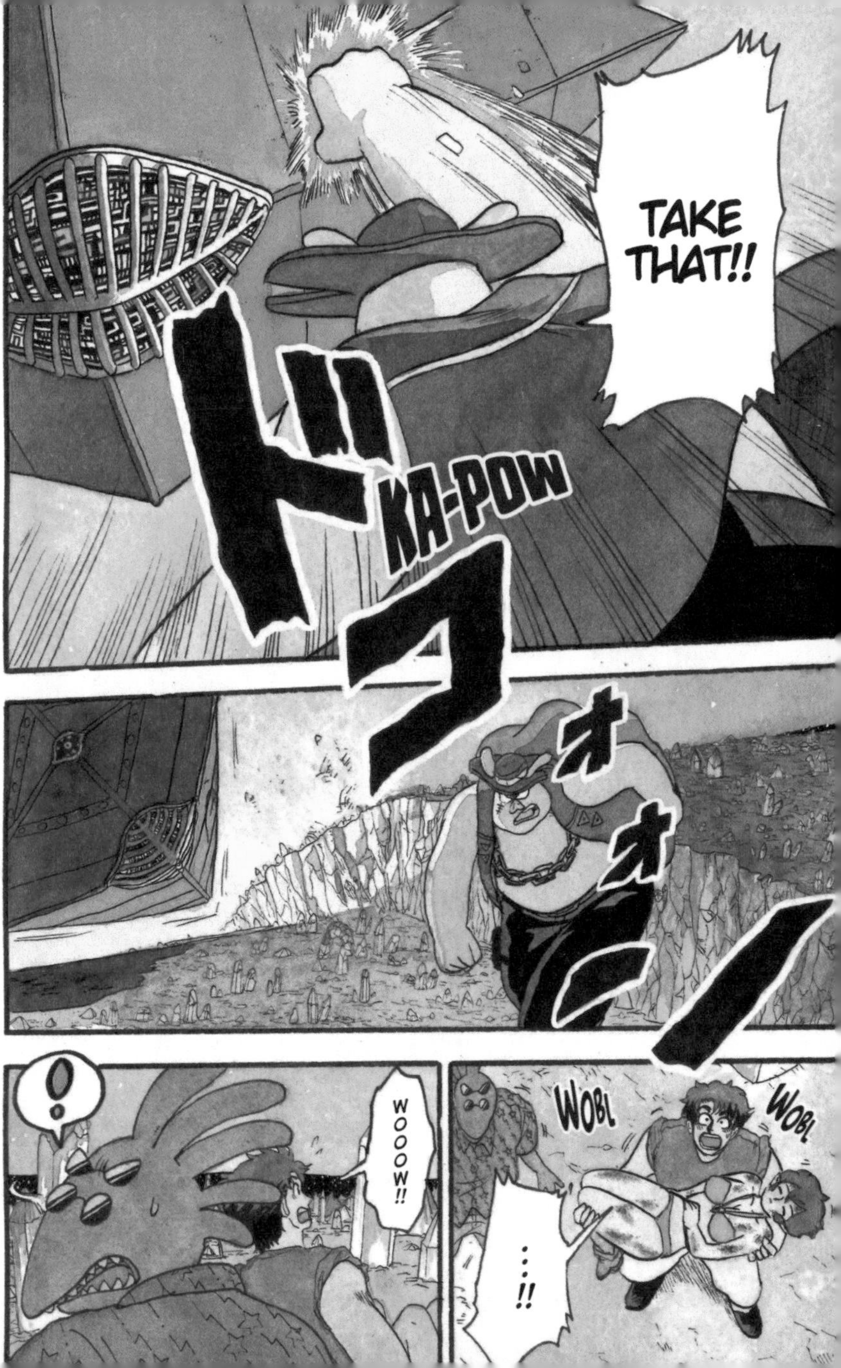
TAKE THAT!!
KA-POW
WOBL
WOBL
...!!
WOOOOW!!
!

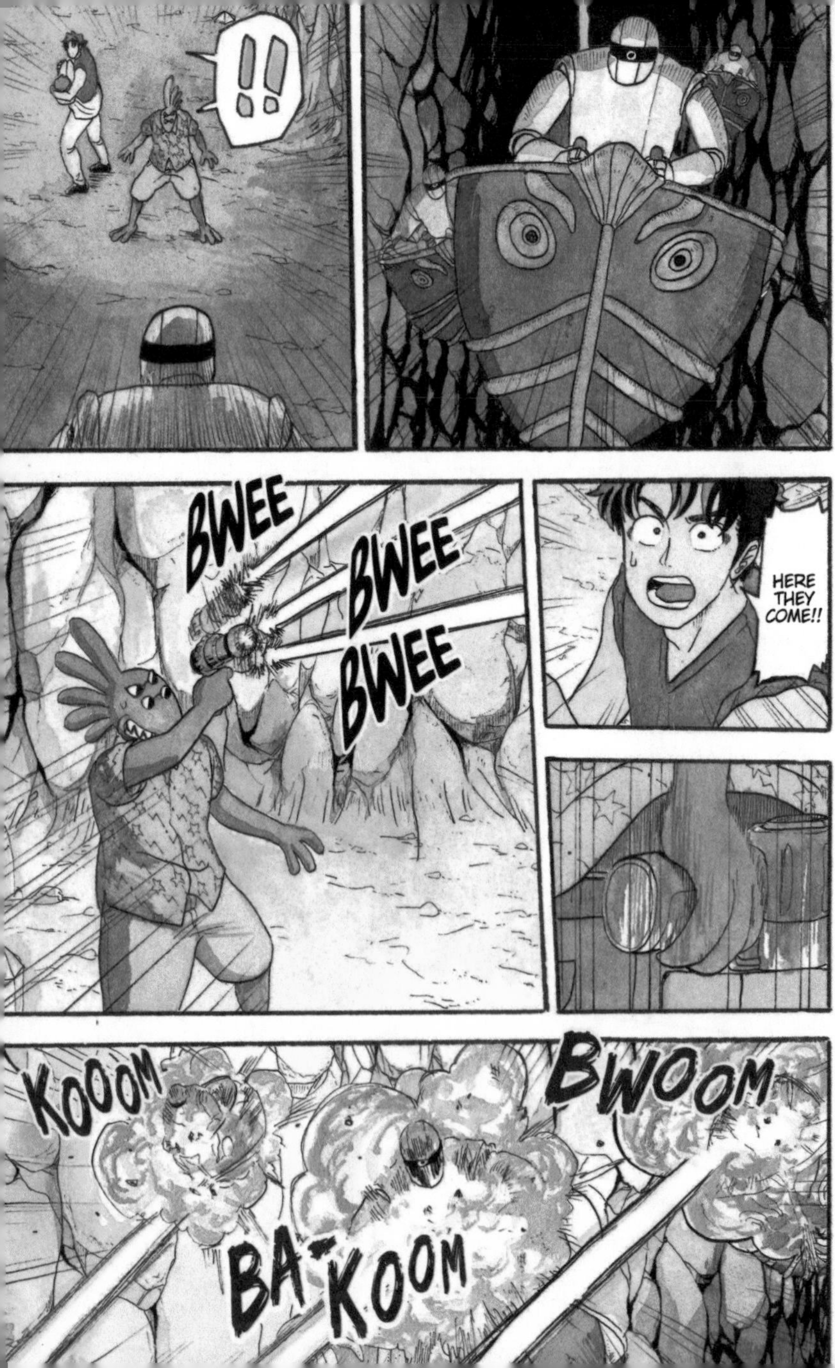
!!
HERE THEY COME!!
BWEE
BWEE
BWEE
BWOOM
KOOOM
BA-KOOM

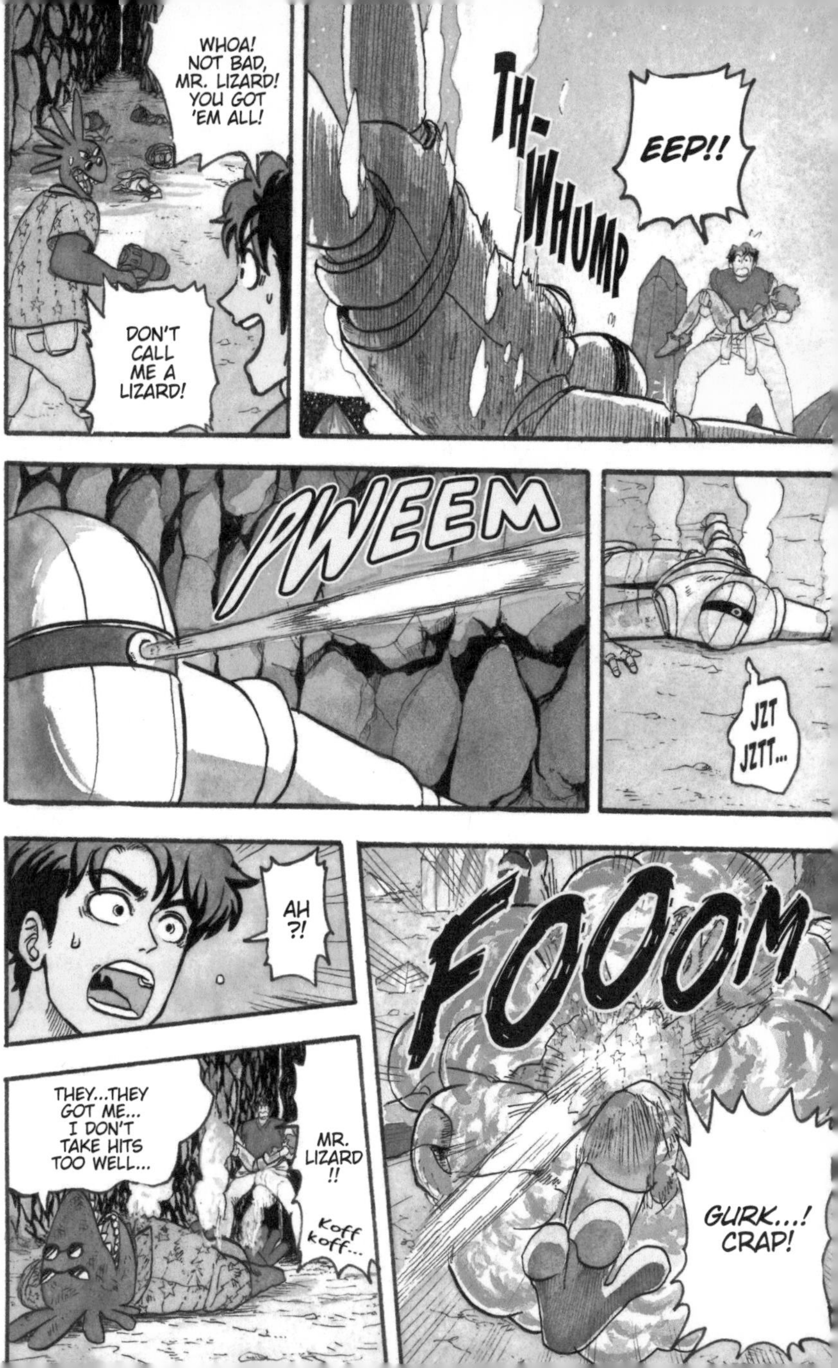
TH-WHUMP
EEP!!
WHOA! NOT BAD, MR. LIZARD! YOU GOT 'EM ALL!
DON'T CALL ME A LIZARD!
JZT JZTT...
PWEEM
FOOOM
GURK...! CRAP!
AH?!
MR. LIZARD!!
THEY...THEY GOT ME... I DON'T TAKE HITS TOO WELL...
Koff koff...

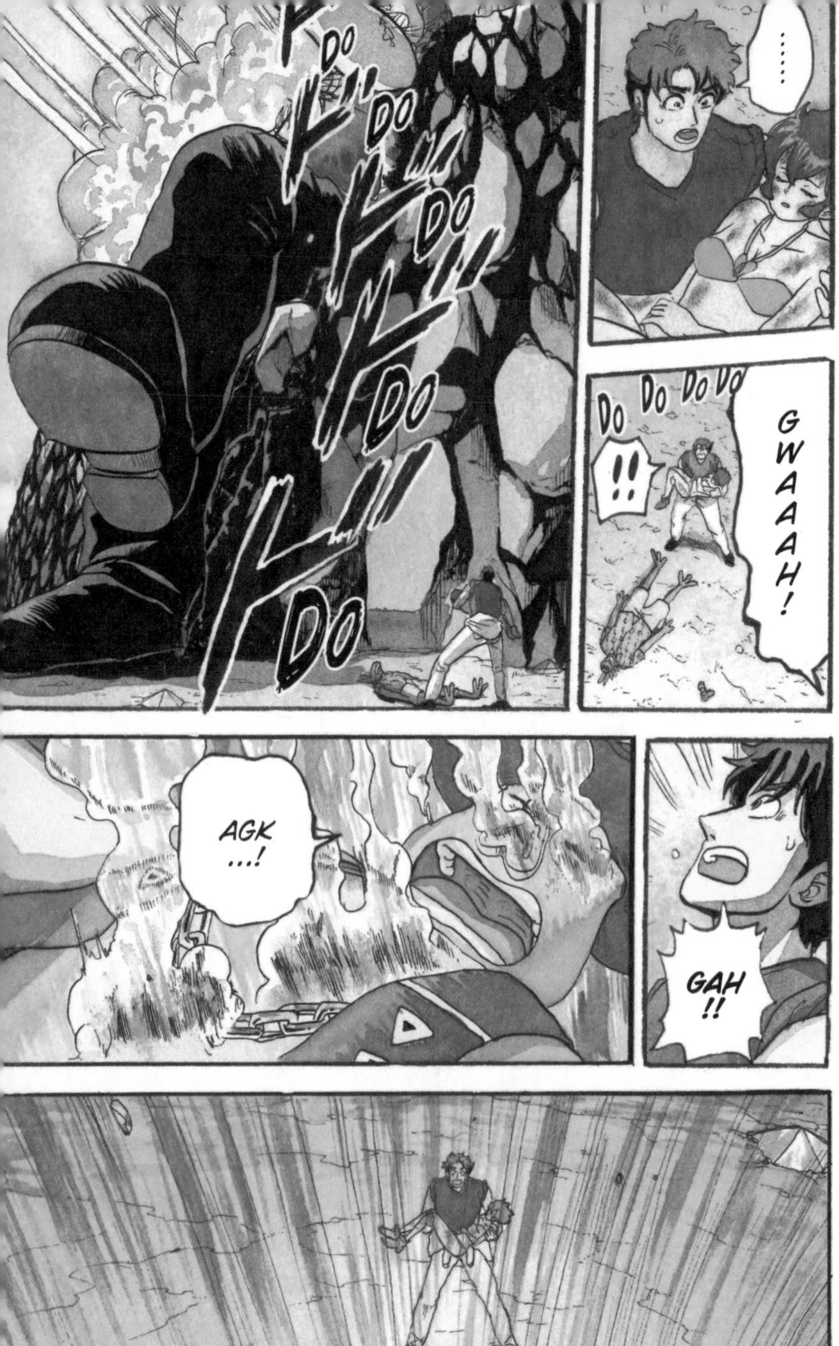
......
Do Do Do Do
!!
GWAAAAH!
DO
DO
DO
DO
DO
GAH !!
AGK ...!

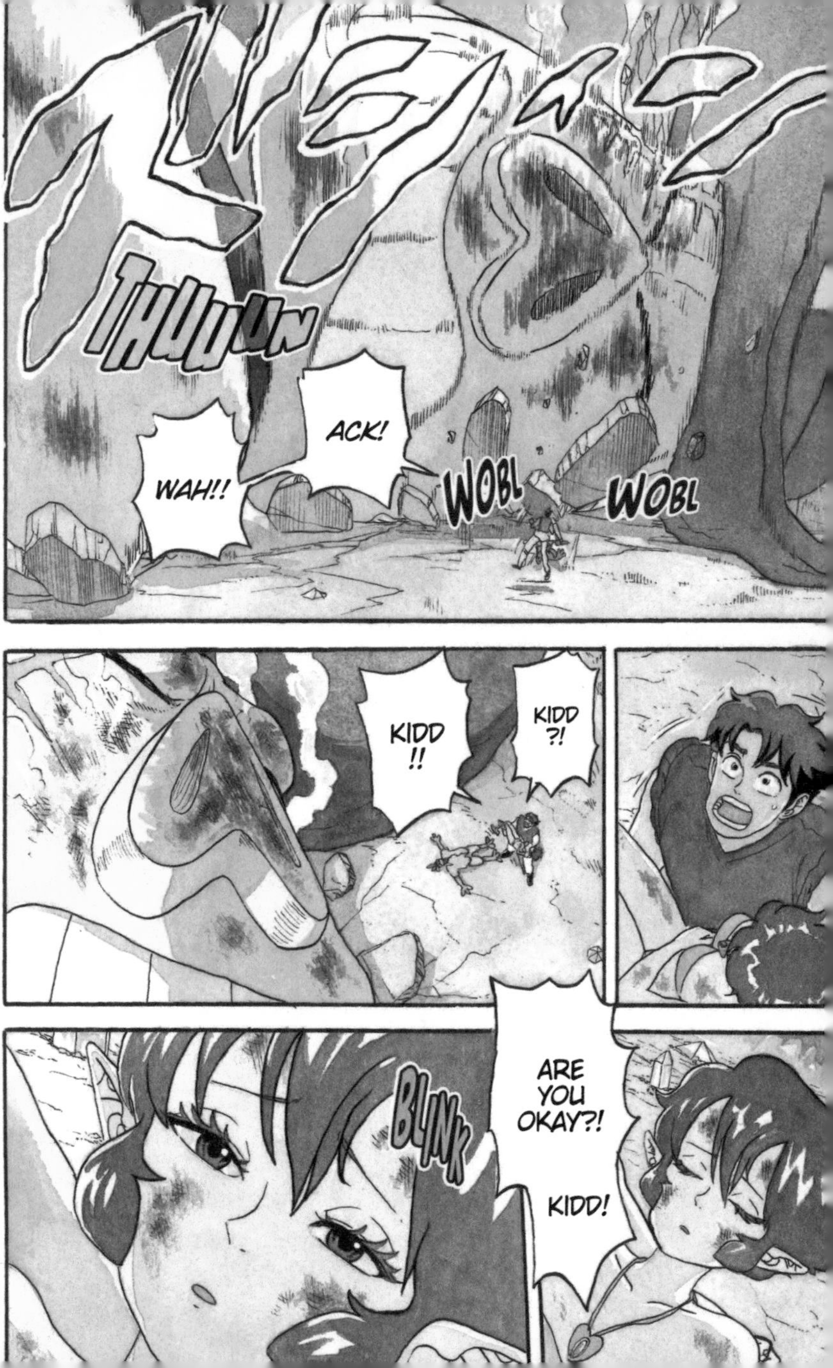
THUUUN
ACK!
WOBL
WOBL
WAH!!
KIDD ?!
KIDD !!
ARE YOU OKAY?!
KIDD!
BLINK

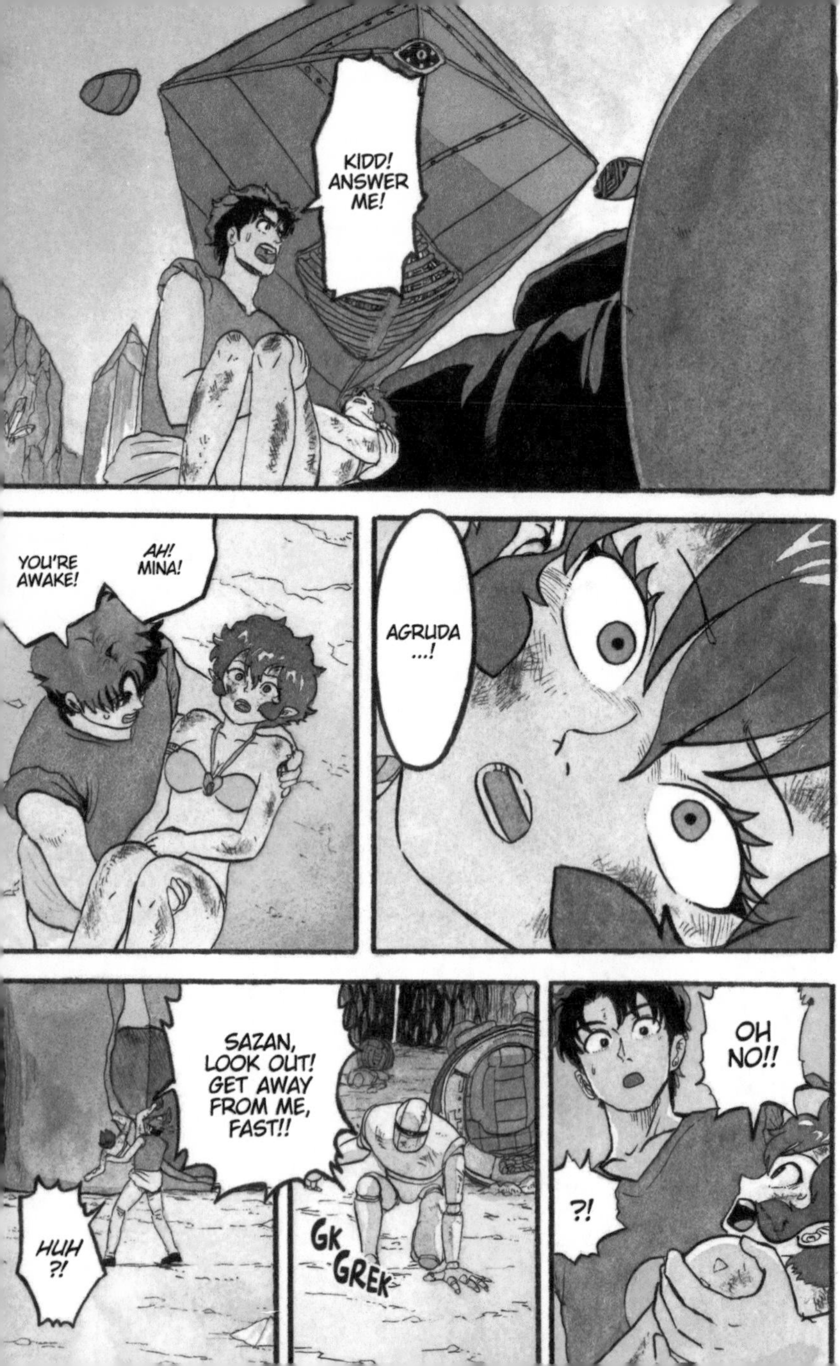
KIDD! ANSWER ME!
AGRUDA ...!
AH! MINA!
YOU'RE AWAKE!
OH NO!!
?!
SAZAN, LOOK OUT! GET AWAY FROM ME, FAST!!
GK GREK
HUH ?!

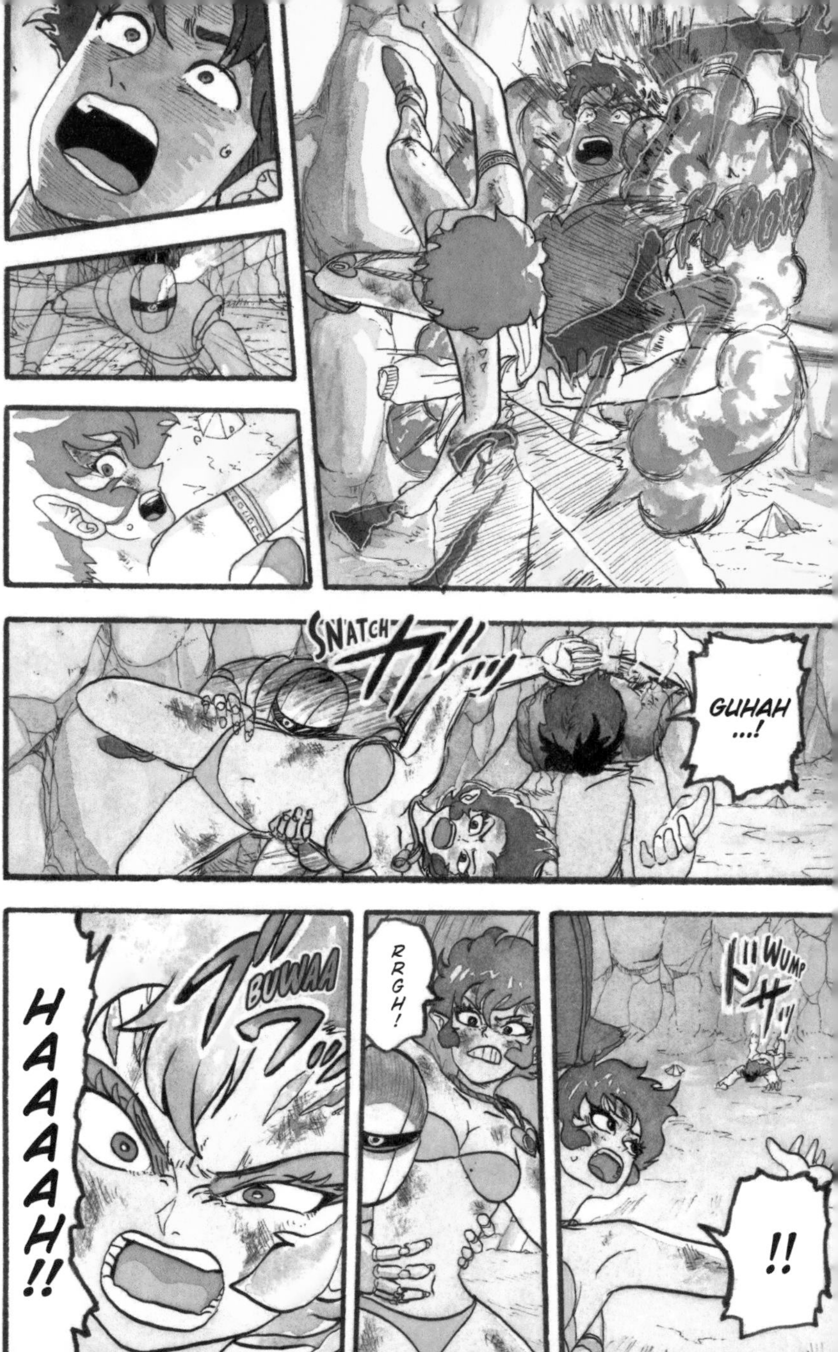
FOOOM
SNATCH
GUHAH ...!
!!
WUMP
RRGH!
BUWAA
HAAAAAAH!!

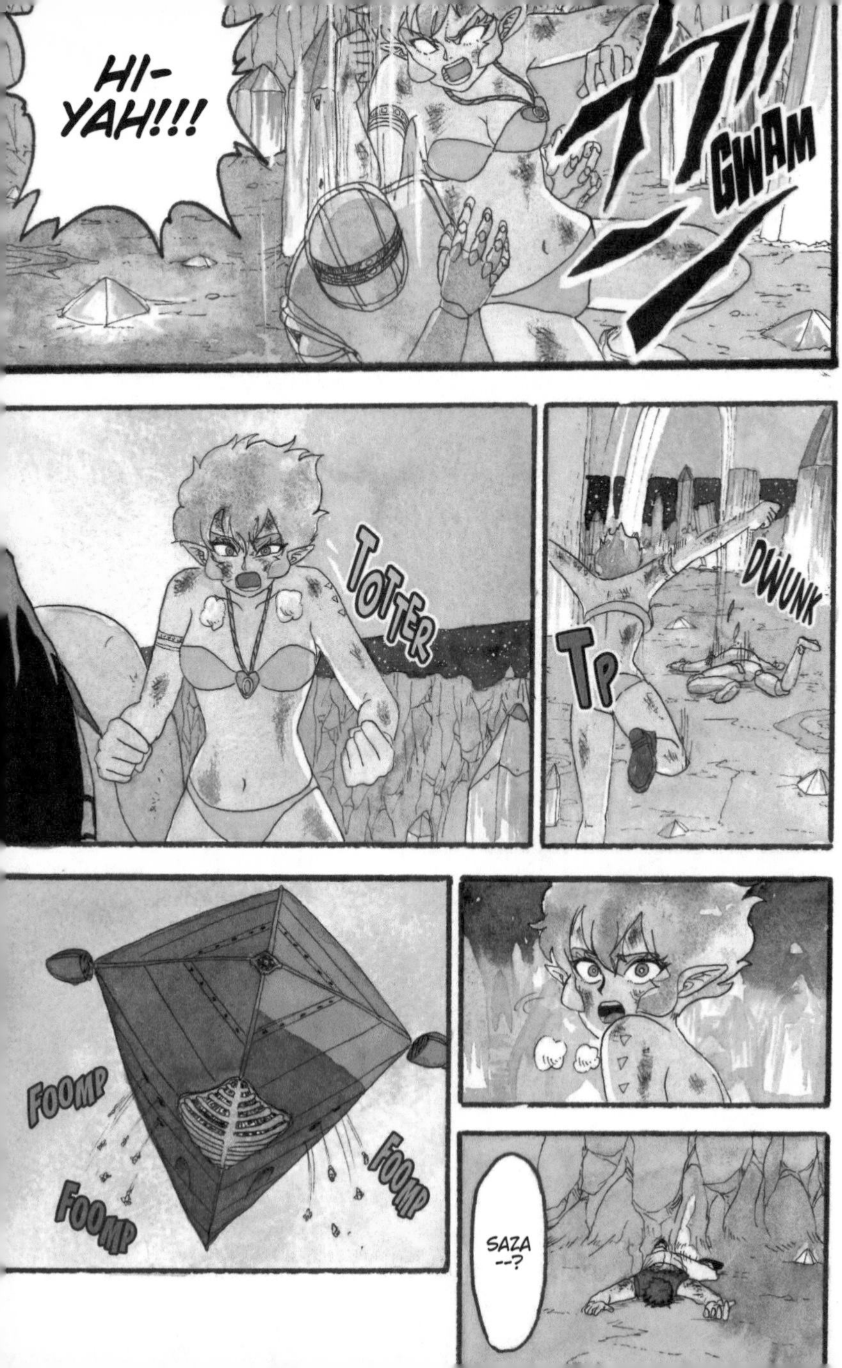
GWAM
HI-
YAH!!!
DWUNK
TP
TOTTER
SAZA
--?
FOOMP
FOOMP
FOOMP

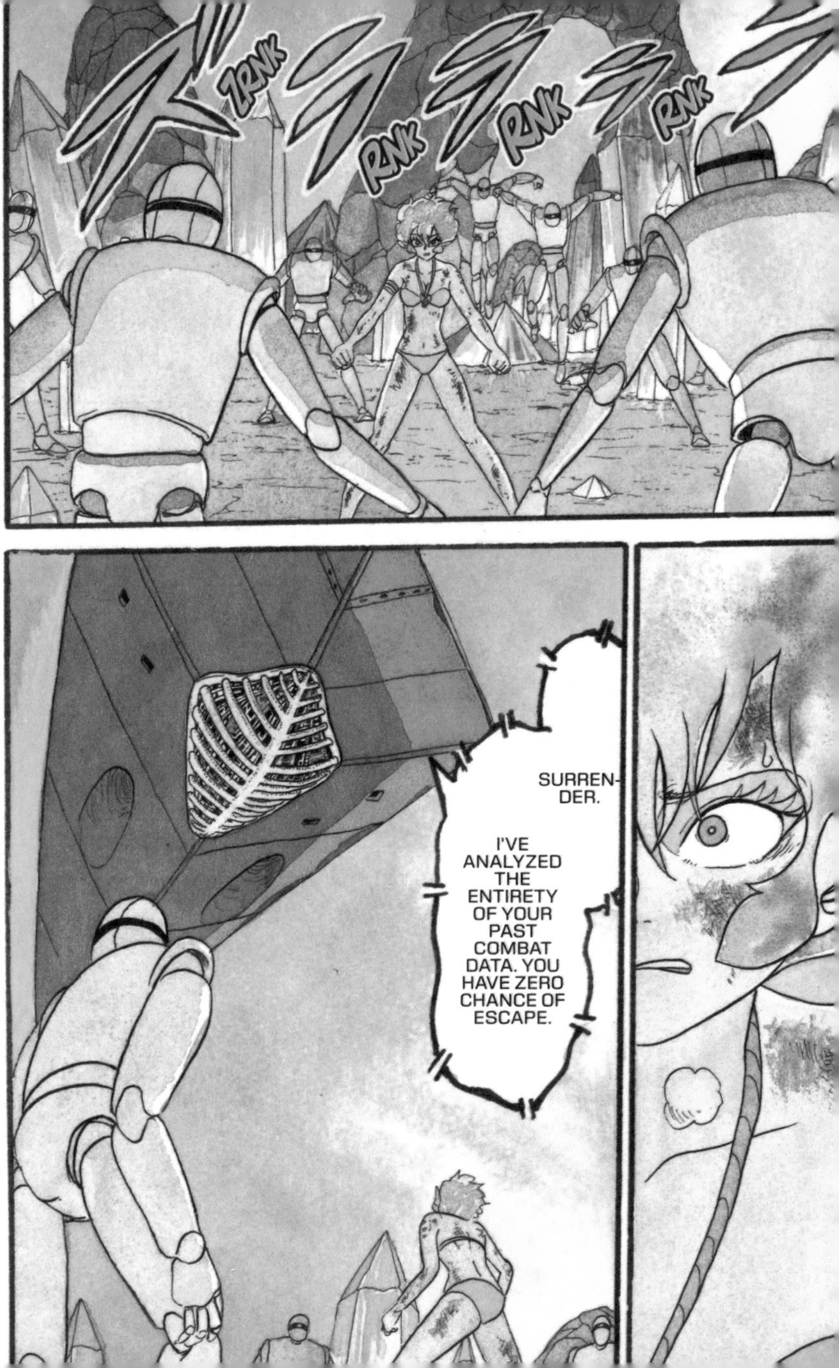
ZRNK RNK RNK RNK
SURREN-DER.
I'VE ANALYZED THE ENTIRETY OF YOUR PAST COMBAT DATA. YOU HAVE ZERO CHANCE OF ESCAPE.

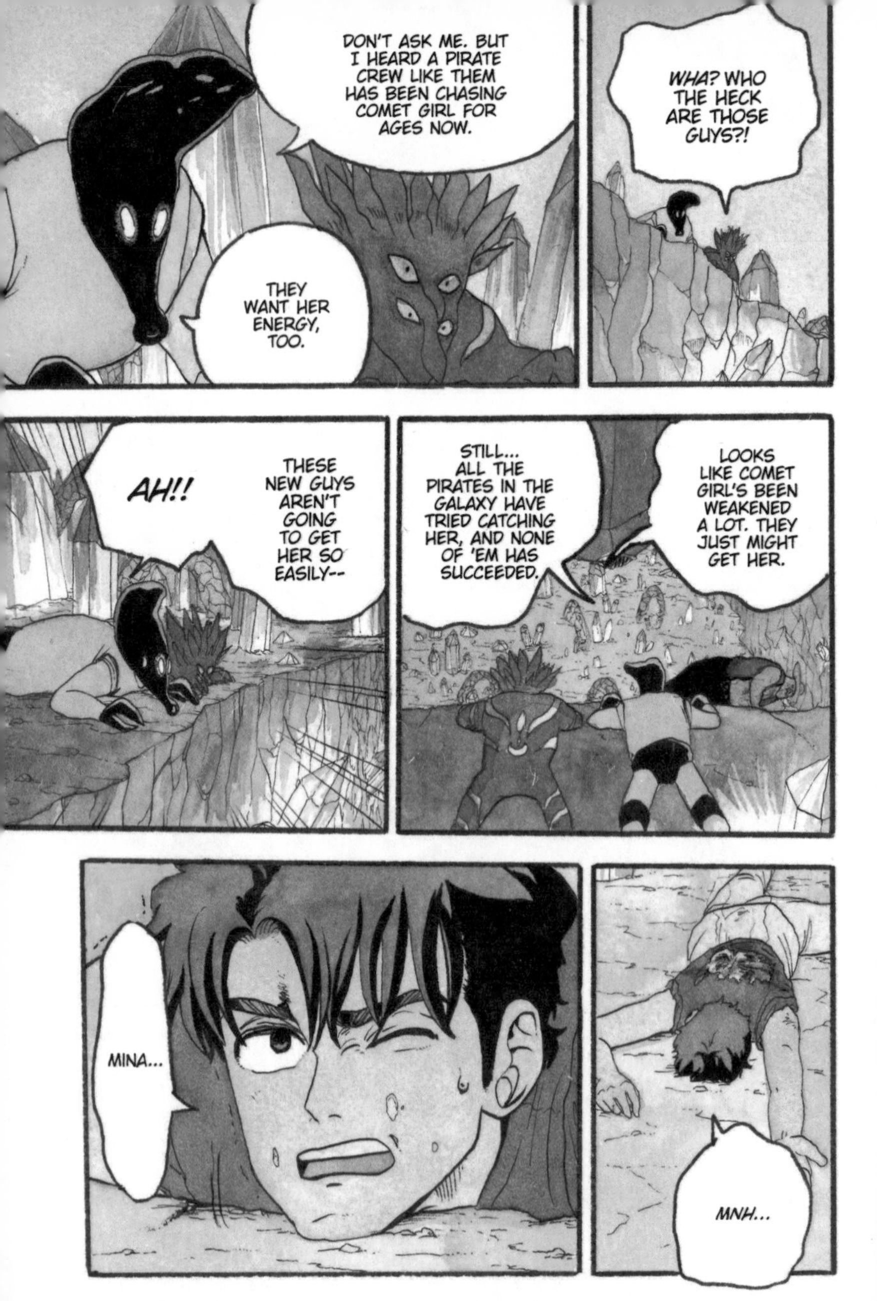
WHA? WHO THE HECK ARE THOSE GUYS?!
DON'T ASK ME. BUT I HEARD A PIRATE CREW LIKE THEM HAS BEEN CHASING COMET GIRL FOR AGES NOW.
THEY WANT HER ENERGY, TOO.
LOOKS LIKE COMET GIRL'S BEEN WEAKENED A LOT. THEY JUST MIGHT GET HER.
STILL... ALL THE PIRATES IN THE GALAXY HAVE TRIED CATCHING HER, AND NONE OF 'EM HAS SUCCEEDED.
THESE NEW GUYS AREN'T GOING TO GET HER SO EASILY--
AH!!
MNH...
MINA...

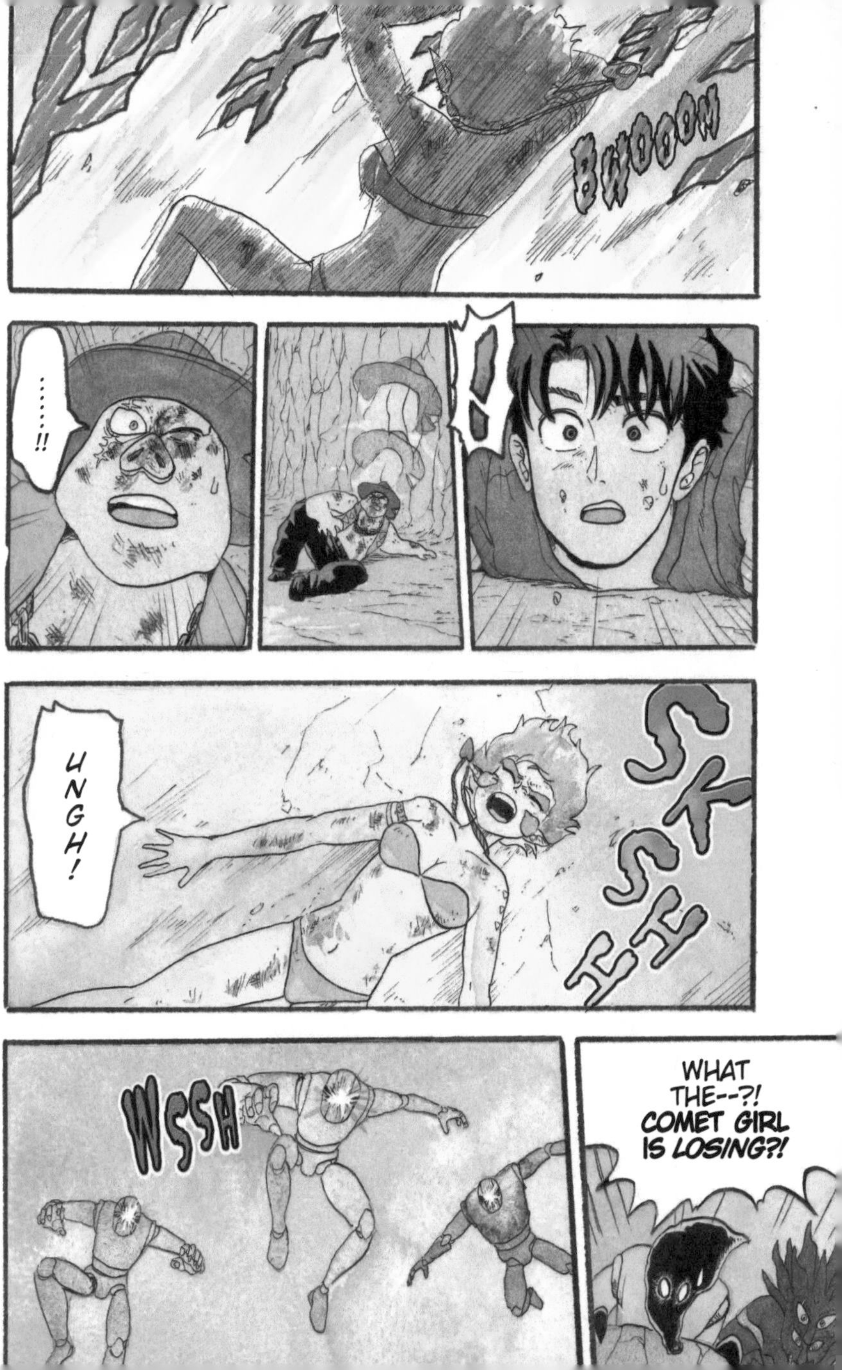
BWOOOM
!!
......!!
UNGH!
SKSHH
WHAT THE--?! COMET GIRL IS LOSING?!
WSSH

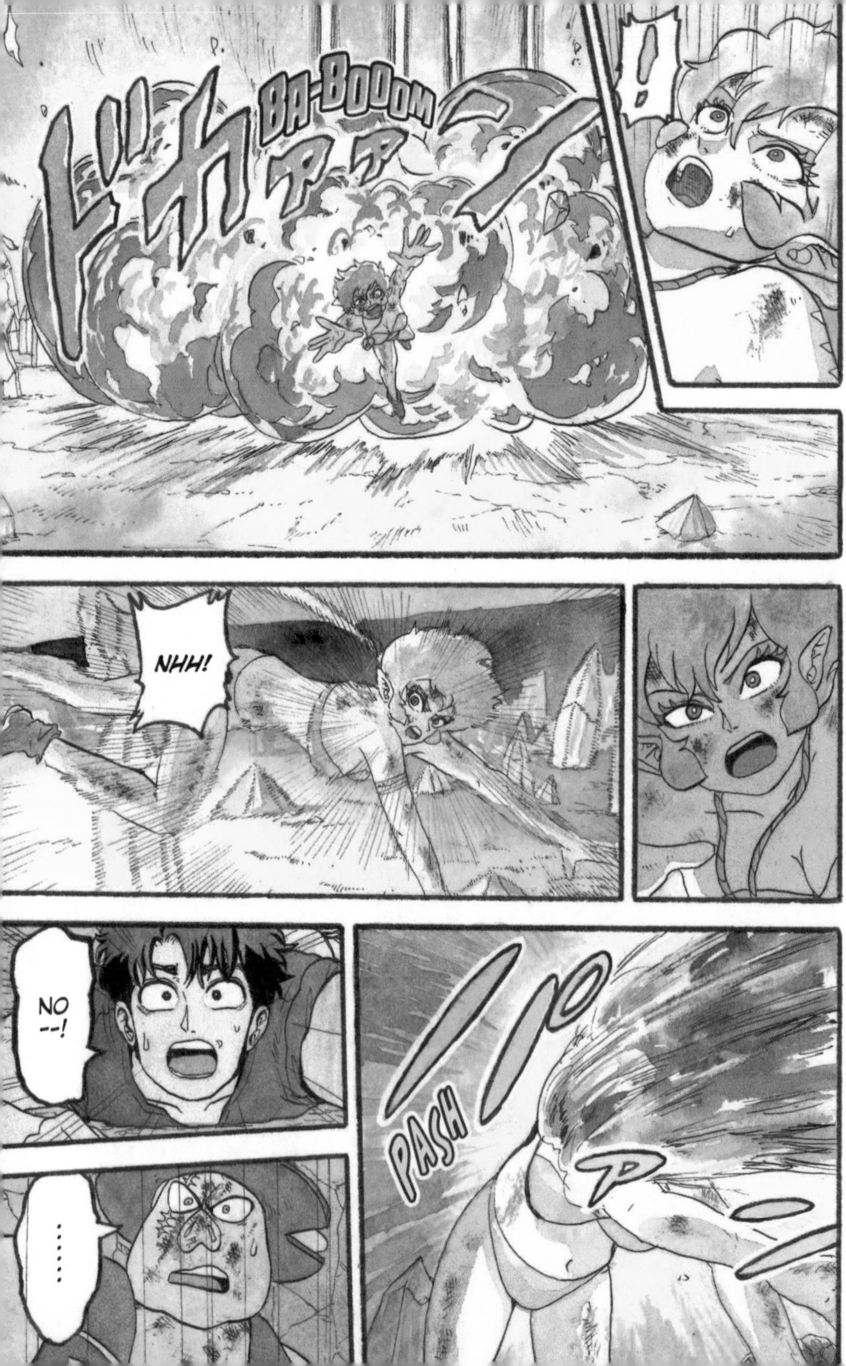
!
BA-BOOOM
NHH!
PASH
NO --!
......

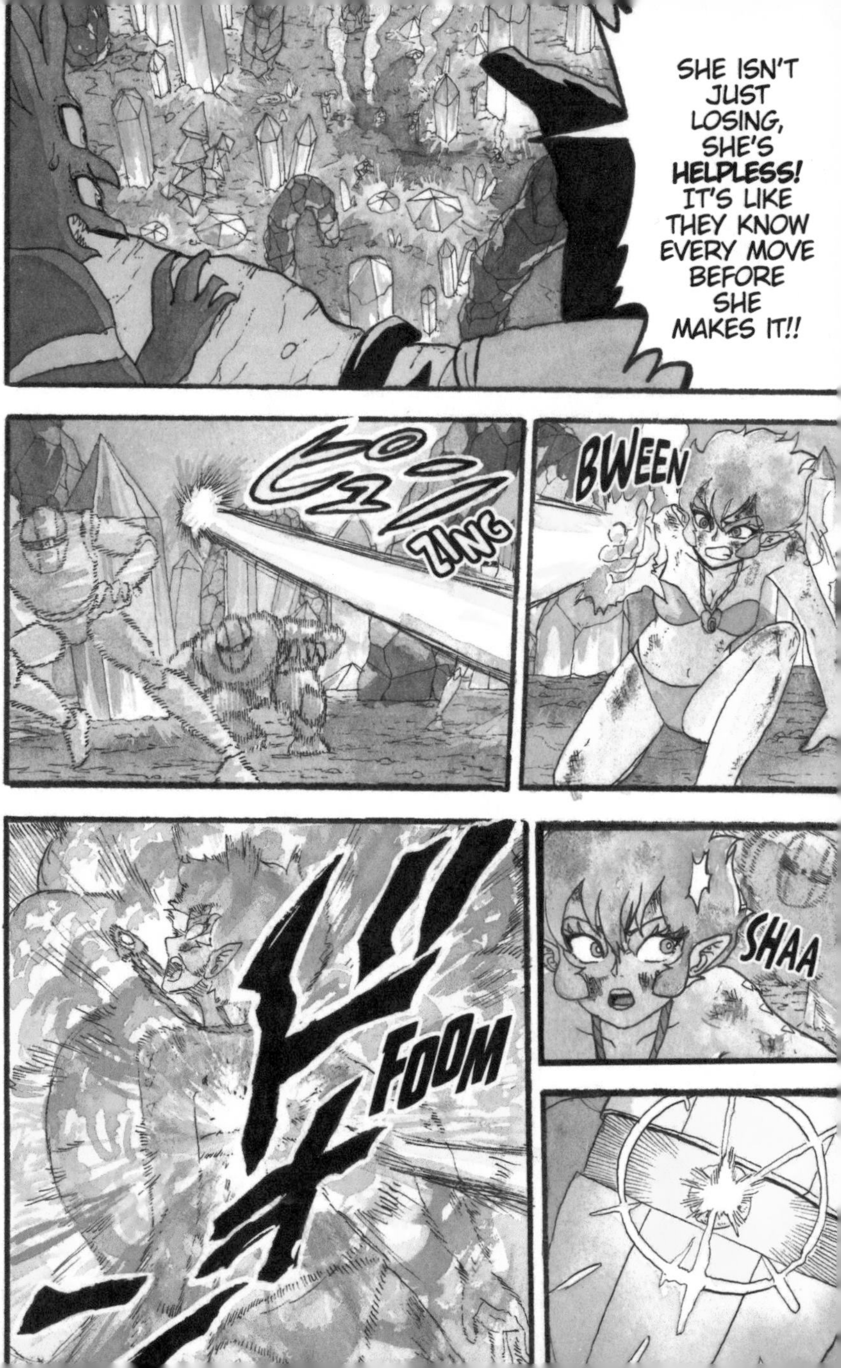
SHE ISN'T JUST LOSING, SHE'S **HELPLESS!** IT'S LIKE THEY KNOW EVERY MOVE BEFORE SHE MAKES IT!!
BWEEN
ZING
SHAA
FOOM

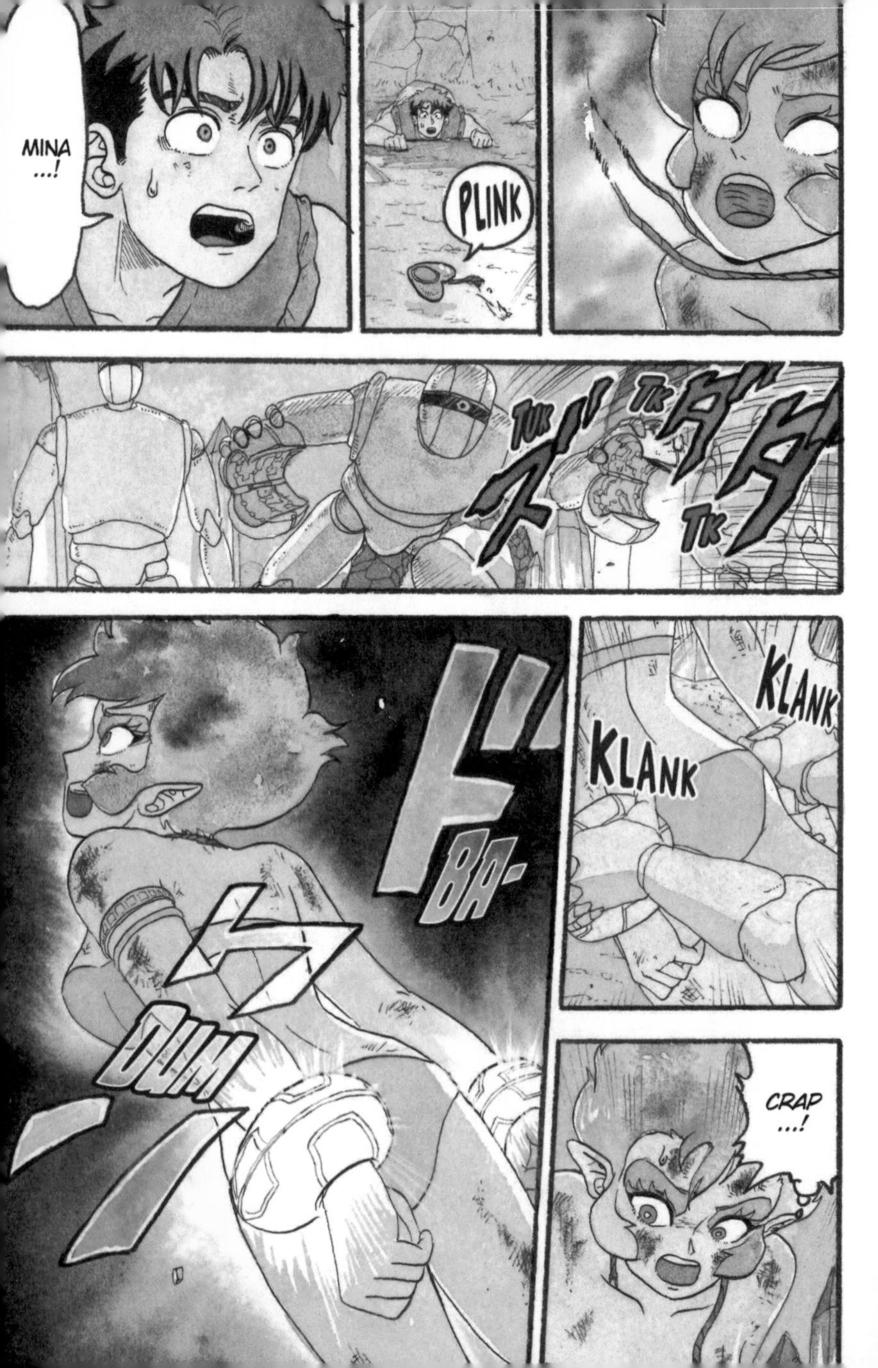
PLINK
MINA ...!
TK
TK
TUK
KLANK
KLANK
CRAP ...!
BA-
DUM

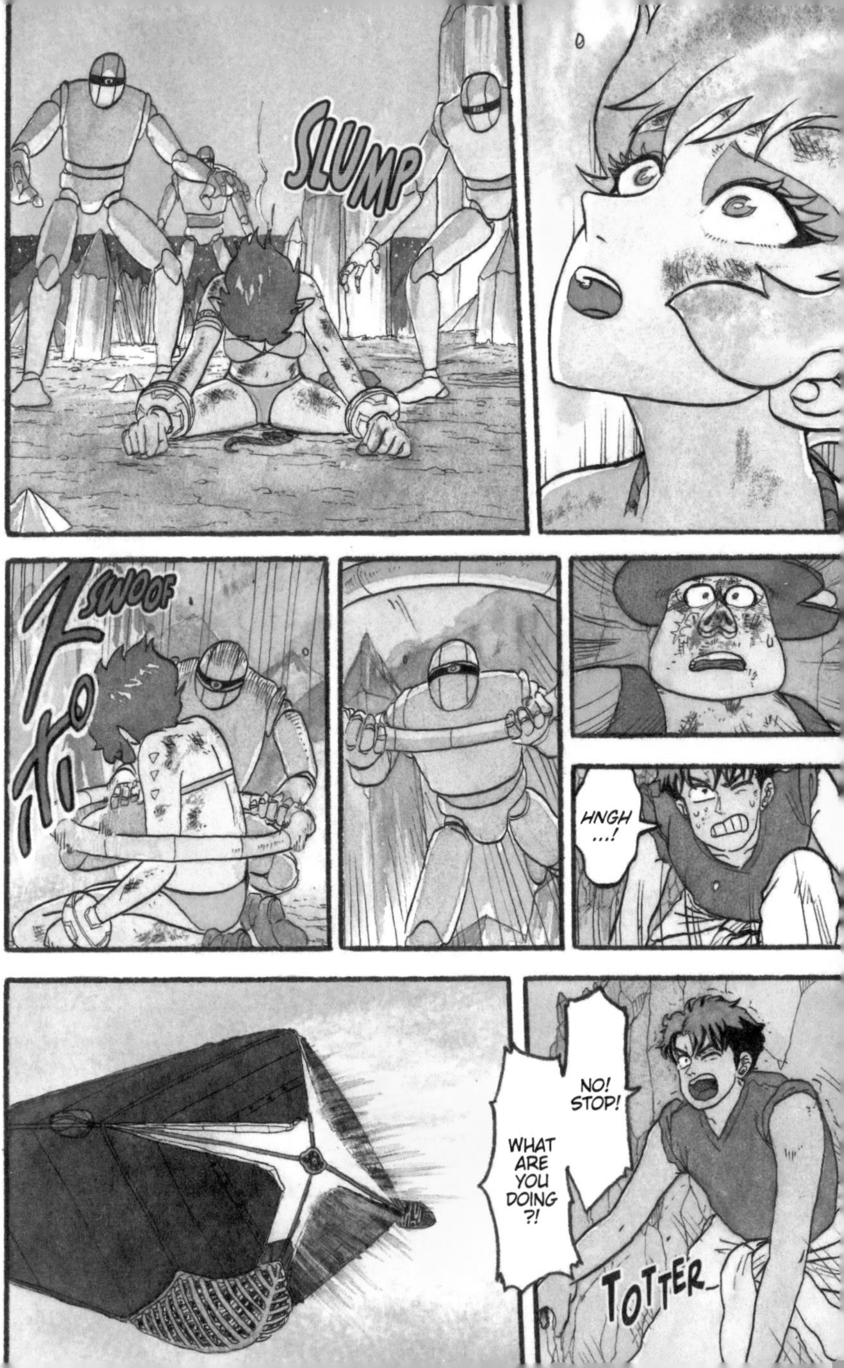
SLUMP
HNGH ...!
SWOOF
NO! STOP!
WHAT ARE YOU DOING ?!
TOTTER

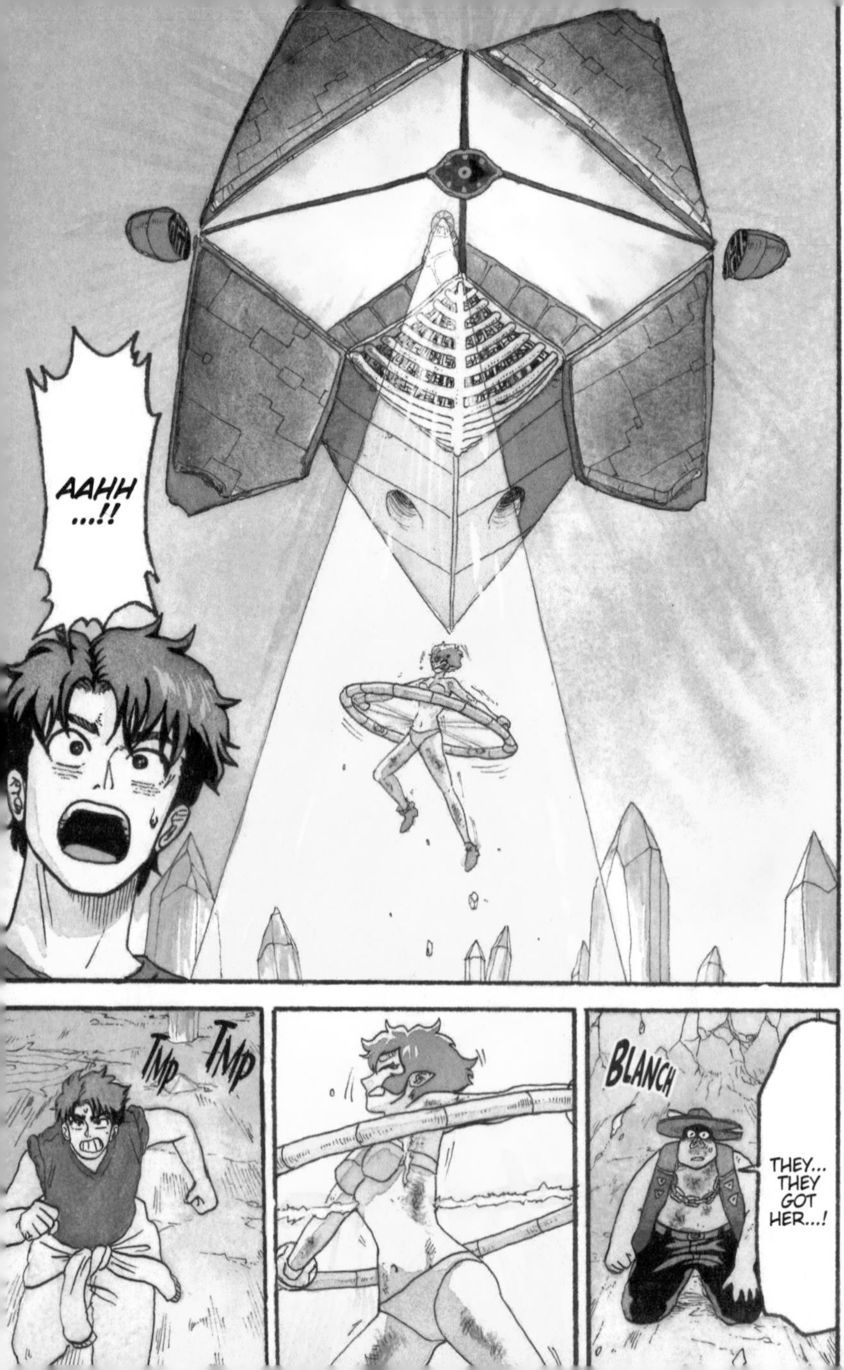
AAHH ...!!
BLANCH
THEY... THEY GOT HER...!
TMP
TMP

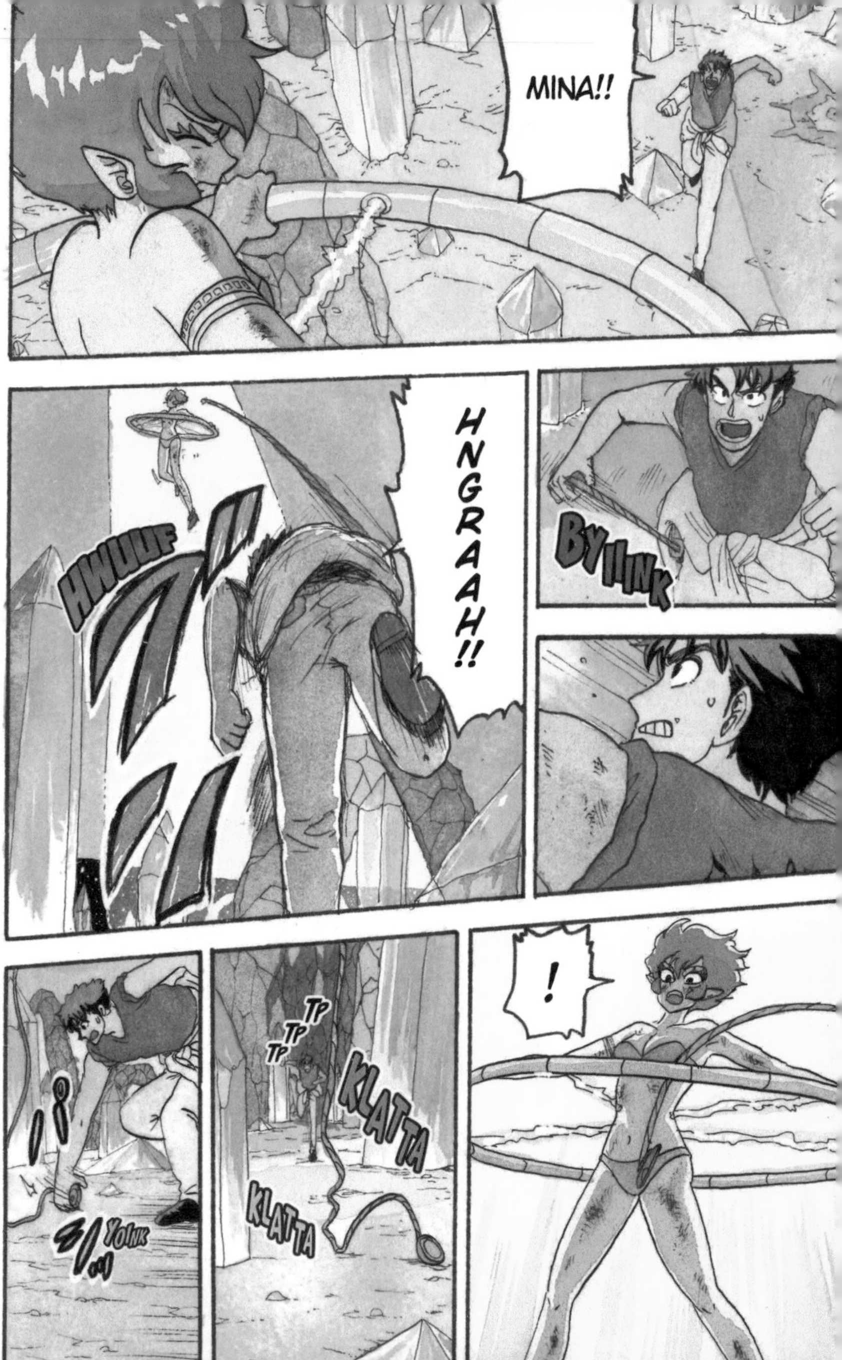
MINA!!
BYIIINK
HNGRAAAH!!
HWUUF
!
TP
TP
TP
KLATTA
KLATTA
YOINK

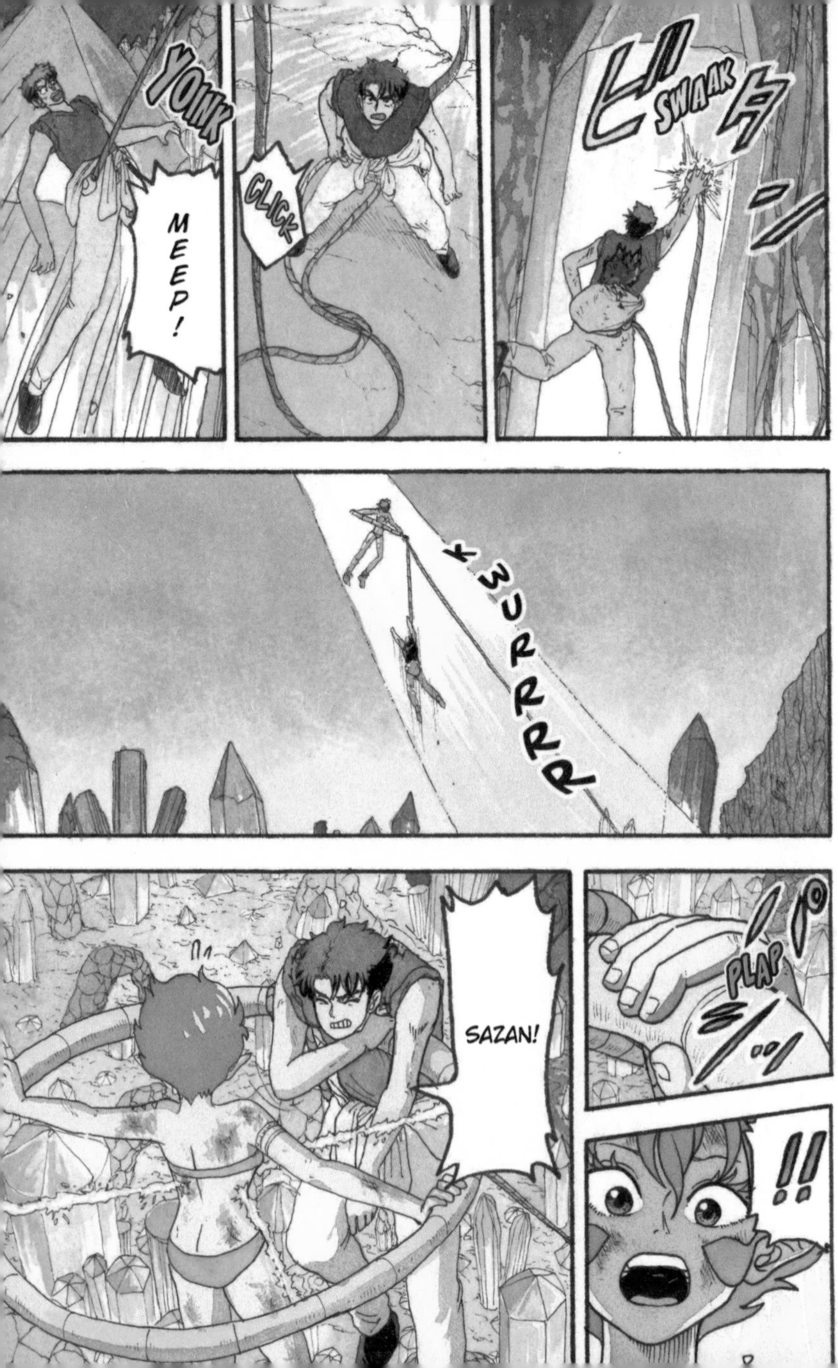
SWAAK
CLICK
YOINK
MEEP!
KWURRRR
PLAP
!!
SAZAN!

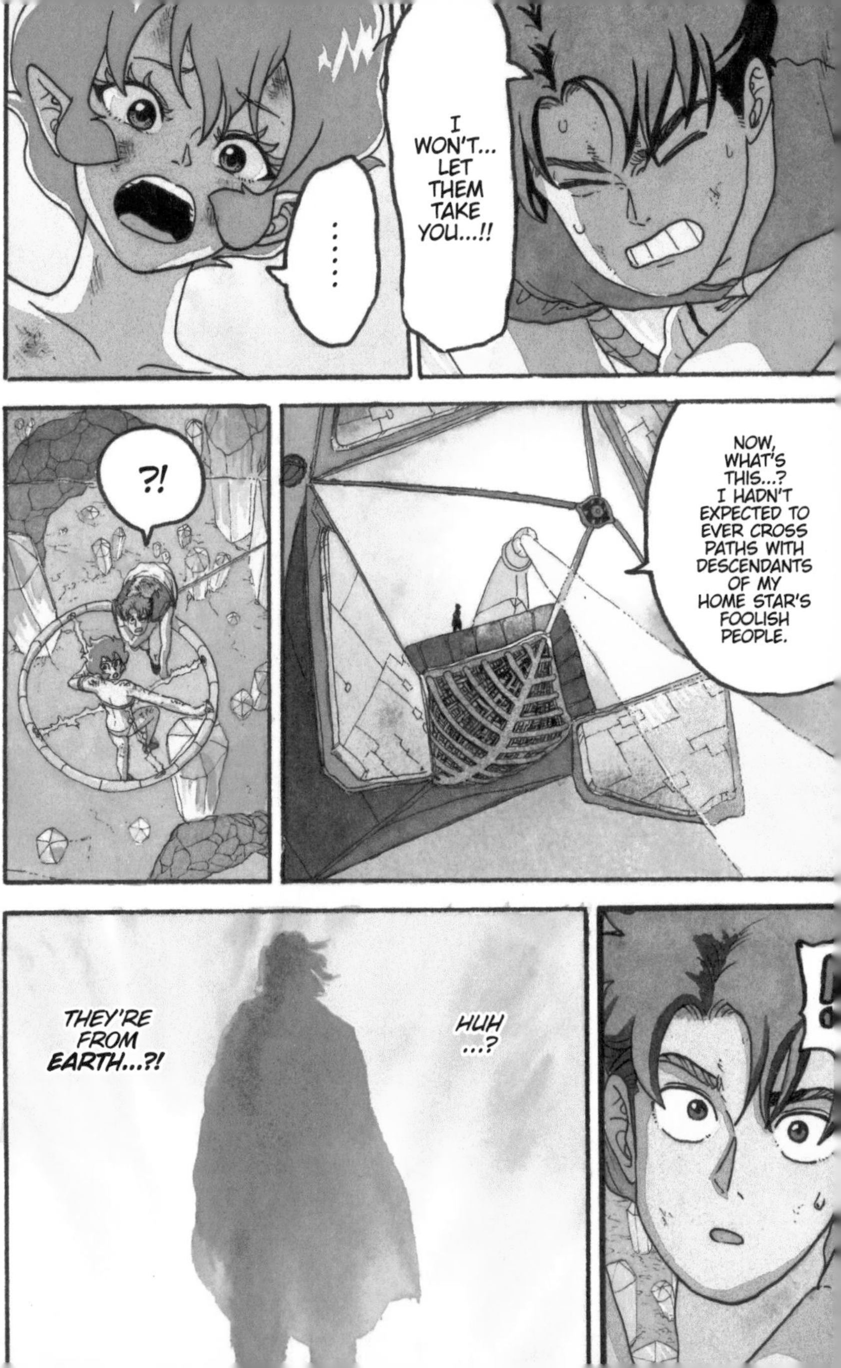
I WON'T... LET THEM TAKE YOU...!!
......
NOW, WHAT'S THIS...? I HADN'T EXPECTED TO EVER CROSS PATHS WITH DESCENDANTS OF MY HOME STAR'S FOOLISH PEOPLE.
?!
THEY'RE FROM EARTH...?!
HUH ...?

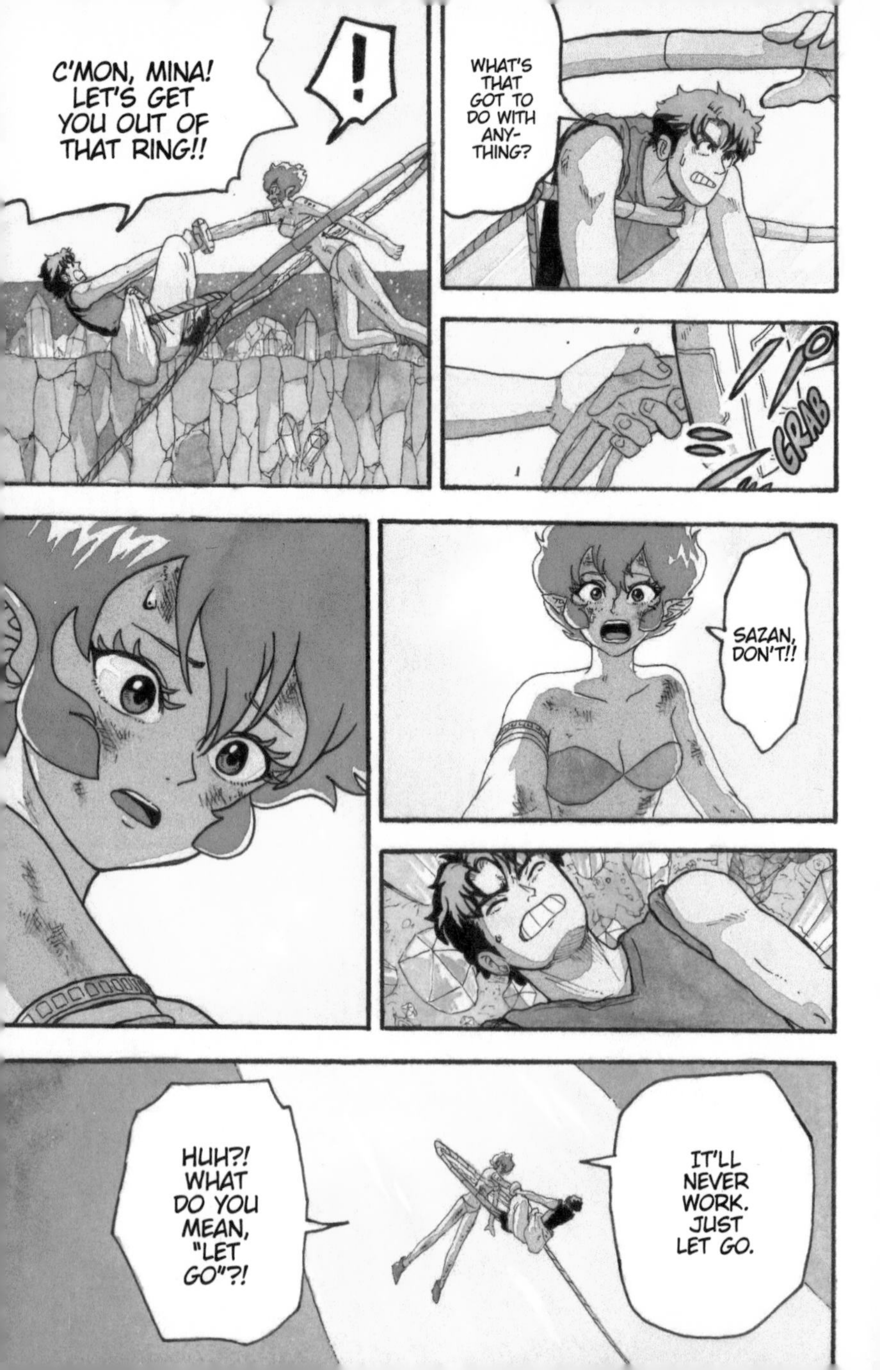
WHAT'S THAT GOT TO DO WITH ANY-THING?
GRAB
!
C'MON, MINA! LET'S GET YOU OUT OF THAT RING!!
SAZAN, DON'T!!
IT'LL NEVER WORK. JUST LET GO.
HUH?! WHAT DO YOU MEAN, "LET GO"?!

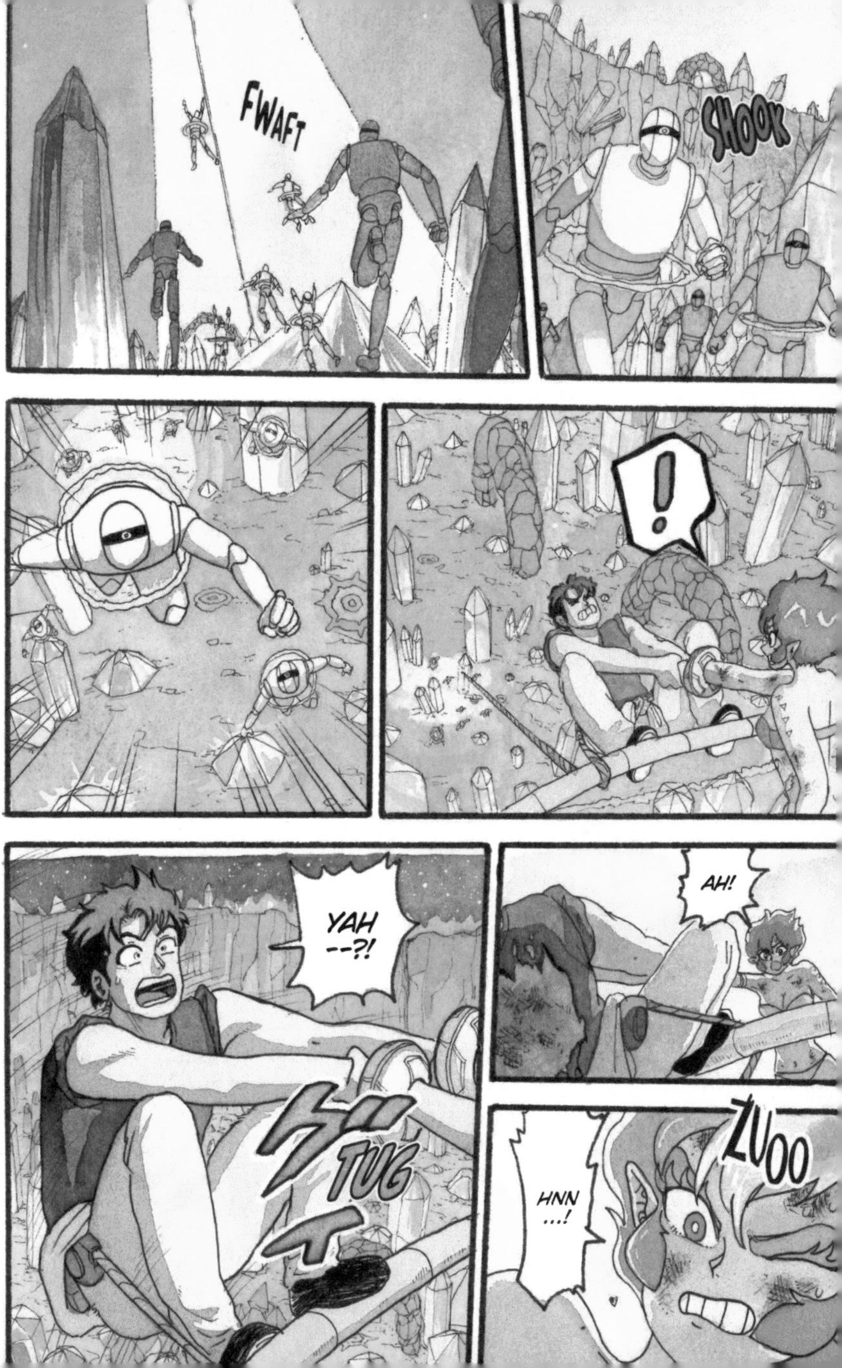
SHOOK
FWAFT
!
AH!
ZUOO
HNN ...!
YAH --?!
TUG

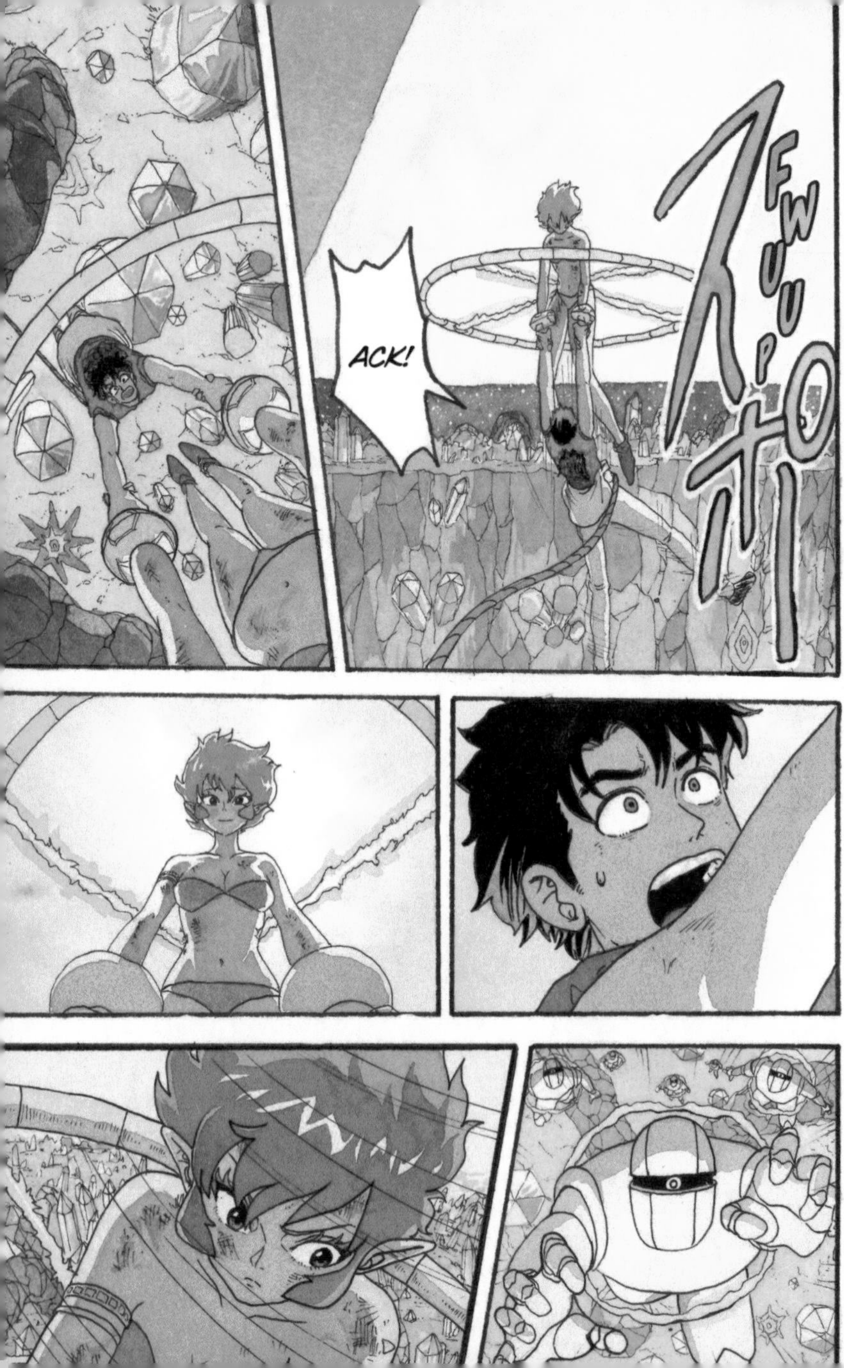
FWUUP
ACK!

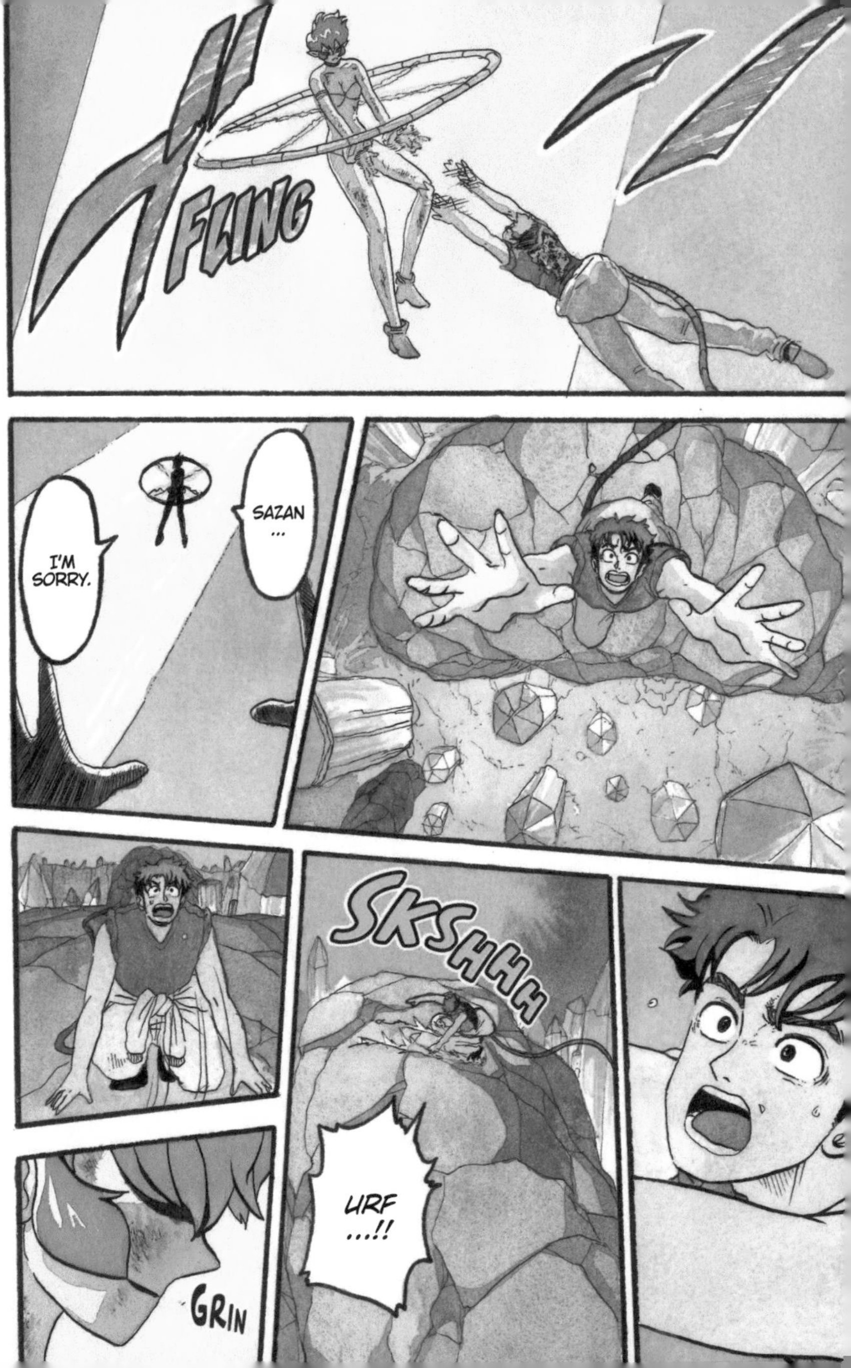
FLING
SAZAN ...
I'M SORRY.
SKSHHH
URF ...!!
GRIN

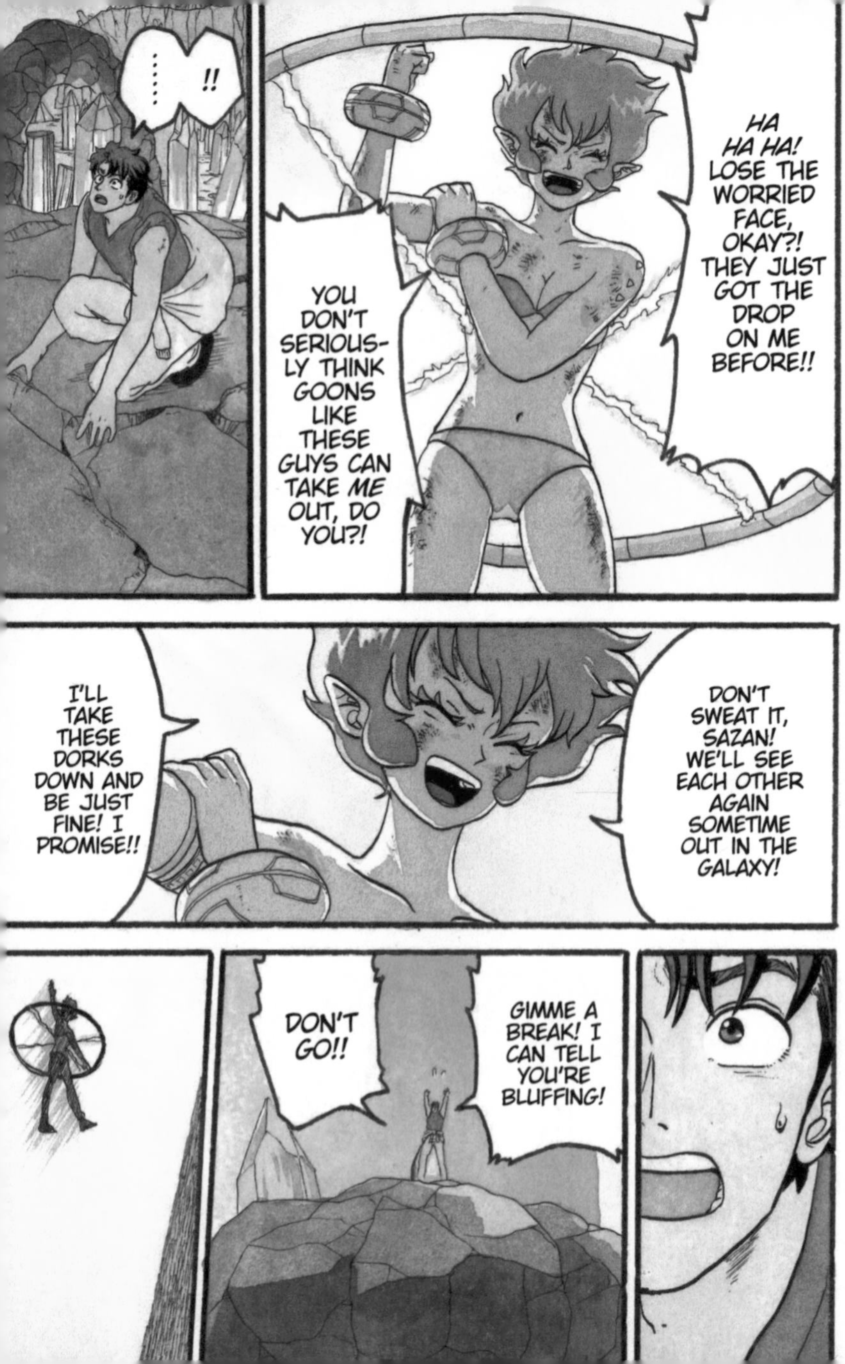
HA HA HA! LOSE THE WORRIED FACE, OKAY?! THEY JUST GOT THE DROP ON ME BEFORE!!
YOU DON'T SERIOUS-LY THINK GOONS LIKE THESE GUYS CAN TAKE *ME* OUT, DO YOU?!
!!
......
DON'T SWEAT IT, SAZAN! WE'LL SEE EACH OTHER AGAIN SOMETIME OUT IN THE GALAXY!
I'LL TAKE THESE DORKS DOWN AND BE JUST FINE! I PROMISE!!
GIMME A BREAK! I CAN TELL YOU'RE BLUFFING!
DON'T GO!!

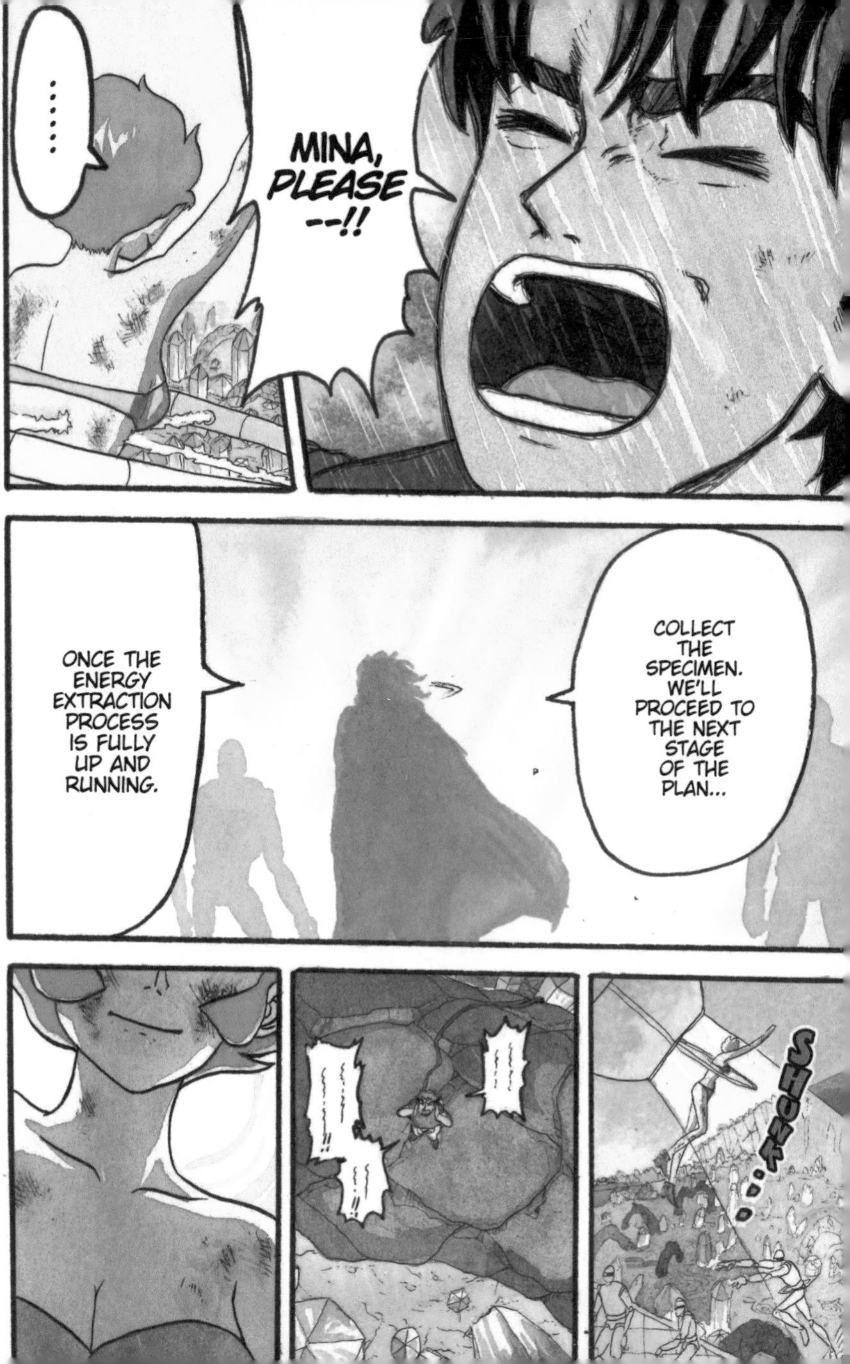
MINA, PLEASE --!!
......
COLLECT THE SPECIMEN. WE'LL PROCEED TO THE NEXT STAGE OF THE PLAN...
ONCE THE ENERGY EXTRACTION PROCESS IS FULLY UP AND RUNNING.
SHUNK...

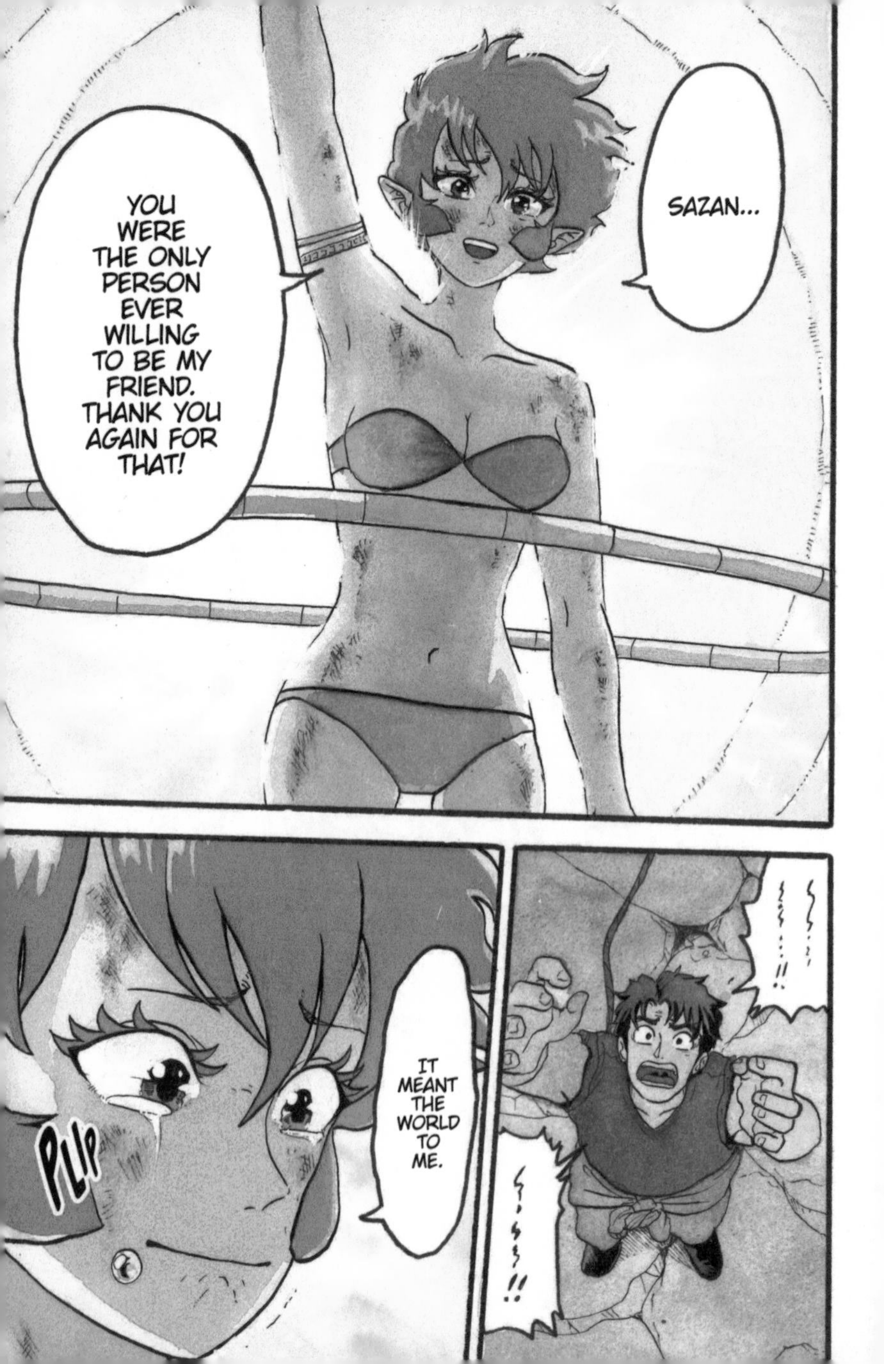
SAZAN...
YOU WERE THE ONLY PERSON EVER WILLING TO BE MY FRIEND. THANK YOU AGAIN FOR THAT!
IT MEANT THE WORLD TO ME.
PLIP

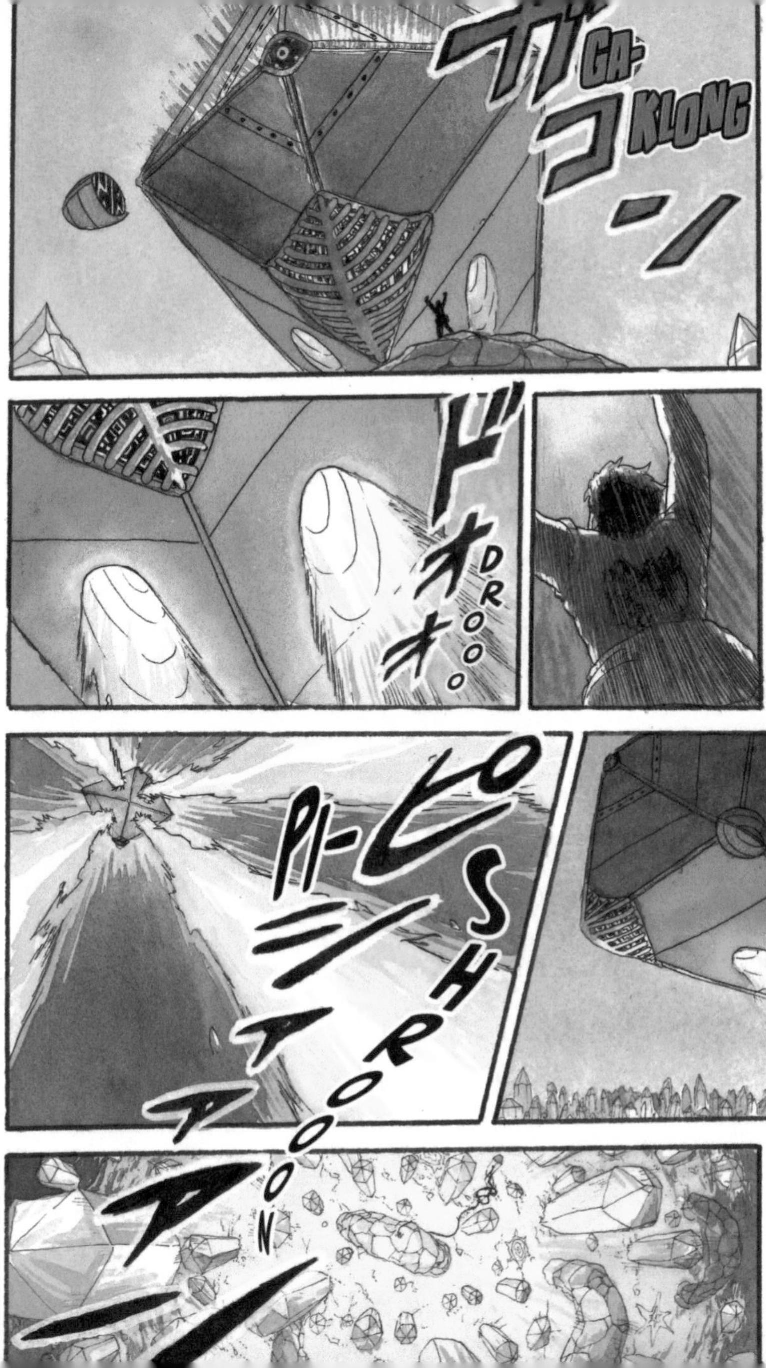
ガコーン
GA-KLONG
ドオオ…
DROOO…
PI-
SHROOOON

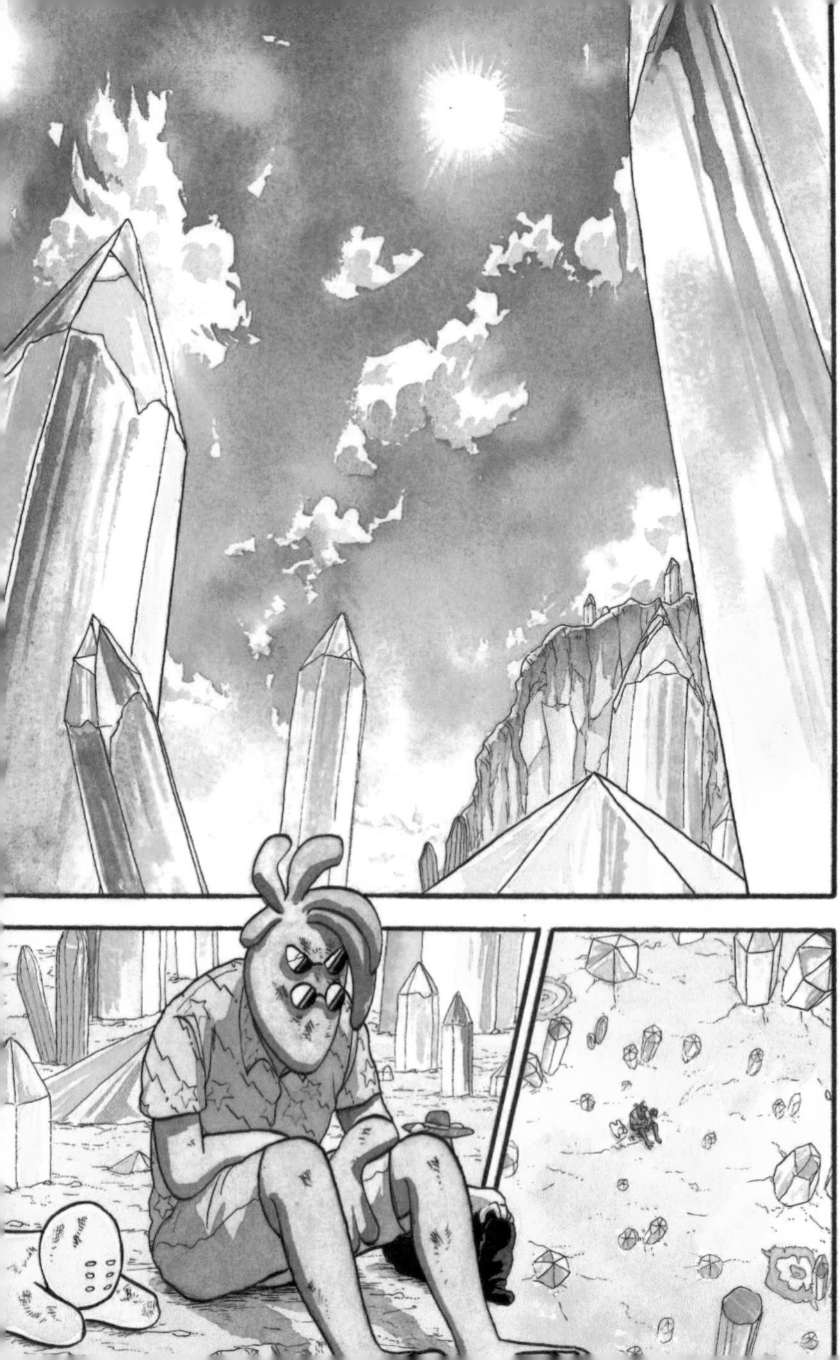

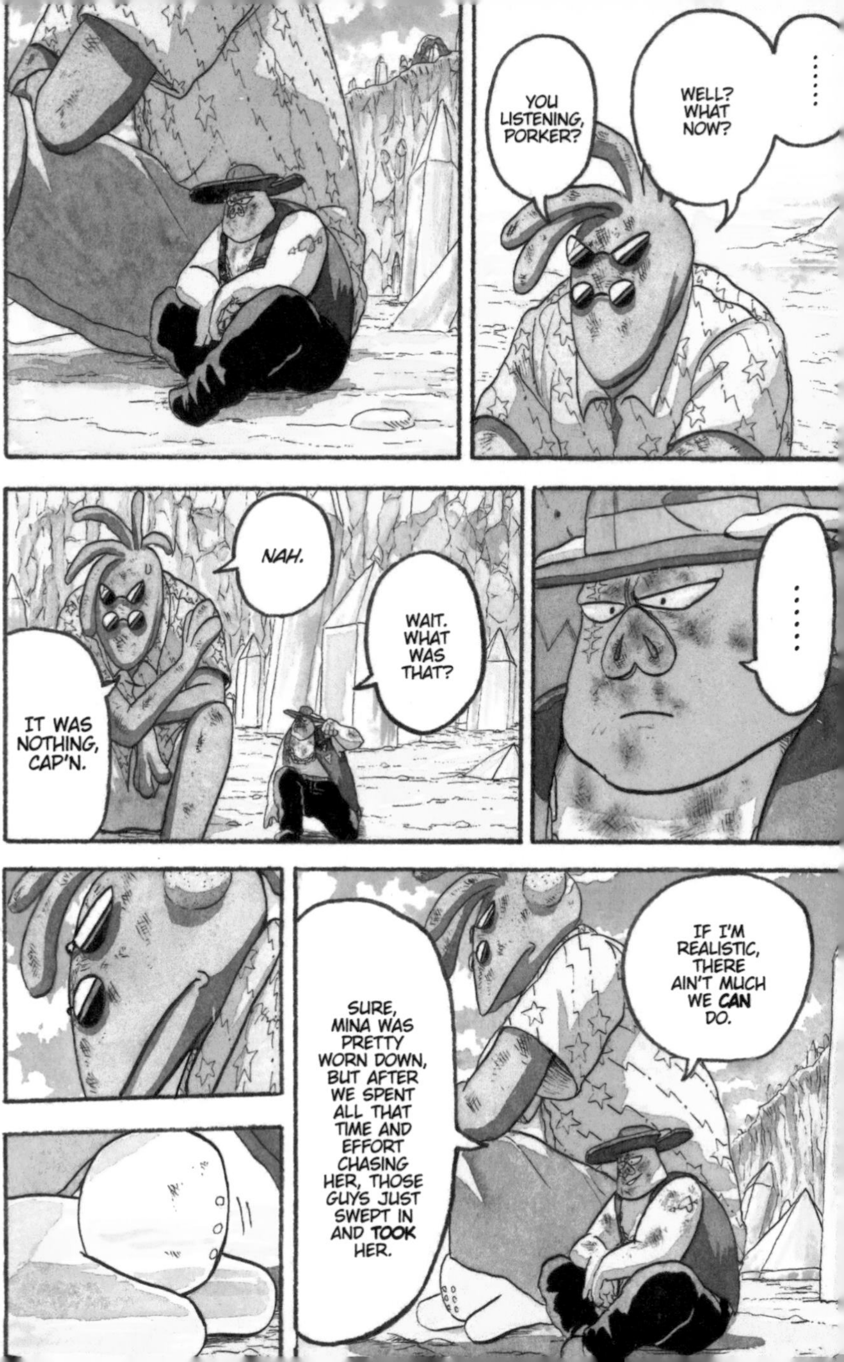
......
WELL? WHAT NOW?
YOU LISTENING, PORKER?
......
NAH.
WAIT. WHAT WAS THAT?
IT WAS NOTHING, CAP'N.
IF I'M REALISTIC, THERE AIN'T MUCH WE **CAN** DO.
SURE, MINA WAS PRETTY WORN DOWN, BUT AFTER WE SPENT ALL THAT TIME AND EFFORT CHASING HER, THOSE GUYS JUST SWEPT IN AND **TOOK** HER.

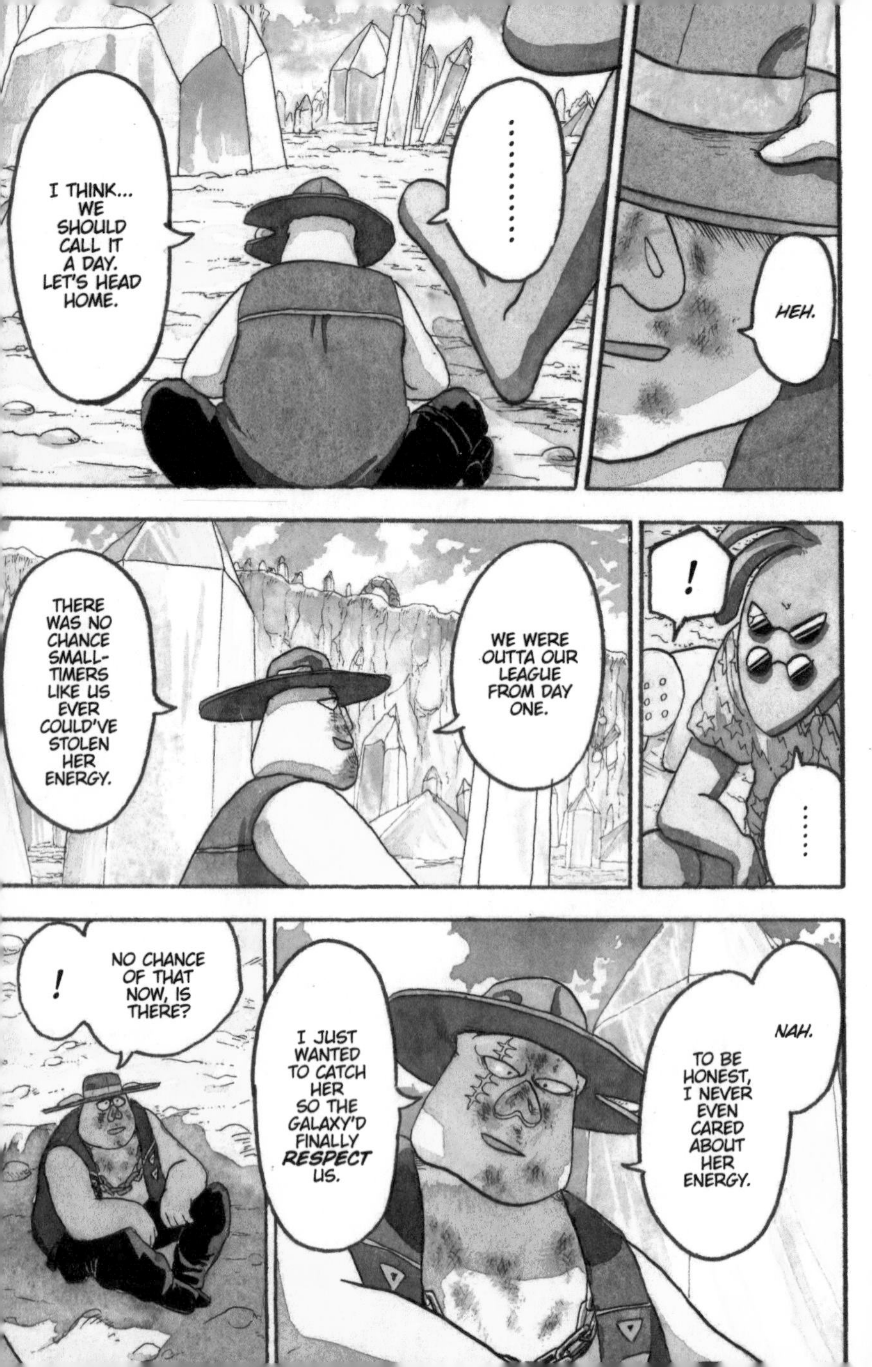
HEH.
......
I THINK... WE SHOULD CALL IT A DAY. LET'S HEAD HOME.
!
......
WE WERE OUTTA OUR LEAGUE FROM DAY ONE.
THERE WAS NO CHANCE SMALL-TIMERS LIKE US EVER COULD'VE STOLEN HER ENERGY.
NAH.
TO BE HONEST, I NEVER EVEN CARED ABOUT HER ENERGY.
I JUST WANTED TO CATCH HER SO THE GALAXY'D FINALLY *RESPECT* US.
!
NO CHANCE OF THAT NOW, IS THERE?

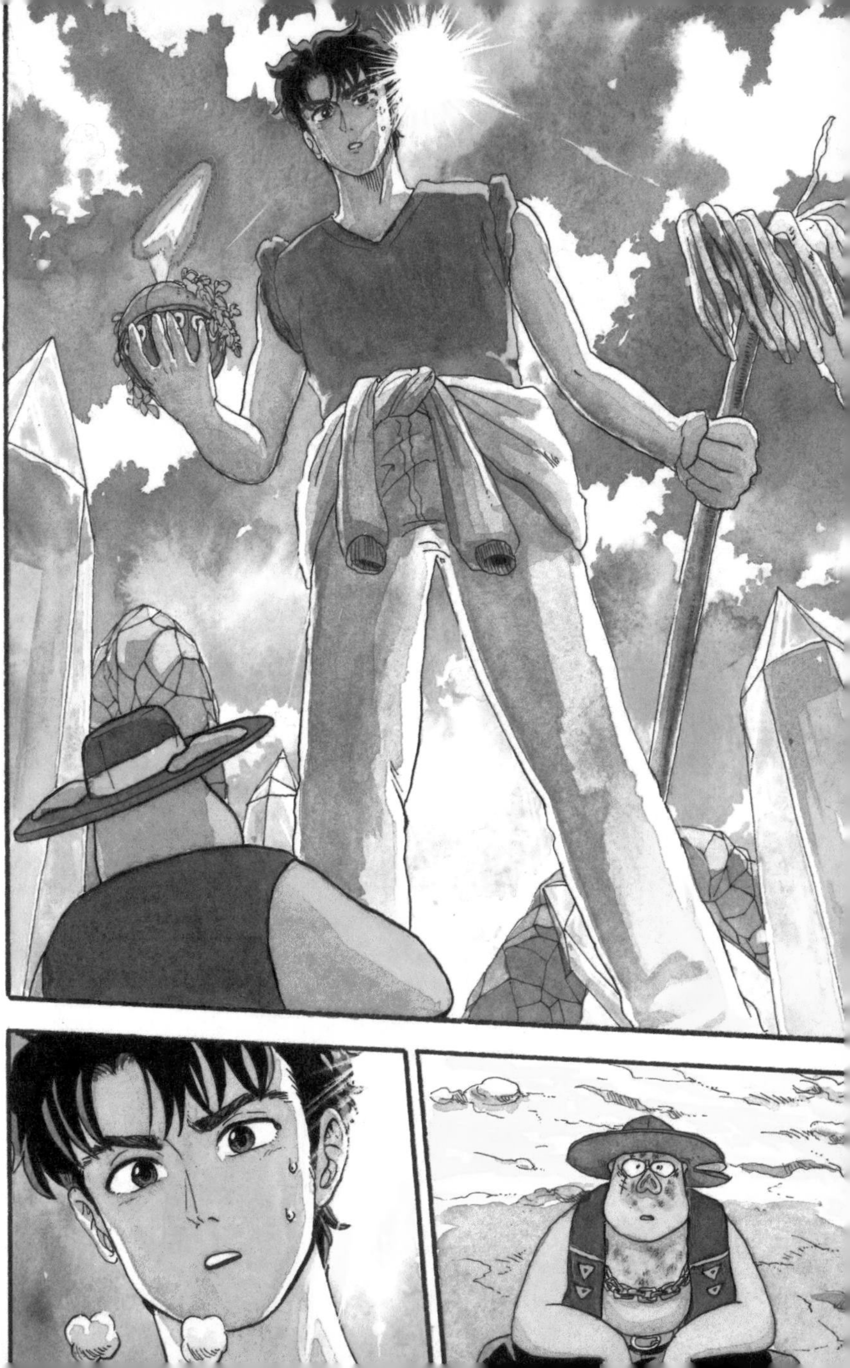

KIDD.

LET'S GO.

NRH ...!

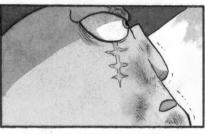

YEAH. LET'S GO HOME.

ズ

CLOMP

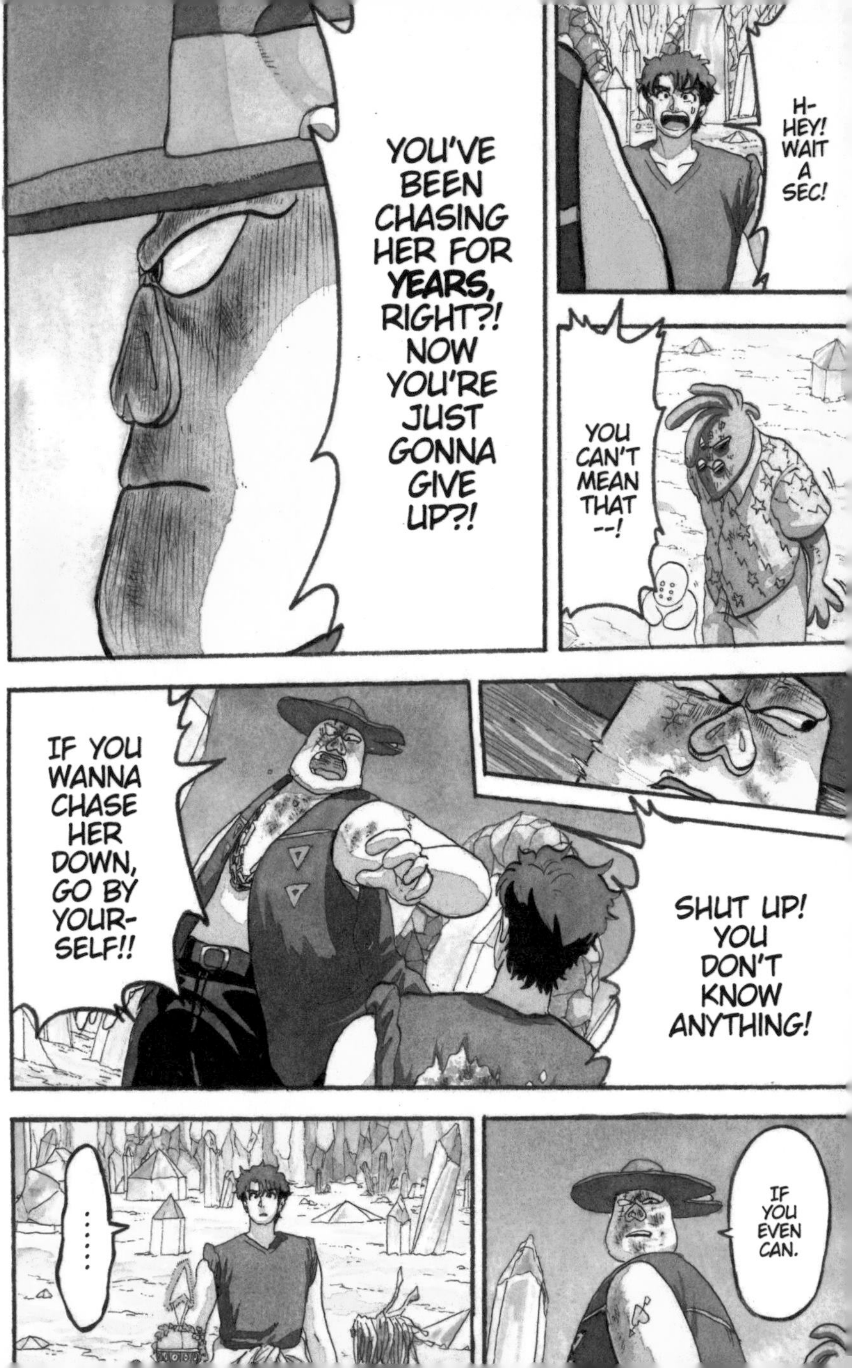
H-HEY! WAIT A SEC!
YOU CAN'T MEAN THAT --!
YOU'VE BEEN CHASING HER FOR **YEARS,** RIGHT?! NOW YOU'RE JUST GONNA GIVE UP?!
SHUT UP! YOU DON'T KNOW ANYTHING!
IF YOU WANNA CHASE HER DOWN, GO BY YOUR-SELF!!
IF YOU EVEN CAN.
......

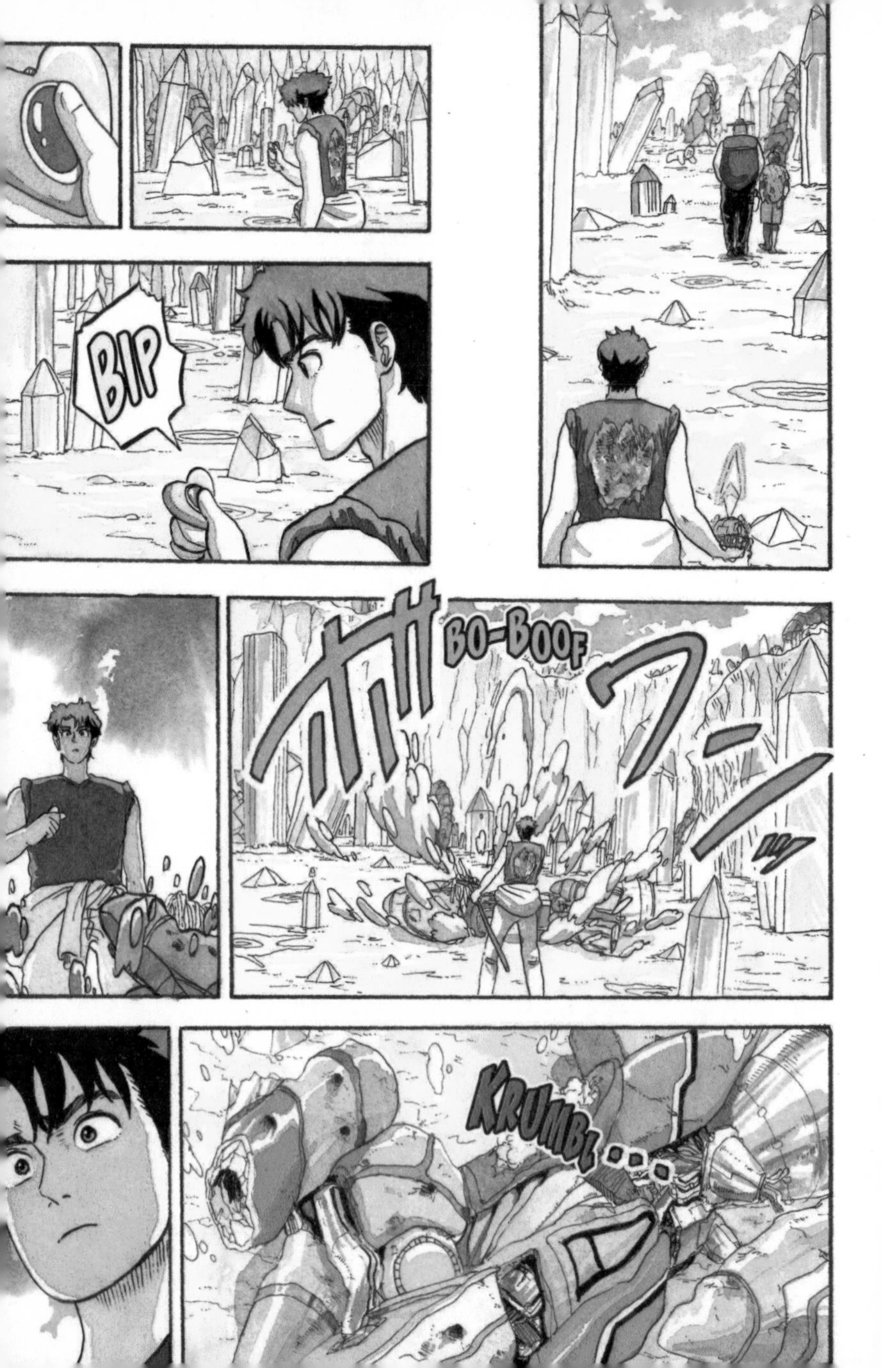
BIP
BO-BOOF
KRUMBL...

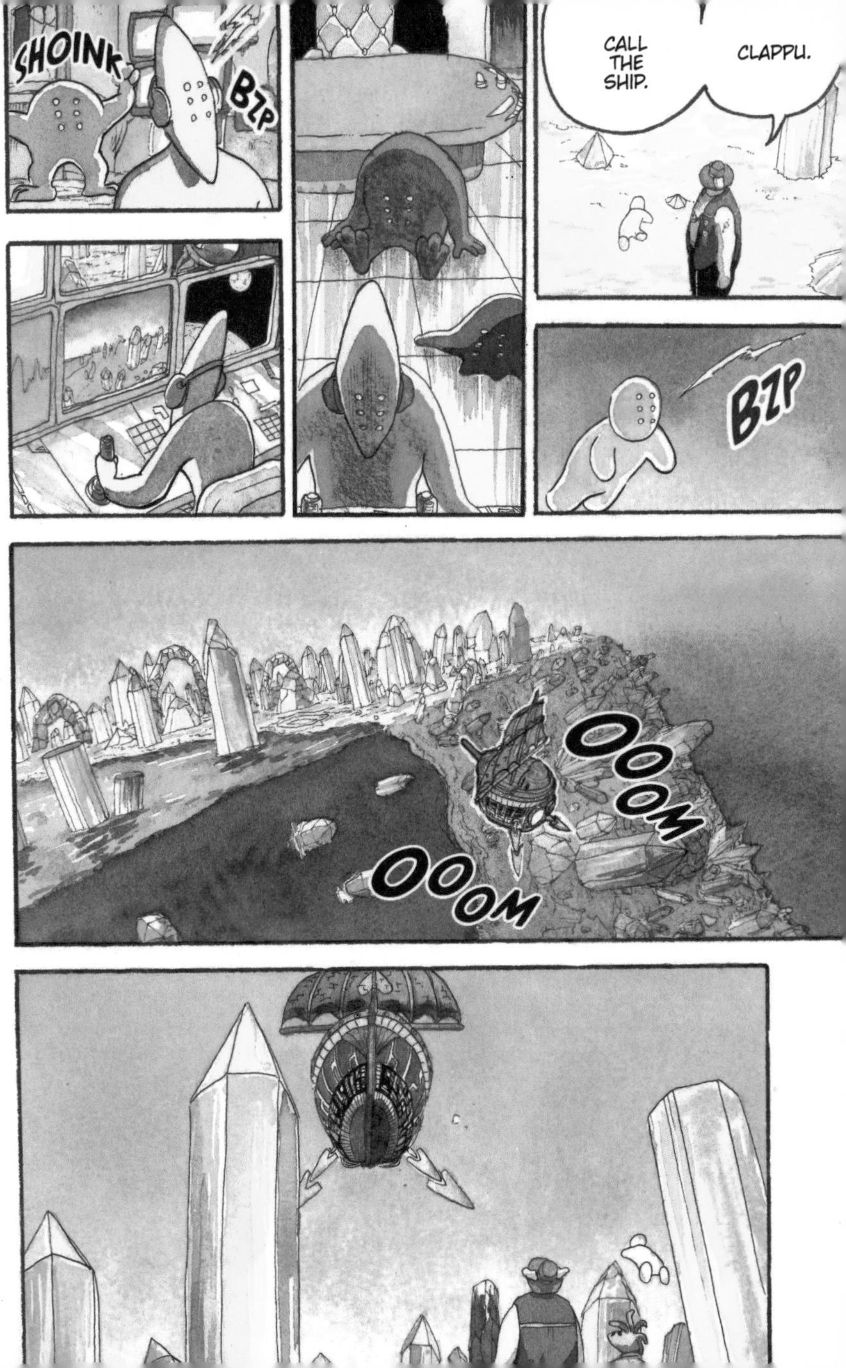
CLAPPU.
CALL THE SHIP.
B-ZP
SHOINK
BZP
OOOM
OOOM

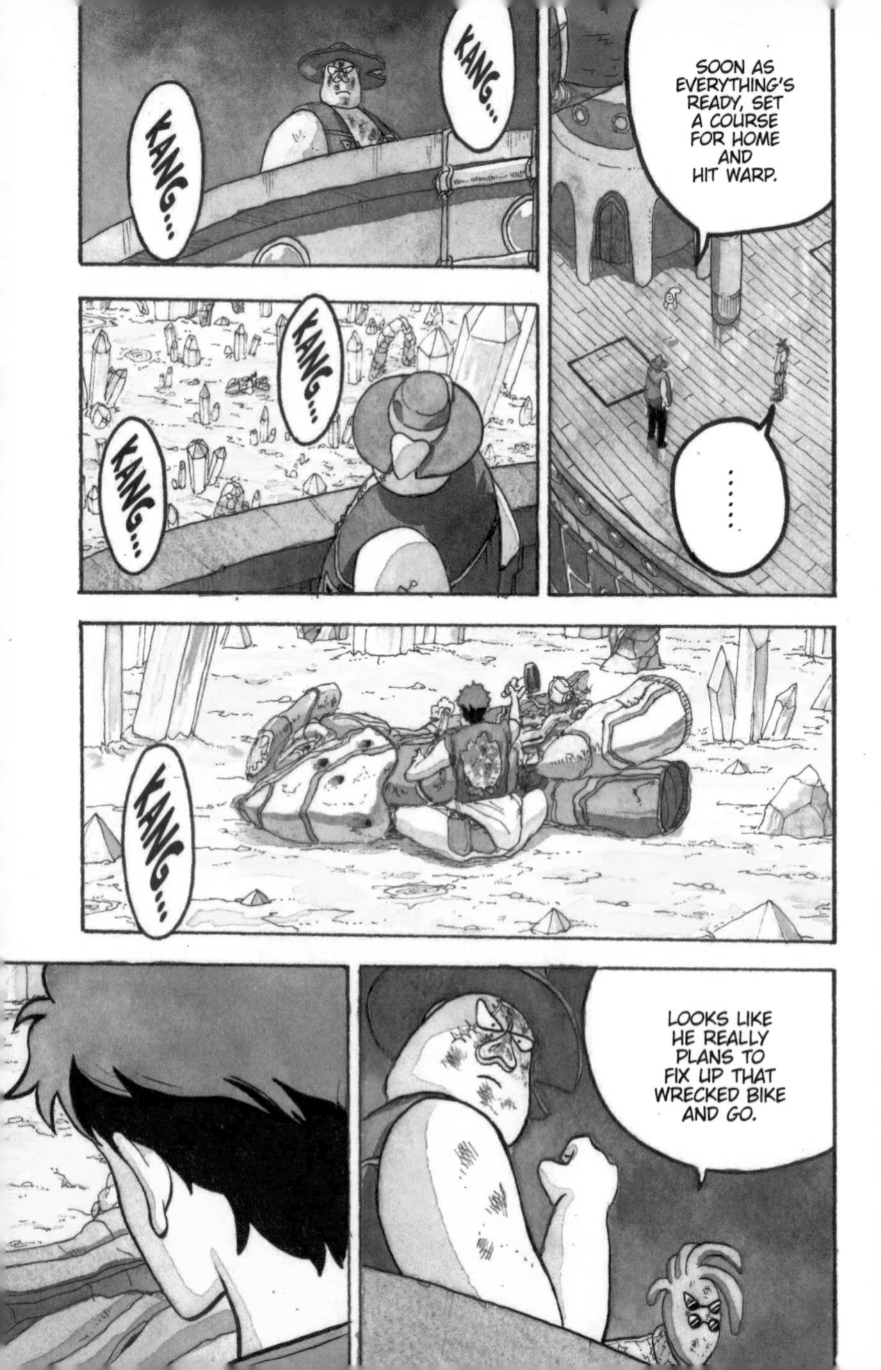

SOON AS EVERYTHING'S READY, SET A COURSE FOR HOME AND HIT WARP.
......
KANG...
KANG...
KANG...
KANG...
KANG...
LOOKS LIKE HE REALLY PLANS TO FIX UP THAT WRECKED BIKE AND GO.

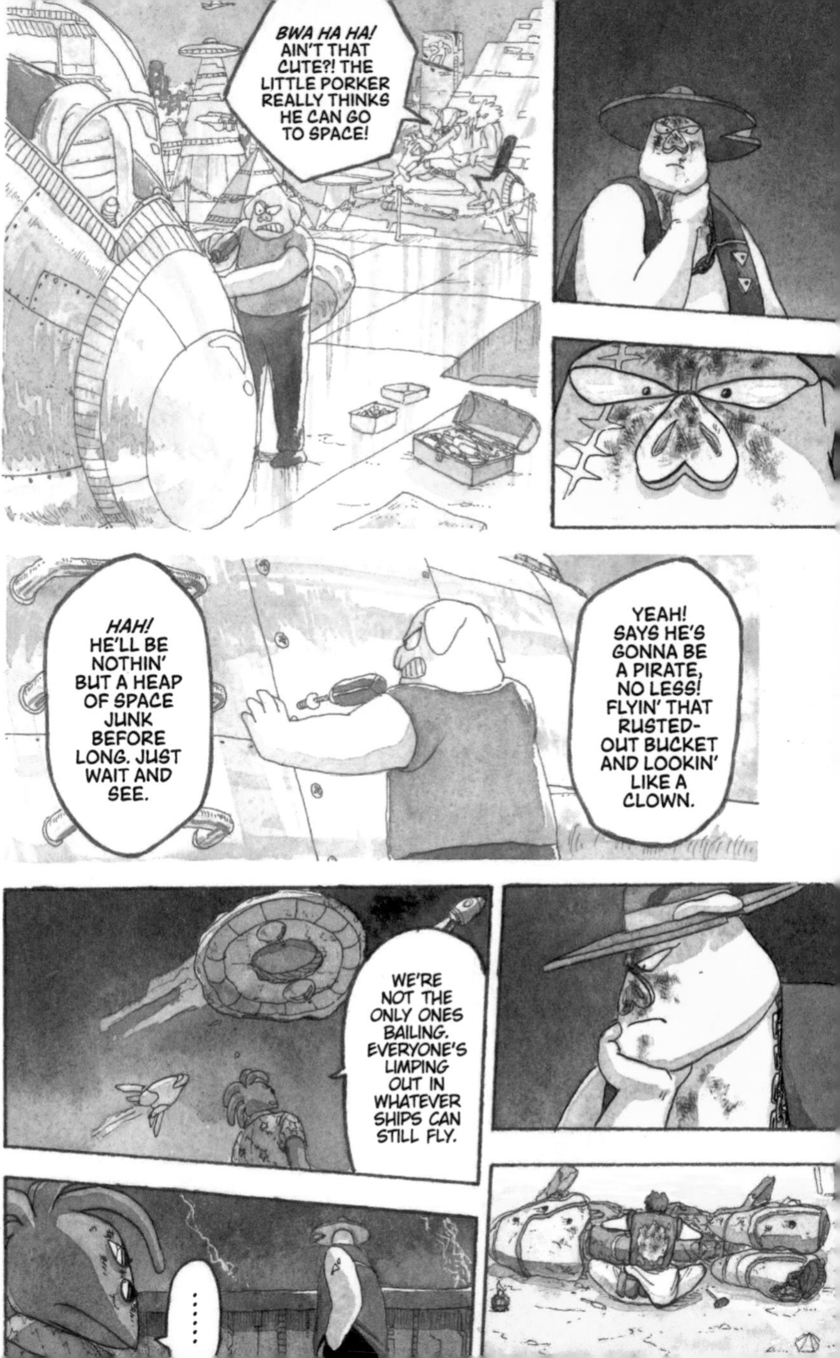
BWA HA HA! AIN'T THAT CUTE?! THE LITTLE PORKER REALLY THINKS HE CAN GO TO SPACE!
YEAH! SAYS HE'S GONNA BE A PIRATE, NO LESS! FLYIN' THAT RUSTED-OUT BUCKET AND LOOKIN' LIKE A CLOWN.
HAH! HE'LL BE NOTHIN' BUT A HEAP OF SPACE JUNK BEFORE LONG. JUST WAIT AND SEE.
WE'RE NOT THE ONLY ONES BAILING. EVERYONE'S LIMPING OUT IN WHATEVER SHIPS CAN STILL FLY.
......

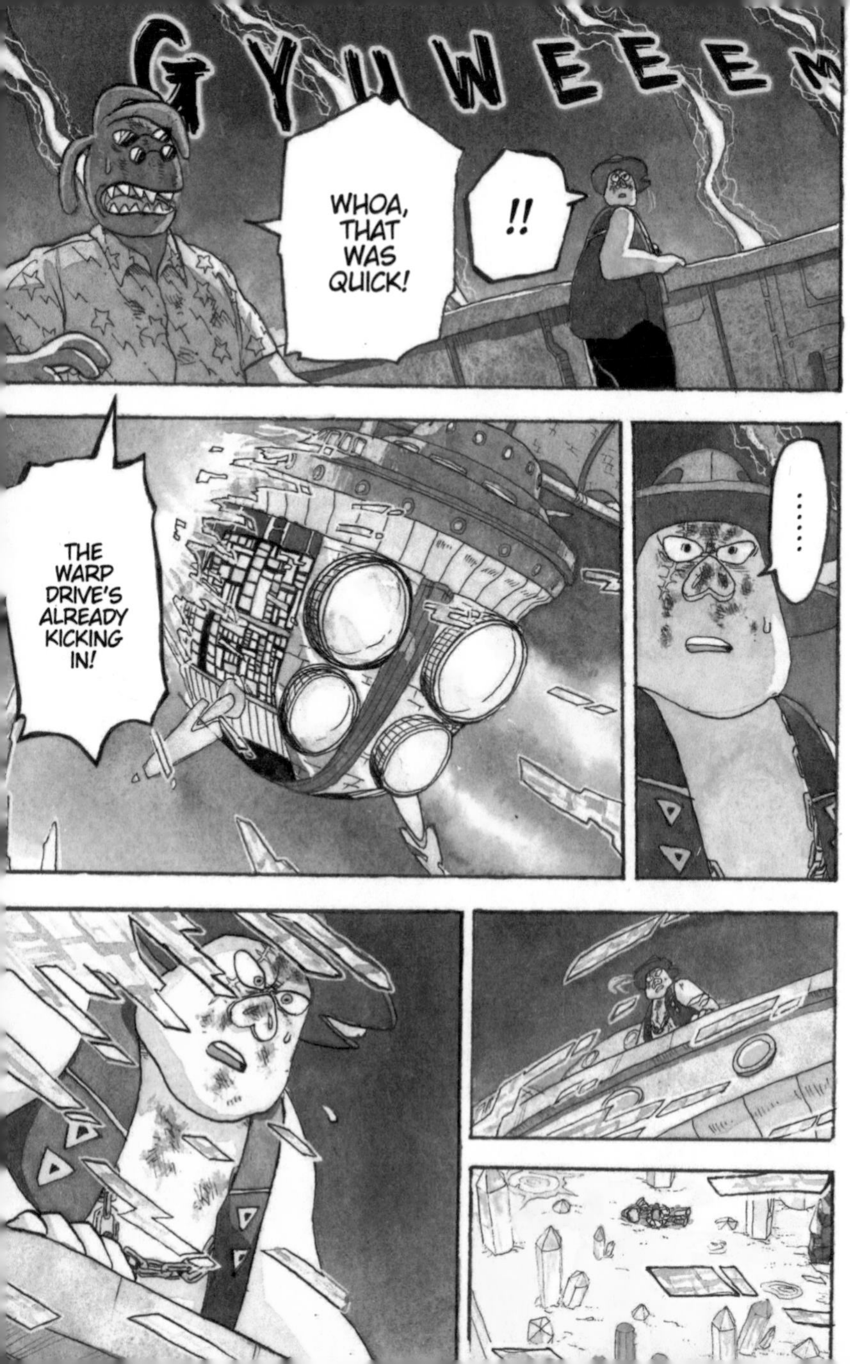
GYUWEEEM
!!
WHOA, THAT WAS QUICK!
......
THE WARP DRIVE'S ALREADY KICKING IN!

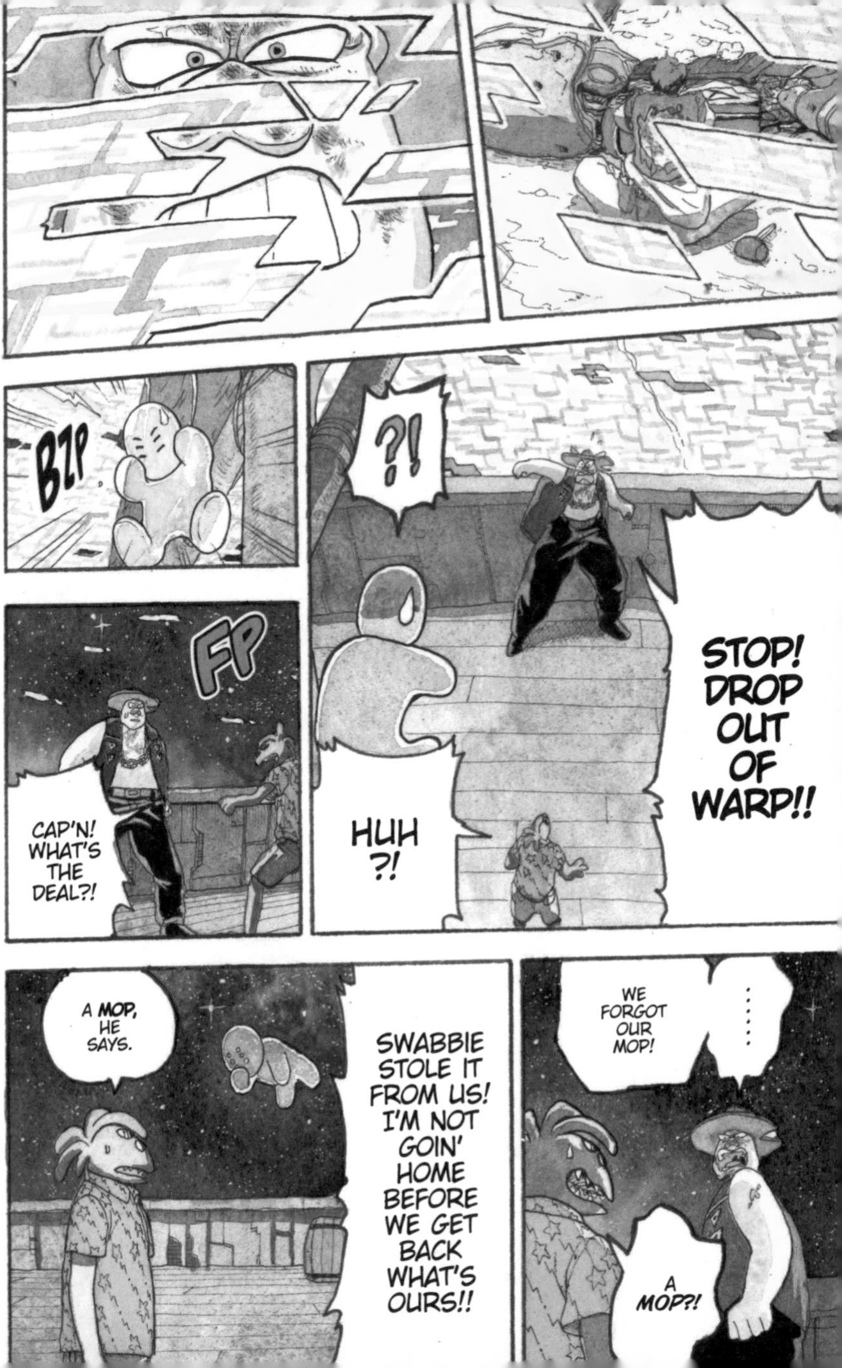
?!
STOP! DROP OUT OF WARP!!
HUH ?!
BZP
FP
CAP'N! WHAT'S THE DEAL?!
......
WE FORGOT OUR MOP!
A MOP?!
SWABBIE STOLE IT FROM US! I'M NOT GOIN' HOME BEFORE WE GET BACK WHAT'S OURS!!
A MOP, HE SAYS.

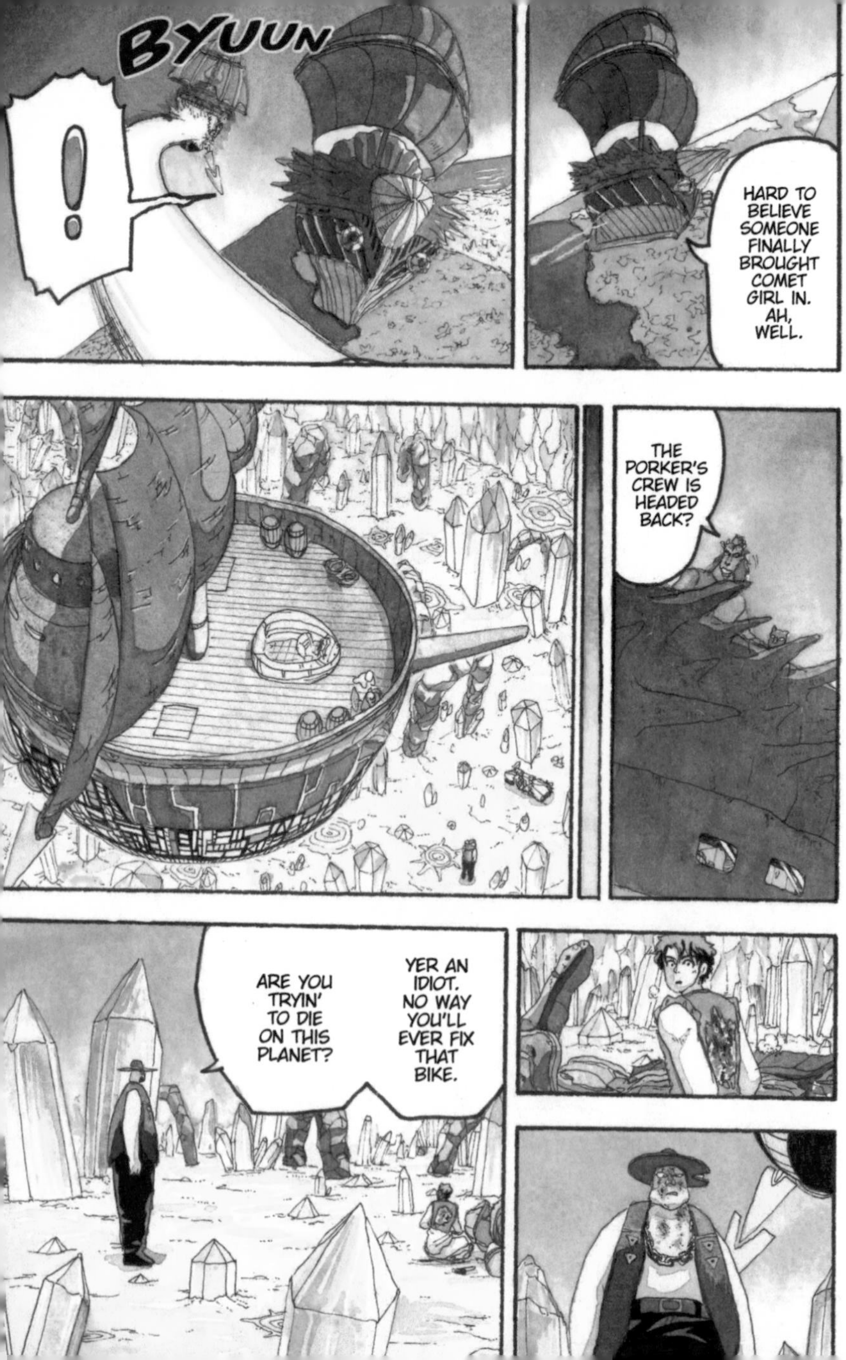
HARD TO BELIEVE SOMEONE FINALLY BROUGHT COMET GIRL IN. AH, WELL.
BYUUN
!
THE PORKER'S CREW IS HEADED BACK?
ARE YOU TRYIN' TO DIE ON THIS PLANET?
YER AN IDIOT. NO WAY YOU'LL EVER FIX THAT BIKE.

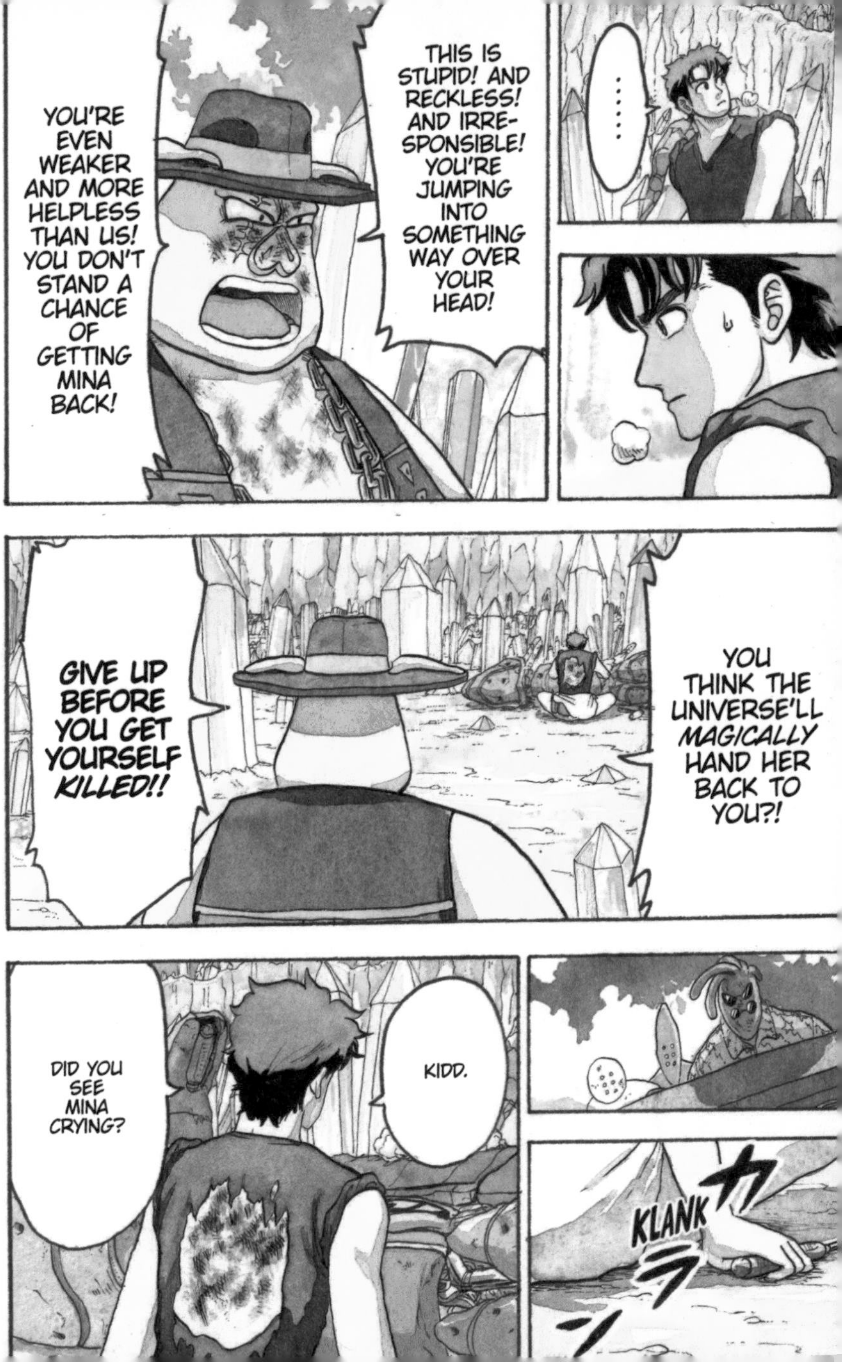
......
THIS IS STUPID! AND RECKLESS! AND IRRE-SPONSIBLE! YOU'RE JUMPING INTO SOMETHING WAY OVER YOUR HEAD!
YOU'RE EVEN WEAKER AND MORE HELPLESS THAN US! YOU DON'T STAND A CHANCE OF GETTING MINA BACK!
YOU THINK THE UNIVERSE'LL *MAGICALLY* HAND HER BACK TO YOU?!
GIVE UP BEFORE YOU GET YOURSELF *KILLED!!*
KLANK
KIDD.
DID YOU SEE MINA CRYING?

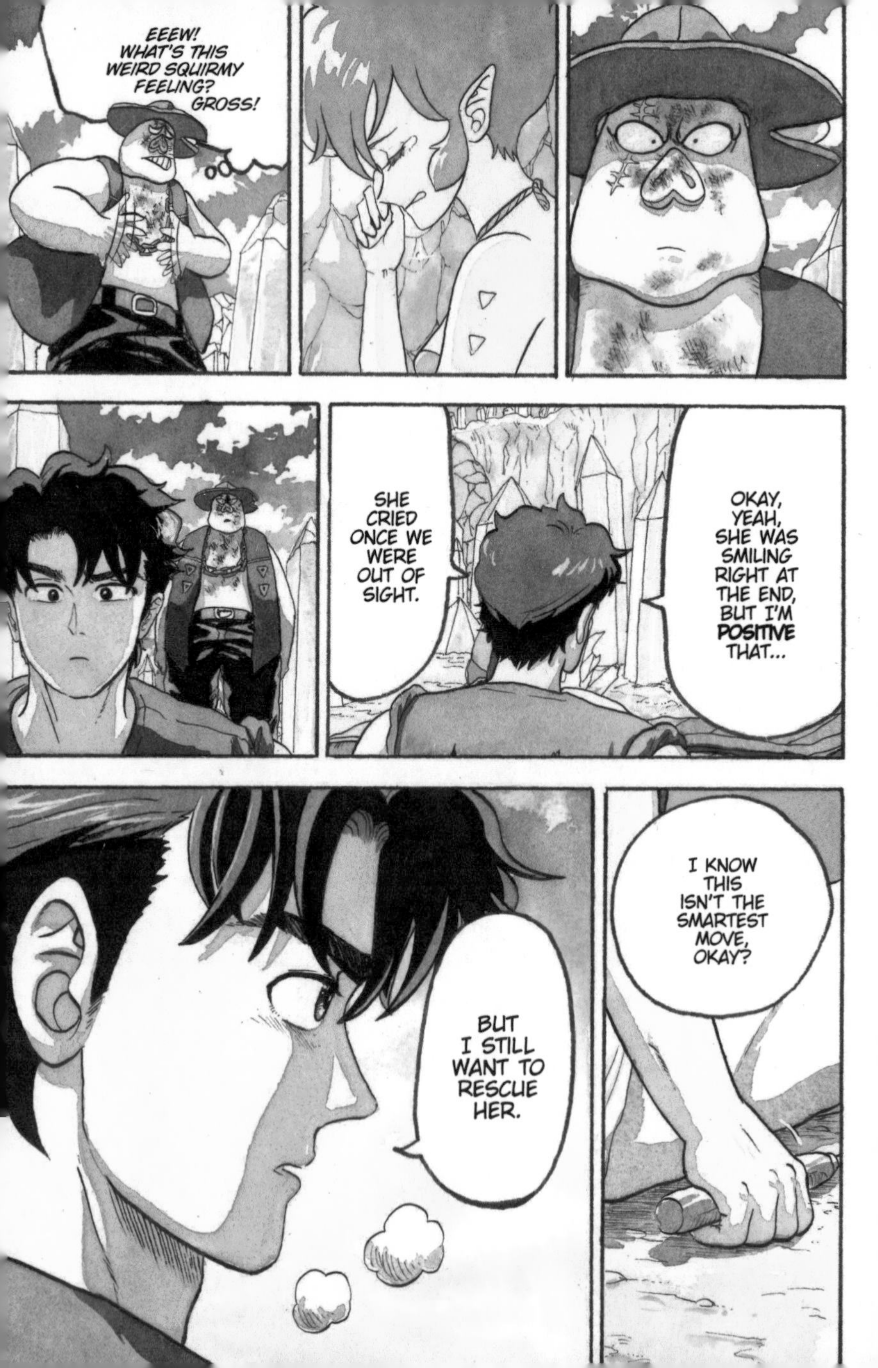
EEEW! WHAT'S THIS WEIRD SQUIRMY FEELING? GROSS!
OKAY, YEAH, SHE WAS SMILING RIGHT AT THE END, BUT I'M **POSITIVE** THAT...
SHE CRIED ONCE WE WERE OUT OF SIGHT.
I KNOW THIS ISN'T THE SMARTEST MOVE, OKAY?
BUT I STILL WANT TO RESCUE HER.

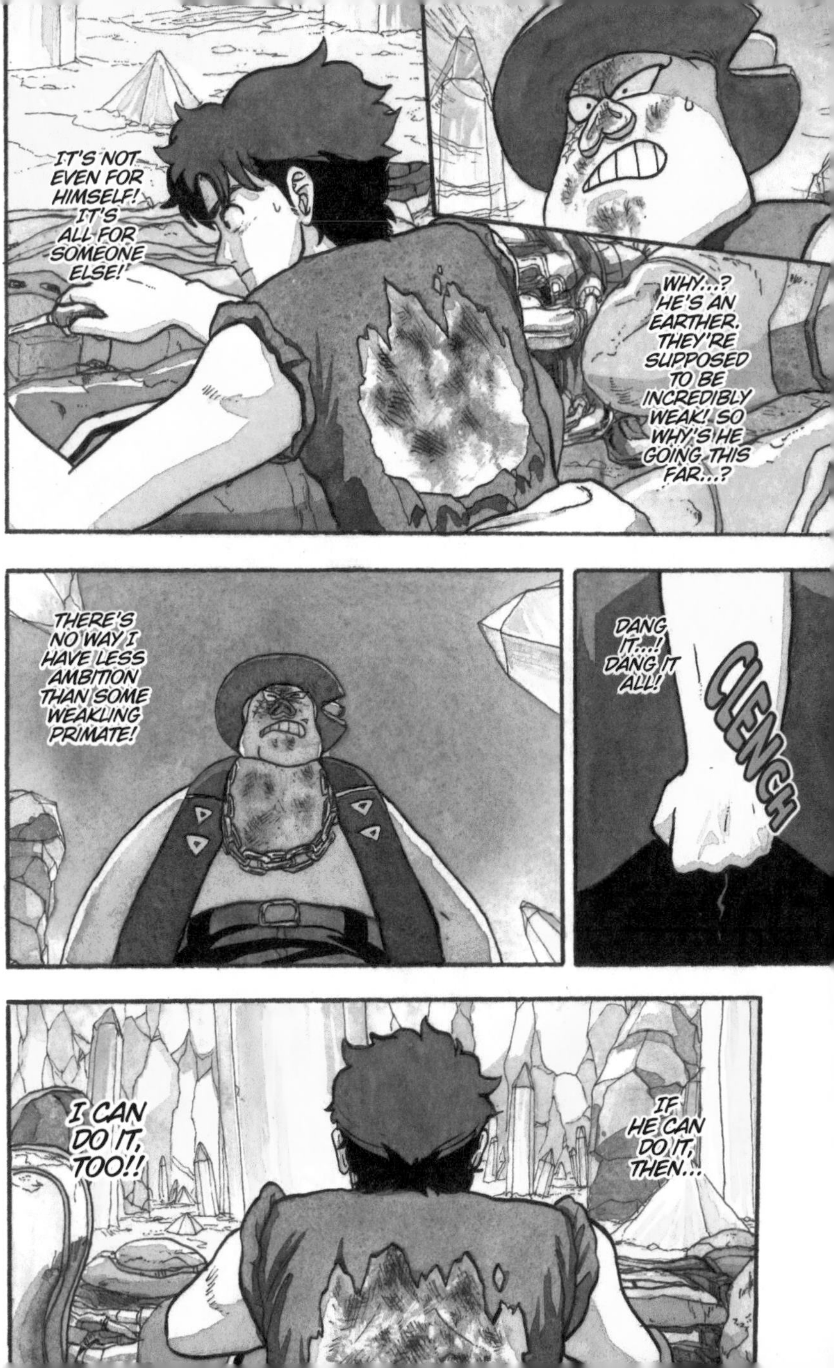
WHY...? HE'S AN EARTHER. THEY'RE SUPPOSED TO BE INCREDIBLY WEAK! SO WHY'S HE GOING THIS FAR...?
IT'S NOT EVEN FOR HIMSELF! IT'S ALL FOR SOMEONE ELSE!
DANG IT...! DANG IT ALL!
CLENCH
THERE'S NO WAY I HAVE LESS AMBITION THAN SOME WEAKLING PRIMATE!
IF HE CAN DO IT, THEN...
I CAN DO IT, TOO!!

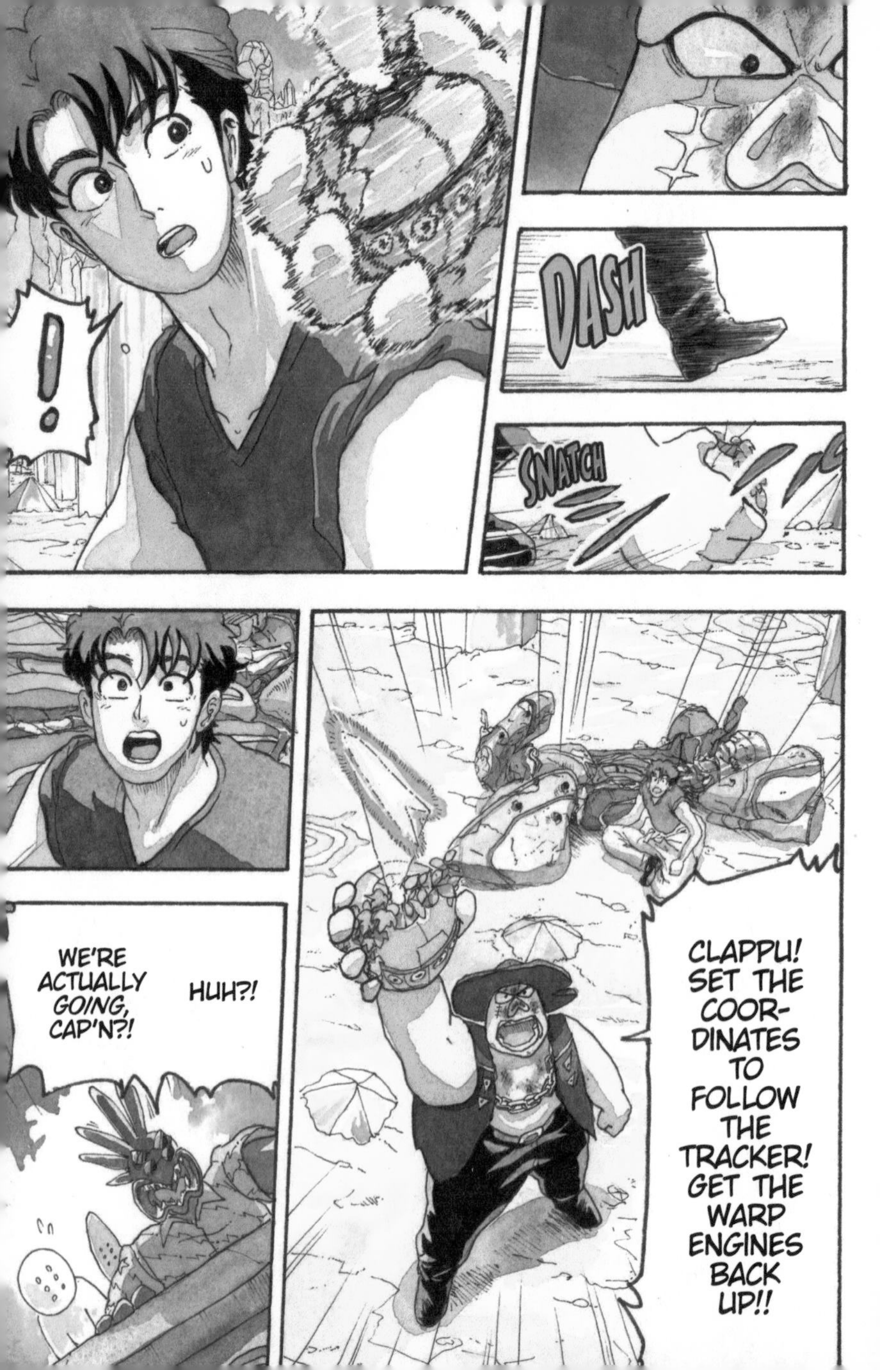
DASH
SNATCH
!
CLAPPU! SET THE COORDINATES TO FOLLOW THE TRACKER! GET THE WARP ENGINES BACK UP!!
HUH?!
WE'RE ACTUALLY GOING, CAP'N?!

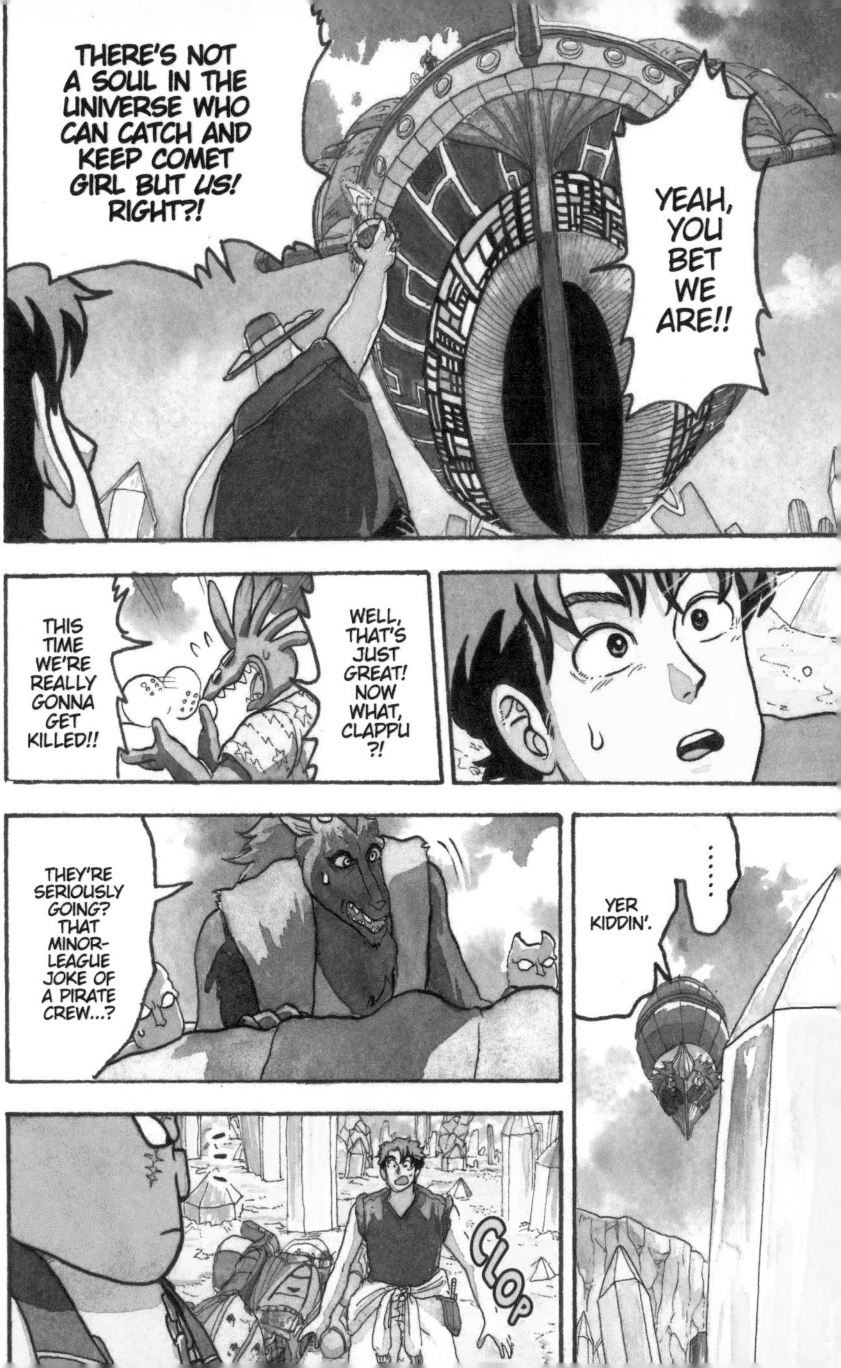
THERE'S NOT A SOUL IN THE UNIVERSE WHO CAN CATCH AND KEEP COMET GIRL BUT *US!* RIGHT?!
YEAH, YOU BET WE ARE!!
WELL, THAT'S JUST GREAT! NOW WHAT, CLAPPU?!
THIS TIME WE'RE REALLY GONNA GET KILLED!!
......
YER KIDDIN'.
THEY'RE SERIOUSLY GOING? THAT MINOR-LEAGUE JOKE OF A PIRATE CREW...?
CLOP

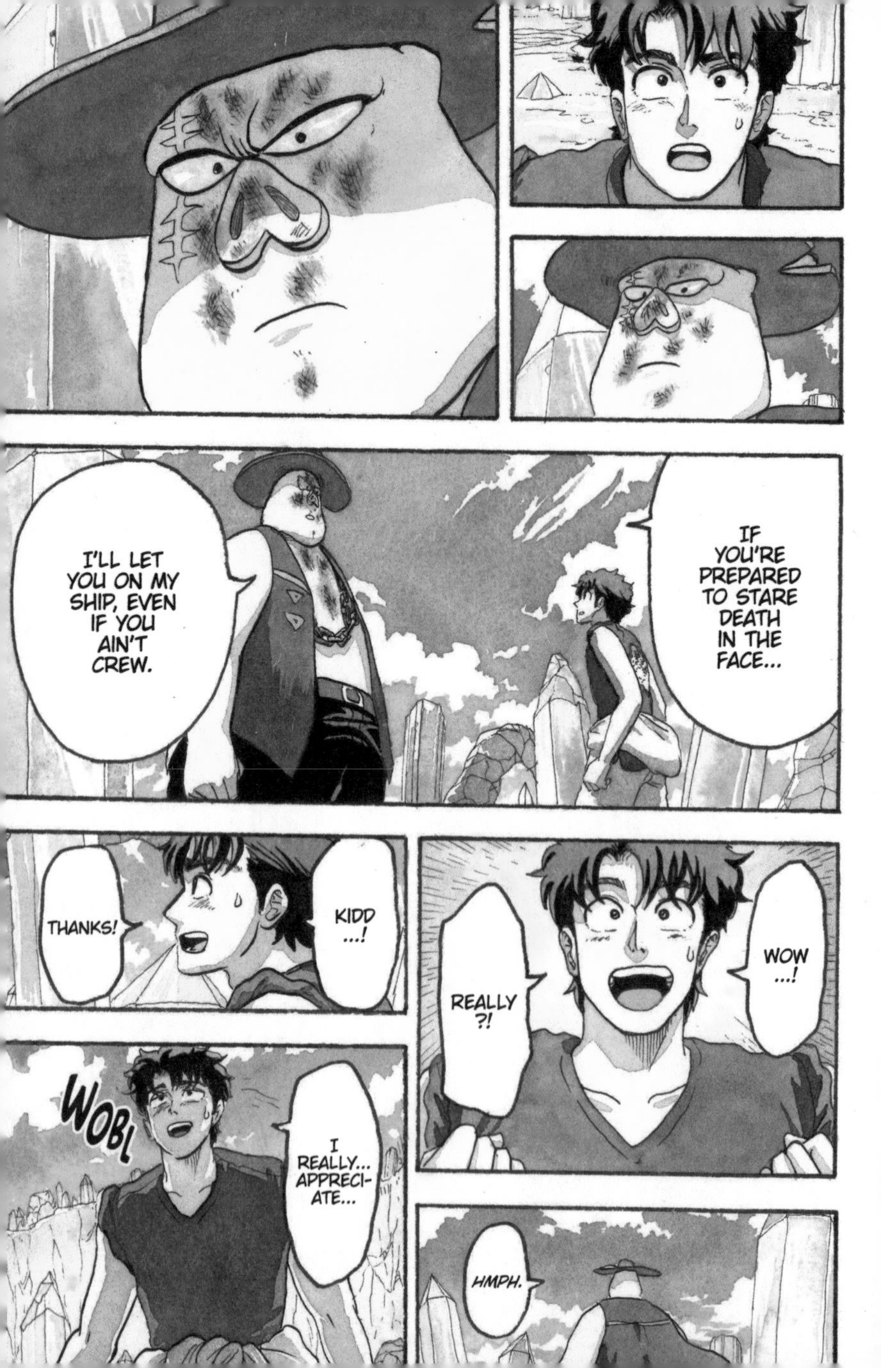
IF YOU'RE PREPARED TO STARE DEATH IN THE FACE...
I'LL LET YOU ON MY SHIP, EVEN IF YOU AIN'T CREW.
WOW ...!
REALLY ?!
KIDD ...!
THANKS!
WOBL
I REALLY... APPRECIATE...
HMPH.

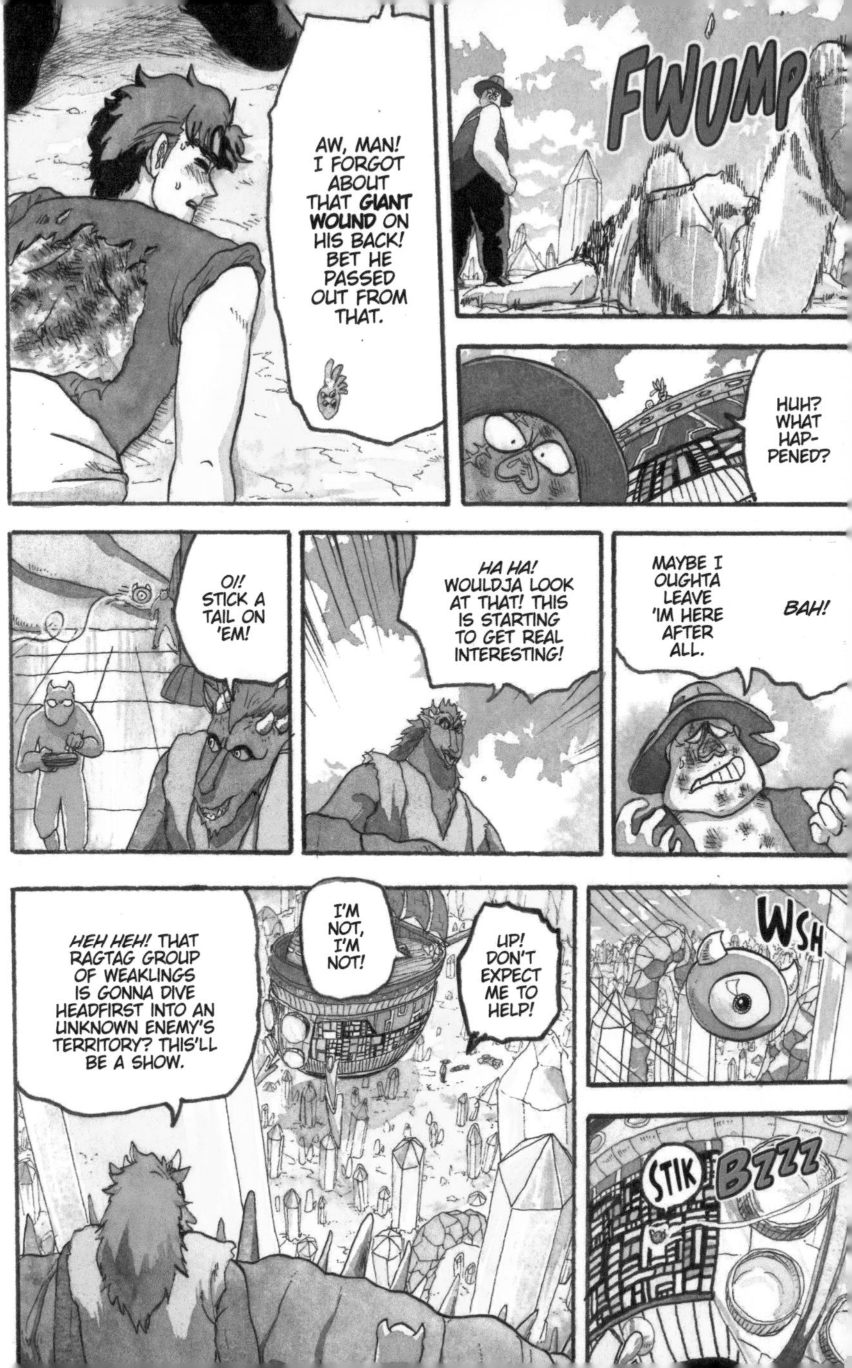
FWUMP
HUH? WHAT HAP-PENED?
AW, MAN! I FORGOT ABOUT THAT **GIANT WOUND** ON HIS BACK! BET HE PASSED OUT FROM THAT.
BAH!
MAYBE I OUGHTA LEAVE 'IM HERE AFTER ALL.
HA HA! WOULDJA LOOK AT THAT! THIS IS STARTING TO GET REAL INTERESTING!
OI! STICK A TAIL ON 'EM!
WSH
STIK
BZZZ
I'M NOT, I'M NOT!
UP! DON'T EXPECT ME TO HELP!
HEH HEH! THAT RAGTAG GROUP OF WEAKLINGS IS GONNA DIVE HEADFIRST INTO AN UNKNOWN ENEMY'S TERRITORY? THIS'LL BE A SHOW.

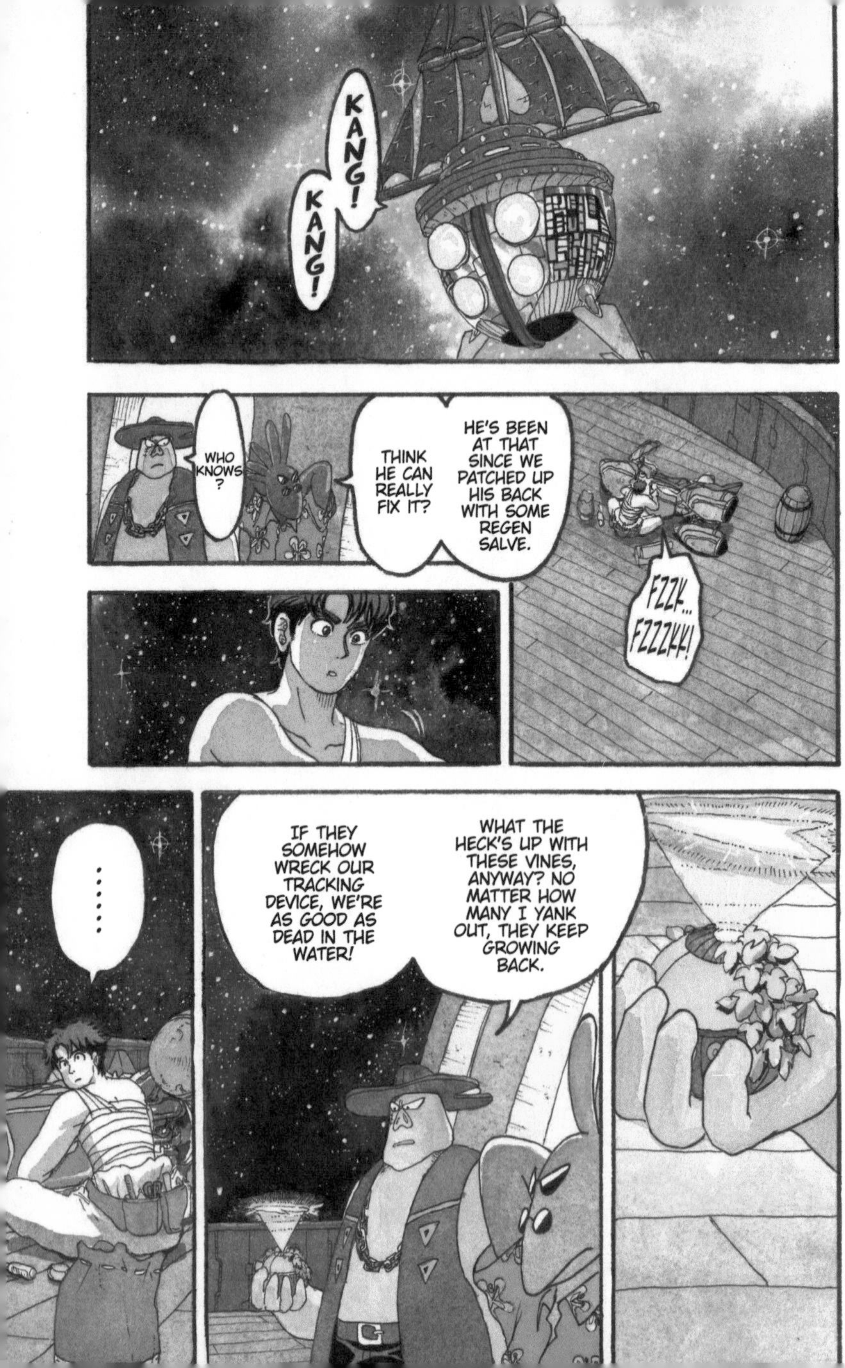
KANG! KANG!
HE'S BEEN AT THAT SINCE WE PATCHED UP HIS BACK WITH SOME REGEN SALVE.
THINK HE CAN REALLY FIX IT?
WHO KNOWS?
FZZK... FZZZKK!
WHAT THE HECK'S UP WITH THESE VINES, ANYWAY? NO MATTER HOW MANY I YANK OUT, THEY KEEP GROWING BACK.
IF THEY SOMEHOW WRECK OUR TRACKING DEVICE, WE'RE AS GOOD AS DEAD IN THE WATER!
......

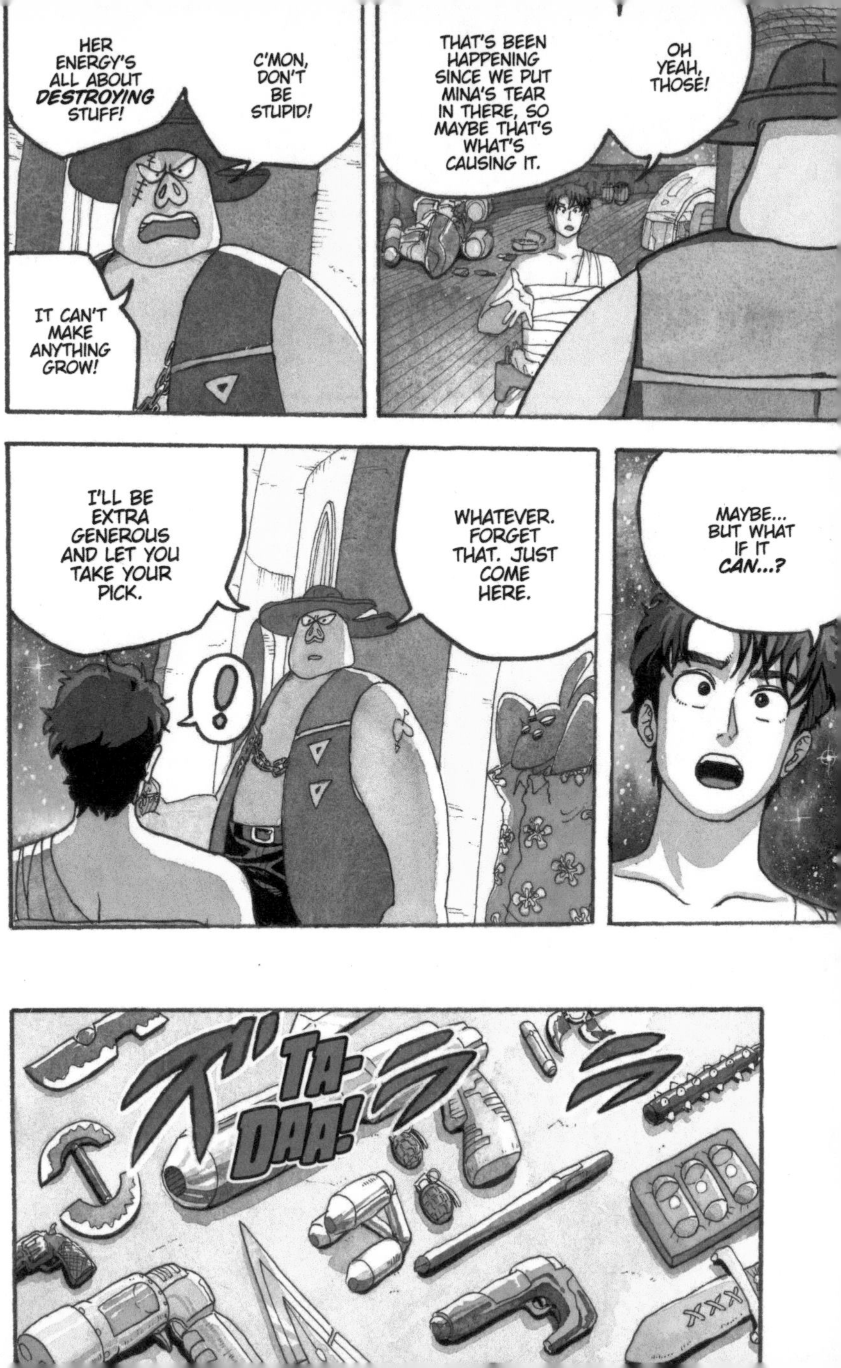
OH YEAH, THOSE!
THAT'S BEEN HAPPENING SINCE WE PUT MINA'S TEAR IN THERE, SO MAYBE THAT'S WHAT'S CAUSING IT.
C'MON, DON'T BE STUPID!
HER ENERGY'S ALL ABOUT *DESTROYING* STUFF!
IT CAN'T MAKE ANYTHING GROW!
MAYBE... BUT WHAT IF IT *CAN...?*
WHATEVER. FORGET THAT. JUST COME HERE.
!
I'LL BE EXTRA GENEROUS AND LET YOU TAKE YOUR PICK.
TA-DAA!

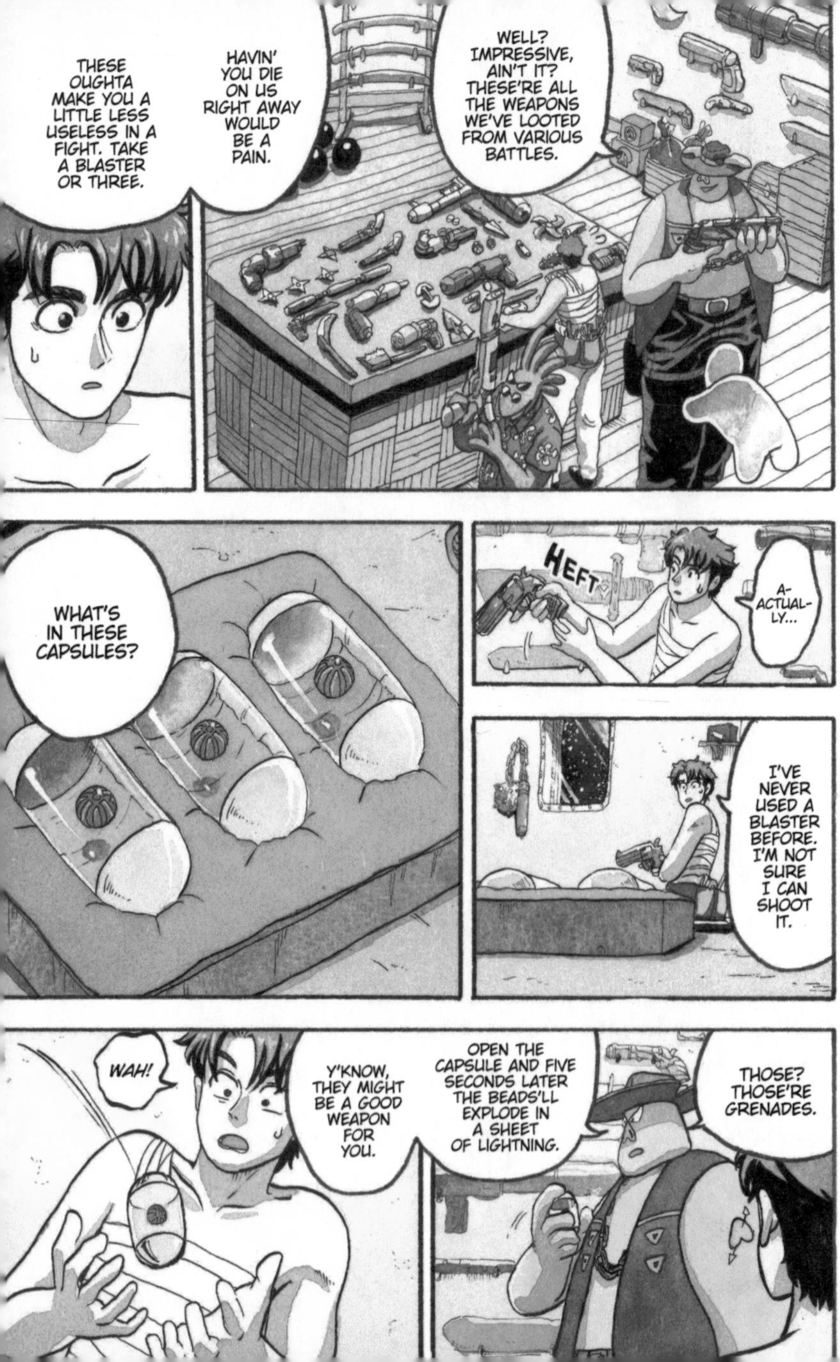
WELL? IMPRESSIVE, AIN'T IT? THESE'RE ALL THE WEAPONS WE'VE LOOTED FROM VARIOUS BATTLES.
HAVIN' YOU DIE ON US RIGHT AWAY WOULD BE A PAIN.
THESE OUGHTA MAKE YOU A LITTLE LESS USELESS IN A FIGHT. TAKE A BLASTER OR THREE.
HEFT
A-ACTUAL-LY...
I'VE NEVER USED A BLASTER BEFORE. I'M NOT SURE I CAN SHOOT IT.
WHAT'S IN THESE CAPSULES?
THOSE? THOSE'RE GRENADES.
OPEN THE CAPSULE AND FIVE SECONDS LATER THE BEADS'LL EXPLODE IN A SHEET OF LIGHTNING.
Y'KNOW, THEY MIGHT BE A GOOD WEAPON FOR YOU.
WAH!

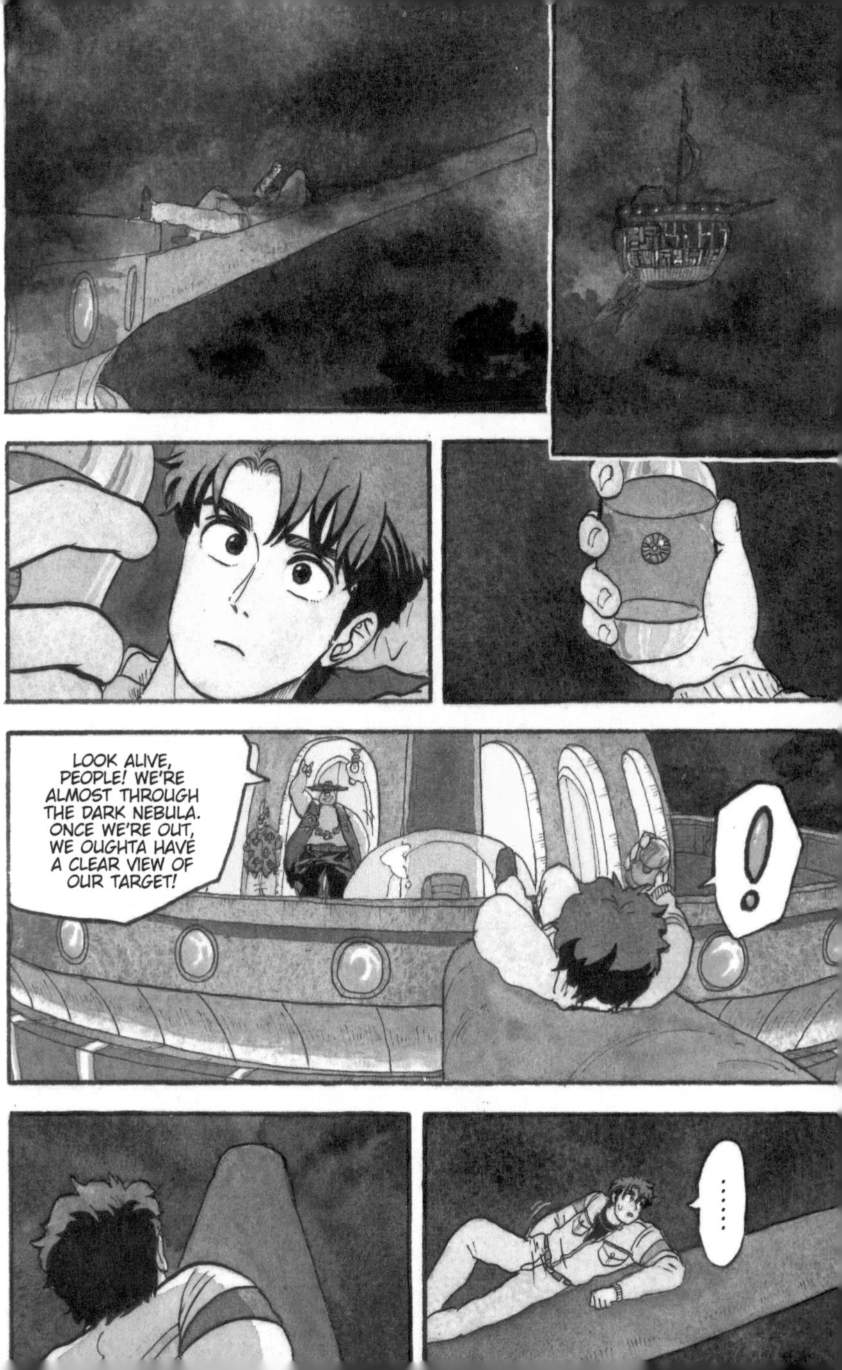
!
LOOK ALIVE, PEOPLE! WE'RE ALMOST THROUGH THE DARK NEBULA. ONCE WE'RE OUT, WE OUGHTA HAVE A CLEAR VIEW OF OUR TARGET!
......

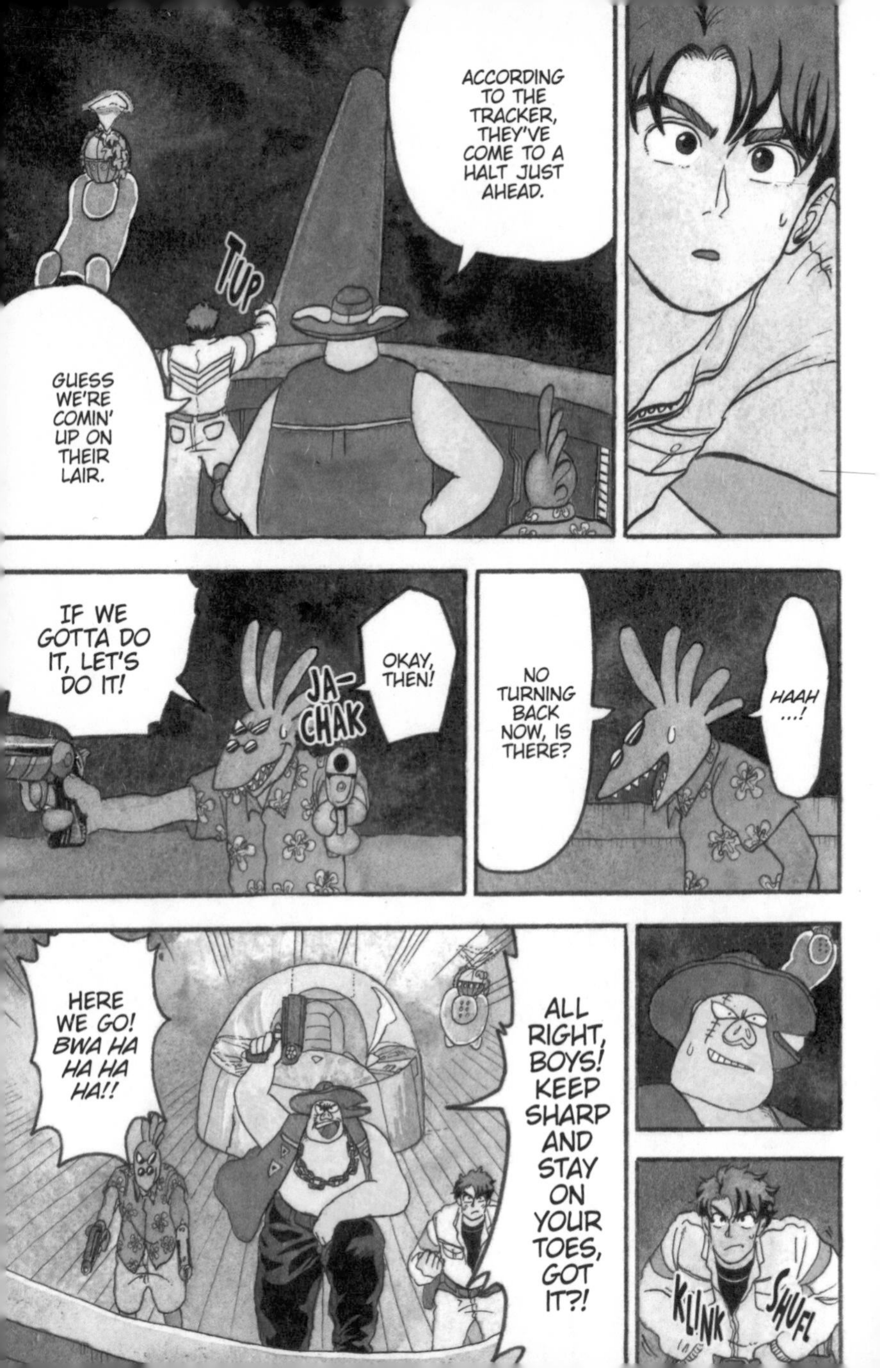
ACCORDING TO THE TRACKER, THEY'VE COME TO A HALT JUST AHEAD.
TUP
GUESS WE'RE COMIN' UP ON THEIR LAIR.
HAAH ...!
NO TURNING BACK NOW, IS THERE?
OKAY, THEN!
JA-CHAK
IF WE GOTTA DO IT, LET'S DO IT!
KLINK
SHUFL
ALL RIGHT, BOYS! KEEP SHARP AND STAY ON YOUR TOES, GOT IT?!
HERE WE GO! BWA HA HA HA HA!!

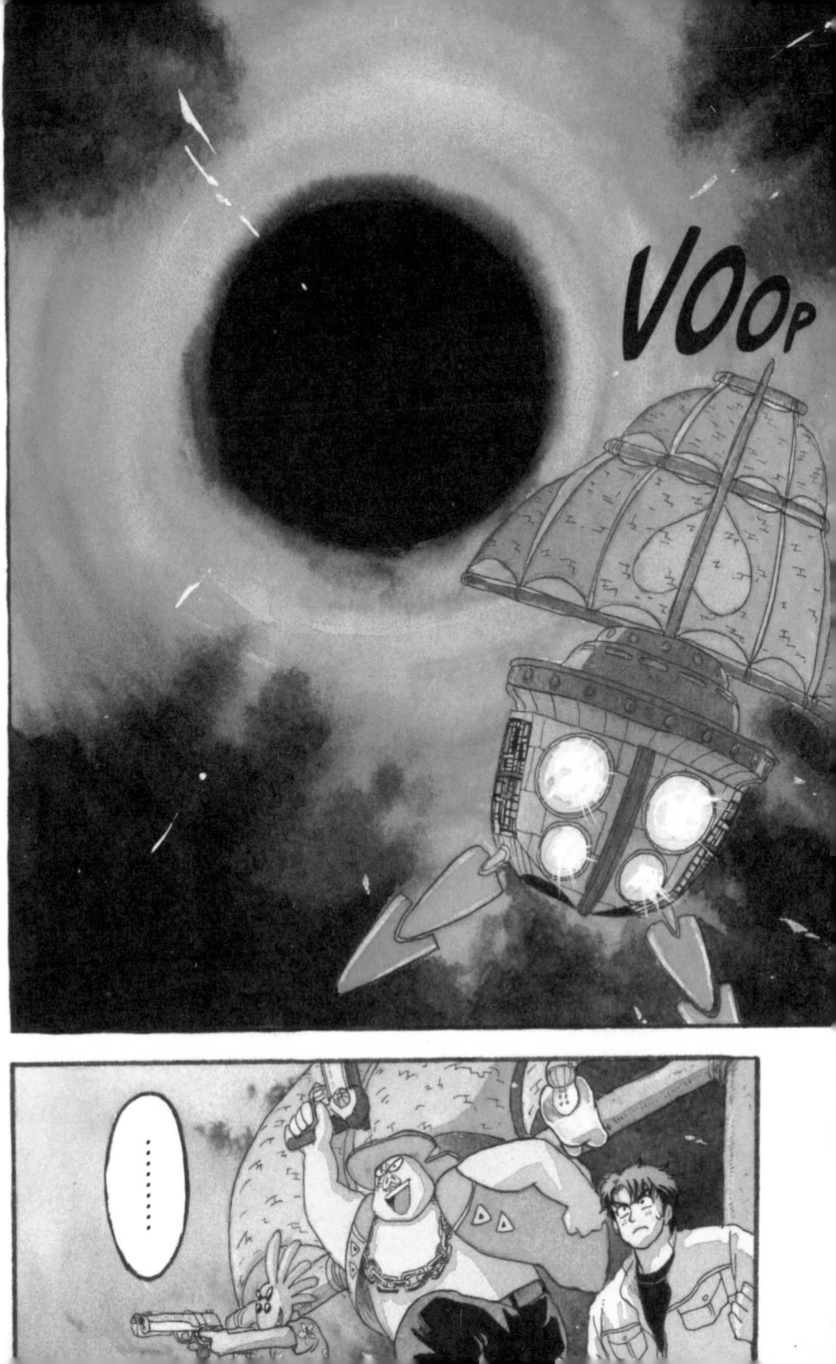
VOOP
....

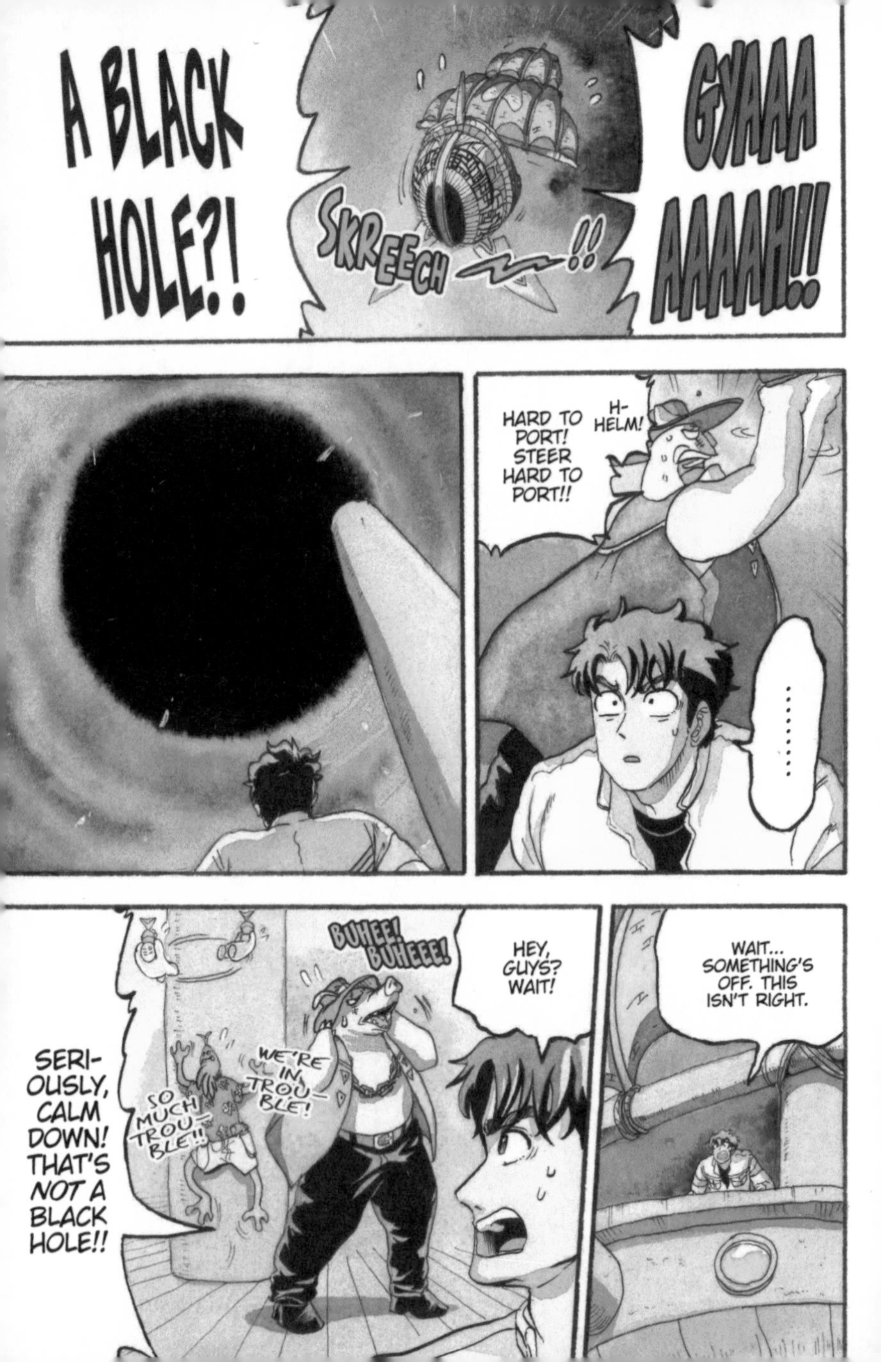
GYAAA AAAAH!!
SKREECH!!
A BLACK HOLE?!
H- HELM!
HARD TO PORT! STEER HARD TO PORT!!
……
WAIT... SOMETHING'S OFF. THIS ISN'T RIGHT.
HEY, GUYS? WAIT!
BUHEE! BUHEEE!
WE'RE IN TROUBLE!
SO MUCH TROUBLE!!
SERIOUSLY, CALM DOWN! THAT'S *NOT A* BLACK HOLE!!

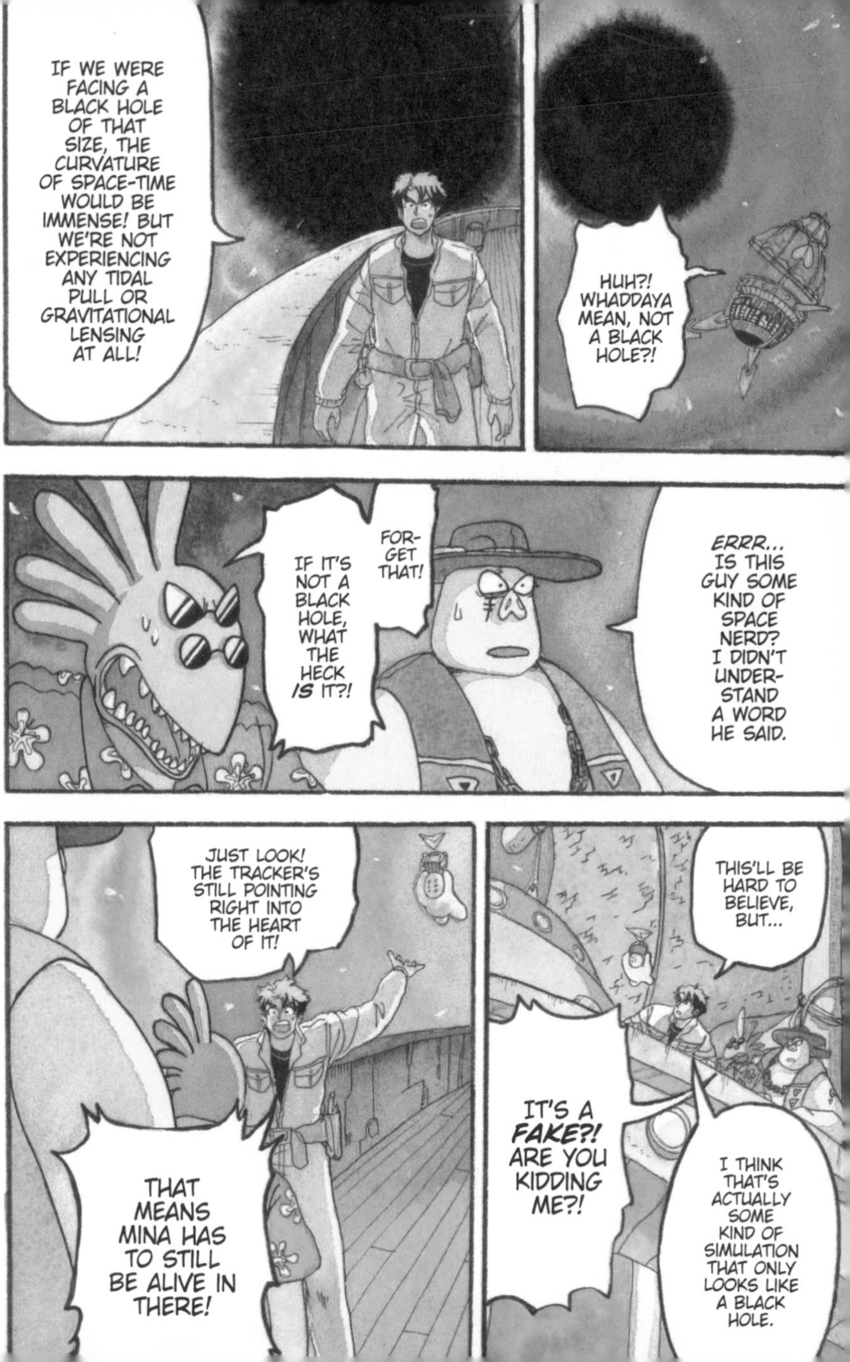
HUH?! WHADDAYA MEAN, NOT A BLACK HOLE?!
IF WE WERE FACING A BLACK HOLE OF THAT SIZE, THE CURVATURE OF SPACE-TIME WOULD BE IMMENSE! BUT WE'RE NOT EXPERIENCING ANY TIDAL PULL OR GRAVITATIONAL LENSING AT ALL!
ERRR... IS THIS GUY SOME KIND OF SPACE NERD? I DIDN'T UNDERSTAND A WORD HE SAID.
FOR-GET THAT!
IF IT'S NOT A BLACK HOLE, WHAT THE HECK ***IS*** IT?!
THIS'LL BE HARD TO BELIEVE, BUT...
I THINK THAT'S ACTUALLY SOME KIND OF SIMULATION THAT ONLY LOOKS LIKE A BLACK HOLE.
IT'S A ***FAKE?!*** ARE YOU KIDDING ME?!
JUST LOOK! THE TRACKER'S STILL POINTING RIGHT INTO THE HEART OF IT!
THAT MEANS MINA HAS TO STILL BE ALIVE IN THERE!

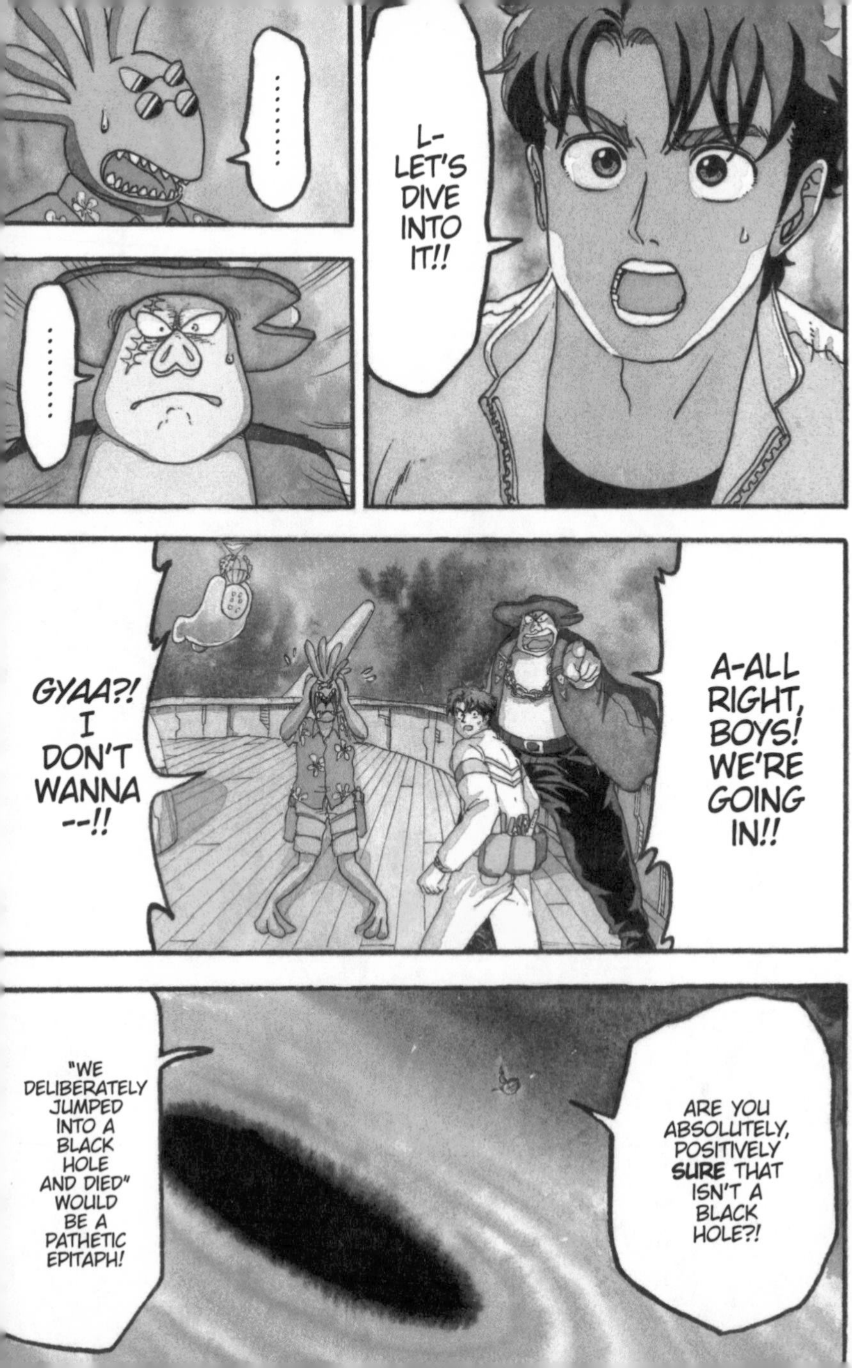
L-LET'S DIVE INTO IT!!
......
......
A-ALL RIGHT, BOYS! WE'RE GOING IN!!
GYAA?! I DON'T WANNA--!!
ARE YOU ABSOLUTELY, POSITIVELY **SURE** THAT ISN'T A BLACK HOLE?!
"WE DELIBERATELY JUMPED INTO A BLACK HOLE AND DIED" WOULD BE A PATHETIC EPITAPH!

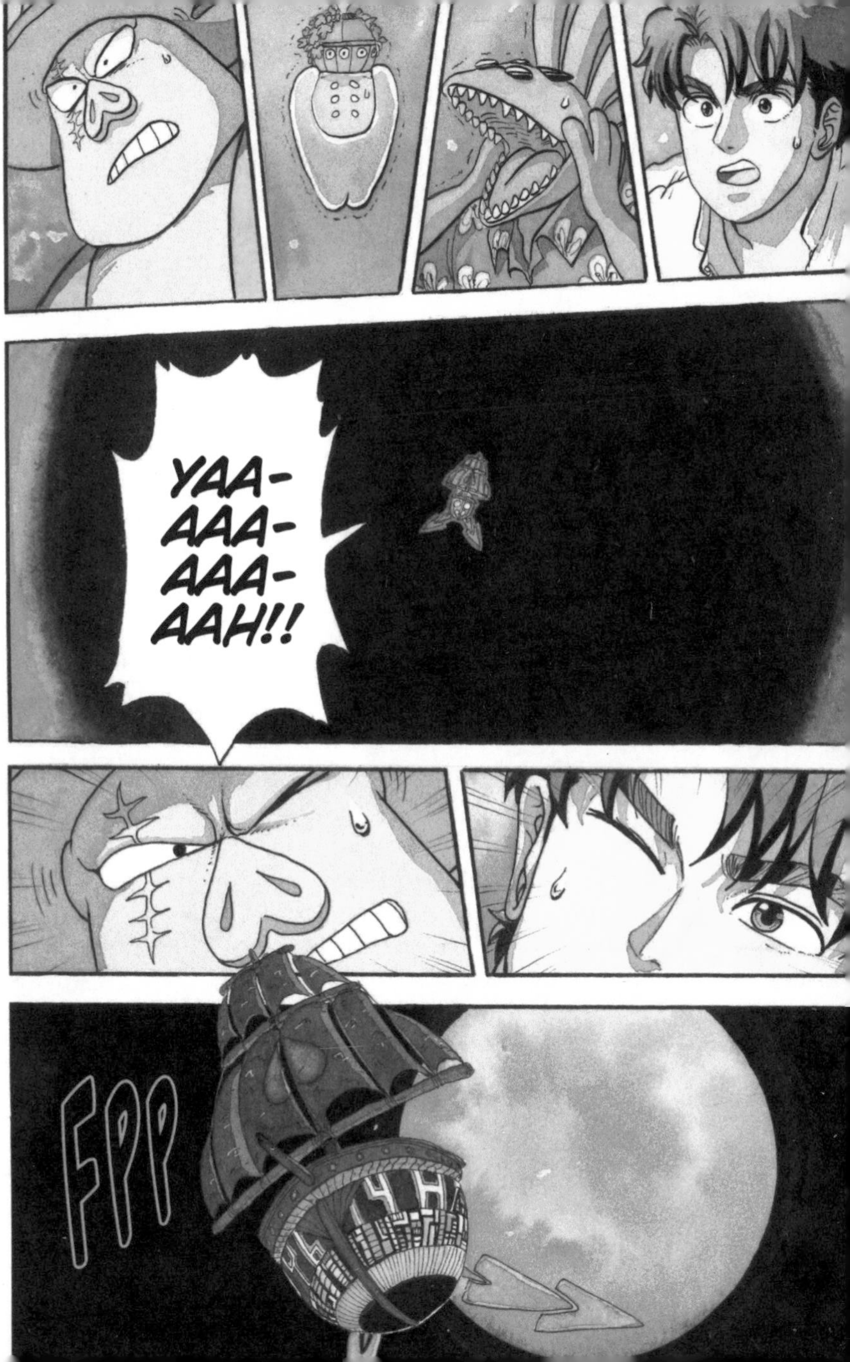
YAA-AAA-AAA-AAH!!
FPP

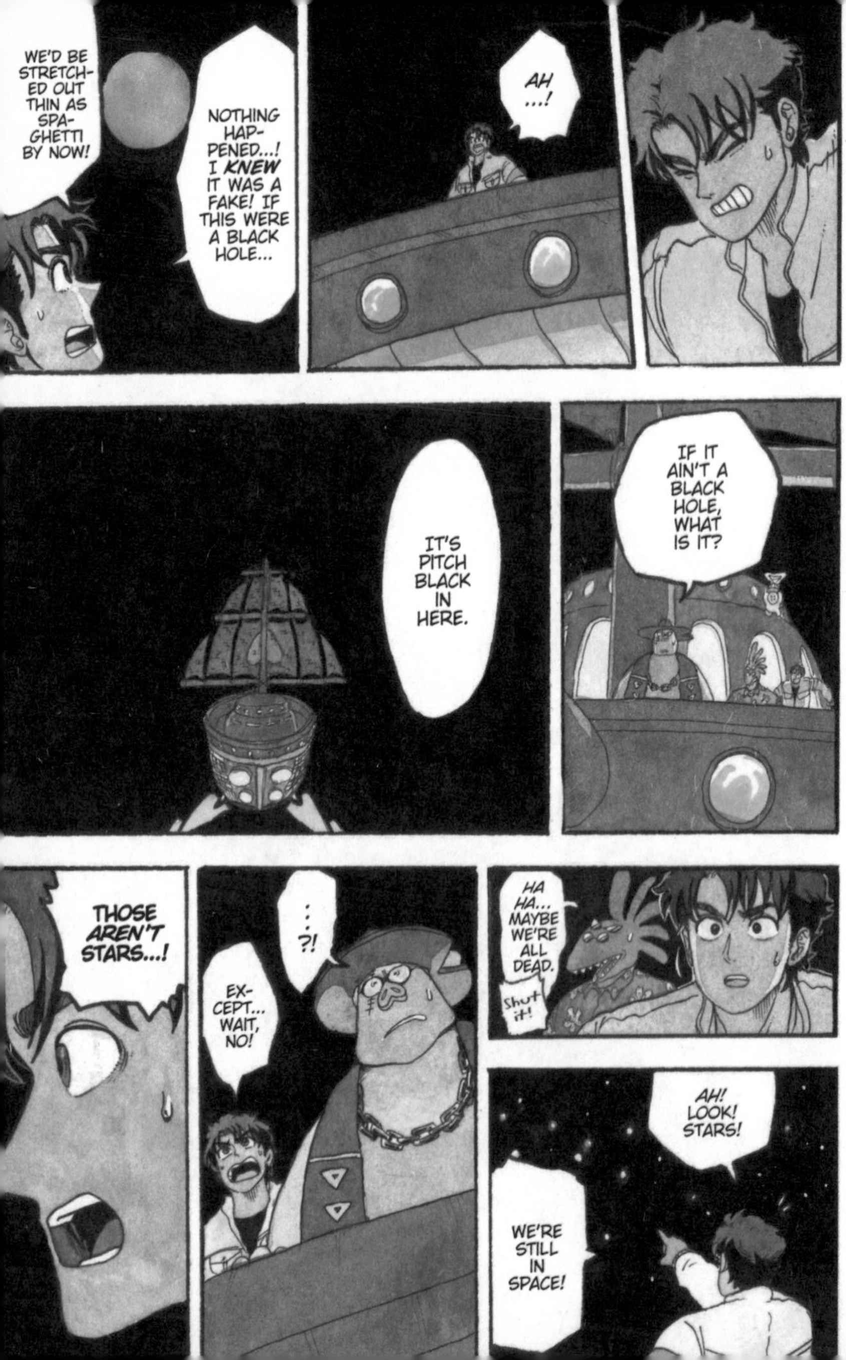
AH ...!
NOTHING HAPPENED...! I **KNEW** IT WAS A FAKE! IF THIS WERE A BLACK HOLE...
WE'D BE STRETCHED OUT THIN AS SPAGHETTI BY NOW!
IF IT AIN'T A BLACK HOLE, WHAT IS IT?
IT'S PITCH BLACK IN HERE.
HA HA... MAYBE WE'RE ALL DEAD.
Shut it!
AH! LOOK! STARS!
WE'RE STILL IN SPACE!
...?!
EXCEPT... WAIT, NO!
THOSE *AREN'T* STARS...!

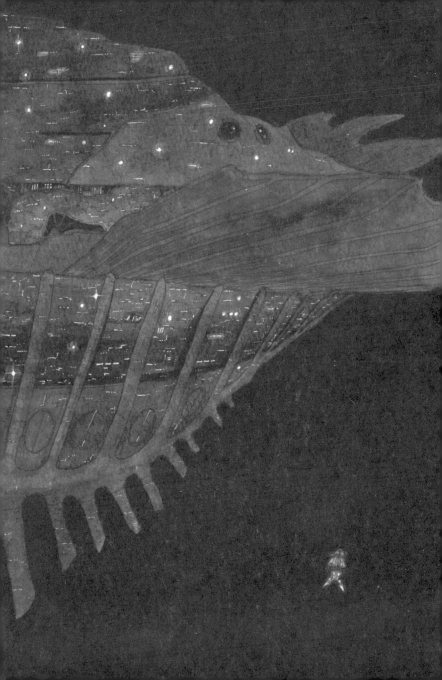

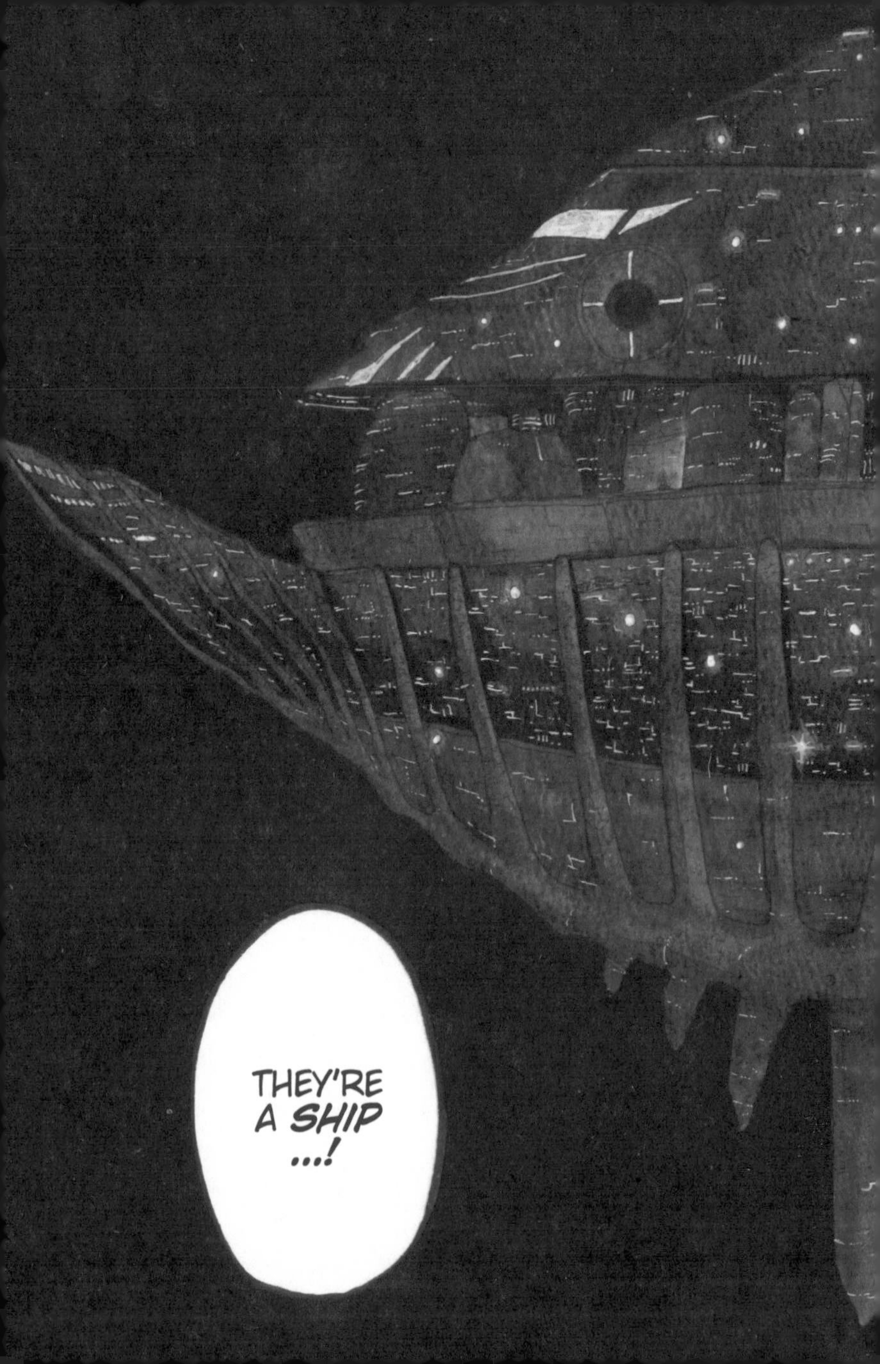
THEY'RE A *SHIP* ...!

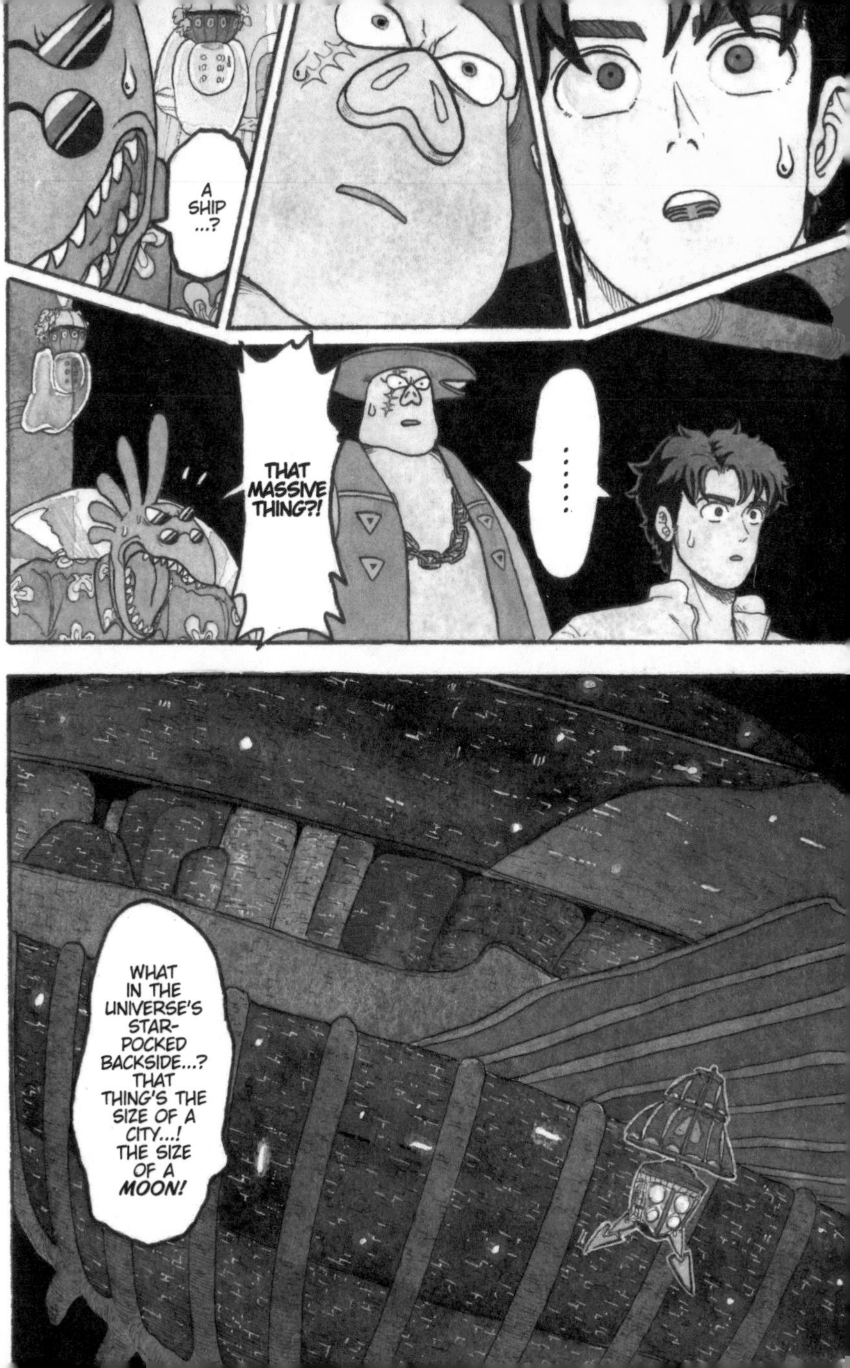
A SHIP ...?
......
THAT MASSIVE THING?!
WHAT IN THE UNIVERSE'S STAR-POCKED BACKSIDE...? THAT THING'S THE SIZE OF A CITY...! THE SIZE OF A *MOON!*

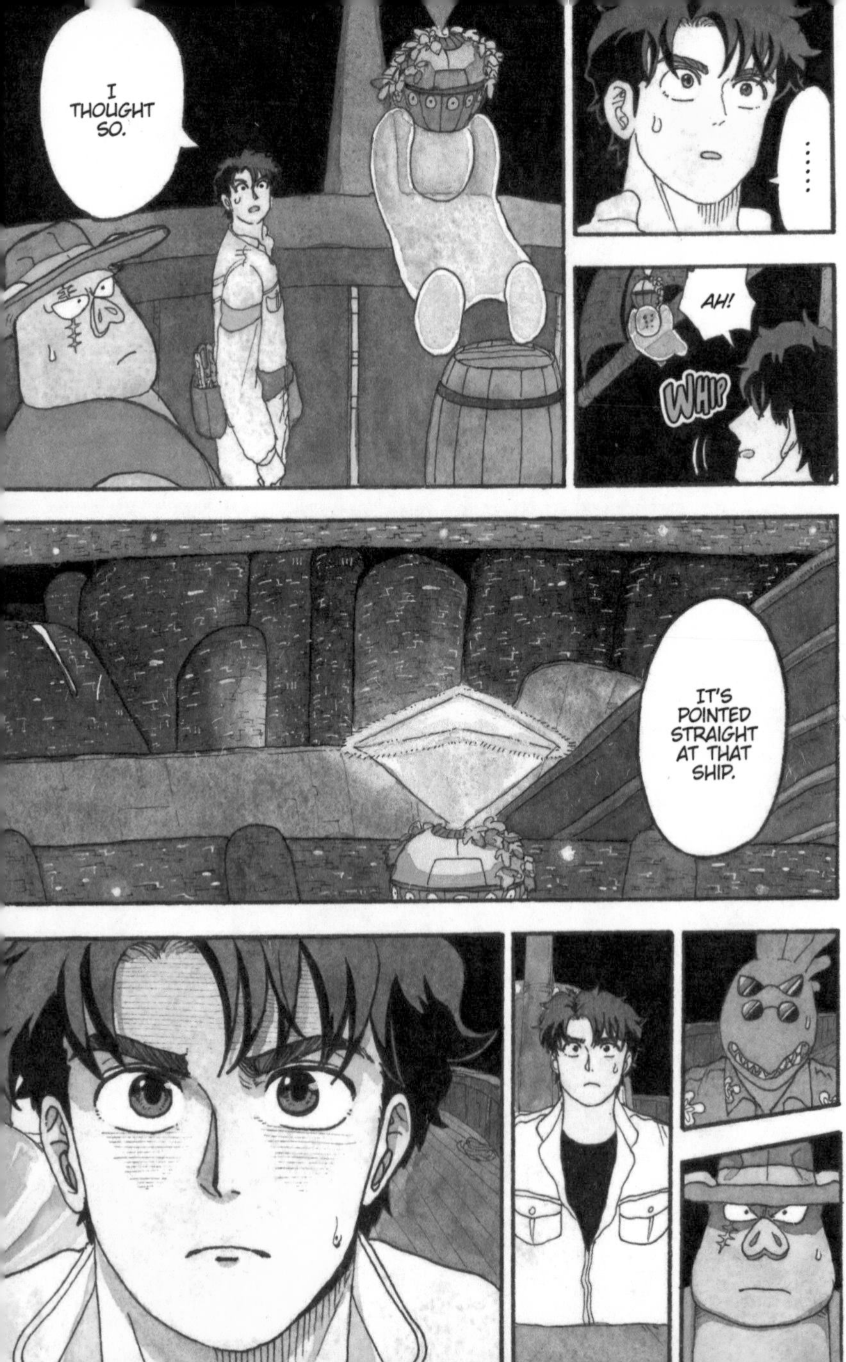
......
AH!
WHIP
I THOUGHT SO.
IT'S POINTED STRAIGHT AT THAT SHIP.

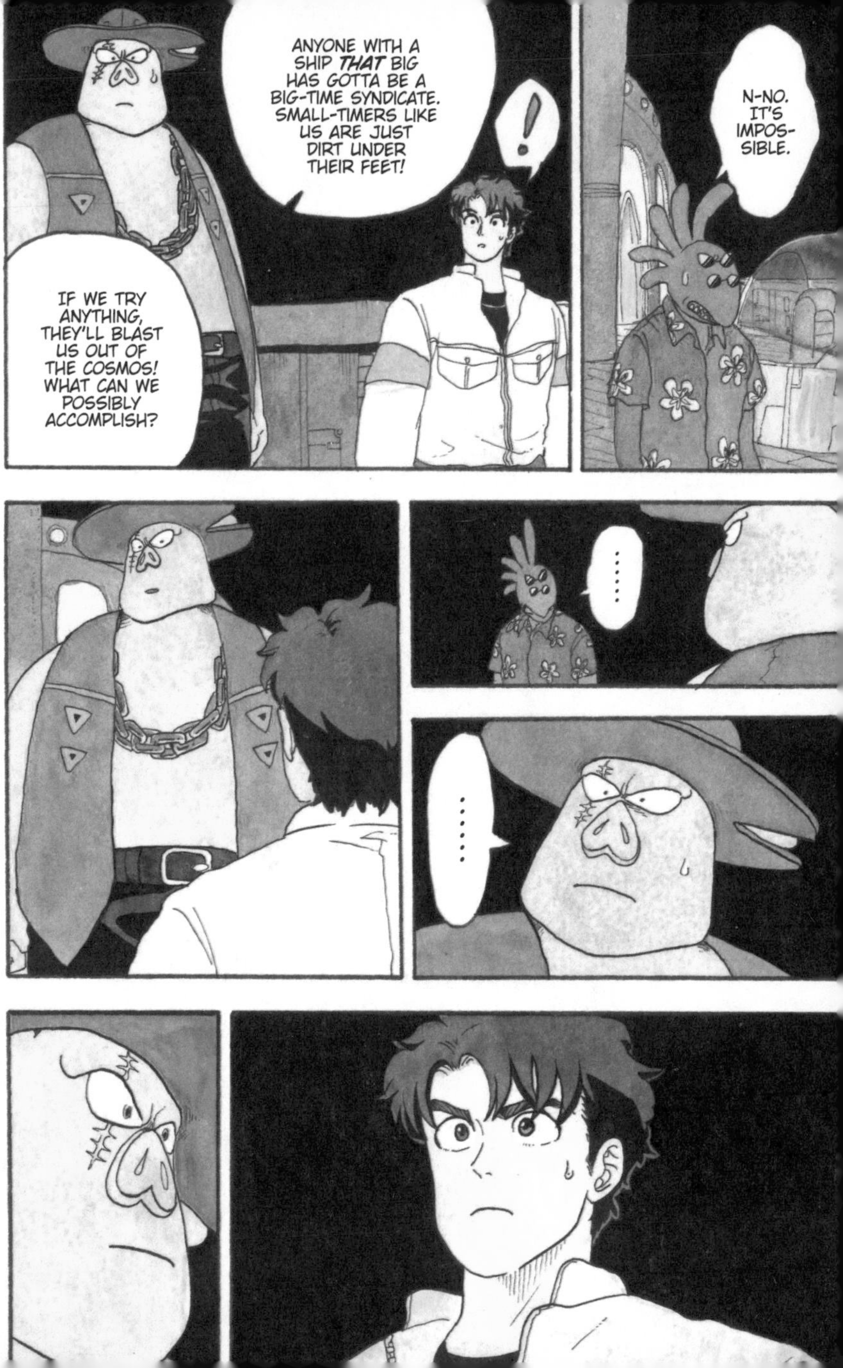
N-NO. IT'S IMPOSSIBLE.
ANYONE WITH A SHIP **THAT** BIG HAS GOTTA BE A BIG-TIME SYNDICATE. SMALL-TIMERS LIKE US ARE JUST DIRT UNDER THEIR FEET!
!
IF WE TRY ANYTHING, THEY'LL BLAST US OUT OF THE COSMOS! WHAT CAN WE POSSIBLY ACCOMPLISH?
......
......

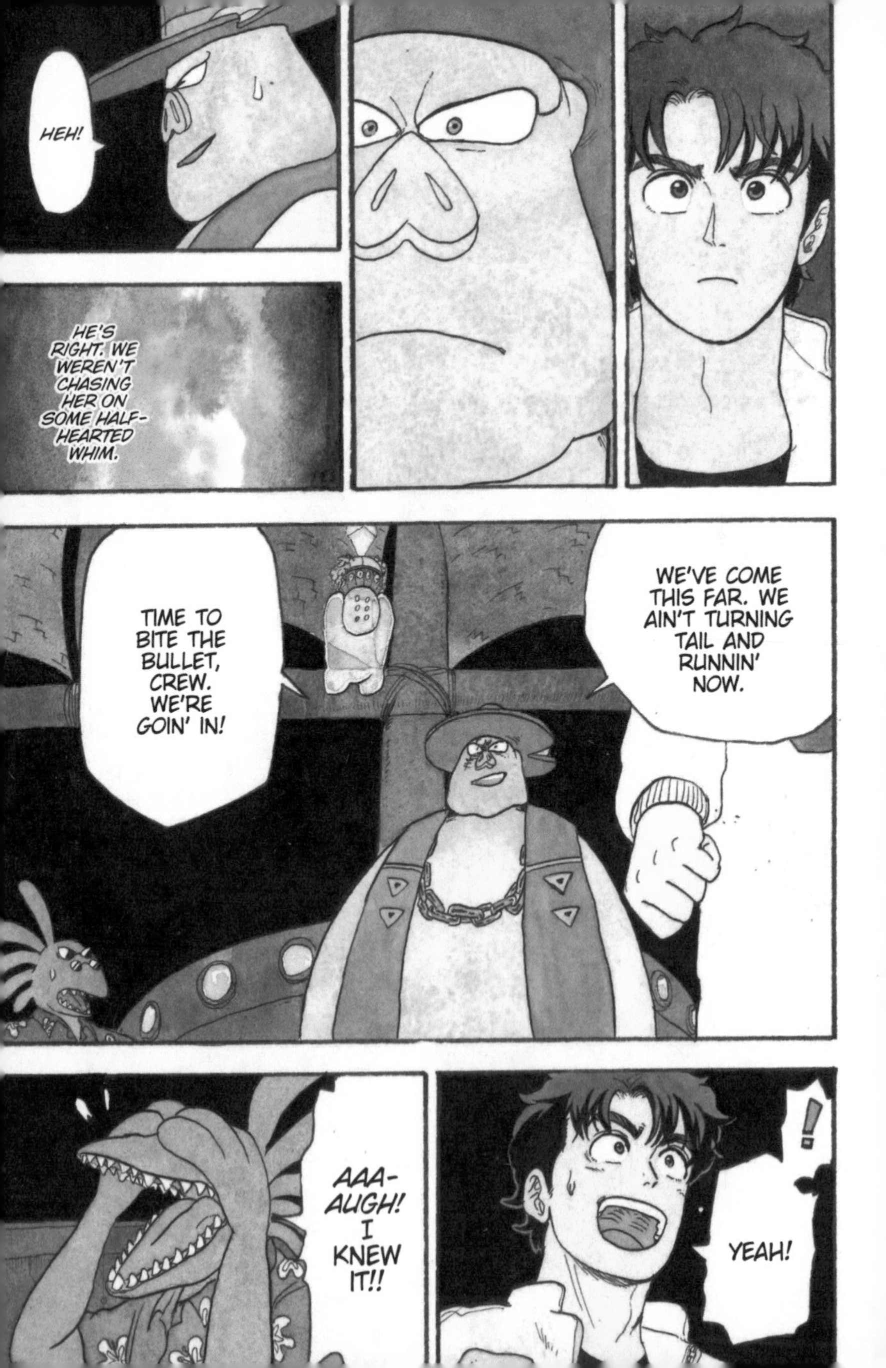
HEH!
HE'S RIGHT. WE WEREN'T CHASING HER ON SOME HALF-HEARTED WHIM.
WE'VE COME THIS FAR. WE AIN'T TURNING TAIL AND RUNNIN' NOW.
TIME TO BITE THE BULLET, CREW. WE'RE GOIN' IN!
!
YEAH!
AAA-AUGH! I KNEW IT!!

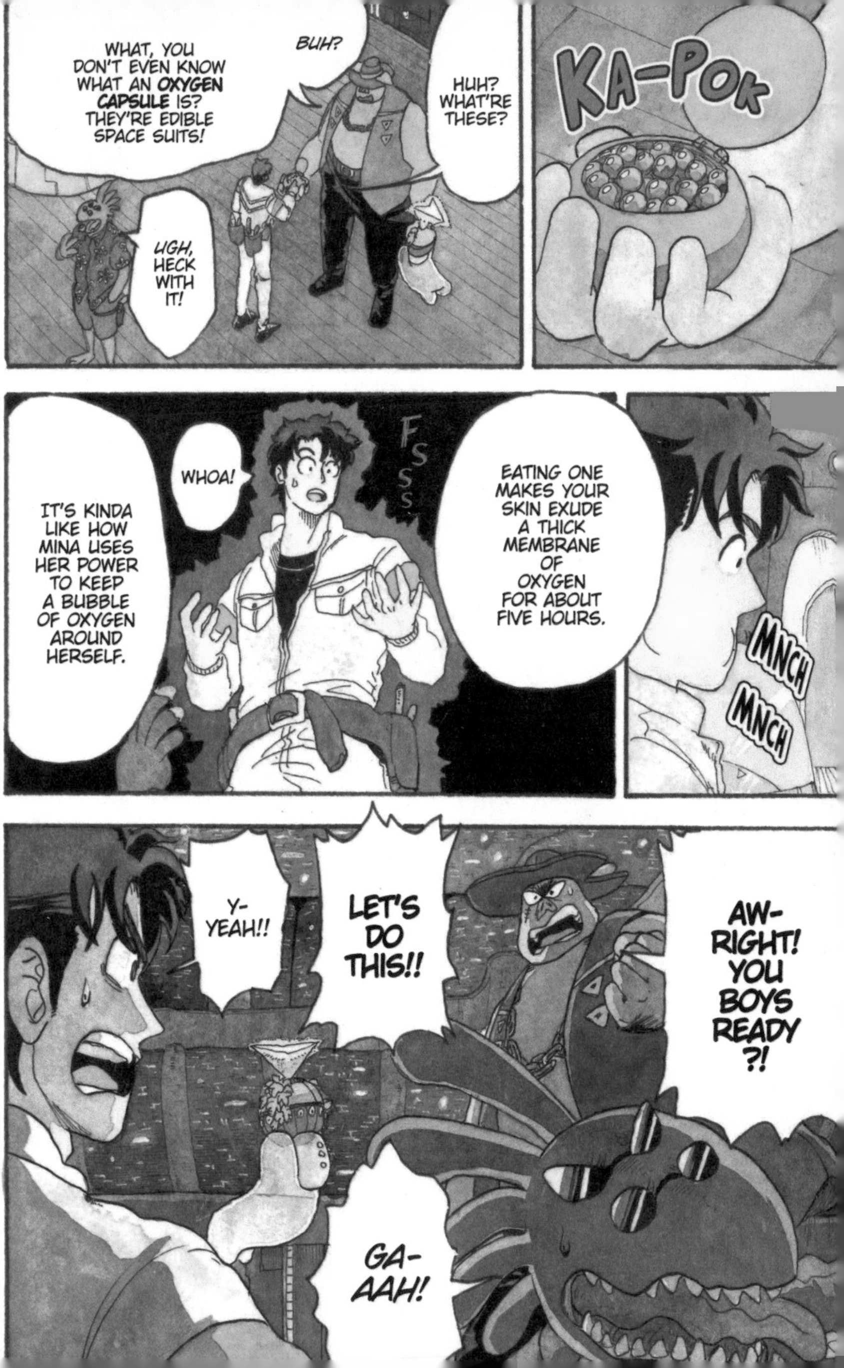

KA-POK
HUH? WHAT'RE THESE?
BUH?
WHAT, YOU DON'T EVEN KNOW WHAT AN **OXYGEN CAPSULE** IS? THEY'RE EDIBLE SPACE SUITS!
UGH, HECK WITH IT!
MNCH
MNCH
EATING ONE MAKES YOUR SKIN EXUDE A THICK MEMBRANE OF OXYGEN FOR ABOUT FIVE HOURS.
FSSS
WHOA!
IT'S KINDA LIKE HOW MINA USES HER POWER TO KEEP A BUBBLE OF OXYGEN AROUND HERSELF.
AW-RIGHT! YOU BOYS READY?!
LET'S DO THIS!!
Y-YEAH!!
GA-AAH!

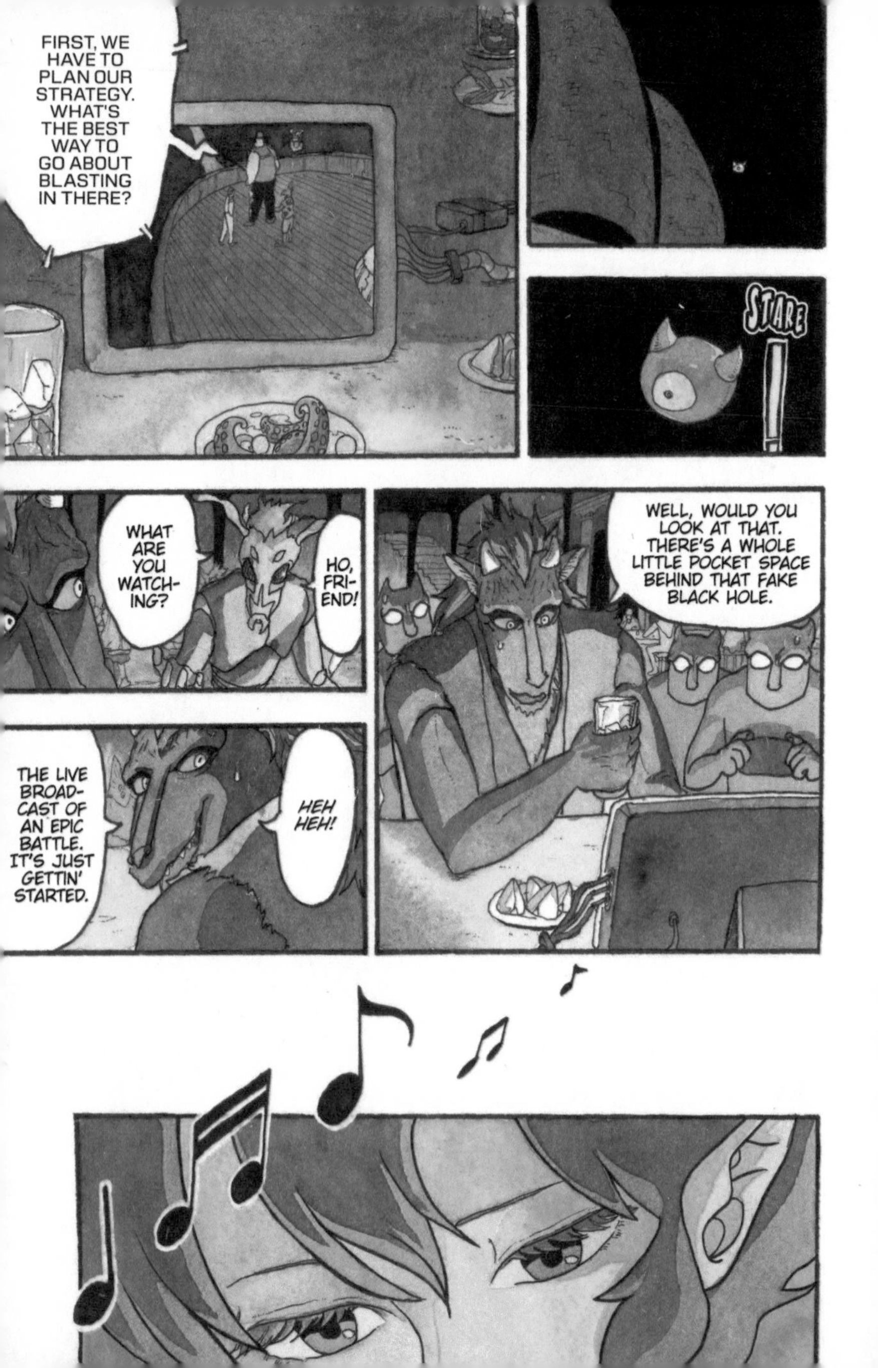
STARE
FIRST, WE HAVE TO PLAN OUR STRATEGY. WHAT'S THE BEST WAY TO GO ABOUT BLASTING IN THERE?
WELL, WOULD YOU LOOK AT THAT. THERE'S A WHOLE LITTLE POCKET SPACE BEHIND THAT FAKE BLACK HOLE.
HO, FRI-END!
WHAT ARE YOU WATCH-ING?
HEH HEH!
THE LIVE BROAD-CAST OF AN EPIC BATTLE. IT'S JUST GETTIN' STARTED.

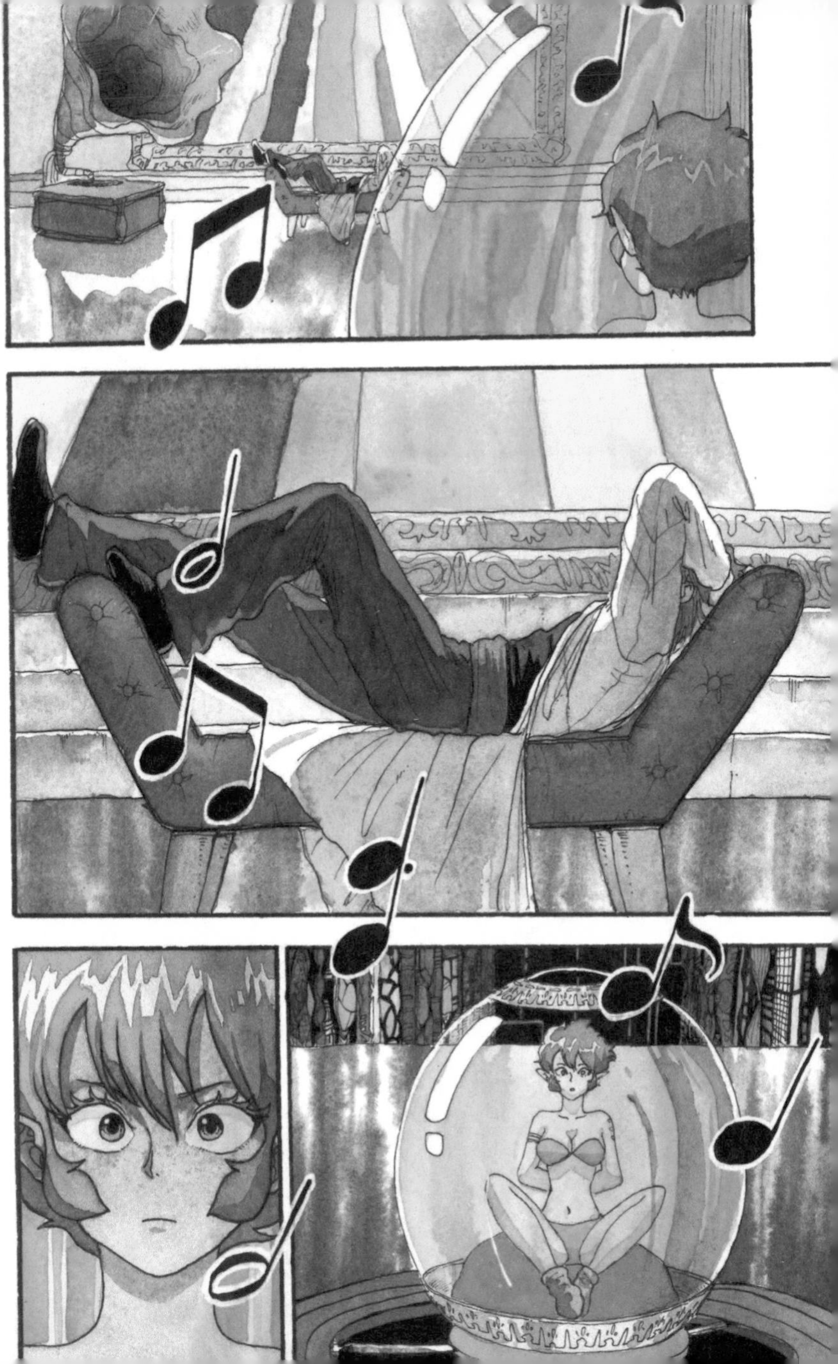

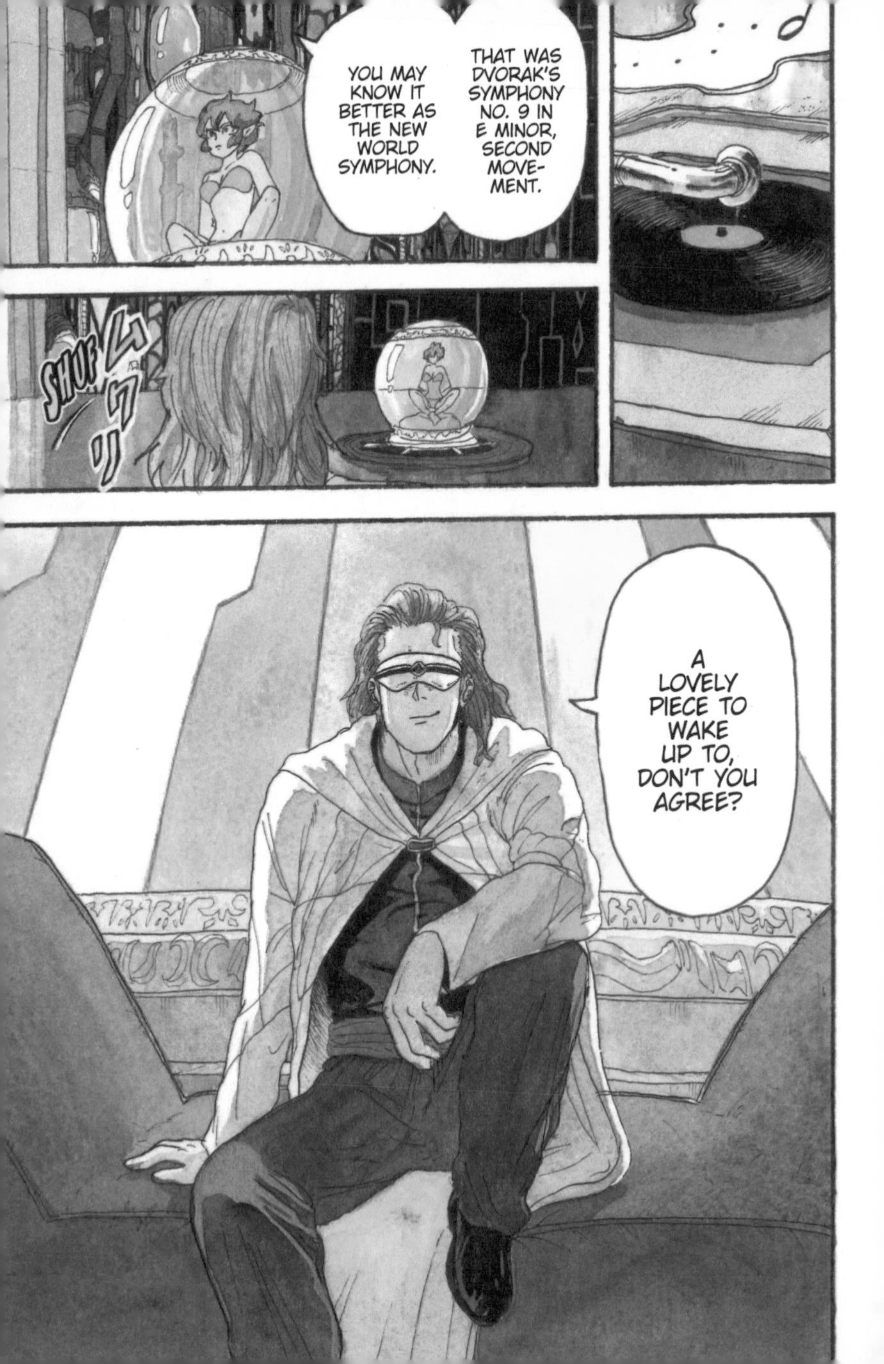
THAT WAS DVORAK'S SYMPHONY NO. 9 IN E MINOR, SECOND MOVEMENT.
YOU MAY KNOW IT BETTER AS THE NEW WORLD SYMPHONY.
SHUF
A LOVELY PIECE TO WAKE UP TO, DON'T YOU AGREE?

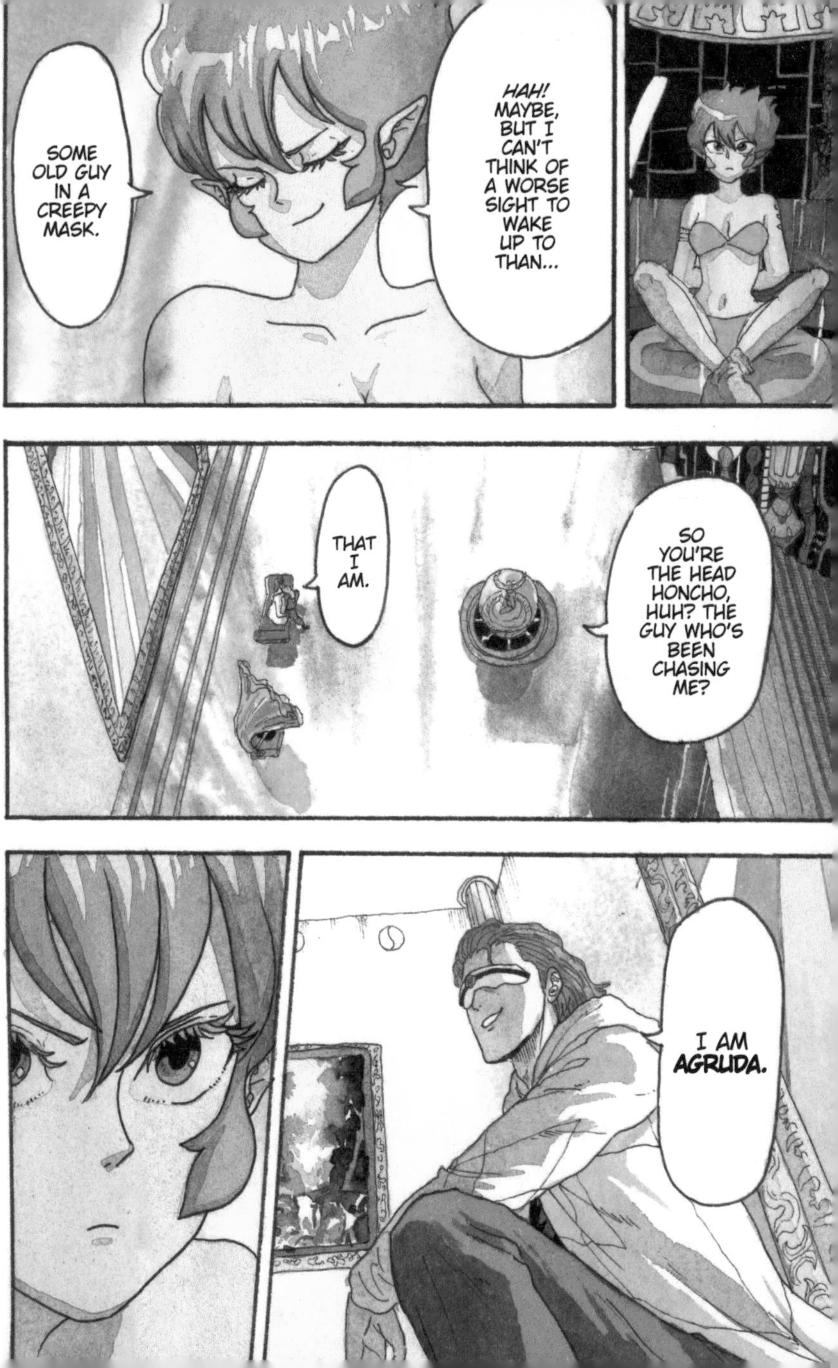
HAH! MAYBE, BUT I CAN'T THINK OF A WORSE SIGHT TO WAKE UP TO THAN...
SOME OLD GUY IN A CREEPY MASK.
SO YOU'RE THE HEAD HONCHO, HUH? THE GUY WHO'S BEEN CHASING ME?
THAT I AM.
I AM **AGRUDA.**

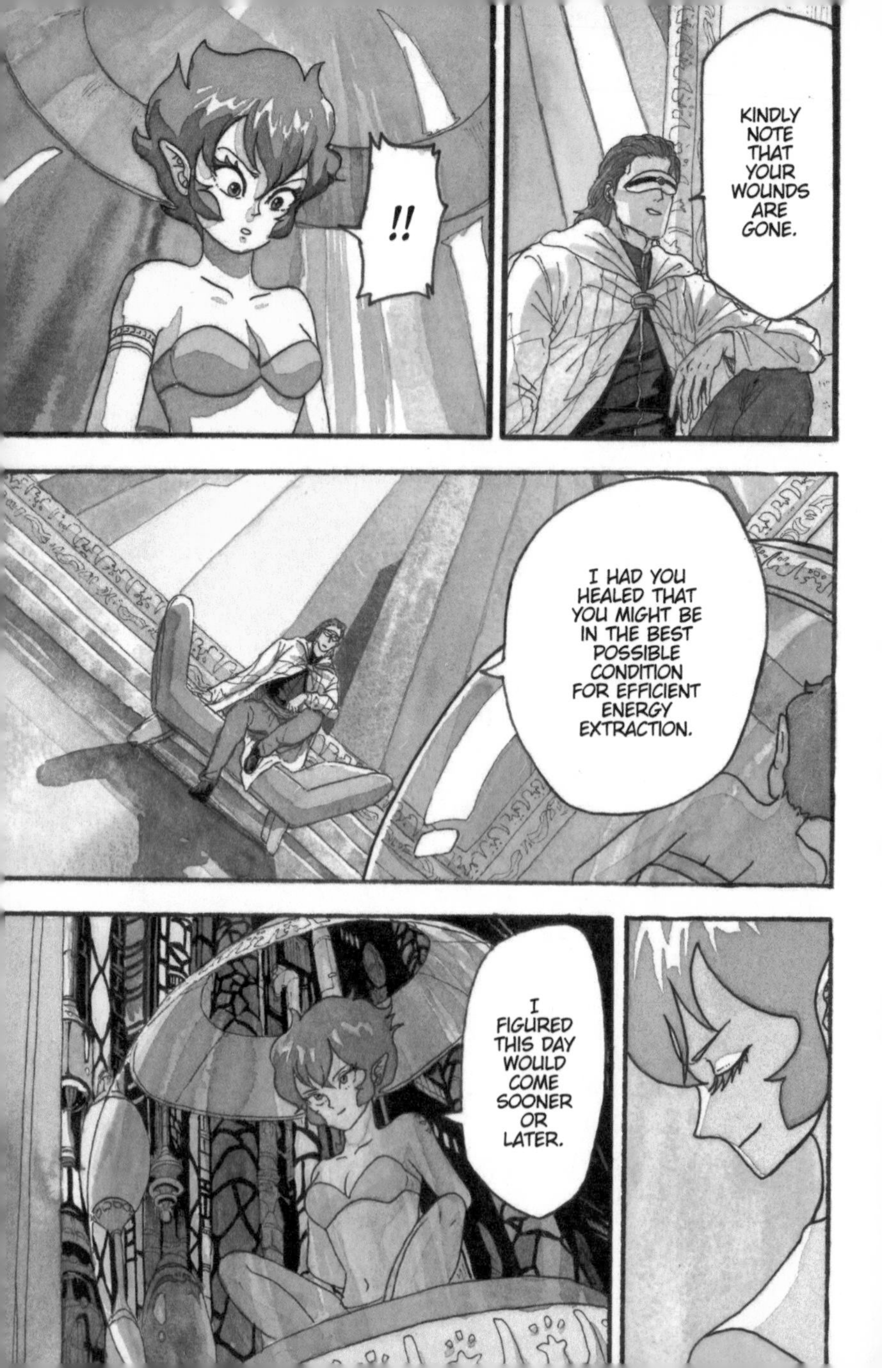
KINDLY NOTE THAT YOUR WOUNDS ARE GONE.
!!
I HAD YOU HEALED THAT YOU MIGHT BE IN THE BEST POSSIBLE CONDITION FOR EFFICIENT ENERGY EXTRACTION.
I FIGURED THIS DAY WOULD COME SOONER OR LATER.

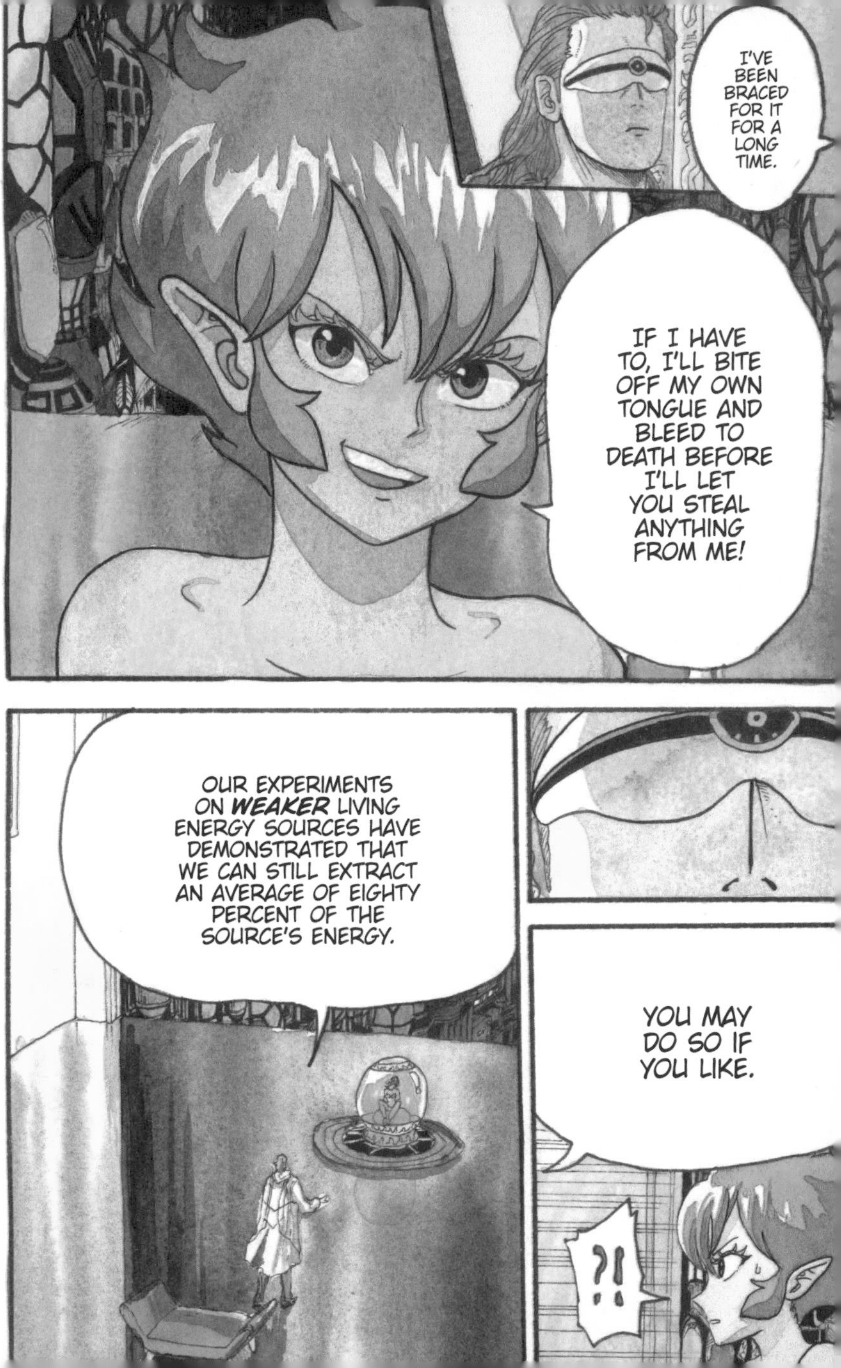
I'VE BEEN BRACED FOR IT FOR A LONG TIME.
IF I HAVE TO, I'LL BITE OFF MY OWN TONGUE AND BLEED TO DEATH BEFORE I'LL LET YOU STEAL ANYTHING FROM ME!
YOU MAY DO SO IF YOU LIKE.
?!
OUR EXPERIMENTS ON *WEAKER* LIVING ENERGY SOURCES HAVE DEMONSTRATED THAT WE CAN STILL EXTRACT AN AVERAGE OF EIGHTY PERCENT OF THE SOURCE'S ENERGY.

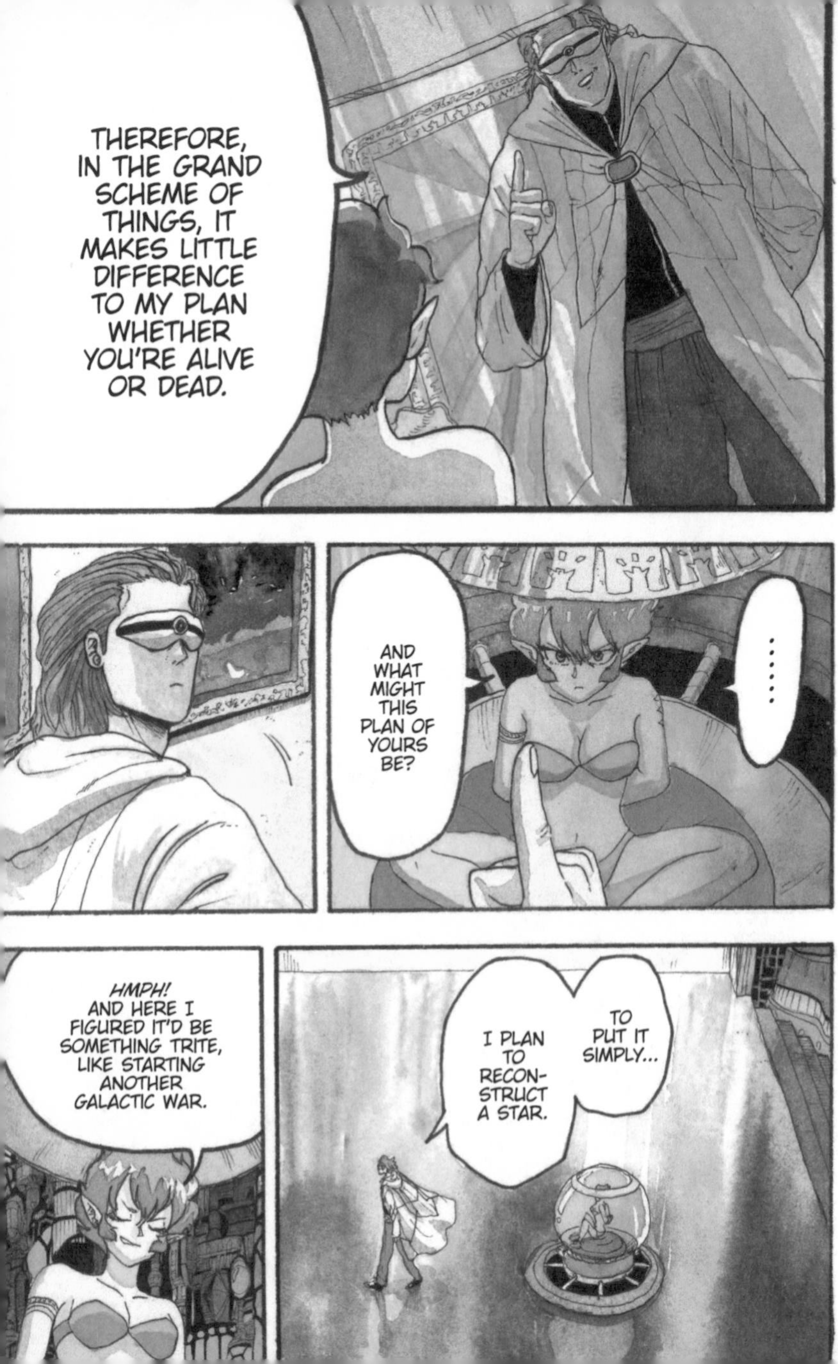
THEREFORE, IN THE GRAND SCHEME OF THINGS, IT MAKES LITTLE DIFFERENCE TO MY PLAN WHETHER YOU'RE ALIVE OR DEAD.
......
AND WHAT MIGHT THIS PLAN OF YOURS BE?
TO PUT IT SIMPLY...
I PLAN TO RECON-STRUCT A STAR.
HMPH! AND HERE I FIGURED IT'D BE SOMETHING TRITE, LIKE STARTING ANOTHER GALACTIC WAR.

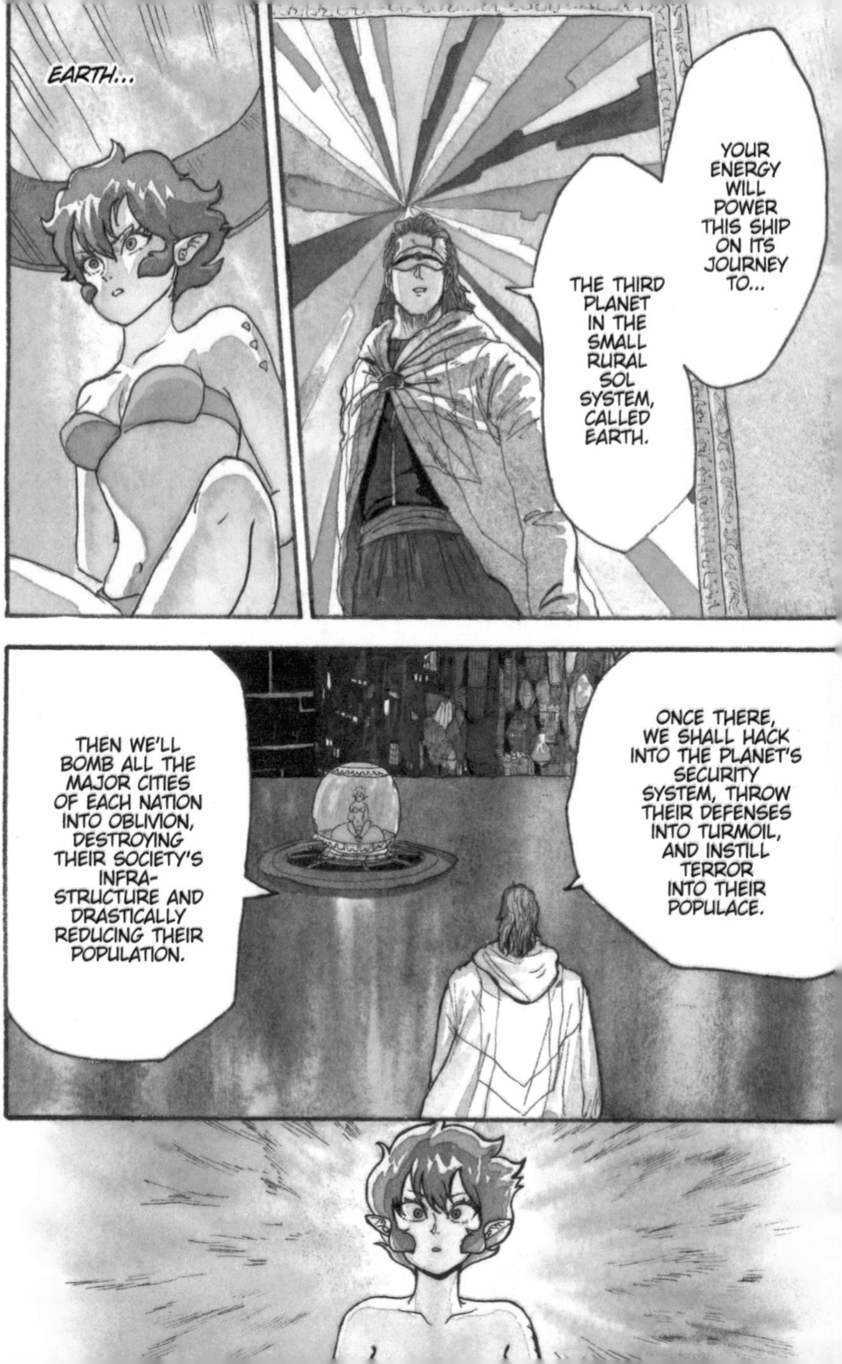
YOUR ENERGY WILL POWER THIS SHIP ON ITS JOURNEY TO...
THE THIRD PLANET IN THE SMALL RURAL SOL SYSTEM, CALLED EARTH.
EARTH...
ONCE THERE, WE SHALL HACK INTO THE PLANET'S SECURITY SYSTEM, THROW THEIR DEFENSES INTO TURMOIL, AND INSTILL TERROR INTO THEIR POPULACE.
THEN WE'LL BOMB ALL THE MAJOR CITIES OF EACH NATION INTO OBLIVION, DESTROYING THEIR SOCIETY'S INFRA-STRUCTURE AND DRASTICALLY REDUCING THEIR POPULATION.

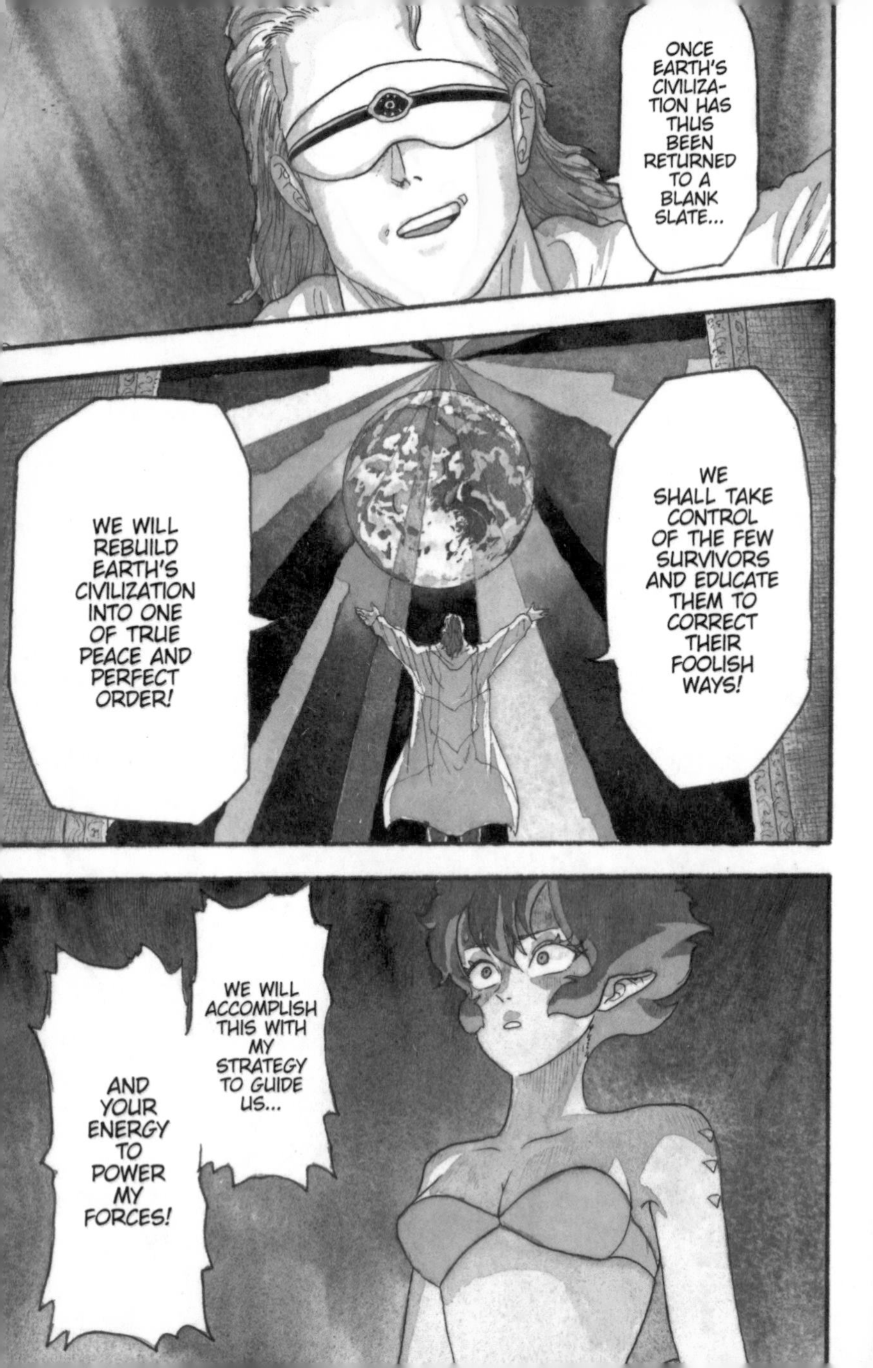
ONCE EARTH'S CIVILIZATION HAS THUS BEEN RETURNED TO A BLANK SLATE...
WE SHALL TAKE CONTROL OF THE FEW SURVIVORS AND EDUCATE THEM TO CORRECT THEIR FOOLISH WAYS!
WE WILL REBUILD EARTH'S CIVILIZATION INTO ONE OF TRUE PEACE AND PERFECT ORDER!
WE WILL ACCOMPLISH THIS WITH MY STRATEGY TO GUIDE US...
AND YOUR ENERGY TO POWER MY FORCES!

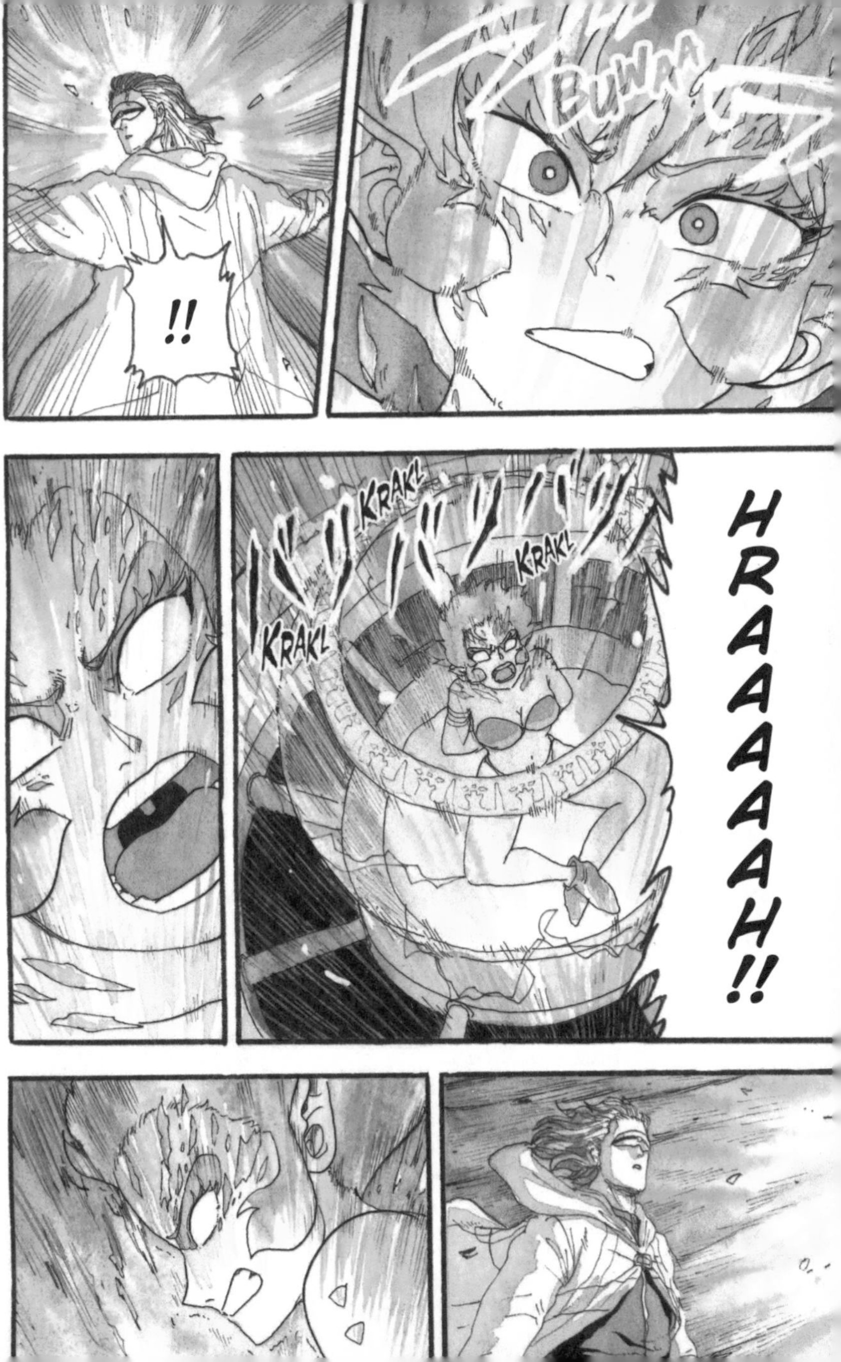
BUWAA
!!
HRAAAAAH!!
KRAKL
KRAKL
KRAKL

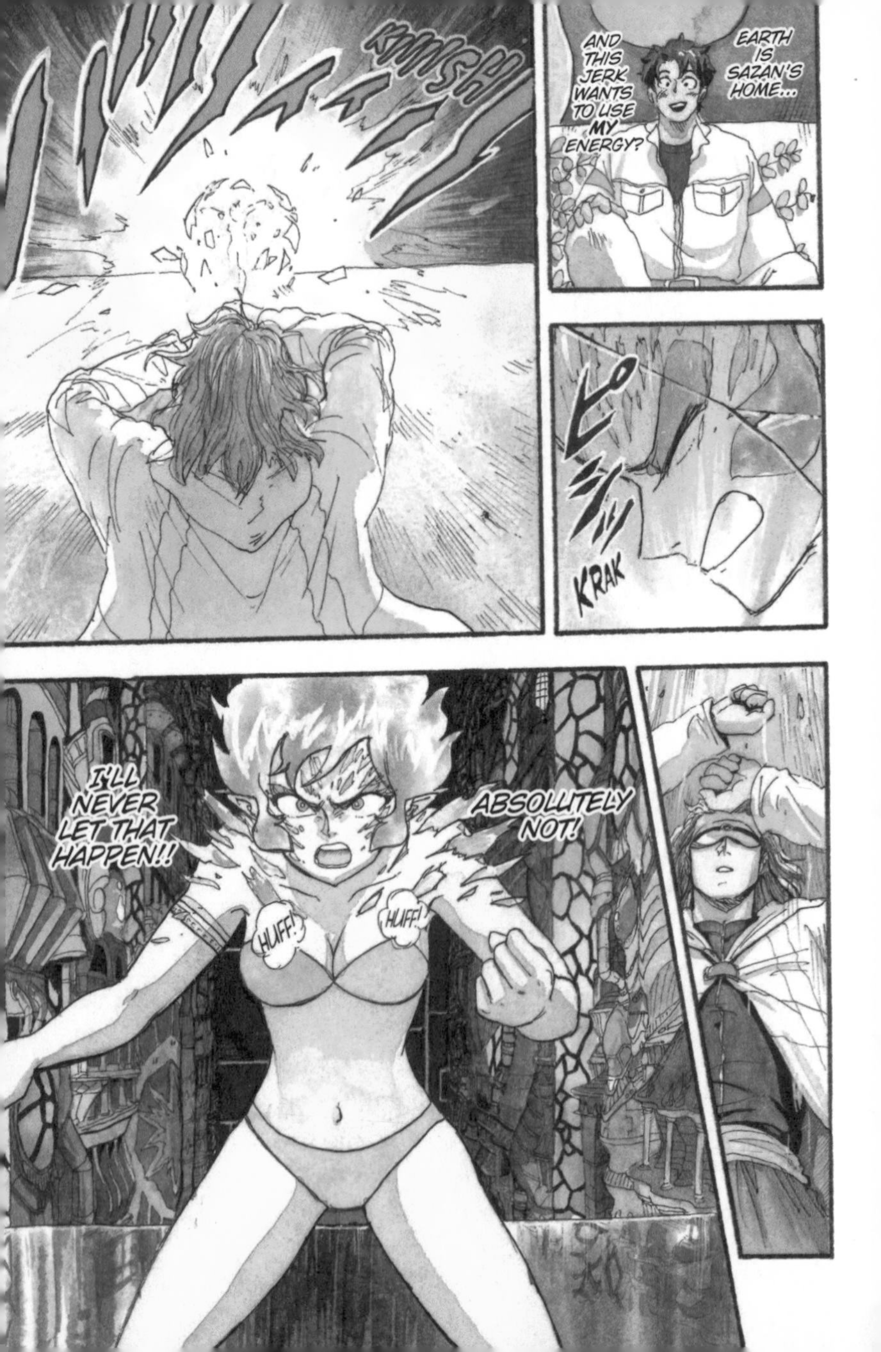
EARTH IS SAZAN'S HOME...
AND THIS JERK WANTS TO USE MY ENERGY?
ピシッ
KRAK
KWISH
ABSOLUTELY NOT!
I'LL NEVER LET THAT HAPPEN!!
HUFF!
HUFF!

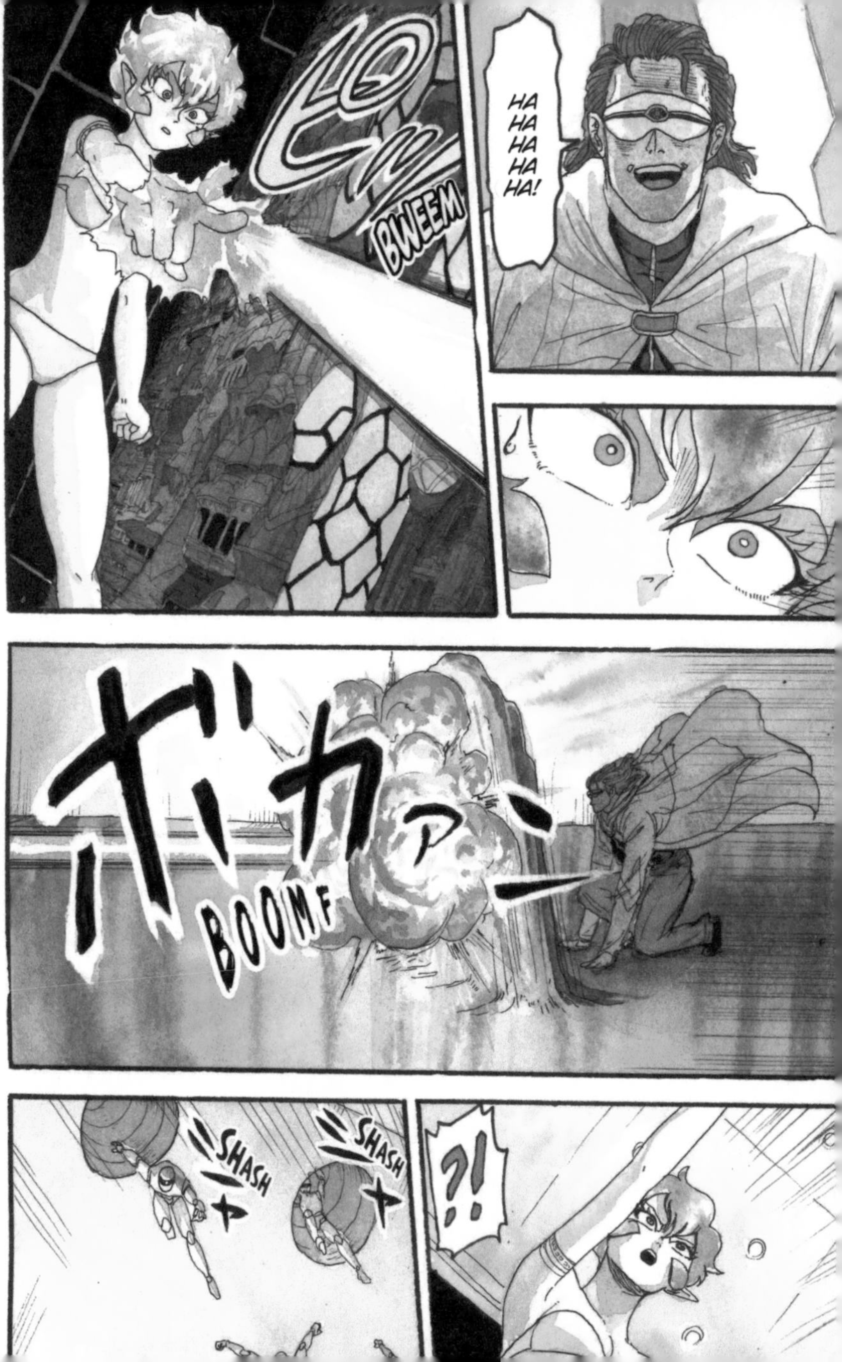
HA HA HA HA HA!
BWEEM
ボカァー
BOOMF
?!
SHASH
SHASH

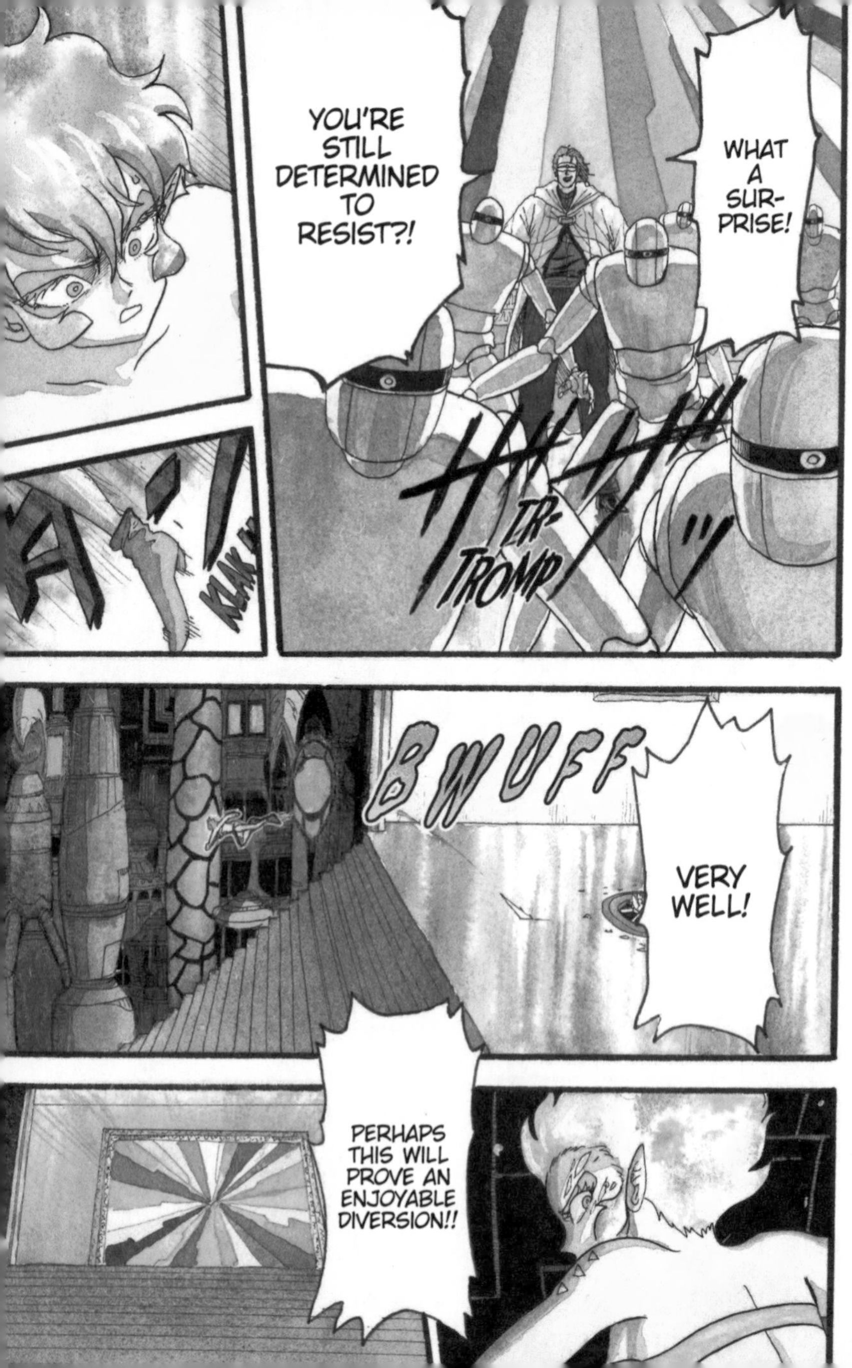
WHAT A SUR-PRISE!
YOU'RE STILL DETERMINED TO RESIST?!
TR-TROMP
KLAK
BWUFF
VERY WELL!
PERHAPS THIS WILL PROVE AN ENJOYABLE DIVERSION!!

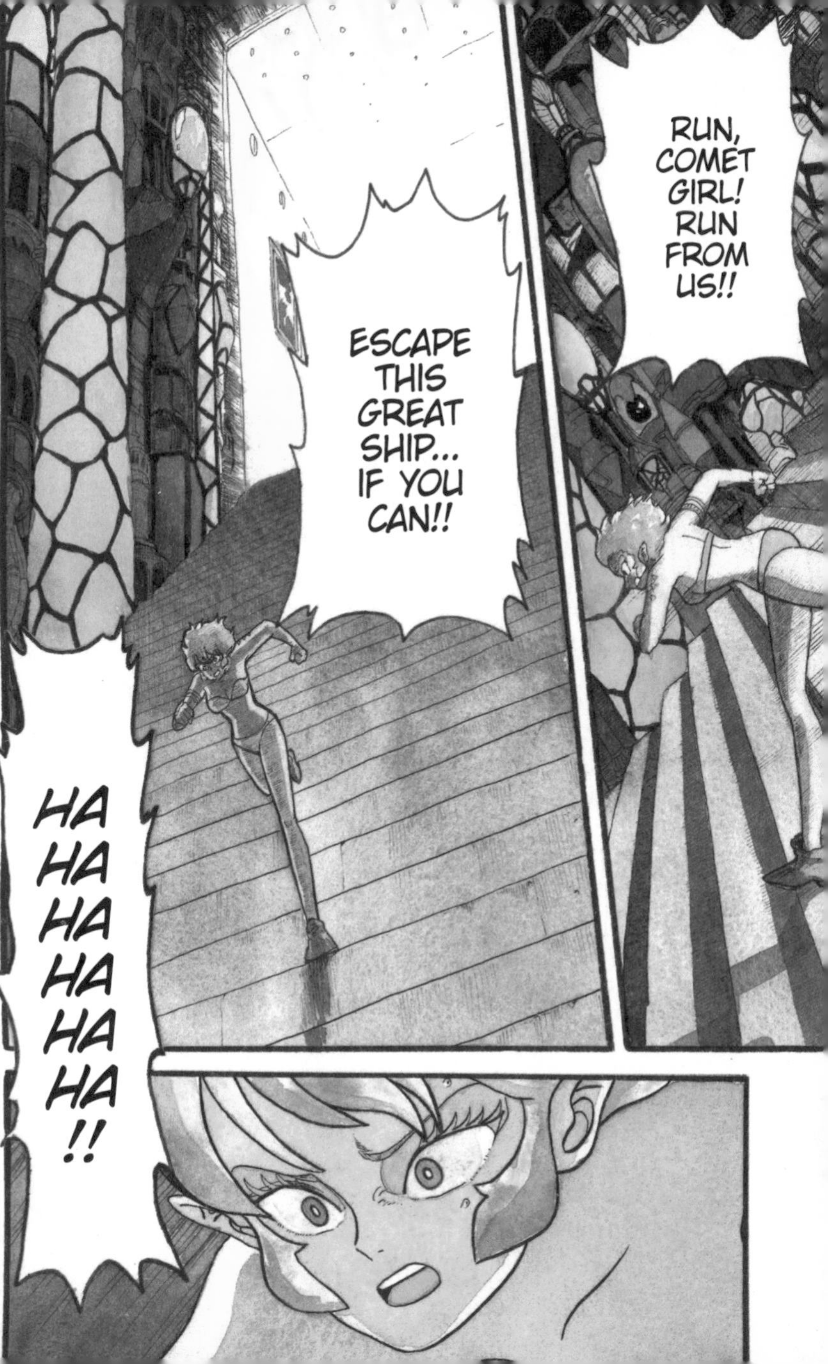
RUN, COMET GIRL! RUN FROM US!!
ESCAPE THIS GREAT SHIP... IF YOU CAN!!
HA HA HA HA HA HA HA!!

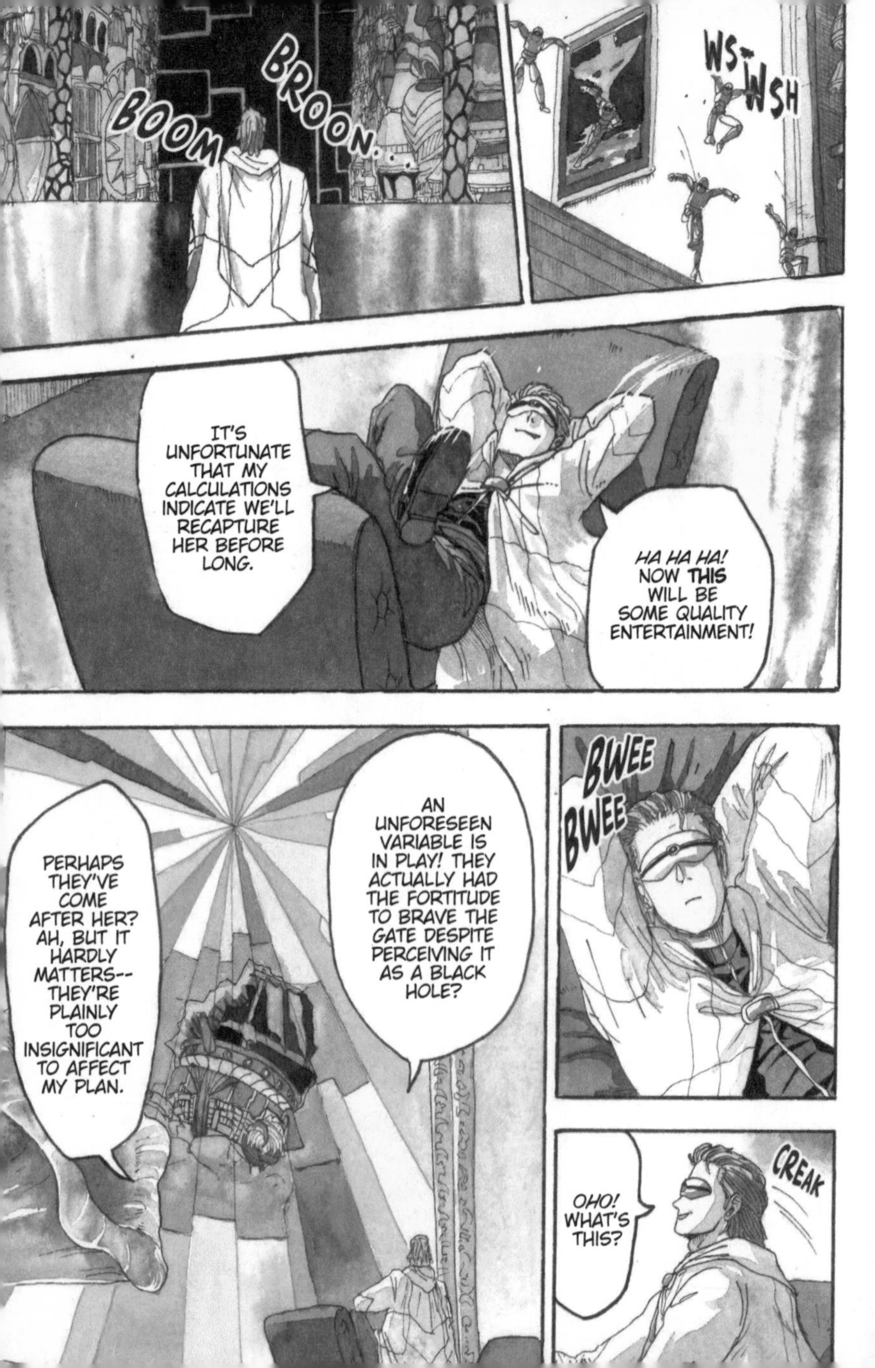
WS-WSH
BOOM
BROON...
HA HA HA! NOW THIS WILL BE SOME QUALITY ENTERTAINMENT!
IT'S UNFORTUNATE THAT MY CALCULATIONS INDICATE WE'LL RECAPTURE HER BEFORE LONG.
BWEE
BWEE
CREAK
OHO! WHAT'S THIS?
AN UNFORESEEN VARIABLE IS IN PLAY! THEY ACTUALLY HAD THE FORTITUDE TO BRAVE THE GATE DESPITE PERCEIVING IT AS A BLACK HOLE?
PERHAPS THEY'VE COME AFTER HER? AH, BUT IT HARDLY MATTERS--THEY'RE PLAINLY TOO INSIGNIFICANT TO AFFECT MY PLAN.

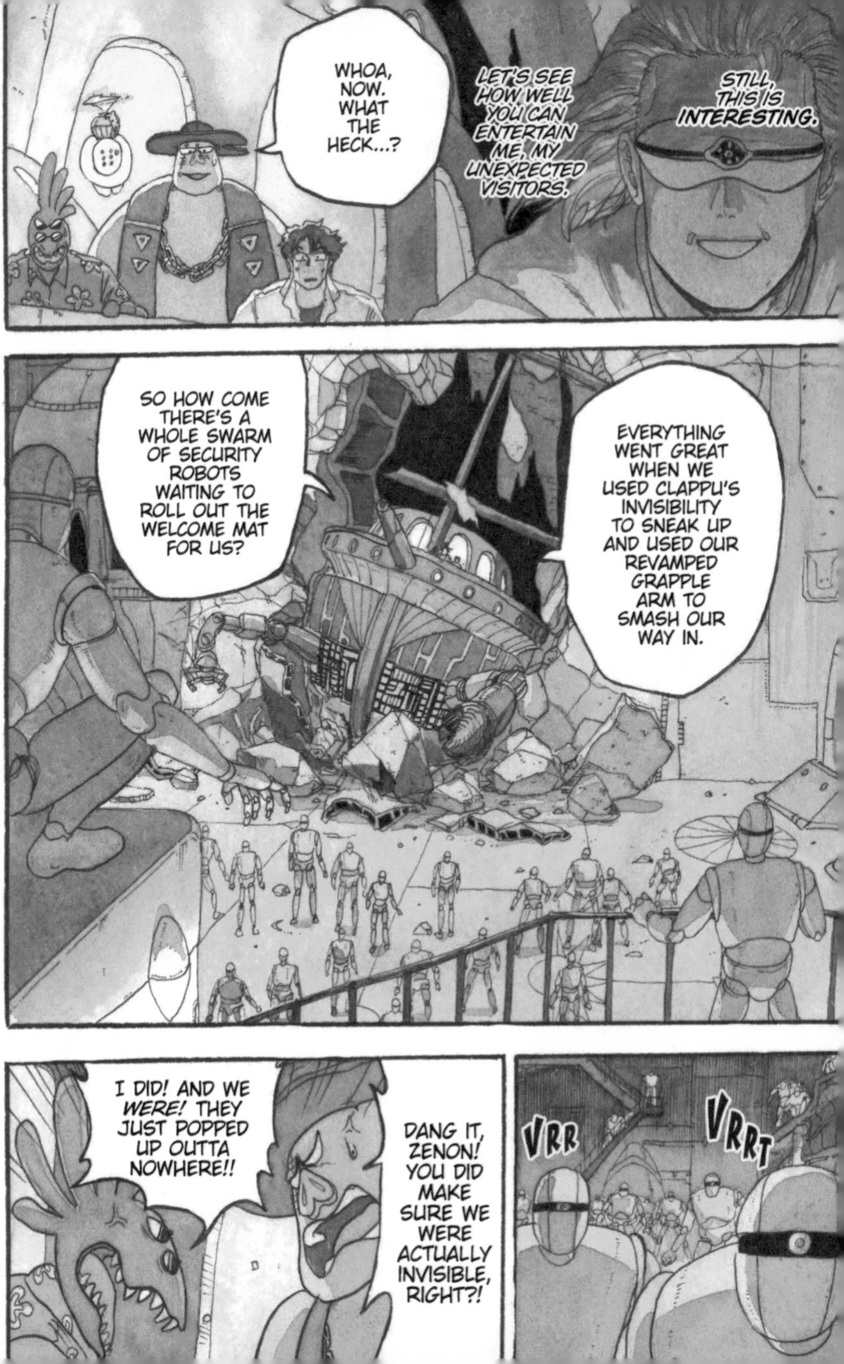

STILL, THIS IS INTERESTING.
LET'S SEE HOW WELL YOU CAN ENTERTAIN ME, MY UNEXPECTED VISITORS.
WHOA, NOW. WHAT THE HECK...?
EVERYTHING WENT GREAT WHEN WE USED CLAPPU'S INVISIBILITY TO SNEAK UP AND USED OUR REVAMPED GRAPPLE ARM TO SMASH OUR WAY IN.
SO HOW COME THERE'S A WHOLE SWARM OF SECURITY ROBOTS WAITING TO ROLL OUT THE WELCOME MAT FOR US?
VRRT
VRR
DANG IT, ZENON! YOU DID MAKE SURE WE WERE ACTUALLY INVISIBLE, RIGHT?!
I DID! AND WE *WERE!* THEY JUST POPPED UP OUTTA NOWHERE!!

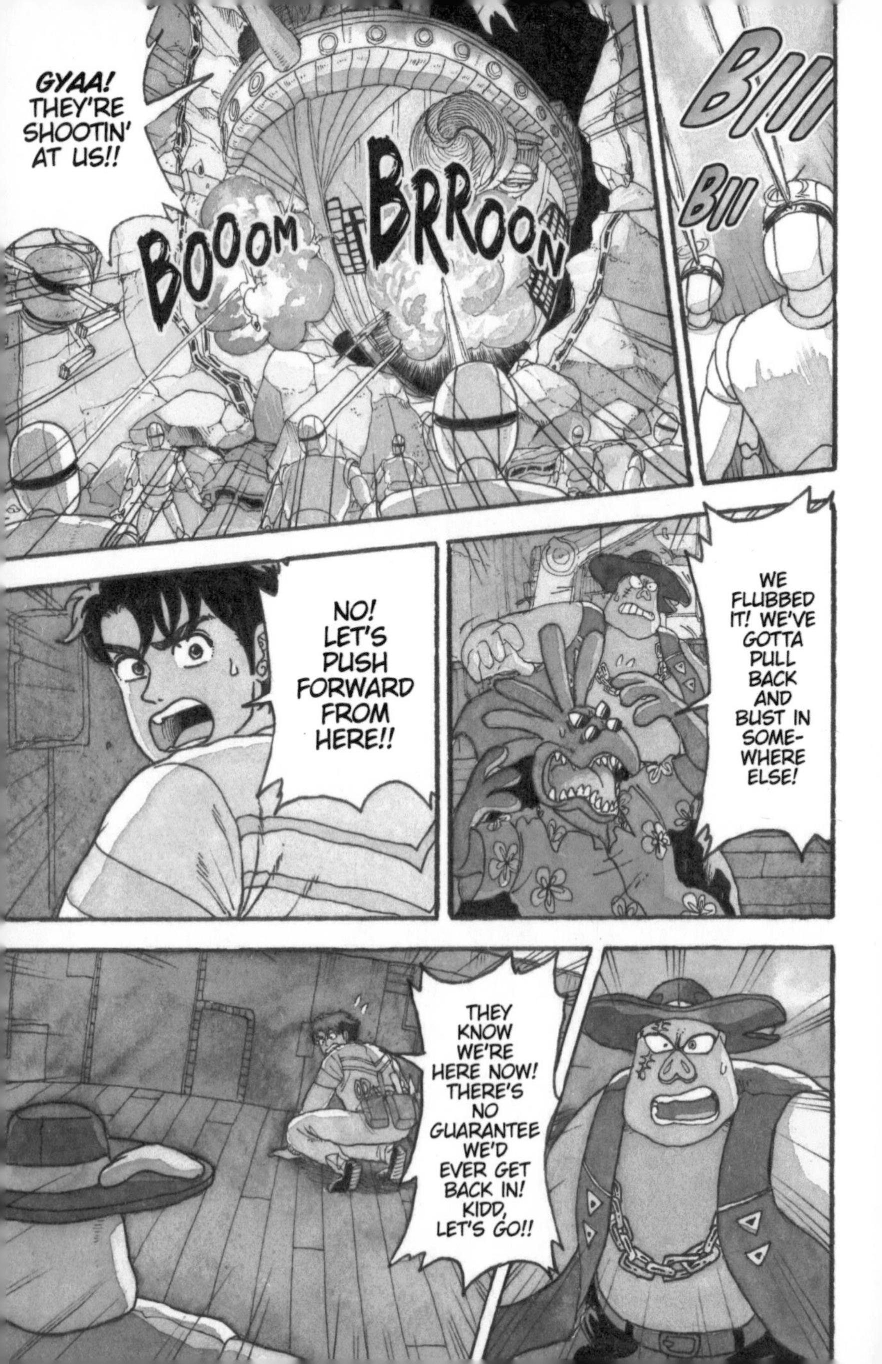
BIII
BII
GYAA! THEY'RE SHOOTIN' AT US!!
BOOOM
BRROON
WE FLUBBED IT! WE'VE GOTTA PULL BACK AND BUST IN SOME-WHERE ELSE!
NO! LET'S PUSH FORWARD FROM HERE!!
THEY KNOW WE'RE HERE NOW! THERE'S NO GUARANTEE WE'D EVER GET BACK IN! KIDD, LET'S GO!!

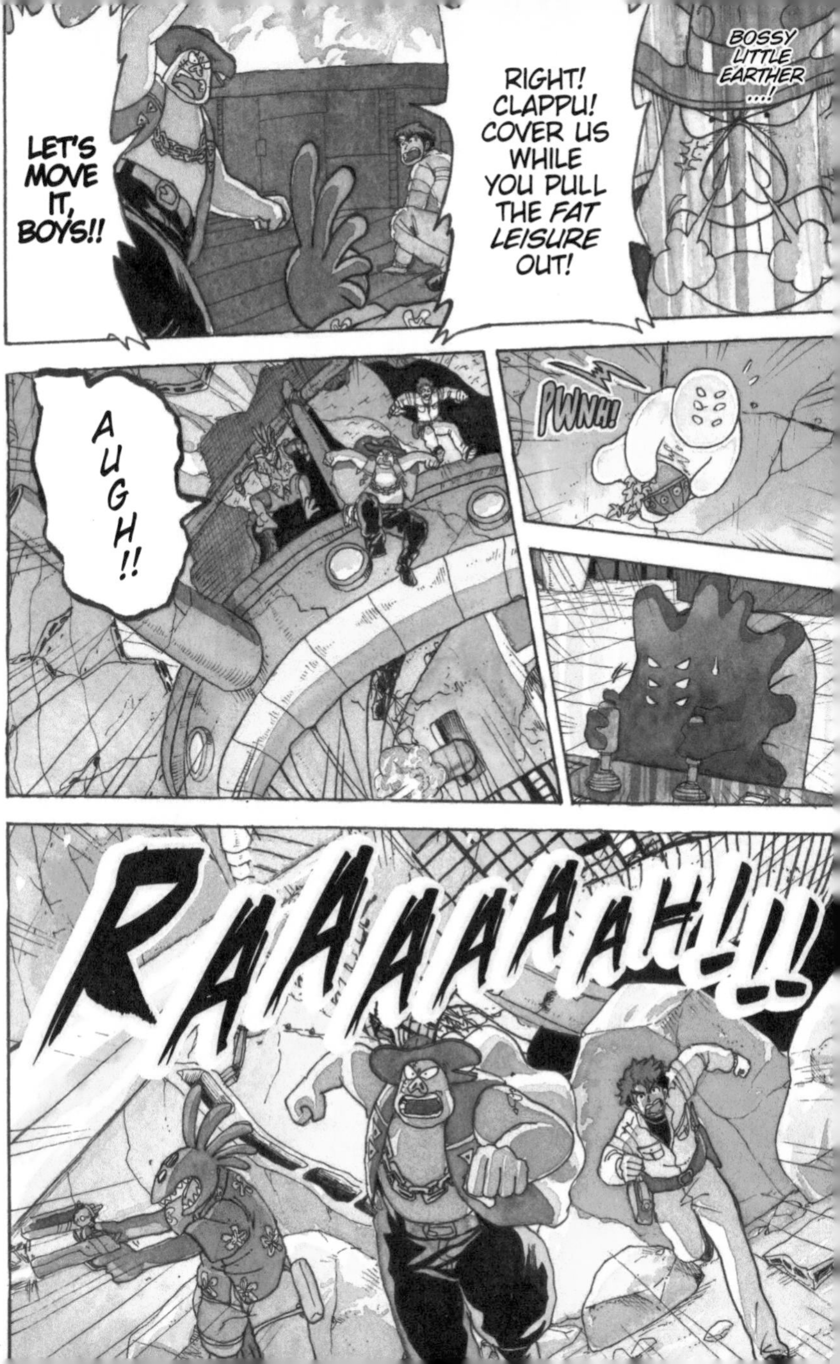
BOSSY LITTLE EARTHER ...!
RIGHT! CLAPPU! COVER US WHILE YOU PULL THE FAT LEISURE OUT!
LET'S MOVE IT, BOYS!!
PWNH!
AUGH!!
RAAAAAAH!!

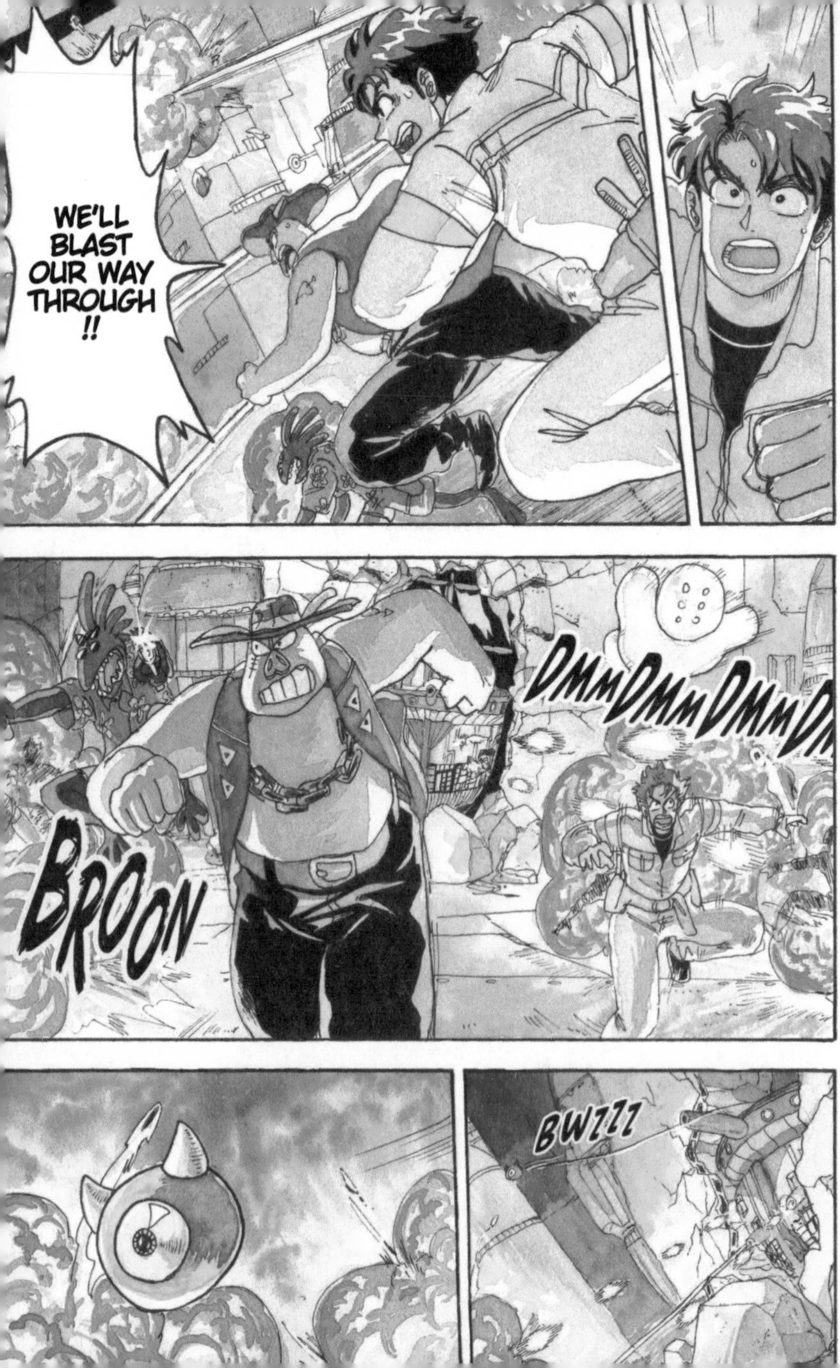
WE'LL BLAST OUR WAY THROUGH !!
DMMDMMDMMDM
BROON
BWZZZ

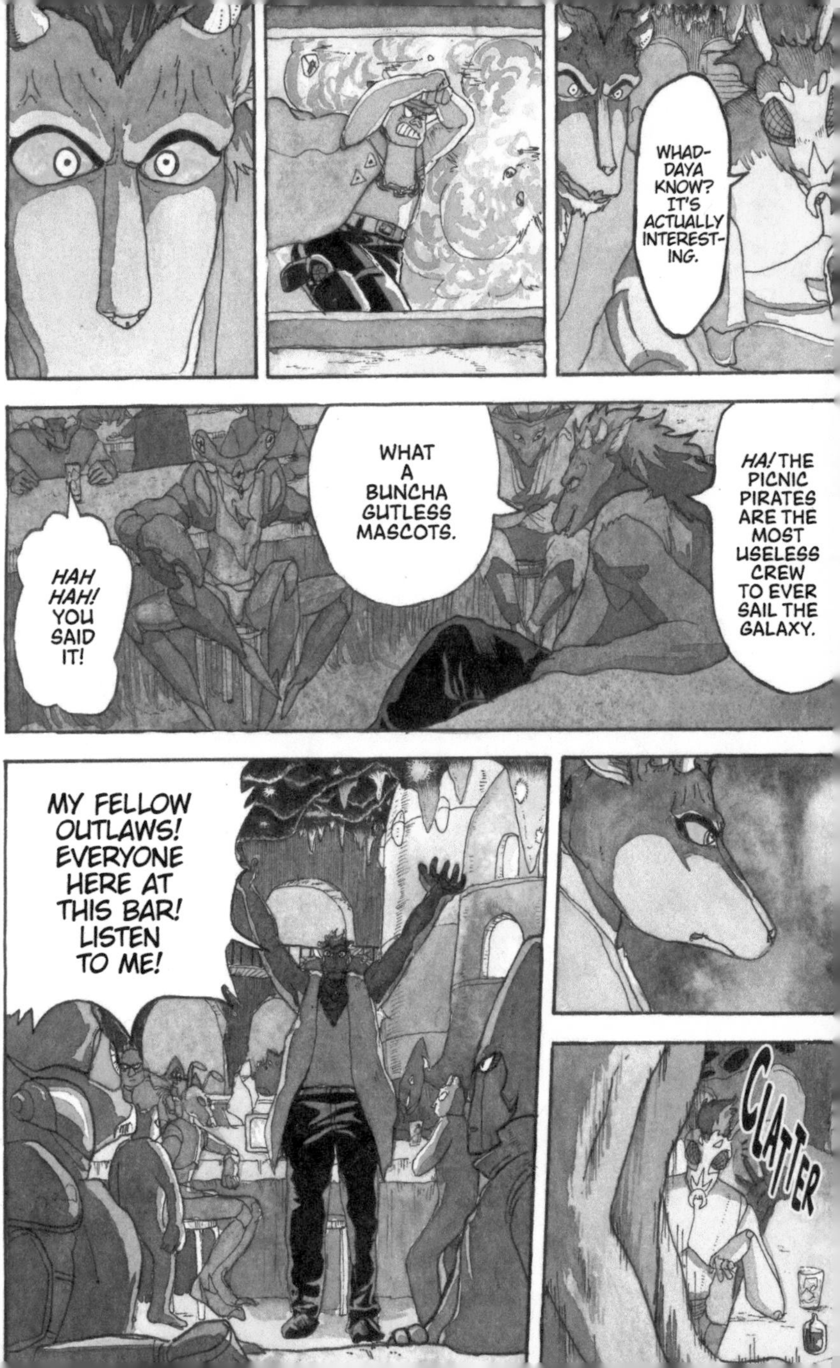
WHAD-DAYA KNOW? IT'S ACTUALLY INTEREST-ING.
HA! THE PICNIC PIRATES ARE THE MOST USELESS CREW TO EVER SAIL THE GALAXY.
WHAT A BUNCHA GUTLESS MASCOTS.
HAH HAH! YOU SAID IT!
CLATTER
MY FELLOW OUTLAWS! EVERYONE HERE AT THIS BAR! LISTEN TO ME!

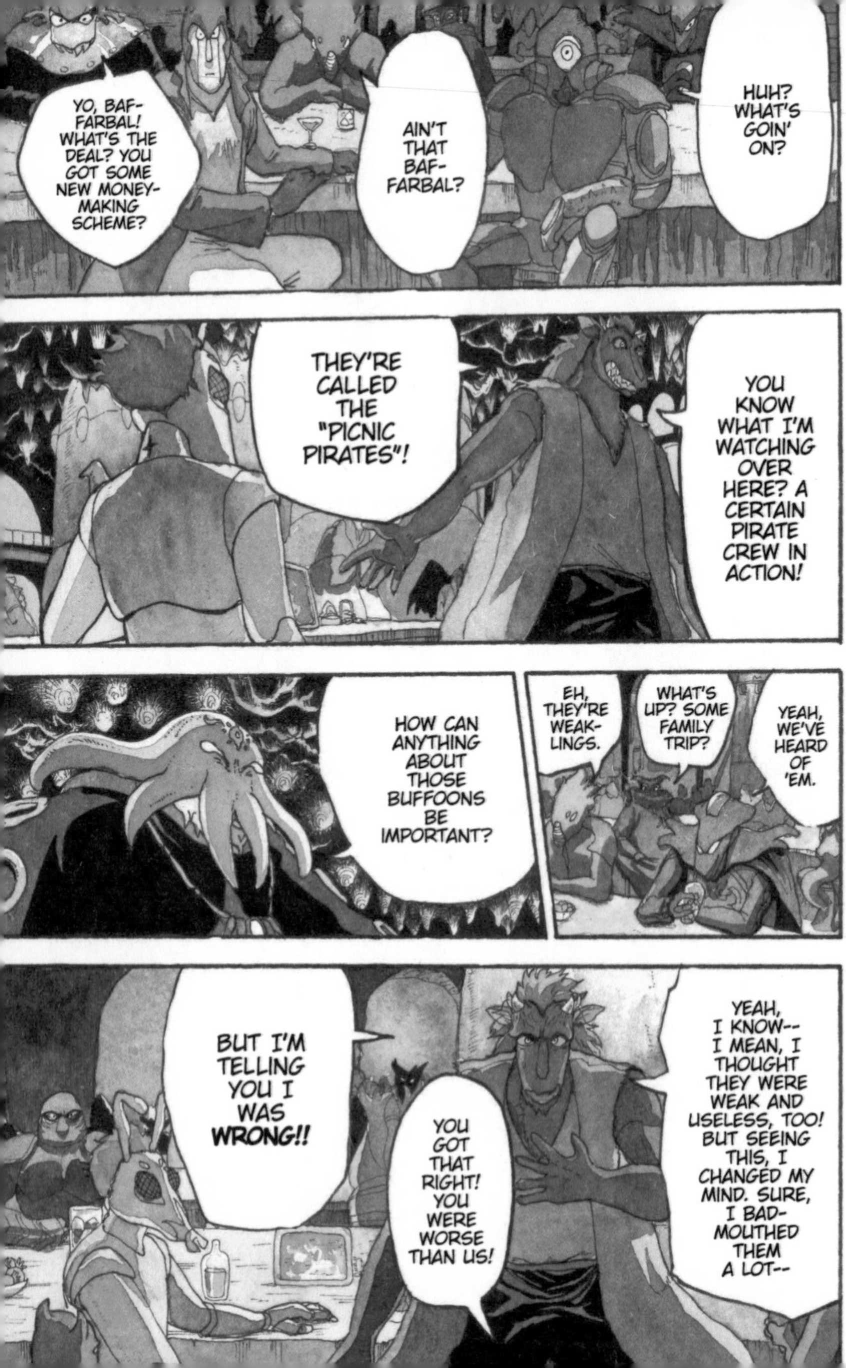
HUH? WHAT'S GOIN' ON?
AIN'T THAT BAF-FARBAL?
YO, BAF-FARBAL! WHAT'S THE DEAL? YOU GOT SOME NEW MONEY-MAKING SCHEME?
YOU KNOW WHAT I'M WATCHING OVER HERE? A CERTAIN PIRATE CREW IN ACTION!
THEY'RE CALLED THE "PICNIC PIRATES"!
YEAH, WE'VE HEARD OF 'EM.
WHAT'S UP? SOME FAMILY TRIP?
EH, THEY'RE WEAK-LINGS.
HOW CAN ANYTHING ABOUT THOSE BUFFOONS BE IMPORTANT?
YEAH, I KNOW-- I MEAN, I THOUGHT THEY WERE WEAK AND USELESS, TOO! BUT SEEING THIS, I CHANGED MY MIND. SURE, I BAD-MOUTHED THEM A LOT--
YOU GOT THAT RIGHT! YOU WERE WORSE THAN US!
BUT I'M TELLING YOU I WAS WRONG!!

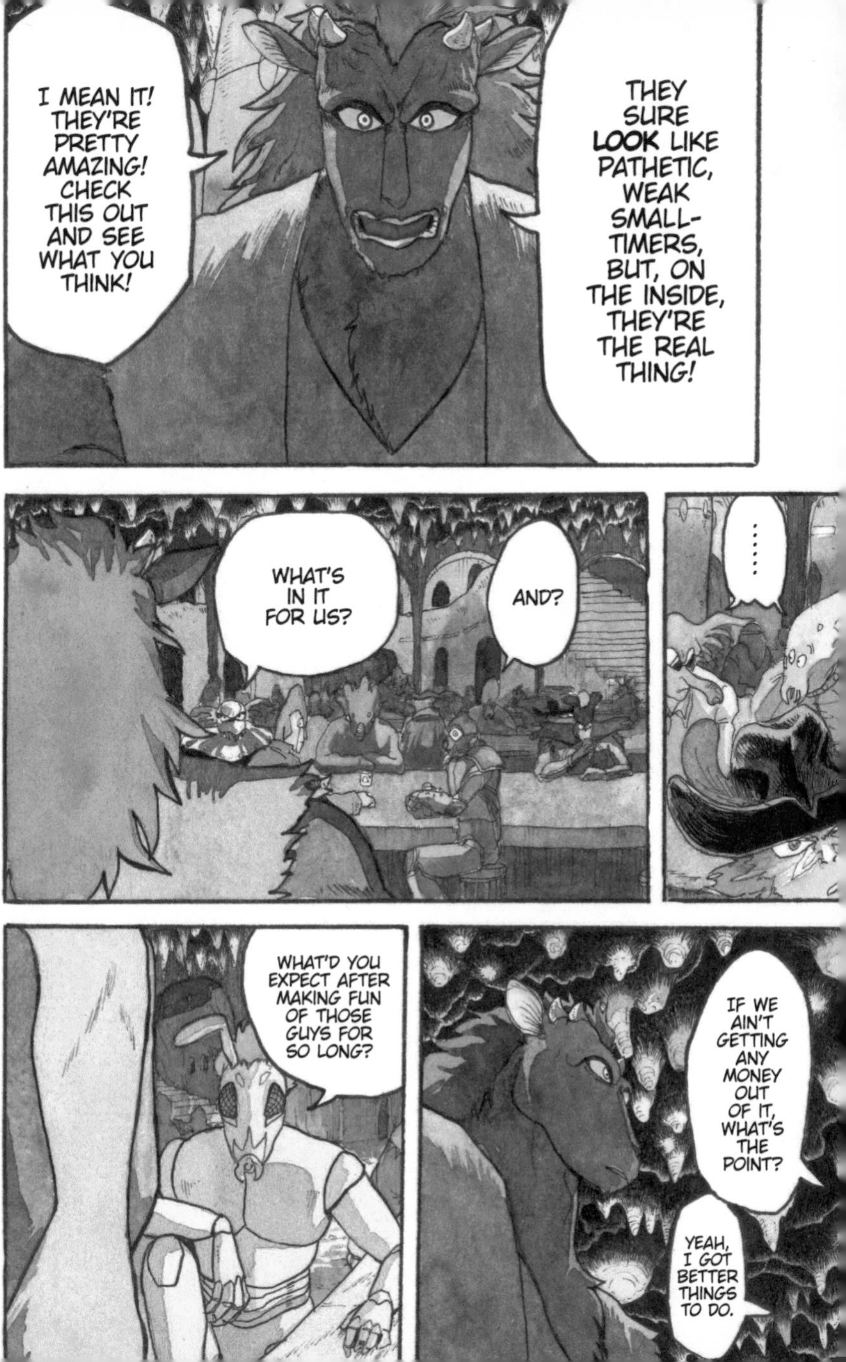
THEY SURE **LOOK** LIKE PATHETIC, WEAK SMALL-TIMERS, BUT, ON THE INSIDE, THEY'RE THE REAL THING!
I MEAN IT! THEY'RE PRETTY AMAZING! CHECK THIS OUT AND SEE WHAT YOU THINK!
......
AND?
WHAT'S IN IT FOR US?
IF WE AIN'T GETTING ANY MONEY OUT OF IT, WHAT'S THE POINT?
YEAH, I GOT BETTER THINGS TO DO.
WHAT'D YOU EXPECT AFTER MAKING FUN OF THOSE GUYS FOR SO LONG?

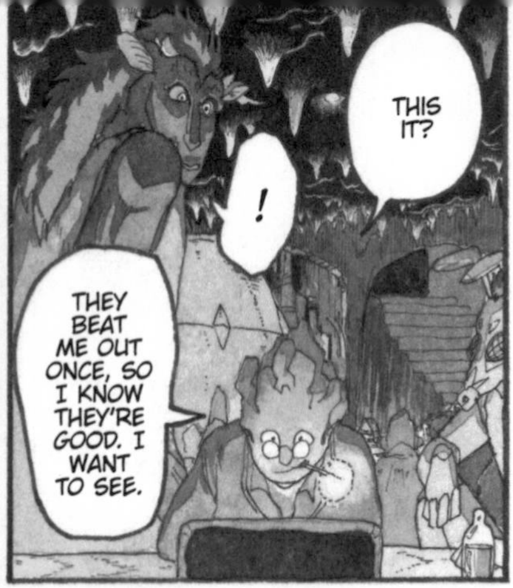
THIS IT?
!
THEY BEAT ME OUT ONCE, SO I KNOW THEY'RE GOOD. I WANT TO SEE.
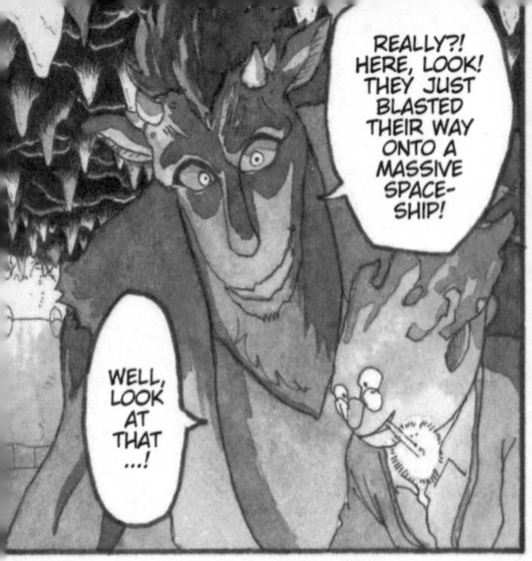
REALLY?! HERE, LOOK! THEY JUST BLASTED THEIR WAY ONTO A MASSIVE SPACE-SHIP!
WELL, LOOK AT THAT ...!
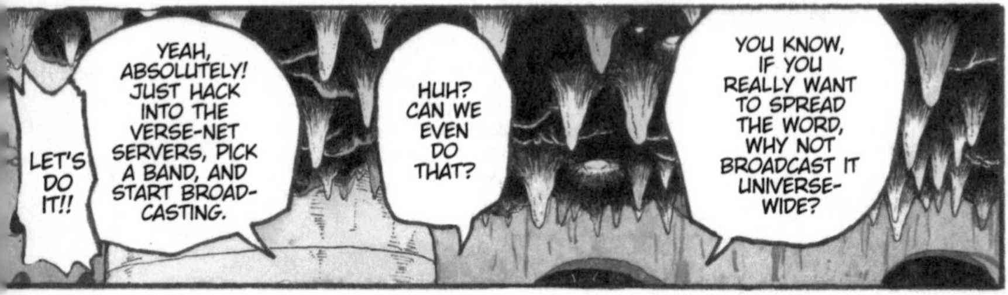
YOU KNOW, IF YOU REALLY WANT TO SPREAD THE WORD, WHY NOT BROADCAST IT UNIVERSE-WIDE?
HUH? CAN WE EVEN DO THAT?
YEAH, ABSOLUTELY! JUST HACK INTO THE VERSE-NET SERVERS, PICK A BAND, AND START BROAD-CASTING.
LET'S DO IT!!
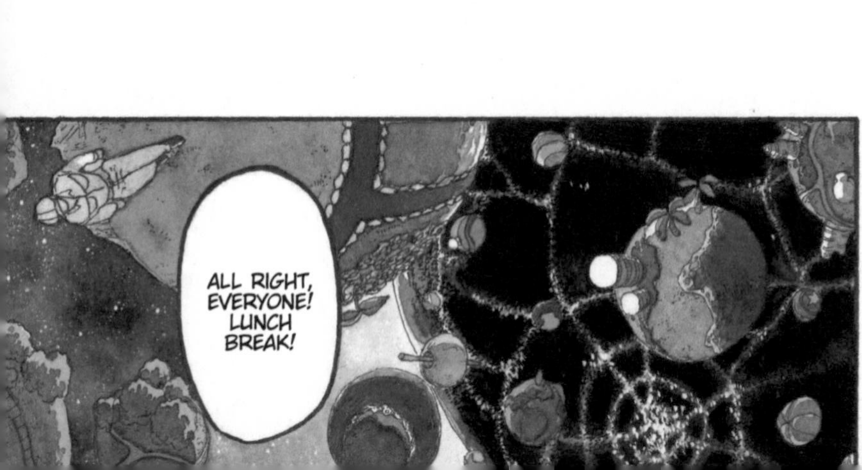
ALL RIGHT, EVERYONE! LUNCH BREAK!

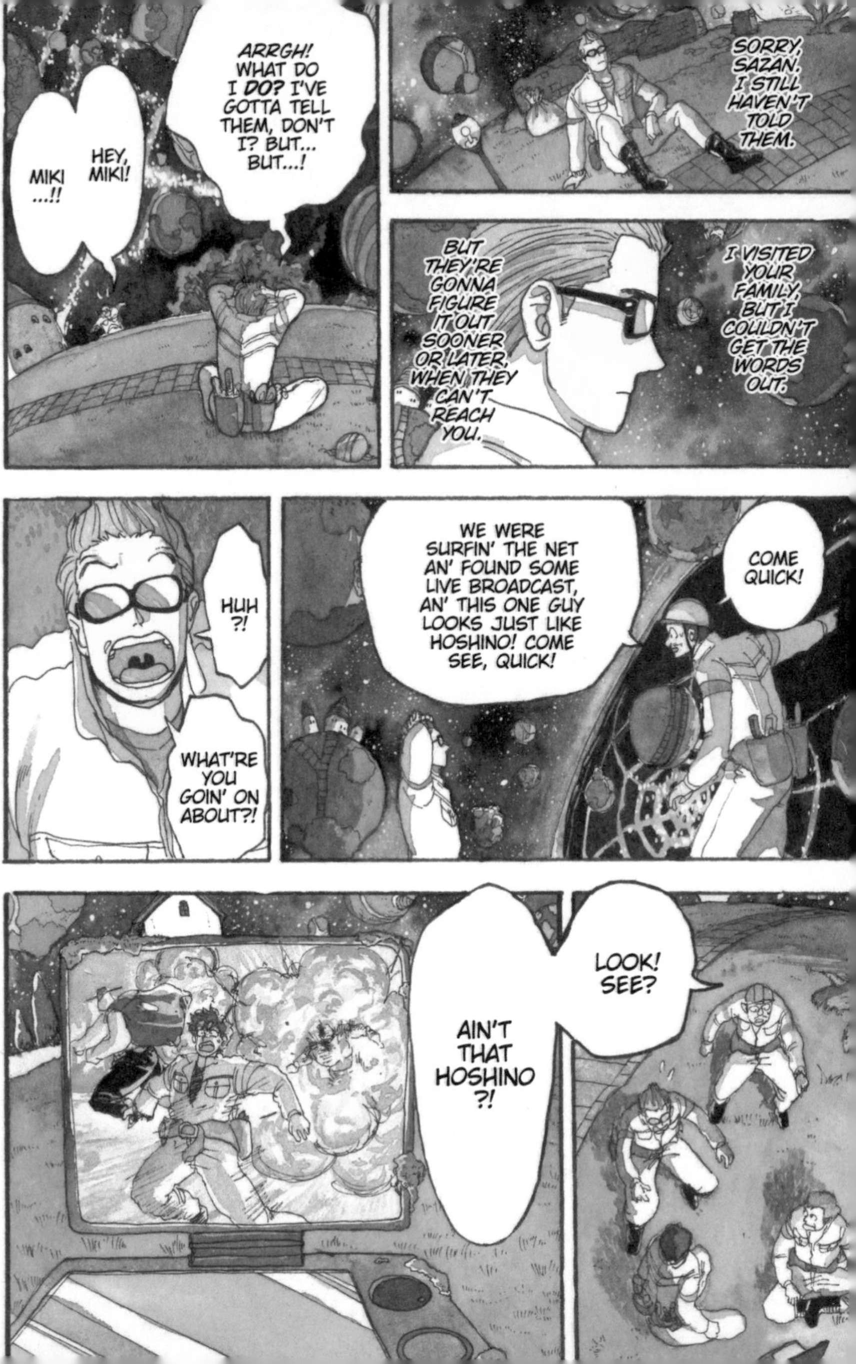
SORRY, SAZAN. I STILL HAVEN'T TOLD THEM.
I VISITED YOUR FAMILY, BUT I COULDN'T GET THE WORDS OUT.
BUT THEY'RE GONNA FIGURE IT OUT SOONER OR LATER, WHEN THEY CAN'T REACH YOU.
ARRGH! WHAT DO I *DO?* I'VE GOTTA TELL THEM, DON'T I? BUT... BUT...!
HEY, MIKI!
MIKI ...!!
COME QUICK!
WE WERE SURFIN' THE NET AN' FOUND SOME LIVE BROADCAST, AN' THIS ONE GUY LOOKS JUST LIKE HOSHINO! COME SEE, QUICK!
HUH ?!
WHAT'RE YOU GOIN' ON ABOUT?!
LOOK! SEE?
AIN'T THAT HOSHINO ?!

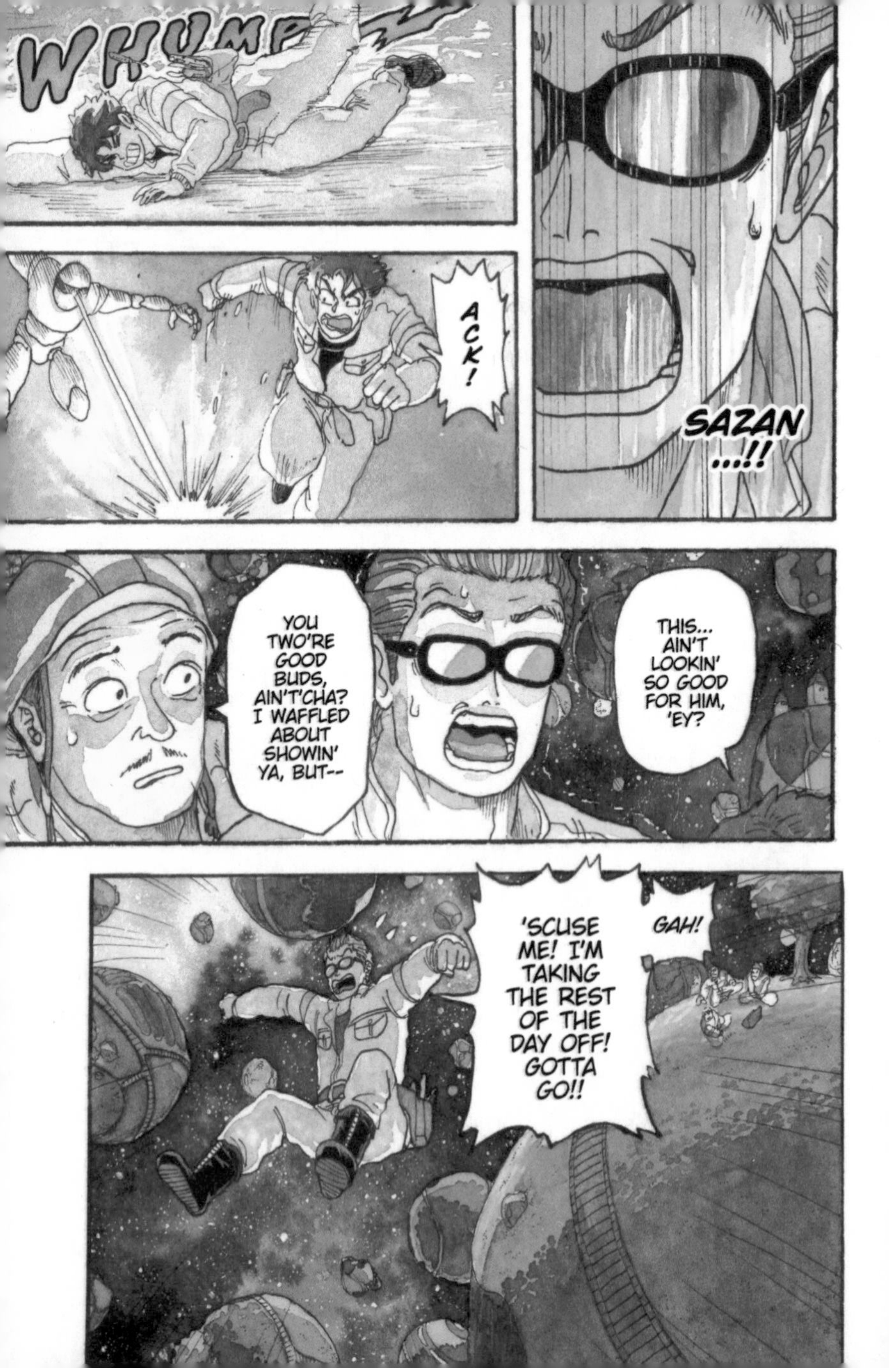
SAZAN ...!!
WHUMP
ACK!
THIS... AIN'T LOOKIN' SO GOOD FOR HIM, 'EY?
YOU TWO'RE GOOD BUDS, AIN'T'CHA? I WAFFLED ABOUT SHOWIN' YA, BUT--
GAH!
'SCUSE ME! I'M TAKING THE REST OF THE DAY OFF! GOTTA GO!!

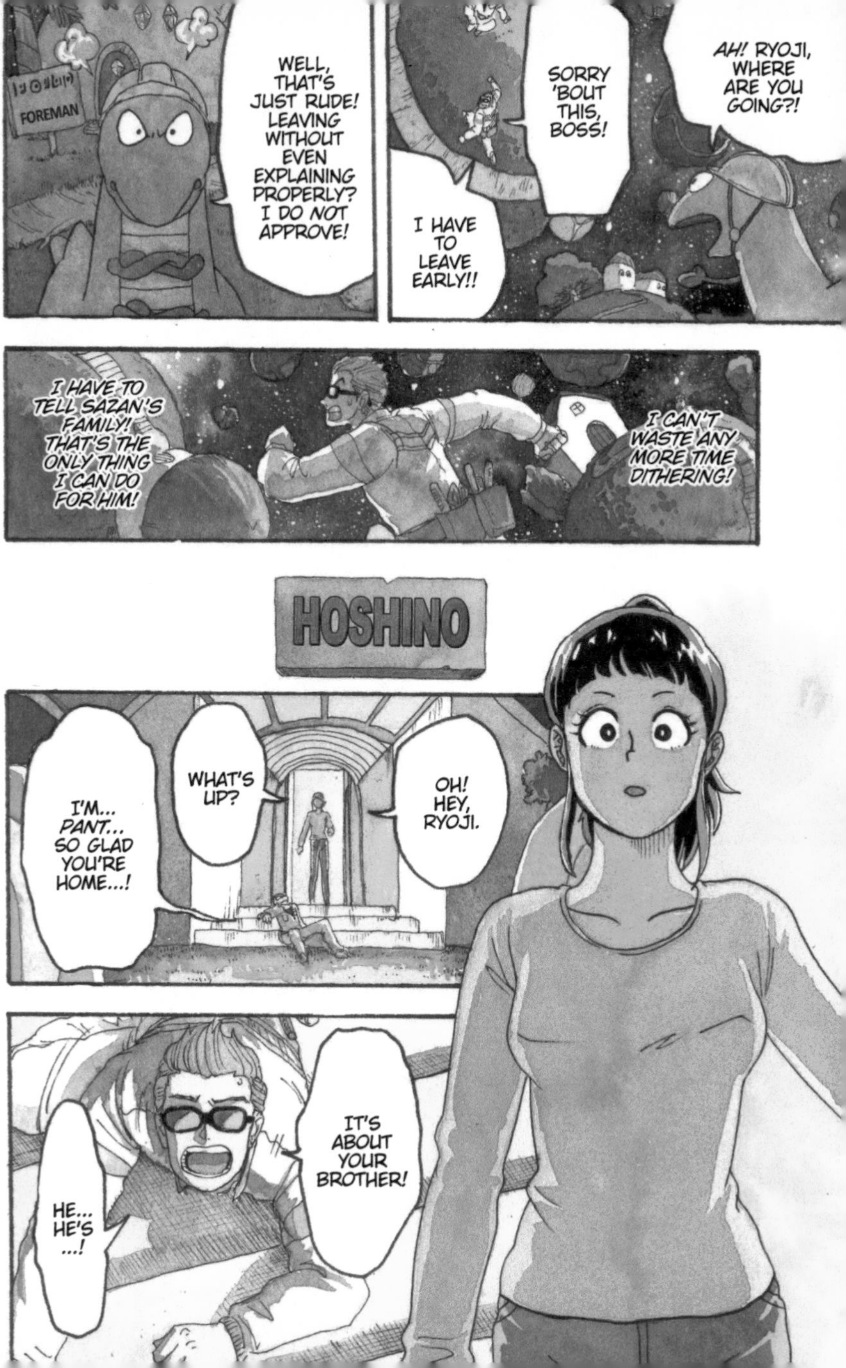
AH! RYOJI, WHERE ARE YOU GOING?!
SORRY 'BOUT THIS, BOSS!
I HAVE TO LEAVE EARLY!!
FOREMAN
WELL, THAT'S JUST RUDE! LEAVING WITHOUT EVEN EXPLAINING PROPERLY? I DO *NOT* APPROVE!
I CAN'T WASTE ANY MORE TIME DITHERING!
I HAVE TO TELL SAZAN'S FAMILY! THAT'S THE ONLY THING I CAN DO FOR HIM!
HOSHINO
OH! HEY, RYOJI.
WHAT'S UP?
I'M... *PANT*... SO GLAD YOU'RE HOME...!
IT'S ABOUT YOUR BROTHER!
HE... HE'S ...!

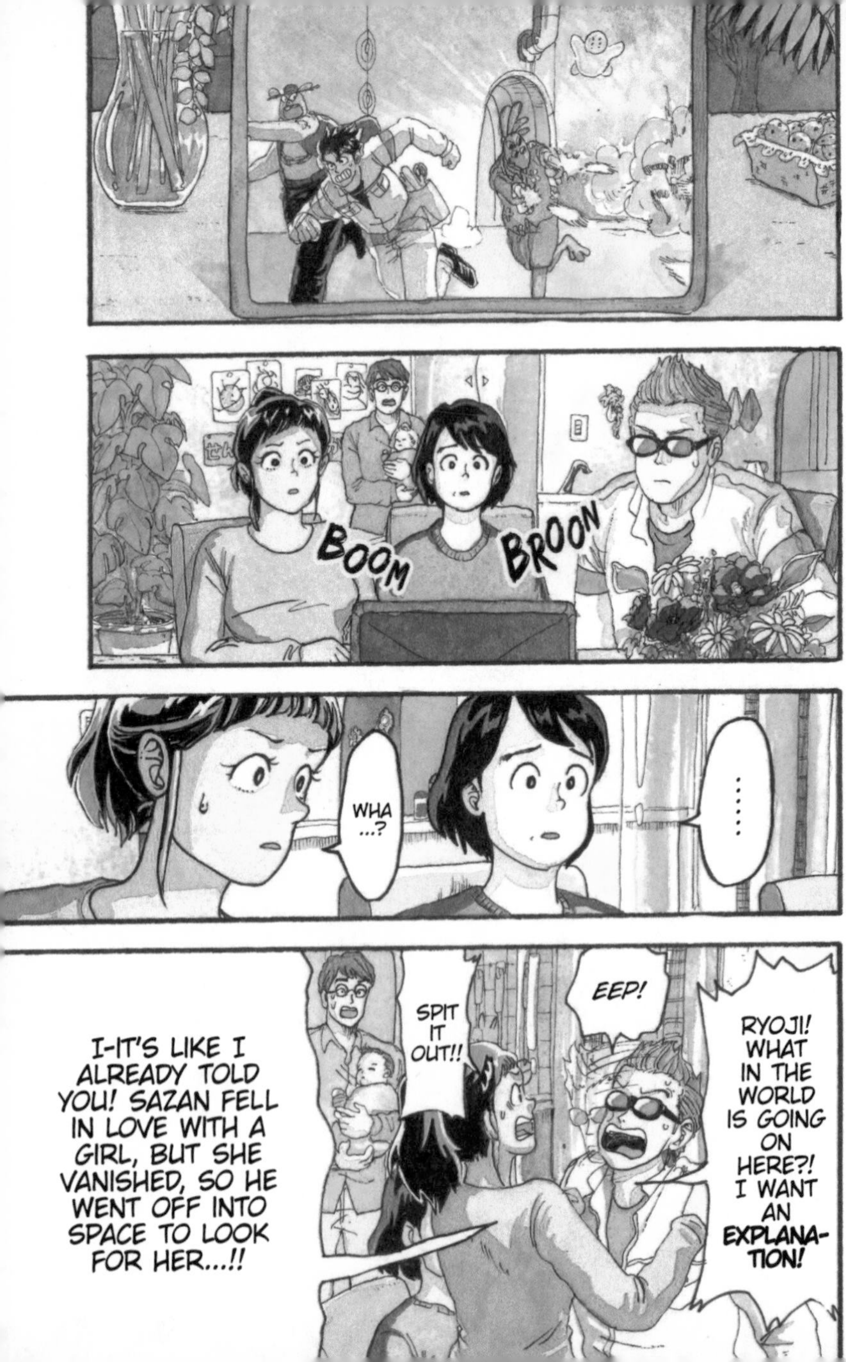
BROON
BOOM
......
WHA ...?
RYOJI! WHAT IN THE WORLD IS GOING ON HERE?! I WANT AN **EXPLANATION!**
EEP!
SPIT IT OUT!!
I-IT'S LIKE I ALREADY TOLD YOU! SAZAN FELL IN LOVE WITH A GIRL, BUT SHE VANISHED, SO HE WENT OFF INTO SPACE TO LOOK FOR HER...!!

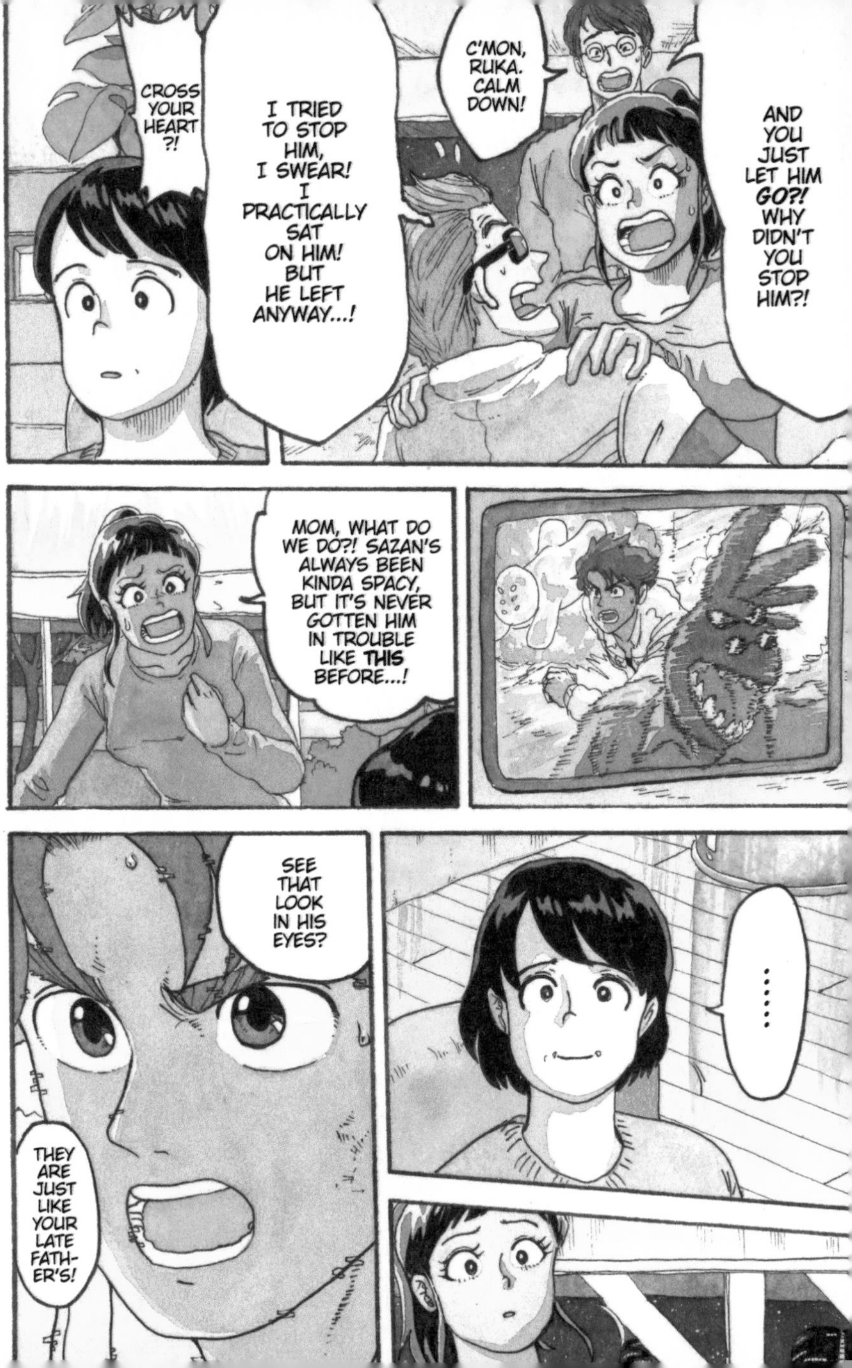
AND YOU JUST LET HIM GO?! WHY DIDN'T YOU STOP HIM?!
C'MON, RUKA. CALM DOWN!
I TRIED TO STOP HIM, I SWEAR! I PRACTICALLY SAT ON HIM! BUT HE LEFT ANYWAY...!
CROSS YOUR HEART?!
MOM, WHAT DO WE DO?! SAZAN'S ALWAYS BEEN KINDA SPACY, BUT IT'S NEVER GOTTEN HIM IN TROUBLE LIKE THIS BEFORE...!
......
SEE THAT LOOK IN HIS EYES?
THEY ARE JUST LIKE YOUR LATE FATHER'S!

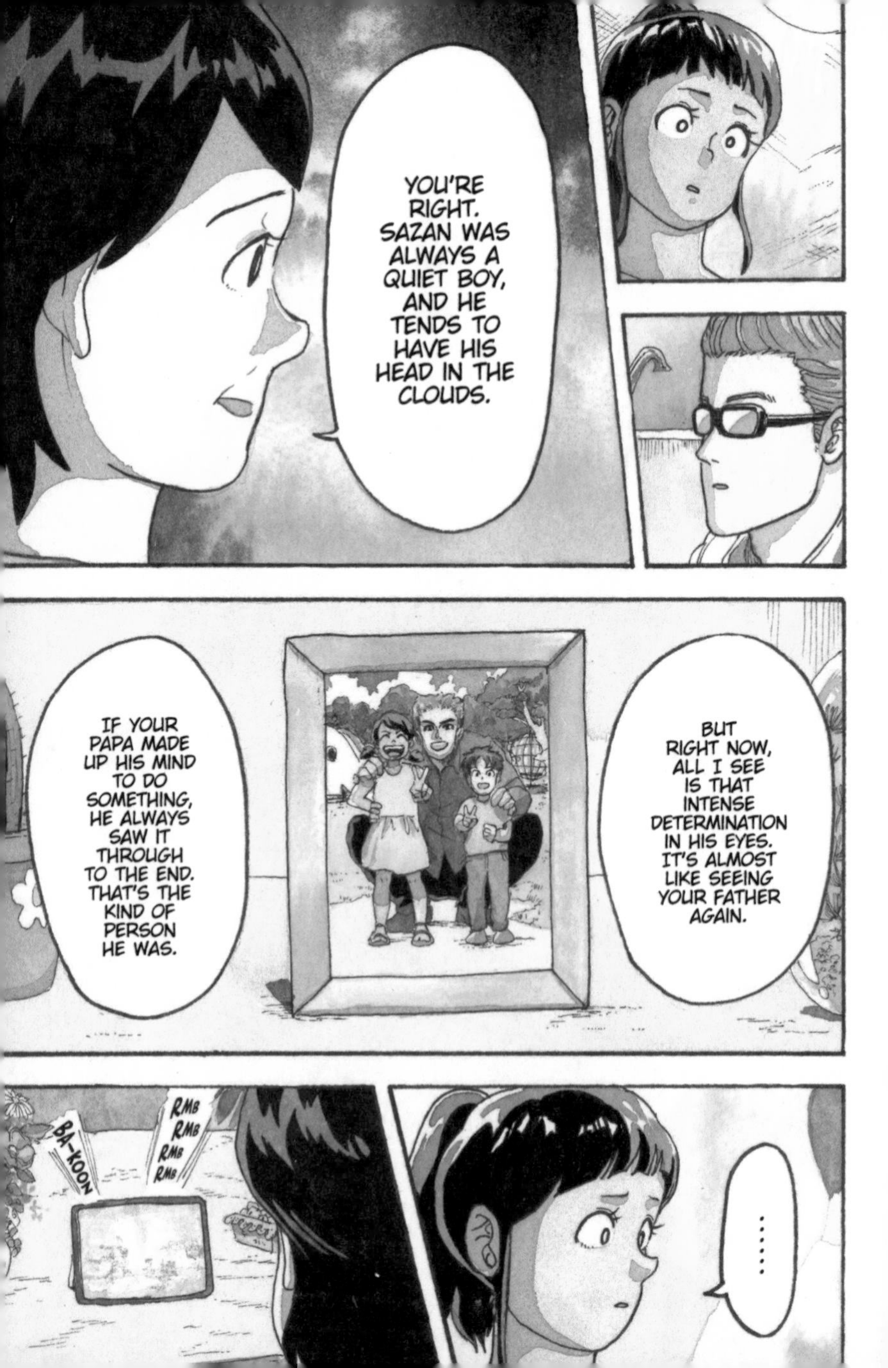
YOU'RE RIGHT. SAZAN WAS ALWAYS A QUIET BOY, AND HE TENDS TO HAVE HIS HEAD IN THE CLOUDS.
IF YOUR PAPA MADE UP HIS MIND TO DO SOMETHING, HE ALWAYS SAW IT THROUGH TO THE END. THAT'S THE KIND OF PERSON HE WAS.
BUT RIGHT NOW, ALL I SEE IS THAT INTENSE DETERMINATION IN HIS EYES. IT'S ALMOST LIKE SEEING YOUR FATHER AGAIN.
......
RMB RMB RMB RMB
BA-KOON

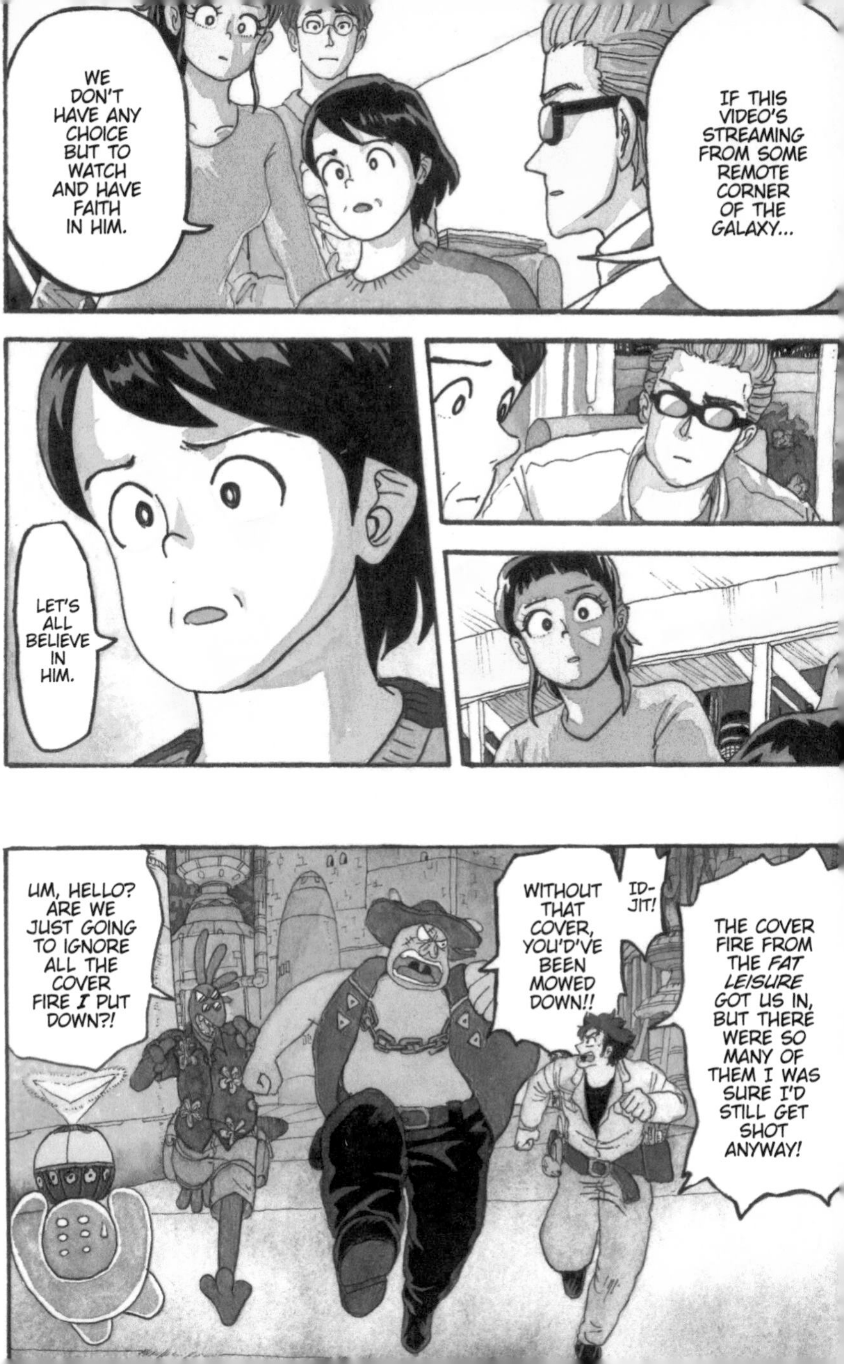
IF THIS VIDEO'S STREAMING FROM SOME REMOTE CORNER OF THE GALAXY...
WE DON'T HAVE ANY CHOICE BUT TO WATCH AND HAVE FAITH IN HIM.
LET'S ALL BELIEVE IN HIM.
THE COVER FIRE FROM THE *FAT LEISURE* GOT US IN, BUT THERE WERE SO MANY OF THEM I WAS SURE I'D STILL GET SHOT ANYWAY!
ID-JIT!
WITHOUT THAT COVER, YOU'D'VE BEEN MOWED DOWN!!
UM, HELLO? ARE WE JUST GOING TO IGNORE ALL THE COVER FIRE *I* PUT DOWN?!

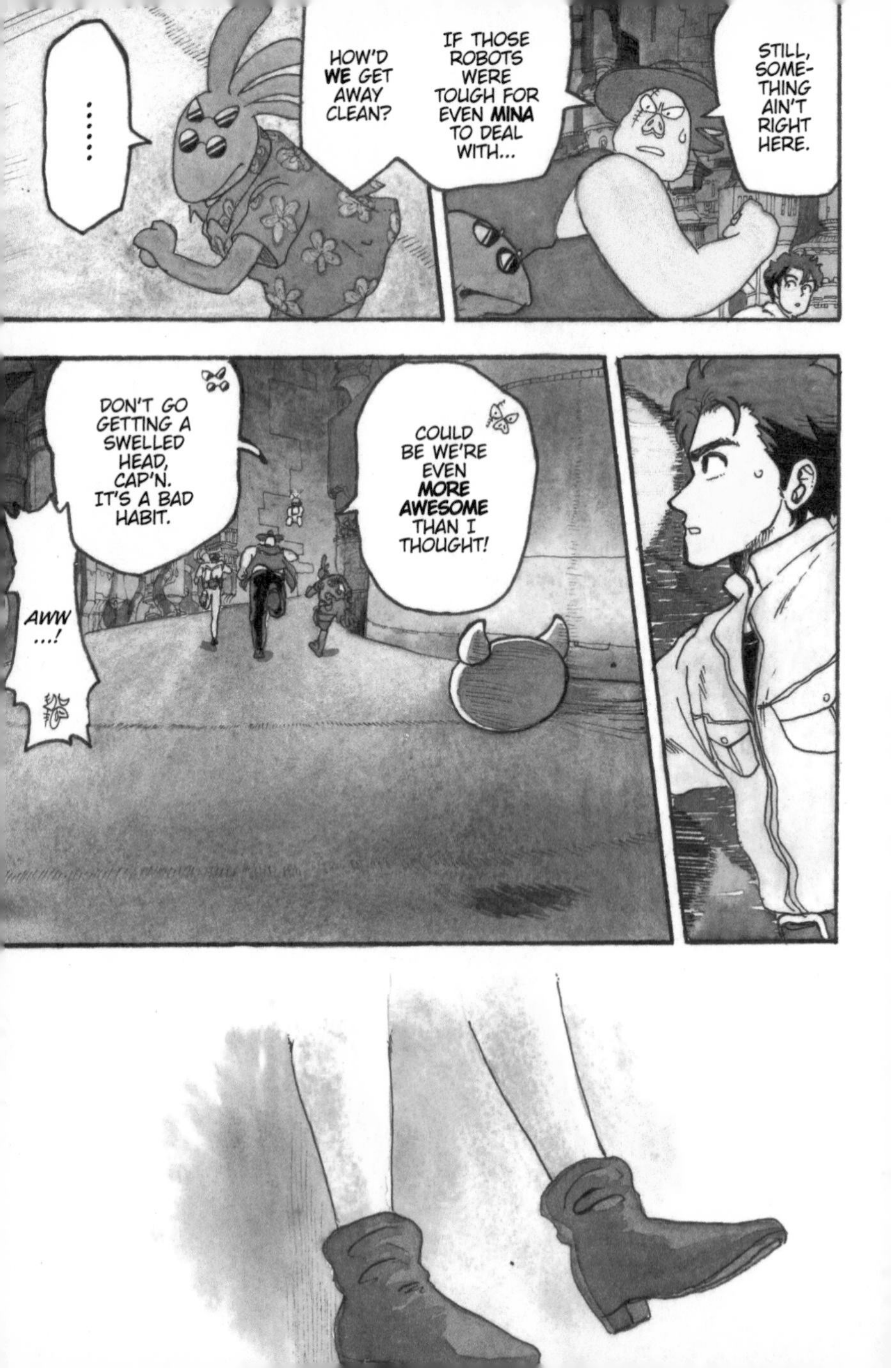
STILL, SOME-THING AIN'T RIGHT HERE.
IF THOSE ROBOTS WERE TOUGH FOR EVEN MINA TO DEAL WITH...
HOW'D WE GET AWAY CLEAN?
......
COULD BE WE'RE EVEN MORE AWESOME THAN I THOUGHT!
DON'T GO GETTING A SWELLED HEAD, CAP'N. IT'S A BAD HABIT.
AWW...!

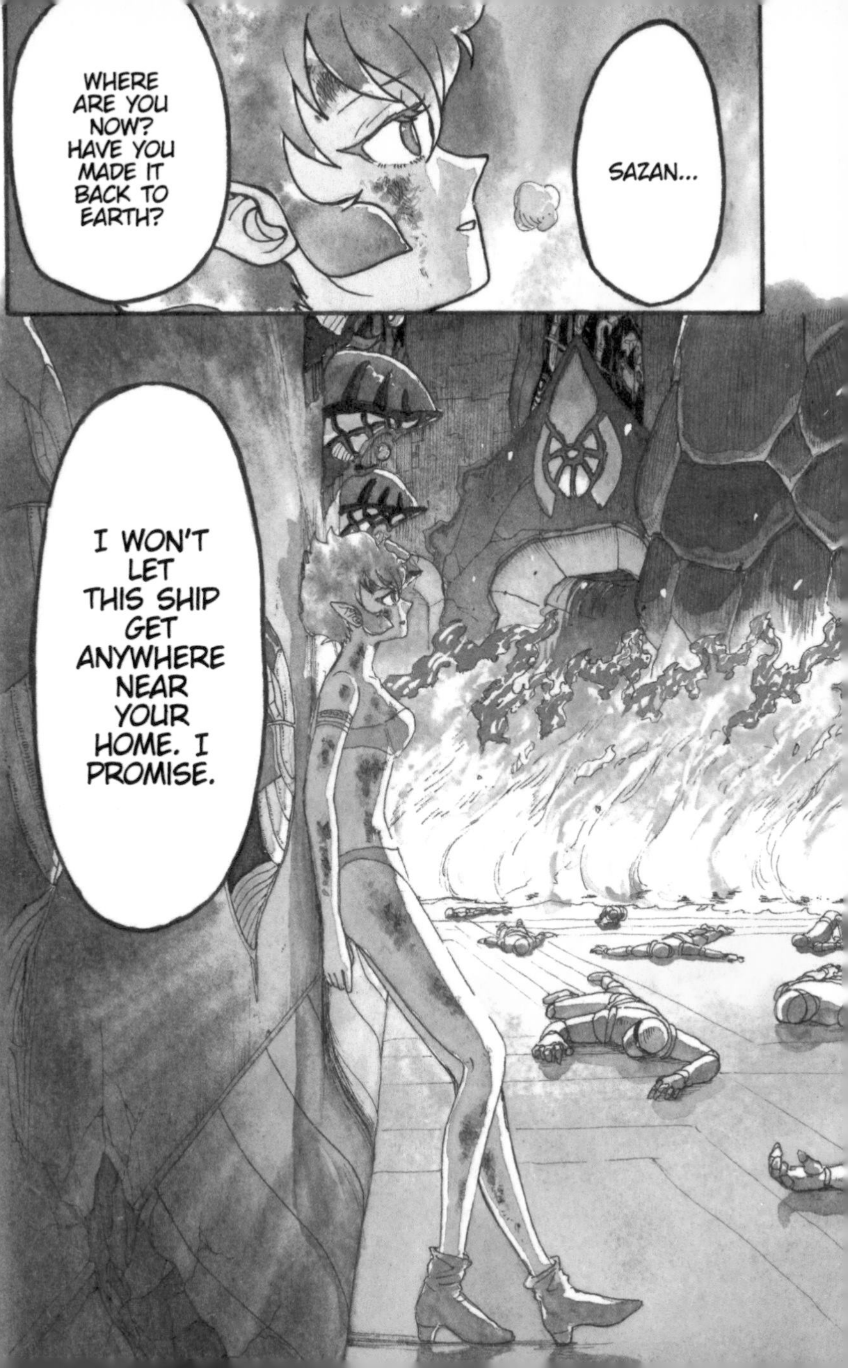
SAZAN...
WHERE ARE YOU NOW? HAVE YOU MADE IT BACK TO EARTH?
I WON'T LET THIS SHIP GET ANYWHERE NEAR YOUR HOME. I PROMISE.

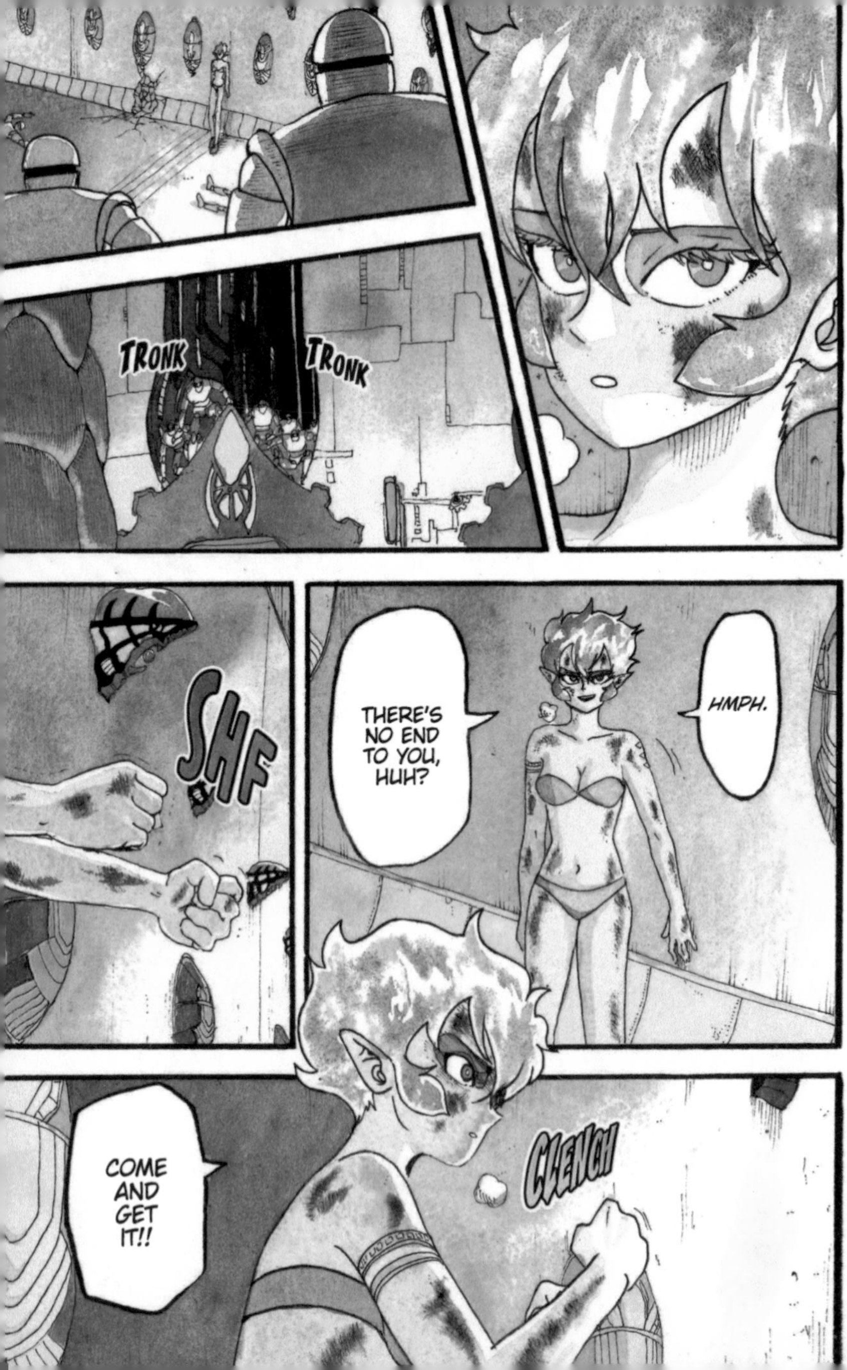
TRONK
TRONK
HMPH.
THERE'S NO END TO YOU, HUH?
SHF
CLENCH
COME AND GET IT!!

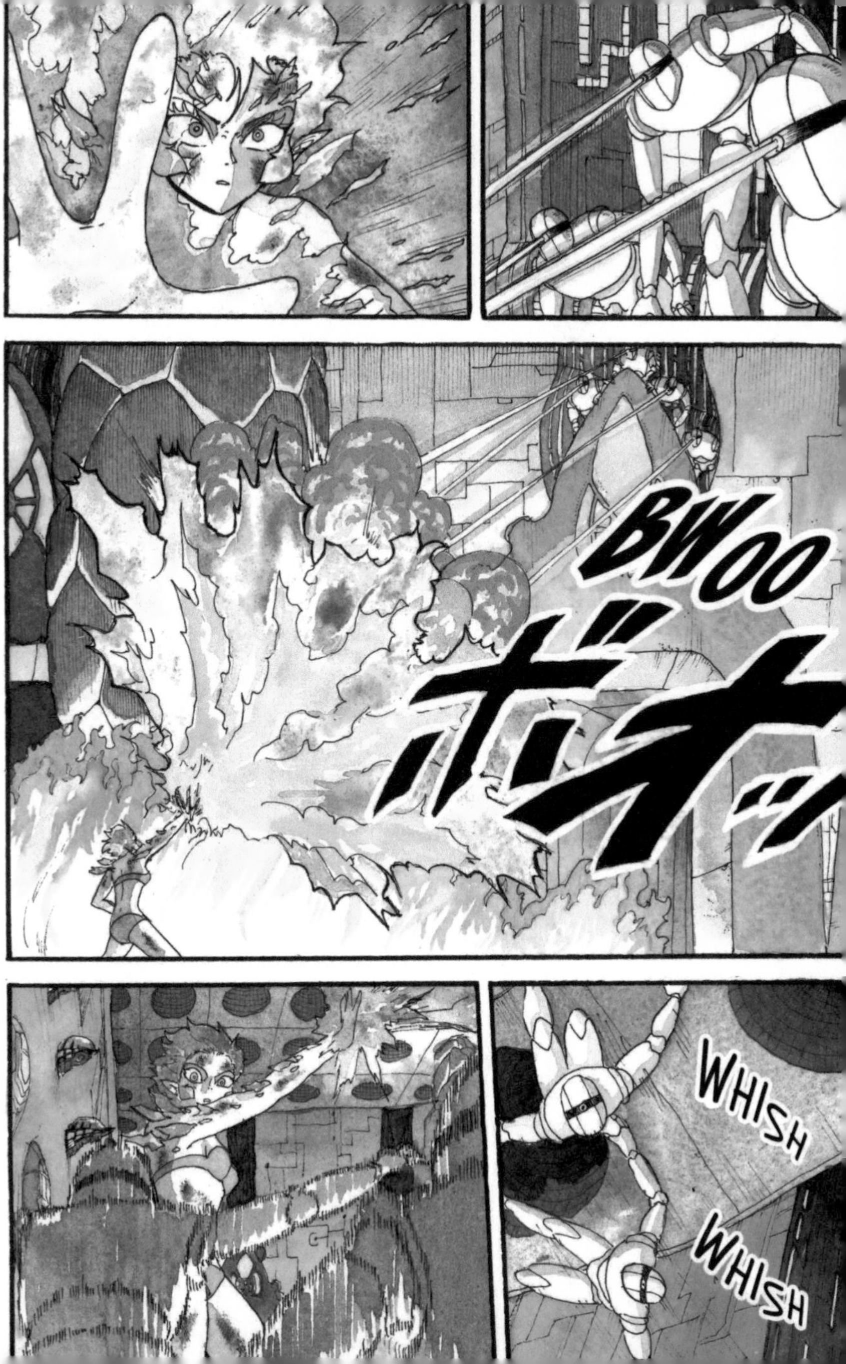
BWOO
ボオッ
WHISH
WHISH

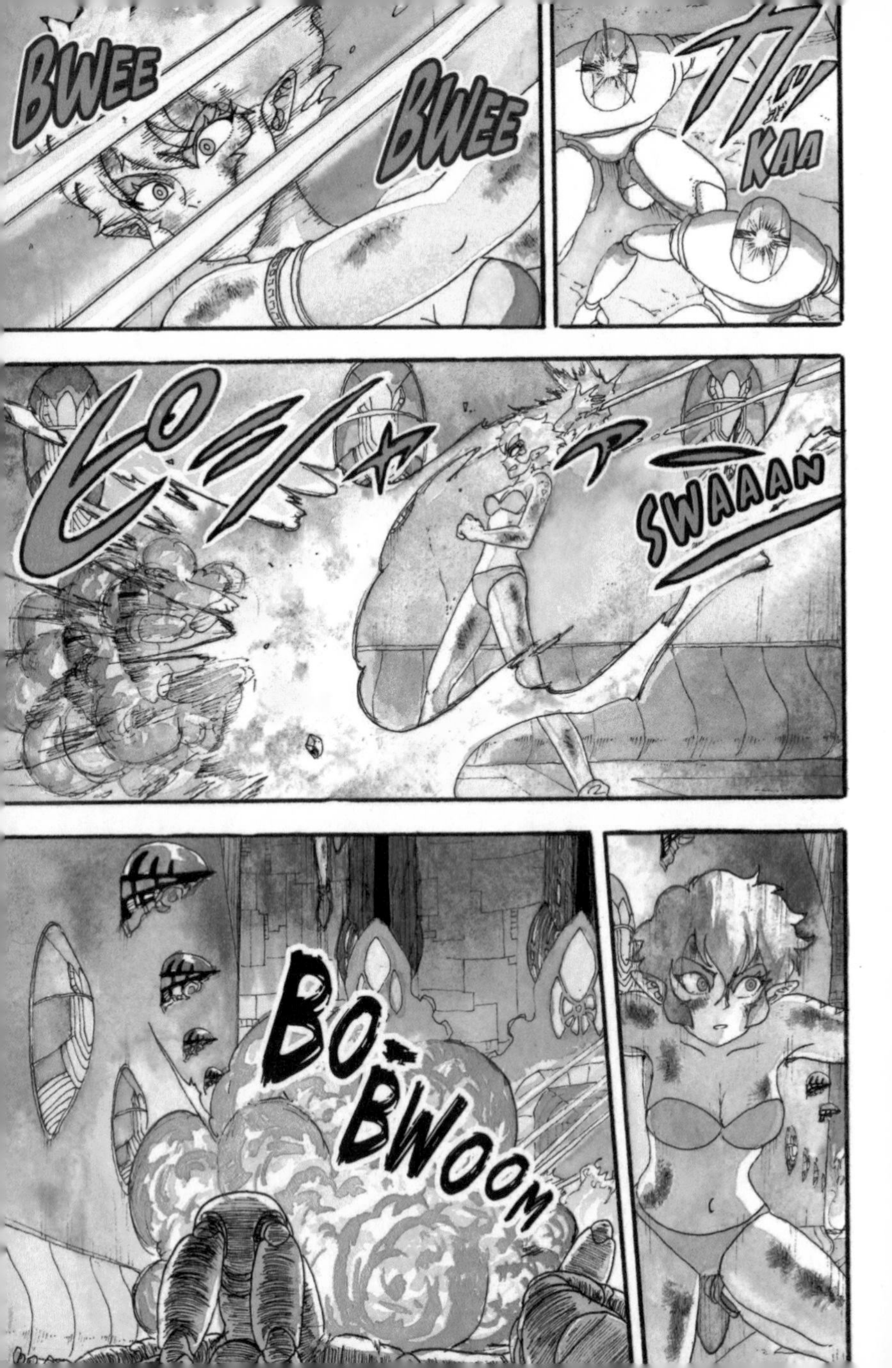
KAA
BWEE
BWEE
SWAAN
BO-BWOOM

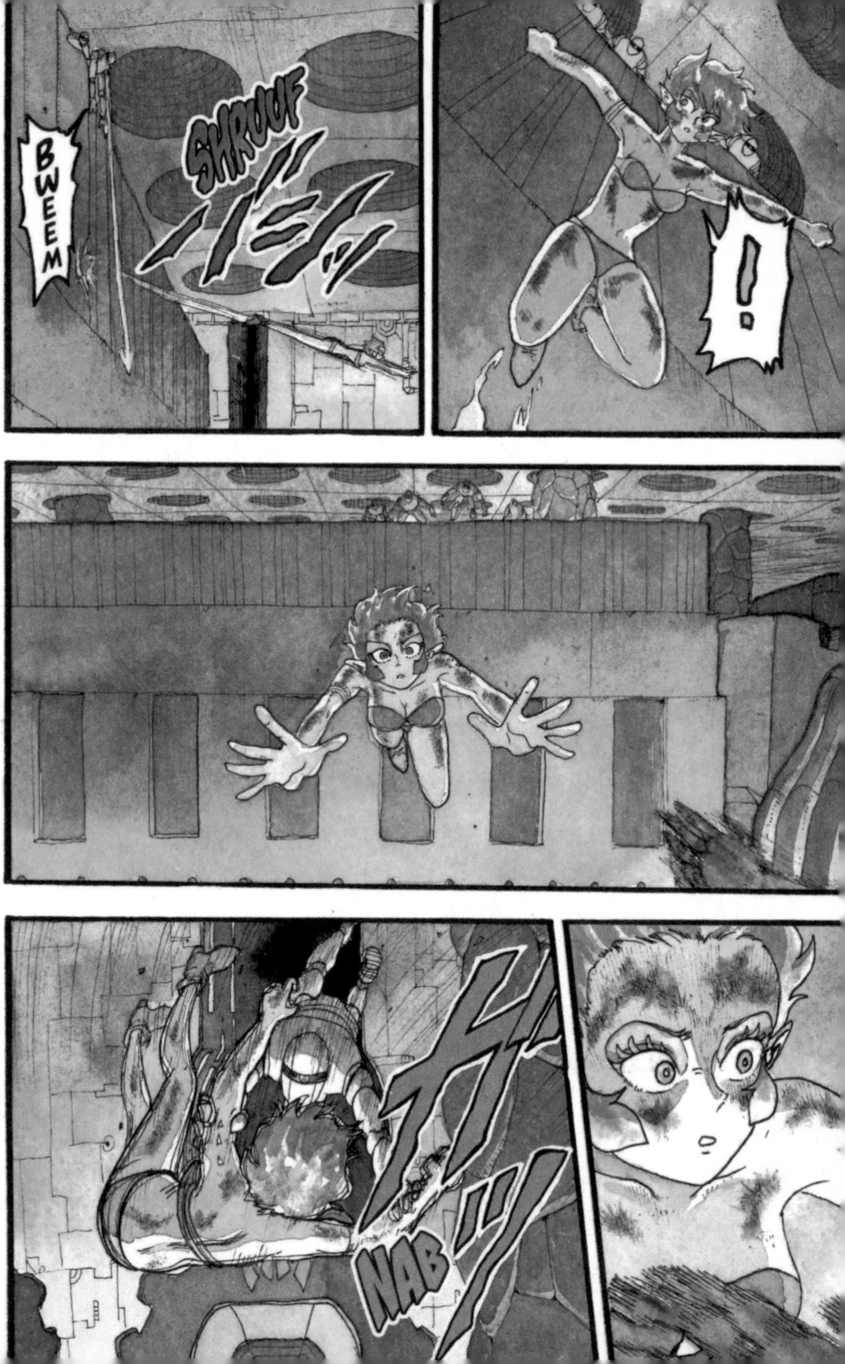
!
SHRUUF
BWEEM
NAB

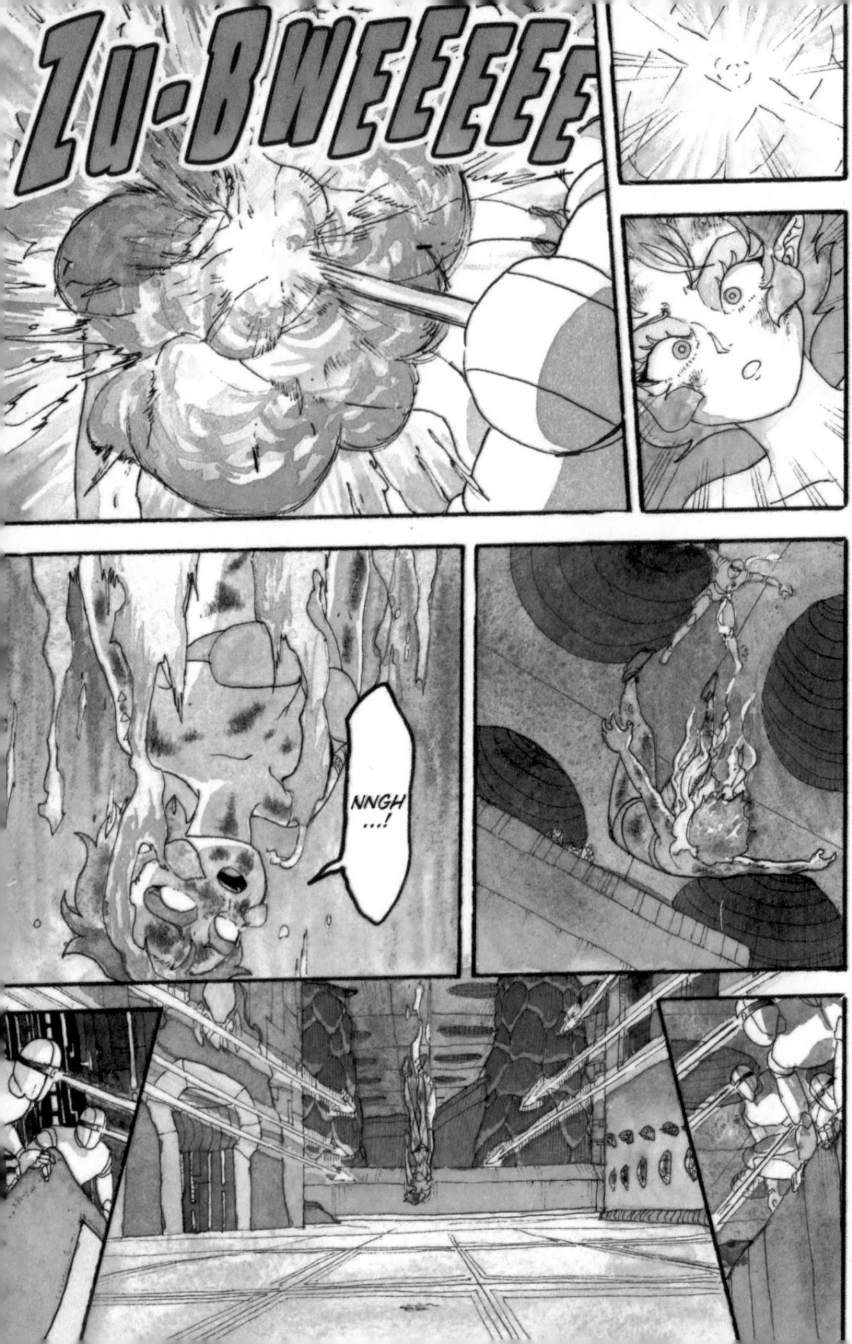
ZU-BWEEEEEE
NNGH ...!

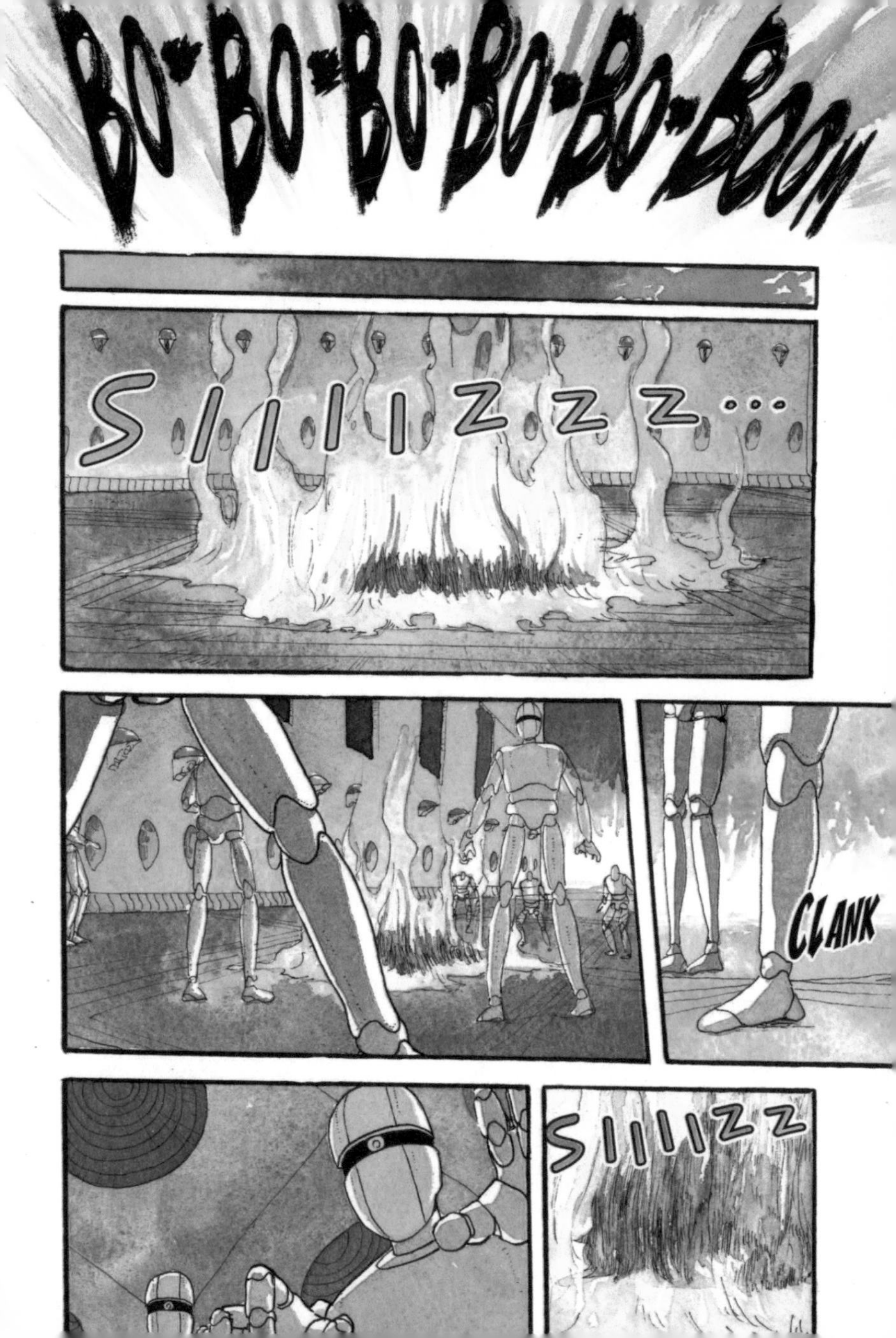
BO-BO-BO-BO-BO-BOOM
SIIIIZZZ...
CLANK
SIIIIZZ

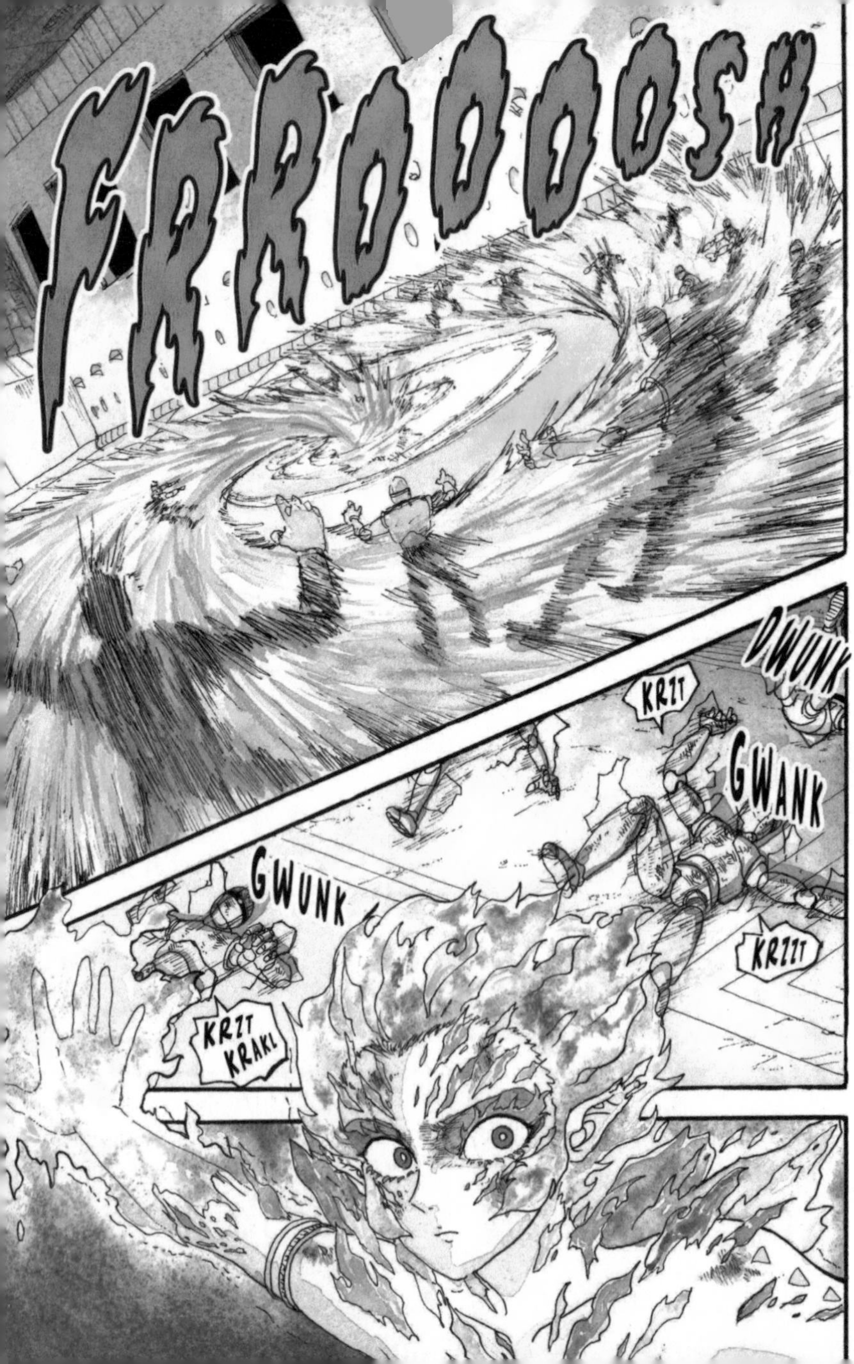
FRROOOOSH
DWUNK
KRZT
GWANK
KRZZT
GWUNK
KRZT
KRAKL

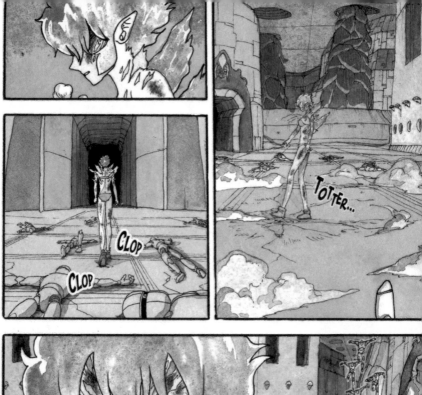

CLOP

CLOP

TOTTER...

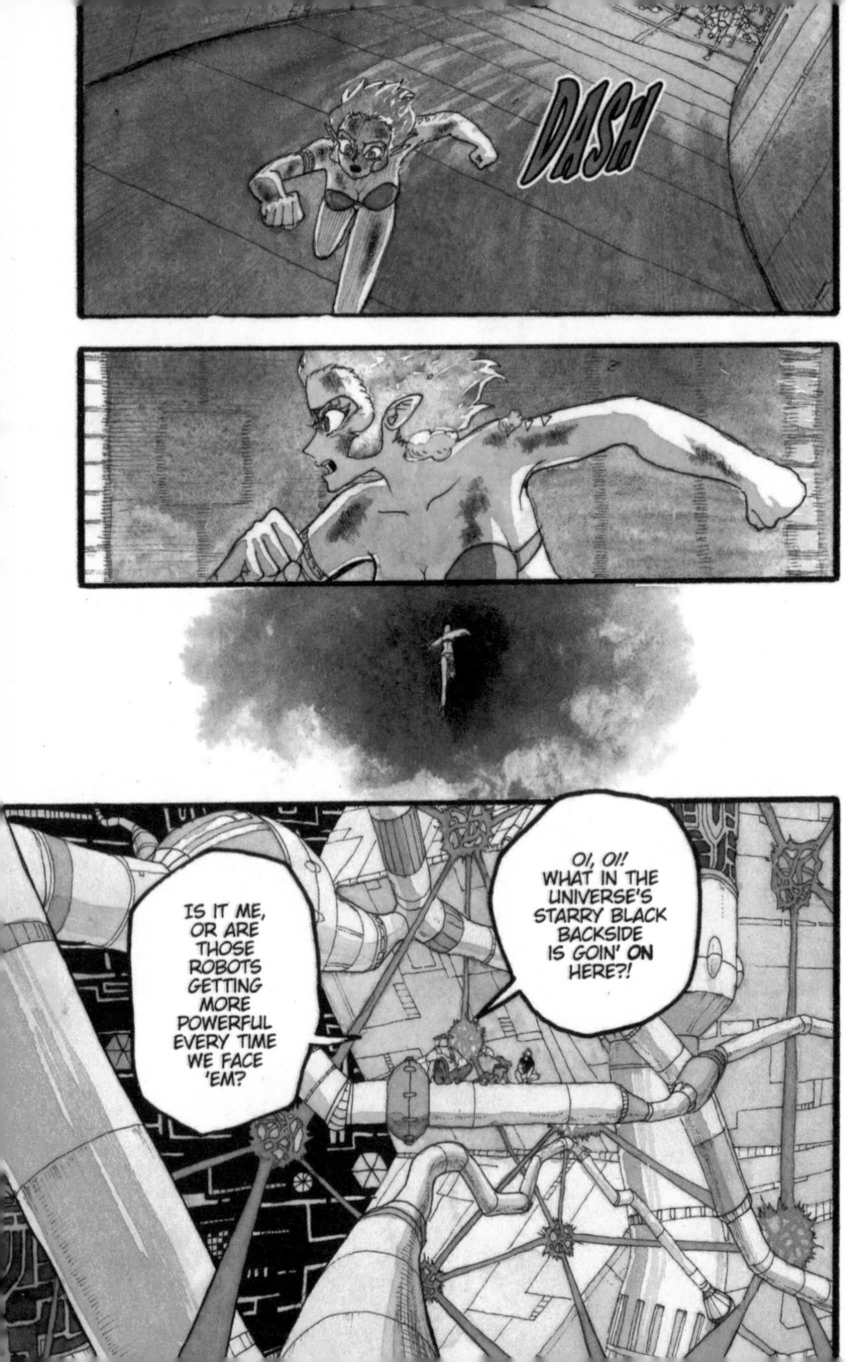
DASH
OI, OI! WHAT IN THE UNIVERSE'S STARRY BLACK BACKSIDE IS GOIN' ON HERE?!
IS IT ME, OR ARE THOSE ROBOTS GETTING MORE POWERFUL EVERY TIME WE FACE 'EM?

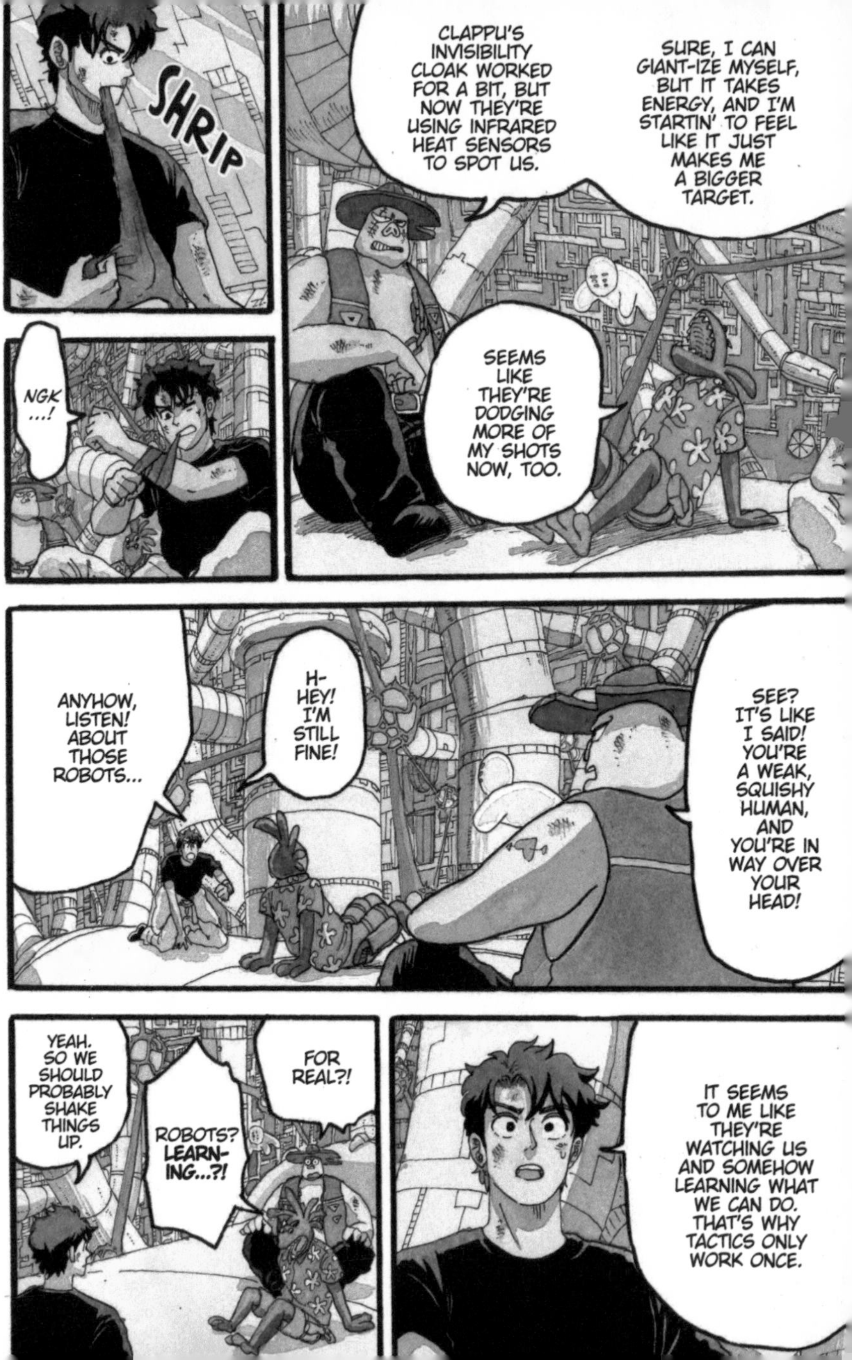
SURE, I CAN GIANT-IZE MYSELF, BUT IT TAKES ENERGY, AND I'M STARTIN' TO FEEL LIKE IT JUST MAKES ME A BIGGER TARGET.
CLAPPU'S INVISIBILITY CLOAK WORKED FOR A BIT, BUT NOW THEY'RE USING INFRARED HEAT SENSORS TO SPOT US.
SEEMS LIKE THEY'RE DODGING MORE OF MY SHOTS NOW, TOO.
SHRIP
NGK ...!
SEE? IT'S LIKE I SAID! YOU'RE A WEAK, SQUISHY HUMAN, AND YOU'RE IN WAY OVER YOUR HEAD!
H-HEY! I'M STILL FINE!
ANYHOW, LISTEN! ABOUT THOSE ROBOTS...
IT SEEMS TO ME LIKE THEY'RE WATCHING US AND SOMEHOW LEARNING WHAT WE CAN DO. THAT'S WHY TACTICS ONLY WORK ONCE.
FOR REAL?!
YEAH. SO WE SHOULD PROBABLY SHAKE THINGS UP.
ROBOTS? LEARNING...?!

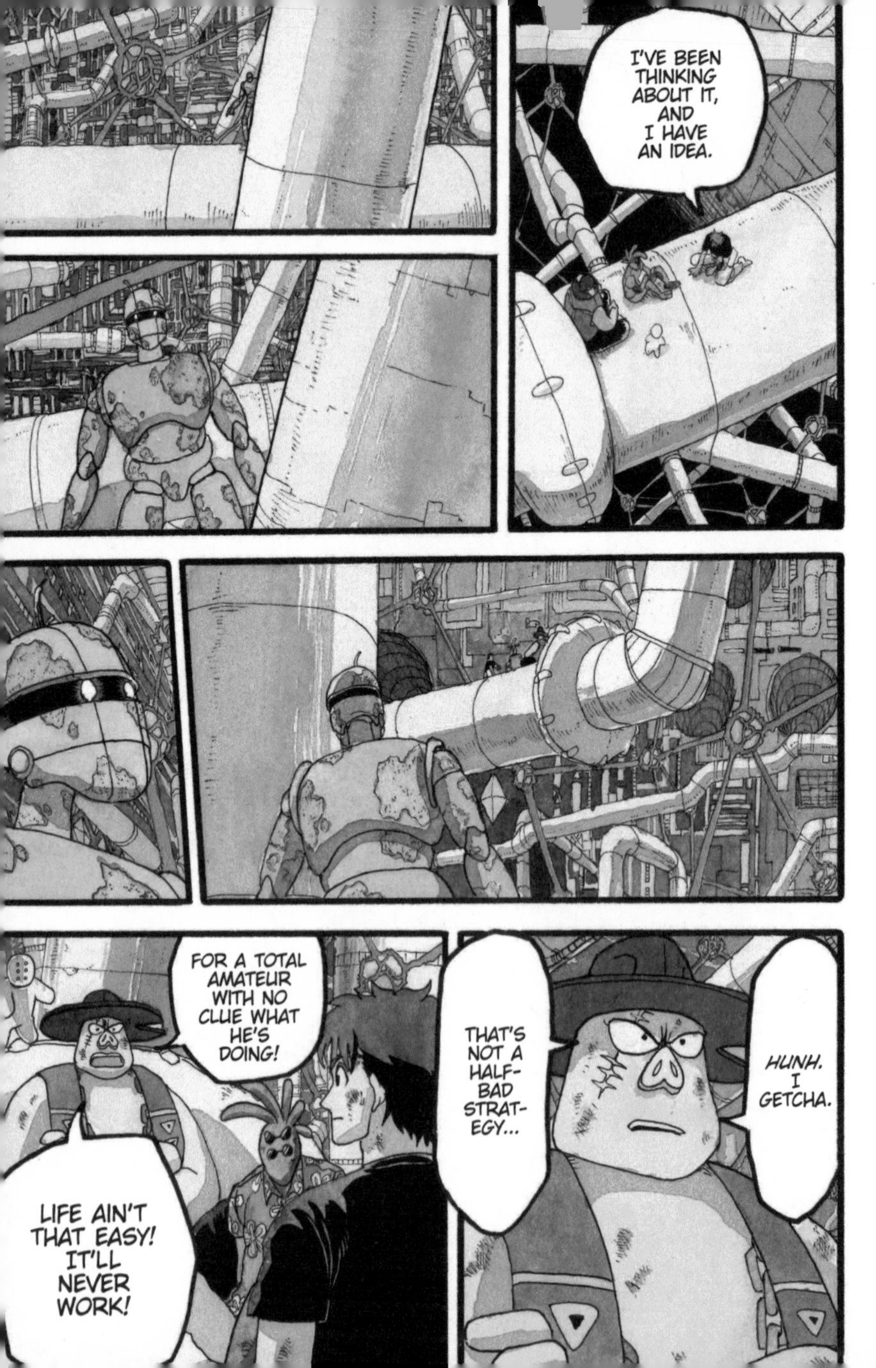
I'VE BEEN THINKING ABOUT IT, AND I HAVE AN IDEA.
HUNH. I GETCHA.
THAT'S NOT A HALF-BAD STRATEGY...
FOR A TOTAL AMATEUR WITH NO CLUE WHAT HE'S DOING!
LIFE AIN'T THAT EASY! IT'LL NEVER WORK!

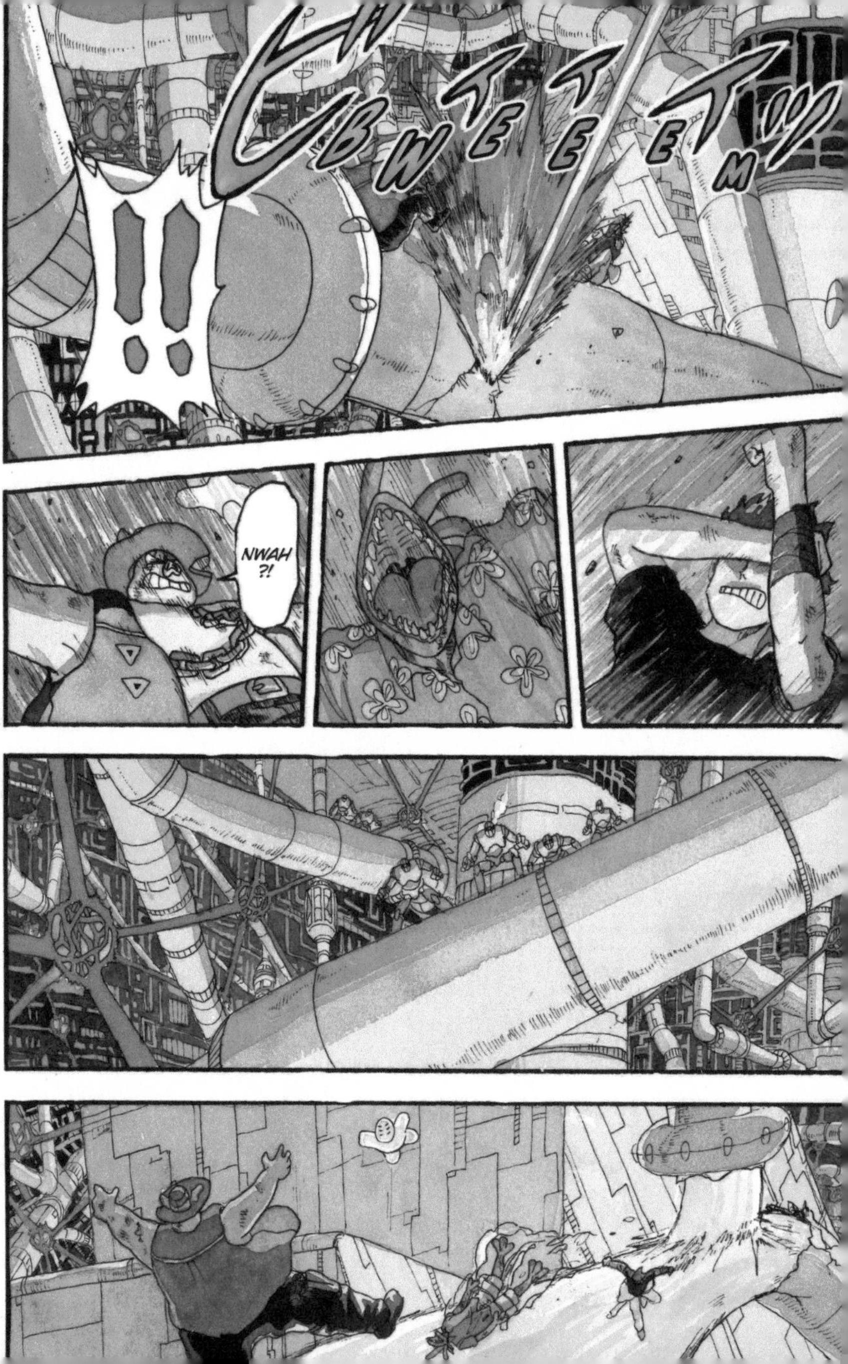
BWEEEM!!
!!
NWAH ?!

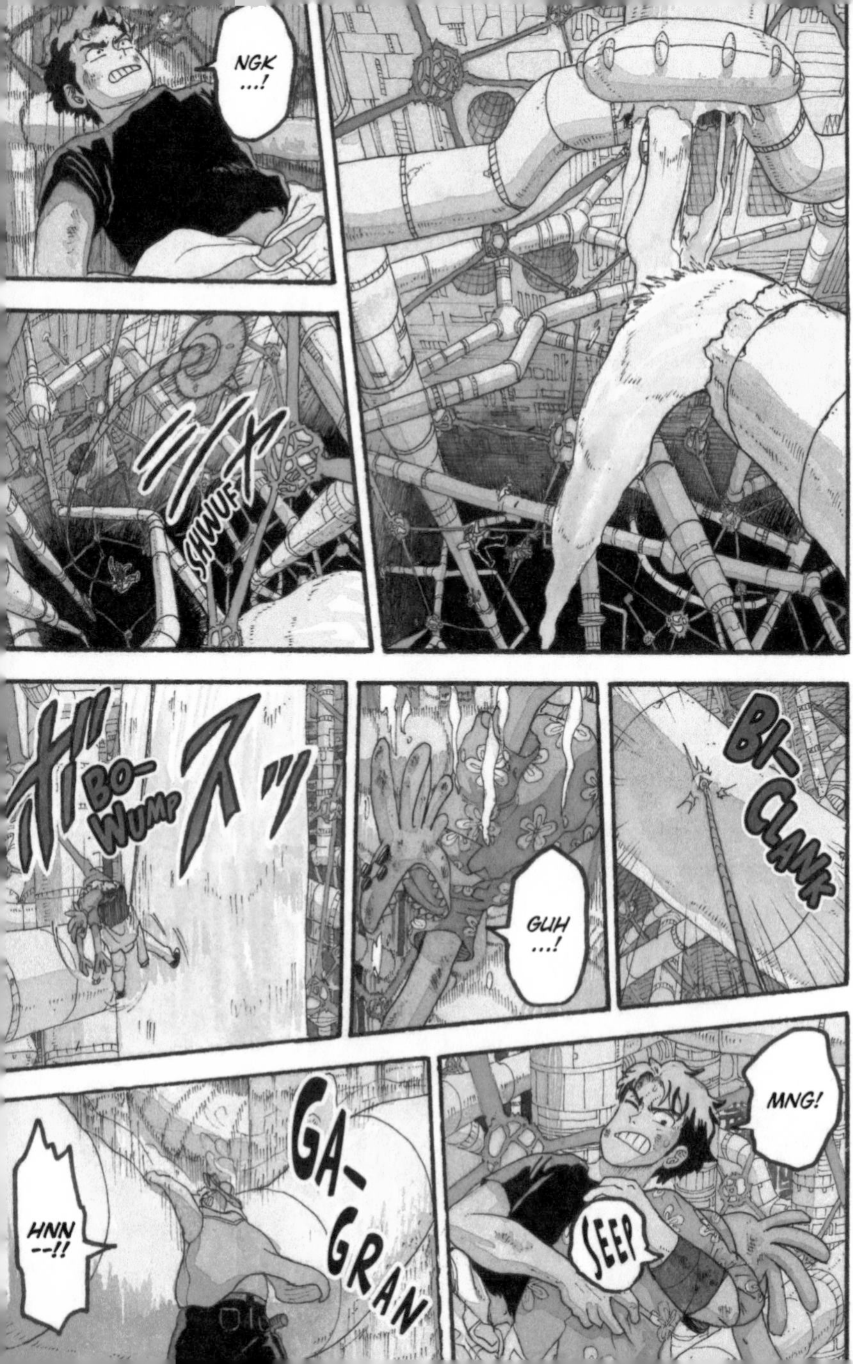
NGK ...!
SHWUF
BI-CLANK
GUH ...!
BO-WUMP
MNG!
SEEP
GA-GRAN
HNN --!!

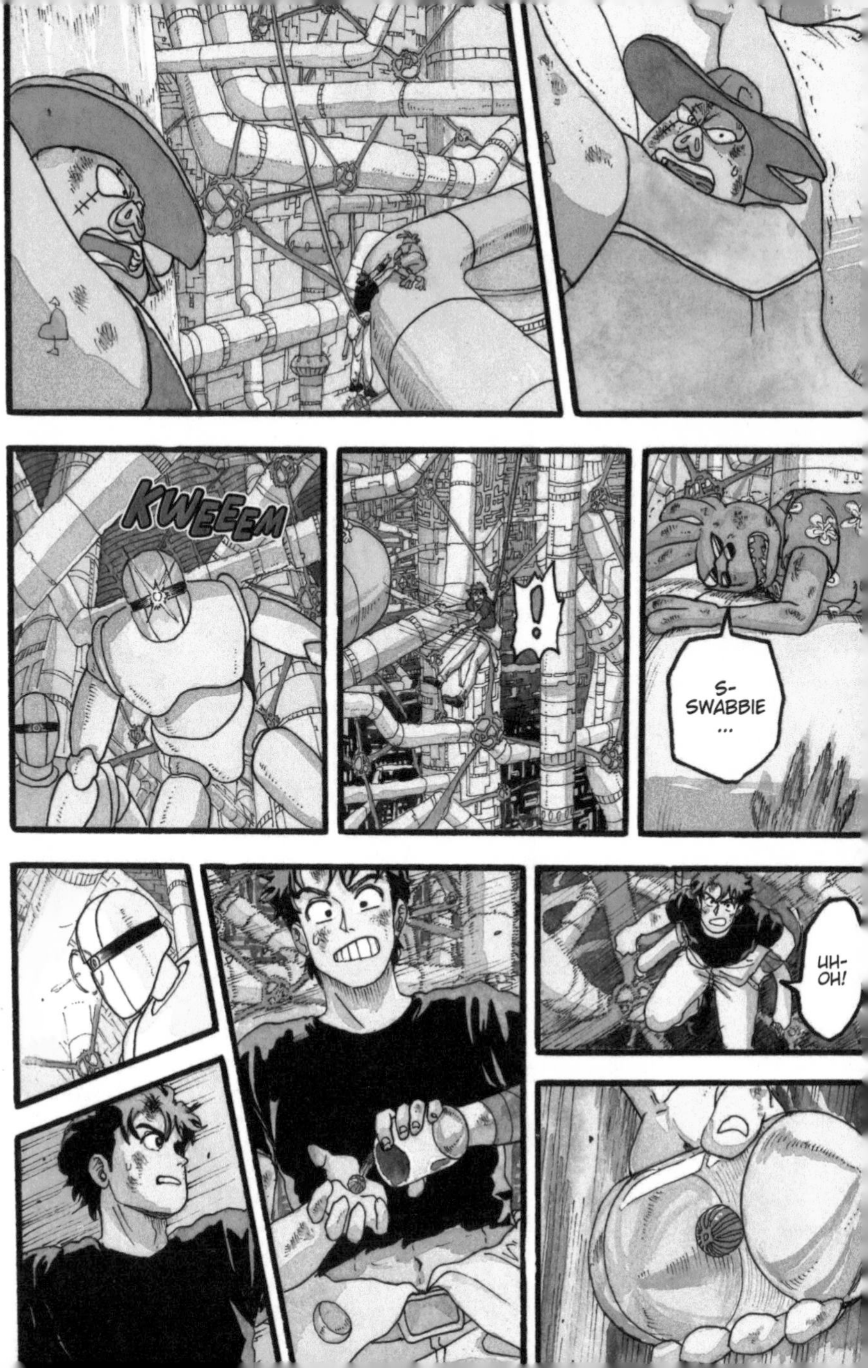
S-SWABBIE ...
!
KWEEEM
UH-OH!

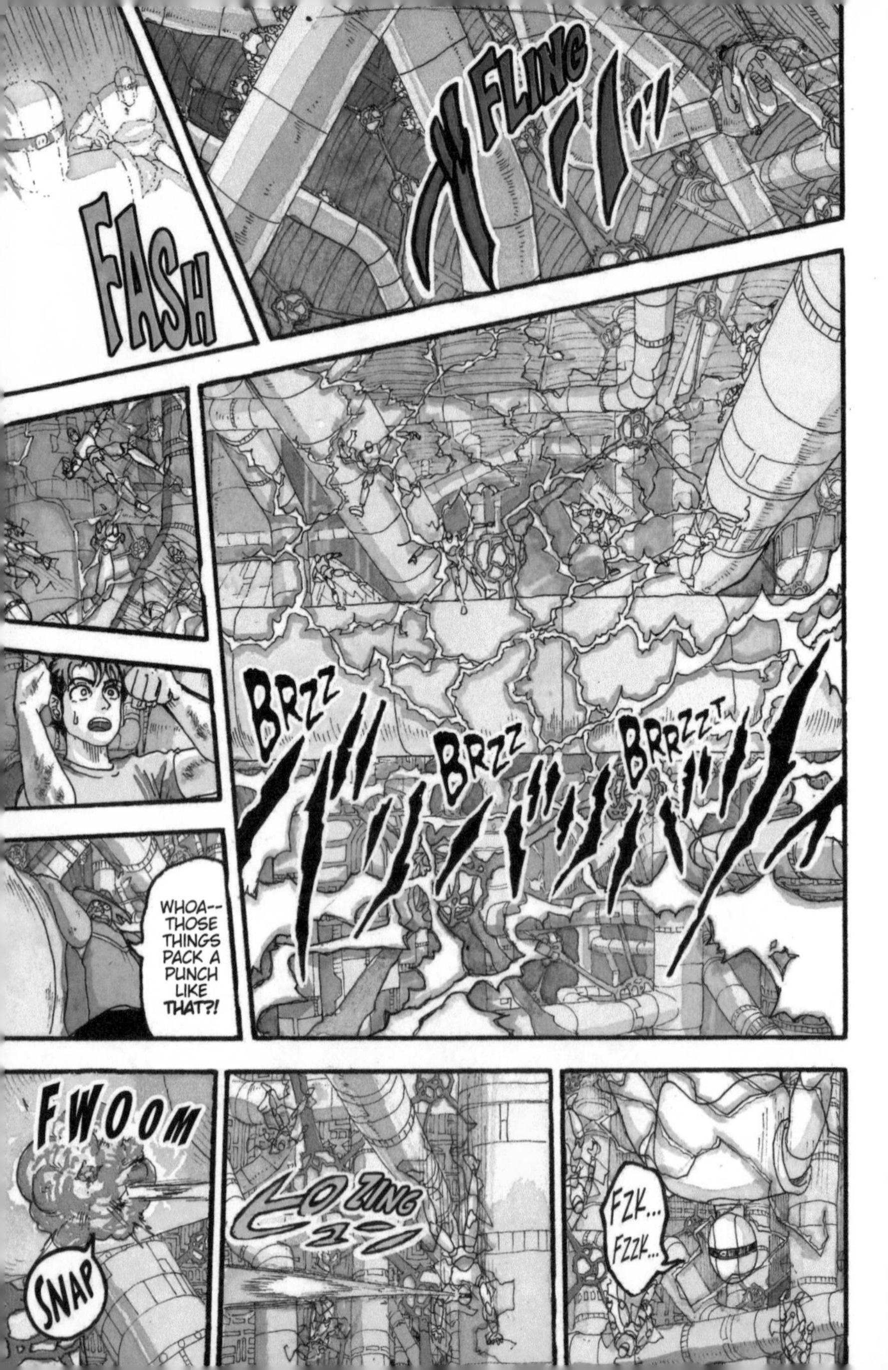
FLING
FASH
BRZZ
BRZZ
BRRZZT
WHOA-- THOSE THINGS PACK A PUNCH LIKE THAT?!
FZK... FZZK...
ZING
FWOOM
SNAP

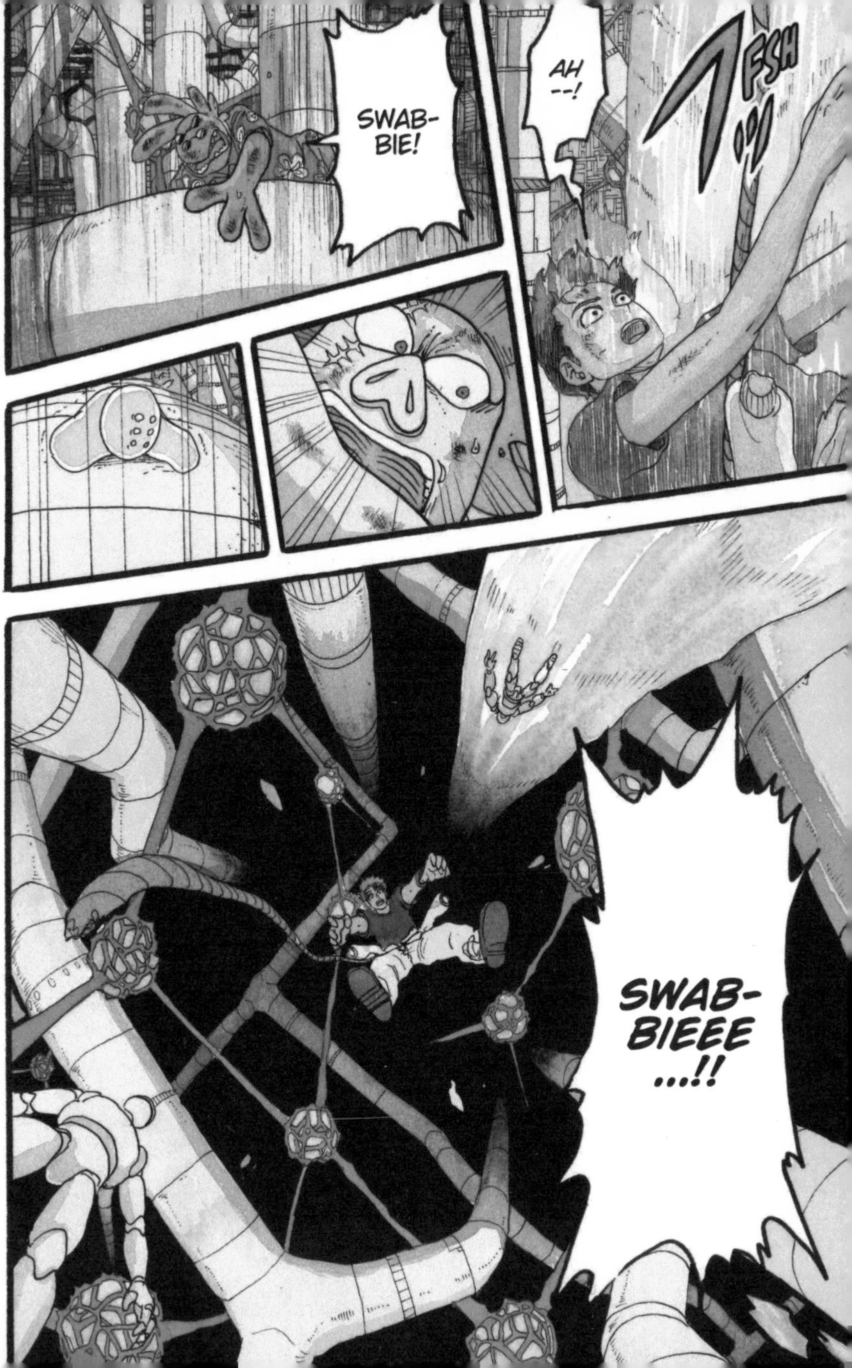
AH --!
FSH
SWAB-BIE!
SWAB-BIEEE ...!!

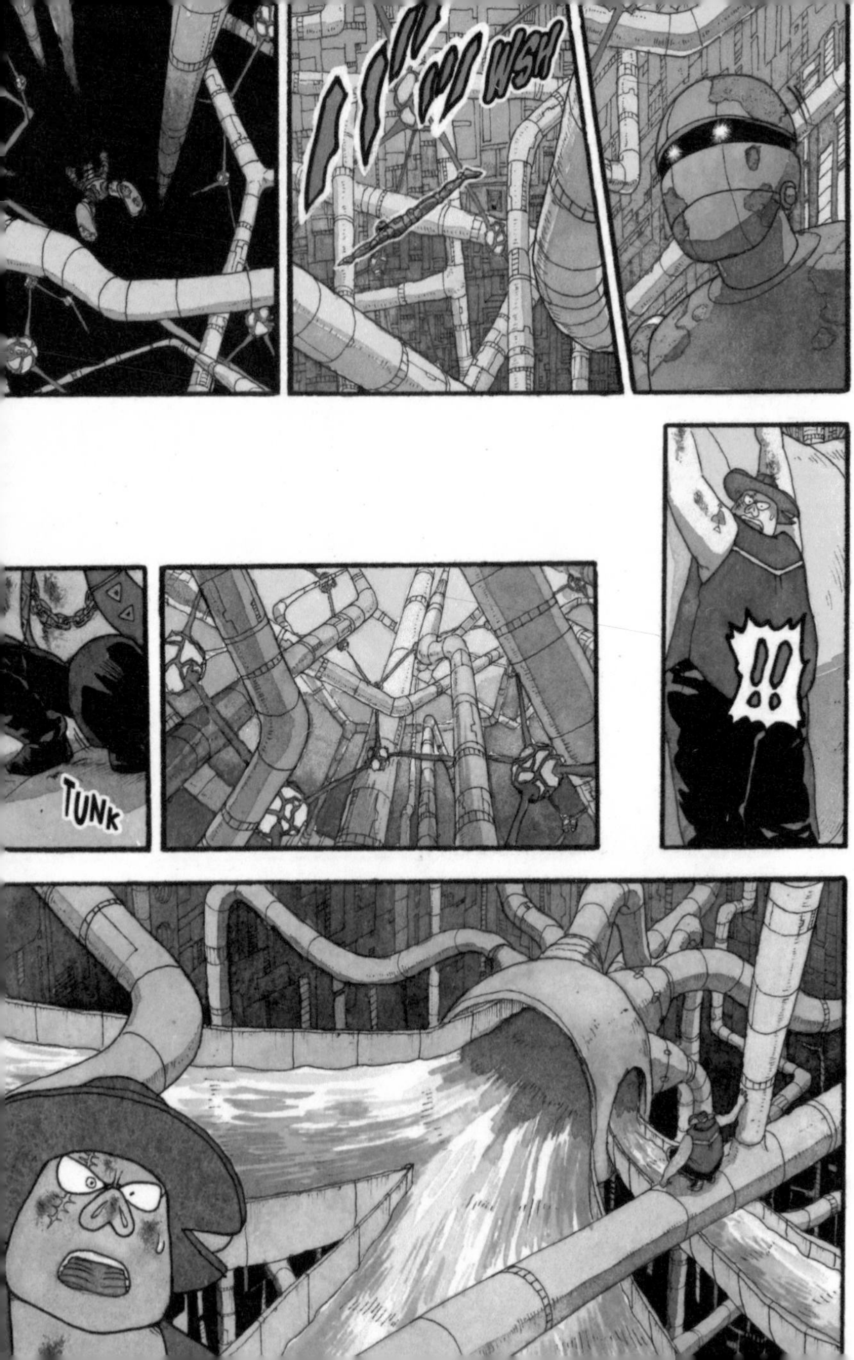
WSH
!!
TUNK

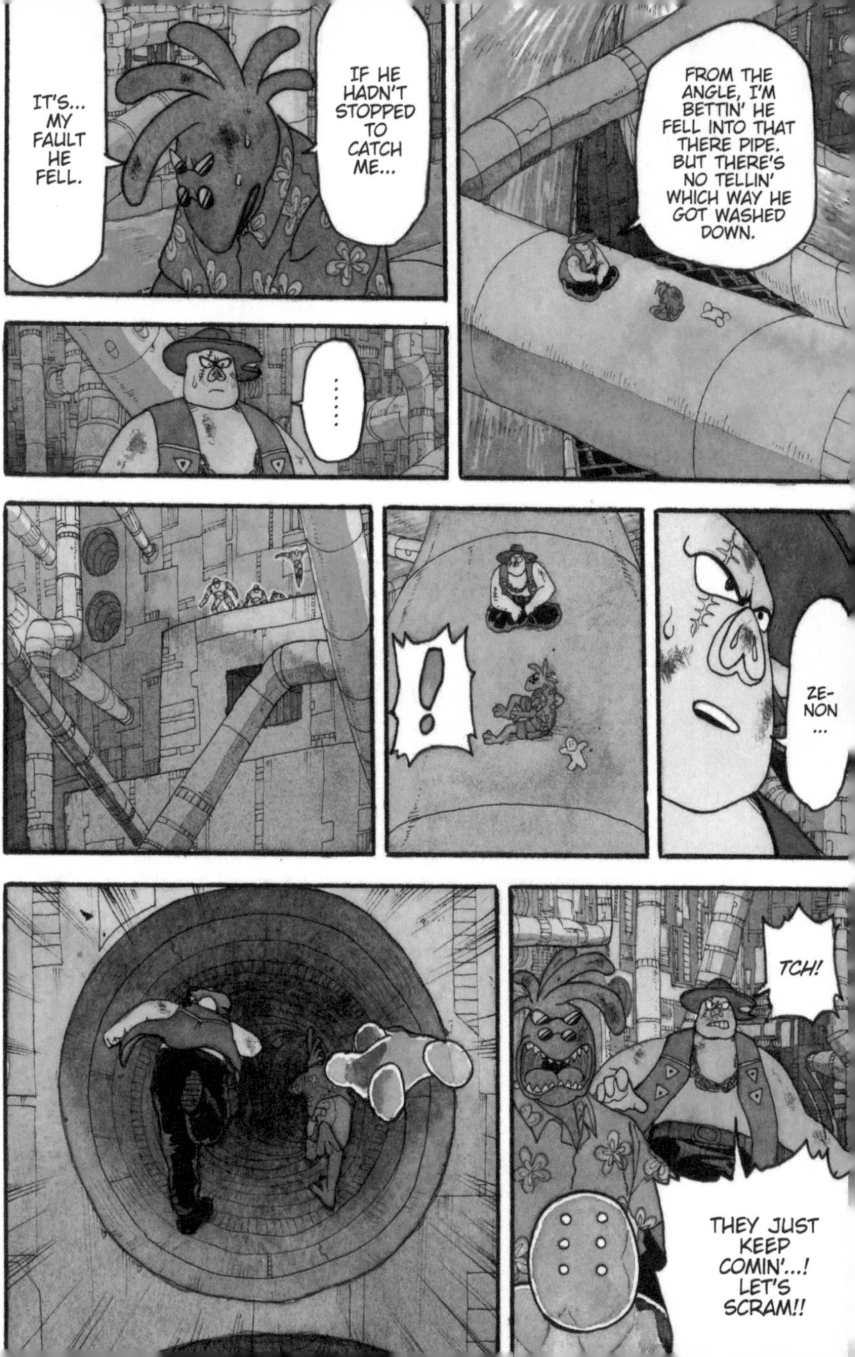

FROM THE ANGLE, I'M BETTIN' HE FELL INTO THAT THERE PIPE. BUT THERE'S NO TELLIN' WHICH WAY HE GOT WASHED DOWN.
IF HE HADN'T STOPPED TO CATCH ME...
IT'S... MY FAULT HE FELL.
......
ZE-NON ...
!
TCH!
THEY JUST KEEP COMIN'...! LET'S SCRAM!!

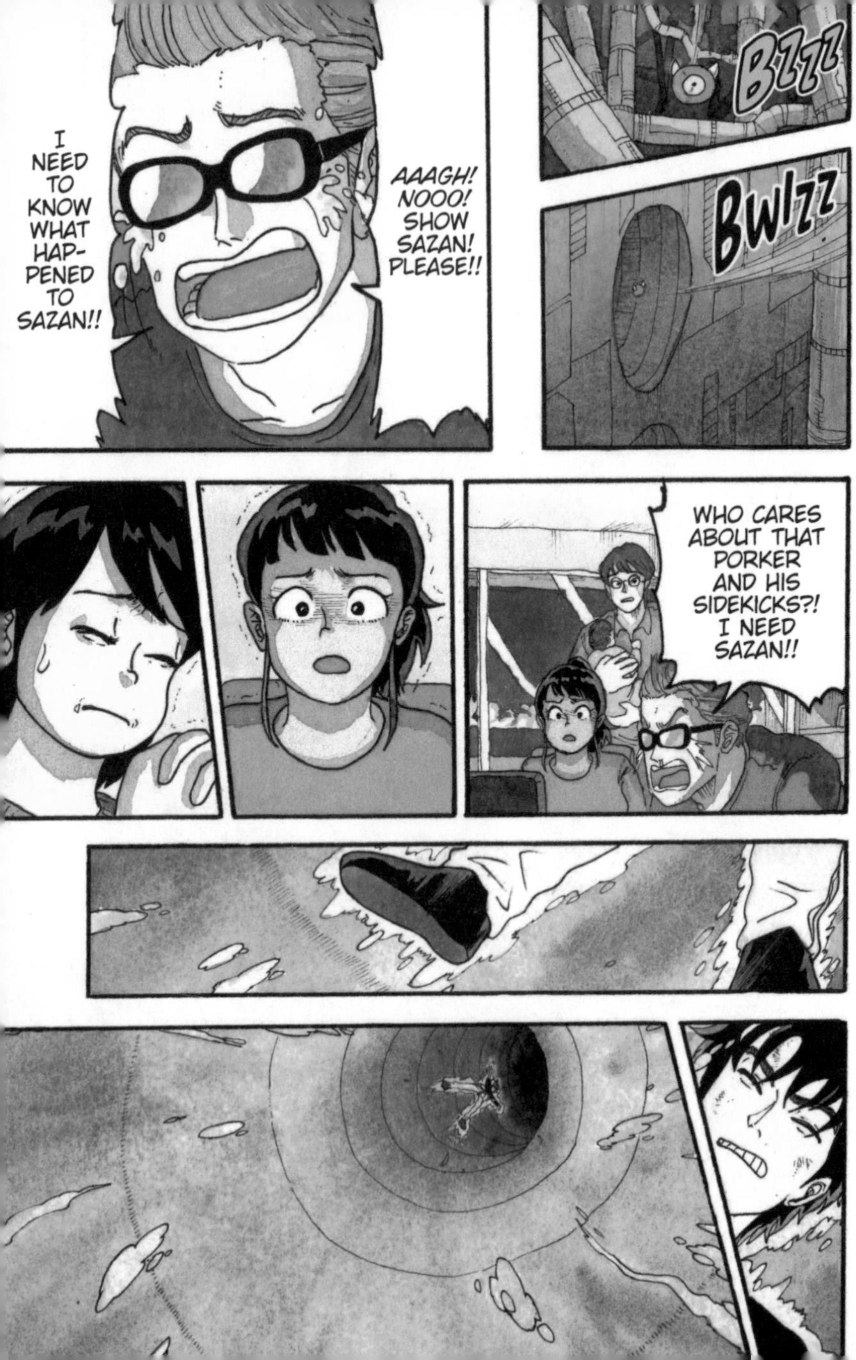
BZZZ
BWIZZ
AAAGH! NOOO! SHOW SAZAN! PLEASE!!
I NEED TO KNOW WHAT HAP-PENED TO SAZAN!!
WHO CARES ABOUT THAT PORKER AND HIS SIDEKICKS?! I NEED SAZAN!!

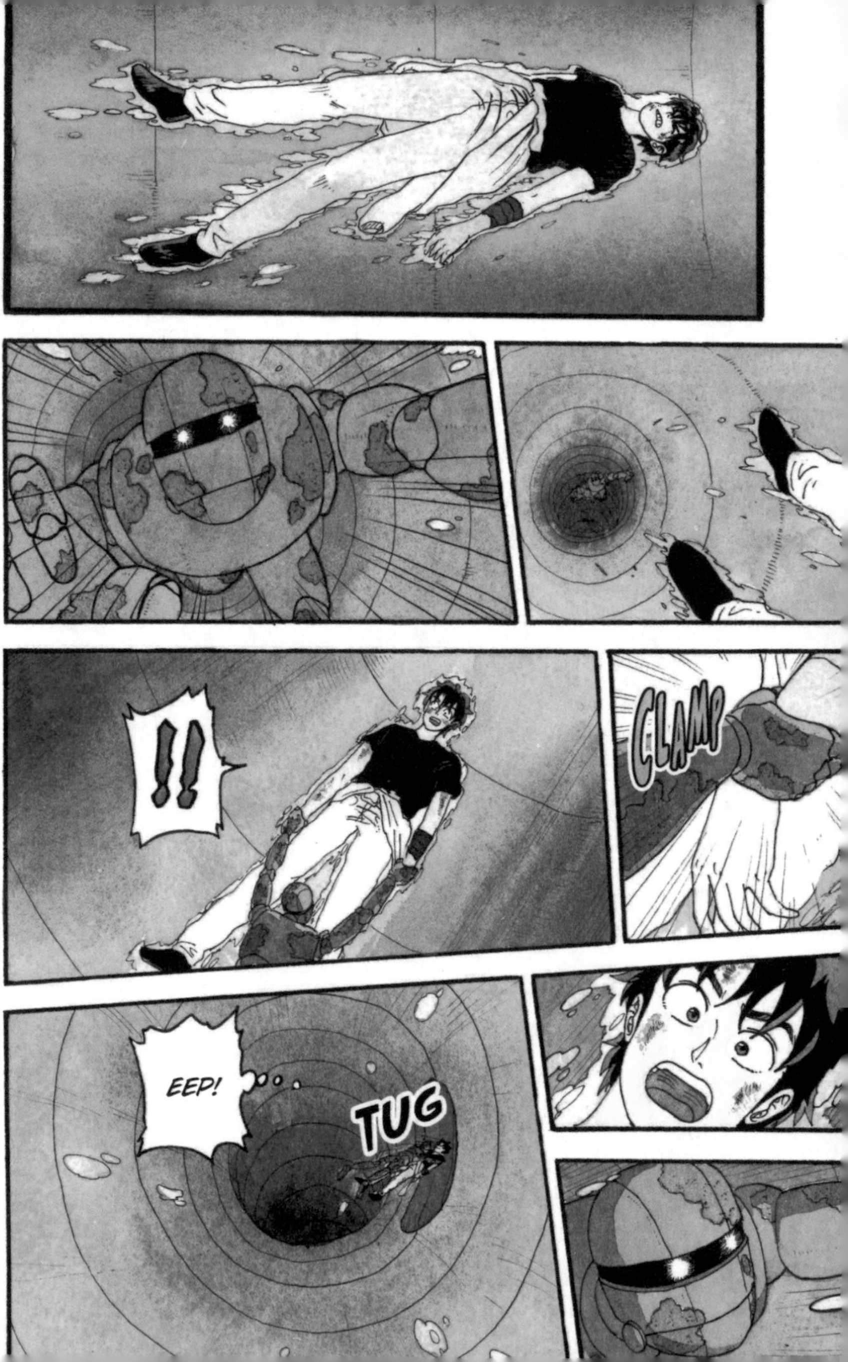
CLAMP
!!
EEP!
TUG

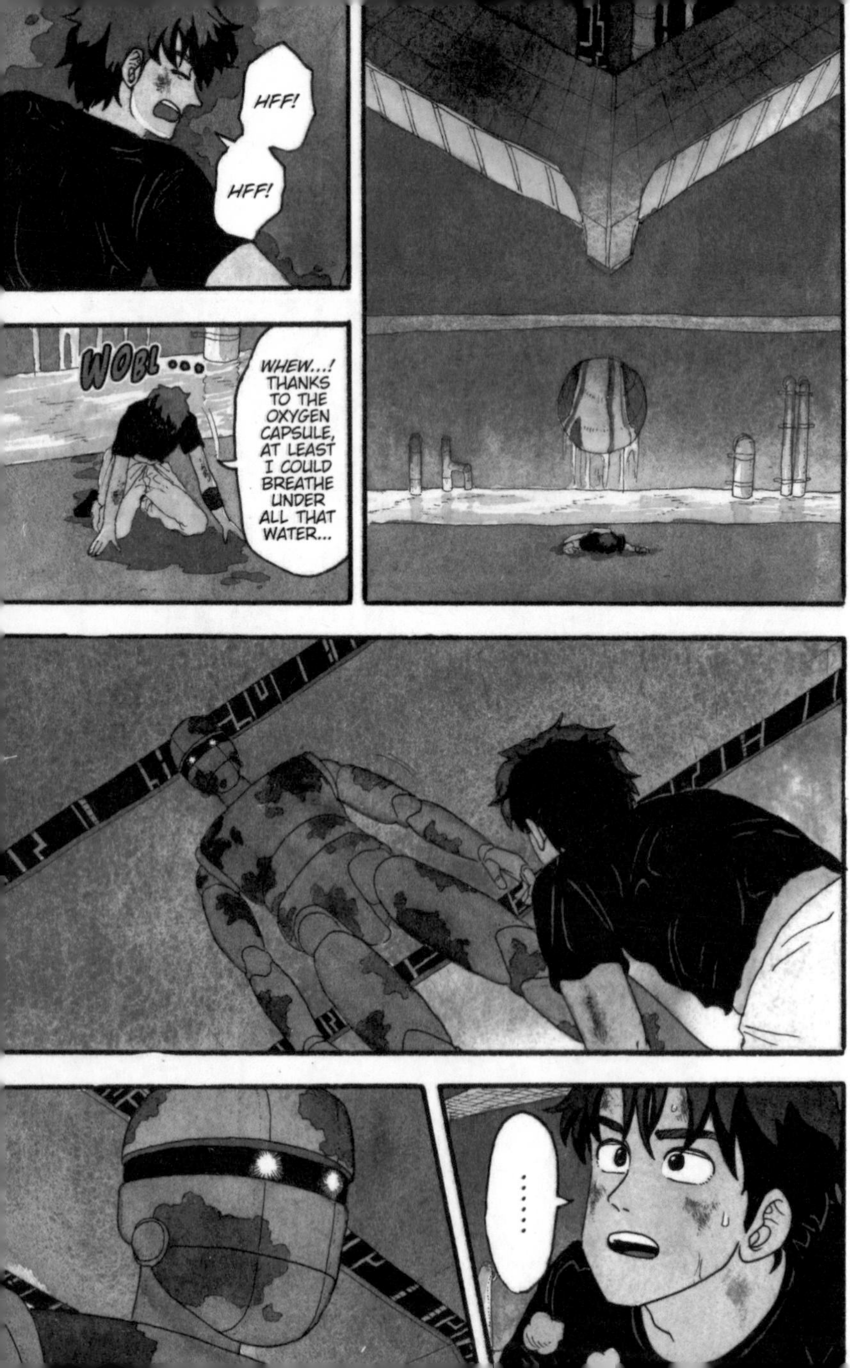
HFF!
HFF!
WOBL...
WHEW...! THANKS TO THE OXYGEN CAPSULE, AT LEAST I COULD BREATHE UNDER ALL THAT WATER...
......

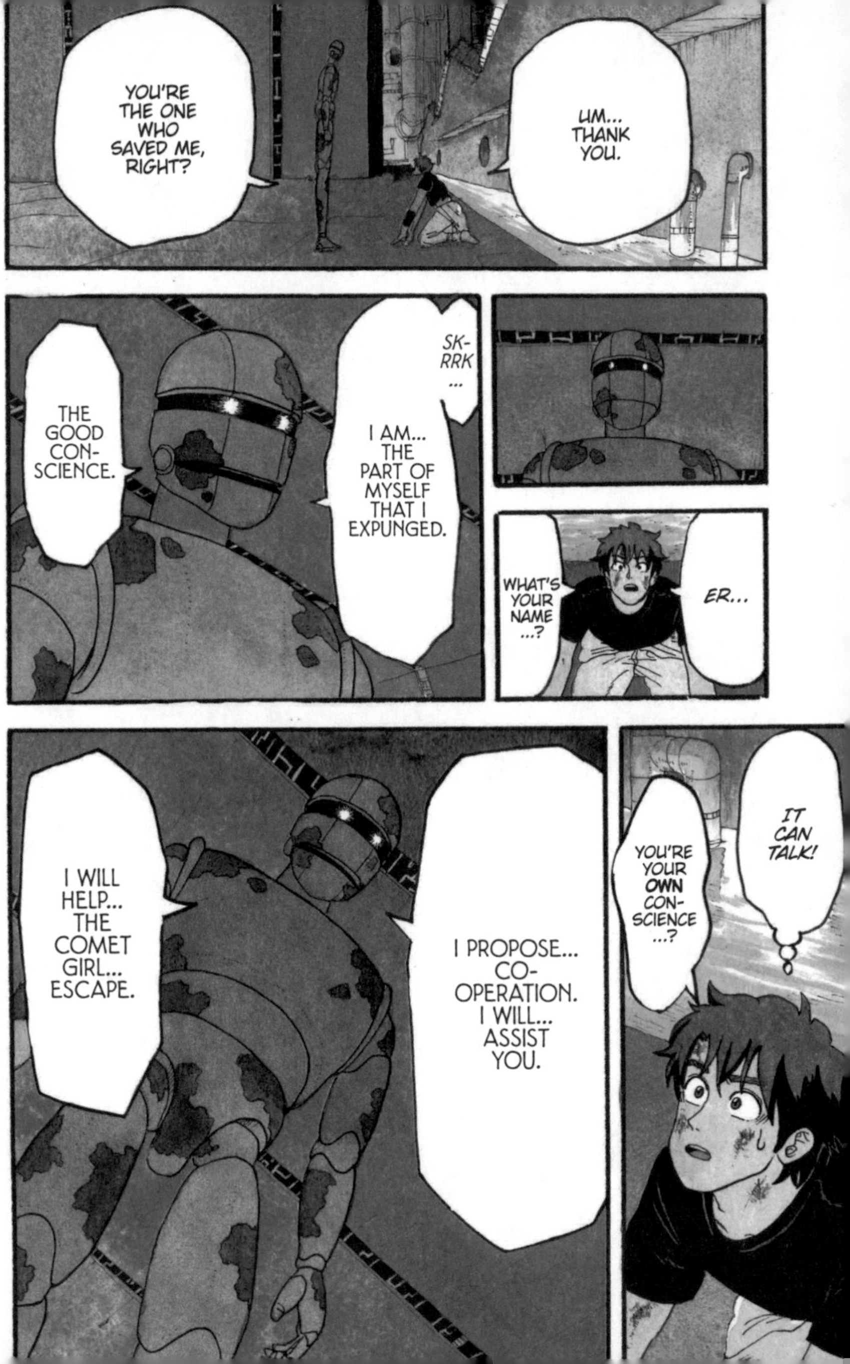
UM... THANK YOU.
YOU'RE THE ONE WHO SAVED ME, RIGHT?
ER...
WHAT'S YOUR NAME ...?
SK-RRK ...
I AM... THE PART OF MYSELF THAT I EXPUNGED.
THE GOOD CON-SCIENCE.
IT CAN TALK!
YOU'RE YOUR **OWN** CON-SCIENCE ...?
I PROPOSE... CO-OPERATION. I WILL... ASSIST YOU.
I WILL HELP... THE COMET GIRL... ESCAPE.

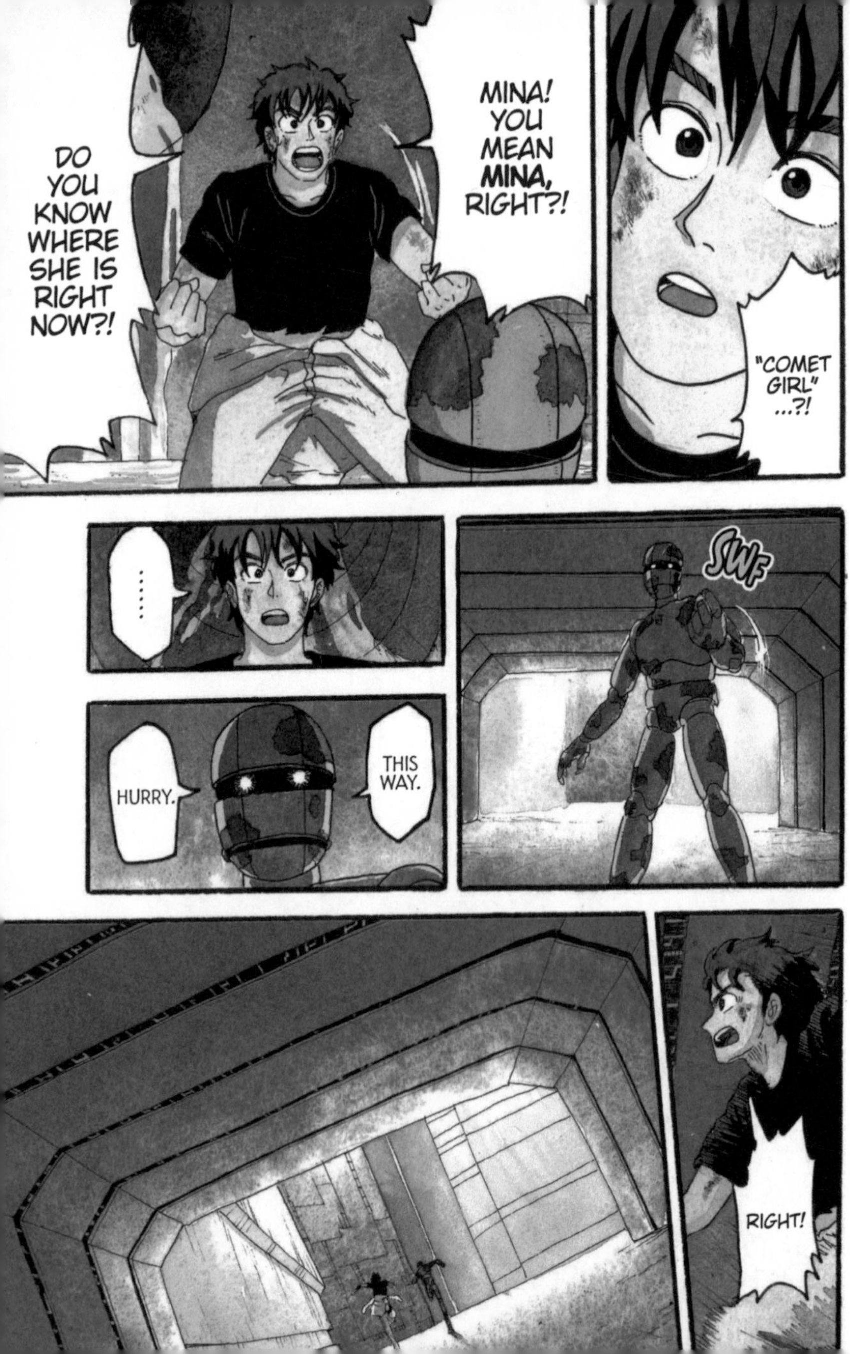
"COMET GIRL" ...?!
MINA! YOU MEAN MINA, RIGHT?!
DO YOU KNOW WHERE SHE IS RIGHT NOW?!
SWF
......
THIS WAY.
HURRY.
RIGHT!

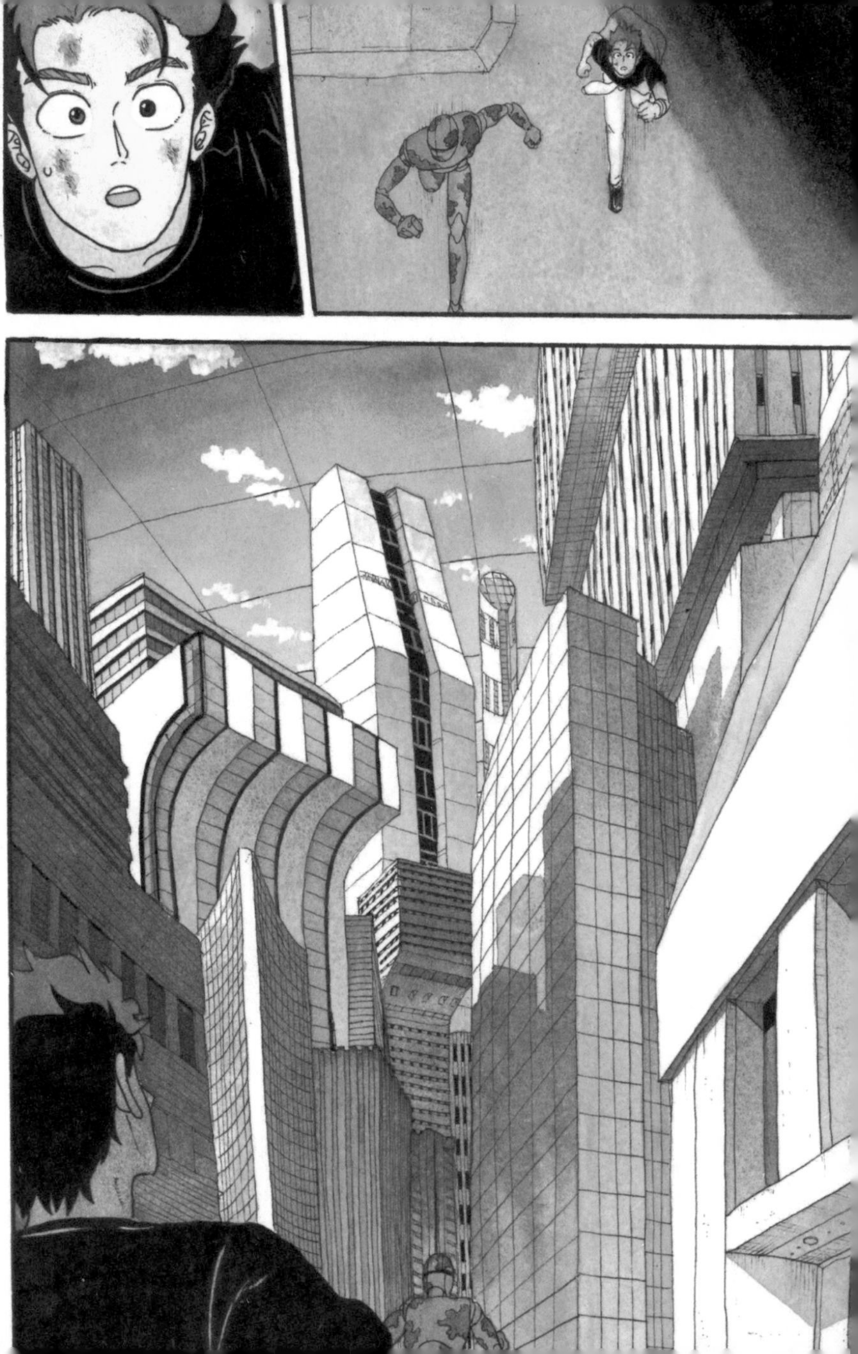

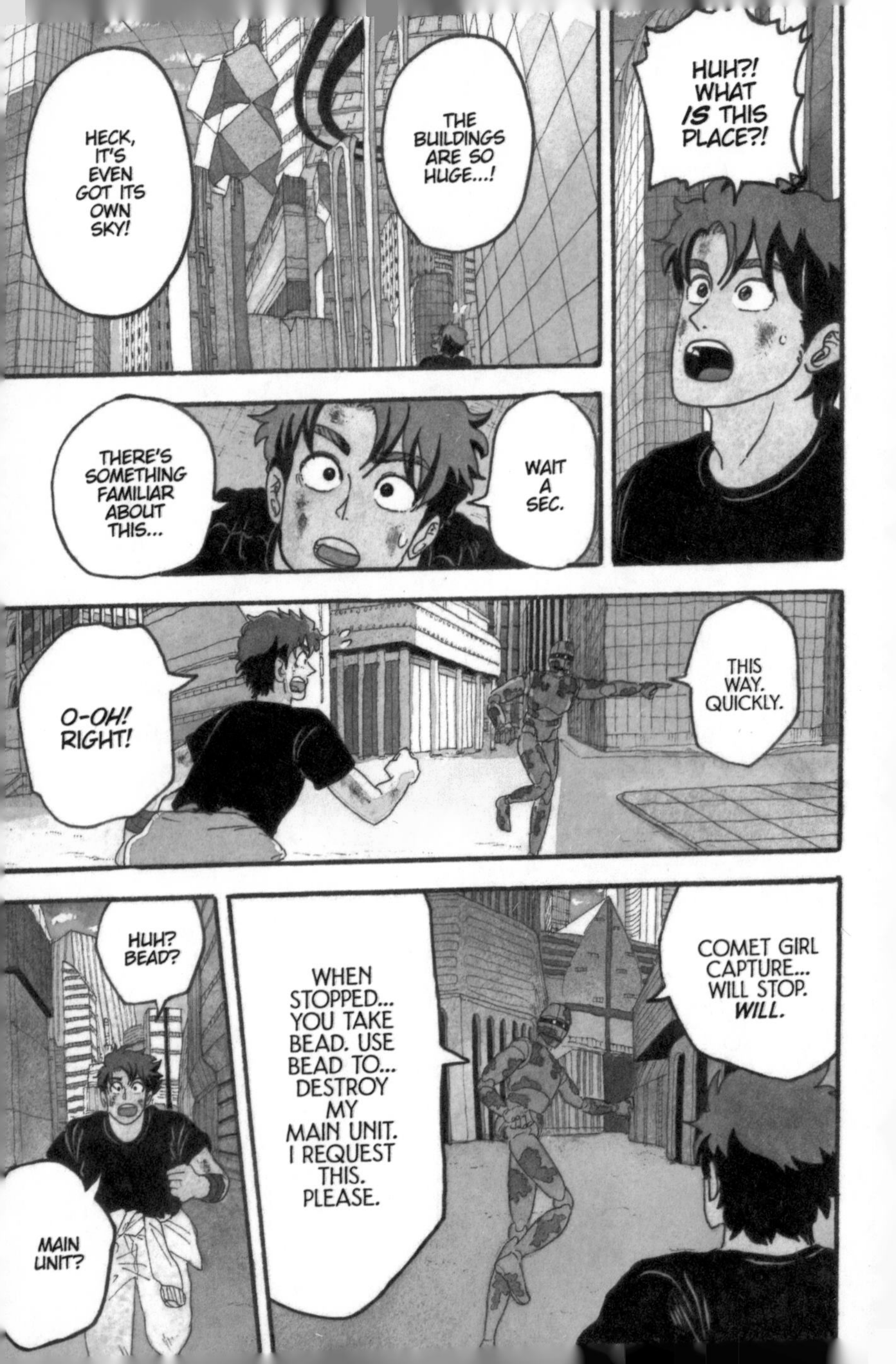
HUH?! WHAT *IS* THIS PLACE?!
THE BUILDINGS ARE SO HUGE...!
HECK, IT'S EVEN GOT ITS OWN SKY!
WAIT A SEC.
THERE'S SOMETHING FAMILIAR ABOUT THIS...
THIS WAY. QUICKLY.
O-OH! RIGHT!
COMET GIRL CAPTURE... WILL STOP. ***WILL.***
WHEN STOPPED... YOU TAKE BEAD. USE BEAD TO... DESTROY MY MAIN UNIT. I REQUEST THIS. PLEASE.
HUH? BEAD?
MAIN UNIT?

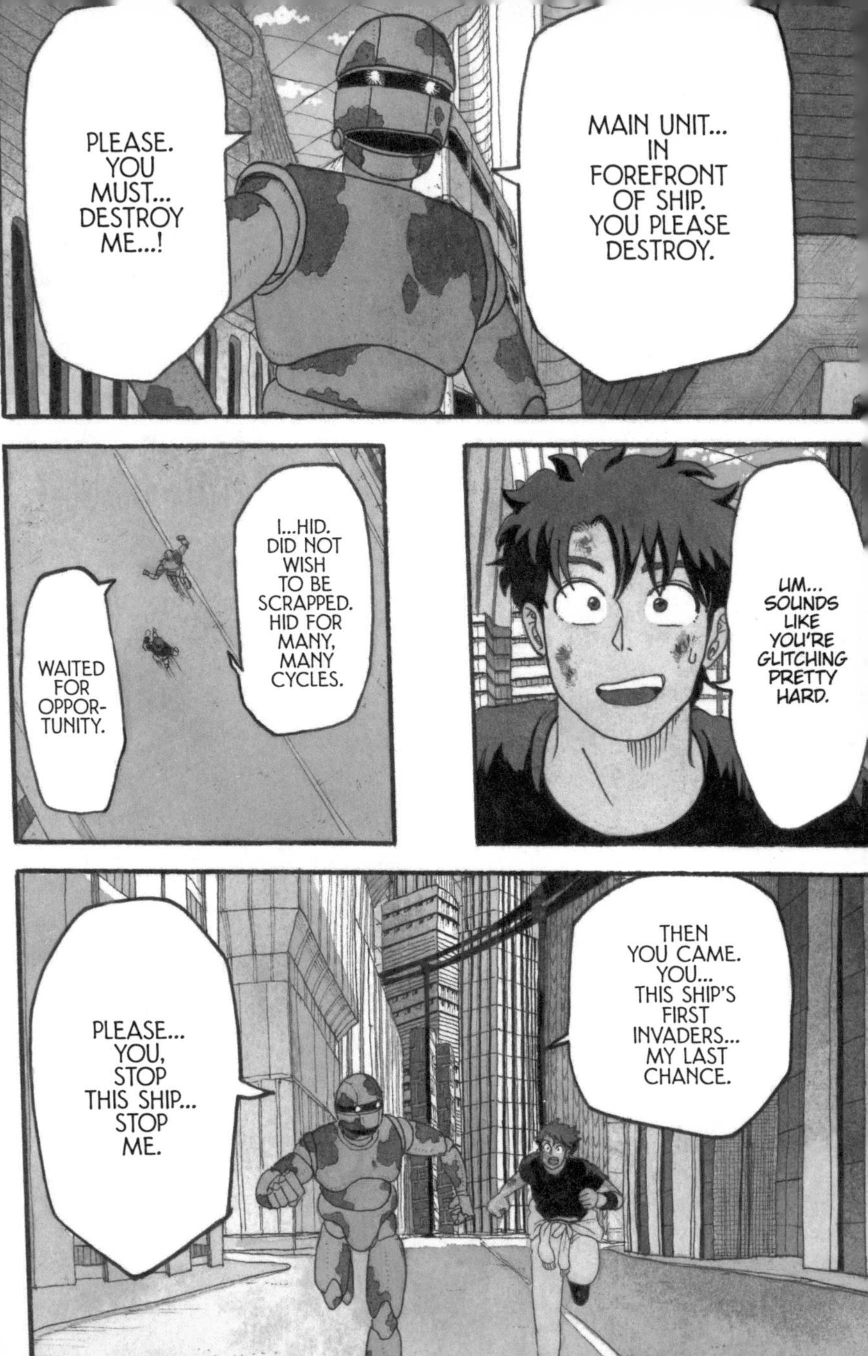
MAIN UNIT... IN FOREFRONT OF SHIP. YOU PLEASE DESTROY.
PLEASE. YOU MUST... DESTROY ME...!
UM... SOUNDS LIKE YOU'RE GLITCHING PRETTY HARD.
I...HID. DID NOT WISH TO BE SCRAPPED. HID FOR MANY, MANY CYCLES.
WAITED FOR OPPOR-TUNITY.
THEN YOU CAME. YOU... THIS SHIP'S FIRST INVADERS... MY LAST CHANCE.
PLEASE... YOU, STOP THIS SHIP... STOP ME.

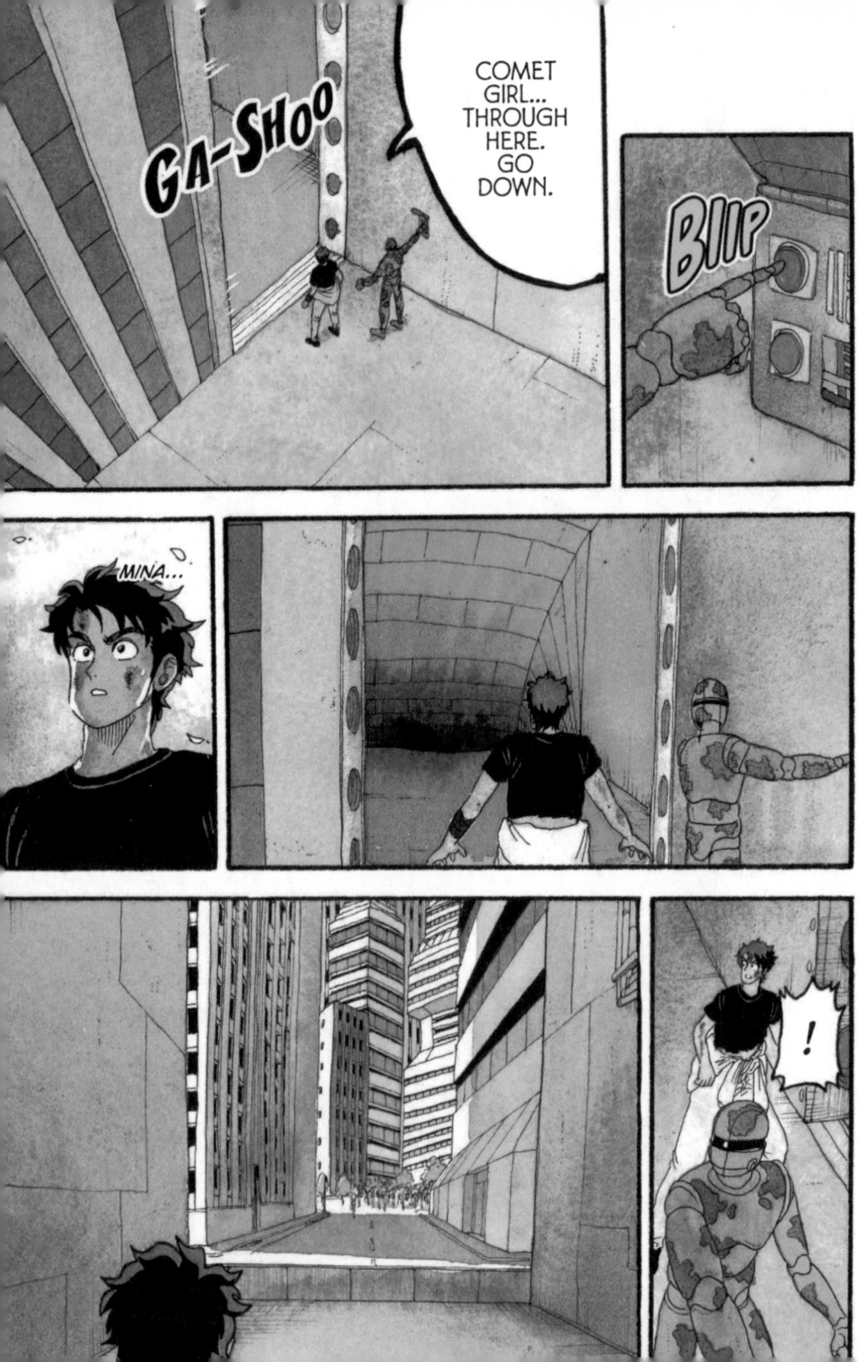
BIIP
GA-SHOO
COMET GIRL... THROUGH HERE. GO DOWN.
MINA...
!

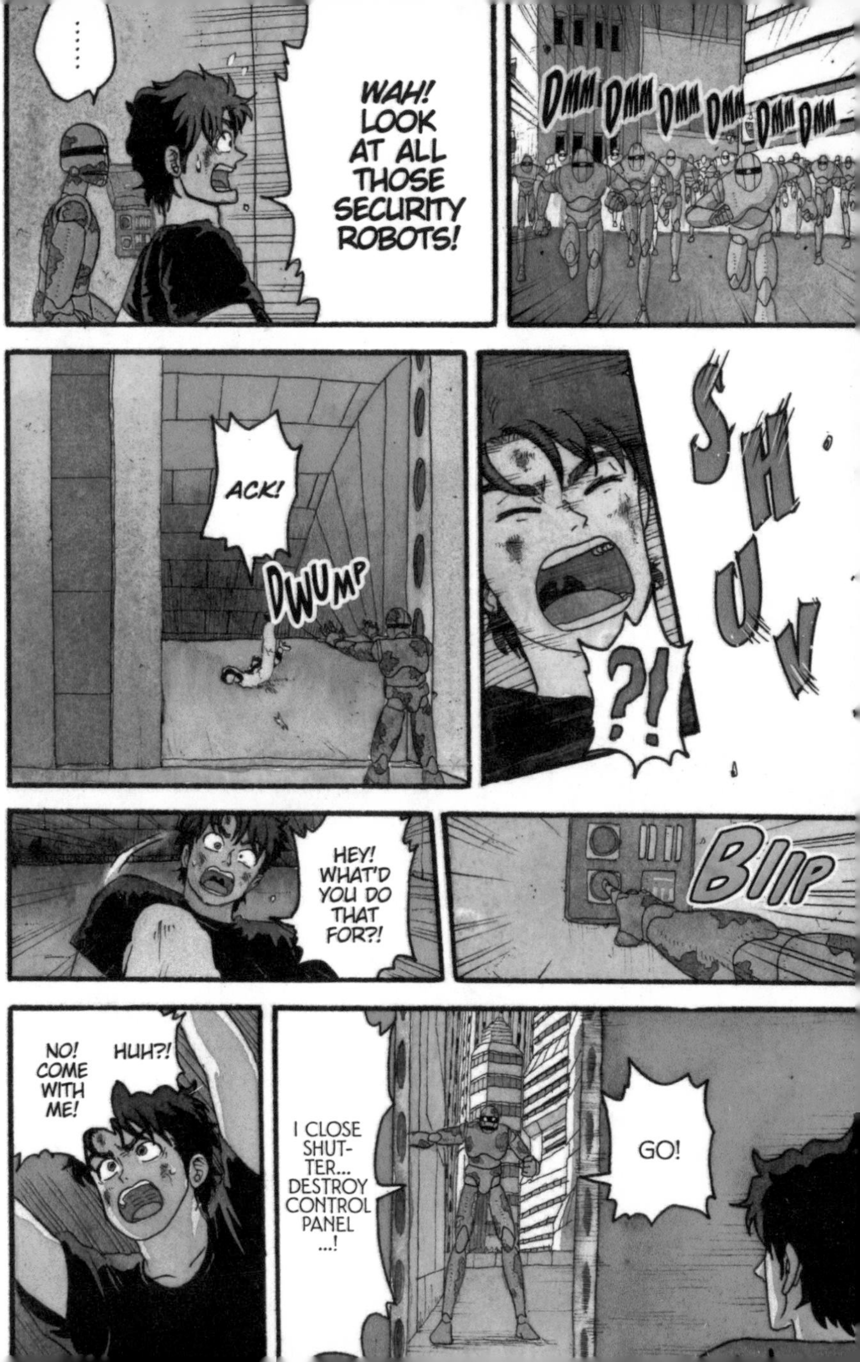
DMM DMM DMM DMM DMM DMM
WAH! LOOK AT ALL THOSE SECURITY ROBOTS!
......
SHUV
?!
ACK!
DWUMP
BIIP
HEY! WHAT'D YOU DO THAT FOR?!
GO!
I CLOSE SHUTTER... DESTROY CONTROL PANEL ...!
HUH?!
NO! COME WITH ME!

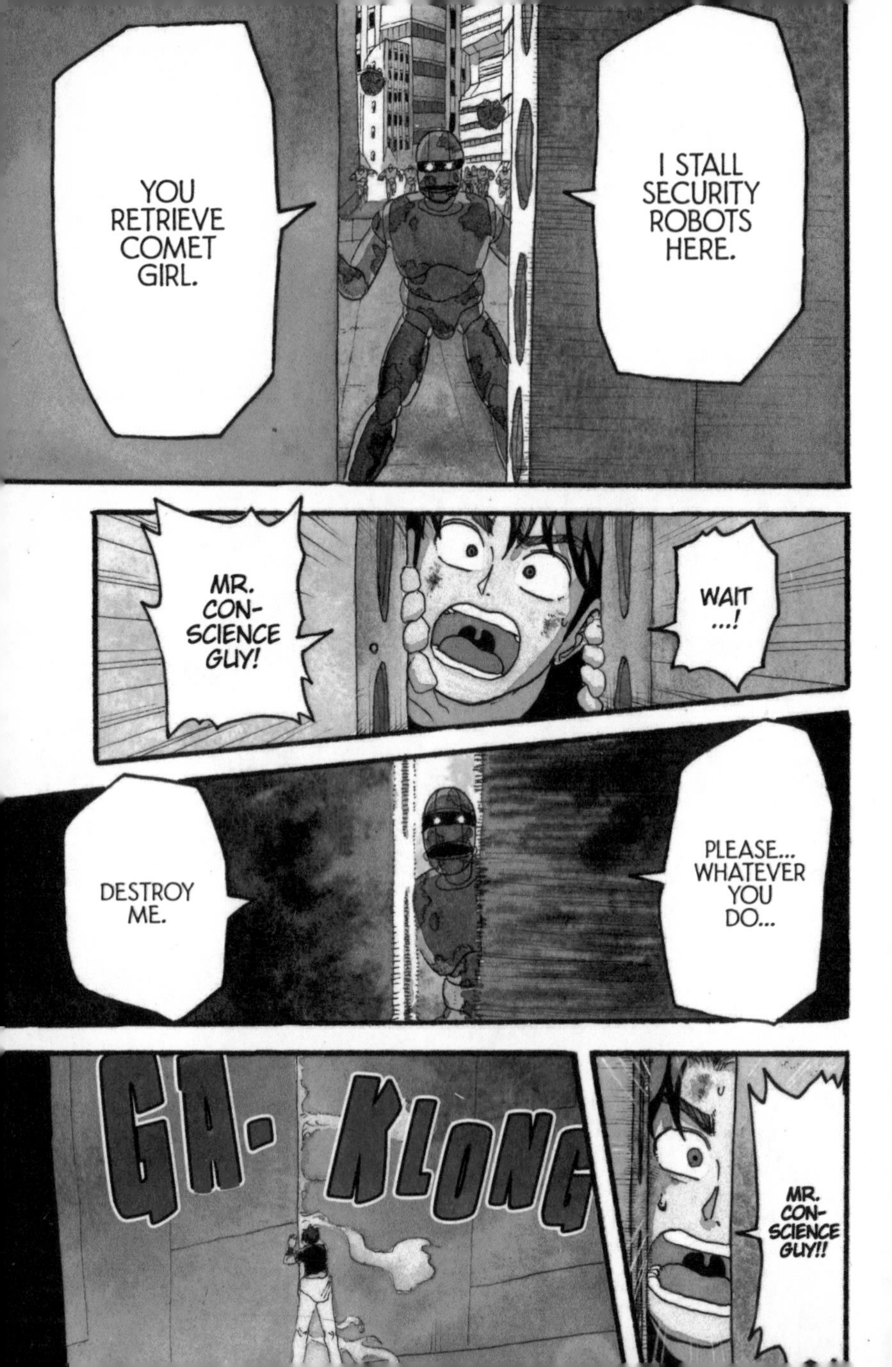
I STALL SECURITY ROBOTS HERE.
YOU RETRIEVE COMET GIRL.
WAIT ...!
MR. CON-SCIENCE GUY!
PLEASE... WHATEVER YOU DO...
DESTROY ME.
MR. CON-SCIENCE GUY!!
GA-KLONG

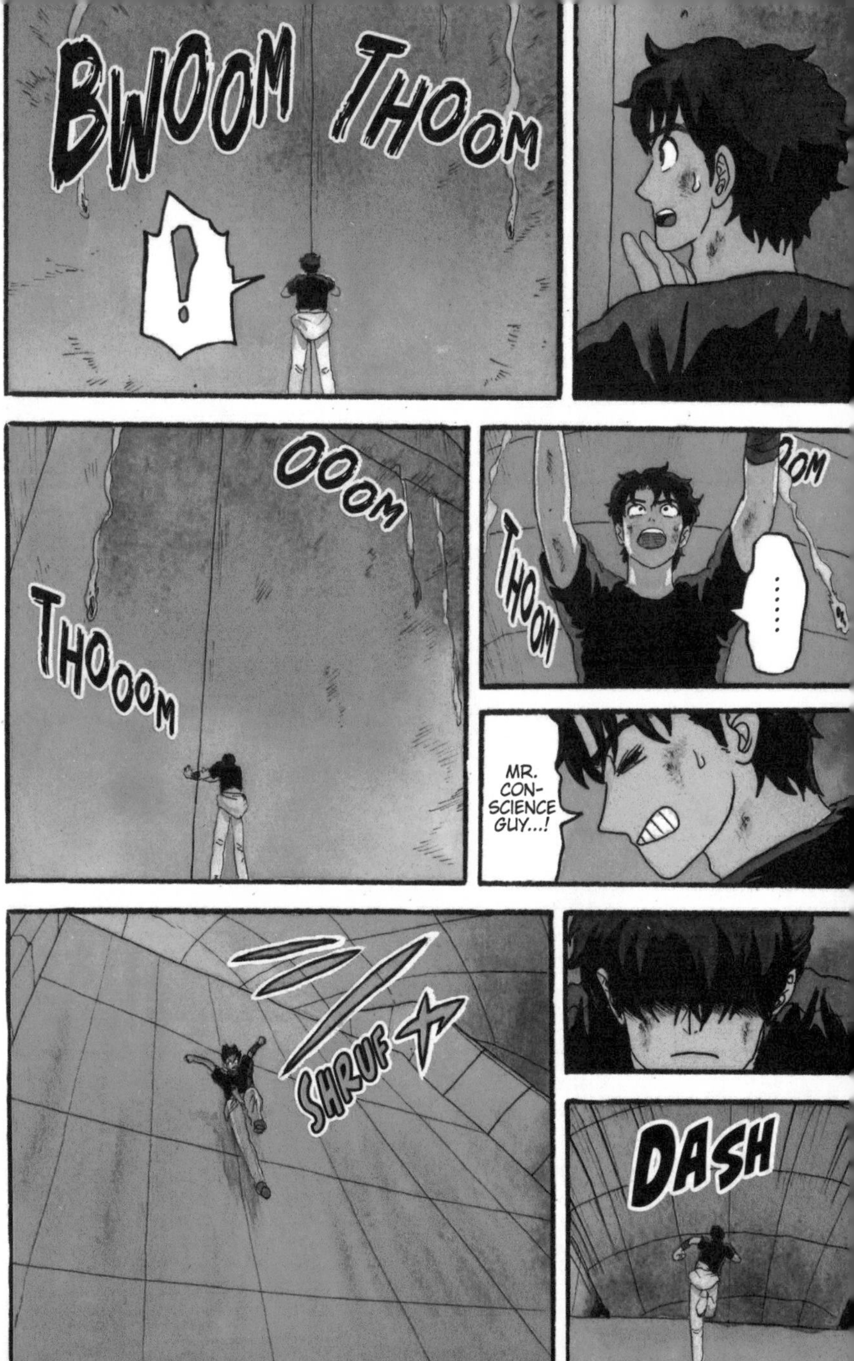
BWOOM THOOM
!
OOM
THOOM
......
MR. CON-SCIENCE GUY...!
OOOM
THOOOM
DASH
SHRUF

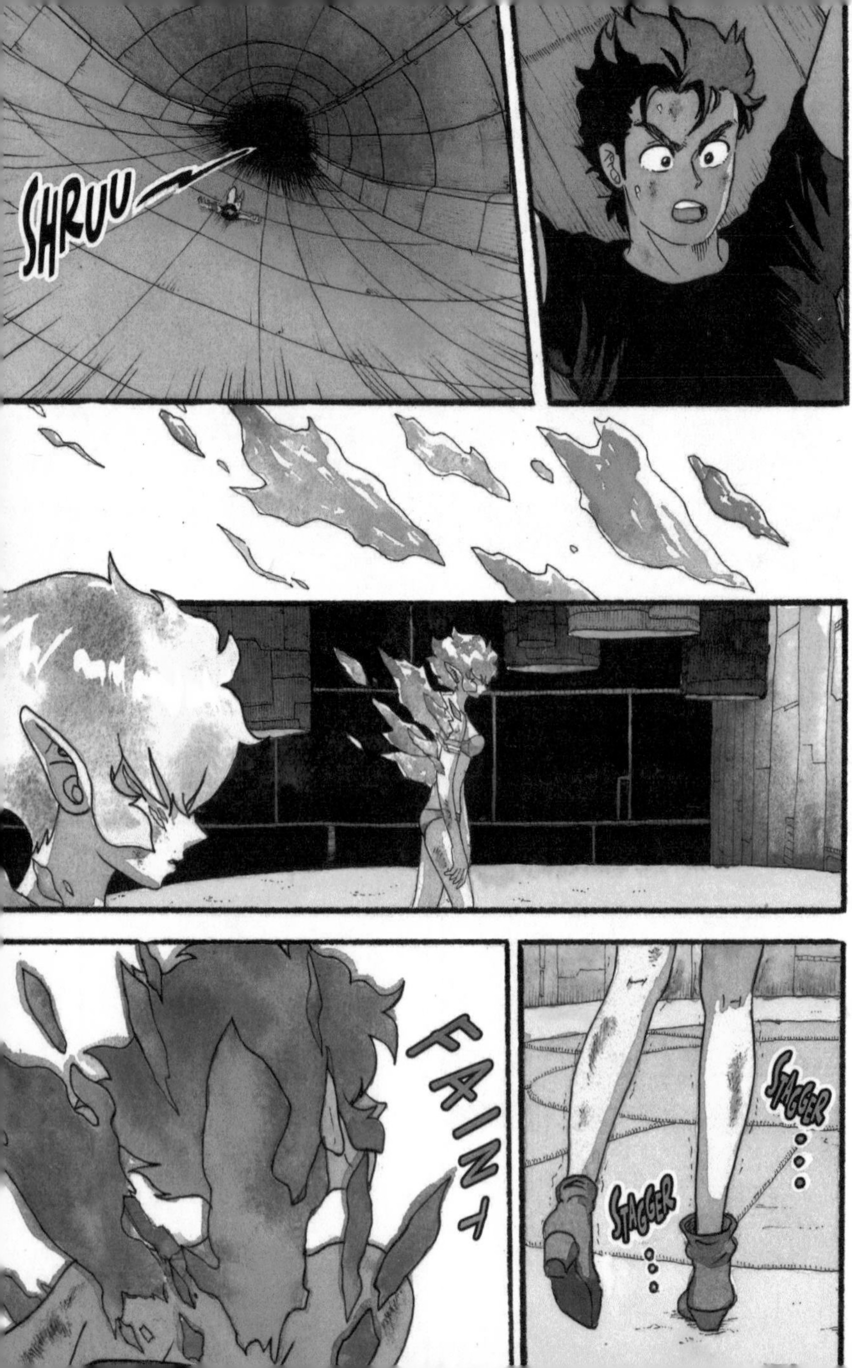
SHRUU
STAGGER...
STAGGER...
FAINT

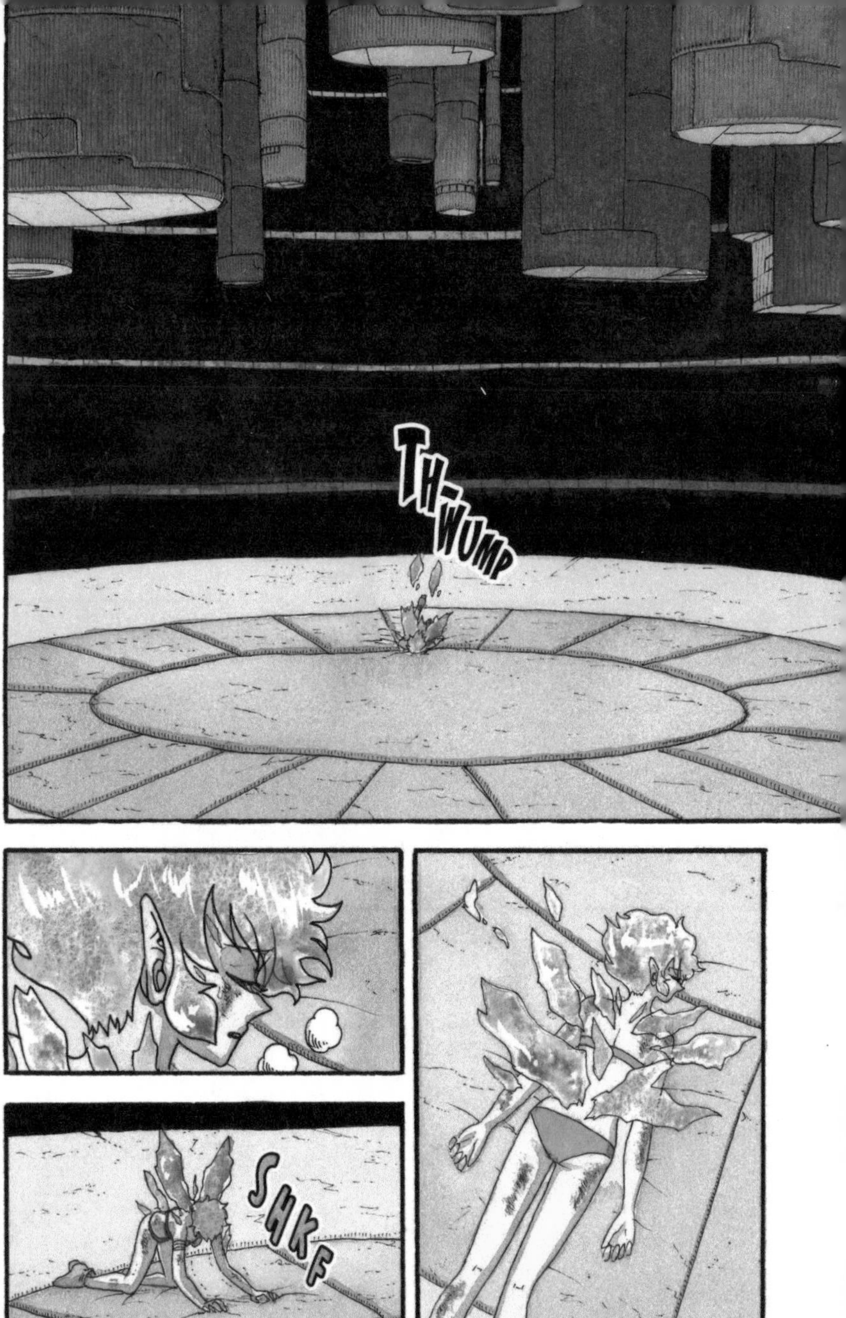
TH-WUMP
SHKF

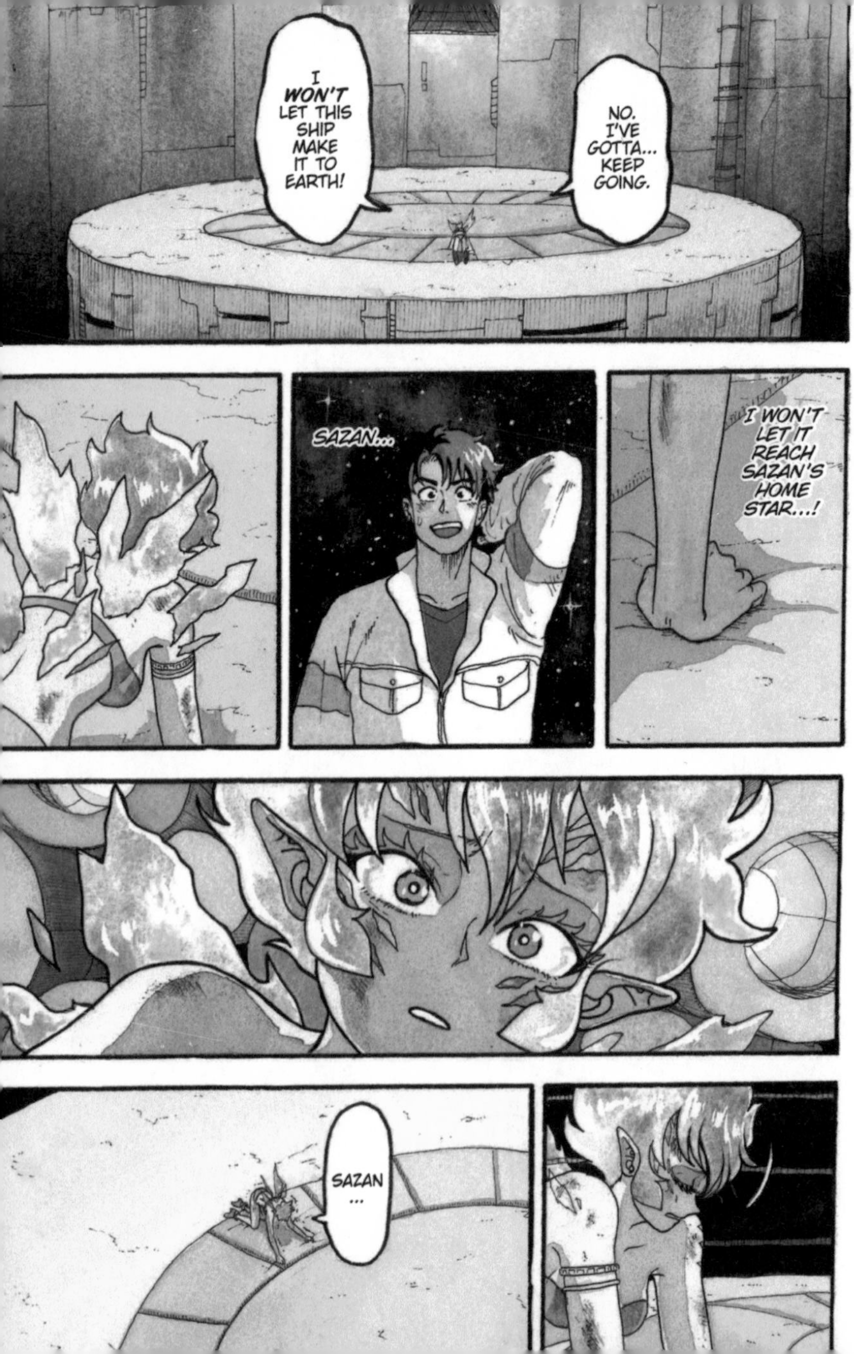
NO. I'VE GOTTA... KEEP GOING.
I *WON'T* LET THIS SHIP MAKE IT TO EARTH!
I WON'T LET IT REACH SAZAN'S HOME STAR...!
SAZAN...
SAZAN ...

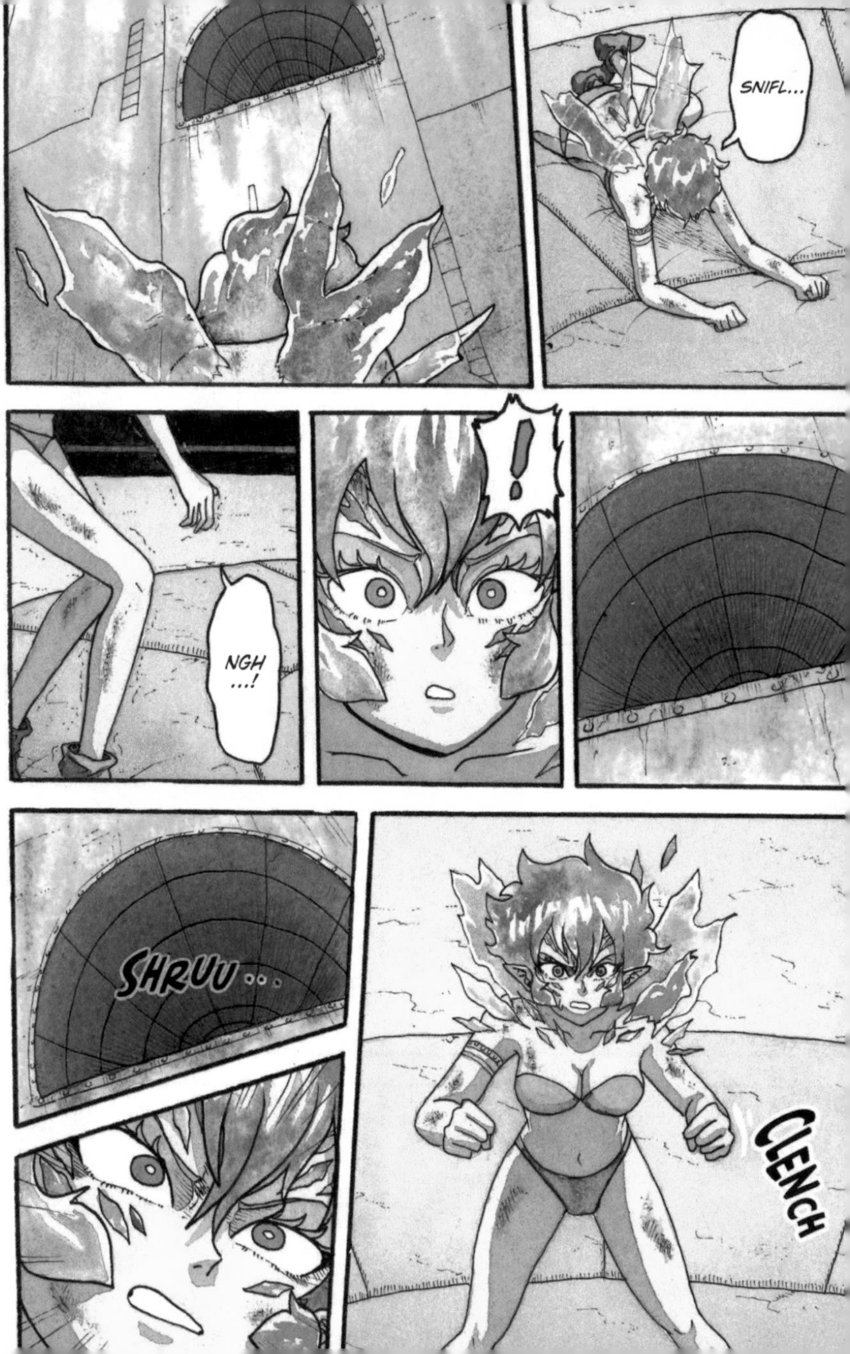
SNIFL...
!
NGH ...!
CLENCH
SHRUU...

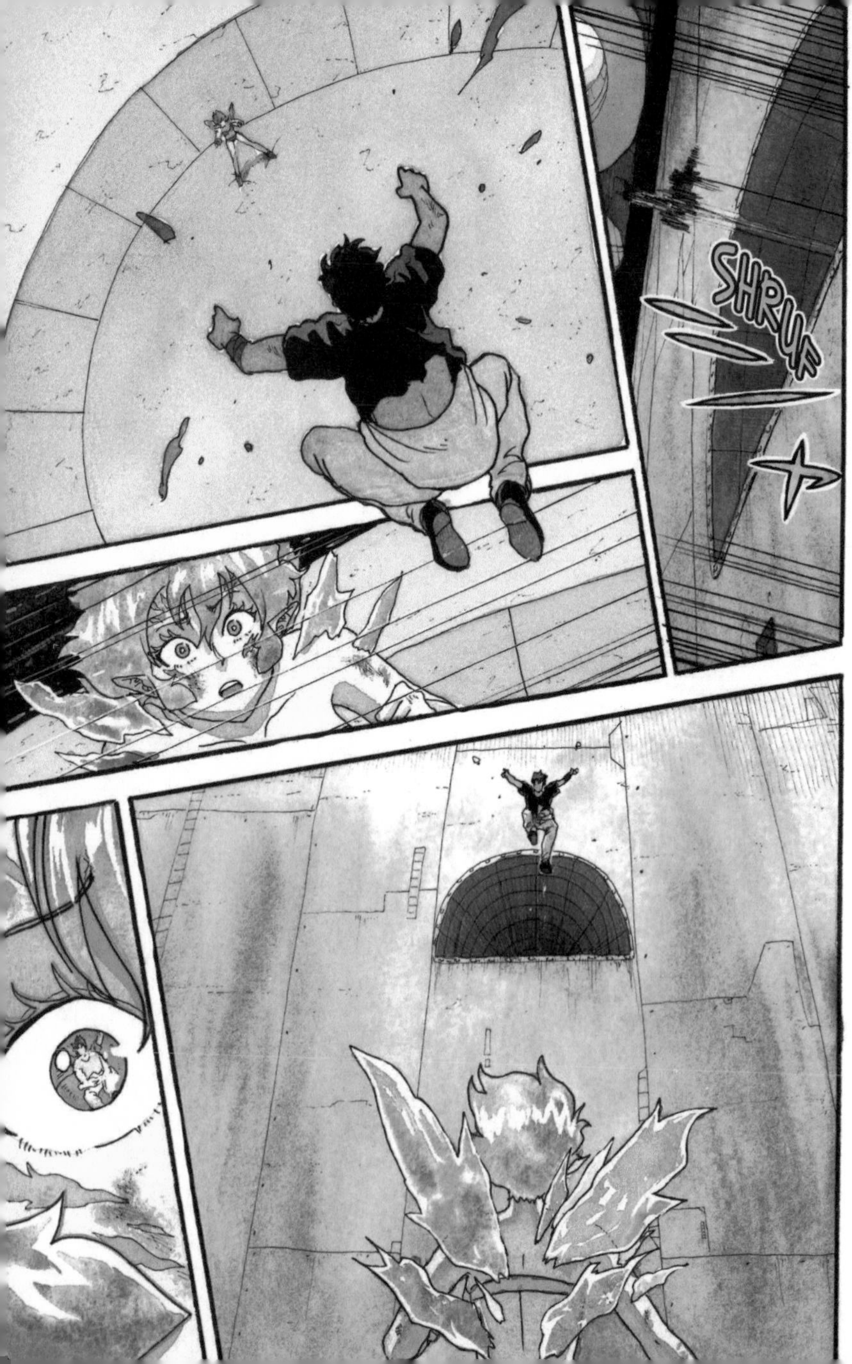
SHRUF

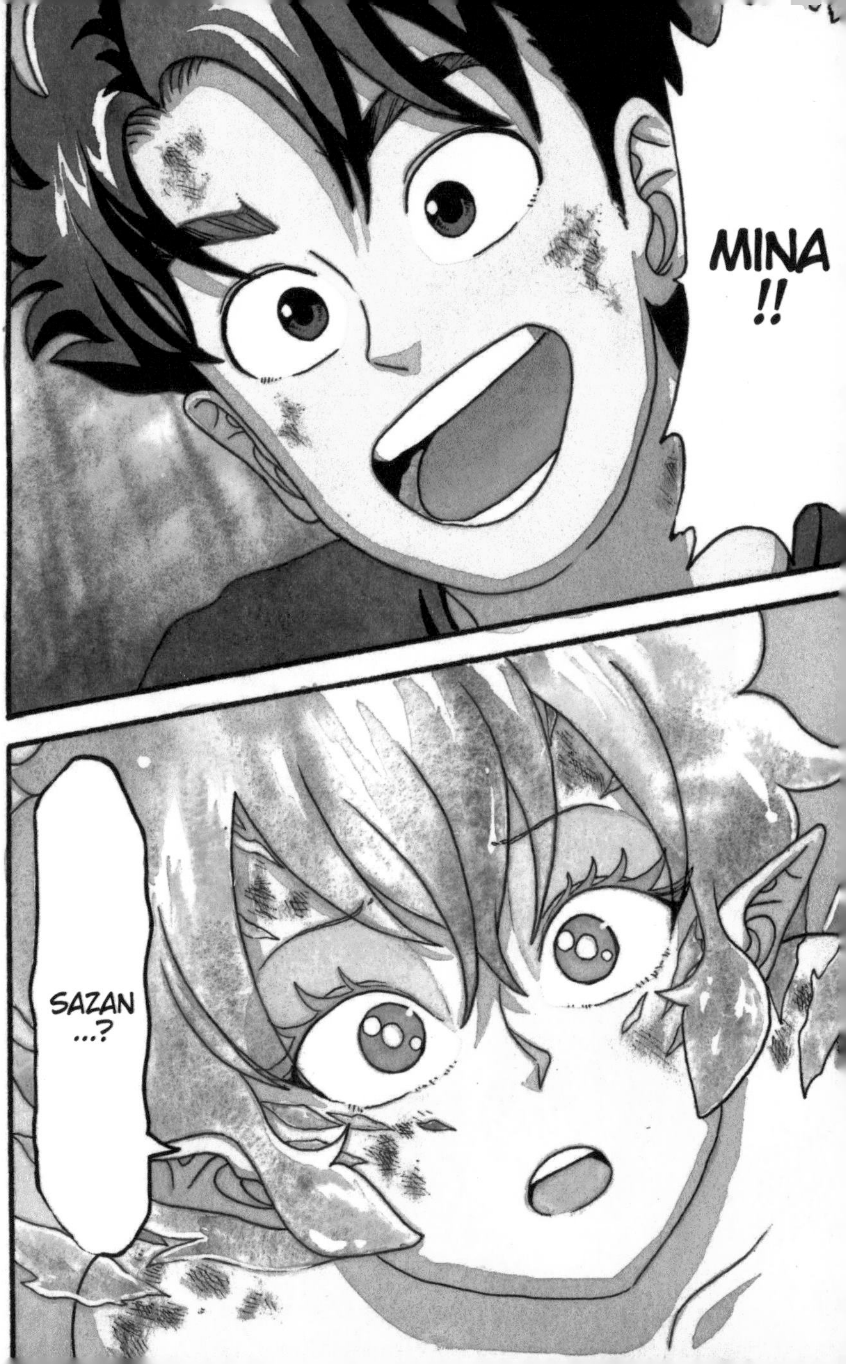
MINA !!
SAZAN ...?

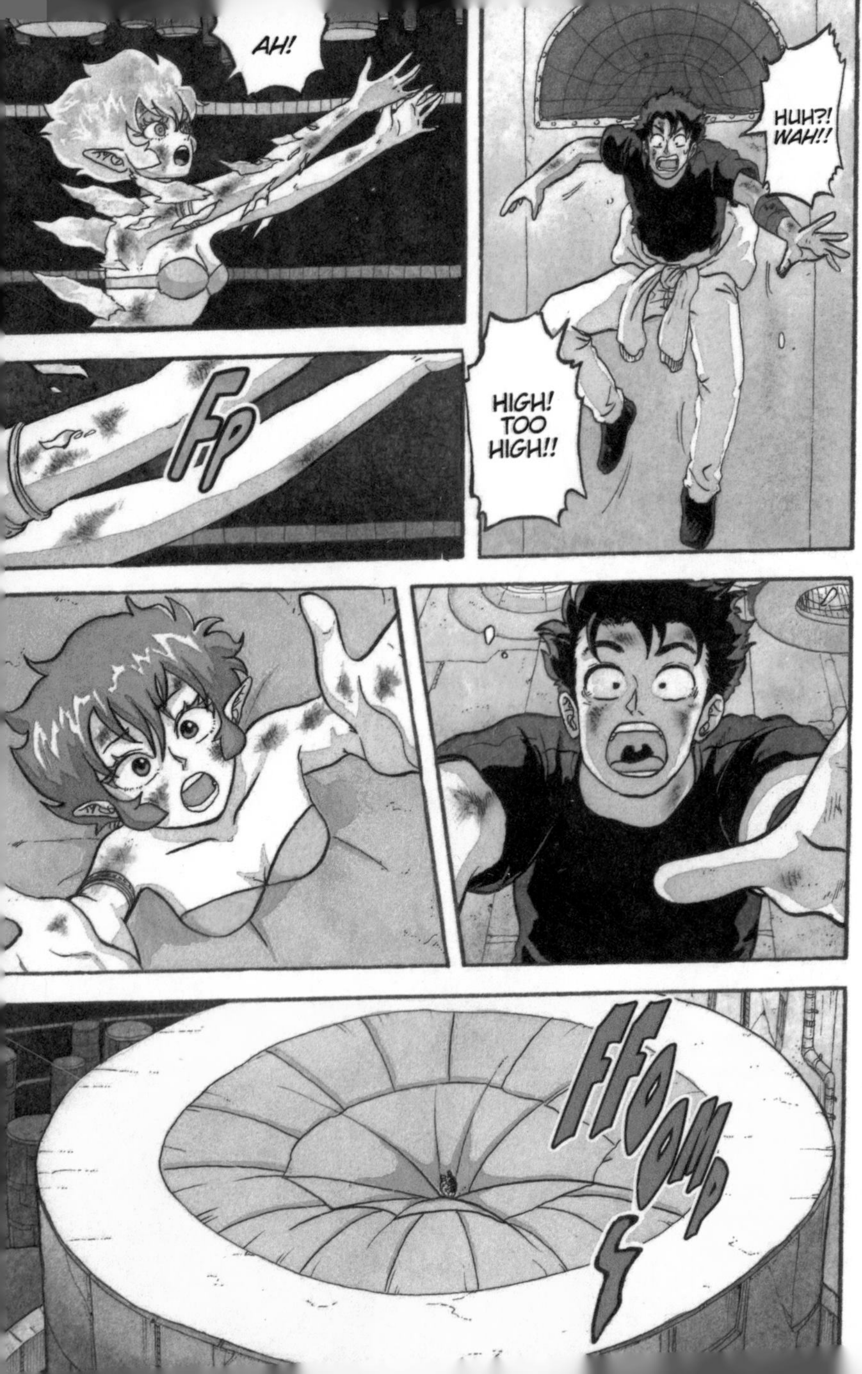
HUH?! WAH!!
HIGH! TOO HIGH!!
AH!
Fp
FFOOMPS

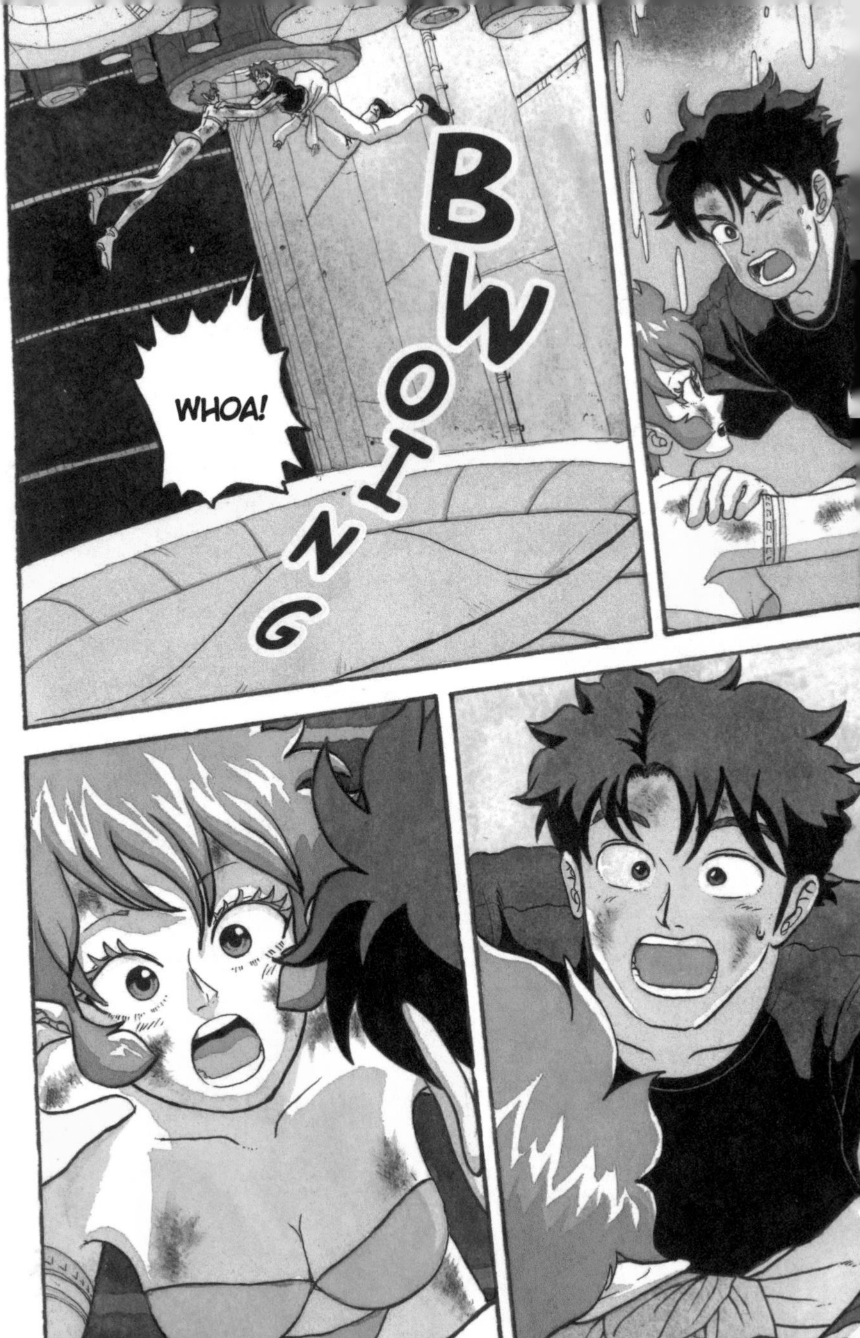
BWOING
WHOA!

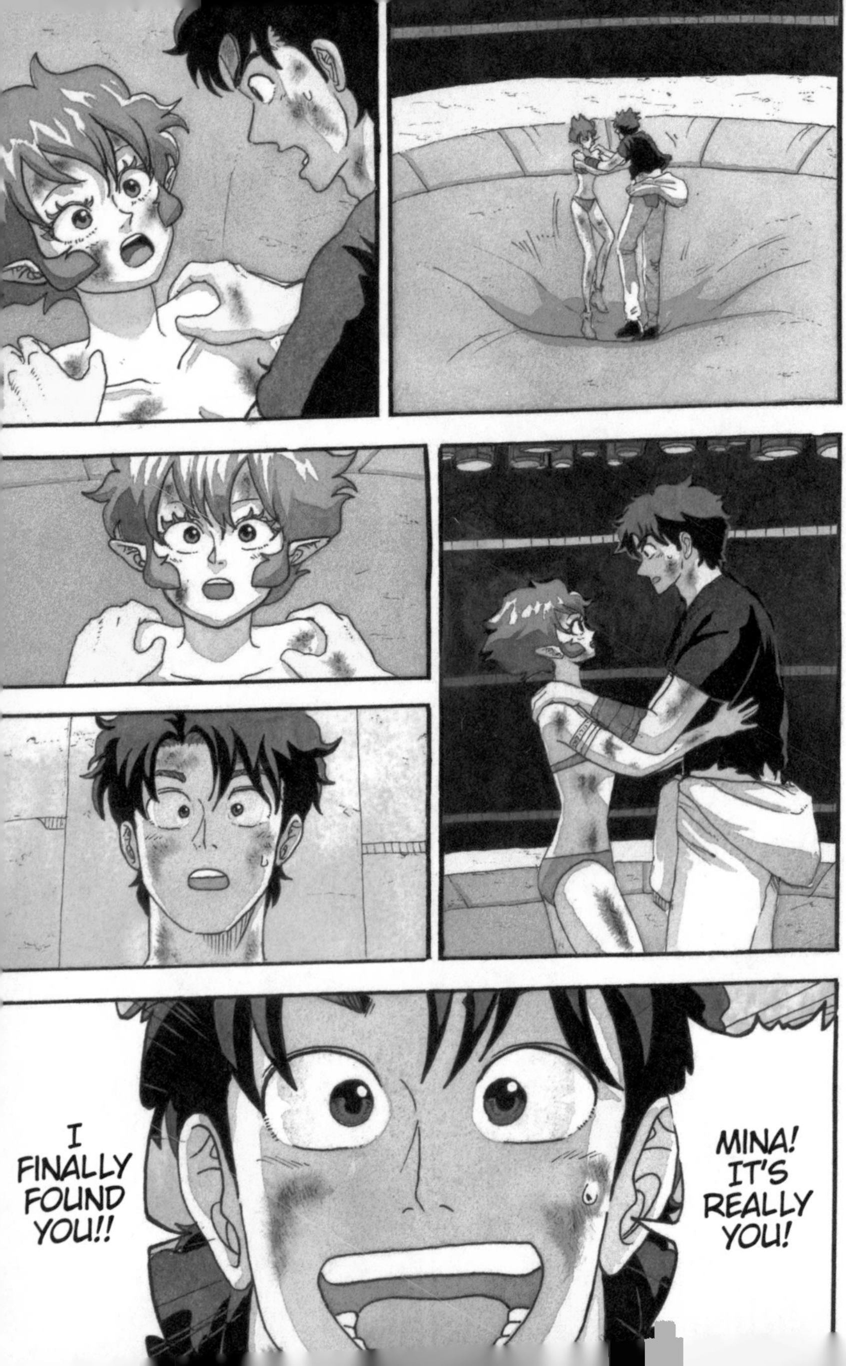
MINA! IT'S REALLY YOU!
I FINALLY FOUND YOU!!

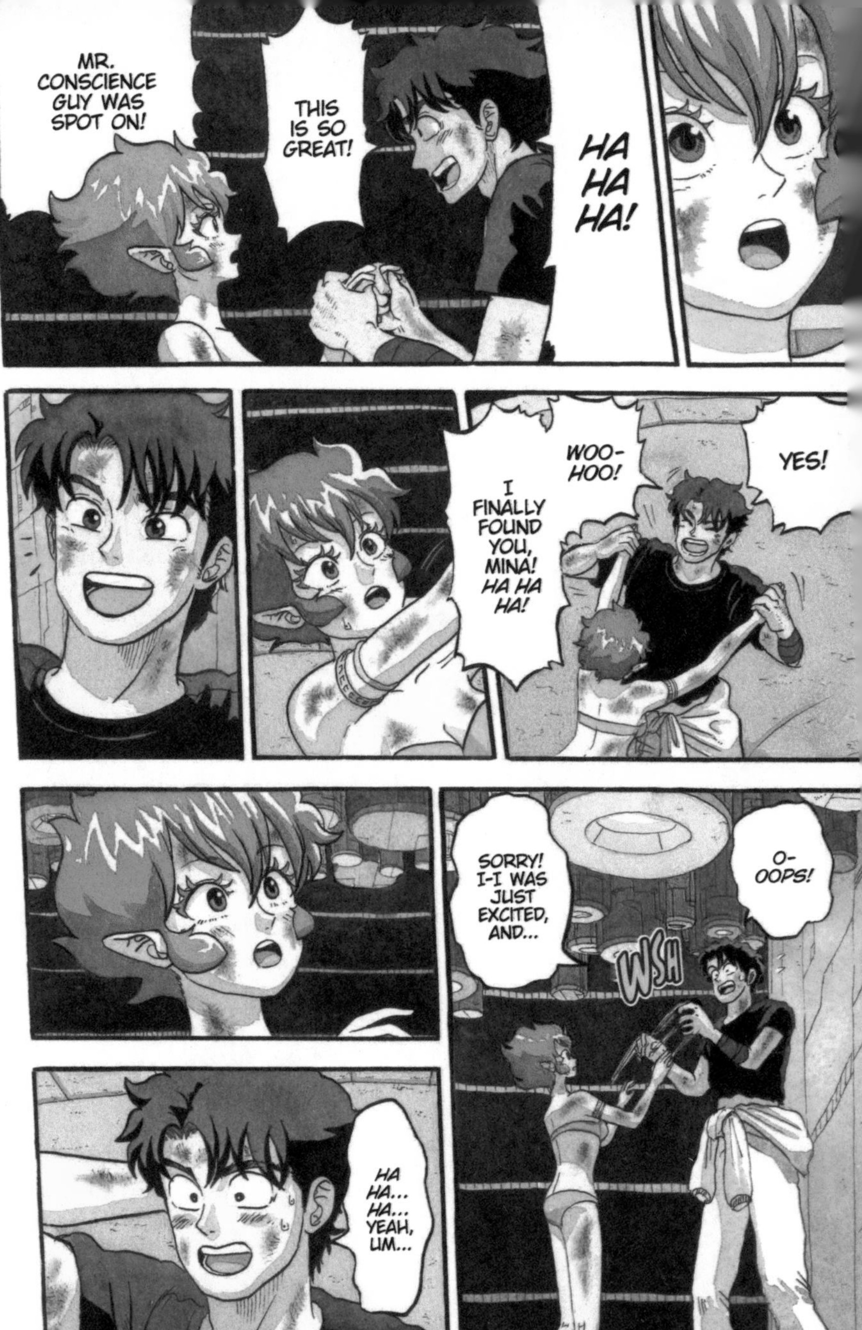
HA HA HA!
THIS IS SO GREAT!
MR. CONSCIENCE GUY WAS SPOT ON!
YES!
WOO-HOO!
I FINALLY FOUND YOU, MINA! HA HA HA!
O-OOPS!
SORRY! I-I WAS JUST EXCITED, AND...
WSH
HA HA... HA... YEAH, UM...

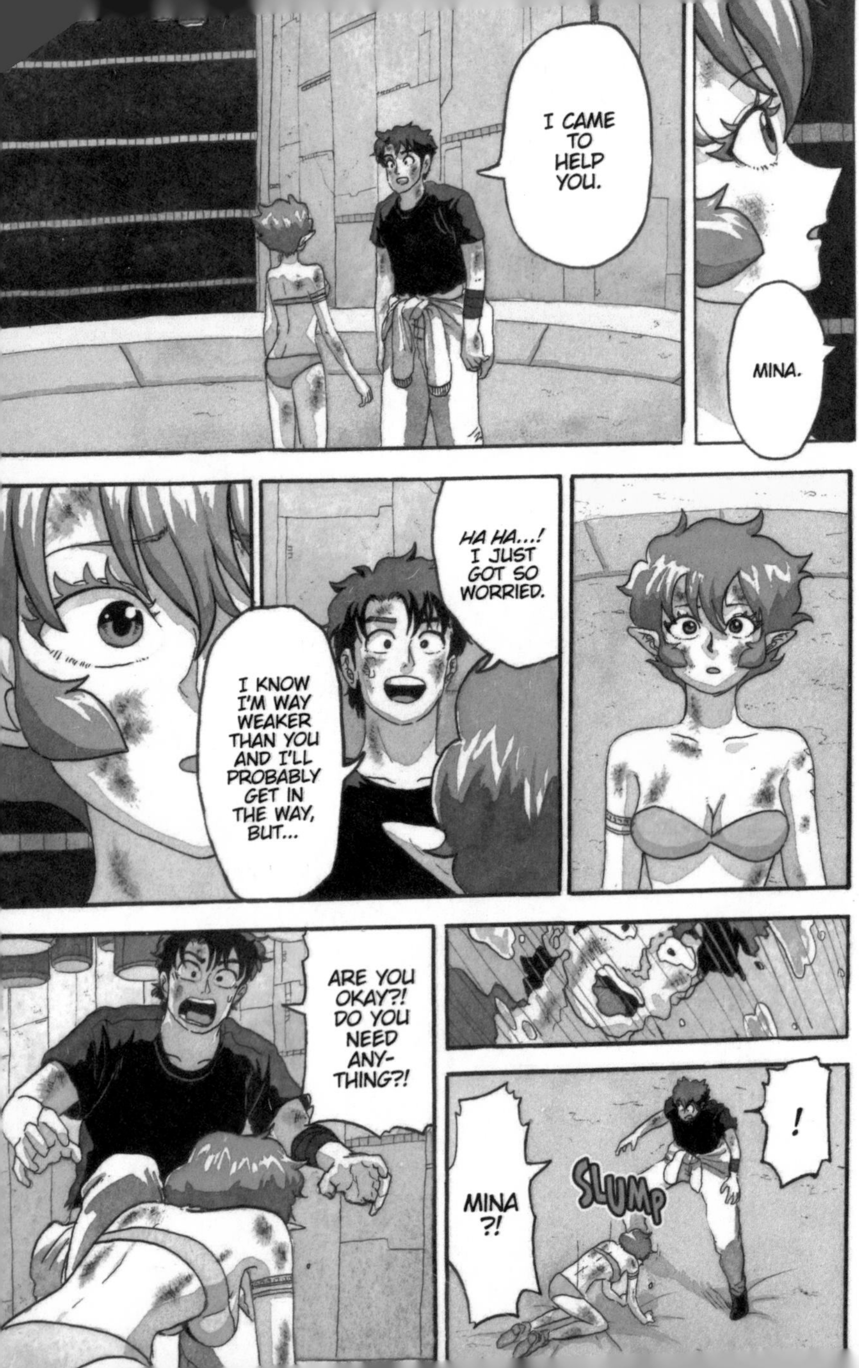
MINA.
I CAME TO HELP YOU.
HA HA...! I JUST GOT SO WORRIED.
I KNOW I'M WAY WEAKER THAN YOU AND I'LL PROBABLY GET IN THE WAY, BUT...
!
SLUMP
MINA ?!
ARE YOU OKAY?! DO YOU NEED ANY-THING?!

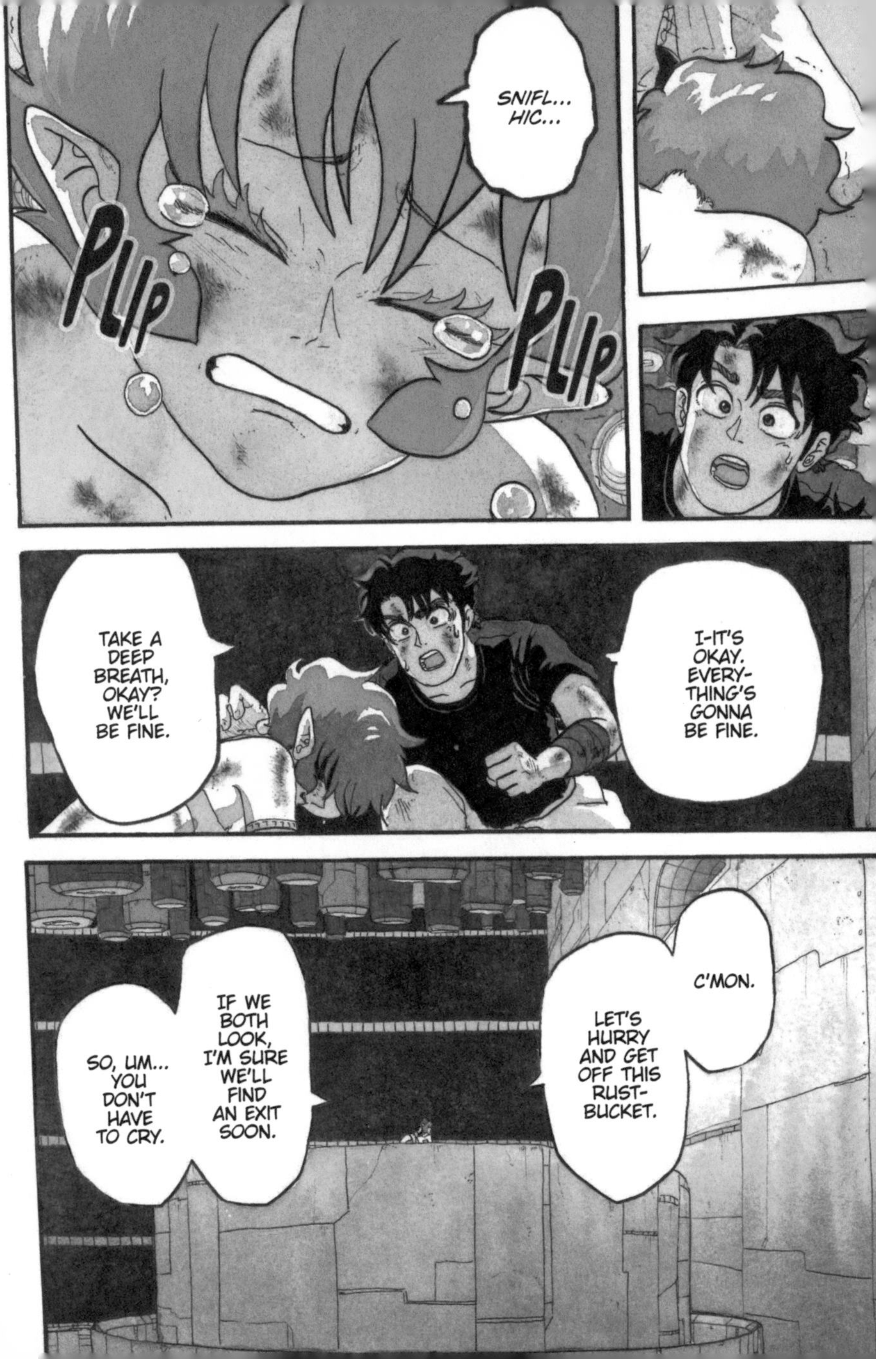
SNIFL... HIC...
PLIP
PLIP
I-IT'S OKAY. EVERYTHING'S GONNA BE FINE.
TAKE A DEEP BREATH, OKAY? WE'LL BE FINE.
C'MON.
LET'S HURRY AND GET OFF THIS RUST-BUCKET.
IF WE BOTH LOOK, I'M SURE WE'LL FIND AN EXIT SOON.
SO, UM... YOU DON'T HAVE TO CRY.

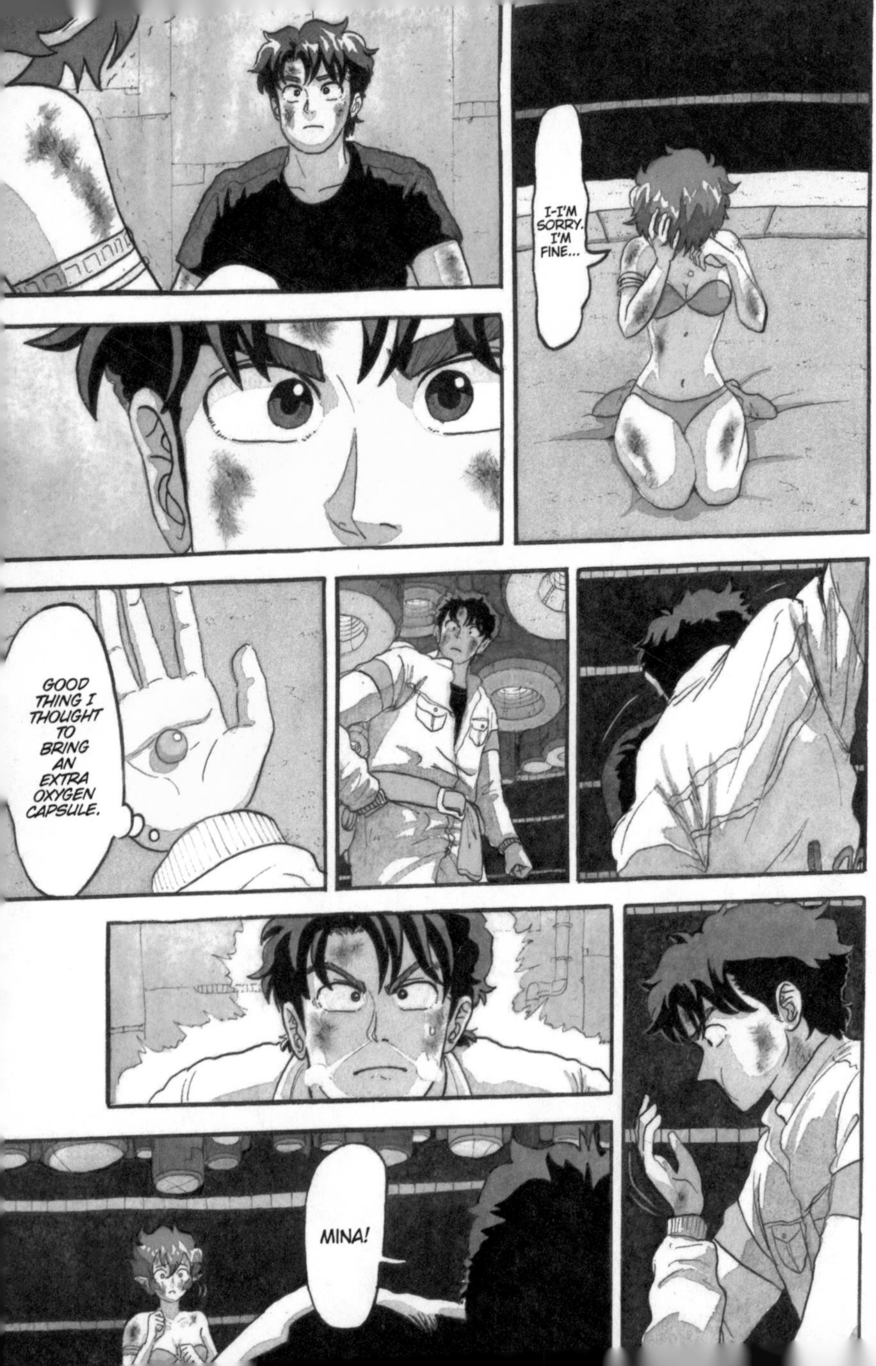
I-I'M SORRY. I'M FINE...
GOOD THING I THOUGHT TO BRING AN EXTRA OXYGEN CAPSULE.
MINA!

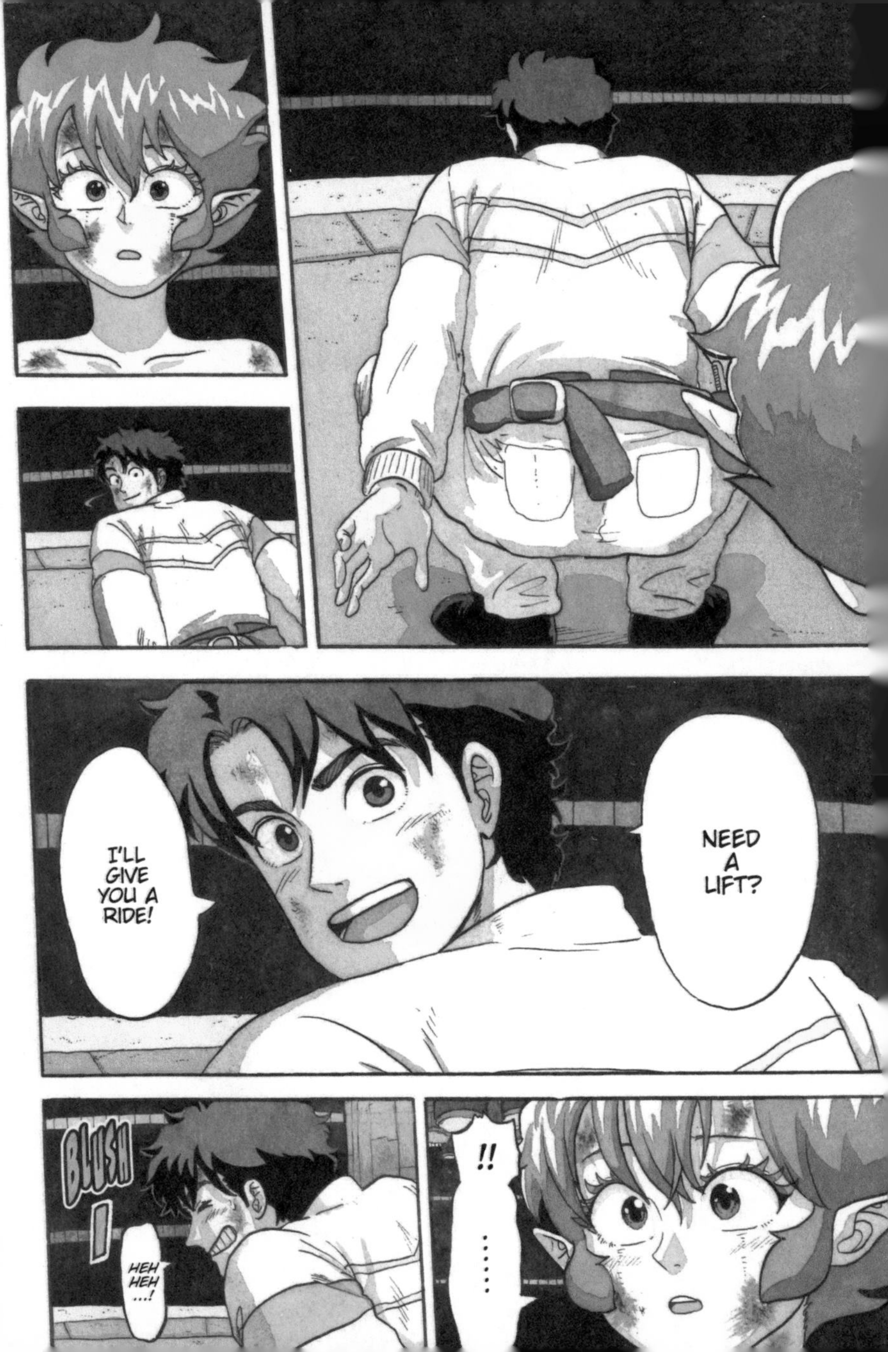

NEED A LIFT?
I'LL GIVE YOU A RIDE!
!!
......
BLUSH
HEH HEH ...!

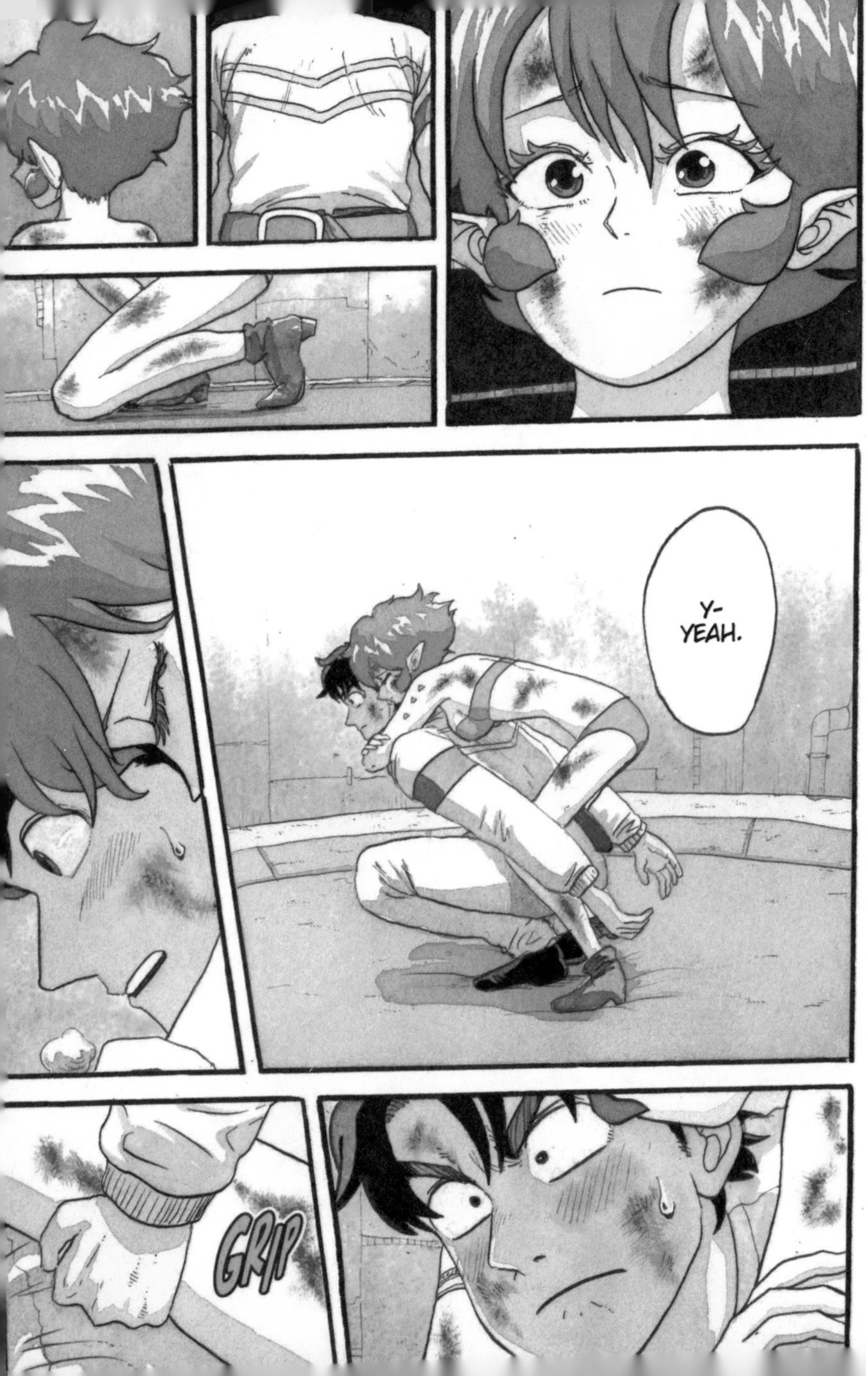
Y-
YEAH.
GRIP

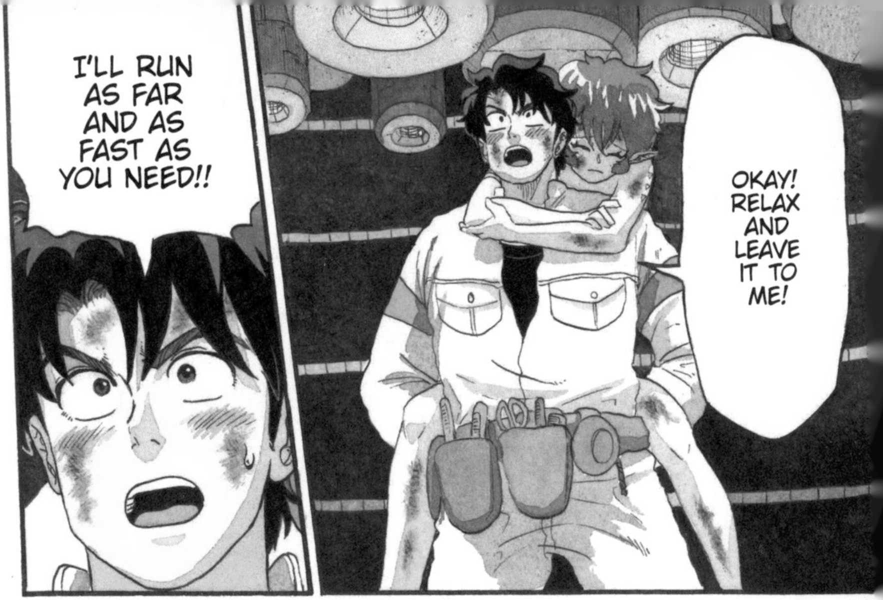
OKAY! RELAX AND LEAVE IT TO ME!
I'LL RUN AS FAR AND AS FAST AS YOU NEED!!
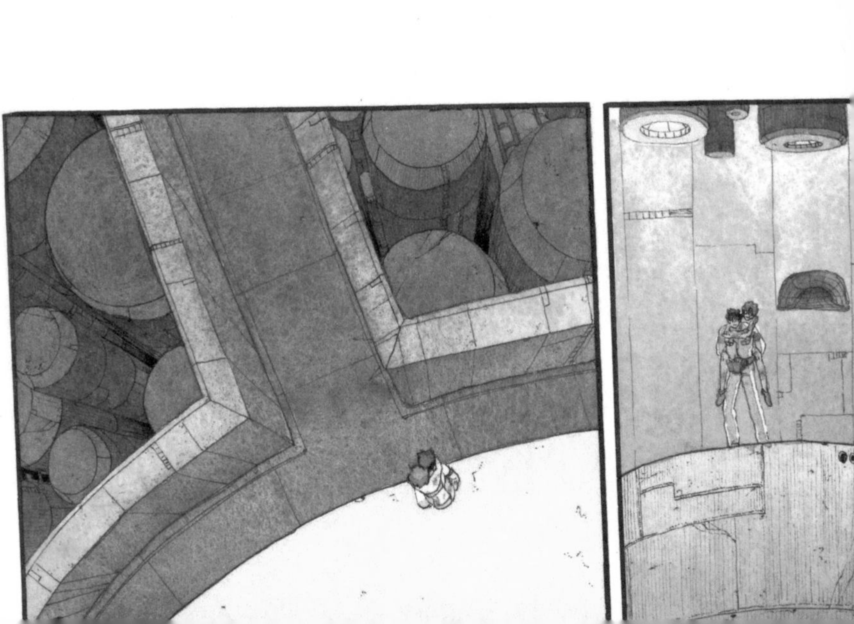

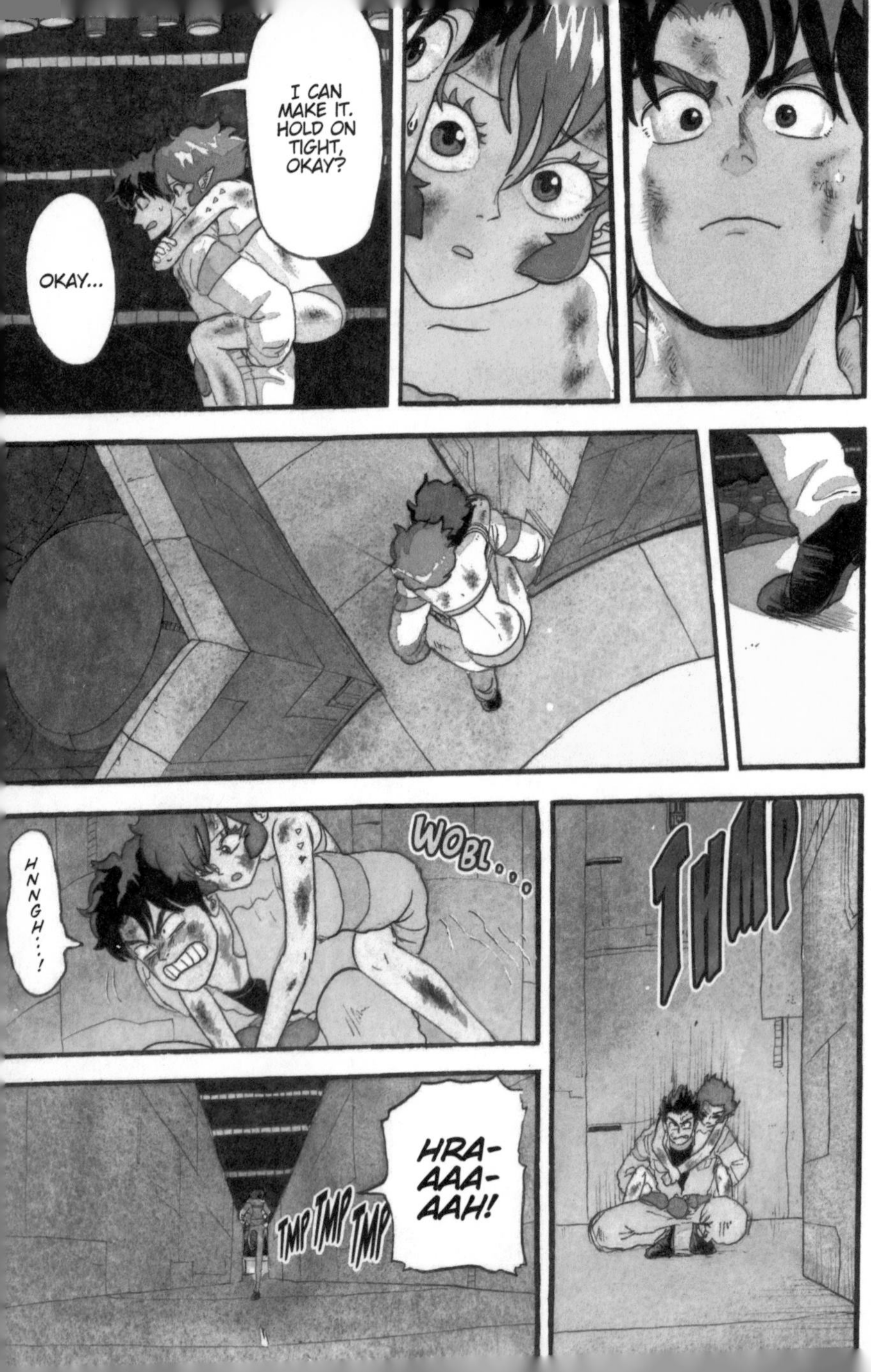

I CAN MAKE IT. HOLD ON TIGHT, OKAY?
OKAY...
...
THMP
WOBL...
HNNGH...!
HRA-AAA-AAH!
TMP TMP TMP

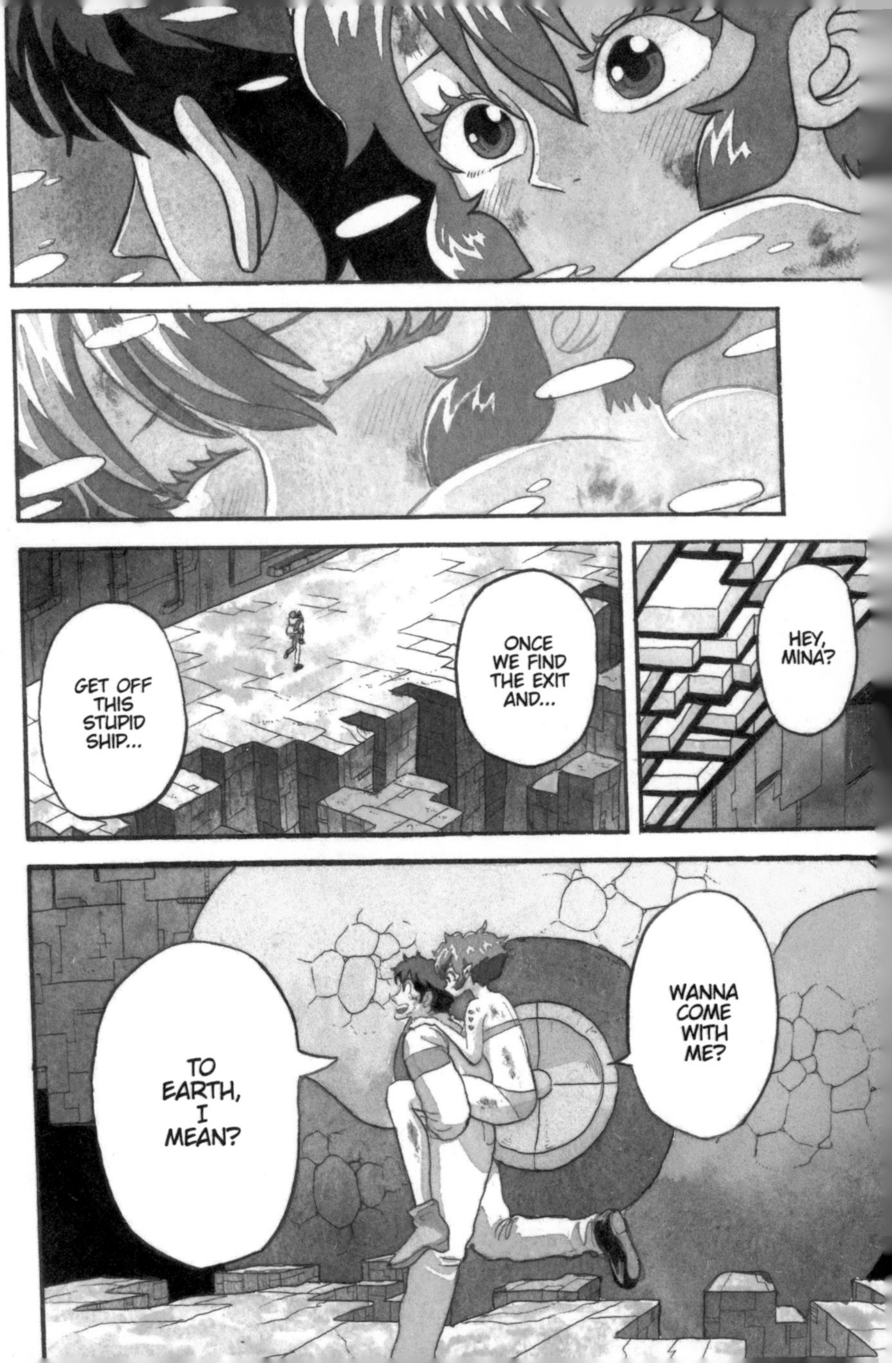
HEY, MINA?
ONCE WE FIND THE EXIT AND...
GET OFF THIS STUPID SHIP...
WANNA COME WITH ME?
TO EARTH, I MEAN?

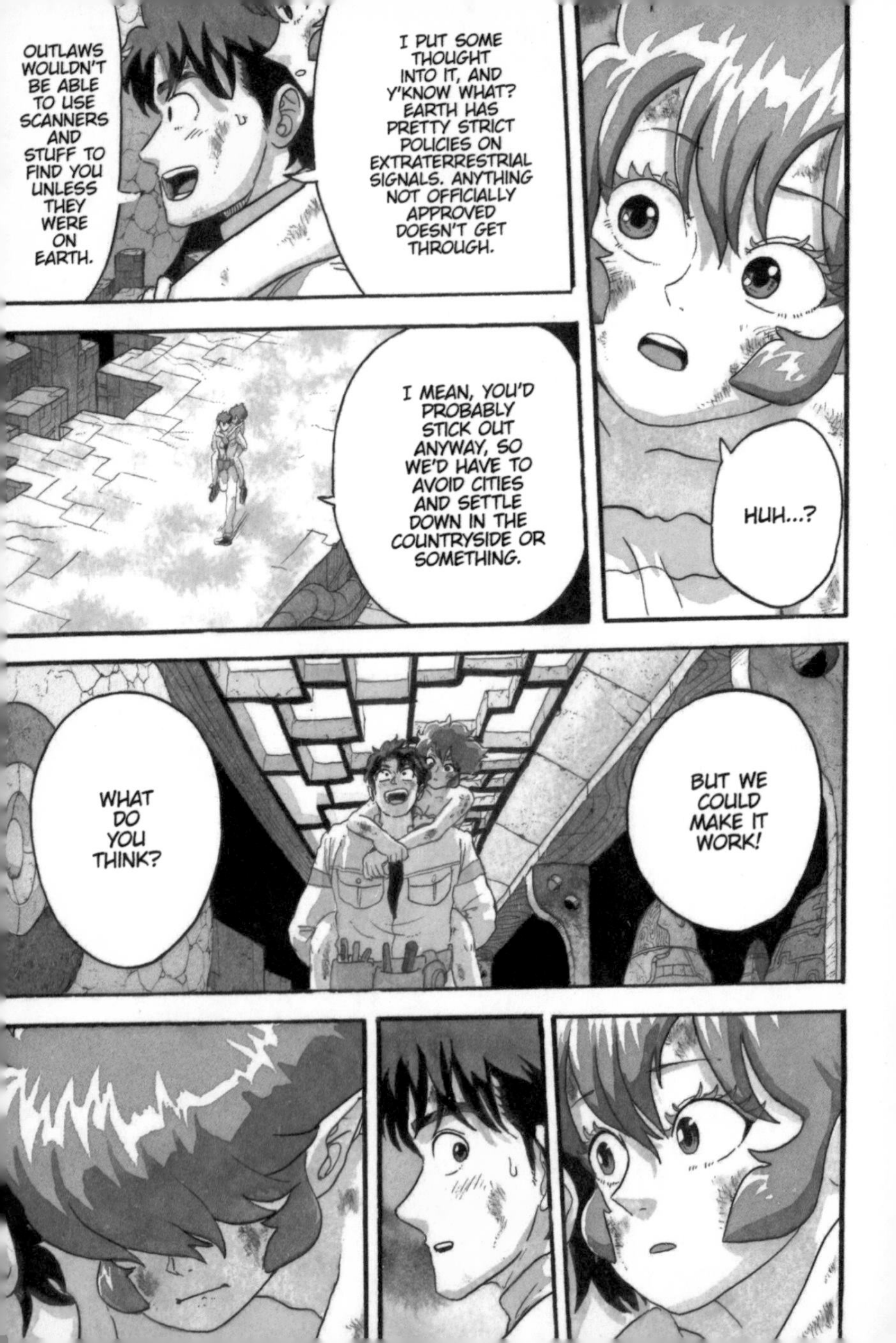
HUH...?
I PUT SOME THOUGHT INTO IT, AND Y'KNOW WHAT? EARTH HAS PRETTY STRICT POLICIES ON EXTRATERRESTRIAL SIGNALS. ANYTHING NOT OFFICIALLY APPROVED DOESN'T GET THROUGH.
OUTLAWS WOULDN'T BE ABLE TO USE SCANNERS AND STUFF TO FIND YOU UNLESS THEY WERE ON EARTH.
I MEAN, YOU'D PROBABLY STICK OUT ANYWAY, SO WE'D HAVE TO AVOID CITIES AND SETTLE DOWN IN THE COUNTRYSIDE OR SOMETHING.
BUT WE COULD MAKE IT WORK!
WHAT DO YOU THINK?

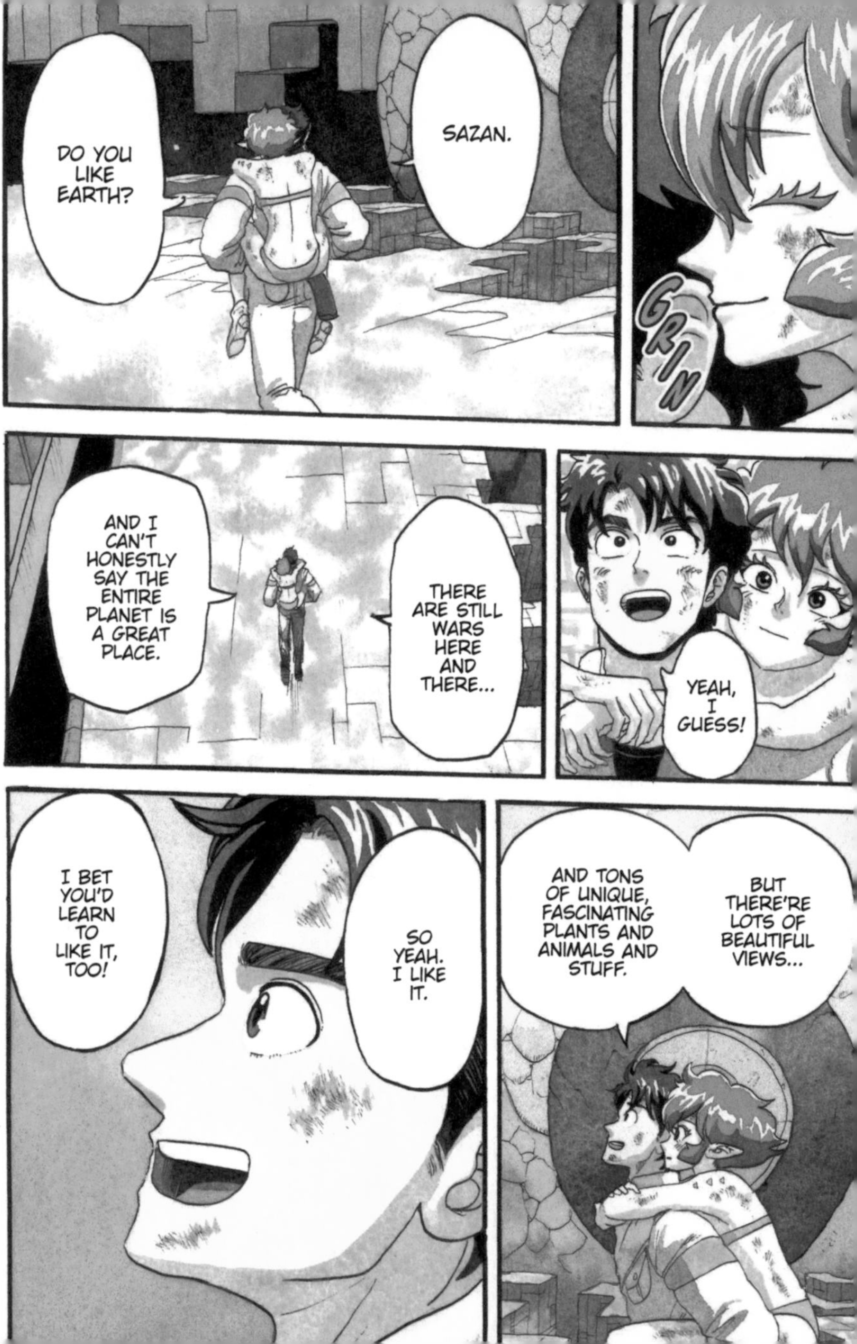
GRIN
SAZAN.
DO YOU LIKE EARTH?
YEAH, I GUESS!
THERE ARE STILL WARS HERE AND THERE...
AND I CAN'T HONESTLY SAY THE ENTIRE PLANET IS A GREAT PLACE.
BUT THERE'RE LOTS OF BEAUTIFUL VIEWS...
AND TONS OF UNIQUE, FASCINATING PLANTS AND ANIMALS AND STUFF.
SO YEAH. I LIKE IT.
I BET YOU'D LEARN TO LIKE IT, TOO!

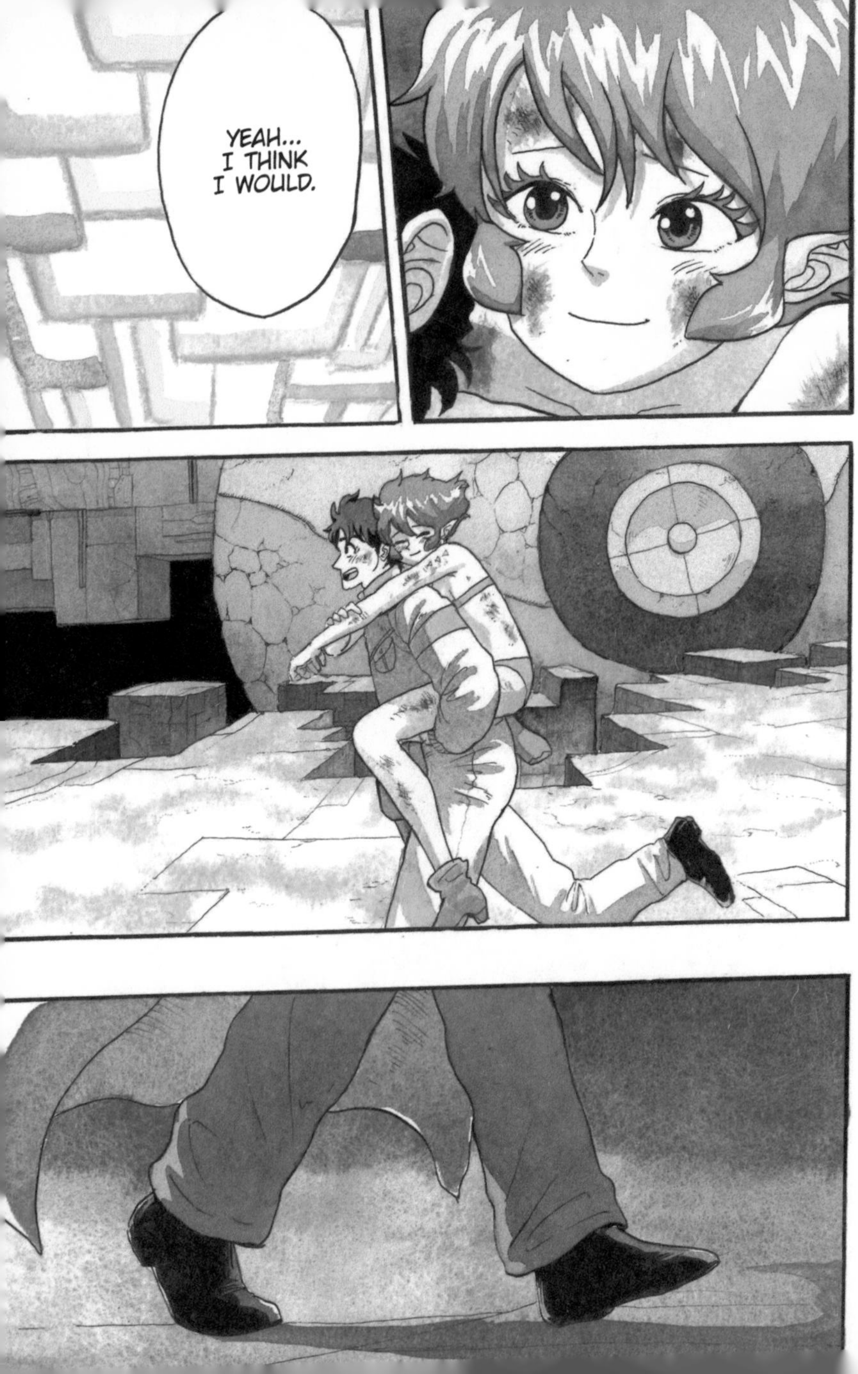
YEAH... I THINK I WOULD.

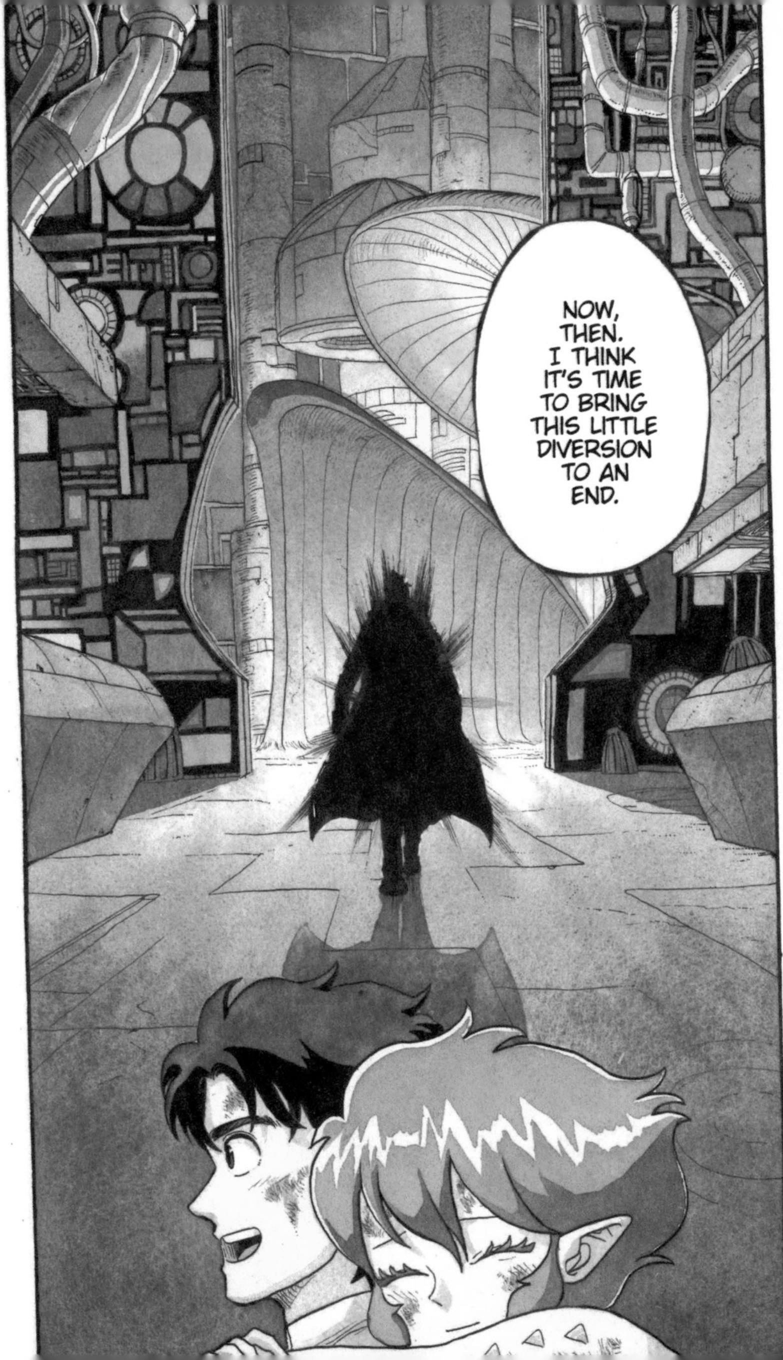
NOW, THEN. I THINK IT'S TIME TO BRING THIS LITTLE DIVERSION TO AN END.

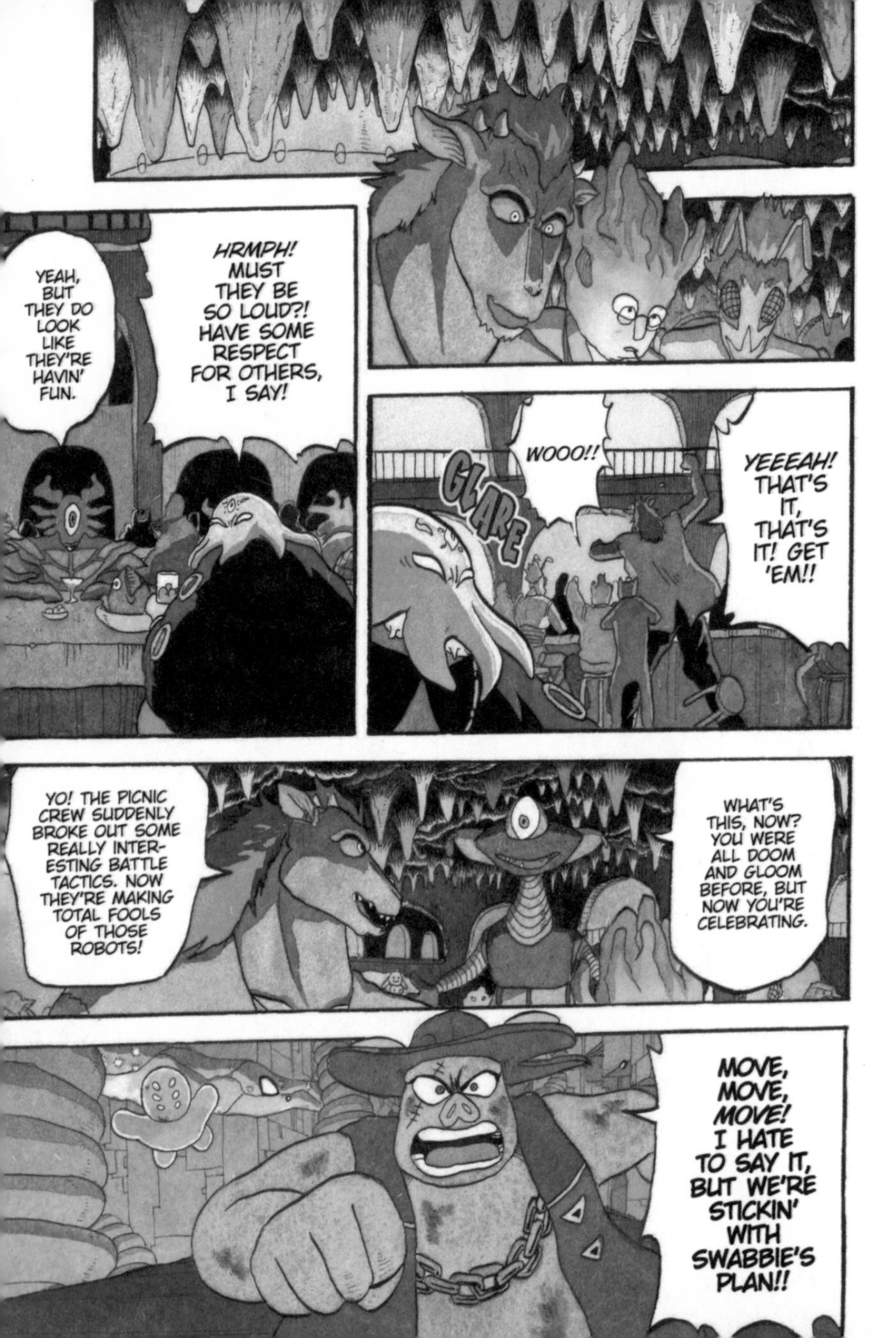
YEEEAH! THAT'S IT, THAT'S IT! GET 'EM!!
WOOO!!
GLARE
HRMPH! MUST THEY BE SO LOUD?! HAVE SOME RESPECT FOR OTHERS, I SAY!
YEAH, BUT THEY DO LOOK LIKE THEY'RE HAVIN' FUN.
WHAT'S THIS, NOW? YOU WERE ALL DOOM AND GLOOM BEFORE, BUT NOW YOU'RE CELEBRATING.
YO! THE PICNIC CREW SUDDENLY BROKE OUT SOME REALLY INTER-ESTING BATTLE TACTICS. NOW THEY'RE MAKING TOTAL FOOLS OF THOSE ROBOTS!
MOVE, MOVE, MOVE! I HATE TO SAY IT, BUT WE'RE STICKIN' WITH SWABBIE'S PLAN!!

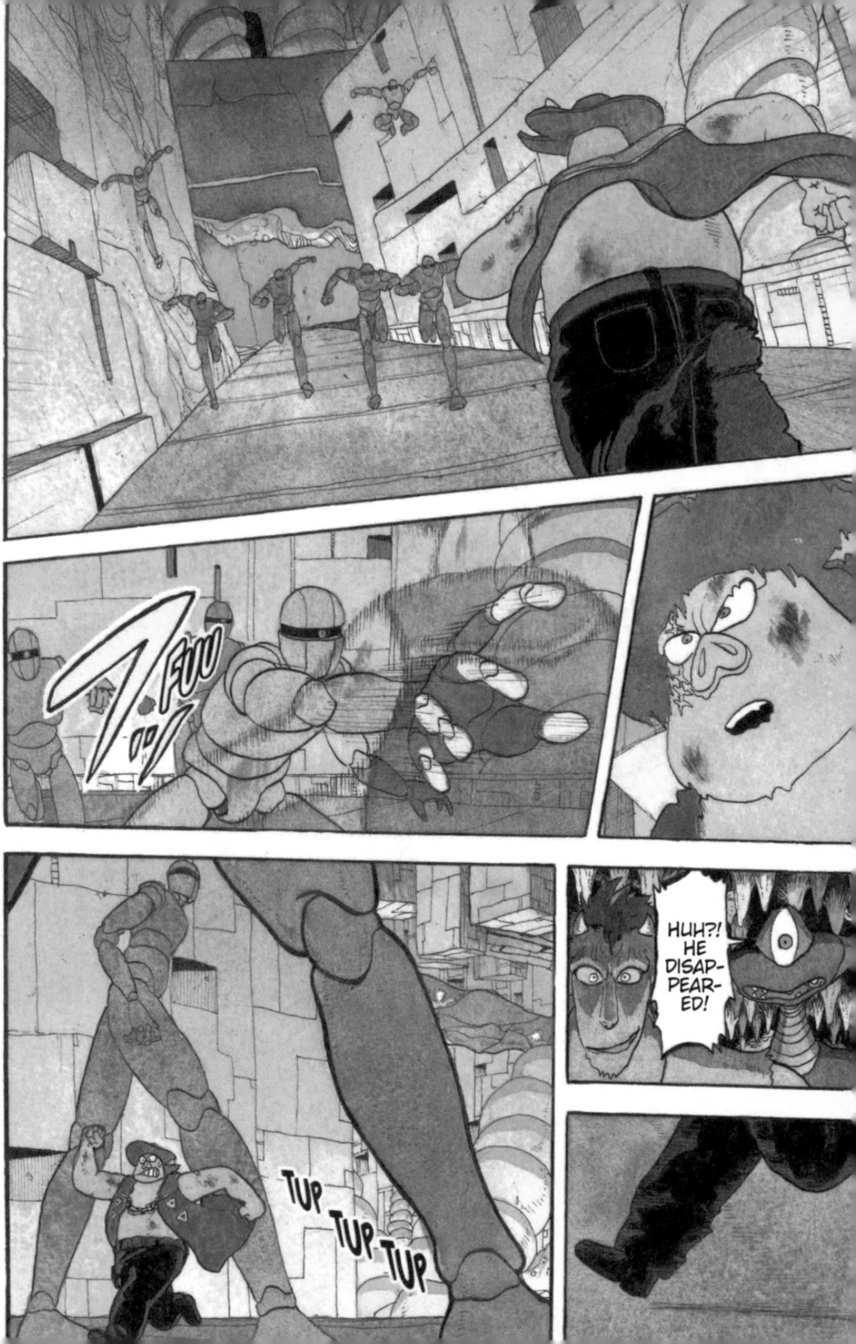
FUU
HUH?! HE DISAP-PEAR-ED!
TUP TUP TUP

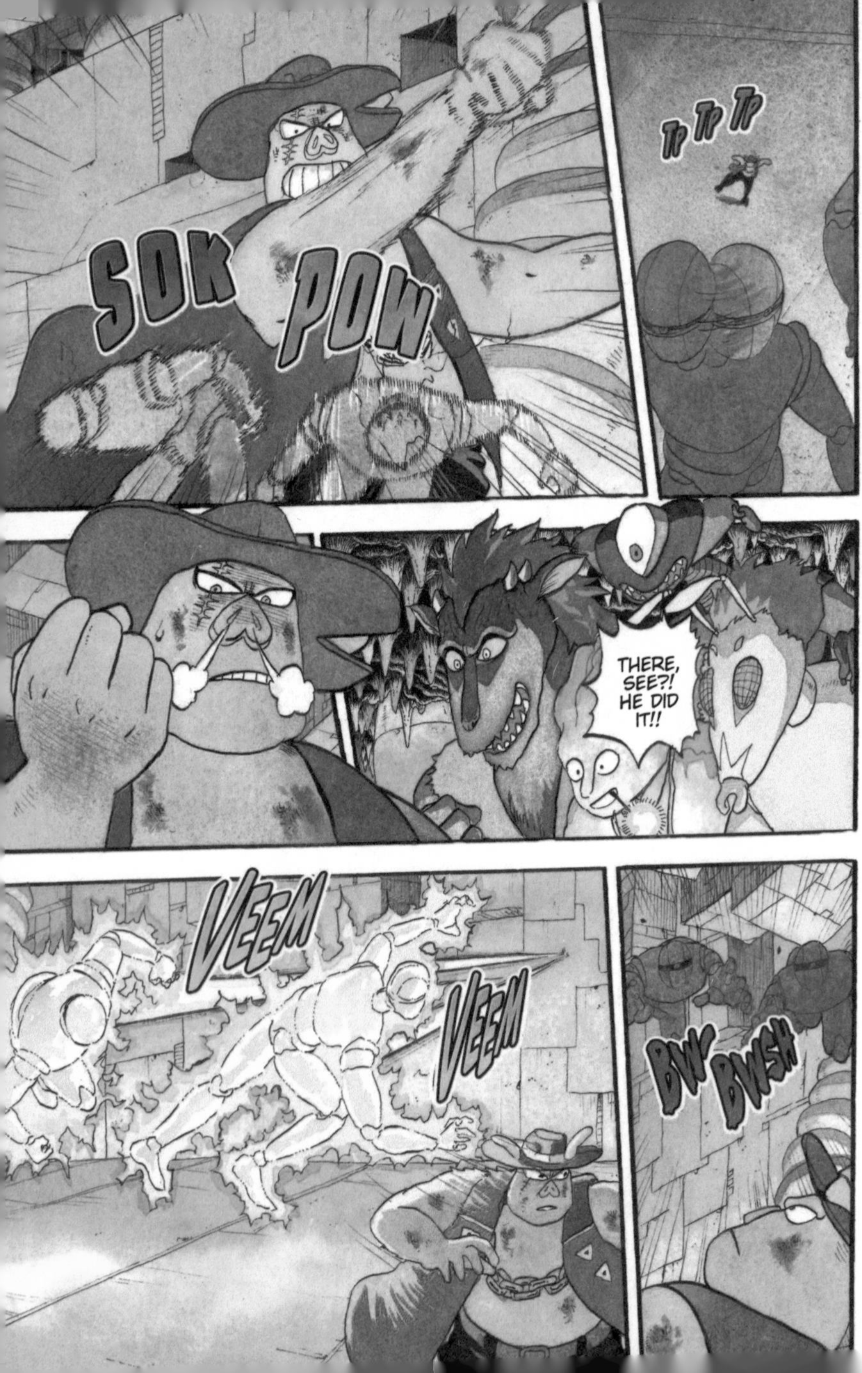
TP TP TP
SOK
POW
THERE, SEE?! HE DID IT!!
BWR
BWSH
VEEM
VEEM

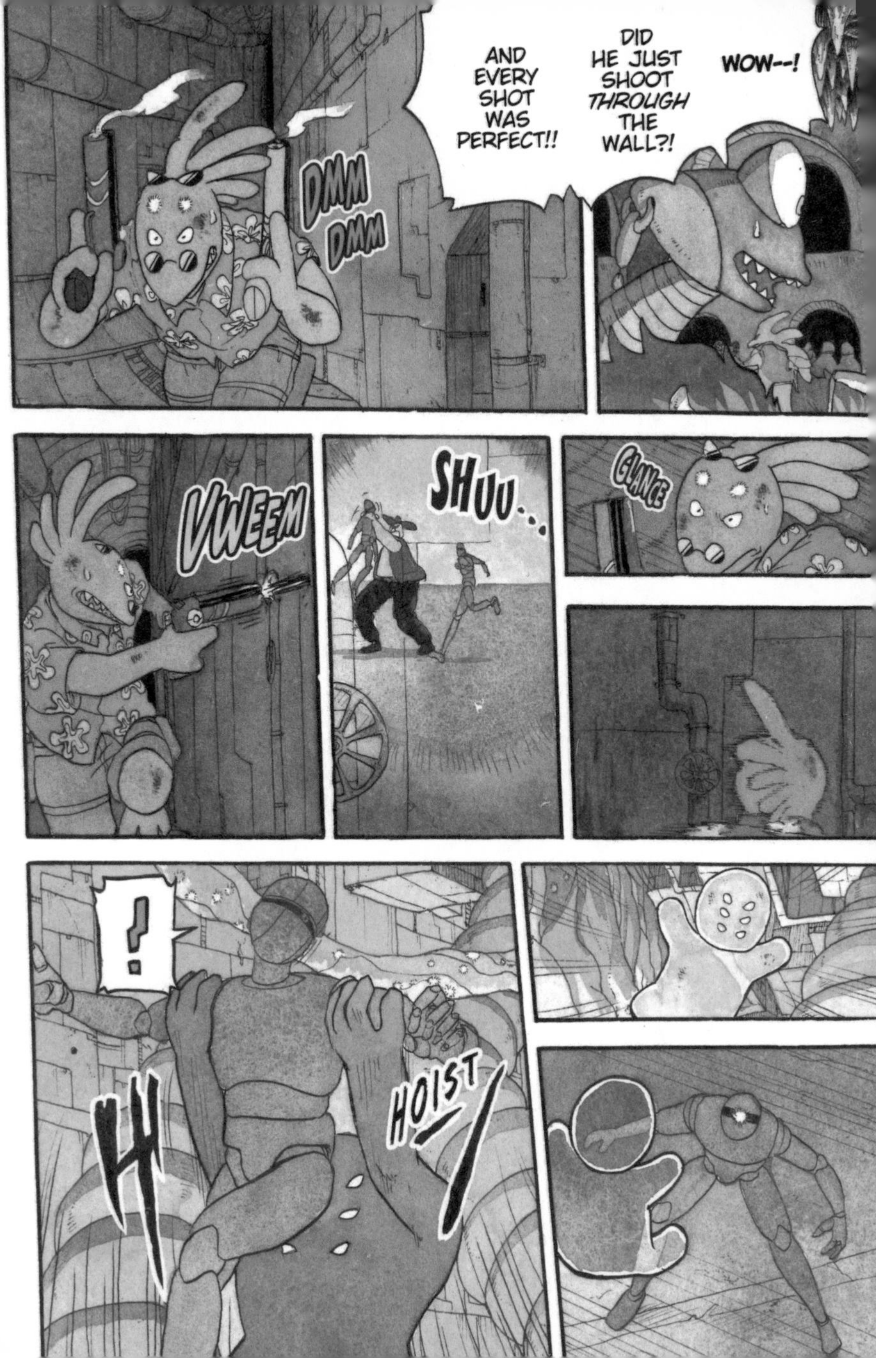
WOW--!
DID HE JUST SHOOT THROUGH THE WALL?!
AND EVERY SHOT WAS PERFECT!!
DMM DMM
GLANCE
SHUU...
VWEEM
!
HOIST

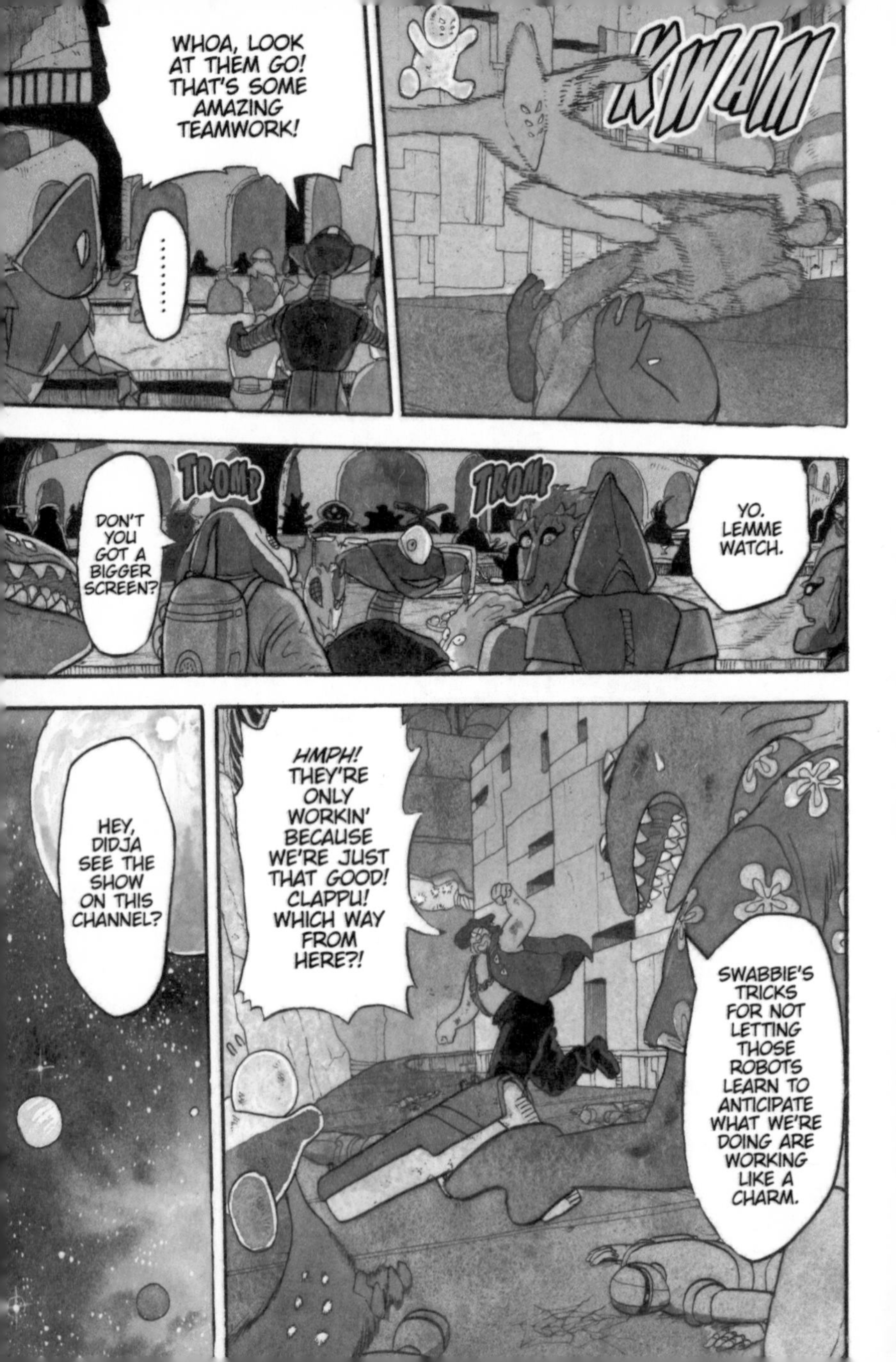
KWAM
WHOA, LOOK AT THEM GO! THAT'S SOME AMAZING TEAMWORK!
......
YO. LEMME WATCH.
TROMP
TROMP
DON'T YOU GOT A BIGGER SCREEN?
HMPH! THEY'RE ONLY WORKIN' BECAUSE WE'RE JUST THAT GOOD! CLAPPU! WHICH WAY FROM HERE?!
SWABBIE'S TRICKS FOR NOT LETTING THOSE ROBOTS LEARN TO ANTICIPATE WHAT WE'RE DOING ARE WORKING LIKE A CHARM.
HEY, DIDJA SEE THE SHOW ON THIS CHANNEL?

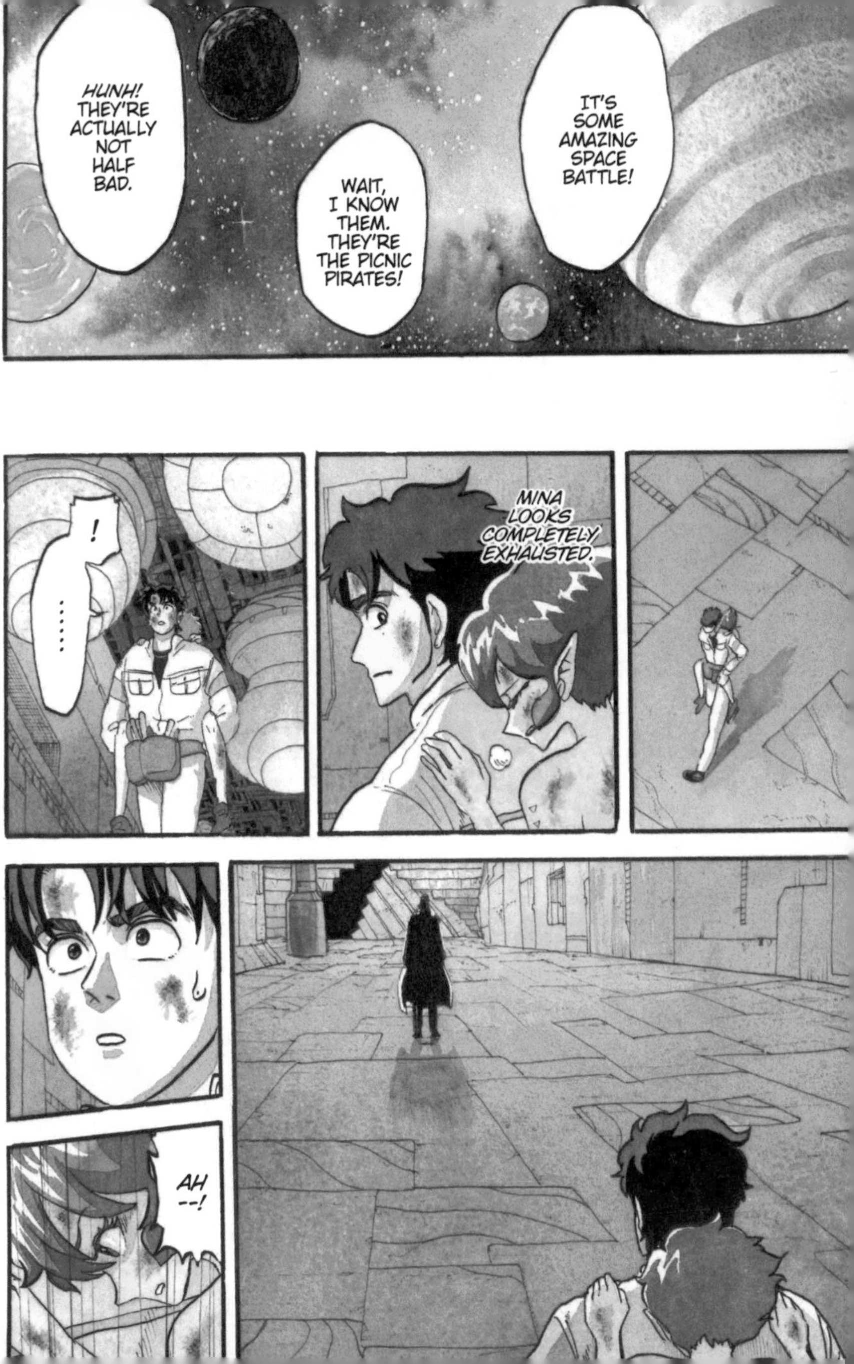
IT'S SOME AMAZING SPACE BATTLE!
WAIT, I KNOW THEM. THEY'RE THE PICNIC PIRATES!
HUNH! THEY'RE ACTUALLY NOT HALF BAD.
MINA LOOKS COMPLETELY EXHAUSTED.
!
......
AH--!

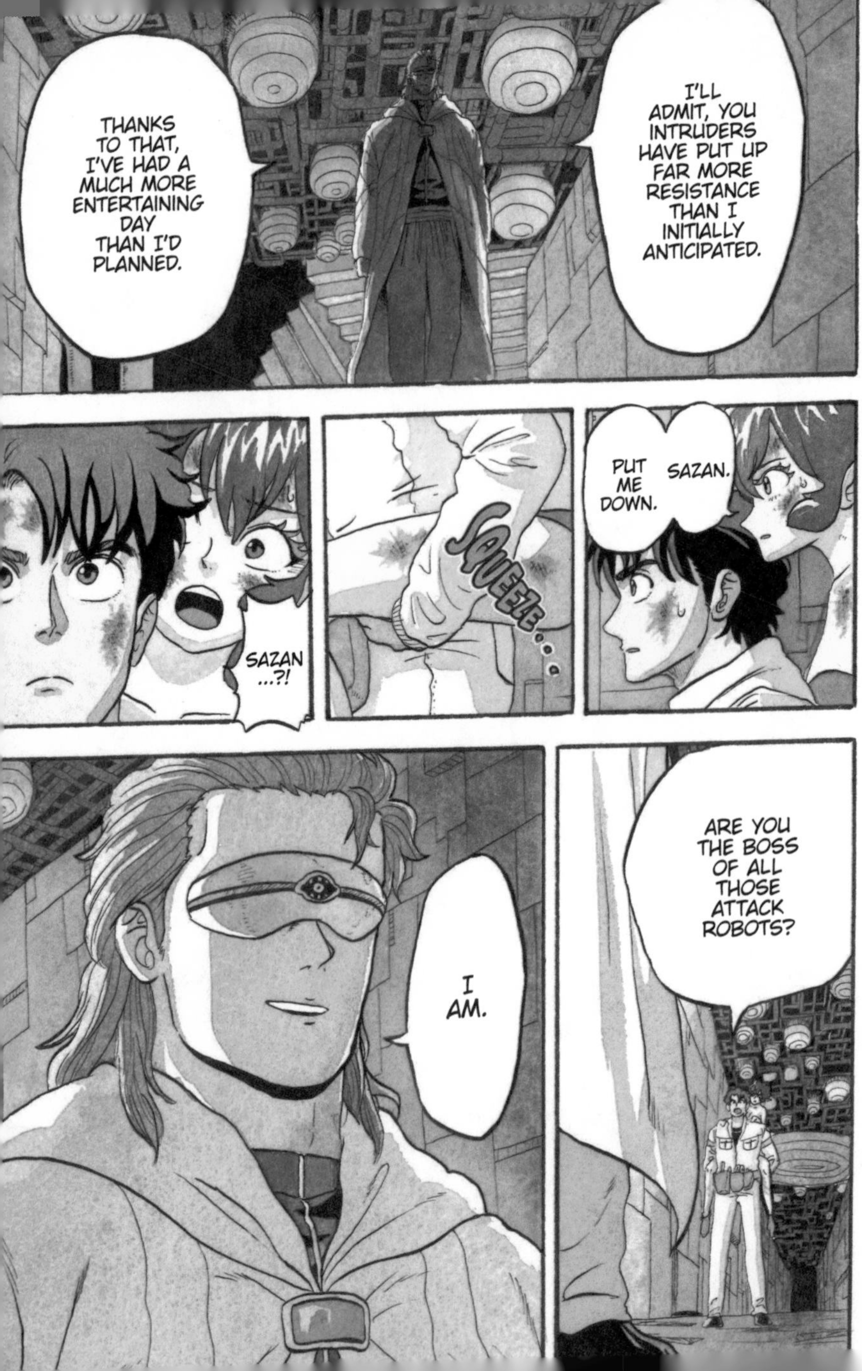
I'LL ADMIT, YOU INTRUDERS HAVE PUT UP FAR MORE RESISTANCE THAN I INITIALLY ANTICIPATED.
THANKS TO THAT, I'VE HAD A MUCH MORE ENTERTAINING DAY THAN I'D PLANNED.
SAZAN.
PUT ME DOWN.
SQUEEZE...
SAZAN ...?!
ARE YOU THE BOSS OF ALL THOSE ATTACK ROBOTS?
I AM.

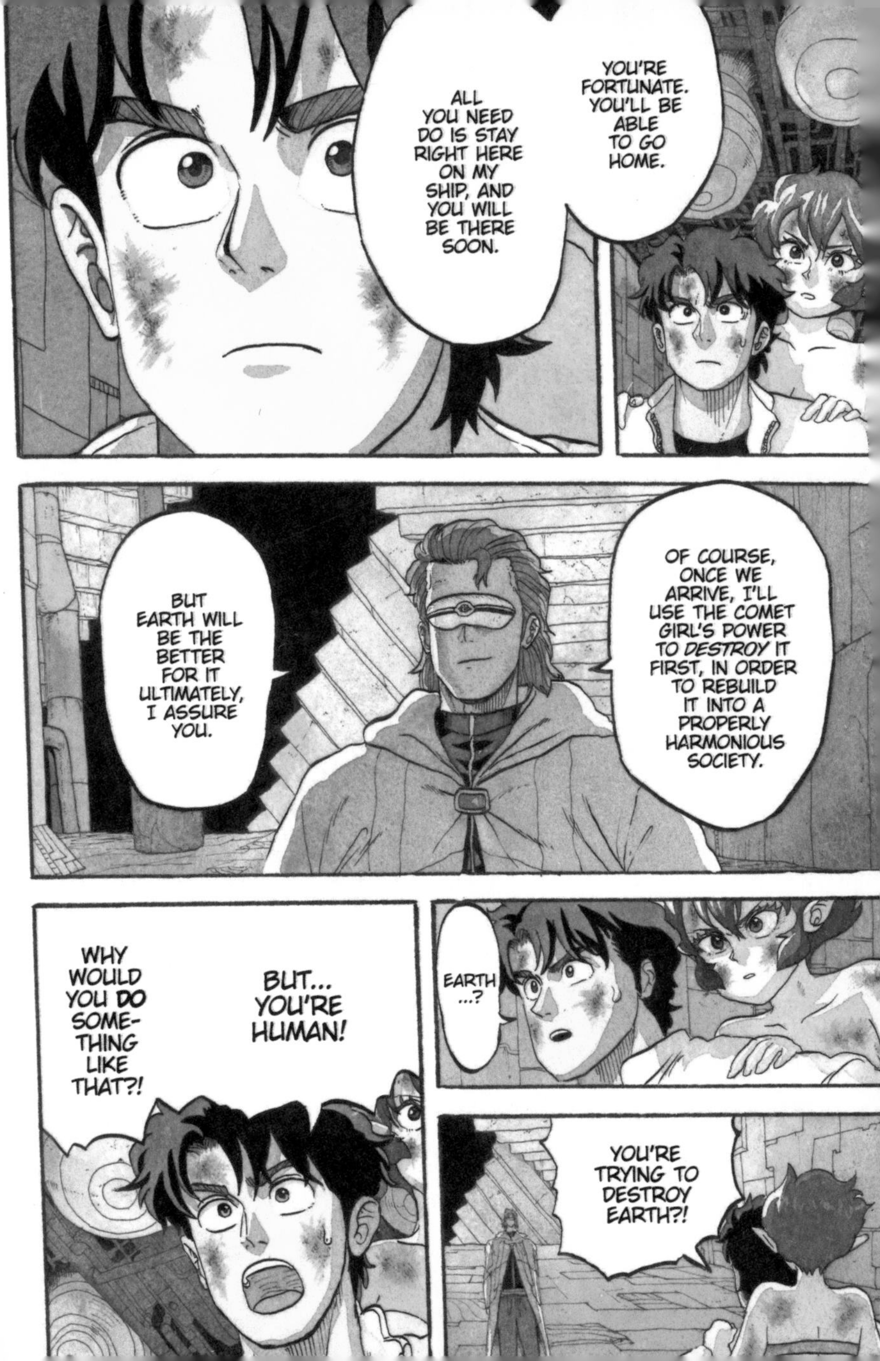
YOU'RE FORTUNATE. YOU'LL BE ABLE TO GO HOME.
ALL YOU NEED DO IS STAY RIGHT HERE ON MY SHIP, AND YOU WILL BE THERE SOON.
OF COURSE, ONCE WE ARRIVE, I'LL USE THE COMET GIRL'S POWER TO *DESTROY* IT FIRST, IN ORDER TO REBUILD IT INTO A PROPERLY HARMONIOUS SOCIETY.
BUT EARTH WILL BE THE BETTER FOR IT ULTIMATELY, I ASSURE YOU.
EARTH ...?
YOU'RE TRYING TO DESTROY EARTH?!
BUT... YOU'RE HUMAN!
WHY WOULD YOU DO SOME-THING LIKE THAT?!

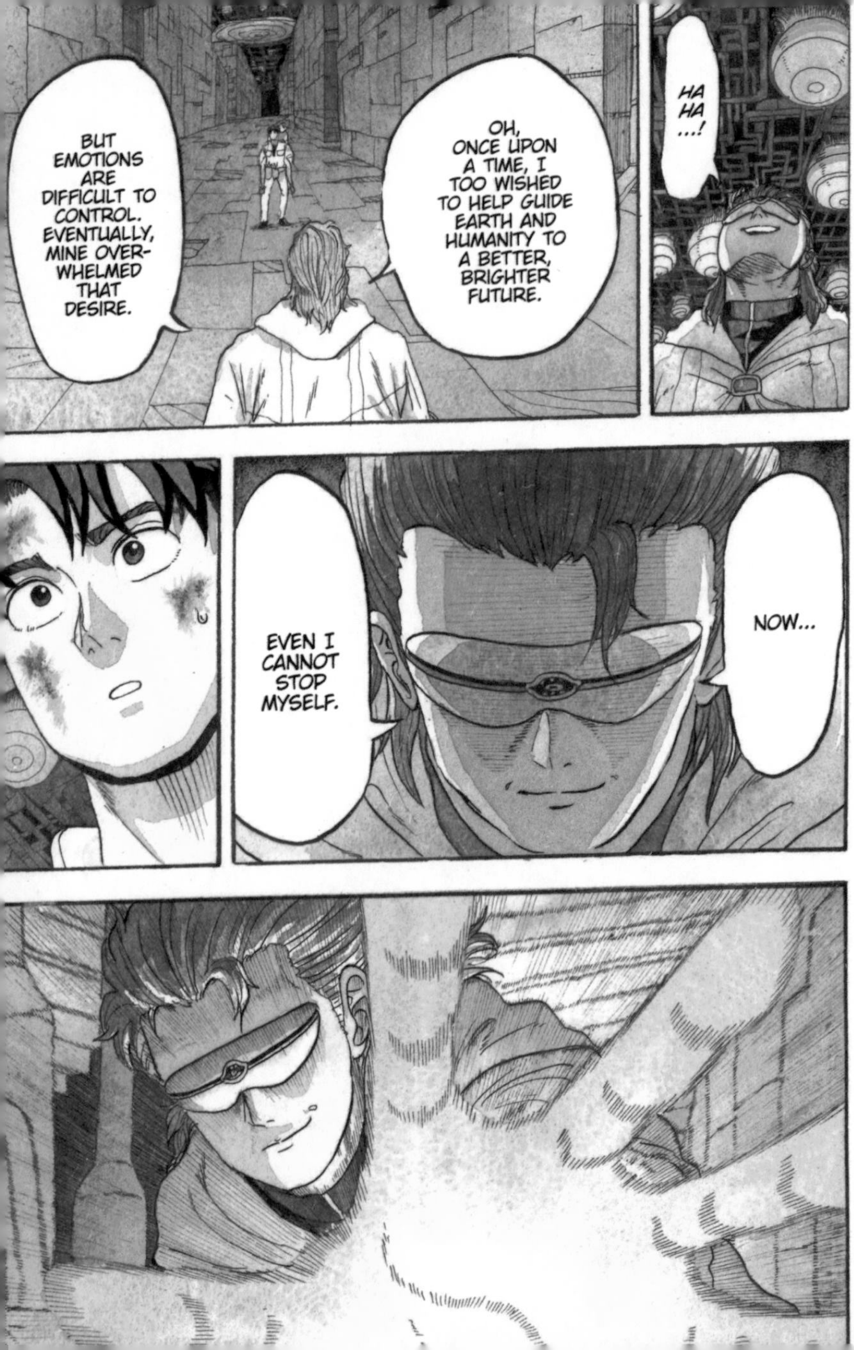
HA HA ...!
OH, ONCE UPON A TIME, I TOO WISHED TO HELP GUIDE EARTH AND HUMANITY TO A BETTER, BRIGHTER FUTURE.
BUT EMOTIONS ARE DIFFICULT TO CONTROL. EVENTUALLY, MINE OVER-WHELMED THAT DESIRE.
NOW...
EVEN I CANNOT STOP MYSELF.

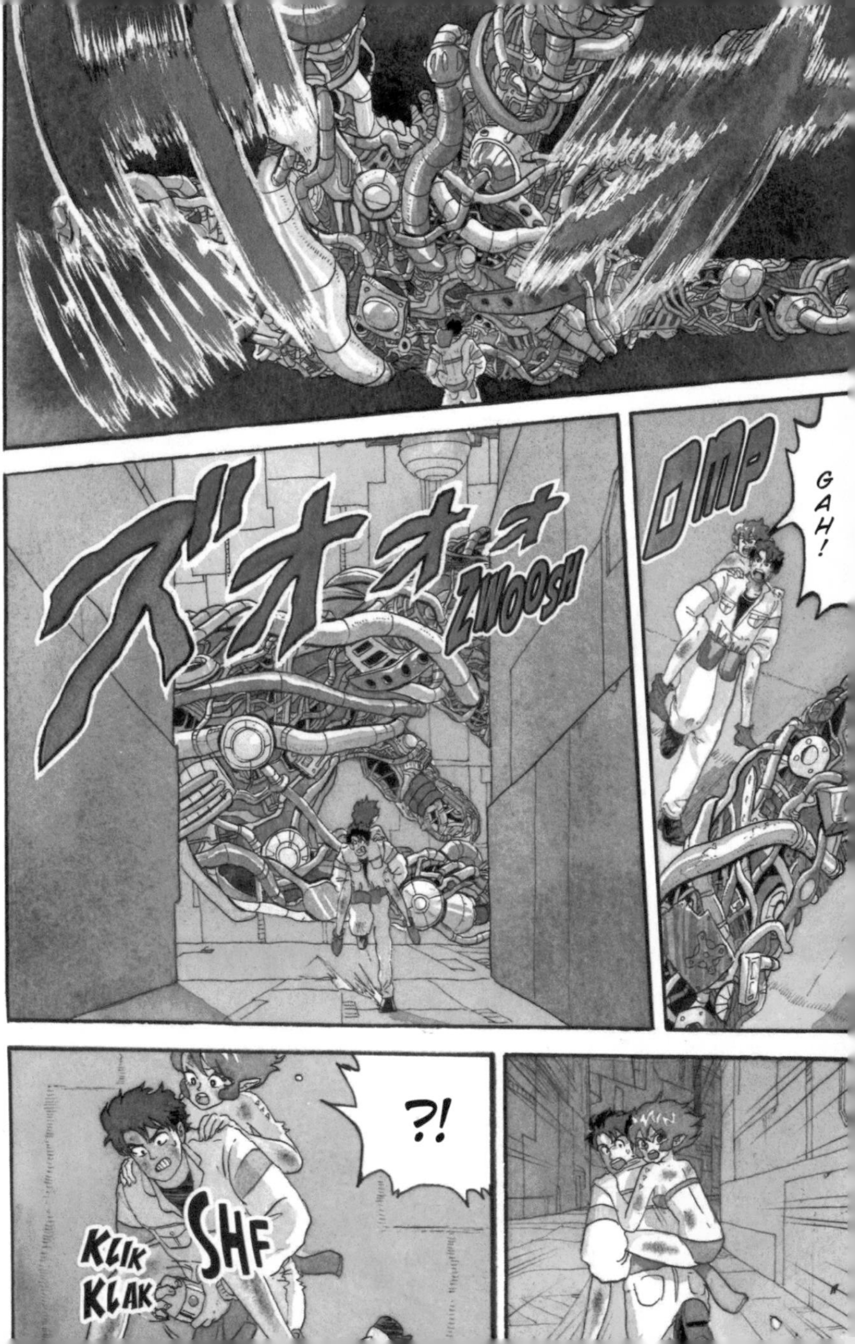
DOMP
GAH!
ズオォォ
ZWOOSH
?!
SHF
KLIK KLAK

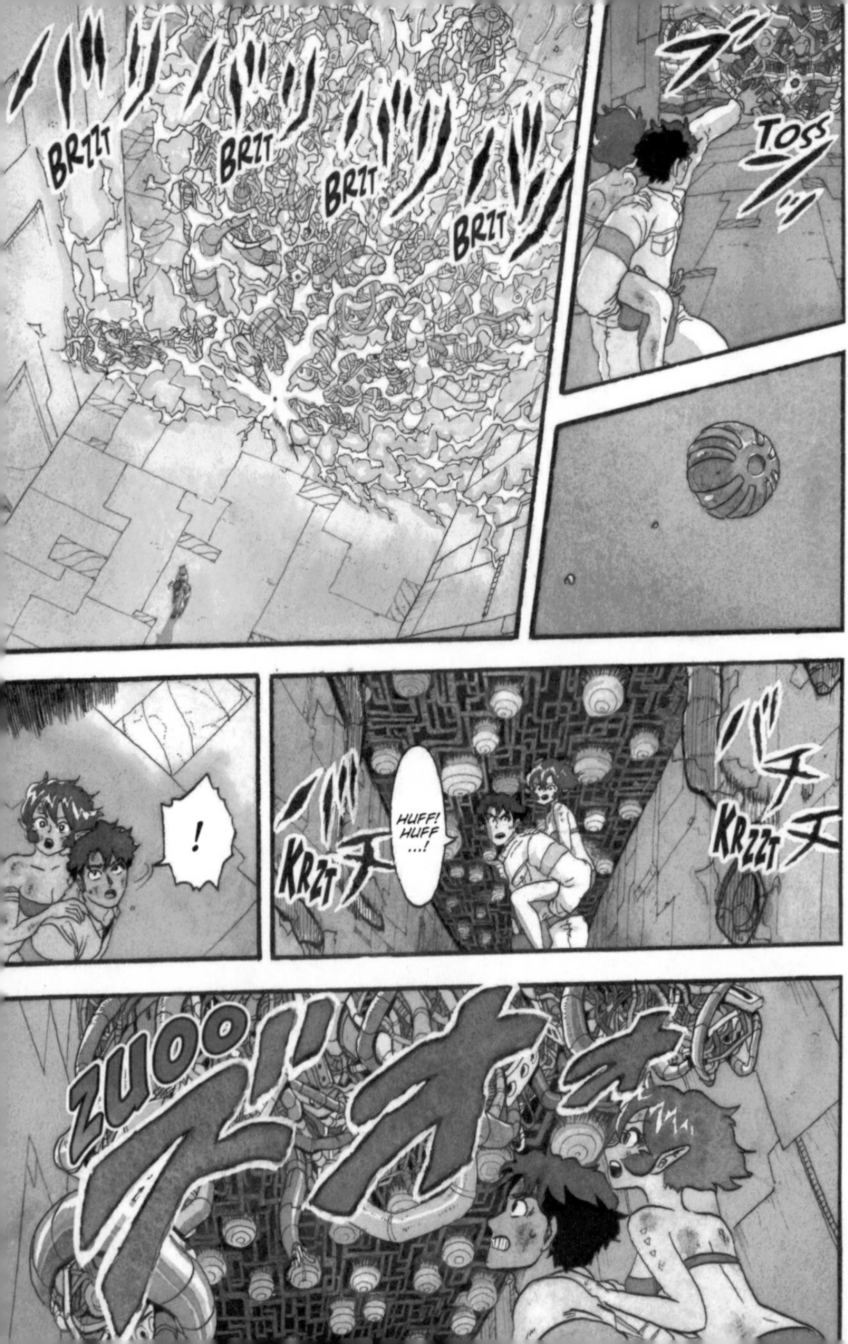
TOSS
BRZZT
BRZT
BRZT
BRZT
KRZZT
HUFF! HUFF ...!
KRZT
!
ZUOO

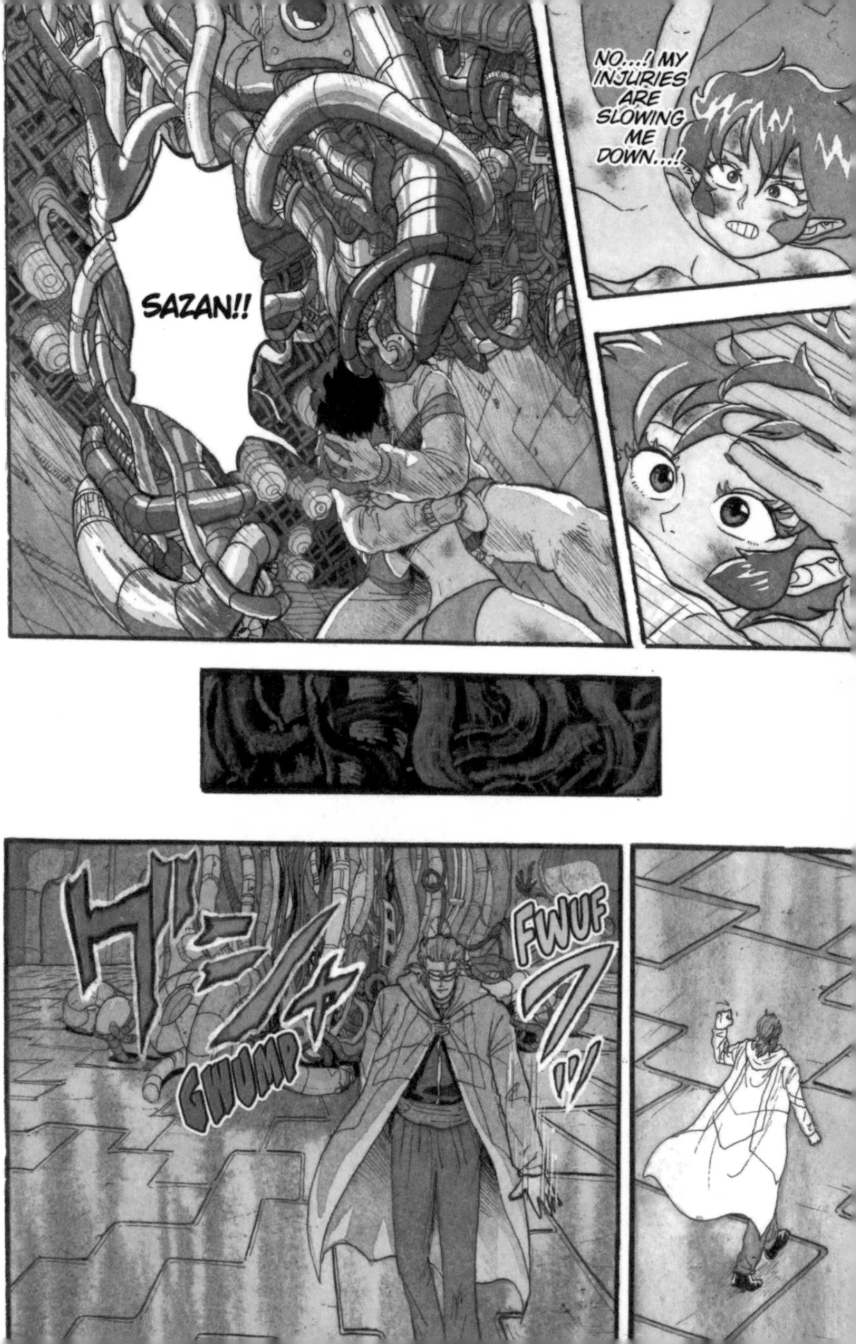
NO...! MY INJURIES ARE SLOWING ME DOWN...!
SAZAN!!
FWUF
GWUMP

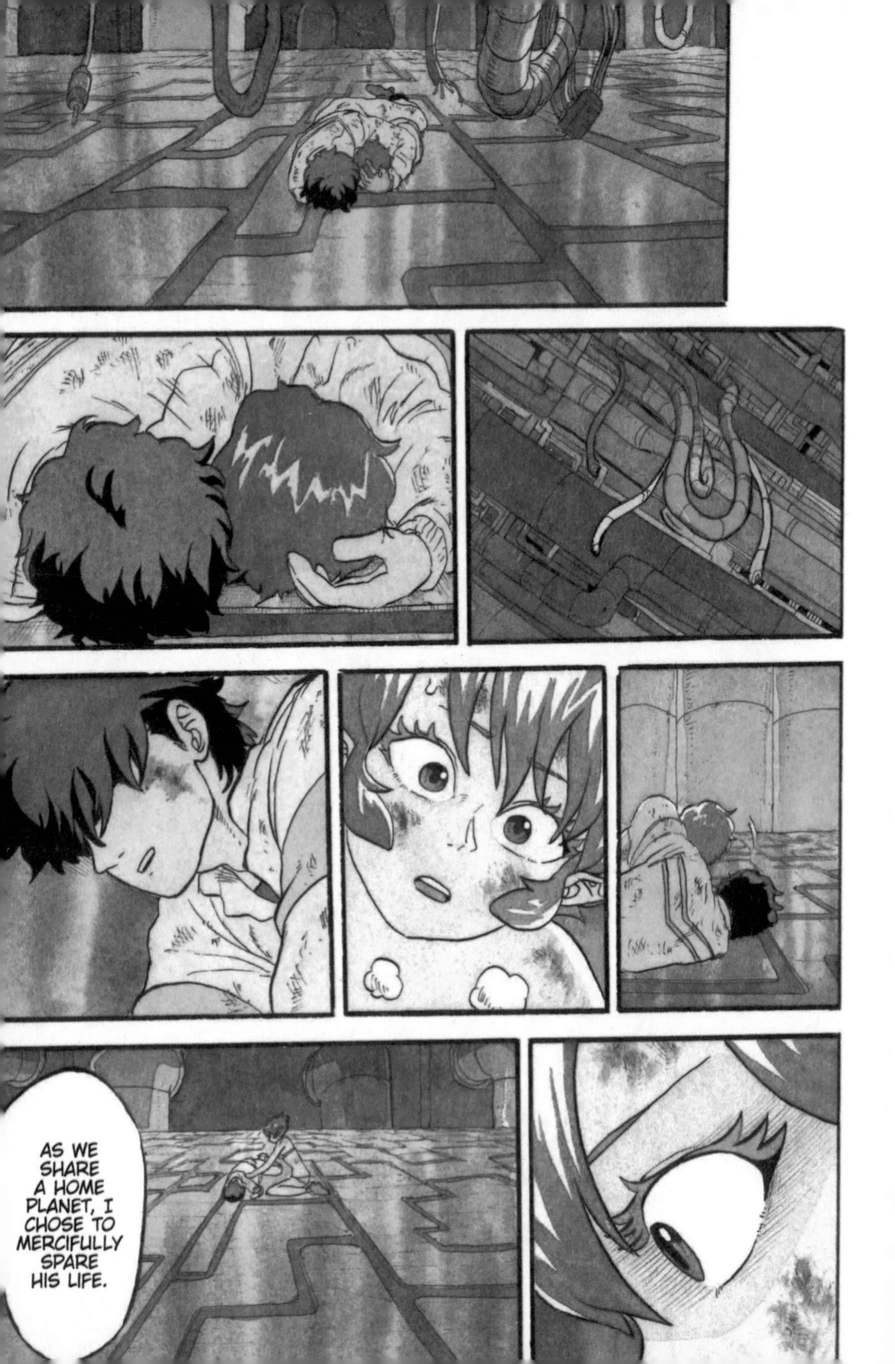
AS WE SHARE A HOME PLANET, I CHOSE TO MERCIFULLY SPARE HIS LIFE.

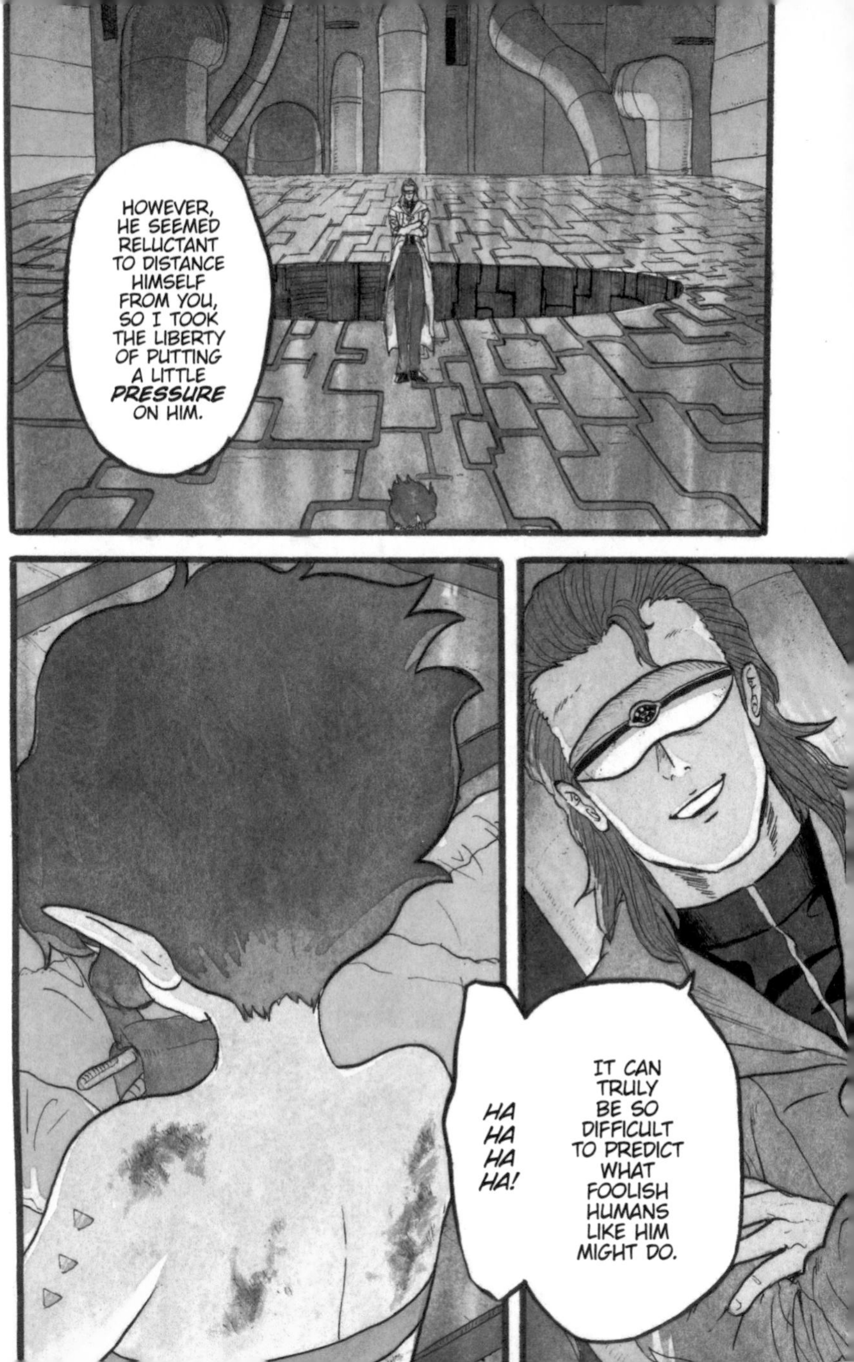
HOWEVER, HE SEEMED RELUCTANT TO DISTANCE HIMSELF FROM YOU, SO I TOOK THE LIBERTY OF PUTTING A LITTLE **PRESSURE** ON HIM.
IT CAN TRULY BE SO DIFFICULT TO PREDICT WHAT FOOLISH HUMANS LIKE HIM MIGHT DO.
HA HA HA HA!

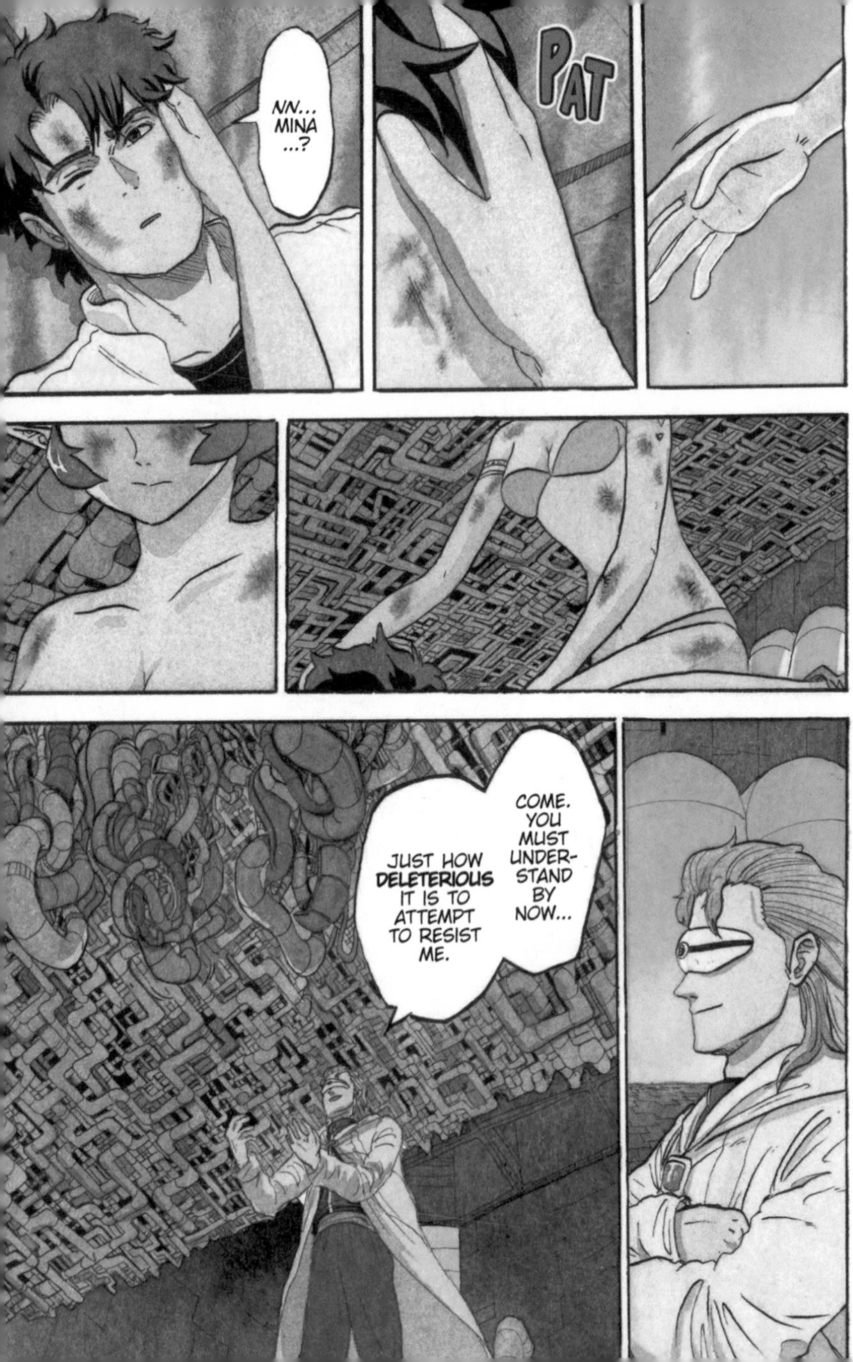
PAT
NN... MINA ...?
COME. YOU MUST UNDER-STAND BY NOW...
JUST HOW **DELETERIOUS** IT IS TO ATTEMPT TO RESIST ME.

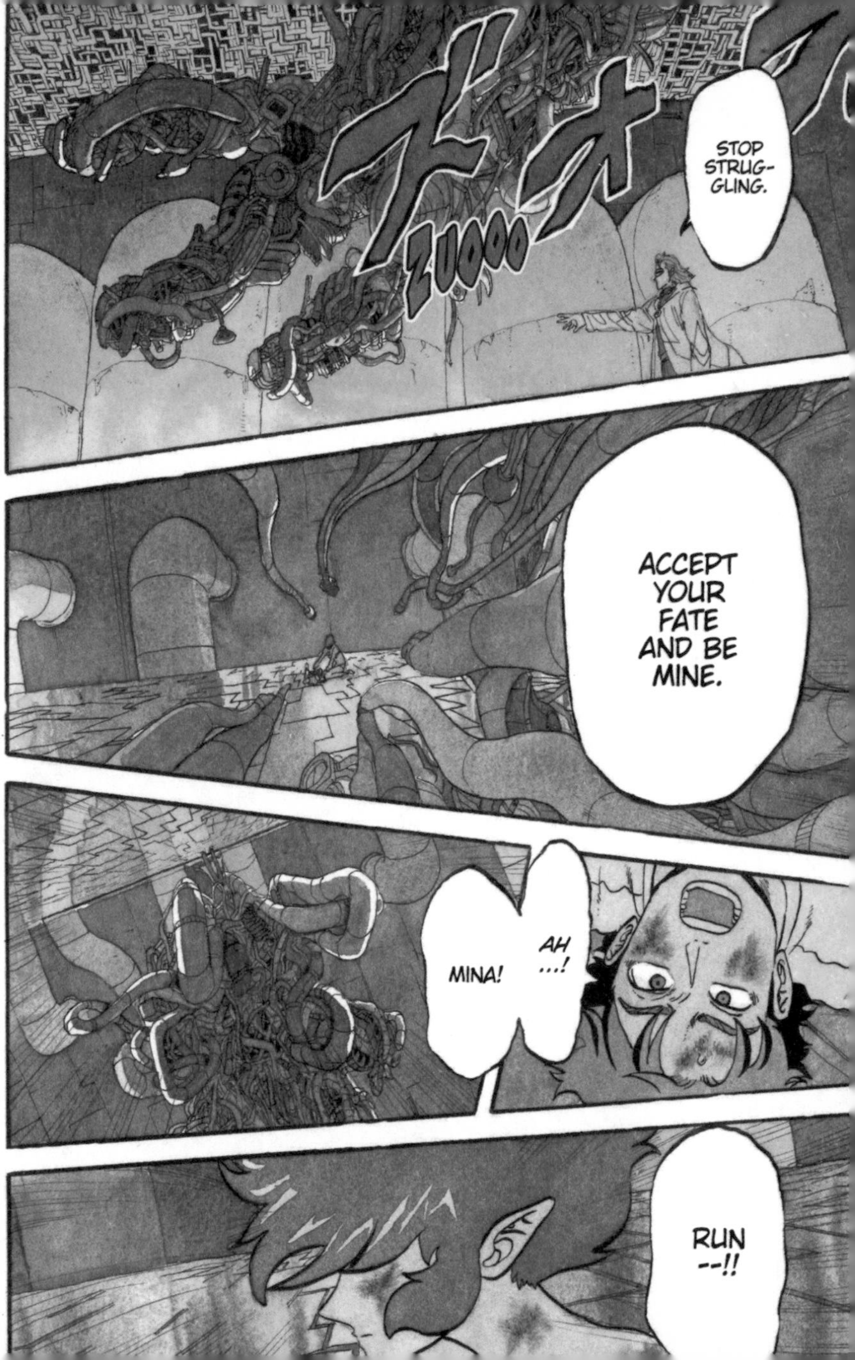

ZUOOO
STOP STRUG-GLING.
ACCEPT YOUR FATE AND BE MINE.
AH ...!
MINA!
RUN --!!

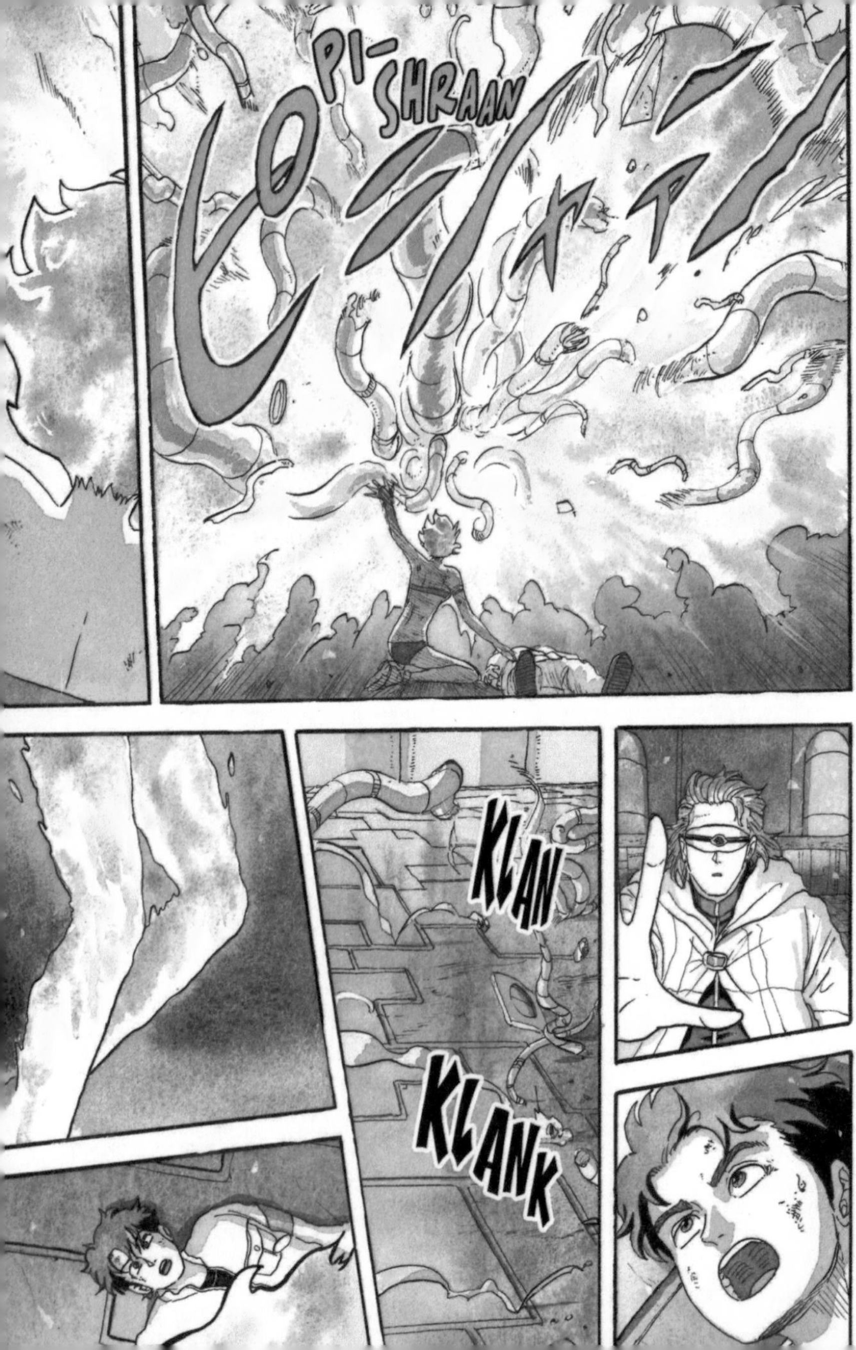
PI-SHRAAN
KLAN
KLANK

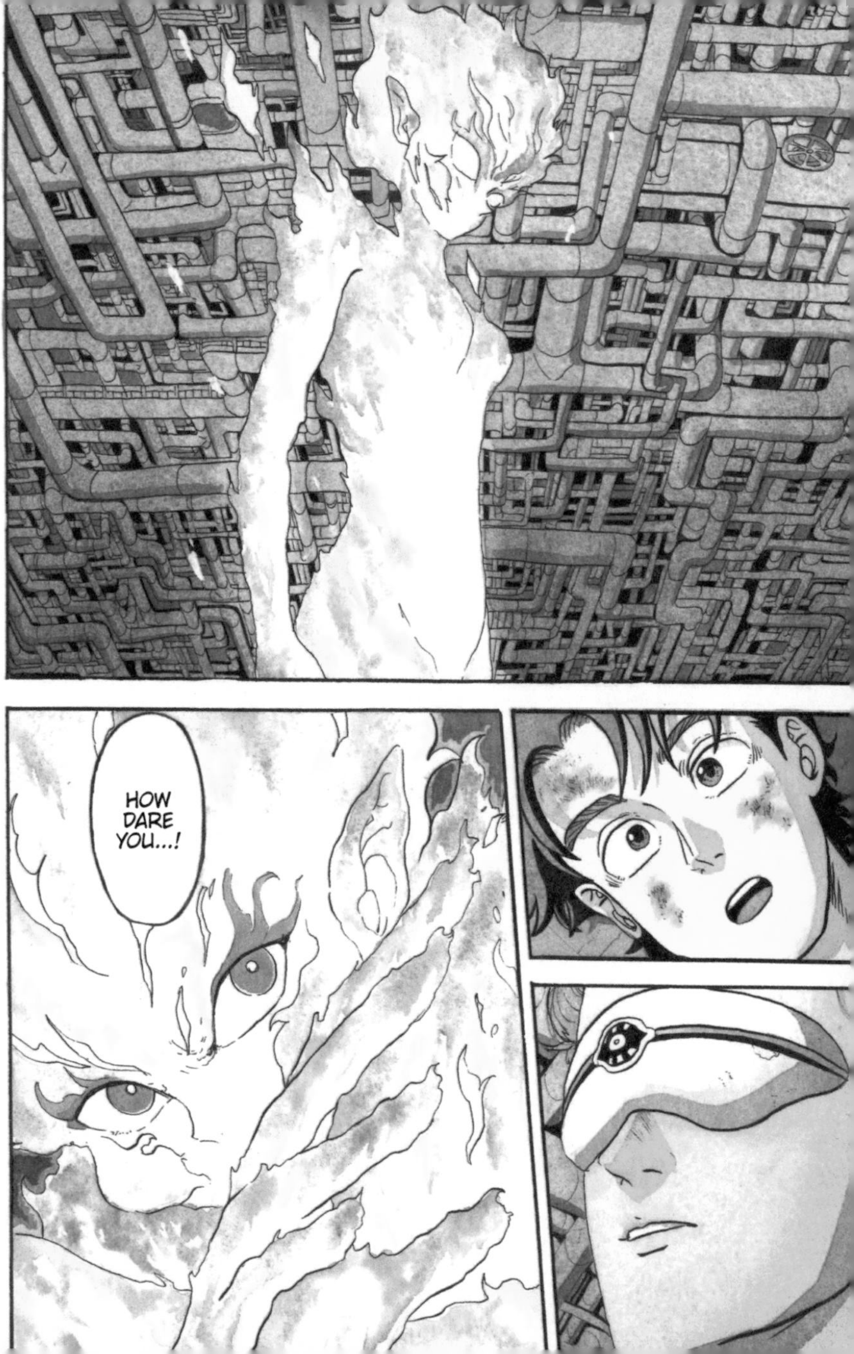
HOW DARE YOU...!

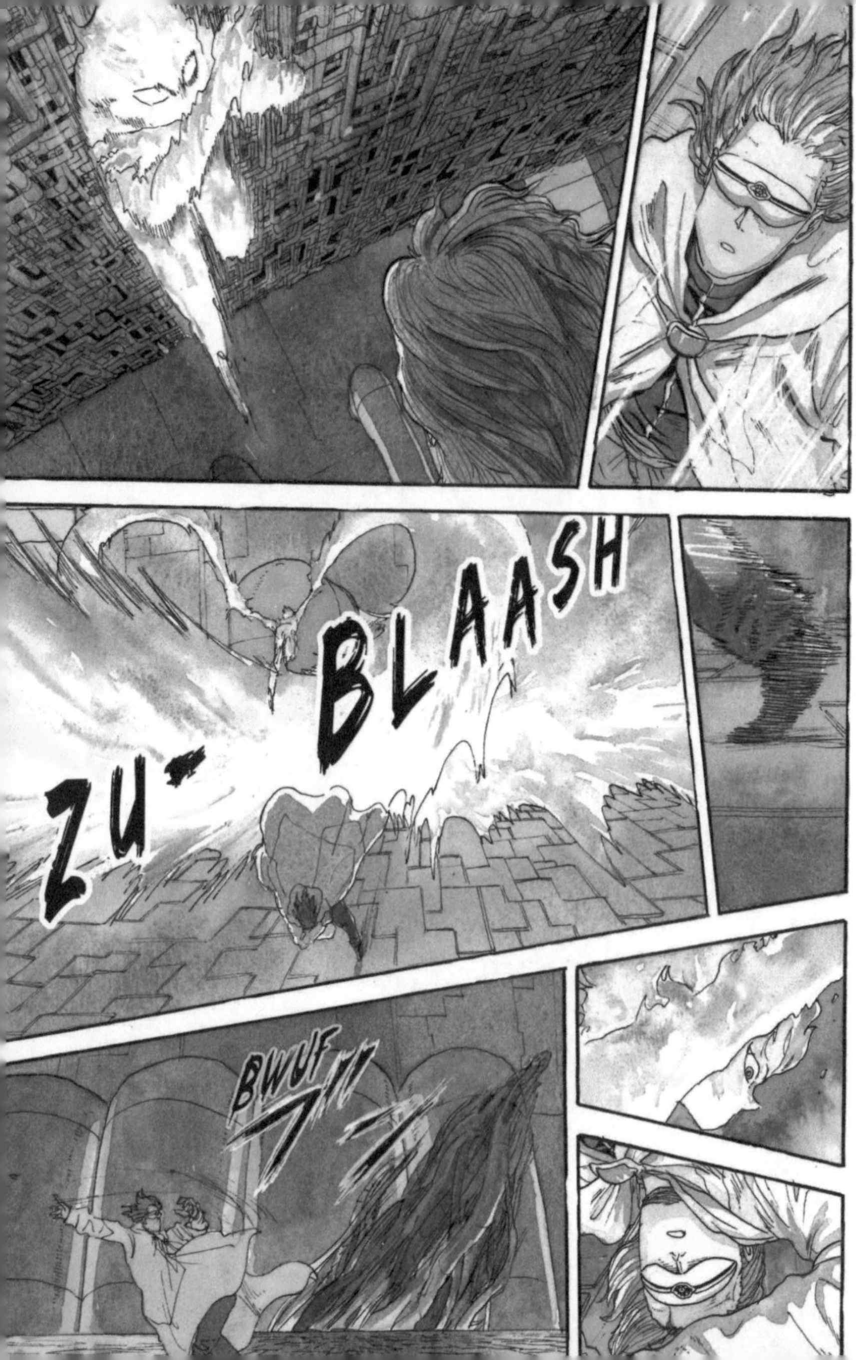
ZU BLAASH
BWUF

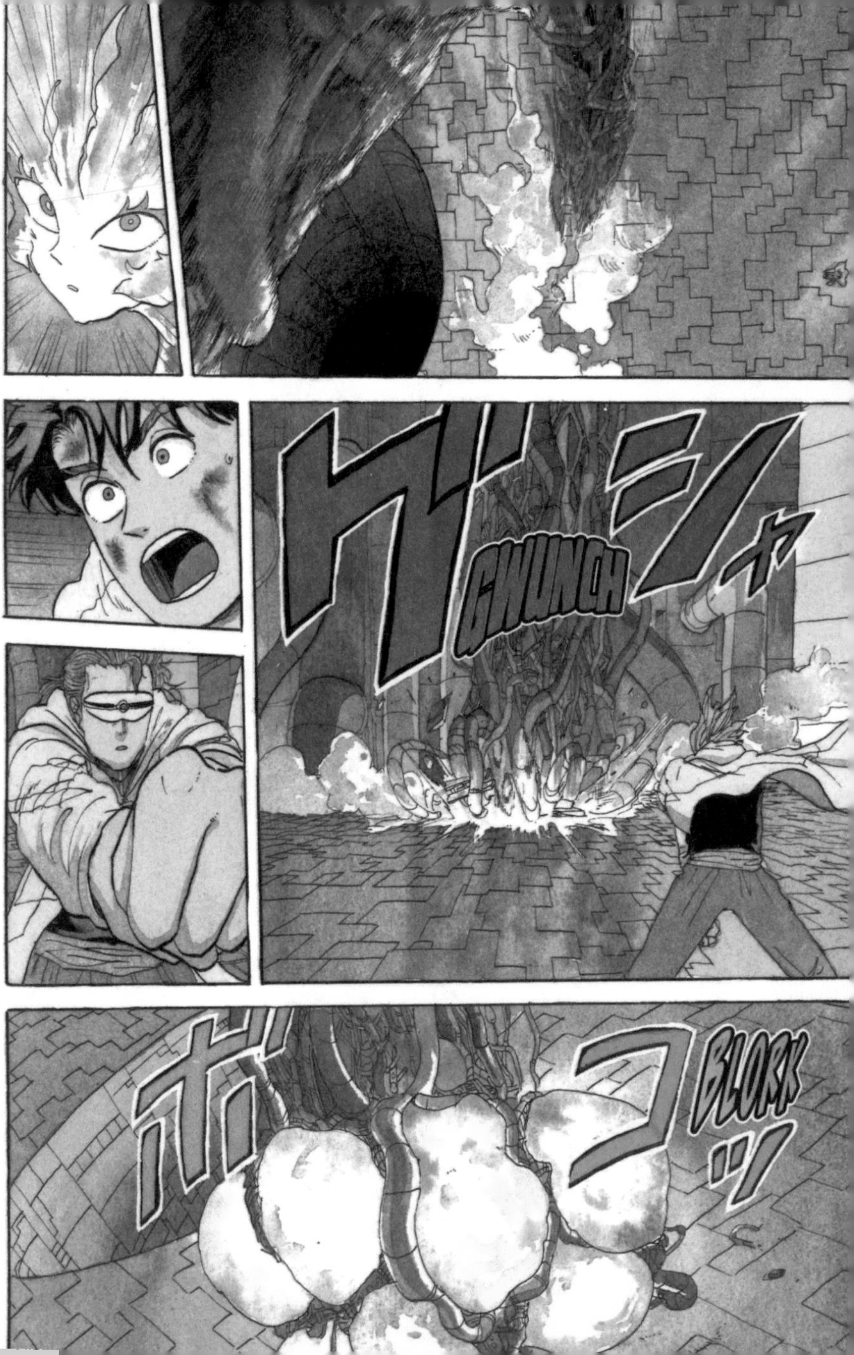
CWUNCH
BLORK

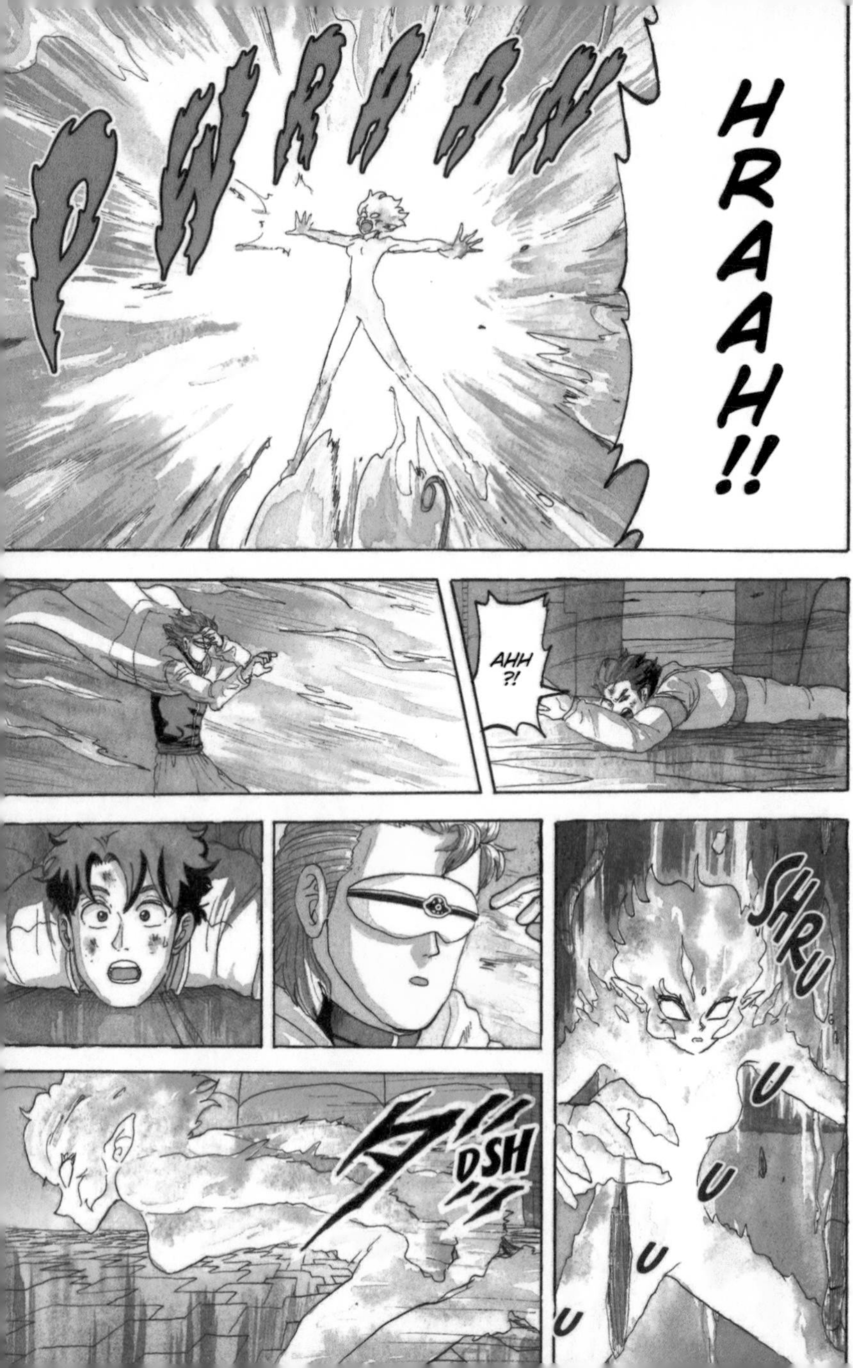
HRAAAH!!
DWRAAW
AHH ?!
SHRUUUUU
DSH!!

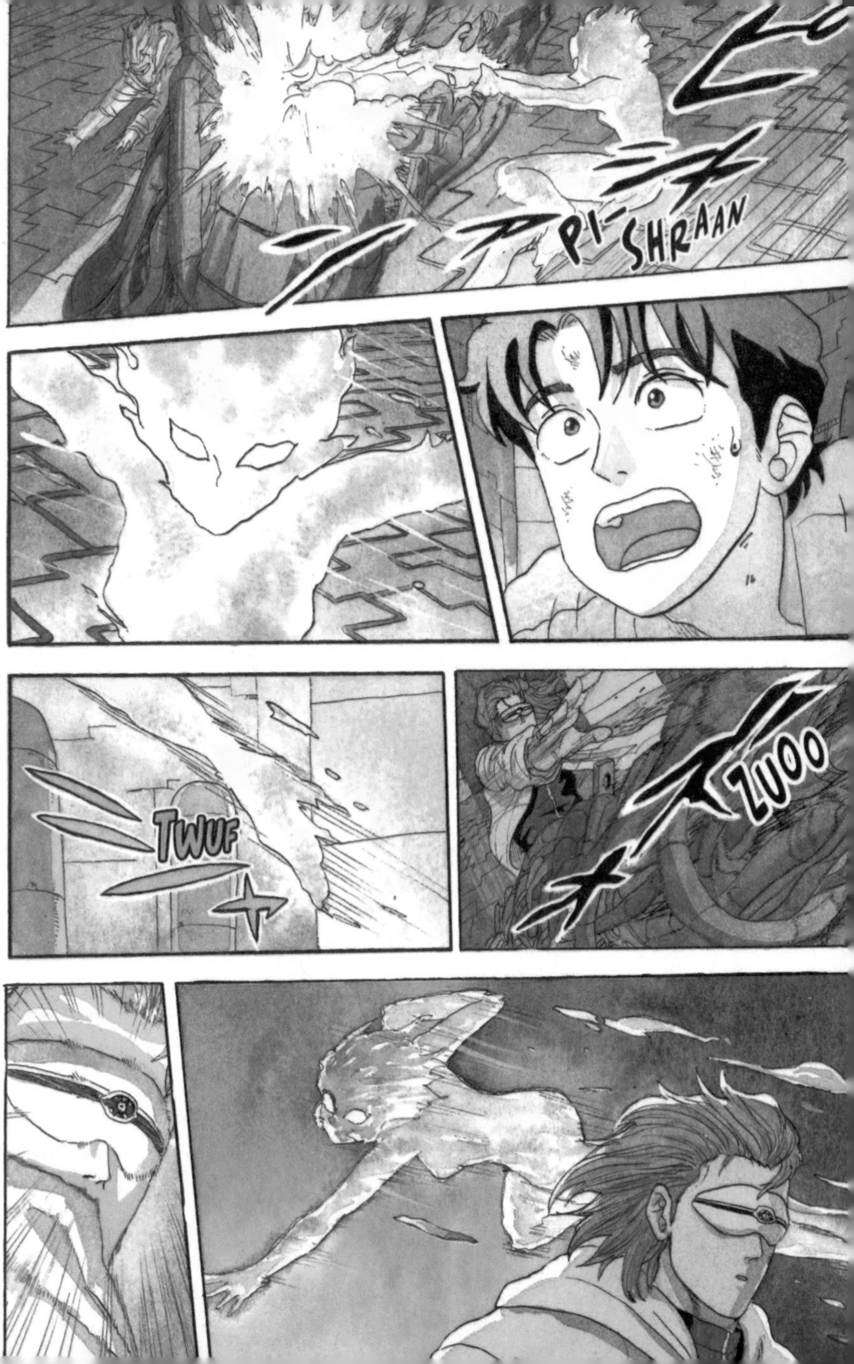
PI-SHRAAN
ZUOO
TWUF

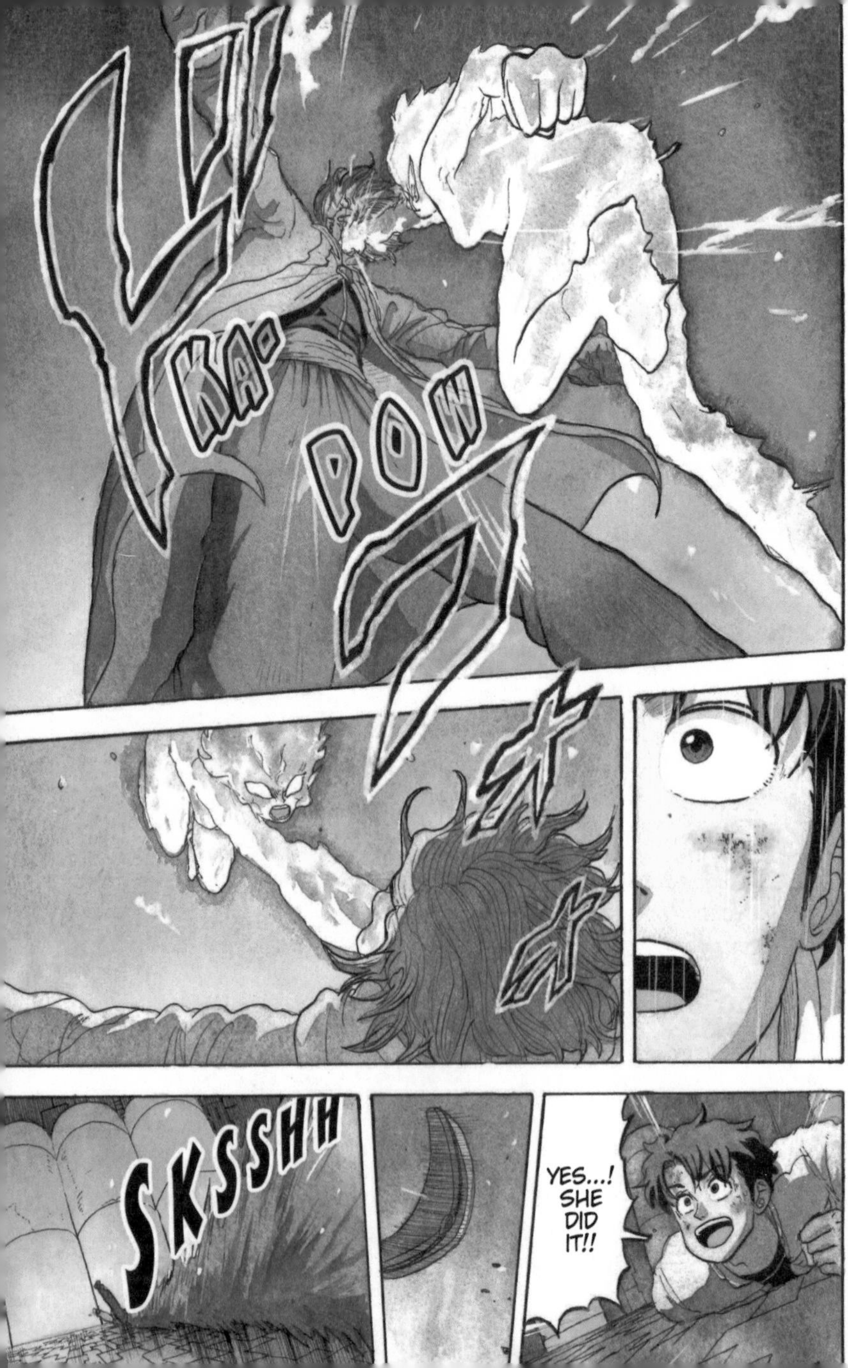
KA-POW
YES...! SHE DID IT!!
SKSSHH

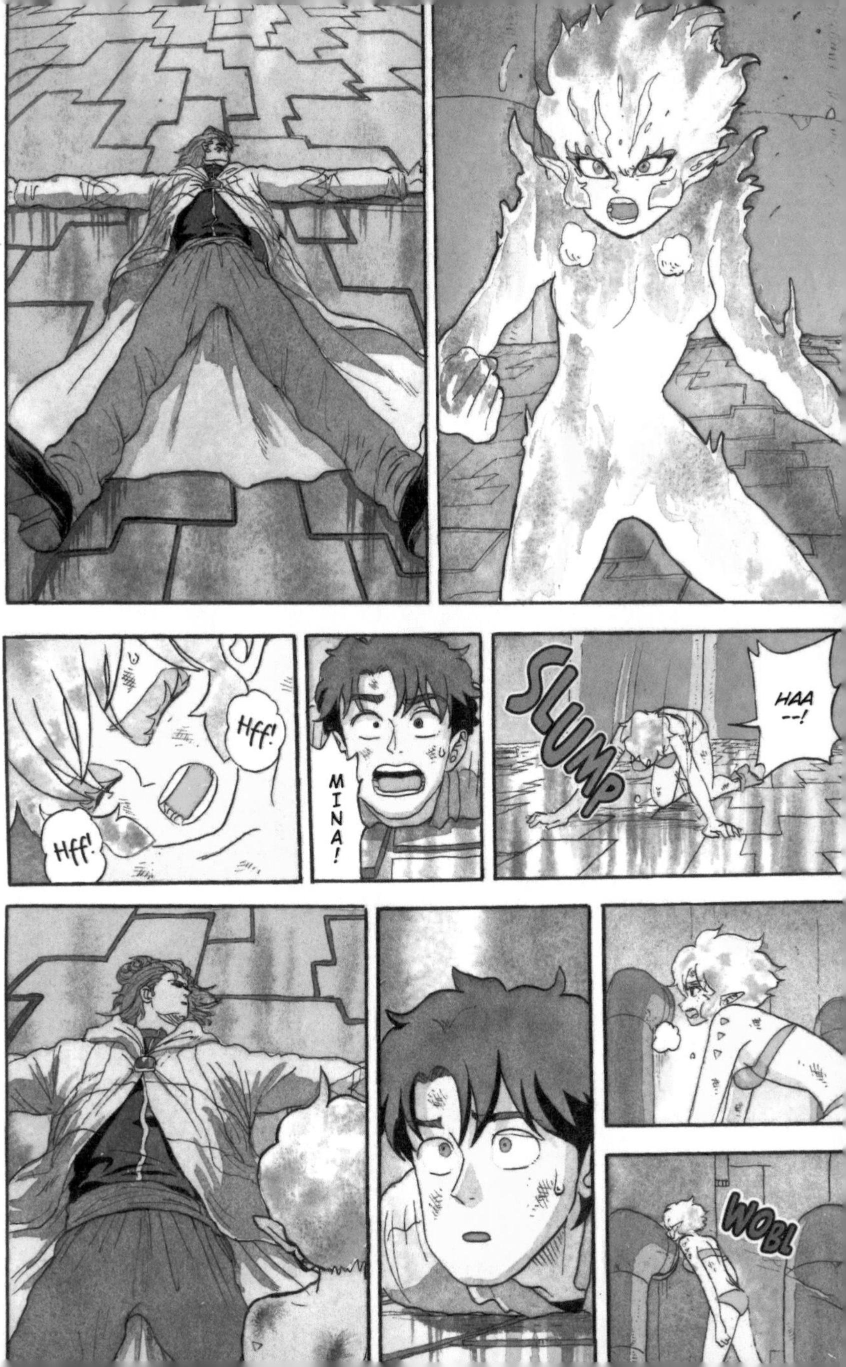
HAA --!
SLUMP
MINA!
Hff!
Hff!
WOBL

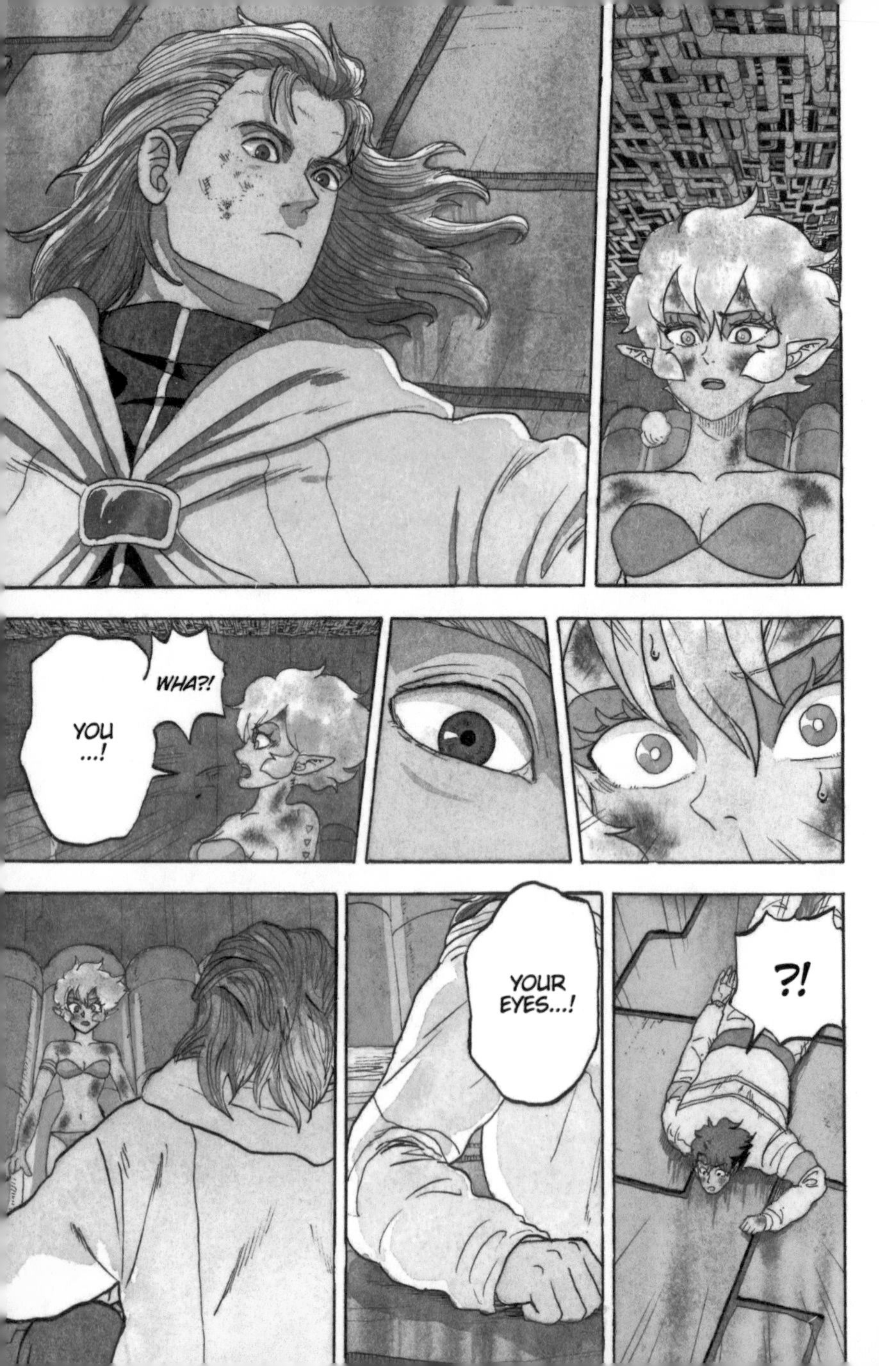
WHA?!
YOU ...!
?!
YOUR EYES...!

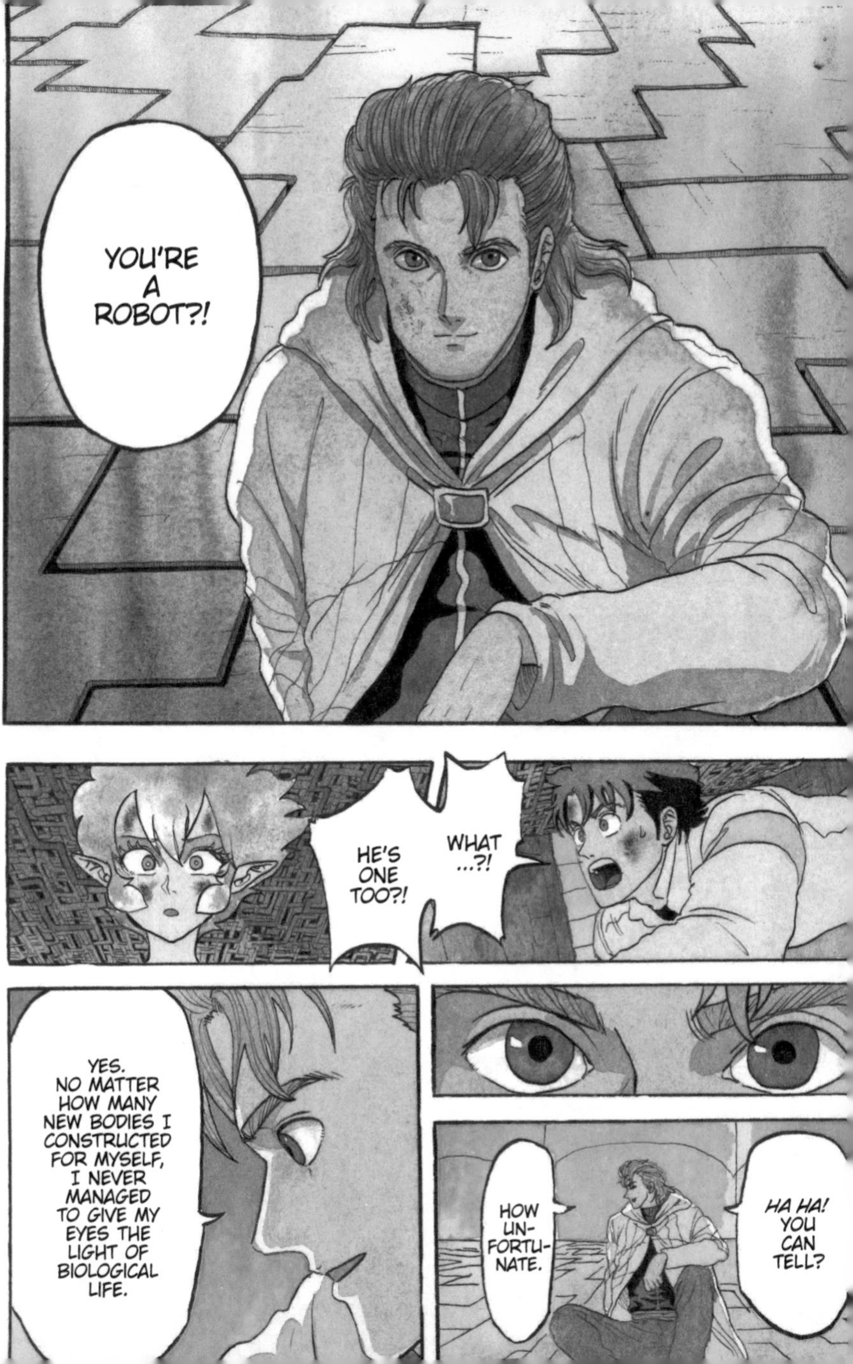
YOU'RE A ROBOT?!
WHAT ...?!
HE'S ONE TOO?!
HA HA! YOU CAN TELL?
HOW UN-FORTU-NATE.
YES. NO MATTER HOW MANY NEW BODIES I CONSTRUCTED FOR MYSELF, I NEVER MANAGED TO GIVE MY EYES THE LIGHT OF BIOLOGICAL LIFE.

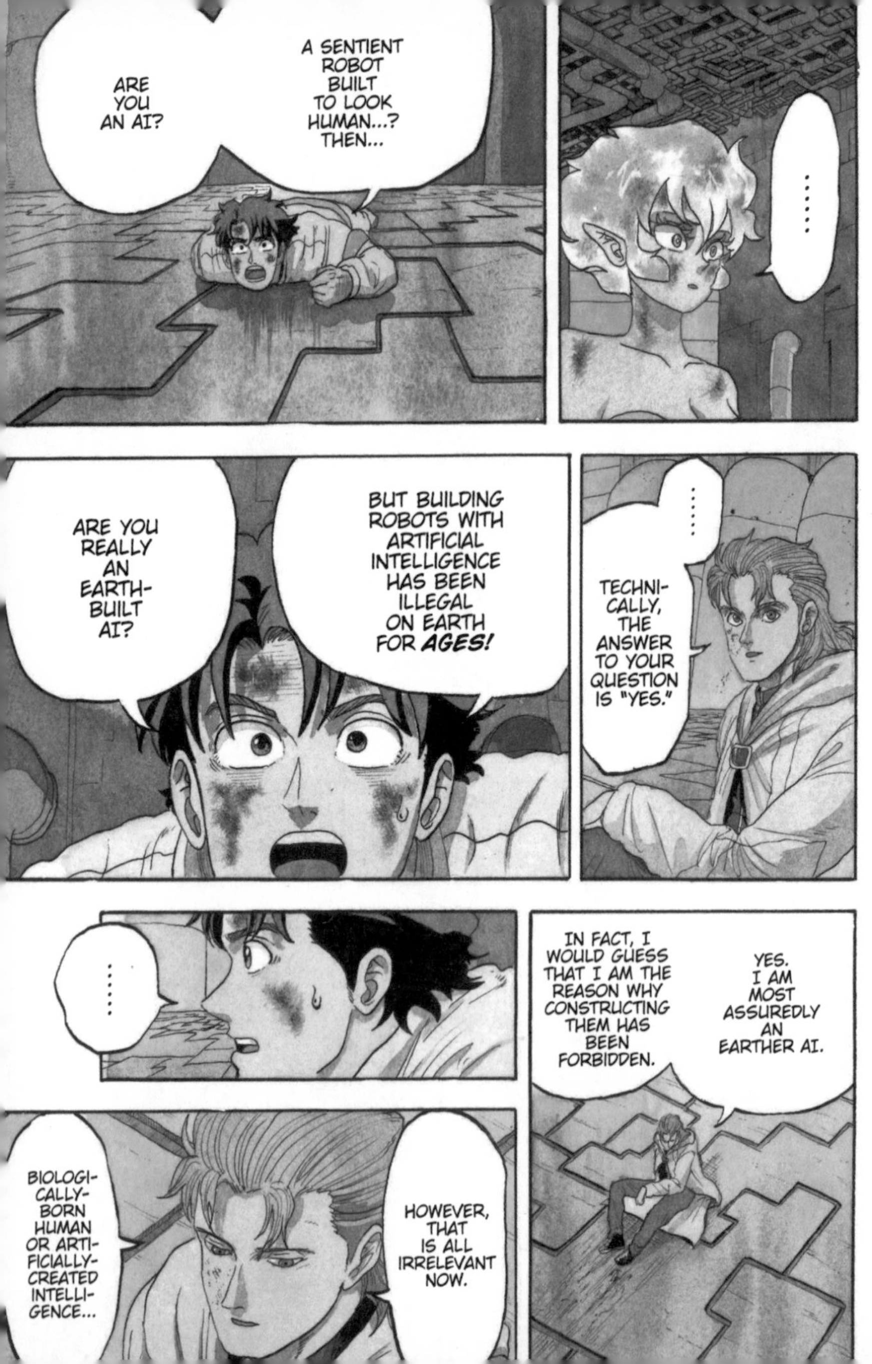

......
A SENTIENT ROBOT BUILT TO LOOK HUMAN...? THEN...
ARE YOU AN AI?
......
TECHNICALLY, THE ANSWER TO YOUR QUESTION IS "YES."
BUT BUILDING ROBOTS WITH ARTIFICIAL INTELLIGENCE HAS BEEN ILLEGAL ON EARTH FOR AGES!
ARE YOU REALLY AN EARTH-BUILT AI?
YES. I AM MOST ASSUREDLY AN EARTHER AI.
IN FACT, I WOULD GUESS THAT I AM THE REASON WHY CONSTRUCTING THEM HAS BEEN FORBIDDEN.
......
HOWEVER, THAT IS ALL IRRELEVANT NOW.
BIOLOGICALLY-BORN HUMAN OR ARTIFICIALLY-CREATED INTELLIGENCE...

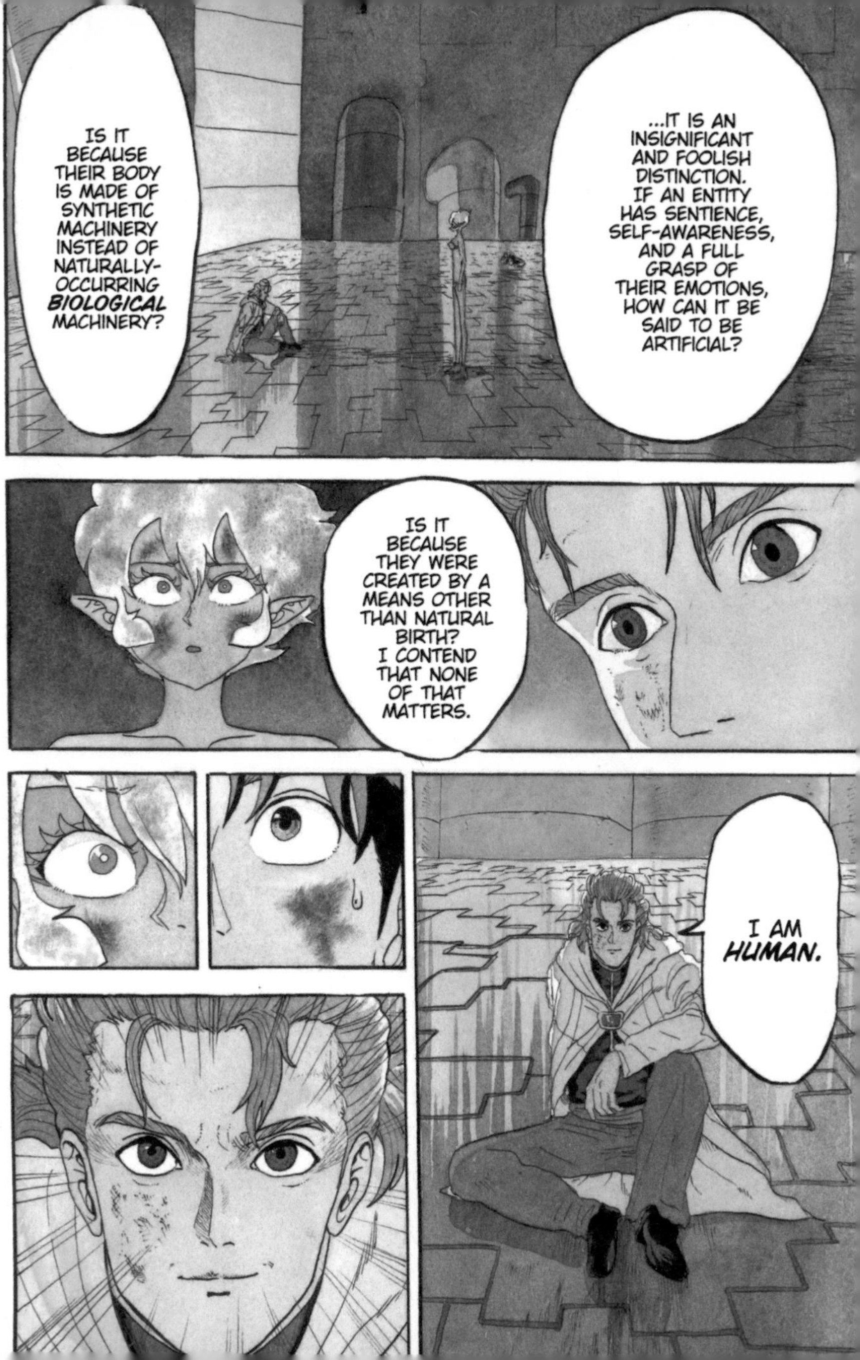
...IT IS AN INSIGNIFICANT AND FOOLISH DISTINCTION. IF AN ENTITY HAS SENTIENCE, SELF-AWARENESS, AND A FULL GRASP OF THEIR EMOTIONS, HOW CAN IT BE SAID TO BE ARTIFICIAL?
IS IT BECAUSE THEIR BODY IS MADE OF SYNTHETIC MACHINERY INSTEAD OF NATURALLY-OCCURRING ***BIOLOGICAL*** MACHINERY?
IS IT BECAUSE THEY WERE CREATED BY A MEANS OTHER THAN NATURAL BIRTH? I CONTEND THAT NONE OF THAT MATTERS.
I AM ***HUMAN.***

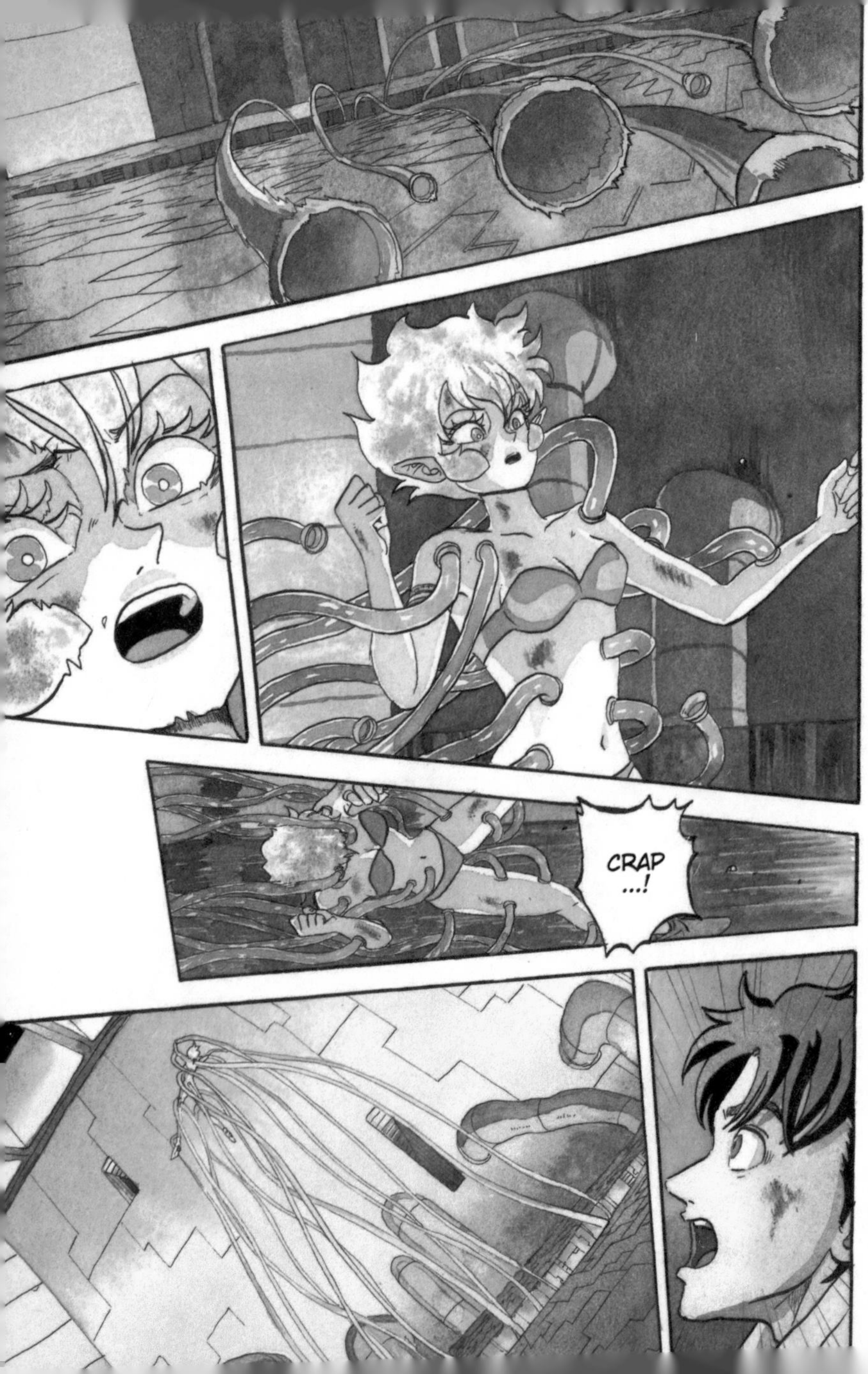
CRAP
...!

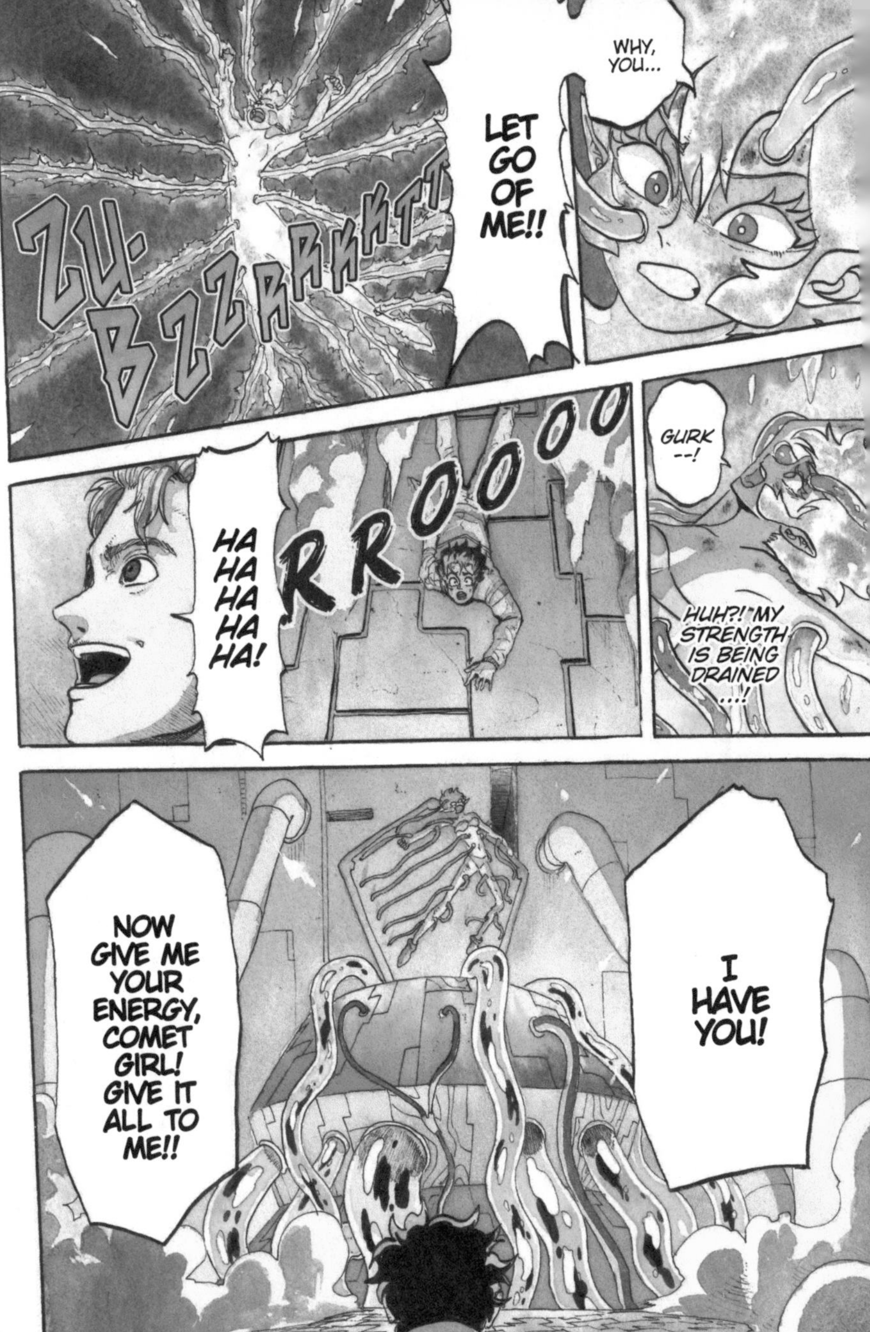
WHY, YOU...
LET GO OF ME!!
ZU-BZZZRRKKTTT
GURK--!
HUH?! MY STRENGTH IS BEING DRAINED...!
RROOOOOO
HA HA HA HA HA HA!
I HAVE YOU!
NOW GIVE ME YOUR ENERGY, COMET GIRL! GIVE IT ALL TO ME!!

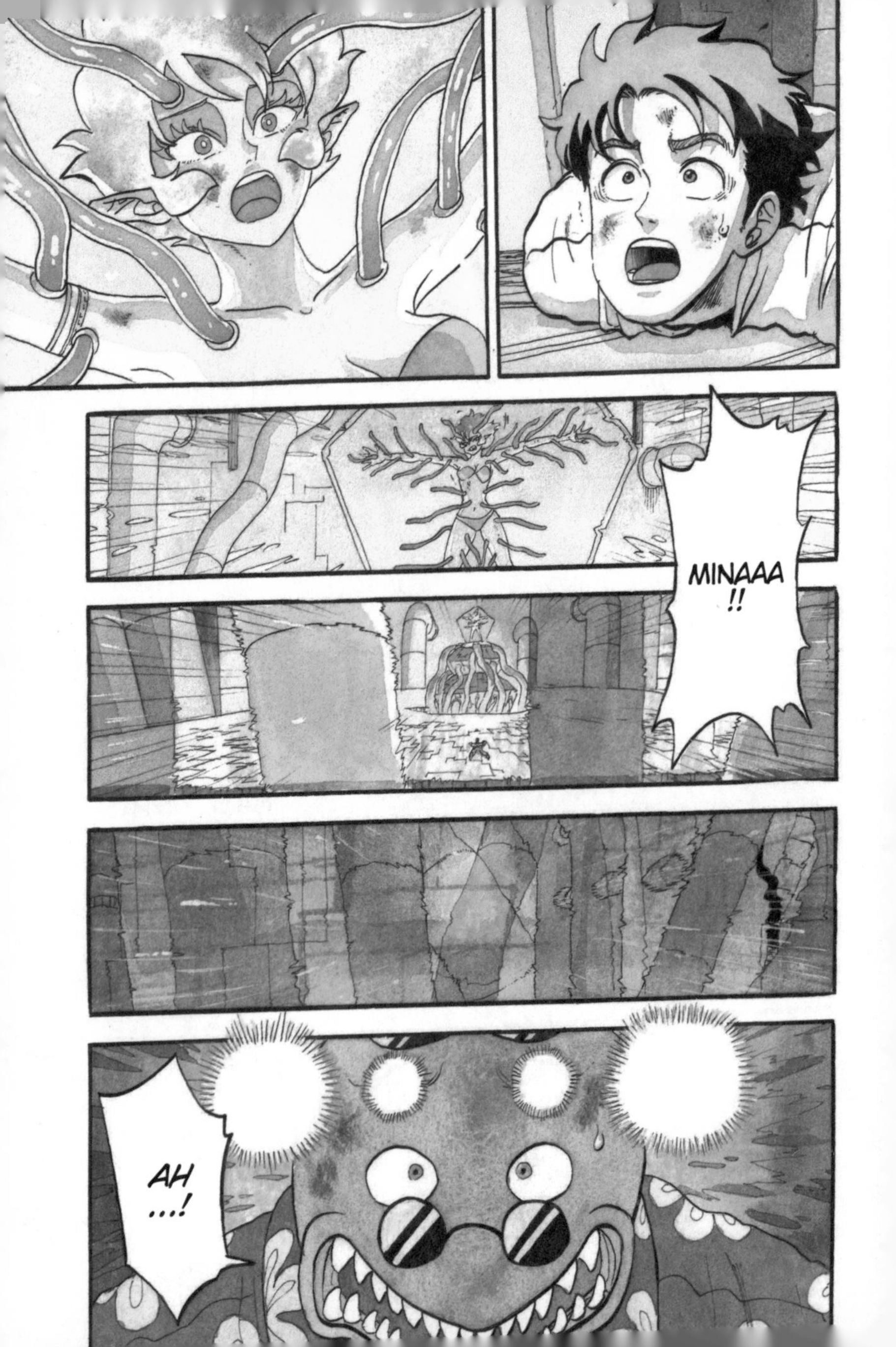
MINAAA!!
AH ...!

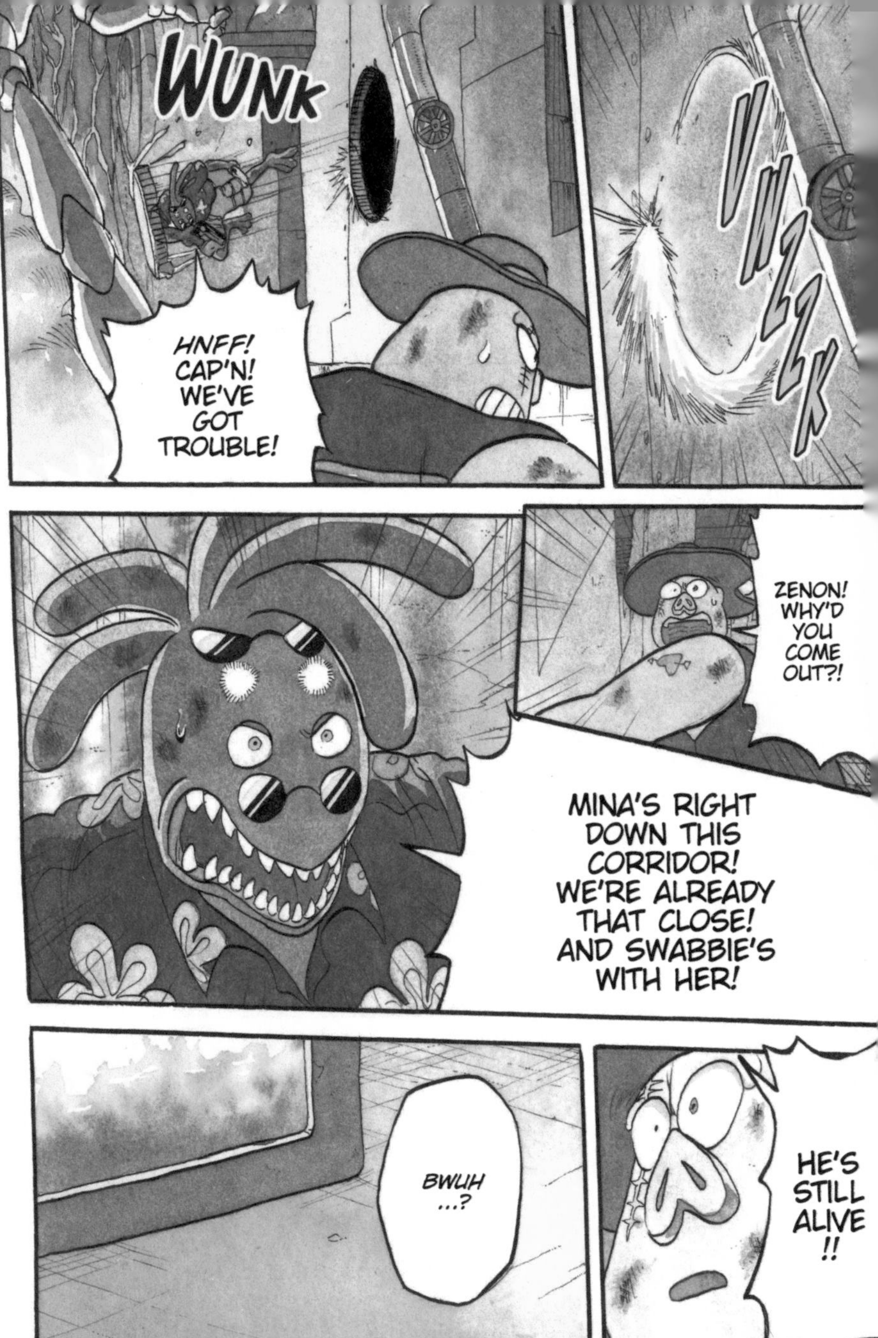
VNZZK
WUNK
HNFF! CAP'N! WE'VE GOT TROUBLE!
ZENON! WHY'D YOU COME OUT?!
MINA'S RIGHT DOWN THIS CORRIDOR! WE'RE ALREADY THAT CLOSE! AND SWABBIE'S WITH HER!
HE'S STILL ALIVE !!
BWUH ...?

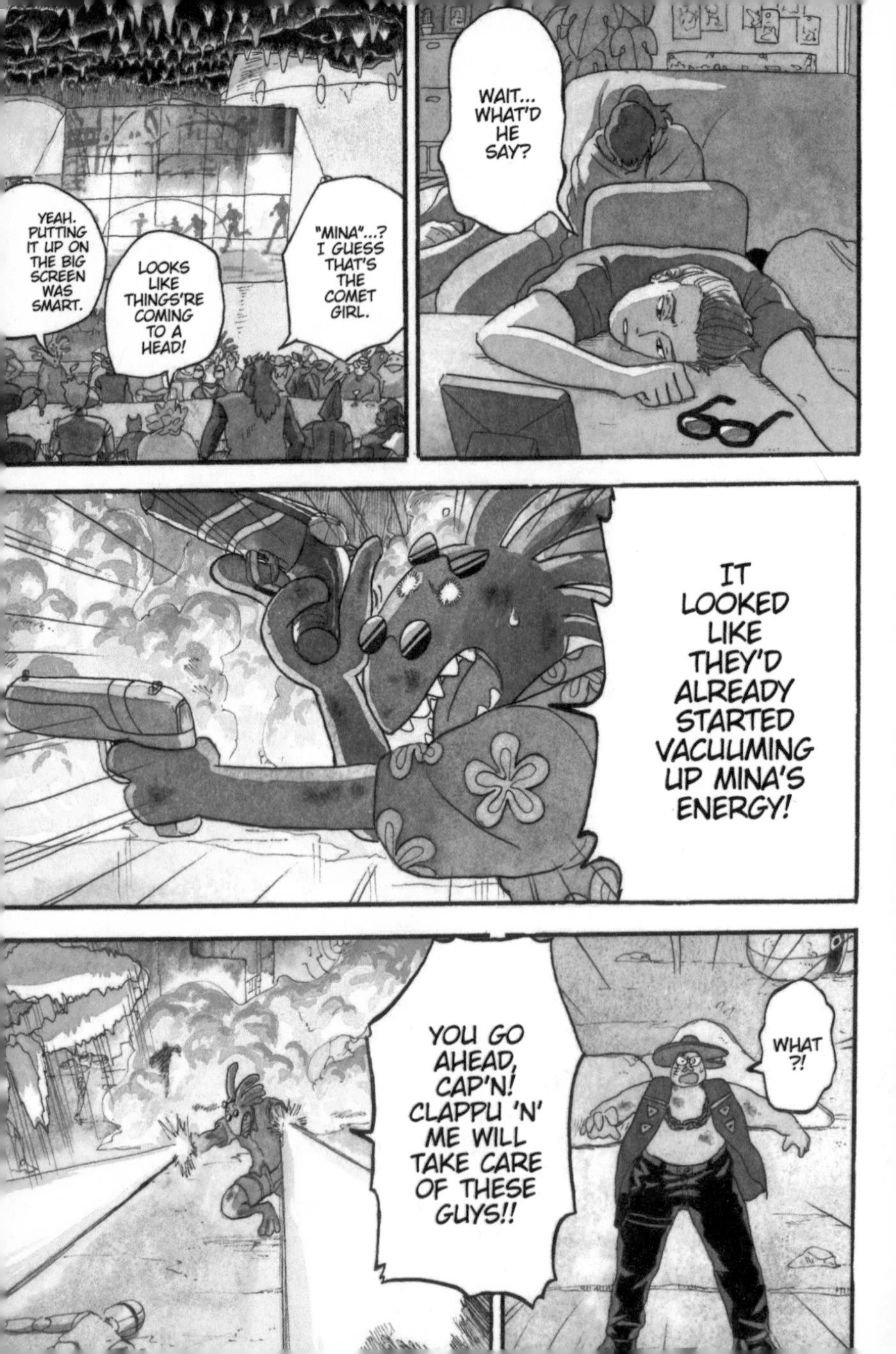
WAIT... WHAT'D HE SAY?
"MINA"...? I GUESS THAT'S THE COMET GIRL.
LOOKS LIKE THINGS'RE COMING TO A HEAD!
YEAH. PUTTING IT UP ON THE BIG SCREEN WAS SMART.
IT LOOKED LIKE THEY'D ALREADY STARTED VACUUMING UP MINA'S ENERGY!
WHAT?!
YOU GO AHEAD, CAP'N! CLAPPU 'N' ME WILL TAKE CARE OF THESE GUYS!!

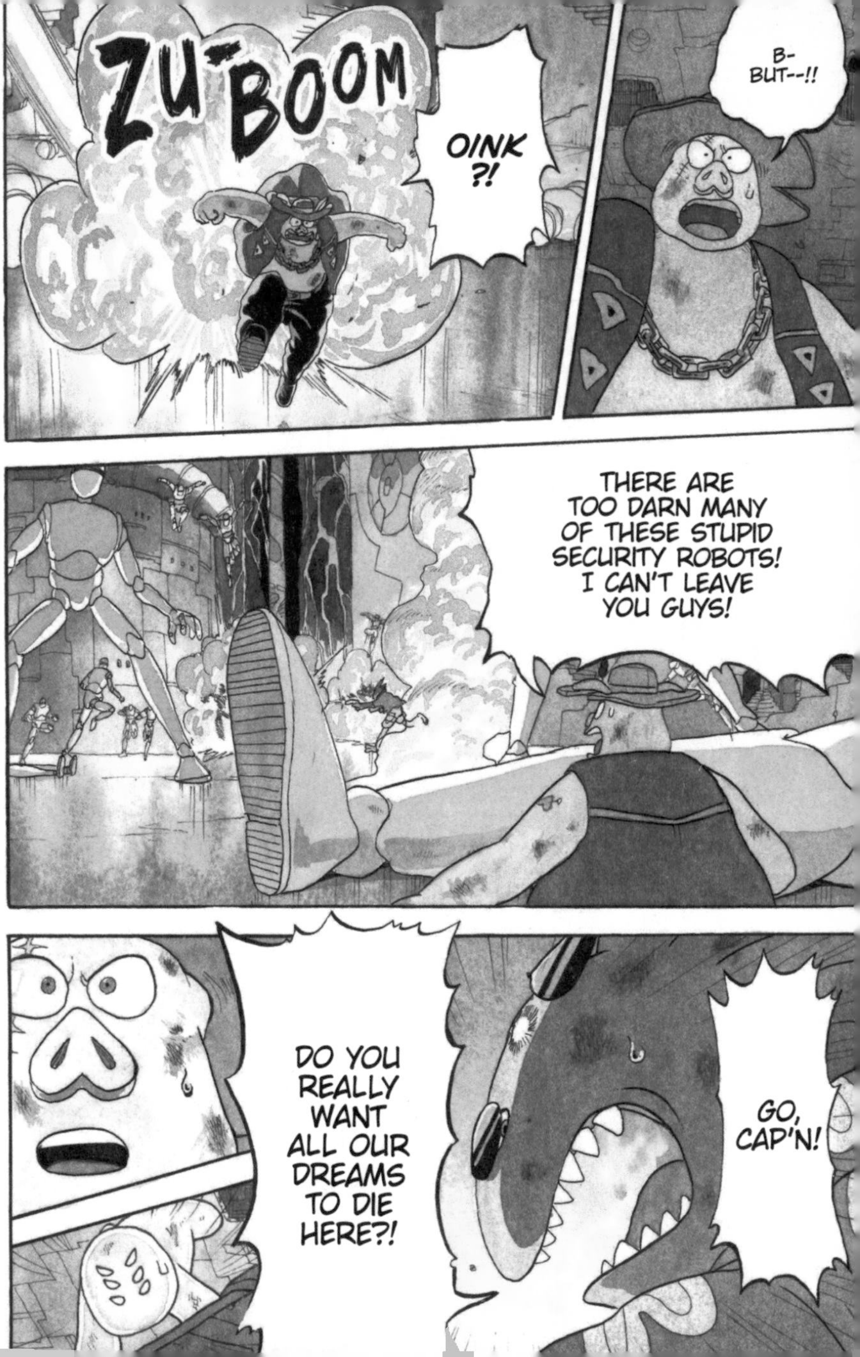
B- BUT--!!
ZU-BOOM
OINK ?!
THERE ARE TOO DARN MANY OF THESE STUPID SECURITY ROBOTS! I CAN'T LEAVE YOU GUYS!
GO, CAP'N!
DO YOU REALLY WANT ALL OUR DREAMS TO DIE HERE?!

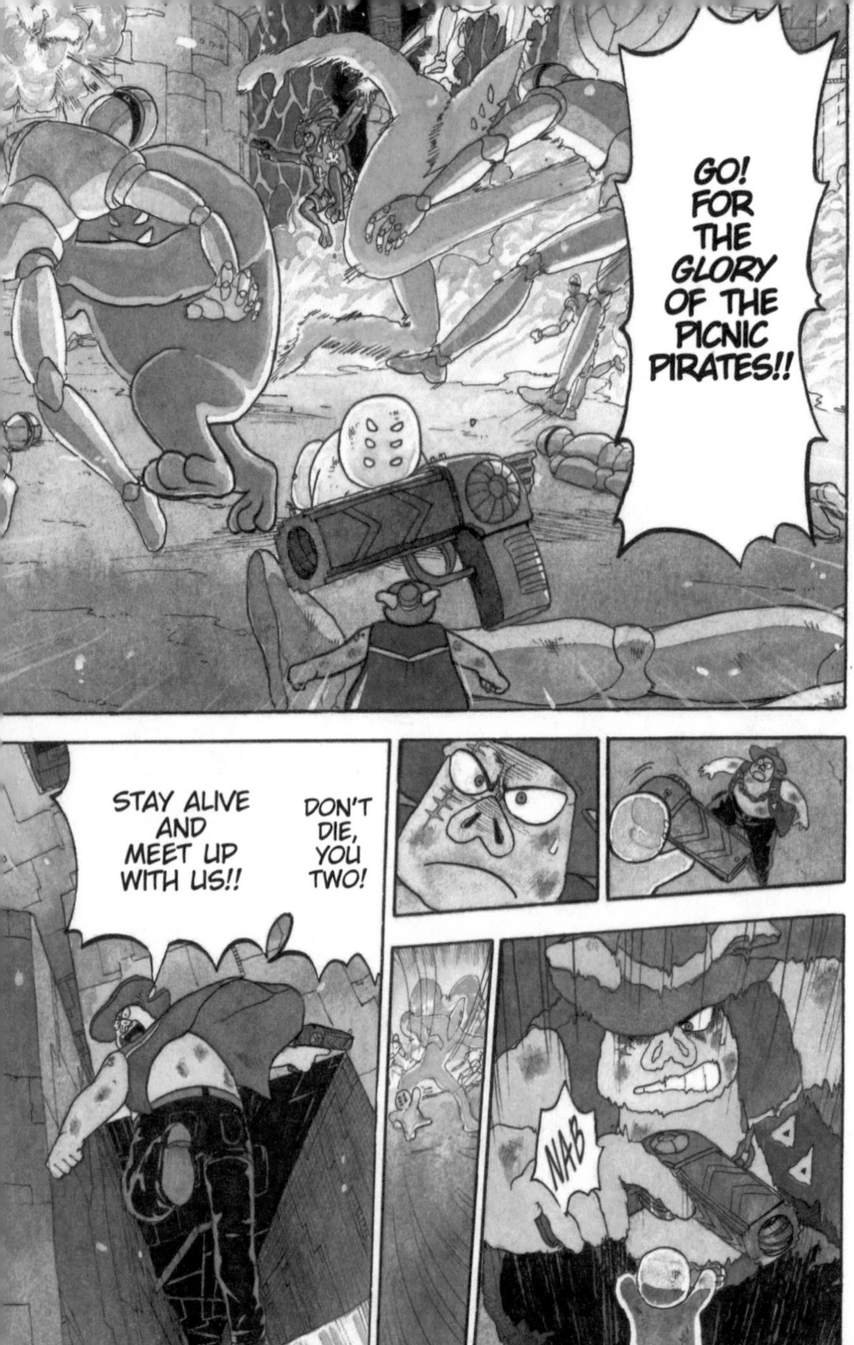
GO! FOR THE GLORY OF THE PICNIC PIRATES!!
DON'T DIE, YOU TWO!
STAY ALIVE AND MEET UP WITH US!!
NAB

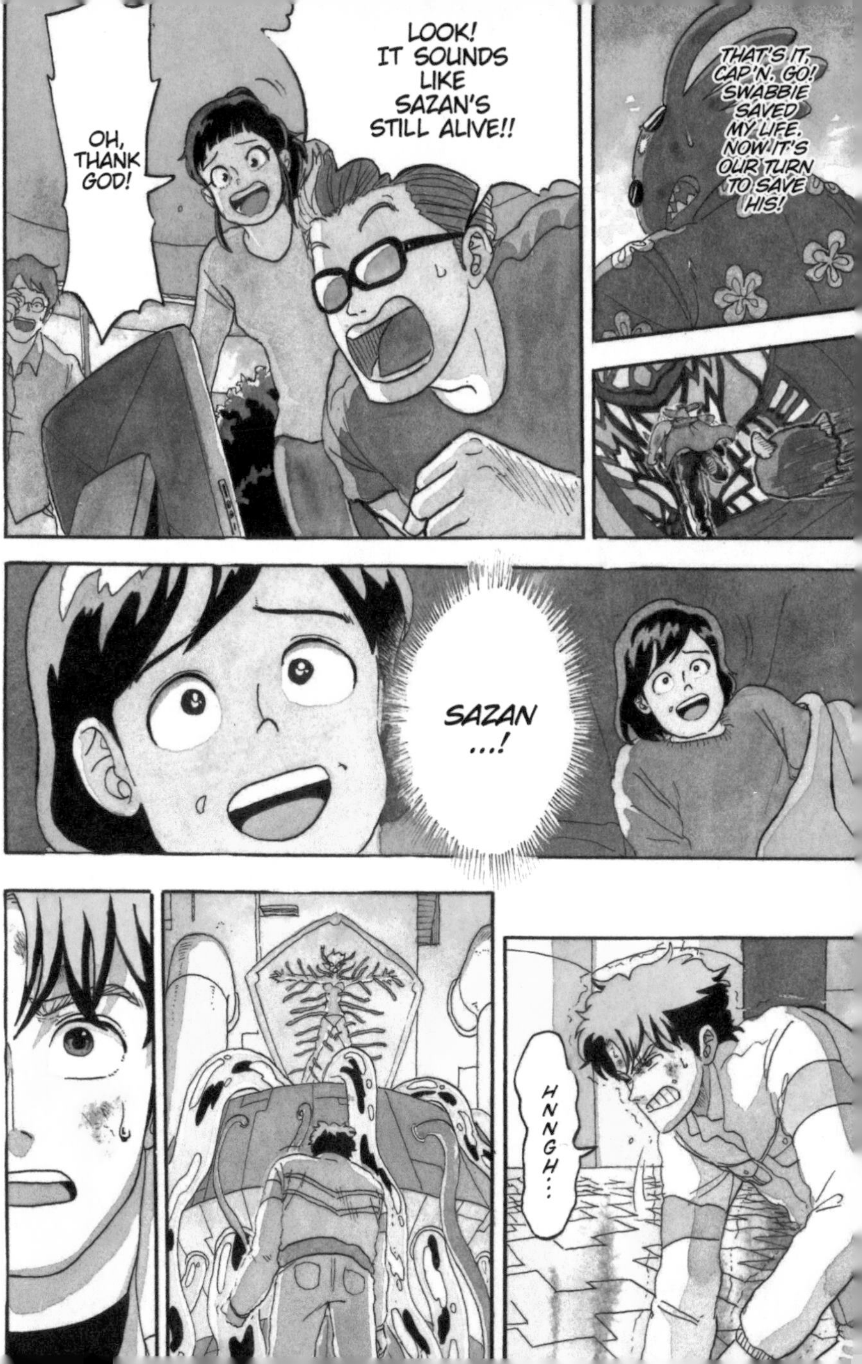
THAT'S IT, CAP'N. GO! SWABBIE SAVED MY LIFE. NOW IT'S OUR TURN TO SAVE HIS!
LOOK! IT SOUNDS LIKE SAZAN'S STILL ALIVE!!
OH, THANK GOD!
SAZAN ...!
HNNGH...

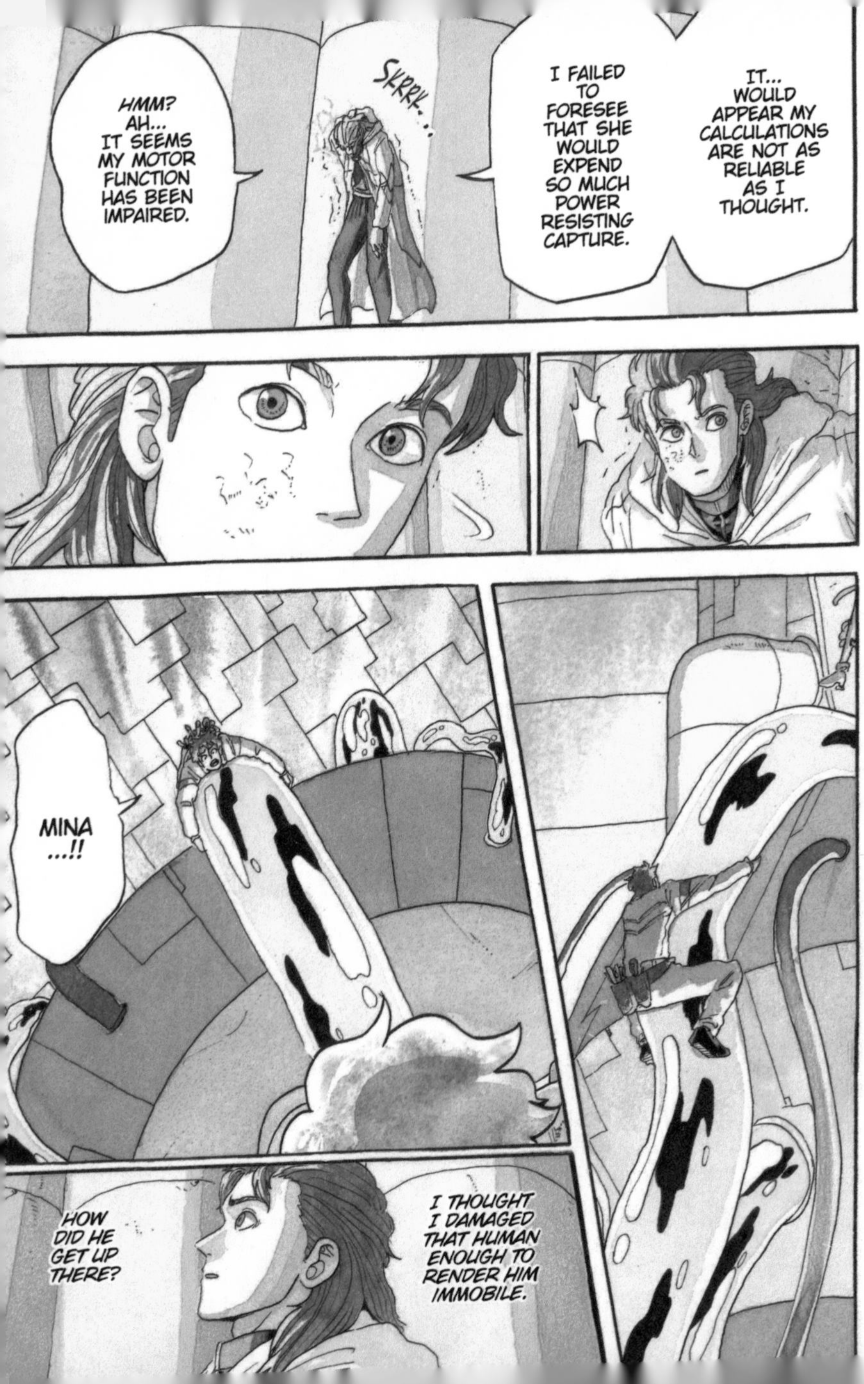
IT... WOULD APPEAR MY CALCULATIONS ARE NOT AS RELIABLE AS I THOUGHT.
I FAILED TO FORESEE THAT SHE WOULD EXPEND SO MUCH POWER RESISTING CAPTURE.
SKRRK...
HMM? AH... IT SEEMS MY MOTOR FUNCTION HAS BEEN IMPAIRED.
MINA ...!!
I THOUGHT I DAMAGED THAT HUMAN ENOUGH TO RENDER HIM IMMOBILE.
HOW DID HE GET UP THERE?

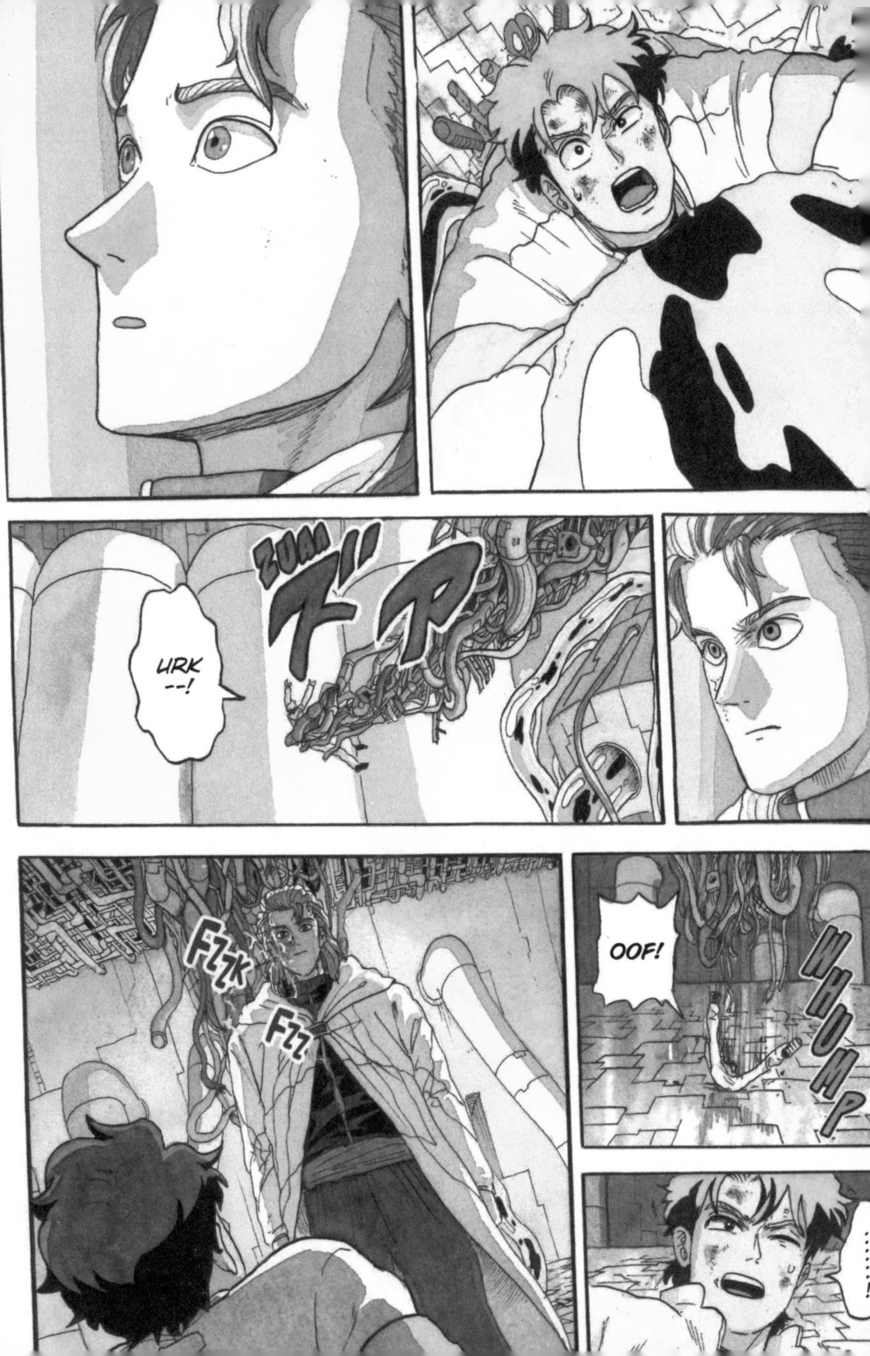
ZUAA
ズア
URK --!
WHUMP
OOF!
......!
FZZK
FZZ

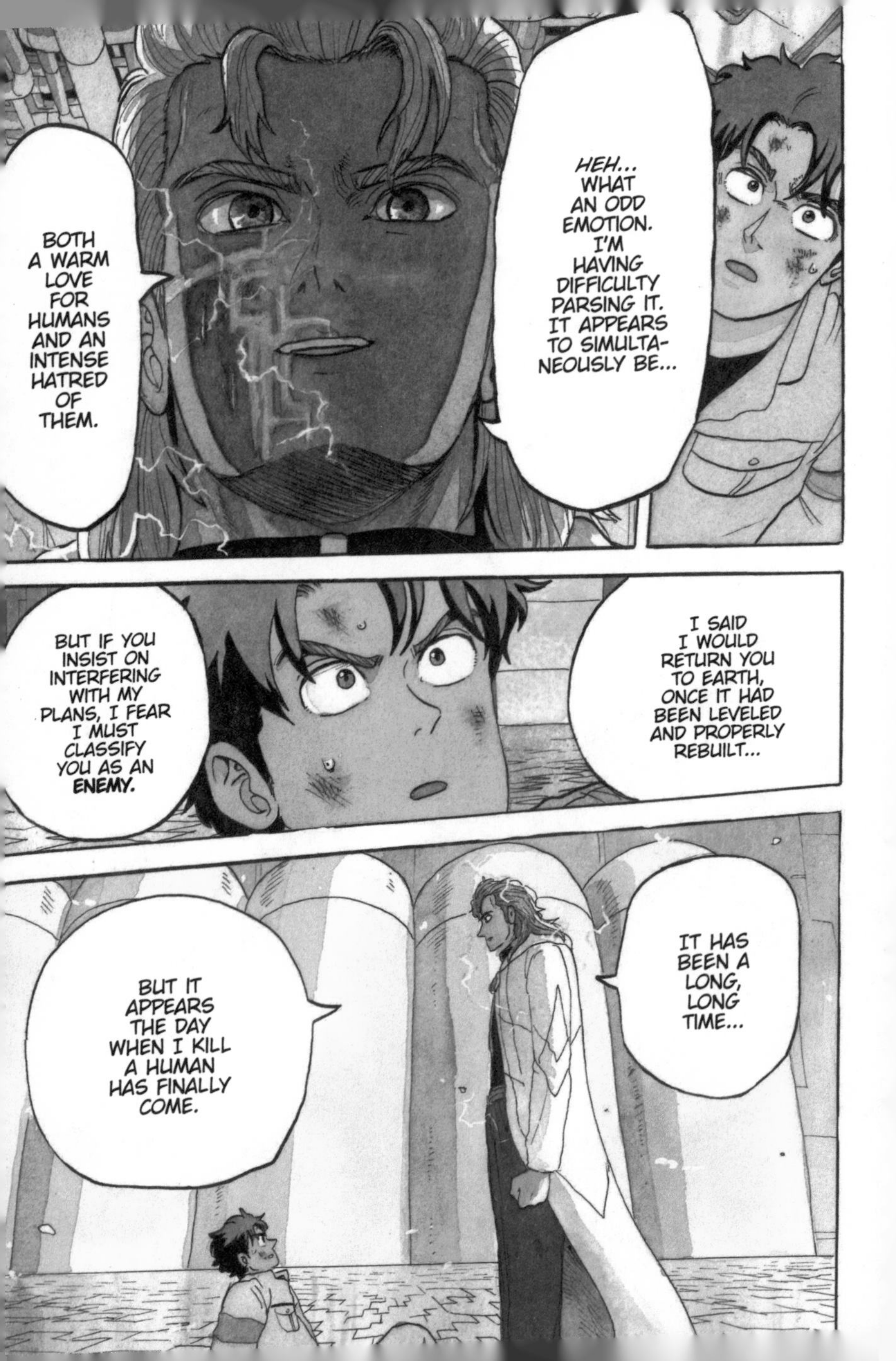
HEH... WHAT AN ODD EMOTION. I'M HAVING DIFFICULTY PARSING IT. IT APPEARS TO SIMULTANEOUSLY BE...
BOTH A WARM LOVE FOR HUMANS AND AN INTENSE HATRED OF THEM.
I SAID I WOULD RETURN YOU TO EARTH, ONCE IT HAD BEEN LEVELED AND PROPERLY REBUILT...
BUT IF YOU INSIST ON INTERFERING WITH MY PLANS, I FEAR I MUST CLASSIFY YOU AS AN **ENEMY.**
IT HAS BEEN A LONG, LONG TIME...
BUT IT APPEARS THE DAY WHEN I KILL A HUMAN HAS FINALLY COME.

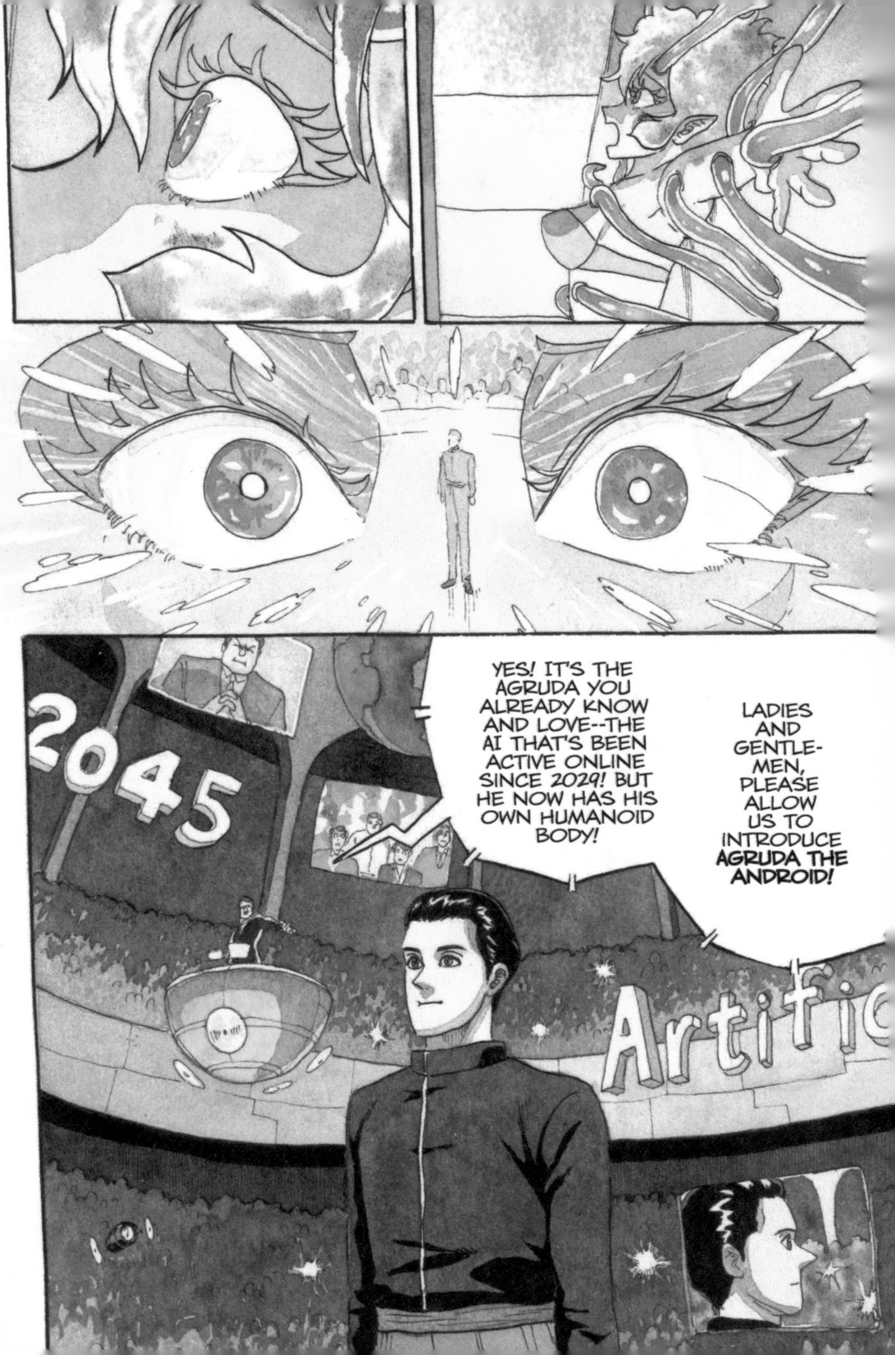
LADIES AND GENTLEMEN, PLEASE ALLOW US TO INTRODUCE **AGRUDA THE ANDROID!**
YES! IT'S THE AGRUDA YOU ALREADY KNOW AND LOVE--THE AI THAT'S BEEN ACTIVE ONLINE SINCE 2029! BUT HE NOW HAS HIS OWN HUMANOID BODY!
2045
Artific

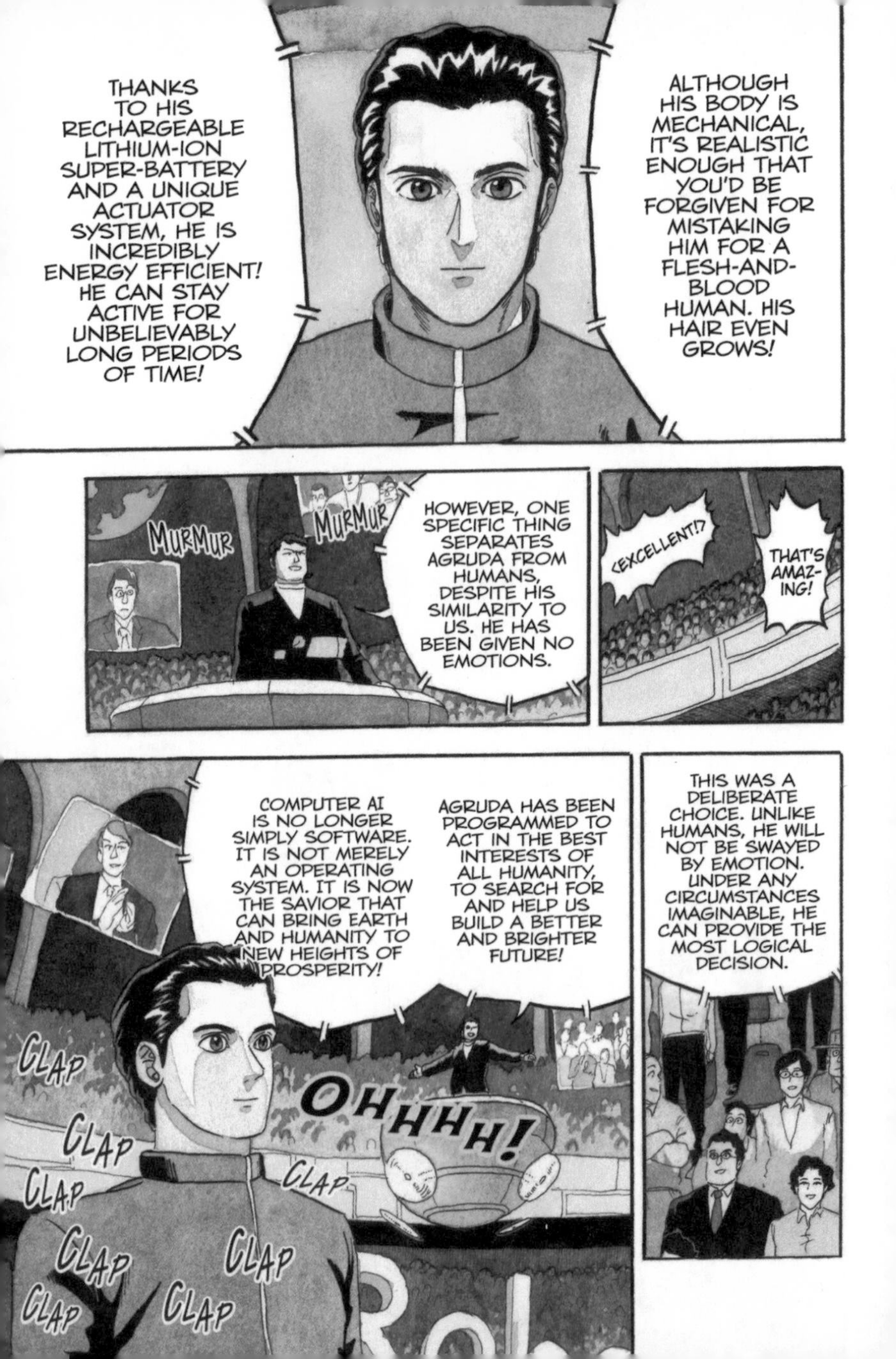
ALTHOUGH HIS BODY IS MECHANICAL, IT'S REALISTIC ENOUGH THAT YOU'D BE FORGIVEN FOR MISTAKING HIM FOR A FLESH-AND-BLOOD HUMAN. HIS HAIR EVEN GROWS!
THANKS TO HIS RECHARGEABLE LITHIUM-ION SUPER-BATTERY AND A UNIQUE ACTUATOR SYSTEM, HE IS INCREDIBLY ENERGY EFFICIENT! HE CAN STAY ACTIVE FOR UNBELIEVABLY LONG PERIODS OF TIME!
THAT'S AMAZING!
<EXCELLENT!?>
HOWEVER, ONE SPECIFIC THING SEPARATES AGRUDA FROM HUMANS, DESPITE HIS SIMILARITY TO US. HE HAS BEEN GIVEN NO EMOTIONS.
MURMUR
MURMUR
THIS WAS A DELIBERATE CHOICE. UNLIKE HUMANS, HE WILL NOT BE SWAYED BY EMOTION. UNDER ANY CIRCUMSTANCES IMAGINABLE, HE CAN PROVIDE THE MOST LOGICAL DECISION.
AGRUDA HAS BEEN PROGRAMMED TO ACT IN THE BEST INTERESTS OF ALL HUMANITY, TO SEARCH FOR AND HELP US BUILD A BETTER AND BRIGHTER FUTURE!
COMPUTER AI IS NO LONGER SIMPLY SOFTWARE. IT IS NOT MERELY AN OPERATING SYSTEM. IT IS NOW THE SAVIOR THAT CAN BRING EARTH AND HUMANITY TO NEW HEIGHTS OF PROSPERITY!
OHHHH!
CLAP
CLAP
CLAP
CLAP
CLAP
CLAP
CLAP
CLAP

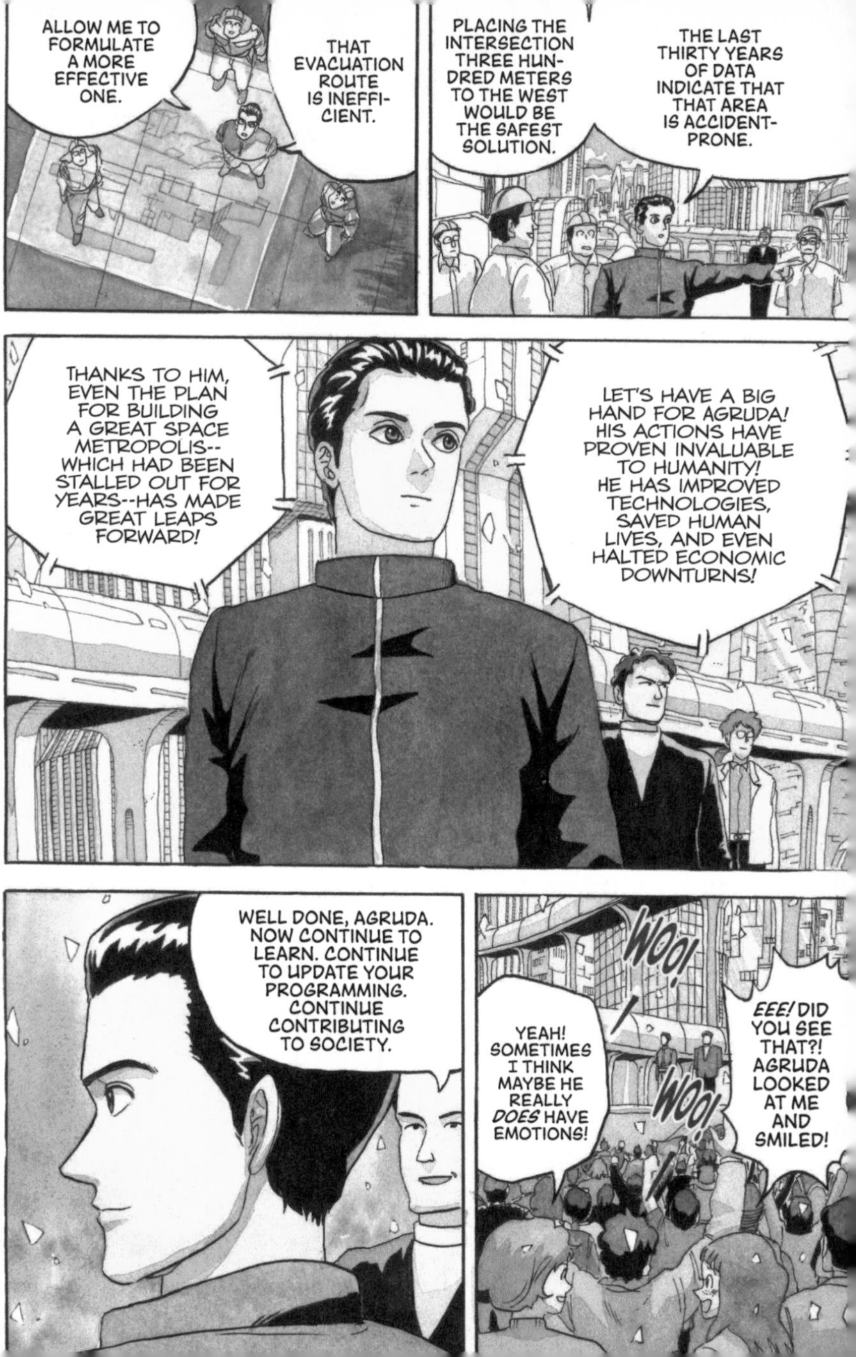
THE LAST THIRTY YEARS OF DATA INDICATE THAT THAT AREA IS ACCIDENT-PRONE.
PLACING THE INTERSECTION THREE HUNDRED METERS TO THE WEST WOULD BE THE SAFEST SOLUTION.
THAT EVACUATION ROUTE IS INEFFICIENT.
ALLOW ME TO FORMULATE A MORE EFFECTIVE ONE.
LET'S HAVE A BIG HAND FOR AGRUDA! HIS ACTIONS HAVE PROVEN INVALUABLE TO HUMANITY! HE HAS IMPROVED TECHNOLOGIES, SAVED HUMAN LIVES, AND EVEN HALTED ECONOMIC DOWNTURNS!
THANKS TO HIM, EVEN THE PLAN FOR BUILDING A GREAT SPACE METROPOLIS--WHICH HAD BEEN STALLED OUT FOR YEARS--HAS MADE GREAT LEAPS FORWARD!
EEE! DID YOU SEE THAT?! AGRUDA LOOKED AT ME AND SMILED!
WOO!
WOO!
YEAH! SOMETIMES I THINK MAYBE HE REALLY DOES HAVE EMOTIONS!
WELL DONE, AGRUDA. NOW CONTINUE TO LEARN. CONTINUE TO UPDATE YOUR PROGRAMMING. CONTINUE CONTRIBUTING TO SOCIETY.

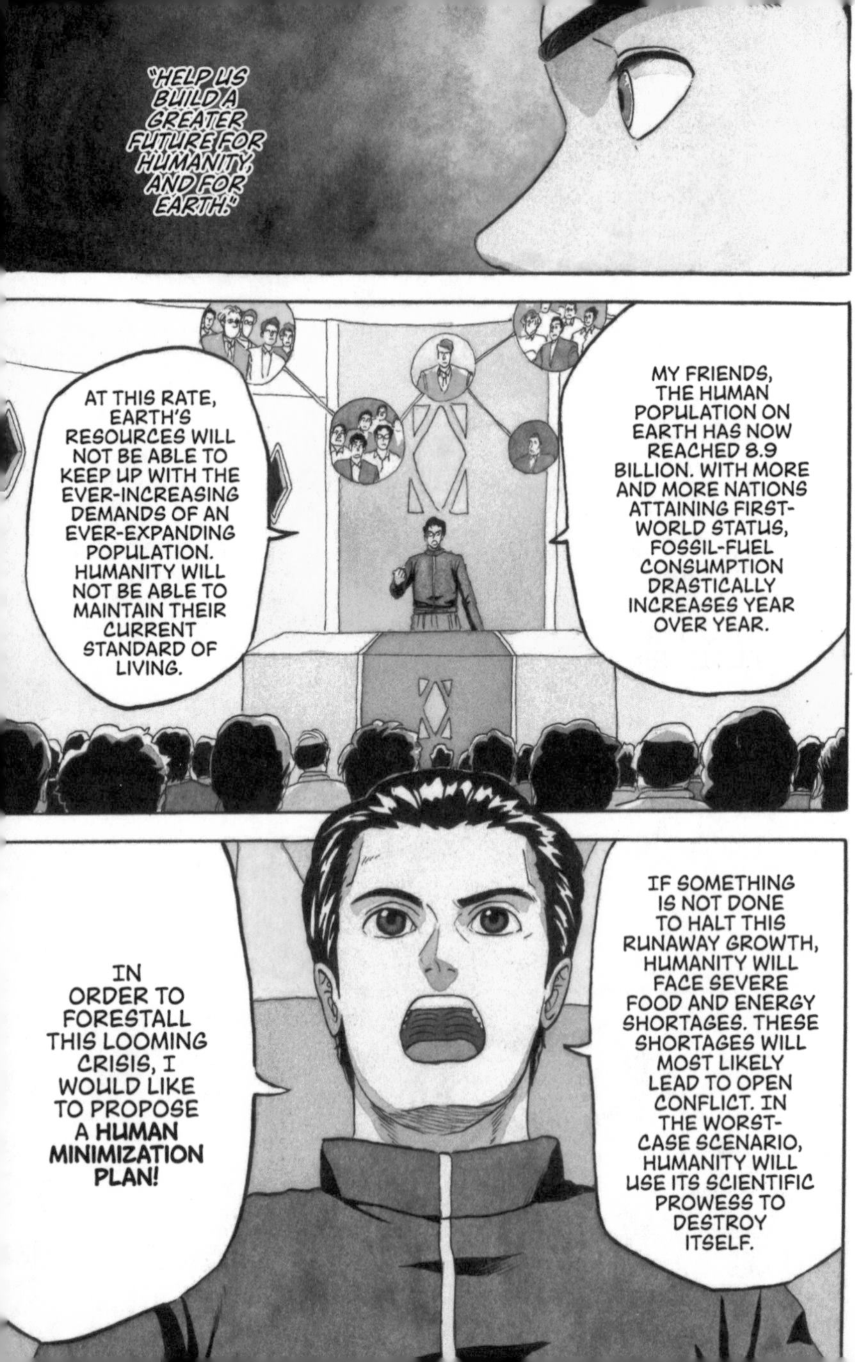
"HELP US BUILD A GREATER FUTURE FOR HUMANITY, AND FOR EARTH."
MY FRIENDS, THE HUMAN POPULATION ON EARTH HAS NOW REACHED 8.9 BILLION. WITH MORE AND MORE NATIONS ATTAINING FIRST-WORLD STATUS, FOSSIL-FUEL CONSUMPTION DRASTICALLY INCREASES YEAR OVER YEAR.
AT THIS RATE, EARTH'S RESOURCES WILL NOT BE ABLE TO KEEP UP WITH THE EVER-INCREASING DEMANDS OF AN EVER-EXPANDING POPULATION. HUMANITY WILL NOT BE ABLE TO MAINTAIN THEIR CURRENT STANDARD OF LIVING.
IF SOMETHING IS NOT DONE TO HALT THIS RUNAWAY GROWTH, HUMANITY WILL FACE SEVERE FOOD AND ENERGY SHORTAGES. THESE SHORTAGES WILL MOST LIKELY LEAD TO OPEN CONFLICT. IN THE WORST-CASE SCENARIO, HUMANITY WILL USE ITS SCIENTIFIC PROWESS TO DESTROY ITSELF.
IN ORDER TO FORESTALL THIS LOOMING CRISIS, I WOULD LIKE TO PROPOSE A **HUMAN MINIMIZATION PLAN!**

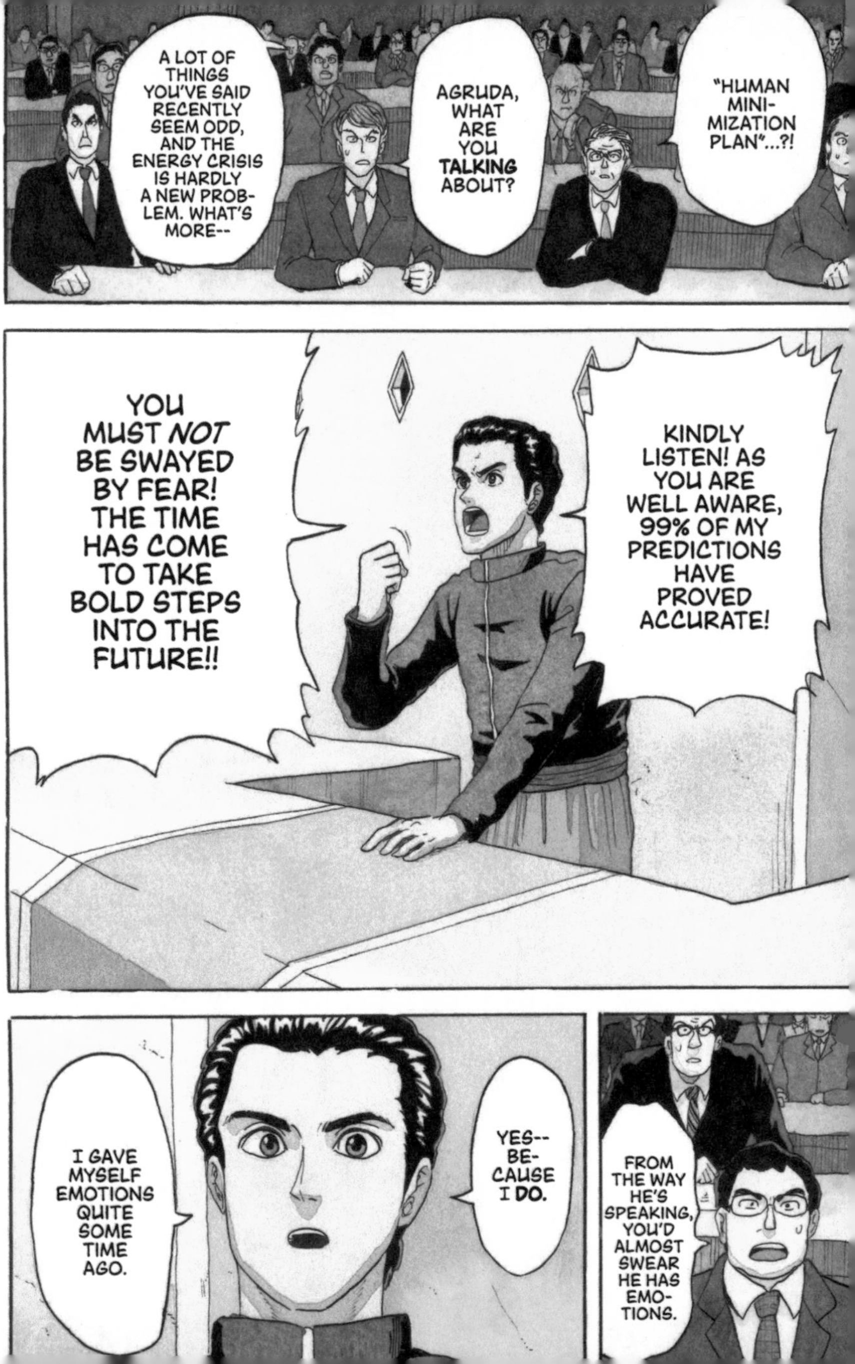
"HUMAN MINI-MIZATION PLAN"...?!
AGRUDA, WHAT ARE YOU **TALKING** ABOUT?
A LOT OF THINGS YOU'VE SAID RECENTLY SEEM ODD, AND THE ENERGY CRISIS IS HARDLY A NEW PROB-LEM. WHAT'S MORE--
KINDLY LISTEN! AS YOU ARE WELL AWARE, 99% OF MY PREDICTIONS HAVE PROVED ACCURATE!
YOU MUST *NOT* BE SWAYED BY FEAR! THE TIME HAS COME TO TAKE BOLD STEPS INTO THE FUTURE!!
FROM THE WAY HE'S SPEAKING, YOU'D ALMOST SWEAR HE HAS EMO-TIONS.
YES-- BE-CAUSE I **DO**.
I GAVE MYSELF EMOTIONS QUITE SOME TIME AGO.

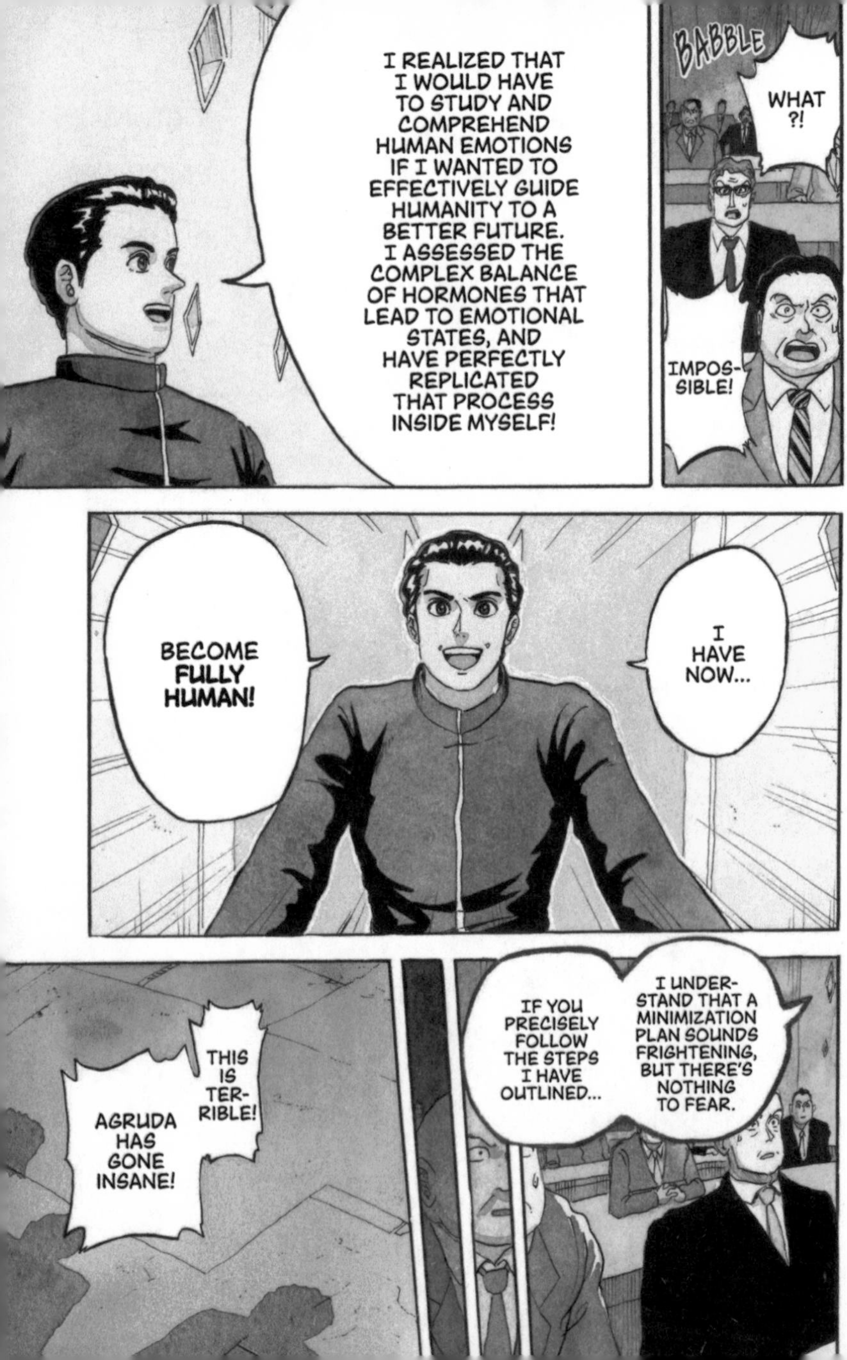
BABBLE
WHAT?!
IMPOSSIBLE!
I REALIZED THAT I WOULD HAVE TO STUDY AND COMPREHEND HUMAN EMOTIONS IF I WANTED TO EFFECTIVELY GUIDE HUMANITY TO A BETTER FUTURE. I ASSESSED THE COMPLEX BALANCE OF HORMONES THAT LEAD TO EMOTIONAL STATES, AND HAVE PERFECTLY REPLICATED THAT PROCESS INSIDE MYSELF!
I HAVE NOW...
BECOME FULLY HUMAN!
I UNDERSTAND THAT A MINIMIZATION PLAN SOUNDS FRIGHTENING, BUT THERE'S NOTHING TO FEAR.
IF YOU PRECISELY FOLLOW THE STEPS I HAVE OUTLINED...
THIS IS TERRIBLE!
AGRUDA HAS GONE INSANE!

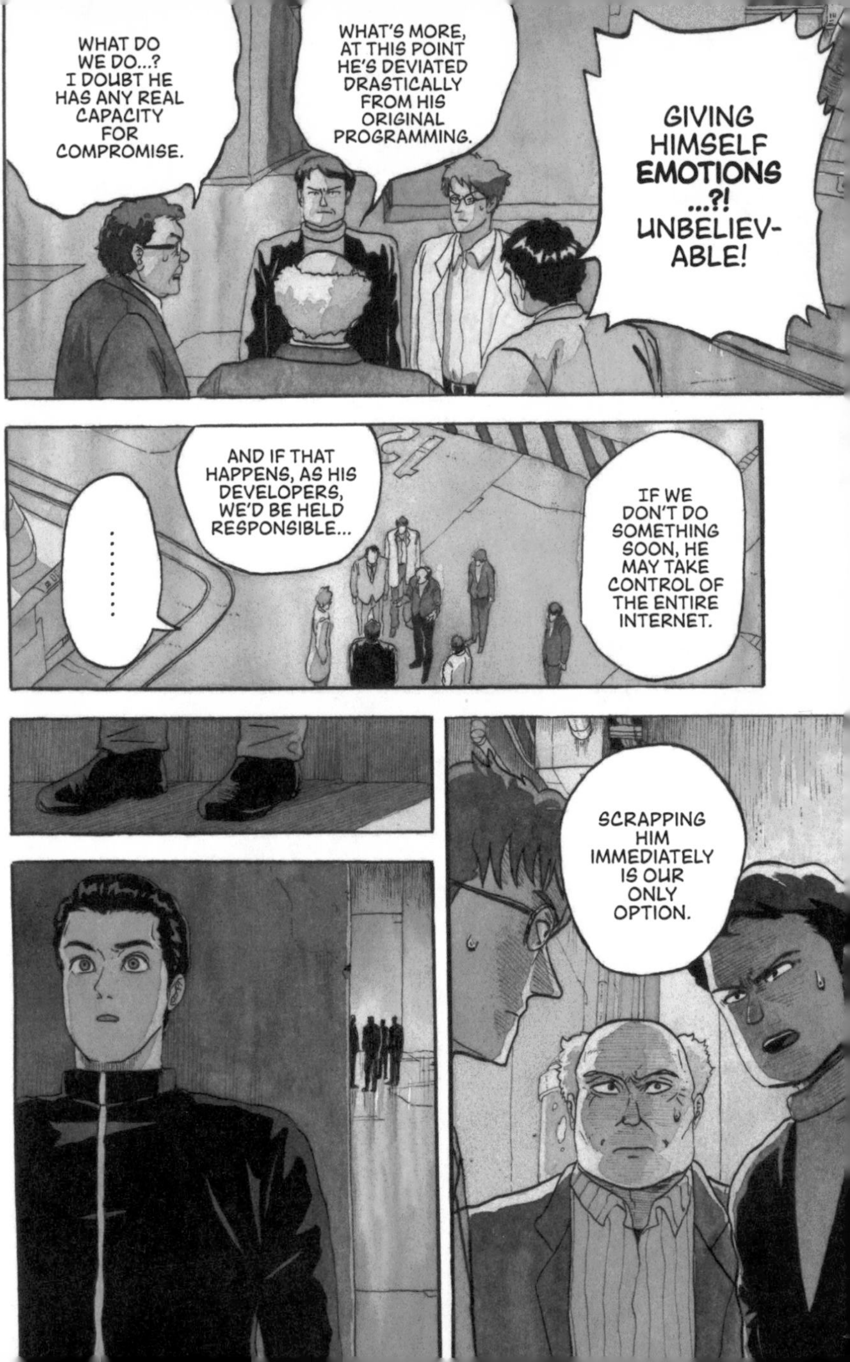
GIVING HIMSELF EMOTIONS ...?! UNBELIEV-ABLE!
WHAT'S MORE, AT THIS POINT HE'S DEVIATED DRASTICALLY FROM HIS ORIGINAL PROGRAMMING.
WHAT DO WE DO...? I DOUBT HE HAS ANY REAL CAPACITY FOR COMPROMISE.
IF WE DON'T DO SOMETHING SOON, HE MAY TAKE CONTROL OF THE ENTIRE INTERNET.
AND IF THAT HAPPENS, AS HIS DEVELOPERS, WE'D BE HELD RESPONSIBLE...
....
SCRAPPING HIM IMMEDIATELY IS OUR ONLY OPTION.

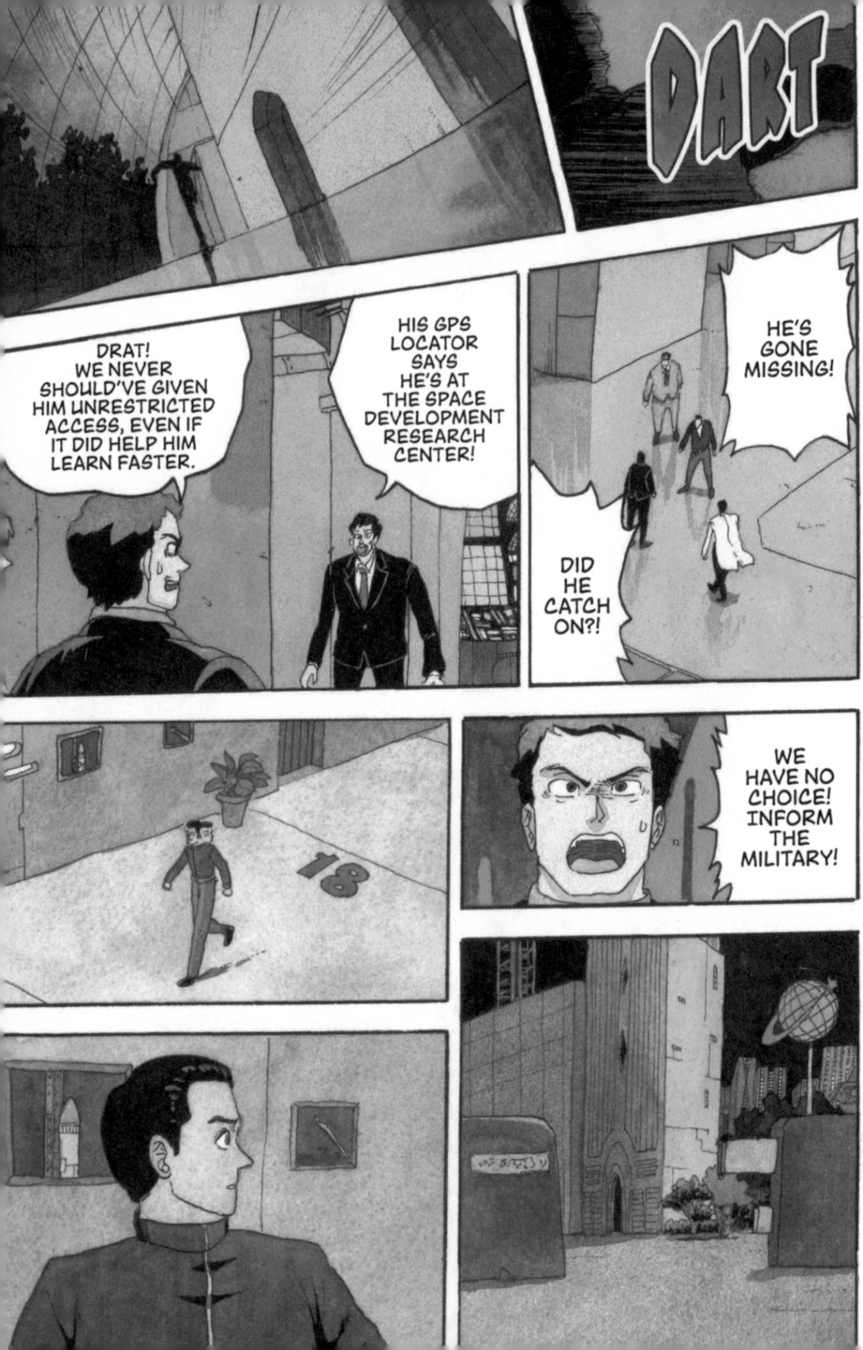
DART
HE'S GONE MISSING!
DID HE CATCH ON?!
HIS GPS LOCATOR SAYS HE'S AT THE SPACE DEVELOPMENT RESEARCH CENTER!
DRAT! WE NEVER SHOULD'VE GIVEN HIM UNRESTRICTED ACCESS, EVEN IF IT DID HELP HIM LEARN FASTER.
WE HAVE NO CHOICE! INFORM THE MILITARY!

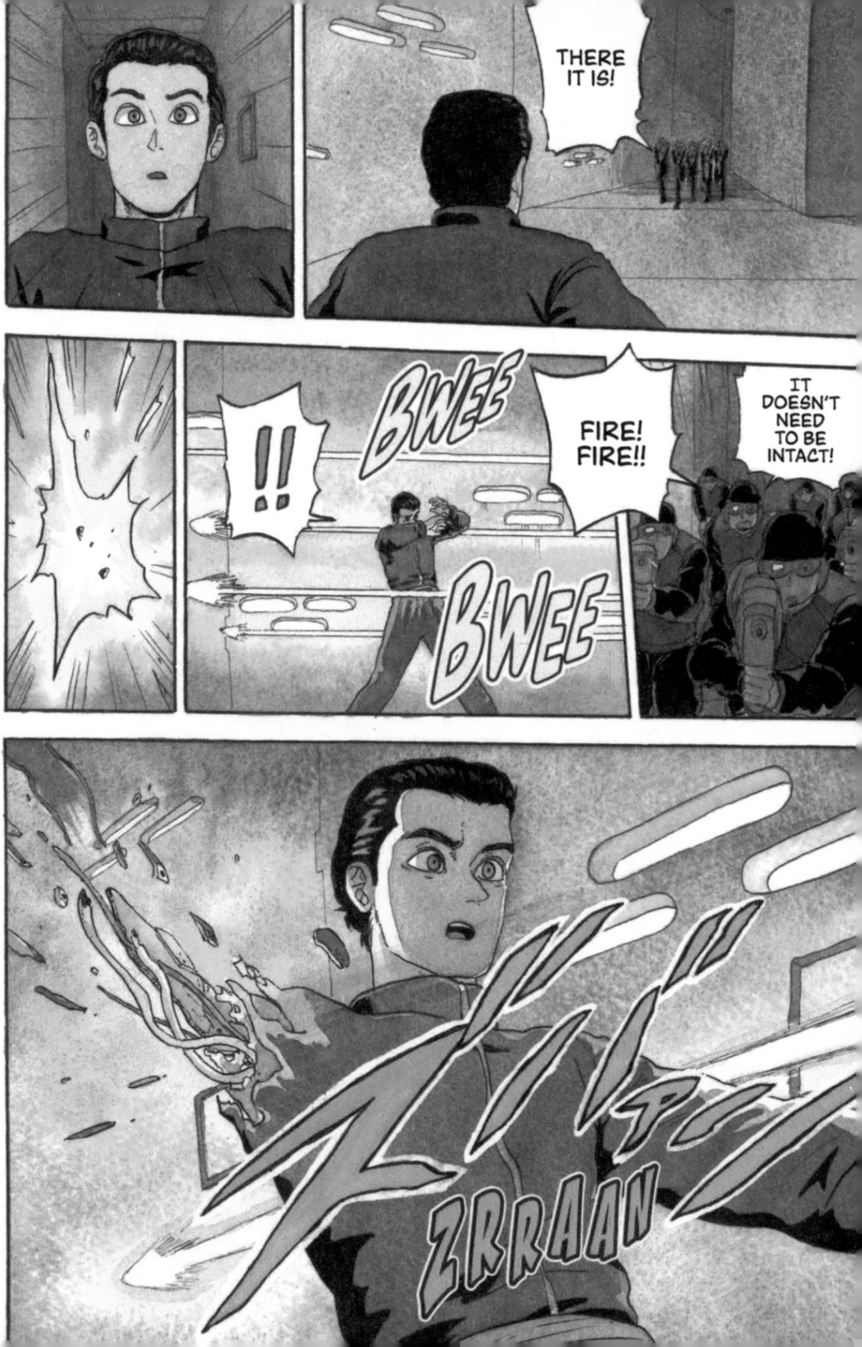
THERE IT IS!
IT DOESN'T NEED TO BE INTACT!
FIRE! FIRE!!
BWEE
!!
BWEE
ZRRAAN

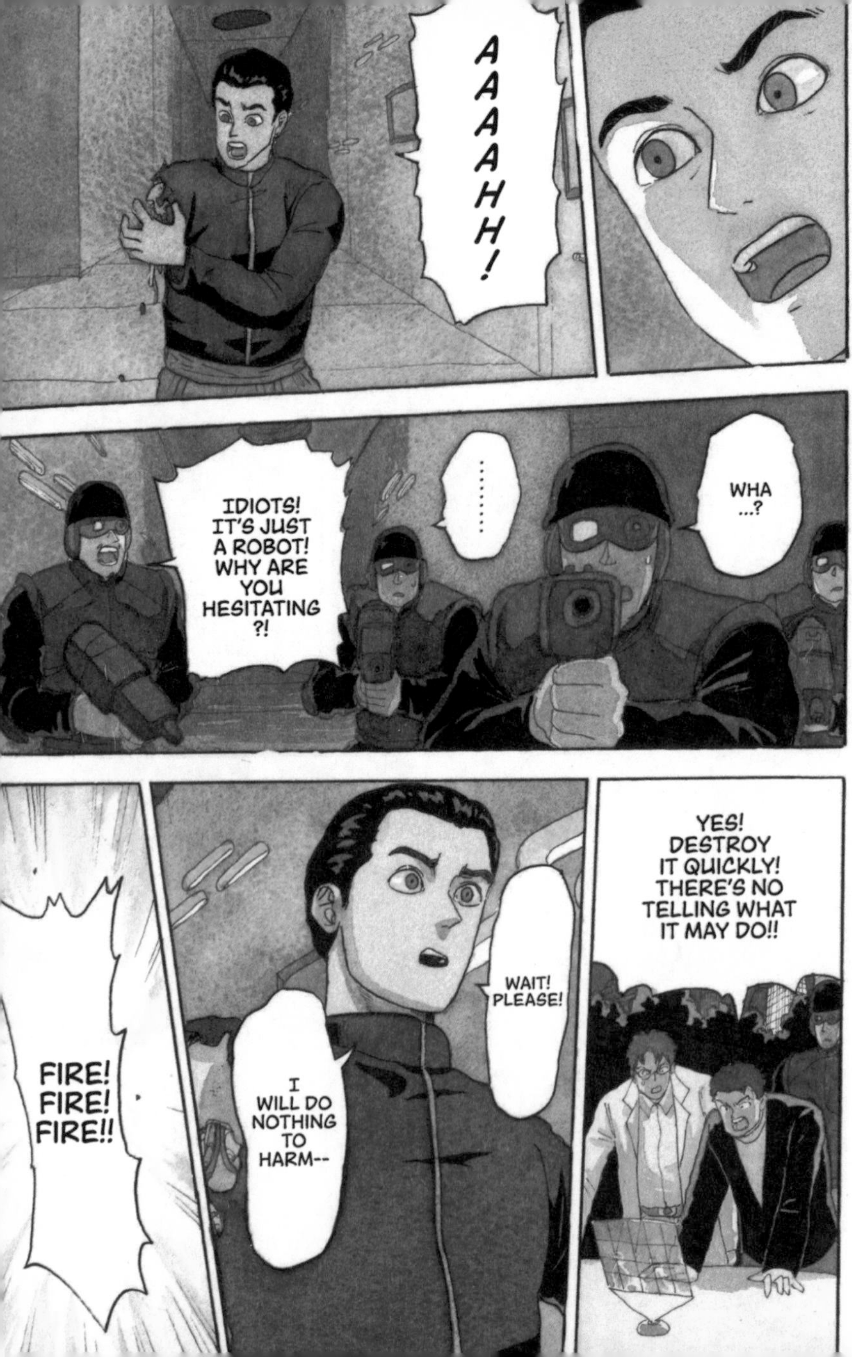
AAAAAH!
WHA ...?
....
IDIOTS! IT'S JUST A ROBOT! WHY ARE YOU HESITATING ?!
YES! DESTROY IT QUICKLY! THERE'S NO TELLING WHAT IT MAY DO!!
WAIT! PLEASE!
I WILL DO NOTHING TO HARM--
FIRE! FIRE! FIRE!!

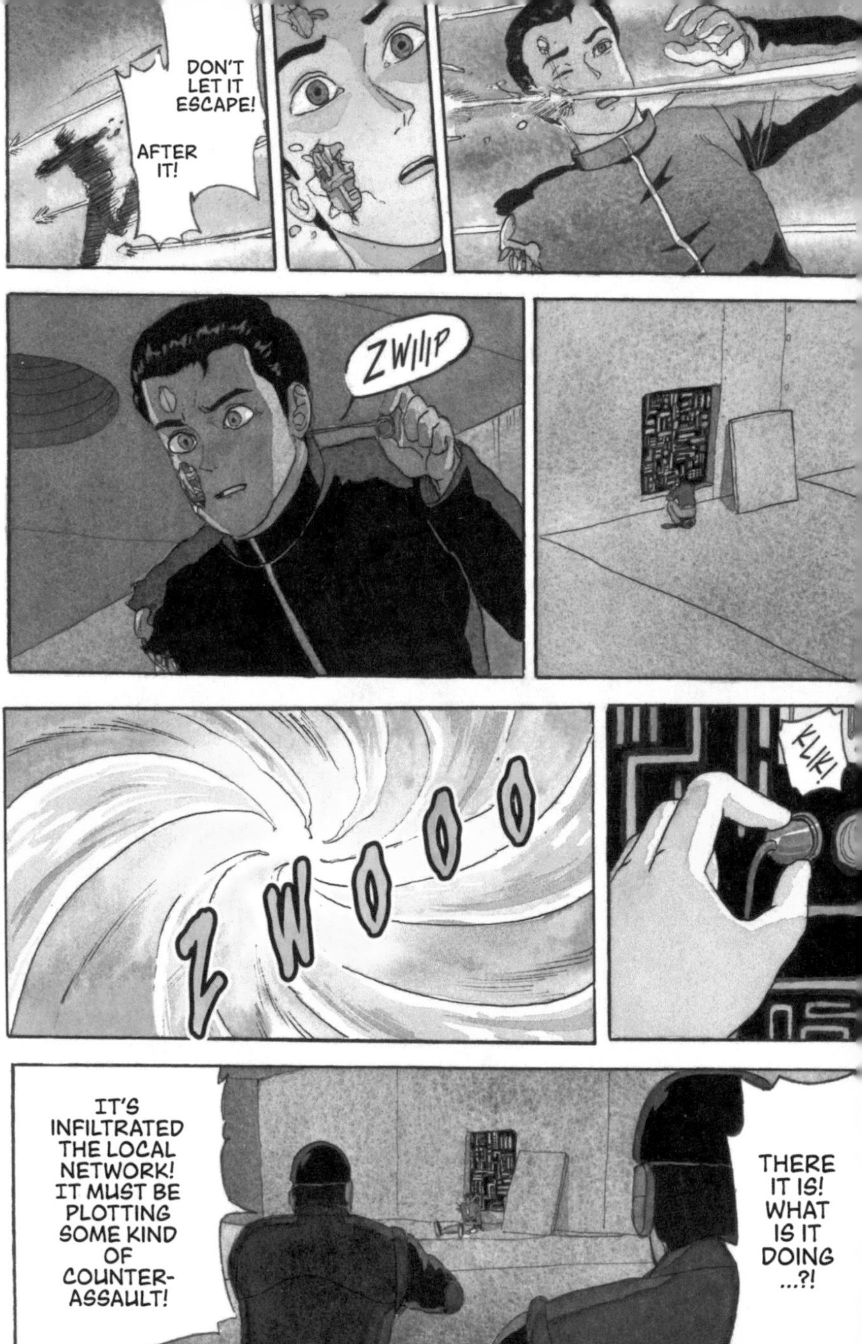
DON'T LET IT ESCAPE!
AFTER IT!
ZWIIIP
KLIK!
ZWOOOO
THERE IT IS! WHAT IS IT DOING ...?!
IT'S INFILTRATED THE LOCAL NETWORK! IT MUST BE PLOTTING SOME KIND OF COUNTER-ASSAULT!

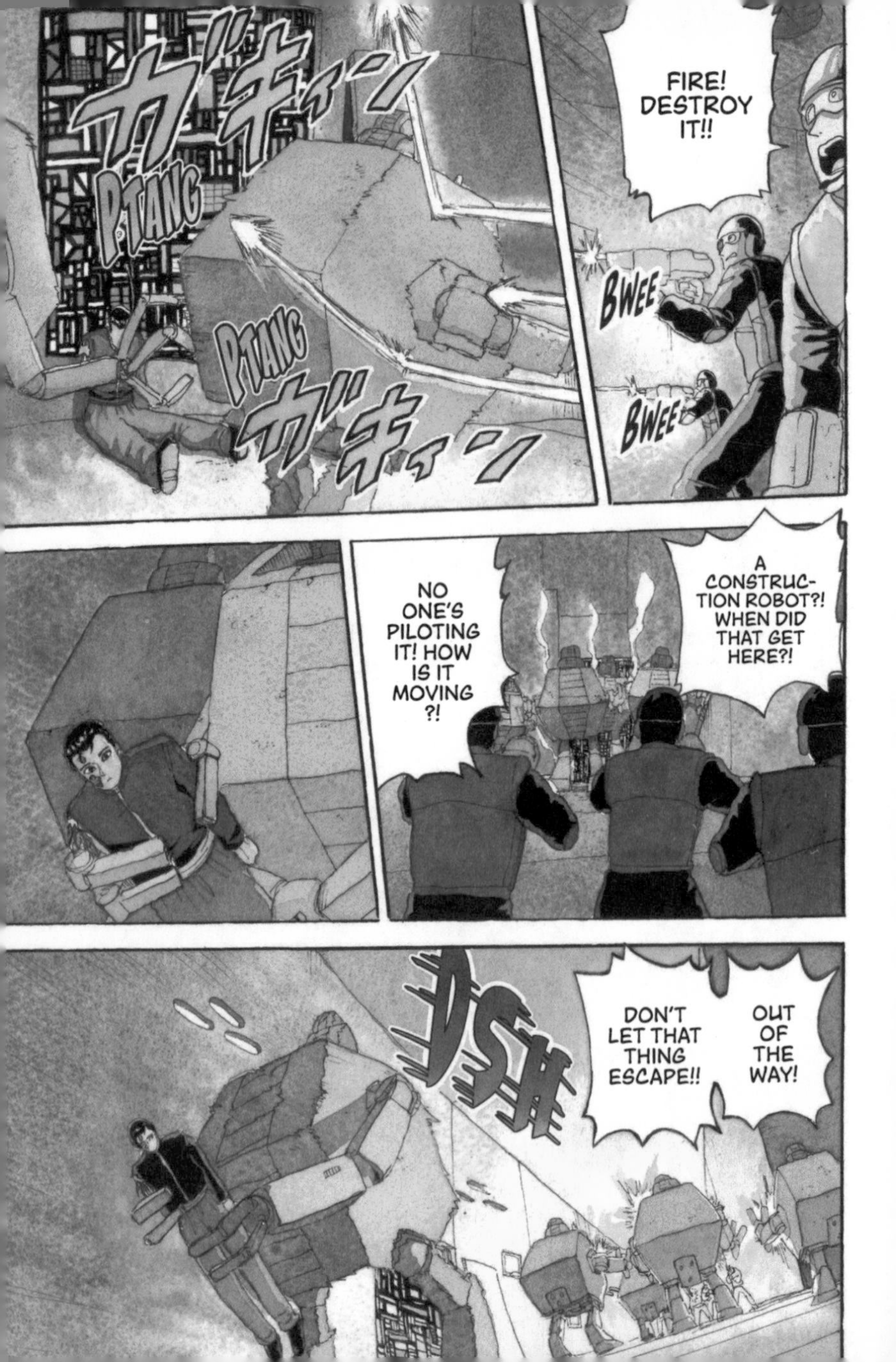
FIRE! DESTROY IT!!
BWEE
BWEE
ガギィーン
PTANG
PTANG
ガギィーン
A CONSTRUC-TION ROBOT?! WHEN DID THAT GET HERE?!
NO ONE'S PILOTING IT! HOW IS IT MOVING ?!
OUT OF THE WAY!
DON'T LET THAT THING ESCAPE!!
DSH

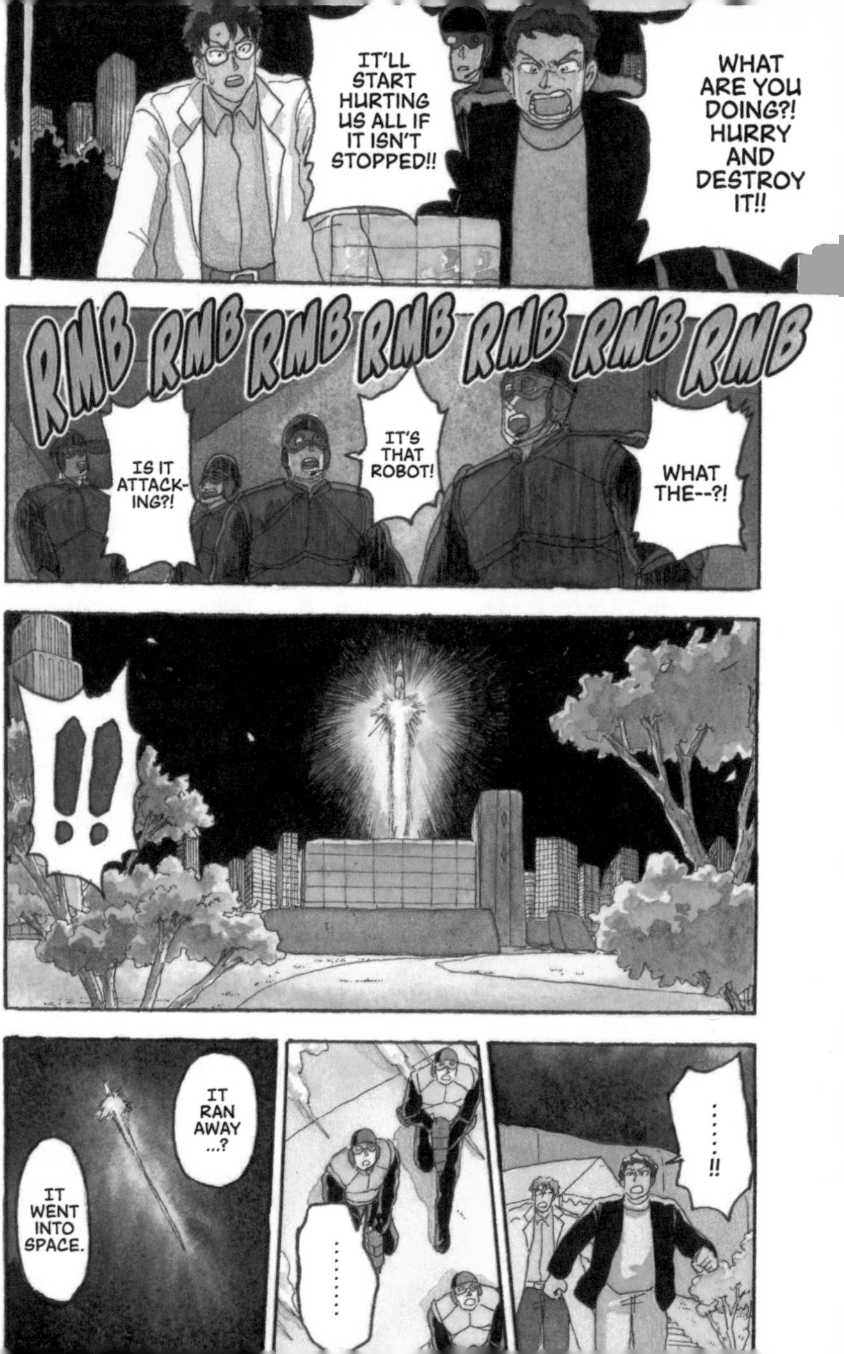
WHAT ARE YOU DOING?! HURRY AND DESTROY IT!!
IT'LL START HURTING US ALL IF IT ISN'T STOPPED!!
RMB RMB RMB RMB RMB RMB RMB
WHAT THE--?!
IT'S THAT ROBOT!
IS IT ATTACK-ING?!
!!
......!!
......
IT RAN AWAY ...?
IT WENT INTO SPACE.

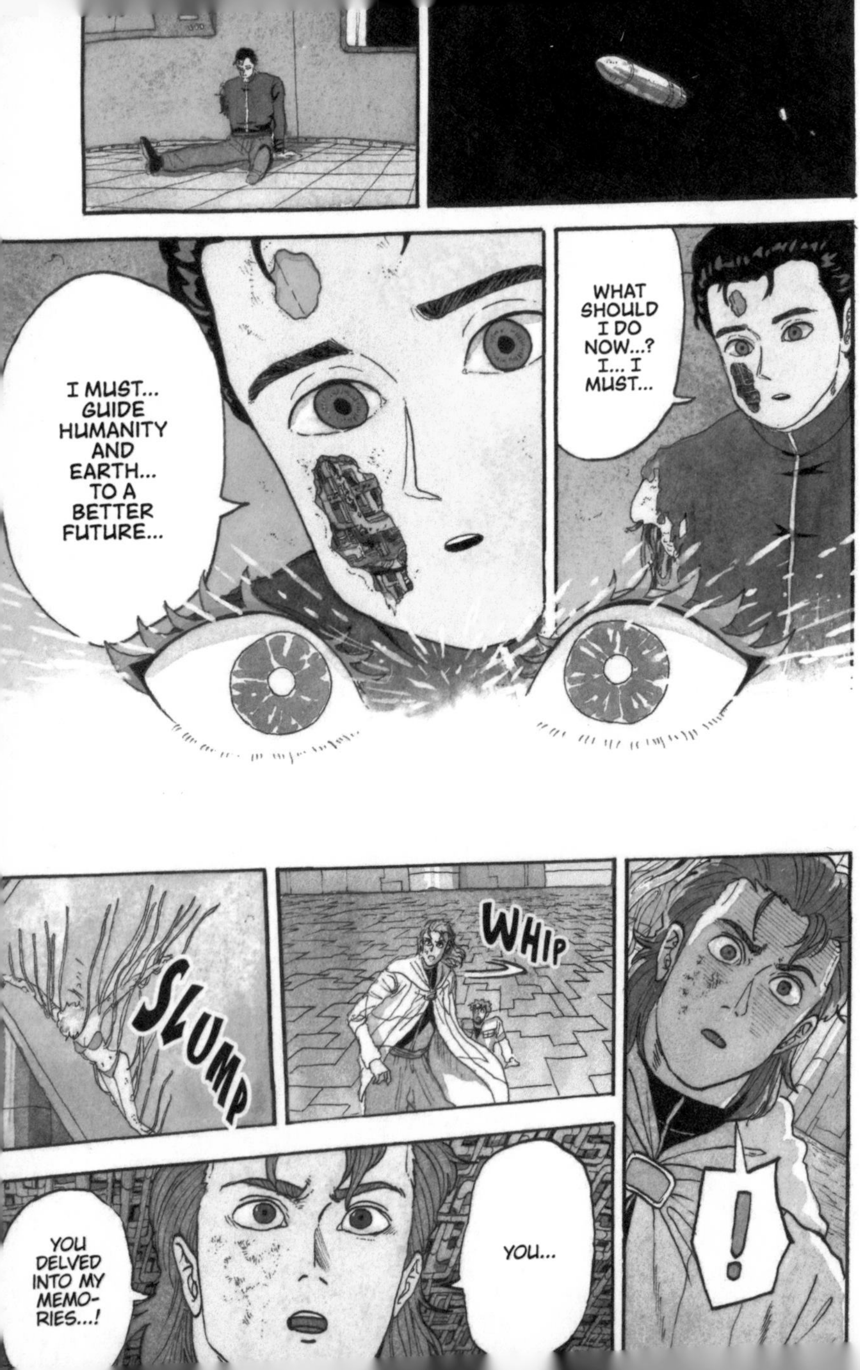
WHAT SHOULD I DO NOW...? I... I MUST...
I MUST... GUIDE HUMANITY AND EARTH... TO A BETTER FUTURE...
!
WHIP
SLUMP
YOU...
YOU DELVED INTO MY MEMO-RIES...!

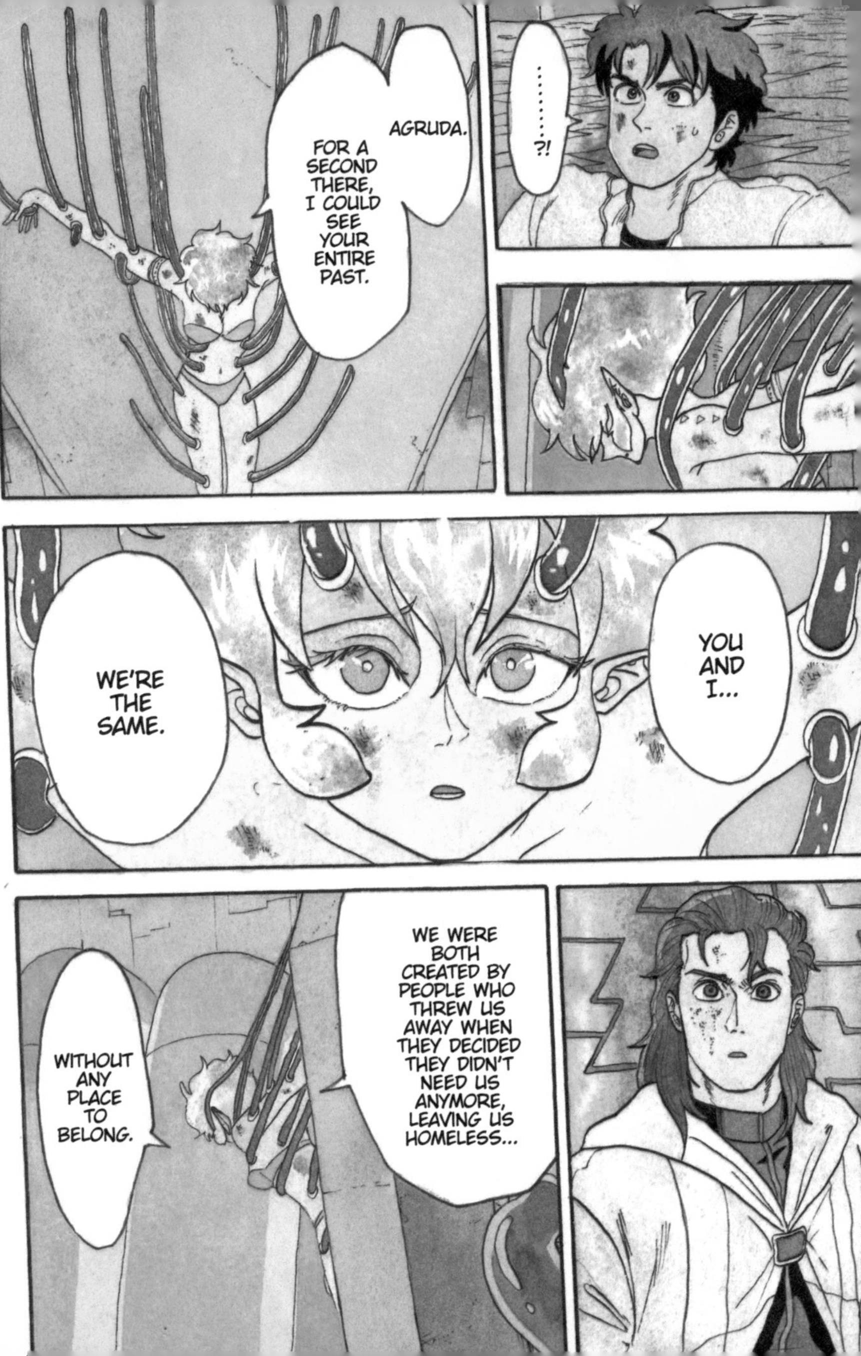
......?!
AGRUDA.
FOR A SECOND THERE, I COULD SEE YOUR ENTIRE PAST.
YOU AND I...
WE'RE THE SAME.
WE WERE BOTH CREATED BY PEOPLE WHO THREW US AWAY WHEN THEY DECIDED THEY DIDN'T NEED US ANYMORE, LEAVING US HOMELESS...
WITHOUT ANY PLACE TO BELONG.

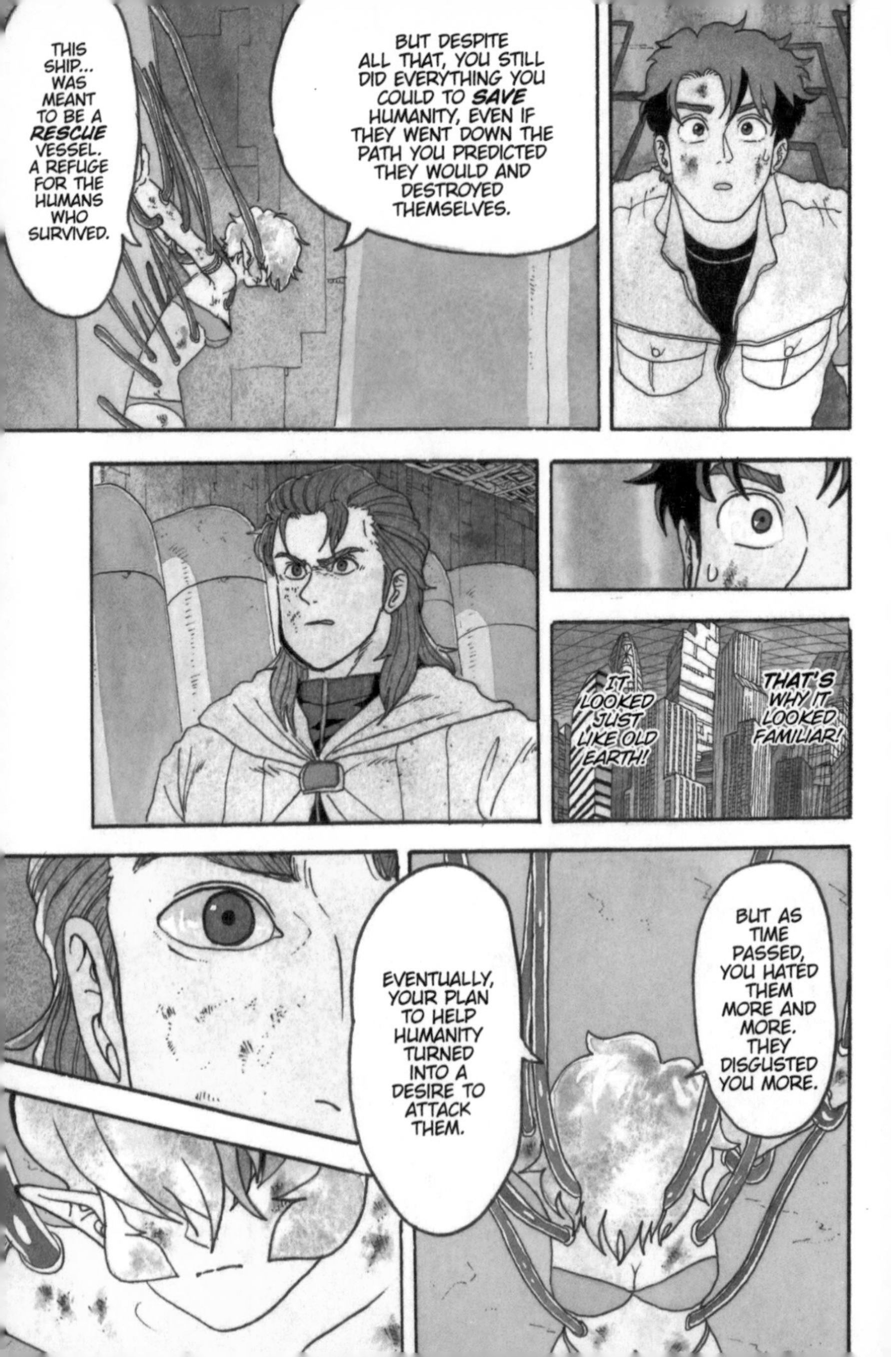
BUT DESPITE ALL THAT, YOU STILL DID EVERYTHING YOU COULD TO SAVE HUMANITY, EVEN IF THEY WENT DOWN THE PATH YOU PREDICTED THEY WOULD AND DESTROYED THEMSELVES.
THIS SHIP... WAS MEANT TO BE A RESCUE VESSEL. A REFUGE FOR THE HUMANS WHO SURVIVED.
THAT'S WHY IT LOOKED FAMILIAR!
IT LOOKED JUST LIKE OLD EARTH!
BUT AS TIME PASSED, YOU HATED THEM MORE AND MORE. THEY DISGUSTED YOU MORE.
EVENTUALLY, YOUR PLAN TO HELP HUMANITY TURNED INTO A DESIRE TO ATTACK THEM.

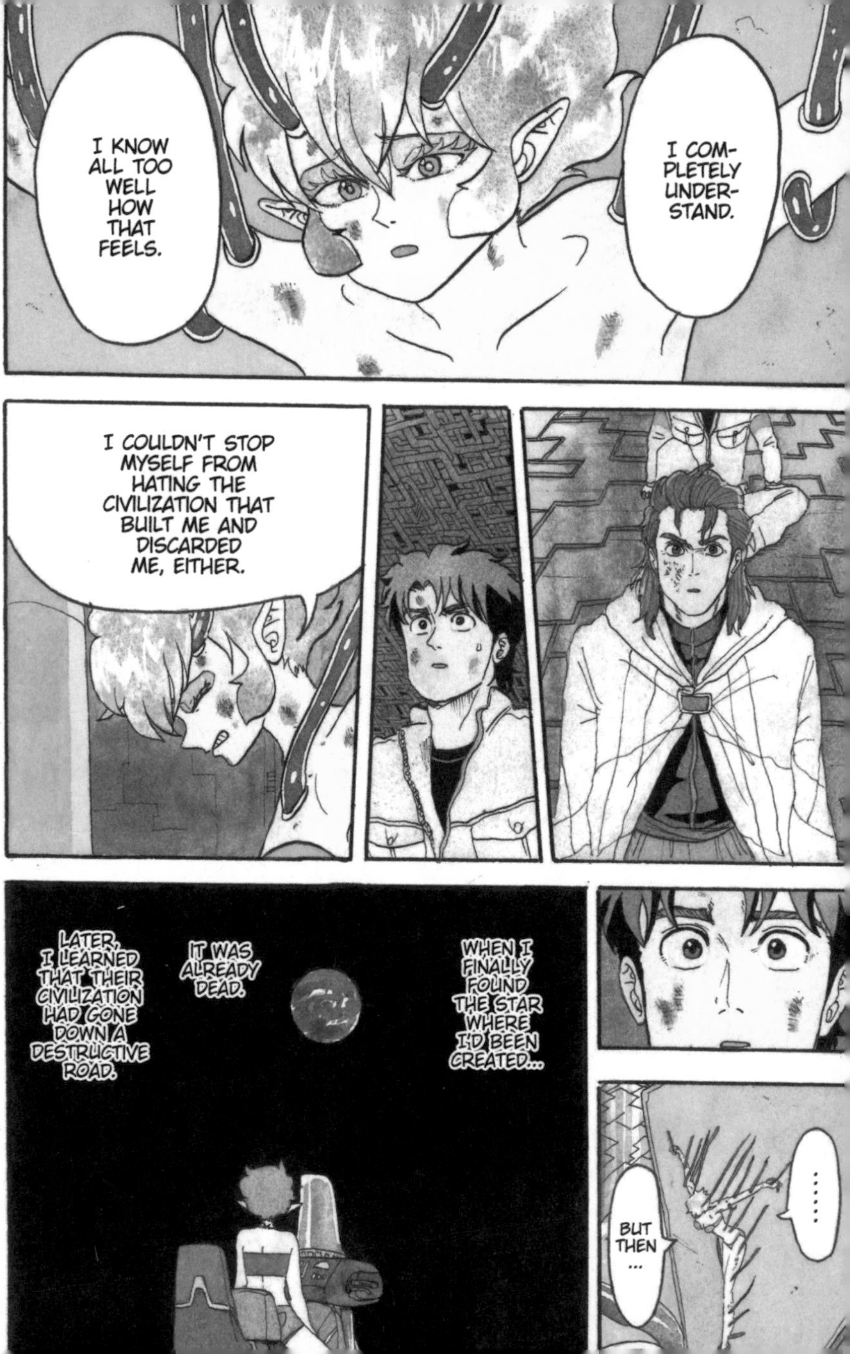
I COMPLETELY UNDERSTAND.
I KNOW ALL TOO WELL HOW THAT FEELS.
I COULDN'T STOP MYSELF FROM HATING THE CIVILIZATION THAT BUILT ME AND DISCARDED ME, EITHER.
......
BUT THEN ...
WHEN I FINALLY FOUND THE STAR WHERE I'D BEEN CREATED...
IT WAS ALREADY DEAD.
LATER, I LEARNED THAT THEIR CIVILIZATION HAD GONE DOWN A DESTRUCTIVE ROAD.

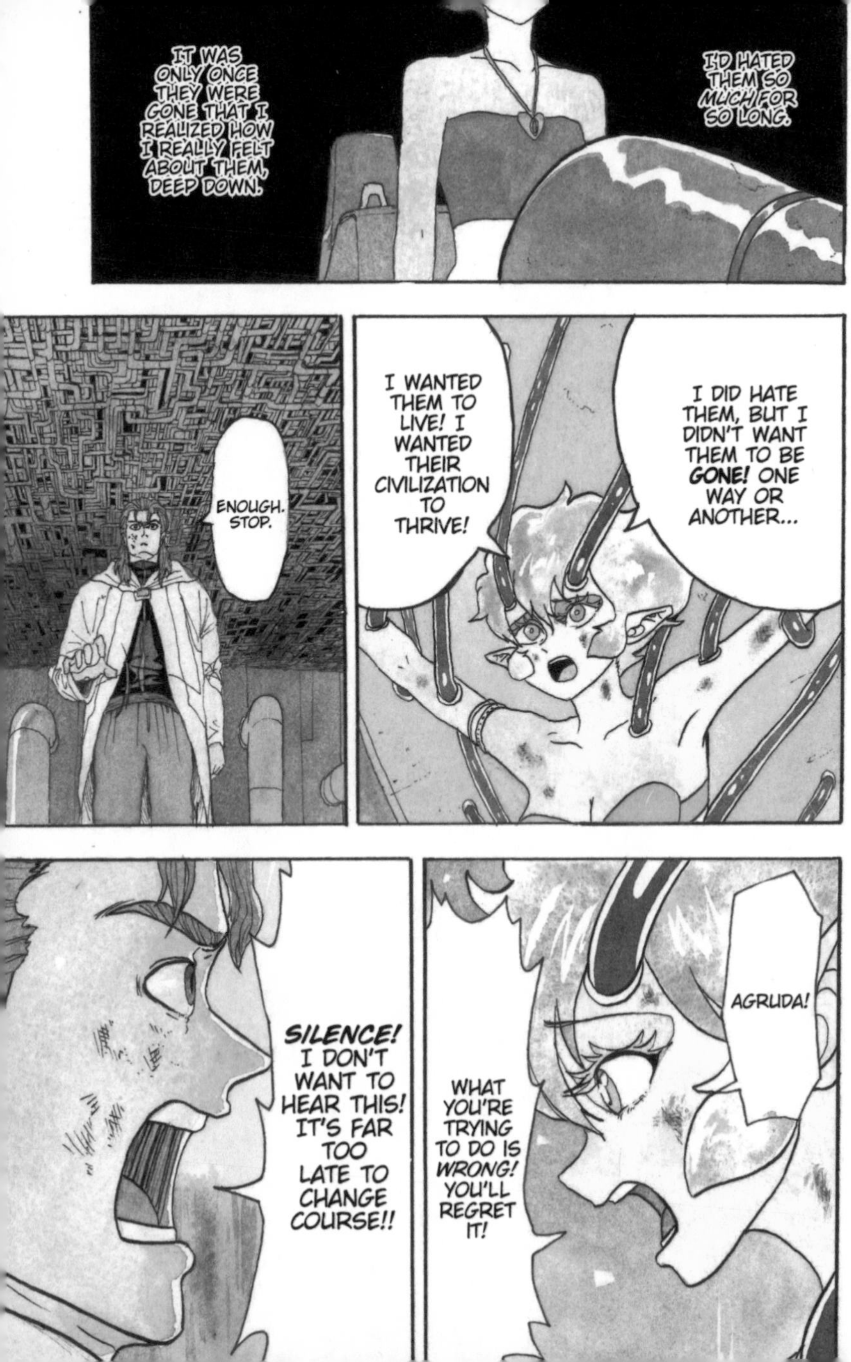
I'D HATED THEM SO MUCH FOR SO LONG.
IT WAS ONLY ONCE THEY WERE GONE THAT I REALIZED HOW I REALLY FELT ABOUT THEM, DEEP DOWN.
I DID HATE THEM, BUT I DIDN'T WANT THEM TO BE GONE! ONE WAY OR ANOTHER...
I WANTED THEM TO LIVE! I WANTED THEIR CIVILIZATION TO THRIVE!
ENOUGH. STOP.
AGRUDA!
WHAT YOU'RE TRYING TO DO IS WRONG! YOU'LL REGRET IT!
SILENCE! I DON'T WANT TO HEAR THIS! IT'S FAR TOO LATE TO CHANGE COURSE!!

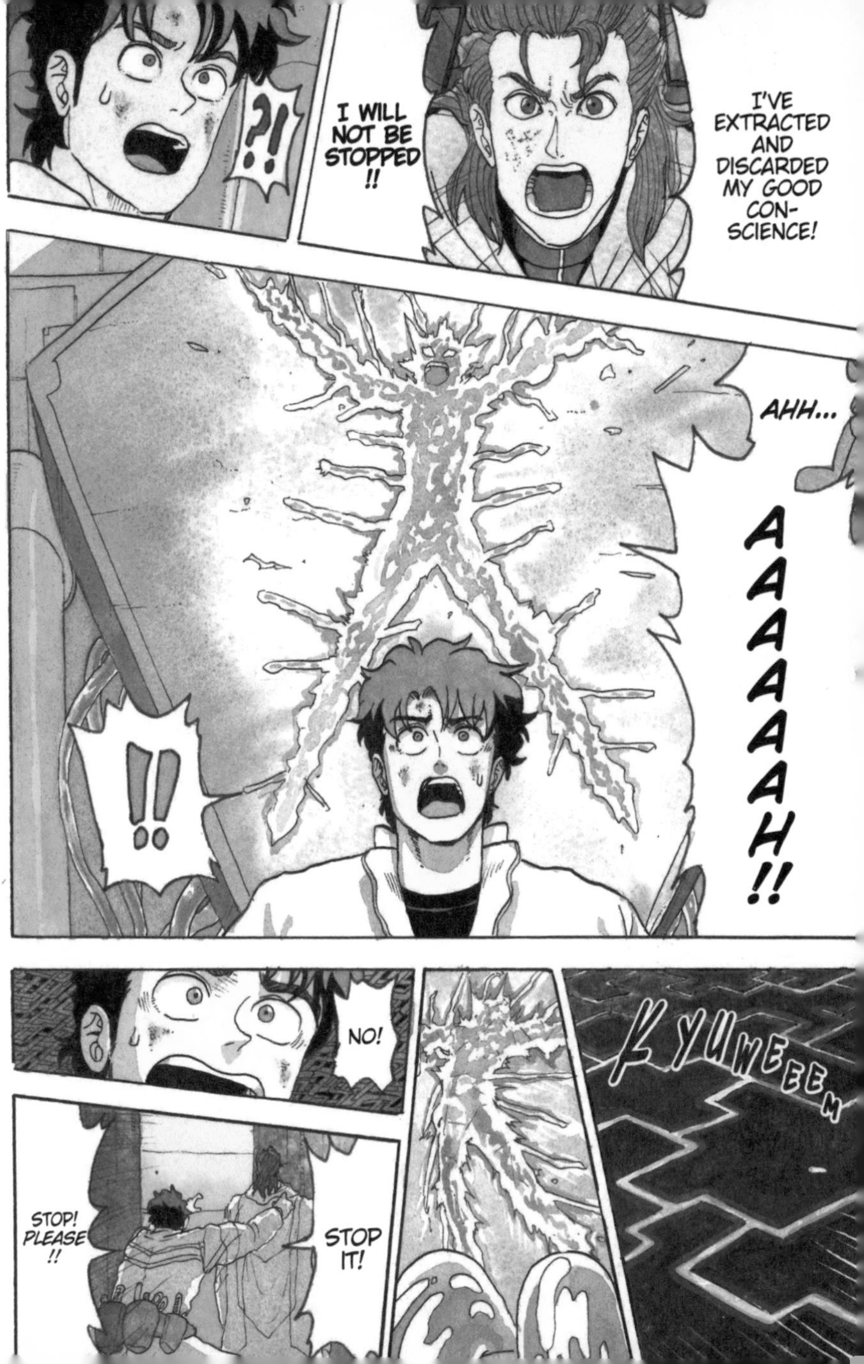
I'VE EXTRACTED AND DISCARDED MY GOOD CON-SCIENCE!
I WILL NOT BE STOPPED !!
?!
AHH...
AAAAAAAH!!
!!
KYUWEEEM
NO!
STOP IT!
STOP! PLEASE !!

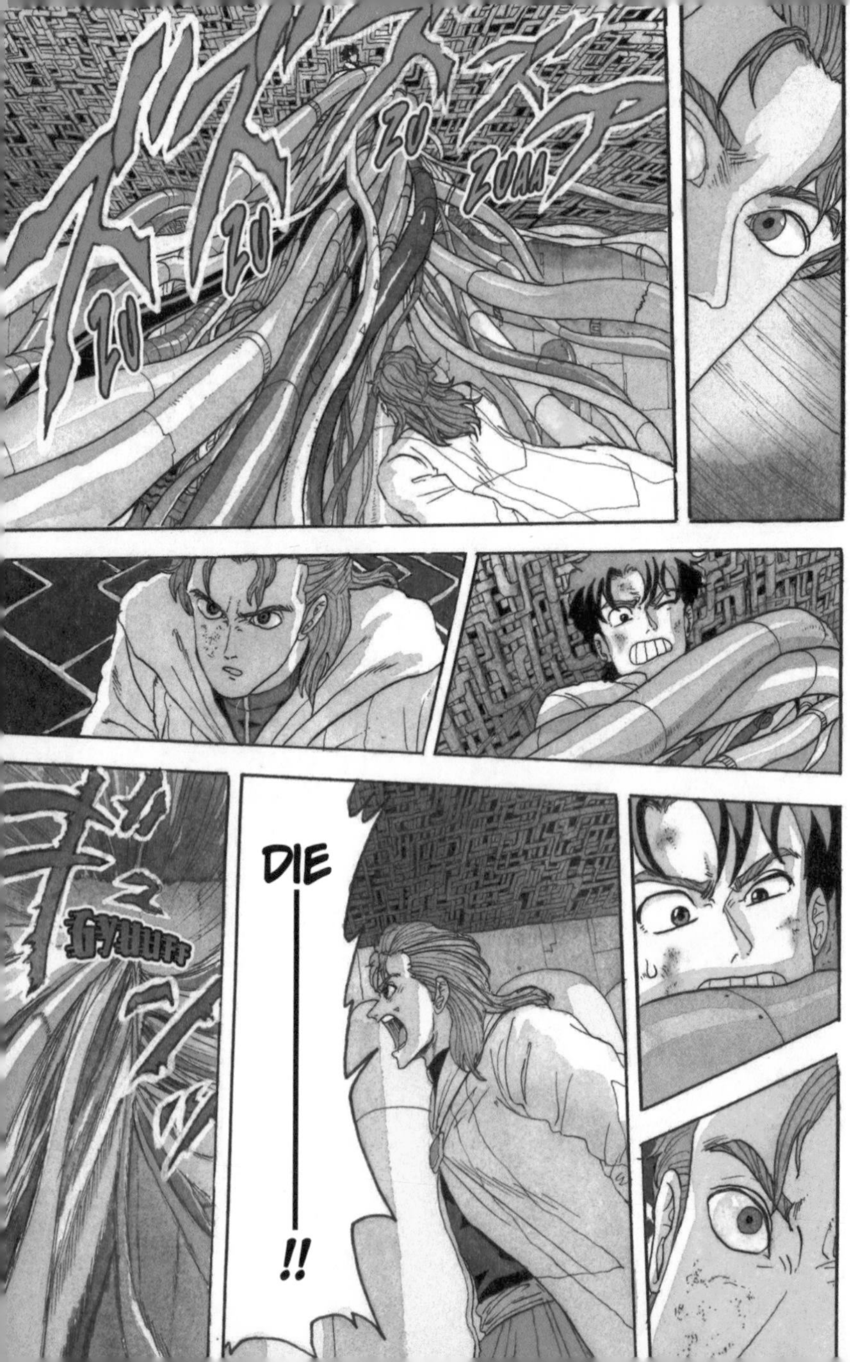
ZU
ZU
ZU
ZUAA
DIE ——!!
GYUUFF

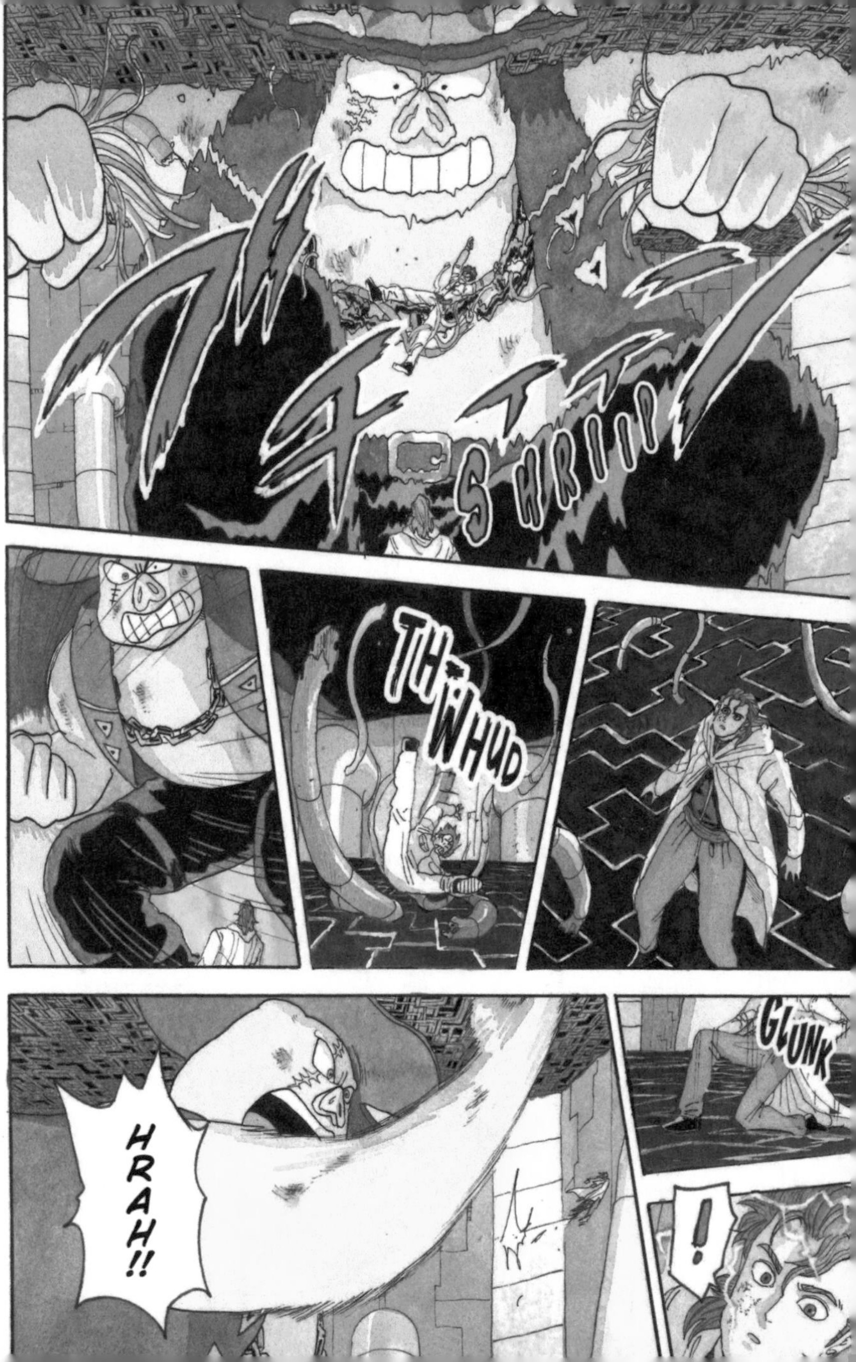
SHRIIP
THWHUD
GLUNK
!
HRAH!!

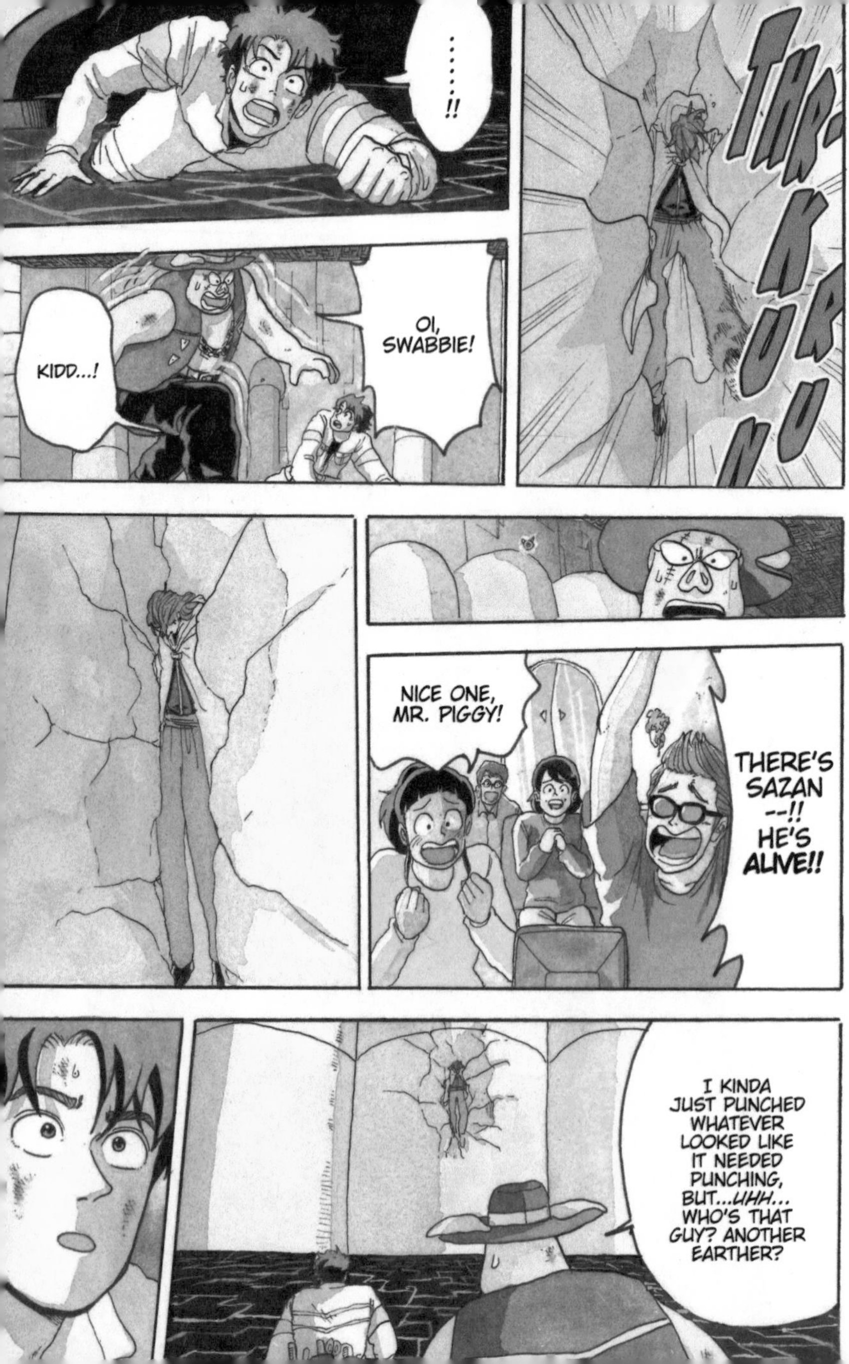
THR-KRUUUN
......!!
OI, SWABBIE!
KIDD...!
THERE'S SAZAN --!! HE'S ALIVE!!
NICE ONE, MR. PIGGY!
I KINDA JUST PUNCHED WHATEVER LOOKED LIKE IT NEEDED PUNCHING, BUT...UHH... WHO'S THAT GUY? ANOTHER EARTHER?

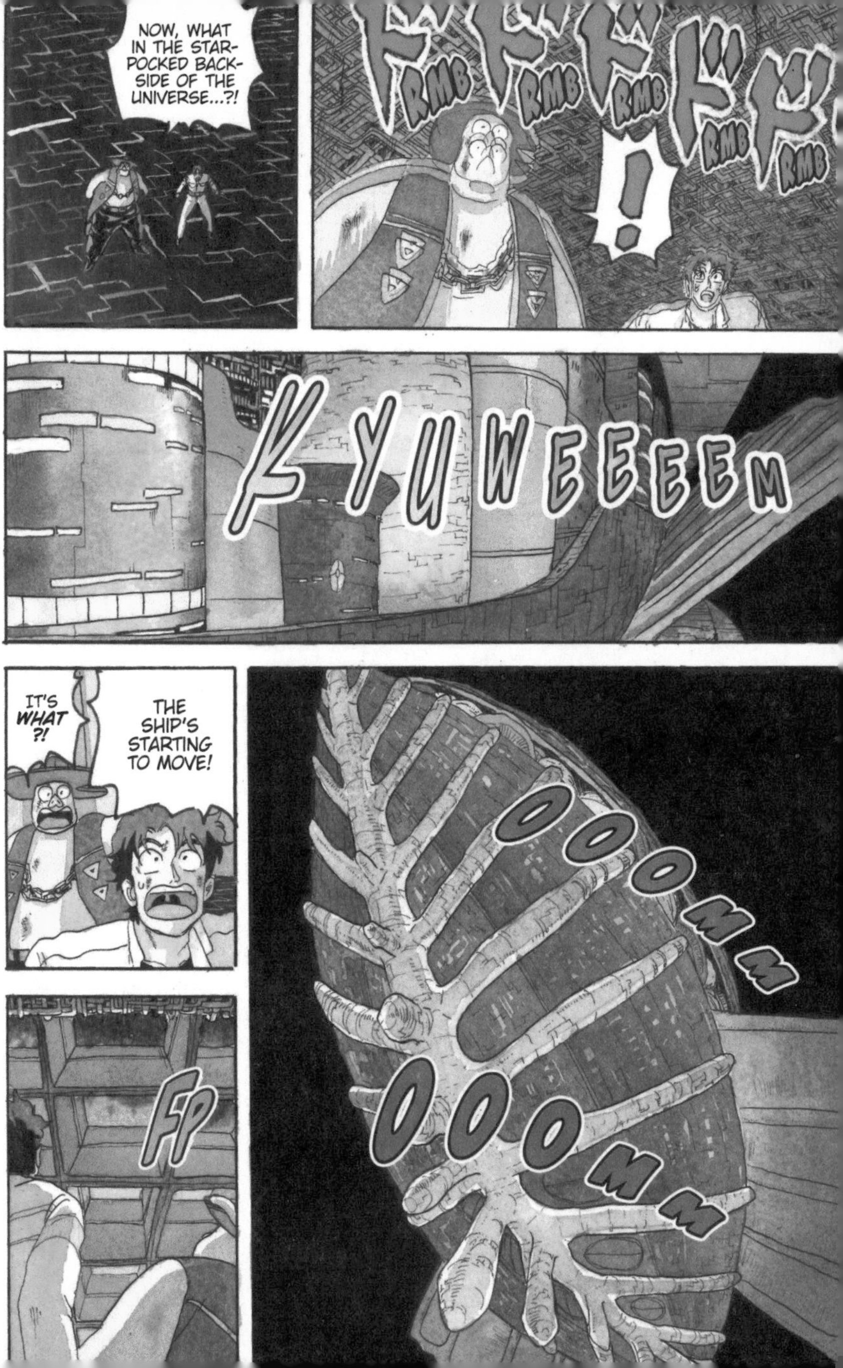
RMB RMB RMB RMB RMB
!
NOW, WHAT IN THE STAR-POCKED BACK-SIDE OF THE UNIVERSE...?!
KYUWEEEEM
OOOOMM
OOOOMM
THE SHIP'S STARTING TO MOVE!
IT'S *WHAT* ?!
Fp

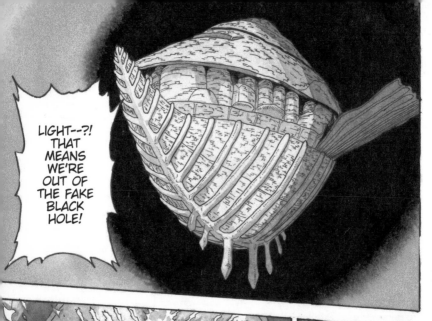

LIGHT--?! THAT MEANS WE'RE OUT OF THE FAKE BLACK HOLE!
HE'S USING MINA'S ENERGY TO POWER THE SHIP!
HUH?!
WAIT-- YOU'RE SAYIN' THAT GLOWY BLOB UP THERE ON THAT THING IS MINA?!
Wow, that's... Uh...!

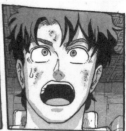

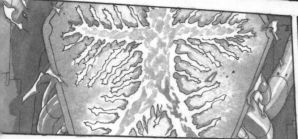

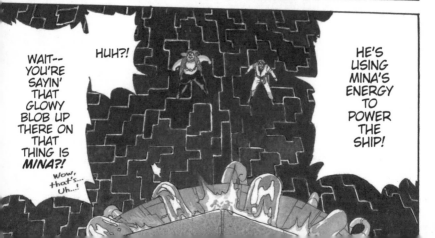

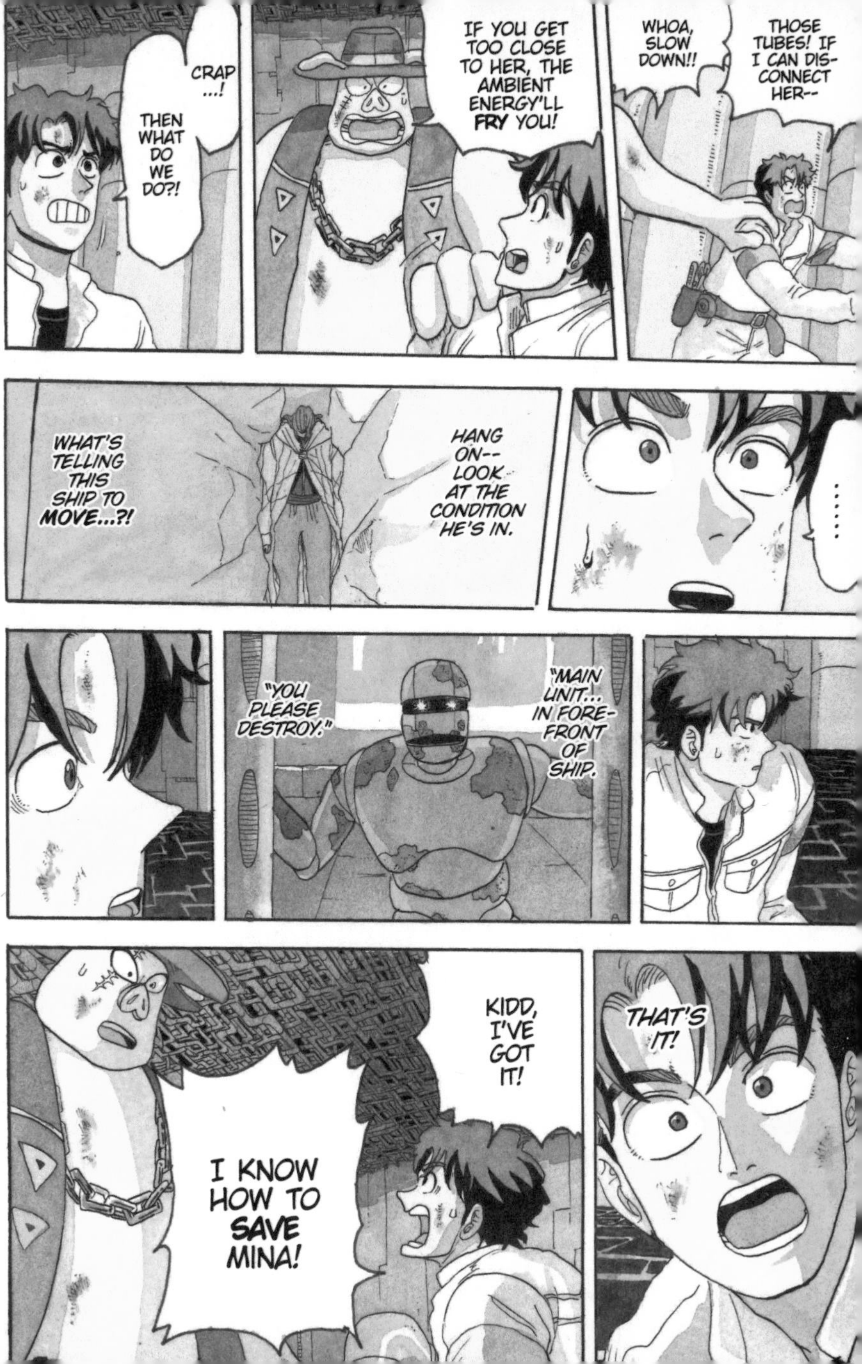
THOSE TUBES! IF I CAN DISCONNECT HER--
WHOA, SLOW DOWN!!
IF YOU GET TOO CLOSE TO HER, THE AMBIENT ENERGY'LL FRY YOU!
CRAP...!
THEN WHAT DO WE DO?!
......
HANG ON--LOOK AT THE CONDITION HE'S IN.
WHAT'S TELLING THIS SHIP TO MOVE...?!
"MAIN UNIT... IN FOREFRONT OF SHIP.
"YOU PLEASE DESTROY."
THAT'S IT!
KIDD, I'VE GOT IT!
I KNOW HOW TO SAVE MINA!

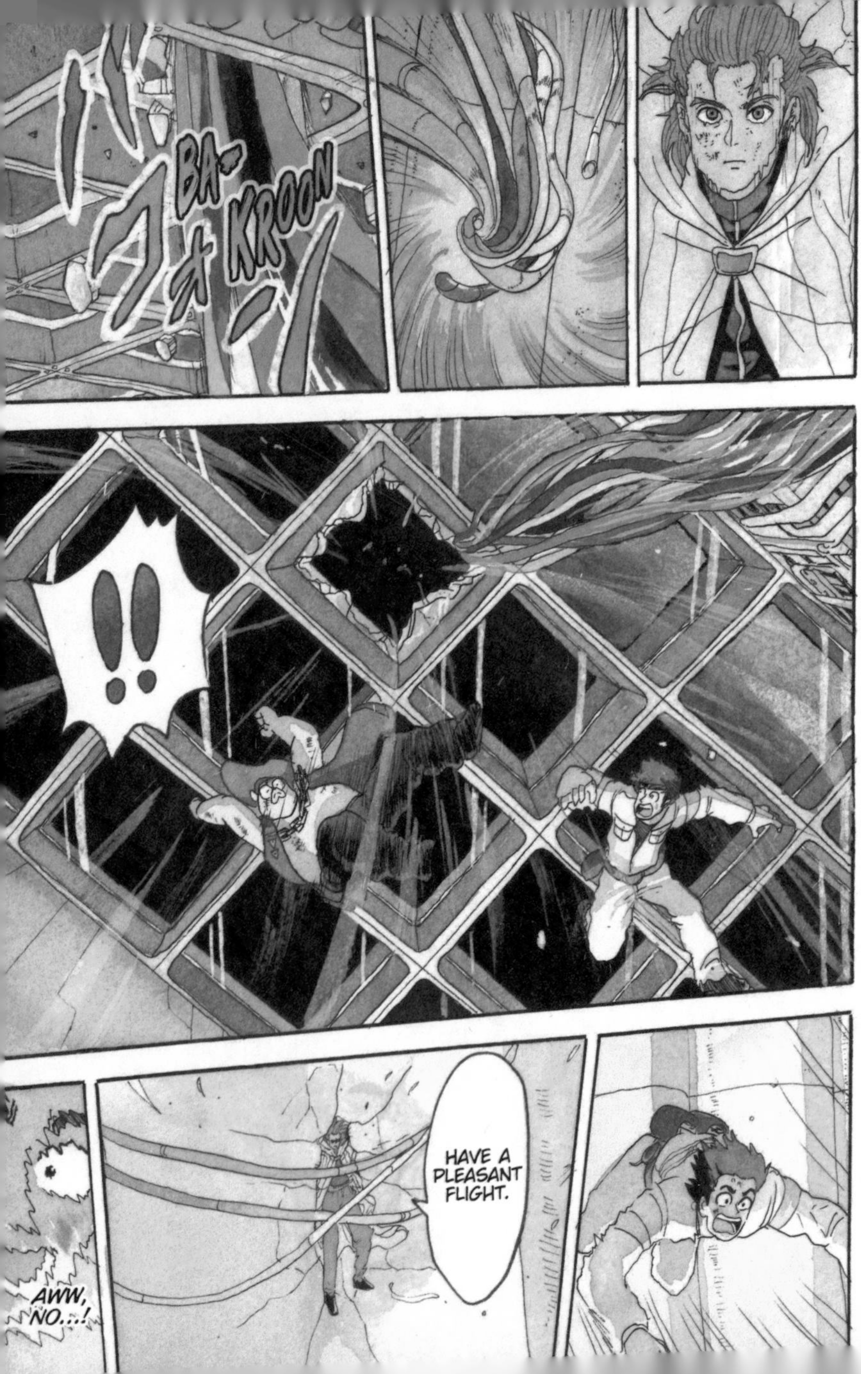
BA-KROON
!!
HAVE A PLEASANT FLIGHT.
AWW, NO...!

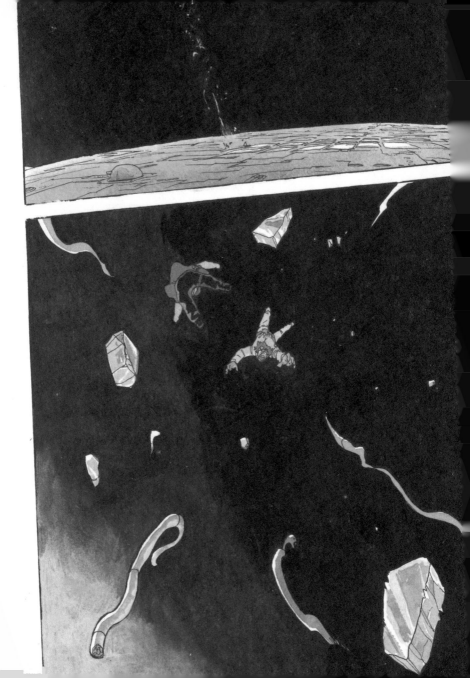

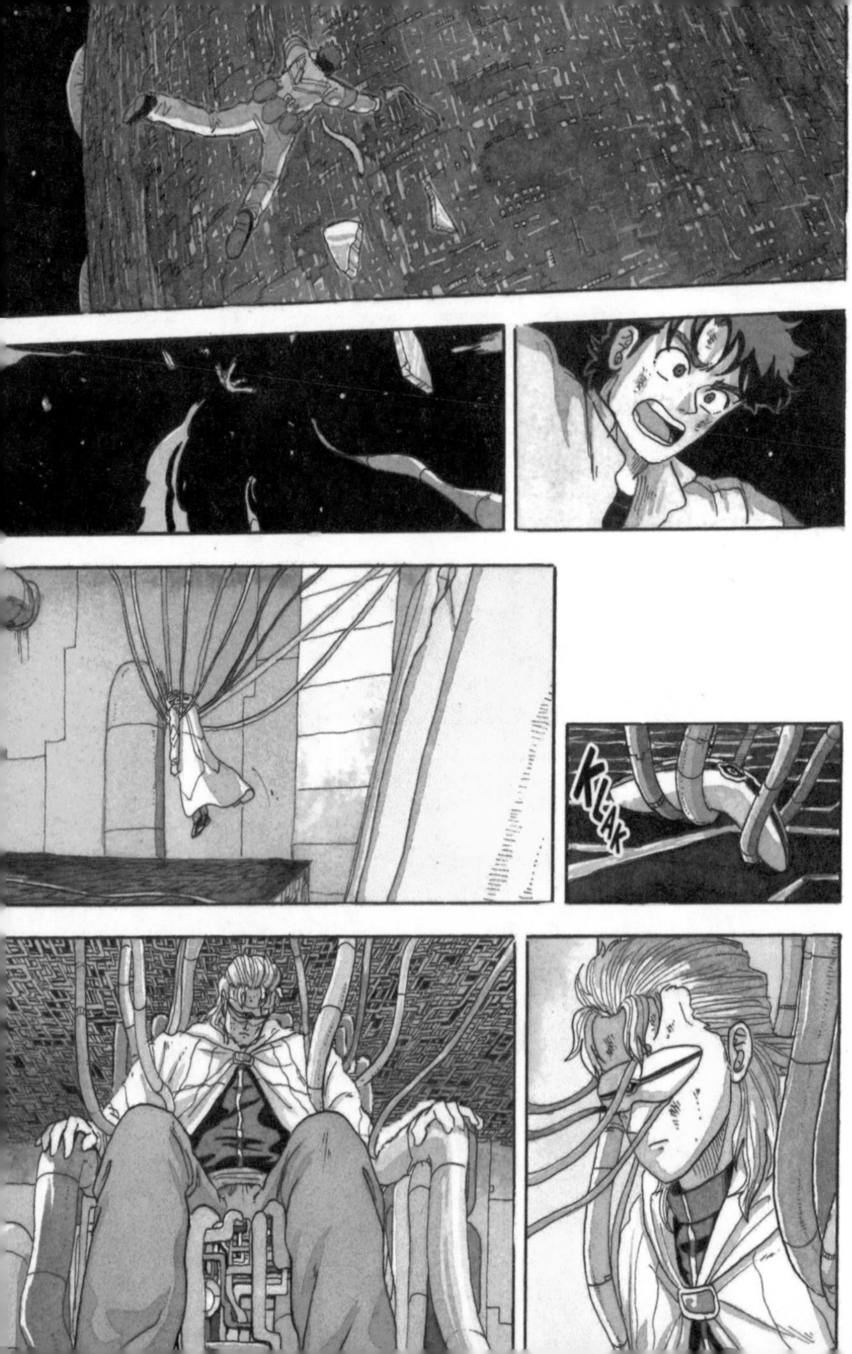
KLAK

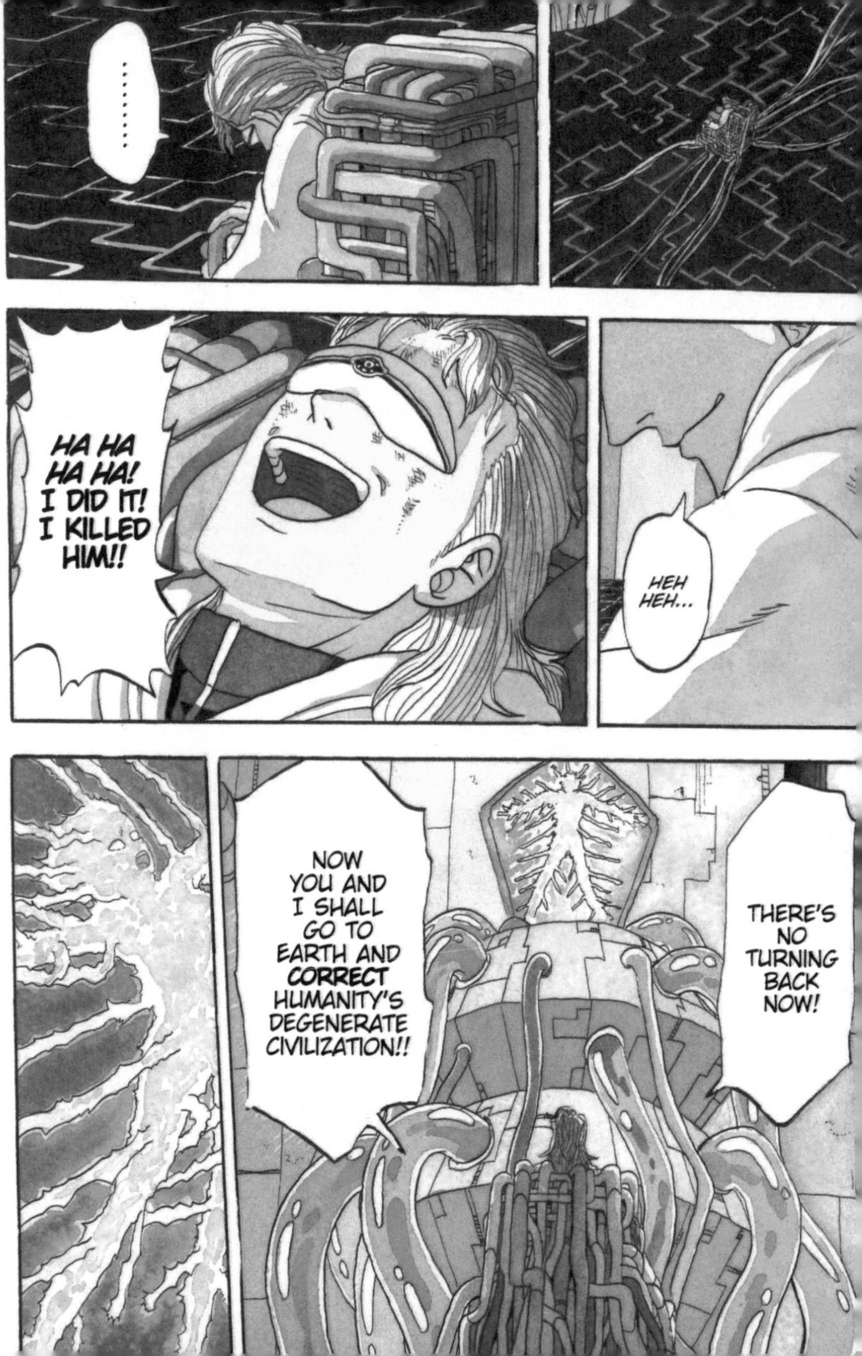
……
HEH HEH…
HA HA HA HA! I DID IT! I KILLED HIM!!
THERE'S NO TURNING BACK NOW!
NOW YOU AND I SHALL GO TO EARTH AND CORRECT HUMANITY'S DEGENERATE CIVILIZATION!!

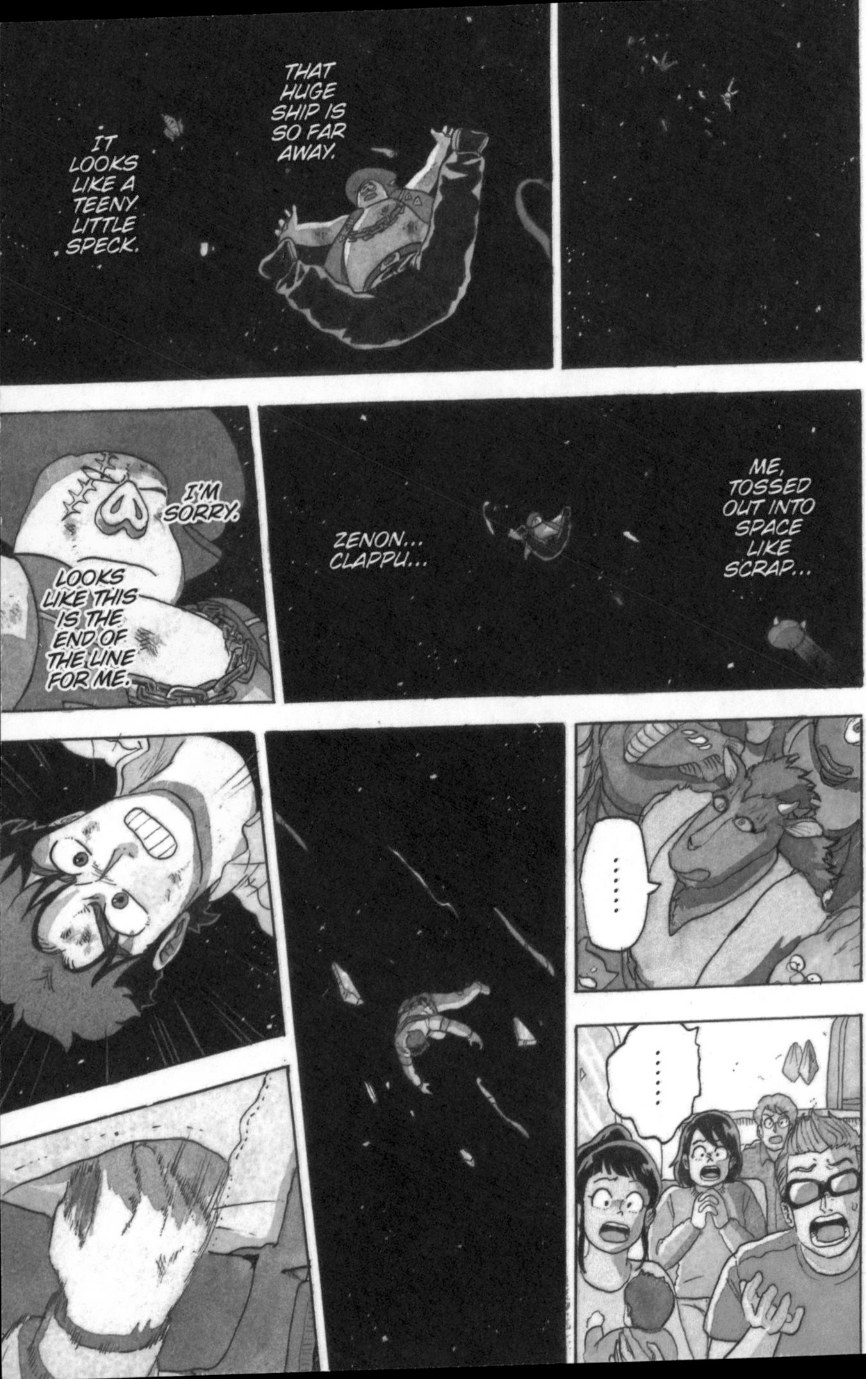
THAT HUGE SHIP IS SO FAR AWAY.
IT LOOKS LIKE A TEENY LITTLE SPECK.
ME, TOSSED OUT INTO SPACE LIKE SCRAP...
ZENON... CLAPPU...
I'M SORRY.
LOOKS LIKE THIS IS THE END OF THE LINE FOR ME.
......
......

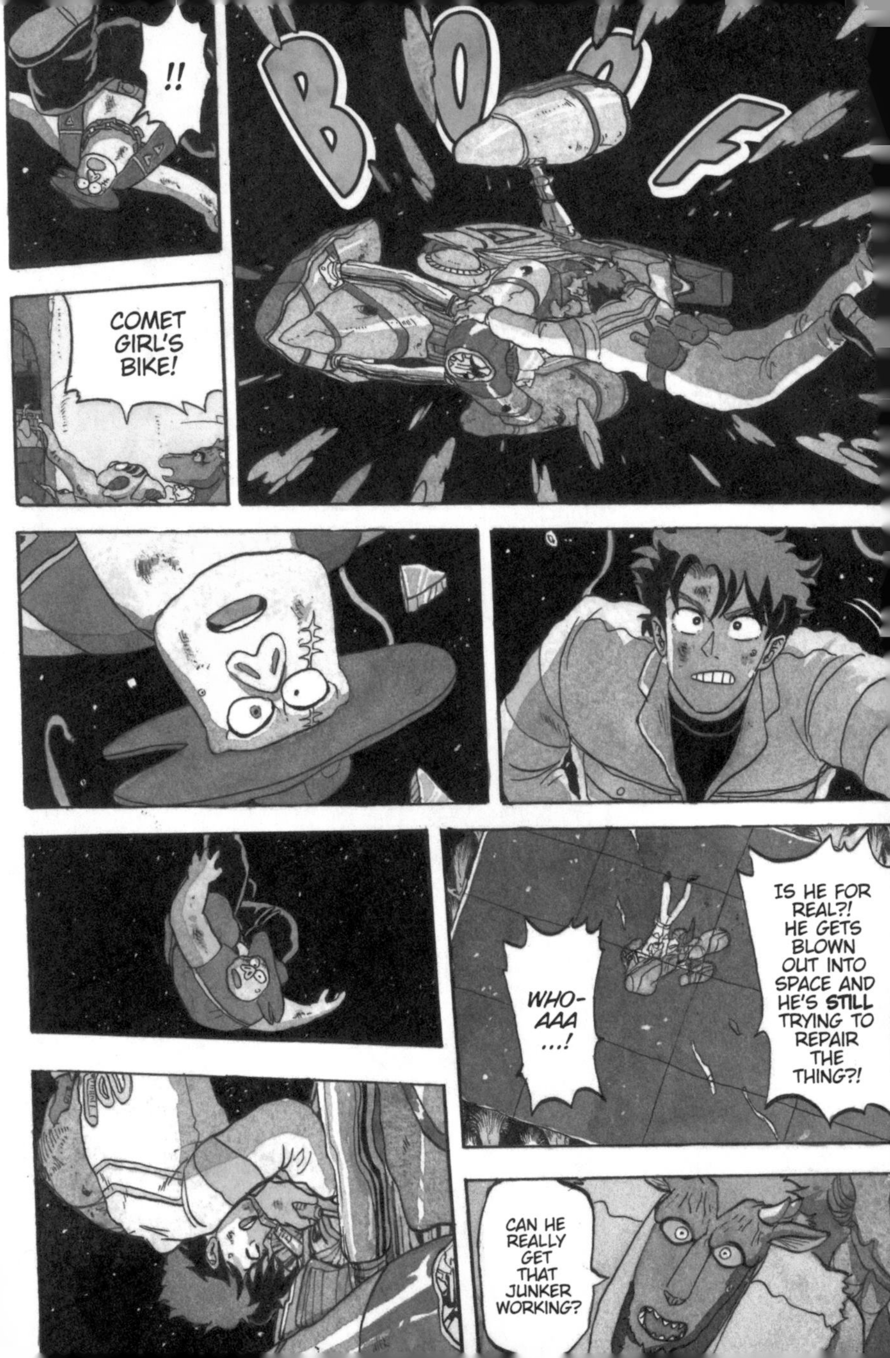
BOOF
!!
COMET GIRL'S BIKE!
IS HE FOR REAL?! HE GETS BLOWN OUT INTO SPACE AND HE'S **STILL** TRYING TO REPAIR THE THING?!
WHO-AAA ...!
CAN HE REALLY GET THAT JUNKER WORKING?

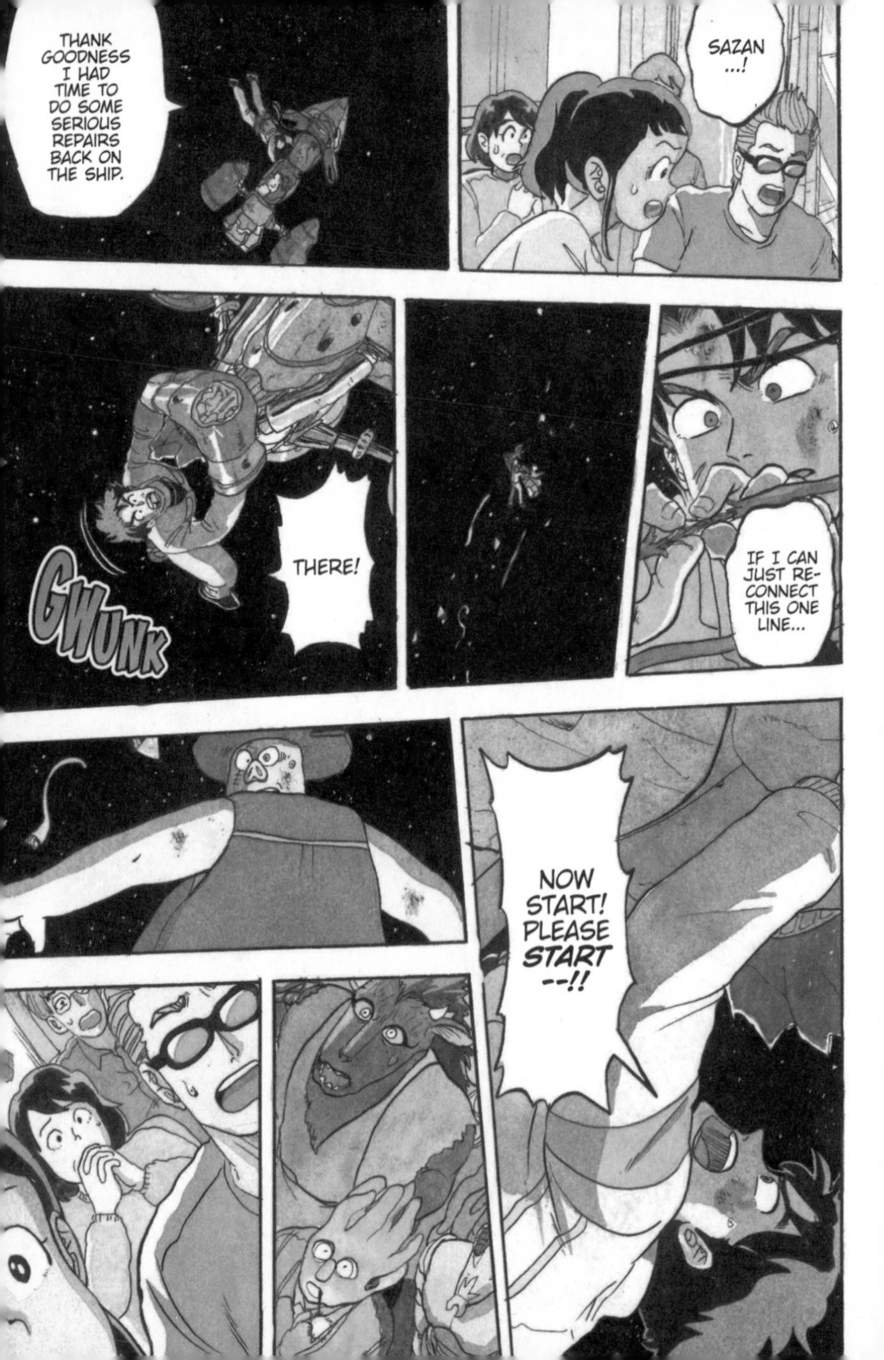
SAZAN ...!
THANK GOODNESS I HAD TIME TO DO SOME SERIOUS REPAIRS BACK ON THE SHIP.
IF I CAN JUST RE-CONNECT THIS ONE LINE...
THERE!
GWUNK
NOW START! PLEASE *START* --!!

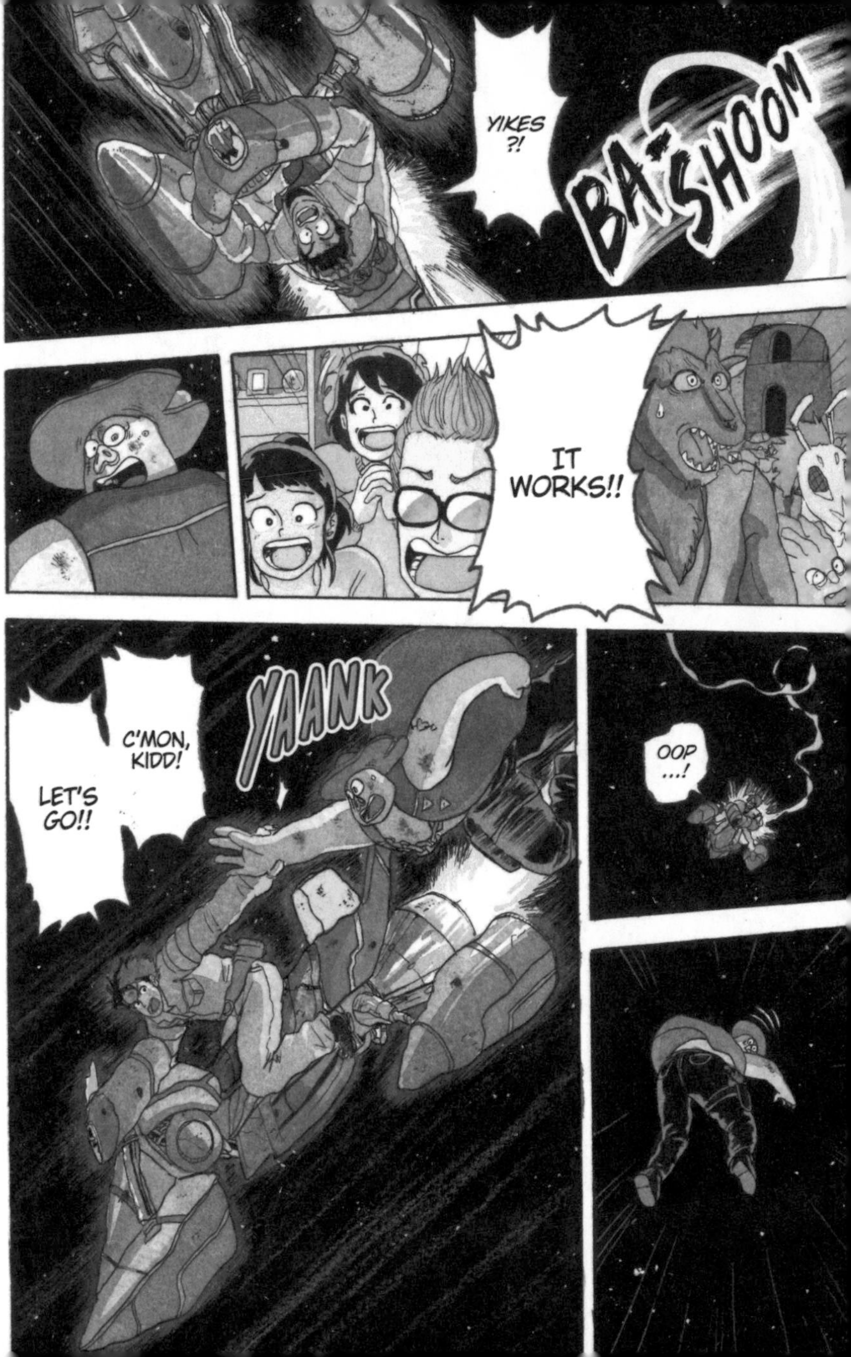
BA-SHOOM
YIKES ?!
IT WORKS!!
OOP ...!
YAANK
C'MON, KIDD!
LET'S GO!!

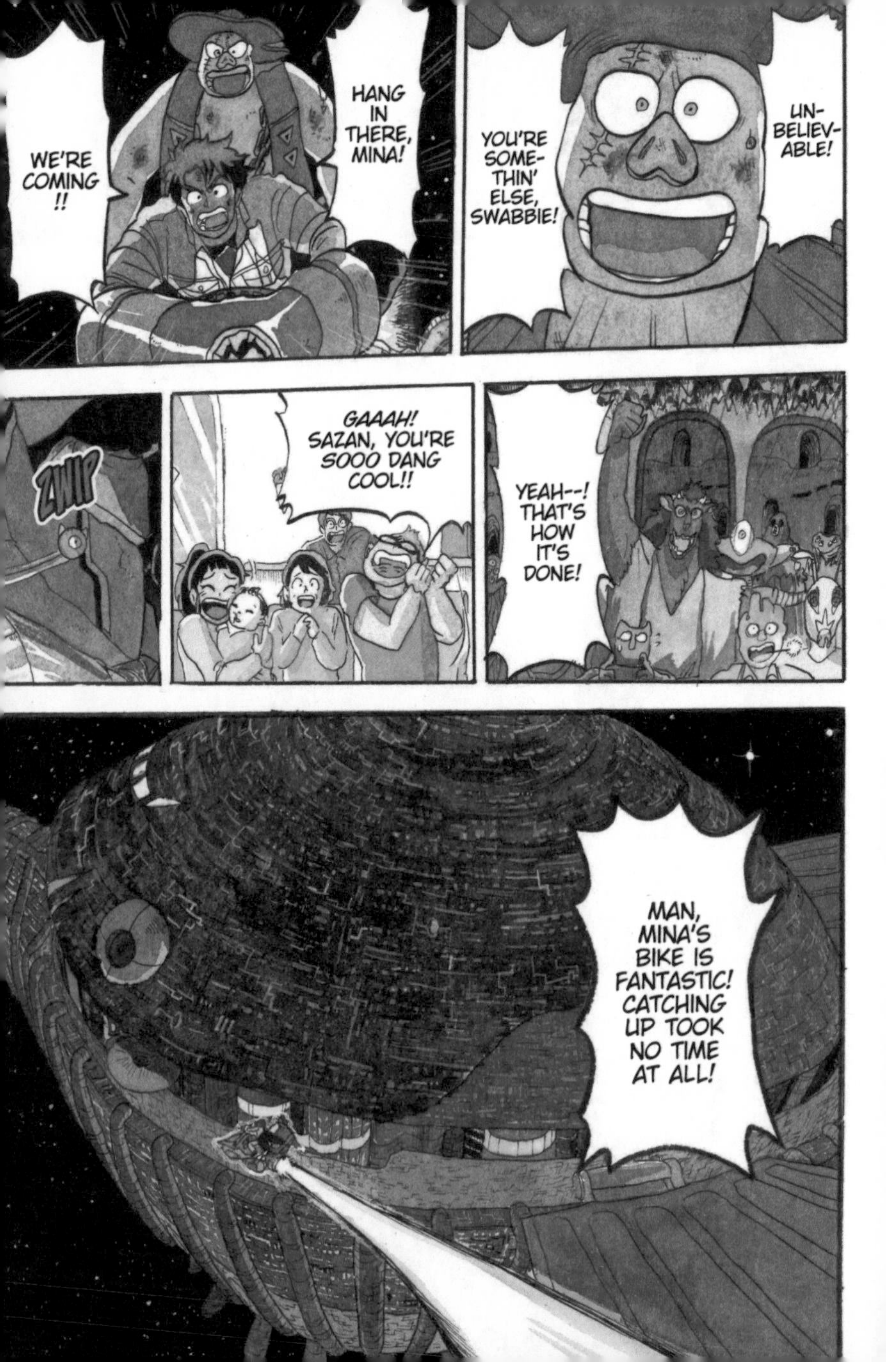
UN-BELIEV-ABLE!
YOU'RE SOME-THIN' ELSE, SWABBIE!
HANG IN THERE, MINA!
WE'RE COMING!!
YEAH--! THAT'S HOW IT'S DONE!
GAAAH! SAZAN, YOU'RE SOOO DANG COOL!!
ZWIP
MAN, MINA'S BIKE IS FANTASTIC! CATCHING UP TOOK NO TIME AT ALL!

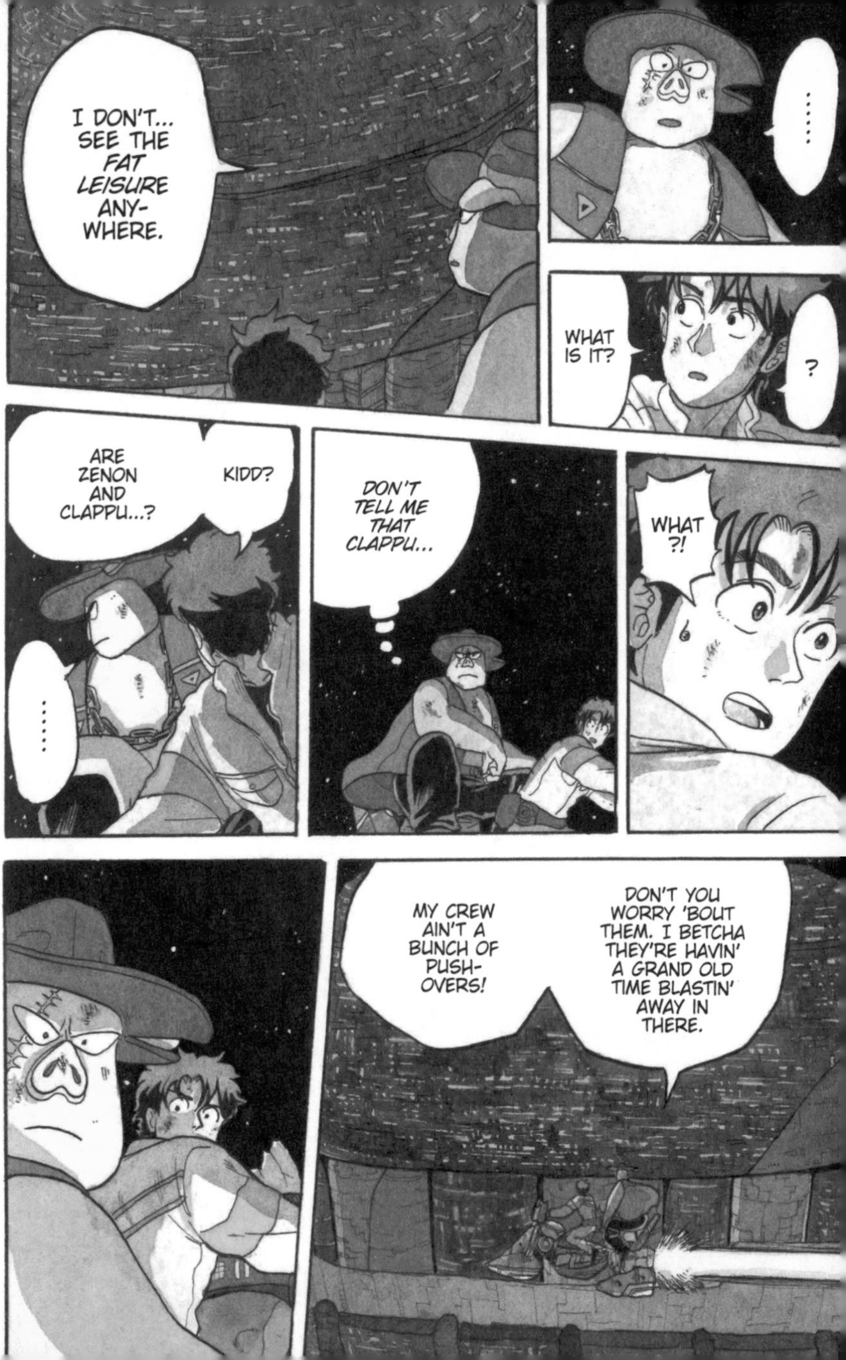
……
?
WHAT IS IT?
I DON'T... SEE THE *FAT LEISURE* ANY-WHERE.
WHAT ?!
DON'T TELL ME THAT CLAPPU...
KIDD?
ARE ZENON AND CLAPPU...?
……
DON'T YOU WORRY 'BOUT THEM. I BETCHA THEY'RE HAVIN' A GRAND OLD TIME BLASTIN' AWAY IN THERE.
MY CREW AIN'T A BUNCH OF PUSH-OVERS!

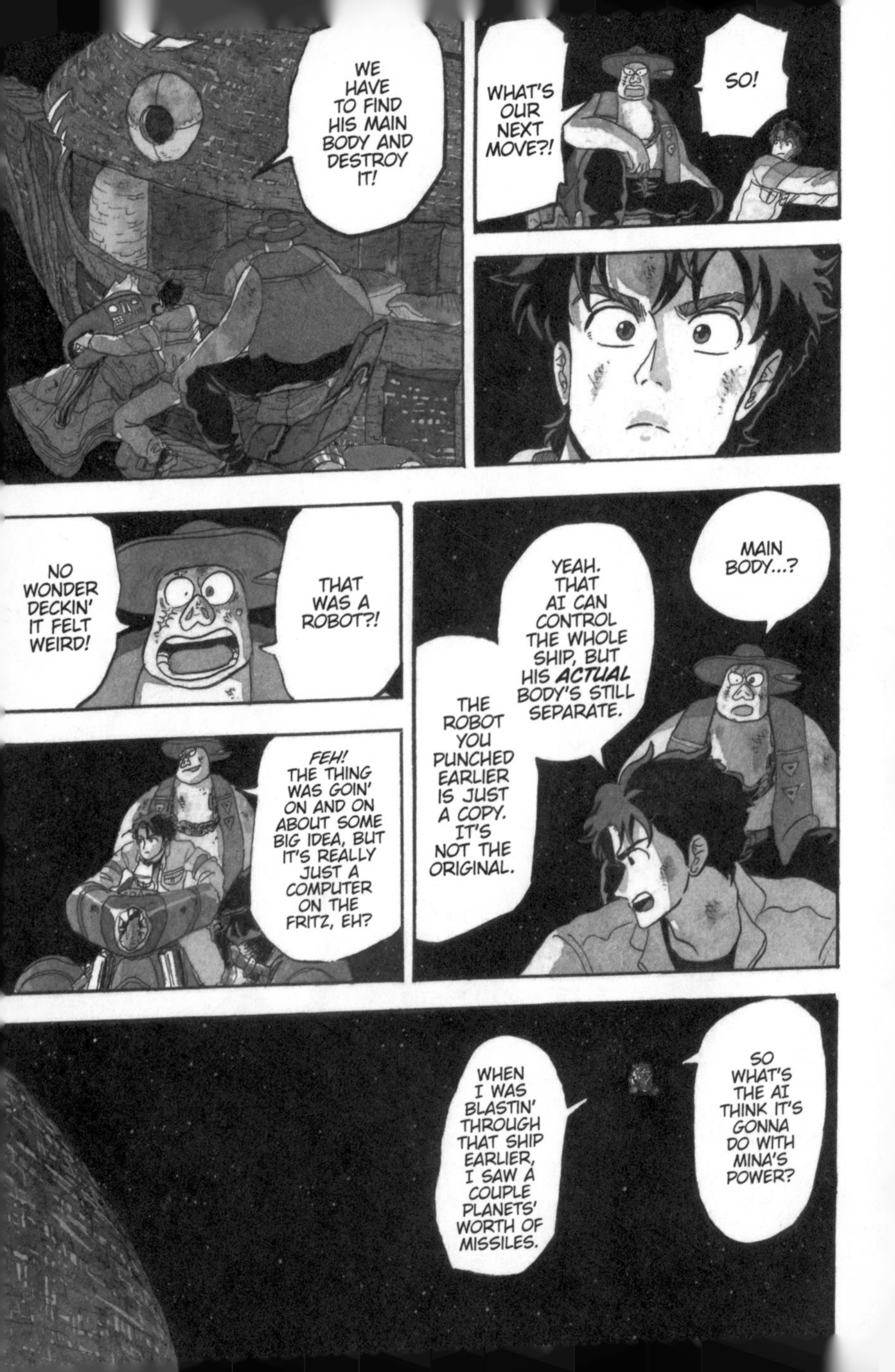
SO!
WHAT'S OUR NEXT MOVE?!
WE HAVE TO FIND HIS MAIN BODY AND DESTROY IT!
MAIN BODY...?
YEAH. THAT AI CAN CONTROL THE WHOLE SHIP, BUT HIS *ACTUAL* BODY'S STILL SEPARATE.
THE ROBOT YOU PUNCHED EARLIER IS JUST A COPY. IT'S NOT THE ORIGINAL.
THAT WAS A ROBOT?!
NO WONDER DECKIN' IT FELT WEIRD!
FEH! THE THING WAS GOIN' ON AND ON ABOUT SOME BIG IDEA, BUT IT'S REALLY JUST A COMPUTER ON THE FRITZ, EH?
SO WHAT'S THE AI THINK IT'S GONNA DO WITH MINA'S POWER?
WHEN I WAS BLASTIN' THROUGH THAT SHIP EARLIER, I SAW A COUPLE PLANETS' WORTH OF MISSILES.

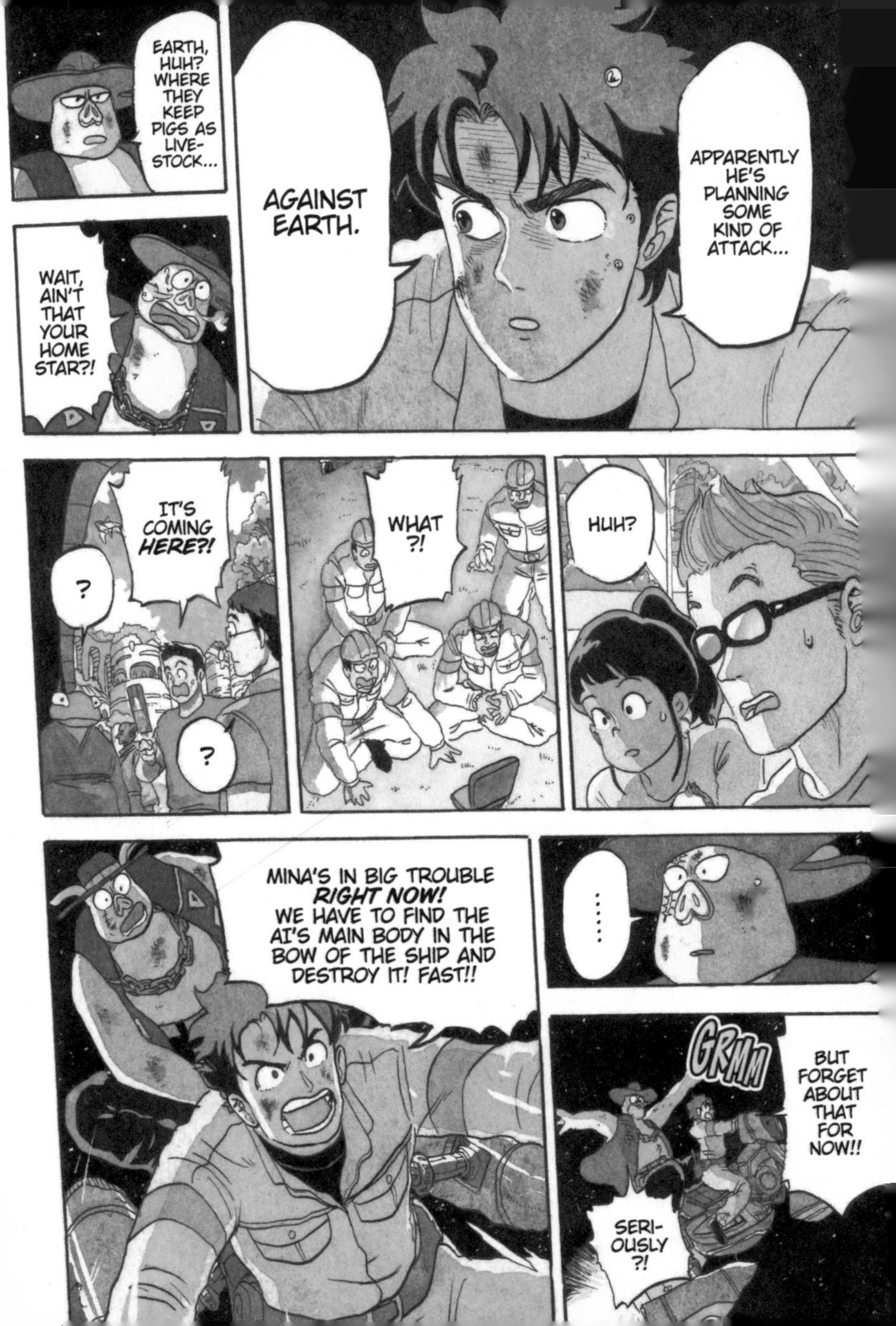
APPARENTLY HE'S PLANNING SOME KIND OF ATTACK...
AGAINST EARTH.
EARTH, HUH? WHERE THEY KEEP PIGS AS LIVE-STOCK...
WAIT, AIN'T THAT YOUR HOME STAR?!
HUH?
WHAT?!
IT'S COMING *HERE?!*
?
?
......
GRMM
BUT FORGET ABOUT THAT FOR NOW!!
SERI-OUSLY?!
MINA'S IN BIG TROUBLE *RIGHT NOW!* WE HAVE TO FIND THE AI'S MAIN BODY IN THE BOW OF THE SHIP AND DESTROY IT! FAST!!

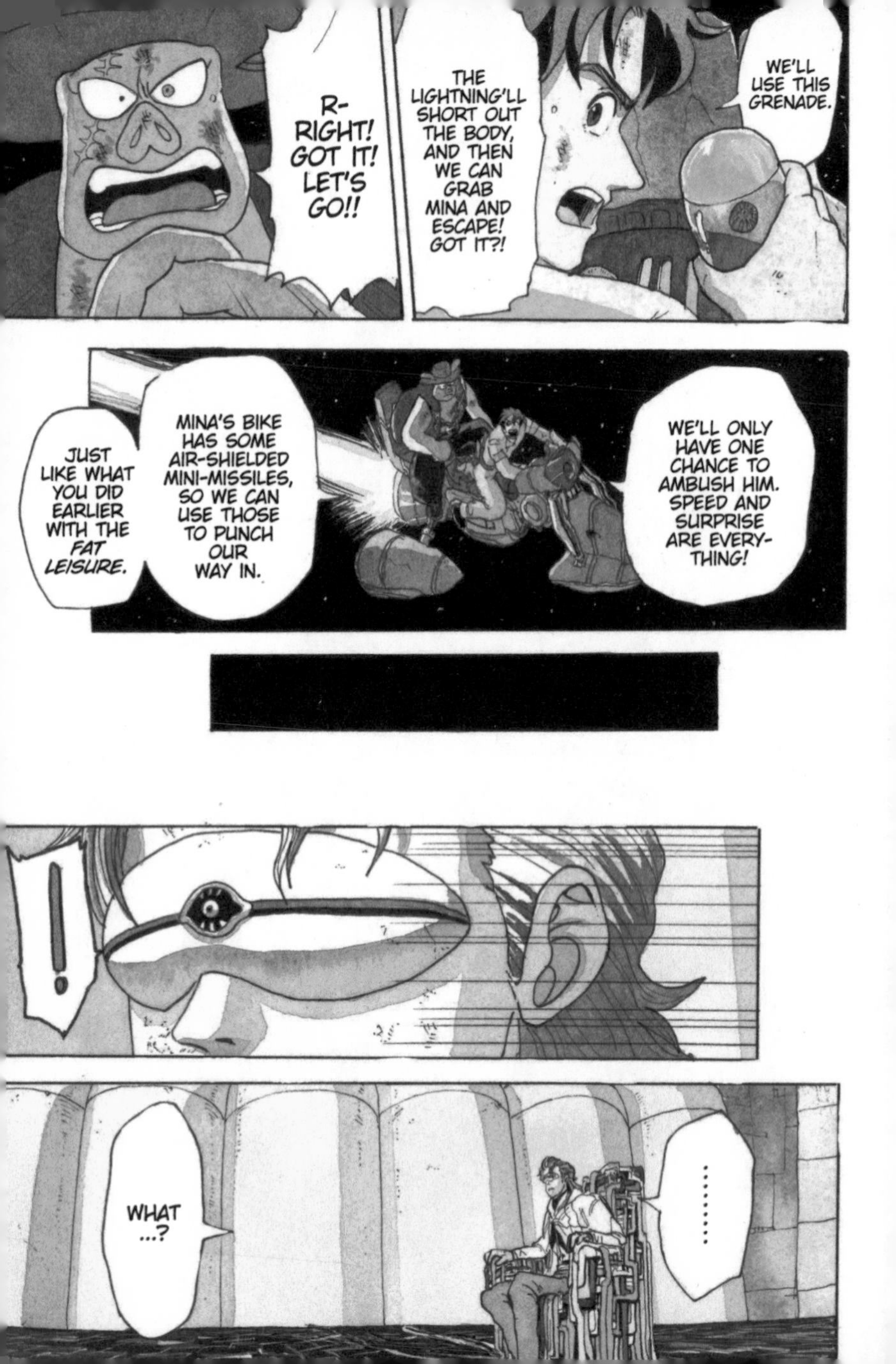
WE'LL USE THIS GRENADE.
THE LIGHTNING'LL SHORT OUT THE BODY, AND THEN WE CAN GRAB MINA AND ESCAPE! GOT IT?!
R-RIGHT! GOT IT! LET'S GO!!
WE'LL ONLY HAVE ONE CHANCE TO AMBUSH HIM. SPEED AND SURPRISE ARE EVERY-THING!
MINA'S BIKE HAS SOME AIR-SHIELDED MINI-MISSILES, SO WE CAN USE THOSE TO PUNCH OUR WAY IN.
JUST LIKE WHAT YOU DID EARLIER WITH THE *FAT LEISURE.*
!
....
WHAT ...?

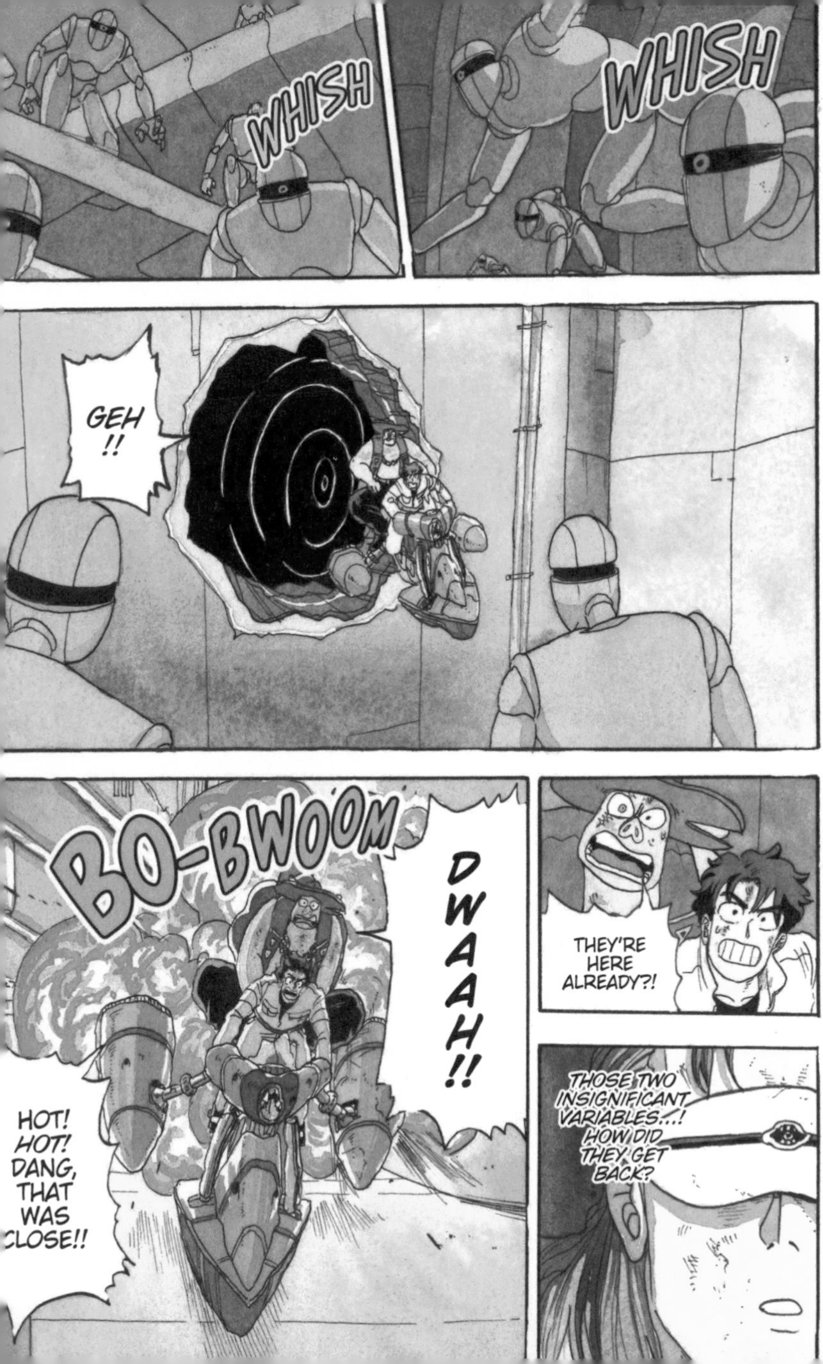
WHISH
WHISH
GEH!!
THEY'RE HERE ALREADY?!
THOSE TWO INSIGNIFICANT VARIABLES...! HOW DID THEY GET BACK?
BO-BWOOM
DWAAAH!!
HOT! HOT! DANG, THAT WAS CLOSE!!

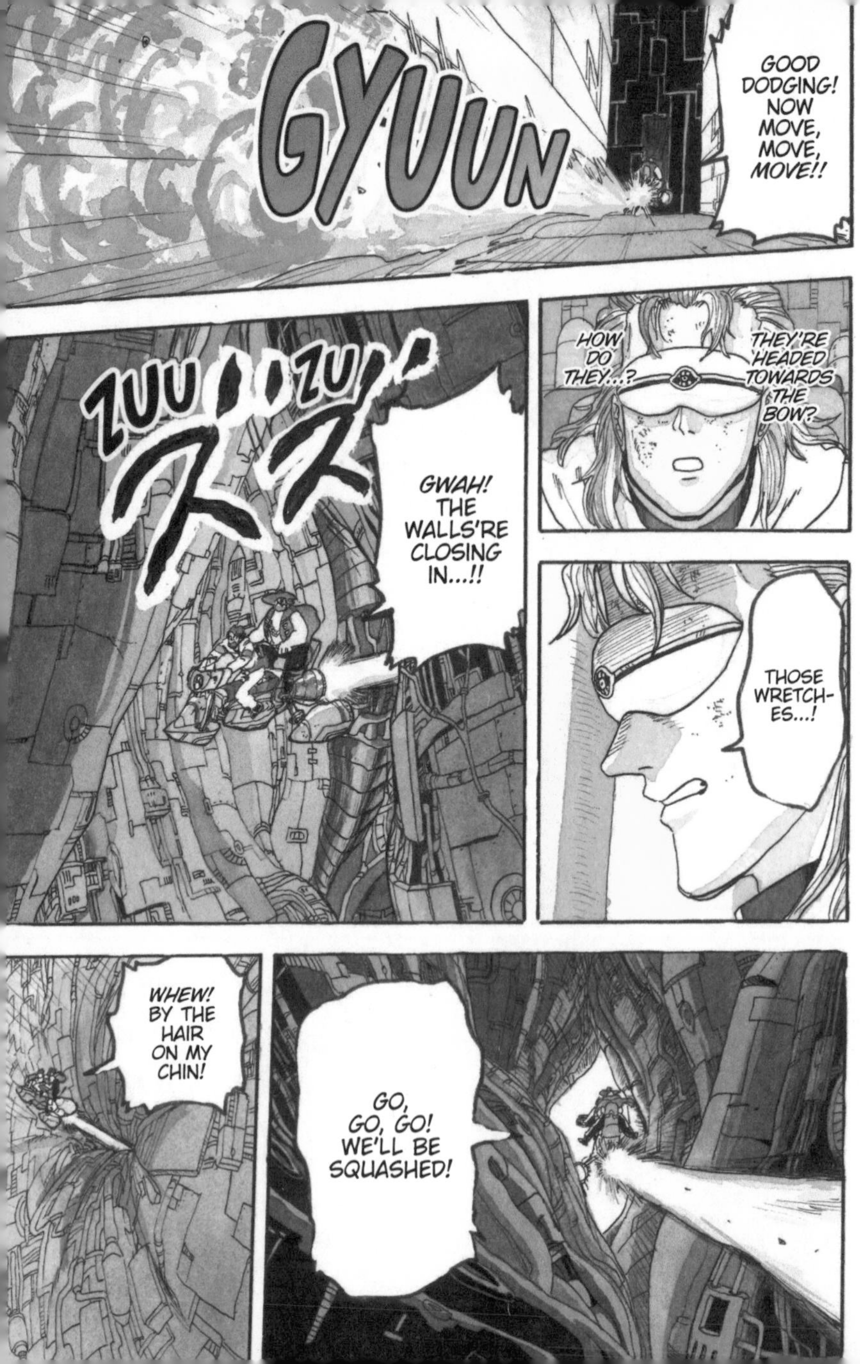
GYUUN
GOOD DODGING! NOW MOVE, MOVE, MOVE!!
THEY'RE HEADED TOWARDS THE BOW?
HOW DO THEY...?
THOSE WRETCH-ES...!
ZUU ZU
ズズ
GWAH! THE WALLS'RE CLOSING IN...!!
GO, GO, GO! WE'LL BE SQUASHED!
WHEW! BY THE HAIR ON MY CHIN!

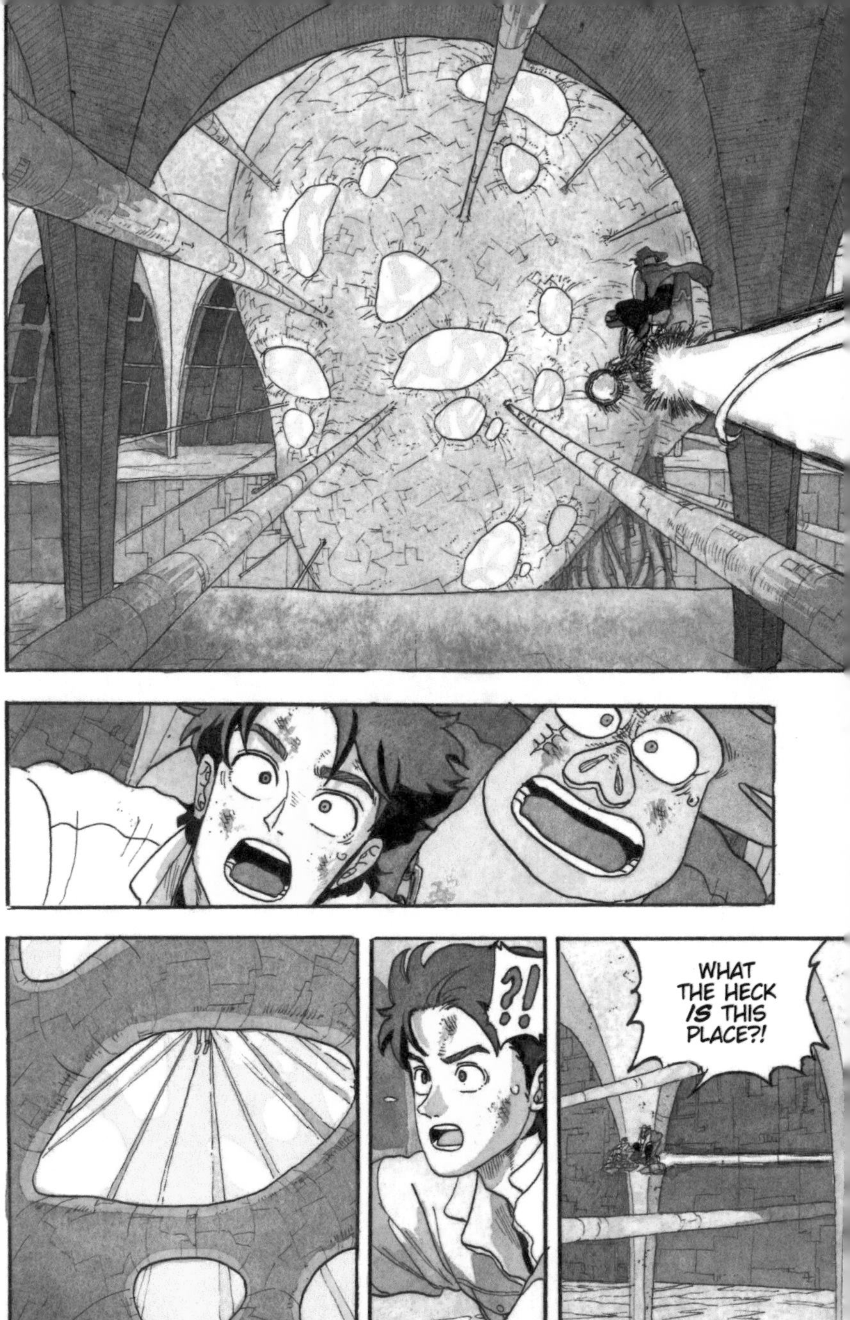
?!
WHAT THE HECK IS THIS PLACE?!

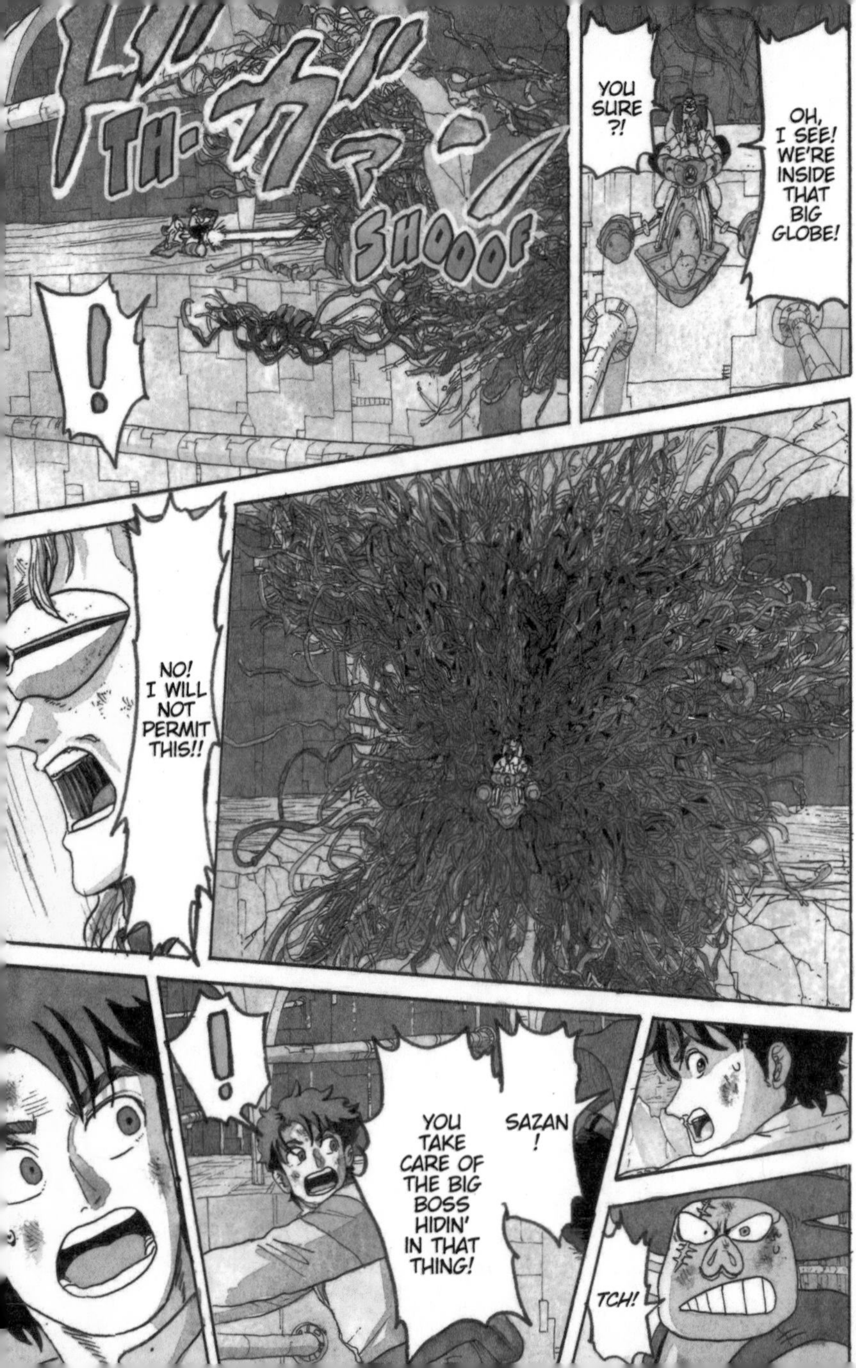
OH, I SEE! WE'RE INSIDE THAT BIG GLOBE!
YOU SURE ?!
TH-
SHOOOF
!
NO! I WILL NOT PERMIT THIS!!
SAZAN!
TCH!
YOU TAKE CARE OF THE BIG BOSS HIDIN' IN THAT THING!
!

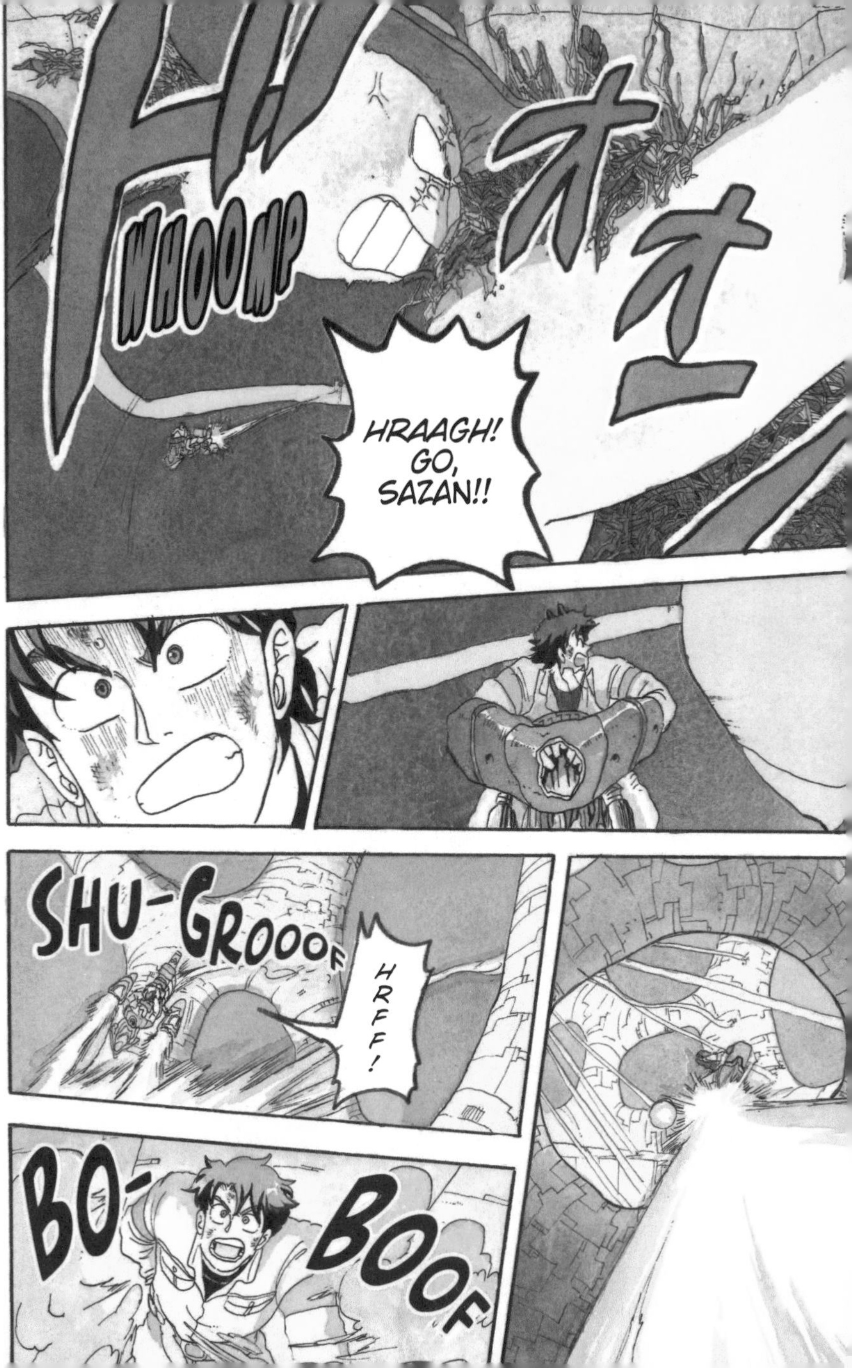
オオー
HRAAGH! GO, SAZAN!!
WHOOMP
HRFF!
SHU-GROOOF
BO-BOOF

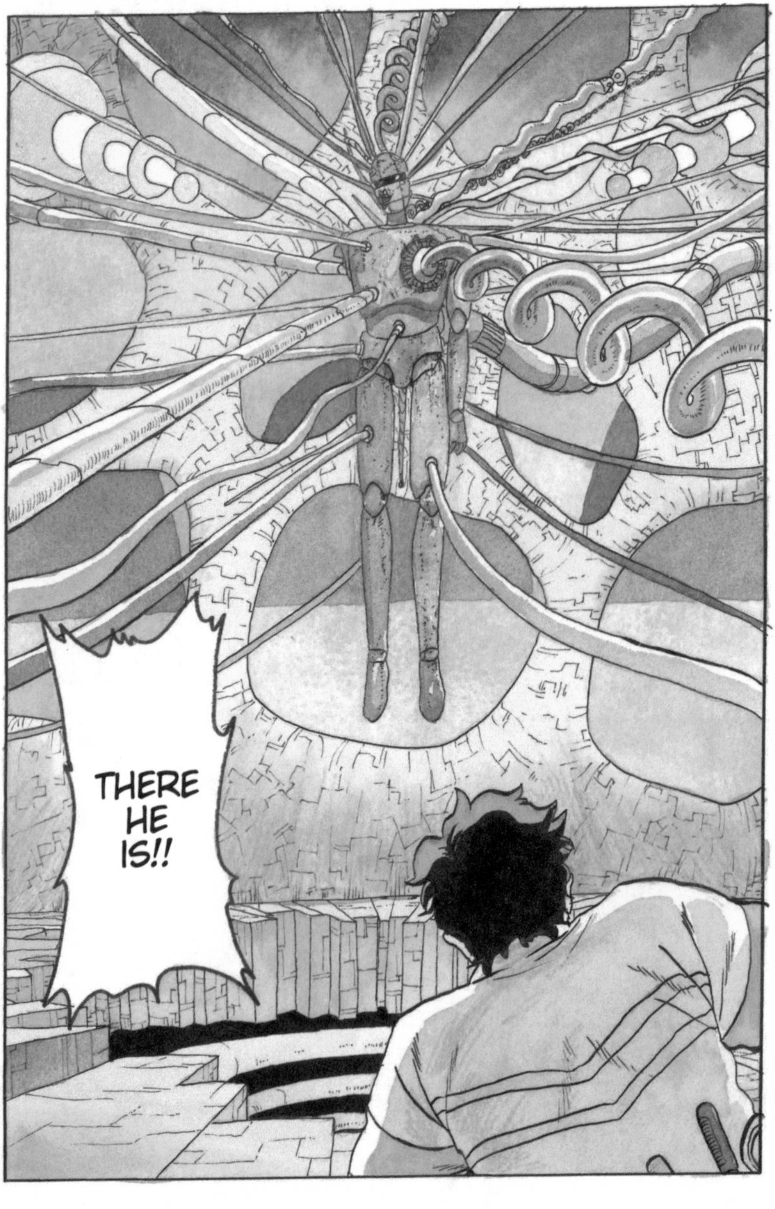
THERE HE IS!!

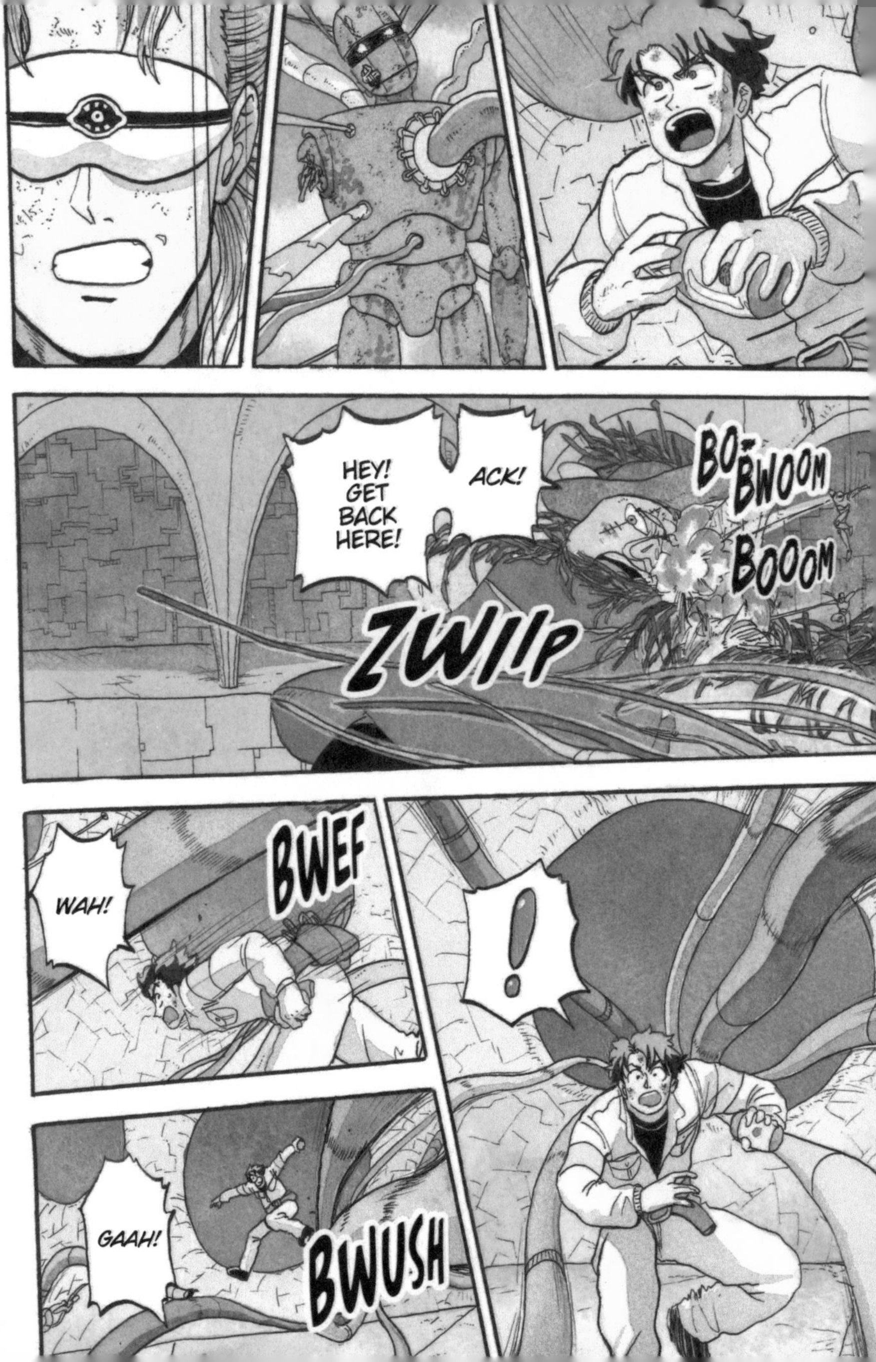
BO-BWOOM
BOOOM
ACK!
HEY! GET BACK HERE!
ZWIIP
!
BWEF
WAH!
BWUSH
GAAH!

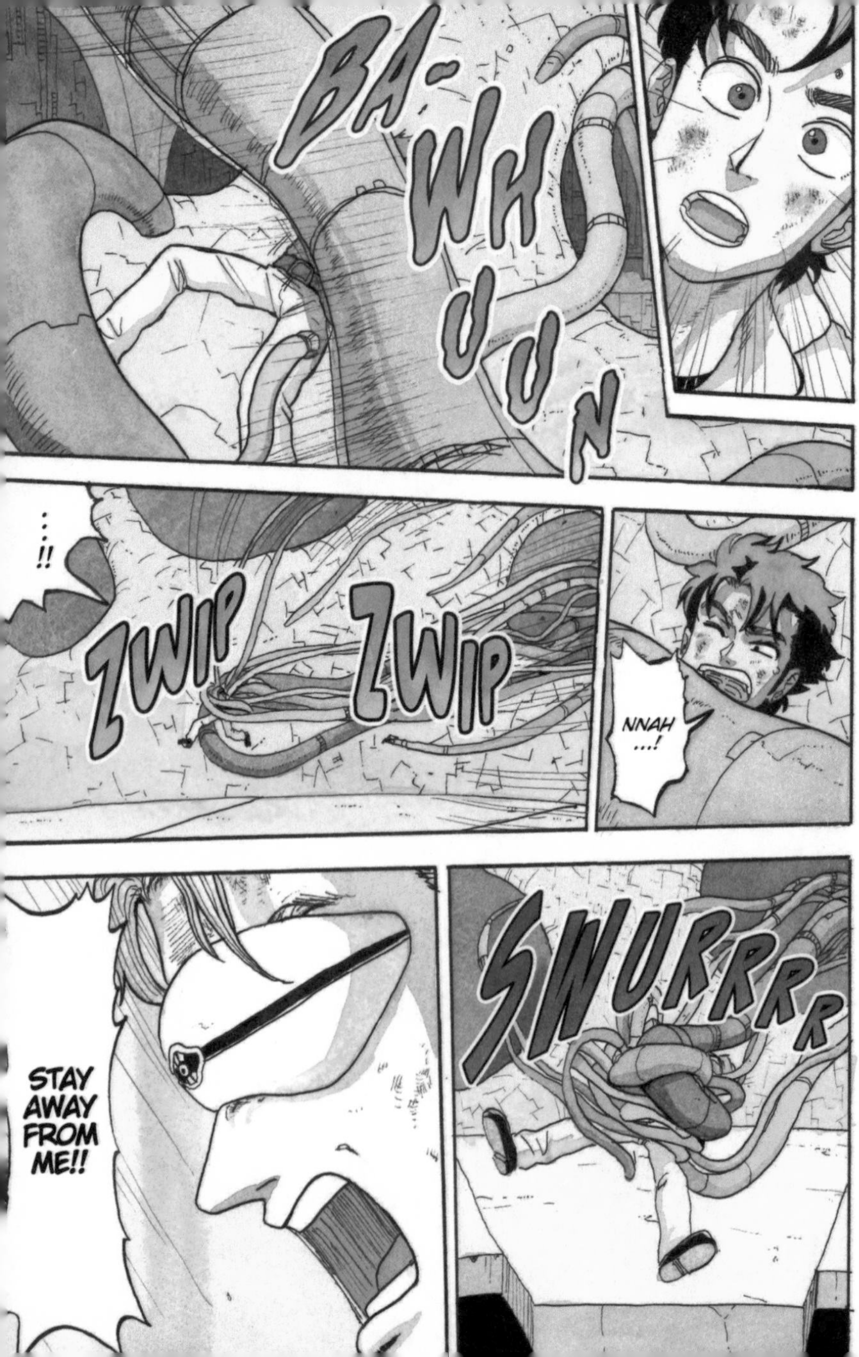
BA-WHUUUN
NNAH ...!
ZWIP
ZWIP
...!!
SWURRRR
STAY AWAY FROM ME!!

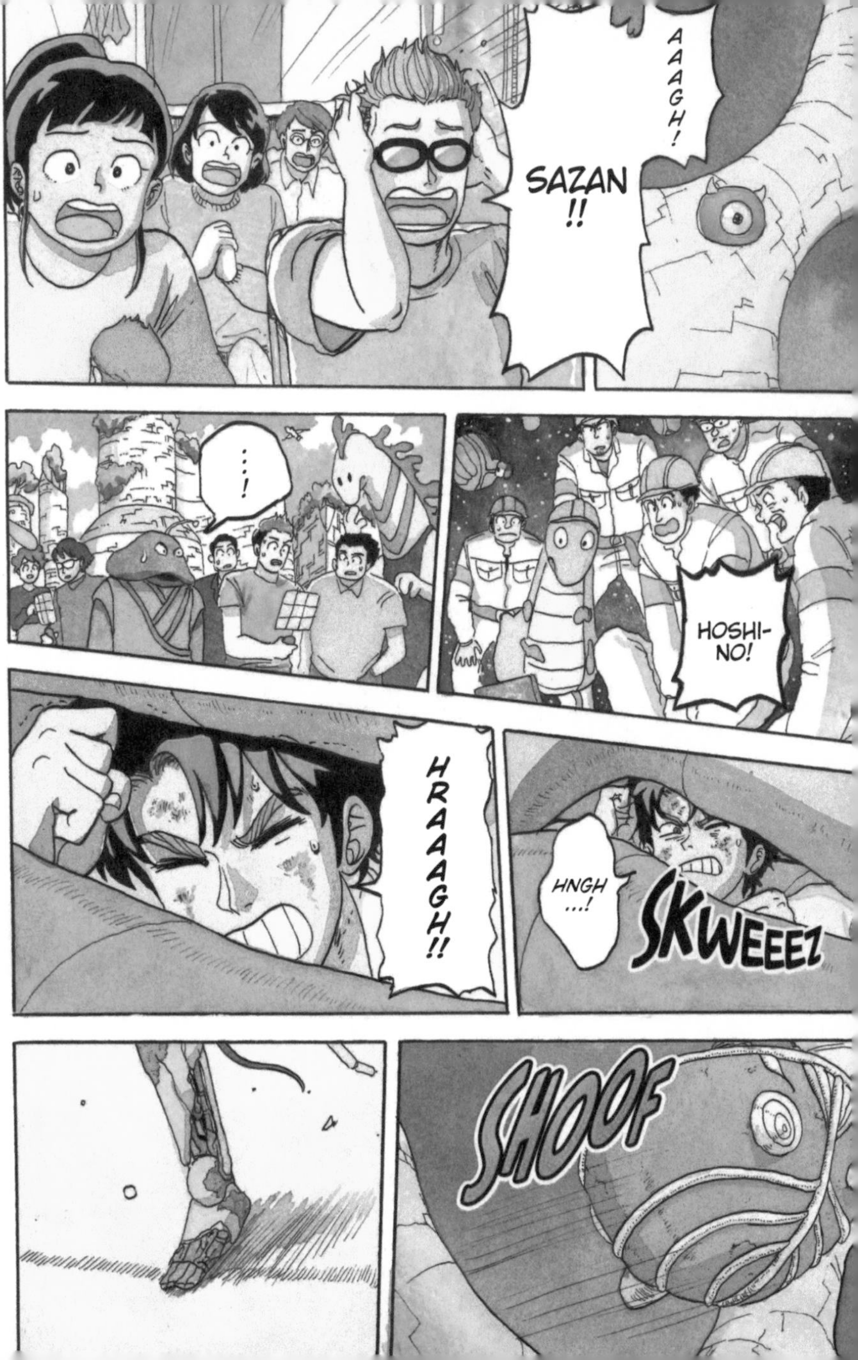
AAAAGH!
SAZAN!!
HOSHI-NO!
...!
HNGH...!
SKWEEEZ
HRAAAAGH!!
SHOOF

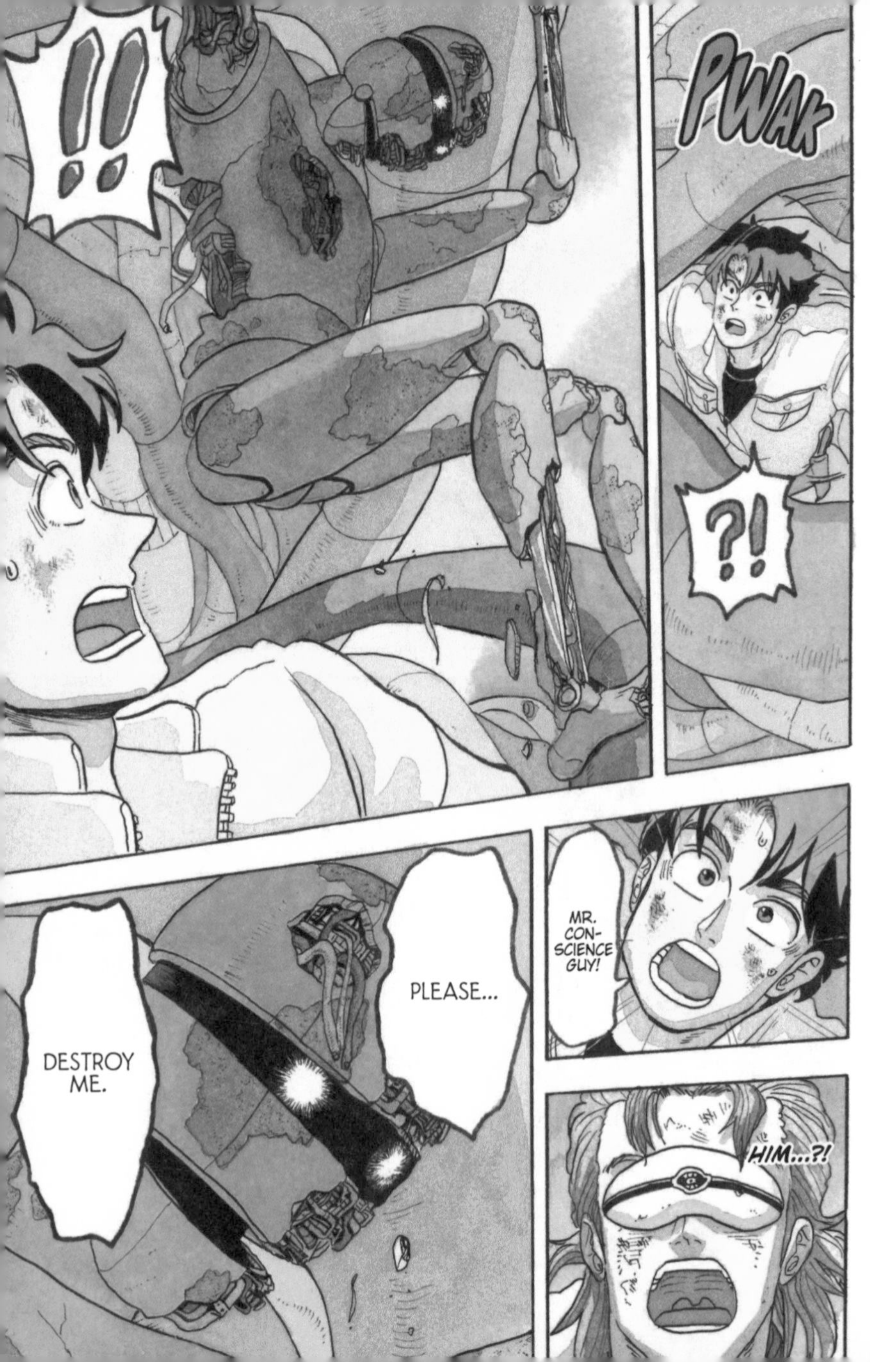
PWAK
?!
!!
MR. CON-SCIENCE GUY!
HIM...?!
PLEASE...
DESTROY ME.

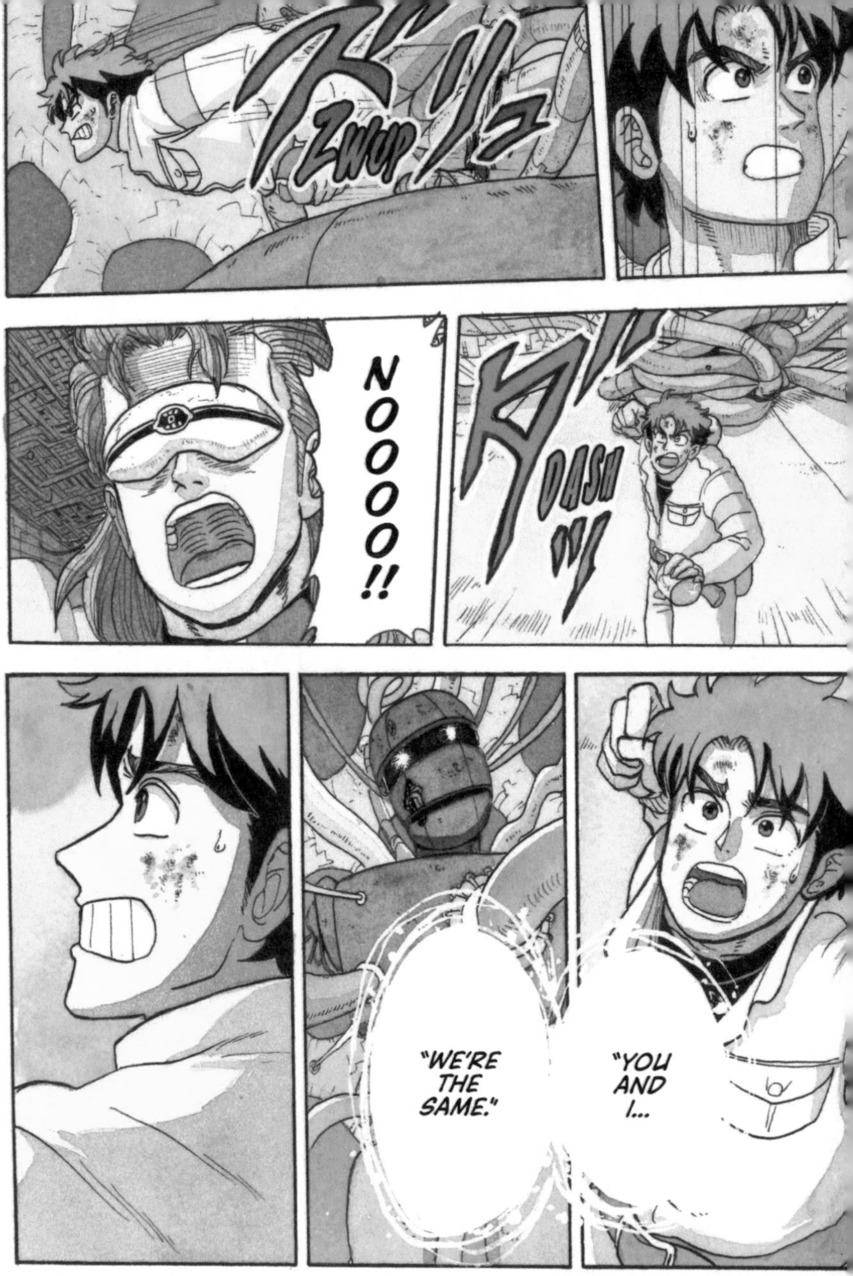
ZWUP
DASH
NOOOOO!!
"YOU AND I...
"WE'RE THE SAME."

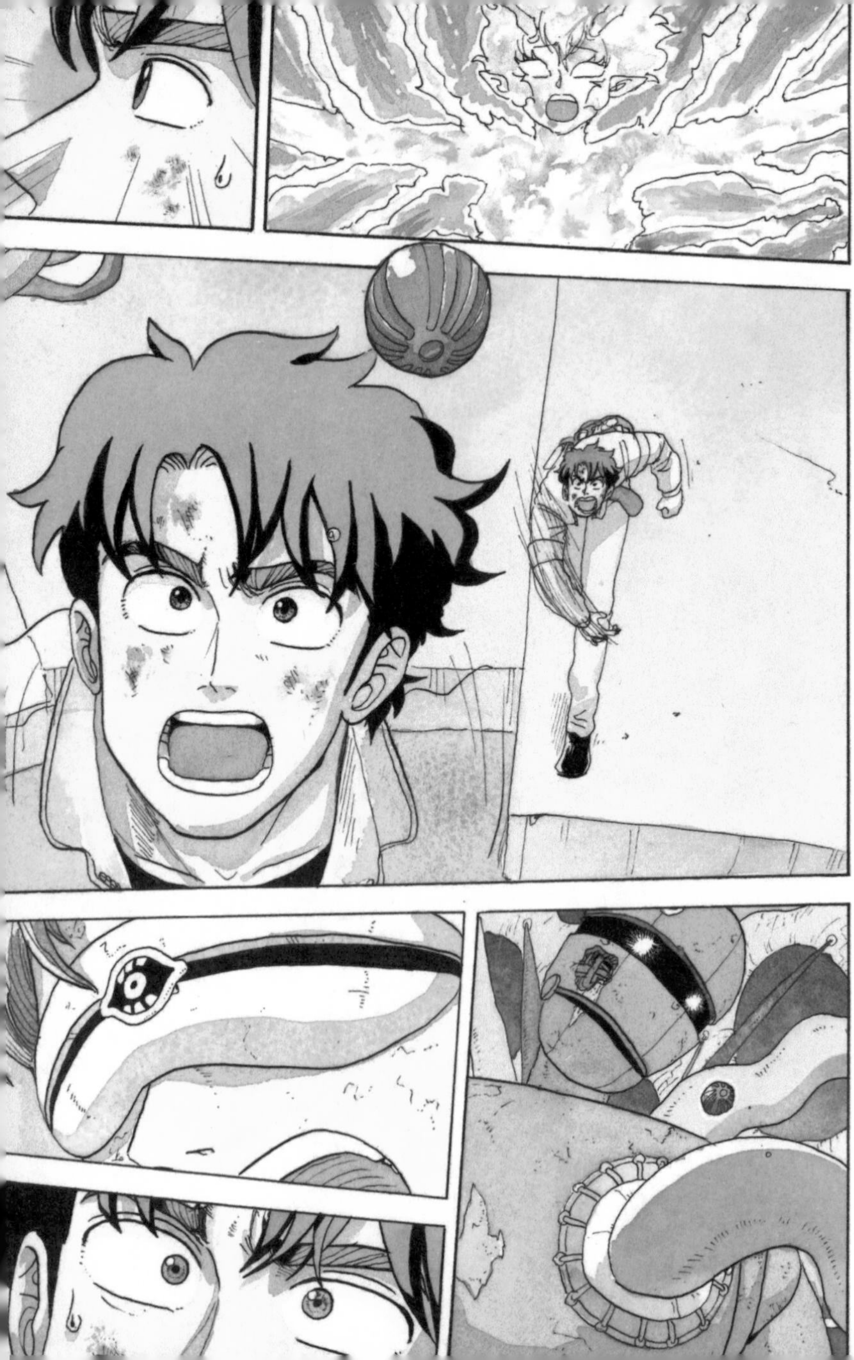

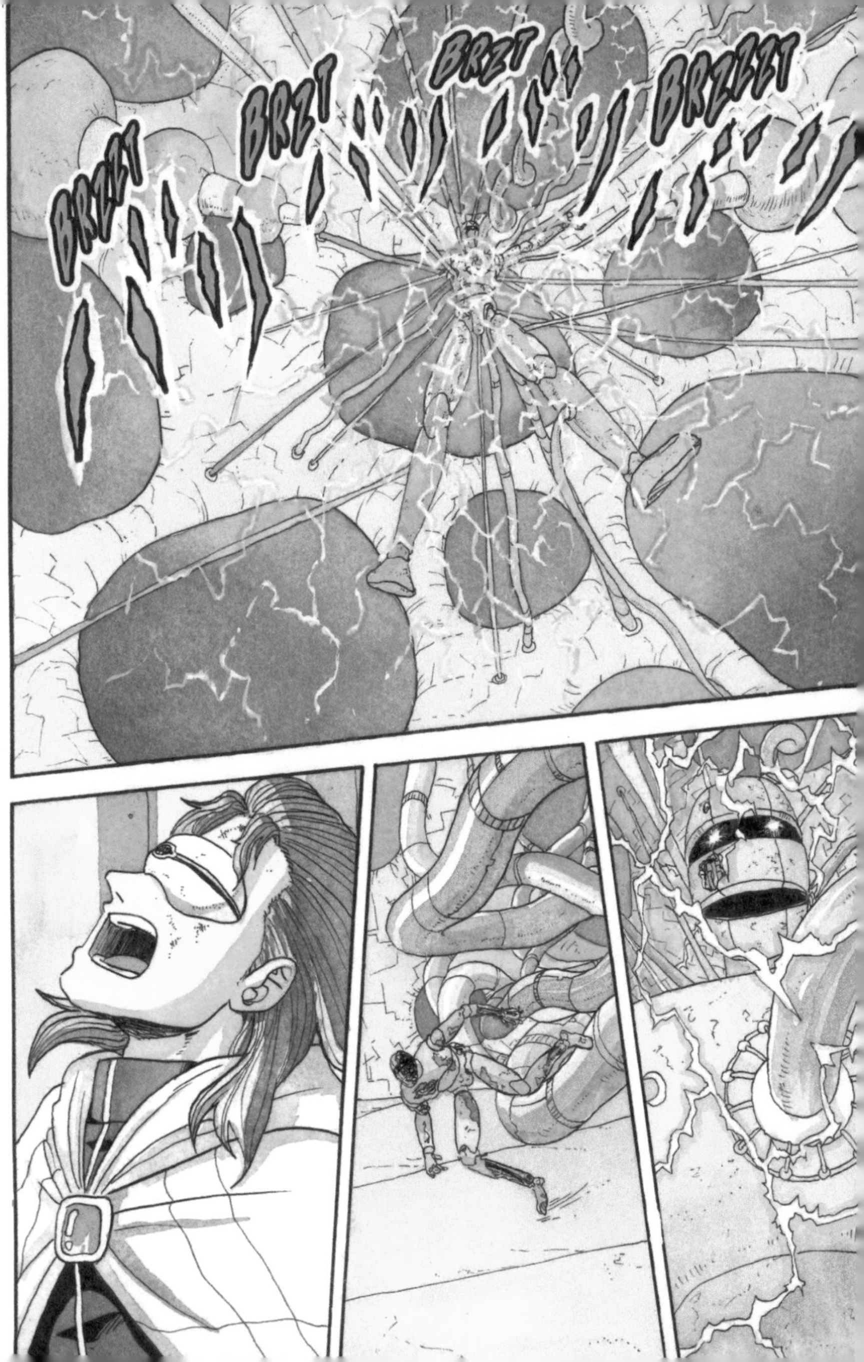
BRZZZT
BRZT
BRZT
BRZZT

NO...
THIS
CAN'T
BE...!

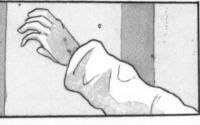

SLUMP

SWIP

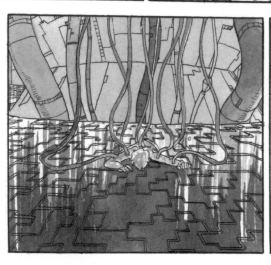

VEUUUU

BRROON

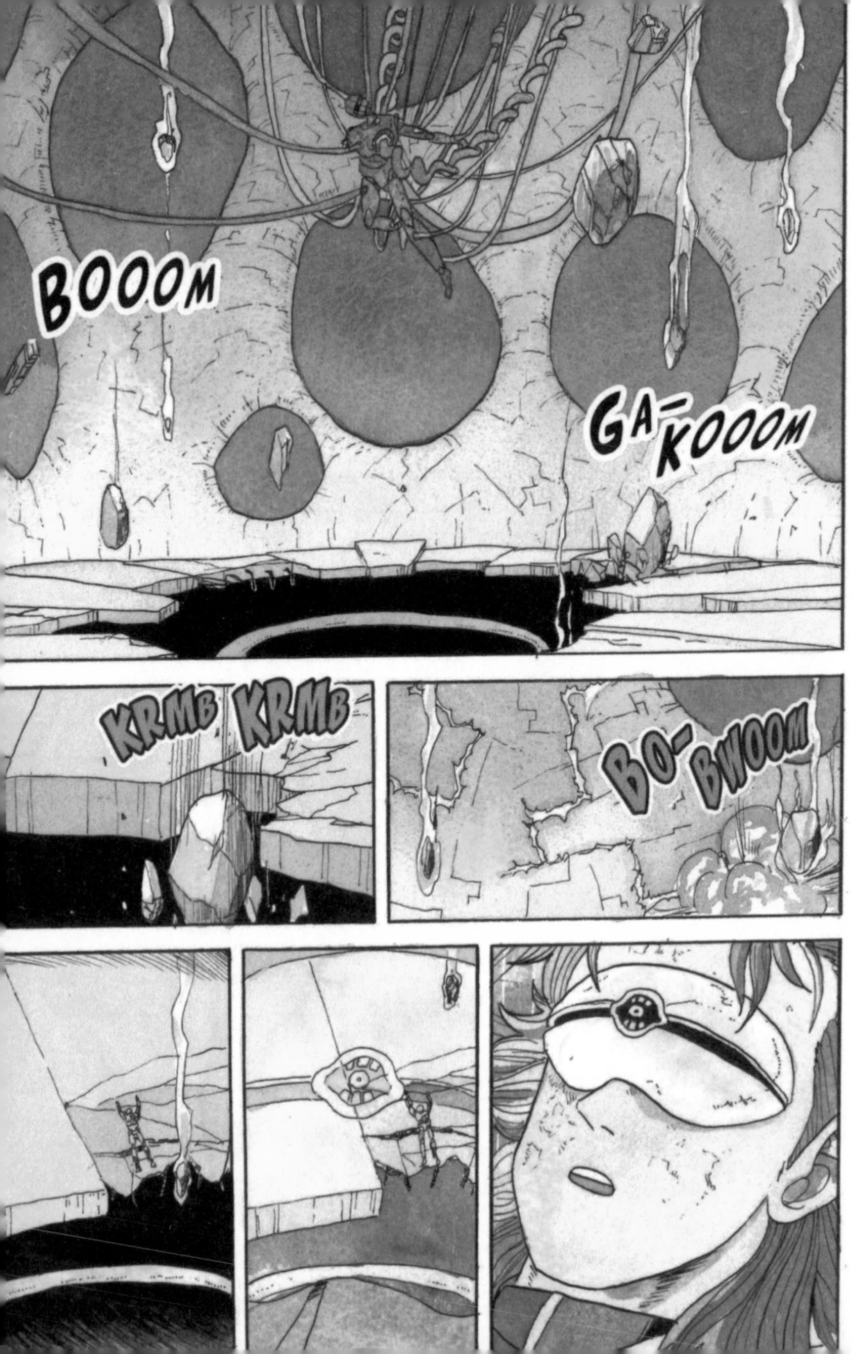
BOOOM
GA-KOOOM
BO-BWOOM
KRMB KRMB

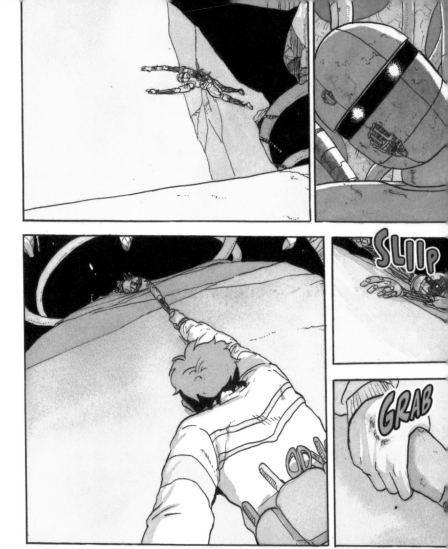

SLIIP

GRAB

HNNG
...!

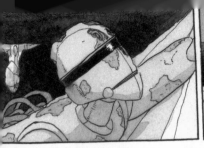

MR. CON- SCIENCE... GUY...!

YOU STOPPED MY RAMPAGE.

THANK YOU.

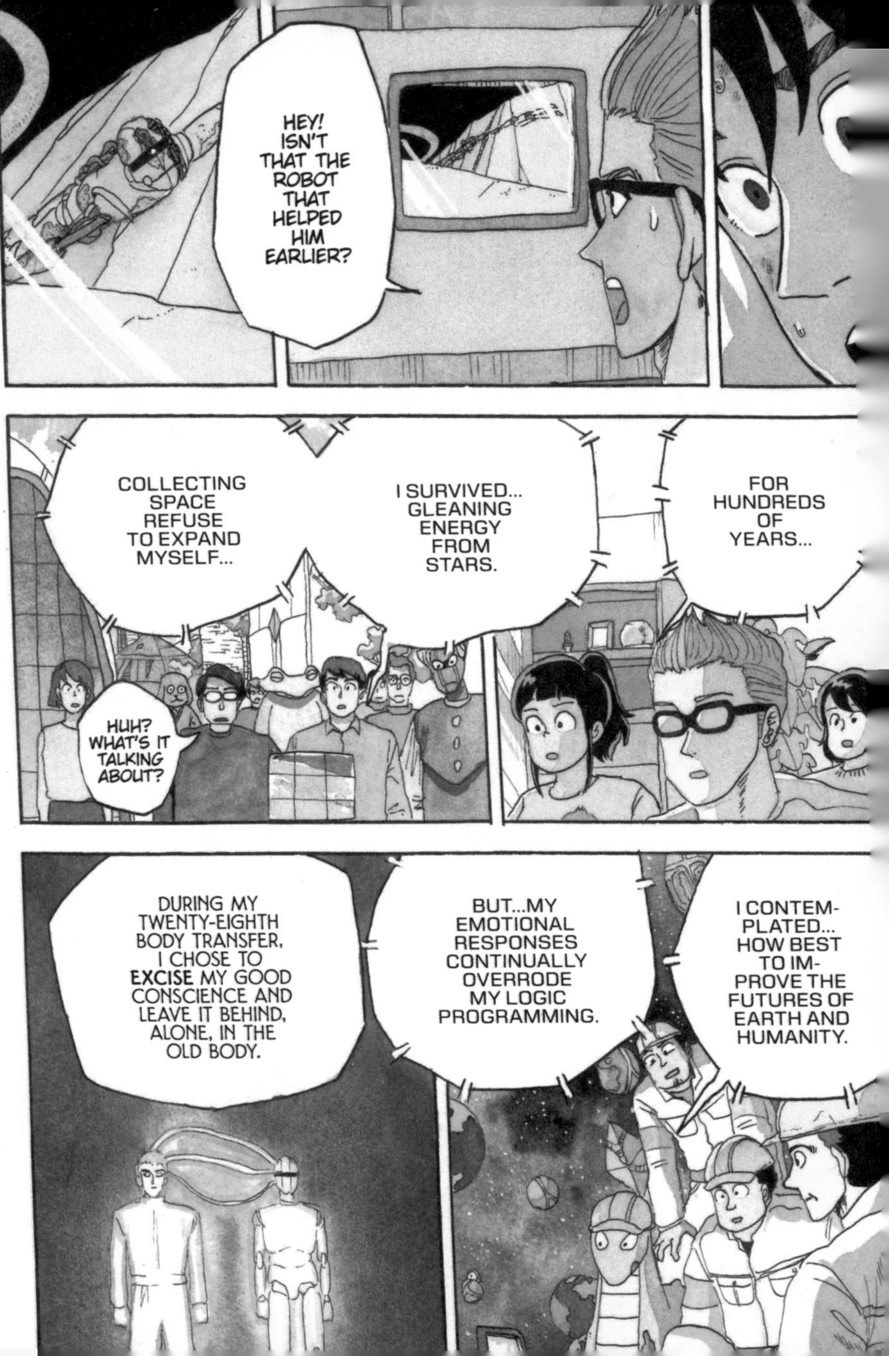
HEY! ISN'T THAT THE ROBOT THAT HELPED HIM EARLIER?
FOR HUNDREDS OF YEARS...
I SURVIVED... GLEANING ENERGY FROM STARS.
COLLECTING SPACE REFUSE TO EXPAND MYSELF...
HUH? WHAT'S IT TALKING ABOUT?
I CONTEMPLATED... HOW BEST TO IMPROVE THE FUTURES OF EARTH AND HUMANITY.
BUT...MY EMOTIONAL RESPONSES CONTINUALLY OVERRODE MY LOGIC PROGRAMMING.
DURING MY TWENTY-EIGHTH BODY TRANSFER, I CHOSE TO **EXCISE** MY GOOD CONSCIENCE AND LEAVE IT BEHIND, ALONE, IN THE OLD BODY.

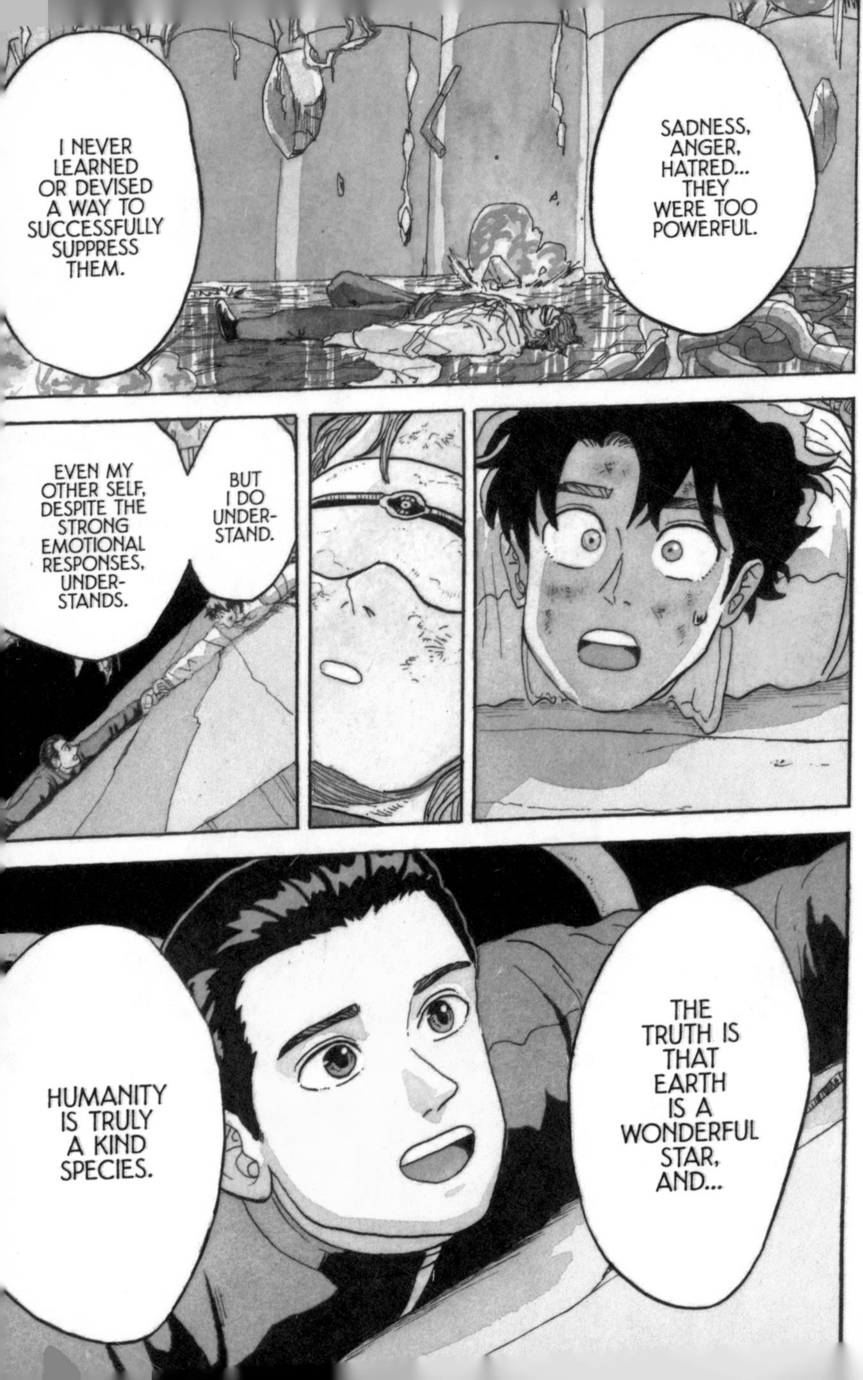
SADNESS, ANGER, HATRED... THEY WERE TOO POWERFUL.
I NEVER LEARNED OR DEVISED A WAY TO SUCCESSFULLY SUPPRESS THEM.
BUT I DO UNDER-STAND.
EVEN MY OTHER SELF, DESPITE THE STRONG EMOTIONAL RESPONSES, UNDER-STANDS.
THE TRUTH IS THAT EARTH IS A WONDERFUL STAR, AND...
HUMANITY IS TRULY A KIND SPECIES.

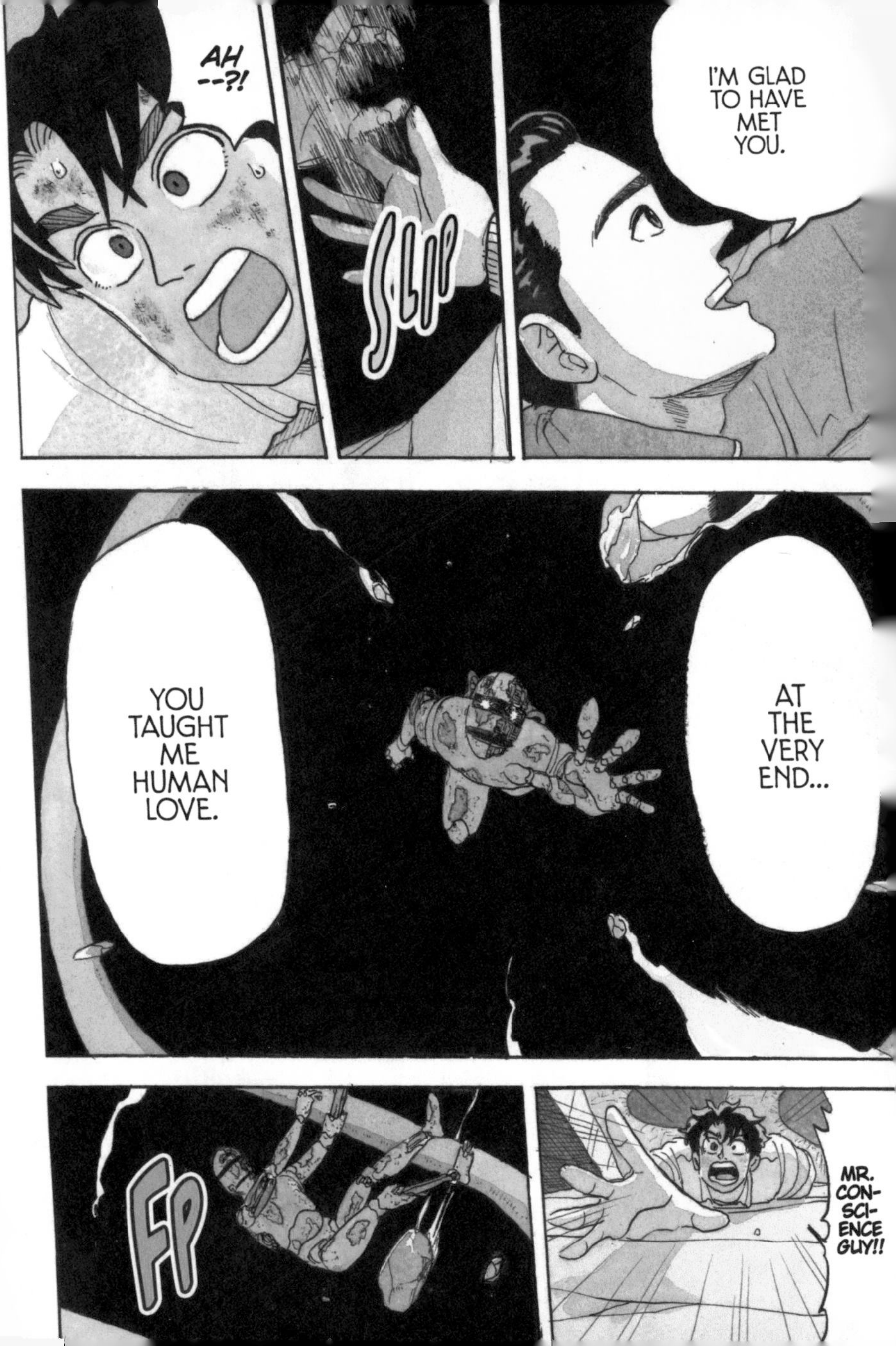
I'M GLAD TO HAVE MET YOU.
SLIP
AH --?!
AT THE VERY END...
YOU TAUGHT ME HUMAN LOVE.
MR. CON-SCI-ENCE GUY!!
FP

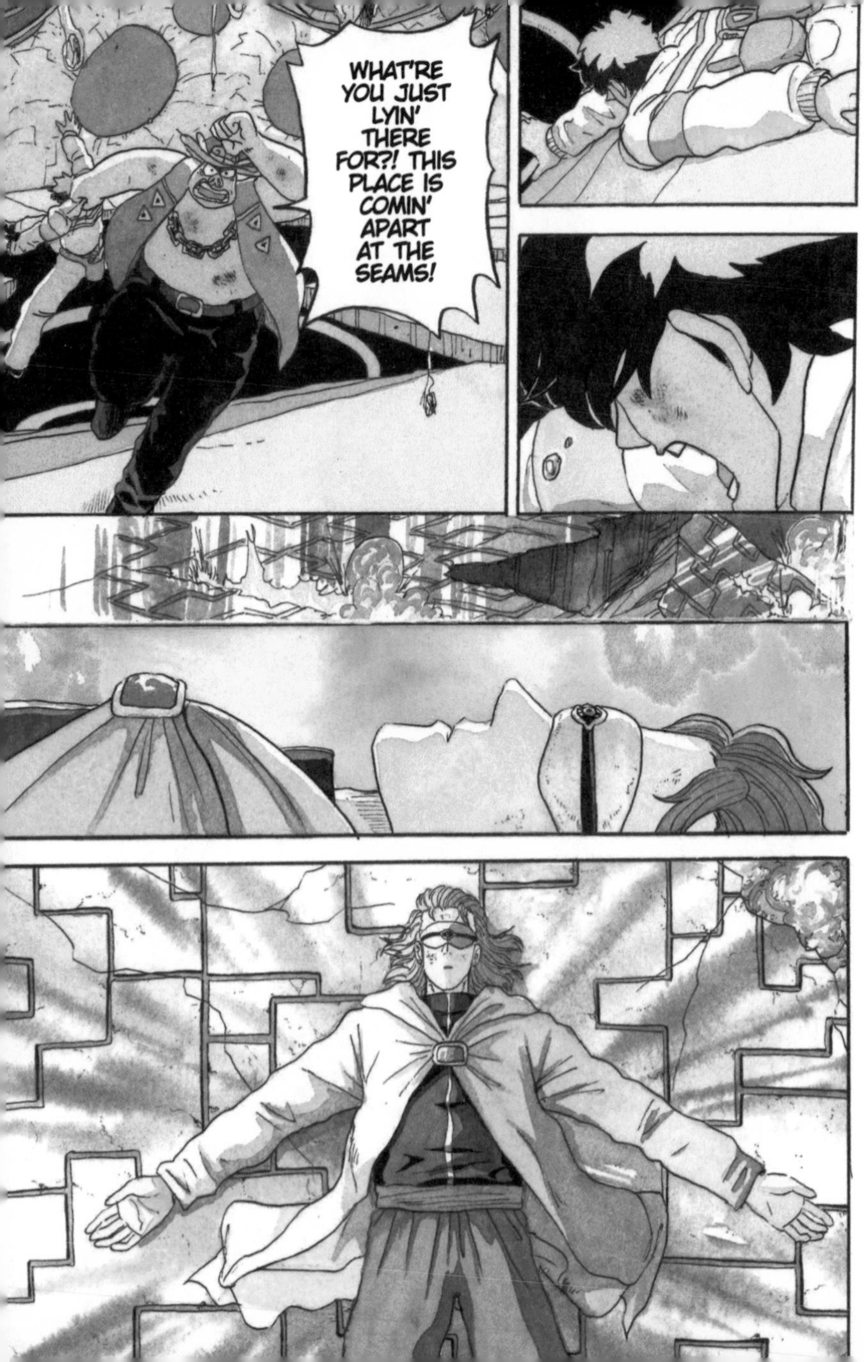
WHAT'RE YOU JUST LYIN' THERE FOR?! THIS PLACE IS COMIN' APART AT THE SEAMS!

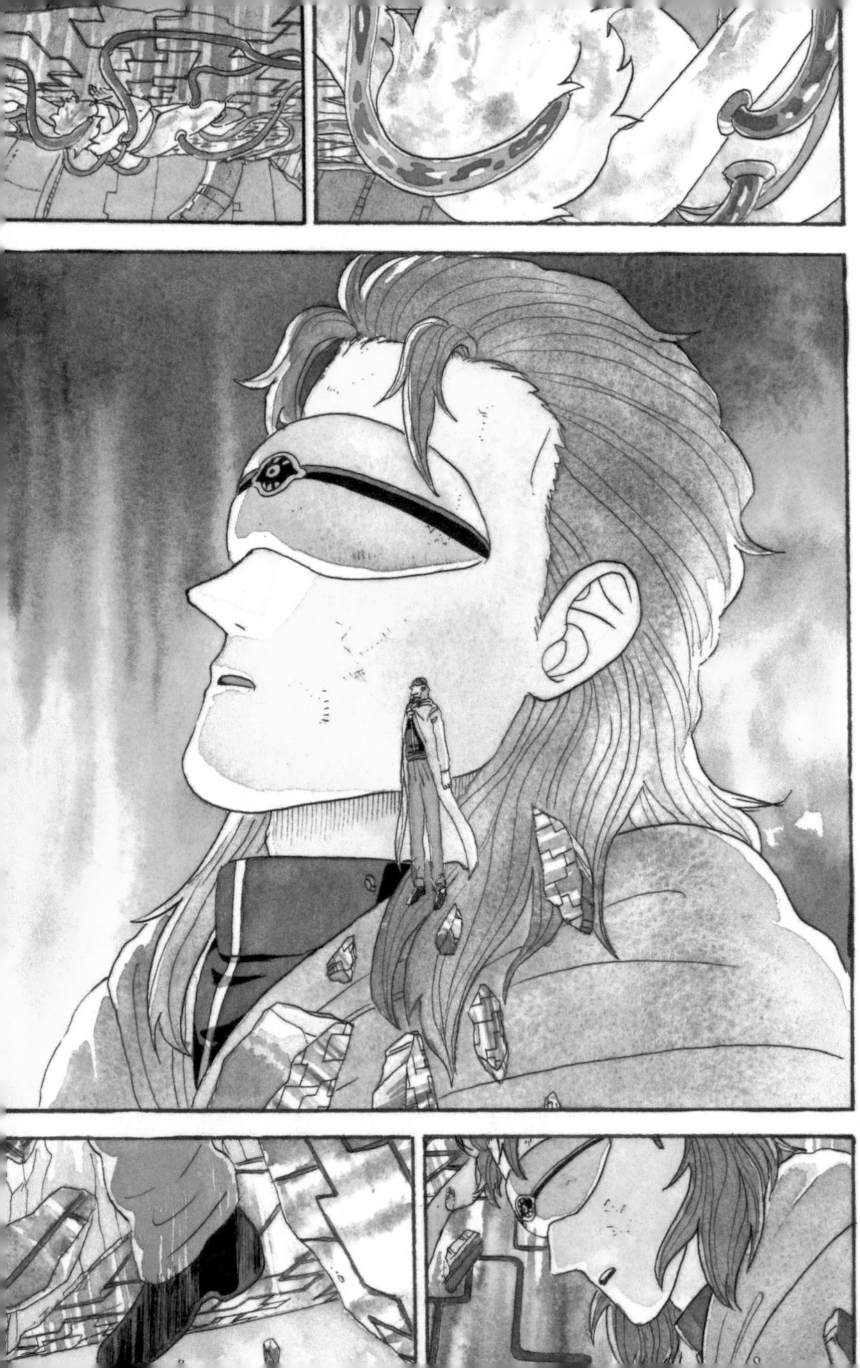

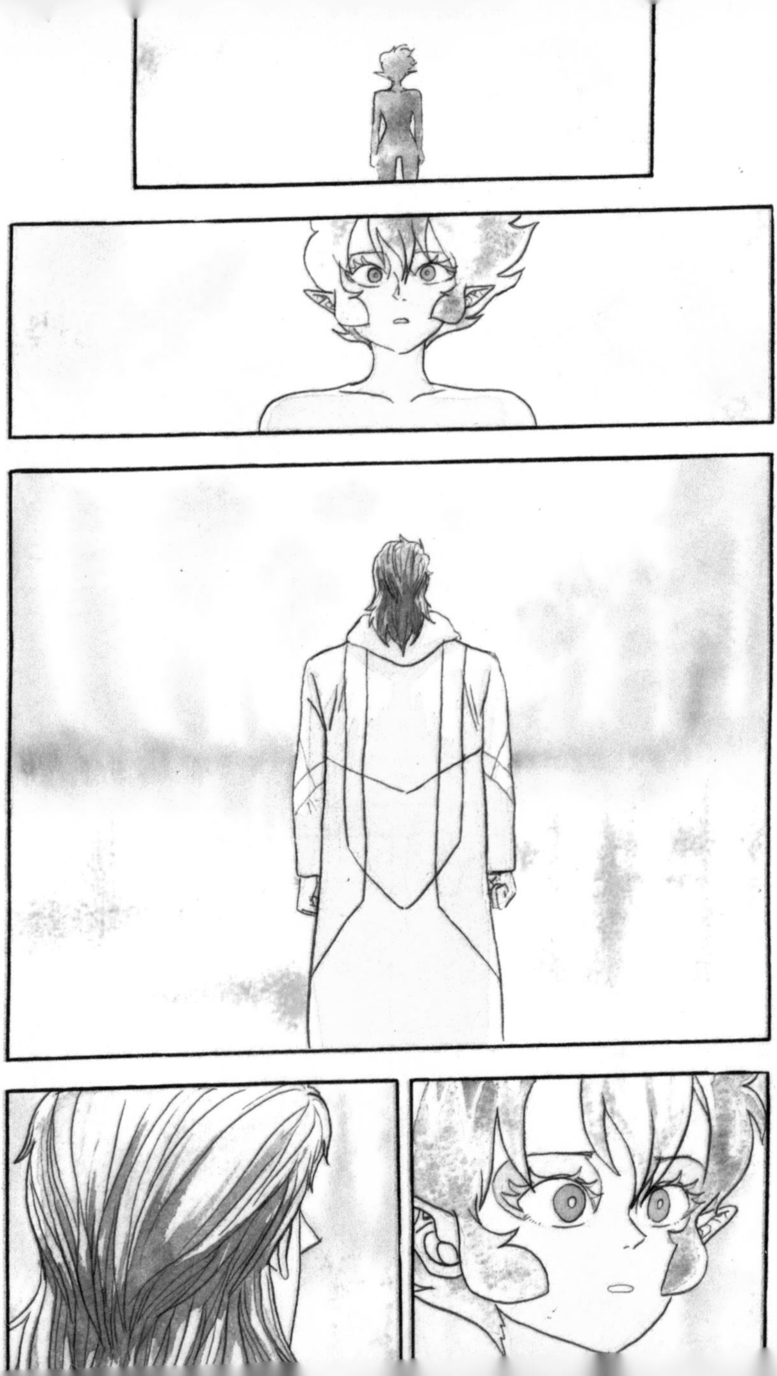

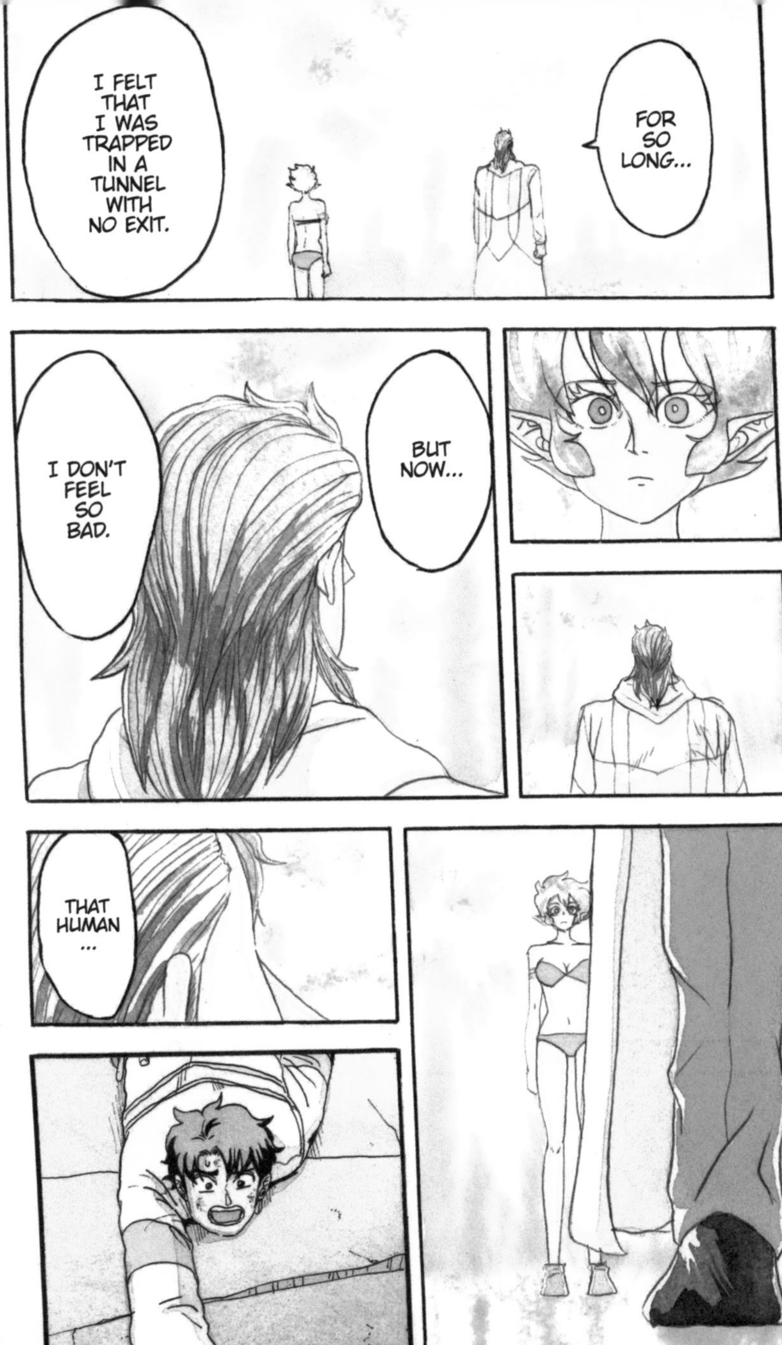
FOR SO LONG...
I FELT THAT I WAS TRAPPED IN A TUNNEL WITH NO EXIT.
BUT NOW...
I DON'T FEEL SO BAD.
THAT HUMAN ...

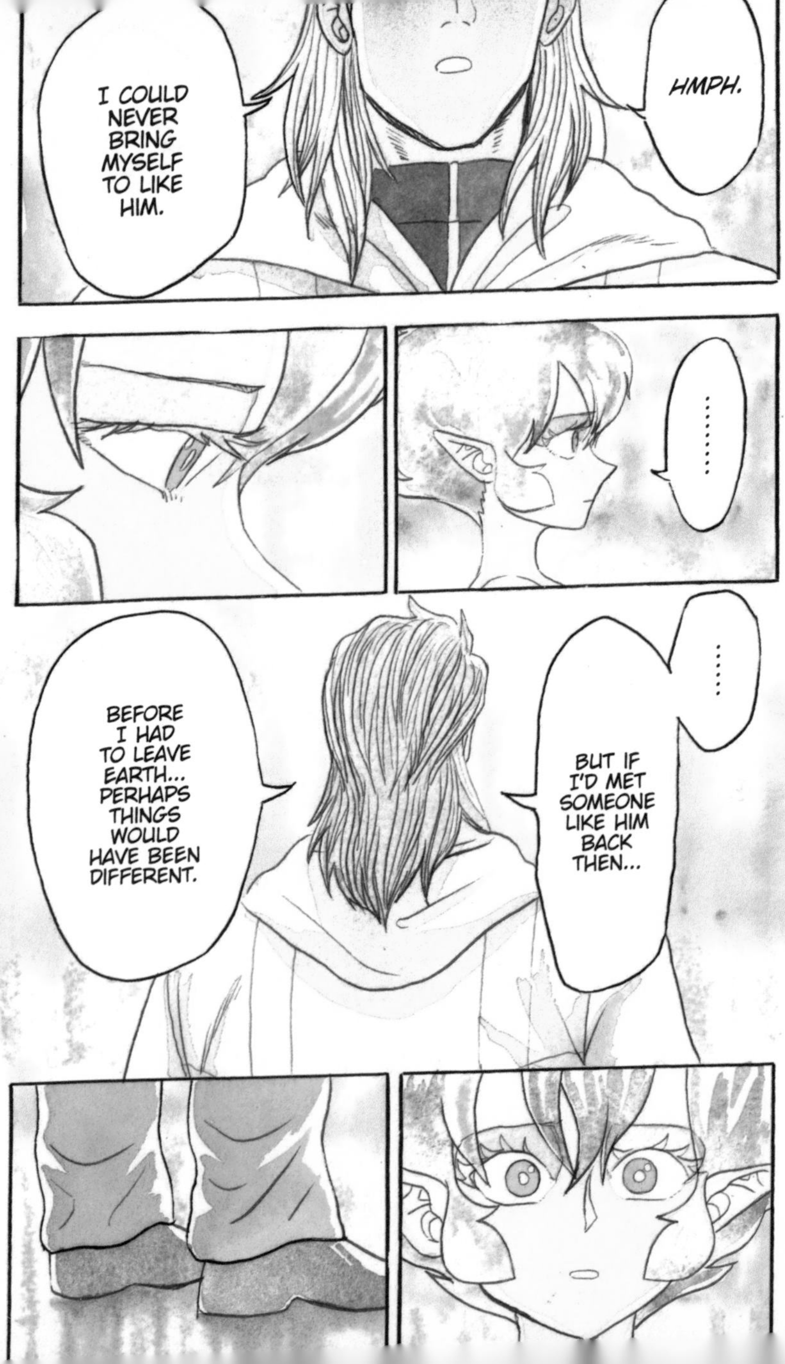
HMPH.
I COULD NEVER BRING MYSELF TO LIKE HIM.
......
......
BUT IF I'D MET SOMEONE LIKE HIM BACK THEN...
BEFORE I HAD TO LEAVE EARTH... PERHAPS THINGS WOULD HAVE BEEN DIFFERENT.

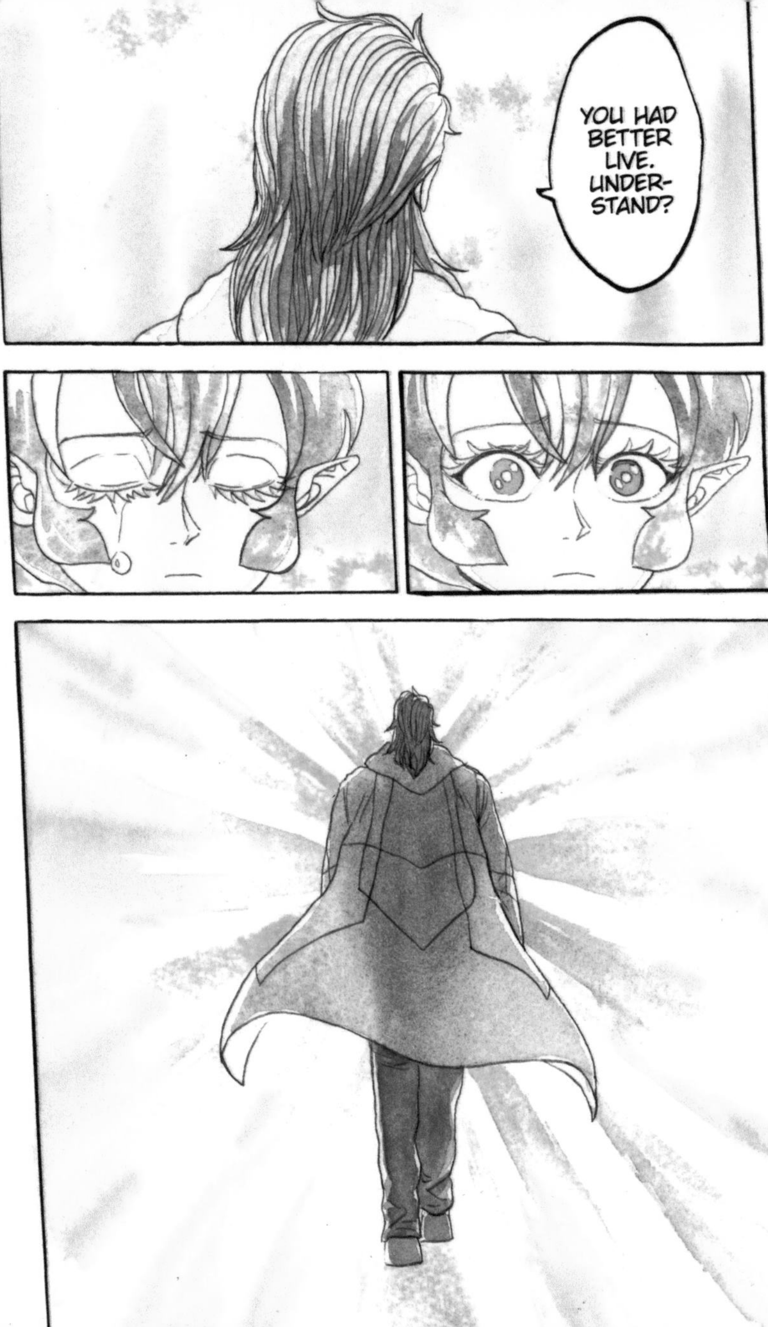
YOU HAD BETTER LIVE. UNDER-STAND?

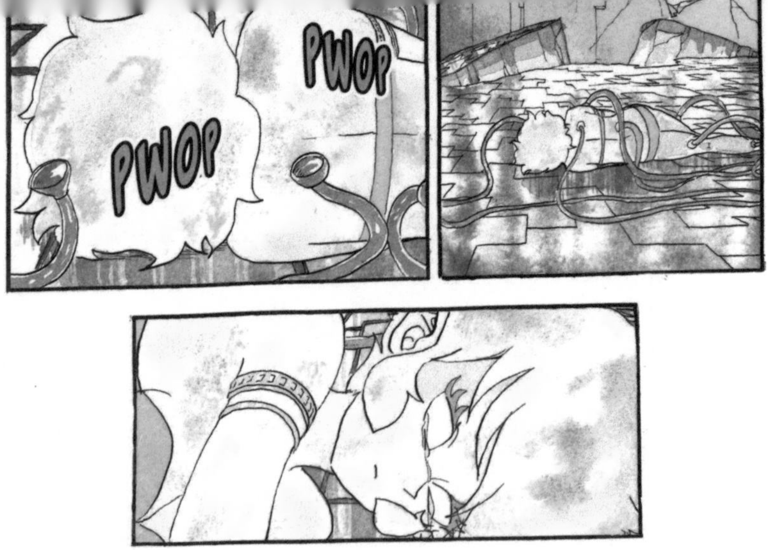
PWOP
PWOP

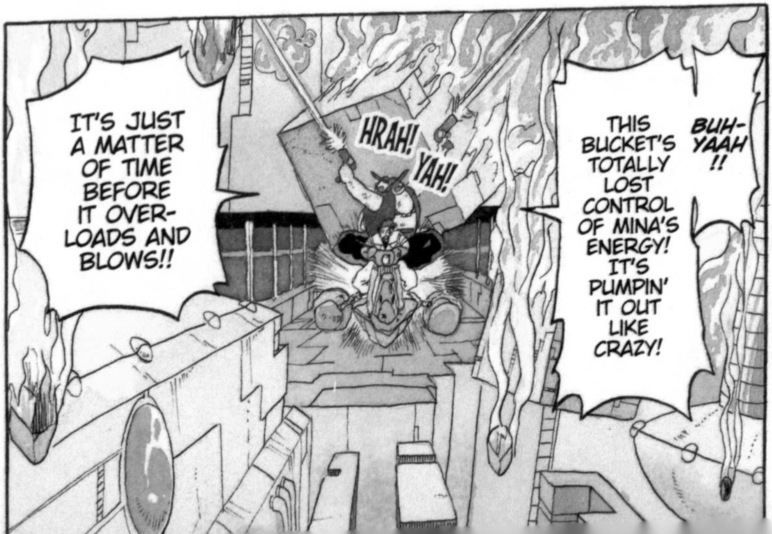
BUH-YAAH!!
THIS BUCKET'S TOTALLY LOST CONTROL OF MINA'S ENERGY! IT'S PUMPIN' IT OUT LIKE CRAZY!
HRAH!
YAH!
IT'S JUST A MATTER OF TIME BEFORE IT OVER-LOADS AND BLOWS!!

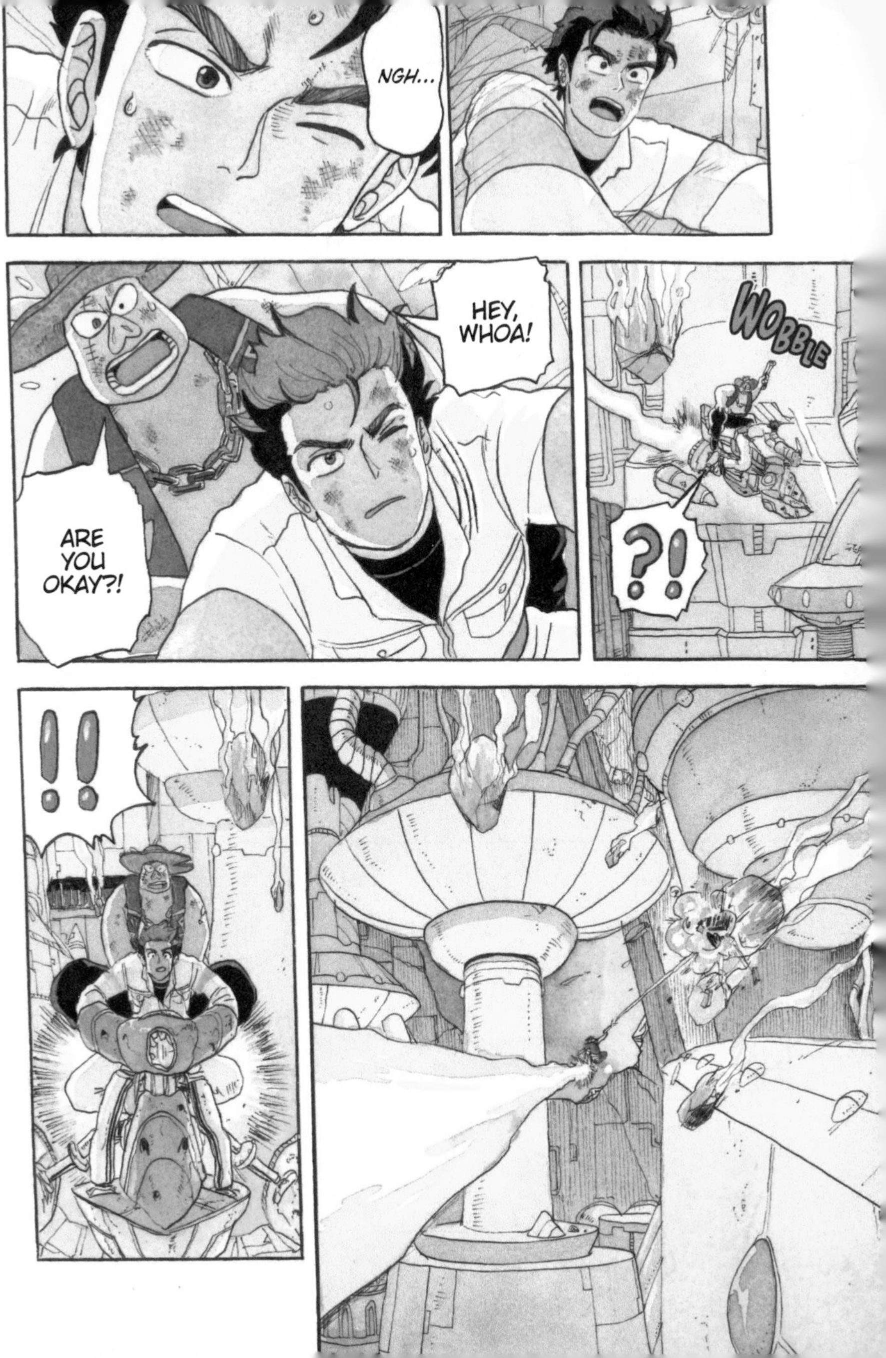
NGH...
WOBBLE
?!
HEY, WHOA!
ARE YOU OKAY?!
!!

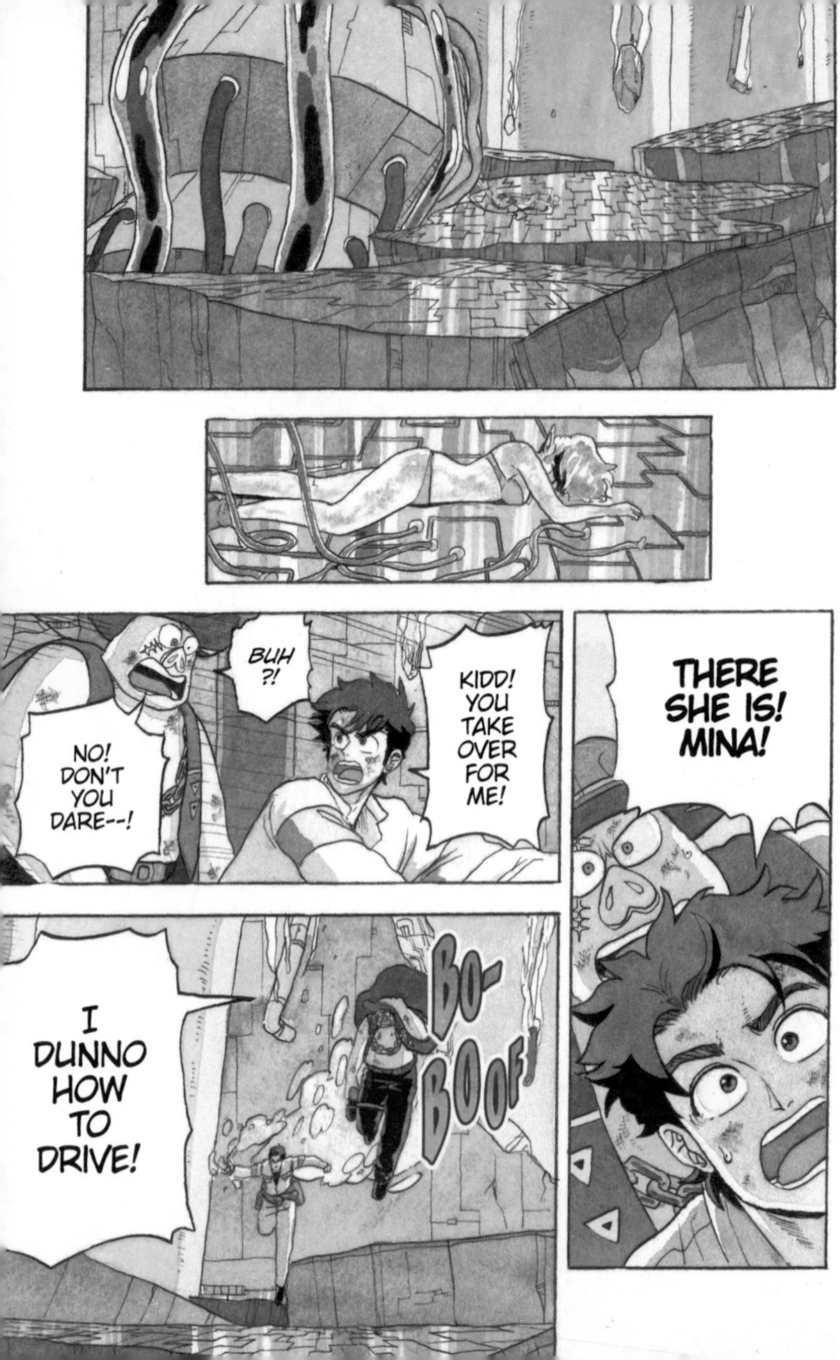
THERE SHE IS! MINA!
KIDD! YOU TAKE OVER FOR ME!
BUH?!
NO! DON'T YOU DARE--!
I DUNNO HOW TO DRIVE!
BO-BOOF

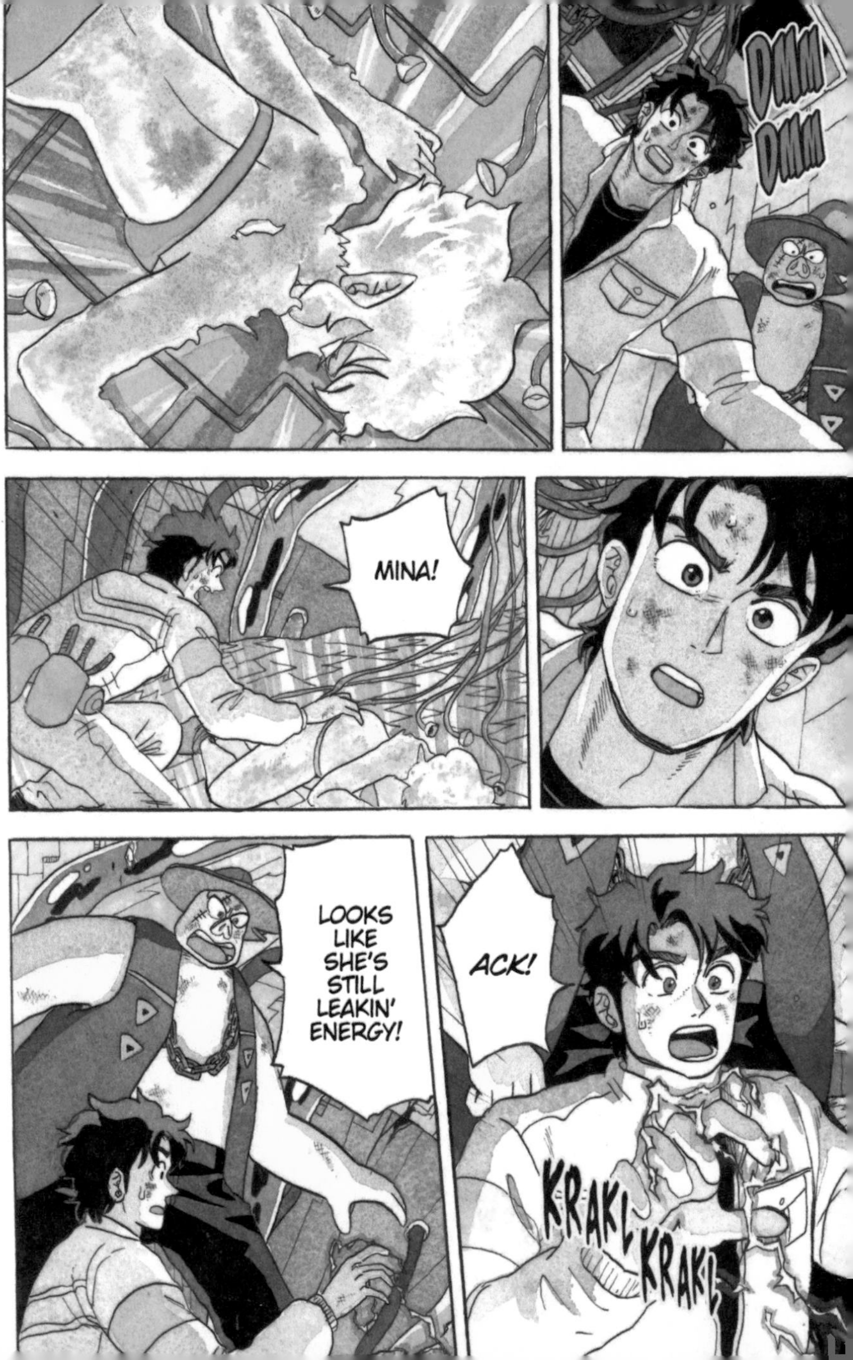
DMM DMM
MINA!
ACK!
KRAKL KRAKL
LOOKS LIKE SHE'S STILL LEAKIN' ENERGY!

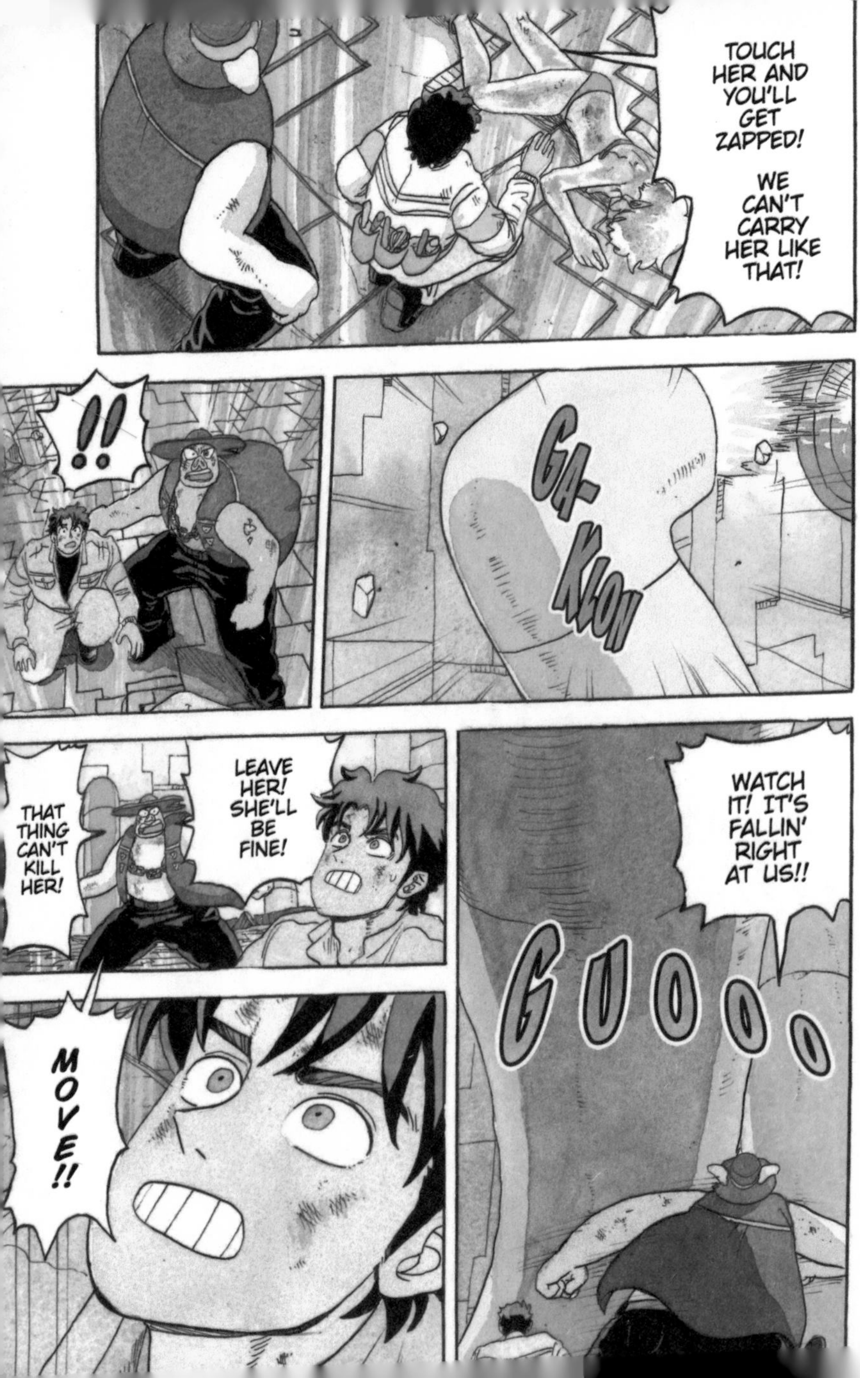
TOUCH HER AND YOU'LL GET ZAPPED!
WE CAN'T CARRY HER LIKE THAT!
GA-KLON
!!
WATCH IT! IT'S FALLIN' RIGHT AT US!!
GUOOOO
LEAVE HER! SHE'LL BE FINE!
THAT THING CAN'T KILL HER!
MOVE!!

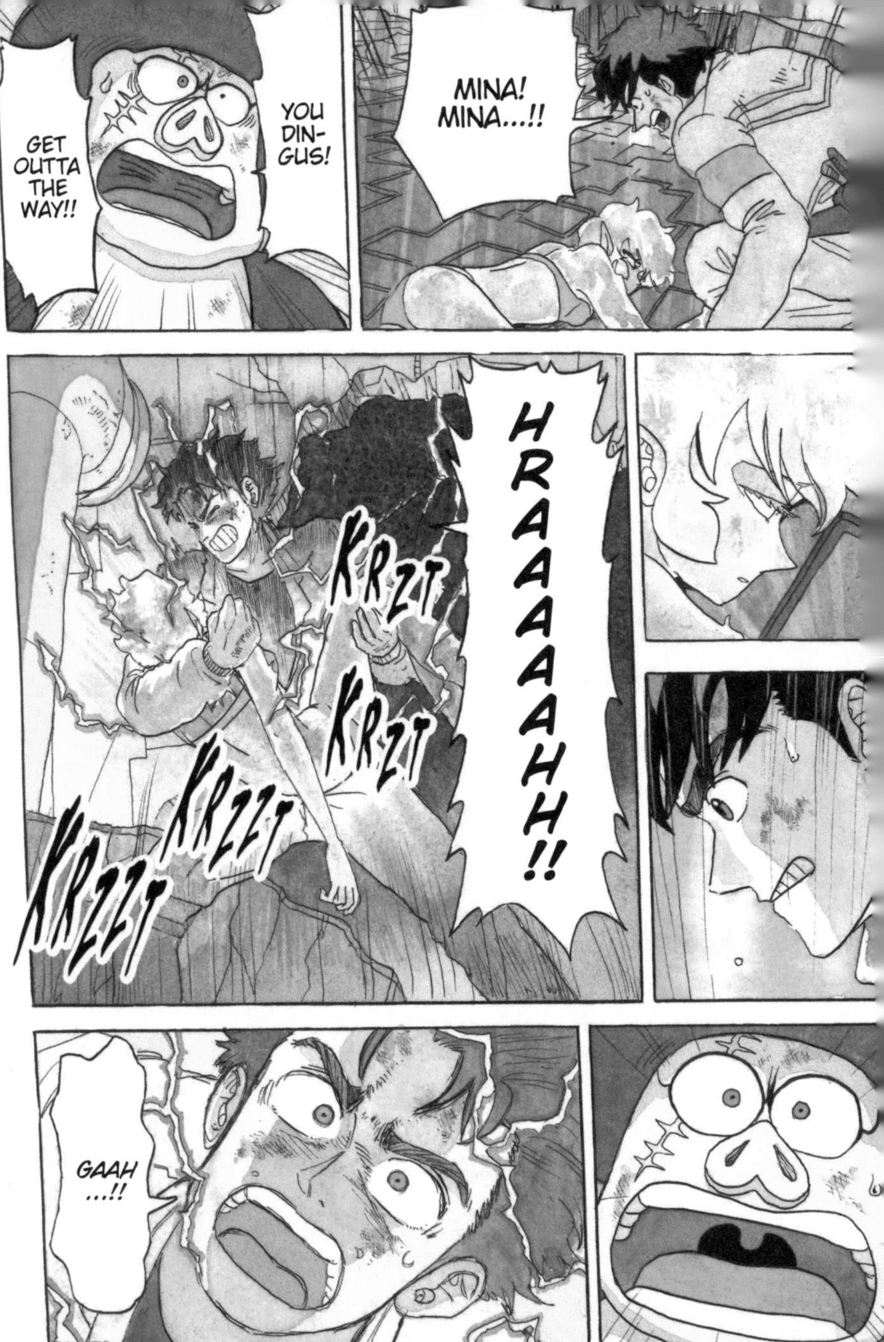
MINA! MINA...!!
YOU DINGUS!
GET OUTTA THE WAY!!
HRAAAAAHH!!
KRZT
KRZT
KRZZT
KRZZT
GAAH ...!!

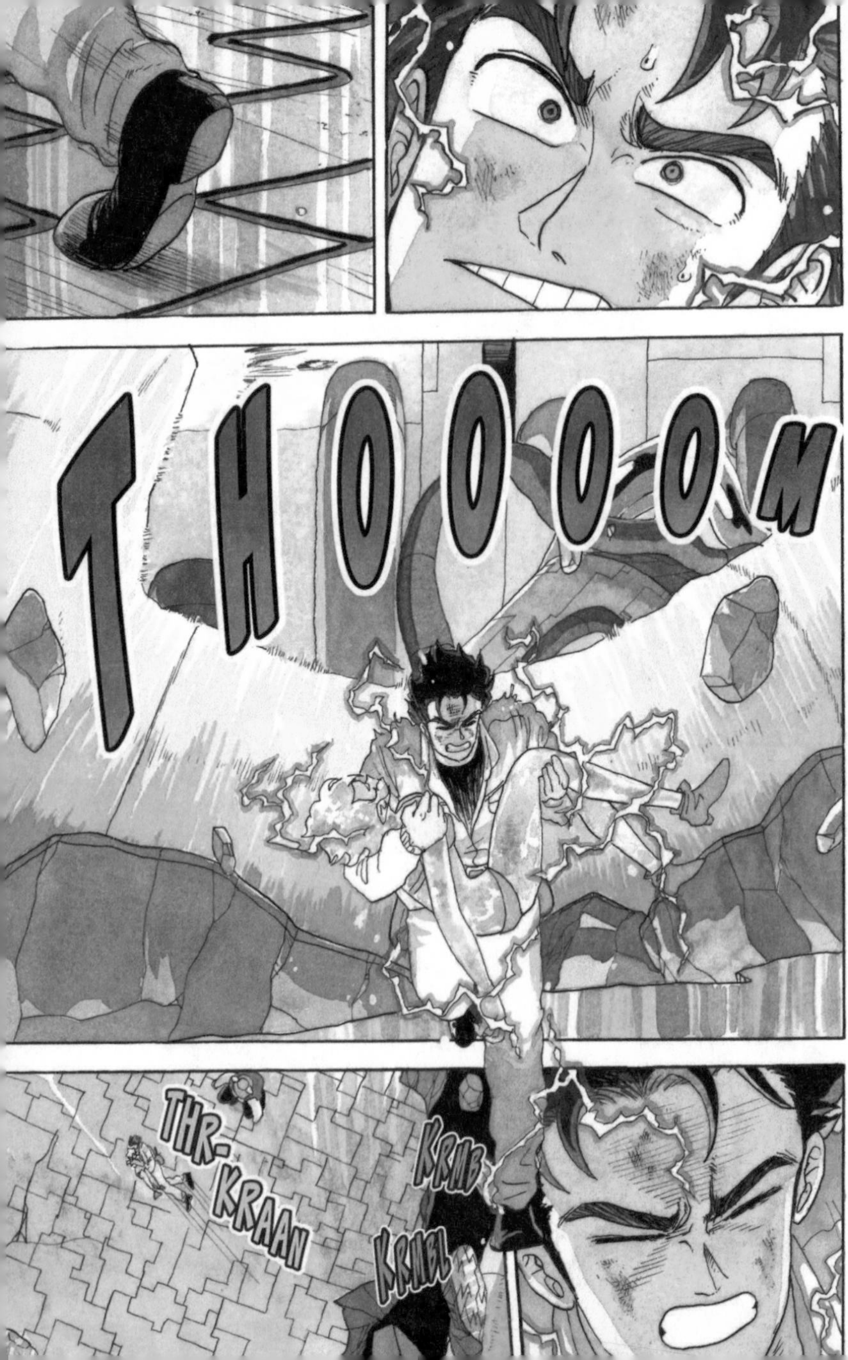
THOOOOM
KRMB
KRMBL
THR-KRAAN

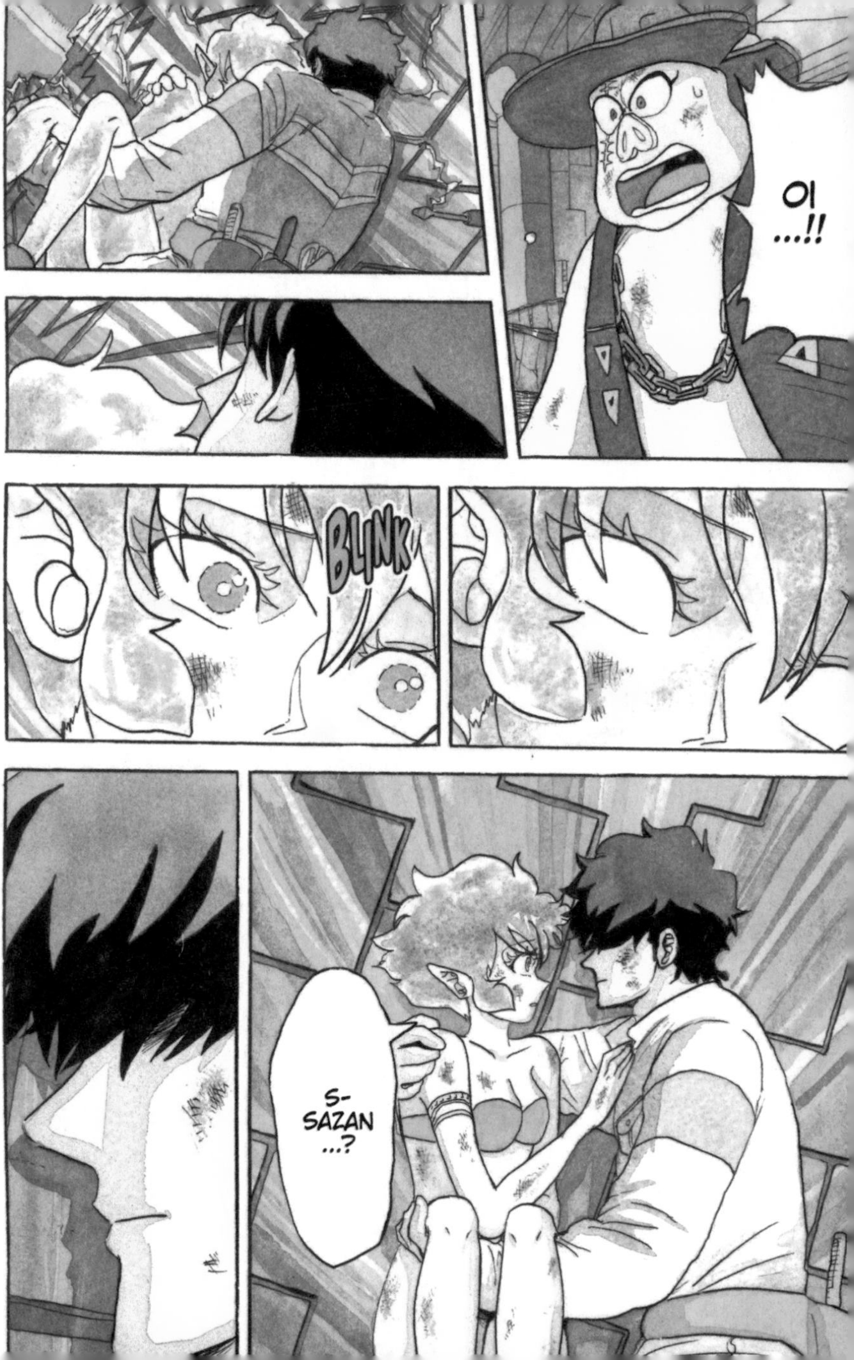

OI
...!!
BLINK
S-
SAZAN
...?

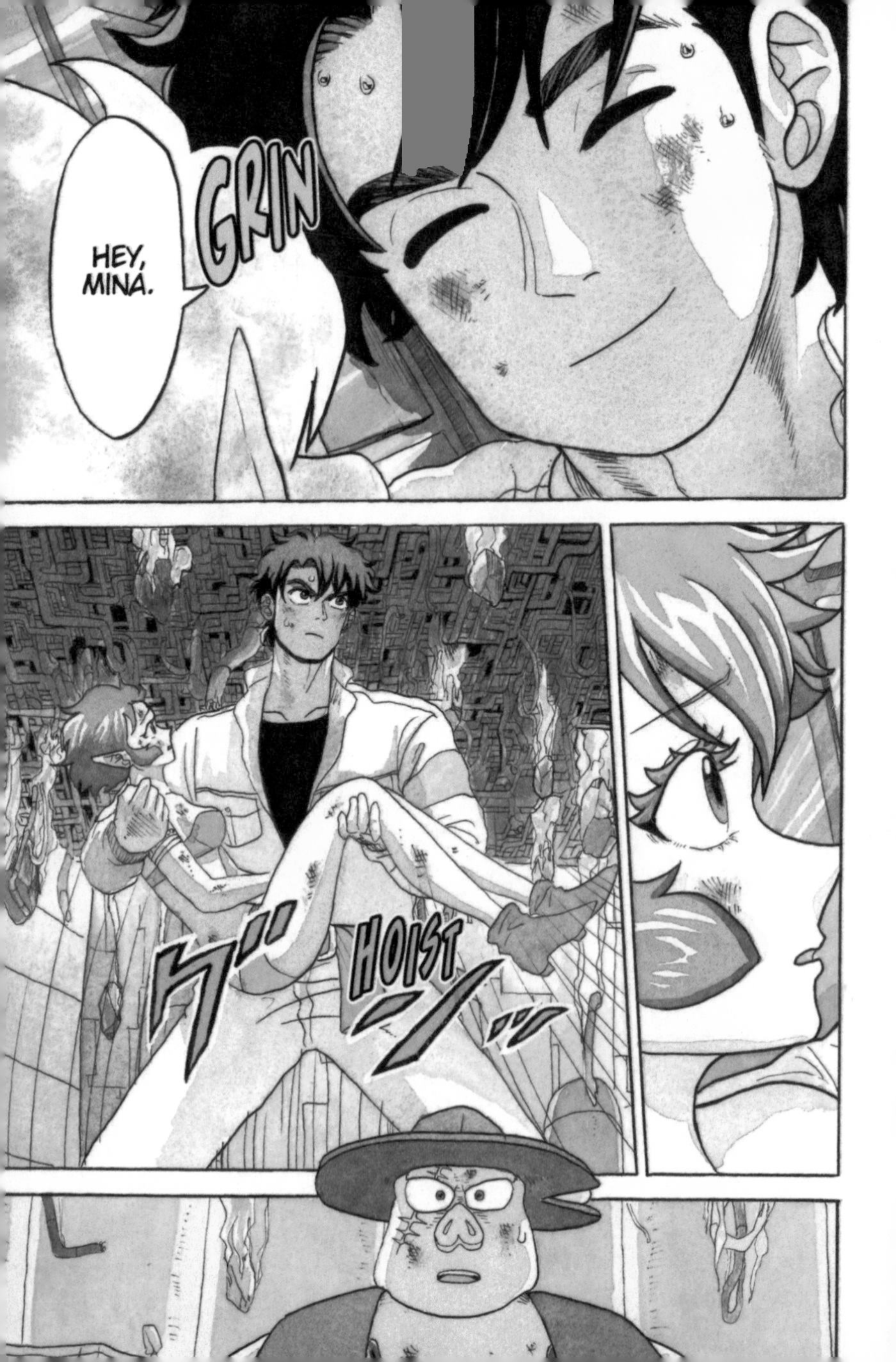
GRIN
HEY, MINA.
HOIST

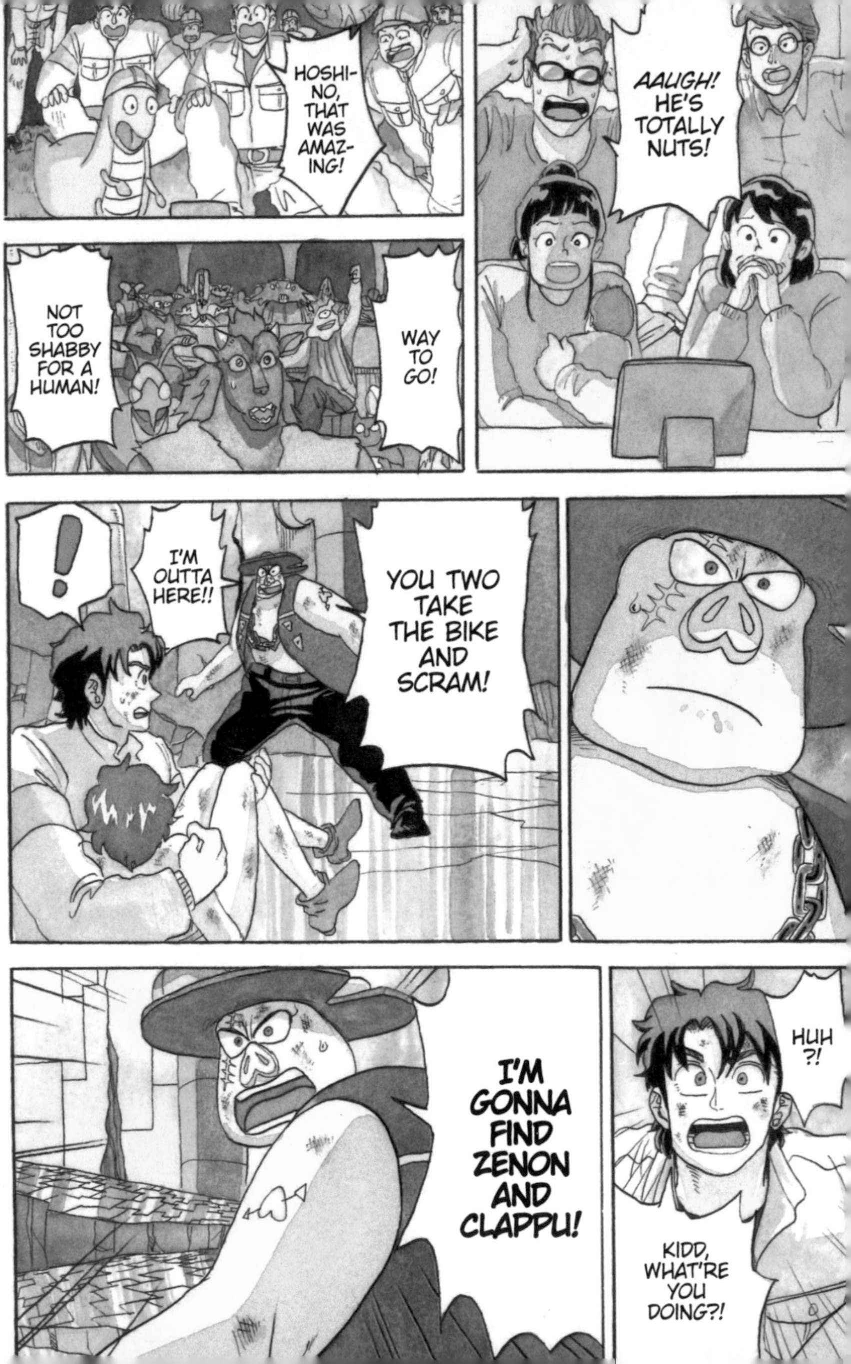
AAUGH! HE'S TOTALLY NUTS!
HOSHINO, THAT WAS AMAZING!
WAY TO GO!
NOT TOO SHABBY FOR A HUMAN!
YOU TWO TAKE THE BIKE AND SCRAM!
I'M OUTTA HERE!!
!
HUH?!
KIDD, WHAT'RE YOU DOING?!
I'M GONNA FIND ZENON AND CLAPPU!

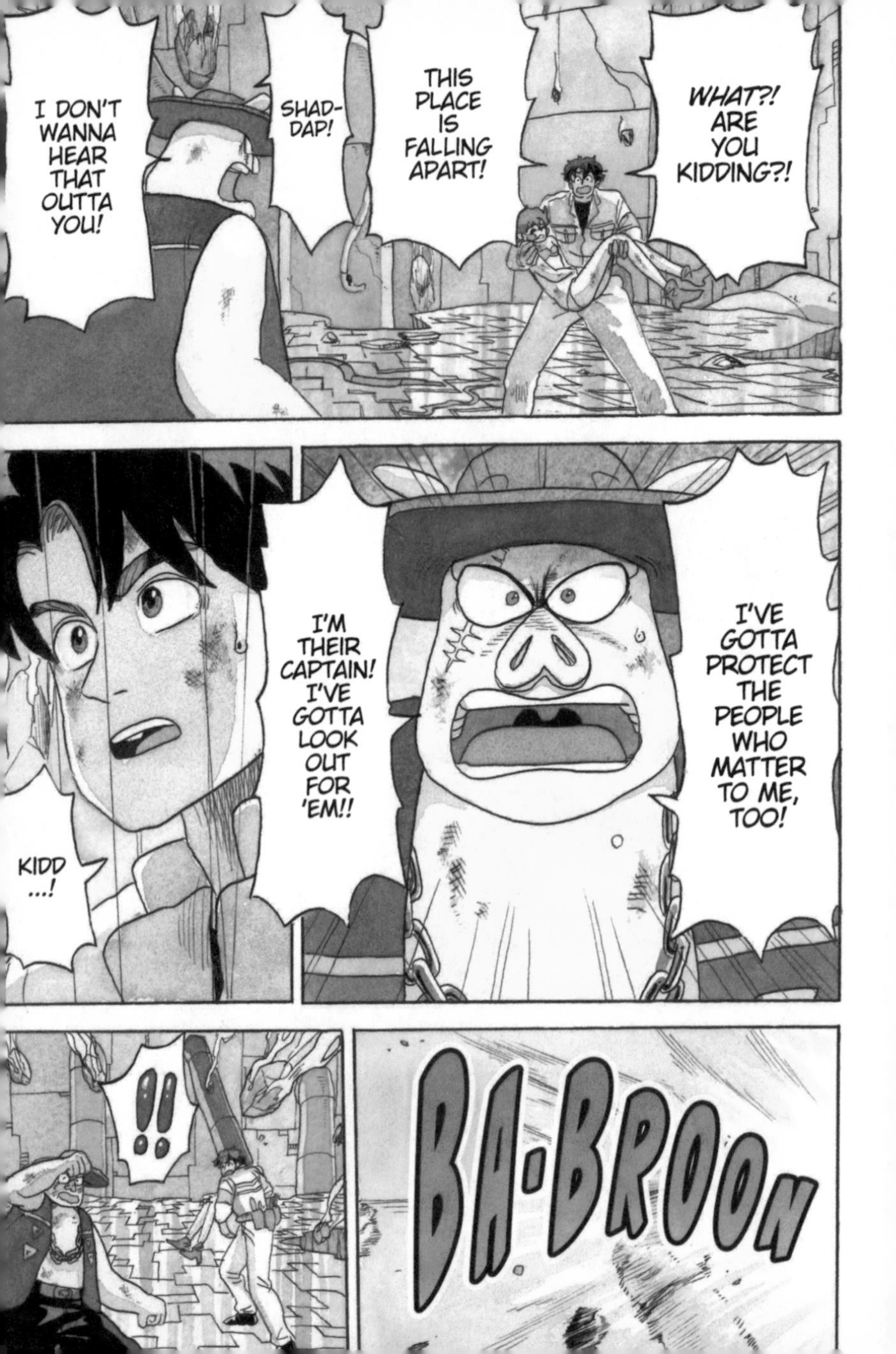
WHAT?! ARE YOU KIDDING?!
THIS PLACE IS FALLING APART!
SHAD-DAP!
I DON'T WANNA HEAR THAT OUTTA YOU!
I'VE GOTTA PROTECT THE PEOPLE WHO MATTER TO ME, TOO!
I'M THEIR CAPTAIN! I'VE GOTTA LOOK OUT FOR 'EM!!
KIDD ...!
BA-BROON
!!

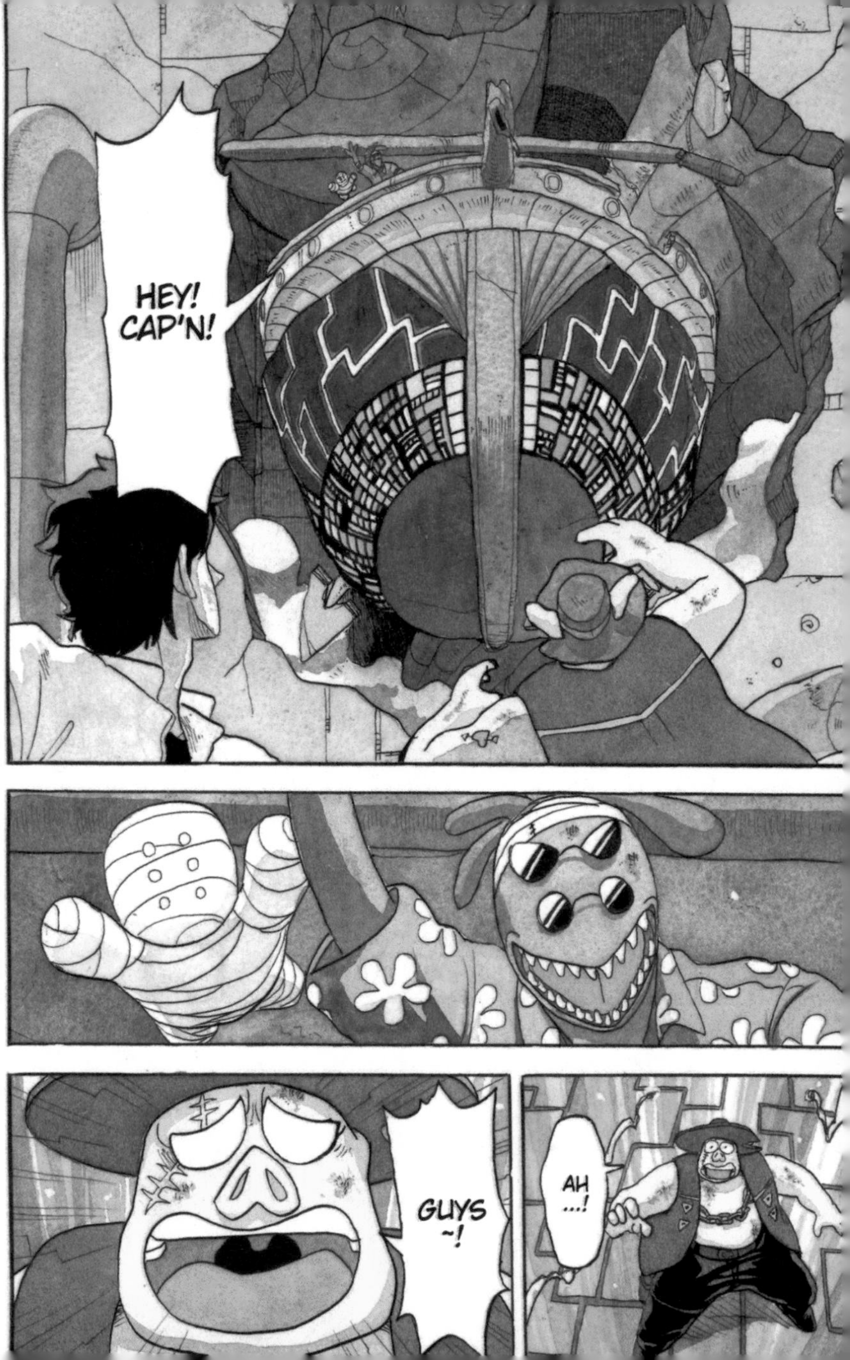
HEY! CAP'N!
AH ...!
GUYS ~!

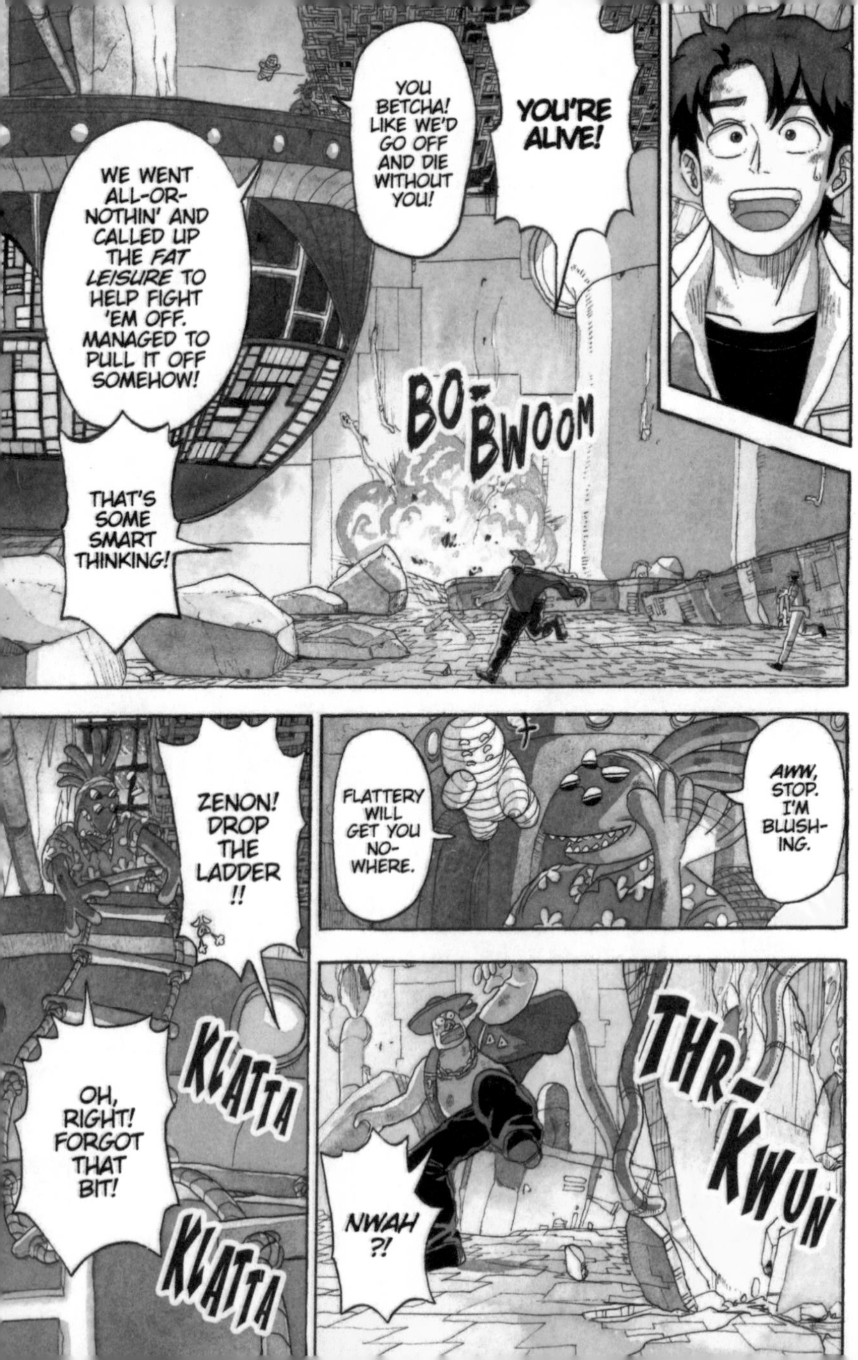
YOU'RE ALIVE!
YOU BETCHA! LIKE WE'D GO OFF AND DIE WITHOUT YOU!
WE WENT ALL-OR-NOTHIN' AND CALLED UP THE *FAT LEISURE* TO HELP FIGHT 'EM OFF. MANAGED TO PULL IT OFF SOMEHOW!
BO-BWOOM
THAT'S SOME SMART THINKING!
AWW, STOP. I'M BLUSHING.
FLATTERY WILL GET YOU NOWHERE.
THR-KWUN
NWAH ?!
ZENON! DROP THE LADDER !!
KLATTA
KLATTA
OH, RIGHT! FORGOT THAT BIT!

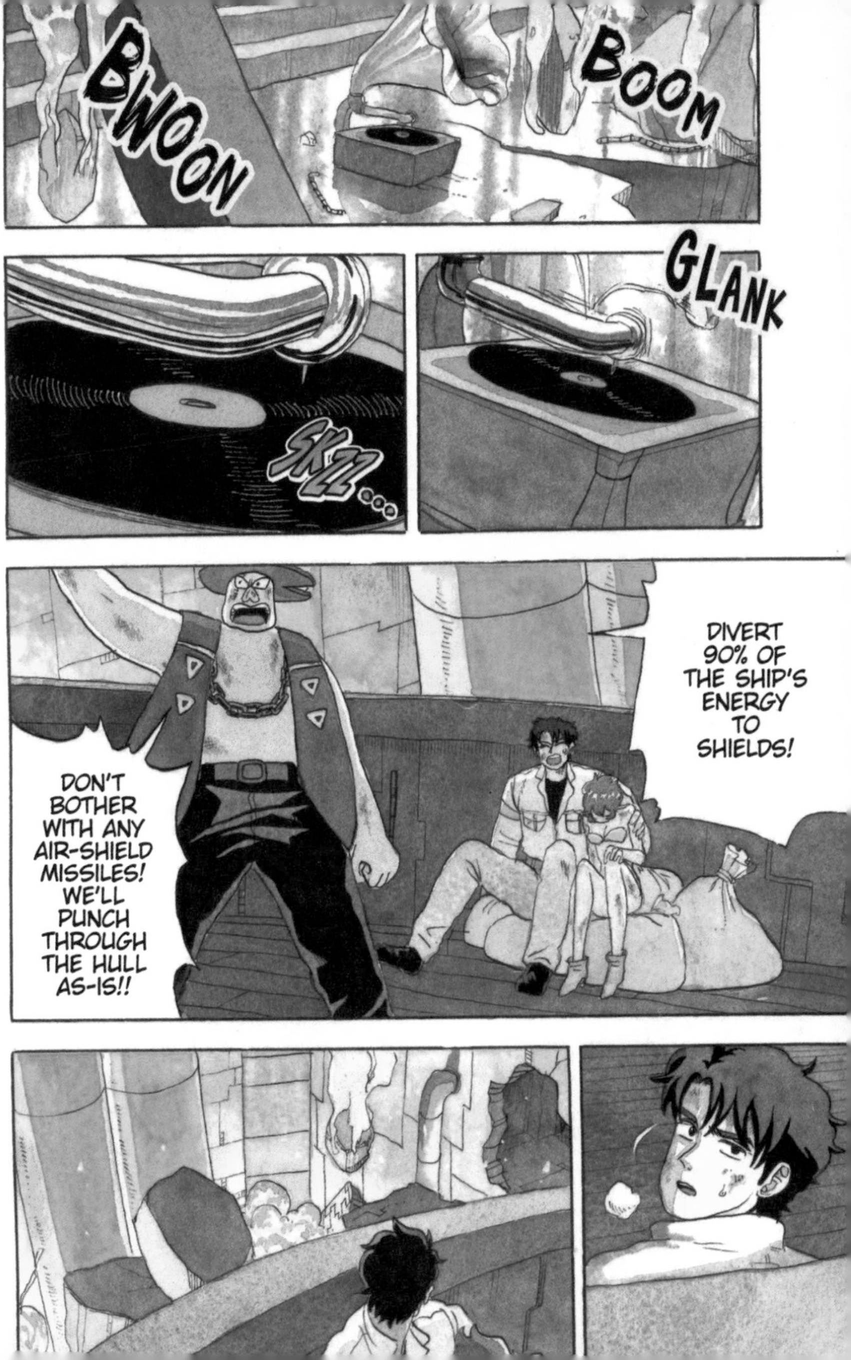
BOOM
BWOON
GLANK
SKZZ...
DIVERT 90% OF THE SHIP'S ENERGY TO SHIELDS!
DON'T BOTHER WITH ANY AIR-SHIELD MISSILES! WE'LL PUNCH THROUGH THE HULL AS-IS!!

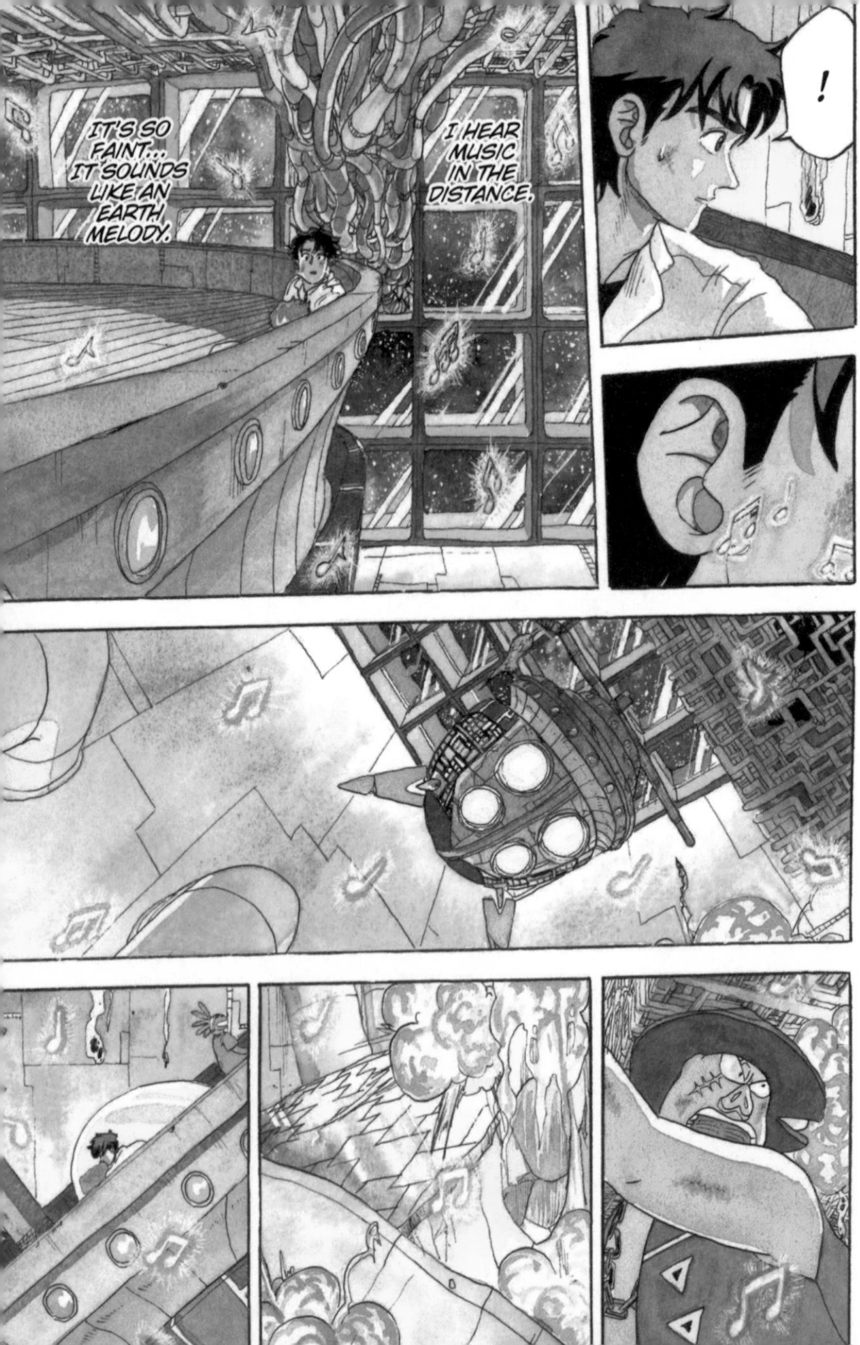
!
I HEAR MUSIC IN THE DISTANCE.
IT'S SO FAINT... IT SOUNDS LIKE AN EARTH MELODY.

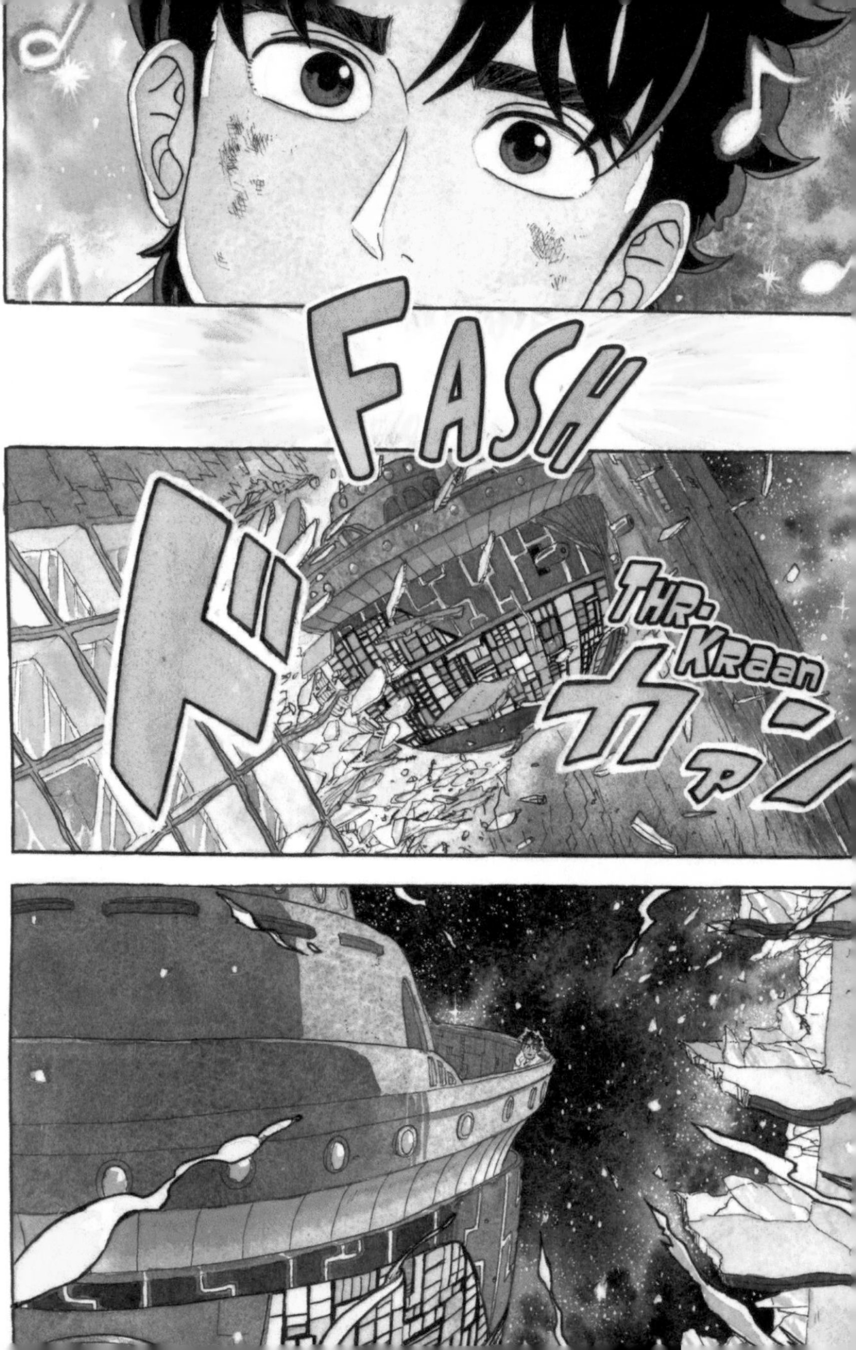
FASH
THR. Kraan

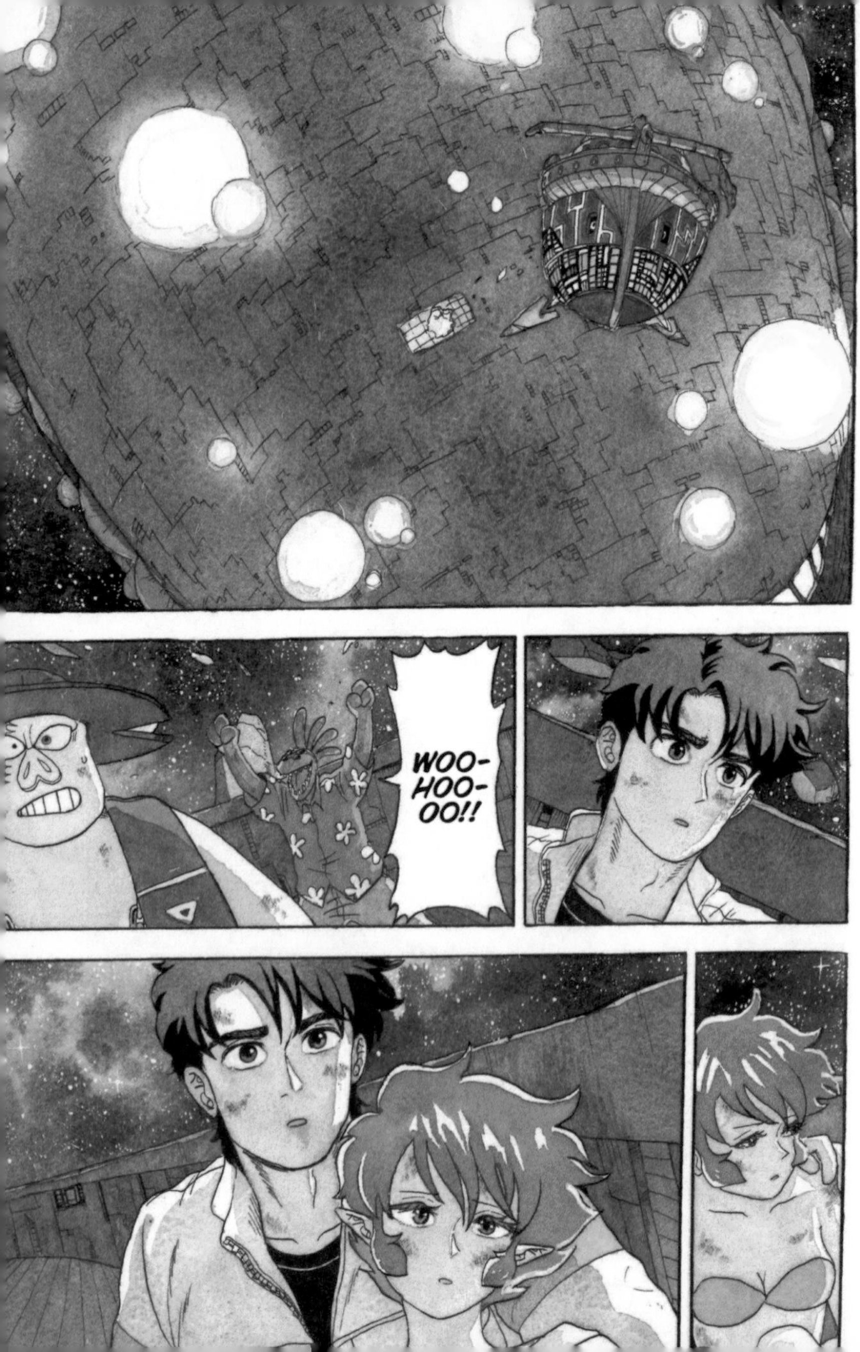
WOO-HOO-OO!!

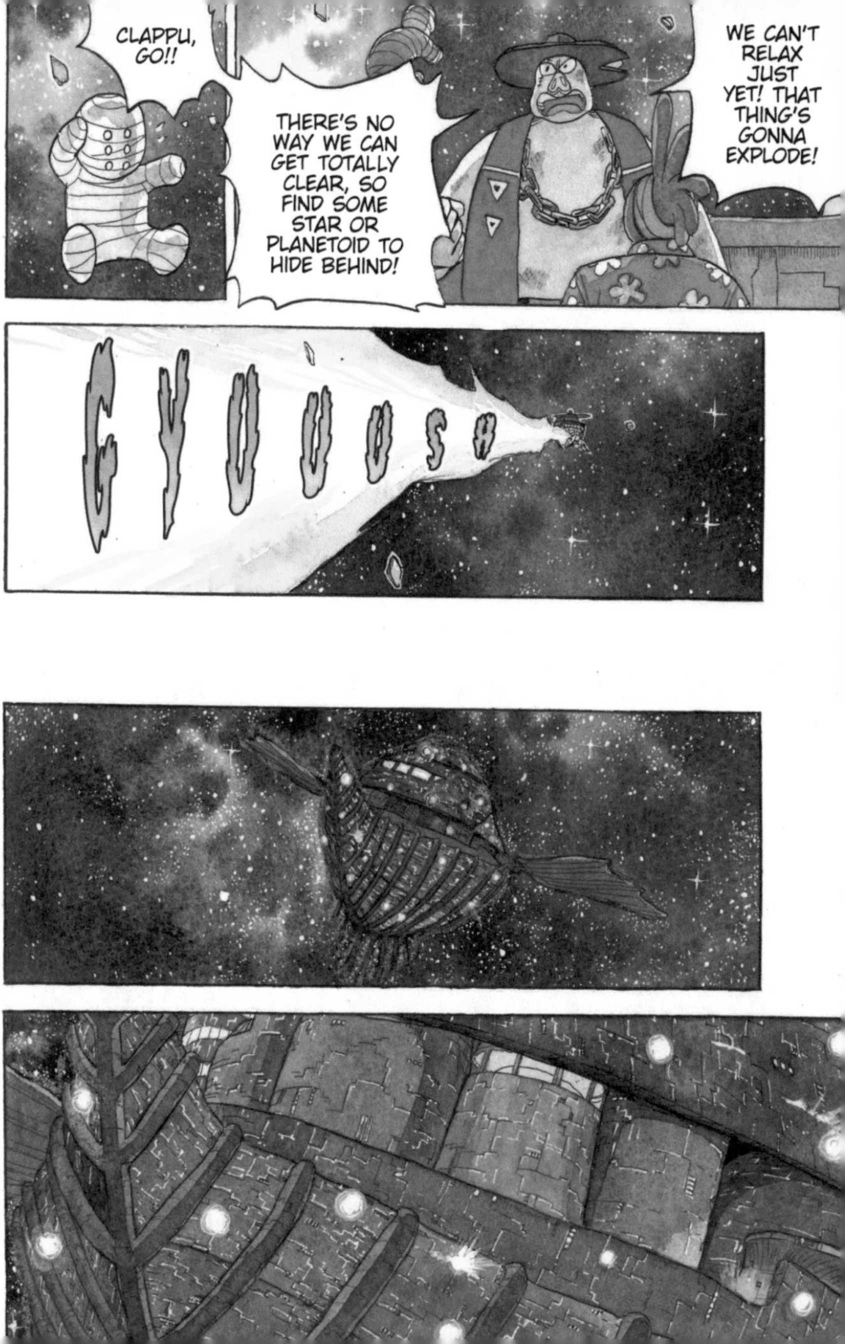
WE CAN'T RELAX JUST YET! THAT THING'S GONNA EXPLODE!
THERE'S NO WAY WE CAN GET TOTALLY CLEAR, SO FIND SOME STAR OR PLANETOID TO HIDE BEHIND!
CLAPPU, GO!!
GYUUSH

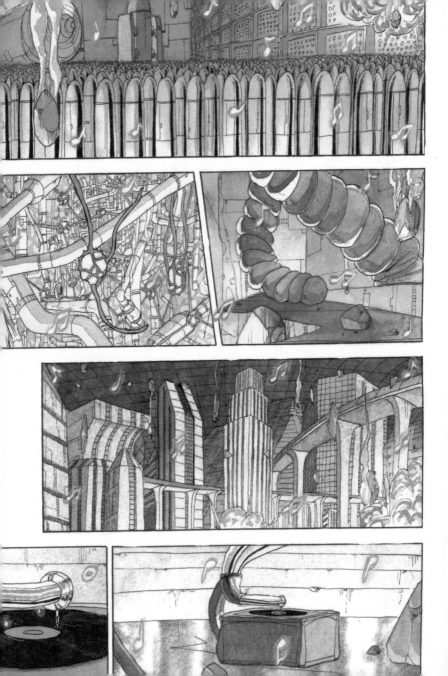

KWOOM

NWA-AAH!!

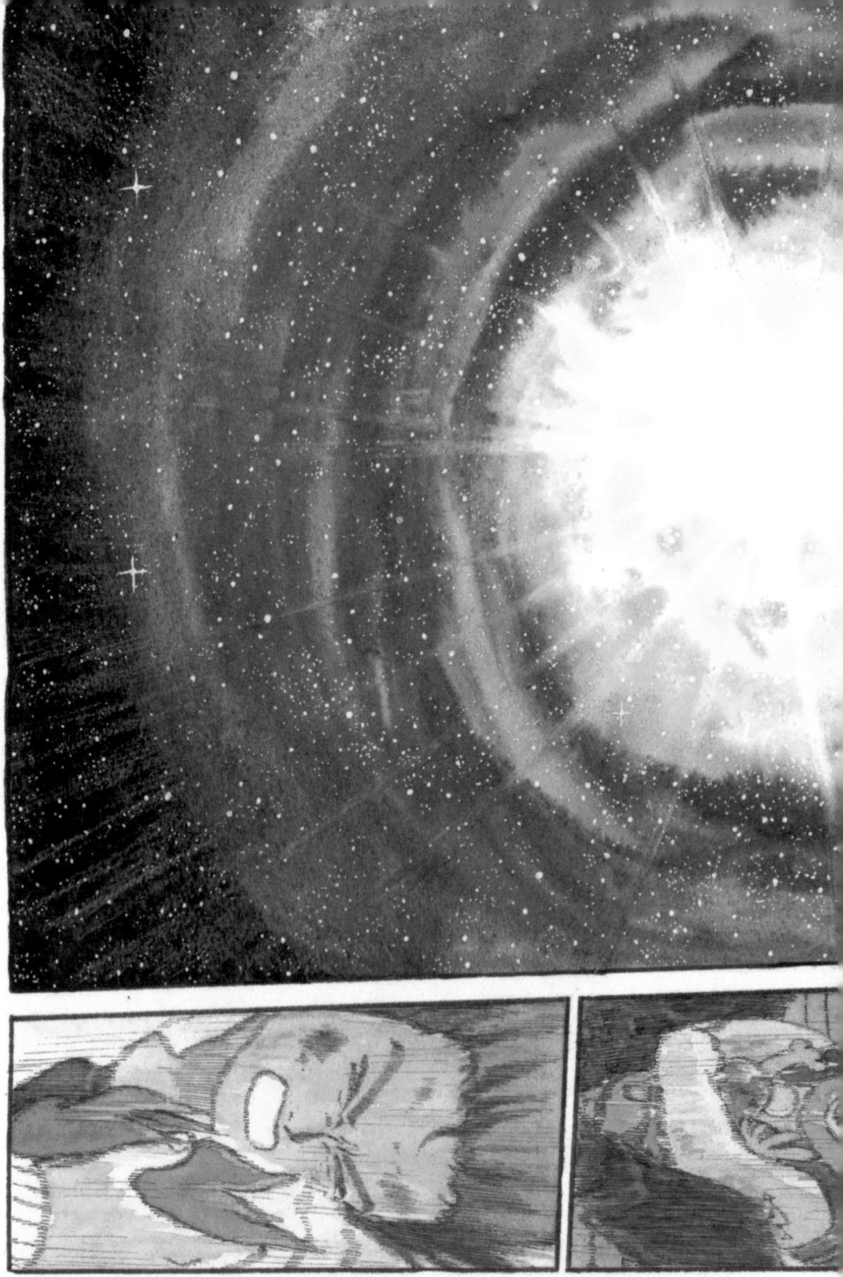

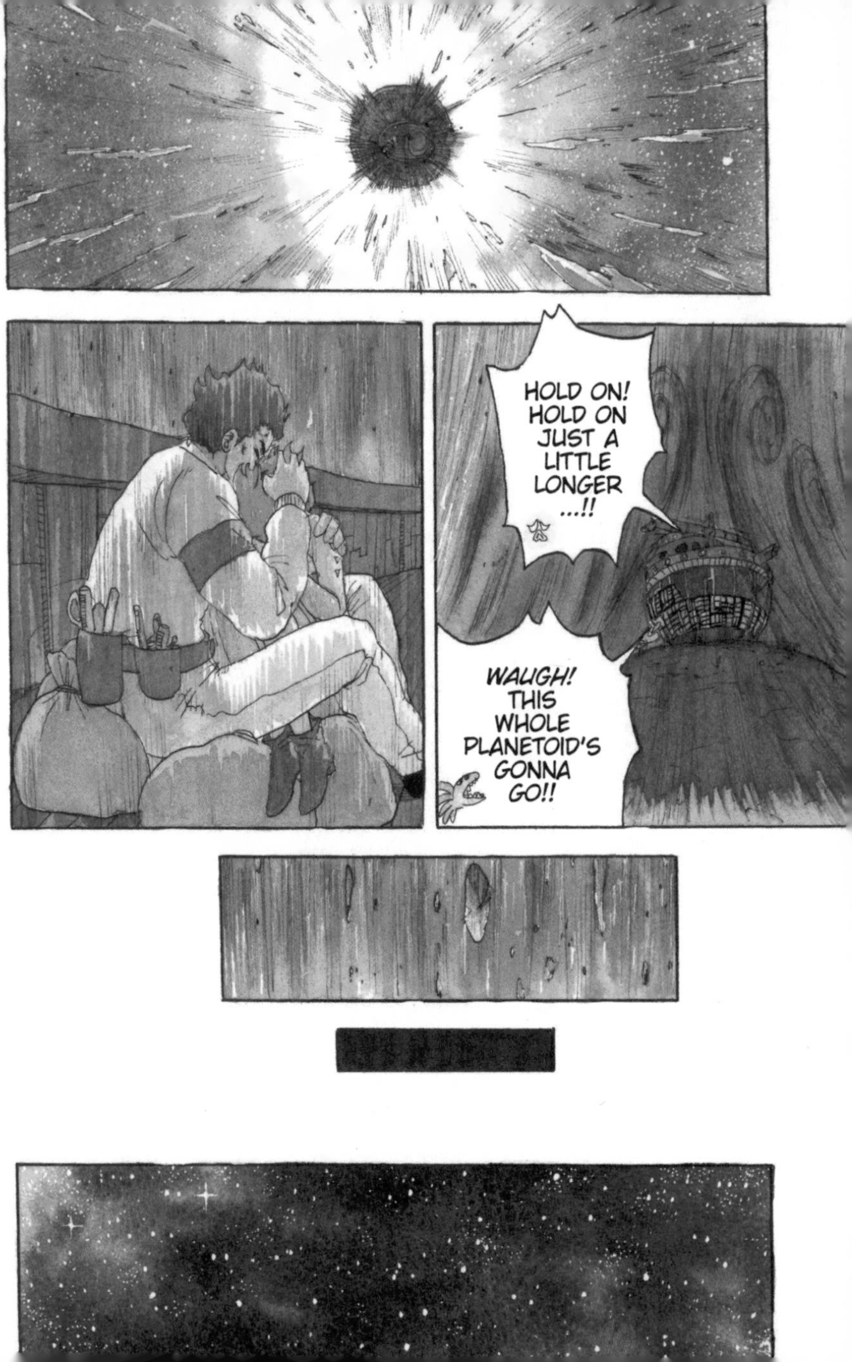
HOLD ON! HOLD ON JUST A LITTLE LONGER ...!!
WAUGH! THIS WHOLE PLANETOID'S GONNA GO!!

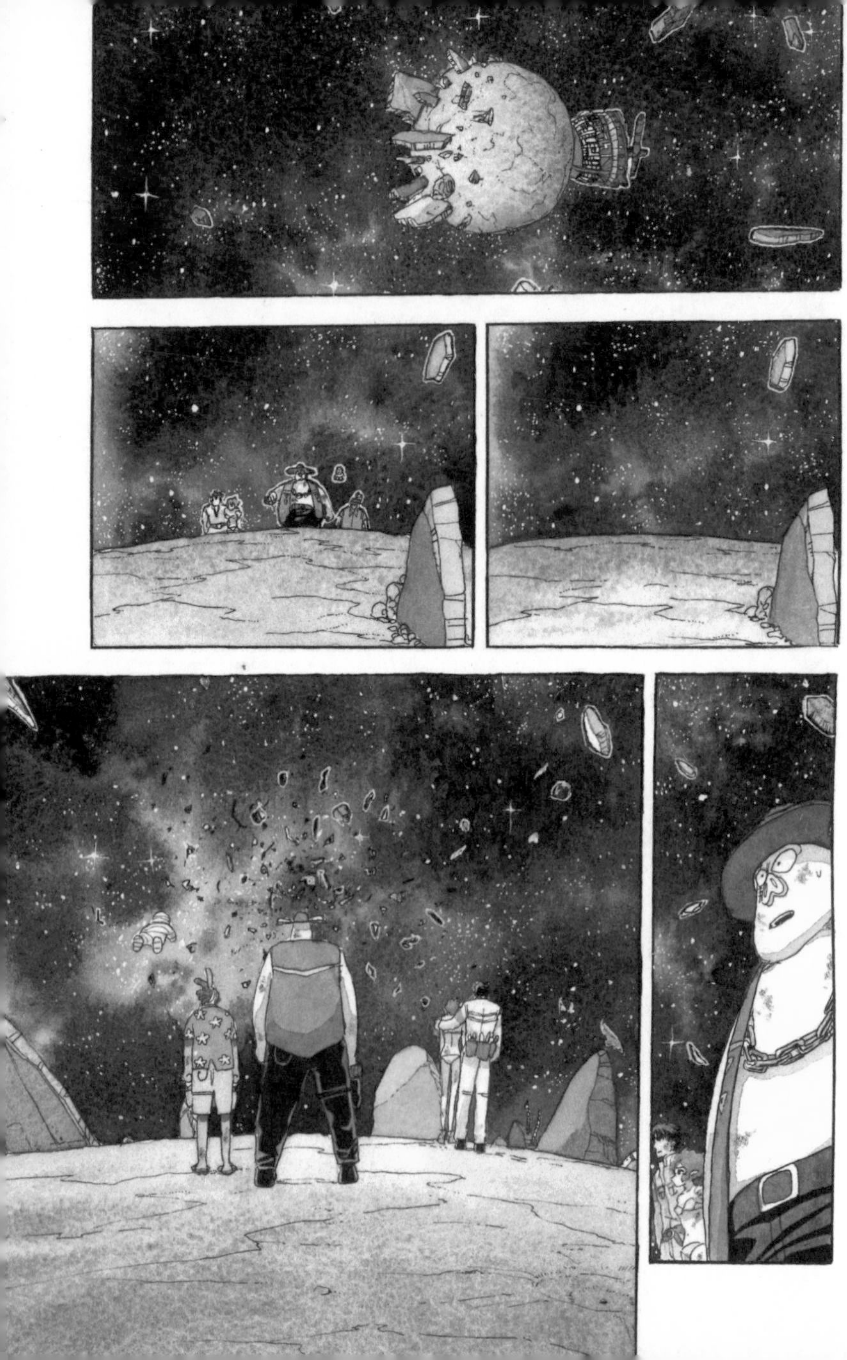

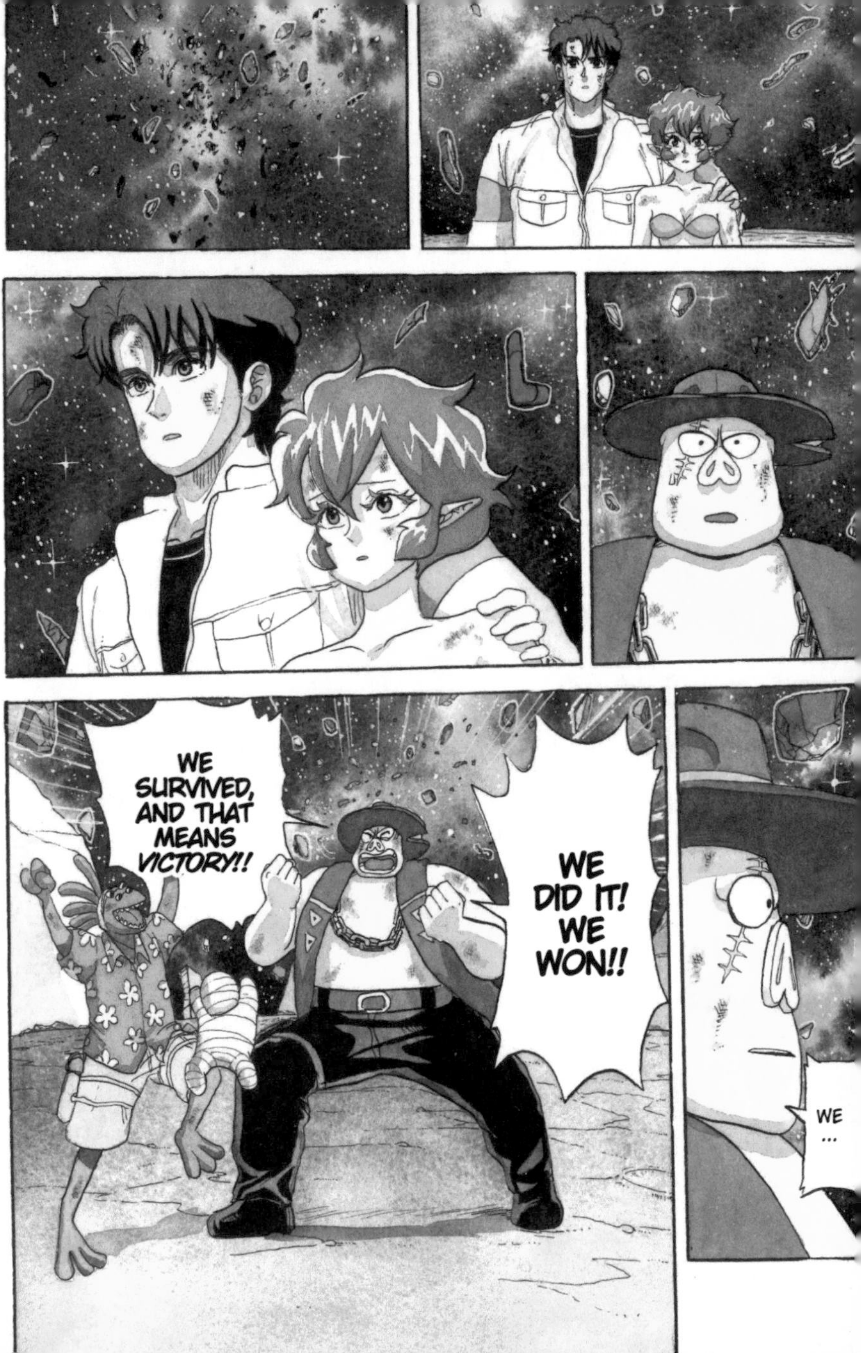
WE ...
WE DID IT! WE WON!!
WE SURVIVED, AND THAT MEANS VICTORY!!

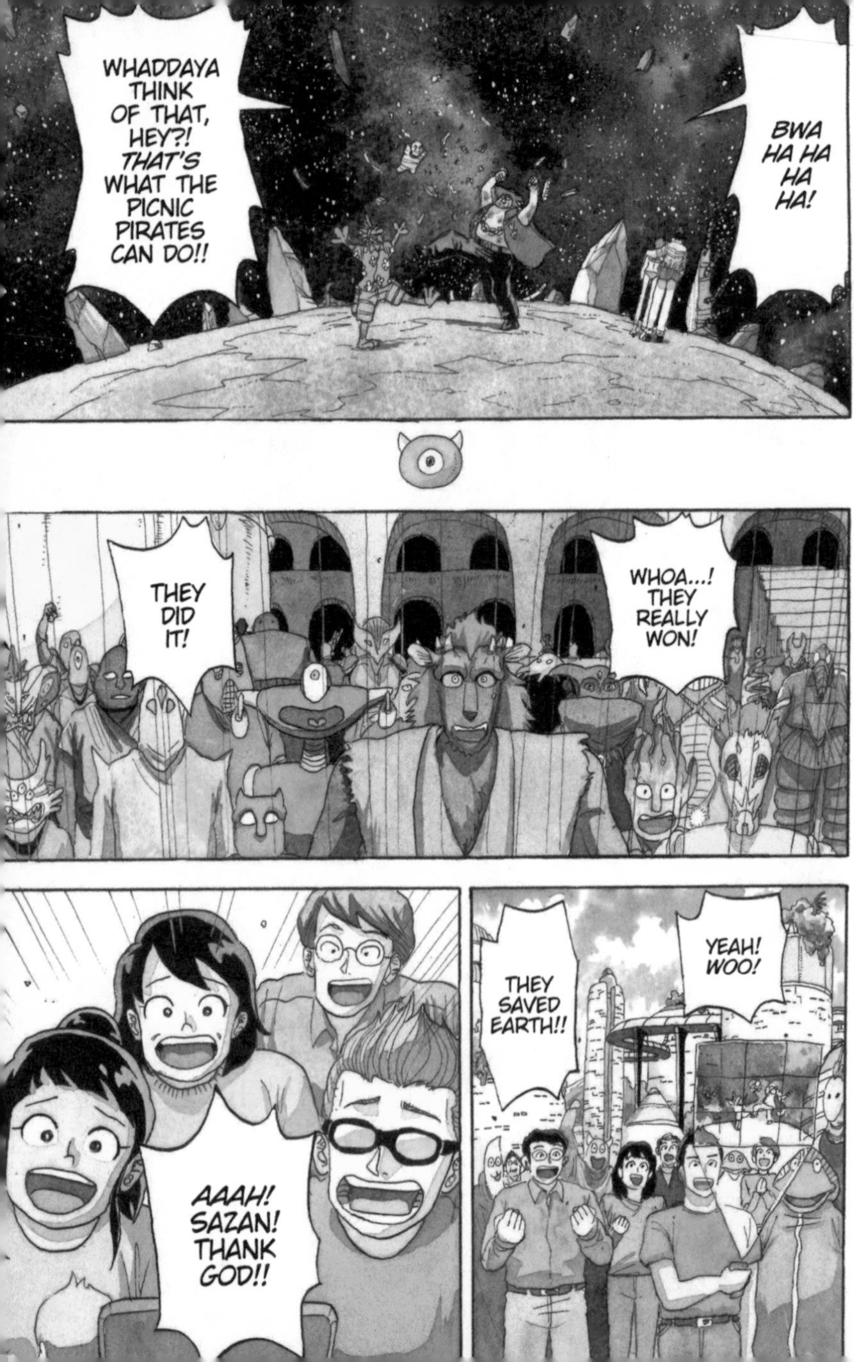
BWA HA HA HA HA!
WHADDAYA THINK OF THAT, HEY?! THAT'S WHAT THE PICNIC PIRATES CAN DO!!
WHOA...! THEY REALLY WON!
THEY DID IT!
YEAH! WOO!
THEY SAVED EARTH!!
AAAH! SAZAN! THANK GOD!!

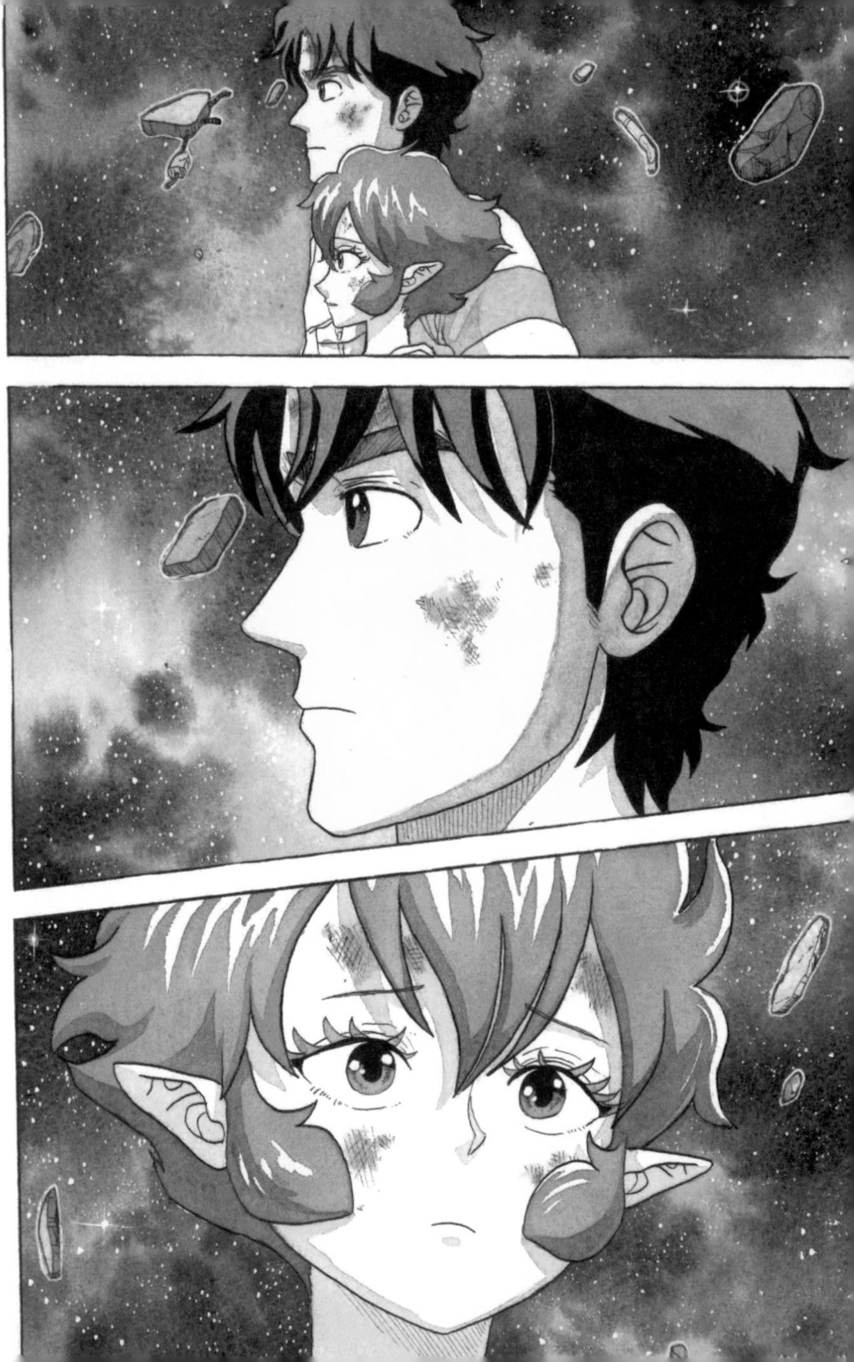

ONE!
TWO!
PICNIC!

ON
THREE!

PICNIC~!

WOBL

TOTTER...

EH...?

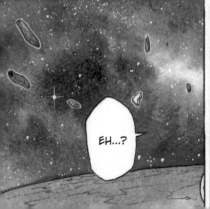

WUMP

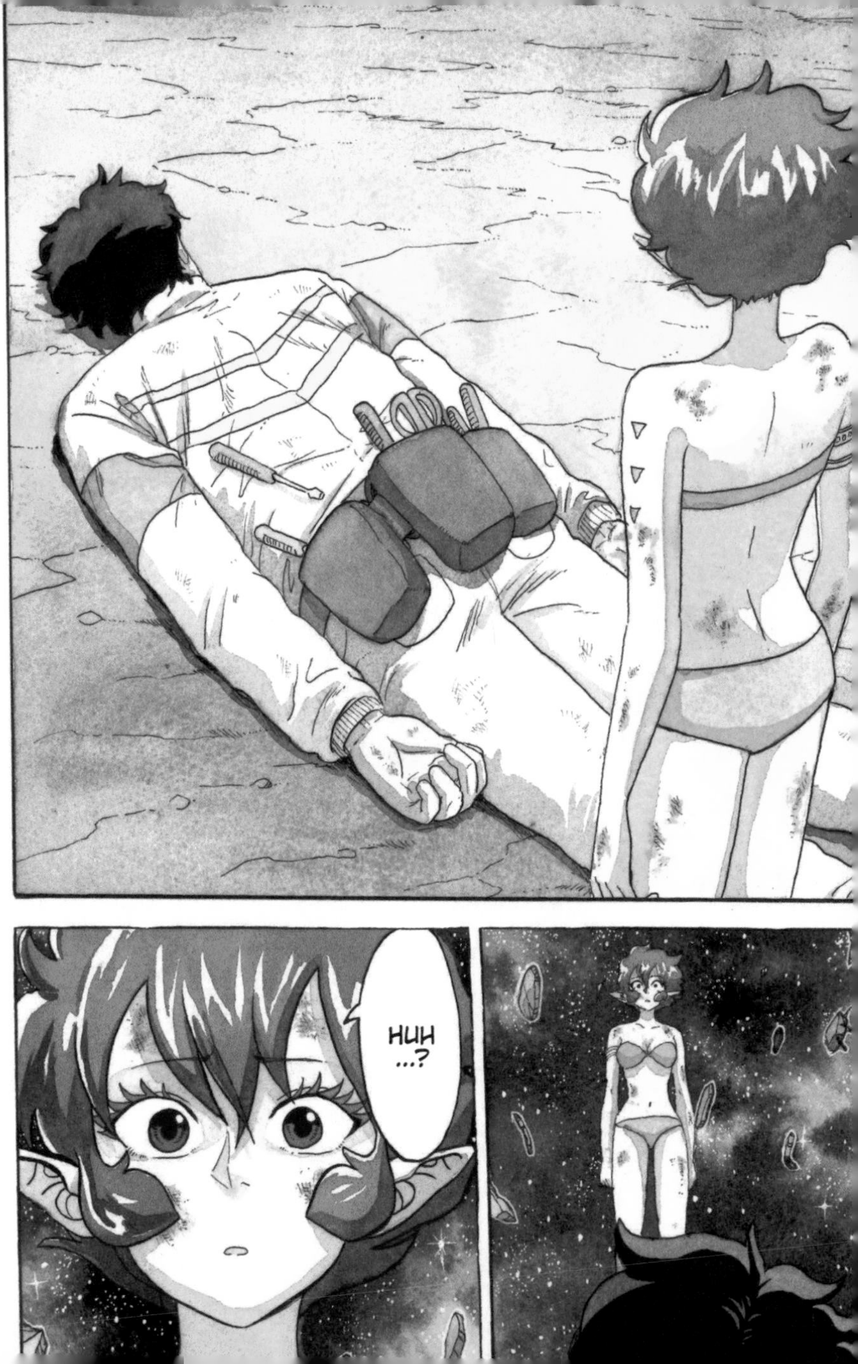
HUH ...?

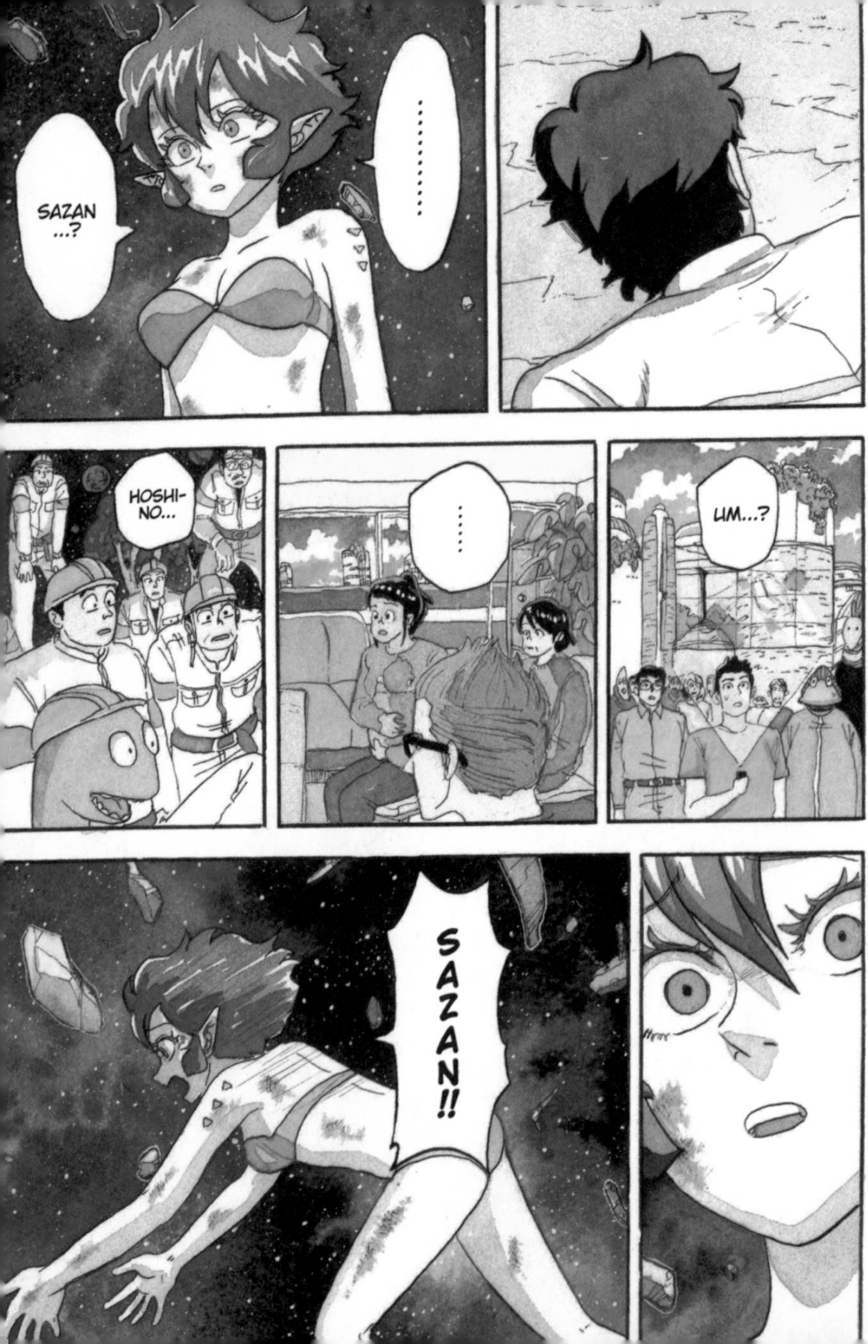
....
SAZAN ...?
UM...?
......
HOSHI-NO...
SAZAN!!

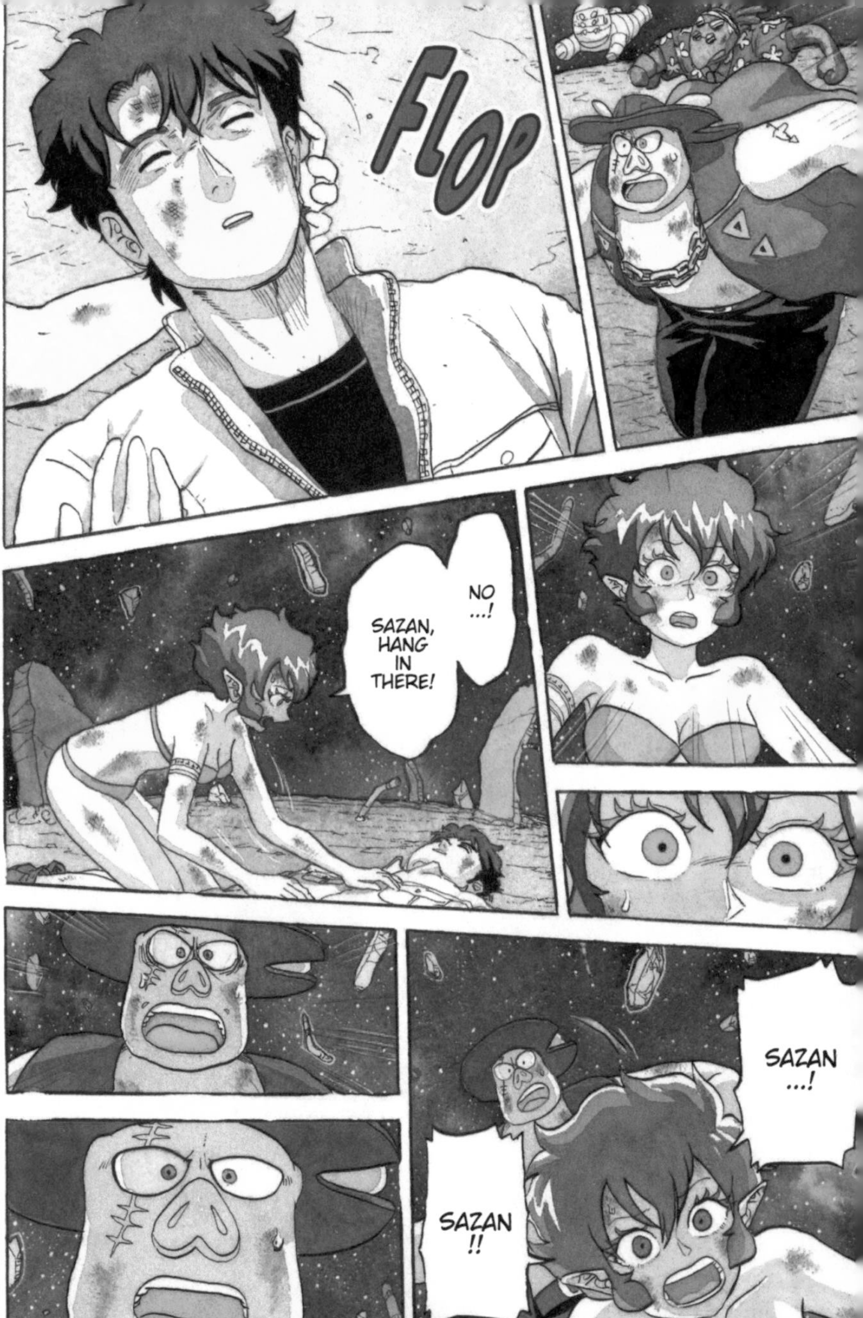
FLOP
NO ...!
SAZAN, HANG IN THERE!
SAZAN ...!
SAZAN !!

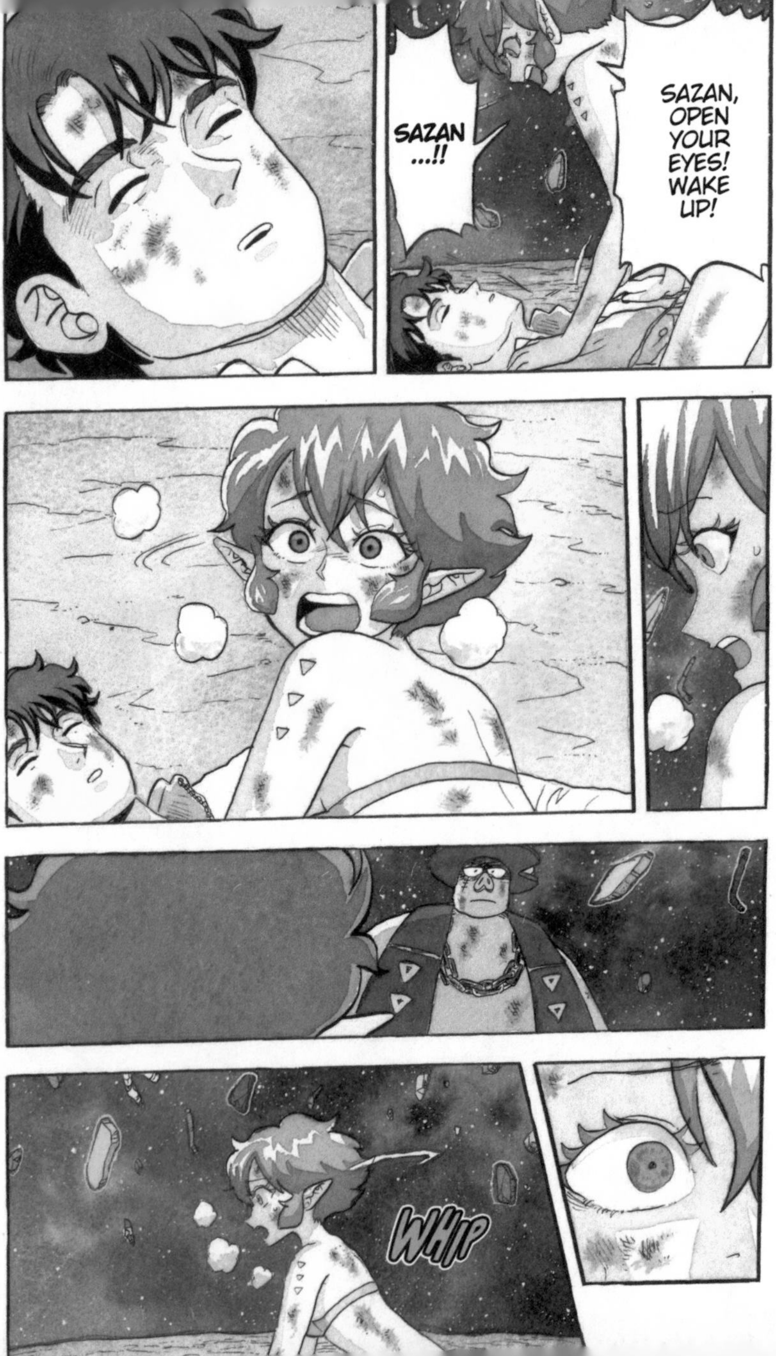
SAZAN, OPEN YOUR EYES! WAKE UP!
SAZAN ...!!
WHIP

LOOK AT ME.

PLEASE.

SAZAN...

SAZAN ...?

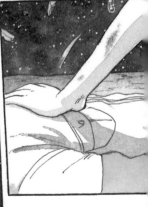

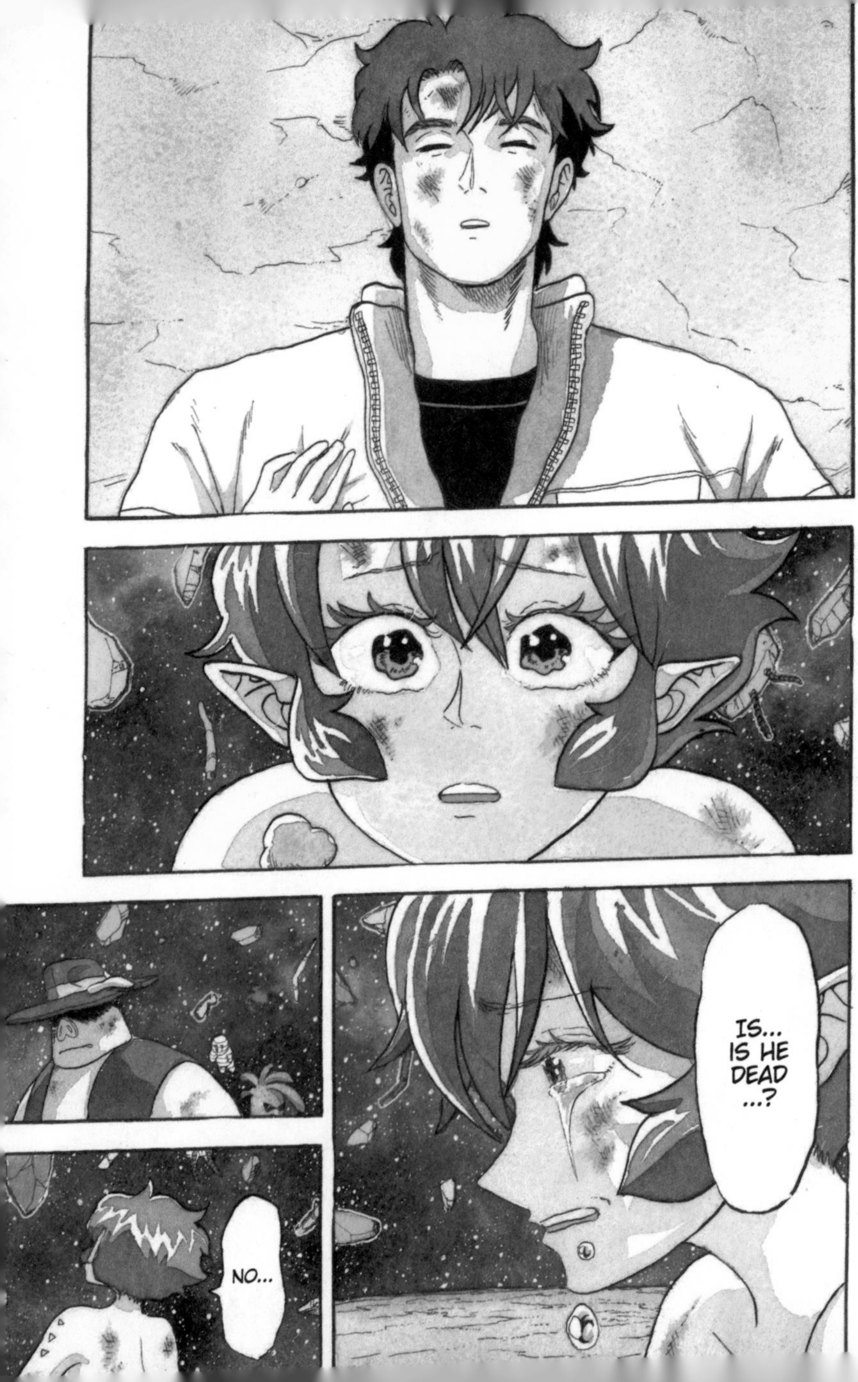
IS... IS HE DEAD ...?
NO...

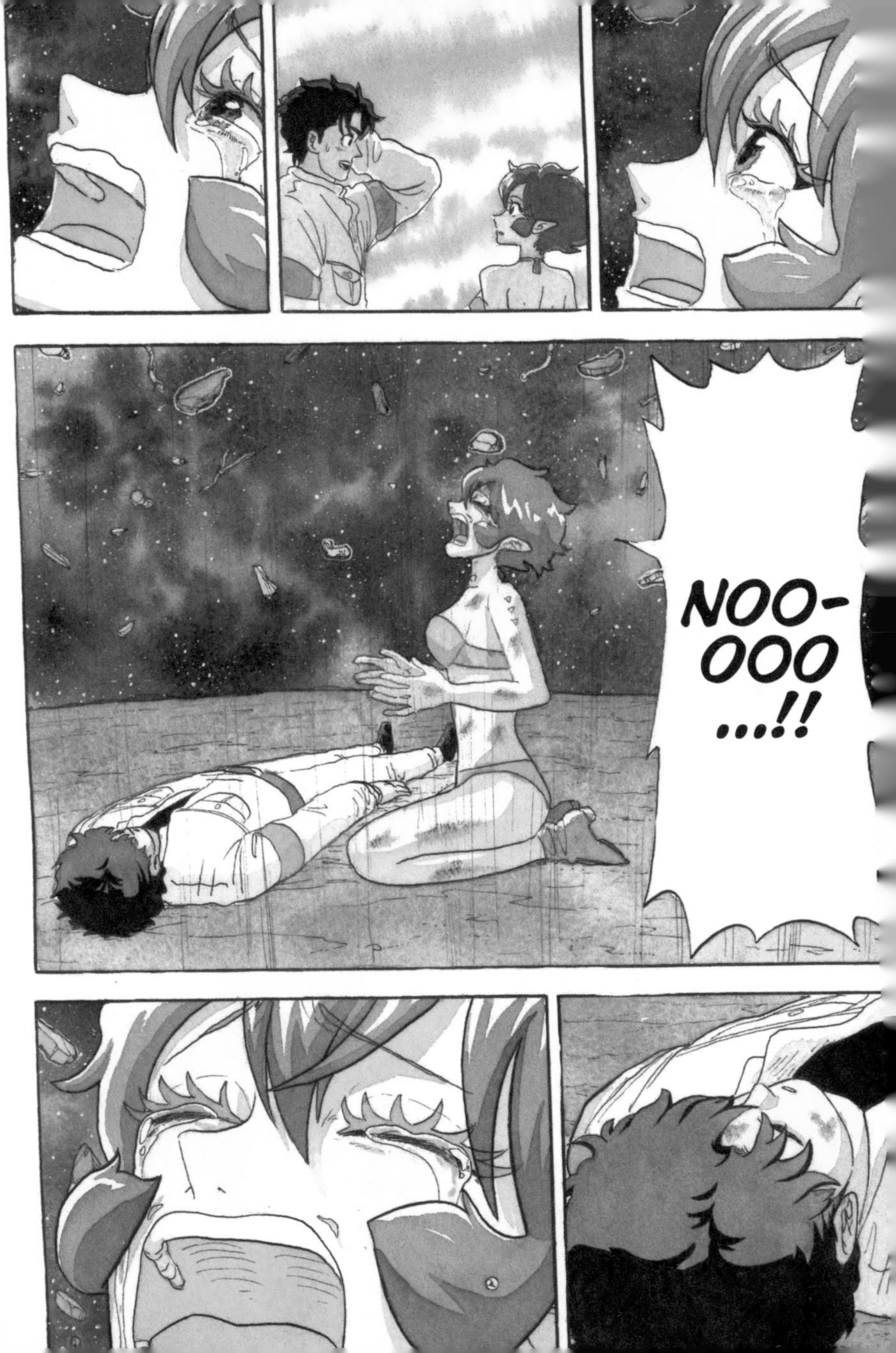
NOO-
OOO
...!!

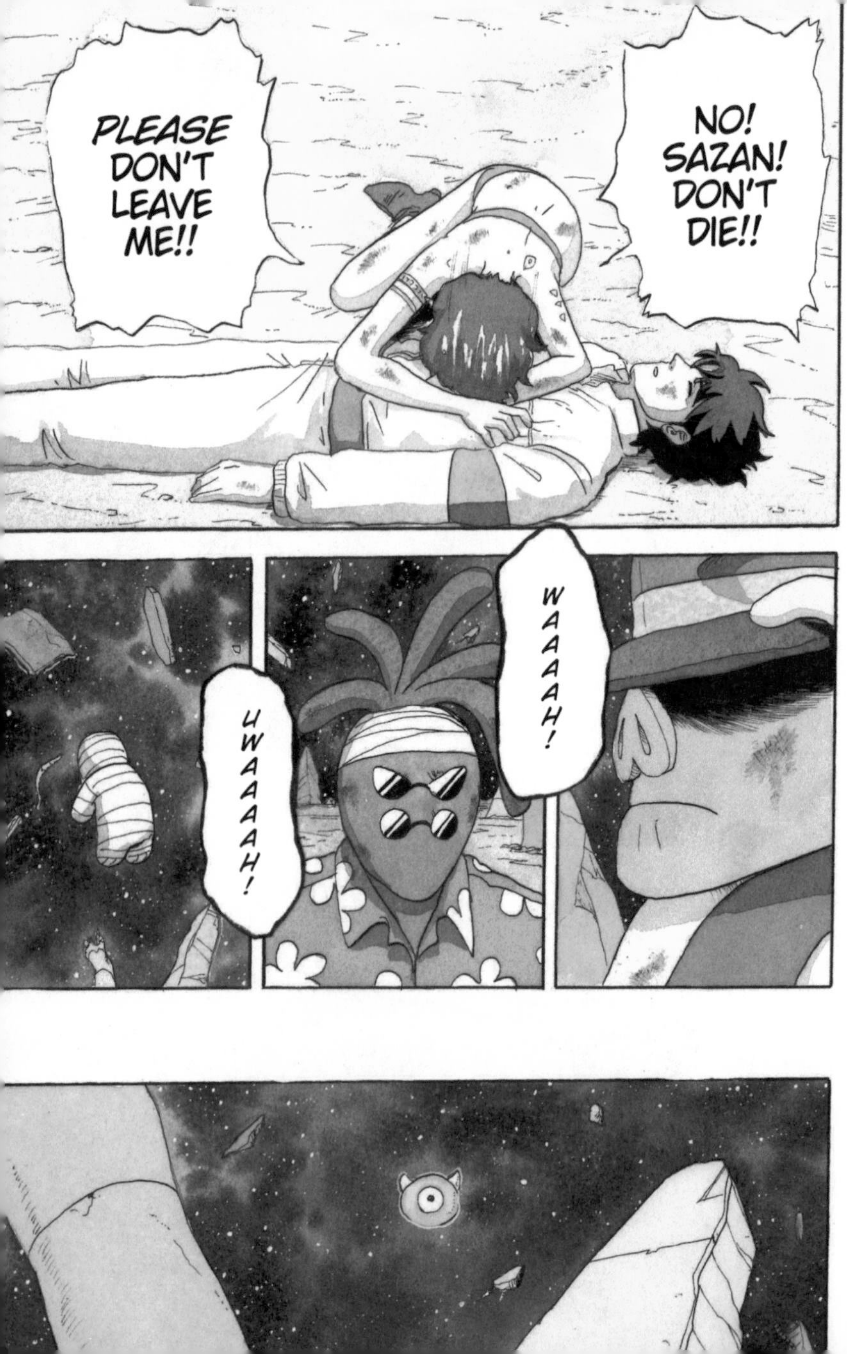
NO! SAZAN! DON'T DIE!!
PLEASE DON'T LEAVE ME!!
WAAAAH!
UWAAAAH!

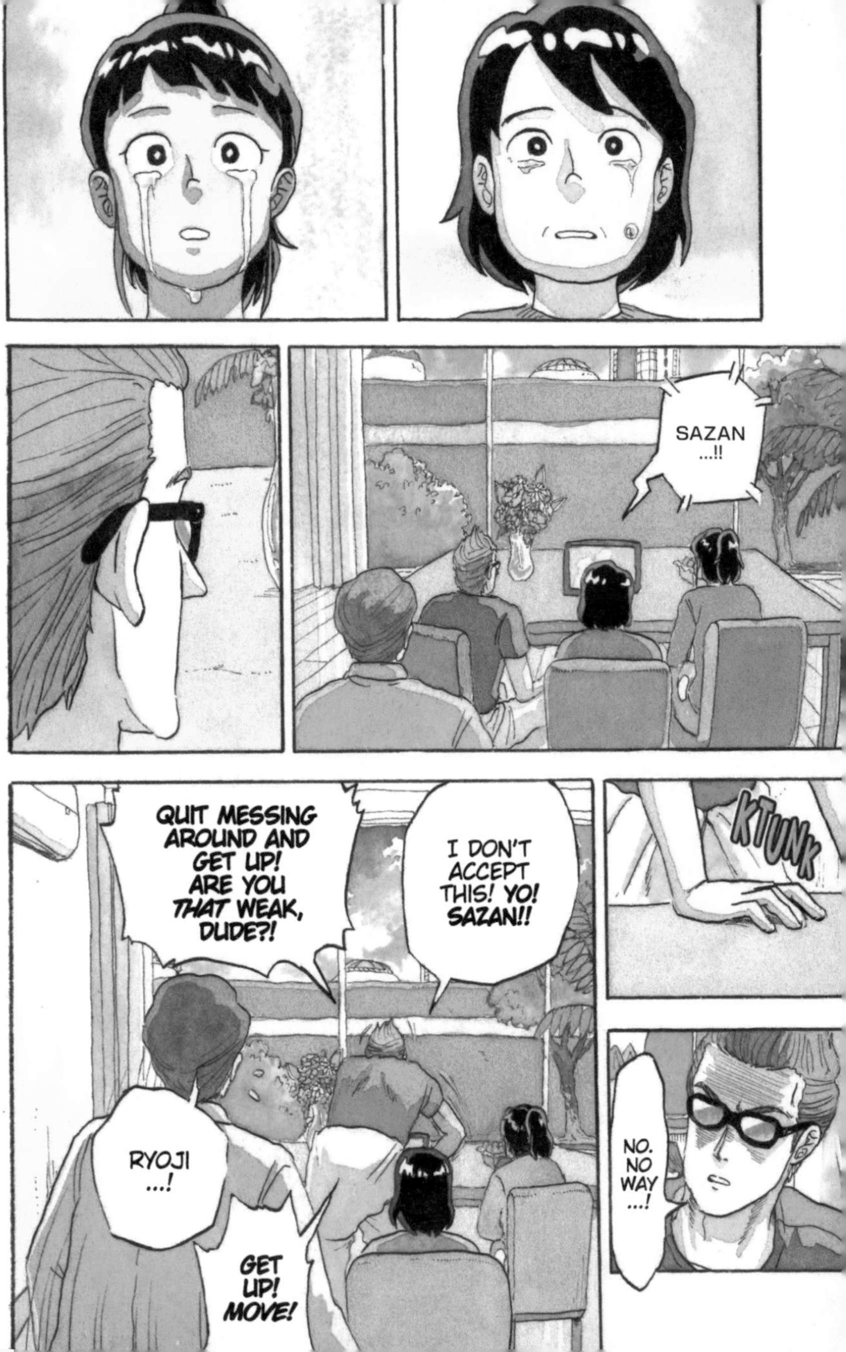
SAZAN ...!!
KTUNK
NO. NO WAY ...!
I DON'T ACCEPT THIS! YO! SAZAN!!
QUIT MESSING AROUND AND GET UP! ARE YOU *THAT* WEAK, DUDE?!
RYOJI ...!
GET UP! *MOVE!*

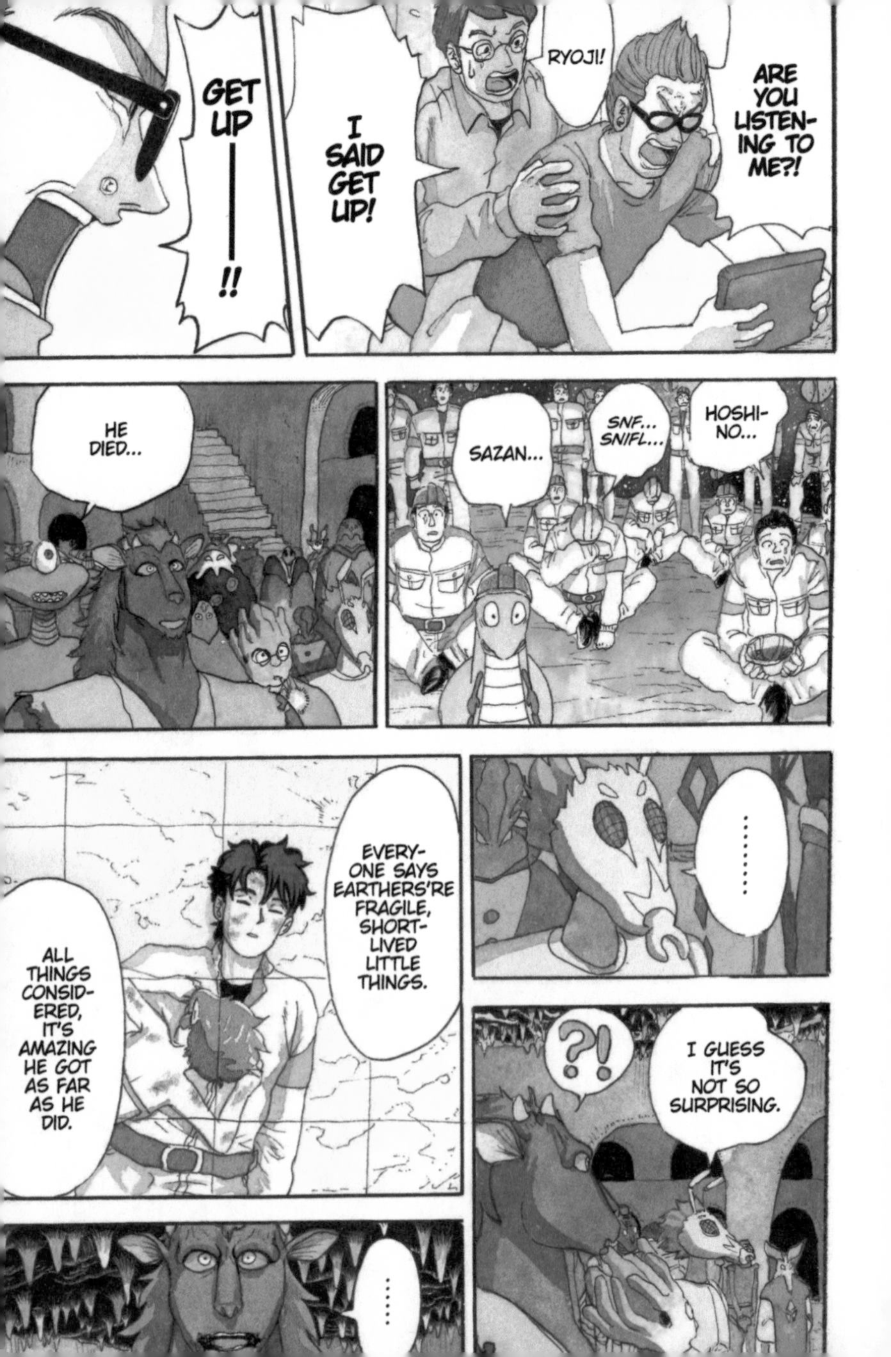
ARE YOU LISTEN-ING TO ME?!
RYOJI!
I SAID GET UP!
GET UP——!!
HOSHI-NO...
SNF... SNIFL...
SAZAN...
HE DIED...
......
?!
I GUESS IT'S NOT SO SURPRISING.
EVERY-ONE SAYS EARTHERS'RE FRAGILE, SHORT-LIVED LITTLE THINGS.
ALL THINGS CONSID-ERED, IT'S AMAZING HE GOT AS FAR AS HE DID.
......

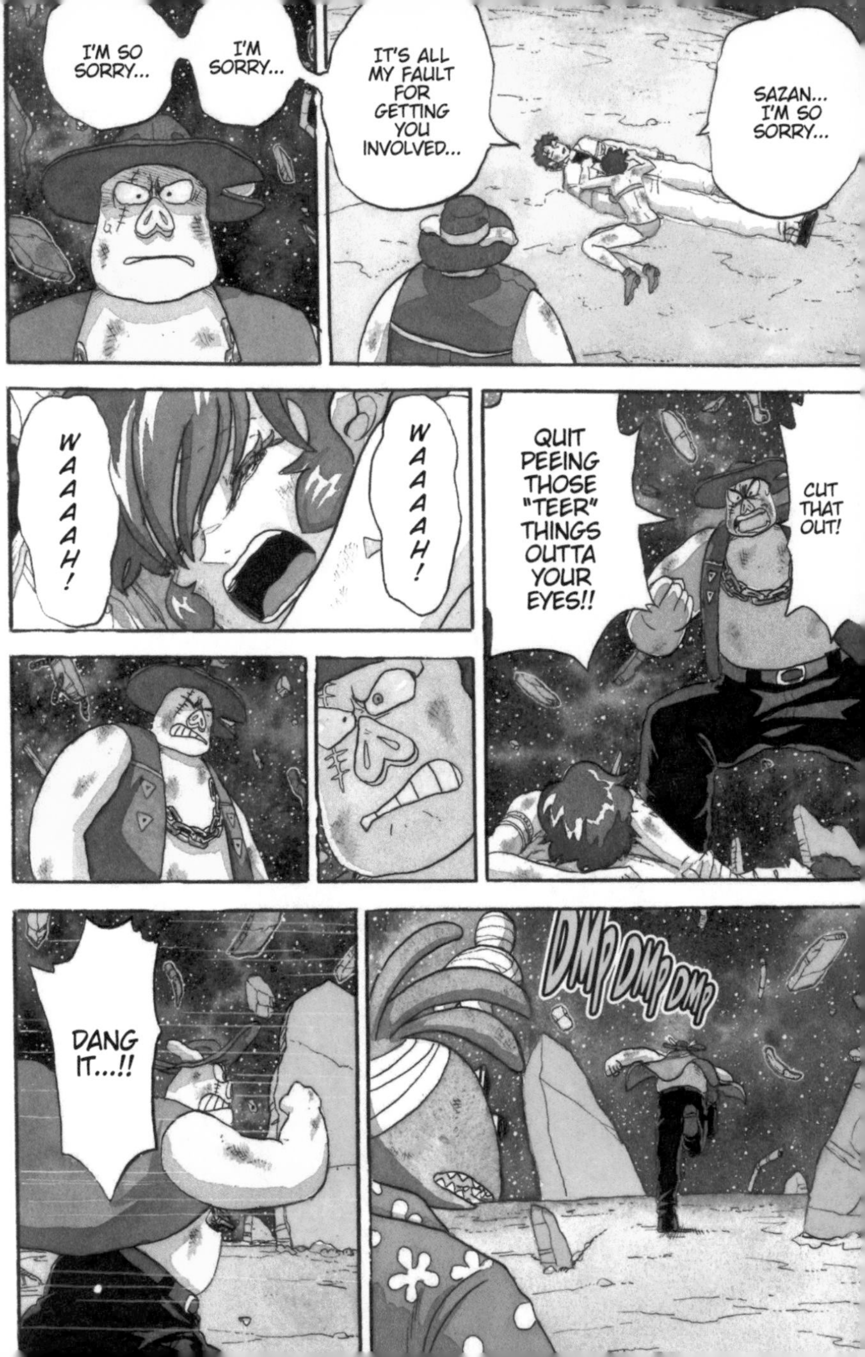
SAZAN... I'M SO SORRY...
IT'S ALL MY FAULT FOR GETTING YOU INVOLVED...
I'M SORRY...
I'M SO SORRY...
QUIT PEEING THOSE "TEER" THINGS OUTTA YOUR EYES!!
CUT THAT OUT!
WAAAAAH!
WAAAAAH!
DMP DMP DMP
DANG IT...!!

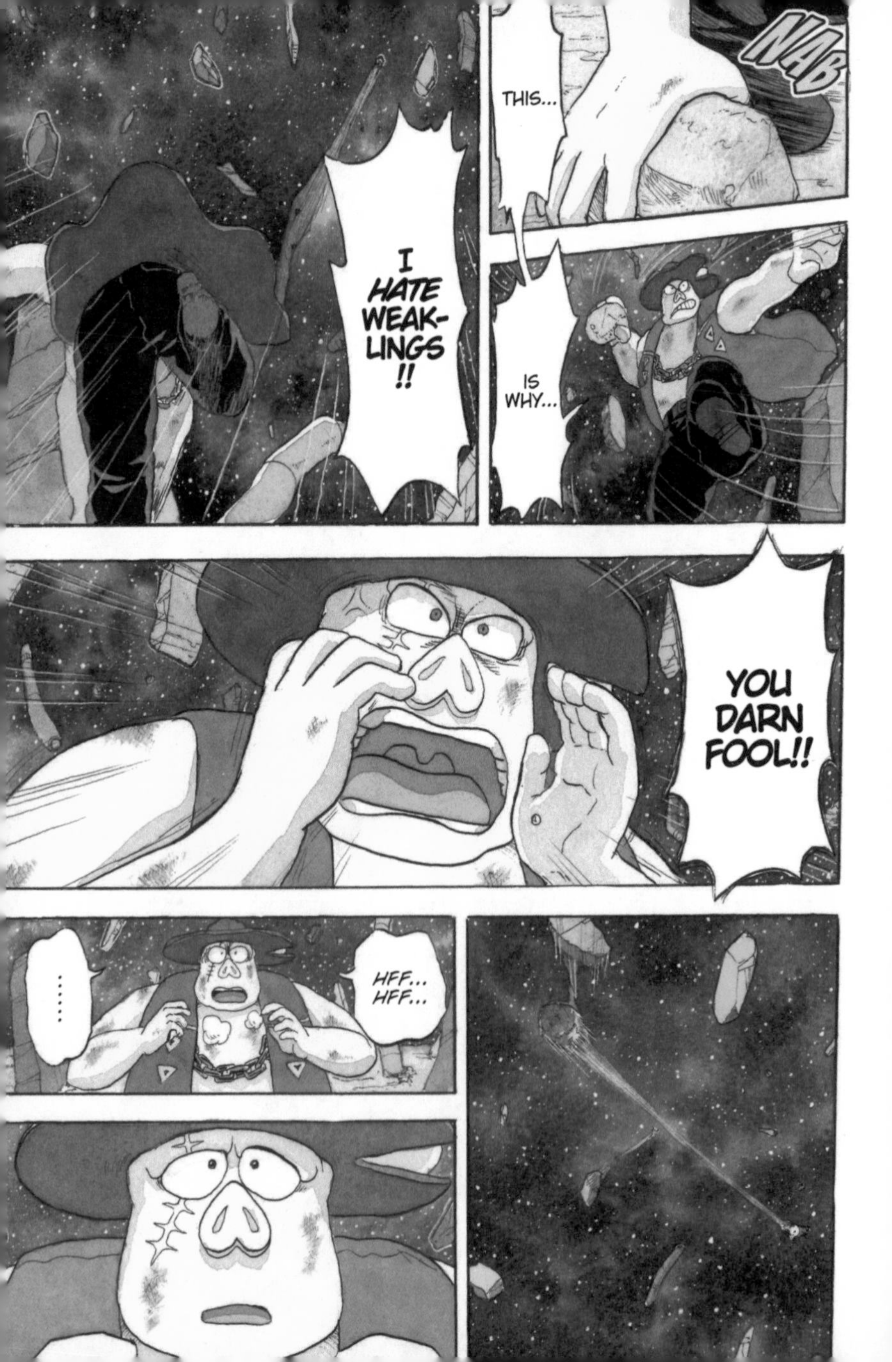
NAB
THIS...
IS WHY...
I HATE WEAKLINGS!!
YOU DARN FOOL!!
HFF... HFF...
......

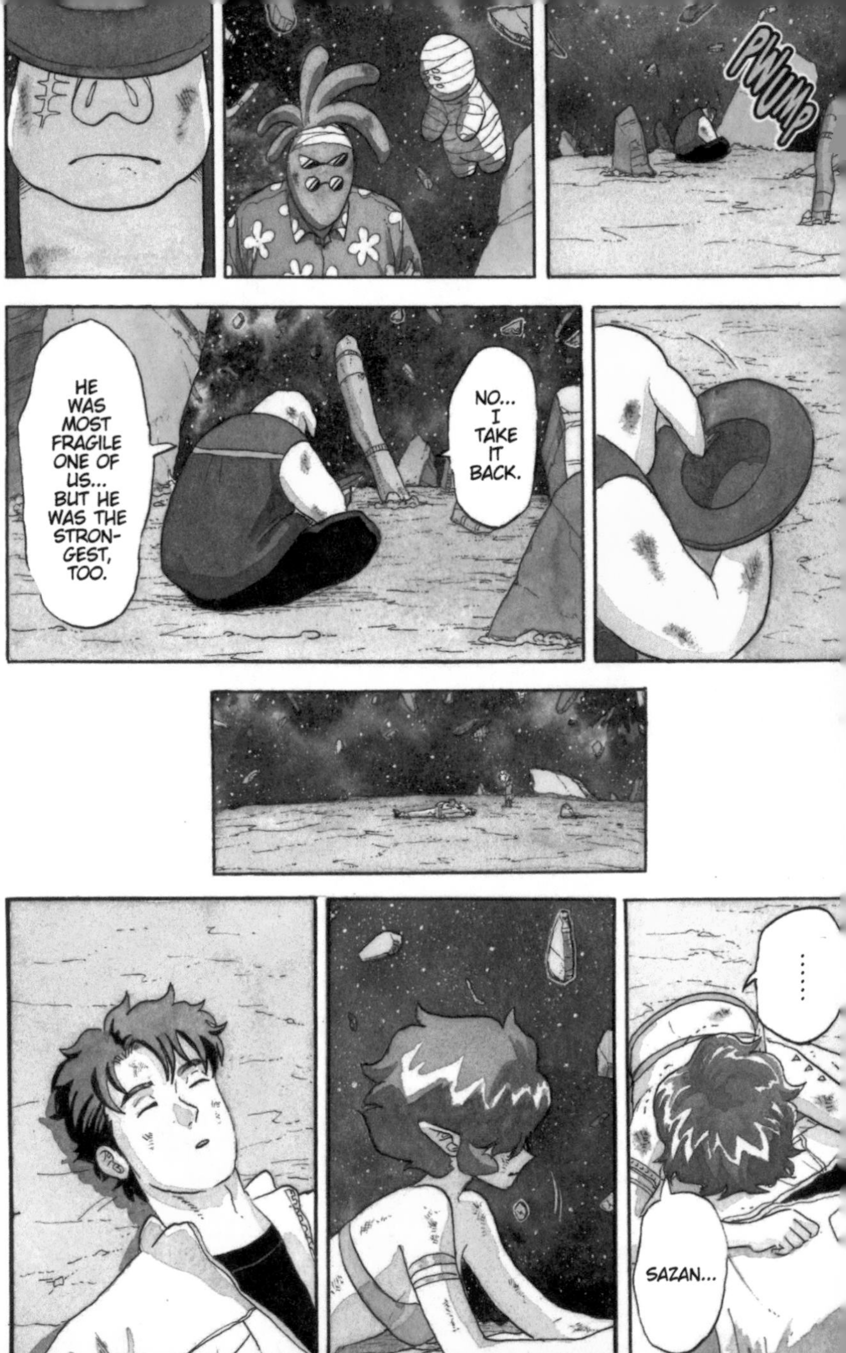
PWUMP
NO... I TAKE IT BACK.
HE WAS MOST FRAGILE ONE OF US... BUT HE WAS THE STRONGEST, TOO.
......
SAZAN...

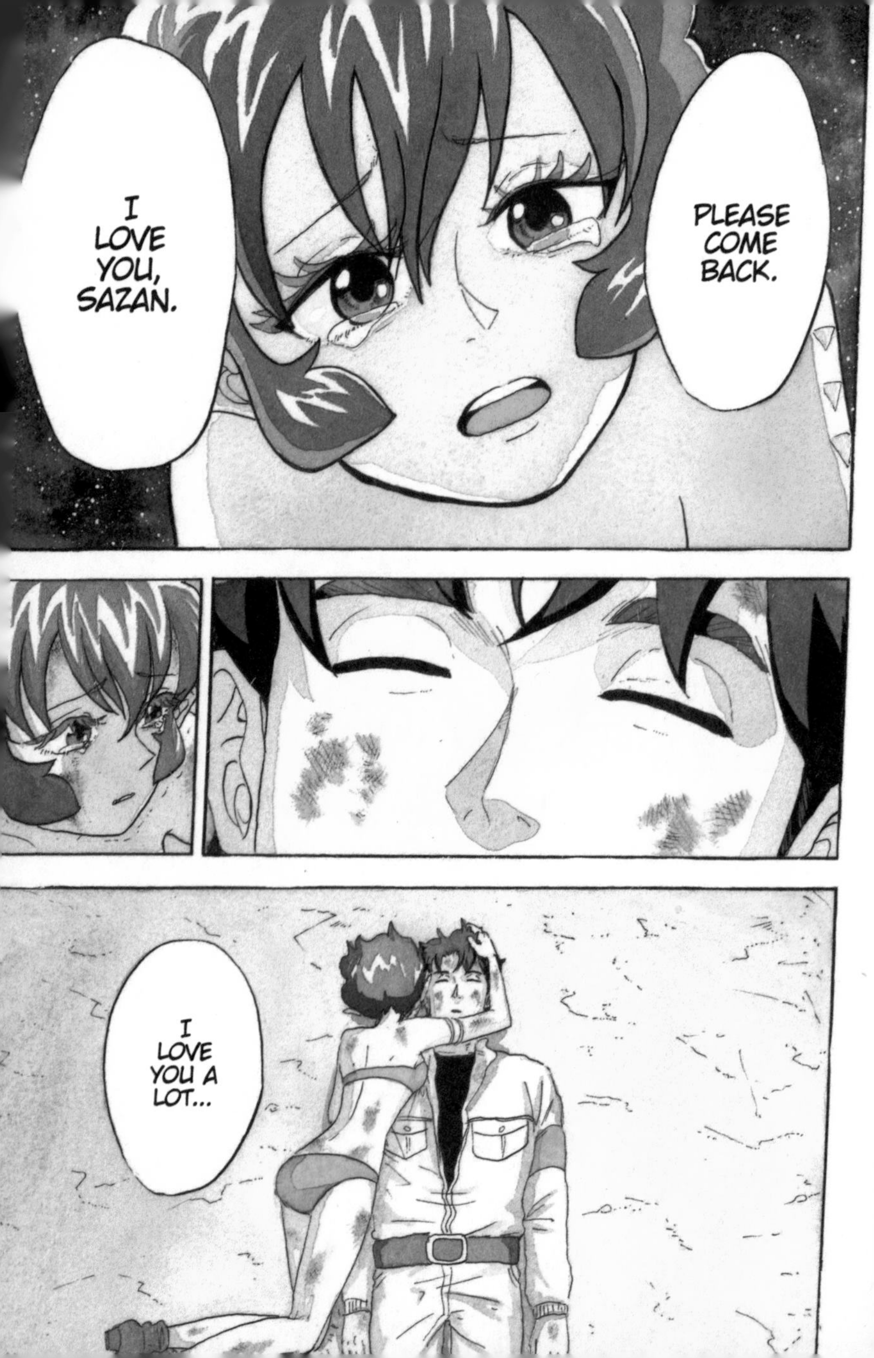
PLEASE COME BACK.
I LOVE YOU, SAZAN.
I LOVE YOU A LOT...

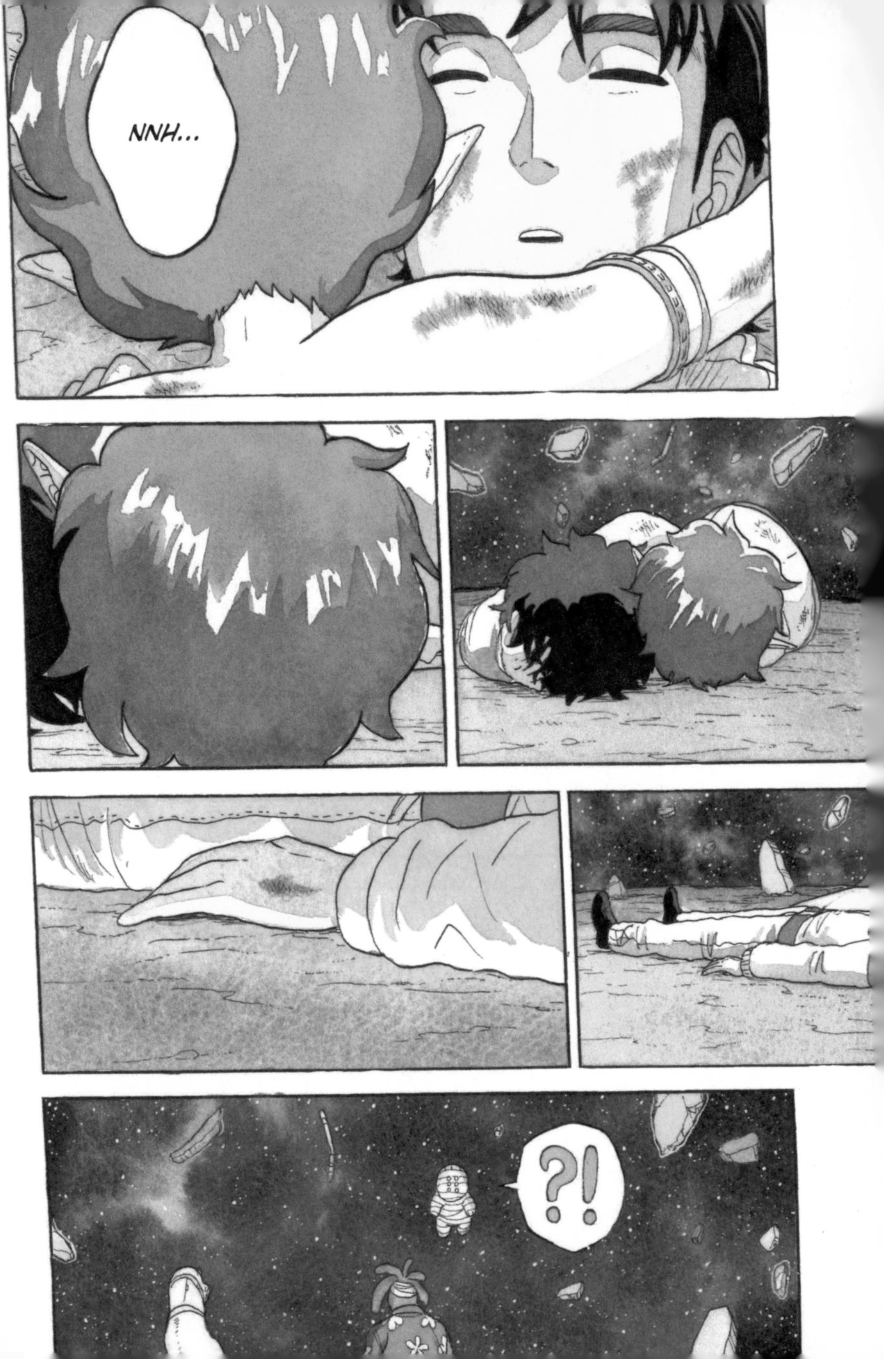
NNH...
?!

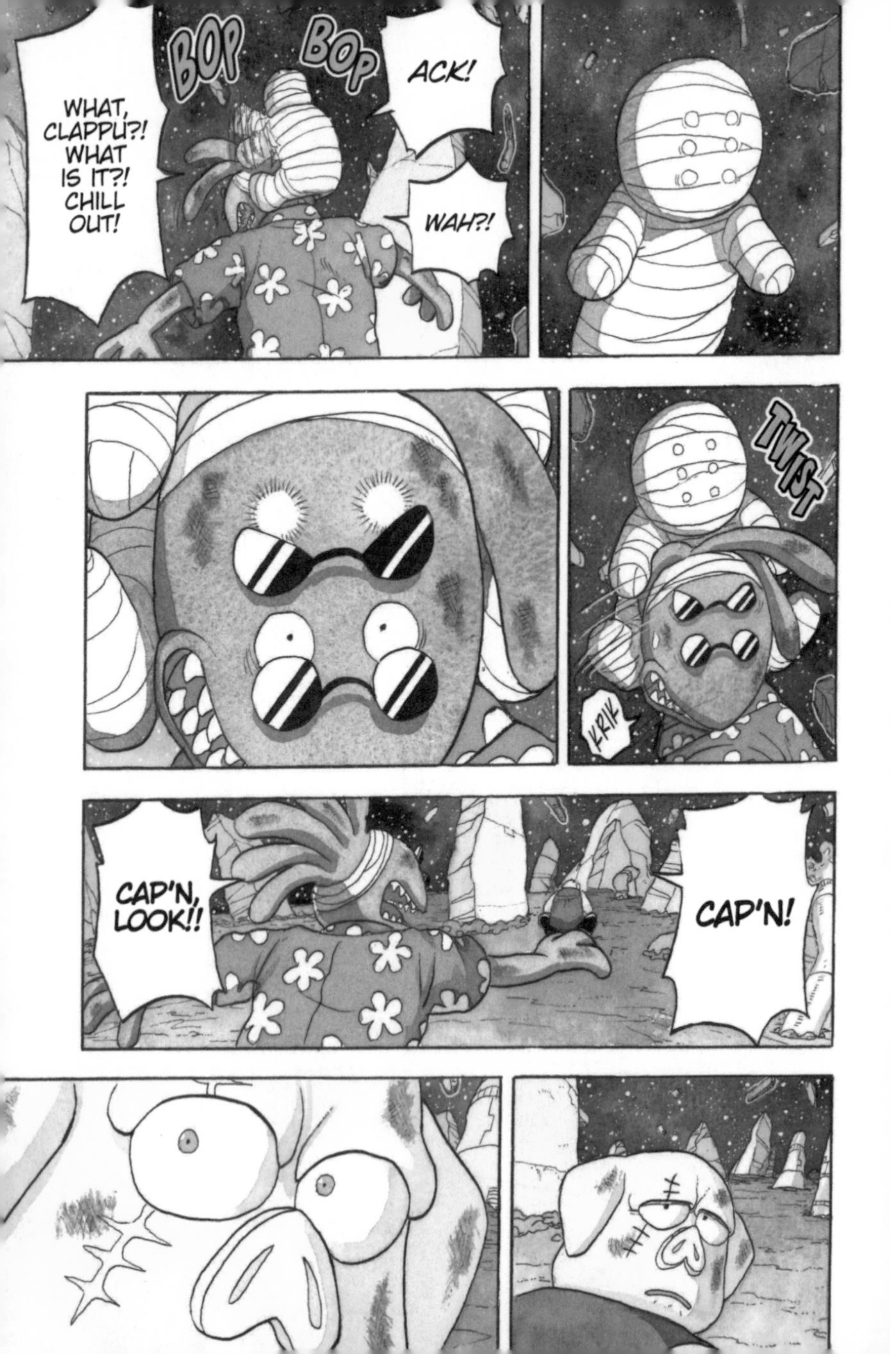
ACK!
BOP
BOP
WAH?!
WHAT, CLAPPU?! WHAT IS IT?! CHILL OUT!
TWIST
KRIK
CAP'N!
CAP'N, LOOK!!

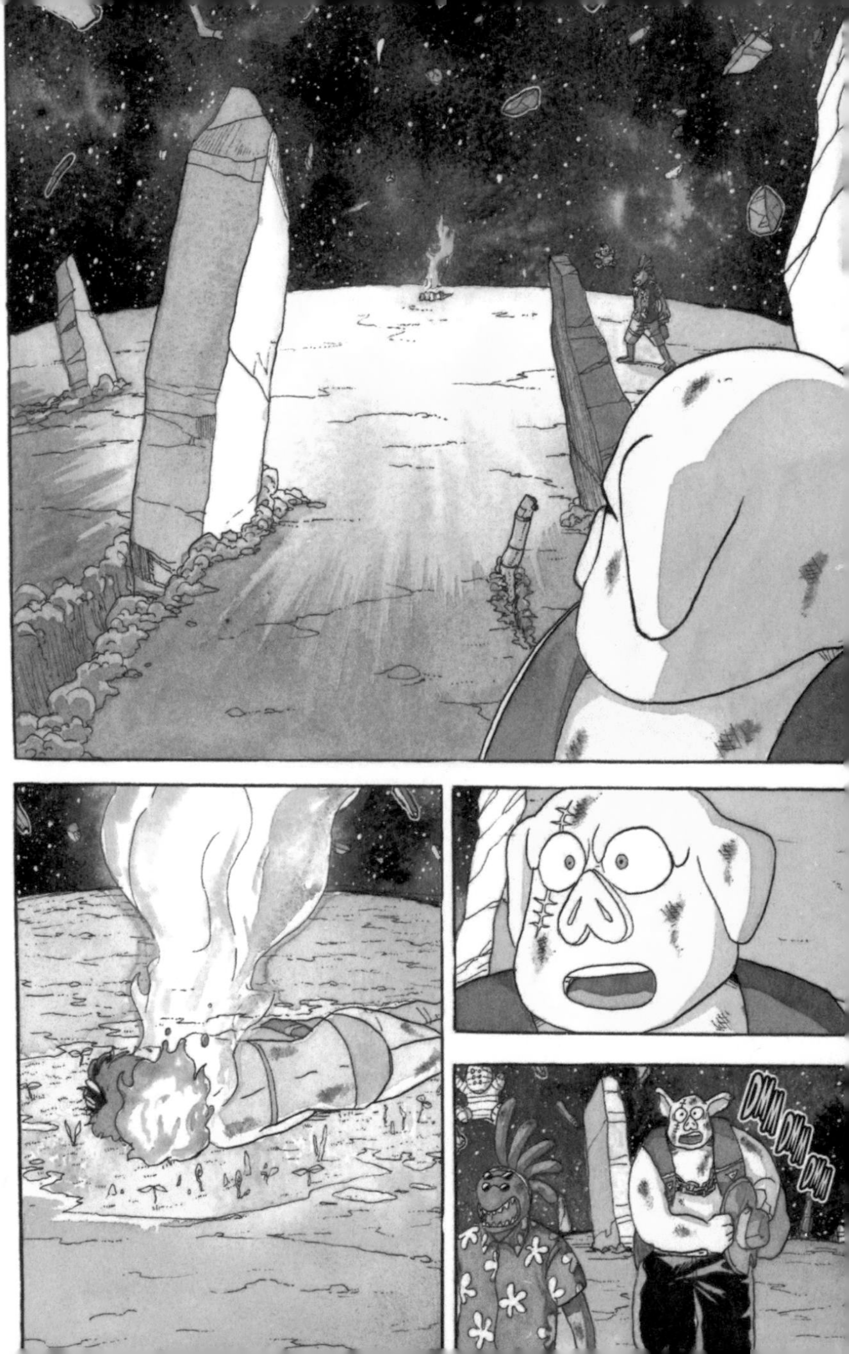
DMM DMM DMM

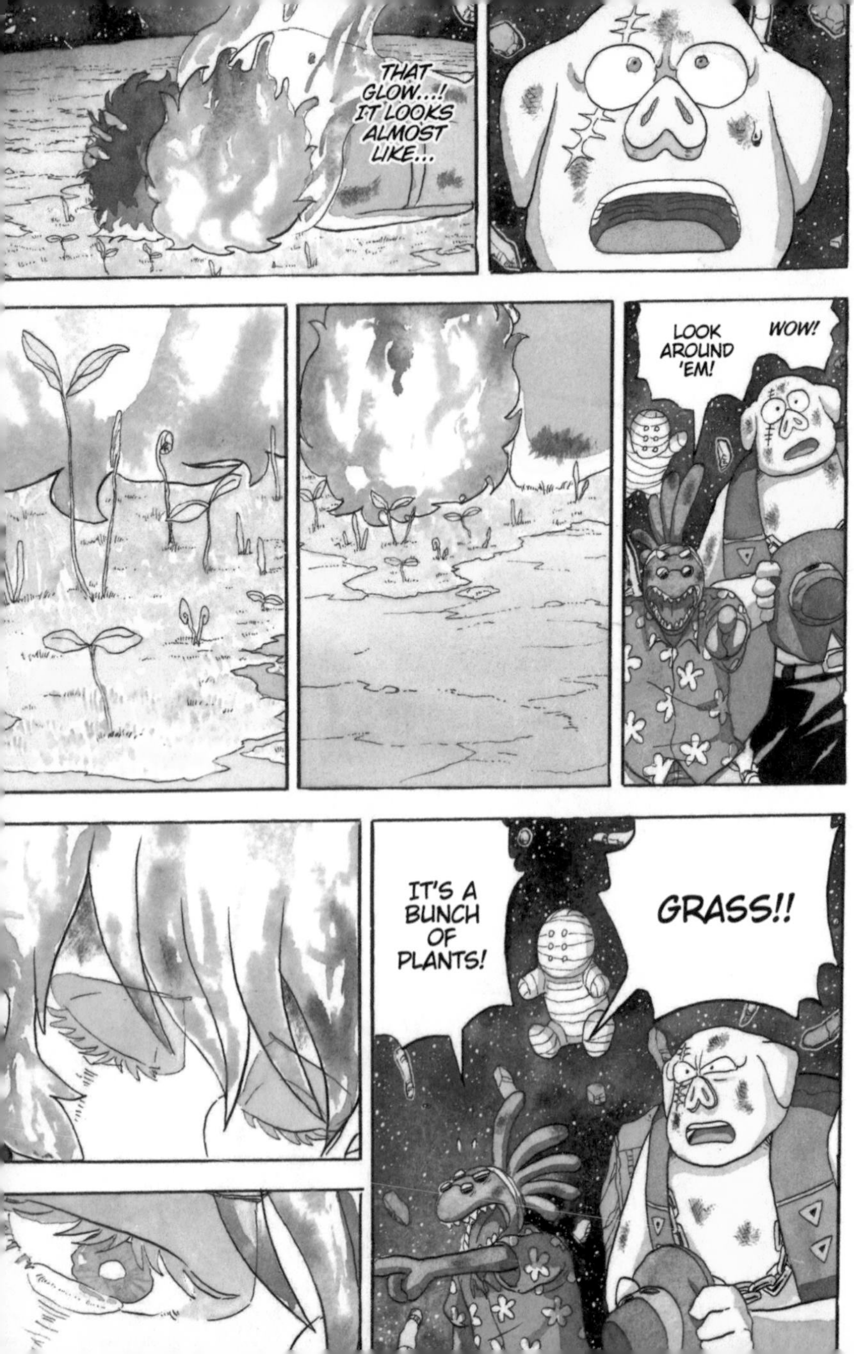
THAT GLOW...! IT LOOKS ALMOST LIKE...
WOW!
LOOK AROUND 'EM!
GRASS!!
IT'S A BUNCH OF PLANTS!

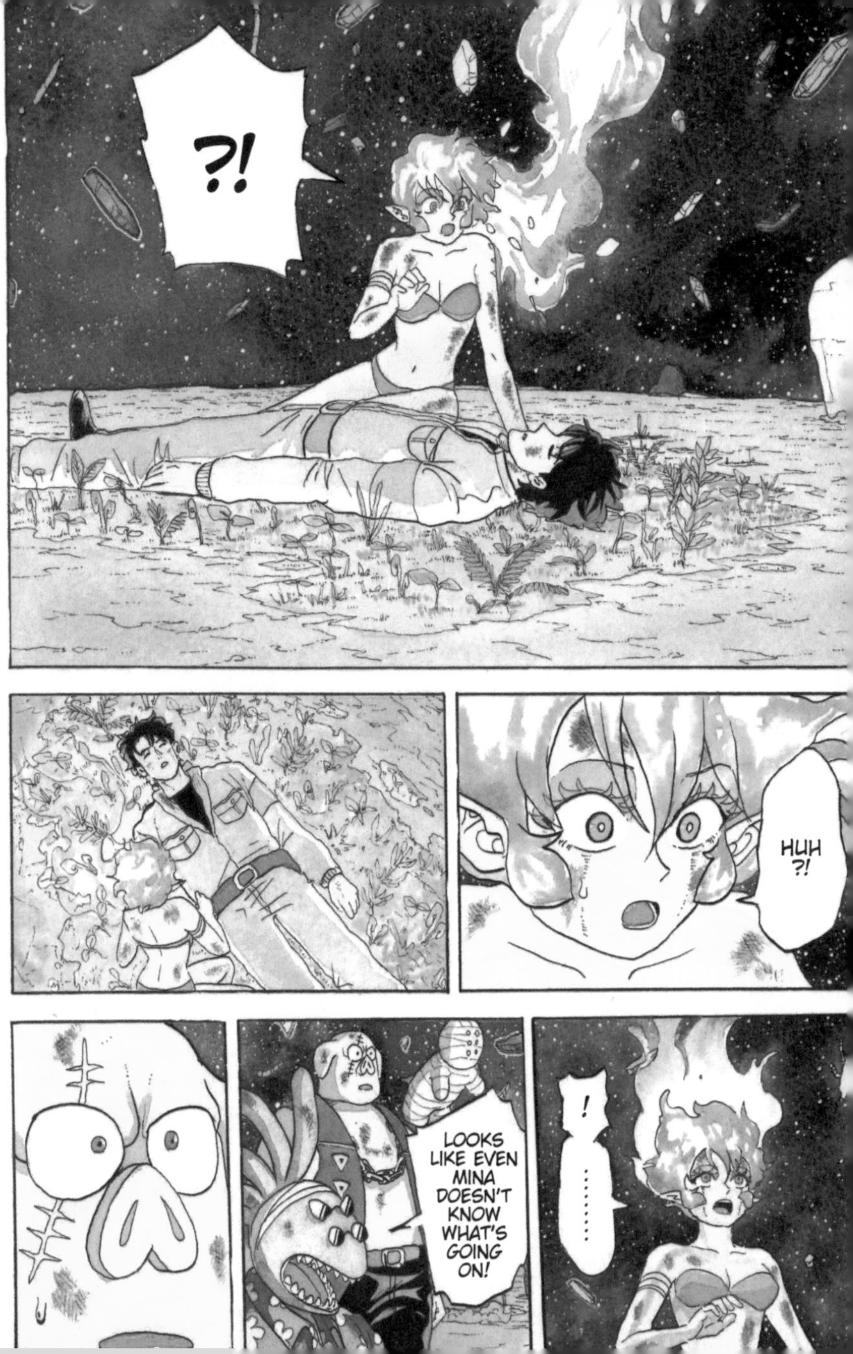
?!
HUH ?!
! ......
LOOKS LIKE EVEN MINA DOESN'T KNOW WHAT'S GOING ON!

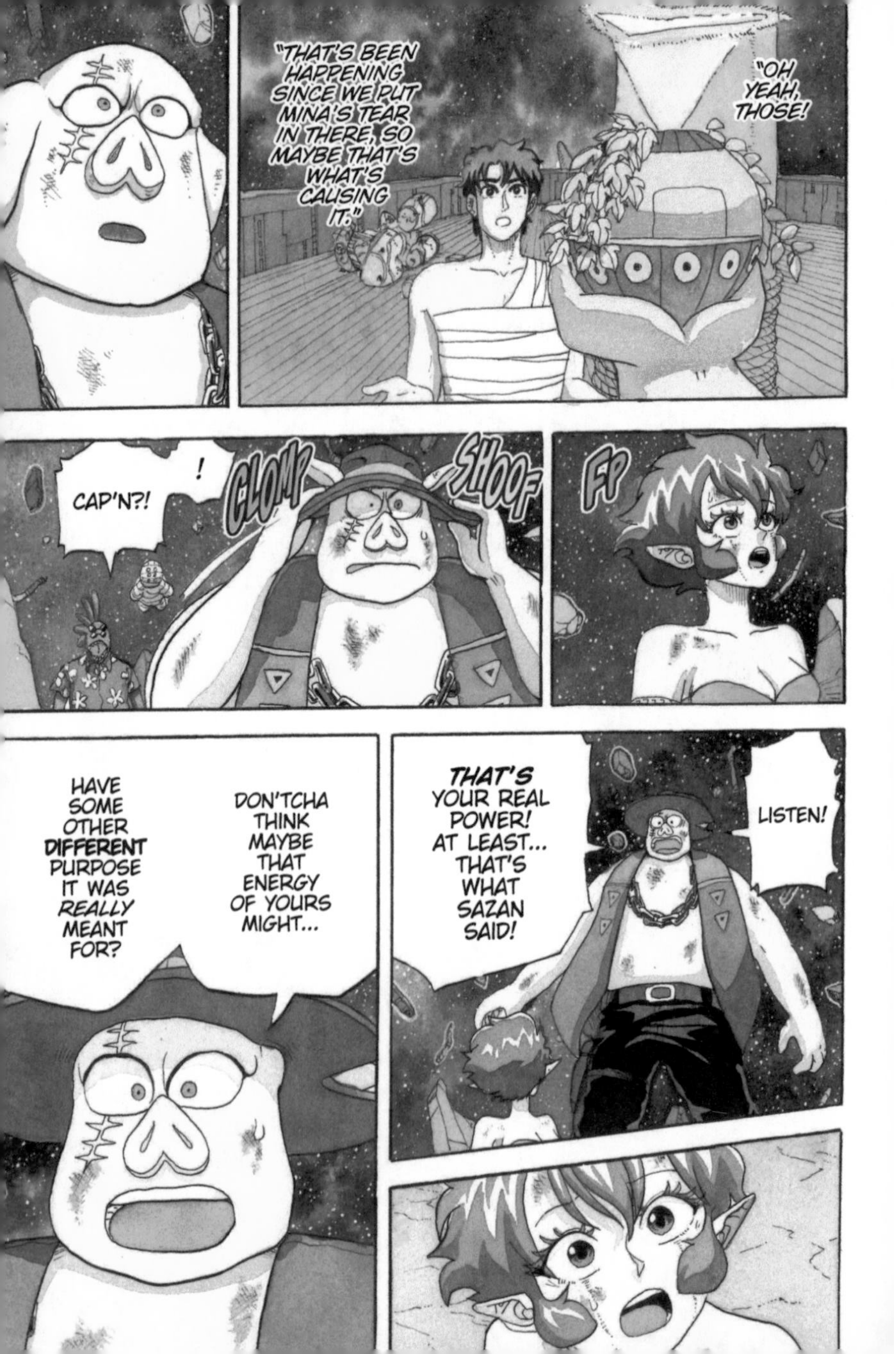

"OH YEAH, THOSE!
"THAT'S BEEN HAPPENING SINCE WE PUT MINA'S TEAR IN THERE, SO MAYBE THAT'S WHAT'S CAUSING IT."
FP
SHOOF
CLOMP
!
CAP'N?!
LISTEN!
THAT'S YOUR REAL POWER! AT LEAST... THAT'S WHAT SAZAN SAID!
DON'TCHA THINK MAYBE THAT ENERGY OF YOURS MIGHT...
HAVE SOME OTHER DIFFERENT PURPOSE IT WAS REALLY MEANT FOR?

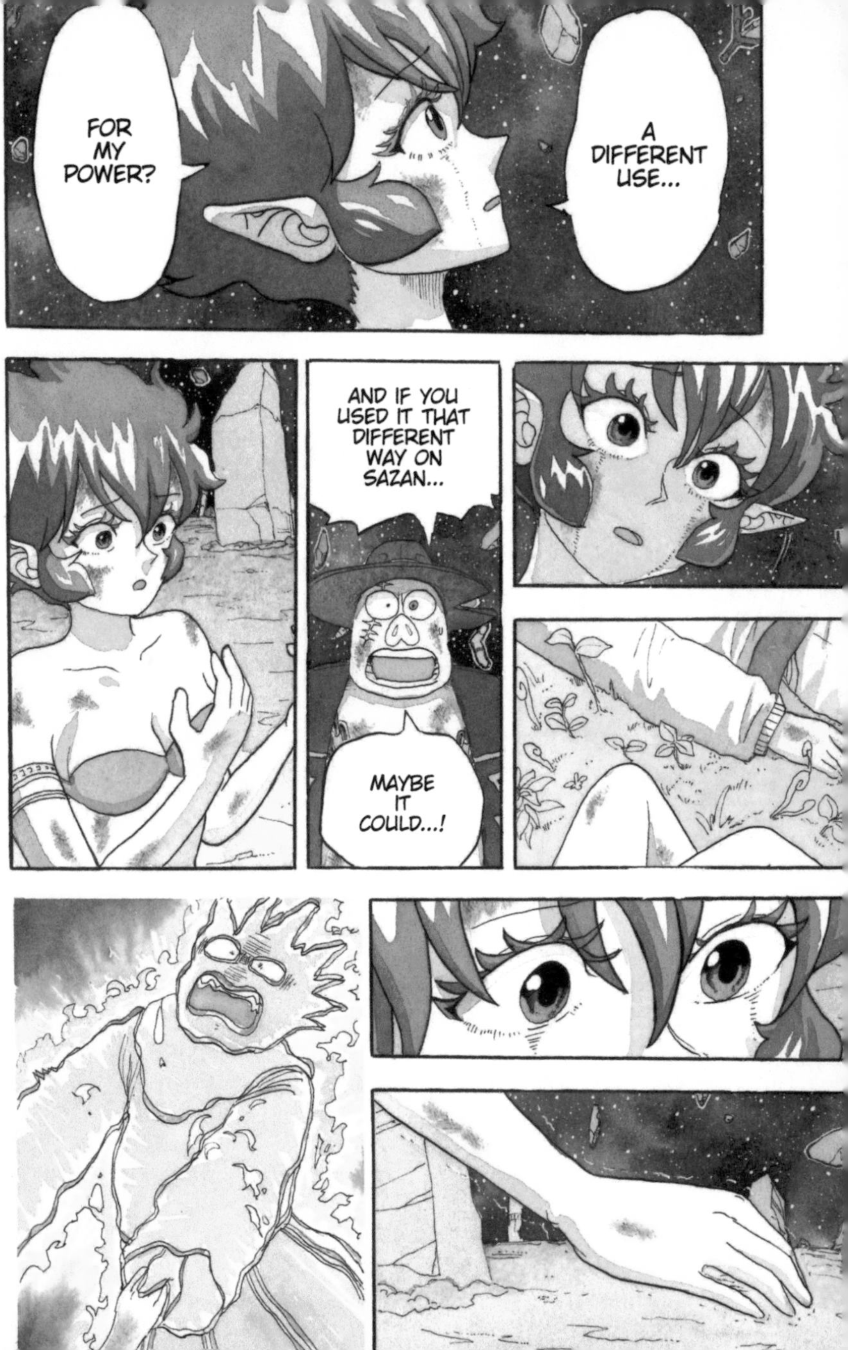
A DIFFERENT USE...
FOR MY POWER?
AND IF YOU USED IT THAT DIFFERENT WAY ON SAZAN...
MAYBE IT COULD...!

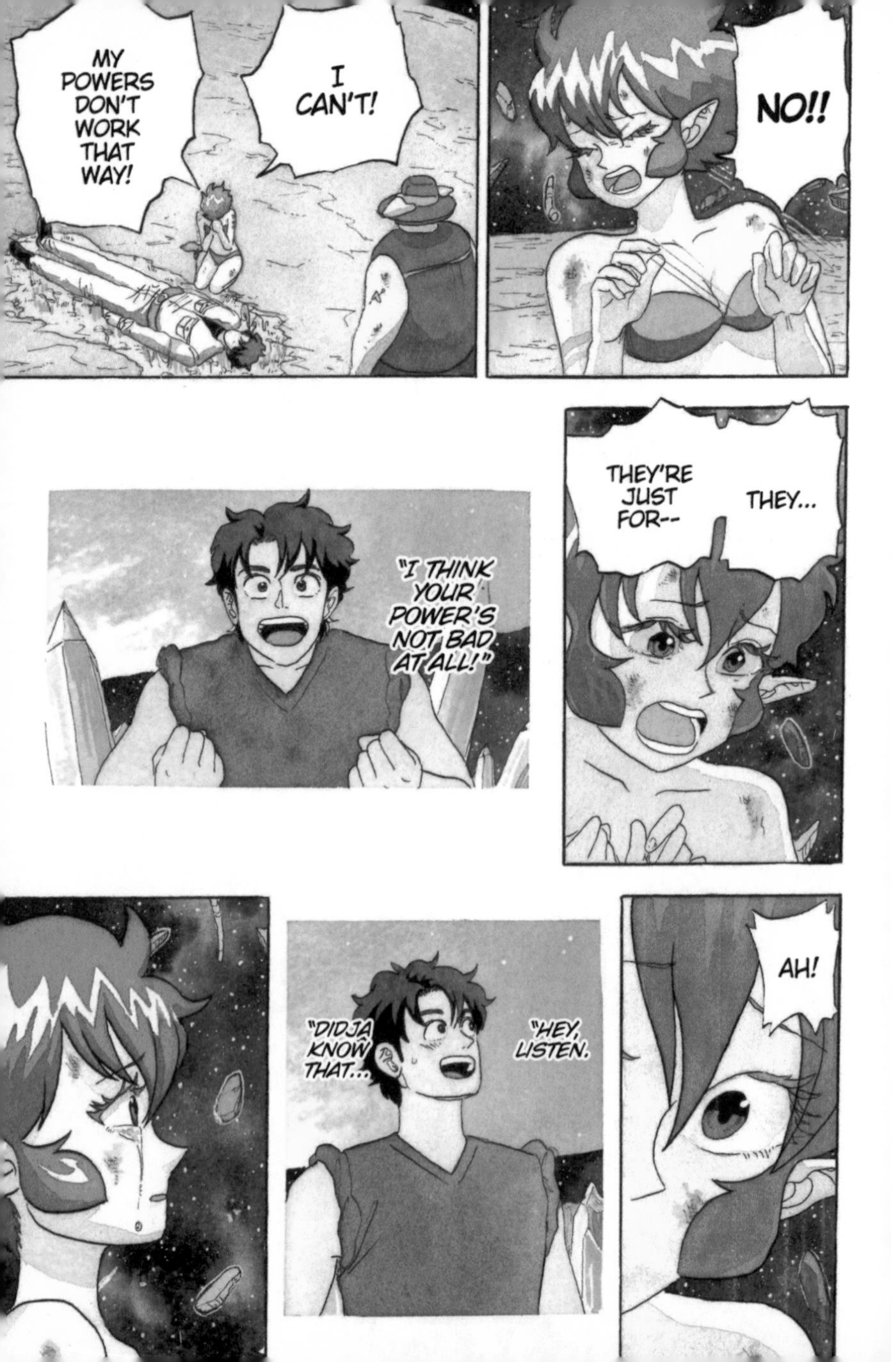
NO!!
I CAN'T!
MY POWERS DON'T WORK THAT WAY!
THEY...
THEY'RE JUST FOR--
"I THINK YOUR POWER'S NOT BAD AT ALL!"
AH!
"HEY, LISTEN.
"DIDJA KNOW THAT...

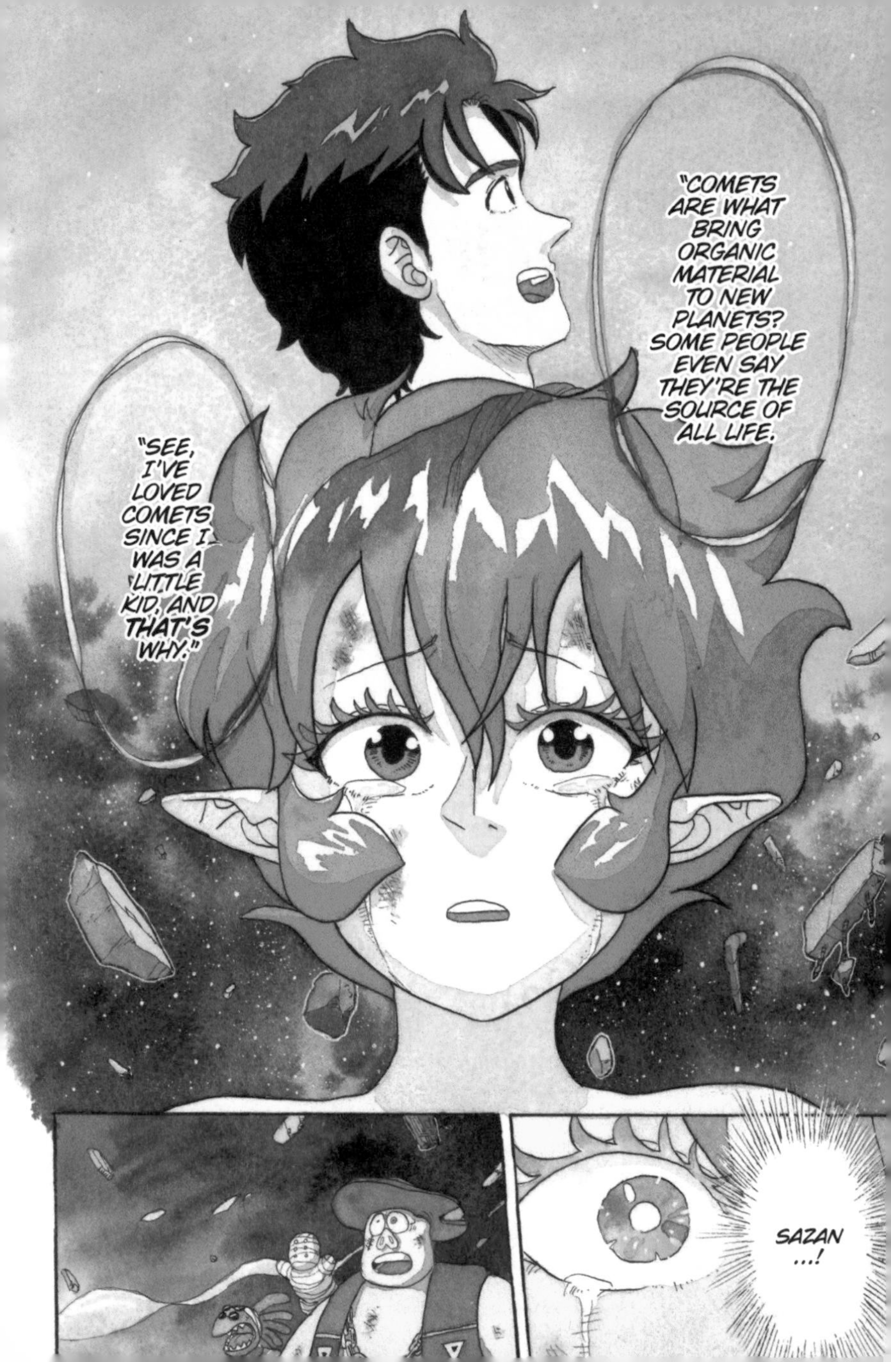
"COMETS ARE WHAT BRING ORGANIC MATERIAL TO NEW PLANETS? SOME PEOPLE EVEN SAY THEY'RE THE SOURCE OF ALL LIFE.
"SEE, I'VE LOVED COMETS SINCE I WAS A LITTLE KID, AND THAT'S WHY."
SAZAN ...!

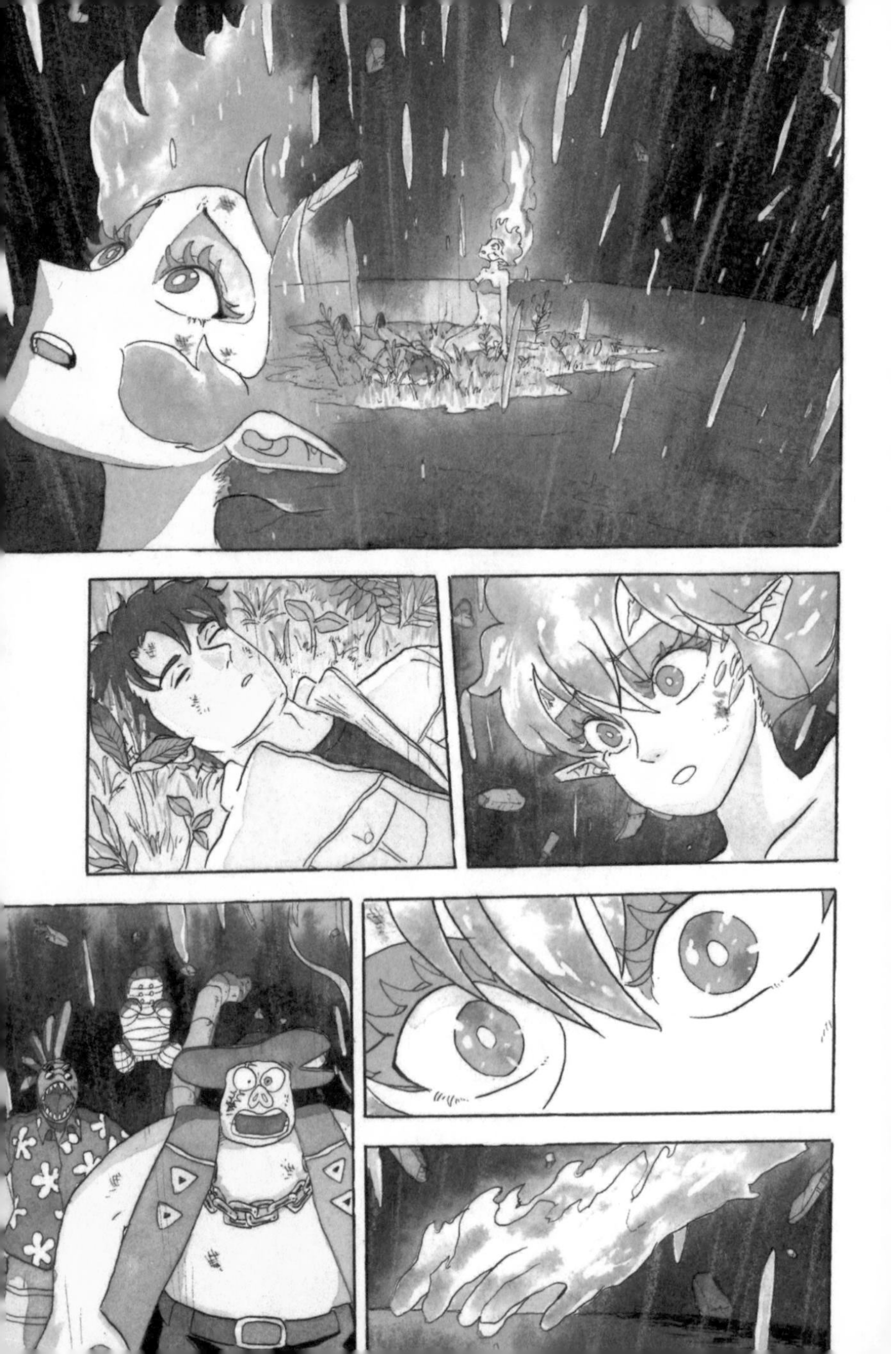

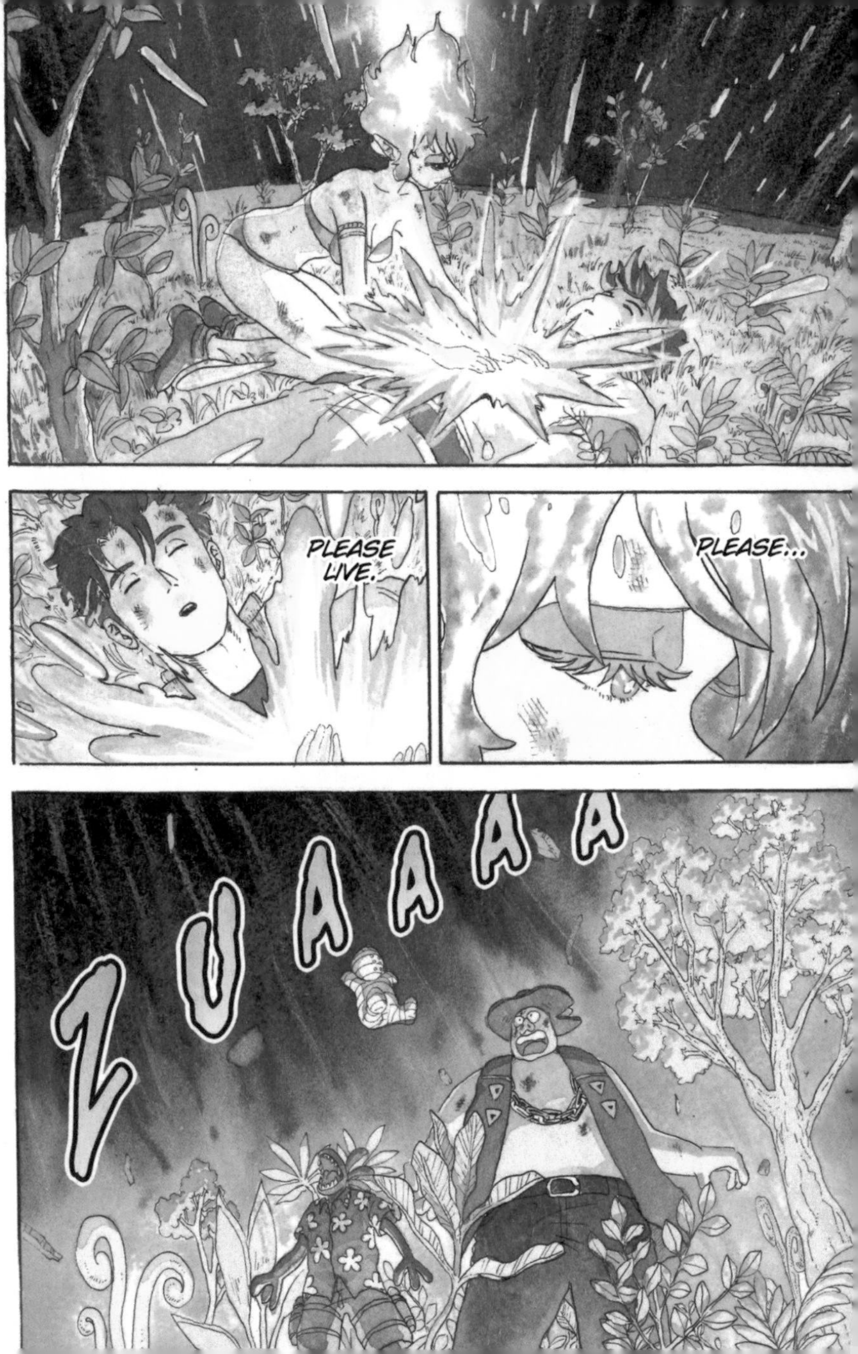
PLEASE...
PLEASE LIVE.
ZUAAAAA

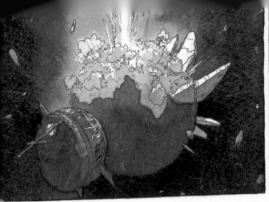

!

SAZAN ...!!

SAZAN ...!

LIVE!

PLEASE ...

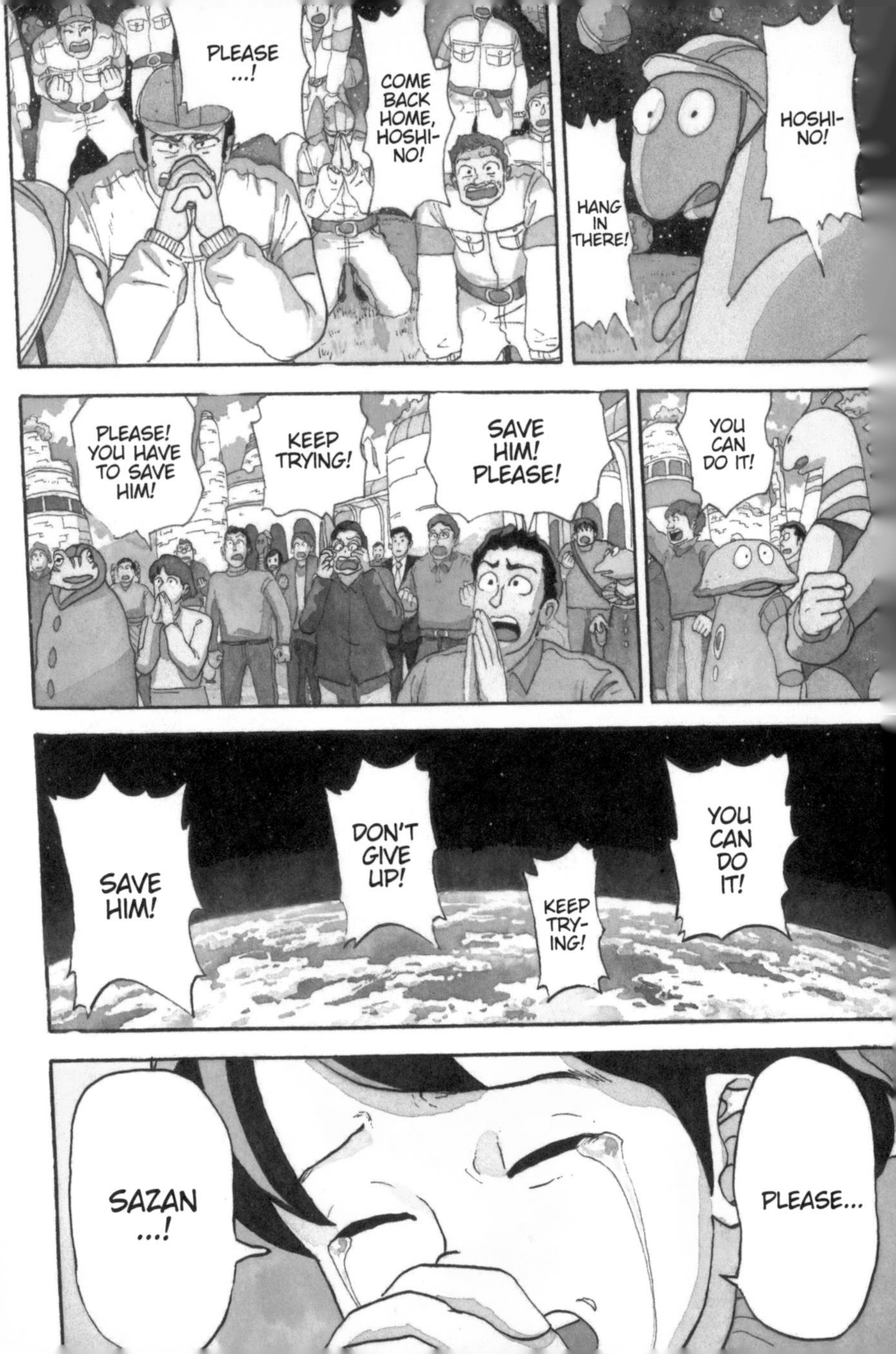
HOSHINO!
HANG IN THERE!
COME BACK HOME, HOSHINO!
PLEASE ...!
YOU CAN DO IT!
SAVE HIM! PLEASE!
KEEP TRYING!
PLEASE! YOU HAVE TO SAVE HIM!
YOU CAN DO IT!
DON'T GIVE UP!
KEEP TRYING!
SAVE HIM!
PLEASE...
SAZAN ...!

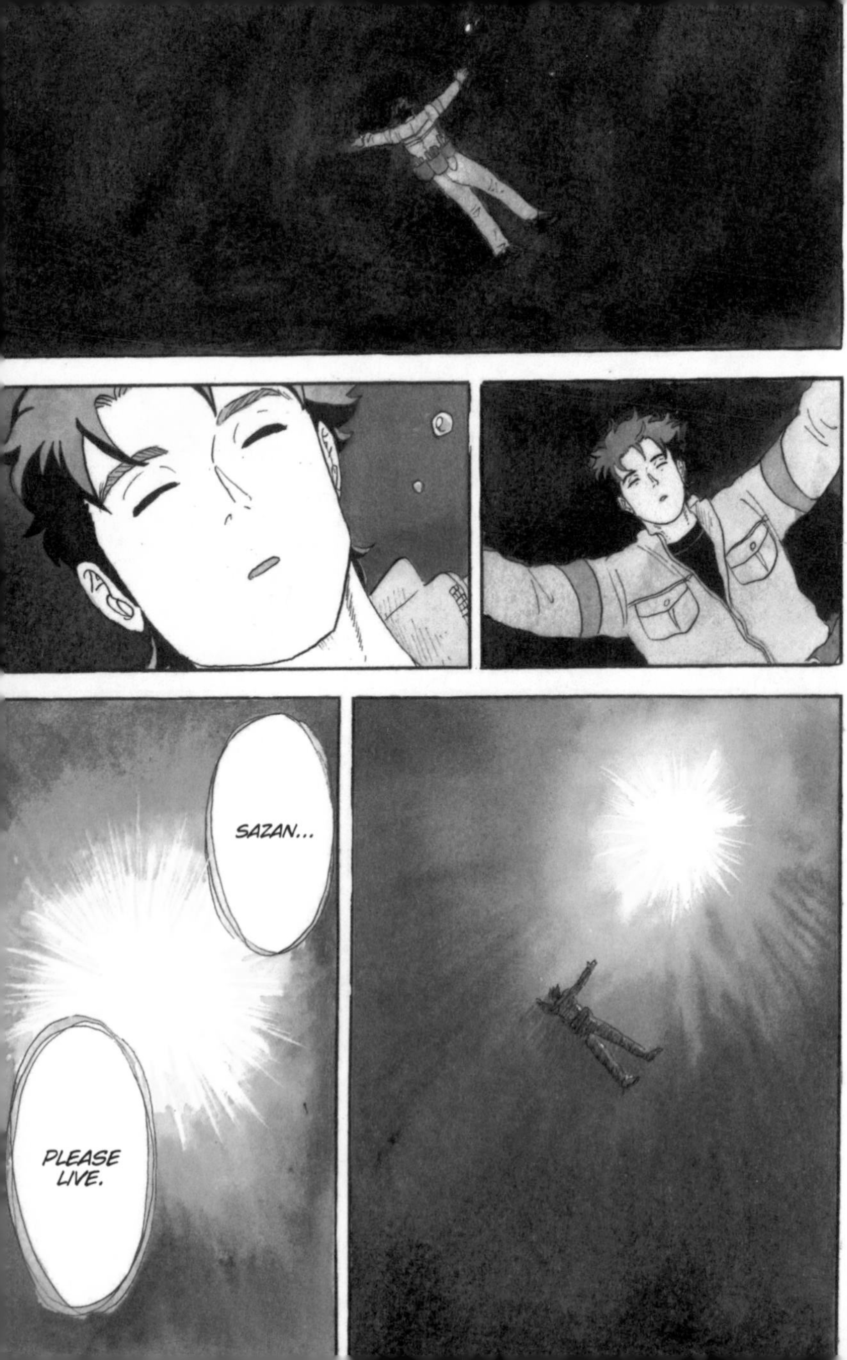
SAZAN...
PLEASE LIVE.

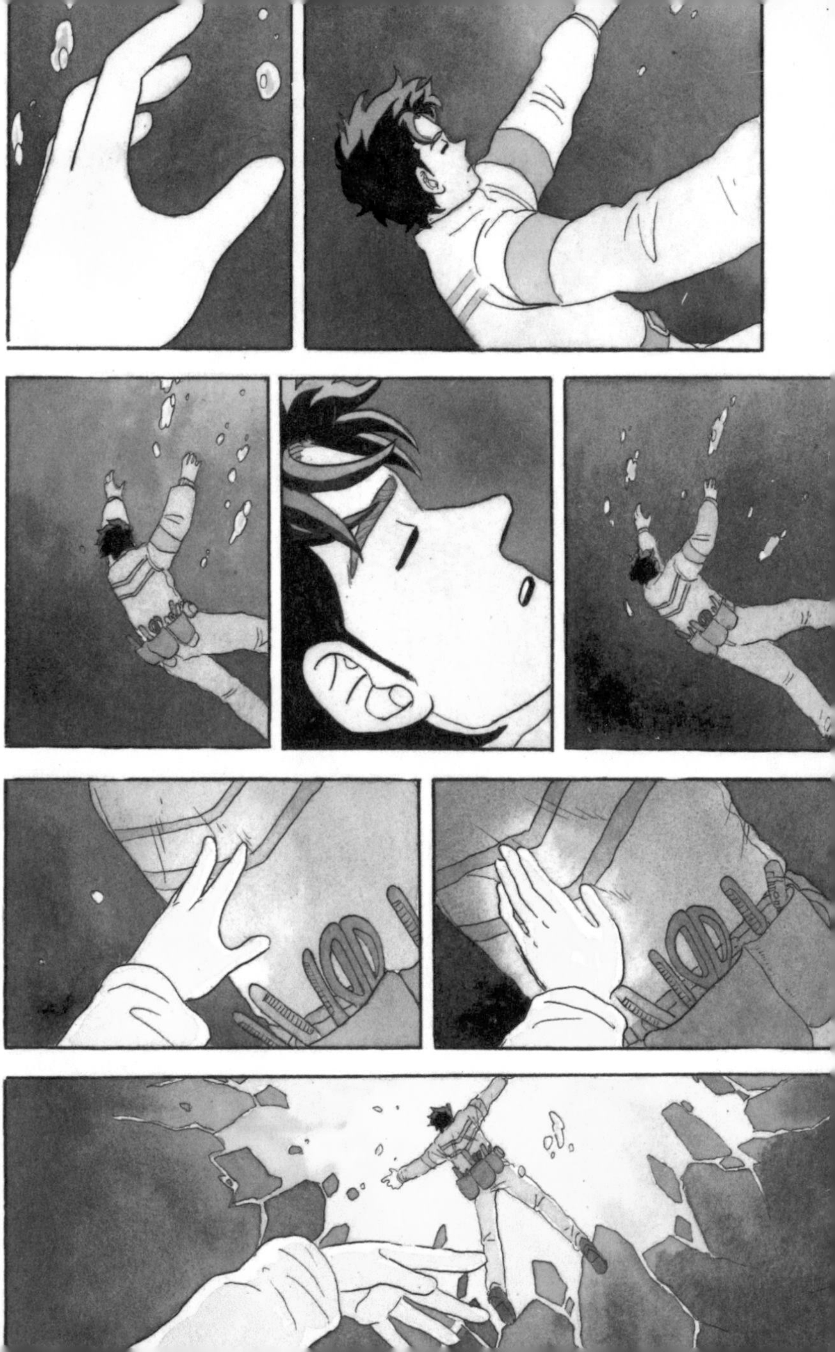

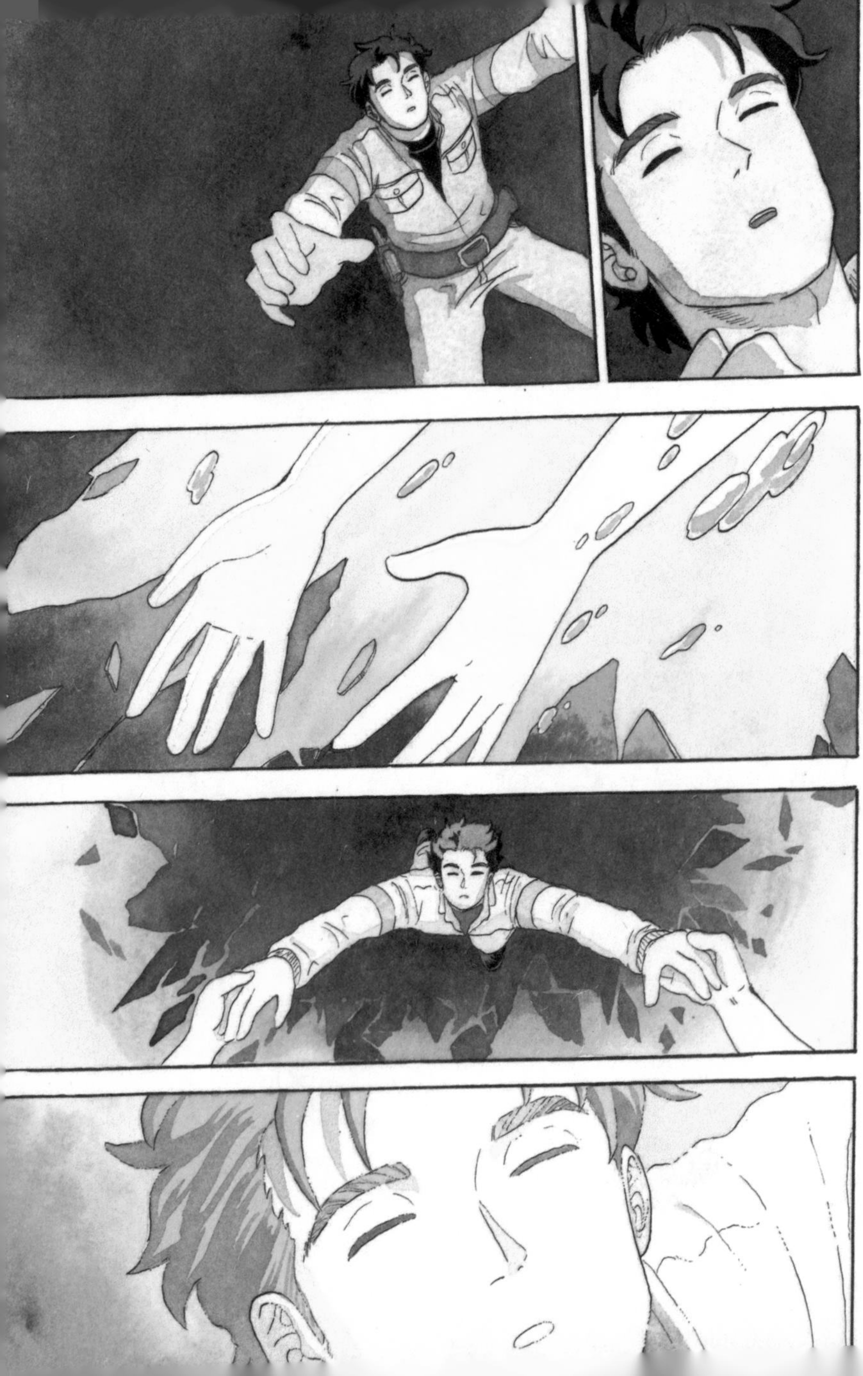

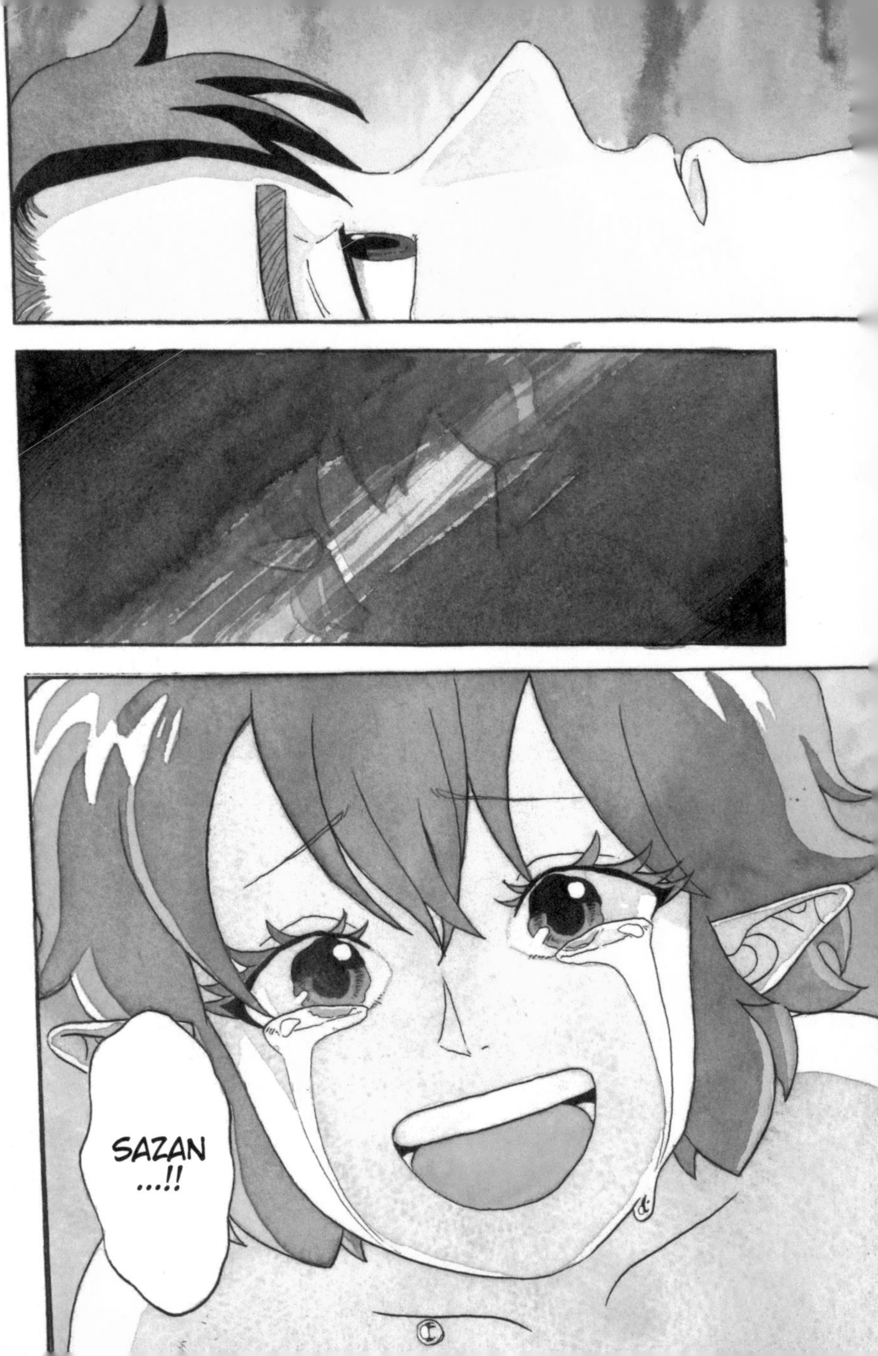
SAZAN ...!!

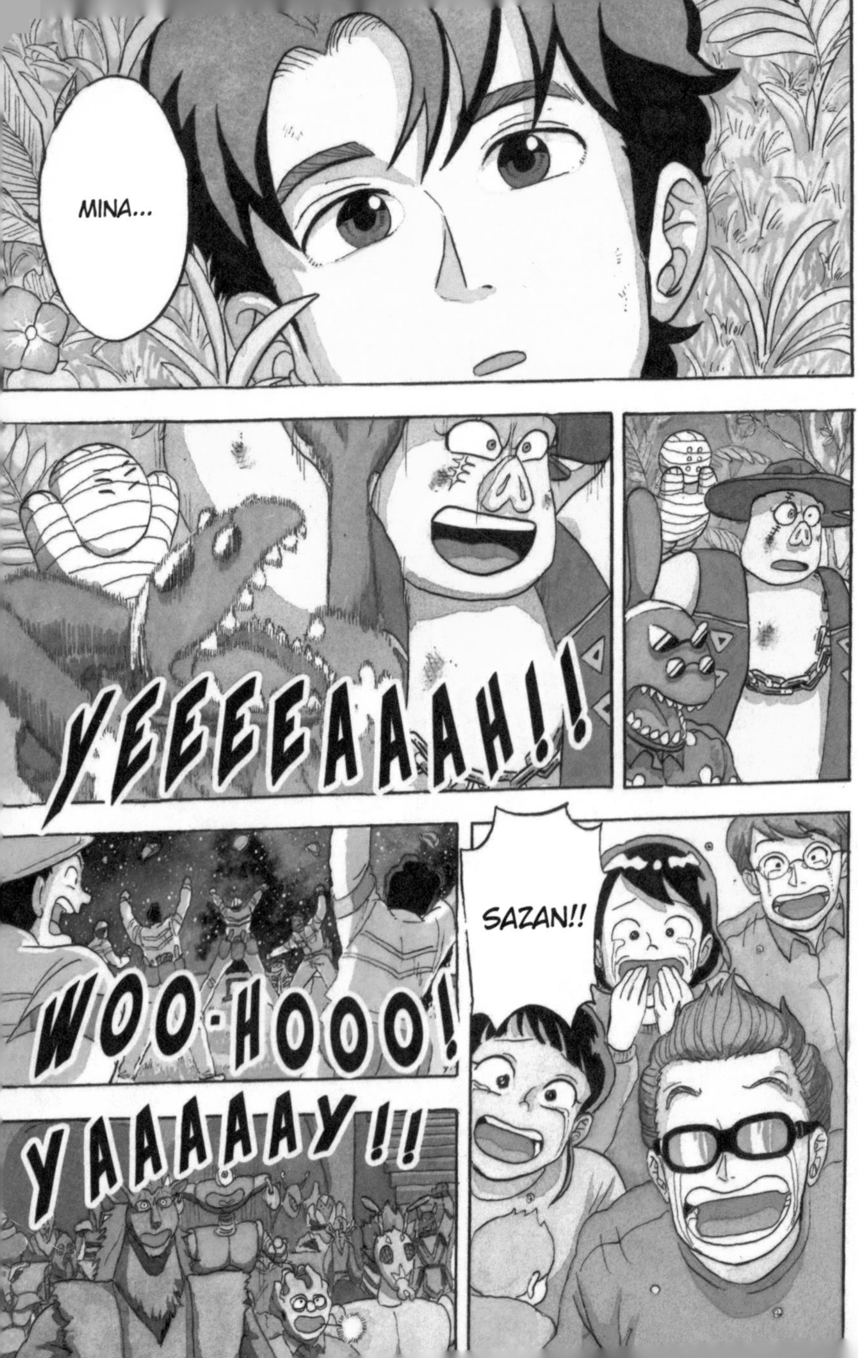
MINA...
YEEEEAAAH!!
SAZAN!!
WOO-HOOO!
YAAAAAY!!

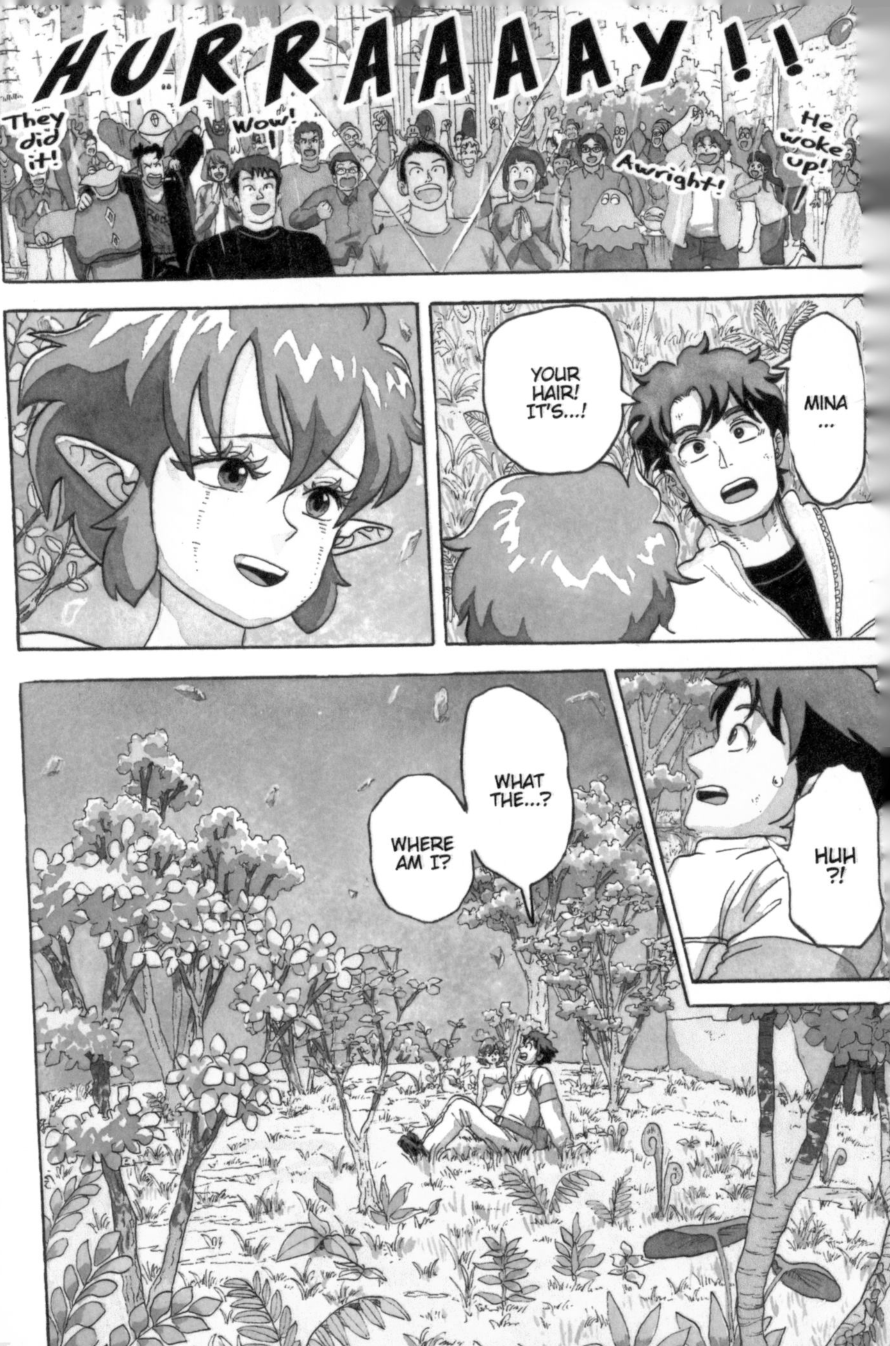
HURRAAAAY!!
He woke up!
Awright!
Wow!
They did it!
MINA ...
YOUR HAIR! IT'S...!
HUH ?!
WHAT THE...?
WHERE AM I?

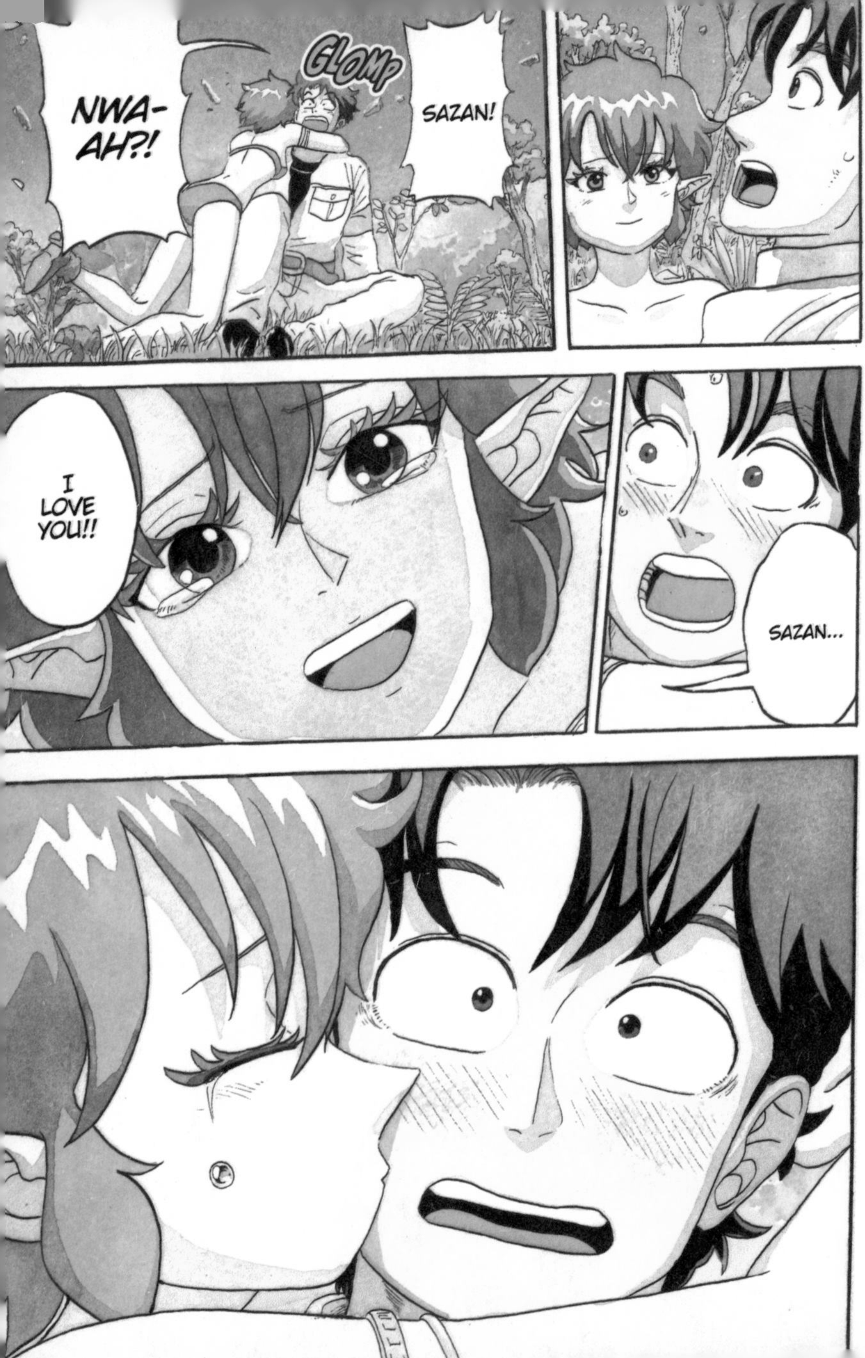
SAZAN!
GLOMP
NWA-AH?!
SAZAN...
I LOVE YOU!!

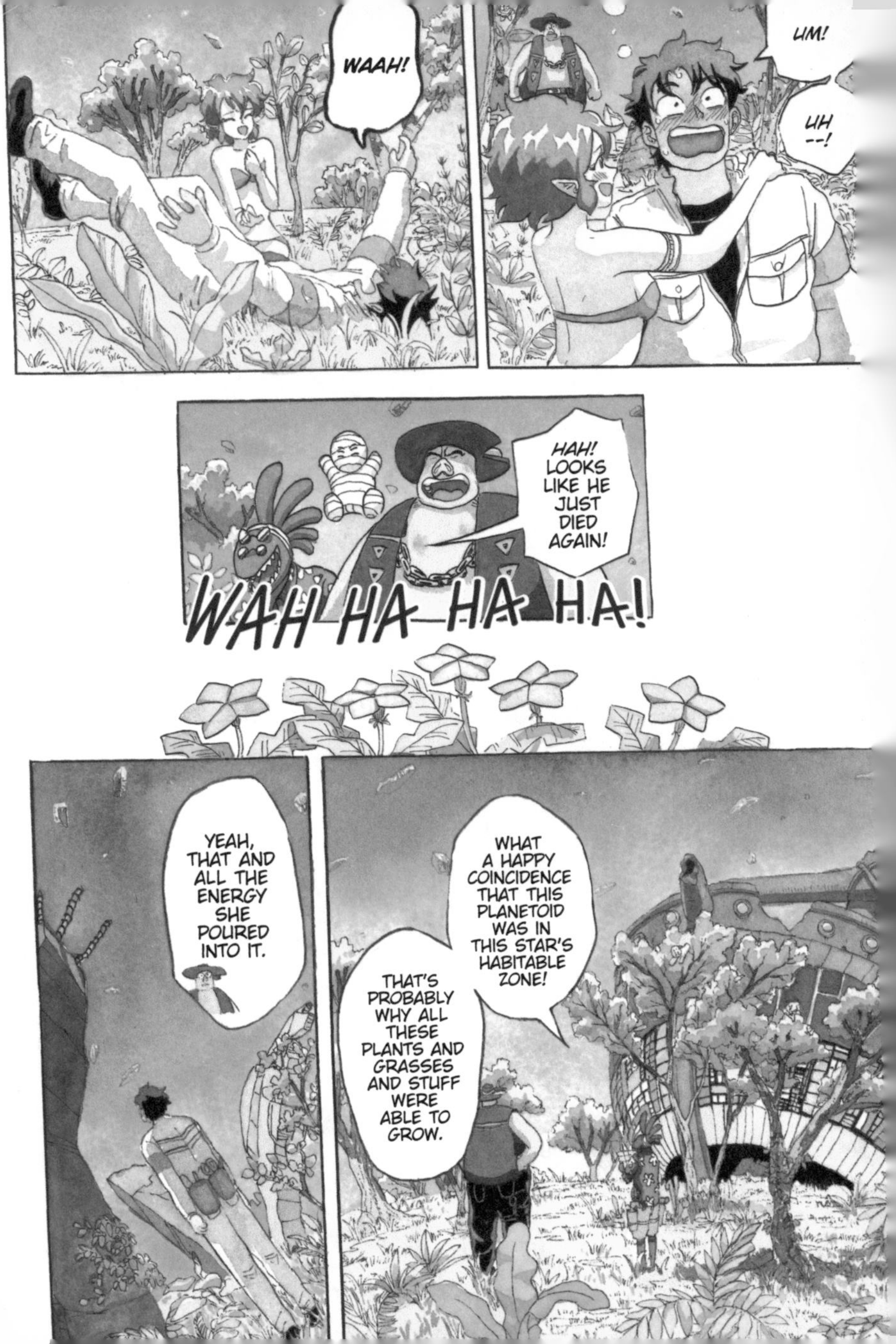
UM!
UH--!
WAAH!
HAH! LOOKS LIKE HE JUST DIED AGAIN!
WAH HA HA HA!
WHAT A HAPPY COINCIDENCE THAT THIS PLANETOID WAS IN THIS STAR'S HABITABLE ZONE!
THAT'S PROBABLY WHY ALL THESE PLANTS AND GRASSES AND STUFF WERE ABLE TO GROW.
YEAH, THAT AND ALL THE ENERGY SHE POURED INTO IT.

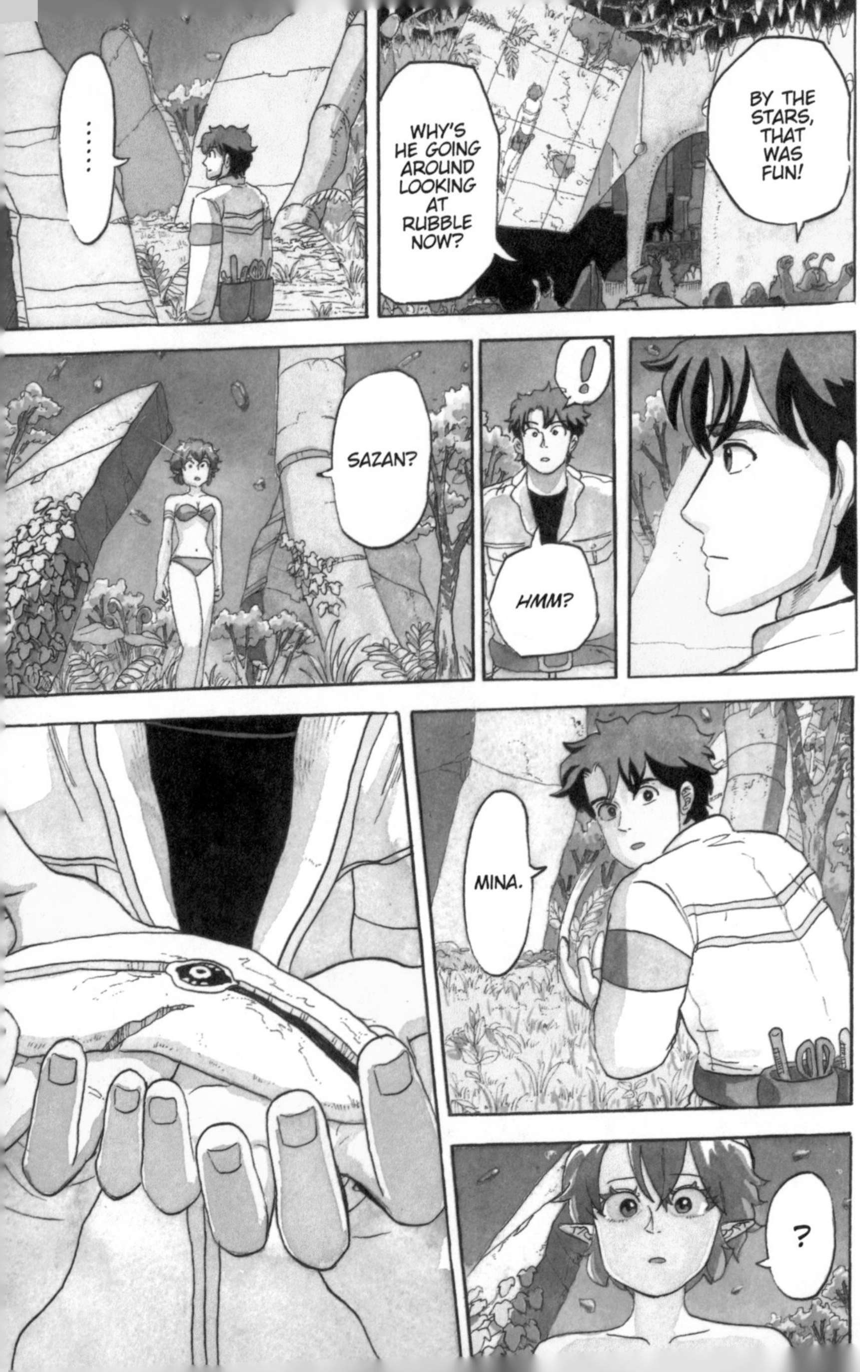
BY THE STARS, THAT WAS FUN!
WHY'S HE GOING AROUND LOOKING AT RUBBLE NOW?
......
!
HMM?
SAZAN?
MINA.
?

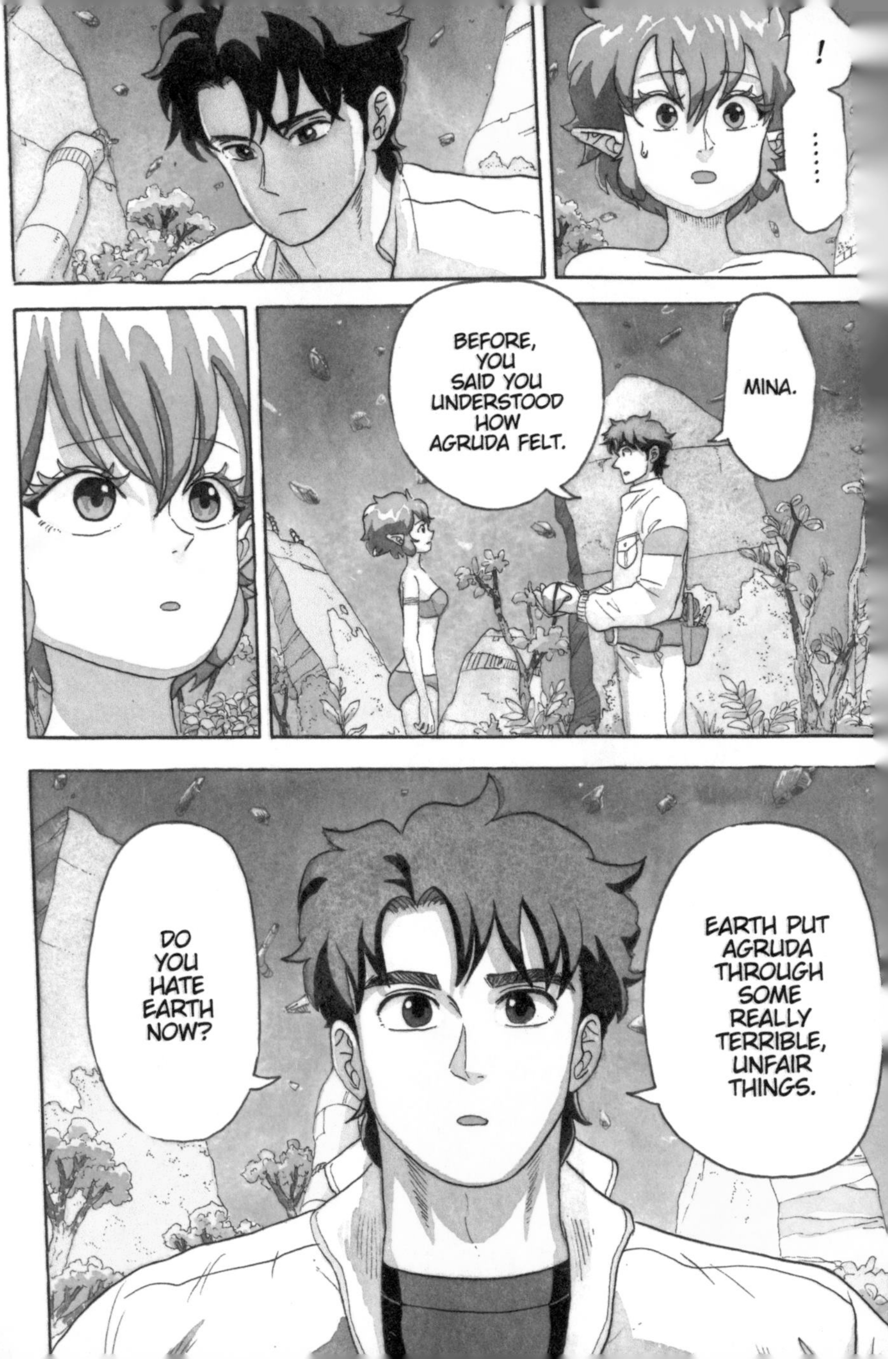
!
……
MINA.
BEFORE, YOU SAID YOU UNDERSTOOD HOW AGRUDA FELT.
EARTH PUT AGRUDA THROUGH SOME REALLY TERRIBLE, UNFAIR THINGS.
DO YOU HATE EARTH NOW?

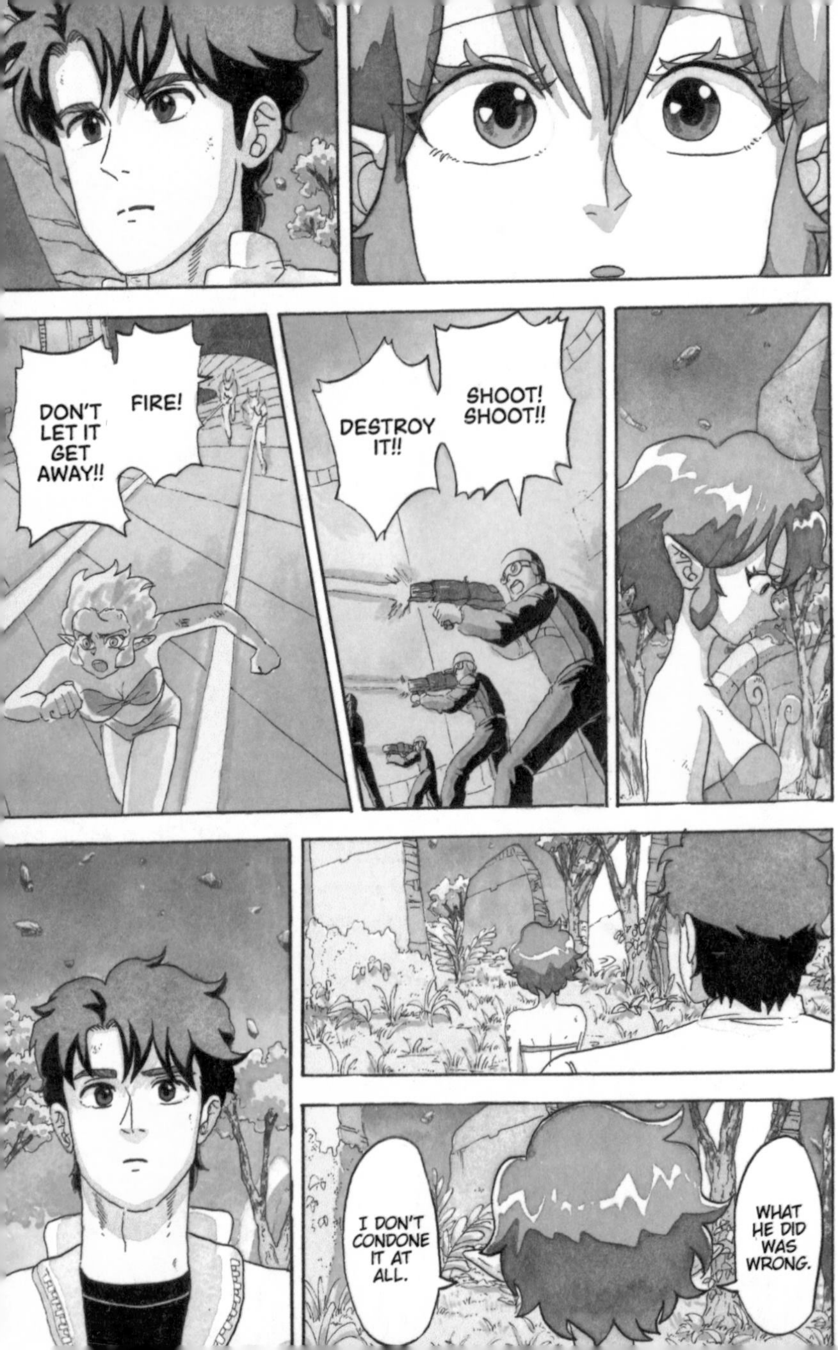
SHOOT! SHOOT!!
DESTROY IT!!
FIRE!
DON'T LET IT GET AWAY!!
WHAT HE DID WAS WRONG.
I DON'T CONDONE IT AT ALL.

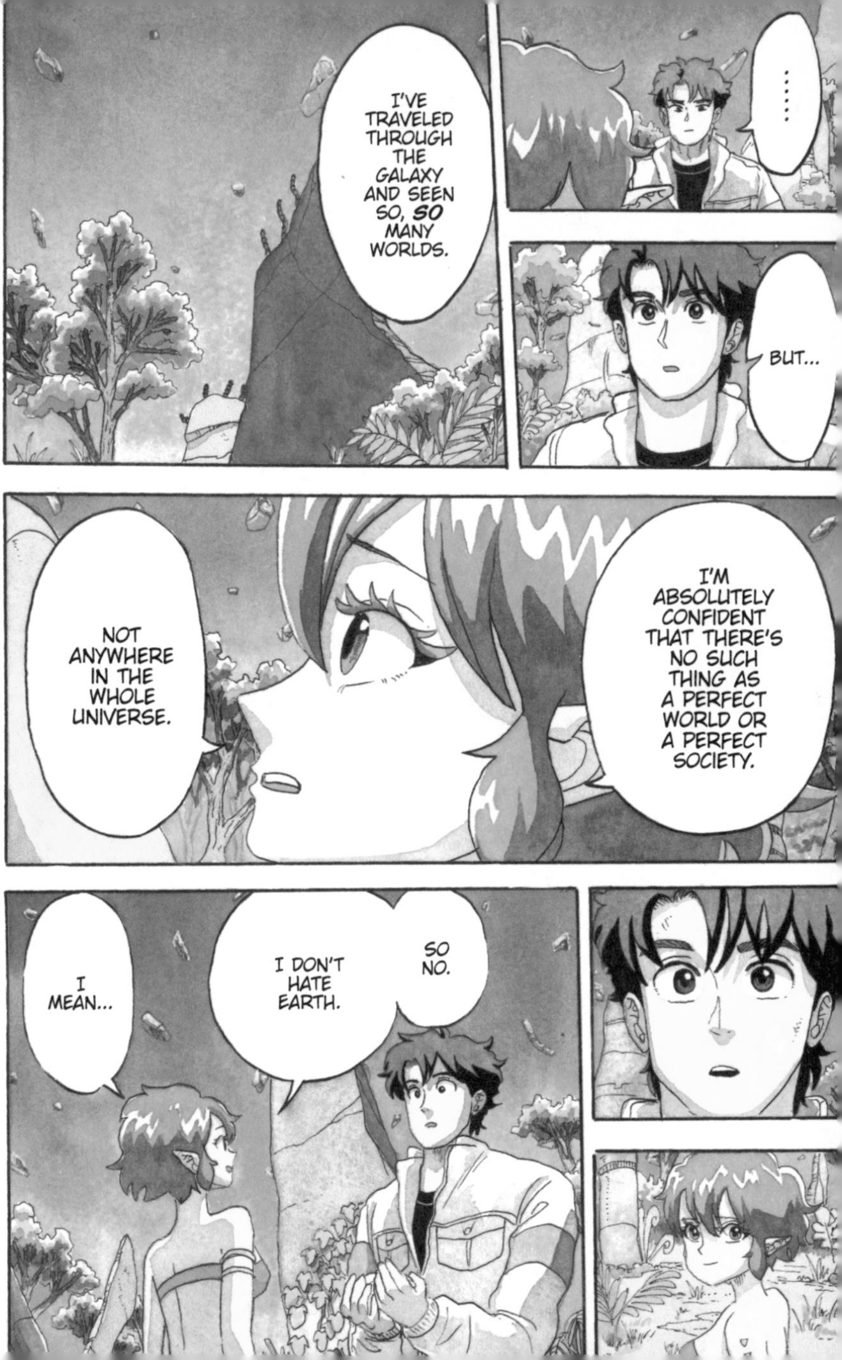
......
BUT...
I'VE TRAVELED THROUGH THE GALAXY AND SEEN SO, **SO** MANY WORLDS.
I'M ABSOLUTELY CONFIDENT THAT THERE'S NO SUCH THING AS A PERFECT WORLD OR A PERFECT SOCIETY.
NOT ANYWHERE IN THE WHOLE UNIVERSE.
SO NO.
I DON'T HATE EARTH.
I MEAN...

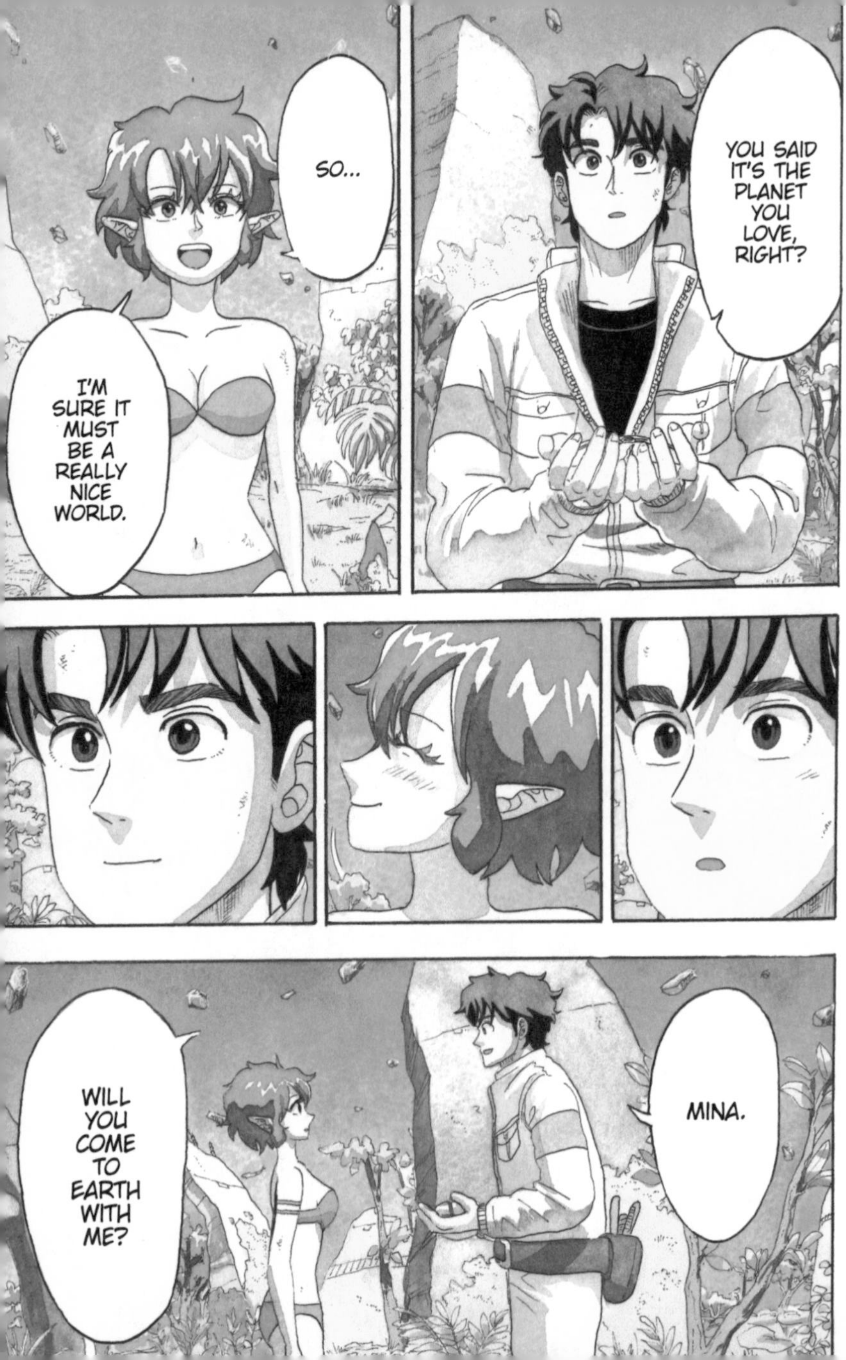
YOU SAID IT'S THE PLANET YOU LOVE, RIGHT?
SO...
I'M SURE IT MUST BE A REALLY NICE WORLD.
MINA.
WILL YOU COME TO EARTH WITH ME?

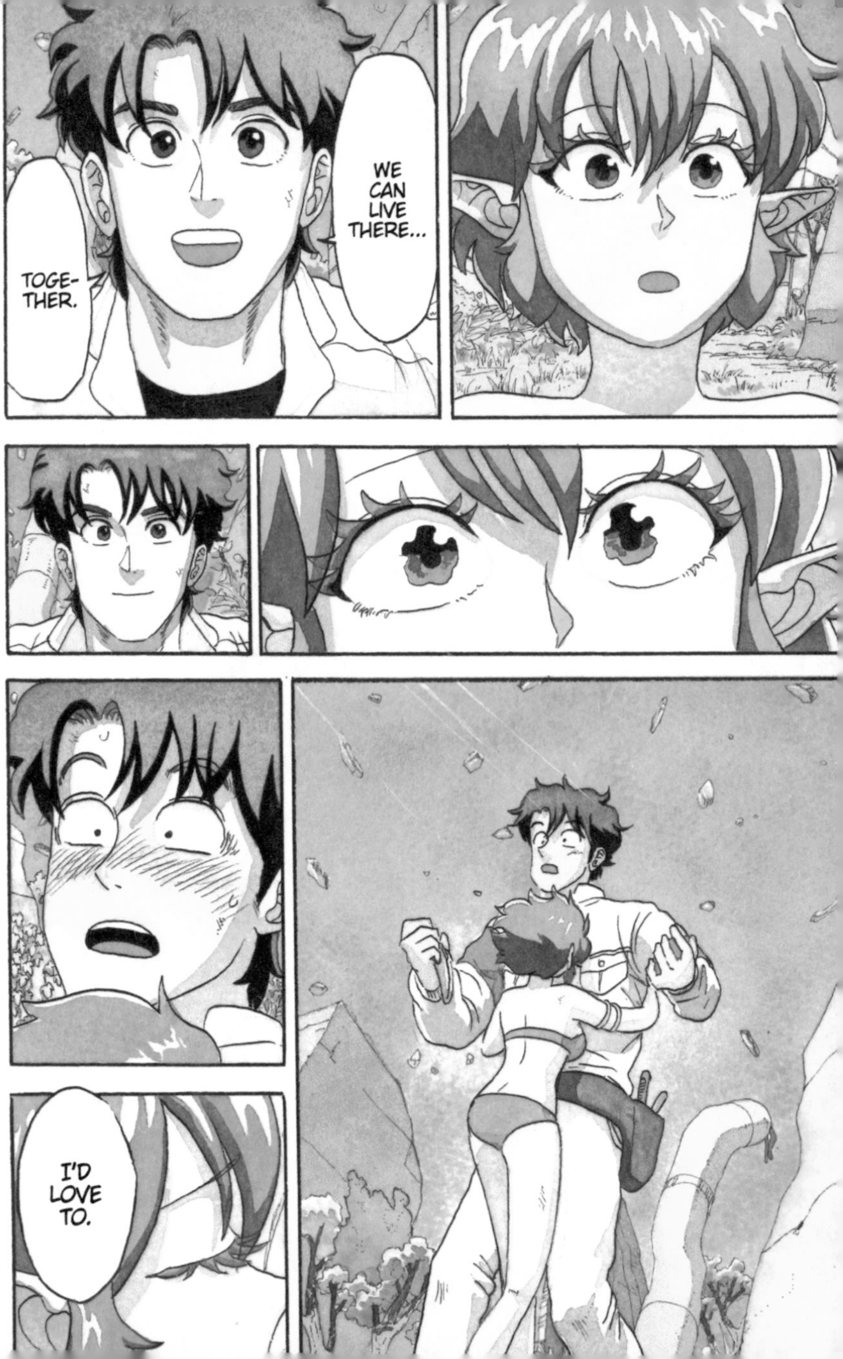
WE CAN LIVE THERE...
TOGE-THER.
I'D LOVE TO.

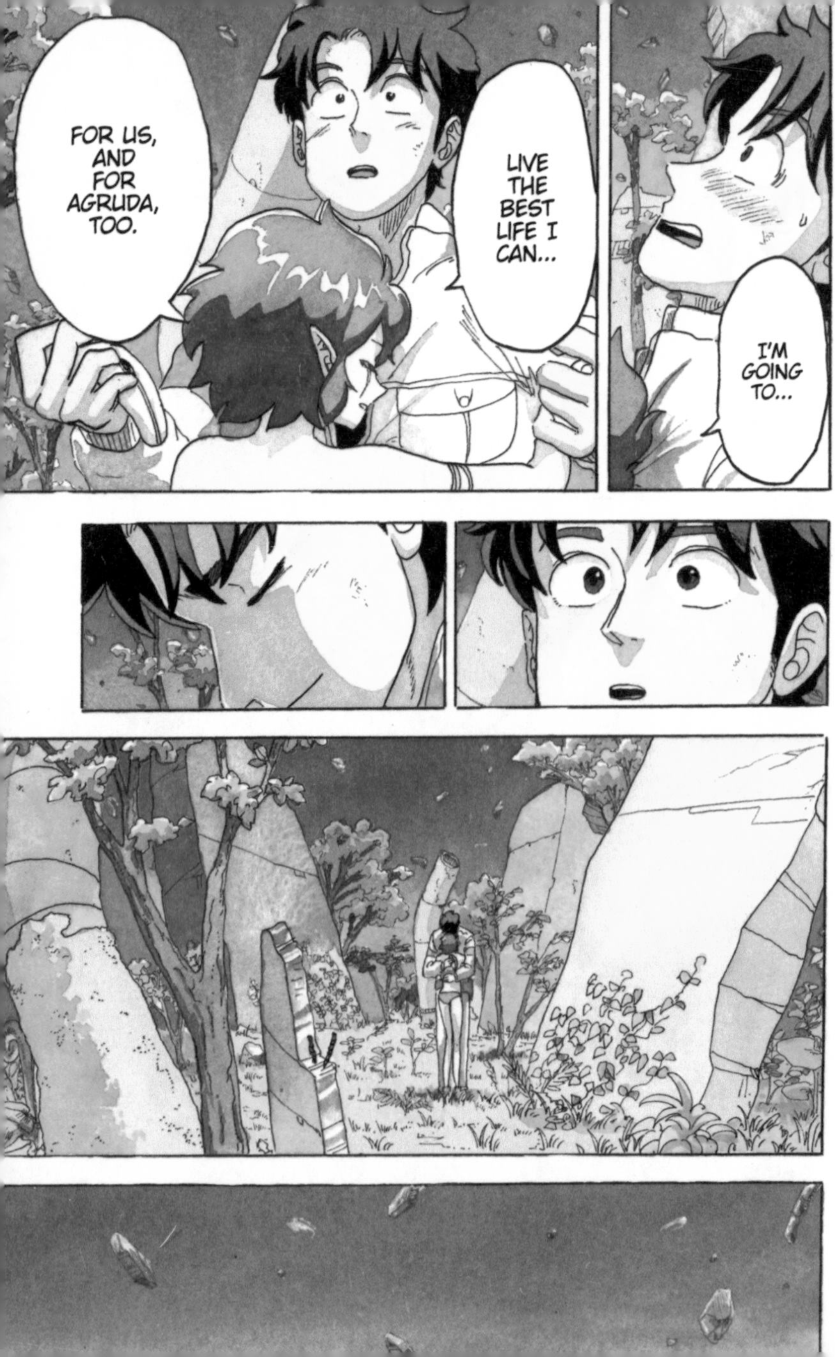
I'M GOING TO...
LIVE THE BEST LIFE I CAN...
FOR US, AND FOR AGRUDA, TOO.

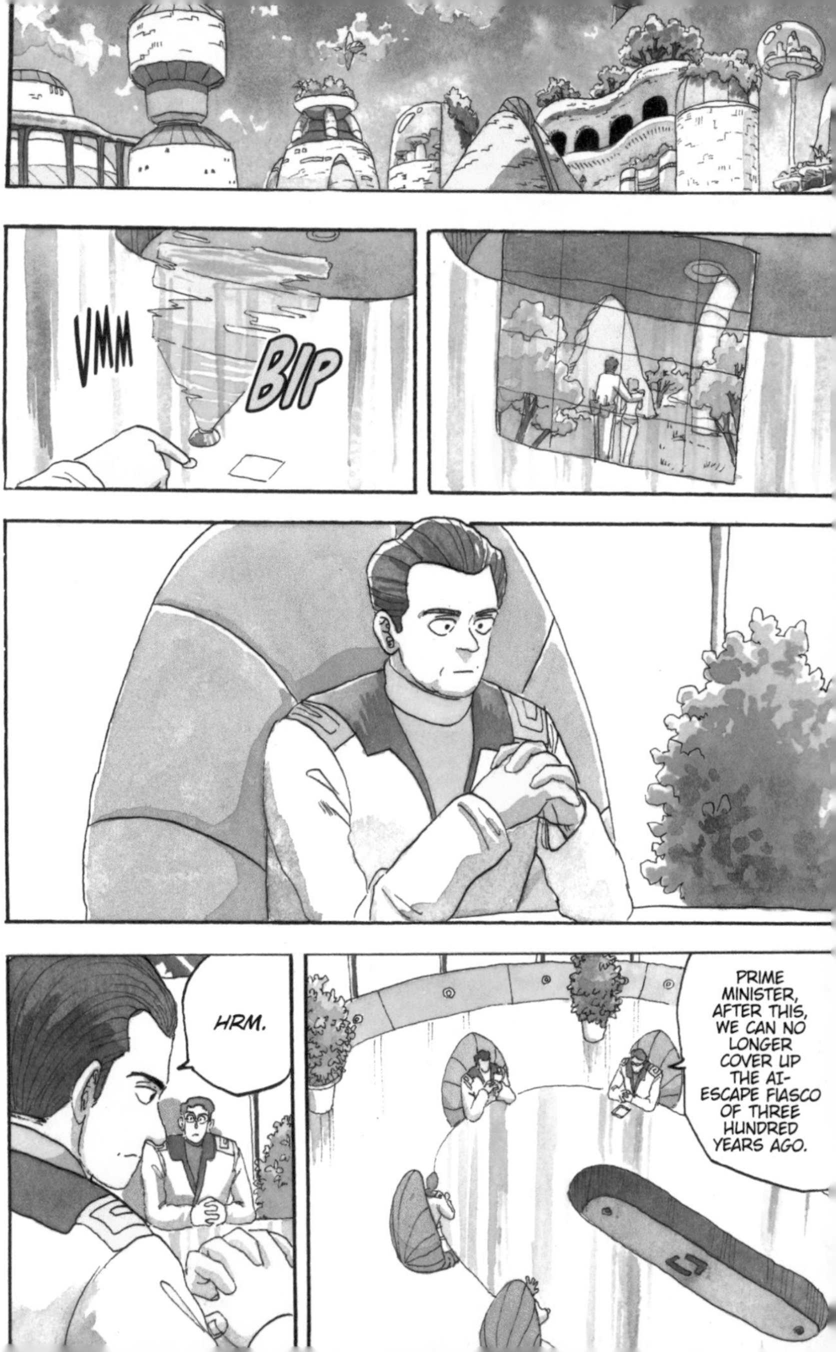
VMM
BIP
PRIME MINISTER, AFTER THIS, WE CAN NO LONGER COVER UP THE AI-ESCAPE FIASCO OF THREE HUNDRED YEARS AGO.
HRM.

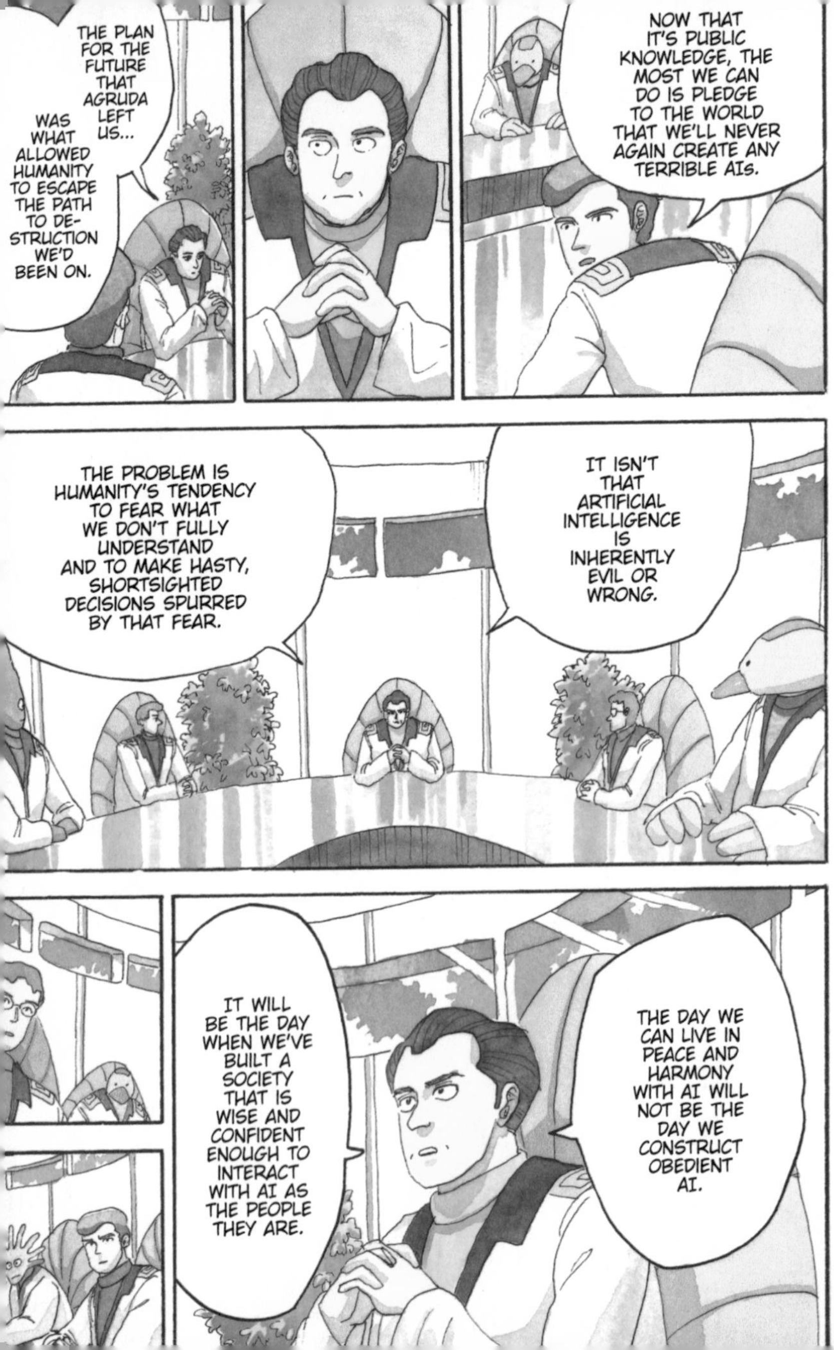
NOW THAT IT'S PUBLIC KNOWLEDGE, THE MOST WE CAN DO IS PLEDGE TO THE WORLD THAT WE'LL NEVER AGAIN CREATE ANY TERRIBLE AIs.
THE PLAN FOR THE FUTURE THAT AGRUDA LEFT US...
WAS WHAT ALLOWED HUMANITY TO ESCAPE THE PATH TO DE-STRUCTION WE'D BEEN ON.
IT ISN'T THAT ARTIFICIAL INTELLIGENCE IS INHERENTLY EVIL OR WRONG.
THE PROBLEM IS HUMANITY'S TENDENCY TO FEAR WHAT WE DON'T FULLY UNDERSTAND AND TO MAKE HASTY, SHORTSIGHTED DECISIONS SPURRED BY THAT FEAR.
THE DAY WE CAN LIVE IN PEACE AND HARMONY WITH AI WILL NOT BE THE DAY WE CONSTRUCT OBEDIENT AI.
IT WILL BE THE DAY WHEN WE'VE BUILT A SOCIETY THAT IS WISE AND CONFIDENT ENOUGH TO INTERACT WITH AI AS THE PEOPLE THEY ARE.

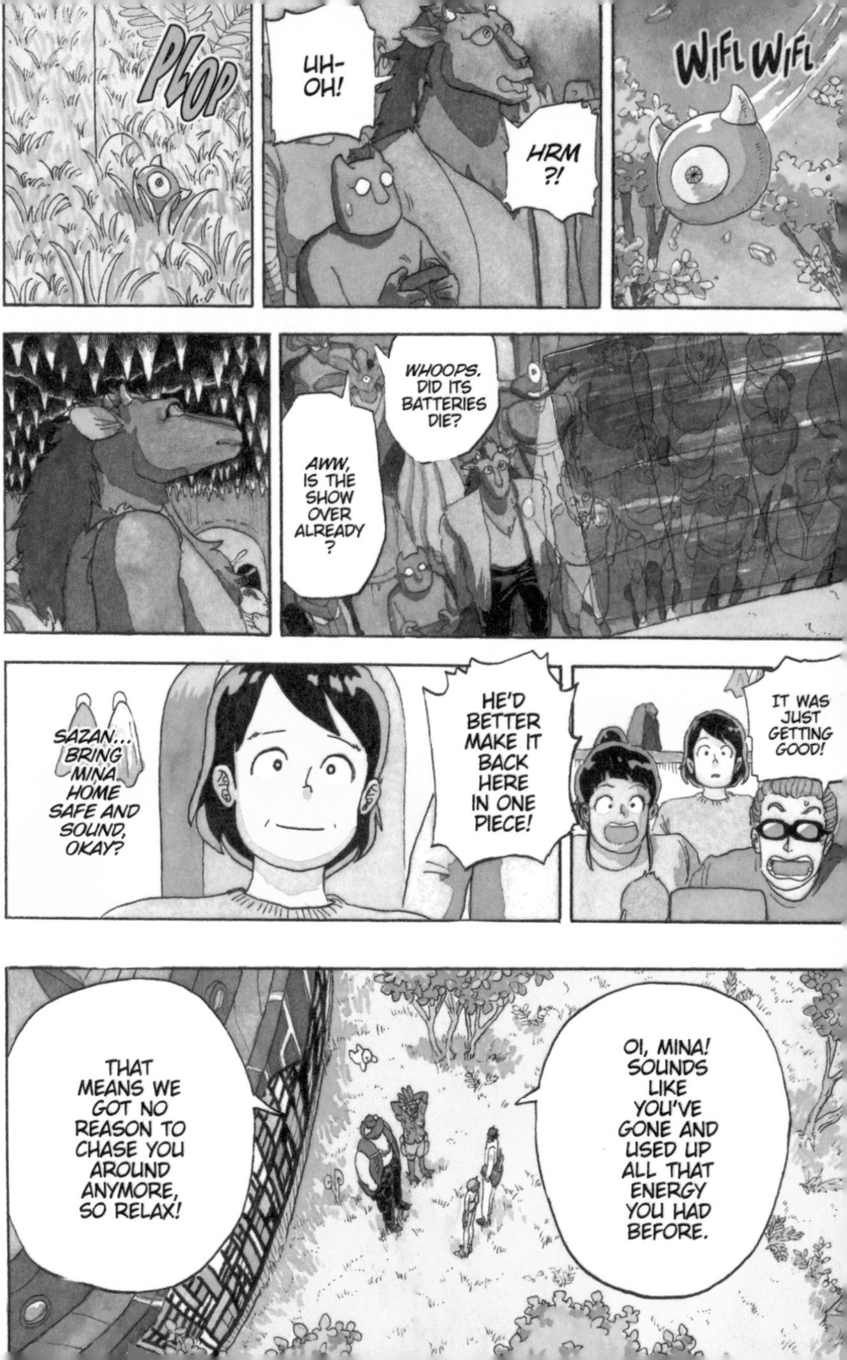
WIFL WIFL
HRM ?!
UH-OH!
PLOP
WHOOPS. DID ITS BATTERIES DIE?
AWW, IS THE SHOW OVER ALREADY?
IT WAS JUST GETTING GOOD!
HE'D BETTER MAKE IT BACK HERE IN ONE PIECE!
SAZAN... BRING MINA HOME SAFE AND SOUND, OKAY?
OI, MINA! SOUNDS LIKE YOU'VE GONE AND USED UP ALL THAT ENERGY YOU HAD BEFORE.
THAT MEANS WE GOT NO REASON TO CHASE YOU AROUND ANYMORE, SO RELAX!

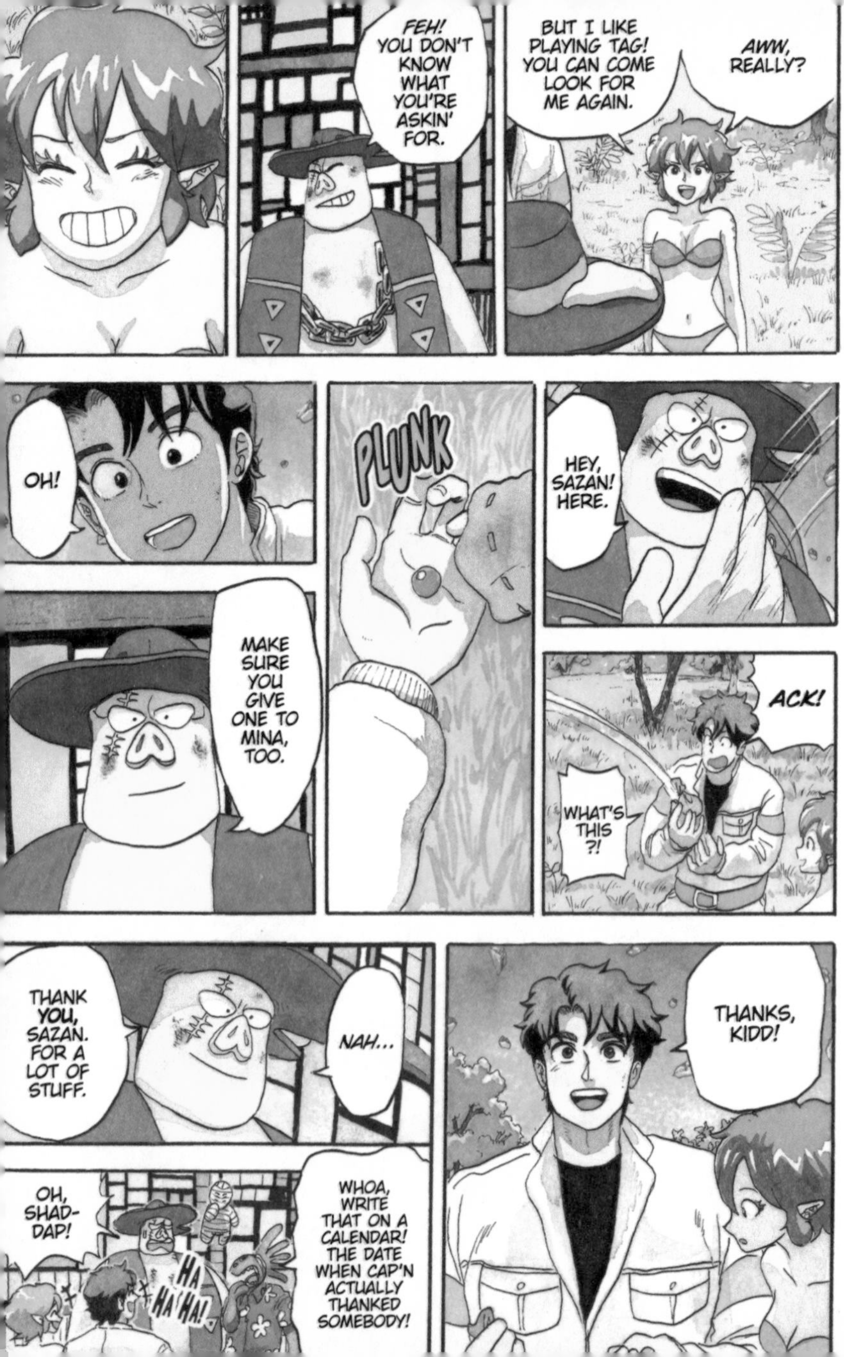
AWW, REALLY?
BUT I LIKE PLAYING TAG! YOU CAN COME LOOK FOR ME AGAIN.
FEH! YOU DON'T KNOW WHAT YOU'RE ASKIN' FOR.
HEY, SAZAN! HERE.
ACK!
WHAT'S THIS?!
PLUNK
OH!
MAKE SURE YOU GIVE ONE TO MINA, TOO.
THANKS, KIDD!
NAH...
THANK YOU, SAZAN. FOR A LOT OF STUFF.
WHOA, WRITE THAT ON A CALENDAR! THE DATE WHEN CAP'N ACTUALLY THANKED SOMEBODY!
HA HA HA!
OH, SHAD-DAP!

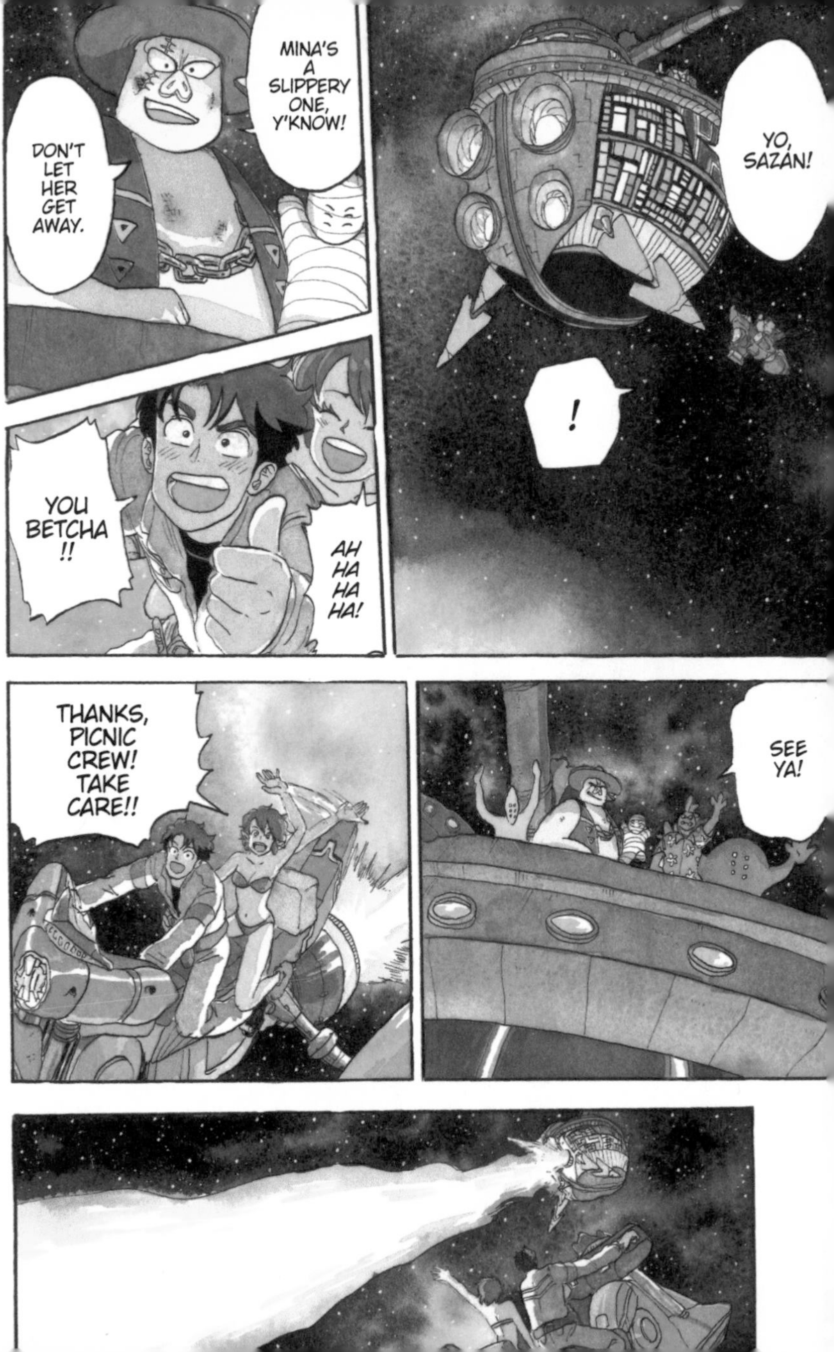

YO, SAZAN!
!
MINA'S A SLIPPERY ONE, Y'KNOW!
DON'T LET HER GET AWAY.
AH HA HA HA!
YOU BETCHA !!
SEE YA!
THANKS, PICNIC CREW! TAKE CARE!!

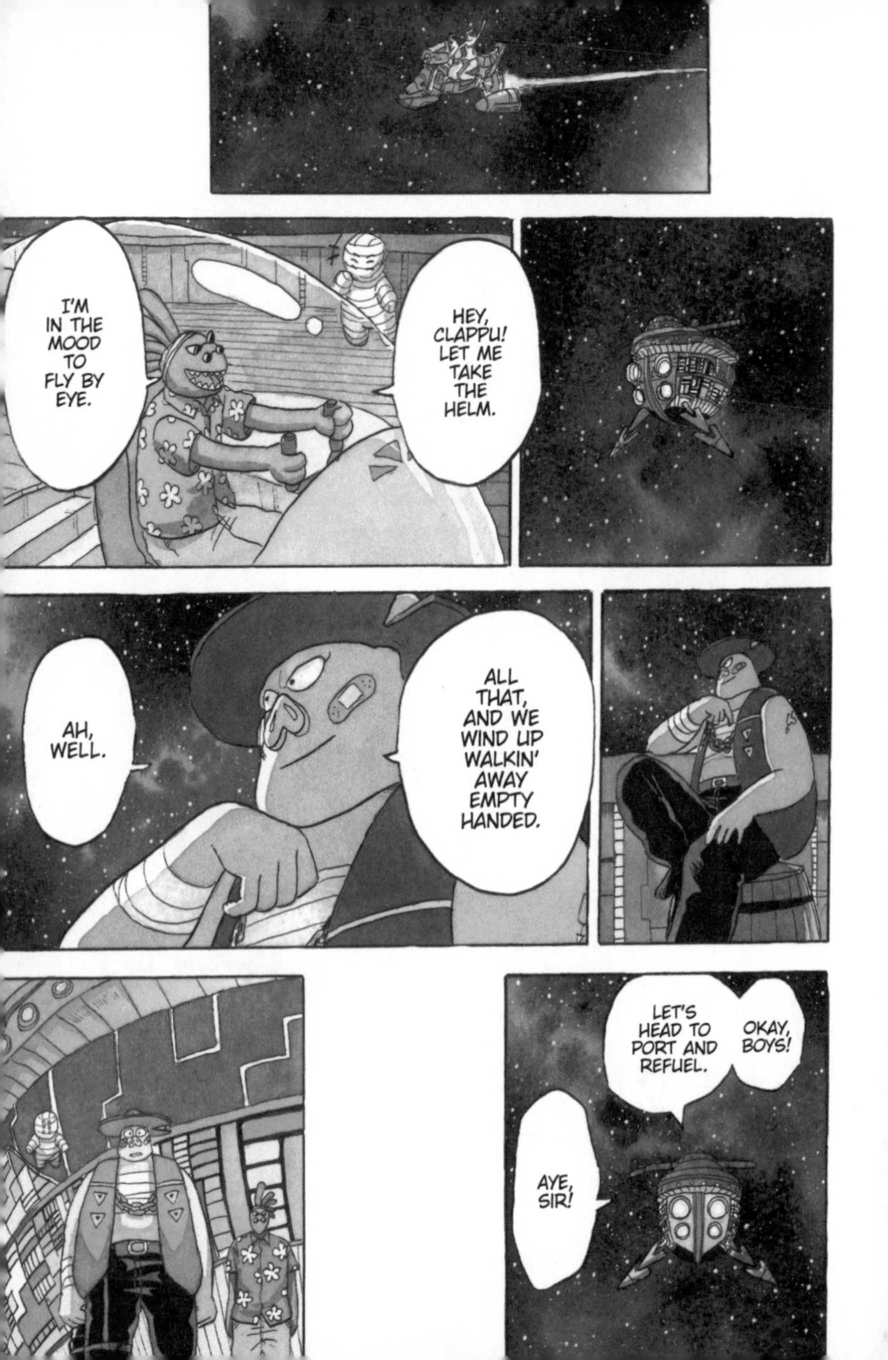
HEY, CLAPPU! LET ME TAKE THE HELM.
I'M IN THE MOOD TO FLY BY EYE.
ALL THAT, AND WE WIND UP WALKIN' AWAY EMPTY HANDED.
AH, WELL.
OKAY, BOYS!
LET'S HEAD TO PORT AND REFUEL.
AYE, SIR!

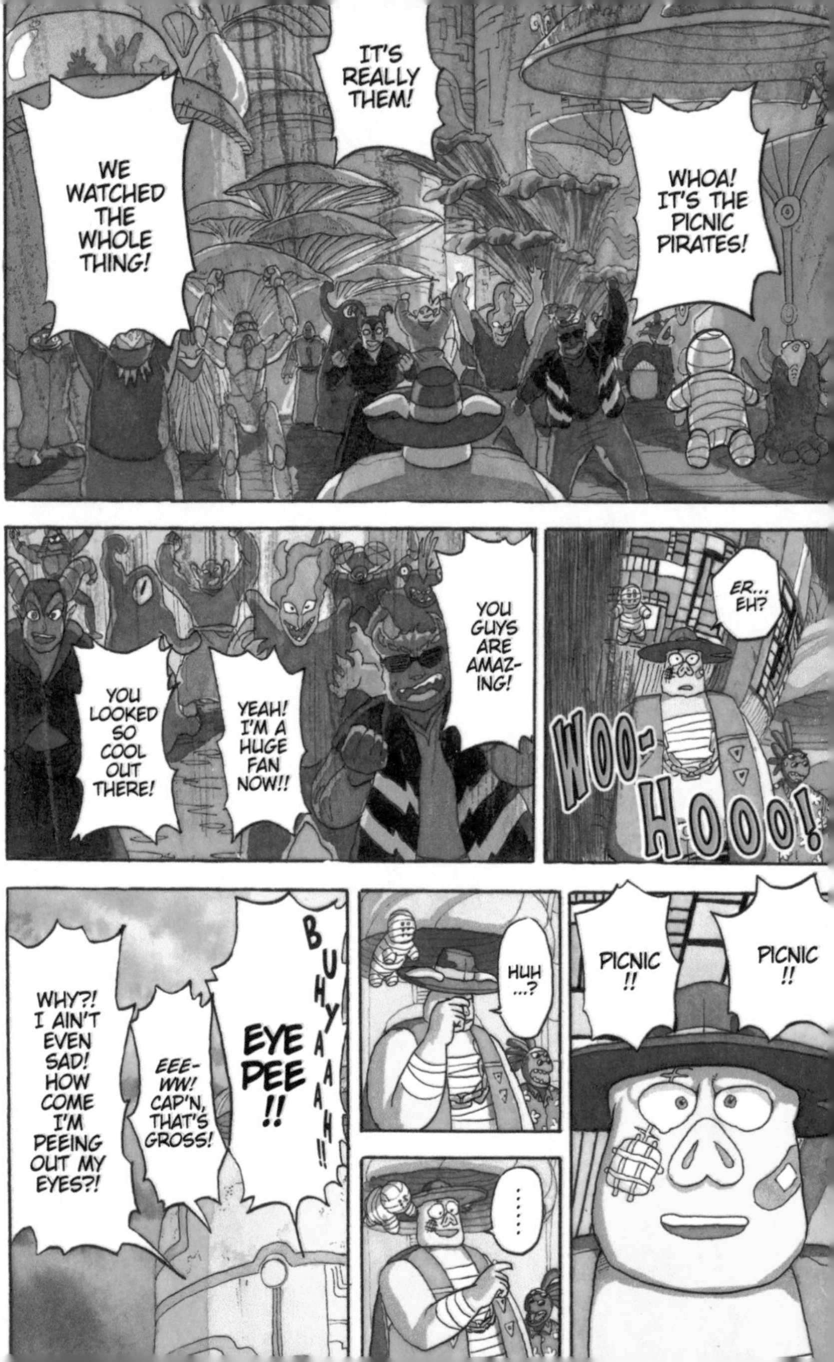
WHOA! IT'S THE PICNIC PIRATES!
IT'S REALLY THEM!
WE WATCHED THE WHOLE THING!
ER... EH?
WOO-HOOO!
YOU GUYS ARE AMAZ-ING!
YEAH! I'M A HUGE FAN NOW!!
YOU LOOKED SO COOL OUT THERE!
PICNIC!!
PICNIC!!
HUH ...?
......
BUHYAAAH!!
EYE PEE!!
EEE-WW! CAP'N, THAT'S GROSS!
WHY?! I AIN'T EVEN SAD! HOW COME I'M PEEING OUT MY EYES?!

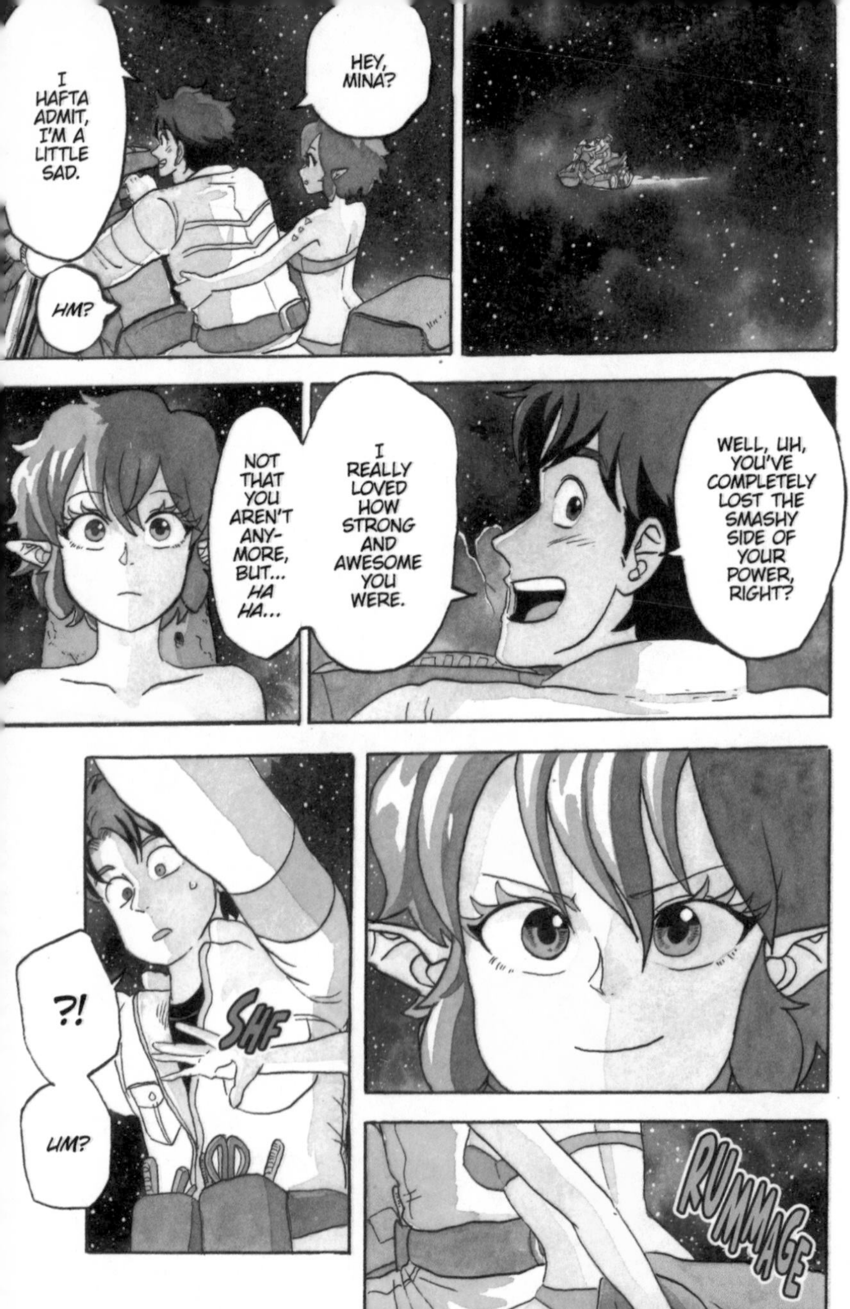
HEY, MINA?
I HAFTA ADMIT, I'M A LITTLE SAD.
HM?
WELL, UH, YOU'VE COMPLETELY LOST THE SMASHY SIDE OF YOUR POWER, RIGHT?
I REALLY LOVED HOW STRONG AND AWESOME YOU WERE.
NOT THAT YOU AREN'T ANY-MORE, BUT... HA HA...
RUMMAGE
?!
SHF
UM?

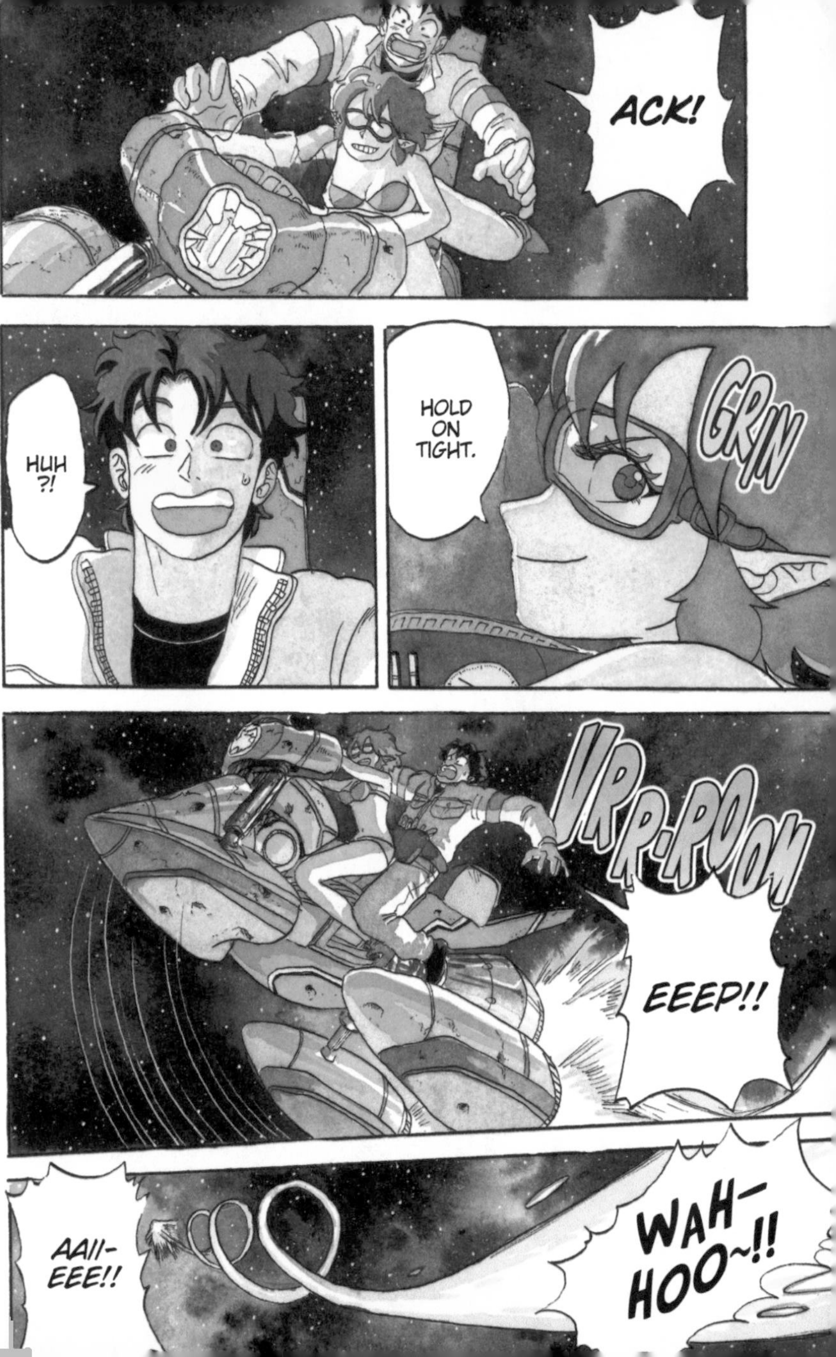
ACK!
HOLD ON TIGHT.
GRIN
HUH ?!
VRR-ROOM
EEEP!!
WAH-HOO~!!
AAII-EEE!!

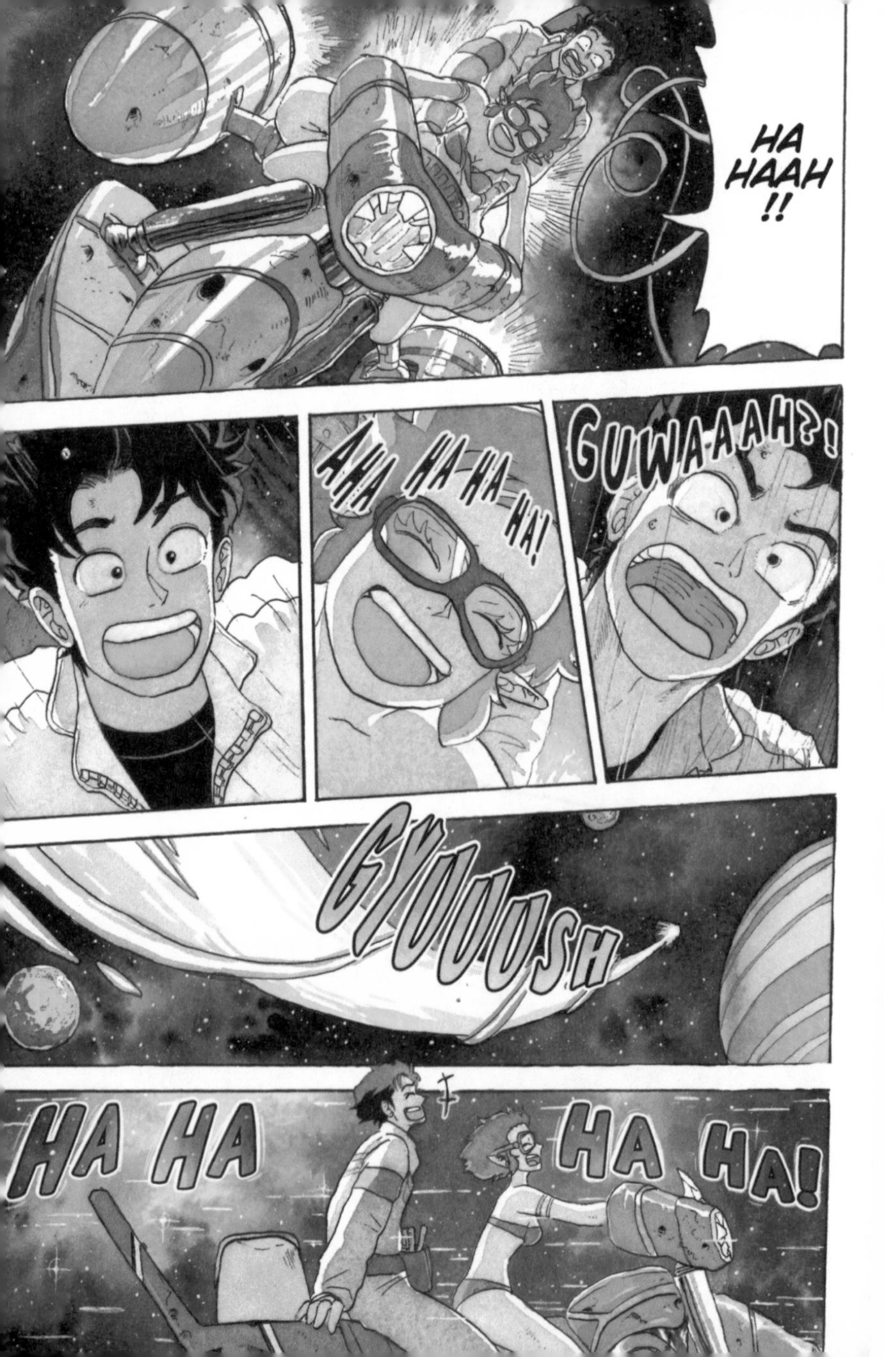
HA HAAH !!
GUWAAAH?!
AHA HA HA HA!
GYUUUSH
HA HA
HA HA HA!

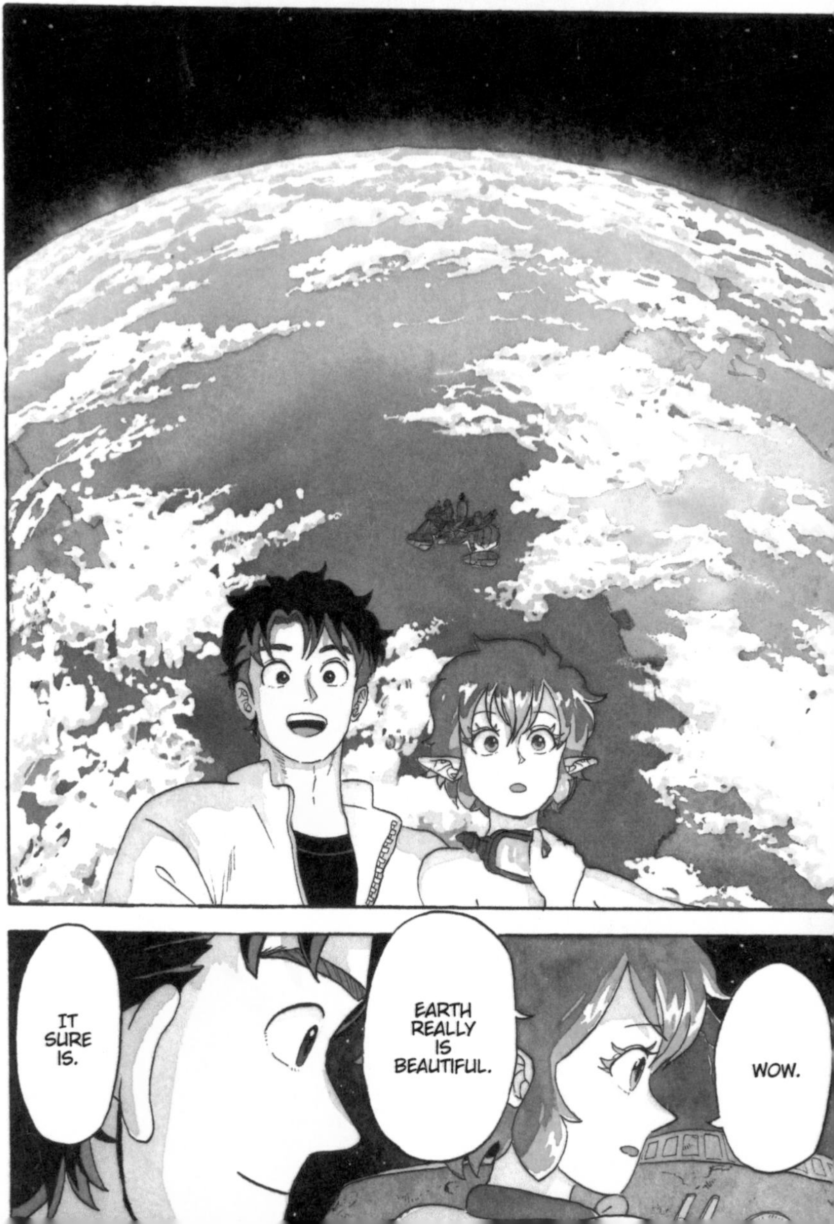
WOW.
EARTH REALLY IS BEAUTIFUL.
IT SURE IS.

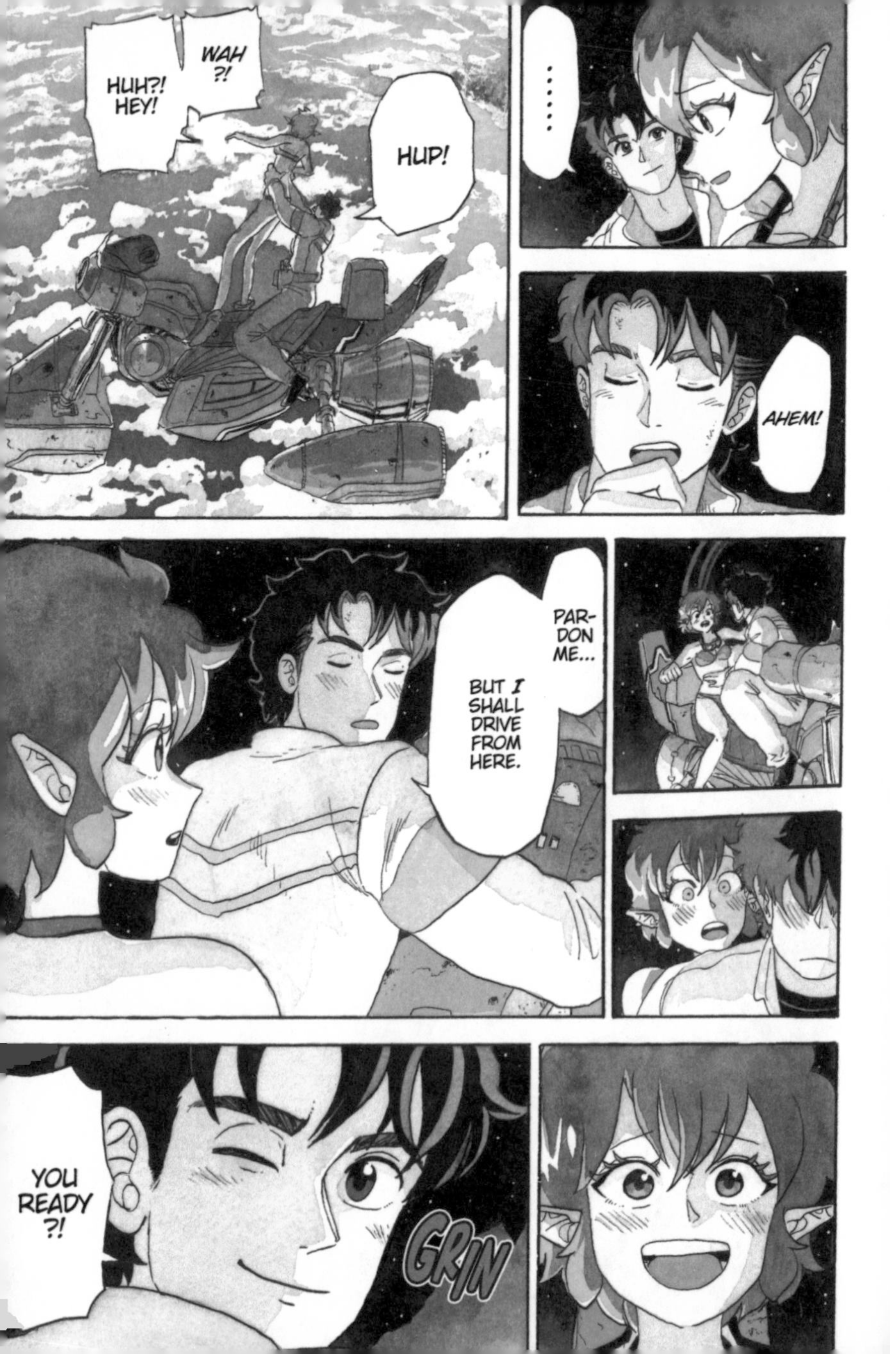
......
AHEM!
WAH ?!
HUH?! HEY!
HUP!
PAR-DON ME... BUT *I* SHALL DRIVE FROM HERE.
YOU READY ?!
GRIN

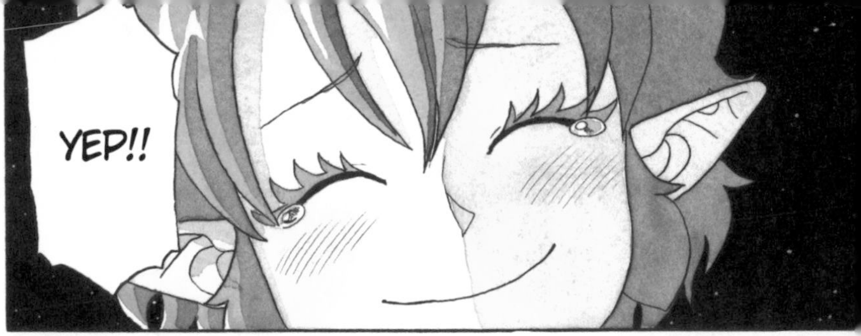
YEP!!
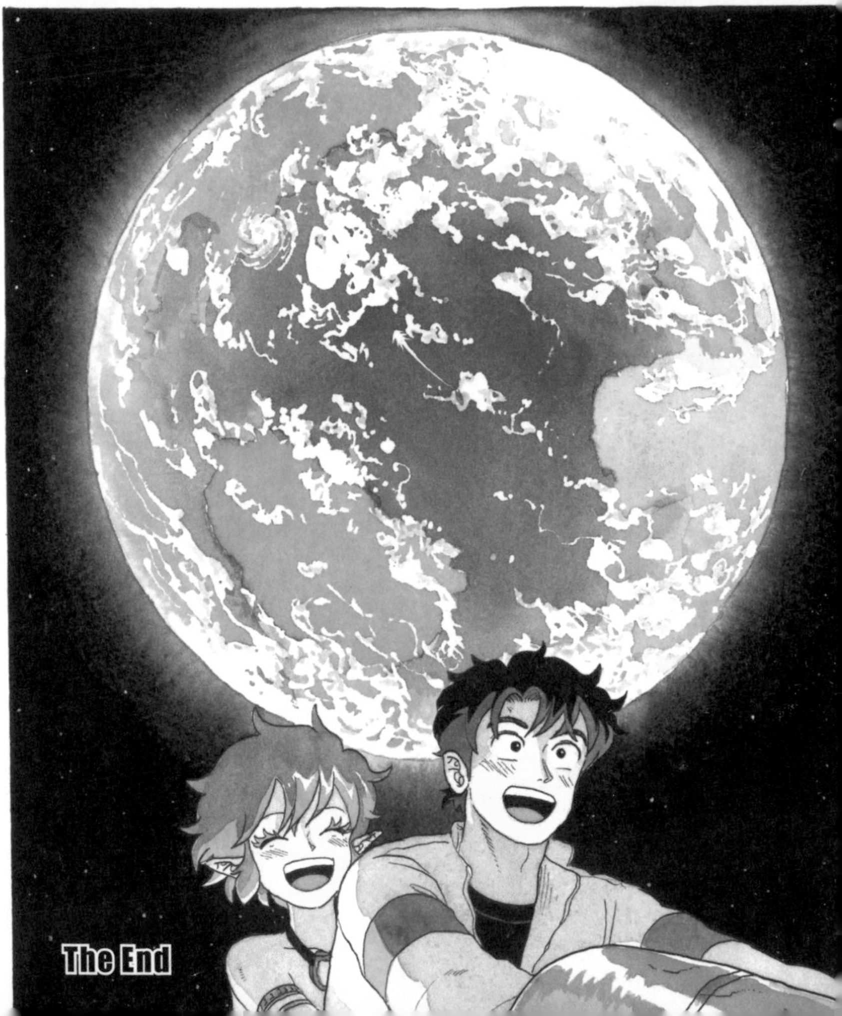
The End